18th IADIS International Conference Information Systems 2025 and 23rd International Conference on e-Society 2025

Madeira Island, Portugal
1-3 March 2025

Editors:

Miguel B. Nunes
Pedro Isaias
Philip Powell
Piet Kommers

ISBN: 979-8-3313-1620-4

Printed from e-media with permission by:

Curran Associates, Inc.
57 Morehouse Lane
Red Hook, NY 12571

Some format issues inherent in the e-media version may also appear in this print version.

Printed with permission by Curran Associates, Inc. (2025)

International Association for Development of the Information Society (IADIS)
Rua Sao Sebastiao Da Pedreira
No. 100, 30, 1050-209
Lisbon, Portugal

Phone: 351 21 3151373
Fax: 351 21 3151244

secretariat@iadis.org

Additional copies of this publication are available from:

Curran Associates, Inc.
57 Morehouse Lane
Red Hook, NY 12571 USA
Phone: 845-758-0400
Fax: 845-758-2633
Email: curran@proceedings.com
Web: www.proceedings.com

INTERNATIONAL CONFERENCES PROCEEDINGS

2025

Information Systems

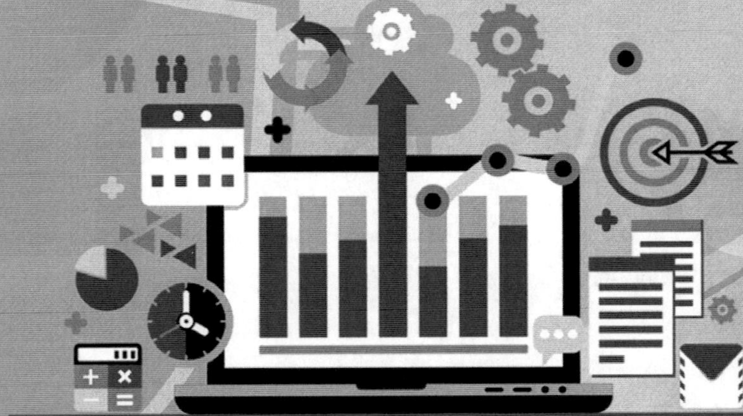

& e-Society

Madeira Island,
Portugal
01-03 March

Edited by:
Miguel Baptista Nunes
Pedro Isaías
Philip Powell
Piet Kommers

INTERNATIONAL CONFERENCES

IADIS INFORMATION SYSTEMS 2025

AND

E-SOCIETY 2025

PROCEEDINGS OF THE INTERNATIONAL CONFERENCES

IADIS INFORMATION SYSTEMS 2025

AND

E-SOCIETY 2025

1 - 3 MARCH, 2025

MADEIRA ISLAND, PORTUGAL

Organised by

iadis

international association for development of the information society

As a member of Crossref (a non-profit membership organization for scholarly publishing working with the purpose to make content easy to find, link, cite and assess) each published paper in this book of proceedings will be allocated a DOI (Digital Object Identifier) number for its fast and easy citation and indexation.

Edited by Miguel Baptista Nunes, Pedro Isaías, Philip Powell and Piet Kommers

Associate Editor: Luís Rodrigues

TABLE OF CONTENTS

e-Society

SHORT PAPERS

Information Systems

e-Society

REFLECTION PAPERS

Information Systems

e-Society

POSTERS

Information Systems

FOREWORD

These proceedings contain the papers and posters of the 18th IADIS International Conference Information Systems 2025 and the 23rd International Conference on e-Society, which was organised by the International Association for Development of the Information Society in Madeira Island, Portugal, from 1 – 3 March 2025.

The IADIS Information Systems Conference 2025 aims to provide a forum for the discussion of IS taking a socio-technological perspective. It aims to address the issues related to design, development and use of IS in organisations from a socio-technological perspective, as well as to discuss IS professional practice, research and teaching. A set of key areas has been identified. However, these do not aim at being prescriptive, or set in stone, and any innovative contributions that do not fit into these areas have also been considered.

The following main tracks have been object of paper submissions:

- IS in Practice, Technology Infrastructures and Organisational Processes
- IS Design, Development and Management Issues and Methodologies
- IS Professional Issues
- IS Research
- IS Learning and Teaching

The e-Society 2025 conference aims to address the main issues of concern within the Information Society. This conference covers both the technical as well as the non-technical aspects of the Information Society. Broad areas of interest are:

- e-Government / e-Governance
- e-Business / e-Commerce
- Technology and Society
- e-Learning
- New Media and E-Society
- e-Health
- Information Systems
- Information Management
- COVID-19 & Digital Transformation

These events received 243 submissions from more than 33 countries. Each submission has been anonymously reviewed by an average of 4 independent reviewers, to ensure the final high standard of the accepted submissions. Out of the papers submitted, 47 got blind referee ratings that published them as full papers, which means that the acceptance rate was 19%. Some other submissions were published as short and reflection papers, posters and doctoral paper. Extended versions of the best papers will be selected to be published in the IADIS Journal on Computer Science and Information Systems (ISSN: 1646-3692) indexed by Emerging Sources Citation Index by Thomson Reuters, and in the IADIS Journal on WWW/Internet (ISSN: 1645-7641).

The conference, besides the papers' presentations, also includes a keynote presentation from an internationally distinguished researcher. We wish to thank Professor Laurence Brooks, Professor of Information Systems, Information School, University of Sheffield, United Kingdom, for accepting our invitation as keynote speaker. Furthermore, it is included a Tutorial entitled "Expanding Your Research with Text Mining and Topic Modelling" by Azar Shahgholian and Eyyüb Can Odacıoğlu (The University of Manchester, United Kingdom).

As we all know, a conference requires the effort of many individuals. We would like to thank all members of the Program Committee for their hard work in reviewing and selecting the papers that appear in the book of the proceedings. We would also like to thank all the authors who have submitted their papers to this conference. We wish to thank all members of our organizing committee.

Last but not the least, we hope that everybody enjoyed the presentations and we invite all participants for the next year edition of the International Conferences on IADIS Information Systems and e-Society.

Philip Powell, University of London, UK
IADIS IS 2025 Conference Chair

Miguel Baptista Nunes, Xi'an Jiaotong-Liverpool University, China
IADIS IS 2025 Program Co-Chair

Pedro Isaias, Universidade Aberta (Portuguese Open University), Portugal
IADIS IS 2025 Program Co-Chair and ES 2025 Conference Chair

Piet Kommers, UNESCO Professor of Educational Technology, The Netherlands
ES 2025 Program Chair

March 2025

PROGRAM COMMITTEE

INFORMATION SYSTEMS

CONFERENCE CHAIR

Professor Philip Powell, University of London, UK

PROGRAM CO-CHAIRS

Miguel Baptista Nunes, Xi'an Jiaotong-Liverpool University, China
Pedro Isaías, Universidade Aberta (Portuguese Open University), Portugal

COMMITTEE MEMBERS

Ali-Reza Montazemi, Mcmaster University, Canada
Amelia Badica, University of Craiova, Romania
Antonios Kaniadakis, Brunel University of London, United Kingdom
Armel Lefebvre, Leiden University, Netherlands
Betim Cico, Epoka University, Tirana, Albania
Binshan Lin, Louisiana State University Shreveport (LSUS), USA
Bo Wen, Swansea University, United Kingdom
Carlos Medina, Technological University of Panama, Panama
Christos Kalloniatis, University of The Aegean, Greece
Ciara Heavin, Cork University Business School, Ireland
David G. Rosado, University of Castilla-la Mancha, Spain
Deisy Chaves, Universidad del Valle, Colombia
Demetrios Sarantis, United Nations University, Portugal
Desireé Cranfield, Swansea University, United Kingdom
Dimitris Kardaras, Athens University of Economics and Business, Greece
Ekaterina Korneeva, University of Bonn, Germany
Eleana Asimakopoulou, University of Bedfordshire, United Kingdom
Euripidis Loukis, University of The Aegean, Greece
Faiez Gargouri, University of Sfax. ISIMS. Miracl Lab, Tunisia
Giacomo Vella, Politecnico di Milano School of Management, Italy
Guoqing Zhao, Swansea University, United Kingdom
Hans-Peter Steinbacher, University of Applied Sciences, Austria
Hariram K. Chavan, K J Somaiya Institute of Technology, India
Huanhuan Xiong, Cork University Business School, Ireland
Ina Kayser, Ist-hochschule, University of Applied Sciences, Germany
Iyad Zoukar, Higher Institute of Applied Sciences and Technologies, Syria
James Thong, HKUST Business School, Hong Kong
Javad Chamanara, L3s Research Center, Germany
Jorge Hochstetter, Universidad de La Frontera, Chile
Jose Antonio Pow Sang Portillo, Pontificia Universidad Catolica del Peru, Peru

E-SOCIETY

PROGRAM CHAIR

Piet Kommers, UNESCO Professor of Educational Technology, The Netherlands

CONFERENCE CHAIR

Pedro Isaías, Universidade Aberta (Portuguese Open University), Portugal

COMMITTEE MEMBERS

Abdelsalam Busalim, Technological University Dublin, Ireland
Adam Wojciechowski, Poznan University of Technology, Poland
Agapito Ledezma, Universidad Carlos III de Madrid, Spain
Albena Antonova, University of Sofia, Bulgaria
Aleksandar Dimov, University of Sofia St. Kliment Ohridski, Bulgaria
Alexandre Veronese, University of Brasilia, Brazil
Ali Fawaz Shareef, The Maldives National University, Maldives
Anastasija Nikiforova, University of Tartu, Estonia
Anna Lewandowska, University of Information Technology and Management, Poland
Boong Yeol Ryoo, Missouri Western State University, USA
Boyan Bontchev, Sofia University St. Kl. Ohridski, Bulgaria
Bruce Chien-ta Ho, National Chung Hsing University, Taiwan
Cesar Alberto Collazos, University of Cauca, Colombia
Christos Georgiadis, University of Macedonia, Greece
Christos Kalloniatis, University of The Aegean, Greece
Chun Kit Lok, The University of Hong Kong, Hong Kong
Daniel Alaez Gomez, Public University of Navarra, Spain
David Cabrero Souto, University of A Coruña, Spain
Dessislava Vassileva, Sofia University “st. Kliment Ohridski”, Bulgaria
Dorina Kabakchieva, University of National and World Economy, Bulgaria
Egbert Sánchez Vanderkast, National Autonomuos University of Mexico, Mexico
Eliza Stefanova, Sofia University, Bulgaria
Elvis Mazzoni, University of Bologna, Italy
Eugenia Kovatcheva, University of Library Studies and Information Technologies, Bulgaria
Faton Shabani, University of Tetova, Albania
Fausto Fasano, Università Degli Studi del Molise, Italy
Gen-Yih Liao, Chang Gung University, Taiwan
George Tsihrintzis, University of Piraeus, Greece
George S. Ioannidis, University of Patras, Greece
Grzegorz Protaziuk, Warsaw University of Technology, Poland
Gunter Saake, Otto-von-Guericke-University Magdeburg, Germany
Haluk Unaldi, Paradigma Consultancy, Turkey
Hans Weigand, Tilburg University, Netherlands
Helen Liu, National Taiwan University, Taiwan
Hiroyuki Mitsuhara, Tokushima University, Japan
Horatiu Dragomirescu, Bucharest University of Economic Studies, Romania
Ida Bifulco, University of Salerno, Italy

KEYNOTE LECTURE

ETHICAL CHALLENGES OF AI

by Professor Laurence Brooks
Information School, University of Sheffield, United Kingdom

Abstract

Artificial Intelligence (AI) is fast becoming one of the issues of the first quarter of the 21st century. It is fast reaching ubiquity, with the technology that supports it developing at an incredibly fast rate and already embedded in every aspect of our lives. At the same time AI is seen as having to potential to be both the liberating force that enables us to live better and more prosperous lives and the 'terminator' style overlord and oppressor that is going to subjugate humanity. The reality is of course that we are still a long way off from AI being able to take on either of those roles. However, as a ubiquitous technology, with it's own failings (notably bias introduced from poor data training sets, or lack of insight into the implications of using these technologies), what is clear is that we have a number of ethical challenges presented by the use of any one AI in any one specific context. Stephen Hawking notably said in 2016 at the inauguration of the Cambridge Leverhulme Centre for the Future of Intelligence "The rise of powerful AI will be either the best, or the worst thing, ever to happen to humanity. We do not yet know which." For me, this shows that we have choices which we can make, in both the development and use of AI technologies. The key issues are how we should be using AI, as opposed to how we can… to make the world a better place, while not making things worse.

TUTORIAL

EXPANDING YOUR RESEARCH WITH TEXT MINING AND TOPIC MODELLING

Azar Shahgholian[1] and Eyyüb Can Odacıoğlu[2]
The University of Manchester, UK
[1]Alliance Manchester Business School
[2]Civil Engineering and Management

Abstract

This tutorial will cover the major techniques for mining and analysing textual data to discover interesting patterns, extract useful knowledge, and support decision-making. We introduce a generic approach that can be applied to any text dataset with a minimum of effort. Attendees will learn the basic concepts, principles, and major algorithms in text mining and their potential applications.
Detailed analysis of textual data requires understanding of natural language processing, data pre-processing and manipulation and finally applying an appropriate text mining technique. The technique we focus on in this tutorial is Topic Modelling such as Latent Dirichlet Allocation (LDA), which is trending in recent research publications. We will use examples in Python since it provides rich libraries for different stages of analysis and optimisation. Having completed the tutorial, you will appreciate the capabilities for enriching the type of research you can conduct and the range of research questions you can answer. Indeed, information extraction and analysis are increasingly becoming mainstream research tools in contemporary science.

The objectives of this tutorial are as follows:

- Understand the concept of text mining and its underlying mechanisms.
- Consider a range of text mining approaches, such as information extraction and name entity identification, suited to extracting different kinds of information from social media data sources.
- Apply basic natural language processing methods as the first step in any text mining project.
- Understand Topic Modelling, the LDA algorithm, and its role in expanding the range of research questions.
- Learn how to interpret the Topic Modelling results.

Keywords: Natural Language Processing, Text Mining, Topic Modeling, Information Extraction, Research

Full Papers

DRIVING INNOVATION THROUGH CUSTOM SOFTWARE ADOPTION IN SME: A CASE STUDY IN THE CONSTRUCTION INDUSTRY

Antonio Miloso[1], Marco De Marco[1], Paolo Fantozzi[2], Luigi Laura[1] and Marco Parrillo[1]
[1]*International Telematic University Uninettuno, Rome, Italy*
[2]*LUMSA University, Rome, Italy*

ABSTRACT

This study examines the adoption of a custom software application for document management in a small-to-medium enterprise (SME) in the construction industry. Using the Unified Theory of Acceptance and Use of Technology (UTAUT), the research identifies key factors influencing adoption, such as performance expectancy, effort expectancy, social influence, and facilitating conditions. While specialists reported increased efficiency, operators found the added tasks burdensome, resulting in mixed adoption outcomes. The study emphasizes the role of technology adoption in fostering digitalization and innovation and highlights the importance of aligning interventions with workflows, responsive technical support, and tailored strategies for different roles. Through qualitative interviews, it provides insights into the benefits and challenges of the software, contributing to the literature on technology adoption in SMEs.

KEYWORDS

Innovation, Digitalization, Technology Adoption, UTAUT, Construction Industry

1. INTRODUCTION

In the construction industry, where adherence to traditional practices has historically prevailed, technology adoption serves as a cornerstone for driving digital transformation. Traditionally characterized by resistance to change and a reliance on established methodologies and manual processes, the construction sector presents a unique opportunity to investigate how digital innovation can overcome entrenched inefficiencies and foster productivity.

Europe's construction sector faces additional challenges, including a fragmented industry structure and limited digital skills among the workforce. These barriers exacerbate the complexity of integrating innovative technologies, particularly within small-to-medium enterprises (SMEs), which often lack the resources and strategic frameworks required to implement comprehensive digital solutions. As a result, understanding the mechanisms and factors influencing technology adoption in this context becomes critical for designing interventions that align with organizational workflows and industry-specific needs.

By leveraging the Unified Theory of Acceptance and Use of Technology (UTAUT) as a framework, this study examines how technology adoption acts as a critical enabler of digital transformation, aligning organizational processes with modern demands for productivity and competitiveness (Ershadi and Lijauco, 2024). The integration of custom IS solutions not only addresses traditional inefficiencies but also catalyzes innovation by transforming workflows, enhancing data accuracy, and fostering cross-functional collaboration. These advancements highlight the potential for digital transformation to reshape an industry often hesitant to adopt new practices, demonstrating that targeted technological interventions can successfully bridge the gap between traditional and modern methodologies.

This study focuses on the adoption of a custom software application within a small-to-medium enterprise (SME) in the construction sector, designed to improve the process of producing certifying documentation. This certifying documentation is a collection of documents provided by the company to its clients, certifying the quality of the interventions performed and justifying the costs. A key element of this documentation is the

Intervention Report, a document created for each intervention that includes specific identifying details and images related to the intervention itself.

Two distinct user groups played critical roles in this adoption process: the specialized on-site technicians, referred to as operators, and the back-office technicians, referred to as specialists. Operators are responsible for completing tasks in the field, while specialists manage the certification process in the office, ensuring that all necessary documentation is accurately produced and delivered to clients.

By applying the UTAUT model, this research investigates how key factors, such as Performance Expectancy, Effort Expectancy, Social Influence, and Facilitating Conditions, impacted the adoption of the new software among operators and specialists. The study highlights the importance of aligning technology solutions with the distinct needs and workflows of these two user groups, as well as the critical role of peer influence and technical support in driving successful technology adoption.

This research aims to address the following research questions:

What are the challenges associated with adopting new technologies in SMEs operating in the construction sector?

1. How do user expectations and organizational support influence technology adoption?
2. What strategies can improve the alignment of technology solutions with business workflows?
3. How does organizational culture impact the success of technology adoption?
4. What role does technical support play in facilitating effective technology integration?

By addressing these questions, this research aims to provide actionable insights for both businesses and scholars, offering strategies for overcoming the barriers to technology integration in the construction industry, where traditional mindsets have often hindered progress.

2. BODY OF PAPER

2.1 Technology Adoption and Its Importance for Businesses

Technology adoption refers to the process by which individuals or organizations decide to start using a particular technology. This phenomenon is crucial for businesses because adopting new technologies often determines their ability to innovate, remain competitive, and optimize processes. As technology permeates every aspect of business operations, understanding the factors that influence its adoption is essential for ensuring that technological investments provide tangible benefits (Hu et al., 1999).

However, technology adoption is not merely about implementing new tools; it is also a critical enabler of innovation. Innovation, in this context, involves the rethinking and redesigning of existing processes, products, or services to create value and drive organizational transformation. Studies have shown that adopting innovative technologies often leads to process improvements, enhanced efficiency, and competitive advantage (Legner et al., 2017; Olanipekun and Sutrisna, 2021). For example, digital transformation initiatives in SMEs have been linked to the ability to integrate customer demands with advanced technological solutions, thereby enabling rapid adaptation to market changes (Chen, 2023).

Furthermore, advanced data-driven methods, such as those leveraging AI applications for business intelligence or operational support, play a crucial role in enhancing decision-making and creating value. For instance, neural networks have been employed to extract complex information from documents, effectively enriching organizational knowledge bases (De Marco et al., 2021; De Marco et al., 2021; Camerlingo et al., 2024).

The adoption process, however, is not automatic. Even efficient technologies may face resistance if users do not perceive a clear value in using them or encounter barriers during implementation. This resistance can be a significant bottleneck in the innovation process, as successfully navigating user perceptions and experiences is critical for ensuring the overall effectiveness of the technology (Venkatesh et al., 2003). Moreover, research highlights that innovation-driven technology adoption often requires a cultural shift within organizations, emphasizing the alignment of organizational goals with technological potential (Mitropoulos and Tatum, 1999).

The significance of technology adoption as a driver of innovation has led researchers to explore the factors influencing user behavior, from psychological aspects to organizational conditions. Among the key models developed to understand this phenomenon is the Unified Theory of Acceptance and Use of Technology (UTAUT), which synthesizes insights from previous models to provide a comprehensive framework for studying technology adoption (Venkatesh et al., 2003). UTAUT not only helps explain user acceptance but also offers insights into how technologies can serve as catalysts for organizational innovation, fostering new ways of working and reshaping traditional business practices.

2.2 The UTAUT Model and Its Variables

The Unified Theory of Acceptance and Use of Technology (UTAUT), developed by Venkatesh and Davis (2003), consolidates various theoretical frameworks to explain how users come to accept and use technology. UTAUT identifies four main constructs that directly influence user behavior: Performance Expectancy, Effort Expectancy, Social Influence, and Facilitating Conditions.

Performance Expectancy refers to the degree to which a person believes that using the technology will help them improve job performance. This is often the most significant factor influencing technology adoption, as users are more likely to adopt a system they perceive as beneficial to their work.

Effort Expectancy relates to the perceived ease of use of the technology. Technologies that are easier to use or require less cognitive effort are more likely to be adopted, as users generally prefer solutions that do not introduce significant barriers to their workflow.

Social Influence addresses how the perceptions of peers, supervisors, or societal expectations affect an individual's decision to adopt a technology. This variable is particularly important in organizational settings, where group norms and managerial endorsement can play a significant role in encouraging or discouraging adoption.

Facilitating Conditions concern the infrastructure and support systems in place to help users implement the technology. These include access to resources, technical support, and training. If users feel that they have sufficient support, they are more likely to adopt the technology.

UTAUT also includes moderating variables, such as age, gender, experience, and voluntariness, which can influence the strength of the relationships between the core constructs and user behavior. The model has proven effective in predicting technology adoption across various settings, from workplace systems to consumer technologies (Alghatrifi and Khalid, 2019; Chand and Kumar, 2024; Has, 2016).

Research on technology adoption in Small and Medium-sized Enterprises (SMEs) within the construction sector has been extensively reviewed in recent literature. A critical gap identified in these studies is the tendency to focus on individual technologies, rather than examining the broader adoption process. This has limited the understanding of the organizational dynamics at play during technology adoption, as most research relies on a diffusion model (let it happen) rather than a dissemination model (make it happen), primarily focusing on customers rather than vendors (Sepasgozar et al., 2016). This highlights a need for research to shift from individual to organizational perspectives, as most decisions related to technology implementation in construction firms occur at the organizational level (Chen, 2023; Mitropoulos and Tatum, 1999).

Studies like those by Mitropoulos and Tatum (1999) have similarly emphasized the critical role of managerial decision-making in the adoption of new technologies by construction firms, often influenced by external pressures such as client demands. However, research also shows that management's conservative attitudes can hinder the adoption of innovations like 3D CAD and BIM (Chen, 2023). This underscores the need for stronger internal push strategies, aligning with Sepasgozar's call for a comprehensive framework that accounts for customer-vendor interactions in technology dissemination (Sepasgozar et al., 2016).

Despite these barriers, success stories from SMEs adopting digital technologies highlight the critical role of management commitment and the strategic use of collaboration. Firms that prioritize digital leadership and foster a culture of innovation are more likely to overcome the initial hurdles associated with technology adoption (Chen, 2023). Furthermore, external factors such as government incentives, regulatory frameworks, and industry standards are key to driving wider adoption among construction SMEs (Mitropoulos and Tatum, 1999). By addressing these gaps, future research can provide more actionable insights into how SMEs in the construction industry can better navigate technology adoption. This shift would enable not just customers but also vendors to effectively engage in the process of innovation dissemination, ultimately leading to higher rates of technological integration in the sector (Sepasgozar et al., 2016).

3. METHODOLOGY

The chosen methodology for analyzing this business case is qualitative, offering deep insights into how a new software tool is perceived and integrated into organizational workflows. This approach enables a nuanced understanding of factors influencing technology adoption in SMEs.

Data collection involved semi-structured interviews with four operators and two specialists, focusing on the adoption of the custom software and its organizational impact. Questions were adapted from the Unified Theory of Acceptance and Use of Technology (UTAUT) framework by Venkatesh et al. (2003) to align with qualitative analysis. Quantitative UTAUT questions were rephrased into open-ended prompts, encouraging detailed responses on Performance Expectancy, Effort Expectancy, Social Influence, and Facilitating Conditions. Redundant questions were eliminated to avoid repetition and ensure participant engagement.

Interviews occurred in two phases: first, operators were interviewed after two months of using the mobile application on tablets for field data input; then, specialists were interviewed after two months of using the desktop version for back-office tasks. Each session lasted 20-35 minutes, was audio-recorded with consent, and transcribed for thematic analysis. Thematic analysis identified recurring themes related to workflow impact, collaboration, and productivity, structured around UTAUT constructs. This qualitative approach, tailored to the interview context, provides a solid foundation for understanding software adoption dynamics in SMEs, ensuring comprehensive and relevant data collection.

4. CASE ANALYSIS

4.1 Company Context and Information Process

In the case study under examination, an experiment was conducted to assess the adoption of a custom software application. The company involved is a small-to-medium enterprise (SME) operating in the construction industry. Its field operations are highly specialized, and the on-site technicians are well-trained to perform these tasks. Moreover, every intervention carried out by the company requires certification to ensure quality, regulatory compliance, and for reporting and accountability purposes.

Each operator, in addition to receiving specific training in material handling, is equipped with a tablet to input the necessary data for the certification of each intervention. To manage the information provided by the operators, the company has a back-office team responsible for analyzing incoming data, handling anomalies, and managing atypical interventions.

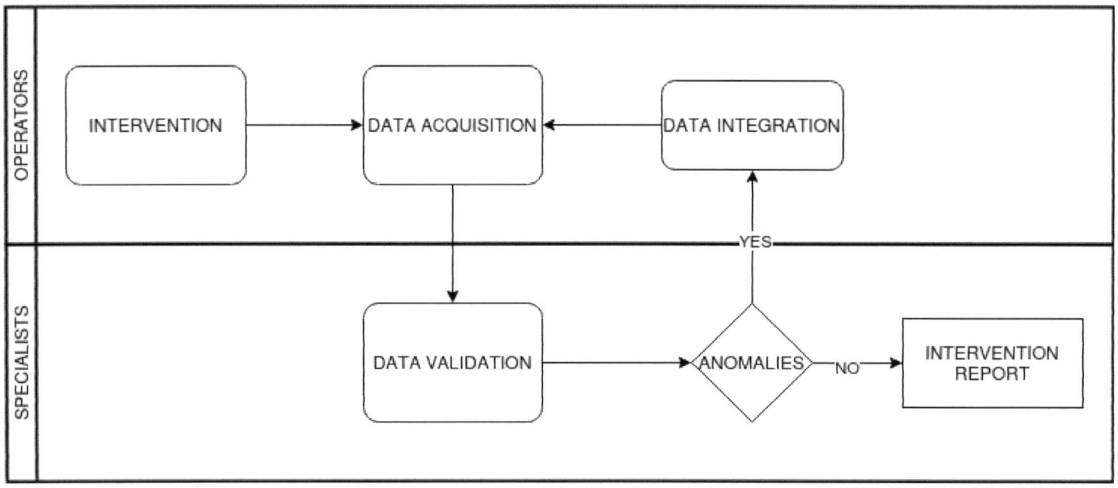

Figure 1. Process before the technology adoption

As depicted in Figure 1, the certification process is structured into several stages:

1. Intervention: Field operators complete an intervention, gathering essential information.
2. Data Acquisition: Operators record the relevant details using a tablet, facilitating the transfer of information to the back-office team.
3. Data Validation: The data received is analyzed by specialists to ensure its accuracy.
4. Data Integration: In cases of anomalies, data is corrected or integrated through collaboration between operators and specialists.
5. Intervention Report: Once no anomalies are detected, specialists generate the final certification documentation.

The frequent occurrence of unique interventions makes full automation of the process challenging. However, the custom application has significantly improved document production efficiency, allowing operators to systematically collect data during the Data Acquisition stage illustrated in the figure. Specialists, in turn, focus on managing anomalies and producing the Intervention Report, thus completing the certification process.

The second critical stage is the data processing required for document production. This phase is only partially automatable, as some of the decisions require human judgment regarding the intervention. This limits the extent to which technology can streamline the process however it can still offer support to the decision making process.

To improve document production efficiency, the chosen solution was the development of a custom application for creating "Intervention Report". These forms are specific documents that must be generated for every intervention and are essential components of the certification documentation.

Data acquisition occurs once an intervention is completed by the operator, meaning that the generation of the Intervention Report can either happen at the moment of data entry by the operator or later during back-office data processing for document production.

The introduction of a custom software application aimed to streamline the certification process within the company. As part of the implementation, we conducted qualitative interviews with both operators and specialists to assess the impact of the new system. By analyzing the feedback from both roles, we aim to evaluate how the software was adopted in practice and how it influenced the division of tasks between operators and back-office specialists. The following section summarizes the key findings from these interviews, providing insights into the adoption process.

4.2 Interviews

The following section summarizes key insights from the qualitative interviews conducted, based on the core constructs of the Unified Theory of Acceptance and Use of Technology (UTAUT). Participants provided detailed feedback regarding their experiences with the application, focusing on usage patterns, challenges, and perceived benefits. The findings are structured according to the latent constructs of UTAUT: Actual Use Behavior, Performance Expectancy, Effort Expectancy, Social Influence, and Facilitating Conditions. The interviewees were divided into two main categories based on their roles within the organization: operators and specialists.

4.2.1 Operators

The operators complete 10 interventions on average, for each of those interventions they perform 5 minutes to collect and send all the required data to the back office. However, the steps following the generation of the form resulted to be more time-consuming since the compilation of the form took approximately between 10 to 15 minutes to complete. Operators must retrieve the form and attach the relevant data, which is then sent to the back-office specialists for documentation production. This additional layer of work was reported as burdensome and extended the time needed to send data.

Contrary to expectations, the application has not improved productivity for operators. Instead, it has lengthened the process of sending data to the back office. While the tool could be helpful if operators were responsible for creating forms from scratch, this is not typically part of their role. As a result, operators feel the application has added complexity without offering significant productivity gains.

The application was considered relatively user-friendly after initial difficulties related to navigating between forms for data entry were addressed. Once users became familiar with the workflow, the process became more streamlined. However, certain elements of the UI were deemed unintuitive, particularly in terms of how the system handled data visualization and user interaction during data uploads. Specifically, issues related to the organization of interactive elements and the overall layout were noted, impacting the UX. These design flaws required additional navigation steps, detracting from the efficiency and accessibility of key functions.

When encountering problems, operators frequently relied on informal peer support within the office. This collaborative approach helped them troubleshoot and resolve issues. However, this reliance on peer assistance also highlighted the limitations of the system's UX, as the need for external guidance indicated areas where the interface failed to facilitate intuitive task completion. Additionally, many operators viewed the application as an added layer of complexity, contributing to workload rather than alleviating it, which negatively impacted the overall perception of the software in the workplace.This collective approach to the tool can be interpreted as a typical challenge in innovation processes, often met with resistance when the organizational culture, shaped in this case by prevailing industry paradigms, is not fully aligned with the adoption of new tools and, consequently, the changes they bring.

Technical support from the dedicated team was reported as slow, with responses typically taking up to a day, which was not conducive to the operators' workflow. The lack of immediate assistance, coupled with the technical team's inability to fully resolve certain issues, led to delays in task completion. These shortcomings in both UI design and technical support infrastructure contributed to user frustration and hindered the smooth adoption of the application.

4.2.2 Specialists

Interviewed specialists varied in their frequency of use of the application since most of the work was handled by a single one of them after the adoption of the software. One user initially used the software daily for over an hour at a time but shifted to more sporadic use after a colleague took over responsibility for the Intervention Report production task. Another user kept the application open throughout the day, using it intermittently for up to two hours depending on the task load. The custom software application significantly reduced the time required for documentation, fostering a paradigm shift in the certification process, which previously relied on manual practices. Despite regular use, minor technical issues, such as occasional system crashes during image uploads, were reported. These crashes, however, were infrequent and did not significantly impact overall productivity.

Both interviewees noted a significant increase in productivity due to the application. One user mentioned that the task of processing 100 Intervention Reports took two and a half days while now it was completed in just 20 minutes. Similarly, the second user highlighted that the application helped halve the time required to complete tasks once they became familiar with it. This accelerated workflow allowed users to handle tasks much more efficiently, allowing the specialists to invest the time gained in other tasks.

The ease of learning the application was universally praised. Users reported that it took very little time to become proficient, with one participant noting they mastered the application in about 20 minutes. Another participant echoed this sentiment, stating that the application was "very intuitive" and required minimal instruction to use effectively.

Social support played a key role in the adoption of the application. One user mentioned receiving initial guidance from a colleague before becoming self-sufficient. Similarly, another participant noted that their early experience was supported by a colleague, after which they independently navigated the system. The application was generally well-received by the broader professional community, with users perceiving it as a major improvement over previous manual processes.

The technical support available to users was highlighted as a critical resource. Both interviewees expressed satisfaction with the support provided, particularly when they encountered technical issues that they could not resolve independently. The presence of a responsive technical support team was instrumental in ensuring the application's smooth operation and quick resolution of any problems, reinforcing its seamless integration into existing workflows.

5. DISCUSSION

This study demonstrates how targeted technological interventions can drive digitalization, helping SMEs overcome operational barriers. However, adoption is influenced by challenges such as organizational resistance, workflow disruptions, and user expectations. While specialists recognized the software's potential, operators faced difficulties, highlighting the need for tailored change management strategies that consider both technical and human factors.

Key challenges in construction-sector SMEs include resistance to change, limited digital skills, and industry fragmentation. Operators experienced increased workloads due to additional software responsibilities, disrupting workflows and causing frustration, exacerbated by delayed technical support. The sector's traditional culture further fueled resistance, emphasizing the importance of addressing both cultural and operational barriers. User expectations and organizational support significantly affected adoption. Specialists, whose tasks aligned with the software's design, reported increased productivity. However, operators expected seamless integration, and unmet expectations led to dissatisfaction. Managing expectations through clear communication, tailored training, and strong organizational support is essential for fostering acceptance and engagement. Aligning technology with business workflows emerged as a crucial factor. Involving end-users in software design ensures practical usability, with simplified interfaces, intuitive navigation, and adaptive features reducing resistance. Feedback loops during early deployment help identify and address pain points, facilitating a smoother transition. Organizational culture plays a pivotal role in adoption. Peer influence among specialists fostered engagement, while operator dissatisfaction, due to increased workloads and workflow disruptions, hindered adoption. Shifting towards an innovation-driven culture through clear communication and incentives can enhance engagement and adoption rates. Technical support is critical in shaping user experiences. While specialists found support adequate, operators required immediate assistance to maintain workflows, revealing gaps in the support structure. More responsive systems, complemented by comprehensive manuals, tutorials, and training sessions, can mitigate these challenges and improve future implementations.

6. CONCLUSION

For construction companies, traditionally characterized by a conservative mindset, technology adoption presents a key opportunity for innovation. This study highlights how applying the UTAUT model can identify critical aspects of technology adoption within corporate contexts. Understanding corporate culture (Social Influence) and analyzing business processes (Performance Improvement) are essential for successfully integrating enabling technologies.

Findings indicate that resistance to change, limited digital skills, and inadequate technical support are major obstacles. Overcoming resistance requires fostering a culture of collaboration, involving stakeholders in decision-making, and clearly communicating benefits and expectations. Structured engagement and transparent dialogue can further ease concerns and encourage organizational buy-in.

Organizational culture plays a dual role, both facilitating and hindering adoption. Peer influence can create a supportive environment, but dissatisfaction may spread if new technologies disrupt workflows. Companies should manage these dynamics by incentivizing early adopters, sharing success stories, and implementing feedback mechanisms to enhance adoption rates.

Technical support is crucial for seamless technology integration. Future implementations should prioritize responsive support systems, particularly for field operators needing timely assistance. Accessible resources like online knowledge bases, video tutorials, and real-time troubleshooting can improve the adoption process. Proactive support measures, such as automated diagnostics, can further enhance user experience.

By demonstrating how tailored software fosters process innovation, this study contributes to SME digitalization. Future strategies should align technology deployment with diverse organizational roles, ensuring tangible benefits. A holistic approach, addressing technical, cultural, and operational aspects, is essential for driving sustained innovation and competitiveness in the construction industry.

REFERENCES

Alghatrifi, I., Khalid, H., (2019). A systematic review of UTAUT and UTAUT2 as a baseline framework of information system research in adopting new technology: a case study of IPV6 adoption, in: 2019 6th International Conference on Research and Innovation in Information Systems (ICRIIS). IEEE, pp. 1–6.

Chand, S.S., Kumar, B.A., (2024). Applying the UTAUT Model to Understand M-payment Adoption. A Case Study of Western Part of Fiji. J. Knowl. Econ. https://doi.org/10.1007/s13132-023-01722-x

Chen, S., (2023). Digital Transformation in the Construction Industry: A Systematic Literature Review, in: Proceedings of the 2023 9th International Conference on Industrial and Business Engineering. Presented at the ICIBE 2023: 2023 the 9th International Conference on Industrial and Business Engineering, ACM, Beijing China, pp. 235–244. https://doi.org/10.1145/3629378.3629431

De Marco, M., Fantozzi, P., Fornaro, C., Laura, L., Miloso, A., (2021a). Cognitive analytics management of the customer lifetime value: an artificial neural network approach. J. Enterp. Inf. Manag. 34, 679–696.

De Marco, M., Fantozzi, P., Laura, L., Miloso, A., (2021b). AI-Powered Curricula Selection: A Neural Network Approach Suited for Small and Medium Companies, in: Ceci, F., Prencipe, A., Spagnoletti, P. (Eds.), Exploring Innovation in a Digital World, Lecture Notes in Information Systems and Organisation. Springer International Publishing, Cham, pp. 11–20. https://doi.org/10.1007/978-3-030-87842-9_2

Camerlingo, G., Fantozzi, P., Laura, L., Parrillo, M. (2024). Teaching Neural Networks Using Comic Strips. In: Herodotou, C., et al. Methodologies and Intelligent Systems for Technology Enhanced Learning, 14th International Conference. MIS4TEL 2024. Lecture Notes in Networks and Systems, vol 1171. Springer, Cham. https://doi.org/10.1007/978-3-031-73538-7_1

Ershadi, M., Lijauco, F., (2024). A framework for digitalizing construction businesses: drivers, barriers and outcomes. Smart Sustain. Built Environ. ahead-of-print. https://doi.org/10.1108/SASBE-01-2024-0003

Has, M.N., (2016). Examining factors influencing webinar adoption using UTAUT model (Case study at distance learning program, ABC University, Bandung-Indonesia 2016), in: 2016 IEEE Asia Pacific Conference on Wireless and Mobile (APWiMob). IEEE, pp. 52–58.

Hu, P.J., Chau, P.Y.K., Sheng, O.R.L., Tam, K.Y., (1999). Examining the Technology Acceptance Model Using Physician Acceptance of Telemedicine Technology. J. Manag. Inf. Syst. 16, 91–112. https://doi.org/10.1080/07421222.1999.11518247

Legner, C., Eymann, T., Hess, T., Matt, C., Böhmann, T., Drews, P., Mädche, A., Urbach, N., Ahlemann, F., (2017). Digitalization: Opportunity and Challenge for the Business and Information Systems Engineering Community. Bus. Inf. Syst. Eng. 59, 301–308. https://doi.org/10.1007/s12599-017-0484-2

Mitropoulos, P., Tatum, C.B., (1999). Technology Adoption Decisions in Construction Organizations. J. Constr. Eng. Manag. 125, 330–338. https://doi.org/10.1061/(ASCE)0733-9364(1999)125:5(330)

Olanipekun, A.O., Sutrisna, M., (2021). Facilitating digital transformation in construction—a systematic review of the current state of the art. Front. Built Environ. 7, 660758.

Sepasgozar, S.M., Loosemore, M., Davis, S.R., (2016). Conceptualising information and equipment technology adoption in construction: A critical review of existing research. Eng. Constr. Archit. Manag. 23, 158–176.

Venkatesh, Morris, Davis, Davis, 2003. User Acceptance of Information Technology: Toward a Unified View. MIS Q. 27, 425. https://doi.org/10.2307/30036540

BLOCKCHAIN DIGITAL TWIN TO MODELING DATA CENTER

Marta Chinnici[1], Davide De Chiara[2], Marco Antonini[3], Guido Guarnieri[2], Giuseppe Santomauro[2], Francesco Genovese[4], Giovanni Ponti[5] and Luigi Telesca[3]
[1]*TERIN-ICT Division, HPC Lab, ENEA, R.C. Casaccia, Italy*
[2]*TERIN-ICT Division, HPC Lab, ENEA, R.C. Portici, Italy*
[3]*Trakti Ltd., United Kingdom*
[4]*TERIN-ICT Division, ENEA, R.C. Casaccia, Italy*
[5]*TERIN-ICT Division, ENEA, Sede, Italy*

ABSTRACT

Data Center (DC) 's energy consumption has skyrocketed due to the surge in digital technology, services, and associated applications. By 2030, they are expected to consume 13% of the global energy demand, potentially up to 21%, and release 8% of the associated global carbon emissions. This can lead to significant operational costs, power security impacts, and environmental threats. Prior heuristics, statistics, and engineering approaches are ineffective in improving energy efficiency because of the sheer number of configurations, non-linear parameter interactions, and vast amounts of operating data. Hence, optimizing a DC, particularly the class of High-Performance Computing (HPC) clusters, is a significant concern. Integrating the IoT, sensors, and intelligent devices has significantly contributed to generating vast operational management data from various aspects of the DC industry. Indeed, effectively modeling and processing this data could improve energy efficiency, ensure reliability, reduce operating costs, and sustainably manage DC. This study proposes a holistic approach based on Blockchain Digital Twin, augmented by Artificial Intelligence (AI) processed data to represent the DC physical complex system in virtual and tokenized models. The objective is to obtain near-real-time prediction, optimization, monitoring, controlling and improved decision-making. In detail, the methodology, the architecture and steps taken to develop a scalable analytical dashboard in Blockchain are shown. The pioneering Blockchain DC Digital Twin approach is experimented with in a real infrastructural setting; ENEA HPC Cluster namely CRESCO7 learns from actual operational data and allows the management, monitoring, and control in real-time visualization of the whole DC, thus allowing coverage of the DC status and the optimization of its functionalities. The authors also aim to show the achieved benefits of the Blockchain Digital Twin DC challenge for various stakeholders.

KEYWORDS

Digital Twin, Data Center, HPC, Energy Efficiency, Data Science, AI

1. INTRODUCTION

Data Centers (DCs) are the backbone of the ever-increasing need for reliable and scalable data processing, storage, and networking capabilities to support businesses and individual users. With the rapid growth in demand for digital services and associated applications, DCs have become ubiquitous, which underpins the ever-growing digitization. In the meantime, they pose significant threats in terms of both energy costs and the associated carbon emissions (Vafamehr et al., 2018). The current global energy consumption of DCs is estimated to be approximately 3%. According to Andrae (Andrae et al., 2015) and the late update in 2019 (Andrae et al., 2019), given the rapid pace of digitization, if necessary, actions are not taken, DCs are expected to consume 21% of the global demand by 2030. Regarding environmental issues, DCs are estimated to contribute 0.3% of global carbon emissions annually (Jones et al., 2018) and are expected to increase to 8% by 2030 (Cao et al., 2022). Optimizing the energy efficiency of DCs, and in particular, High-Performance Computing (HPC) clusters, is, therefore, a significant concern. Demand for computing resources and thus energy demand for High HPC is steadily increasing while the energy market transforms to renewable energy and faces significant price increases (Kostenko et al, 2020; Gartner, 2019; Uddin et al., 2015; Shuja et al., 2026; Liu et al., 2014). This paper presents the creation of a Blockchain Digital Twin framework for analyzing and reducing energy consumption and computing resources optimization of a real-world HPC system. The Digital Twin approach leverages the innovative HPC cluster at the Italian National Agency for New Technologies, Energy and Sustainable Economic Development (ENEA)- HPC cluster called Cresco7 in R.C. Portici, Italy. The Digital Twin framework receives information from multiple internal and external data sources to cover the different optimization opportunities, to represent physical assets and intangible resources in Blockchain and to tokenize the infrastructure favoring more accountable and sustainable consumption of the HPC resources. The Digital Twin also consists of a scheduling simulation framework that uses the data from the Digital Twin and real-world job traces to test the influence of the different parameters on the HPC cluster. The authors develop an analytical reporting system, "Analytical Dashboard", for operation and energy management based on a data-driven AI-based framework for modeling DC efficiency that learns from actual operational data (Chinnici et al, 2023; Chinnici et al., 2022; Grishina et al., 2020; Chinnici et al., 2020). The dashboard will allow the management, monitoring, and (near) real-time visualization of data related to real DC using Blockchain technology. Technology solution to implement the analytical dashboard: the hardware and software resources have been modelled as a Digital Twin. Blockchain and Tokenization technologies will be used to allocate computing resources (HPC loads) to optimize or efficiently distribute infrastructure energy consumption across various activities. Our approach, which is exhaustively trained and tested using real operational data obtained from the ENEA-HPC DC, CRESCO7 cluster, leverages the unique features of the Digital Twin approach. This promising method not only provides physical characteristics of the DC system but also dynamically adjusts scene parameters through programming. As a result, it generates numerous samples to assist model training and improve fault tolerance. According to Gartner (Gartner, 2019), the proliferation of Digital twins in industries, especially when combined with AI technology, will enable open, connected, and coordinated intelligent spaces. The seamless connection and real-time data exchange between the physical and Digital Twin allow us to conduct real-time energy consumption simulation and energy-saving control. Therefore, the combination of AI technology and Blockchain technology to build the Digital Twin is conducive to researching adaptive, intelligent, and fault-tolerant DCs energy saving schemes in a more flexible and dynamic way. To realize green and safe DCs, a novel energy-saving solution is proposed in this paper. With its real-time management, monitoring, and control capabilities, the Digital Twin DC approach provides a comprehensive visualization of the entire DC, enabling the coverage of the DC status and the optimization of its functionalities. We also aim to demonstrate the potential benefits of the Digital Twin DC challenge to stakeholders. Utilizing Blockchain to tokenize High-Performance Computing (HPC) assets and implement Smart Contracts has significantly enhanced transparency, demonstrated by a 40% increase in cost visibility for shared resources. This technology enables real-time resource accounting and robust process control, aligning HPC operations with strict Environmental, Social, and Governance (ESG) criteria, essential for organizations committed to meeting rigorous ESG standards. The remainder of this paper is organized as follows: Section 2 describes the methodology and architecture for building the Digital Twin Data Center using a holistic approach and results; Section 3 provides the authors' conclusions.

1.1 Digital Twin: An Enabler for Holistic Approach

Data Center, for its complex nature, has a dual role in the implementation of Digital Twins:

1. To support the creation and management of Digital Twin (DT)

b. To become a Digital Twin to provide a virtual representation of the whole process within to manage data consumption and optimizing processing.

Using the Digital Twin definition - "Digital twin can be defined as a virtual representation of a physical asset enabled through data and simulators for real-time prediction, optimization, monitoring, controlling, and improved decision-making" – the holistic approach, illustrated in Figure 1, is proposed. The baseline of Data Center HPC.

In detail, the approach consists of 3 pillars:

1. Virtual Twin: Creation of a virtual representation of a physical asset or a device – mathematical models &computer science are used to support the creation.

2. Predictive Twin: Physics-based data-driven or hybrid models operating on the virtual twin to predict the behavior of the physical asset – AI&ML techniques are used to analyze the data coming to the physical model.

3. Twin Projection: Integration of insight generated by the predictive twin in operations and processes – value additions of digital twin are identified, e.g. predictive maintenance, operational strategy, optimization strategy, energy efficiency, and also time-remote monitoring and control, more excellent safety, risk assessment, more efficient and informed decision support system.

The proposed Digital Twin is an enabler for a holistic approach to improve energy efficiency and sustainability issues in HPC data centers using Blockchain technology. To address the overfitting problem caused by insufficient samples, the authors implemented a holistic approach based on asset Tokenization, analytic Blockchain solution and AI. The experimental phase is conduct on ENEA-HPC Cluster namely CRESCO 7 with 1,4 PetaFLOPS.

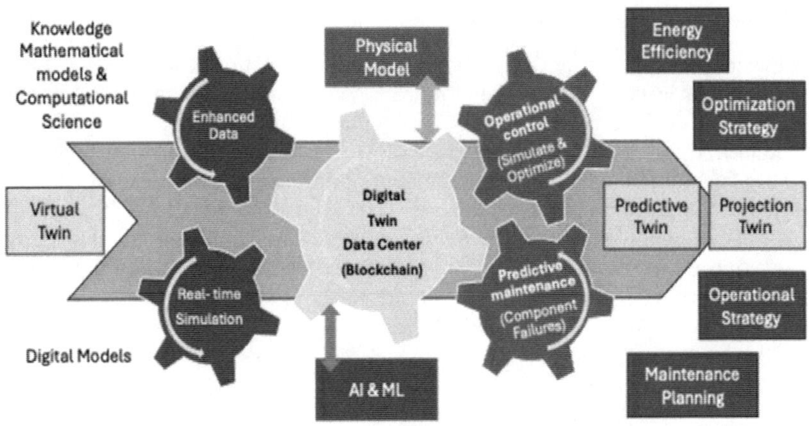

Figure 1. Digital Twin an enabler for holistic approach

2. METHODOLOGY

The methodology adopted in this work for creating a more advanced Digital Twin model involved the usage of AI to enhance and refine raw data from ENEA HPC (CRESCO7) systems for integration into a Blockchain framework, culminating in a tokenized representation of HPC resources.

The holistic, multifaceted approach is based on has been broken down into several key phases:

- **Data Collection and Preprocessing**
- **AI-Driven Data Augmentation**
- **Tokenization of HPC Resources**
- **Validation and Testing**
- **Ethical and Regulatory Compliance**

Our methodology enhances the utility of HPC data and facilitates a more granular and dynamic representation of HPC resources. This has the potential to revolutionize how these powerful computing platforms are managed and utilized, offering stakeholders a glimpse into the future of HPC resource management.

2.1 Digital Twin Data Collection and Pre-processing: Augmented Data an Enabler for Holistic Approach

The virtualization of whole data centers (DCs) is becoming increasingly essential to optimize performance and reduce energy consumption. In this context, the ENEA has launched an innovative project to create a state-of-the-art HPC system, a Digital Twin of the CRESCO 7 cluster. This ambitious initiative involves extensive data collection and, for the first time, the implementation of sophisticated AI algorithms to enhance raw data and accurately simulate the real behaviors and operations of the cluster. Since 2018, we have meticulously collected data from the CRESCO 7 cluster, including:

- **Energy consumption**: Detailed records of energy use for each compute node.
- **Cooling systems**: Monitoring of performance and energy consumption of cooling units.
- **Environmental conditions**: Data on temperature and humidity around the cluster, gathered through a sensor network.
- **Meteo data**: Data coming from external climatic factors like ambient temperature, humidity, and other weather conditions
- **Workload** data: Job accounting data

Although this data collection provides a holistic view of the cluster's operations and environmental impact, more was needed to improve the efficiency, reliability, and sustainability of our HPC infrastructure.

2.1.1 Data Collection and Pre-Processing

The authors enhanced data precision by designing a data acquisition system based on Python scripts on a dedicated machine. This system processes and uploads the collected data into a MongoDB database. Python scripts leverage advanced libraries for statistics, concurrent programming, database connectivity, and data science. Data collection for CRESCO 7 employs an IPMItools utility that enables high-performance readings. Python allows for telemetry acquisition from compute nodes using multithreading and multiprocessing. The authors utilized concurrent programming because the data acquisition for CRESCO 7's compute nodes involve long-running tasks and potentially parallelizable operations. This approach enables multiple threads to read data from groups of compute nodes simultaneously, completing an entire cycle (covering all cluster nodes) in under one second. For job data (completed and running), we rely on data provided by the SLURM job scheduler using commands such as "sacct", "control", "info", and "queue". These daemons manage entities like nodes (compute resources), partitions (logical sets of nodes), jobs (user-assigned resource allocations), and job steps (sets of tasks within a job). The SLURM daemons provide real-time insights into completed and running jobs. Completed jobs, stored in MongoDB, include details on energy consumption and user data, while running jobs temporarily store instantaneous power consumption measurements, providing a snapshot of the cluster's current state. Command outputs are intercepted, processed, and encoded before being saved as MongoDB documents.

2.1.2 Environmental Monitoring

The authors evaluate environmental conditions, such as temperature and humidity, every 15 seconds in both the hot and cold aisles of the cluster, using a network of 12 professional sensors near the cluster. MongoDB stores the historical data for CRESCO 7 nodes. The authors use a professional weather station to decouple energy consumption from external climatic factors like ambient temperature, humidity, and other weather conditions (Davis Vantage PRO2). This station provides weather updates every five minutes, storing data in MongoDB. Sensors measure air temperature, humidity, rainfall, wind speed and direction, barometric pressure, and hygrometric heat indices.

2.1.3 AI for Data Analysis

Artificial intelligence has been instrumental in transforming raw data into actionable insights. Sophisticated AI algorithms, including regression analysis and random forest models, are employed to:

- **Identify patterns**: Detect trends and anomalies in energy consumption and environmental conditions.
- **Predictive modeling**: Forecast future energy consumption and optimize cooling requirements.
- **Workload optimization**: Allocate resources efficiently to balance workloads and enhance performance.

These AI models have created highly reliable simulations of the CRESCO 7 cluster's real behavior.

2.1.4 Digital Twin and Advanced Analytics

The data collection and AI analysis efforts culminated in the creation of a Digital Twin of the CRESCO 7 cluster, which performs critical functions such as:

- **Performance simulation**: Mimicking real-time operations to identify potential issues before they occur.
- **Energy optimization**: Testing configurations and cooling strategies to minimize energy consumption.

- **Resource management**: Providing insights into resource utilization and suggesting improvements for greater efficiency.

Job accounting data is constantly updated with snapshots and historical records, displayed on a Grafana dashboard designed for this purpose.

Figure 2. Real-time power consumption Dashboard

2.1.5 Thermal Imaging for Cluster Analysis

The authors use a professional thermal camera for real-time imaging, processed with custom-designed software, to:

1. Detect and prevent faults by identifying overheating risks in HPC systems.
2. Improve energy efficiency by locating hot spots and cooling and energy distribution inefficiencies.
3. Conduct advanced thermal analysis to examine HPC components and infrastructure, optimizing layouts and designs.
4. Support decision-making with accurate thermal data for maintenance, upgrades, or optimization.

Inefficient air distribution in data centers can create localized hot spots during IT equipment operations. Reducing supply/return air temperatures can eliminate hot spots but may lead to excessive energy consumption and cold spots, wasting energy. We focus on AI-driven energy consumption strategies for HPC data centers to define a holistic approach for green, automated, secure, and efficient HPC-DC operations. Continuous monitoring with a thermal camera provides a clear view of heat distribution among compute nodes.

2.2 Tokenized Digital Twin HPC-Data Center: Architecture Methodology

Thanks to the work done and data augmentation, we got very advanced data to start the design of the Digital Twin. To further enhance the management and allocation of HPC computing resources, we decided to digitize hardware and software resources using Blockchain technology for the secure representation and creation of the Digital Twin, leveraging augmented data provided by AI components. Due to its decentralized, transparent, and immutable nature, Blockchain is an ideal platform for creating digital twins. When applied to HPC resources, Blockchain provides a robust and secure way to represent the physical state and behavior of the HPC, adding usage rules via Smart Contracts and new intangible elements so we can monitor and manage computational assets comprehensively and efficiently. The use of a distributed Blockchain infrastructure and Tokenization techniques is more than just theoretical. We are actively using these tools to tokenize and account for computing resources (HPC loads) in a way that optimizes infrastructure energy consumption for the various activities (HPC jobs) activated by users. Our innovative approach involves tokenizing resources and allocating them based on workload and request patterns. This method ensures efficient and transparent resource management, aligning with the dynamic demands of modern DC operations. It's a unique solution that will revolutionize the management of HPC computing resources. In this context, to correctly represent the HPC's Digital Twin, we had to embed three main Blockchain concepts: Identity, Tokenization, and Certification. First, each physical asset, such as an HPC scheduler or node, was assigned a unique Digital Identity, which is made immutable and tamper-proof thanks to the innate properties of the Blockchain and allows precise tracking and management of each asset, facilitating high accountability and traceability. Secondly, with Tokenization, we have been converting physical assets into digital tokens that represent ownership or usage rights. This meant creating tokens representing computational power, storage capacity, and energy consumption for HPC resources. Each token can be traded, tracked, and managed on the Blockchain, transforming the otherwise intangible HPC resources into tangible digital assets. This Tokenization not only enables efficient allocation of resources but also provides a high degree of flexibility, empowering you to manage and control resource usage as per your needs, enabling us to implement a real-time, rule-based, smart-contract-centric accounting methodology that abstracts away all the complexity related to a standard accounting method with the transparency only a blockchain can provide on top of that (European Commission, 2020; European Commission, 2021). In fact, through the smart contracts, we defined the algorithm and model used to calculate the energy consumption of every single job launched on the HPC, which then gets converted into the corresponding token amount, which is then automatically charged to the user. This whole operation is done automatically as soon as the job terminates its execution, and the results are forever stored on the blockchain, easily verifiable by everyone, with clear parameters on how the calculation was done. As for the model used to calculate the consumption for each job, a custom one was thought out and tailored to this use case; the algorithm isn't a simple static mathematical formula, but it's an algorithm that also takes into consideration the nature of the environment it's being implemented in. It's reflective of the status the HPC finds itself in at runtime. This algorithm was finely tuned to promote and incentivize the user to utilize the resources being provided more efficiently and thoughtfully through a combination of incentives and penalties entirely dependent on the behavior of the job and, thus, by proxy, the behavior of the user who launched it. At a more practical and in-depth level, this translates into a calculation model that, given the unstoppable nature of the HPC nodes, aims at redistributing part of the upkeeping cost (energy consumed by the nodes themselves, energy for the cooling system, the switches and the storage stack) back to the user following the logic of common good with limited resources. On top of that, the job's behavior is also taken into account and plays a crucial role in the calculation of the final amount that the user has to pay, putting particular focus on how the resources are utilized; for example, part of the algorithm consists in calculating the CPU utilization efficiency of a job and assign a penalty if deemed too low because it's considered a waste of resources. The end goal of this algorithm is to create an independent and autonomous HPC from an economic point of view while also teaching the users how to utilize the resources more efficiently and thoughtfully. Finally, Certification refers to the issuance of digital certificates that testify to the compliance and authenticity of an asset, a computation byproduct, or, like in this case, a reward for a specific behavior. In particular, certificates are minted as a reward to the HPC for the execution of what we consider net-positive jobs; we define "net-positive jobs" as jobs that leveraged all the resources they requested (e.g. high CPU and memory efficiency) and that contributed positively to an environmental or social cause, for example, what could be a job that contributed towards medical research, to attest to the jobs' energy efficiency, operational performance, ESG criteria, and adherence to regulatory standards. For each of these jobs, we mint a certificate that stores and attests the total amount of grams of CO2 emitted by the HPC to execute the job. Afterwards, once these certificates are minted, the goal is to create a global market driven by the need of the companies to increase their own ESG score; the principle is simple, a company looking to lower their CO2 emissions is allowed to buy the ones that were generated by the HPC, for the execution of those particular jobs, as a way of offloading thus emissions from their own lowering their total CO2 emissions. At the same time, they contribute directly to the upkeep and maintenance of the HPC.

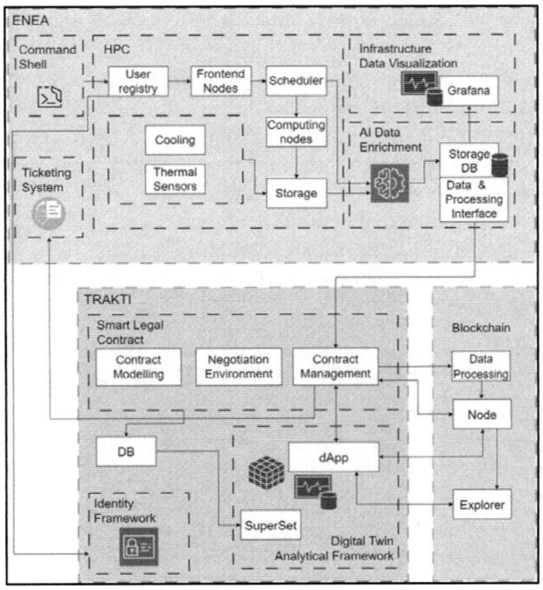

Figure 3. Digital Twin architecture

These certificates are now stored on the Blockchain, making them immutable and easily verifiable in such a way that there will never be a doubt about when the certificate was minted, as a result of what job, and how the total amount of CO2 emitted was calculated. Solidity Smart Contracts have been used to define and automate the issuance and validation of these certificates, ensuring that all stakeholders have access to reliable and trustworthy information stored using the popular ERC721 standard to represent each certificate as a Non-Fungible Token (NFT). The programmable components in Blockchain are the Smart Contracts, self-executing, distributed applications representing agreements coded on the Blockchain. They play a crucial role in this system. They automate the execution of logic and definitions, ensuring that operations such as resource allocation, cost calculation, and compliance verification are carried out automatically and transparently. This automation reduces administrative overhead and ensures that the management of HPC resources is conducted securely and verifiable. Considering all of the above, to represent the HPC architecture digitally in the Blockchain, we had to start from its core component, the scheduler. The scheduler is a pivotal component of the HPC and is responsible for managing job queues, allocating resources, and optimizing workload distribution. By replicating the scheduler's functions within a Smart Contract, we can achieve a transparent and automated system for tracking job submissions, managing execution timelines, and dynamically allocating computational resources based on availability, job priority and, potentially, a priority fee, similar to how most transaction queuing algorithm work in Blockchain. This Digital Twin of the scheduler ensures that all operations are recorded immutably on the Blockchain, allowing for real-time auditing and verification of resource usage. The transparency of this system is a testament to its trustworthiness and integrity. Furthermore, we considered additional Smart Contracts to address the intangible aspects of HPC resource management, such as job quality, efficiency, and energy consumption. By creating contracts that evaluate and rate jobs based on performance metrics like computational efficiency and execution time, we can incentivize optimal usage of HPC resources. For instance, energy efficiency contracts can monitor jobs' real-time energy consumption and reward those operating within predefined efficiency benchmarks. This promotes sustainable practices and provides tangible metrics that can be audited and verified. Certification and Tokenization further enhance the management of HPC resources. We designed Smart Contracts to issue digital certificates to jobs that meet specific efficiency and performance criteria, which are then stored on the Blockchain for transparency and verification. These certificates prove compliance with best practices, facilitating stakeholder trust and accountability. As illustrated in Figure 3, the proposed Digital Twin architecture consists of the physical space of the ENEA HPC with all the cooling and thermal sensors included, the AI engine, the infrastructure Data Visualization dashboard, the Smart Legal Contract Framework (Trakti, 2024) and finally the Blockchain node where the Digital Twin is tokenized and all the jobs are rated scored and certified. Trakti handles HPC data integration, acting as a middle layer, processing the data from MongoDB, and preparing it to be stored in the

Blockchain. It offers a way to model and deploy smart legal contracts (citation to the job) in Blockchain that are responsible for the Blockchain Digital Twin. In this specific implementation, the Smart Legal Contract not only automates and enforces the terms of resource usage but also provides a transparent and immutable record of all transactions and interactions with the HPC.

This dual role enhances the visibility and management of HPC resources, transforming intangible computational power into tangible, tokenized assets. Smart Contracts automatically enforce terms related to resource usage, such as job execution limits, cost calculations, and penalty enforcement. This automation reduces administrative overhead and ensures compliance with predefined agreements. Blockchain acts as the registry of the HPC Digital Twins, maintaining an immutable and decentralized record of all HPC resources and their utilization. This registry ensures that the digital representation of each HPC resource is accurate, up-to-date, and tamper-proof.

2.3 Operational Consideration Data Structure and Data Flow for the Creation of the Tokenized HPC Digital Twin

A comprehensive example of this system in action involves the following steps: a user submits a job to the HPC system after authenticating through the shell, and the SLURM scheduler is then responsible for the allocation of the available resources for the execution of the job or storing the job in a queue if there aren't enough resource available to execute such job. Once the job is finally executed and terminates, either positively (job terminates because he reached his goal and gracefully exits) or with an error (out of memory, a bug in the code, etc.…), the result is stored inside a MongoDB table. Throughout the execution of the said job, SLURM also gathers the energy the nodes consumed to execute the job; this data is also stored inside the same mongoDB table. Once done, the data is transferred to Trakti, which processes the raw data and prepares it to be stored in the blockchain. Then, it pushes the data to the blockchain node, which will store it in the Smart Contract. There, the Smart Contract completes the cycle, calculates the total amount of energy consumed, and retrieves the tokens from the user.

2.4 HPC Digital Twin Visualization

The Digital Twin is seamlessly integrated with an advanced dashboard system that visualizes data, providing an immersive and interactive environment for monitoring and managing the cluster. Modern DCs leverage these integrated dashboard systems to visualize collected data comprehensively. These dashboards (Figure 4) offer a holistic view of the DCs' operations, encompassing performance metrics, energy consumption, and user activity. By integrating Blockchain technology, these systems can create a Digital Twin of hardware and software resources, facilitating Tokenization and efficient resource allocation based on real-time demands. This integration enhances operational efficiency and ensures transparency and security in resource management. The Digital Twin of the ENEA HPC system offered a complete simulation and real-time monitoring of computational processes, energy consumption, and cost estimations. Integrating Blockchain technology and smart legal contracts introduces a solid framework for the secure, transparent, and automated management of HPC resources. By providing these two levels of representation, we ensure comprehensive management of HPC resources, from overarching system operations to detailed node-level monitoring. This dual approach enhances optimizing resource usage, improving energy efficiency, and ensuring compliance with best practices.

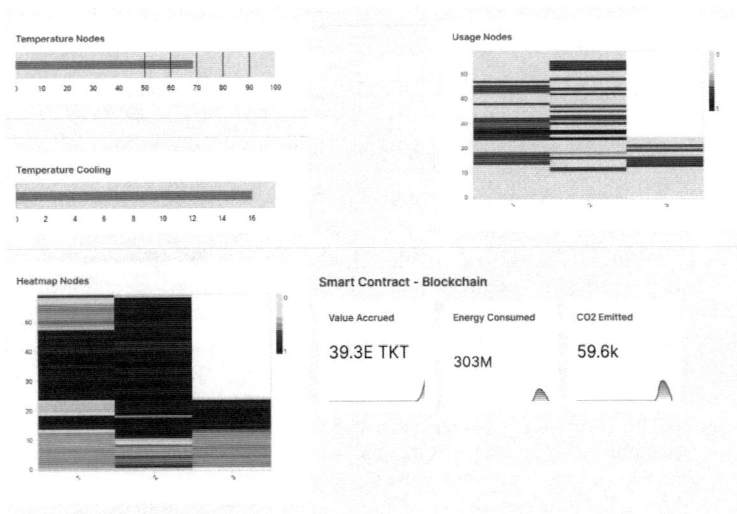

Figure 4. A detail of CRESCO7 Dashboard

3. CONCLUSION

In this work, the authors aim to create a comprehensive, self-sustaining system that optimizes the performance of the ENEA HPC CRESCO 7 cluster and sets a benchmark for sustainable DC operations worldwide. Based on blockchain technology watch, we would like to conclude our work by summarizing our most important contributions. Utilizing Blockchain technology to tokenize HPC assets and implementing efficiency-based Smart Contracts has delivered several significant benefits. Firstly, it has enhanced transparency, demonstrated by a 40% increase in the visibility of costs associated with using shared resources. This improvement helps users better understand and manage their resource consumption. Secondly, Blockchain enables the nearly instantaneous accounting of all resources used within the HPC environment, allowing for seamless, real-time tracking and management of computational assets. Lastly, it provides robust end-to-end control and process certification. This ensures that every computational job can be audited and validated, which is particularly valuable when aligning HPC operations with Environmental, Social, and Governance (ESG) criteria. This capability allows for the precise measurement and certification of the impact and efficiency of HPC tasks, which is essential for organizations committed to meeting rigorous ESG standards. To conclude, the Digital Twin DC concept offers many new perspectives on our rapidly digitalized society and its seamless interactions with many different elders. Combining complementary strengths in physics-based and data-driven modeling approaches, the hybrid analysis and Blockchain framework becomes particularly appealing for developing robust digital twin platforms. It enables us to make more informed decisions and ask better questions to mitigate challenges relevant to big data cybernetics, security, digitalization, automatization, and cognition. This approach is scalable and replicable in other HPC contexts. In the future, we will refine our models further and integrate additional data sources to improve the AI engine's accuracy and functionality, enhancing the Digital Twin's detail.

ACKNOWLEDGEMENT

Project ECS 0000024 Rome Technopole, – CUP B83C22002820006, PNRR Mission 4 Component 2 Investment 1.5, Funded by the European Union – NextGenerationEU".

REFERENCES

Andrae, A. S., (2019). Projecting the chiaroscuro of the electricity use of communication and computing from 2018 to 2030. Preprint. 504, 1-23.

Andrae, A. S., Edler, T., (2015). On global electricity usage of communication technology: trends to 2030. Challenges, 6(1):117-57.

Cao, Z., Zhou, X., Hu, H., Wang, Z., and Wen, Y., (2022). Toward a systematic survey for carbon neutral data centers, IEEE Communications 507 Surveys & Tutorials, vol. 24, no. 2, pp. 895–936.

Chinnici, M., Telesca, L., Mahfuzul, I., Georges, J.-P., (2023). Scalable and Transparent Blockchain Multi-layer Approach for Smart Energy Communities", Lecture Notes in Networks and Systems Volume 595 LNNS, Pages 183 - 1972023 4th International Congress on Blockchain and Applications, Blockchain 2022. ISBN 978-303121228-4

De Chiara, D., Chinnici, M., Kor, A.-L., (2020). Data mining for big dataset-related thermal analysis of high-performance computing (HPC) data center, Lecture Notes in Computer Science, Volume 12143 LNCS, Pages 367 – 38, ISSN: 03029743, ISBN: 978-303050435-9, DOI: 10.1007/978-3-030-50436-6_27.

European Commission (2020). Directorate-General for Justice and Consumers. Telesca, L., Islam, M., Jukka Huhtamäki, J., & Hazard, J., Modelling the EU economy as an ecosystem of contracts, Volume 1, Feasibility study. Publications Office of the European Union. https://data.europa.eu/doi/10.2838/28184.

European Commission (2021). Directorate-General for Justice and Consumers, Telesca, L., Islam, M., Jukka Huhtamäki, J., Guyer, S., Furner, A., Stamboglis, N., Lafond, F., Pichler, A., Farmer, D., & Hazard, J., Modelling the EU economy as an ecosystem of contracts. Volume 2, Methodology study, Publications Office of the European Union. https://data.europa.eu/doi/10.2838/594001

Gartner, (2019). Top 10 strategic technology trends for 2020, Stamford, CT, USA.

Grishina, A., Chinnici, M., Kor, A.-L., De Chiara, D. , Guarnieri, G., Rondeau, E. , Georges, J.-P., (2022). Thermal Awareness to Enhance Data Center Energy Efficiency, Cleaner Engineering and Technology, V.16, https://doi.org/10.1016/j.clet.2022.100409.

Grishina, A., Chinnici, M., Kor, A.-L., Rondeau, E., Georges, J.-P., (2020). A machine learning solution for data center thermal characteristics analysis", Energies, 13(17), ISSN: 19961073, DOI: 10.3390/en13174378.

Jones, N., et al., (2018). The information factories, Nature, vol. 561, no. 7722, pp.163–166.

Kostenko, W. P., Torok, J. G. and Demetriou, D.W., (2020). IBM z15: Improved data center density and energy efficiency, new system packaging, and modeling, IBM Journal of Research and Development, vol. 64, no. 5/6, pp. 16:1-16:10.

Liu, Y., Draper, S. C., and Kim, N. S., (2014). SleepScale: Runtime joint speed scaling and sleep states management for power efficient data centers, ACM Sigarch Computer Architecture News, vol. 42, no. 3, pp. 313-324.

Shuja, J., Bilal, K., Madani, S. A., et al., (2016). Survey of Techniques and Architectures for Designing Energy-Efficient Data Centers, IEEE Systems Journal, vol. 10, no. 2, pp. 507-519.

Trakti (2024). Smart Legal Contract platform. https://www.trakti.com/

Uddin, M., Darabidarabkhani, Y., Shah, A., and Memon, J., (2015). Evaluating power efficient algorithms for efficiency and carbon emissions in cloud data centers: A review, Renewable and Sustainable Energy Reviews, vol. 51, pp. 1553-1563.

Vafamehr, A., Khodayar, M. E., (2018). Energy-aware cloud computing. The Electricity Journal, 31(2):40-9.

EXAMINING CRITICAL FACTORS IN FCA-SAPO FRAMEWORK: A QUALITATIVE AND QUANTITATIVE STUDY ON THE ADOPTION OF FOG COMPUTING IN SAUDI ARABIAN PUBLIC ORGANISATIONS BY IT EMPLOYEES

Mohammed Alyami[1,2], Natalia Beloff[1] and Martin White[1]
[1] *Dept. of Informatics, University of Sussex, Brighton, United Kingdom*
[2] *Dept. of Computer Science, Jazan University, Jazan, Saudi Arabia*

ABSTRACT

Fog computing is a rapidly evolving domain within information technology and enterprise computing, providing organisations with the opportunity to greatly improve efficiency and productivity. This is particularly pertinent in developing countries, where effective resource utilisation is critical. Despite its potential, there has been limited research on the factors influencing the adoption of fog computing in Saudi Arabia, as well as the associated benefits and challenges. This study seeks to fill this gap by examining the various factors, advantages, and obstacles related to fog computing adoption within Saudi Arabian public organisations. To address the absence of a context-specific model, we employed a mixed-methods approach, gathering qualitative data through semi-structured interviews with 15 IT managers, revealing that complexity was the sole factor hindering adoption. Quantitative data was then collected from 665 IT managers and employees to validate the framework's constructs, showing that privacy, complexity, awareness, and senior management support were insignificant among 12 factors in influencing adoption intention. The quantitative analysis complements these findings, indicating that while the majority of factors significantly influence the adoption process, a portion of the factors were found to be insignificant. Findings from both qualitative and quantitative analyses highlight the importance of technical, organisational, environmental, and financial contexts in the adoption process. These insights provide valuable guidance for IT managers in the Saudi public sector, emphasising the need to consider these factors comprehensively to achieve successful fog computing implementation.

KEYWORDS

FCA-SAPO Framework, Fog Computing, Saudi Arabia

1. INTRODUCTION

By focusing on the public sector in Saudi Arabia, Examining Critical Factors in FCA-SAPO Framework provides a detailed understanding of fog computing adoption, addressing the unique challenges and strategic needs of public IT employees. Fog computing, a transformative technology, allows users to access computing resources locally without depending on centralised data centres, facilitating real-time data processing across various geographical locations (Wöbker *et al.*, 2018; Donno and Dragoni, 2019). As technological advancements, particularly in AI, reshape daily life, fog computing stands out as a promising solution for regions where efficient resource utilisation is crucial. This study investigates fog computing adoption in Saudi Arabian public organisations, a setting where challenges like service efficiency, data security, and regulatory compliance are heightened, particularly in alignment with Saudi Arabia's Vision 2030 goals.

Fog computing extends cloud capabilities by decentralising data processing, bringing it closer to data sources. This architectural shift improves latency and allows real-time decision-making, making it highly suitable for IoT, autonomous vehicles, and smart cities (Chiang and Zhang, 2016). The demand for decentralised systems has grown significantly as IoT devices produce increasing amounts of data, which centralised cloud solutions struggle to process efficiently (Bonomi *et al.*, 2012). Despite fog computing's promise, it faces adoption challenges such as security, privacy, interoperability, and resource management

(Stojmenovic and Wen, 2014; Yi, Qin and Li, 2015). In developing nations like Saudi Arabia, fog computing offers substantial potential for enhanced service delivery, yet organisations often face obstacles tied to organisational readiness, workforce technical skills, and compliance requirements (Alqahtani, 2016; Alfaifi, 2022). Research in Saudi Arabia on the adoption of fog computing and similar technologies has highlighted issues related to the cultural and regulatory contexts, which can slow technology uptake and complicate adoption frameworks (Al Mudawi, Beloff and White, 2022). Notably, few studies have developed adoption models for the Saudi public sector, leaving a gap in the understanding of factors that could drive or hinder fog computing implementation in this context. Addressing this gap, the present study introduces a framework proposed to Saudi Arabian public organisations—the fog computing Adoption in Saudi Arabian Public Organisations (FCA-SAPO) framework, first proposed by Alyami, Beloff and White (2023).

The primary objective of this research is to identify the key technical, organisational, environmental, and financial factors influencing fog computing adoption in Saudi Arabia's public sector and to validate the FCA-SAPO framework designed for this purpose. To explore these objectives, this study uses twelve hypotheses to test the significance of various factors, including Quality of Service, Security, Technology Readiness, and Compliance with Regulations, hypothesising that these factors positively influence adoption. It also explores the potential barrier posed by Privacy, alongside other variables such as Complexity, Awareness, and Senior Management Support.

The scope of this research is limited to public sector organisations in Saudi Arabia, focusing on their specific challenges and benefits in adopting fog computing. While this context provides valuable insights, it also limits the study's applicability to other countries or sectors. The use of a mixed-methods approach, combining qualitative interviews with IT managers and quantitative surveys with both IT managers and employees, allows for a comprehensive analysis. However, the reliance on data from Saudi Arabian public organisations may not fully capture the broader organisational dynamics present in other settings.

The structure of this paper is as follows: Section 2 outlines the related work on the adoption of fog computing. Section 3 details the mixed-methods research methodology used to test the framework. Section 4 presents qualitative results from interviews with IT managers, and the quantitative survey findings. Section 5 discusses the implications of the findings, then finally, Section 6 closes with concluding with recommendations and potential directions for future research.

2. RELATED WORK

Fog computing represents a transformative paradigm that enhances computational efficiency by reducing latency and facilitating real-time data processing closer to data sources (Bonomi *et al.*, 2012). Unlike conventional Cloud computing, which is reliant on centralised data centres, fog computing distributes computational resources across multiple layers positioned between the Cloud and end-user devices. This architecture supports faster data processing and decision-making at the network edge, essential for applications requiring low-latency responses, such as the Internet of Things (IoT), autonomous vehicles, and smart cities (Chiang and Zhang, 2016). The rise in IoT devices has amplified the need for decentralized computing infrastructures, highlighting the crucial role of fog computing in managing the significant amounts of real-time data produced (Gubbi *et al.*, 2013; Mahmood and Ramachandran, 2018). However, while fog computing offers several benefits, its adoption also presents challenges, including issues of security, privacy, interoperability, and resource management (Stojmenovic and Wen, 2014; Yi, Qin and Li, 2015; Roman, Lopez and Mambo, 2018).

In developing countries, including Saudi Arabia, the adoption of fog computing presents both promising opportunities and obstacles. While potential benefits include enhanced service delivery and reduced latency, barriers to adoption remain significant, including organisational readiness, staff technical expertise, and regulatory constraints (Al-Mashari, 2002; Alharthi *et al.*, 2015). Additionally, cultural considerations and resistance to change pose further challenges (Alfaifi, 2022). Currently, a lack of a cohesive model to guide fog computing adoption within Saudi Arabia's public sector further complicates its implementation. Although considerable research has explored the technical and operational aspects of fog computing, there remains a lack of focus on a comprehensive adoption framework designed to public sector needs in Saudi Arabia. Much of the literature addresses general barriers to fog computing without examining factors specific to the region, such as regulatory readiness and the particular organisational characteristics of Saudi public institutions. Moreover, previous studies have tended to overlook the importance of financial considerations in the adoption process, a gap that is increasingly relevant given the significant investments required for infrastructure and technical training.

This study adopts and expands upon the Technology-Organisation-Environment (TOE) framework proposed by Tornatzky and Fleischer (1990) to examine fog computing adoption within Saudi public organisations. The TOE framework is ideal for the FCA-SAPO framework due to limitations in other theories. UTAUT omits key factors like privacy and regulation, TRA focuses narrowly on attitudes and norms, TAM overlooks organisational concerns like finance and policy, and DOI fails to address trust and contextual differences. Thus, TOE's comprehensive focus on technology, organisation, and environment makes it more suitable. Building on the FCA-SAPO framework introduced by Alyami, Beloff and White (2023), which identified critical factors influencing the adoption process in the public sector, this research integrates a financial context into the TOE model to address the economic factors influencing adoption. This framework includes four contextual domains: Technical, Organisational, Environmental, and Financial, each with unique influencing factors tailored to the Saudi context. By refining the FCA-SAPO framework, this study seeks to support fog computing adoption in Saudi Arabia's public sector by providing a structured approach for understanding and managing these key contextual elements. This current research validates the expanded framework, aiming to address the identified barriers and promote fog computing adoption across Saudi public organisations.

3. METHODOLOGY

This study employed a mixed-methods approach to explore the factors influencing the intention to adopt fog computing, as outlined in the proposed FCA-SAPO framework. Figure 1 illustrates the framework's approach, identifying the intention to adopt fog computing as the dependent variable. The independent variables incorporated into the framework include Quality of Service, Security, Privacy, Compatibility, Complexity, Awareness, Senior Management Support, Technology Readiness, Competitive Pressures, Compliance with Regulations, Cost, and Maintenance. By integrating qualitative and quantitative research techniques, the methodology enabled a comprehensive analysis of the data gathered (Creswell, 2013; Neuman, 2014; Ishtiaq, 2019).

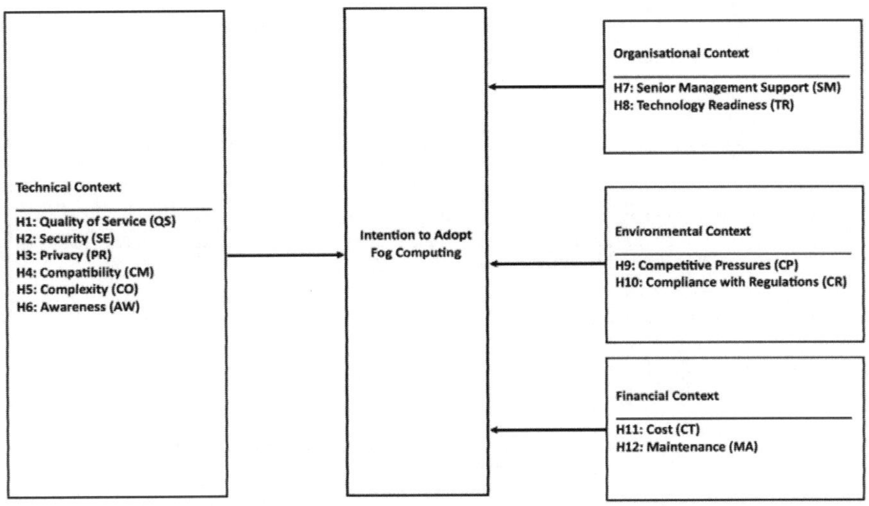

Figure 1. The conceptual research model of fog computing Adoption in Saudi Arabian Public Organisations (FCA-SAPO) (Alyami, Beloff and White, 2023)

The selection of participants for this study focused on IT managers from various ministries within Saudi Arabian public organisations, all of whom possess relevant experience and knowledge of e-government systems. A total of 15 semi-structured interviews were conducted, providing rich, descriptive data. For the quantitative aspect, the survey targeted IT employees across public organisations, with a final sample size of

383 respondents determined, achieving a confidence level of 95% and a margin of error of 5%. In total, 665 individuals participated in the study, ensuring a solid data set.

Qualitative data were gathered through a series of 15 semi-structured interviews, each consisting of 10 open-ended questions that were carefully validated by subject matter experts. This interactive method aimed to produce descriptive insights regarding the impact of FCA-SAPO factors on the intention to adopt fog computing. The quantitative data collection involved the development of a structured survey, based on the theoretical framework of FCA-SAPO, that included Technical, Organisational, Environmental, and Financial factors as key variables. A 5-point Likert scale was employed, ranging from 5 (strongly agree) to 1 (strongly disagree), to quantify responses.

Data analysis was conducted using SPSS and SmartPLS 3 software. The qualitative interviews were recorded and securely stored in compliance with the Research Data Management and Protection guidelines of the University of Sussex. Ethical measures were meticulously observed throughout the study, ensuring participant confidentiality and voluntary participation. Unique identifiers were assigned to interview participants, and all research data were stored in password-protected files approved by the university's ethical committee (ER/MA2282/2). This complete approach allowed for the effective analysis of both qualitative and quantitative data, thereby enriching the understanding of factors influencing fog computing adoption in Saudi Arabian public organisations.

4. RESULTS

The interviews with IT managers revealed nine main themes: enhancing service quality, security and privacy concerns, awareness initiatives, internal complexity, governmental challenges, organisational size variances, crucial compliance, financial complexity, and importance of considerations, see Figure 2. These themes highlight key factors for fog computing adoption, supporting the FCA-SAPO framework evaluation.

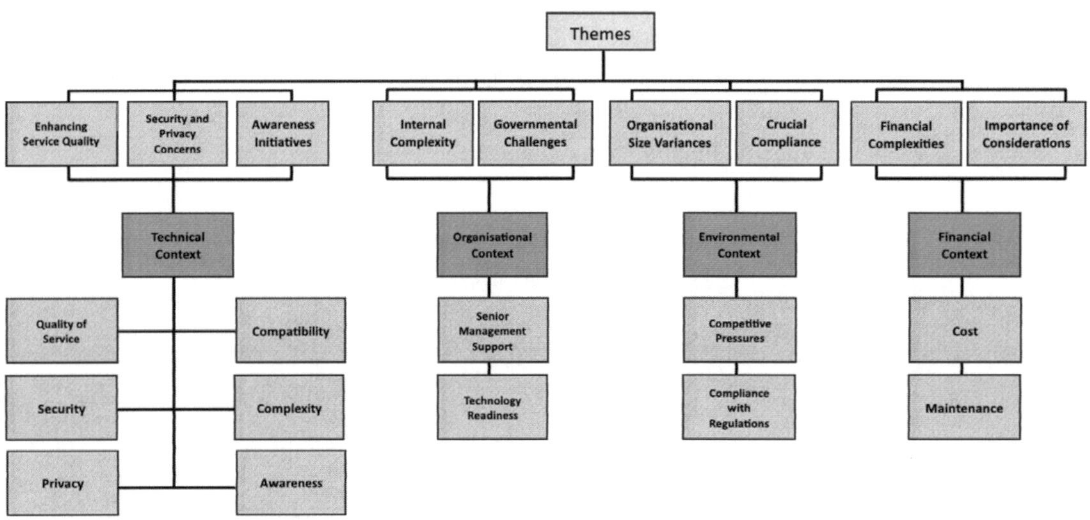

Figure 2. Identified themes from thematic analysis

Quantitative analysis was conducted to understand fog computing adoption in Saudi Arabia's public organisations, surveying IT managers and employees via Qualtrics. Data were analysed with descriptive statistics (frequency, percentages, bar charts) and advanced statistical methods for model validation. Structural Equation Modeling (SEM) tested the FCA-SAPO framework's fit, and SPSS 26 and SmartPLS 3 were used for data analysis, ensuring normality, skewness, and other statistical prerequisites.

For technical factors, it includes quality of service (QS), security (SE), privacy (PR), compatibility (CM), complexity (CO), and awareness (AW). Organisational factors focus on senior management support (SM), and technology readiness (TR). Environmental factors are influenced by competitive pressures (CP) and compliance with regulations (CR). Financial factors cover cost (CT) and maintenance (MA).

4.1 Thematic Analysis

A comprehensive overview of the factors influencing the adoption of fog computing is provided in Figure 2 which illustrates the various factors that will be driving the adoption of fog computing in the context of the proposed framework (FCA-SAPO).

4.1.1 Quality of Service (QS)

QS enhances service quality of user experience and performance. An IT director stated:

"Fog computing is intended to provide a higher quality of service when retrieving data, reducing Internet slowness, slow support, and data analysis." [MOI] This highlights its role in addressing specific challenges and enhancing overall service quality.

4.1.2 Security (SE)

SE ensures data protection and mitigates security concerns. An IT manager stated:

"Organisations must take care of security and privacy concerns to ensure that data and information will be secure and properly protected while using this technology." [KAU] Highlighting security and privacy concerns considerations as a foundational requirement for maximising the benefits of fog computing.

4.1.3 Privacy (PR)

PR protects sensitive data within public organisations. An IT manager remarked:

"Privacy is very influential and useful; fog computing is important for protecting patient data and preventing unreliable access attempts." [NEC] Safeguarding privacy addresses concerns about data misuse.

4.1.4 Compatibility (CM)

CM with existing systems allows for seamless integration. An IT director highlighted:

"The compatibility between new and old technology through networks and operating systems in the public sector is very important to make services fast and easy to use for system users." [NCA] Compatibility reduces disruptions in public organisations.

4.1.5 Complexity (CO)

CO can lead to resistance to change. An IT manager stated:

"Complexity may be considered a negative aspect because fog computing is a new electronic services system and will often face resistance to change among the organisation's employees in the IT sector and other sectors." [NEC] Reducing complexity through training can ease adoption.

4.1.6 Awareness (AW)

Raising awareness initiatives is crucial for successful adoption. An IT director noted:

"I think when adopting any technology, we will need workshops, which in turn raise awareness among fog computing users." [NCA] Awareness initiatives provides employees with the necessary knowledge.

4.1.7 Senior Management Support (SM)

SM supports adoption. An IT director mentioned:

"The support of senior management is very important, as they are responsible for enacting regulations and legislation to adopt any new technology." [NCA] Support from management enables faster decision-making.

4.1.8 Technology Readiness (TR)

High technology readiness is essential. An IT director noted:

"*It is worth noting that our technical readiness is there and there is no problem regarding compatibility, as we can successfully use fog computing without major problems*". [MHRSD] Adequate readiness reduces technical challenges.

4.1.9 Competitive Pressures (CP)

CP encourages adoption to align with national goals. An IT manager stated:

"Competitive pressure is crucial for keeping pace with Saudi Arabia's Vision 2023. Adopting fog computing ensures operational speed and security of user data." [MOF] Responding to competitive pressures aligns with Saudi's Vision 2030.

4.1.10 Compliance with Regulations (CR)

Compliance is necessary to secure public sector data especially when they have enormous number of employees. An IT director stressed:

"Organisations with big number of employees must ensure that their use of fog computing complies with these regulations and laws." [KAU] This ensures compliance with laws, reducing work-related problems and potential security threats in large scale organisations.

4.1.11 Cost (CT)

CT considerations impact adoption feasibility. An IT manager stated:

"The cost of fog computing definitely requires financial statements and studying previous financial statements when implementing new technologies." [MOI] Addressing costs supports sustainable adoption.

4.1.12 Maintenance (MA)

MA planning is crucial for continued functionality. An IT manager noted:

"Maintenance operations must be carefully considered, including determining its cost and allocating personnel and financial resources to it." [MRM] A strong maintenance plan ensures system reliability.

The main factors influencing fog computing adoption in Saudi public organisations include QS, SE, PR, CM, AW, SM, TR, CP, CR, CT, and MA. While CO may hinder adoption, training and support can help mitigate this. Adopting fog computing aligns with Vision 2030, enhancing service standards and operational security.

4.2 Descriptive Statistics

The FCA-SAPO framework, covering Technical, Organisational, Environmental, and Financial contexts, offers valuable insights. Table 1 summarises key demographic variables and their potential correlations with adoption factors across the four contexts. To enhance its practical relevance, exploring these correlations is significant. For instance, in the Technical Context, IT staff with different experience levels may perceive security or compatibility challenges differently. In the Organisational Context, technology readiness might vary by age group, revealing readiness gaps. Environmental factors, like compliance with regulations, could highlight differences in awareness across roles or sectors (e.g., education, finance, public health). Financially, cost perceptions may differ by organisational size, workforce, or education. These correlations can uncover group-specific patterns, offering actionable strategies to support fog computing adoption.

Table 1 provides a detailed breakdown of the respondents' demographic characteristics, highlighting patterns that influence fog computing adoption. This analysis lays the foundation for understanding contextual factors.

Table 1. Respondents' descriptive characteristics (N= 665)

Constructs	Categories	Number	Percentage
Gender	Male	553	83.2
	Female	112	16.8
Age	31-45 Years	471	70.8
	18-30 Years	178	26.8
	46-60 Years	16	2.4
Education level	Bachelor`s Degree	390	58.6
	Master`s Degree	272	40.9
	Diploma	2	0.3
	Doctorate Degree	1	0.2
Business nature of your organisation	Education	215	32.3
	Financial	163	24.5
	Public Health	142	21.4
	Other	117	17.6
	Retail	28	4.2
Number of employees in your organisation	10-49 Employees	412	62.0
	50-250 Employees	206	31.0
	More than 250 Employees	43	6.5
	1-9 Employees	4	0.6
Organisation's location	Southern Province	318	47.8
	Central Province	274	41.2
	Northern Province	73	11.0
Occupation in the organisation	IT Staff	489	73.5
	IT Director	158	23.8
	Director of the Governmental Organisation	10	1.5
	Other	8	1.2
Years of experience	Less than 10 Years	337	50.7
	More than 10 Years	223	33.5
	Less than 3 Years	104	15.6
	Less than 1 Year	1	0.2
Does your organisation adopt fog computing?	No	636	95.6
	Yes	29	4.4

4.3 Data Analysis and Confirmatory Factor Analysis (CFA)

Confirmatory Factor Analysis (CFA) was performed to validate the measurement model and test relationships between observed variables and latent constructs, following Hair et al. (2010). This approach confirmed the reliability of factors influencing fog computing adoption in Saudi Arabian public organisations, including Quality of Service (QS), Security (SE), Privacy (PR), Compatibility (CM), Complexity (CO), Awareness (AW), Senior Management Support (SM), Technology Readiness (TR), Competitive Pressures (CP), Compliance with Regulations (CR), Cost (CT), Maintenance (MA), and Adoption Intention (AI). The CFA findings support the robustness of these factors in the context of fog computing adoption.

4.4 Measures of the Model Validity

CFA, using SEM and SmartPLS 3, was applied to ensure unidimensionality, reliability, and discriminant validity. Constructs met the thresholds for Cronbach's Alpha (>0.7), Composite Reliability (>0.7), and AVE (>0.5), as shown in Table 2, ensuring model reliability and validity. Discriminant validity was established by AVE square roots exceeding inter-construct correlations, and all HTMT values were below 0.9, as recommended by Hair et al. (2010); Hair, Ringle and Sarstedt (2013). These results indicate that the model is statistically sound and valid for further analysis.

Table 2. Validity and reliability of constructs

Constructs	Cronbach's Alpha	Composite Reliability	AVE
Quality of Service	0.715	0.823	0.54
Security	0.743	0.834	0.557
Privacy	0.716	0.816	0.529
Compatibility	0.718	0.82	0.533
Complexity	0.713	0.75	0.500
Awareness	0.742	0.836	0.561
Senior Management Support	0.717	0.816	0.528
Technology Readiness	0.760	0.847	0.581
Competitive Pressures	0.747	0.838	0.565
Compliance with Regulations	0.803	0.871	0.628
Cost	0.762	0.847	0.582
Maintenance	0.814	0.878	0.643
Adoption Intention to fog computing	0.736	0.828	0.500

4.5 Model Good Fit

R-squared (R^2) analysis in Table 3, following Cohen (1988), showed an R^2 of 0.346 (33.4%) for (AI) which is greater than 0.25 reflecting a strong goodness of fit (based on R-square limits for SEM), indicating the model's substantial explanatory power for fog computing adoption intentions in Saudi public organisations, supporting its robustness (Hair, Ringle and Sarstedt, 2013). This R^2 value signifies that the model effectively explains a significant portion of the variance in adoption intentions.

Table 3. R-Square measure for goodness of fit

Dependent Variable	R Square	R Square Adjusted
Adoption Intention to fog computing	0.346	0.334

4.6 Discriminant Validity

Discriminant validity ensures constructs are distinct, with low correlations among them. Using the Fornell-Larcker criterion and HTMT ratio, all values fell below 0.85, validating distinctness among constructs (Hair *et al.*, 2010; Hair, Ringle and Sarstedt, 2013). Table 4 summarises the HTMT matrix. The analysis confirms that each construct is unique and independent within the model.

Table 4. Hetero-Trait Mono-Trait (HTMT) for discriminant validity

Constructs	AI	AW	CM	CP	CO	CR	CT	MA	PR	QS	SE	SM	TR
AI													
AW	0.294												
CM	0.286	0.133											
CP	0.44	0.381	0.088										
CO	0.079	0.153	0.091	0.067									
CR	0.415	0.187	0.191	0.336	0.1								
CT	0.455	0.27	0.114	0.349	0.073	0.382							
MA	0.46	0.234	0.137	0.355	0.073	0.315	0.398						
PR	0.328	0.177	0.146	0.321	0.056	0.28	0.367	0.262					
QS	0.527	0.348	0.126	0.378	0.115	0.308	0.427	0.306	0.349				
SE	0.323	0.181	0.219	0.179	0.052	0.208	0.264	0.328	0.242	0.231			
SM	0.313	0.387	0.178	0.338	0.148	0.26	0.352	0.202	0.342	0.312	0.176		
TR	0.459	0.237	0.217	0.326	0.052	0.378	0.436	0.365	0.423	0.403	0.317	0.284	

4.7 Structural Equation Model

SEM was utilised to assess the relationships within the FCA-SAPO model (Hair et al., 2010). Table 5 summarises results: significant predictors of (AI) included QS ($\beta=0.205$, $p=0.0001$), SE ($\beta=0.067$, $p=0.017$), CM ($\beta=0.113$, $p=0.001$), TR ($\beta=0.09$, $p=0.008$), CP ($\beta=0.128$, $p=0.001$), CR ($\beta=0.102$, $p=0.006$), CT ($\beta=0.103$, $p=0.002$), and MA ($\beta=0.137$, $p=0.0001$). Non-significant predictors were PR ($\beta=0.027$, $p=0.424$), CO (β=-0.003, p=0.957), AW (β=0.023, p=0.472), and SM (β=0.037, p=0.219), suggesting their limited role in fog computing adoption in the public sector. These results highlight key factors that are statistically significant in influencing Adoption Intention.

Table 5. Summary of hypotheses` results

Hypotheses	Paths	Coefficient	P-value	Results
H1	Quality of Service -> Adoption Intention to fog computing	0.205	0.0001	Supported
H2	Security -> Adoption Intention to fog computing	0.067	0.017	Supported
H3	Privacy -> Adoption Intention to fog computing	0.027	0.424	Rejected
H4	Compatibility -> Adoption Intention to fog computing	0.113	0.001	Supported
H5	Complexity -> Adoption Intention to fog computing	-0.003	0.957	Rejected
H6	Awareness -> Adoption Intention to fog computing	0.023	0.472	Rejected
H7	Senior Management Support -> Adoption Intention to fog computing	0.037	0.219	Rejected
H8	Technology Readiness -> Adoption Intention to fog computing	0.09	0.008	Supported
H9	Competitive Pressure -> Adoption Intention to fog computing	0.128	0.001	Supported
H10	Compliance with Regulations -> Adoption Intention to fog computing	0.102	0.006	Supported
H11	Cost -> Adoption Intention to fog computing	0.103	0.002	Supported
H12	Maintenance -> Adoption Intention to fog computing	0.137	0.0001	Supported

5. DISCUSSION

The **qualitative findings**, collected from IT managers, reveal that technical, organisational, environmental, and financial factors all influence the adoption of fog computing in Saudi Arabian public organisations.

Technical Factors: The majority of IT managers agreed that technical factors supported FC adoption, except for Complexity (CO). Quality of Service (QS), Security (SE), Privacy (PR), Compatibility (CM), and Awareness (AW) were beneficial, enhancing data speed, user experience, and data protection. Compatibility with legacy systems was manageable, though Complexity (CO) posed a challenge, with resistance due to unfamiliarity with new technology, underscoring the need for thorough training.

Organisational Factors: Senior Management Support (SM) and Technology Readiness (TR) were essential. SM ensured strategic direction and resources, while TR, including infrastructure and workforce skills, facilitated smoother fog computing adoption.

Environmental Factors: Competitive Pressures (CP) and Compliance with Regulations (CR) were influential. CP, aligned with Saudi's Vision 2030, motivated fog computing adoption for efficiency, while CR ensured legal and data protection compliance.

Financial Factors: Cost (CT) and Maintenance (MA) were critical concerns, particularly for smaller organisations. While larger entities managed expenses more easily, effective maintenance planning was essential for long-term FC sustainability.

This section discusses the **quantitative analysis** of the FCA-SAPO framework, which examines factors influencing fog computing adoption in Saudi Arabian public organisations. Path coefficients from statistical tests support hypotheses on technical, organisational, environmental, and financial factors, validated with supporting literature and feedback from IT managers who participated in interviews, see Figure 3.

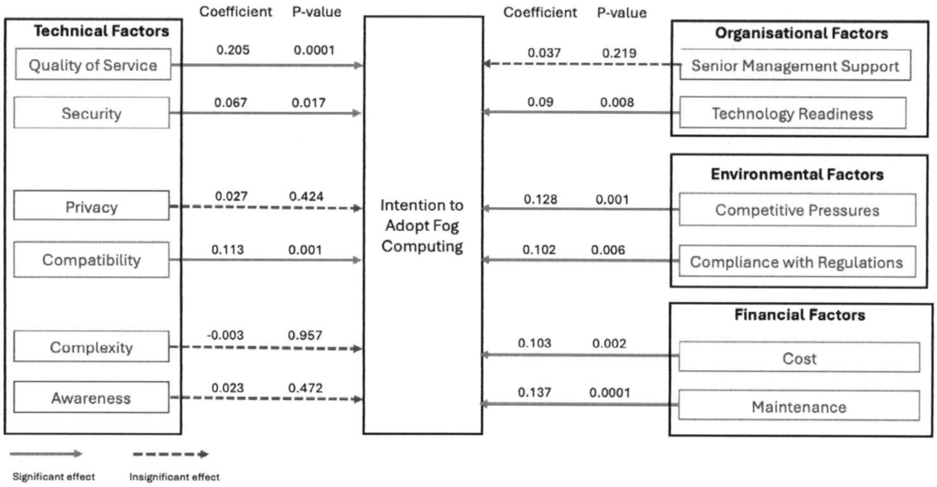

Figure 3. The updated FCA-SAPO framework

Technical Factors: Quality of Service (QS) shows a significant positive impact on adoption intention (AI) (path coefficient = 0.205, p = 0.0001), supporting Hypothesis 1. This aligns with studies emphasising QS in technology adoption (Alkhater, Walters and Wills, 2018). Also, it is confirmed by IT managers who noted service quality as essential for adoption. Security (SE) also shows a significant correlation with AI (path coefficient = 0.067, p = 0.017), confirming Hypothesis 2. Enhanced security perceptions are key for adoption (Hashizume *et al.*, 2013), which is echoed by IT managers who emphasised the importance of security for organisational readiness. Privacy (PR), however, is insignificant (path coefficient = 0.027, p = 0.424), rejecting Hypothesis 3. Privacy, while important, may not drive adoption alone (Pearson, 2013). One participant reflected this: *"Privacy is important, but without other supporting factors like efficiency and data handling, it won't be enough to drive adoption alone"* [KAU]. Compatibility (CM) is significant (path coefficient = 0.113, p = 0.001), supporting Hypothesis 4, with studies and IT managers highlighting its importance for seamless integration with existing systems (Rogers, Singhal and Quinlan, 2019). Complexity (CO) and Awareness (AW) are both insignificant (path coefficients -0.003, p = 0.957 and 0.023, p = 0.472), rejecting Hypothesis 5 and Hypothesis 6. Some IT managers observed that while complexity can be managed through preparation, it remains a barrier: *"I see the complexity of the technology affecting our ability to embrace fog computing in government"* [MHRSD], while others noted awareness gaps [JU]. In summary, QS, SE, and CM support adoption, while PR, CO, and AW do not.

Organisational Factors: Senior Management Support (SM) is insignificant (path coefficient = 0.037, p = 0.219), rejecting Hypothesis 7. Although crucial, participants and IT managers noted challenges with management support in regulatory processes: *"the support of senior management is very important... But top management support is a challenge..."* [NCA]. Literature highlights management's role in resource allocation, yet technical staff may perceive it as less critical (Ifinedo, 2011). Technology Readiness (TR) is significant (path coefficient = 0.09, p = 0.008), supporting Hypothesis 8, with studies and IT managers linking technological readiness to increased adoption likelihood (Parasuraman and Colby, 2015). In conclusion, TR positively impacts adoption, while SM shows limited influence.

Environmental Factors: Competitive Pressures (CP) significantly impacts adoption intention (path coefficient = 0.128, p = 0.001), supporting Hypothesis 9. Competitive pressures are a recognised driver for adoption (Zhu and Kraemer, 2005), as also highlighted by IT managers who noted it as a key factor.

Compliance with Regulations (CR) also shows a positive impact (path coefficient = 0.102, p = 0.006), supporting Hypothesis 10, with IT managers affirming that regulatory adherence influences adoption decisions (Mell and Grance, 2011). To summarise, both CP and CR support fog computing adoption.

Financial Factors: Cost (CT) positively impacts adoption intention (path coefficient = 0.103, p = 0.002), supporting Hypothesis 11, with studies and IT managers noting that reduced costs favour adoption (Oliveira, Martins and Martins, 2011). Maintenance (MA) is significant (path coefficient = 0.137, p = 0.0001), supporting Hypothesis 12, as lower maintenance requirements facilitate adoption (Thong, 1999). In short, lower costs and reduced maintenance needs support fog computing adoption.

To enhance fog computing adoption, IT managers and policymakers should prioritise service quality, security, and compatibility with existing systems while aligning with regulatory requirements to ensure compliance. Budgeting for implementation and maintenance, simplifying complexity through training, and incorporating privacy measures can build trust and reduce resistance. Including diverse perspectives and addressing cultural factors will refine strategies and ensure successful integration.

6. CONCLUSION

This study has provided a comprehensive analysis of the critical factors influencing the adoption of fog computing within the Saudi Arabian public sector, a field of research that has garnered significant attention and requires further exploration due to its adoption challenges (Aazam, Zeadally and Harras, 2018; Brogi *et al.*, 2018). The qualitative findings underscored the importance of quality of service, security, privacy, compatibility, and awareness as vital elements for successful adoption, while also identifying complexity as a significant barrier. Furthermore, organisational factors such as senior management support, and technology readiness were revealed to be crucial, alongside environmental factors like competitive pressures and compliance of regulations, and financial considerations related to cost and maintenance. The quantitative analysis affirmed these relationships, demonstrating significant positive correlations for most factors, while privacy, complexity, awareness, and senior management support did not significantly influence adoption intentions.

The significance of this study lies in its contribution to the understanding of technology adoption in developing regions, particularly within the context of the Saudi Arabian public sector. By utilising the FCA-SAPO framework, this research sheds light on the detailed dynamics of fog computing adoption, offering practical insights for IT managers and policymakers aimed at enhancing implementation strategies.

Future work should focus on expanding fog computing research in developing countries to strengthen the understanding of adoption drivers in similar socio-economic contexts. Broader qualitative sampling that includes a diverse range of public sector representatives can enrich perspectives across organisational levels. Additionally, integrating views from both IT managers and employees in quantitative analyses would provide a more balanced view of organisational factors, including senior management support.

Lastly, incorporating cultural and social contexts into the FCA-SAPO model can clarify factors influencing technology acceptance in Saudi public sector, while longitudinal studies on fog computing can reveal evolving challenges and enablers, refining the model further.

REFERENCES

Aazam, M., Zeadally, S. and Harras, K.A. (2018) 'Deploying fog computing in Industrial Internet of Things and Industry 4.0', IEEE Transactions on Industrial Informatics, 14(10), pp. 4674–4682. Available at: https://doi.org/10.1109/TII.2018.2855198.

Al Mudawi, N., Beloff, N. and White, M. (2022) 'Developing a Framework of Critical Factors Affecting the Adoption of Cloud Computing in Government Systems (ACCE-GOV)', in, pp. 520–538. Available at: https://doi.org/10.1007/978-3-030-80119-9_32.

Alfaifi, Y. (2022) Benefits and Challenges of the Adoption of Cloud Computing in Telecommunications Companies in Saudi Arabia. Available at: https://www.researchgate.net/publication/378941441.

Alharthi, A. et al. (2015) 'An Overview of Cloud Services Adoption Challenges in Higher Education Institutions', in Proceedings of the 2nd International Workshop on Emerging Software as a Service and Analytics. SCITEPRESS - Science and and Technology Publications, pp. 102–109. Available at: https://doi.org/10.5220/0005529701020109.

Alkhater, N., Walters, R. and Wills, G. (2018) 'An empirical study of factors influencing cloud adoption among private sector organisations', Telematics and Informatics, 35(1), pp. 38–54. Available at: https://doi.org/10.1016/j.tele.2017.09.017.

Al-Mashari, M. (2002) 'Enterprise resource planning (ERP) systems: a research agenda', Industrial Management & Data Systems, 102(3), pp. 165–170. Available at: https://doi.org/10.1108/02635570210421354.

Alqahtani, F. (2016) 'Identifying the critical factors that impact on the Development of Electronic Government using TOE Framework in Saudi E-Government Context: A Thematic Analysis', in.

Alyami, M., Beloff, N. and White, M. (2023) 'FCA-SAPO: A New Comprehensive fog computing Adoption Model for Saudi Arabian Public Organisations', in, pp. 69–85. Available at: https://doi.org/10.1007/978-3-031-37717-4_6.

Bonomi, F. et al. (2012) 'fog computing and its role in the internet of things', in MCC'12 - Proceedings of the 1st ACM Mobile Cloud Computing Workshop, pp. 13–15. Available at: https://doi.org/10.1145/2342509.2342513.

Brogi, A. et al. (2018) 'Bonsai in the Fog: An active learning lab with fog computing', in 2018 Third International Conference on Fog and Mobile Edge Computing (FMEC). IEEE, pp. 79–86. Available at: https://doi.org/10.1109/FMEC.2018.8364048.

Chiang, M. and Zhang, T. (2016) 'Fog and IoT: An Overview of Research Opportunities', IEEE Internet of Things Journal. Institute of Electrical and Electronics Engineers Inc., pp. 854–864. Available at: https://doi.org/10.1109/JIOT.2016.2584538.

Cohen, J. (1988) Statistical Power Analysis for the Behavioral Sciences Second Edition. Academic press.

Creswell, J.W. (2013) 'Research Design (International Student Edition): Qualitative, Quantitative, and Mixed Methods Approaches (4th ed).', SAGE Publications [Preprint].

Donno, M. De and Dragoni, N. (2019) 'Combining antibiotic with fog computing: Antibiotic 2.0', 2019 IEEE 3rd International Conference on Fog and Edge Computing, ICFEC 2019 - Proceedings [Preprint]. Available at: https://doi.org/10.1109/CFEC.2019.8733144.

Gubbi, J. et al. (2013) Internet of Things (IoT): A Vision, Architectural Elements, and Future Directions. Available at: www.buyya.com.

Hair, J.F. et al. (2010) Multivariate data analysis: A global perspective. New Jersey: Pearson Prentice Hall.

Hair, J.F., Ringle, C.M. and Sarstedt, M. (2013) 'Partial Least Squares Structural Equation Modeling: Rigorous Applications, Better Results and Higher Acceptance', Long Range Planning, 46(1–2), pp. 1–12. Available at: https://doi.org/10.1016/j.lrp.2013.01.001.

Hashizume, K. et al. (2013) 'An analysis of security issues for cloud computing', Journal of Internet Services and Applications, 4(1), pp. 1–13. Available at: https://doi.org/10.1186/1869-0238-4-5.

Ifinedo, P. (2011) 'Internet/e-business technologies acceptance in Canada's SMEs: An exploratory investigation', Internet Research, 21(3), pp. 255–281. Available at: https://doi.org/10.1108/10662241111139309.

Ishtiaq, M. (2019) 'Book Review Creswell, J. W. (2014). Research Design: Qualitative, Quantitative and Mixed Methods Approaches (4th ed.). Thousand Oaks, CA: Sage', English Language Teaching, 12(5), p. 40. Available at: https://doi.org/10.5539/elt.v12n5p40.

Mahmood, Z. and Ramachandran, M. (2018) 'fog computing: Concepts, Principles and Related Paradigms', in Z. Mahmood (ed.) fog computing: Concepts, Frameworks and Technologies. Cham: Springer International Publishing, pp. 3–21. Available at: https://doi.org/10.1007/978-3-319-94890-4_1.

Mell, P.M. and Grance, T. (2011) 'The NIST definition of cloud computing', National Institute of Standards and Technology, Information Technology Laboratory, 145(7), pp. 6–8. Available at: https://doi.org/10.6028/NIST.SP.800-145.

Neuman, W. (2014) Social Research Methods: Qualitative and Quantitative Approaches. Essex, UK.: Pearson.

Oliveira, T., Rosario Oliveira Martins, M. and Fraga Martins, M. (2011) 'Literature Review of Information Technology Adoption Models at Firm Level', The Electronic Journal Information Systems Evaluation, 14, p. 110.

Parasuraman, A. and Colby, C.L. (2015) 'An Updated and Streamlined Technology Readiness Index: TRI 2.0', Journal of Service Research, 18(1), pp. 59–74. Available at: https://doi.org/10.1177/1094670514539730.

Pearson, S. (2013) 'Privacy, Security and Trust in Cloud Computing', in, pp. 3–42. Available at: https://doi.org/10.1007/978-1-4471-4189-1_1.

Rogers, E.M., Singhal, A. and Quinlan, M.M. (2019) 'Diffusion of innovations', An Integrated Approach to Communication Theory and Research, Third Edition, pp. 415–433. Available at: https://doi.org/10.4324/9780203710753-35.

Roman, R., Lopez, J. and Mambo, M. (2018) 'Mobile edge computing, Fog et al.: A survey and analysis of security threats and challenges', Future Generation Computer Systems, 78, pp. 680–698. Available at: https://doi.org/10.1016/j.future.2016.11.009.

Stojmenovic, I. and Wen, S. (2014) 'The fog computing paradigm: Scenarios and security issues', in 2014 Federated Conference on Computer Science and Information Systems, FedCSIS 2014. Institute of Electrical and Electronics Engineers Inc., pp. 1–8. Available at: https://doi.org/10.15439/2014F503.

Thong, L. (1999) An Integrated Model of Information Systems Adoption in Small Businesses on JSTOR. Available at: https://www.jstor.org/stable/40398410 (Accessed: 22 May 2024).

Tornatzky, M. and Fleischer, L. (1990) 'The processes of technological innovation', Lexington, Mass [Preprint].

Wöbker, C. et al. (2018) 'Fogernetes: Deployment and management of fog computing applications', IEEE/IFIP Network Operations and Management Symposium: Cognitive Management in a Cyber World, NOMS 2018, pp. 1–7. Available at: https://doi.org/10.1109/NOMS.2018.8406321.

Yi, S., Qin, Z. and Li, Q. (2015) 'Security and privacy issues of fog computing: A survey', in Lecture Notes in Computer Science (including subseries Lecture Notes in Artificial Intelligence and Lecture Notes in Bioinformatics). Springer Verlag, pp. 685–695. Available at: https://doi.org/10.1007/978-3-319-21837-3_67.

Zhu, K. and Kraemer, K.L. (2005) 'Post-adoption variations in usage and value of e-business by organizations: Cross-country evidence from the retail industry', Information Systems Research. INFORMS Inst.for Operations Res.and the Management Sciences, pp. 61–84. Available at: https://doi.org/10.1287/isre.1050.0045.

AI INTEGRATION IN SMART FACTORIES: A SYSTEMATIC REVIEW OF SUCCESS FACTORS AND CHALLENGES IN OPERATIONAL EFFICIENCY AND WORKFORCE DEVELOPMENT

Ammaarah Omar and Lizette Weilbach
Department of Informatics, University of Pretoria, Pretoria 0001, South Africa

ABSTRACT

In the ongoing transition towards Industry 4.0, the increasing adoption of artificial intelligence (AI) is driving smart manufacturing and digital transformation. AI holds the potential to enhance operational efficiency, workforce capabilities, and sustainability, but its implementation in factories presents significant challenges. It is crucial to understand both the critical success factors and obstacles to successfully implement AI in factories. This paper conducts a systematic literature review (SLR) to identify the success factors and challenges associated with AI integration in smart manufacturing. A total of 34 peer-reviewed articles were analysed and mapped to the Technology-Organization-Environment (TOE) framework to provide a structured evaluation of technological enablers, organizational readiness, and environmental factors. Key findings include the importance of a robust technological infrastructure, such as IoT devices and data analytics systems, strong management commitment, clear strategic vision, workforce upskilling, and adherence to data governance frameworks. Challenges such as high initial costs, interoperability issues, cybersecurity risks, and workforce resistance were also identified. The paper offers practical recommendations for smart factory owners, including investing in scalable technologies, fostering leadership support, implementing robust data security measures, and incentivizing workforce development. These insights provide a comprehensive roadmap for successfully navigating the complexities of AI integration in smart factories. By leveraging the actionable strategies, industry leaders can enhance operational efficiency, drive innovation, and ensure sustainable growth in the era of Industry 4.0.

KEYWORDS

Artificial Intelligence (AI), Smart Factories, Industry 4.0, Manufacturing Optimization, Critical Success Factors, Workforce Development, Operational Efficiency, TOE Framework, Technological Infrastructure, Data Security

1. INTRODUCTION

The increasing adoption of Artificial Intelligence (AI) is transforming manufacturing by enhancing operational efficiency, sustainability, and workforce development (Blinova et al., 2024; Chernigovskaya et al., 2024). AI-driven smart manufacturing enables real-time decision-making, predictive maintenance, and process optimization, contributing to improved production flexibility and product quality (Wan et al., 2020; Jamwal et al., 2022; Psarommatis et al., 2023). Research indicates that organizations leveraging AI achieve higher profitability and efficiency by aligning with technological advancements (Jamwal et al., 2022).

Smart factories integrate key technologies such as machine learning, big data analytics, and the Internet of Things (IoT) to create adaptive, interconnected production environments (Ryalat et al., 2023; Dorneanu et al., 2022). These advancements enhance decision-making and resource allocation while reducing downtime and waste (Khan et al., 2022). However, AI adoption presents challenges, including high implementation costs, workforce skill gaps, cybersecurity risks, and interoperability issues with legacy systems (Elahi et al., 2023; Othman and Yang, 2023). Moreover, AI's full potential remains underutilized due to organizational resistance and data management limitations (Othman and Yang, 2023).

This study conducts a systematic literature review (SLR) to identify key success factors and challenges in AI integration for smart manufacturing (Sun, 2024). The research explores AI's role in optimizing efficiency, sustainability, and human-robot collaboration while providing industry leaders with a structured roadmap for implementation. The guiding research question is: *What are the critical success factors and challenges in integrating AI to optimize operational efficiency, sustainability, and workforce development in smart factories?*

The paper is structured as follows: Section 2 presents the background and literature review, Section 3 outlines the research methodology, Section 4 details key findings, Section 5 applies the Technology-Organization-Environment (TOE) framework, and Section 6 analyzes findings through this lens. Section 7 concludes with insights, recommendations, and future research directions.

2. BACKGROUND AND LITERATURE REVIEW

Smart manufacturing, a key aspect of Industry 4.0, integrates AI with advanced processes to transform traditional systems into intelligent, adaptive, and efficient operations (Blinova et al., 2024). Beyond operational improvements, this shift impacts economic, environmental, and social dimensions, drawing substantial academic and industrial attention (Dorneanu et al., 2022). Emerging technologies such as big data and machine learning drive efficiency, enabling real-time decision-making and predictive maintenance (Dorneanu et al., 2022; Blinova et al., 2024).

AI also plays a crucial role in sustainable manufacturing, optimizing processes to reduce waste and energy consumption while aligning with global sustainability efforts (Jamwal et al., 2022). However, high initial costs, complex data management, and workforce adaptation present significant adoption challenges. Additionally, human-robot collaboration is essential for improving productivity while ensuring worker safety and ergonomic benefits, requiring a balance between automation and human oversight (Othman and Yang, 2023).

This SLR explores these dynamics, providing a structured roadmap for understanding AI's role in smart manufacturing. By identifying critical success factors and challenges, it offers valuable insights for industry leaders and researchers to navigate AI adoption effectively.

3. RESEARCH METHOD

This study employs a SLR to assess AI integration in smart factories, ensuring a structured, transparent, and replicable approach (Riaño-Casallas and Rojas-Berrio, 2024). The methodology involves a multi-step process of data collection, selection, thematic analysis, and synthesis to ensure academic rigor and the identification of critical success factors and challenges.

Data collection was conducted through three major databases—ScienceDirect, Scopus, and Elsevier—using targeted search terms such as *"manufacturing," "AI," "smart factories," "workforce upskilling," "data management,"* and *"technological infrastructure."* The PRISMA (Preferred Reporting Items for Systematic Reviews and Meta-Analyses) framework was applied to ensure a systematic selection process. The initial search returned 210 articles. After eliminating 36 duplicates, 174 papers remained. Screening of abstracts, introductions, and conclusions led to the exclusion of 61 papers that lacked direct relevance to AI in smart factories, leaving 113 articles for full-text review. After applying inclusion and exclusion criteria, 34 peer-reviewed studies were selected for final analysis. The inclusion criteria required papers to be peer-reviewed journal articles or conference papers published in English, directly addressing AI's role in operational efficiency, sustainability, and workforce development in smart manufacturing. Exclusion criteria removed duplicate studies, non-English papers, those unrelated to the research question, and those lacking full-text availability.

A structured data extraction table was used to categorize selected papers based on their key themes. Thematic analysis, following Braun and Clarke's (2012) six-phase approach - familiarization, coding, theme generation, theme review, theme definition, and final synthesis - was employed to identify patterns in AI implementation, success factors, and challenges. The extracted data was then mapped to the Technology-Organization-Environment (TOE) framework (Tornatzky and Fleischer, 1990), categorizing insights into three dimensions: technology, organization, and environment. The **technology dimension** examined AI enablers such as IoT device integration, data analytics, and IT infrastructure. The **organization dimension** focused on leadership commitment, workforce upskilling, and strategic resource allocation. The **environment dimension** included regulatory compliance, cybersecurity concerns, and market-driven pressures.

By structuring findings within the TOE framework, this study provides a comprehensive perspective on AI adoption in smart factories, ensuring alignment between technological capabilities, organizational readiness, and external industry demands.

4. FINDINGS

This section analyzes the critical success factors and challenges of AI integration in smart manufacturing, focusing on its impact on **efficiency, sustainability, and human-robot collaboration**. The findings are categorized into **management commitment, technological infrastructure, workforce upskilling, data management, and strategic integration**, providing a comprehensive framework for understanding AI adoption challenges.

4.1 Management Commitment Factors

Management commitment plays a pivotal role in the successful implementation of AI technologies in smart factories, encompassing both strategic and operational support from senior leadership. This category is divided into four key sub-themes: resource allocation, leadership support, clear vision and strategy, and involvement in AI projects. Together, these sub-themes provide a comprehensive understanding of how management contributes to transforming traditional manufacturing into smart manufacturing.

The first sub-theme, **resource allocation**, ensures that adequate financial (Blinova et al., 2024; Dorneanu et al., 2022; Elahi et al., 2023; Riaño-Casallas and Rojas-Berrio, 2024; Minarro-Viseras et al., 2005) and material resources (Blinova et al., 2024; Elahi et al., 2023; Peretz-Andersson et al., 2024; Othman and Yang, 2023; Khan et al., 2022; Jamwal et al., 2022; Minarro-Viseras et al., 2005) are dedicated to AI initiatives. This allocation is essential for driving efficiency, fostering innovation, and achieving the scalability needed in manufacturing environment. **Leadership support** focuses on the involvement of senior management in AI projects, emphasizing top-level backing (Chernigovskaya et al., 2024; Othman and Yang, 2023) and cultural alignment (Chernigovskaya et al., 2024; Othman and Yang, 2023) to prioritize AI initiatives (Othman and Yang, 2023). Strong leadership not only reflects organizational commitment but also drives innovation and enhances overall manufacturing efficiency. The sub-theme **clear vision and strategy** underlines the importance of a well-defined roadmap for AI integration (Dorneanu et al., 2022; Liang et al., 2024). It includes setting clear objectives, identifying potential challenges, and ensuring alignment among stakeholders to create a unified approach to AI implementation (Ryalat et al., 2023; Pozzi et al., 2023). Lastly, **involvement in AI projects** highlights the need for active management participation in decision-making processes. This involvement ensures that AI initiatives are closely aligned with broader business goals, thereby enhancing both their effectiveness and long-term sustainability (Dorneanu et al., 2022).

4.2 Technological Infrastructure Factors

Technological infrastructure factors encompass the essential technological systems and elements that support the effective implementation of AI in smart manufacturing. These factors are organized into three primary sub-themes: the **integration of IoT devices**, **data analytics systems**, and **robust IT infrastructure**.

The first sub-theme, **integration of IoT devices**, highlights the importance of IoT sensors and devices in collecting real-time data in manufacturing environments (Dorneanu et al., 2022; Muruganandam et al., 2023; Ryalat et al., 2023; Soori et al., 2023; Hu et al., 2024). IoT facilitates continuous data flow and environmental monitoring, forming a critical foundation for AI algorithms to function effectively and without interruption. Additionally, IoT devices enable predictive maintenance, reducing downtime and optimizing resource allocation by identifying potential system failures in advance (Soori et al., 2023; Jamwal et al., 2022; Pozzi et al., 2023; Hu et al., 2024). **Data analytics systems** are pivotal for processing large datasets and identifying trends that enhance decision-making (Muruganandam et al., 2023; Koot et al., 2021; Bojana et al., 2017; Yu, 2023; Tang et al., 2022; Ryalat et al., 2023; Peretz-Andersson et al., 2024). These systems enable manufacturers to extract actionable insights, optimize resources, and ensure smooth transitions to smart manufacturing (Pozzi et al., 2023). Robust analytic capabilities facilitate better planning and execution, contributing to the successful implementation of AI technologies. **Robust IT infrastructure** underpins the computational demands of AI applications. It includes elements such as cloud computing for scalable data storage and processing (Shahbazi and Byun, 2021; Othman and Yang, 2023; Zhuang et al., 2021), as well as secure network infrastructures to protect sensitive manufacturing data (Pozzi et al., 2023; Dorneanu et al., 2022; Ryalat et al., 2023; Sun, 2024; Bojana et al., 2017). A reliable IT framework is crucial, as its absence can lead to failed implementation efforts and operational inefficiencies. The core technologies identified as essential for AI integration in smart factories, include IoT (Peretz-Andersson et al., 2024; Ryalat et al., 2023; Shahbazi and Byun, 2021; Othman and Yang, 2023; Tang et al., 2022; Soori et al., 2023; Fryer et al., 2007; Muruganandam et al., 2023; Hu et al., 2024), cloud computing (Shahbazi and Byun, 2021; Othman and Yang, 2023; Wan et al., 2020), and advanced analytics (Ryalat et al., 2023; Shahbazi and Byun, 2021; Othman and Yang, 2023; Pozzi et al., 2023; Minarro-Viseras et al., 2005; Ma et al., 2023), which collectively enable data-driven decision-making and sustainable manufacturing practices. Other technologies include robotics (Wan et al., 2020; Tang et al., 2022; Othman and Yang, 2023; Shahbazi and Byun, 2021; Ryalat et al., 2023; Hu et al., 2024), Augmented Reality (AR) (Othman and Yang, 2023; Pozzi et al., 2023), Cyber-Physical System (CPS) (Pozzi et al., 2023; Ryalat et al., 2023; Shahbazi and Byun, 2021; Dyba, 2005), Blockchain (Shahbazi and Byun, 2021; Othman and Yang, 2023), digital twins (Wan et al., 2020; Xie and Wan, 2023), and Machine Learning (ML) (Pozzi et al., 2023; Shahbazi and Byun, 2021).

This categorization provides a foundation for understanding how technological infrastructure supports AI integration, emphasizing the need for robust systems, advanced analytics, and seamless data flows to drive operational efficiency and innovation

4.3 Workforce Upskilling and Training Factors

Workforce upskilling and training are critical for developing employees' skills to effectively adapt to AI-driven manufacturing environments. This category is divided into four sub-themes: **regular training programs**, **skill development workshops**, and **incentive programs**.

Regular training programs are essential for equipping employees with the knowledge and skills to utilize the latest AI tools and techniques effectively. These programs foster a culture of continuous learning (Elahi et al., 2023; Fryer et al., 2007; Pozzi et al., 2023; Trkman, 2010), enabling employees to stay updated with advancements in AI (Wan et al., 2020; Elahi et al., 2023; Pozzi et al., 2023) and contribute to the organization's success. **Skill development workshops** focus on providing hands-on experience and practical knowledge (Pokorni et al., 2021; Trkman, 2010; Fryer et al., 2007; Pozzi et al., 2023; Wang et al., 2024), allowing employees to develop specialized capabilities in AI-related areas. These workshops bridge knowledge gaps and enable employees to undertake more complex and critical tasks (Othman and Yang, 2023). **Incentive programs** motivate employees to actively engage in upskilling activities by offering rewards for learning and applying new skills. Recognition and rewards serve as key drivers for continuous improvement, ensuring that employees remain committed to their professional growth and aligned with organizational goals (Muruganandam et al., 2023; Pozzi et al., 2023).

This structured approach to workforce development ensures that employees are prepared to navigate the evolving technological landscape, enhancing organizational adaptability and innovation.

4.4 Data Management and Security Factors

Data management and security factors are essential for ensuring the integrity, security, and usability of data used in AI technologies. This category comprises three sub-themes: **data security measures**, **data quality assurance**, and **governance frameworks**. **Data security measures** focus on implementing robust security protocols to protect AI systems from cyber threats, unauthorized access, and potential exploits. Key elements include cybersecurity protocols which safeguard data confidentiality and integrity (Othman and Yang, 2023; Ryalat et al., 2023; Bojana et al., 2017; Noiki et al., 2023), (Othman and Yang, 2023; Ryalat et al., 2023; Bojana et al., 2017; Noiki et al., 2023), and access control, which ensures that sensitive data is available only to authorized personnel (Elahi et al., 2023; Othman and Yang, 2023; Ryalat et al., 2023; Trkman, 2010; Xu et al., 2024). Preventative measures are critical to minimizing security breaches and maintaining trust in AI systems (Othman and Yang, 2023). **Data quality assurance** is vital for maintaining the accuracy, reliability, and completeness of data, which directly impacts AI performance (Pozzi et al., 2023). Quality assurance frameworks and procedures ensure that data remains consistent and dependable, enhancing the overall effectiveness of AI operation (Sun, 2024). **Governance frameworks** provide the structural support necessary to manage data responsibly and align with organizational policies. These frameworks encompass policy development to establish data management standards and compliance monitoring to ensure adherence to internal and external regulations. Effective governance is essential for maintaining high standards, achieving organizational goals, and fostering trust among stakeholders (Pozzi et al., 2023; Ryalat et al., 2023).

By addressing these factors, organizations can enhance the security, quality, and governance of their data, enabling reliable and ethical use of AI technologies in smart manufacturing.

5. THE TECHNOLOGY-ORGANIZATION-ENVIRONMENT (TOE) FRAMEWORK

The TOE framework (Tornatzky and Fleischer, 1990) provides a structured approach to analyzing factors that influence the adoption of new technologies in organizations, categorized into three dimensions: **Technology, Organization, and Environment**. The **Technology dimension** addresses the capabilities, complexity, and compatibility of AI with existing systems. Key enablers in smart manufacturing include **IoT devices, data analytics, and IT infrastructure**, which support AI-driven operations and real-time decision-making. The **Organization dimension** examines internal factors such as **management commitment, resource allocation, and workforce readiness**, which are critical for AI implementation. Leadership support and upskilling initiatives ensure that employees can adapt to AI-driven manufacturing processes. The **Environment dimension** includes external pressures such as **regulatory compliance, market competition, and cybersecurity standards**. Organizations must align with industry regulations, maintain data security, and adapt to market demands to ensure sustainable AI adoption.

Applying the TOE framework to AI integration in smart factories provides a holistic understanding of technological, organizational, and environmental influences. This structured approach helps industry leaders navigate AI adoption, enhance efficiency, and address implementation challenges in Industry 4.

6. ANALYSIS OF FINDINGS THROUGH THE LENS OF THE TOE FRAMEWORK

Mapping the identified success factors and challenges to the TOE framework provides a comprehensive understanding of the multi-dimensional influences shaping AI adoption in smart manufacturing.

6.1 Technological Factors

Technological factors influence AI adoption in smart manufacturing, including **IoT device integration, data analytics, IT infrastructure,** and **interoperability**. IoT devices enable real-time data collection and predictive maintenance, improving equipment monitoring and operational efficiency (Koot et al., 2021). However, deployment is costly and complex, requiring standardization for seamless integration.

Data analytics supports decision-making by processing vast datasets and optimizing resource allocation (Dorneanu et al., 2022). Yet, significant investment in software and hardware is required, and compatibility with legacy systems presents additional challenges. Robust IT infrastructure, including cloud computing and network security, is essential for AI-driven manufacturing (Elahi et al., 2023). Cloud computing enhances scalability, while security measures protect data integrity. However, maintaining these systems demands ongoing investment and updates.

Interoperability is crucial for integrating AI with existing technologies, ensuring smooth automation and data exchange. The lack of standardization can create barriers, requiring custom solutions or middleware (Ryalat et al., 2023). Collaboration with technology vendors is necessary to align AI systems with industry standards, enhancing long-term scalability and effectiveness.

6.2 Organizational Factors

Organizational factors influence AI adoption through **management commitment** and **workforce upskilling**. Strong management support ensures adequate resource allocation, leadership involvement, and a clear strategic vision. Financial and material resources are essential for scalable AI implementation (Yu, 2023), while leadership fosters a pro-innovation culture aligned with operational goals (Othman and Yang, 2023). A well-defined roadmap helps unify stakeholders in AI adoption (Dorneanu et al., 2022). However, high initial costs and inconsistent leadership support can hinder progress, risking incomplete implementation.

Workforce upskilling is critical for AI integration, requiring regular training programs, skill development workshops, and incentive structures. Continuous learning enhances employee proficiency with AI tools (Wan et al., 2020), while hands-on training bridges skill gaps (Pozzi et al., 2023). Incentive programs further motivate engagement and innovation (Muruganandam et al., 2023). However, sustaining investment in training and keeping pace with evolving AI technologies remain key challenges, necessitating alignment with broader organizational objectives.

6.3 Environmental Factors

Environmental factors influencing AI adoption include **data security measures, data quality assurance, and data governance frameworks**. AI systems rely on vast data volumes, making cybersecurity protocols and access control essential to prevent cyber threats and unauthorized access (Othman and Yang, 2023). However, maintaining robust security requires ongoing updates to counter evolving risks, as AI systems become increasingly critical to daily operations. Ensuring data accuracy and reliability is crucial for optimizing AI performance. High-quality data enhances predictive analytics and decision-making, while poor data management can lead to biases and inaccuracies (Sun, 2024). Organizations must invest in data quality practices to maintain AI effectiveness. Governance frameworks establish standards for responsible data management, ensuring transparency, accountability, and regulatory compliance (Pozzi et al., 2023). However, implementing these frameworks is resource-intensive and requires continuous monitoring to adapt to changing regulations. Proactively addressing these factors is essential for aligning AI adoption with industry regulations, safeguarding data integrity, and ensuring long-term success in smart manufacturing.

6.5 Recommendations for Smart Factory Owners and Industry Leaders

Based on the study's findings, the following recommendations offer actionable strategies for smart factory owners and industry stakeholders to improve AI integration, aligned with the TOE framework, to address key success factors and challenges.

6.5.1 Technological Recommendations

To address IoT deployment complexities, organizations should: **invest in interoperable IoT devices** aligned with industry standards, reducing compatibility challenges and ensuring seamless integration (Dorneanu et al., 2022); **collaborate with vendors and adopt modular IoT designs** to improve flexibility (Ryalat et al., 2023); **enhance data analytics infrastructure** by adopting scalable, cloud-based analytics systems to manage large datasets efficiently and lower costs (Muruganandam et al., 2023); **strengthen IT security protocols** by implementing real-time monitoring, multi-factor authentication, and encrypted data storage to protect sensitive manufacturing data from cyber threats (Othman and Yang, 2023); and **collaborate with vendors for interoperability** by ensuring AI systems integrate smoothly with legacy infrastructure and comply with evolving industry standards (Ryalat et al., 2023).

6.5.2 Organizational Recommendations

Organizations should **prioritize leadership support** by ensuring active involvement from senior management to sustain long-term AI projects, drive a pro-innovation culture, and align AI initiatives with organizational goals (Othman and Yang, 2023); **develop a strategic AI roadmap** by creating a clear, actionable plan that defines objectives, milestones, and resource needs, ensuring alignment across departments and stakeholders (Dorneanu et al., 2022); **expand workforce training programs** by implementing regular training and skill development workshops to equip employees with both technical and soft skills for effective AI adoption (Wan et al., 2020; Pozzi et al., 2023); and **introduce incentive-based learning** by establishing reward systems that encourage employees to engage in continuous upskilling, improving engagement and fostering innovation (Muruganandam et al., 2023).

6.5.3 Environmental Recommendations

Organizations should **establish robust governance frameworks** by developing comprehensive data governance policies to ensure regulatory compliance, promote ethical AI use, and enhance accountability through regular audits and monitoring (Pozzi et al., 2023); **focus on data quality management** by implementing automated tools to continuously monitor data accuracy and reliability, ensuring high-quality data for effective AI operations (Sun, 2024); **adapt to evolving regulations** by creating a compliance team to stay updated on changing legal and regulatory requirements related to AI and data security, mitigating risks and ensuring alignment with global standards (Ryalat et al., 2023); **leverage industry collaboration** by engaging with industry consortiums and technology partners to share best practices, co-develop standards, and accelerate progress in AI adoption (Dorneanu et al., 2022).

7. CONCLUSION

AI-driven smart manufacturing is essential for enhancing operational efficiency, sustainability, and human-robot collaboration, yet its integration remains complex. This systematic literature review analyzed 34 papers to identify critical success factors and challenges, organizing the findings using the Technology-Organization-Environment (TOE) framework. Technological factors, including IoT, data analytics, IT infrastructure, and interoperability, enable real-time monitoring and predictive maintenance but face challenges such as high costs and interoperability issues. Organizational readiness depends on management commitment, strategic planning, and workforce upskilling, though sustaining training investments remains a challenge. Environmental factors, including regulatory compliance, data security, and governance frameworks, are crucial for protecting data and meeting industry standards. A balanced approach across these dimensions is key to successful AI adoption. The TOE framework serves as a roadmap for navigating challenges and optimizing manufacturing processes. Future research should explore AI-driven predictive maintenance, human-centric AI design, and advanced cybersecurity to ensure sustainable and resilient AI integration in smart factories.

REFERENCES

Blinova, T., Pant, R., Nijhawan, G., Prakash, A. & Sharma, A. Innovations in Smart Manufacturing: An Experimental Assessment of Emerging Technologies. BIO Web of Conferences, 2024. EDP Sciences, 01064.

Bojana, N., Jelena, I., Suzic, N., Branislav, S. & Aleksandar, R. Predictive manufacturing systems in industry 4.0: Trends, benefits and challenges. Proceedings of 28th DAAAM International Symposium on Intelligent Manufacturing and Automation, 2017. DAAAM International, Vienna, Austria, 796-802.

Braun, V. & Clarke, V. (2012). *Thematic analysis*, American Psychological Association.

Chernigovskaya, M., Nahhas, A., Kharitonov, A. & Turowski, K. (2024). Hyper-parameter Optimization in the context of Smart Manufacturing: a Systematic Literature Review. *Procedia Computer Science,* 232, 804-812.

Dorneanu, B., Zhang, S., Ruan, H., Heshmat, M., Chen, R., Vassiliadis, V. S. & Arellano-Garcia, H. (2022). Big data and machine learning: A roadmap towards smart plants. *Frontiers of Engineering Management,* 9, 623-639.

Dyba, T. (2005). An empirical investigation of the key factors for success in software process improvement. *IEEE transactions on Software Engineering,* 31, 410-424.

Elahi, M., Afolaranmi, S. O., Martinez Lastra, J. L. & Perez Garcia, J. A. (2023). A comprehensive literature review of the applications of AI techniques through the lifecycle of industrial equipment. *Discover Artificial Intelligence,* 3, 43.

Fryer, K. J., Antony, J. & Douglas, A. (2007). Critical success factors of continuous improvement in the public sector: A literature review and some key findings. *The TQM magazine,* 19, 497-517.

Hu, Y., Jia, Q., Yao, Y., Lee, Y., Lee, M., Wang, C., Zhou, X., Xie, R. & Yu, F. R. (2024). Industrial Internet of Things Intelligence Empowering Smart Manufacturing: A Literature Review. *IEEE Internet of Things Journal.*

Jamwal, A., Agrawal, R. & Sharma, M. (2022). Deep learning for manufacturing sustainability: Models, applications in Industry 4.0 and implications. *International Journal of Information Management Data Insights,* 2, 100107.

Khan, A. N., Iqbal, N., Rizwan, A., Malik, S., Ahmad, R. & Kim, D. H. (2022). A criticality-aware dynamic task scheduling mechanism for efficient resource load balancing in constrained smart manufacturing environment. *IEEE Access,* 10, 50933-50946.

Koot, M., Mes, M. R. & Iacob, M. E. (2021). A systematic literature review of supply chain decision making supported by the Internet of Things and Big Data Analytics. *Computers & industrial engineering,* 154, 107076.

Liang, P., Sun, X. & Qi, L. (2024). Does artificial intelligence technology enhance green transformation of enterprises: Based on green innovation perspective. *Environment, Development and Sustainability,* 26, 21651-21687.

Ma, L., Zhang, J., Lin, L., Wang, T., Ma, C., Wang, X., Li, M., Qiao, Y., Wang, Y. & Zhang, G. (2023). Data-driven engineering framework with AI algorithm of Ginkgo Folium tablets manufacturing. *Acta Pharmaceutica Sinica B,* 13, 2188-2201.

Minarro-Viseras, E., Baines, T. & Sweeney, M. (2005). Key success factors when implementing strategic manufacturing initiatives. *International Journal of Operations & Production Management,* 25, 151-179.

Muruganandam, S., Salameh, A. A., Pozin, M. a. A., Manikanthan, S. & Padmapriya, T. (2023). Sensors and machine learning and AI operation-constrained process control method for sensor-aided industrial internet of things and smart factories. *Measurement: Sensors,* 25, 100668.

Noiki, A. A., Salawu, E. Y., Afolalu, S. A., Kayode, F. J. & Lawal, S. L. Leveraging Modelling and Simulation to address Manufacturing Challenges. 2023 International Conference on Science, Engineering and Business for Sustainable Development Goals (SEB-SDG), 2023. IEEE, 1-9.

Othman, U. & Yang, E. (2023). Human–robot collaborations in smart manufacturing environments: review and outlook. *Sensors,* 23, 5663.

Peretz-Andersson, E., Tabares, S., Mikalef, P. & Parida, V. (2024). Artificial intelligence implementation in manufacturing SMEs: A resource orchestration approach. *International Journal of Information Management,* 77, 102781.

Pokorni, B., Volz, F., Zwerina, J. & Hämmerle, M. Development of a holistic method to implement artificial intelligence in manufacturing areas. Advances in Artificial Intelligence, Software and Systems Engineering: Proceedings of the AHFE 2020 Virtual Conferences on Software and Systems Engineering, and Artificial Intelligence and Social Computing, July 16-20, 2020, USA, 2021. Springer, 3-8.

Pozzi, R., Rossi, T. & Secchi, R. (2023). Industry 4.0 technologies: critical success factors for implementation and improvements in manufacturing companies. *Production Planning & Control,* 34, 139-158.

Psarommatis, F., May, G. & Azamfirei, V. (2023). Envisioning maintenance 5.0: Insights from a systematic literature review of Industry 4.0 and a proposed framework. *Journal of Manufacturing Systems,* 68, 376-399.

Riaño-Casallas, M. I. & Rojas-Berrio, S. (2024). How to Report Systematic Literature Reviews in Management Using SyReMa. *Innovar: Revista de ciencias administrativas y sociales,* 34, 1-16.

Ryalat, M., Elmoaqet, H. & Alfaouri, M. (2023). Design of a smart factory based on cyber-physical systems and Internet of Things towards Industry 4.0. *Applied Sciences,* 13, 2156.

Shahbazi, Z. & Byun, Y.-C. (2021). Integration of blockchain, IoT and machine learning for multistage quality control and enhancing security in smart manufacturing. *Sensors,* 21, 1467.

Soori, M., Arezoo, B. & Dastres, R. (2023). Internet of things for smart factories in industry 4.0, a review. *Internet of Things and Cyber-Physical Systems,* 3, 192-204.

Sun, Y. (2024). Research on the trend and optimization path of China's older adult service industry. *Journal of Infrastructure, Policy and Development,* 8, 2826.

Tang, Q., Yu, F. R., Xie, R., Boukerche, A., Huang, T. & Liu, Y. (2022). Internet of intelligence: A survey on the enabling technologies, applications, and challenges. *IEEE Communications Surveys & Tutorials,* 24, 1394-1434.

Tornatzky, L. & Fleischer, M. (1990). The process of technology innovation, Lexington, MA. Lexington books.

Trkman, P. (2010). The critical success factors of business process management. *International journal of information management,* 30, 125-134.

Wan, J., Li, X., Dai, H.-N., Kusiak, A., Martinez-Garcia, M. & Li, D. (2020). Artificial-intelligence-driven customized manufacturing factory: key technologies, applications, and challenges. *Proceedings of the IEEE,* 109, 377-398.

Wang, X., Hu, X. & Wan, J. (2024). Digital-twin based real-time resource allocation for hull parts picking and processing. *Journal of Intelligent Manufacturing,* 35, 613-632.

Xie, J. & Wan, J. (2023). Digital Twin Four-Dimension Fusion Modeling Method Design and Application to the Discrete Manufacturing Line. *Big Data and Cognitive Computing,* 7, 89.

Xu, F., Yin, Z., Han, G., Li, Y., Zhang, F. & Bi, Y. (2024). Multi-objective fog node placement strategy based on heuristic algorithms for smart factories. *Wireless Networks,* 30, 5407-5424.

Yu, Y. (2023). Packaging design of virtual manufacturing products based on computer vision and big data. *The International Journal of Advanced Manufacturing Technology*, 1-13.

Zhuang, M., Li, G., Ding, K. & Xu, G. (2021). Optimized design of mechanical chain drive based on a wireless sensor network data algorithm. *Journal of Sensors,* 2021, 2901624.

FROM CATALOGUES TO E-COMMERCE: UNDERSTANDING PROCUREMENT IN DAYCARE CENTERS

Marcel Patalon, Christian Paul and Peter Weber
South Westphalia University of Applied Sciences
Lübecker Ring 2, 59494 Soest, Germany

ABSTRACT

This study explores the organizational buying behavior (OBB) of daycare centers in Germany, focusing on how technological, organizational, and environmental factors shape procurement practices. Using the Technology-Organization-Environment (TOE) framework, it analyzes how daycare centers navigate digital procurement within regulatory constraints, limited resources, and mission-driven priorities. A quantitative survey of 857 daycare centers shows that, although digital tools like e-commerce platforms are gradually being adopted, many centers remain cautious due to concerns about trust, data security, and digital competencies. Traditional procurement methods, including in-store purchases, continue to be highly trusted. The findings indicate that daycare centers prioritize child safety, pedagogical quality, and regulatory compliance over cost-efficiency in procurement decisions. These results challenge traditional OBB models by underscoring the significance of non-economic factors in decision-making processes for smaller, resource-constrained entities. By applying the TOE framework, this study offers a nuanced understanding of the complexities surrounding digital adoption in daycare centers, contributing to both OBB and digital transformation literature. It also suggests practical measures, such as targeted digital literacy training and support programs, to encourage digital tool adoption in this sector. Future research should examine digital adoption's long-term impacts, cross-national differences, and barriers, offering insights for adaptive strategies and tailored support in daycare procurement.

KEYWORDS

Organizational Buying Behavior, Procurement, Technology-Organization-Environment Framework

1. INTRODUCTION

The digital transformation of organizational buying behavior (OBB) has deepened the divide between resource-rich and resource-constrained organizations, particularly in regulated sectors like early childhood education (Aditya & Andrisyah, 2023; Joseph et al., 2024). While large organizations utilize advanced digital procurement tools to enhance operational efficiency, smaller, mission-driven organizations face challenges in balancing technological adoption with regulatory compliance and social responsibilities (Müller et al., 2018). Traditional OBB frameworks, which emphasize resource availability and economic efficiency, often overlook these mission-driven contexts, where social priorities outweigh profit motives (Johnston & Lewin, 1996; Makkonen et al., 2012). This theoretical tension is particularly evident in daycare centers (Ljunggren, 2024). Daycare centers operate under strict regulatory requirements, balancing child safety and pedagogical quality while managing digital transformation with limited resources, technological competency gaps, and data security concerns (Biedinger, 2019; German Federal Ministry of Justice, 1990). Although digital procurement tools can streamline access to suppliers and products, thereby improving efficiency (Strohmer et al., 2020), their adoption remains inconsistent, as many centers continue to rely on traditional methods (Abu-ELSamen et al., 2010). These challenges necessitate a reevaluation of conventional OBB assumptions.

This study applies the Technology-Organization-Environment (TOE) framework by Tornatzky and Fleischer (1990) to analyze procurement behavior in German daycare centers. Unlike traditional OBB models, the TOE framework offers a comprehensive lens by integrating technological capabilities, organizational constraints, and environmental pressures (Baker, 2012). Therefore, our central research question asks: *How do technological, organizational, and environmental factors shape procurement decisions in daycare centers?* Specifically, we aim to (a) identify key factors influencing procurement behavior and (b) develop an empirical understanding of procurement practices. Using data from a quantitative survey of 857 daycare centers in Germany, we analyze procurement decisions for items such as educational materials, safety equipment, and operational supplies.

This research extends OBB literature by applying the TOE framework to an underexplored context, demonstrating that daycare procurement decisions are driven not only by economic factors but also by child safety, pedagogical quality, and digital trust. It highlights the role of non-economic factors in procurement and contributes to digital transformation literature by showing that successful adoption of digital tools depends on trust and regulatory alignment. The paper is organized as follows: first, we integrate OBB theory with the TOE framework. Next, we outline the methodology, present findings, and conclude with discussions of theoretical and practical implications, limitations, and future research directions.

2. THEORETICAL BACKGROUND

OBB is a complex field that has evolved significantly over time, shifting from classical economic models to frameworks that account for behavioral, social, and relational factors. Early models, such as Marshall's (1890) principles of economics, focused on rational, cost-based decision-making, assuming that firms make purchasing decisions to maximize utility. However, this perspective was challenged by Simon's (1955) concept of bounded rationality, which suggested that organizations often operate under constraints, making decisions that are satisfactory rather than optimal due to limited information and cognitive limitations. This paved the way for more nuanced theories, such as Cyert's et al. (1959) behavioral theory of the firm, which highlighted the role of internal routines and external pressures in shaping decision-making processes. Building on these foundational theories, Sheth's (1973) model of industrial buyer behavior emphasized the importance of psychological and social factors, proposing that organizational purchasing is influenced by individual decision-makers' preferences and relationships with suppliers. Robinson's et al. (1967) Buygrid framework further categorized buying decisions into various tasks, highlighting that different types of purchases—ranging from straight rebuys to new tasks—require varying levels of effort and complexity.

These models collectively recognize that OBB is not solely a rational process but one influenced by a range of factors, including organizational context and external environments. Prior (2021) argues that traditional OBB models inadequately capture the non-linear nature of modern purchasing decisions, particularly in resource-constrained organizations. This limitation is especially evident in sectors like early childhood education, where organizations must balance multiple competing priorities beyond cost efficiency, including regulatory compliance, safety standards, and educational outcomes. Therefore, Prior's (2021) critique underscores the need for a more comprehensive framework that can accommodate the dynamic nature of digital adoption.

2.1 TOE Framework as a Lens for Understanding Daycare Procurement

The TOE framework, introduced by Tornatzky and Fleischer (1990), is widely used in technology adoption studies due to its comprehensive structure (Baker, 2012). Unlike traditional OBB models that primarily focus on economic factors, this framework accounts for technological, organizational, and environmental factors. Alternative models, such as the Technology Acceptance Model (TAM) and the Unified Theory of Acceptance and Use of Technology (UTAUT), focus on individual user attitudes and perceived ease of use (Davis, 1989; Venkatesh et al., 2003). However, these models are less effective in addressing the broader organizational and environmental factors critical in regulated sectors like early childhood education. For example, TAM's focus on perceived usefulness neglects regulatory compliance and trust concerns central to daycare procurement. Similarly, UTAUT's emphasis on user intentions overlooks structural and policy constraints faced by small organizations. In contrast, the TOE framework's multidimensional approach offers a comprehensive lens for examining procurement behavior in daycare centers. By tailoring the TOE framework to daycare procurement, we gain deeper insights into how internal capabilities, constraints, external compliance mandates, and sector-specific challenges shape technology adoption. Figure 1 illustrates the adapted Technology, Organization, and Environment contexts, highlighting their roles in digital procurement decisions within daycare settings.

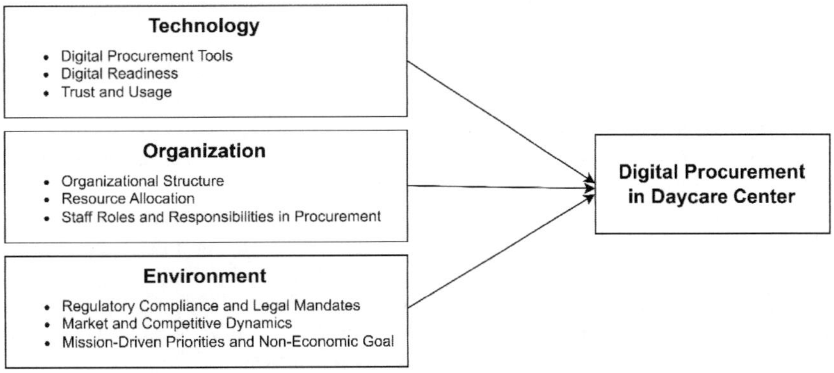

Figure 1. Digital procurement daycare center framework based on Tornatzky and Fleischer (1990)

In the original TOE framework, the technology context refers to available and emerging technologies that shape an organization's capacity for innovation (Tornatzky & Fleischer, 1990). For daycare centers, this includes digital procurement tools such as e-commerce platforms, online catalogs, and digital marketplaces, as well as the organization's readiness to adopt them. Digital tools enhance supplier access and decision-making efficiency (Motaung & Sifolo, 2023). However, daycare centers often face barriers like limited digital literacy and data security concerns (Müller et al., 2018). Trust and perceived risks, such as concerns over platform reliability and data security, influence adoption decisions as organizations balance these factors against potential efficiency gains (Cho & Choi, 2022; Karanatova & Kulev, 2020). Thus, the technological context must consider the availability of digital procurement tools, digital readiness, and the perceived trustworthiness necessary for their adoption.

The organization context in the TOE framework encompasses internal factors like structure, resources, and processes that influence technology adoption (Tornatzky & Fleischer, 1990). In daycare centers, decentralized structures often distribute procurement responsibilities across administrators, educators, and support staff, complicating decision-making and creating inefficiencies (Müller et al., 2018). Limited financial and human resources further hinder the adoption of digital tools, as tight budgets and staff workloads prioritize caregiving and operational needs over technological investments (Biedinger, 2019; Strohmer et al., 2020). Therefore, this context must consider the organizational structure, resource allocation, and staff roles in procurement.

The environmental context of the TOE framework addresses external pressures, such as regulatory frameworks, competitive dynamics, and industry standards, that shape technology adoption (Oliveira & Martins, 2011; Tornatzky & Fleischer, 1990). Regulatory compliance plays a pivotal role in daycare center procurement, driven by legal mandates and standards focused on child safety and care quality (German Federal Ministry of Justice, 1990). Daycare centers operate in a reputation-sensitive environment, where adherence to standards often complicates the adoption of digital tools, particularly when platforms are perceived as misaligned with regulations or organizational values (Prior, 2021). Market and competitive dynamics further influence this landscape, as centers compete on cost and quality to attract parents. Balancing affordability with priorities such as safety standards, pedagogical goals, and regulatory compliance heightens competition and shapes procurement decisions (Biedinger, 2019; Strohmer et al., 2020). Unlike larger organizations, daycare centers prioritize social missions, including child welfare and education, which frequently conflict with cost-driven procurement approaches (Walker et al., 2020). This context includes regulatory compliance, competitive dynamics, and the balance of cost, quality, and mission priorities.

3. METHODOLOGY

This study employs a quantitative approach, guided by the TOE framework, to examine factors influencing procurement behavior in German daycare centers.

Data were gathered via a web-based survey using LimeSurvey, a platform widely recognized for its reliability, security, and adaptability in academic research (Vehovar & Manfreda, 2017). The survey was distributed via email to 9,701 daycare centers across eight German federal states to ensure broad geographic diversity (Dillman et al., 2014). Of the 1,018 daycare centers that participated, 161 incomplete responses were excluded, leaving 857 fully completed surveys for analysis. To reach this sample, email addresses were compiled through web crawling techniques, allowing for extensive outreach and minimizing selection bias (Schäfer, 2016). The survey was open for responses from June to July 2024. This distribution strategy was chosen to mitigate non-response bias and to enhance the study's generalizability (Groves et al., 2009). A stratified random sampling technique was applied to ensure representation of the diverse daycare centers in Germany. Stratification was based on organization type (public, private, non-profit), geographic location (North, South, East, West), and size (number of children enrolled) (Cochran, 1977). This stratified approach allowed the study to capture potential variations in procurement practices across different institutional contexts, improving the representativeness and reliability of the results (Yin, 2017).

All participants were informed of the study's purpose, confidentiality measures, and data usage, in compliance with ethical standards in research (Williams & Pigeot, 2017). Participation was voluntary, and respondents were assured that their responses would be anonymized and used solely for academic purposes.

The survey was designed around the key dimensions of the TOE framework, with items tailored to the specific context of daycare procurement. Drawing on insights from the literature and the theoretical background, the instrument focused on the acquisition of essential children's items, including toys, learning materials, musical instruments, hygiene products, and furnishings (DeVellis, 2017).

It comprised three key domains:

1. **Technological Factors:** 18 items assessed information sourcing, procurement channels, and trust levels, evaluating digital readiness and technology adoption.
2. **Organizational Characteristics:** 9 items explored internal structures, resource availability, and staff roles in procurement decisions.
3. **Environmental Factors:** 14 items examined external pressures, including regulatory requirements and market conditions, highlighting compliance as a key driver.

Questions specific to procurement channels and trust levels utilized five-point Likert-type scales to gauge both the frequency of channel use (ranging from "never" to "always") and the level of trust in each channel (from "no trust" to "full trust"). Additionally, psychographic factors related to the importance of tangible asset procurement were surveyed using a similar scale (from "not at all important" to "very important") (Harpe, 2015; Likert, 1932).

The survey was validated with input from early childhood education experts and counseling leaders for 58 daycare centers, ensuring that it accurately reflected the procurement challenges encountered by these institutions. This validation ensured content relevance and clarity, enhancing the survey's reliability (Luque-Vara et al., 2020).

Data analysis was conducted using SPSS 29, applying a range of descriptive statistical techniques to summarize and interpret the responses (Pallant, 2020). Key descriptive measures, such as frequencies, percentages, means, standard derivation, variance, and skewness for each factor were used to summarize the data and to provide an overview of the procurement practices of the daycare centers (Grant et al., 2016). Likert-scale responses were treated as ordinal data and analyzed using appropriate descriptive statistics to summarize trends in procurement behaviors, trust in procurement channels, and decision-making factors (Jamieson, 2004). This approach aligns with best practices in survey analysis and allows for accurate interpretation of how procurement behaviors vary across institutional contexts (Fowler, 2014).

4. RESULTS

The survey received responses from 857 daycare centers, achieving an 84.1% completion rate from the participating sample. The geographical distribution of respondents varied significantly across German federal states. Baden-Wuerttemberg had the highest representation with 284 participants (33.14%), followed by Bavaria with 198 (23.10%) and Saxony with 132 (15.40%). Other notable states included Schleswig-Holstein (111, 12.95%) and North Rhine-Westphalia (79, 9.22%). The remaining states—Lower Saxony, Rhineland-Palatinate, Saarland, and Thuringia—contributed 53 respondents (6.17%).

Figure 2 presents detailed information on the organizational characteristics of the daycare providers. Most providers were private non-profit (44.46%), followed closely by public providers (40.61%). A smaller proportion included parent initiatives (5.95%) and private for-profit institutions (2.92%). The typical institution size included 50-57 children (24.97%), with 20.54% serving 75-99 children and 22.52% accommodating 25-50 children. A minority of providers managed fewer than 25 children (11.20%). The annual material budget reveals varied financial resources. Most respondents reported budgets under 5,000€ (24.27%) or in unspecified "other" categories (24.15%), followed by budgets under 3,000€ (17.39%), 2,000€ (21.94%), and 1,000€ (11.44%).

Figure 3 illustrates that 95.1% of respondents had direct procurement responsibilities. Managers were the primary decision-makers, representing 82.85% of the roles, while 5.25% were deputy managers, and 1.4% were daycare group leaders. Regarding the number of people involved in procurement, 37.81% managed it in teams of two, while 31.39% handled procurement individually.

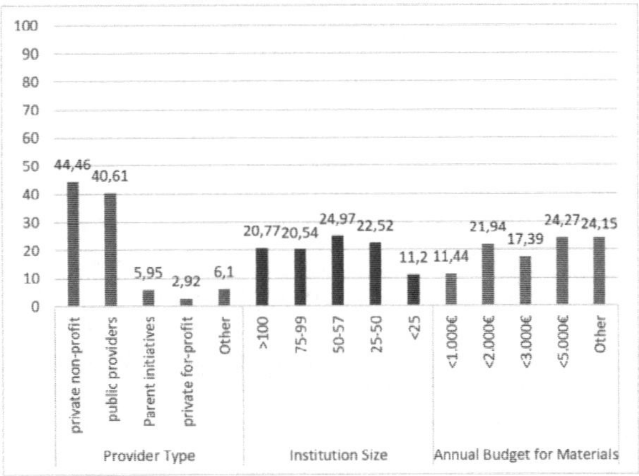

Figure 2. Organizational characteristics of daycare centers in Germany

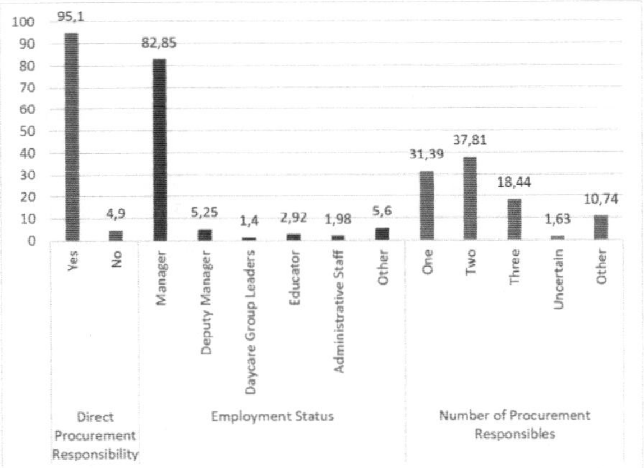

Figure 3. Procurement responsibilities of daycare centers in Germany

As illustrated in Figure 4, the gender distribution showed a predominance of female respondents (95.68%), with a smaller proportion identifying as male (23.57%) or diverse (0.58%). Most respondents were aged 35–44 (47.02%) and 45–54 (46.09%), while younger (18–24: 6.53%) and older (65+: 2.22%) age groups were underrepresented.

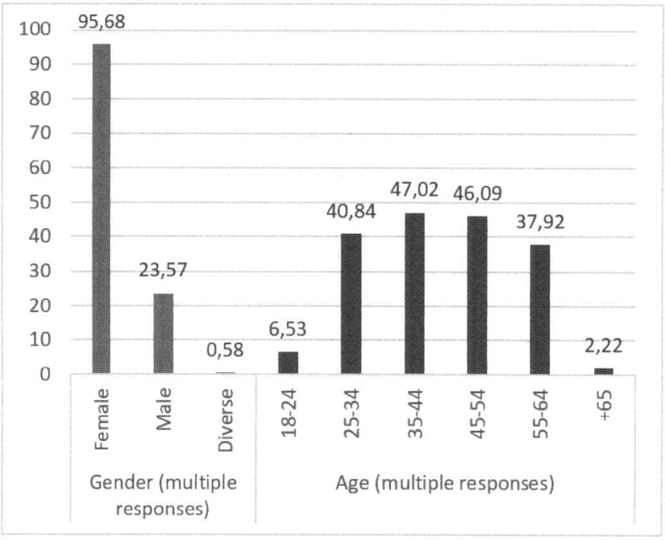

Figure 4. Gender and age distribution of daycare centers in Germany

This data reveals that procurement responsibilities are concentrated in managerial roles, with managers being the predominant decision-makers. The involvement of multiple individuals in procurement across many institutions suggests a collaborative approach. Additionally, the variation in annual budgets indicates a range of resource availability, which may influence procurement strategies and choices. Furthermore, the significant representation of female procurement-responsible individuals aligns with the demographic trends in the daycare sector, emphasizing the gendered nature of roles in early childhood care.

4.1 Trust, Usage, and Environmental Influences in Procurement Channels

In analyzing trust in procurement channels, we observed the highest trust in in-store purchasing, with a mean of 4.06 ± 0.754, variance of 0.568, and skewness of -0.465, indicating a slightly left-skewed distribution of responses. Catalogs followed with a mean of 3.90 ± 0.731, variance of 0.534, and a skewness of -0.166, reflecting a more symmetrical distribution. Trust in company websites showed a mean of 3.95 ± 0.714, variance of 0.509, and a skewness of -0.479, suggesting a preference for this digital option as well. As shown in Table 1, respondents most frequently used online search engines for information, with a mean of 3.69 ± 0.858, variance of 0.735, and a skewness of -1.04, indicating a strong preference among many respondents. Company websites followed with a mean of 3.50 ± 0.899, variance of 0.808, and skewness of -0.842. Social media was the least used channel, with a mean of 1.63 ± 0.773, variance of 0.774, and a positive skewness of 1.30, suggesting a concentration of responses at the lower end. E-commerce platforms had a mean usage of 3.01 ± 1.19, variance of 1.41, and skewness of -0.429, reflecting moderate variability in usage.

These results indicate a dual preference for both digital and traditional information channels in procurement, with Online Search Engines and Company Websites leading in information gathering, while In-Store interactions and Company Websites dominate in terms of trust. This suggests that while digital tools are pivotal in the initial stages of procurement, trust is still strongly associated with physical interactions and established traditional channels. The lower trust in E-Commerce Platforms compared to other digital sources could point to ongoing concerns about reliability and transparency in online transactions. Moreover, the relatively low usage and trust in Social Media for procurement suggest that it is not yet a mainstream channel for professional decision-making in this context. This presents an opportunity for further exploration into how these platforms could potentially enhance their role in the procurement landscape.

Table 1. Descriptive statistics of technological factors: Information, Usage and Trust in Procurement Channels

Factors	Categories	Mean	SD	Variance	Skewness
Information Channels for Procurement	Catalog	3.36	0.883	0.780	-0.549
	Online Search Engines	3.69	0.858	0.735	-1.04
	Company Websites	3.50	0.899	0.808	-0.842
	Social Media	1.63	0.773	0.774	1.30
	E-Commerce Platforms	2.99	1.169	1.36	-0.362
	Newsletters	2.02	0.881	0.882	0.580
	Sales Representatives	2.26	0.985	0.970	0.290
	In-Store	2.77	0.913	0.835	-0.190
Procurement Channels usage	Catalog	3.02	1.06	1.12	-0.472
	Company Websites	3.59	0.844	0.713	-0.887
	E-Commerce Platforms	3.01	1.19	1.41	-0.429
	Sales Representatives	2.20	0.992	0.984	0.416
	In-Store	2.86	0.868	0.753	-0.205
Trust in Procurement Channels	Catalog	3.90	0.731	0.534	-0.166
	Company Websites	3.95	0.714	0.509	-0.479
	E-Commerce Platforms	3.03	0.922	0.851	-0.181
	Sales Representatives	3.42	1.00	1.01	-0.334
	In-Store	4.06	0.754	0.568	-0.465

Table 2 highlights the environmental factors influencing procurement decisions. Providers prioritized pedagogical value, with a mean of 4.84 ± 0.366, variance of 0.134, and skewness of -1.98, indicating a strong preference for this criterion. Quality and durability followed with a mean of 4.74 ± 0.467, variance of 0.218, and skewness of -1.41. Price considerations, with a mean of 4.26 ± 0.726, variance of 0.527, and skewness of -0.727, were also important. Brand importance was rated lower, with a mean of 2.61 ± 0.976, variance of 0.952, and skewness of 0.159, showing a more evenly distributed view among respondents. Perceptions influencing procurement decisions included budget constraints, with a mean of 4.32 ± 0.932, variance of 0.869, and skewness of -1.65, highlighting its critical role. Stakeholder feedback had a mean of 4.38 ± 0.625, variance of 0.391, and skewness of -0.700. The increasing role of e-commerce in procurement decisions showed a mean of 4.22 ± 0.771, variance of 0.594, and skewness of -1.19, suggesting that many providers are adapting to digital procurement.

The findings highlight that pedagogical considerations, safety, and product quality are the primary drivers of procurement decisions in daycare centers, underscoring the focus on providing a safe and enriching environment for children. The growing importance of eco-friendly products also reflects an increasing awareness of sustainability in the sector. While digital transformation is making headway, as evidenced by the importance of e-commerce and digitalization, traditional factors like stakeholder feedback and budget constraints remain central to the decision-making process. The relatively lower emphasis on brand and obtaining multiple quotes suggests that daycare providers may prioritize product functionality and alignment with educational goals over brand prestige or formalized procurement procedures.

Table 2. Descriptive statistics of environmental factors influencing Procurement Decisions

Factors	Categories	Mean	SD	Variance	Skewness
Importance	Safety	4.47	0.709	0.502	-1.35
	Eco-friendly	4.18	0.701	0.492	-0.537
	Pedagogical Value	4.84	0.366	0.134	-1.98
	Quality and Durability	4.74	0.467	0.218	-1.41
	Price	4.26	0.726	0.527	-0.727
	Brand	2.61	0.976	0.952	0.159
	Innovation	3.20	0.831	0.691	-0.164
Perception	Efficiency	3.30	0.939	0.883	-0.315
	Budget Constraints	4.32	0.932	0.869	-1.65
	Stakeholder Feedback	4.38	0.625	0.391	-0.700
	Obtaining three quotes	2.45	1.10	1.21	0.456
	Payment on Invoice	3.83	1.15	1.34	-0.810
	increasing role of e-commerce	4.22	0.771	0.594	-1.19
	Increasing role of digitalization	3.63	1.00	1.01	-0.424

5. DISCUSSION

This study examined the OBB of daycare centers in Germany, focusing on how procurement practices are shaped by technological, organizational, and environmental factors. By applying the TOE framework, we provide a nuanced understanding of procurement processes in smaller, resource-constrained institutions. The findings contribute to the broader literature on OBB and digital adoption, particularly in highly regulated, mission-driven environments.

Our results highlight the critical yet uneven role of technology in shaping procurement behaviors in daycare centers. While digital tools such as e-commerce platforms (3.01 ± 1.19) and company websites (3.50 ± 0.89) are moderately utilized, traditional procurement channels continue to dominate. In-store purchasing (4.06 ± 0.75) and catalogs (3.90 ± 0.73) remain the most trusted channels, indicating a persistent reluctance to fully transition to digital procurement. These findings align with prior studies emphasizing the importance of trust in smaller organizations' technology adoption (Cho & Choi, 2022). Trust emerged as a decisive factor in digital adoption, with respondents exhibiting a clear preference for established procurement methods over newer digital channels. This reluctance is reinforced by the low trust in social media as a procurement tool (1.63 ± 0.77), underscoring concerns over security, reliability, and transparency. These barriers are consistent with previous research indicating that trust remains a significant determinant of technology adoption in smaller organizations (Cho & Choi, 2022). However, the moderate usage of e-commerce platforms and search engines (3.69 ± 0.86) suggests a gradual shift towards digital solutions, albeit at a slower pace compared to larger organizations with greater technological capabilities (Müller et al., 2018). To foster trust in digital procurement, suppliers should enhance transparency with certified safety labels, clear pricing, and regulatory compliance assurances. These measures reassure daycare centers about product quality and safety while establishing credibility. Nevertheless, trust concerns extend beyond supplier actions. Procurement personnel need training in cybersecurity, fraud prevention, and digital tool navigation to mitigate risks and confidently use digital platforms. At the same time, regulatory bodies can strengthen credibility by introducing certified procurement platforms that meet compliance standards, offering daycare centers reliable, pre-vetted solutions. Combined, these efforts reduce uncertainty, drive adoption, and create a more secure, transparent procurement environment.

Organizational structure significantly influences procurement behavior in daycare centers. Procurement responsibilities are highly centralized, with 95.1% of respondents directly involved in procurement decisions. Managers (82.85%) play the primary role, while procurement is less frequently handled by deputy managers (5.25%) or daycare group leaders (1.4%). This hierarchical structure is consistent with findings by Baker (2012), which demonstrate that resource-constrained organizations tend to centralize decision-making to maintain control over procurement activities. Despite this centralization, purchasing decisions often involve collaboration. While 31.39% of respondents handle procurement individually, 37.81% manage procurement in teams of two, reflecting a balance between centralized authority and stakeholder input. Resource limitations constrain the extent to which smaller daycare centers can explore innovative procurement strategies such as cooperative purchasing or digital procurement platforms. Variations in procurement budgets further reinforce these disparities. While 24.27% of daycare centers operate with budgets under 5,000€, a substantial proportion (21.94%) manage budgets under 2,000€. This financial constraint limits their ability to invest in digital procurement solutions, leading many centers to continue relying on traditional procurement methods. Therefore, improving procurement efficiency in daycare centers requires collaboration, administrative support, and digital tools. Strengthening collaborative decision-making enhances purchasing power, enabling better supplier negotiations and resource allocation. Providing procurement training and sharing best practices equip teams to navigate purchasing processes effectively. Meanwhile, automating workflows with digital platforms and integrated approval systems streamlines decision-making, ensuring efficiency, compliance, and cost control. These strategies collectively reduce administrative burdens while optimizing procurement outcomes.

Environmental factors, particularly regulatory requirements, exert a profound influence on procurement decisions, often outweighing cost considerations. Compliance with Germany's Social Code (1990) mandates high standards for child safety, pedagogical quality, and environmental sustainability, which strongly shape procurement priorities. The results highlight this regulatory influence, as pedagogical value (4.84 ± 0.37) and quality/durability (4.74 ± 0.47) ranked significantly higher than price considerations (4.26 ± 0.73). These findings support prior research (Magnuson et al., 2004), indicating that early childhood education institutions prioritize quality over cost-efficiency when child welfare is at stake. Additionally, environmental concerns are increasingly shaping procurement choices. The preference for eco-friendly products (4.18 ± 0.70) suggests that daycare centers are incorporating sustainability considerations into procurement decisions. However, regulatory complexity and budget constraints often hinder their ability to consistently prioritize sustainable purchasing. These findings challenge traditional OBB models that emphasize cost-efficiency, suggesting that frameworks like TOE, which account for regulatory and social dimensions, are better suited to analyzing procurement behavior in daycare centers. This aligns with Magnuson et al. (2004), who noted similar prioritization of quality over cost in educational settings, particularly when decisions impact child outcomes. That implies that, a certification system for suppliers could ensure access to pre-vetted, high-quality products while reducing administrative burdens. Implementing this as a government-backed or industry-driven initiative would streamline procurement. To further support sustainability, policymakers could offer subsidies, tax reductions, or special funding, enabling daycare centers to adopt eco-friendly practices without compromising quality or cost efficiency.

By applying the TOE framework, this study provides a holistic perspective on how daycare centers navigate procurement challenges, demonstrating the interplay between technological readiness, organizational characteristics, and environmental pressures. Unlike traditional OBB models focused on economic efficiency, the TOE framework captures the unique constraints and priorities of highly regulated, mission-driven organizations. Our findings reinforce Baker's (2012) argument that the TOE framework is adaptable to diverse settings, including small service-oriented institutions. Furthermore, this research highlights that while digital tools offer significant opportunities for efficiency and innovation, their adoption requires overcoming trust barriers and building digital competencies within these organizations.

Despite offering valuable insights, this study has also limitations. The study's focus on daycare centers in Germany limits the generalizability of findings, as procurement behavior may differ in countries with varying regulations, cultural norms, and digital infrastructures. Its cross-sectional design captures procurement practices at a single point in time, preventing insights into changes over time; longitudinal studies could better track adaptation to digital tools and evolving regulations. Internal decision-making dynamics, such as organizational culture and individual preferences, remain underexplored, yet these factors likely influence procurement behavior. Qualitative methods, such as interviews, could provide deeper insights. Reliance on self-reported data poses risks of bias, such as over-reporting digital tool usage to conform to industry norms; incorporating objective data sources, like procurement records, would enhance accuracy. While the TOE framework is valuable, it may overlook sector-specific nuances, such as psychological and relational factors in purchasing; integrating additional theories could offer a more comprehensive understanding. Additionally, advanced statistical methods, such as linear regression, logistic regression, or structural equation modeling, were not employed in this study but could provide a more detailed examination of the relationships between independent and dependent variables. Lastly, barriers to digital adoption, such as limited digital literacy or infrastructure challenges, are not fully addressed.

Future research should address several areas to deepen the understanding of OBB in daycare centers. Longitudinal studies could track the evolution of procurement practices, examining how centers adapt to digital tools and regulatory changes over time. Such studies would shed light on the long-term impacts of digital adoption and the factors sustaining or hindering these changes. Expanding beyond the German context, cross-national comparisons could explore how varying regulatory frameworks and digital infrastructures shape procurement behaviors, providing a global perspective on challenges and opportunities in the childcare sector. Qualitative approaches, such as case studies or interviews with managers and staff, could offer deeper insights into internal decision-making processes. These methods can reveal how organizational culture, individual attitudes, and power dynamics influence procurement decisions, complementing broader quantitative findings. Research should also focus on specific barriers to digital adoption in smaller centers, such as digital literacy gaps, security concerns, and budget constraints. Understanding these obstacles could guide the development of tailored support programs to bridge the digital divide between resource-rich and resource-constrained centers. Finally, future studies could explore the potential of emerging technologies like artificial intelligence and machine learning to optimize procurement. Investigating how these tools can address the unique needs of daycare centers may open new pathways for efficiency and cost-effectiveness, further modernizing procurement practices in this sector.

6. CONCLUSION

This study highlights that daycare centers prioritize child safety, pedagogical quality, and regulatory compliance over purely economic considerations in procurement decisions. These priorities are shaped by regulatory frameworks like Germany's Social Code, which emphasize safety and educational outcomes. While digital tools such as e-commerce platforms are gaining traction, adoption remains uneven. Trust concerns, resource constraints, and data security issues pose significant barriers, particularly for smaller, resource-limited centers. Larger centers, with greater capacity, are more likely to integrate digital solutions. The study also found that decision-making is highly centralized, with managers playing a pivotal role in procurement processes. This centralized structure reflects the need for experienced leadership to navigate regulatory complexities and align decisions with mission-driven goals. By applying the TOE framework, the research underscores its value in analyzing procurement behaviors within regulated, mission-oriented environments. The framework effectively captures the interplay between technological readiness, organizational factors, and external pressures, demonstrating its applicability beyond traditional business contexts. Looking ahead, the digital procurement landscape for daycare centers will likely evolve with advancements in technology and shifts in regulatory standards. Addressing the digital divide between larger and smaller providers will require targeted initiatives, including training programs, government support, and collaborative procurement models. Emerging technologies like artificial intelligence and automation offer further opportunities to streamline procurement while maintaining high safety and educational standards. Future research should explore how these innovations can be tailored to the unique needs of daycare centers, ensuring efficiency without compromising their core mission.

REFERENCES

Abu-ELSamen, A., Chakraborty, G., & Warren, D. (2010). A Process-Based Analysis of e-Procurement Adoption. Journal of Internet Commerce, 9(3-4), 243–259. https://doi.org/10.1080/15332861.2010.526489

Aditya, B. R., & Andrisyah (2023). Digital Transformation in Early Childhood Education: Teachers' Self-regulated Model for Digital Learning. International Journal of Information and Education Technology, 13(2), 329–334. https://doi.org/10.18178/ijiet.2023.13.2.1811

Baker, J. (2012). The Technology–Organization–Environment Framework. In Y. K. Dwivedi, M. R. Wade, & S. L. Schneberger (Eds.), Integrated Series in Information Systems. Information Systems Theory (Vol. 28, pp. 231–245). Springer New York. https://doi.org/10.1007/978-1-4419-6108-2_12

Biedinger, N. (Ed.). (2019). Was Eltern und Fachkräfte bewegt: Ein Überblick über die vorschulische Bildung in Deutschland. Verlag Barbara Budrich. https://elibrary.utb.de/doi/book/10.3224/9783847414766

Cho, W.-J., & Choi, I.-S. (2022). Validation of the digital competence assessment tool for early childhood teachers. The Korea Association for Early Childhood Education and Educare Welfare, 26(4), 33–55. https://doi.org/10.22590/ecee.2022.26.4.33

Cochran, W. G. (1977). Sampling Techniques (3rd Edition). John Wiley & Sons.

Creswell, J. W., & Plano Clark, V. L. (2018). Designing and conducting mixed methods research (Third edition, international student edition). Sage.

Cyert, R. M., Feigenbaum, E. A., & March, J. G. (1959). Models in a behavioral theory of the firm. Behavioral Science, 4(2), 81–95. https://doi.org/10.1002/bs.3830040202

Davis, F. D. (1989). Perceived Usefulness, Perceived Ease of Use, And User Acceptance. MIS Quarterly, 13(3), 319.

DeVellis, R. F. (2017). Scale development: Theory and applications (Fourth edition). Applied social research methods series: Vol. 26. Sage.

Dillman, D. A., Smyth, J. D., & Christian, L. M. (2014). Internet, phone, mail, and mixed-mode surveys: The tailored design method (Fourth edition). Wiley.

Fowler, F. J. (2014). Survey research methods (5. ed.). Applied social research methods series: Vol. 1. Sage.

German Federal Ministry of Justice. (1990). Sozialgesetzbuch (SGB) - Achtes Buch (VIII) - Kinder- und Jugendhilfe. https://www.gesetze-im-internet.de/sgb_8/

Grant, A., Ries, R., & Thompson, C. (2016). Quantitative approaches in life cycle assessment—part 1—descriptive statistics and factor analysis. The International Journal of Life Cycle Assessment, 21(6), 903–911. https://doi.org/10.1007/s11367-016-1099-4

Groves, R. M., Fowler, F. J., Couper, M., Lepkowski, J. M., Singer, E., & Tourangeau, R. (2009). Survey methodology (Second edition). Wiley series in survey methodology. Wiley.

Harpe, S. E. (2015). How to analyze Likert and other rating scale data. Currents in Pharmacy Teaching and Learning, 7(6), 836–850. https://doi.org/10.1016/j.cptl.2015.08.001

Jamieson, S. (2004). Likert scales: How to (ab)use them. Medical Education, 38(12), 1217–1218. https://doi.org/10.1111/j.1365-2929.2004.02012.x

Johnston, W. J., & Lewin, J. E. (1996). Organizational buying behavior: Toward an integrative framework. Journal of Business Research, 35(1), 1–15. https://doi.org/10.1016/0148-2963(94)00077-8

Joseph, O. B., Onwuzulike, O. C., & Shitu, K. (2024). Digital transformation in education: Strategies for effective implementation. World Journal of Advanced Research and Reviews, 23(2), 2785–2799. https://doi.org/10.30574/wjarr.2024.23.2.2668

Karanatova, L., & Kulev, A. (2020). Innovative Development of the Contract System: Transition to Smart Procurement. Administrative Consulting, 22–31. https://doi.org/10.22394/1726-1139-2020-2-22-31

Likert, R. (1932). A technique for the measurement of attitudes. Archives of Psychology, 22 140, 55.

Ljunggren, B. (2024). Hybridity and Leadership In Norwegian Early Childhood Education and Care Organizations. Nordisk Barnehageforskning, 21(2), 266–286. https://doi.org/10.23865/nbf.v21.483

Luque-Vara, T., Linares-Manrique, M., Fernández-Gómez, E., Martín-Salvador, A., Sánchez-Ojeda, M. A., & Enrique-Mirón, C. (2020). Content Validation of an Instrument for the Assessment of School Teachers' Levels of Knowledge of Diabetes through Expert Judgment. International Journal of Environmental Research and Public Health, 17(22). https://doi.org/10.3390/ijerph17228605

Magnuson, K., Ruhm, C., & Waldfogel, J. (2004). Does Prekindergarten Improve School Preparation and Performance? https://doi.org/10.3386/w10452

Makkonen, H., Olkkonen, R., & Halinen, A. (2012). Organizational buying as muddling through: A practice–theory approach. Journal of Business Research, 65(6), 773–780. https://doi.org/10.1016/J.JBUSRES.2010.12.015

Marshall, A. (1890). Principles of Economics. Macmillan.

Motaung, J. R., & Sifolo, P. P. S. (2023). Benefits and Barriers of Digital Procurement: Lessons from an Airport Company. Sustainability, 15(5), 4610. https://doi.org/10.3390/su15054610

Müller, J. M., Kiel, D., & Voigt, K.-I. (2018). What Drives the Implementation of Industry 4.0? The Role of Opportunities and Challenges in the Context of Sustainability. Sustainability, 10(1), 247. https://doi.org/10.3390/su10010247

Oliveira, T., & Martins, M. F. (2011). Literature Review of Information Technology Adoption Models at Firm Level. Electronic Journal of Information Systems Evaluation, 14, 110–121.

Pallant, J. (2020). SPSS Survival Manual. Routledge. https://doi.org/10.4324/9781003117452

Preston, A. E. (1993). Efficiency, quality, and social externalities in the provision of day care: Comparisons of nonprofit and for-profit firms. Journal of Productivity Analysis, 4(1-2), 165–182. https://doi.org/10.1007/BF01073472

Prior, D. D. (2021). The Organisational Buying Process Revisited. In D. D. Prior (Ed.), Organisational Buying (pp. 41–57). Springer International Publishing. https://doi.org/10.1007/978-3-030-67414-4_3

Robinson, P., Faris, C., & Wind, Y. (1967). Industrial Buying and Creative Marketing. Allyn & Bacon.

Schäfer, R. (2016). On Bias-free Crawling and Representative Web Corpora. In P. Cook, S. Evert, R. Schäfer, & E. Stemle (Eds.), Proceedings of the 10th Web as Corpus Workshop (pp. 99–105). Association for Computational Linguistics. https://doi.org/10.18653/v1/W16-2612

Sheth, J. N. (1973). A Model of Industrial Buyer Behavior. Journal of Marketing, 37(4), 50. https://doi.org/10.2307/1250358

Simon, H. A. (1955). A Behavioral Model of Rational Choice. The Quarterly Journal of Economics, 69(1), 99. https://doi.org/10.2307/1884852

Strohmer, M. F., Easton, S., Eisenhut, M., Epstein, E., Kromoser, R., Peterson, E. R., & Rizzon, E. (2020). Digital in Procurement. In M. F. Strohmer, S. Easton, M. Eisenhut, E. Epstein, R. Kromoser, E. R. Peterson, & E. Rizzon (Eds.), Disruptive Procurement (pp. 49–76). Springer International Publishing. https://doi.org/10.1007/978-3-030-38950-5_3

Tai, Y.-M., Ho, C.-F., & Wu, W.-H. (2010). The performance impact of implementing Web-based e-procurement systems. International Journal of Production Research, 48(18), 5397–5414. https://doi.org/10.1080/00207540903117915

Tornatzky, L. G., & Fleischer, M. (1990). The Processes of Technological Innovation. Lexington Books.

Vehovar, V., & Manfreda, K. L. (2017). Overview: Online Surveys. In N. G. Fielding, R. M. Lee, & G. Blank (Eds.), The SAGE Handbook of Online Research Methods (pp. 143–161). SAGE Publications Ltd. https://doi.org/10.4135/9781473957992.n9

Venkatesh, Morris, & Davis (2003). User Acceptance of Information Technology: Toward a Unified View. MIS Quarterly, 27(3), 425. https://doi.org/10.2307/30036540

Walker, T., Esmene, S., Colebrooke, L., Leyshon, C., & Leyshon, M. (2020). Digital possibilities and social mission in the voluntary sector: the case of a community transport organisation in the UK. Voluntary Sector Review, 11(1), 59–77. https://doi.org/10.1332/204080520x15787076882640

Williams, G., & Pigeot, I. (2017). Consent and confidentiality in the light of recent demands for data sharing. Biometrical Journal. Biometrische Zeitschrift, 59(2), 240–250. https://doi.org/10.1002/bimj.201500044

Yin, R. K. (2017). Case Study Research and Applications: Design and Methods. Sage Publications.

ANALYSIS OF THE MODELING PHASE IN THE OSEMN METHODOLOGY

Ketjona Shameti and Betim Çiço
Epoka University, Department of Computer Engineering
Highway Tiranë-Rinas, km. 12, 1000, Albania

ABSTRACT

With an emphasis on data-driven approaches, this study investigates the use of the OSEMN framework—Obtain, Scrub, Explore, Model, and iNterpret—in several fields. The study emphasizes the modeling stage, which is where forecasting models are created and assessed, and stresses the significance of structured processes in data science. The study does thorough Exploratory Data Analysis (EDA) on a COVID-19 dataset that includes cases and deaths from several regions in order to identify trends and connections in the information. Python is used to create three predictive models in a Google Colab environment: Linear Regression, Random Forest, and Gradient Boosting Machines (GBM).

To ascertain the models' effectiveness in managing intricate datasets, performance metrics such as Mean Squared Error (MSE) and R-squared values are used for comparison. Findings show that ensemble models outperform conventional linear models, offering guidance on model selection for practical data science applications. This study of the literature also looks at previous research that uses the OSEMN approach in a variety of settings, including real-time sentiment analysis, IoT-driven precision agriculture, and scalable IT infrastructures for scholarly research. The results provide a path for further study and real-world applications, adding to the expanding corpus of information on data science best practices.

KEYWORDS

OSEMN, Exploratory Data Analysis (EDA), Data Science, Linear Regression, Random Forest, Gradient Boosting Machines (GBM)

1. INTRODUCTION

Organized frameworks are now required due to the quick development of data science approaches, to manage data-driven projects efficiently. The OSEMN method, which comprises five essential steps—Obtain, Scrub, Explore, Model, and Interpret—is one example of such a framework (Kumari et al., 2020). Mason and Wiggins initially proposed the acronym OSEMN in 2010 as a useful procedure for data scientists to methodically manage challenging data-related tasks (Dineva et al., 2018). A crucial component of the data science lifecycle is covered by each stage of the OSEMN process, which makes sure that data is appropriately gathered, cleansed, examined, modeled, and interpreted in order to produce insightful findings (Martínez-Plumed et al., 2021).

The modeling stage of the OSEMN process is the main focus of this investigation. In order to assess how well three prediction models—Linear Regression, Random Forest, and Gradient Boosting Machines (GBM)—handle complex data sets, the experiment compares their performances. The research guarantees that every stage of the data science process is meticulously followed by using the OSEMN methodology, producing accurate and comprehensible results. Because it directly affects the results' understanding and forecast accuracy, the modeling phase is essential. Performance indicators such as Mean Squared Error (MSE), R-squared values, and feature importance are used to assess the chosen models. By offering insights into each model's suitability for various kinds of data-driven challenges, these metrics aid in identifying each model's advantages and disadvantages (Wirth & Hipp, 2000). Finding the model that best strikes a compromise between computing efficiency and forecast accuracy—a crucial factor in practical data science applications—is the goal of the experiment.

By concentrating on the modeling stage, this study advances our knowledge of how various machine learning models function inside the organized workflow that the OSEMN framework offers. The findings of this study will improve the overall efficacy of data-driven decision-making processes by assisting data scientists in choosing the best models for their responsibilities. Investigating the application of the OSEMN framework to COVID-19 data analysis is the aim of this project. In terms of prediction efficiency and model fit, among these three mentions models the study suggest which performs better.

2. RELATED WORK

We have analyzed three papers that have impacted most of our study. According to Dineva et al. the application of the OSEMN technique to data gathered from Internet of Things devices installed in beehives is the main topic of this article (Dineva et al., 2018). The application of the OSEMN technique to data gathered from Internet of Things devices installed in beehives is the main topic of this article. Sensors both within and outside the hive are used to gather data on variables like weight, humidity, and temperature (Dineva et al., 2018). In data preprocessing, columns of data are combined, invalid values are eliminated, and min-max scaling is used to normalize the data (Laser et al., 2020). Patterns in beehive behavior, like variations in humidity and temperature, can be found using exploratory data analysis, or EDA. To help with early management, predictive models are created to identify abnormalities and forecast the beehives' future conditions. A web-based platform is used to visualize the results, allowing beekeepers to make informed decisions (Dineva et al., 2018). The study offers a unified method for data processing and analysis in precision agriculture by illustrating how the OSEMN framework can be successfully applied to actual IoT applications.

According to Kumari et al. the use of the OSEMN methodology in real-time data analysis, with an emphasis on sentiment evaluation, is shown in this study. It emphasizes the significance of real-time data processing and contrasts machine learning algorithms for multilingual sentiment categorization (Kumari et al., 2020). Web APIs are used to collect data from social media networks, with a special emphasis on Twitter data. To guarantee high-quality input for the models, data cleaning entails lemmatization, stemming, and handling values that are lacking (Kumari et al., 2020). Important characteristics in text information, such as sentiment-bearing sentences, are found through exploratory analysis (Boudreau, 2019). For sentiment classification, machine learning methods such as Support Vector Machines (SVM) and Naive Bayes are employed. English and French are the two languages used to contrast the results of the models. Pie charts and other representations are used to display the outcomes, demonstrating the model's precision and sentiment dispersion (Mariscal et al., 2010). The OSEMN process's adaptability in managing real-time data streams and applying machine learning models for instant insights is highlighted in the report.

According to Laser et al., the creation of a scalable IT infrastructure to facilitate data-driven research in an academic setting is the main topic of this study. It incorporates the FAIR data principles and standards for reproducible research into the OSEMN architecture (Laser et al., 2020). Tools such as CKAN are utilized for handling metadata-driven search and retrieval of data from a variety of sources, including unorganized files and structured databases (Laser et al., 2020). Docker containers provide a uniform runtime environment while Jupyter Notebooks are used for data manipulation and cleaning. With the help of extra tools like Superset for interactive visualizations, JupyterHub is utilized for exploratory data research. Python libraries such as Scikit-learn are used to create machine learning models (Edelstein, 1998). Kubernetes-based automated model deployment and scaling are supported by the network. Displays and analyses are used to display the findings, guaranteeing the research process's traceability and reproducibility. In order to ensure reproducibility, scalability, and adherence to data management norms, the study offers a plan for developing a strong data science platform in an academic setting (Cao, 2017). An example of the OSEMN process's real-world use in expansive settings is the combination of open-source platforms and cloud-native solutions (Pang & Lee, 2008).

3. HYPOTHESIS AND RESEARCH QUESTIONS

H1 – The Mean Squared Error (MSE) of the Random Forest and GBM models is lower than that of the Linear Regression model.

- RQ1: How have the Linear Regression, Random Forest, and GBM models performed when considering the metrics of MSE?

H2 – Greater explanatory power is indicated by the higher R-squared values of the Random Forest and GBM models.

- RQ2: How have the Linear Regression, Random Forest, and GBM models performed when considering the metrics of R-squared?

4. METHODOLOGY

The dataset employed in this work is extremely useful for assessing real-world public health statistics since it includes information regarding COVID-19 cases and deaths across several regions. The date of record, geographic location, cumulative number of COVID-19 cases, and cumulative number of deaths are among the dataset's important characteristics. Because it includes time-series data with innate trends and variances, this dataset offers a useful foundation for assessing predictive models.

Before moving on to the modeling stage, exploratory data analysis, or EDA, was done to learn more about the dataset. To see the patterns of COVID-19 cases and fatalities over time, several visualizations were made. To comprehend the distribution of important variables, summary statistics were computed, incorporating metrics for principal tendency and dispersion. Additionally, the association between the total number of cases and deaths was investigated using correlation analysis, which gave preliminary clues regarding the predictive power of the information.

The correlation matrix is clearly displayed in the heatmap created with Seaborn and Matplotlib, emphasizing the degree of association between various characteristics. Strong correlations provide important information about the relationships between variables in the dataset, especially between total cases and total deaths. A comprehensive overview of the central tendencies and variability of important characteristics, including mean, median, and standard deviation, is provided by statistical summary. Significant trends, including the occurrence of certain death counts and the overall dispersion of the data, are also revealed by the histogram showing the distribution of COVID-19 deaths. Identifying the underpinning probability distribution is further aided by the addition of a kernel density estimate (KDE).

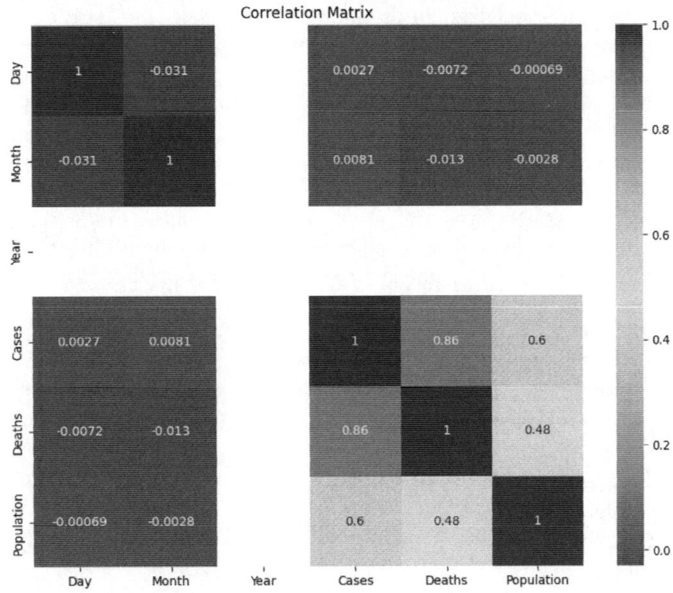

Figure 1. Correlation Matrix for the OSEMN methodology

As shown above at Figure. 1 we can clearly notice that the relationships among variables as not all linear relationships. Only two variables have a linear relationship as the value of correlation is near 1. The other relationships are represented either by a negative value or a value close to 0.

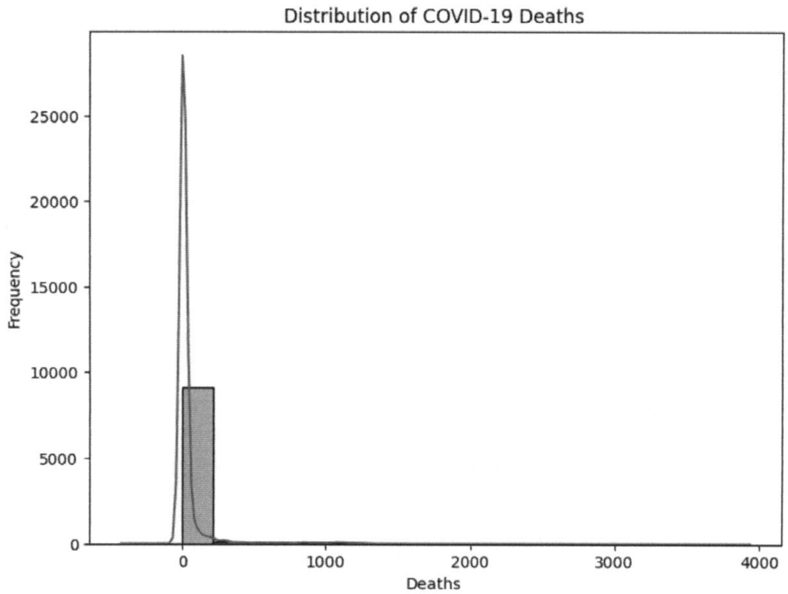

Figure 2. Distribution of COVID-19 deaths representing the occurrence of certain death counts

An essential component of the EDA process involves handling missing values (Martínez-Plumed et al., 2021). As shown in Figure. 2 the data distribution representing the occurrence of death counts is presented. To maintain data integrity, some rows were either eliminated completely or interpolated using mean values, depending on the degree of missing data. Furthermore, new variables like daily new cases and daily new deaths were derived via feature engineering, which improved the models' prediction power and added insightful perspectives to the analysis.

Google Colab, a cloud-based platform that provides an interactive Python environment, was used to implement the OSEMN process in its entirety, including EDA and modeling. The investigation made use of a number of Python libraries. Matplotlib and Seaborn were utilized to create visualizations, while Pandas was utilized for data cleanup and modification. Scikit-learn, a powerful toolkit that offers a variety of tools for model construction and assessment, was used to implement machine learning models.

The dataset was used to evaluate three predictive models: Random Forest, Gradient Boosting Machines (GBM), and Linear Regression. A baseline for comparison was provided by linear regression, which is an easy-to-understand approach. Because of its capacity to identify intricate patterns in the data, Random Forest, an ensemble technique that blends several decision trees, was chosen. Due to its high accuracy in a variety of predicting tasks, GBM— the ensemble method renowned for its sequential approach to error reduction—was included. Performance indicators including Mean Squared Error (MSE) and R-squared values were used to assess the models, while significance of features analysis shed light on the relative importance of various predictors.

This study highlights the significance of fully comprehending the dataset prior to deploying predictive models by concentrating on EDA and model assessment. This study's methodical approach guarantees that the findings are trustworthy and comprehensible, providing useful information for data-driven decision-making in public health situations.

5. COMPARATIVE ANALYSIS

In this section of the paper, we have conducted an experiment that would answer the research questions raised at the hypotheses. The data utilized are from Covid-19 Deaths and Cases dataset. We are utilizing the values generated from the implementation of three prediction models at the model part of OSEMN methodology. The results are presented also by using graphical visualization. We have organized the experiment section into one study case analyzing the metrics and comparing them among three models.

5.1 Case Study

The metrics utilized for analyzing the models are MSE and R-Squared values. One of the most important metrics for assessing how well predictive models' function is the Mean Square Error (MSE). It calculates the average squared difference between a dataset's actual target values and its anticipated values. The MSE's main goal is to evaluate the model's forecasting accuracy by calculating the extent to which it matches the ground truth. The MSE is sensitive to outliers because it squares the differences, giving greater mistakes a higher weight. Greater overall performance is indicated by a lower MSE, which shows that the predictions made by the model are closer to the actual values.

Linear Regression model MSE: 5781.475

Random Forest model MSE: 1081.531

Gradient Boosting Machines (GBM) model MSE: 918.312

The R-squared formula, often known as the coefficient of determination, describes the way a dependent variable change when the independent variable changes. A 30% R squared value indicates that the dependent variable deviates by 30% from the expected value. It appears from 0 to 1, with 1 indicating that the model fits the data perfectly. A value of 1 indicates that the independent variables explain all of the variability in the dependent variable, whereas a value of 0 indicates that the independent variables explain none of it.

Linear Regression model R-Squared: 0.7765

Random Forest model R-Squared: 0.9504

Gradient Boosting Machines (GBM) model R-Squared: 0.9579

As shown in Figure. 3 the graph represents the predicted versus the actual values for the Linear Regression model. The model did not predict accurately most of the data. While at Figure. 2 we observe a considerable improvement in predicting the data when comparing it to the Linear Regression. At Figure. 3 we can observe that most of the data has been predicted accurately and better than the previous models. A regression coefficient indicates the amount and direction of a predictor's association with the response variable. The coefficient for a variable describes an alteration in the mean response caused by a change in that term, while the other factors in the model remain constant. Feature importance is calculated by assigning a rating to all the input characteristics in a machine learning model to determine the value of each feature in the course of decision-making.

Linear Regression model Coefficient: 0.0163671; Intercept = 6.9506

Random Forest model Feature Importances: [0.91488451, 0.08511549]

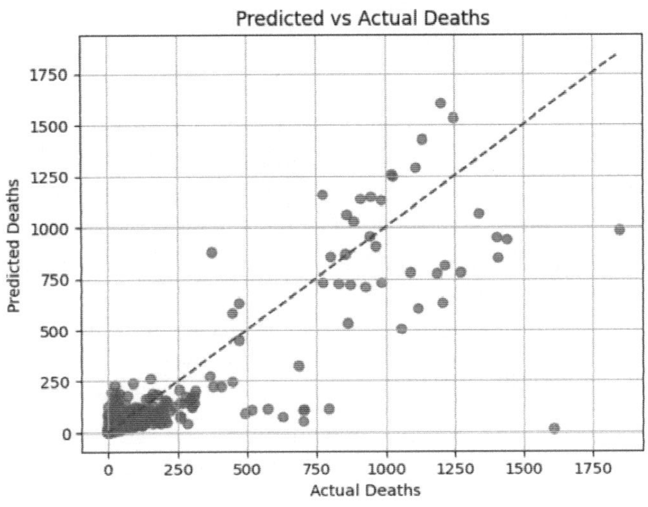

Figure 3. Predicted versus actual values for the linear regression model

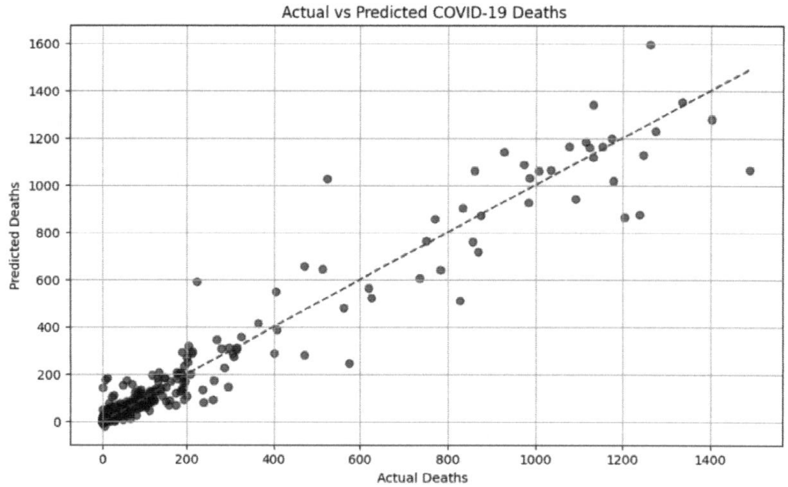

Figure 4. Predicted versus actual values for the random forest model

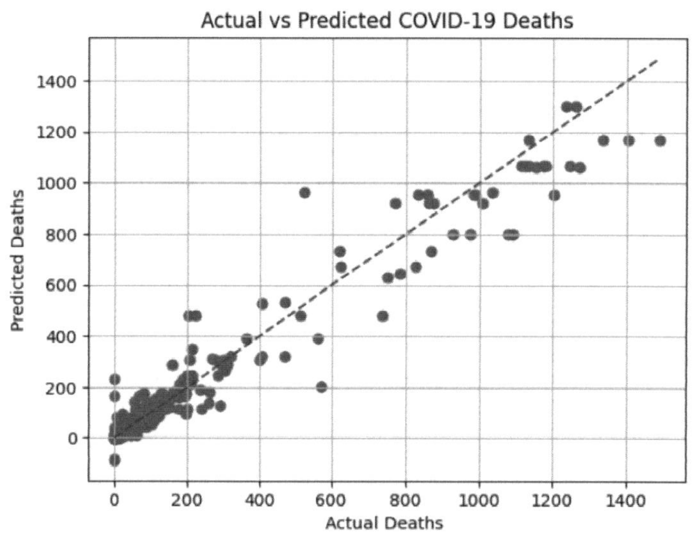

Figure 5. Predicted versus actual values for the gradient boosting machines model

As shown in Table. 1 we have presented all the predictive models' results regarding MSE and R-Squared values to have a better understanding.

Table 1. MSE and R-Squared Values for three predictive models

Metric	Linear Regression	Random Forest	Gradient Boosting Machines
MSE	5781.475	1081.531	918.312
R-squared	0.7765	0.9504	0.9579

6. DISCUSSIONS OF RESULTS

Linear regression model has the largest MSE value among all the models. The forecasts made by the model are more likely to diverge from the actual outcomes when the MSE is higher. This implies that, in this instance, linear regression is less reliable than the other models. It has a large difference comparing to random forest and gradient boosting machines. Compared to Linear Regression, Random Forest's MSE is substantially lower, suggesting higher accuracy in forecasting. More intricate connections between the features and the target variable are handled by this model. GBM is the most accurate of the three models, as evidenced by its lowest MSE. GBM mostly has a great performance when the relationships among variables are non-linear and can optimize the accuracy of the model by correcting previously encountered issues.

The R-squared score of 0.7765 indicates that the linear regression model explains around 77.65% of the variance in the target variable. This is a good fit, but not optimal for capturing intricate patterns. The Random Forest model accounts for around 95% of the variation in the data, which is a major improvement over linear regression. This illustrates that Random Forest detects more underlying patterns in the data. Amongst the three models, GBM has the greatest r-squared value, explaining 95.79% of the variance. This shows that GBM has the best fit to the data and makes the most accurate forecasts.

The coefficient of linear regression model indicates that the model is simple, with a very low value for the feature. It indicates that there is a poor linear correlation between the independent and dependent variables. The intercept shows where the line intersects the y-axis while every attribute is zero. The Random Forest model shows that one feature is significantly more essential than the other, with the first feature has a 91.5% of the importance. This shows that the model makes a lot of predictions based on one attribute, but it also takes into account another.

As shown above in figure 1, figure 2 and figure 3 we can notice that the values are predicted more accurately at random forest and gradient boosting machines model, with very few differences favoring the GBM model. Gradient Boosting Machines (GBM) is the most accurate approach, outperforming other models in MSE and R^2 and visual representation. Random Forest is a powerful candidate that achieves a great equilibrium among complexity and predicted accuracy. While linear regression is fundamental and simple to understand, it falls short in terms of predicting accuracy when compared to Random Forest and GBM models. If interpretability is important, Linear Regression may be preferable; nonetheless, Gradient Boosting Machines provide the best prediction results.

7. CONCLUSION

With an emphasis on model performance assessment, this study sought to investigate the use of the OSEMN framework in COVID-19 data analysis. In terms of model correctness, explanatory power, and significance of features, the study aimed to address three main questions. In terms of both prediction accuracy and explanation ability, the experiment showed that ensemble approaches—more especially, Random Forest and Gradient Boosting Machines (GBM)—performed noticeably better than the Linear Regression approach.

In response to RQ1 and RQ2, the Mean Squared Error (MSE) and R-squared values showed that the Random Forest and GBM models outperformed Linear Regression in terms of predictions. The accuracy of the ensemble models was confirmed by the significantly decreased MSE values. Furthermore, compared to Linear Regression (0.7765), Random Forest (0.9504) and GBM (0.9579) had substantially greater R-squared values, suggesting superior model fit and predictive ability.

The significance of features analysis showed that, in contrast to linear regression, ensemble models provided more meaningful readings of the information. Random Forest and GBM emphasized feature significance, showing that cases had a significantly more influence on deaths than other factors, but the Linear Regression model only provided one coefficient and an intercept.

In relation to accuracy, resilience, and comprehension, ensemble models performed better than the conventional linear regression approach. The findings imply that ensemble models are better suited for predicting tasks in intricate, real-world datasets such as COVID-19 cases and fatalities.

In conclusion, by showcasing the effectiveness of the OSEMN methodology in addressing practical data science issues, this study adds to the expanding corpus of knowledge on data-driven approaches. The study emphasizes how crucial EDA is to make accurate forecasts and how to choose the right models. This research could be expanded in the future by adding more variables, investigating different ensemble approaches, and using the OSEMN framework in various fields like environmental monitoring, healthcare, and finance.

REFERENCES

Wirth, R., & Hipp, J. (2000). CRISP-DM: Towards a standard process model for data mining.

Martínez-Plumed, F., García-Sánchez, F., & Pomares, H. (2021). CRISP-DM twenty years later: From data mining processes to data science trajectories. IEEE Transactions on Knowledge and Data Engineering, 33(8), 3048–3061. https://doi.org/10.1109/tkde.2019.2962680

Kumari, K., Bhardwaj, M., & Sharma, S. (2020). OSEMN approach for real-time data analysis. International Journal of Engineering and Management Research, 10(2), 107–110. https://doi.org/10.31033/ijemr.10.2.11

Dineva, K., & Atanasova, T. (2018). OSEMN process for working over data acquired by IoT devices mounted in beehives. Current Trends in Natural Sciences. Retrieved from http://natsci.upit.ro/media/1641/paper-7.pdf

Laser, H., Ram, S., & Ku, Y. (2020). Data science as a service: Integrated IT infrastructure. Journal of Advanced Computing Systems, 13(12), 112–125. https://doi.org/10.xxxx/jacs.2020.1312.112

Boudreau, P. (2019). Applying artificial intelligence to project management. ISBN: 9781687550941

Mariscal, G., Marbán, O., & Fernández, C. (2010). A survey of data mining and knowledge discovery process models and methodologies. The Knowledge Engineering Review, 25(2), 137–166.

Edelstein, H. A. (1998). Introduction to data mining and knowledge discovery. Two Crows.

Pang, B., & Lee, L. (2008). Opinion mining and sentiment analysis. Foundations and Trends in Information Retrieval, 2(1-2), 1-135.

Cao, L. (2017). Data science: A comprehensive overview. ACM Computing Surveys (CSUR), 50(3), 43. https://doi.org/10.1145/3083686.3083690

A GENERAL METHODOLOGY ENABLING DATA ANALYSIS OF CORPORATION CAREERS

Yinglei Han[1], Dario Colazzo[1] and François-Xavier Dudouet[2]
Université Paris Dauphine – PSL, Paris, France
[1]CNRS, LAMSADE
[2]CNRS, IRISSO

ABSTRACT

This paper introduces a systematic methodology that facilitates the data analysis of corporate careers. We establish a workflow that begins with the collection and storage of CVs in JSON format within our CV store. Utilising database and machine learning techniques, we then organise this information within a relational database and a graph database. This system enables us to perform comprehensive analyses, such as sequence analysis, to explore the career trajectories of managers to deepen our understanding of business elites and their career progression. Our approach is designed to serve as a replicable model for future researchers.

KEYWORDS

Corporate Career Analysis, Top Managers, Relational Database, Graph Database, Sequence Analysis

1. INTRODUCTION

Big businesses play an increasingly important role in our world, making it crucial to understand who leads them and how. More and more often, the leaders of large corporations attain their positions through their careers rather than their wealth. To better grasp the mechanisms of power within these corporations, it is essential to study their career systems, which often reveal shared career paths. However, significant challenges hinder such analysis (Koyuncu et al., 2017). First, the collection, organization, cleaning, and automatic enrichment of web-based career data remain formidable tasks for social science researchers, who frequently rely on time-consuming manual methods. Second, the lack of publicly available database architectures in this domain limits opportunities for shared learning, replicability, and scientific accumulation. This creates a gap in systematic and scalable approaches to studying corporate career data. To address these issues, this paper proposes a comprehensive model for automating the collection, storage, and cleansing of career-related data in the social sciences. It also introduces a database architecture designed specifically for processing and analyzing the career paths of corporate managers. For the sake of simplicity, this paper is not in the context of massive data. Instead, we focus on detailed descriptions of our workflow, as in the future, each step implemented in the workflow can be scaled up today by solutions (i.e., Hadoop, Spark, etc.) to cope with massive data analysis.

We develop a reproducible approach, intended to serve as a replicable model for future social scientists for work including CV analysis, career analysis, and so on. Specifically, we create one workflow framework (Figure 1) for corporate manager career data analysis. To start, the workflow includes a JSON CV store to save new CV input. Following information reconstruction, we have created a relational database in PostgreSQL and a graph database in Neo4j. By means of these two databases, we could conduct further analysis such as sequence analysis, network analysis, ad-hoc analysis, etc.

Section 2 is related work. We briefly review systematic career analysis in the field of top managers, including data preparation methods and sequence analysis, serving as one way of further analysis. Section 3 describes our data source (i.e., top managers from CAC 40 corporations in 2019 in our paper) and data collection method in this paper. We present how we create a relational database in Section 4, where we discuss how to conceptualize career trajectories collectively and introduce a term called "Arena" to conceptualize executive and non-executive positions. In Section 5, we describe a combination of rule-based and machine-learning methods to label career hierarchy "Rank" in our database. Section 6 is about sequence analysis to show how we apply our database to conduct further analysis, and this section also presents our findings obtained by cluster analysis of career paths. Section 7 summarises our approach and future work.

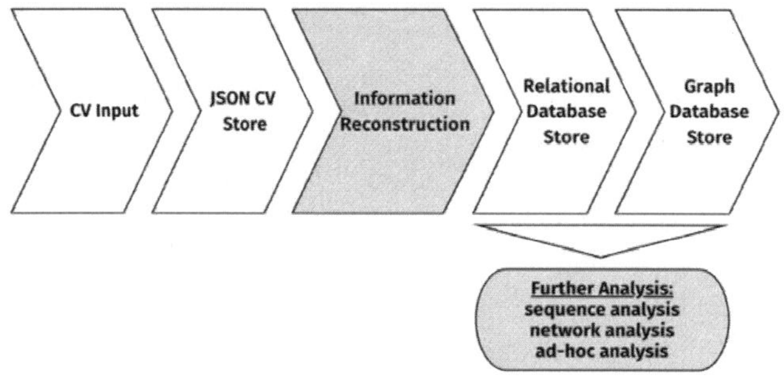

Figure 1. Workflow enabling data analysis of corporation careers

2. RELATED WORK

Elites exert disproportionate control over diverse social resources, including economic, social, cultural, political, and knowledge capital (Khan, 2012). Thus, the study of elite recruitment is crucial (Reeves et al., 2017). Recent literature has systematically explored career progression patterns and social relations of elites from a collective perspective. For example, Koch et al. (2017) analysed the career moves of Fortune 100 CEOs across various dimensions of job mobility, such as status, function, and employer. Davoine and Schmid (2022) reviewed key characteristics of top managers' careers, while Bühlmann et al. (2022) identified three career hubs that shape the global corporate elite. Henriksen and Seabrooke (2016) developed a two-level network for organisations and professionals. Specific studies within industries include Araujo's diachronic analysis of 301 Swiss banking elites during the 20th century through manual work (Araujo, 2022), and his study on the transnational corporate elite network, identifying three career paths (Araujo, 2018). These studies collect data either from an existing database (Araujo, 2022, 2018), manually (Studer Matthias and Ritschard Gilbert, 2014), or do not disclose the collection process ((Bühlmann et al., 2022).

During the data preprocessing, since job titles from resumes are typically human-written and un- structured, normalization is necessary for effective data analysis. Common methods include semantic analysis using NLP techniques and the segmentation of titles or extraction of keywords. For instance, Zhang et al. (2019) utilised an online API, MonkeyLearn, to categorize original job titles into 26 classes based on resume descriptions, although their analysis primarily maintained domain-specific information. Extending this, Singh et al. (2023) included both domain and position information, while Zhang et al. (2021) extracted function and responsibility from titles, aggregating them by keywords based on the manually annotated IPOD dataset (Liu et al., 2019).

Sequence analysis has become an increasingly popular method in the social sciences (Abbott, 1983), but not many studies have been carried out on the careers of corporate executives. Henriksen and Seabrooke (2016) conducted sequence analysis to examine longitudinal corporate careers over different dimensions. Koch et al. (2017) studied status, employer, and function. They coded CEOs who held multiple positions within a year for the highest status held in that year. However, this approach relies on manual labelling of statuses and excludes non-executive positions. Our paper addresses these limitations by utilising automatic rank labelling and information reconstruction during database reconstruction.

3. DATA COLLECTION

Top managers are people who belong to the top arenas of these big corporations. The two top arenas of joint- stock companies are the Board of Directors and the Executive Committee. So in our paper, we define top leaders as members of the Board of Directors and Executive Committees. While the latter is often absent in many Anglo-Saxon firms, where executive directors fulfill similar roles, various terms such as "Executive management", "Management Team", "Management Committee" are used interchangeably to denote this group. In Germany and German-speaking regions, equivalent entities are known as the Supervisory Board and the management board. All these terms essentially refer to the top tiers of corporate governance, including roles such as Chief Executive Officer, Chief Financial Officer, Chief Operating Officer, and so on.

Since we are studying the career trajectories of executives in large corporations based in France, our data source is CAC 40 Company executives (CAC 40 a stock index of the 40 highest-capitalized companies on the French market). We find members of Board of Directors and Executive Committees from those large corporations according to their financial report of 2019. Then, we retrieve their profiles from Linkedin, as this seems to be one of the most popular and most frequently used websites for public resume information. This approach consistent with methodologies in existing job mobility research (Li et al., 2017; Singh et al., 2023; Vafa et al., 2022; Zhang et al., 2021).

In our research, CV collection is crucial for developing a robust database. We identify 845 Board and Executive Committee members from the 2019 annual report. Using Phantombuster, we gather LinkedIn URLs by name and institution, then leverage iScraper API to extract LinkedIn profile data, prioritizing legality, ethics, and efficiency. APIs, unlike web scraping, align with LinkedIn's terms and offer structured, accurate data collection. We opt for JSON format for its readability, language independence, and efficient data transmission qualities. Out of 845 targeted profiles, we successfully obtained 363 usable CVs.

4. RELATIONAL DATABASE CREATION

Our database comprises 11 tables, each tailored to store distinct data types from LinkedIn CVs, facilitating comprehensive career path analysis. Specifically, there are tables to store fixed information (locations, certificates, skills, etc.), but the main entities are an individual defined by, a surname, a first name, a gender and a date of birth, an institution defined by a name and a type of institution (firm, public administration, NGO, etc.), a professional position (CEO, Chairman, executive vice-president, head of, etc.), an arena (board of directors, executive committee, etc.), a professional or educational trajectory with time intervals to connect with different entities. Primary keys (e.g., "id individual" in the individual table) uniquely identify records, while foreign keys create relational links between tables (e.g., "ID institution" in the education table references the institution ID). This relational structure, enhanced by primary and foreign keys, connects various tables (e.g., the career table links individuals and institutions to specific career trajectories). Overall, this design ensures that data across different entities is interconnected and accessible for detailed analysis. Apart from original information from Linkedin CVs, we also enrich this database in following aspects.

4.1 Arena

An arena is a structured social setting where individuals regularly gather, typically to orchestrate organisational activities. It's a formal, collegial space conducive to open dialogue and debate, often housing confrontations. Examples include boards of directors and executive committees. Not all roles, such as CEO or Professor, are tied to a specific arena. For simplicity, "Executive position" is used as a default arena, distinguishing primary (executive) and secondary (other arenas) career trajectories.

4.2 Job Title Reconstruction

The "Job title" from resumes often includes vague information covering job responsibilities, positions, arenas, and other details such as subsidiary involvement. Normalising job titles is crucial to address challenges like the following: the vast diversity of over 1000 different positions without normalising, language discrepancies (e.g., "Director General" vs. "CEO"; varying responsibilities under the same title (e.g., a chief officer might manage finance or technology), and inconsistent naming (e.g., "Global CEO"; To tackle these issues, we categorize the raw data from LinkedIn into three attributes as shown in Figure 2: "position", "arena", and "title description" where "title description" captures additional details beyond standardised "position" and "arena" categories. This structured approach aids in accurately interpreting and grouping job titles for analysis.

4.3 Education

We supplement LinkedIn data by searching public records for educational details, so far 823 entries in Table t-education. Education data, categorized by "degree name" and "field of study", includes undefined descriptions under "Grande École", labelled as "Master's Degree and Equivalent". Executive education such as Executive MBAs are noted separately, while standard MBAs are also classified under "Master's Degree and Equivalent".

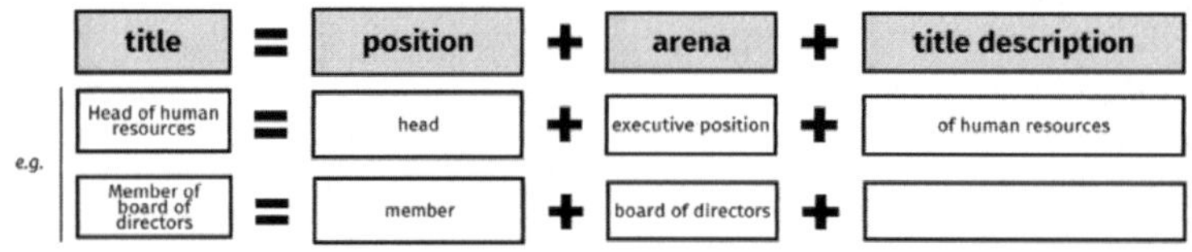

Figure 2. Title_reconstruction

4.4 Institution

Our database includes over 1,000 institutions, which we categorize by nature, type, scope level, and parent institution when applicable. There are two main types: educational and professional. Nature is divided into five categories: non-profit, corporations, academic institutions, government entities, and others. We initially employ a heuristic-based Python script using specific keywords to classify these institutions—for example, "inc", "ltd", "corporation", and "GmbH" for corporations; "ministry", "department", and "federation" for government entities; "foundation", "institute", "society", and "association" for non-profits. Institutions marked as "others" are re-evaluated using already labelled institutions as new keywords. For further refinement, we utilise the latest capabilities of ChatGPT (as of April 2023) to assist in categorization. However, some institutions remain uncategorized due to insufficient details. Regarding scope, corporations are classified into four levels: group, area, country, and division, with "area level" encompassing multiple countries or large countries like the US. ChatGPT also supports this aspect of our categorization effort.

4.5 Rank

One significant variable we include in this table is rank, which is used to show professionals' progression in their careers. We classify all positions into executive and non-executive ones. There are 10 ranks for executive positions (i.e., 1 - Entry-level or specialist, 2 - Middle-level management, 3 - Senior management, 4 - Executive committee, 5 - Deputy CEO, 6 - CEO, 7 - Chairman and CEO, 8 - Founder, 9 - Job outside of big corporations, 10 - High civil servant) and 7 ranks for non-executive positions (i.e., a - Chairman of the board of directors, b - Vice chairman, independent leader director of the board, c - Chairman of committee of the board of directors (or supervisory board), d - Member of committee of the board of directors (or supervisory board), e - Member of the board of directors, f - Non-executive member of the board of directors, g – Advisory arena).

5. AUTOMATIC RANK LABELLING

Rank labelling is a classification task. As we are incorporating the career hierarchy variable "rank", it is necessary to label this feature for all career trajectories according to Table 1 and Table 2. Traditionally, this task has been performed manually. However, in our paper, we aim to reduce the amount of manual work and automate the process to the maximum extent possible.

5.1 Method

We employ a combination of rule-based and machine-learning methods to address the rank labelling task. Specifically, the rule-based method is suitable for clearer situations in rank labelling, while machine-learning methods are adapted to more complex scenarios. Machine learning is particularly applicable due to the presence of textual data ("title description") and ordered data ("career step"). For example, the job title "CEO American" and "CEO" in a subsidiary may not denote a CEO in the true sense. Therefore, we utilise machine learning methods to classify such complex situations when executive ranks are 1, 2, 3. As mentioned in previous sections, the criteria for rule-based methods are clear. Thus, this section focuses on selecting variables in complex situations using machine learning techniques. There are four factors to consider: the title description provides additional information for job titles; positions; scope levels, and the specific step of this trajectory in the professional's career. Therefore, the four relevant variables are "id position", "scope level", "title description", and "career step".

5.2 Use of Classification Models

The target variables in this classification task are Rank 1, 2, and 3. We have considered five models to build the classifiers: (a) K-Nearest Neighbors (KNN) is a non-parametric, lazy learning algorithm that predicts the class of a data point based on the majority class among its k nearest neighbors, suitable for irregular decision boundaries. (b) Support Vector Machine (SVM) with an RBF kernel optimally separates classes in high-dimensional spaces by maximizing the margin between them, ideal when dimensions outnumber samples. (c) XGBoost, a fast and efficient implementation of gradient boosted decision trees, offers flexibility across various predictive modeling problems. (d) Decision Trees provide a simple, interpretable tree-like graph of decisions, though prone to overfitting. (e) Random Forest, an ensemble method using multiple decision trees, excels in accuracy for both categorical and continuous data.

5.3 Implementation

To train this classifier and predict other unlabelled records using this classifier, we follow the workflow outlined in Figure 3. Step 1: data preprocessing. Textual data ("title description") is vectorized using TF-IDF, categorical features ("id position", "scope level") are One-Hot Encoded, and ordered data ("career step") is standardized. Due to class imbalance (Class 1: 56, Class 2: 140, Class 3: 479), we use SMOTE to balance the dataset. Step 2: training and 10-fold cross-validation. We utilise 676 labelled career trajectories to build the classifier. The SVM model with an RBF kernel demonstrates the best performance among all, achieving an average accuracy of 86%. For the SVM method, we generate an overall confusion matrix for all cross-validation folds. This is accomplished by employing "cross val predict" to obtain predictions for each instance when it is in the test set, and then calculating the confusion matrix for these predictions against the actual labels. According to Confusion Matrix result, 42 instances (75.0%) in Class 1, 102 instances (73%) in Class 2, and 438 instances (91%) in Class 3 are predicted correctly. Class 3 exhibits the highest number of correct predictions, indicating robust classifier performance for this class. Before employing the classifier rank prediction for unlabelled records, to ensure the accuracy of rank predictions for unlabelled records, in Step 3, we identify 100 mismatched records by comparing actual and predicted ranks during the cross- validation process. Using the k-means method, analysed by the elbow method and silhouette scores, we select the number of components as 20, with a cumulative explained variance of 0.7. We identify two clusters: Cluster 0 contains 68 records, and Cluster 1 contains 32 records. These clusters have a commonality; the scope level is at the group level, but the actual ranks for more advanced career steps are higher in Cluster

0, and for earlier to mid-stage career steps are lower in Cluster 1. Step 4: we extract 344 similar records from the 1370 unlabelled records by calculating distance. These selected records are likely mislabelled by machine learning classifiers, thus we update them manually. But the remaining 1026 records are predicted by the classifier directly.

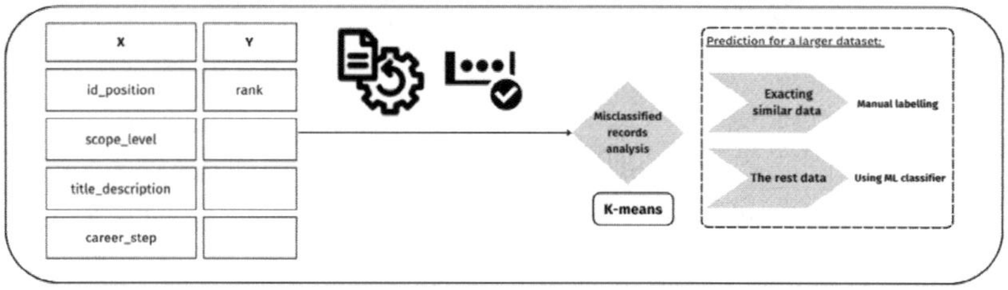

Figure 3. Rank labelling automation

6. SEQUENCE ANALYSIS

Sequence analysis is used to explore social and behavioral phenomena like career paths and educational trajectories, focusing on how elements are temporally ordered. This method facilitates the examination of patterns and transitions across various industries and educational backgrounds. We also perform parallel analyses for executive and non-executive positions, acknowledging that top managers might occupy positions in both categories. For these analyses, we employ "TraMineR", an R-package designed for sequence data.

6.1 Data Preparation

While TraMineR supports various ways of organising sequence data, in this analysis, we opt for one of the most popular forms—the STS format. In this format, each sequence is presented as a (row) vector of consecutive states. Consequently, it is necessary to reshape the data first, which involves reorganising the data so that each individual's career states over time are laid out across columns. This method requires a continuous sequence of "career-year" values for each individual without overlapping or gaps. To address the issue of overlapping, we transform the records into along format by extending the start-year and the end-year into different career years. For the first scenario of overlapping issues, if the end-year of one record is the same as the start-year of the subsequent record, we maintain the subsequent one. For other scenarios of overlapping issues, we choose a higher rank among multiple career trajectories in the same career year. At this stage, we focus on the main trajectory analysis, so we set a "rank" map in Python. This mapping assigns numeric ranks from 1 to 7, where 7 represents the highest and 1 the lowest within this subgroup. Ranks 8, 9, and 10 are treated as equivalent and less significant than ranks 1–7, though they remain higher than any alphabetic ranks. Alphabetic ranks are considered the lowest overall. This approach ensures that executive positions are assigned higher ranks for prioritization in the analysis.

6.2 Exploring Trajectories

We analysed career trajectories of 324 individuals, defining 11 distinct states across two dimensions: executive vs. non-executive roles, and positions within vs. outside large corporations. According to our result (Figure 4), 73.4% of individuals start their careers in executive roles within corporations, with 26.8% at entry-level or as specialists, 32.4% in middle management, and 14.2% in senior management. Additionally, 14.5% start in government roles, while 12.1% begin from jobs outside big corporations, founders or others. Our analysis, focusing on career lengths up to 37 years (Figure 5), reveals a trend where top positions such as CEO and Chairman become more common over time, whereas lower positions decrease.

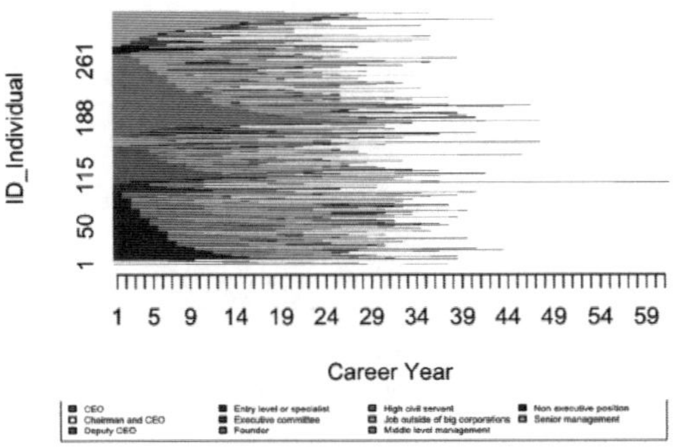

Figure 4. Index plot

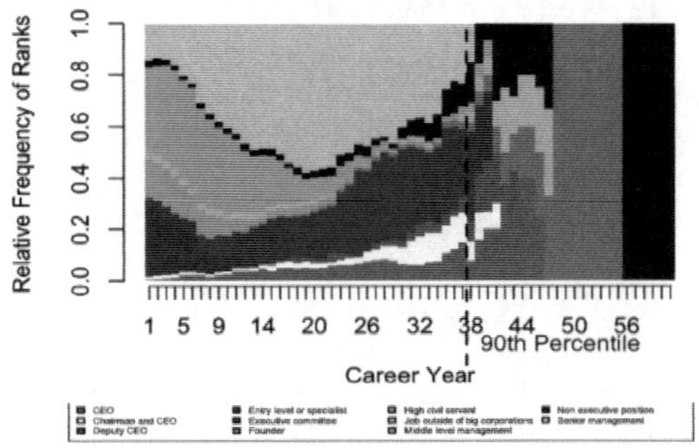

Figure 5. Rank distribution

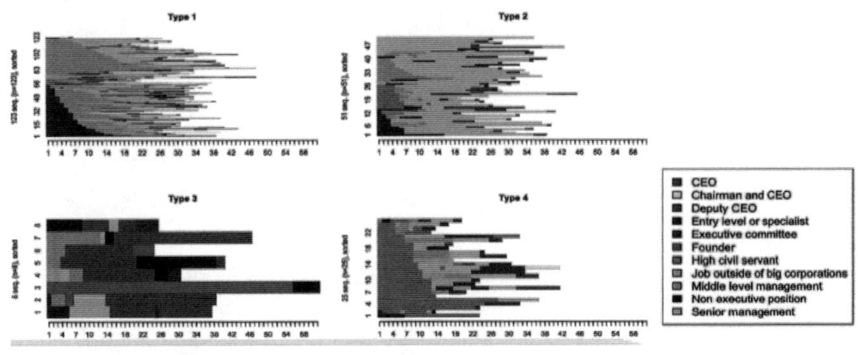

Figure 6. Optimal matching for people whose career information starting before 30

6.3 Typology Analysis

Optimal matching calculates dissimilarities between sequences to detect patterns (Studer Matthias and Ritschard Gilbert, 2014). We applied this method to 207 individuals in our database, excluding those whose career information starts after age 30 to ensure accuracy, as most sequences begin with senior roles. Clustering (Figure 6) reveals four types of path. Type 1 involves long careers starting in lower positions, progressing to executive roles after 15-20 years; Type 2 shows rapid progression from junior management to top positions within a decade; Type 3 includes individuals who have been CEOs for most of their careers, warranting qualitative analysis; and Type 4 reflects executives transitioning from the French civil service ("pantouflage"). It is interesting to compare Types 1 and 2, as they present the same career structures but at different paces. Comparatively, Type 2 has fewer women (21.1%) and non-French individuals (7.81%) than Type 1 (31.7% and 11.38%, respectively), with 76% of Type 2 attending Grande École, slightly above Type 1's 73%, but with a significantly higher attendance at the most prestigious institutions such as École Polytechnique, and ENA (37.3% vs. 24.4%).

7. CONCLUSION AND FUTURE WORK

In this paper, we presented a workflow for analyzing corporate careers, integrating three stores: the CV store, the relational database, and the graph database. This framework is designed for applications in organizational studies, HR analytics, and social science research. We showcased sequence analysis as a method to uncover patterns in career progression, such as gender-specific leadership barriers or executive pathways. Future work includes refining sequence typology analysis to identify distinct career types and advancing network analysis with the graph database. For example, temporal visualizations can track evolving professional connections, providing insights into talent flows and organizational dynamics. Additionally, we are exploring career hubs to examine trajectories leading to CAC 40 firms.

ACKNOWLEDGEMENT

Parts of this research were carried within the European Union's Horizon 2020 research and innovation programme under the Marie Skłodowska-Curie grant agreement No 945304 - Cofund AI4theSciences hosted by PSL University.

REFERENCES

Abbott, A., (1983). Sequences of Social Events: Concepts and Methods for the Analysis of Order in Social Processes. Historical Methods: A Journal of Quantitative and Interdisciplinary History.

Araujo, P., (2018). Dynamics of internationalization: a sequential analysis of the careers of Swiss banking elites. pp. 73–89. https://doi.org/10.4324/9781315163796-4

Araujo, P., (2022). Continuity and discontinuity in the capitals legitimating business elites – a diachronic analysis of the Swiss banking elites during the 20th century (1890-2020) 32.

Bühlmann, F., Ellersgaard, C.H., Larsen, A.G., Lunding, J.A., n.d. How career hubs shape the global corporate elite. Global Networks n/a. https://doi.org/10.1111/glob.12430

Constantinov, C., Dogaru, D., Mocanu, M., (2020). Graph Model Proposals for Capturing Meta-information Within Professional Network Data, in: 2020 Seventh International Conference on Social Networks Analysis, Management and Security (SNAMS).

Davoine, E., Schmid, S., (2022). Career patterns of top managers in Europe: Signs of further globalisation? European Management Journal, 40, 467–474. https://doi.org/10.1016/j.emj.2022.05.007

Henriksen, L.F., Seabrooke, L., (2016). Transnational organizing: Issue professionals in environmental sustainability networks. Organization, 23, 722–741. https://doi.org/10.1177/1350508415609140

Khan, S.R., (2012). The Sociology of Elites. Annual Review of Sociology, 38, 361–377. https://doi.org/10.1146/annurev-soc-071811-145542

Koch, M., Forgues, B., Monties, V., (2017). The Way to the Top: Career Patterns of Fortune 100 CEOS: The Way to the Top: Career Patterns of Fortune 100 CEOs. Human Resource Management, 56, 267–285. https://doi.org/10.1002/hrm.21759

Koyuncu, B., Hamori, M., Baruch, Y., (2017). Guest Editors' Introduction: CEOs' Careers: Emerging Trends and Future Directions. Human Resource Management, 56, 195–203. https://doi.org/10.1002/hrm.21760

Li, L., Jing, H., Tong, H., Yang, J., He, Q., Chen, B.-C., (2017). NEMO: Next Career Move Prediction with Contextual Embedding, in: Proceedings of the 26th International Conference on World Wide Web Companion - WWW '17 Companion.

Liu, J., Guo, C., Ng, Y.C., Wood, K.L., Lim, K.H., (2019). IPOD: CORPUS OF 190,000 Industrial Occupations.

Reeves, A., Friedman, S., Rahal, C., Flemmen, M., 2017. The Decline and Persistence of the Old Boy: Private Schools and Elite Recruitment 1897 to 2016. American Sociological Review, 82, 1139–1166. https://doi.org/10.1177/0003122417735742

Singh, S., Gupta, A., Baraheem, S.S., Nguyen, T.V., (2023). Multi-Output Career Prediction: Dataset, Method, and Benchmark Suite, in: 2023 57th Annual Conference on Information Sciences and Systems (CISS).

Studer Matthias, Ritschard Gilbert, (2014). A comparative review of sequence dissimilarity measures. https://doi.org/10.12682/LIVES.2296-1658.2014.33

Vafa, K., Palikot, E., Du, T., Kanodia, A., Athey, S., Blei, D.M., (2022). CAREER: Transfer Learning for Economic Prediction of Labor Sequence Data.

Zhang, C., Wang, H., Wu, Y., (2019). ResumeVis: A Visual Analytics System to Discover Semantic Information in Semi-structured Resume Data. ACM Transactions on Intelligent Systems and Technology, 10, 1–25. https://doi.org/10.1145/3230707

Zhang, L., Zhou, D., Zhu, H., Xu, T., Zha, R., Chen, E., Xiong, H., (2021). Attentive Heterogeneous Graph Embedding for Job Mobility Prediction, in: Proceedings of the 27th ACM SIGKDD Conference on Knowledge Discovery & Data Mining.

MM4PV: A METHOD TO DESIGN BUSINESS PROCESS VERSIONS

Fatma Ellouze[1,2], Mohamed Amine Chaabane[1], Eric Andonoff[3] and Rafik Bouaziz[1]
[1]MIRACL, University of Sfax, Route de l'aéroport, BP 1088, 3018 Sfax, Tunisia
[2]ENIG, University of Gabes, Rue Omar Ibn el Khattab, CP 6029 Gabès, Tunisia
[3]IRIT, University of Toulouse 1-Capitole, Rue du Doyen Gabriel Marty, 31042 Toulouse, France

ABSTRACT

This paper presents a new method based-on the Model-Driven Architecture (MDA) approach to support designers in modeling and reusing business process versions and their associated entities. The method, called MM4PV (Modeling Method for Process Versions), offers (i) a modeling language comprising key concepts, models, and construction rules, (ii) a structured modeling process that guides designers through the appropriate steps, and (iii) a computer-aided software tool that supports both the modeling language and process, assisting designers in creating new business process versions. Finally, the paper highlights a case study to demonstrate how the method can be applied practically, showing its usability, effectiveness and potential benefits in real-world scenarios.

KEYWORDS

BPM Method, Business Process Version, Context, Ontology, Version Retrieval using Context

1. INTRODUCTION

The version-based approach is widely used to cope with process flexibility, which is an important issue in the Business Process Management (BPM) field. The version-based approach allows handling, at the same time, different versions of a given Business Process (BP).

However, designers of BP can encounter some difficulties in modeling process versions in a multi-version environment. Indeed, to model a new process version, a designer may have to both model new versions of the process entities (e.g., activities, operations, informational resources, roles, …), and reuse already existing ones, in accordance with the use context of the new modeled process version. The lack of assistance methods makes such design more difficult.

In a previous work (Ellouze et al., 2016), we advocated to use versioning for BP flexibility and we have proposed the Version of Process Meta-Model (VP2M) according to which we propose modeling versions of processes. VP2M considers versions for all levels of granularity (i.e., process, activity, role and information), and for both individual and collective (intra and inter-organisational) processes. Then, we have proposed a VP2M extension (Ellouze et al., 2017; Ellouze et al., 2020) using an appropriate ontology to provide support for the context modeling of process versions. The new meta-model, Onto-VP2M, takes advantages of the ontology's capabilities to describe the context of the different components of versions modeled according to VP2M (i.e., versions of a process, an individual process, a collective process, an atomic activity, an event, a role, an organizational unit or an informational resource). Moreover, Onto-VP2M helps search a possible process version suitable for a given context.

To sum up, our previous works deal with (1) modeling of both process versions and their corresponding contexts, and (2) context-based querying of process versions.

Despite the above advantages, the version-based approach has drawbacks, notably the problem of version proliferation and the problem of lack of supports for designers in modeling BP versions. Thus, this paper aims to present a novel method that assists the designer in modeling new process versions and reusing already modeled ones. More precisely, this method allows assisting the designer in searching and reusing an already existing process version that is appropriate to a given context, and, if such a version does not exist, in modeling a new version he/she needs.

Therefore, this paper introduces the method MM4PV (Modeling Method for Process Versions) that assists BP designers to deal with the modeling of process versions. A running example is presented to evaluate MM4PV and illustrate its usability, effectiveness and potential for real-world application. MM4PV follows the Model-Driven Architecture (MDA) approach. It consists of three components:

- Component 1: a modeling language describing the models, concepts and rules, that we present as we describe the method steps, allowing the designer to define his/her process version models.
- Component 2: a modeling process as guidelines that the designer has to follow.
- Component 3: a CAiS (Computer-Aided Software) useful to reach the goal of modeling and retrieval of process versions.

The first component is already done in our previous works cited previously (Ellouze et al., 2020; Chaabane et al., 2020; Ellouze et al., 2017; Ellouze et al., 2016). So this paper will consider only the second and the third components.

The remainder of the paper is organized as follows. Section 2 introduces the modeling process of MM4PV and illustrates its use within a case study. Section 3 introduces the CAiS we have developed for MM4PV support. Section 4 reviews related work about methods in use and positions our contribution with respect to the literature. Finally, Section 5 concludes the paper and gives some directions for our future work.

2. THE MODELING PROCESS OF MM4PV

In this section, we describe the modeling process (i.e., guidelines) of our method MM4PV which is intended for assisting BP designers to successfully and ecologically model entity versions (i.e., modeling only the necessary versions and reusing existing ones).

The modeling process of MM4PV considers two scenarios according to the MDA approach. The first scenario corresponds to the case where the first version must be modeled, while the second scenario corresponds to the case of modeling subsequent versions, starting with the second one. We refer to these versions as derived versions, i.e., versions that are modeled from an existing one.

We explain in the two following sub-sections the running of the two scenarios, with an illustration on the case study of the Subsea Pipeline Installation business process.

2.1 First Scenario: Creating the First Version

Figure 1 depict the process of the first scenario, which includes seven steps.

Step 1- Ontology creation. In this step, the designer creates an application context ontology that defines the context elements relevant to their domain of processes. For example, in the case of the Subsea Pipeline Installation (SPI) business process, the designer defines context elements such as sea depth, pipeline length, installation technique, transported substance, and so on. For more details on how to create ontologies, refer to our previous work in [Ellouze et al., 2017].

Step 2- Process modeling. In this step, the designer must respect construct rules of MM4PV language [Ellouze et al., 2016]. For example, according to the construct rules, an individual process obviously starts with a composite activity having a start event, at least one activity (composite or atomic activity) and an end event, and using a control pattern.

Step 3- Context modeling. The designer describes the process model with an appropriate context using concepts from the application context ontology. More precisely, he/she specifies all the context conditions.

Steps 1, 2 and 3 constitute the CIM layer steps.

Step 4- Process version modeling including modeling the first versions of its components.

Step 5- Context modeling for entity versions. The context defined for the process model (at the CIM layer, step 3) will be automatically added in the application context ontology as a new context rule for the new defined process version model. For each context rule, a deduction rule is generated and stored in the application context ontology. The deduction rules facilitate the retrieval of process versions.

Steps 4 and 5 constitute the PIM layer steps.

Step 6- Generating the pivot model. Modeled versions of the PIM model will be transformed into XML files along with their context. Step 6 constitutes the first PSM layer step.

Step 7- Generating executable specifications. In this step, the designer generates from the pivot model one or more descriptions, each adapted to a specific used technology platform. A description can be a BPMN description for BPMN-based Business Process Management Systems (BPMS), a Petri-net-based BPMS, or others. Step 7 constitutes the second PSM layer step.

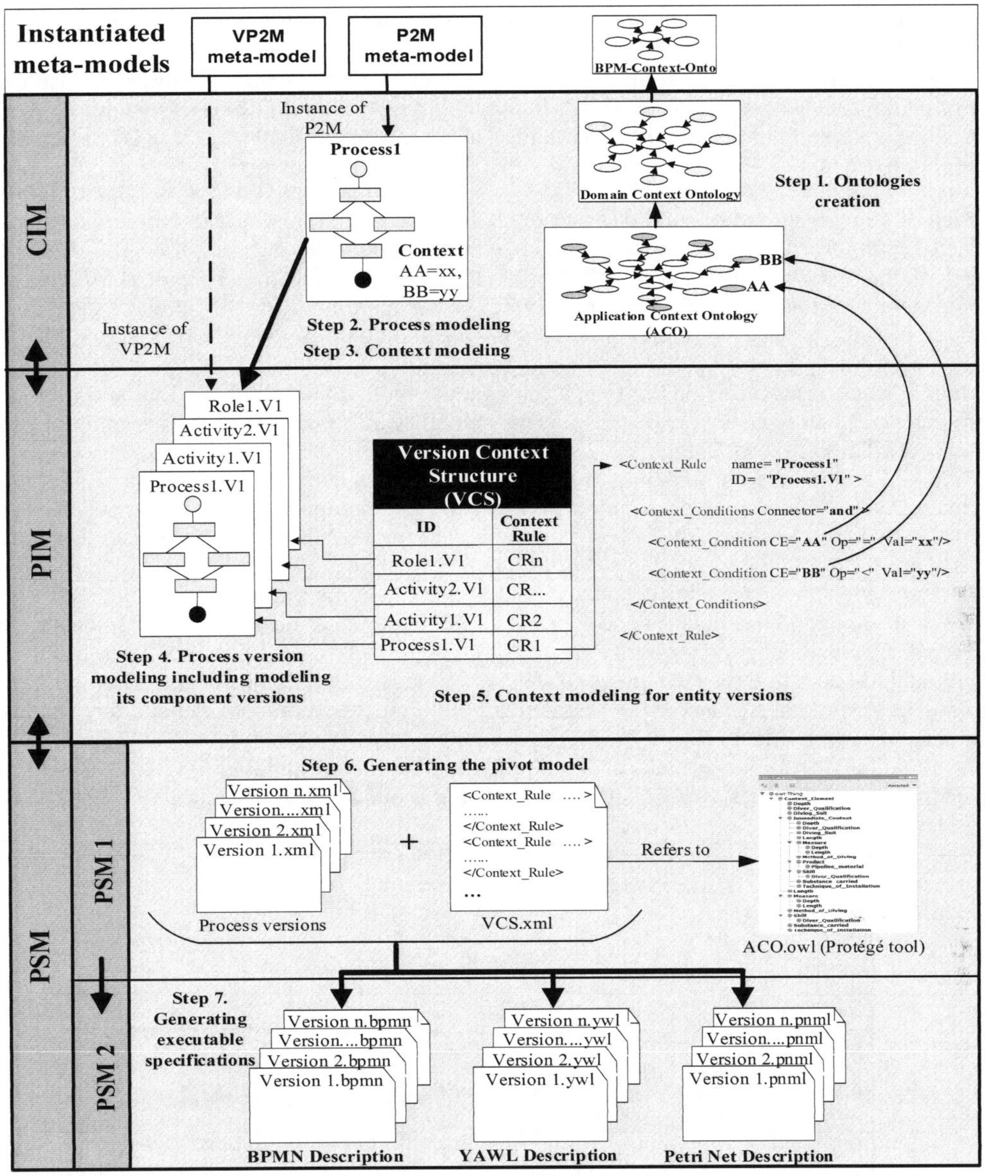

Figure 1. Synoptic schema of MM4PV for the modeling process in the first scenario

To show how put the modeling process of the first scenario of MM4PV into practice, we use a real case study, namely the Subsea Pipeline Installation (SPI) process from the marine domain.

The SPI is a collective process; its main partner is SAROST, which is a Tunisian company committed to subsea pipeline installation and maintenance. The SPI process is the following. SAROST receives an installation order from a Client company. Once the order is received, SAROST specifies the necessary team and equipment. Then, it proceeds with the assembling and the control of pipes on shore by welders, pipefitters and controllers. The next activity is the laying of pipes offshore by the divers. Finally, when the installation is over, a test campaign has to be performed. It should be noted that the assembling, control and laying have to be repeated until reaching the pipeline length. After the test campaign, SAROST prepares an acceptance certificate and sends it to the Client. According to the SAROST domain experts, this process is almost executed when the sea depth is less than 50 meters, the pipeline length is less than 10 km, the installation technique is floating, and the transported substance is water.

We recall that according to the first scenario, the SPI process is new and has not been modeled before. Thus we follow the steps (from step 1 to step 5) as presented in Figure 1.

Step 1- Ontologies creation. We use the SPI context ontology from GitHub (https://github.com/Onto-VP2M/context-BPM/blob/master/myOnto.owl). In this ontology, we have also defined the business rules useful for inference mechanisms. As an example, a rule is given below in the form of if-then statement.

```
Business Rule: If pipeline_length < 5 then transported_substance = "water".
```

Step 2- Process modeling. According to the P2M meta-model presented in our previous work [Ellouze et al., 2016], the designer has to model the SPI collective process involving two partners: SAROST and Client. Therefore, the designer models an individual process, the activities, the events, the roles and the informational resources without considering the concept of version. Figure 2 shows the SPI process involving these two partners. In fact, we only report on SAROST's private and public activities along with public activities of Client's individual process.

Step 3- Context modeling. In this step, the designer chooses from the SPI application context ontology the appropriate elements of context to describe the context of the SPI process model. This context is described by context conditions as shown in Figure 2.

Step 4- Process version modeling including modeling its component versions. This step is handled automatically. After describing the process model and its appropriate context, a first version is defined automatically for each entity of the SPI process model. Thus all the SPI entities (activities, events…) are stored as first versions of corresponding entity. For example, the public atomic activity of the Client process "Send order" is stored as the first version denoted as "SO.1", the Client process is stored as the first version denoted as "Client.1", and consequently the collective process SPI is stored as the first version denoted as "SPI.1".

Step 5- Context modeling for entity versions. As for the context modeling of the new entity versions, the context initially described for the process model SPI (cf. Figure 2) is automatically added in the SPI context ontology as a new context rule for the new defined SPI.1 process version model and for all the versions of individual processes Client.1 and SAROST.1. In addition, context rules are automatically added in the SPI context ontology for all first versions of atomic activities of Client.1 and SAROST.1. However, the designer can update the context rules of these versions by deleting or adding context elements.

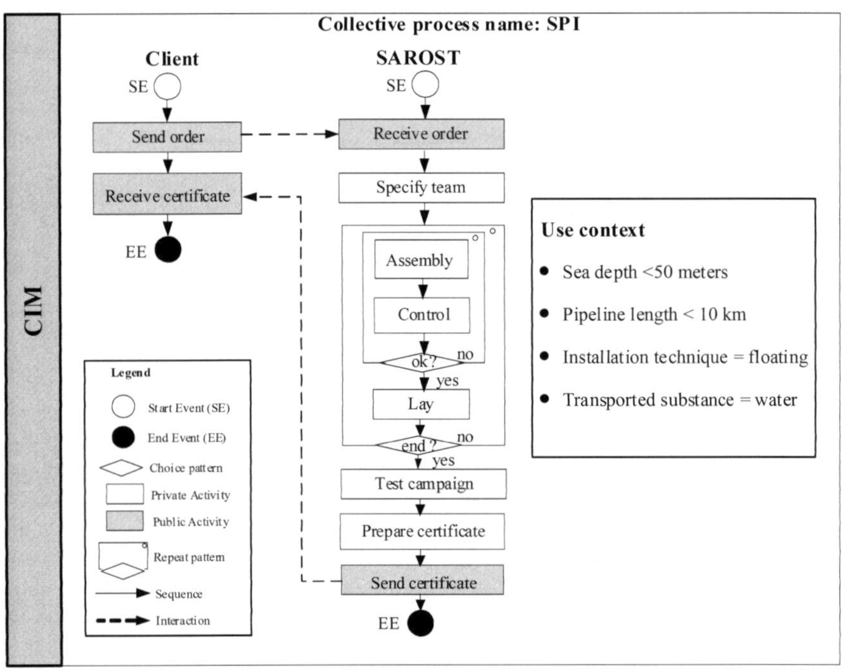

Figure 2. SPI process model at the CIM level (before versioning)

2.2 Second Scenario: Deriving Versions

In the second scenario, the designer has to model a new version of an existing process, for which one or more versions have already been modeled.

Step 1- The designer queries the system by specifying the current situation in terms of context elements. According to the query result, three cases can be met:

(i) Only one version is retrieved; thus this version has exactly the same context as the current situation specified by the BP designer in its query: it is well suited to the current situation. So, as a convenient version already exists, the designer will not model a new one.

(ii) Several versions that have a close context to the described situation are retrieved. In this case, the designer has to check if one of them is suitable to the current situation given in the initial query. If so, the designer will not model a new version; instead, he/she selects the most suitable version and can update its use context by adding new values for existing context elements from the current situation. If the designer does not find a suitable version to his/her situation, he/she must follow the modeling process in the following Step 2.

(iii) No retrieved version or no suitable version. In this case, the designer follows the modeling process in the following Step 2.

Step 2- Deriving a new version. To derive a new process version from an existing one, the designer has to choose the source process version that will serve as a basis for the derivation. The source process version is a version that has a close context to the described situation of the designer.

For this illustration, we suppose that three versions of SPI collective process have been already modeled along with three versions of SAROST individual process and two versions of Client individual process. Table1 shows the use context of each version.

SPI.2, visualized in Figure 3(a), is defined for oil or gas transportation, and for a pipeline length that does not exceed 50 km. In this case, SAROST only proceeds to the installation without making the test campaign and the certification activities. These two activities are subcontracted to an external company, such as the Bureau Veritas (BV) company. The latter will be contacted by SAROST, which justifies the presence of public activities RRC.1, RC.1, and SC.1.

SPI.3, visualized in Figure 3(b), is defined in case of installation of long and deep-water pipelines. In this case, SAROST only proceeds with the installation. Once the installation is over, it sends back a report to the Client and ends the process. Then, the Client contact BV to perform the activities of the test campaign and the certification.

Table 1. Context of SPI, SAROST and Client versions

VERSION ID	CONTEXT ELEMENTS			
	Sea depth	**Pipeline length**	**Installation technique**	**Transported substance**
SPI.1	<50	<10	floating	water
SPI.2	<50	<10	floating	gas or oil
SPI.3	<50	>50	floating	gas or oil
SAROST.1	<50	<10	floating	water
SAROST.2	<50	<10	floating	gas or oil
SAROST.3	<50	>50	floating	gas or oil
Client.1	>=50	10 to 50	sliding	gas or oil
Client.2	>90	10 to 50	sliding	gas or oil

In what follows, we show how to model a new version of SPI according to the modeling process of MM4PV. First of all, let us consider the following new situation: the BP designer is interested in finding SPI versions appropriate for a 70 kilometers long subsea pipeline, transporting gas at a depth of 47 meters and using the sliding technique for the installation.

Step 1- The first step consists in querying the system with the following context elements (Sea depth=47, Pipeline length=70, Installation technique=Sliding and Transported substance=gas).

Thanks to the reasoning mechanism of the ontology, SPI.3 version will be retrieved and displayed to the designer. Interested readers can consult (Ellouze et al., 2017) to get additional information on how the query is executed. According to the designer, the returned version SPI.3 is not well suited to the current situation as he/she wants to use another Installation technique, namely sliding instead of floating. So the designer decides to derive a new version of SPI appropriate for its current situation.

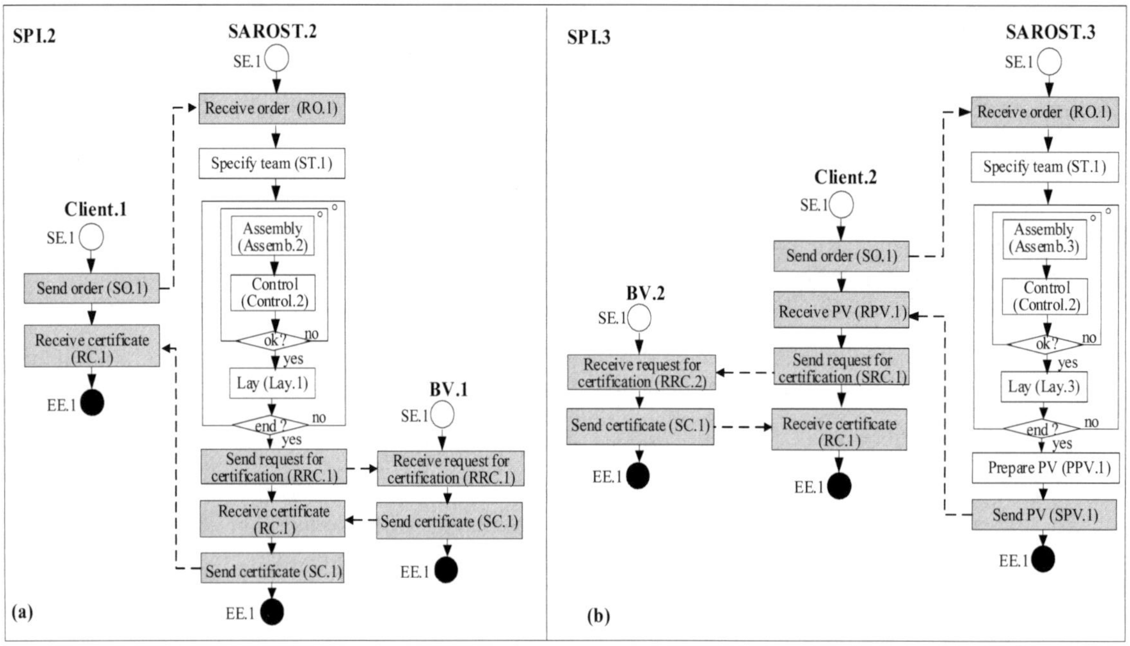

Figure 3. SPI.2 and SPI.3 process versions

Step 2- Deriving a new version. The designer firstly chooses the source of derivation, namely SPI.3 (which is the retrieved version). Secondly, he/she derives a new version from SPI.3 identified by SPI.4 that has the same schema of SPI.3. Thirdly, the designer proceeds to update SPI.4 according to his/her needs.

The update of SPI.4 addresses the replacement of the existing individual process version(s) by other ones that are more adequate to the designer situation.

Therefore, the designer proceeds recursively by querying the system to search for versions of SAROST, Client and BV that are adequate to the current situation. For example, the designer starts by searching SAROST version appropriate for a 70 kilometers long subsea pipeline, transporting gas at a depth of 47 meters and using the sliding technique for the installation. However, as shown in Table 1, no version of SAROST can be retrieved. In this case, the designer has to derive a new version of SAROST process identified by SAROST.4. Recursively, the designer proceeds again to define SAROST.4. Once SAROST.4 is defined, the designer selects this new version to replace SAROST.3 (cf. Figure 3(b)). On the other hand, the designer queries the system to search versions for the Client process and the BV process that are suitable to his/her current situation. As Client.2 and BV.2 are appropriate to the new situation, the designer uses these two versions to make up SPI.4.

3. CAiS OF MM4PV

Let us recall that a CAiS is defined as the software system that automates number of the tasks required to develop information systems. The CAiS we propose for MM4PV, entitled BPV-CAiS, is a computer-based system aimed at supporting the modeling of BP versions. Figure 4 gives the architecture of BPV-CAiS. In this architecture, we give the components needed to perform the different steps of MM4PV.

The process version modeler component supports version entity modeling. The Retrieval Version Artifact & The Context Modeler component supports the retrieval of entity versions and the context modeling of entity versions. The Process Version Generator component supports the automatic generation of all defined models into XML files. The BPV-CAiS is available online at (BPV-CAiS, 2023).

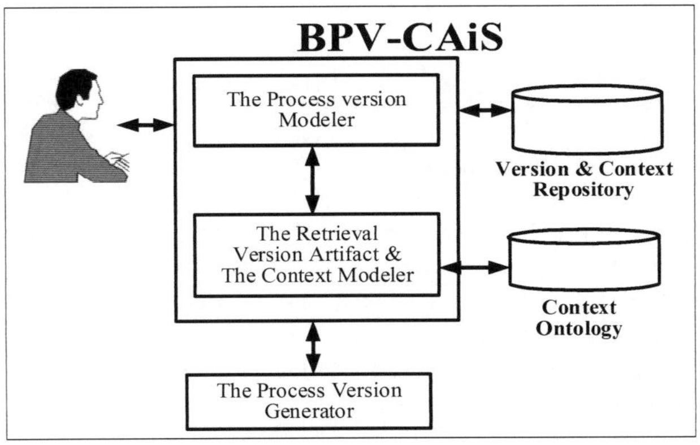

Figure 4. BPV-CAiS architecture

4. RELATED WORK

We first mention works that introduced specific meta-models to capture the process changes over time using a version-based approach. The authors of (Ekanayake et al., 2011) and (Zhao and Liu, 2013) proposed version-based meta-models to support the modeling of versions only at the process and activity granularity level. (Silveira, D. et al, 2020) defines an approach to build and configure a process-oriented feature model aiming at representing a family of business process models by means of its reusable process modules. However, these authors did deal neither with the modeling of the contexts for versions nor with solutions to retrieve versions. As for the authors of (Ellouze et al., 2016), (Lassoued et al., 2016) and (Ben Said et al., 2018), they have proposed version-based meta-models that support the modeling of versions for all the granularity levels. Moreover, they have proposed solutions to model contexts of versions. However, we can find only in (Ellouze et al., 2017) and (Lassoued et al., 2016) a solution to query process versions in order to retrieve the adequate version for a specific situation according to its context. Yet there is no proposed method to model BP versions.

We also mention works investigating context modeling and process version retrieval. Context modeling for processes is addressed to characterize the situation in which a version can be used (Ellouze et al., 2017; Lassoued et al., 2016; Anastassiu et al., 2016; Hallerbach et al., 2010). As for the process version retrieval, we distinguish the structural querying and the contextual querying. The former corresponds to queries defined as a sub-graph of the process to be selected. The relevant works about structural querying are especially discussed in (Awad et al., 2008) and (Beeri et al., 2008). The contextual querying is based on given descriptive information (i.e., metadata describing the context) about a particular (version) process. However, the contextual querying is less investigated than the structural querying (Polyvyanyy et al., 2017). The authors of (Chaâbane et al., 2020) and (Ellouze et al., 2017) have proposed an ontology-based approach to query versions of process using their context of use.

We finally mention works addressing BPM tools such as YAWL which is one of the powerful process modeling languages due to its support of the most frequent control-flow patterns found in the current business process modeling (Traganos, k. 2024; Aalst and Hofstede, 2005). YAWL language is supported by a software system that includes an execution engine, a graphical editor and a worklist handler. It is worth saying that YAWL already proposed a language and a CAiS, which we can considered as two parts of a method. But it fails in providing the modeling process intended for the designer to ease the process modeling task. Recently, (Kourani, H., et al, 2024) introduced a BPM tool that uses Large Language Models (LLMs) and generative AI to automate and refine process modeling in BPM. By converting textual descriptions into process models, the framework makes modeling more accessible to non-experts and more efficient for experts. It supports standard notations like BPMN and Petri nets. However, the generated process models did not depend on a meta-model and there is no proposed solution to query process models.

We notice a real missing of a method that assists the BP designer to model business process versions including the modeling of their contexts. For these reasons, we have proposed, in this paper, the new method MM4PV.

5. CONCLUSION

The new proposed method, entitled MM4PV (Modeling Method for Process Versions), has successfully delivered the following benefits:

- Addressing the versioning for all the granularity levels of processes thanks to the use of the VP2M meta-model.
- Modeling the context of process versions and retrieving the appropriate process versions according to their specific contexts, by adopting the ontology-based approach.
- Offering guidelines in terms of actions that designers should do to model business process versions, according to the MDA-based approach.

The interest and the practical feasibility of the design under MM4PV are illustrated through a real case study from the marine domain.

Our future work includes two axes. Firstly, as the paper does not sufficiently deal with the MM4PV transformations between the three layers of MDA, we would like to improve our method by considering the modeling of transformations between models. Secondly, we plan to introduce design patterns in order to facilitate the modeling of process versions. Thus, we need to examine how to integrate design patterns in MM4PV.

REFERENCES

Anastassiu, M. et al, (2016). The quest for organizational flexibility: driving changes in business processes through the identification of relevant context. *Business Process Management Journal.* Vol. 22 No. 4, pp 763-790.

Awad, A. et al, (2008). Semantic querying of business process models. *In Proceedings of the 12th International Conference on Enterprise Distributed Object Computing*, München, Germany, pp 85-94.

Beeri, C. et al, (2008). Querying business processes with BP-QL. *Journal of Information Systems*, Vol. 33 No. 6, pp 477–507.

Ben Said I. et al, (2018). BPMN4VC-modeller: easy-handling of versions of collaborative processes using adaptation patterns. *Information Systems and Change Management*, Vol. 10 No. 2, pp140-189.

BPV-CAiS, (2023) https://github.com/Onto-VP2M/Onto_VP2M_Fw.

Chaâbane, M. et al, (2020). A context-based approach for modelling and querying versions of BPMN processes. *International Journal of Business Process Integration and Management*, pp 62-86.

Ekanayake C. et al, (2011). Fragment-based version management for repositories of business process models. *International Conferences OTM Confederated on the Move to Meaningful Internet Systems*, Hersonissos, Crete, Greece, pp 20-37.

Ellouze F. et al, (2016). Addressing inter-organisational process flexibility using versions: The VP2M approach. *In: Proceedings of the 10th International Conference on Research Challenges in Information Science*, Grenoble, France, pp 1-12.

Ellouze F. et al, (2017). Onto-VP2M: A New Approach to Model and Manage Collaborative Process Versions using Contexts and Ontologies. *International Journal of e-Collaboration*, Vol. 13 No. 3, pp 39-62.

Ellouze, F. et al, (2020). A Version and Context-based Approach to easily Model Flexible Collaborative Processes, *Collaborative Convergence and Virtual Teamwork for Organizational Transformation*, IGI Global, pp 18-45.

Hallerbach A. et al, (2010). Capturing variability in business process models: the PROVOP approach. *Journal of Software: Evolution and Process*, Vol. 22 No. 67, pp 519-546.

Kourani, H. et al, (2024). Process modeling with large language models. *Enterprise, Business-Process and Information Systems Modeling*, Springer Nature Switzerland, pp 229–244.

Lassoued Y. et al, (2016). Context-aware business process versions management. *International Journal of e-Collaboration,* Vol. 12 No. 3, pp 7-33.

Polyvyanyy, A. et al, (2017). Process Querying: Enabling Business Intelligence through Query-Based Process Analytics. *Journal of Decision Support Systems*, 2017, pp 41-56.

Silveira, D. et al, (2020). Towards a reusable business process modelling approach. *International Journal of Business Process Integration and Management* (IJBPIM), Vol. 10, No. 2, pp104 – 114.

Traganos, k. et al, (2024). Business process management engines. *Handbook on Business Process Management and Digital Transformation.* Edward Elgar.

Van Der Aalst, W. M., and Ter Hofstede, A. H., (2005). YAWL: yet another workflow language. *Information systems*, Vol. 30 No. 4, pp 245-275.

Zhao X. and Liu C. (2013). Version management for business process schema evolution. *International Journal of Information Systems*, Vol. 38 No. 8, pp1046-1069.

APPLYING GPT-4O AND PROMPT ENGINEERING IN AUTOMATED FINANCIAL SURVEYS AND FINANCIAL ADVICE

Senye Pan
Shanghai University, Shanghai, 201800, China

ABSTRACT

This paper explores the application of GPT-4o and Prompt Engineering in automating financial surveys and delivering personalized financial advice. By utilizing pre-stored prompt files and a modular system of multiple agents, this research demonstrates that virtual agents based on large language models (LLMs) can simulate and replace real human actions in financial decision-making processes. The system includes distinct agents for generating virtual personas (Agent-C), creating tailored surveys (Agent-S), configuring persona knowledge using Retrieval-Augmented Generation (RAG) and web searches (Agent-0 to Agent-(n-1)), and evaluating results to generate actionable financial recommendations (Agent-E). This flexible architecture supports the parallel execution of virtual personas answering surveys, simulating diverse investor profiles. With a robust Python implementation, the system provides scalable and reliable financial advisory capabilities, demonstrating the significant role of AI in modern financial decision-making. Furthermore, this approach utilizes RLHF-like Agentic Automation, enhancing the adaptability and personalization of financial advice by simulating real-time decision-making processes in a dynamic financial environment.

KEYWORDS

RLHF-Like Agentic Automation, GPT-4o, Prompt Engineering, RAG (Retrieval-Augmented Generation), Financial Surveys

1. INTRODUCTION

1.1 Research Background

The financial sector relies heavily on accurate data collection and analysis to provide reliable investment advice (Gautam and Bhimavarapu, 2022; Gartner, Inc., 2022). Traditional methods of survey generation and data analysis are time-consuming and often lack real-time relevance, making them less adaptable to the rapidly changing market conditions. The emergence of large language models, such as GPT-4o, combined with techniques like Prompt Engineering, presents new opportunities to automate and enhance these processes. Through the use of pre-stored prompt files and intelligent frameworks, this research shifts the focus from traditional approaches to more dynamic and efficient solutions.

A significant advancement in this field is the integration of Agentic Automation—a technology that creates virtual agents capable of simulating human-like behaviors and decisions. By mapping real human personas into the Agentic system, these agents can evolve through continuous learning, using Retrieval-Augmented Generation (RAG) and real-time web searches to adapt and make decisions akin to those of actual investors. This system holds promise for automating financial decision-making in a way that closely mimics human decision-making patterns, providing a more accurate and personalized investment advisory service.

Furthermore, cognitive automation plays a critical role in streamlining data processing and integration, enhancing both the reliability and scalability of automated financial solutions (Merchia, 2024; Ye et al., 2023). In recent discussions about AI advancements in the financial sector, particularly with the application of large language models (LLMs) in China's financial landscape, notable examples include Ant Group's Zhixiaobao, which has already served over 43 million individual investors (Lu and Chen, 2024). The service offers portfolio assessments, market analysis, and investment advice, demonstrating the potential of AI in delivering actionable insights to users. This example highlights the practical applications, as well as the challenges of AI-powered financial assistants, underscoring the importance of precise data integration, response simulation, and continuous enhancement through Agentic and cognitive automation technologies.

1.2 Research Objectives

The primary objective of this research is to apply GPT-4o and Prompt Engineering to automate financial surveys and generate reliable financial advice. Specific goals include:

1. The primary objective of this research is to apply GPT-4o and Prompt Engineering to automate financial surveys and generate reliable financial advice. The specific goals of this study include:
2. Building a Retrieval-Augmented Generation (RAG) knowledge base, prioritizing materials directly related to portfolio management and risk control, such as:
   - Macroeconomic and regulatory policies.
   - Industry research reports and broker research.
   - Publicly listed company financial reports and announcements.
   - Market and product data.
   - Financial media reports and market trends.
   - Risk case studies and regulatory enforcement data.
   - Prioritizing the collection of materials relevant to the Chinese market, especially from domestic regulatory bodies (e.g., the People's Bank of China, China Banking and Insurance Regulatory Commission, China Securities Regulatory Commission), domestic brokerage research, and major Chinese financial media outlets.
3. Using GPT-4o to extract, analyze, and synthesize the data from these materials, ensuring that the information is up-to-date, reliable, and relevant for financial surveys and decision-making.
4. Integrating principles of Agentic Automation to enhance the virtual persona's ability to process and respond to data, evolving through real-time knowledge retrieval and dynamic learning.
5. Generating customized survey questions based on the insights drawn from the RAG knowledge base, ensuring alignment with various investor personas and their financial contexts.
6. Simulating investor survey responses through GPT-4o to reflect diverse financial preferences, risk appetites, and investment goals.
7. Analyzing the survey responses to generate insights, detect patterns, and enhance decision-making processes for personalized financial advice.
8. Leveraging GPT-4o to make informed financial decisions based on the survey responses, integrating the insights derived from the RAG knowledge base to tailor advice to individual investor profiles.

2. LITERATURE REVIEW

2.1 Importance of Financial Data and Application of Surveys

Financial data, including market data, macroeconomic indicators, and corporate financial statements, is essential for effective analysis and decision-making in the financial sector. This data helps evaluate market conditions, assess company performance, and make informed investment decisions. According to Gartner, leveraging data, analytics, and artificial intelligence (AI) can significantly enhance decision-making processes, driving strategic outcomes and operational efficiency (Gartner, Inc., 2022).

Surveys have traditionally been used to collect insights from investors and market participants. However, they face challenges in scalability and real-time relevance. Modern techniques, including the application of AI and advanced analytics, are transforming survey processes, making them more efficient, timely, and adaptable to dynamic market conditions. Data-driven decision-making in finance highlights the importance of continuous and contextual analysis to improve the accuracy and relevance of insights collected (Gautam and Bhimavarapu, 2022).

2.2 Current Applications of GPT-4o and Prompt Engineering

2.2.1 GPT-4o's Artificial General Intelligence (AGI) Capabilities

The GPT-4o model, as detailed by Bubeck et al. (2023), represents significant progress toward artificial general intelligence (AGI). This model excels in tasks that require deep understanding, nuanced context interpretation, and human-like response generation. These capabilities make GPT-4o an invaluable tool for financial applications such as automating surveys and providing reliable financial advice. This research leverages GPT-4o to enhance the efficiency and accuracy of financial data collection and decision-making processes (Bubeck et al., 2023).

2.2.2 GPT-4o and Prompt Engineering

Prompt engineering, as discussed by Giray (2023), involves the creation and optimization of prompts to effectively utilize large language models like GPT-4o. This process is crucial for tailoring GPT-4o's outputs to specific tasks, such as financial analysis and survey generation. The ability to craft precise prompts is key to harnessing GPT-4o's full potential, ensuring relevant and accurate responses. Extance (2023) further explores the integration of Retrieval-Augmented Generation (RAG) with GPT-4o, enhancing its ability to access up-to-date information and improve the reliability of generated responses. This approach is particularly valuable for financial surveys, where timeliness and accuracy are essential (Giray, 2023; Extance, 2023).

2.2.3 Integration with Dynamic Agentic Automation

Unlike traditional methods that rely on static systems, Agentic Automation introduces a dynamic approach by integrating intelligent agents capable of learning, adapting, and executing tasks autonomously. These agents leverage large language models, such as GPT-4o, and incorporate principles of cognitive automation to handle complex, unstructured tasks in real time. This study replaces static workflows with dynamic, context-driven agentic execution, which facilitates the automated handling of financial surveys, portfolio management, and risk assessment (Ye et al., 2023).

Merchia (2024) discusses Agentic Automation as a paradigm that empowers AI agents to bridge the gap between natural language inputs and actionable outputs. By incorporating technologies like RAG and GPT-4o into this framework, systems can dynamically adjust to evolving investor needs and make informed, personalized financial decisions. The integration of Agentic Automation with advanced AI tools enables a seamless and efficient process for automating financial tasks and enhancing decision-making accuracy.

2.3 Agentic Automation and Related Concepts

Agentic Automation marks an evolution from traditional Robotic Process Automation (RPA) by incorporating intelligent agents capable of complex decision-making and dynamic adaptation. While RPA is effective for automating repetitive tasks, it is limited in scenarios requiring human-like reasoning and flexibility (Lacity and Willcocks, 2018). Cognitive automation, which merges RPA with AI, further extends automation capabilities by allowing systems to handle more complex, unstructured tasks (Syed et al., 2020).

Agentic Automation builds upon these advancements by using AI-driven agents that can interpret user instructions, reason through tasks, and make decisions based on real-time data and context. This approach is exemplified in Agentic Process Automation (APA), which shifts the focus from static, rule-based workflows to dynamic, context-aware task execution (Ye et al., 2023).

In the context of financial decision-making, Agentic Automation enables AI agents to simulate and adapt to the roles of human investors, taking into account factors such as risk tolerance, investment goals, and market conditions. This allows the system to simulate diverse investor personas and generate tailored financial advice that evolves with real-time market data and individual preferences.

3. TECHNICAL FRAMEWORKS AND METHODOLOGY

3.1 Setup of GPT-4o API

The GPT-4o model is deployed within the Azure AI Foundry project, which integrates several advanced Azure AI services to optimize the system's functionality. This deployment includes the Azure AI Search service, which allows for the efficient indexing and retrieval of relevant financial data from a variety of sources. Additionally, the text-embedding-ada-002 model service is used to enhance the search capabilities by providing high-quality text embeddings, enabling the system to better understand and process large amounts of financial text data.

By configuring the API endpoints and handling authentication keys for seamless operation, GPT-4o is fully integrated into the application, allowing it to automate financial survey generation, simulate responses, and analyze data effectively. The combination of these advanced Azure services ensures that the system is capable of handling large datasets and adapting to dynamic financial conditions, facilitating more accurate and personalized financial decision-making.

3.2 Retrieval-Augmented Generation (RAG)

Retrieval-Augmented Generation (RAG) plays a pivotal role in this methodology by enhancing the capabilities of GPT-4o with real-time access to vast external datasets. The RAG process involves retrieving relevant information from a knowledge base, followed by the generation of contextually appropriate and accurate responses.

To ensure that the information used by the system is always up-to-date, the Azure AI Search service is used to query comprehensive financial datasets that include:

- Macroeconomic policies
- Industry research reports
- Corporate financial disclosures
- Market data
- Regulatory case studies and enforcement actions

The text-embedding-ada-002 model service is then employed to process and generate embeddings for the extracted data, allowing GPT-4o to better understand and incorporate complex financial contexts into its outputs.

3.3 Agentic Automation and Dynamic Persona Configuration

The integration of Agentic Automation enables the creation of dynamic virtual personas that simulate real-world investor profiles. These personas are initialized using data from RAG, and their responses evolve as they "learn" from the latest market conditions and external information.

The process includes the following steps:

1. Persona Creation: Agent-C generates virtual personas, each with unique attributes like age, income, investment goals, and risk tolerance.
2. Agent Initialization: Agent-0 to Agent-(n-1) agents receive their persona data and are configured by using RAG and real-time web searches to adapt their knowledge and enhance their decision-making capabilities.
3. Survey Generation: Agent-S creates tailored financial surveys, ensuring the questions align with the personas' characteristics and the current market environment.
4. Simulated Responses: GPT-4o generates realistic and diverse survey responses by referencing the RAG knowledge base, providing insights into different investor perspectives.
5. Analysis of Responses: The system analyzes the survey responses, extracting valuable insights into investor sentiment and preferences.
6. Informed Decision-Making: GPT-4o synthesizes the survey data and provides actionable financial recommendations, enhancing the decision-making process for investors.

The system's adaptability is key to maintaining its relevance and accuracy. As the virtual agents interact with more data, they refine their responses, improving the overall decision-making process. The use of Azure AI Search and text-embedding-ada-002 ensures that the system can efficiently process and integrate new financial information, keeping it in line with real-time market conditions.

4. EXPERIMENTS AND RESULTS

4.1 Data Set Description

The data set includes information from a custom-built RAG database that aggregates a wide range of financial data relevant to portfolio management and risk control. This data is sourced from reliable financial channels, including macroeconomic indicators, industry reports, and publicly available financial statements. The process begins with the creation of virtual investor personas and the generation of corresponding survey templates by the Agentic System. These personas simulate real-world investor profiles, including risk preferences, financial goals, and market sentiment.

4.2 Experimental Setup

Subsequently, virtual agents use the survey templates to simulate answers, reflecting diverse investment profiles. The responses are then analyzed and aggregated by Agent-E, which uses advanced decision-making models to derive actionable financial advice from the collected data. This multi-step process from data extraction to decision-making is illustrated in Figure 1.

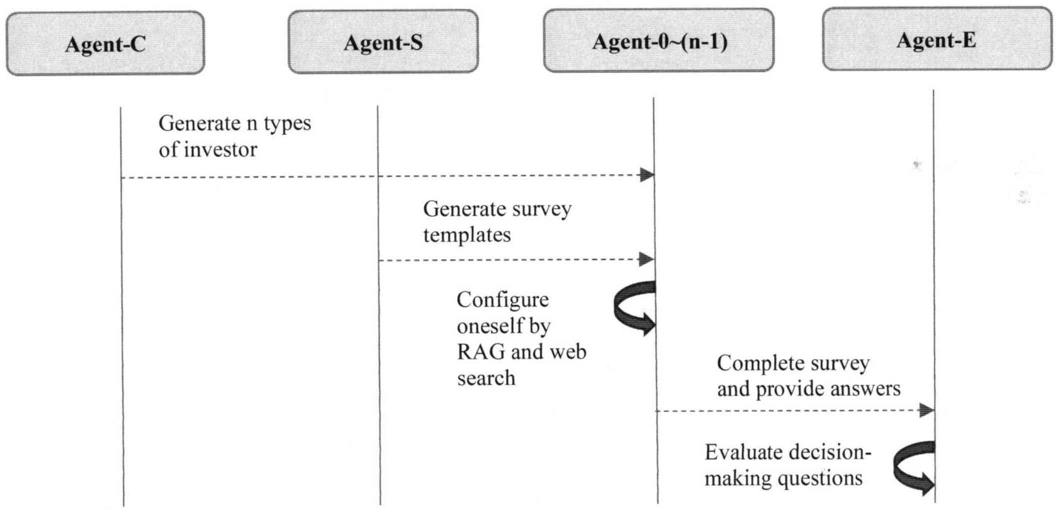

Figure 1. This figure illustrates the integration of the RAG system and GPT-4o with the Agentic System, demonstrating the process from data extraction to decision-making

4.3 Automated Decision Making

In our experiments, we aimed to evaluate the effectiveness of GPT-4o in providing automated answers to financial decision-making questions. We tested 20 financial decision questions by generating automated responses using our system and then manually asking the same questions by the author. The results of this comparison are shown in Table 1.

Table 1. Comparison of Automated Responses by GPT-4o System and author's choices

Metric	Number of Questions Tested	Number of Matching Responses	Match Rate (%)
Total Questions	20	16	80%

5. DISCUSSION: NECESSITY AND LONG-TERM UTILITY OF THE PROPOSED APPROACH

Although large language models (LLMs) like GPT-4o have demonstrated remarkable capabilities in instruction-following, question-answering, and reasoning chain generation, their application in complex and dynamic financial decision-making processes remains a challenge. While LLMs can efficiently perform basic tasks, they are generally constrained by their static workflows, which struggle to adapt in real-time to evolving market conditions and personalized needs. This limitation is especially evident in the realm of financial advisory, where real-time data, multiple investor personas, and contextual adaptability are essential.

5.1 Enhancing LLM Utility through Agentic Automation

The method proposed in this paper, integrating Agentic Automation with Retrieval-Augmented Generation (RAG) and GPT-4o, enhances the utility of LLMs in this domain. The key differences between traditional LLM approaches and the proposed method include:

1. Dynamic Adjustment to Market Conditions:
   - Traditional LLMs typically rely on static workflows.
   - Agentic Automation continuously adapts to evolving market data and investor profiles, ensuring timely and personalized financial advice.
2. Multi-agent System for Simulation:
   - Unlike traditional approaches, which involve a single-task model, our system uses multiple agents simulating diverse investor personas. These agents generate dynamic, real-time surveys and personalized recommendations.

5.2 Integration of RLHF-like Agentic Automation for Improved Reasoning

Recent advancements, such as those demonstrated by DeepSeek in incentivizing reasoning capabilities in LLMs (DeepSeek-AI, 2025), highlight the potential of Reinforcement Learning with Human Feedback (RLHF) in improving model performance. RLHF has been shown to enhance reasoning by guiding model behaviors based on human feedback, encouraging more effective decision-making processes. Although our proposed approach draws on similar principles, it utilizes RLHF-like Agentic Automation, which provides further refinement and adaptability. While RLHF and the actor-critic mechanism in reinforcement learning are focused on individual model behavior, RLHF-like Agentic Automation introduces the ability to simulate a diverse set of financial personas that interact with real-time data and adjust autonomously.

1. Continuous Refinement of Reasoning Ability:
   - The integration of RLHF-like Agentic Automation allows virtual agents to continuously improve their reasoning capabilities through real-time data interaction and autonomous adaptation.
   - The actor-critic mechanism, similar to RLHF, is reflected in the feedback loop where agents autonomously adjust their strategies, learning from new market data and refining decision-making over time.
2. Enhanced Decision-making:
   - While RLHF focuses on improving reasoning by incentivizing model behaviors using human feedback, our approach provides a more nuanced, context-aware solution tailored specifically for financial advisory.

- Unlike traditional RLHF, our multi-agent system allows agents to simulate diverse investor profiles and dynamically adjust decision-making strategies according to evolving market conditions, offering a scalable and adaptable solution.

5.3 Comparison with Traditional Training and Fine-tuning of LLMs

In addition to enhancing the core capabilities of GPT-4o, our approach stands out in comparison to the traditional training and fine-tuning of LLMs. The key distinctions include:

1. Real-time Adaptation vs. Static Fine-tuning:
   - Traditional LLMs typically undergo training on a fixed dataset followed by fine-tuning for specific tasks, without adapting to new, real-time information.
   - In contrast, Agentic Automation allows for dynamic, real-time learning and decision-making, ensuring that the system stays relevant to the current market conditions.
2. Single-agent vs. Multi-agent Systems:
   - Training and fine-tuning LLMs generally use a single agent or model to process data and perform tasks.
   - Our method incorporates a multi-agent system that simulates a wide range of financial personas and adapts to personalized financial needs, resulting in more robust and diverse recommendations.

5.4 Long-term Utility of the Proposed Approach

The long-term utility of the proposed approach lies in its ability to:

1. Integrate Real-time Knowledge Retrieval:
   - The system's dynamic nature allows it to continually adjust to new financial data, improving its responsiveness and decision-making.
2. Simulate Diverse Investor Behaviors:
   - As financial markets evolve, the virtual agents in this system learn from continuous data streams, adapting to changing investor needs and financial landscapes.
3. Provide Personalized, Scalable Financial Advice:
   - The flexibility of the Agentic Automation framework ensures its continued relevance as it evolves alongside market trends, offering a future-proof solution for AI-driven financial advisory services.

By enabling real-time adjustment and continuous learning, this method presents both a present-day solution for dynamic financial decision-making and a future-proof approach to AI-driven financial advisory.

6. CONCLUSION

This paper presents the integration of GPT-4o, Retrieval-Augmented Generation (RAG), and Agentic Automation in automating financial surveys and decision-making. By leveraging virtual investor personas and dynamically generated surveys, the system simulates a wide range of investor profiles and delivers tailored financial advice. Our experiments show that the system effectively generates actionable insights, improving the efficiency and accuracy of financial decision-making. This approach provides a scalable solution for the evolving financial advisory landscape, where personalization and adaptability are critical. The code for this project is publicly available on GitHub (https://github.com/psenye/Agentic).

7. FUTURE WORK

Future research should focus on enhancing the flexibility and adaptability of the Agentic Automation framework, particularly in terms of improving real-time decision-making capabilities. Expanding the RAG knowledge base with additional data sources, such as real-time financial indicators and market reports, will enable the system to generate even more personalized and context-aware financial recommendations. Further refinements to the learning processes of the virtual agents will also be necessary to increase the model's ability to simulate complex investor behaviors across different scenarios. Additionally, testing the system in real-world financial advisory applications will be a crucial step in validating its practical utility and expanding its potential across various financial sectors.

REFERENCES

Bubeck, S. et al., (2023). Sparks of artificial general intelligence: Early experiments with GPT-4. *arXiv preprint* arXiv:2303.12712.

DeepSeek-AI, (2025). DeepSeek-R1: Incentivizing Reasoning Capability in LLMs via Reinforcement Learning. arXiv preprint arXiv:2501.12948.

Extance, A., (2023). ChatGPT has entered the classroom: how LLMs could transform education. *Nature*, 623, pp. 474-477.

Gartner, Inc., (2022). Identifying Which Decisions to Reengineer and Why. Guides for Effective Business Decision Making. Available at: https://www.gartner.com/en/information-technology [Accessed 8 July 2024].

Gautam, R.S. and Bhimavarapu, V.M., (2022). Data Driven Decision Making: Application in Finance. *IRE Journals*, 5(12), pp. 52-56.

Giray, L., (2023). Prompt Engineering with ChatGPT: A Guide for Academic Writers. *Annals of Biomedical Engineering,* 51, pp. 2629–2633.

Lacity, M. and Willcocks, L.P., (2018). Robotic Process and Cognitive Automation: The Next Phase. SB Publishing.

Lu, X. and Chen, H., (2024). Dialogue with the Ant Zhixiaobao Team: Intensified Domestic Competition of Large Models, How AI Financial Butler Releases Greater Value? WAIC 2024, presented in July 4, 2024. Available at: https://baijiahao.baidu.com/s?id=1803604684091445390&wfr=spider&for=pc [Accessed 8 July 2024].

Merchia, A., (2024). Agentic AI: Introducing a new era of automation. Moveworks Blog, 1 October. Available at: https://www.moveworks.com/us/en/resources/blog/agentic-automation-is-next-step-in-ai-revolution [Accessed 5 November 2024].

Microsoft, (2024). Introduction to Semantic Kernel. Available at: https://learn.microsoft.com/en-us/semantic-kernel/overview/ [Accessed 8 July 2024].

Syed, R., Suriadi, S., Adams, M., Bandara, W., Leemans, S.J., Ouyang, C., ... and Reijers, H.A., (2020). Robotic process automation: contemporary themes and challenges. Computers in Industry, 115, p.103162. Available at: https://doi.org/10.1016/j.compind.2019.103162

Ye, Y., Cong, X., Tian, S., Cao, J., Wang, H., Qin, Y., Lu, Y., Yu, H., Wang, H., Lin, Y., Liu, Z. and Sun, M., (2023). ProAgent: From Robotic Process Automation to Agentic Process Automation. arXiv preprint arXiv:2311.10751.

ELEMENTS OF DIGITAL ACCESSIBILITY ON THE .HR DOMAIN

Anja Labak[1] and Tomislav Jakopec[2]
[1]*Mono d.o.o., Croatia*
[2]*Faculty of Humanities and Social Sciences in Osijek/Department of Information Sciences, Croatia*

ABSTRACT

The purpose of this paper is to present the research on digital accessibility conducted in the Republic of Croatia on the entire .hr domain homepage registry in January 2024. The aim of this paper is to present the extent to which .hr domain homepages adhere to the Web Content Accessibility Guidelines (WCAG) developed by The Web Accessibility Initiative (WAI). The paper also analyzes previous research on the topic of digital accessibility, to gain insight into the most commonly used tools for analysis and the situation in other countries. For research purposes, the Google Lighthouse tool was adopted to successfully analyze 95,153 .hr domains using a custom solution developed with the Python, JavaScript and PHP programming languages. The data from the analysis were stored in the database and were analyzed using Structure Query Language (SQL). The main result of the digital accessibility research into the entire .hr domain is that 77.47% of .hr domain homepages successfully implement the minimum level of digital accessibility based on the guidelines, so one can conclude that the situation is satisfactory. As a result of the research, it is proposed that the implementation of digital accessibility as well as the use of various tools for its analysis be monitored closely. In the future, the conducted research may be the basis for closer monitoring of the implementation of digital accessibility in the Republic of Croatia.

KEYWORDS

Digital Accessibility, .HR Domain, WCAG, WAI, Google Lighthouse

1. INTRODUCTION

Kulkarni (2018) defines digital accessibility as a measure of the accessibility of technological products, resources and services on devices and software, as well as a measure of the accessibility of digital content. Digital accessibility creates perception, understanding and easier navigation of digital content for people with disabilities. Digital accessibility is important for the inclusion of people with disabilities in educational, economic, political and other forms of activities. To ensure proper digital accessibility of online content, the Web Accessibility Initiative (WAI), developed by the World Wide Web Consortium (W3C), is developing standards and supporting materials to better understand and implement digital accessibility when creating digital content (W3C, 2024). The digital accessibility project first began in the fall of 1996 as the initiative of W3C staff and several enthusiasts from within the professional community, among whom Tim Berners-Lee stands out. After 9 months, the project was officially presented to the public for the first time, after which the W3C proposed the digital accessibility project as an official project. The main reason for the proposal was the lack of official guidelines for the implementation of digital accessibility. The Web Accessibility Initiative (WAI) project began under the leadership of Daniel Dardailler and officially commenced in February 1997 with the support of IBM, Microsoft and others (Dardailler, 2009). Today, WAI continues to develop the WCAG Content Accessibility Guidelines in collaboration with individuals and organizations around the world, with the goal of providing a single common standard for digital content accessibility that meets the needs of individuals, organizations and governments internationally. WCAG 2.2 guidelines are currently in place (W3C, 2023).

In the Republic of Croatia, there are still numerous obstacles for individuals when accessing digital content, although the principles of digital accessibility are prescribed by the Act on the Accessibility of Websites and Software Solutions for Mobile Devices of Public Sector Bodies (Central State Office for the Development of Digital Society, n.d.). The Croatian Parliament adopted a decision on the Act on the Accessibility of Websites and Software Solutions for Mobile Devices of Public Sector Bodies pursuant to Article 89 of the Constitution of the Republic of Croatia at its session on 8 February 2019. This Act provides accessibility measures for websites and software solutions to all users, especially people with disabilities (Act on the Accessibility of Websites, 2019). The Act was created based on Directive (EU) 2016/2102 of the European Parliament and of the Council on the accessibility of the websites and mobile applications of public sector bodies, which was adopted on 26 October 2016; however, in the Republic of Croatia it entered into force in 2019 (Official Journal of the European Union, 2019). Digital accessibility research conducted in the Republic of Croatia on the .hr domain homepage registry in January 2024 gives us an insight into how much digital accessibility is implemented on the .hr domain, and whether the .hr domain adheres to the guidelines for achieving digital accessibility.

2. DIGITAL ACCESSIBILITY

According to W3C (2023), digital accessibility is the accessibility of websites, tools and technologies that were developed in such a way as to enable their use by people with disabilities. In other words, it allows them to perceive, understand, navigate, contribute and communicate with the online network. The field of digital accessibility includes the following disabilities that affect website access: visual, auditory, physical, cognitive, neurological and speech-related. In addition to providing accessibility for people with disabilities, digital accessibility also facilitates access to websites for people without disabilities. For example, individuals who use mobile devices, smartwatches and other devices with small screen dimensions, different input methods, etc.

To ensure everyone can easily access digital content, the WAI initiative develops digital accessibility solutions through technical specifications, guidelines, techniques and ancillary resources. WAI thus develops international standards for digital accessibility such as WCAG 2. WCAG is an international standard that contains guidelines for creating accessible digital content for users with disabilities. Digital content is any information on a website or app, which includes content such as text, images and audio, as well as content such as program code or tags. The WCAG Guidelines were developed in collaboration with individuals and organizations around the world to create standards for digital accessibility that meet the needs of individuals, organizations and countries. Currently, the most current version of the said standard is WCAG 2.2. WCAG 2 consists of a total of 13 guidelines. The digital accessibility guidelines are distributed into 4 principles: Perceivable, Operable, Understandable and Robust. These 4 principles are the foundation for users who want to access and use digital content. Each guideline has success criteria at three levels: A (minimum), AA (recommended) and AAA (excellent) (W3C, 2023).

According to W3C (2023), WAI-ARIA (Accessible Rich Internet Applications) is a specification that defines how online content and applications can be more accessible to people with disabilities. It focuses on improving the digital accessibility of dynamic content, as well as advanced user interface features developed in HTML, JavaScript and other similar technologies. The specification contains three main features: Roles, Properties and States.

3. PREVIOUS RESEARCH

In the Republic of Croatia, the official report on the compliance of websites and mobile applications of public sector bodies with accessibility requirements was published for the first time in December 2021. Based on the data provided by the Information Commissioner, the Central State Office for the Development of Digital Society (CSODDS) submitted the first report on the compliance of websites and mobile applications of public sector bodies with accessibility requirements to the European Commission. For the purposes of this paper, we will refer to the part that refers to websites. The monitoring of websites took place in the period from 1 January 2020 to 22 December 2021. The analysis was conducted by manual testing on a sample of 158 websites, where only the homepages were analyzed. Digital accessibility was based on the monitoring of the requirements issued by the European standard EN 301 549 "Accessibility Requirements for ICT Products and Services". The monitoring was carried out by external associates, representatives of national umbrella associations of persons with disabilities, one person with a motor disorder and one person with a visual impairment.

Monitoring was carried out using Google Chrome and the NVDA screen reader for websites, v. 2021.2 and 2. The results of the monitoring show that the highest average accessibility value was recorded in healthcare (86%) and social welfare (82%). The lowest average values were recorded in transport (31%), environmental protection, recreation and culture (31%) and improvement of housing and communities (33%). The highest values awarded to individual websites of public sector bodies across all branches of the public sector were between 90% and 100% (Central State Office for the Development of Digital Society, 2021).

Although the tool used for accessibility analysis in this paper is from 2016, Brajnik (2004) compared tools for evaluating accessibility. Akgül and Vatansever (2016) conducted 2016 research in Turkey where they analyzed the digital accessibility of the Turkish government's websites. The research analyzed the digital accessibility of 25 Turkish government websites based on WCAG standards 1.0 and 2.0 using automatic digital accessibility analysis tools. The homepages were analyzed on the same day to avoid changes from different points of view, including digital accessibility. To analyze digital accessibility, the authors Akgül and Vatansever used the following tools: AChecker, eXaminator, TAW, Total Validator, WAVE, Web Accessibility Assessment Tool, EvalAccess, Cynthia Says, MAGENTA, HERA, Amp and Sort Site. Based on the results, the authors Akgül and Vatansever concluded that the Turkish government did not meet the minimum requirements for digital accessibility. They urged organizations caring for people with disabilities to spread awareness of the importance of digital accessibility when it came to the Turkish government's websites. It is important to point out that there was no top-rated website in terms of accessibility, as each tool resulted in a different analysis (Yakup).

Acosta-Vargas et al. (2019) conducted research on 40 websites using a modified heuristic method with the integration of the assessment of the severity of digital accessibility barriers according to WCAG standard 2.1. Research results showed that high-ranking websites still did not fully meet all digital accessibility guidelines. They emphasized that even though a page was highly ranked, this did not mean that it was accessible. In addition, the authors emphasized the need for improved methods of assessing digital accessibility.

N. Alajarmeh (2021) analyzed the digital accessibility of public health websites in 25 different countries. The research was conducted during the COVID-19 pandemic in 2020. The following tools were used to collect digital accessibility data: AChecker, WAVE, W3C HTML Validator and W3C CSS Validator. The results of the research showed that most of the pages analyzed were not in accordance with the WCAG AA level, which results in serious difficulties for people with disabilities when accessing the pages in question. Only one website had an average number of accessibility issues.

M. Campoverde-Molina et al. (2021) provided a systematic review of the literature analyzing the digital accessibility of university websites in the world. The systematic review was based on the analysis, synthesis and interpretation of 42 papers to determine standards for website accessibility. The authors used three different methods: automated tools, expert assessment and testing with users of the most commonly-used techniques according to the literature. The results of the research showed that university websites made similar mistakes when it comes to digital accessibility according to the WCAG criteria. The results of the research showed similar types of violations on university websites over time in accordance with the WCAG performance criteria. The evolution of the use of WCAG standards from version 1.0 to 2.1 in the evaluation of the accessibility of university websites is highlighted. It is concluded that certain digital accessibility analytics tools such as AChecker, Bobby, TAW and WAVE were preferred in the research. With the COVID-19 pandemic disrupting the global education system, there was an emphasis on the accessibility of technology tools for learning and teaching. The authors suggested that university website development teams should have integrated the concept of accessibility from the very beginning of the process of creating or redesigning websites, using available resources and testing with real users and experts.

S. Kumar et al. (2021) conducted research comparing 10 WCAG tools for the analysis of the digital accessibility of websites by the World Wide Web Consortium (W3C). To compare all 10 tools, they analyzed two websites. The tools they compared were: Access Assistant Community Edition by Level, A-Checker by the Inclusive Design Research Centre, Functional Accessibility Evaluator 2.0 by the University of Illinois at Urbana-Champaign, QualWeb by Faculdade de Ciências da Universidade de Lisboa, WAVE by WebAIM, Accessibility Insights for Web by Microsoft, Button Contrast Checker by Aditus, Siteimprove Accessibility Checker by Siteimprove, Utilitilia Validator by Utilitia SP. Z O.O and IBM Accessibility Equal Access Toolkit: Accessibility Checker by IBM. The conclusion based on the research was that all of these tools are easy to use; however, the end results produced by each of these tools were different when analyzing the same websites. The tools also differ when it comes to their audit syntax, and there is no ideal tool to analyze digital accessibility. More recent research includes papers by McGill (2023) and Nguyen (2024), which evaluate the effectiveness of Google Lighthouse in identifying website accessibility issues, with one comparing it to other automated tools and the other focusing specifically on Lighthouse's potential and limitations for accessibility audits.

4. RESEARCH

The aim of this research is to gain insight into the state of compliance with digital accessibility standards on the homepages of websites with the Croatian domain (.hr). The research was conducted in January 2024. Based on the previous papers, the following hypothesis was proposed:

H1. Homepages of websites with a Croatian domain do not meet the minimum requirements for digital accessibility

To conduct research into digital accessibility on the homepages of websites with the .hr domain, it was necessary to obtain a list of all websites with a Croatian domain (.hr) from the Registry of all .hr domains, which was obtained from CARNET (the Croatian Academic and Research Network). To successfully scan the entire .hr domain registry, it was necessary to either create a tool for measuring digital accessibility or to use an existing open access tool. For the purposes of this research, we used the open access tool Google Lighthouse, version 11.3.0. An accessibility score is a weighted average of all accessibility audits, which is based on axe user impact assessments. Since the tool is mainly used for manual scanning of a single page, it was necessary to adjust the tool to automatically scan the entire .hr domain registry. For the purposes of this research, only the homepages of the .hr domain were scanned. The tool was customized using the Python, PHP and JavaScript programming languages. Google Lighthouse stores the results of digital accessibility in the JSON format, which needs to be stored in a database. The library Chrome Launcher, which enables the launching of the Google Chrome browser via a command line, was used. For the purposes of this research, Chrome Launcher was used to automate tools and quickly launch Google Lighthouse. Chrome Launcher version 1.1.0 was used. Figure 1 shows infographics of the .hr domain homepage digital accessibility measurement tool architecture and an ERA diagram of the database used to successfully store and interpret data. The MariaDB relational database management system was used.[1]

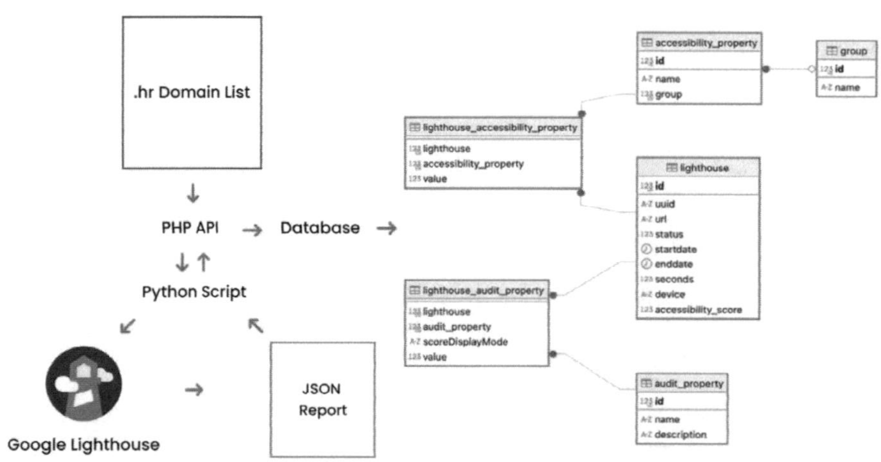

Figure 1. Architecture infographics with ERA diagram

Prior to the main .hr domain homepage harvesting, a 10-page test harvesting was conducted to test the digital accessibility measurement tool. Test harvesting was successful with 10 JSON reports returned. All the anonymous data are stored on PUH: https://puh.srce.hr/s/xQ4kHJXk7qy9ywF https://puh.srce.hr/s/Yb9AREXQTYtxPyq.

[1] Source code available on https://github.com/alabak48/accessibility-webcrawler-lighthouse

5. RESULTS

To conduct the research, it was necessary to find unique, real .hr domains. The total number of actual domains is 95,153. From the total actual domains, it was necessary to reach the domains and subdomains. For example, the domain of the University of Josip Juraj Strossmayer is unios.hr. The University consists of several faculties, so the website of the Faculty of Humanities and Social Sciences in Osijek is its subdomain. The total number of occurrences of all domains found was 1,158,577. This number was filtered, and a total of 111,121 unique domains and subdomains was obtained. So, this number was filtered down to the number of homepages only, without any further redirects within the .hr domain.

A total of 23,914 websites was not analyzed. At the time of collection, these websites were not available. The domains/subdomains exist, but their content is not accessible. An example of a website that was not analyzed is http://www.joriside.hr/. After the website had been automatically analyzed, this website was further analyzed through a report that can be generated using Google Lighthouse located in the browser. The results of the analysis showed a problem with First Contentful Paint (FCP) and NO_FCP. Walton (2023) defines FCP as a metric for a perceived loading measure. It indicates the first loading point during website analysis. The website was not loaded during the analysis. The next example is http://www.absulo.hr/. This website also had a NO_FCP error, however, the website had an expired domain, so there was no content on the homepage. The next example is the website http://www.transactioncub.hr/. The specified website could not be analyzed because the page could not be found. When loading it, the error "This page is not available" occurred.

In all of these cases, it is not possible to analyze digital accessibility. Other websites could not be analyzed because they had access problems or were redirected to domains other than .hr. Some of them were in the maintenance phase, while a few took too long to analyze, so the analysis was interrupted for this reason. The total number of websites where results for digital accessibility can be obtained is 87,207.

The analysis of each website leads to the generation of a total digital accessibility percentage for its homepage. Thus, when all automated tests are performed, the analysis provides the overall digital accessibility percentage for the page in the form of JSON reports. The results of the analysis of the digital accessibility percentage of homepages with the .hr domain show that a total of 4,955 (4.46%) homepages score 100%. A total of 17,709 (15.94%) pages have a score of 90%-99%, 33,701 (30.33%) have 80%-89%, 18,193 (16.37%) have 70%-79%, 7,757 (6.98%) have 60%-69% and 3,773 (3.39%) have 50%-59%. 1,036 (0.93%) .hr domains have less than 50% digital accessibility. Finally, only 83 (0.07%) pages have 0% digital accessibility (Figure 2).

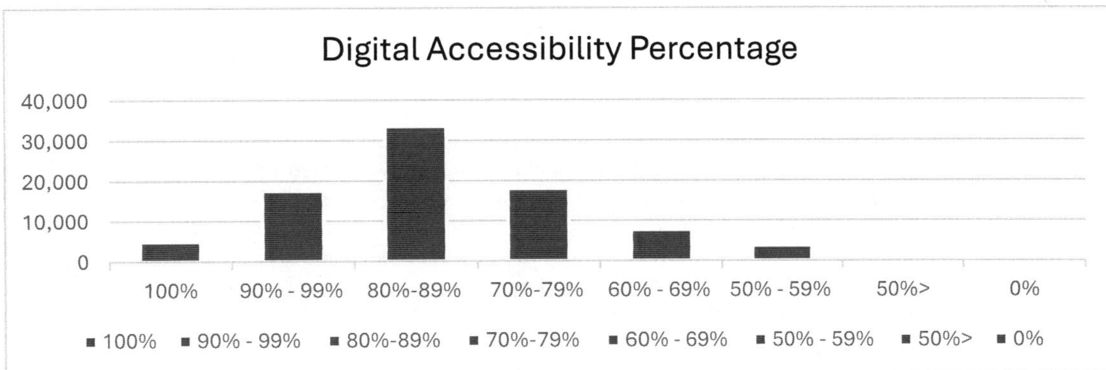

Figure 2. Digital accessibility percentage of homepages with the .hr domain

The results of the research do not support the hypothesis that websites with a Croatian domain will not meet the minimum level of requirements for achieving digital accessibility. The results of the analysis, which yield the total digital accessibility percentage, show that the majority of pages, a total of 33,701 (30.33%), are in the range of 80%-89.99% when it comes to accessibility scores. Of the total websites analyzed, only 83 (0.007%) pages have 0% digital accessibility. Only 4,955 (4.46%) pages have a 100% digital accessibility result. Looking at the results of the overall digital accessibility percentage on an individual domain, as many as 86,088 (77.47%) domains successfully pass more than 50% of audits for the implementation of digital accessibility elements.

If we observe the audits of the analysis of digital accessibility separately, the most common audit is document-title, which is represented on a total of 87,196 pages and which has a total pass rate of 97.22%. Although most hr. domains contain more than 50% of digital accessibility elements, it is important to note that most HTML elements contain them. For example, if we speak of semantic HTML, the digital accessibility percentage increases greatly because semantic HTML is weighted highly in audits. Audits such as document-title have the highest representation on pages and the highest pass rate percentage. Document-title is a property that serves as the title of the page and is an indispensable part of the page. Some code editors, such as Visual Studio Code, already set this property in the header when creating an HTML page. Other properties such as html-lang-valid, html-has-lang and meta-viewport are likewise included. If we do not count the audits that were not carried out on any page, the lowest representation is the aria-text audit, which was audited on a total of 6 pages and which had a 100% pass rate. The results also highlight audits that have a high pass rate. Among them we can find aria attributes and properties: accesskeys (99.49%), aria-allowed-attr (95.85%), aria-allowed-role (93.87%), aria-command-name (94.31%), aria-dialog-name (88.47%), aria-hidden-body (99.99%), aria-hidden-focus (90.50%), aria-required-attr (99.57%), aria-required-parent (88.61%), aria-roles (99.67%), aria-text (100%), aria-toggle-field-name (76.75%), aria-tooltip-name (72.22%), aria-valid-attr-value (98.42%) and aria-valid-attr (99.92%). Certain aria properties and attributes are not represented on a large number of homepages; however, we can conclude that when developers decide to implement them, they do so properly. We must consider that certain aria attributes and properties are subject to change. For example, certain audits were not represented when the latest version of Google Lighthouse was created, so these attributes and properties were not implemented. However, while this may be considered a reason for not implementing it, outdated digital accessibility applications also undermine digital accessibility.

Separate audits that were not performed because they were not found on any of the homepages are as follows: aria-meter-name, bypass, empty-heading, duplicate id-aria, form-field-multiple-labels, identical-link-same-purpose, landmark-one-main, target-size, th-has-dana-cells and video-caption. aria-meter-name is an attribute that associates with a <meter> HTML element. This element is used to express scalar values within a known range, for example, part of the total storage capacity (Accessibility Insights, n.d.). The assumption is that the homepages do not contain sufficiently complex data to express scalar values, so this audit was not carried out on any page. The bypass rule ensures that there is a mechanism for skipping content blocks on each page. For this audit to pass, it is necessary to implement bypassing blocks, remove blocks of repeated content, and place the repeated content at the end, so that it can be avoided by means of user agents, for example, avoid the content by pressing the Escape key. So, simply determining the language and its empty-heading understanding checks whether the page contains a title element that is empty. The duplicate id-aria audit dictates that each id-aria attribute should be unique. form-field-multiple-labels ensures that each field within the form has only one label, that is, the <label> element. The identical-link-same-purpose rule analyzes whether links with identical accessible names resolve to the same resource or equivalent resources. The landmark-one-main audit ensures that the page contains a main landmark marked with the HTML element <main>. If the page contains multiple main landmarks, they should be marked with a separate identifier. The target-size audit ensures that the content on the website is of the target size so that users can interact with it even when they access the content through smaller screens. th-has-dana-cells analyzes the content within the columns in the tables. With this audit, it is important that the table does not have an empty column. Finally, video-caption is an audit for the textual form of information, i.e., subtitles in videos and animations. It includes spoken words, who speaks, when this is not visible, and important sounds relevant to the context of the video itself (W3C, 2024).

6. CONCLUSION

Digital accessibility has become an imperative for today's websites. Equality and inclusion when accessing a website are the right of every individual. Thanks to WCAG, today there is a set of guidelines that can be followed to make content accessible to everyone. Successful implementation of digital accessibility results in the inclusion of all persons, adaptation to their needs, and gradual improvement of digital content. The importance of digital accessibility of websites began in the 90s, and it is still implemented today. Research into digital accessibility elements on the homepages of the .hr domain shows that the .hr domain adheres to the minimum requirements for digital accessibility, although expectations based on previous research were the opposite.

In the Republic of Croatia, in December 2021, an official report on monitoring digital accessibility was submitted for the first time, based on a sample of 158 websites. The highest recorded average accessibility percentage is found in healthcare (86%) and social welfare (82%). The lowest average values were recorded in the fields of transport (31%), environmental protection, recreation and culture (31%) and improvement of housing and communities (33%). By analyzing previous international research on digital accessibility, we can see that the most commonly used tools for analyzing digital accessibility are AChecker, SiteImprove and WAVE. Research clearly shows that other countries' websites do not adhere to the minimum guidelines for digital accessibility. Moreover, it is often advised to use several approaches to analyze digital accessibility. The results of this research show that developers stick to the fundamentals of digital accessibility implementation, but there are exceptions such as aria attributes and properties. Most authors insist on improving the digital accessibility of the pages studied.

The results of the research into digital accessibility elements on the .hr domain reject the hypothesis according to which it was expected that websites with the Croatian domain do not meet the minimum level of requirements for digital accessibility. Out of a total of 111,121 pages analyzed, a total of 23,914 pages were not included in further analysis. The digital accessibility report shows that 4,955 (4.46%) score 100%, while only 83 (0.07%) score 0%. Most pages, a total of 86,088 (77.47%), successfully pass more than 50% of the audits for the implementation of digital accessibility elements.

Individual digital accessibility audits also demonstrate the successful implementation of digital accessibility elements. The most common digital accessibility element is document-title. The document-title audit was conducted on a total of 87,196 pages with a total pass rate of 97.22%. The following audits have a high pass rate: accesskeys (99.49%), aria-allowed-attr (95.85%), aria-allowed-role (93.87%), aria-command-name (94.31%), aria-dialog-name (88.47%), aria-hidden-body (99.99%), aria-hidden-focus (90.50%), aria-required-attr (99.57%), aria-required-parent (88.61%), aria-roles (99.67%), aria-text (100%), aria-toggle-field-name (76.75%), aria-tooltip-name (72.22%), aria-valid-attr-value (98.42%) and aria-valid-attr (99.92%). Certain aria properties and attributes have not been implemented on many pages, but when developers decide to implement them, they implement them properly. These audits are an example of well-implemented digital accessibility elements. Of the other audits that were half-implemented, alternative text in pictures stands out. This is located on 76,127 domains; however, the pass rate of this audit is 68%. Out of a total of 31,649 pages containing the form, 77.54% have a properly implemented <label> element or title for the input field. When analyzing the homepages of the .hr domain, only 9 audits were not performed on any .hr domain, including the video-caption audit. Today, media content on pages is regularly implemented, however, the audit that checks the video-caption elements was not carried out successfully on a single page. Also, the bypass audit used to skip recurring content was not found on any of the pages.

The majority of .hr domain homepages successfully implement the minimum level of digital accessibility guidelines; therefore, based on the .hr domain homepages studied, we can conclude that the situation is satisfactory. To improve this percentage in the future, it is necessary to emphasize the importance of digital accessibility and raise awareness among designers, developers and website owners about the need for accessible design and development of digital content, as this can ultimately attract new users and clients, and improve their user experience. Moreover, the successful implementation of digital accessibility reflects ethical and moral values that promote equality and respect for diversity at the national and international levels.

These research findings can serve as a comprehensive overview of web accessibility in the Republic of Croatia, enabling future comparisons that highlight areas for improvement. This research should raise awareness about the importance of digital accessibility and emphasize the need for equality and inclusion. Given the lack of existing evaluations of web accessibility in the Republic of Croatia, this research can serve as a support for legislators when designing regulations that promote web accessibility compliance, as well as identifying where current laws or guidelines are not being followed.

REFERENCES

Accessibility Principles. (2023). https://www.w3.org/WAI/fundamentals/accessibility-principles/

Acosta-Vargas, P., Salvador-Ullauri, L. A., & Luján-Mora, S. (2019). *Heuristic Method to Evaluate Web Accessibility for Users with Low Vision*. IEEE, Vol. 7, pp. 125639–125647. http://dx.doi.org/10.1109/ACCESS.2019.2939068

Act on the Accessibility of Websites and Software Solutions for Mobile Devices of Public Sector Bodies. (2019). Official Gazette, NN 17/2019. https://narodne-novine.nn.hr/clanci/sluzbeni/2019_02_17_358.html

ACT Rules: Bypass Blocks of Repeated Content. (2024). https://www.w3.org/WAI/standards-guidelines/act/rules/cf77f2/proposed/

Akgül, Y., & Vatansever, K. (2016). *Web Accessibility Evaluation of Government Websites for People with Disabilities in Turkey*. Journal of Advanced Management Science, Vol. 4, No. 3, pp. 205–208. http://dx.doi.org/10.12720/joams.4.3.201-210 (7 March 2024).

Alajarmeh, N. (2021). *Evaluating the Accessibility of Public Health Websites: An Exploratory Cross-Country Study*. Universal Access in the Information Society, Vol. 21, pp. 777–778.

Brajnik, G. (2004). *Comparing accessibility evaluation tools: a method for tool effectiveness*. Universal Access in the Information Society 3(3-4):252-263. http://dx.doi.org/10.1007/s10209-004-0105-y

Central State Office for the Development of Digital Society. (2021). *Report on the Compliance of Websites and Mobile Applications of Public Sector Bodies with Accessibility Requirements for the Period of 1 January 2020 to 22 December 2021 (Websites) and the Period of 23 June 2021 to 22 December 2021 (Mobile Applications).* Zagreb, December 2021. https://pristupinfo.hr/wp-content/uploads/2021/12/2021-12-22-1.-IZVJESCE-REPUBLIKE-HRVATSKE-O-DIGITALNOJ-PRISTUPACNOSTI.pdf?x57830

Central State Office for the Development of Digital Society. (n.d.). *Digital Accessibility*. https://rdd.gov.hr/digitalna-pristupacnost

Dardailler, D. (2009). *WAI Early Days*. World Wide Web Consortium (W3C). https://www.w3.org/WAI/history

Directive (EU) 2016/2102 of the European Parliament and of the Council of 26 October 2016 on the Accessibility of the Websites and Mobile Applications of Public Sector Bodies. (2016). Official Journal of the European Union, 327/2016. https://eur-lex.europa.eu/legal-content/HR/TXT/?uri=CELEX%3A32016L2102

Form Field Must Not Have Multiple Label Elements. (n.d.). https://dequeuniversity.com/rules/axe/4.7/form-field-multiple-labels

Heading Has a Non-Empty Accessible Name. (n.d.). https://www.w3.org/WAI/standards-guidelines/act/rules/ffd0e9/proposed/#accessible-name

IDs Used in ARIA and Labels Must Be Unique. (n.d.). https://dequeuniversity.com/rules/axe/4.3/duplicate-id-aria

Introduction to Web Accessibility: What Is Web Accessibility. URL: https://www.w3.org/WAI/fundamentals/accessibility-intro/#:~:text=products%20and%20services.-,What%20is%20Web%20Accessibility,contribute%20to%20the%20Web

Kulkarni, M. (2019). *Digital Accessibility: Challenges and Opportunities*. IIMB Management Review, Vol. 31, Issue 1, pp. 91–98.

McGill, T., Bamgboye, O., Liu, X. and Kalutharage, C. S. *Towards Improving Accessibility of Web Auditing with Google Lighthouse.* 2023 IEEE 47th Annual Computers, Software, and Applications Conference (COMPSAC), Torino, Italy, 2023, pp. 1594-1599. https://doi.org/10.1109/COMPSAC57700.2023.00246

Nguyen, T, *Evaluating Automated Accessibility Checker Tools* (2024). WWU Honors College Senior Projects. 805. https://cedar.wwu.edu/wwu_honors/805

Understanding the Four Principles of Accessibility. (2023). https://www.w3.org/WAI/WCAG21/Understanding/intro#understanding-the-four-principles-of-accessibility

WAI-ARIA Overview: Introduction. (2023). https://www.w3.org/WAI/standards-guidelines/aria/

Walton, P. (2023). *First Contentful Paint (FCP).* https://web.dev/articles/fcp

WCAG 2 Overview. (n.d.). https://www.w3.org/WAI/standards-guidelines/wcag/

World Wide Web Consortium (W3C). (4 May 2024). *Making the Web Accessible*. https://www.w3.org/WAI/

EXPLORING CHALLENGES AND SUCCESS FACTORS IN ERP SYSTEMS IMPLEMENTATION — A SYSTEMATIC LITERATURE REVIEW

Aleksandra Hornjak, Teodora Vuckovic and Darko Stefanovic
Faculty of Technical Sciences, University of Novi Sad,
Trg Dositeja Obradovica 6, Novi Sad, Serbia

ABSTRACT

In response to the increasing need for organizational efficiency and streamlined business operations, enterprises worldwide are adopting ERP systems as integral tools for digital transformation. This paper investigates the challenges, user acceptance, and success factors influencing the implementation of ERP systems. ERP systems aim to optimize processes and enhance decision-making by integrating data across business functions. The study employs a systematic literature review to evaluate the existing research landscape, focusing on technical, organizational, and financial barriers, as well as strategies for overcoming these challenges. The findings provide insights into improving ERP adoption, aligning systems with organizational needs, and achieving operational efficiency.

KEYWORDS

ERP Systems, Challenges, User Acceptance, Implementation, Systematic Literature Review

1. INTRODUCTION

Enterprise Resource Planning (ERP) systems are standardized software packages that integrate all business functions into a single database, providing a wide range of benefits and capabilities across an organization, starting around the 1960s. (Jovičić and Vlajić, 2007; Klaus et al., 2000). ERP systems facilitate data and information exchange between all functional units within and outside the organization, enhancing various aspects of business operations and supporting the achievement of diverse goals (Addo-Tenkorang and Helo, 2011; Martins and Belfo, 2023).

Implementing ERP systems transforms business processes and organizational structure, requiring thoughtful adaptation in human resources and operations. Though numerous challenges may emerge throughout the ERP lifecycle, careful planning and a strategic approach can help organizations successfully navigate the complexities of ERP adoption, making implementation a key focus for many businesses today (Mahraz, 2018).

This paper theoretically investigates the challenges in ERP systems implementation within enterprises, examining overall success, user resistance, and acceptance of the systems.

This study aims to thoroughly explore and analyze the ERP implementation process in companies, focusing on the obstacles and challenges encountered and the critical factors for successful implementation. Special emphasis is placed on examining the impact of ERP systems on business processes and overall organizational efficiency, including user satisfaction with the system.

This paper systematically reviews existing literature to evaluate the obstacles and challenges, as well as the success factors of ERP system implementation. Following Kitchenham's guidelines for systematic literature reviews (Kitchenham and Charters, 2007) this study is organized as follows: Section 2 describes the background of ERP systems, while Section 3 explores similar literature. Section 4 outlines the methodology of the systematic literature review, covering its planning and execution. Section 5 presents the findings derived from the review, with a discussion in Section 6. The paper concludes with a summary of the key insights and implications in Section 7.

2. BACKGROUND

Since the 1990s, ERP systems have become the primary software choice for companies and have increasingly played a key role in business modernization (Klaus et al., 2000). With rapid technological advancements, ERP systems continuously evolve, enabling organizations to automate business processes and significantly improve data collection, analysis, and presentation. Technologies such as e-commerce, Customer Relationship Management (CRM), and Supply Chain Management (SCM) further enhance ERP functionalities (Dakic et al., 2020; Krneta and Marjanović, 2011). ERP software solutions must meet three core requirements (Krneta and Marjanović, 2011): efficient management of various business activities, a centralized database, and responsiveness to operational rules.

The primary goal of implementing an ERP system is to integrate all business functions within an organization. To be classified as an ERP system, software must possess attributes that ensure effectiveness and adaptability across diverse business environments. The following characteristics make ERP systems agile tools for improving efficiency and productivity in organizations of various sizes and industries (Rejman Petrović, 2009): flexibility, independence, comprehensiveness, modularity, openness, adaptability, and experience.

They serve as a foundation for managing resources, improving data handling, and streamlining operations, which collectively contribute to increased efficiency and productivity within an organization (Beric et al., 2020; Klaus et al., 2000). ERP systems have evolved to accommodate modern technological advancements, such as cloud computing, offering improved flexibility and scalability that supports remote access and enhanced user interfaces (Alhayek and Abu Odeh, 2020; Beric et al., 2018; Mahraz, 2018).

Key challenges in ERP implementation include high initial costs, complex integration with existing infrastructure, and resistance from employees to adopt new systems (Mahraz, 2018). These challenges often stem from the substantial organizational changes ERP systems introduce, affecting workflows and requiring adaptation from staff. Critical success factors for ERP adoption include strong management support, effective project management, user training, and thorough analysis of business needs to ensure system alignment with organizational goals (Pabedinskaitė, 2010; Stankić, 2014)

ERP providers continue to update systems, providing real-time data processing and facilitating decision-making processes. This makes ERP systems crucial for modern enterprises, yet also underscores the importance of addressing the challenges and critical factors impacting successful implementation (Addo-Tenkorang and Helo, 2011; Martins and Belfo, 2023).

3. RELATED WORK

The evolution of ERP, especially with cloud technology, is evident as providers increasingly offer ERP as SaaS or PaaS solutions, with adoption rates rising. ERP implementations are more automated and integrate critical resources like HR, sales, distribution, and finance (Singh and Nagpal, 2014).

ERP implementation at the University of Indonesia faced challenges like incompatibility with legacy systems, poor communication with vendors, lack of internal advocates, and low employee awareness. Externally, the absence of best practices and regulations further hindered adoption. However, strong IT infrastructure, management support, and training helped overcome obstacles. Gradually, benefits like transparency and standardization became evident, highlighting the need for planning, collaboration, and effective change management (Setyawan et al., 2020).

The study examines ERP implementation in manufacturing and production industries, focusing on challenges, user acceptance, and success factors. It highlights issues like complex customization, communication gaps, and employee resistance to new systems. The absence of best practices in some industries further complicates the process. User acceptance is identified as critical, and supported by training and involvement. Success depends on strong management support, reliable IT infrastructure, careful vendor selection, and phased or hybrid rollouts to reduce risks. Effective change management and clear communication are essential for smooth transitions and maximizing ERP benefits (Sri Ranjini. S and TJPRC, 2017).

This SLR provides a comprehensive synthesis of the challenges, factors, and user acceptance critical to ERP system implementation, drawn from research. It highlights actionable solutions, essential for improving ERP adoption. This work equips organizations with practical strategies to enhance efficiency, reduce risks, and achieve successful ERP integration.

4. METHODOLOGY

This paper follows Barbara Kitchenham's guidelines for conducting a systematic literature review (Kitchenham and Charters, 2007) The study consists of three key phases: planning, conducting, and reporting the review. The literature review is based on research questions and the inclusion and exclusion criteria for selecting studies.

Planning the review

In the initial stage of this SLR, it is necessary to identify the need for a review of the chosen topic. This can be determined by evaluating existing literature reviews in the chosen field, as Kitchenham's guidelines propose (Kitchenham and Charters, 2007).

Based on these guidelines (Kitchenham and Charters, 2007) the primary research questions were defined as follows:

- RQ1: What challenges do companies encounter during ERP system implementation?
- RQ2: How does user acceptance affect the success of ERP implementation in organizations?
- RQ3: What are the key factors that influence successful ERP adoption and implementation?

After defining the research questions, the next step is to search a database to gather relevant literature. In this study, the Scopus database was used. Scopus is recognized as one of the leading bibliographic resources, providing access to abstracts and citations of peer-reviewed works, including scholarly articles, conference papers, and books. Scopus was launched in 2004 by the publisher Elsevier (Pranckutė, 2021)

The database search query for this research is structured as follows:

("ERP systems" OR "Enterprise Resource Planning")
AND
(challenges OR obstacles OR barriers)
AND
(company OR enterprise OR business)
AND
(acceptance OR adoption)
AND
(implementation)

The inclusion criteria formulated for this paper are:

IC1: The paper has to be published as a conference paper or journal article.

IC2: The paper has to be written in English.

IC3: The paper must have been published after 2013.

IC4: The paper has to focus on ERP systems and the challenges of their implementation.

IC5: The paper has to be an open access paper.

The exclusion criteria formulated for this paper are:

EC1: Papers that focus solely on ERP systems, without addressing ERP implementation and its challenges, will not be considered for the research.

Conducting and reporting the review

The second phase of this literature review focuses on primary studies met the defined inclusion and exclusion criteria, as shown below in Table 1. The search process is also outlined in the table, emphasizing the systematic approach taken to select relevant studies for review.

Table 1. Flow of the exclusion and inclusion process

Database	Results found	Language and type	Year	Duplicated content	Unavailable	Initial selection	Second selection	Final selection
Scopus	150	39	41	0	13	57	40	29

In the first phase of the SLR, the inclusion and exclusion criteria were defined, along with the database search query. After using the search query in Scopus, 150 results were obtained. The next step involved filtering these papers based on the inclusion and exclusion criteria, removing duplicates, non-English papers, inaccessible content, and papers published before 2013. This process excluded 93 papers.

After further screening by title and abstract, 17 more papers were eliminated, leaving 40 papers. A detailed review of these papers led to removing 11 additional papers unrelated to the topic, resulting in a final selection of 29 relevant studies.

Data Extraction and Summarisation

Through the data extraction process, the studies selected in the previous phases of SLR were further analyzed, and the results are presented in this subsection. The presentation of results consists of figures that visually represent the selected papers, aligned with the established criteria for data extraction.

The primary studies are distributed across continents and countries, with contributions from Asia representing 27.59%, Europe at 20.69%, Africa at 13.79%, North America at 6.90%, and Australia at 3.45%. Figure 1 presents a total of 21 countries from these continents. India leads with 4 studies (Bhadra et al., 2019; Chatterjee, 2015; Mukti and Rawani, 2016; V and Ranjini S, 2018), followed by Saudi Arabia with 3 studies (Althonayan and Althonayan, 2017; Bamufleh et al., 2021; Salih et al., 2022), then the United Kingdom (Alaskari et al., 2021; Lewandowski et al., 2013), Australia (Seethamraju, 2015; Venkatraman and Fahd, 2016), and China (Shao et al., 2016; Xu et al., 2018) with 2 studies each, while the remaining 16 countries contributed one study each, referenced respectively according to the Figure 1 (Achargui and Zaouia, 2016; Ali et al., 2020; Falagara Sigala et al., 2020; Fernandez et al., 2018; Gabryelczyk, 2020; Garefalakis et al., 2016; Govindaraju et al., 2015; Kaluarachchi et al., 2019; Kulikov et al., 2020; Mamoghli and Cassivi, 2019; Meissonier et al., 2013; Soliman and Noorliza, 2020; Soobrayen et al., 2019; Van Vuuren and Seymour, 2013; Verdouw et al., 2015; Zadeh et al., 2018).

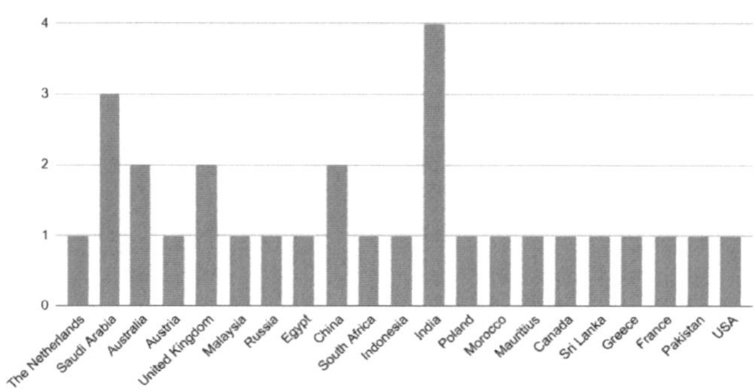

Figure 1. Distribution of primary studies by continent and country

Figure 2 presents the primary studies examined in the context of the core topic. The key questions addressed were the type of research (whether the study is empirical or theoretical), whether it proposes a framework or model for ERP system implementation, and whether it combines multiple approaches, such as a mix of theoretical and empirical research, alongside proposing a framework or model.

The results show that 44.83% or 13 of the studies are empirical (Ali et al., 2020; Althonayan and Althonayan, 2017; Chatterjee, 2015; Falagara Sigala et al., 2020; Fernandez et al., 2018; Govindaraju et al., 2015; Kaluarachchi et al., 2019; Lewandowski et al., 2013; Mamoghli and Cassivi, 2019; Mukti and Rawani, 2016; Salih et al., 2022; Van Vuuren and Seymour, 2013; Xu et al., 2018), relying on surveys or case studies. A total of 27.8% or 8 studies are predominantly empirical, supported by theoretical frameworks (Achargui and Zaouia, 2016; Bhadra et al., 2019; Gabryelczyk, 2020; Kulikov et al., 2020; Meissonier et al., 2013; Soobrayen et al., 2019; V and Ranjini S, 2018; Zadeh et al., 2018). Studies at the highest level of detail, combining theoretical and empirical research while proposing a framework or model, rank third, with 17.24%, or 5 studies (Bamufleh et al., 2021; Seethamraju, 2015; Shao et al., 2016; Soliman and Noorliza, 2020; Verdouw et al., 2015). Empirical studies that propose a framework or model represent 6.90%, or 2 studies (Alaskari et al., 2021; Venkatraman and Fahd, 2016) while purely theoretical studies represent only 3.45% of the total (Garefalakis et al., 2016).

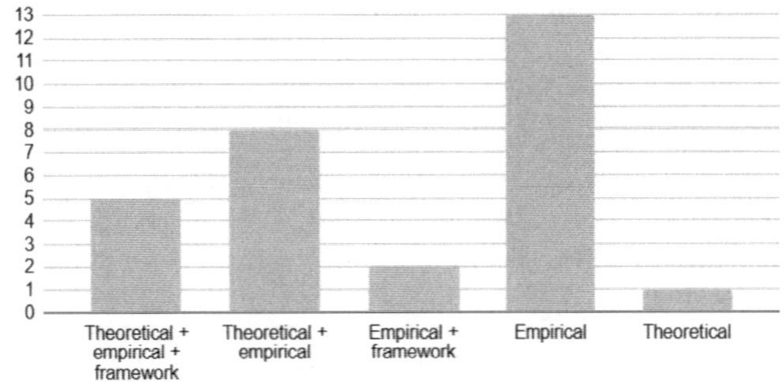

Figure 2. Distribution of primary studies by the type of research

5. RESULTS AND DISCUSSION

The results collected and extracted in the previous subsection will be analyzed and further discussed in the following chapter.

As the answer to RQ1, the challenges faced by companies, higher education institutions, and public enterprises when implementing ERP systems are grouped into seven categories: technical, organizational, financial, HR, adaptation challenges, measuring success - lack of clear criteria for evaluating ERP effectiveness, and other challenges like legal issues and problems with vendors. Most studies focus on small and medium-sized enterprises, highlighting technical, organizational, and financial challenges as critical obstacles to ERP implementation. Key issues include system complexity, requiring customization through detailed process analysis and consulting, and employee resistance, mitigated by early involvement and training.

Financial challenges, especially high initial costs, can be addressed with phased implementation and budgeting. Cloud ERP systems are cost-effective upfront but may incur higher long-term costs, while on-premise systems have significant initial expenses, making cloud ERP more suitable for smaller businesses (Alhayek and Abu Odeh, 2020).

Integration issues can be minimized through pilot projects and testing before full deployment.

The second research question addresses user resistance to ERP adoption, which is often linked to implementation challenges.

User acceptance is crucial for successful ERP implementation, yet common challenges that are mentioned in both empirical and theoretical studies include resistance to change, insufficient training, and poor communication about the system's benefits. Users often struggle to adapt to new workflows and mistrust the system's suitability. Predefined functionalities that fail to meet specific needs, cultural misalignment, and inadequate vendor support further hinder acceptance. Addressing user acceptance issues requires comprehensive training, active user involvement, effective change management, and strong management support to ensure smooth adoption and system effectiveness. Also, maintaining communication with ERP providers and ensuring available technical support is crucial to reducing frustration and promoting adoption.

The results are also obtained for RQ3, what are the key factors that influence successful ERP adoption and implementation. As studies suggest, successful ERP implementation depends on strong management support, effective planning, quality user training, and clear team communication. Flexible, scalable systems that integrate with existing processes and offer ongoing support enhance adoption.

Successful ERP implementation relies on top management support, clear goals, and effective project management to reduce risks. Comprehensive training, system customization, and efficient communication ensure user adoption and seamless integration. Data quality, organizational readiness, and vendor support are critical for success, while effective change management and smooth transitions between phases enhance outcomes and user satisfaction.

The largest number of papers on ERP systems implementation was published in 2016, which may be attributed to technological innovations such as the transition to cloud-based solutions, improvements in user interfaces, and integration with mobile technologies. These advancements may have spurred greater interest among researchers in analyzing these new trends and their impact on business operations. A time lag in the scientific publishing process could explain the lack of relevant papers from 2023 and 2024. Additionally, it may reflect shifts in research priorities or a focus on different topics considered more relevant at that time.

The second figure examined the geographical distribution of studies on ERP system implementation. The research indicates that the largest amount of published papers originates from developing countries, with the highest number from India. India has recently emerged as one of the fastest-growing economies, with numerous enterprises undergoing digital transformation. This is reflected in the significant number of studies from India. With growing competition and the need for efficiency, Indian companies are focused on optimizing their business processes, facilitated by ERP systems, further driving interest in research in this area.

Thirteen studies are classified as only empirical. ERP systems rely heavily on real-world practices, organizational contexts, and challenges, making empirical research, such as case studies and surveys, highly valued for providing practical insights and solutions. Theoretical research is less common as it lacks direct practical implications. However, many studies combine theoretical frameworks with empirical evidence to validate models and proposed solutions. This combination strengthens the relevance and applicability of research findings, and these studies are more valuable, as they provide information from empirical and theoretical aspects.

As business needs and technologies evolve, there is a constant demand for new models and frameworks for ERP implementation. Studies integrating empirical research with framework development offer innovative solutions to improve implementation processes.

6. CONCLUSION

The implementation of ERP systems significantly transforms business operations, offering numerous advantages, but also a range of challenges. Key obstacles include technical, organizational, financial, and human resource-related issues, as well as resistance to change. Successful ERP adoption requires strong management support, effective communication, comprehensive training, and careful planning.

However, some potential limitations should be considered. Further research could include expanding the database scope, to enhance the comprehensiveness and balance of the findings. Also, in further study, the user acceptance of ERP implementation and key factors that influence successful ERP adoption could be more structured by country or type of research.

The limited number of recent studies highlights the need for further research on this topic. This study can serve as a foundation for future research that will update and expand existing insights. Added references address fundamental challenges in ERP system implementation that remain relevant in contemporary practice.

Addressing these barriers through strategic planning, and phased implementation can ensure smoother integration, enhanced user acceptance, and improved organizational efficiency.

ACKNOWLEDGEMENT

This research has been supported by the Ministry of Science, Technological Development and Innovation (Contract No. 451-03-65/2024-03/200156) and the Faculty of Technical Sciences, University of Novi Sad through the project "Scientific and Artistic Research Work of Researchers in Teaching and Associate Positions at the Faculty of Technical Sciences, University of Novi Sad" (No. 01-3394/1).

REFERENCES

Achargui, A., Zaouia, A., (2016). Hosted, Cloud and SaaS, Off-premises ERP Systems Adoption by Moroccan SMEs.

Addo-Tenkorang, R., Helo, P., (2011). Enterprise Resource Planning (ERP): A Review Literature Report, Proceedings of the World Congress on Engineering and Computer Science (WCECS 2011). https://doi.org/10.13140/2.1.3254.7844

Alaskari, O., Pinedo-Cuenca, R., Ahmad, M.M., (2021). Framework for implementation of Enterprise Resource Planning (ERP) Systems in Small and Medium Enterprises (SMEs): A Case Study. Procedia Manuf. 55, 424–430. https://doi.org/10.1016/j.promfg.2021.10.058

Alhayek, W., Abu Odeh, R., (2020). Cloud ERP VS On-Premise ERP12, 10 .

Ali, I., Van Groenendaal, W.J.H., Weigand, H., (2020). Enterprise Resource Planning Systems Implementation and Firm Performance: An Empirical Study. J. Inf. Syst. Eng. Manag. 5. https://doi.org/10.29333/jisem/7822

Althonayan, M., Althonayan, A., (2017). E-government system evaluation: The case of users' performance using ERP systems in higher education. Transform. Gov. People Process Policy 11, 306–342. https://doi.org/10.1108/TG-11-2015-0045

Bamufleh, D., Almalki, M.A., Almohammadi, R., Alharbi, E., (2021). User Acceptance of Enterprise Resource Planning (ERP) Systems in Higher Education Institutions: A Conceptual Model. Int. J. Enterp. Inf. Syst. 17, 144–163. https://doi.org/10.4018/IJEIS.20210101.oa1

Beric, D., Havzi, S., Lolic, T., Simeunovic, N., Stefanovic, D., (2020). Development of the MES software and Integration with an existing ERP Software in Industrial Enterprise, in: 2020 19th International Symposium INFOTEH-JAHORINA (INFOTEH). Presented at the 2020 19th International Symposium INFOTEH-JAHORINA (INFOTEH), IEEE, East Sarajevo, Bosnia and Herzegovina, pp. 1–6. https://doi.org/10.1109/INFOTEH48170.2020.9066345

Beric, D., sekulić, D., Vučković, T., Stefanović, D., (2018). Evolution of ERP Systems in SMEs – Past Research, Present Findings and Future Directions.

Bhadra, S., Sanyal, M.K., Biswas, B., (2019). Cloud ERP Adoption Pitfalls and Challenges – A Fishikawa Analysis in the Context of the Global Enterprises, in: Mandal, J.K., Mukhopadhyay, S., Dutta, P., Dasgupta, K. (Eds.), Computational Intelligence, Communications, and Business Analytics, Communications in Computer and Information Science. Springer Singapore, Singapore, pp. 331–342. https://doi.org/10.1007/978-981-13-8581-0_27

Chatterjee, S., (2015). ERP failure in developing countries: A case study in India, in: 2015 Annual IEEE India Conference (INDICON). Presented at the 2015 Annual IEEE India Conference (INDICON), IEEE, New Delhi, India, pp. 1–6. https://doi.org/10.1109/INDICON.2015.7443222

Dakic, D., Stefanovic, D., Lolic, T., Narandzic, D., Simeunovic, N., (2020). Event Log Extraction for the Purpose of Process Mining: A Systematic Literature Review, in: Prostean, G., Lavios Villahoz, J.J., Brancu, L., Bakacsi, G. (Eds.), Innovation in Sustainable Management and Entrepreneurship. Springer International Publishing, Cham, pp. 299–312. https://doi.org/10.1007/978-3-030-44711-3_22

Falagara Sigala, I., Kettinger, W.J., Wakolbinger, T., (2020). Digitizing the field: designing ERP systems for Triple-A humanitarian supply chains. J. Humanit. Logist. Supply Chain Manag. 10, 231–260. https://doi.org/10.1108/JHLSCM-08-2019-0049

Fernandez, D., Zaino, Z., Ahmad, H., (2018). An Investigation of Challenges in Enterprise Resource Planning (ERP) Implementation: The Case of Public Sector in Malaysia 7.

Gabryelczyk, R., (2020). Is BPM truly a critical success factor for ERP adoption? An examination within the public sector. Procedia Comput. Sci. 176, 3389–3398. https://doi.org/10.1016/j.procs.2020.09.058

Garefalakis, A., Mantalis, G., Vourgourakis, E., Spinthiropoulos, K., Lemonakis, Ch., (2016). Healthcare Firms and the ERP Systems. J. Eng. Sci. Technol. Rev. 9, 139–144. https://doi.org/10.25103/jestr.091.021

Govindaraju, R., Salajar, R.T., Chandra, D.R., Sudirman, I., (2015). Acceptance and usage of ERP systems: The role of institutional factors in ERP post-implementation, in: 2015 IEEE International Conference on Industrial Engineering and Engineering Management (IEEM). Presented at the 2015 IEEE International Conference on Industrial Engineering and Engineering Management (IEEM), IEEE, Singapore, Singapore, pp. 1292–1296. https://doi.org/10.1109/IEEM.2015.7385856

Jovičić, B., Vlajić, S., (2007). EVOLUCIJA ERP SISTEMA. ИнфоМ - Часопис За Информационе Технологије И Мултимедијалне Системе 2007.

Kaluarachchi, T.R., Weerabahu, W.M.S.K., Nanayakkara, L.D.J.F., (2019). Factors influencing Enterprise Information Systems adoption of Small and Medium Enterprises (SMEs): A case study on Sri Lankan manufacturing sector, in: 2019 International Research Conference on Smart Computing and Systems Engineering (SCSE). Presented at the 2019 International Research Conference on Smart Computing and Systems Engineering (SCSE), IEEE, Colombo, Sri Lanka, pp. 220–227. https://doi.org/10.23919/SCSE.2019.8842777

Kitchenham, B., Charters, S., (2007). Guidelines for performing Systematic Literature Reviews in Software Engineering 2.

Klaus, H., Rosemann, M., Gable, G.G., (2000). What is ERP? Inf. Syst. Front. 2, 141–162. https://doi.org/10.1023/A:1026543906354

Krneta, D., Marjanović, Z., (2011). Possibility Integration of Methodological Approaches Information Systems Development And Implementation ERP Solutions. Presented at the INFOTEH-JAHORINA Vol. 10, Ref. E-I-7, pp. 423-427, March 2011.

Kulikov, I., Semin, A., Skvortsov, E., Ziablitckaia, N., Skvortsova, E., (2020). Challenges of enterprise resource planning (ERP) implementation in agriculture. Entrep. Sustain. Issues 7, 1847–1857. https://doi.org/10.9770/jesi.2020.7.3(27)

Lewandowski, J., Salako, A.O., Garcia-Perez, A., (2013). SaaS Enterprise Resource Planning Systems: Challenges of Their Adoption in SMEs, in: 2013 IEEE 10th International Conference on E-Business Engineering. Presented at the 2013 IEEE 10th International Conference on e-Business Engineering (ICEBE), IEEE, Coventry, United Kingdom, pp. 56–61. https://doi.org/10.1109/ICEBE.2013.9

Mahraz, M.-I., (2018). Implementation and Management of ERP Systems: A Literature Review.

Mamoghli, S., Cassivi, L., (2019). Agile ERP Implementation: The Case of a SME:, in: Proceedings of the 21st International Conference on Enterprise Information Systems. Presented at the 21st International Conference on Enterprise Information Systems, SCITEPRESS - Science and Technology Publications, Heraklion, Crete, Greece, pp. 188–196. https://doi.org/10.5220/0007700501880196

Martins, E.J., Belfo, F.P., (2023). Major concerns about Enterprise Resource Planning (ERP) systems: A systematic review of a decade of research (2011-2021). Procedia Comput. Sci. 219, 378–387. https://doi.org/10.1016/j.procs.2023.01.303

Meissonier, R., Lapointe, L., HouzÃ, E., (2013). “Cultural Intelligence” as a Concept to Apprehend Resistance to ERP Implementation.

Mukti, S.K., Rawani, A.M., (2016). ERP System Implementation Issues and Challenges in Developing Nations 11.

Pabedinskaitė, A.O., (2010). Factors of successful implementation of ERP systems.

Pranckutė, R., (2021). Web of Science (WoS) and Scopus: The Titans of Bibliographic Information in Today’s Academic World. Publications 9, 12. https://doi.org/10.3390/publications9010012

Rejman Petrović, D., (2009). ERP SYSTEMS AS SUPPORT IN BUSINESS QUALITY IMPROVEMENT.

Salih, S., Abdelsalam, S., Hamdan, M., Ibrahim, A.O., Abulfaraj, A.W., Binzagr, F., Husain, O., Abdallah, A.E., (2022). The CSFs from the Perspective of Users in Achieving ERP System Implementation and Post-Implementation Success: A Case of Saudi Arabian Food Industry. Sustainability 14, 15942. https://doi.org/10.3390/su142315942

Seethamraju, R., (2015). Adoption of Software as a Service (SaaS) Enterprise Resource Planning (ERP) Systems in Small and Medium Sized Enterprises (SMEs). Inf. Syst. Front. 17, 475–492. https://doi.org/10.1007/s10796-014-9506-5

Setyawan, A., Hermita, E.S., Putri, M.E., Putra, P.K., Shihab, M.R., (2020). Challenges and Supporting Factors in Adopting ERP in Higher Education: Insights From UI, in: 2020 6th International Conference on Computing Engineering and Design (ICCED). Presented at the 2020 6th International Conference on Computing Engineering and Design (ICCED), IEEE, Sukabumi, Indonesia, pp. 1–6. https://doi.org/10.1109/ICCED51276.2020.9415814

Shao, Z., Feng, Y., Hu, Q., (2016). Effectiveness of top management support in enterprise systems success: a contingency perspective of fit between leadership style and system life-cycle. Eur. J. Inf. Syst. 25, 131–153. https://doi.org/10.1057/ejis.2015.6

Singh, A., Nagpal, S., (2014). Implementation Of ERP In Cloud Computing 3.

Soliman, M.S., Noorliza, K., (2020). Explaining the Competitive Advantage of Enterprise Resource Planning Adoption: Insights Egyptian Higher Education Institutions. J. Inf. Technol. Manag. 12. https://doi.org/10.22059/jitm.2020.292788.2424

Soobrayen, S., Khan Jaffur, M.Z.A., Cadersaib, B.Z., (2019). An ERP Adoption Evaluation Framework, in: Satapathy, S.C., Bhateja, V., Somanah, R., Yang, X.-S., Senkerik, R. (Eds.), Information Systems Design and Intelligent Applications, Advances in Intelligent Systems and Computing. Springer Singapore, Singapore, pp. 357–365. https://doi.org/10.1007/978-981-13-3338-5_33

Sri Ranjini. S, S.Ranjini.S., TJPRC, (2017). An Examination of the Essential Aspects in Execution of Enterprise Resource Planning in Manufacturing and Production Industries. Int. J. Mech. Prod. Eng. Res. Dev. 7, 395–402. https://doi.org/10.24247/ijmperddec201744

Stankić, R., (2014). Key Success Factors for Implementation of Business Information System.

V, K., Ranjini S, S., (2018). Investigation and Study of Vital Factors in Selection, Implementation and Satisfaction of ERP in Small and Medium Scale Industries. Int. J. Electr. Comput. Eng. IJECE 8, 1150. https://doi.org/10.11591/ijece.v8i2.pp1150-1155

Van Vuuren, I.J., Seymour, L.F., (2013). Towards a model for user adoption of enterprise systems in SMEs, in: Proceedings of the First International Conference on Enterprise Systems: ES 2013. Presented at the 2013 Enterprise Systems Conference (ES), IEEE, Cape Town, South Africa, pp. 1–9. https://doi.org/10.1109/ES.2013.6690079

Venkatraman, S., Fahd, K., (2016). Challenges and Success Factors of ERP Systems in Australian SMEs. Systems 4, 20. https://doi.org/10.3390/systems4020020

Verdouw, C.N., Robbemond, R.M., Wolfert, J., (2015). ERP in agriculture: Lessons learned from the Dutch horticulture. Comput. Electron. Agric. 114, 125–133. https://doi.org/10.1016/j.compag.2015.04.002

Xu, Z., Brown, D., Stevenson, M., (2018). Enterprise Systems Adoption and Implementation in Chinese SMEs: Exploring relationships between user firms and technology providers through ANT.

Zadeh, A.H., Akinyemi, B.A., Jeyaraj, A., Zolbanin, H.M., (2018). Cloud ERP Systems for Small-and-Medium Enterprises: A Case Study in the Food Industry. J. Cases Inf. Technol. 20, 53–70. https://doi.org/10.4018/JCIT.2018100104

THE ROLE OF SOCIAL MEDIA INFLUENCERS IN ENHANCING E-BUSINESS: A CULTURAL PERSPECTIVE

Ghadeer R. Alsaeed
Department of MIS, Business School, King Faisal University, Al-Ahsa, Saudi Arabia

ABSTRACT

Social media influencer (SMI) marketing has become one of the most prominent strategies in digital marketing, particularly in the Middle East and North Africa MENA region where social media usage is growing rapidly. This study investigates the cultural dynamics that influence the selection of influencers in the MENA context. The findings highlight the significance of cultural authenticity in influencer selection with particular emphasis on factors such as cultural representation, regional diversity, linguistic identity, and social reputation. These elements highlight the necessity of a localised approach to ensure that influencers effectively resonate with local values and engage target audiences. In the MENA region, where social credibility and public image are critical, influencers who align with societal values are more likely to succeed in fostering positive consumer engagement and brand responses. Additionally, reputation management plays a crucial role in establishing trust and cultivating long-term relationships with consumers in this context. The study provides valuable insights for brands seeking to design influencer marketing strategies that are tailored to the unique cultural of the MENA market.

KEYWORDS

E-Business, Social Media Marketing, Influencer Marketing, MENA Region, Cultural Dynamics

1. INTRODUCTION

Social media influencers (SMIs) marketing has become one of the most dynamic and rapidly growing advertising strategies in recent years, gaining widespread adoption across various sectors. Unlike traditional brand-generated content, influencer marketing relies on user-generated content that naturally aligns with the style and format of social media platforms, enhancing its appeal and engagement (De Jans et al., 2020; Munnukka et al., 2019). SMIs are perceived as more relatable and credible, often leading consumers to find influencer-generated content more authentic, engaging, and persuasive compared to traditional advertisements (De Jans et al., 2020; Ki & Kim, 2019; Kim & Kim, 2021). As a result, Influencer Marketing (IM) has demonstrated positive impacts on E-business by enhancing brand recall, increasing brand engagement, and fostering stronger emotional connections with consumers (Eisend et al., 2020; Lee & Watkins, 2016; Munnukka et al., 2019). However, the impact of influencer marketing is not entirely positive. While many consumers respond positively to influencer endorsements, there are also potential negative consequences. For example, research has shown that sponsored content can provoke resistance and brand negative evaluations when consumers perceive the content as commercial or misleading (Eisend et al., 2020; Liu & Zhao, 2024).

Furthermore, concerns about transparency in sponsorship disclosure have led to regulatory examination, with efforts aimed at improving consumer protection (Federal Trade Commission, 2021). Blending of entertainment and advertising in influencer marketing can blur boundaries, making it difficult for consumers to recognise sponsored content which can negatively affect brand perceptions (Eisend et al., 2020; Liu & Zhao, 2024).

Despite these challenges, influencer marketing remains a powerful tool for E-business, particularly in the MENA region, where social media usage is growing rapidly. Users in the UAE and Saudi Arabia, for example, have significantly increased their engagement with platforms like Instagram (VeraContent, 2024), and the influencer marketing market in MENA is expected to grow by 8.44% from 2025 to 2029 (Statista, 2025).

Prior research has explored the impact of culture on consumer responses to advertising and shows significant cultural differences in reactions to sponsored content (Zimand-Sheiner et al., 2020). However, the role of culture in influencer marketing remains underexplored. Zimand-Sheiner et al., (2020) call for further investigation into cultural influences on consumer responses to advertising. In light of the exponential growth of influencer marketing in the MENA region, this research seeks to answer the following question: *What are the most important criteria for selecting social media influencers in the MENA context?*

2. LITERATURE REVIEW

2.1 Influencer Marketing Effectiveness

Given the widespread popularity of social media influencers, numerous empirical studies have been conducted to examine their effectiveness and identify the factors that enhance or diminish their credibility and their content (See Table1). These studies offer valuable insights into how businesses can optimise the persuasion process. For instance, Shamim and Azam, (2025) found that vicarious expressions and informational value in influencers' content significantly influence consumer trust, which mediates the relationship between content characteristics and the urge to purchase impulsively. Influencer-generated content also has been shown to lead to higher brand liking compared to brand-generated content (De Jans et al., 2020), as well as to prompt positive brand perceptions and purchase intentions (Lee & Watkins, 2016). Kim and Kim (2021) further found that a strong fit between an influencer and the endorsed product enhances the impact of the promotion, effectively positioning the marketing message as a personal recommendation. Similarly, Ki and Kim (2019) demonstrated that influencers' attributes such as attractiveness, prestige, expertise, and their ability to provide informative and interactive content, shape consumers' attitudinal responses to influencer posts. These responses influence consumers' desire to mimic influencers which ultimately affects their intention to engage in word-of-mouth behaviour and increase purchase intentions. While these studies predominantly focus on the role of influencers in shaping consumer responses and brand evaluations, very few studies have examined the role of culture in the effectiveness of social media influencers. This calls for an in-depth investigation to explore the cultural aspects that influences the credibility and effectiveness of social media influencers.

2.2 Source Credibility Theory

Source Credibility Theory (SCT) explains how the persuasiveness of a message is influenced by the perceived credibility of its source (Hovland, Janis & Kelley, 1953). Source credibility has emerged as one of the most extensively studied constructs in user-generated content research (Ayeh, 2015; Alsaeed et al., 2023), including influencer marketing research (Banerjee et al., 2017; De Jans et al., 2020) and has been demonstrated to significantly impact consumer responses and brand evaluations (Kim & Kim, 2014). Based on SCT, trustworthiness and expertise are fundamental construct of credibility (Hovland, Janis & Kelley, 1953). *Expertise* is defined as an individual's perception of a source's ability to provide accurate and valid information, while *trustworthiness* reflects the perception of the source as dependable, sincere, honest, and reliable (Hovland, Janis & Kelley, 1953). Based on the current literature, trustworthiness and expertise dimensions of source credibility are shown to have differential importance in affecting attitude and behavioural intention. For instance, existing research on source credibility presents conflicting perspectives regarding its influence on consumer behaviour. Ayeh (2015) argues that source credibility does not exert a direct effect on consumer behaviour and that source expertise is neither significant nor relevant in the context of user-generated content. Conversely, other studies emphasize the pivotal role of source credibility in shaping consumer decisions and brand assessments. For instance, Watts and Zhang (2008) highlight its significant impact and Banerjee et al., (2017) assert that reviewer trustworthiness positively moderates the relationship between review-based online reputation and business patronage. Additionally, Kim and Kim (2014) found that perceived source credibility enhances consumer attitudes, increases visit intention, and fosters engagement in environmentally friendly behaviours. Although prior studies have examined the influence of perceived credibility on consumer decision-making and brand evaluations, they have not sufficiently addressed the role of cultural factors in shaping perceptions of social media influencers as credible sources of information. This study bridges this gap by investigating how culture affects influencers' credibility, contributing to a more comprehensive understanding of credibility assessment in social media marketing.

Table 1 Review of Literature on Influencer Marketing

Study	Method	Theory	Main Finding(s)
Shamim and Azam, (2025)	Survey	The persuasion theory and social capital theory	Vicarious expressions and informational value are identified as key features of influencers' content that significantly influence consumer trust in influencers' posts. Trust in influencers' posts mediates the relationship between content characteristics and the urge to purchase impulsively. Contrary to expectations, persuasion knowledge does not moderate the relationship between content characteristics and trust or urge to buy impulsively.
Kim and Kim, (2021)	Online self-administered, cross-sectional survey	The social exchange theory	Perceived trustworthiness mediated the effects of expertise, authenticity, and homophily on loyalty, product attitude, and purchase intention.
De Jans et al., (2020)	Experiment	The source credibility theory	Influencer posts lead to higher brand liking. Influencers are more greatly admired, whereas brands are perceived as more credible.
Ki and Kim, (2019)	Survey	The influence framework	The attractiveness, prestige, expertise, and informative, interactive qualities of SMIs positively influence consumer attitudes, leading to favourable behavioural outcomes through the desire to mimic SMIs.
Munnukka et al., (2019)	Experiment	The para-social interaction	Audience participation in vlogs strengthens para-social relationships with the vlogger, and vlogs with higher participation increase brand endorsement acceptance through enhanced credibility perceptions.
Lee and Watkins, (2016)	Survey (Study 1) Experiment (Study 2 & 3)	The para-social interaction and social comparison theory	Influencer Marketing on YouTube significantly increases purchase intention and positive perceptions of luxury brands through perceived para-social attachment with the influencer.

3. METHODOLOGY

The researcher conducted 15 in-depth semi-structured interviews with marketing experts in the MENA region. Participants were not compensated for their involvement in the study. The sample size was determined based on the principle of saturation, with the aim of capturing variability among respondents (Guest, Namey, & Chen, 2020). This sample size is considered sufficient as it provides a robust understanding of the phenomenon under investigation (Sandelowski, 1995). Given the exploratory nature of this research, a purposive, theoretical, and snowball sampling approach was employed to recruit participants (Morse, 2020). All interviews were conducted virtually and recorded in audio format for subsequent analysis. Table 2 shows the participants' demographic information.

Table 2. Participants' Demographic Information

Pseudonyms	Country	Position	Experiences in Years
Ali	Saudi Arabia	Digital marketing manager	5
Basel	Saudi Arabia	Marketing campaigns manager	11
Sara	Saudi Arabia	International digital marketing manager	3
Dana	Kuwait	Marketing consultant	5
Emad	Saudi Arabia	Marketing consultant	5
Gazi	Saudi Arabia	Digital marketing manager	4
Hamad	Saudi Arabia	Marketing consultant	3
Esam	Saudi Arabia	Marketing campaigns manager	8
Jassim	Algeria	Marketing manager	10
Fares	Sudan	Marketing specialist	15
Lara	Saudi Arabia	Marketing consultant	1
Mohammed	Saudi Arabia	Marketing campaigns manager	2
Nasser	Saudi Arabia	Marketing manager	5
Omar	Jordan	Marketing consultant	7
Basma	Egypt	Digital marketing manager	6

4. DATA ANALYSIS

In terms of data analysis, the researcher adopted a recursive and systematic process, iteratively moving between co-developed constructs, existing literature, and the collected data (Braun & Clarke, 2006). A thematic analysis approach was employed to code, identify, and organise emergent themes, offering in-depth explanations of the key findings regarding how culture influences the credibility of influencers (Braun & Clarke, 2006). The following outlines the phases of thematic analysis conducted:

1. *Familiarisation with the Data:* The researcher reviewed all interview transcripts thoroughly, taking detailed notes to ensure immersion in the data. Each interview was read individually as it was collected, followed by a comprehensive reading across all interviews upon completion of data collection. This process was guided by an exploratory approach to ensure an in-depth understanding of the dataset.
2. *Generating Initial Codes:* The interview transcripts were coded line by line to extract meaningful insights. These codes were then systematically organised into a cohesive group to facilitate further analysis.
3. *Searching for Themes:* At this stage, similar codes were grouped together to construct preliminary themes. Abductive analysis was also considered to allow for the integration of theoretical insights with emerging patterns in the data.
4. *Reviewing Themes:* The data assigned to each theme were rigorously assessed for internal consistency and to ensure clear distinctions between themes. Interview transcripts were revisited to confirm that no relevant data had been overlooked and that the identified themes accurately reflected the dataset.
5. *Defining and Naming Themes:* Each theme was refined and clearly defined, with appropriate names assigned to reflect their meaning. This step ensured that the themes were both coherent and representative of the data.
6. *Producing the Report:* Representative quotations were selected to illustrate each theme, and careful consideration was given to the presentation of findings, including both verbal and visual data. The findings were then discussed in relation to existing theory and literature, providing a comprehensive interpretation of the results.

To ensure the quality of the research, the researcher followed the quality assessment criteria proposed by Lincoln and Guba (1985) and Wallendorf and Belk (1989). Specifically, (1) Credibility (internal validity) was ensured through prolonged engagement and peer debriefings, (2) Transferability (external validity) was achieved by providing a detailed and explicit description of the examined phenomenon and offering sufficient detail in the findings and discussion, and (3) Integrity was maintained by safeguarding the anonymity of informants and following ethical research standards.

5. FINDINGS

5.1 Cultural Representation as a Key Factor in Influencer Selection

One of the most striking findings from the interviews is the critical role that cultural representation plays in influencer selection within the MENA region. Influencers who actively promote their cultural heritage and identity resonate strongly with brands looking to emphasise local values, history, and national pride. For instance, Sara highlights the importance of an influencer's cultural representation when she states, *"[Influencer's name], when she promotes herself, I see how much she cares about culture, about history, and how she highlights her country's heritage."* This illustrates that in the context of national branding and tourism, the culture serves as a powerful tool for marketing campaigns. Influencers who engage with their audience on a cultural level can significantly enhance the effectiveness of campaigns, particularly those focused on promoting tourism or local products. Brands must tailor their influencer choices to reflect the values and heritage that resonate with local audiences. This approach not only strengthens brand recall but also fosters stronger emotional connections with consumers, which are critical in influencer marketing.

5.2 Regional and Local Differences in Influence

Another key finding relates to the significance of regional and local differences within the MENA region, particularly in Saudi Arabia. Ali's observation that, *"The Saudi market follows its own unique ways for purchasing decisions. If you look more closely, each region in Saudi Arabia has its own distinct characteristics,"* reveals the need for brands to adapt their influencer selection strategies to the cultural and consumer preferences of each region. This insight highlights that influencer effectiveness is not identical across the country. For example, Ali further explains *"...there are influencers who specifically impact Riyadh, and if you delve even deeper, you'll find some influencers are particularly influential in North Riyadh, while others are more impactful in the East."* Thus, brands must take into account these regional distinctions when selecting influencers. This finding supports Zimand-Sheiner et al.,'s (2020) argument that understanding cultural differences is essential when executing successful marketing campaigns. In the case of Saudi Arabia, brands must recognise the cultural diversity within the kingdom and carefully select influencers whose regional identity and appeal match the specific audience they intend to target. Tailoring influencer selection to regional cultural preferences can significantly enhance the relevance of the brand message, ensuring that it resonates with local consumers on a deeper level. This strategy reflects the need for a hyper-localised approach to influencer marketing to understand regional cultural preferences in influencing consumer behaviour.

5.3 The Role of Linguistic Identity and Credibility

Ali's insight into the importance of linguistic identity further reinforces how cultural factors such as accents and dialects affect an influencer's credibility. He notes, *"During a marketing campaign for dates at the Date Festival, the influencer's accent plays an important role in their credibility when promoting dates."* This observation highlights that in the MENA region, linguistic characteristics, including dialect and accent are crucial in shaping an influencer's trustworthiness. In MENA, the authenticity of an influencer's accent can be a deciding factor in their credibility, particularly when promoting region-specific products like dates as the MENA region is known for its diverse varieties of dates, including in Saudi Arabia, the UAE, Egypt, and Tunisia. The impact of linguistic identity on trust and credibility is consistent with previous research showing that consumers are more likely to engage with influencers who share similarity which fosters a sense of credibility (Yuan & Lou, 2020). In the MENA context, linguistic cues not only signal regional identity but also serve as an indication of authenticity, making it an essential consideration in influencer selection.

5.4 Social Reputation and Societal Values

A critical aspect of influencer selection in the MENA region is the influencer's reputation and alignment with societal values. As Lara emphasises, *"I advise staying away from influencers with a bad reputation, as they can harm the business and damage your product. It's better to seek an influencer who adds value to the brand and has a positive impact on society."* This perspective reflects the conservative nature of many MENA societies where influencers must align not only with brand values but also with broader societal expectations. The desire for influencers who positively contribute to society aligns with the ethical considerations outlined in the introduction where concerns about the transparency and authenticity of influencer content are critical.

Reputation management is especially crucial in MENA region where consumers are highly engaged with social media influencers. Hence, influencers' actions and public image can significantly influence public opinion and shape brand perception. Thus, brands in the MENA region must carefully assess an influencer's social reputation, ensuring that they align with cultural values and avoid influencers who might harm the brand's image due to their controversial behaviour. Influencers with a negative reputation can lead to negative consumer and brand responses. In the MENA region, the societal values hold significant importance and an influencer's reputation is a pivotal factor in shaping the effectiveness of marketing campaigns.

6. DISCUSSION

The findings from this study provide valuable insights into the cultural dynamics that affect influencer selection in the MENA region. Cultural representation, regional diversity, linguistic identity, and social reputation all play significant roles in determining an influencer's suitability for marketing campaigns. These factors must be carefully considered to ensure that influencers align with local values and resonate with target audiences. The importance of cultural authenticity and the need for a localised approach to influencer selection are particularly evident in the findings. As brands expand their influencer marketing efforts in the MENA region, they must adopt strategies that are tailored to the region's cultural and social diversity. Influencers who can authentically represent local identities, whether through language, regional affiliations, or cultural narratives, are likely to engage consumers more effectively and enhance brand recall and engagement.

Furthermore, the growing importance of reputation management highlights the need for brands to assess an influencer's societal impact. In the MENA region, where public image and social credibility are critical, influencers who align with societal values are more likely to build trust and foster long-term relationships with their followers.

7. IMPLICATIONS

From a theoretical perspective, this study advances the literature on influencer marketing by highlighting the critical role of cultural factors in influencer selection. It extends source credibility theory by demonstrating how cultural representation, linguistic identity, and social reputation shape the perceived credibility of influencers in the MENA region. Unlike prior applications of source credibility theory which primarily emphasise expertise, trustworthiness, and attractiveness factors, this study reveals that cultural alignment is a key determinant of an influencer's persuasiveness in culturally diverse markets. These findings contribute to a more nuanced understanding of how consumers in the MENA region assess influencer authenticity and credibility within a culturally embedded context.

From a practical perspective, this research offers actionable insights for businesses and marketers navigating the evolving influencer marketing landscape in the MENA region. As brands seek to engage local audiences, a culturally informed approach to influencer selection becomes imperative. Marketers should prioritise influencers who authentically represent local identities through language, regional affiliations, and cultural narratives to enhance consumer engagement and brand trust. Additionally, given the significance of social reputation in the region, brands must conduct thorough evaluations of an influencer's public image, values, and societal impact to ensure alignment with their target audience. Implementing these culturally oriented strategies will not only improve the effectiveness of influencer campaigns but also foster long-term brand loyalty in the region's highly connected digital marketplace.

8. LIMITATIONS AND FUTURE WORK

While this research offers valuable insights into the role of cultural factors in influencer selection within the MENA region, several limitations present opportunities for future studies. This study is context-specific to the MENA region, which has unique socio-cultural dynamics that may not be generalisable to other global markets. To address this, future studies could conduct cross-cultural comparative analyses to examine whether cultural influences on influencer selection differ across diverse digital marketing landscapes. Such comparative research would contribute to a more comprehensive understanding of influencer marketing strategies in varying cultural and geographical contexts. Additionally, this research primarily relies on qualitative insights, which provide depth but may limit the generalisability of the findings. Future research could employ mixed-method approaches, integrating survey-based or experimental studies to validate and quantify the impact of cultural factors on influencer credibility and audience engagement. Furthermore, given the dynamic nature of digital marketing and shifting consumer behaviours, longitudinal studies would be beneficial in tracking how cultural preferences evolve over time. As digital platforms continue to shape and redefine consumer-brand interactions, a longitudinal perspective could offer valuable insights into the changing role of cultural representation and social reputation in influencer marketing. While this study focuses primarily on cultural dynamics, there remains an opportunity to explore the ethical and religious dimensions of influencer marketing, which are particularly significant in the MENA region. Future research could examine how ethical considerations, religious values, and societal norms influence consumer trust and brand-influencer partnerships. Investigating these dimensions would provide a more holistic perspective on influencer marketing within culturally and religiously markets.

REFERENCES

Alsaeed, G. R., Keeling, K. A., Sarantopoulos, P., & Gadalla, E. (2023). Source, message and medium? The role of personal values in forming credibility perceptions of non-sponsored product review videos. *European Journal of Marketing*, 57(5), 1272-1297.

Ayeh, J. K. (2015). Travellers' acceptance of consumer-generated media: An integrated model of technology acceptance and source credibility theories. *Computers in Human Behavior*, *48*, 173–180.

Banerjee, S., Bhattacharyya, S. & Bose, I. (2017). Whose online reviews to trust? Understanding reviewer trustworthiness and its impact on business. *Decision Support Systems*, 96, 17–26.

Braun, V., & Clarke, V. (2006). Using thematic analysis in psychology. *Qualitative research in psychology*, 3(2), 77-101.

De Jans, S., Van de Sompel, D., De Veirman, M., & Hudders, L. (2020). # Sponsored! How the recognition of sponsoring on Instagram posts affects adolescents' brand evaluations through source evaluations. *Computers in Human Behavior*.

Eisend, M., Van Reijmersdal, E. A., Boerman, S. C., & Tarrahi, F. (2020). A meta-analysis of the effects of disclosing sponsored content. *Journal of Advertising, 49*(3), 344-366.

Federal Trade Commission. (2021). *How To Evaluate Online Reviews.* Retrieved Jan 12, 2024, from https://www.consumer.ftc.gov/articles/how-evaluate-online-reviews

Guest, G., Namey, E., & Chen, M. (2020). A simple method to assess and report thematic saturation in qualitative research. *PloS one*, 15(5), e0232076.

Hovland, C. I., Janis, I. L., & Kelley, H. H. (1953). *Communication and persuasion*. Yale University Press.

Ki, C. W., & Kim, Y. K. (2019). The effects of perceived online justice on relational bonds and engagement intention: Evidence from an online game community. *Computers in Human Behavior, 84*, 410–419.

Kim, D. Y., & Kim, H. Y. (2021). Trust me, trust me not: A nuanced view of influencer marketing on social media. *Journal of Business Research, 134*, 223-232.

Kim, S. B. & Kim, D. Y. (2014). The Effects of Message Framing and Source Credibility on Green Messages in Hotels. *Cornell Hospitality Quarterly*.

Lee, J. E., & Watkins, B. (2016). YouTube vloggers' influence on consumer luxury brand perceptions and intentions. *Journal of Business Research, 69*(12), 5753–5760.

Lincoln, Y. S. & Guba, E. G. (1985). *Naturalistic Inquiry*. Beverly Hills, CA: Sage.

Liu, X., & Zhao, H. (2024). A meta-analysis of the effects of sponsorship disclosure in influencer marketing. *Marketing Letters*, 35(1), 1–14.

Morse, J. (2020). The changing face of qualitative inquiry. *International Journal of Qualitative Methods, 19*.

Munnukka, J., Maity, D., Reinikainen, H., & Luoma-aho, V. (2019). "Thanks for watching." The effectiveness of YouTube vlog endorsements. *Computers in Human Behavior, 93*, 226-234.

Sandelowski M. One is the liveliest number: the case orientation of qualitative research. *Res Nurs Health*. 1996;19(6): 525–9.

Shamim, K. and Azam, M. (2025), "The power of the content of the influencers in inducing impulse buying: mediating role of trust", *Asia Pacific Journal of Marketing and Logistics*, Vol. ahead-of-print No. ahead-of-print.

Statista. (2025). *Influencer advertising market in MENA*. Retrieved from https://www.statista.com/statistics/1052290/mena-influencer-advertising-market-size/

VeraContent. (2024). *Social media usage trends in the MENA region*. Retrieved from https://www.veracontent.com

Wallendorf, M., & Belk, R. (1989). Assessing trustworthiness in naturalistic consumer research. In E. C. Hirschman (Ed.), *Interpretive consumer research* (pp. 69-84). *Association for Consumer Research.*

Watts, S. A. & Zhang, W. (2008). Capitalizing on content: Information adoption in two online communities. *Journal of the Association for Information Systems, 9(2), 3.*

Yuan, S., & Lou, C. (2020). How Social Media Influencers Foster Relationships with Followers: The Roles of Source Credibility and Fairness in Parasocial Relationship and Product Interest. *Journal of Interactive Advertising, 20*(2), 133–147.

Zimand-Sheiner, D., Ziegler, A., & Schmiedel, H. (2020). Cultural dimensions in influencer marketing: The role of cultural differences in sponsored content engagement. *Journal of Interactive Marketing, 52*, 1-15.

GREEN INFORMATION TECHNOLOGY: A KNOWLEDGE MANAGEMENT APPROACH TO ORGANIZATIONAL SUSTAINABILITY

Hanlie Smuts
University of Pretoria
Lynnwood Road, Hatfield, Pretoria, 0083, South Africa

ABSTRACT

In the ubiquitous computing environment within which organizations operate, they depend significantly on information technology (IT) to drive business value and economic success. However, organizational sustainability is more than just economics; it also includes environmental and social aspects that, in the context of IT, require organizational attention since the disposal of IT equipment, the way software solutions are developed, and the amount of data generated all impact organizational sustainability. The data centers required to process generated data are energy-intensive and contribute significantly to carbon emissions. This study aimed to consider key knowledge management (KM) strategies and tactics that support green IT initiatives to advance organizational sustainability. Five hundred and thirty-nine (539) responses collected through an online questionnaire were analyzed in two ways. First, three KM strategies, namely performance tracking and measurement, dark data management, and knowledge exchange, were identified through factor analysis. Second, the role of different stakeholders, namely KM practitioners, organizational learning practitioners, data analysts, and data scientists, was analyzed through an individual multiple-factor analysis, highlighting a significant difference between KM and learning practitioners on the one hand and data analysts and scientists on the other. The findings were visualized in a KM strategies and tactics work system to guide KM efforts in organizations seeking to reach their sustainability goals.

KEYWORDS

Green Information Technology, Knowledge Management, Organizational Stability, Dark Data Management

1. INTRODUCTION

The United Nations adopted 17 sustainable development goals (SDGs) in 2015 in the context of the three pillars of sustainability: environmentally sound, economically viable, and socially equitable (Depken and Zeman 2018, Carlsen and Bruggemann 2022). Furthermore, given the recognition that natural resources are limited, the environment cannot be controlled, and people and organizations must work within these constraints over the long term, organizations are under growing pressure to implement sustainability strategies and programs (Rosati and Faria 2019).

However, organizational sustainability objectives represent a paradoxical situation regarding information technology (IT) (Liang and Li 2023). On the one hand, the dependence of organizations on IT has contributed significantly to environmental degradation, as building and disposing of hardware, such as servers, monitors, cellular phones, laptops, and personal computers, present environmental challenges; moreover, the rising energy demands to run data centers contribute to increased carbon emission (Liang and Li 2023). On the other hand, advanced IT and information systems (IS) can play a key role in promoting environmental sustainability, while organizations derive business value from high-performance data processing (Zeng, Lee et al. 2020). Organizations can apply several tactics to address their sustainability concerns, such as customer analysis based on big data analytics (Kitchens, Dobolyi et al. 2018), knowledge management (Zyngier and Burstein 2012), electronic commerce (O'Reilly and Finnegan 2010), supply chain collaboration systems (Cui, Gao et al. 2022), and enterprise architecture (Liao and Wang 2021).

Therefore, due to the increasing attention on organizational sustainability and the requirement to balance economic, environmental, and social factors, this study investigates the question: "*What key knowledge management strategies support green information technology initiatives to advance organizational sustainability?*". By gaining insight into effective knowledge management strategies that enhance green IT practices, organizations can prioritize sustainable practices and ultimately improve their sustainability impact. Section 2 provides background to the research study, followed by the research methodology in Section 3. Section 4 contains the data analysis and findings, Section 5 the contribution, and Section 6 concludes the paper.

2. BACKGROUND

Despite advancements in IT and IS, along with innovations in business models, digitalization, and digital transformation (Bresciani, Ciampi et al. 2021, Adama and Okeke 2024), the rapid growth of data driving transformative changes has also created significant challenges for organizations striving to meet their sustainability objectives (Imamov and Semenikhina 2021, Vermesan and Friess 2022). Hence, organizations should prioritize and apply different organizational strategies and tactics to address and manage their sustainability objectives (Lau 2021).

2.1 Sustainability and Green Information Technology

Green Information technology refers to the process of minimizing the negative environmental effects of information and communication technologies (ICT) while maximizing the positive organizational impacts and engaging with people, processes, and technologies related to the environment (Jain 2011, Göçen and Kurubacak 2023). For organizational strategies related to the environment, the most often used definition is: "*Sustainable development is development that meets the needs of the present without compromising the ability of future generations to meet their own needs,*" as suggested by the Brundtland Commission (Brundtland 1987:41). Improving sustainability is an increasingly important environmental, social and commercial organizational imperative, and because IT is a material contributor to the overall environmental footprint of an organization, adopting green computing can lower the carbon emissions of IT significantly, thereby substantially helping an organization meet its emission reduction goals (Yadav, Samadhiya et al. 2023, Sharanya, Vijayalakshmi et al. 2024).

However, as the demand for digital storage and processing solutions leads to higher energy consumption, IT and its associated processes in an organization can increase the carbon footprint of the organization, which, in turn, results in higher carbon emissions (Masanet, Shehabi et al. 2020). The key to addressing this chain of events may lie in how organizations use and reuse knowledge and data in their daily activities and operations (Jackson and Hodgkinson 2023). IBM (2024) has estimated that more than 50% of an organization's data is considered dark data, referring to collected and stored yet unused data and information sources (IBM 2024). Therefore, the use and reuse of knowledge within knowledge management (KM) processes can improve dark data management, thus contributing to reduced carbon emissions (Ajis and Baharin 2019, Zhong, Jackson et al. 2024).

According to Jackson and Hodgkinson (2023), KM scholars should explore the relationship between responsible management and organizational knowledge reuse, thereby supporting the global effort to mitigate the impact of digital practices on carbon production. Therefore, organizations should opt for environmentally friendly practices to develop organizational knowledge-based capabilities in responding to complex workplace dynamics (Chopra, Saini et al. 2021).

2.2 Knowledge Management

KM refers to the people, processes, content, culture, and enabling technologies necessary to capture, manage, share, and find information as well as harvest all the insights and experience required for organizational functioning (Alavi and Leidner 2001, Sarayreh, Mardawi et al. 2012). KM has been applied as an essential resource for storing, finding, sharing, and using knowledge to realize and consolidate competitive advantages for organizations (Bolisani and Bratianu 2017). In this context, addressing sustainability incorporates multidisciplinary, heterogeneous knowledge and requires acquiring knowledge and skills (the learning organization), developing new behaviors, and cultivating sustainability-oriented norms and values (Sánchez and Mitchell 2017). Applying KM within the context of sustainability and social and environmental responsibility now holds equal priority to economic viability in organizations. This paradigm shift positions KM as a foundation for sustainable development practices (Klingenberg and Rothberg 2020, Van Zyl and Smuts 2021). Therefore, organizations should rely increasingly on their knowledge-generating resources (people and data) and treat KM as a means to enhance compliance with the guidelines of economic, environmental, and social sustainability (Van Reijsen, Helms et al. 2015, Chang, Sabatini-Marques et al. 2018). Furthermore, KM and its range of KM practices provide a way to drive insight from data by transforming data into information and knowledge (Jennex 2009). Organizations must determine the volume of data they need to process to generate useful information and knowledge. As data are converted into information and knowledge, carbon emissions may rise. Therefore, managing data—specifically, what is captured, stored, and processed—is a key consideration for organizations (Jennex 2020, Jackson and Hodgkinson 2023).

3. RESEARCH METHODOLOGY

The study utilized a survey research strategy with a questionnaire as the data collection instrument (Fetters, Curry et al. 2013). The questionnaire contained a demographic section, a content section using a 5-point Likert scale, and a general section with two open-ended questions to capture any additional comments from respondents. The questionnaire was captured on SurveyMonkey (https://www.surveymonkey.com/), and a URL to the questionnaire was shared via LinkedIn networks, such as KM practitioner, data analytics, and organizational learning groups. Six-hundred and six (606) respondents accessed the survey; however, 11 did not provide consent, 23 provided consent but did not begin the questionnaire, and 33 respondents did not complete the questionnaire, leaving 539 complete responses for analysis.

The data were analyzed in two ways: first, through statistical analysis in SPSS v29.0.0.0, including reliability tests applying Cronbach's alpha, one-way analysis of variance, and factor analysis. The purpose of the factor analysis was to identify the factor groupings that could be used to represent relationships among sets of the many interrelated variables (Purwono, Sulasmiyati et al. 2023, Field 2024). Second, a multiple-factor analysis was executed using R version 4.4.1 and two libraries: "FactoMineR" and "factoextra." Two variables were defined for the analysis. Dimension 1 consisted of Role 1, comprising a learning practitioner, KM practitioner, and data analyst/ scientist, and Role 2, comprising decision-making or decision-implementation. Dimension 2 consisted of green IT and KM factors derived from the literature review and incorporated into the questionnaire.

Tables 1 and 2 present the respondent profiles consisting of their operating roles and decision profiles. For the "Other" category, respondents indicated roles such as C-level roles and consulting roles.

Table 1. Operating roles of respondents
(Source: own analysis)

Operating role	Count	%
Data analyst or data scientist	107	19.9
Knowledge management practitioner	225	41.7
Organizational learning practitioner	107	19.9
Other	100	18.6
Total	539	100.0

Table 2. Decision profiles of respondents
(Source: own analysis)

Decision profile	Count	%
Decision implementation	158	29.3
Decision-making	345	64.0
Other	36	6.7
Total	539	100.0

Knowledge management practitioners represented 41.7% (225) of the respondents, followed by data analysts and organizational learning practitioners at 19.9% (107) respondents, respectively. Sixty-four percent (345) of respondents indicated decision-making accountability, while 29.3% (158) indicated decision-implementation accountability.

4. DATA ANALYSIS AND FINDINGS

The Cronbach's alpha reliability for the factors is 0.969, suggesting that the 11 green IT KM (GITKM) strategies have excellent internal reliability and are closely correlated (Izah, Sylva et al. 2023, Tibeica, Baciu et al. 2024). After the Varimax rotation presented in Table 3, Factor Grouping 1 (interpreted as *performance tracking and measurement*) accounts for 30.73% of the total variances between GITKM factors, Factor Grouping 2 (interpreted as *dark data management*) accounts for 25.40% of variances, and Factor Grouping 3 (interpreted as *knowledge exchange*) accounts for 21.37% of the total variances between GITKM factors. These three factor groupings account for 77.50% of the total variances among GITKM factors.

Table 3. Rotated component matrix of GITKM factors (Source: own analysis)

	Component		
Rotated Component Matrix[a]	1	2	3
We regularly conduct workshops and training sessions where employees share strategies to support our sustainability objectives.	0.777		
We have integrated digital decarbonization targets into our KM and operational policies.	0.763		
Employees are provided with guidelines on sustainable software development, including how to write energy-efficient code and minimize computational waste.	0.752		
Our KM system includes tools and protocols for analyzing energy consumption data across all IT systems, helping us identify areas for improvement in energy efficiency.	0.737		
Our organization has implemented a centralized database that tracks carbon emissions from all digital operations.	0.729		
Our organization is aware of the potential risks and challenges associated with managing dark data.		0.798	
We prioritize the secure and compliant handling of dark data to ensure it does not pose a threat to our organization.		0.752	
We have implemented effective strategies to identify and manage dark data within our data storage systems.		0.738	
Our organization effectively shares and exchanges tacit knowledge among employees to improve dark data management.			0.786
We effectively manage dark data at each level of the Knowledge Pyramid (Data to Information to Knowledge to Wisdom), ensuring a seamless flow from data to wisdom.			0.624
Our organization effectively transforms raw data into useful information within the context of dark data management.			0.615

Extraction Method: Principal Component Analysis.
Rotation Method: Varimax with Kaiser Normalization.
a. Rotation converged in six (6) iterations.

Factor Grouping 1, *performance tracking and measurement*, consists of five (5) GITKM factors, all reflecting high factor loadings (Williams, Onsman et al. 2010). The factors with the strongest association are: conducting employee workshops and training sessions, sharing strategies to support our sustainability objectives (0.777), integrating digital decarbonization targets into KM and operational policies (0.763), providing employee guidelines on sustainable software development (0.752), incorporating tools and protocols for analyzing energy consumption data across all IT systems (0.737), and implementing a carbon emissions tracking centralized database (0.729). A strong focus on measuring and tracking green IT initiatives could empower organizations to evaluate their environmental impact and ensure compliance with sustainability goals. By institutionalizing this practice as part of the organization's KM practice, organizations can identify areas for improvement, enhance operational efficiency, and foster a culture of environmental responsibility.

Factor Grouping 2, *dark data management*, comprises three (3) GITKM factors with strong associations and includes potential risks and challenges awareness associated with managing dark data (0.798), prioritizing secure and compliant handling of dark data (0.7520, and implementing effective dark data management strategies (0.738). By recognizing the potential risks and challenges associated with managing dark data, which might lead to compliance issues and security vulnerabilities, organizations can incorporate effective KM strategies to identify, categorize, and manage dark data within data storage systems, thus ensuring its secure and compliant handling towards creating business value.

Factor Grouping 3, *knowledge exchange*, encompasses three (3) GITKM factors with strong associations, i.e., tacit knowledge sharing for dark data management improvement (0.786), strategies to manage and transform dark data into information and knowledge (0.624 and 0.615, respectively), and effectively sharing and exchanging tacit knowledge among employees to enhance dark data management. By creating mechanisms to enable effective knowledge sharing among employees, the seamless transformation of data, information, and knowledge can support insight generation, data-driven decision-making, and, ultimately, implementing innovative practices to support organizational sustainability goals.

The second analysis executed was an individual multiple-factor analysis, creating a factor map (shown in Figure 1) to determine the different stakeholders' opinions. The "habillage" parameter in the "factoextra" library was used to color the individuals' observations. Dimension 1 explains 50.1% of the variance in the data, and Dimension 2 explains 14.6%, indicating that these two dimensions capture 64.7% of the total variance.

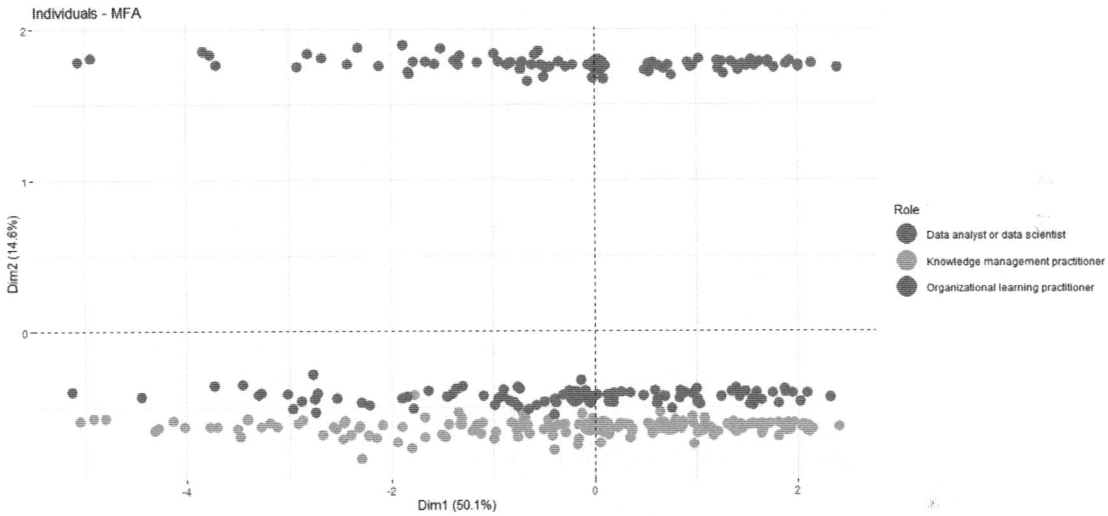

Figure 1. Individual multiple-factor analysis (MFA) (Source: own analysis)

The clusters—data analysts or data scientists (blue cluster), knowledge management practitioners (yellow cluster), and organizational learning practitioners (orange cluster)—indicate significant differences across the two dimensions, suggesting distinct characteristics for each group. The blue cluster is well-separated along Dimension 2, suggesting that data analysts or data scientists have unique attributes compared with other roles. The yellow and orange clusters are more densely clustered along Dimension 1, meaning knowledge management practitioners and organizational learning practitioners have more similarities in the characteristics associated with Dimension 1. The clear separation implies that data analysts or data scientists could have different skill sets, tools, or methodologies compared to the other two roles—as understood in practice in an organizational context and role allocation. The close clustering of knowledge management practitioners and organizational learning practitioners along Dimension 1 suggests that these roles share common ground in KM practices but have some distinct aspects, perhaps in methodologies or focus areas, as represented along Dimension 2.

5. KM STRATEGIES TOWARDS GREEN IT AND ORGANIZATIONAL SUSTAINABILITY

According to Alavi and Leidner (2001), at least four basic KM processes of creating, storing/retrieving, transferring, and applying knowledge must be considered in an organizational context. In addition, specifically related to dark data management and the outcome presented in Figure 1, the role of data science and deriving insight from unstructured and big data datasets must be an additional consideration.

To visualize and operationalize the findings, Figure 2 depicts the different organizational processes relevant to the three (3) role clusters (Figure 1) driven and guided by social, economic, and environmental organizational goals and objectives, which are also applied to measure and track performance. The workforce is supported in the organizational sustainability effort by awareness training and guidelines while executing the transformation of data to actionable insight and business value within a secure and compliant IT environment. Through continuous knowledge exchange, organizational agility, innovation, and decision-making are enhanced by allowing employees to access and build on shared insights, preventing redundancy and fostering a culture of collaboration. This KM strategy based on the GITKM factors not only supports employee development and retention but also preserves institutional knowledge, thus making organizations more resilient and adaptable, especially in the context of their sustainable development goals.

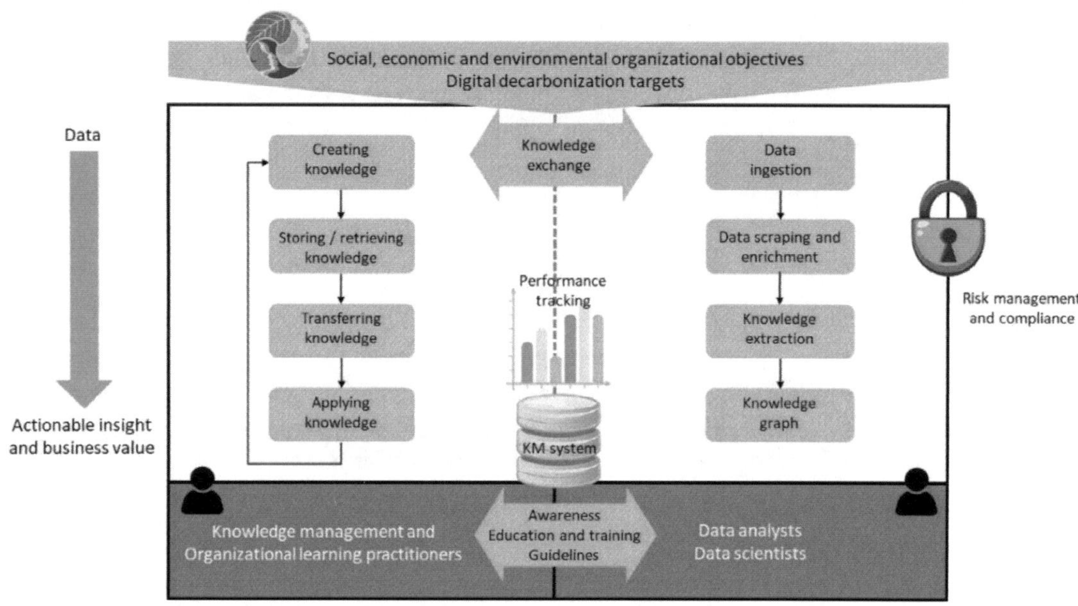

Figure 2. KM strategies and tactics work system (based on the GITKM factors and MFA analysis)

In terms of their qualitative comments, the respondents emphasized that the responsible and efficient use of knowledge and data within organizations is essential for achieving sustainability, highlighting the fundamental role of data in KM strategies and processes. This effort can only be successful based on data governance, and the respondents highlighted data accuracy, data analysis, data science, data cleaning, and data pre-processing as important. Apart from creating awareness and training, the respondents accentuated the need for departmental collaboration to ensure knowledge management and digital decarbonatization efforts are integrated across the organization. This holistic approach can lead to more sustainable practices and better utilization of organizational knowledge. The respondents highlighted that leadership plays a critical role in prioritizing digital decarbonization and dark data management; they further stated that leaders should communicate the importance of these initiatives, aligning them with the organization's broader sustainability goals. Such communication can include setting clear targets for reducing the digital waste and carbon emissions associated with data storage and processing. Several respondents highlighted the importance of goal setting, tracking, and measuring against organizational sustainability goals, but even more so, evaluating the impact of digital operations. Finally, several respondents highlighted that by leveraging artificial intelligence (AI) capabilities to access vast amounts of data and thus use a lot of processing power to process the data, adequate strategies to address dark data and digital decarbonization risks must be considered.

6. CONCLUSION

This study aimed to consider key KM strategies and tactics supporting green IT initiatives to advance organizational sustainability. This objective was achieved by collecting 539 responses through an online questionnaire and analyzing the responses using factor analysis and an individual multiple-factor analysis. Three KM strategies were identified, namely performance tracking and measurement, dark data management, and knowledge exchange. A key finding highlighted the difference in approach and consideration between knowledge management and organizational learning practitioners, as well as between data analysts and data scientists. The findings were visualized and presented in a conceptual work system.

The implementation of the identified KM strategies and tactics towards organizational sustainability could be investigated in future research, thereby contributing to a more detailed implementation of the conceptualized work system. In addition, there is potential to investigate and analyze the contributions of different role players and functional roles, e.g., decision-makers instead of decision-implementers.

REFERENCES

Adama, H. E. and C. D. Okeke (2024). "Digital transformation as a catalyst for business model innovation: A critical review of impact and implementation strategies." Magna Scientia Advanced Research and Reviews 10(02): 256-264.

Ajis, A. F. M. and S. H. Baharin (2019). Dark data management as frontier of information governance. 2019 IEEE 9th Symposium on Computer Applications & Industrial Electronics (ISCAIE), IEEE.

Alavi, M. and D. E. Leidner (2001). "Knowledge management and knowledge management systems: Conceptual foundations and research issues." MIS quarterly: 107-136.

Bolisani, E. and C. Bratianu (2017). "Knowledge strategy planning: an integrated approach to manage uncertainty, turbulence, and dynamics." Journal of Knowledge Management 21(2): 233-253.

Bresciani, S., F. Ciampi, F. Meli and A. Ferraris (2021). "Using big data for co-innovation processes: Mapping the field of data-driven innovation, proposing theoretical developments and providing a research agenda." International Journal of Information Management 60: 102347.

Brundtland, G. H. (1987). Our Common Future: World Commission on Environment and Development. Oxford, Oxford University Press.

Carlsen, L. and R. Bruggemann (2022). "The 17 United Nations' sustainable development goals: A status by 2020." International Journal of Sustainable Development & World Ecology 29(3): 219-229.

Chang, D. L., J. Sabatini-Marques, E. M. da Costa, P. M. Selig and T. Yigitcanlar (2018). "Knowledge-based, smart and sustainable cities: a provocation for a conceptual framework." Journal of Open Innovation: Technology, Market, and Complexity 4(1): 5.

Chopra, M., N. Saini, S. Kumar, A. Varma, S. K. Mangla and W. M. Lim (2021). "Past, present, and future of knowledge management for business sustainability." Journal of Cleaner Production 328: 129592.

Cui, L., M. Gao, J. Dai and J. Mou (2022). "Improving supply chain collaboration through operational excellence approaches: an IoT perspective." Industrial Management & Data Systems 122(3): 565-591.

Depken, D. and C. Zeman (2018). "Small business challenges and the triple bottom line, TBL: Needs assessment in a Midwest State, U.S.A." Technological Forecasting and Social Change 135: 44-50.

Fetters, M. D., L. A. Curry and J. W. Creswell (2013). "Achieving integration in mixed methods designs—principles and practices." Health services research 48(6pt2): 2134-2156.

Field, A. (2024). Discovering statistics using IBM SPSS statistics, Sage publications limited.

Göçen, S. and G. Kurubacak (2023). From Black to Green: Eco-Friendly Learning With Blockchain Technology. Glocal Policy and Strategies for Blockchain: Building Ecosystems and Sustainability, IGI Global: 80-99.

IBM. (2024). "What is dark data?", from https://www.ibm.com/topics/dark-data.

Imamov, M. and N. Semenikhina (2021). "The impact of the digital revolution on the global economy." Linguistics and Culture Review 5(S4): 968-987.

Izah, S. C., L. Sylva and M. Hait (2023). "Cronbach's Alpha: A Cornerstone in Ensuring Reliability and Validity in Environmental Health Assessment." ES Energy & Environment 23: 1057.

Jackson, T. and I. R. Hodgkinson (2023). "Is there a role for knowledge management in saving the planet from too much data?" Knowledge Management Research & Practice 21(3): 427-435.

Jain, H. (2011). Green ICT organizational implementations and workplace relationships. Handbook of Research on Green ICT: Technology, Business and Social Perspectives, IGI Global: 146-168.

Jennex, M. E. (2009). Re-visiting the knowledge pyramid. 2009 42nd Hawaii International Conference on System Sciences, IEEE.

Jennex, M. E. (2020). Knowledge management, innovation, and entrepreneurship in a changing world, IGI Global.

Kitchens, B., D. Dobolyi, J. Li and A. Abbasi (2018). "Advanced customer analytics: Strategic value through integration of relationship-oriented big data." Journal of Management Information Systems 35(2): 540-574.

Klingenberg, B. and H. N. Rothberg (2020). "The Status quo of Knowledge Management and Sustainability Knowledge." Electronic Journal of Knowledge Management 18(2): 136-148.

Lau, E. K.-W. (2021). Relationship Between a Company's Knowledge Management Strategy and Its Business Sustainability. Knowledge Management in Organizations. L. Uden, I. H. Ting and K. Wang. Cham, Springer International Publishing: 187-196.

Liang, L. and Y. Li (2023). "The double-edged sword effect of organizational resilience on ESG performance." Corporate Social Responsibility and Environmental Management 30(6): 2852-2872.

Liao, M.-H. and C.-T. Wang (2021). "Using enterprise architecture to integrate lean manufacturing, digitalization, and sustainability: A lean enterprise case study in the chemical industry." Sustainability 13(9): 4851.

Masanet, E., A. Shehabi, N. Lei, S. Smith and J. Koomey (2020). "Recalibrating global data center energy-use estimates." Science 367(6481): 984-986.

O'reilly, P. and P. Finnegan (2010). "Intermediaries in inter-organisational networks: building a theory of electronic marketplace performance." European Journal of Information Systems 19(4): 462-480.

Purwono, Y., S. Sulasmiyati, H. Susiana, A. Setiawan, R. Roslaini, D. Harefa and Y. Prihatni (2023). "The development of an attidude measurement instrument of responsibility for primary school students." Arisen: Assessment and Research on Education 5(1): 1-9.

Rosati, F. and L. G. D. Faria (2019). "Addressing the SDGs in sustainability reports: The relationship with institutional factors." Journal of Cleaner Production 215: 1312-1326.

Sánchez, L. E. and R. Mitchell (2017). "Conceptualizing impact assessment as a learning process." Environmental Impact Assessment Review 62: 195-204.

Sarayreh, B., A. Mardawi and R. Dmour (2012). "Comparative study: The Nonaka model of knowledge management." International Journal of Engineering and Advanced Technology 1(6): 45-48.

Sharanya, S., V. Vijayalakshmi and R. Radha (2024). Achieving Green Sustainability in Computing Devices in Machine Learning and Deep Learning Techniques. Computational Intelligence for Green Cloud Computing and Digital Waste Management, IGI Global: 172-186.

Tibeica, S. C., E. R. Baciu, I. C. Lupu, C. Balcos, I. Luchian, D. G. Budala, A. Tibeica, Z. Surlari and E. M. Carausu (2024). "Creating and Validating a Questionnaire for Assessing Dentists' Self-Perception on Oral Healthcare Management—A Pilot Study." Healthcare 12(9): 933.

van Reijsen, J., R. Helms, R. Batenburg and R. Foorthuis (2015). "The impact of knowledge management and social capital on dynamic capability in organizations." Knowledge Management Research & Practice 13(4): 401-417.

van Zyl, A. and H. Smuts (2021). An Indoor Farming Framework for Decision Support Towards Food Security in Society 5.0. Society 5.0. A. Gerber and K. Hinkelmann. Cham, Springer International Publishing: 116-128.

Vermesan, O. and P. Friess (2022). Digitising the Industry Internet of Things Connecting the Physical, Digital and VirtualWorlds, CRC Press.

Williams, B., A. Onsman and T. Brown (2010). "Exploratory factor analysis: A five-step guide for novices " Journal of Emergency Primary Health Care 8(3): 1-13.

Yadav, S., A. Samadhiya, A. Kumar, A. Majumdar, J. A. Garza-Reyes and S. Luthra (2023). "Achieving the sustainable development goals through net zero emissions: Innovation-driven strategies for transitioning from incremental to radical lean, green and digital technologies." Resources, Conservation and Recycling 197: 107094.

Zeng, F., S. H. N. Lee and C. K. Y. Lo (2020). "The Role of Information Systems in the Sustainable Development of Enterprises: A Systematic Literature Network Analysis." Sustainability 12(8): 3337.

Zhong, K., T. Jackson, A. West and G. Cosma (2024). Building a Sustainable Knowledge Management System from Dark Data in Industrial Maintenance. International Conference on Knowledge Management in Organizations, Springer.

Zyngier, S. and F. Burstein (2012). "Knowledge Management Governance: The Road to Continuous Benefits Realization." Journal of Information Technology 27(2): 140-155.

AI-DRIVEN DIGITAL TRANSFORMATION: THE NEW INSIGHTS IN AI ADOPTION MODELS

Leila Gluszak
Dr., IAE de Nice
5 rue du 22e B.C.A, 06300 Nice, France

ABSTRACT

As we delve deeper into Digital Transformation, the integration of Artificial Intelligence becomes a pivotal element in driving innovation and efficiency. AI, one of the most disruptive technologies of recent decades, holds immense potential to transform both business operations and societal dynamics. The importance of the research lies in its potential to help organization to overcome implementation challenges and maximize the benefits of AI systems. This research aims to bridge the gap between theoretical insights and practical applications of AI systems, providing a valuable resource for business leaders, technology strategists, and policymakers seeking to leverage AI for competitive advantage.

This research provides a comprehensive review of the existing literature on DT and AI adoption, culminating in the development of a prescriptive framework for the implementation of AI systems. It explores strategic models for deploying AI within enterprises, identifies key drivers and barriers to AI adoption in business environments, and examines how organizations are strategically preparing. The integration AI systems into better navigate the complexities of AI deployment, enhance their innovative capabilities. The study offers valuable insights and recommendations for enterprises considering the adoption of generative AI technologies.

KEYWORDS

Information Systems, Digital Transformation, Artificial Intelligence, Gen AI, AI Adoption

1. INTRODUCTION

Digital Transformation is driving significant changes in organizational operations through automation, data-driven decision-making, and new business models. Generative AI (Gen AI) is a powerful and disruptive technology that is reshaping organizations by enhancing efficiency, driving innovation, and providing a competitive advantage (Rezkinov, 2024). Gen AI models, such as ChatGPT, DALL-E, Google's Bard, and Microsoft's Copilot, represent a significant advancement in artificial intelligence by enabling the generation of entirely new content rather than merely analyzing or classifying existing data (Brown et al., 2020).

Post-Chat GPT, research highlight the growing integration of the high potential of Gen AI within organizations, emphasizing its role in enhancing efficiency and innovation. The technology's applications are expanding across diverse sectors, from creative industries like art and entertainment to more technical fields such as healthcare, finance, and manufacturing.

Nevertheless, the introduction of disruptive AI and other innovative technologies in organizations, and specifically by organizational employees, is a complex phenomenon (Cubric, 2020) owing to the complexity of human decision-making processes. In addition, Gen AI adoption faces notable barriers, particularly in organizations, including high costs, technical skill shortages, and employee resistance. These transformations highlight the need for comprehensive strategies that address the multifaceted challenges of Gen AI adoption, ensuring that organizations can fully leverage AI's transformative potential (Nadkarni and Prüg, 2021) in preparation phase of AI adoption.

In this regard, individuals and organizations readiness for the adoption of innovation is critical to the success of technological change (Kadosh & Chalutz-Ben Gal, 2021). Therefore, the full success of AI adoption depends on a complex set of various conditions and factors.

While organizations start to recognize the value of Gen AI in the DT, most struggle to implement it at scale. The failure to prepare adequately for AI adoption whether through a lack of infrastructure, strategic alignment, or workforce readiness leads to fragmented AI applications and limited improvements, ultimately impeding full-scale transformation efforts (Kalibsa and Altman, 2021; ERC, 2023) which makes it more difficult to implement AI at scale later on. Existing studies on the adoption of AI in organizations have mainly relied on established models like Technology-Organization-Environment (TOE) (Polisetty et al., 2024), TAM (Rahman et al., 2023), or People-Process-Technology Model (Uren & Edwards, 2023). While these models provide valuable explanatory insights into the factors influencing AI adoption, they fall short in offering practical, actionable guidelines that managers can directly apply in their organizational contexts. These models are primarily theoretical and do not sufficiently address the specific challenges faced by organizations, which often have limited resources and unique operational constraints. This ties into a common observation in Gen AI adoption research: the lack of preparation or strategic integration leads to difficulties in expanding AI beyond small, isolated projects. The failure to adequately prepare for AI adoption can result in fragmented efforts, limited improvements, and an inability to scale AI initiatives effectively. As a result, achieving enterprise-wide AI-driven transformation becomes harder because of insufficient infrastructure, lack of expertise, or poorly aligned goals (ERC, 2023). This pattern highlights the importance of creating a robust foundation for AI adoption, including a clear vision, the right infrastructure, and a focus on workforce readiness to fully realize the benefits of AI in digital transformation.

The breach in preparation and execution of AI projects poses significant challenges to maximizing AI's transformative potential, particularly when organizations face difficulties scaling AI beyond pilot projects. Without a comprehensive framework of Gen AI adoption the intended efficiencies and innovations from digital transformation remain elusive (ERC, 2023). We propose the following research questions to explore the impact of lack of preparation the absence of strategic preparation leads to critical failures in scaling AI-driven initiatives. This provides a deeper understanding of the preparatory phase of AI adoption in where the technologies are disruptive.

Research Question: How does the lack of strategic preparation for Gen AI adoption affect the ability of organizations to scale AI-driven digital transformation, and what critical factors contribute to overcoming these barriers?

To address this gap, we aim to provide a comprehensive state-of-the-art review of the literature on DT and to explore the organizational shortcomings in AI adoption and investigate the essential factors are necessary to scale AI across the organization for effective digital transformation. Based on our analysis of the literature, we propose a prescriptive theoretical framework that views AI adoption. This framework fundamentally alters an AI adoption by leveraging the convergence of information, computing, communication, and connectivity technologies.

Responding to this research questions offer a variety of contributions to academic and practical knowledge. The study deepens (i) the theoretical understanding of DT and AI adoption by focusing on the strategic preparation phase and its importance in scaling AI-driven transformation and offer practical guidelines for establishing leadership and governance frameworks that align AI with business strategy, creating a blueprint for other organizations to follow.

The remainder of this paper is set as follows: Sect. 1 proposes state-of-the-art review of DT and AI adoption. Section 2 and 3 presents the methodology and prescriptive framework. Section 4 is dedicated to the discussion. Section 5 concludes the paper.

2. LITERATURE REVIEW

2.1 Digital Transformation Driven by AI

In recent years, digital transformation (DT) has emerged as an important phenomenon in strategic IS research (Bharadwaj et al., 2013; Piccinini et al., 2015) as well as for practitioners (Fitzgerald et al., 2014; Westerman et al., 2011). DT encompasses the profound changes taking place in society and industries using digital technologies (Agarwal et al., 2010; Majchrzak et al., 2016).

Digital transformation, as described by Vial (2019), is a process focused on enhancing organizations by driving significant changes through the adoption of information, computing, communication, and connectivity technologies. It allows companies to become more flexible and efficient, streamline production processes, create innovative value propositions, and respond swiftly to market demands (Alcácer & Cruz-Machado, 2019;

Queiroz et al., 2020; Chen et al., 2018; Dedehayir et al., 2017; Rachinger et al., 2019). As a result, recent academic attention has concentrated on the mechanisms and processes that leverage digital technologies to transform businesses activities, boundaries, and goals (Wessel et al., 2020; Wimelius et al., 2021). Therefore, stakeholders involved in business processes must grasp the significance of each adopted technology and understand the growing importance of digital transformation as technology evolves. Digital transformation reinvigorates industries and empowers the adoption of emerging technologies, reshaping lifestyles and creating new business models (Feliciano-Cestero et al., 2023). Alcacer and Cruz-Machado (2019) emphasize that Industry 4.0 ushers in the digitalization era, influencing commercial activities by fostering collaboration, improving operational processes, product design, and manufacturing services (Haddud & Khare, 2020), implementing digital ecosystems with customers and suppliers (Alcacer & Cruz-Machado, 2019; Salvi et al., 2021), and enhancing and automating supply chain processes (Patrucco et al., 2020).

Very few businesses have undergone successful digital transformations. For instance, Kane et al. (2017) found in a global study that only 25% of organizations had transformed into digital businesses, that 41% were on transformative journeys, and that 34% invested more time talking about the digital transformation trend than they did acting on it. What is noteworthy form this study, however, is that 85% of executives stated that attaining digital maturity is critical to organizational success.

Digital transformation presents challenges, particularly related to AI adoption. By understanding and mitigating these challenges, companies can better leverage AI to achieve their goals. While various conceptualizations of digital transformation (Vial, 2019; Wessel et al., 2020), it is widely agreed that digital technologies, especially using AI, can massively transform organizations (Constantinides et al., 2018; Davenport, 2018) and organization can be overwhelmed. Over the past decade, growing attention has been directed toward the complexities and tensions involved in deploying AI within organizational operations (Agarwal et al., 2010; Hinings et al., 2018). The deployment process is highly intricate, requiring organizations to navigate technical, operational, and cultural challenges as they integrate AI technologies into their workflows. Managers, they also face pressures to change rapidly to keep up with competitors and investors demands while avoiding rash decisions and carefully considering long-term shifts in the business environment and society (Perlow et al., 2002). Added to that, Gen AI is considered as a key driver of change, enabling businesses and to rethink and revamp their operations, customer relationships, and innovation strategies (Khrais & Shidwan, 2020). By leveraging AI's disruptive capabilities, organizations can accelerate DT, resulting in improved efficiency, innovation, and competitiveness.

2.2 Literature Review on AI Adoption Models

The adoption of AI has been a significant area of research, reflecting its transformative potential across various sectors. Dwivedi et al. (2021) define AI adoption as the process through which organizations embrace AI technologies in various functions such as automation, decision-making, and customer engagement, which necessitates technological readiness, organizational transformation, and human adaptation.

A systematic literature review by Kabalisa and Altmann (2021) highlights the economic impacts of AI adoption. The study identifies that AI adoption can significantly influence economic growth by enhancing productivity and efficiency. For instance, AI-driven predictive maintenance in manufacturing can reduce downtime and maintenance costs, leading to significant economic benefits. Companies like Siemens use AI to predict equipment failures before they occur, optimizing maintenance schedules and reducing operational costs.

New challenges face adopters of AI, such as determining how much responsibility to delegate to autonomous systems (Berente et al., 2021). Information management researchers need to address these challenges by conducting empirical socio-technical research that contributes to understanding AI technology, its synergy with Big Data, and the process of adopting it (Cybulski and Scheepers, 2021, Duan et al., 2019, Huysman, 2020, Schuetz and Venkatesh, 2020). For practitioners, such research would help them to formulate strategies for AI development, identified as a gap by Dwivedi et al. (2021).

The research on the adoption of innovative information systems has primarily followed two well-established frameworks: models that focus on individual technology use, such as the Technology Acceptance Model (TAM) and its derivatives like the Unified Theory of Acceptance and Use of Technology (UTAUT), and models that take an organizational perspective, such as the Technology Organization Environment (TOE) framework. Studies like Chatterjee et al. (2021) have applied both TAM and TOE to explore the adoption of Industry 4.0 technologies, including AI, highlighting factors like perceived ease of use, a concept rooted in TAM. The TOE model has been widely utilized to analyze AI adoption in various sectors, as seen in studies by Alsheibani et al. (2018) and Pumplun et al. (2019).

However, researchers have pointed out that current models do not fully capture the disruptive potential of AI. For example, Chi et al. (2020) argue that existing models fail to account for the anthropomorphism of AI service agents. Cao et al. (2021) extended TAM/UTAUT by incorporating societal concerns that might influence managerial decisions regarding AI adoption. Similarly, Khanijahani et al. (2022) emphasized the perceived threat of AI to medical professionals autonomy. In another extension of TAM, Sánchez-Prieto et al. (2020) included factors such as trust in AI in the context of university assessments. Given these limitations, a socio-technical approach is proposed to better understand AI adoption, recognizing the need to incorporate both technological and social factors to address the broader implications of AI in various sectors.

What about Maturity Model for Gen AI adoption? Is it sufficient to a adopt Gen AI? In fact, the objective of the maturity model is to enable companies to determine their own readiness for AI systems as precisely as possible (Sonntag, 2024). In doing so, the model can be applied to individual organizational units as well as the entire company. The resulting findings are to be used to identify areas where there is a greater need for action regarding the safe, efficient and target-oriented use of AI systems (Sonntag, 2024). The focus is on the current state of AI.AI Maturity Models, focus on organizational readiness and capability for adopting and scaling AI, assessing not just the acceptance of AI but how well AI is integrated into an organization's processes, infrastructure, and strategic goals. Based on the 11 maturity models. Many maturity models currently lack consideration and control of implementation costs as part of the introduction of AI in manufacturing companies (Akhtar et al., 2022). The AI Maturity Model often suffers from a lack of theoretical basis, leading to weak analysis due to untested assumptions and arbitrary decision-making. Additionally, organizations face challenges such as insufficient expertise, AI safety concerns, lack of governance, and resistance to change.

However, research still lacks a comprehensive understanding of this phenomenon and its implications across different levels of analysis (Gray & Rumpe, 2017; Kane, 2017; Matt et al., 2015; Vial, 2019). The strategic-operational preparation phase is critical for the successful adoption and scaling of AI-driven transformation within organizations. This phase establishes the foundation for AI initiatives by ensuring the organization is well-prepared to integrate AI technologies effectively and sustainably. Strategic preparation involves aligning business goals, processes, and technology with AI capabilities, creating a roadmap for seamless integration. It ensures that the necessary infrastructure is built, a culture of innovation is fostered, and the organization develops the skills needed to manage and operate AI systems. By doing so, this phase reduces the risk of fragmented implementation, enhances scalability, and ensures that AI initiatives are aligned with broader business strategies maximizing their potential for driving long-term transformation.

3. METHODOLOGY

We have utilized a reflection and synthesis methodology to develop a prescriptive framework for AI adoption, which integrates insights from diverse sources such as theoretical models, empirical research, and practical experiences. This approach aligns with Jaakkola's (2020) emphasis on drawing from multiple knowledge sources to create comprehensive solutions. By reflecting on perspectives across the literature, including models like the TAM, the TOE, framework, and studies on DT (Chatterjee et al., 2021; Vial, 2019), we aim to construct a practical, cohesive guide that is tailored to the unique challenges and requirements of organizations undergoing AI integration.

The strength of this methodology lies in its ability to capture the multifaceted nature of AI adoption. Theoretical insights provide an understanding of technology acceptance and organizational readiness (Davis, 1989; Venkatesh et al., 2003). The prescriptive framework is structured to provide step-by-step guidance for overcoming common obstacles, such as ensuring alignment with organizational strategy, promoting employee upskilling, and developing a supportive data infrastructure (Lee & Shin, 2021). This framework not only addresses technical challenges but also incorporates strategies for fostering a culture of innovation and change management that encourages employee engagement and acceptance of AI (Sánchez-Prieto et al., 2020). By doing so, it facilitates effective AI implementation that is both sustainable and scalable.

4. FRAMEWORK

The adoption of Generative AI is characterized by diverse patterns that reflect the varying strategic goals and operational needs of different industries. Many organizations initially adopt Generative AI through pilot projects that focus on specific applications, such as automated content creation, customer service enhancement, and predictive analytics. These pilot projects often serve as a proof of concept, demonstrating the technology's potential before scaling up to broader implementations. For instance, companies in the retail sector use Generative AI to personalize marketing campaigns and optimize inventory management, while healthcare providers deploy AI to assist in diagnostic procedures and patient care management (Smith et al., 2020; Johnson & Brown, 2021).

This Gen AI adoption framework provides a structured, phased approach for organization to integrate Generative AI and AI multi-agents systems into their business operations. It is designed to guide organizations from initial leadership awareness and the use of general-purpose AI tools to the development of in-house AI solutions tailored to their specific needs. The framework is divided into strategic and operational phases.

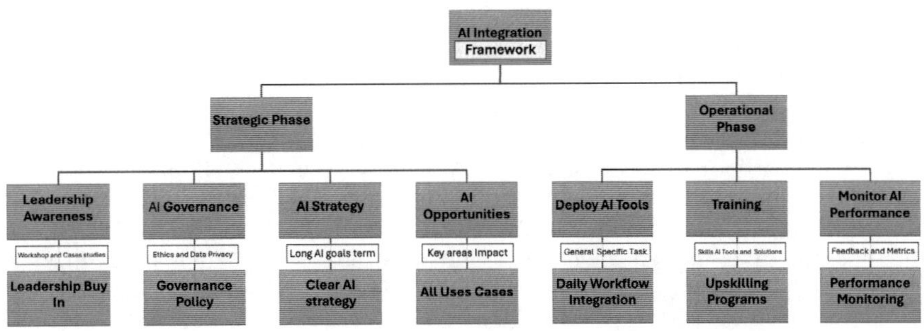

Figure 1. Prescriptive Framework of AI Integration

To analyze the adaptability of this proposed AI adoption framework to disruptive technologies like Generative AI, we need to assess how well the framework handles the unique characteristics, challenges, and opportunities presented by Gen AI. This includes understanding the capabilities of Gen AI, its disruptive nature, and how the framework's phases accommodate the specific requirements of this technology (Chen et al., 2023). Based on the theory of disruptive innovation, Karimi and Walter (2015) found that dynamic responsiveness can improve an enterprise's ability to respond to digital disruption, build digital platforms, and accelerate DT. Meanwhile, Park and El Sawy (2013), from the perspective of digital eco dynamics, studied various configurations of IT systems, organizational dynamic capabilities, and environmental turbulence to help organizations choose the strategies that best suit their environments.

Strategic AI adoption refers to the long-term, deliberate integration of AI technologies into an organization's overall business strategy, with the goal of driving innovation, improving efficiency, and maintaining competitive advantage. Unlike short-term or ad-hoc AI projects, strategic AI adoption is embedded in the organization's core objectives and operational processes. It involves a structured, phased approach that ensures alignment with business goals, ethical governance, and scalability.

The strategic phase of our AI adoption framework focuses on high-level planning, ensuring that AI initiatives are fully aligned with the organization's long-term goals. This phase emphasizes leadership engagement, policy formation, and governance, laying the foundation for ethical and effective AI integration. By aligning leadership with AI objectives, the organization can ensure a unified vision for AI's role in driving business transformation (Harris & White, 2022). Our framework is organized into two phases strategic and operational one. Each phase consists of a set of steps to be followed to be align with our approach.

The first key objective of strategic phase is to establish leadership buy-in by cultivating a deep understanding of AI's potential through workshops and case studies, which highlight AI's strategic value. The leadership plays a pivotal role in driving AI adoption within organizations. Research has consistently highlighted the need for top management to champion AI initiatives, aligning AI goals with the broader strategic objectives of the organization. Leadership commitment is crucial for securing resources, guiding organizational change, and fostering an AI-friendly culture. This phase also includes forming an AI Governance Committee to oversee ethical AI use, set strategic goals, and ensure compliance with legal and ethical standards (Kim & Park, 2023). Ethical considerations surrounding AI, including fairness, transparency, and accountability, have gained increasing attention in the academic literature. The development of ethical AI frameworks that emphasize responsible AI use can help organizations navigate these challenges while maintaining a positive public image.

The next objective key is to define a clear AI strategy that aligns with the organization's goals. To define a clear AI strategy, organizations must establish a comprehensive roadmap that aligns AI initiatives with their overarching business objectives and operational goals. This involves identifying the specific areas where AI can create value, such as improving customer experiences, enhancing operational efficiency, or driving product innovation. A well-defined AI strategy should also outline measurable goals and performance indicators to track progress and evaluate the impact of AI investments over time. This involves too creating AI ethics and governance policies early in the process, addressing critical issues such as data privacy, AI bias, and regulatory compliance (e.g., GDPR). These policies ensure responsible AI use as the organization moves forward (Zhang et al., 2021). Cao et al. (2021) and Khanijahani et al. (2022) argue that addressing ethical concerns is essential for fostering trust and legitimacy in AI adoption. Issues such as algorithmic bias, data privacy, and the societal impact of AI need to be carefully managed.

Finally, the strategic phase involves prioritizing AI opportunities by assessing where Generative AI and other AI technologies can have the most significant impact. Globally, prioritizing AI opportunities is a crucial step in building a sustainable AI strategy. It ensures that AI initiatives are aligned with strategic priorities, achievable within current constraints, and capable of delivering measurable value across the organization. This approach allows organizations to harness the transformative potential of AI effectively while managing risks and fostering a supportive culture for AI adoption. Areas like content generation, customer service automation, and task-specific optimizations are identified for innovation, and measurable goals such as improved productivity, customer satisfaction, and cost savings are set to track AI's impact (Williams & Taylor, 2021). Overall, this phase ensures that AI adoption is guided by leadership alignment, ethical governance, and a well-defined strategy, positioning the organization to leverage AI effectively (Chen et al., 2023).

The operational phase focuses on the execution of AI initiatives, including the integration of AI tools into daily workflows, employee training, and continuous monitoring of AI systems. This phase turns strategic plans into practical applications by selecting, deploying, and refining AI solutions.

The first critical objective is employee training and skills development, which involves conducting hands-on workshops to help employees effectively use Generative AI tools and task-specific solutions (Chui, et al, M,2018; Sutton & Barto, 2019). Upskilling employees and providing training are foundational for AI adoption, enabling organizations to build an AI-literate workforce that is ready to integrate and innovate with AI technologies.

The second key objective is to deploy AI tools starting with general-purpose technologies, such as ChatGPT, for everyday tasks and task-specific solutions to automate key business functions, including customer service, content creation, and supply chain optimization (Heimberger and al, 2024). Regular usage reviews are implemented to measure the effectiveness of these tools and gather employee feedback. Additionally, businesses begin to implement the in-house AI tools developed during the strategic phase, ensuring they are tailored to meet specific operational needs (Khanfar and al, 2024). Beyond technical expertise, AI literacy is essential across all organizational levels to ensure that employees understand AI's capabilities and limitations, fostering greater collaboration between technical and non-technical teams.

Our framework highlights monitoring AI performance and refining its integration into the business. Feedback loops are implemented to continuously assess AI systems efficiency, while user feedback is gathered, and adjustments made as necessary. Regular assessments using metrics like productivity improvements, cost savings, and customer engagement ensure that AI tools are delivering value and driving operational efficiency.

Once the employees are used to Gen AI topics, we can shift to the adoption of task-specific AI tools. Key business functions such as marketing, HR, and customer service are identified where AI-powered tools can enhance efficiency. These tools are integrated into workflows (e.g., automating customer support or generating marketing content), with specialized training provided to ensure employees can effectively use them. After that, RD businesses begin the in-house development of generative AI tools, ensuring these custom solutions are seamlessly integrated into existing business processes. Feedback loops are used to continuously monitor performance, improving tool accuracy and usability over time.

5. CONCLUSION

This research underscores the critical importance of strategic preparation in enabling organizations to scale AI for DT. The findings reveal that a lack of strategic foresight and planning often leads to fragmented and siloed AI implementations, preventing organizations from fully leveraging AI's potential across their operations. Organizations that fail to align AI adoption with business goals often experience limited impact from AI initiatives, which remain isolated within specific departments or projects (Davenport & Ronanki, 2018). The framework introduced in this study offers a structured approach to AI adoption, emphasizing the role of leadership engagement, clear governance policies, and phased implementation to overcome these barriers. Strategic alignment between leadership and operations, combined with the creation of AI governance structures and feedback loops, enables organizations to adopt AI in a sustainable and scalable manner (Chui et al., 2018).

This research highlights that Generative AI technologies can significantly disrupt traditional business processes, but only when integrated into a broader strategic framework that prioritizes long-term objectives and cross-functional integration. Furthermore, organizations that invest in upskilling their workforce and building robust data infrastructure are better positioned to move beyond AI pilot projects and achieve enterprise-wide AI transformation (Bender et al., 2021). For SMEs in particular, this incremental approach allows for cost-effective AI adoption without overwhelming their financial or operational resources (Lee & Shin, 2021).

The evolving nature of AI and its applications presents multiple opportunities for future research. First, industry-specific studies could investigate how sectors like healthcare, finance, and manufacturing manage AI scaling and governance, given their distinct regulatory environments and operational demands (Ransbotham et al., 2018). For example, in healthcare, where data privacy regulations such as HIPAA play a critical role, understanding how AI models are integrated into patient care while complying with regulations would provide valuable insights.

Another promising area for future research is the exploration of how emerging technologies such as edge computing, blockchain, and quantum computing influence AI adoption at scale.

While this research contributes significantly to the understanding of strategic AI adoption, there are several limitations to acknowledge. First, the study's industry focus may limit the generalizability of the findings across different sectors. For instance, the AI adoption framework may not fully account for the unique challenges faced by highly regulated industries, such as healthcare or finance, where compliance requirements may dictate a more cautious and complex approach to AI scaling (Fichman et al., 2011).

Finally, the study did not deeply explore the long-term sustainability of AI systems once adopted. As AI technologies continue to evolve, organizations may face increasing costs related to AI system maintenance, model updates, and the integration of new technologies. Future research could focus on the lifecycle management of AI systems, exploring how organizations can sustain AI performance over time while balancing costs, governance, and ethical considerations (Sutton et al., 2019).

REFERENCES

Agarwal, R., et al. (2010). The digital transformation of healthcare: Current status and the road ahead. *Information Systems Research*, *21*(4), 796-809.

Agrawal, A., et al. (2018). Prediction machines: The simple economics of artificial intelligence. Harvard Business Review Press.

Alcácer, V., & Cruz-Machado, V. (2019). Scanning the Industry 4.0: A literature review on technologies for manufacturing systems. *Engineering Science and Technology, an International Journal*, *22*(3), 899-919.

Brown, T. B., Mann, B., Ryder, N., Subbiah, M., Kaplan, J., Dhariwal, P., Neelakantan, A., et al. (2020). Language Models are Few-Shot Learners. *Proceedings of the 34th Conference on Neural Information Processing Systems (NeurIPS 2020).*

c, S., Rana, N. P., Dwivedi, Y. K., & Baabdullah, A. M. (2021). Industry 4.0 adoption.

Chui, M., Manyika, J., & Miremadi, M. (2018). What AI Can and Can't Do (Yet) for Your Business. *McKinsey Quarterly*.

Constantinides, P., et al. (2018). The impact of digital technology on business models: Insights from the digital transformation of the newspaper industry. *Journal of Business Research*, *89*, 1-10. JPMorgan Chase AI Applications :

Davenport, T. H., & Ronanki, R. (2018). Artificial Intelligence for the Real World. *Harvard Business Review*.

Davis, F. D. (1989). Perceived usefulness, perceived ease of use, and user acceptance of information technology. *MIS Quarterly*.

Heimberger, H., Horvat, D. & Schultmann, F. Exploring the factors driving AI adoption in production: a systematic literature review and future research agenda. *Inf Technol Manag*(2024). https://doi.org/10.1007/s10799-024-00436-z

Hinings, B., et al. (2018). Digital innovation and transformation: An institutional perspective. *Information and Organization*, 28(1), 52-61.

Jaakkola, E. (2020). Designing conceptual articles: four approaches. *AMS Review*.

Kabalisa, R., & Altmann, J. (2021). AI Technologies and Motives for AI Adoption by Countries and Firms: A Systematic Literature Review. In Economics of Grids, Clouds, Systems, and Services (pp. 39-51).

Kane, G. C., et al. (2017). Strategy, not technology, drives digital transformation. *MIT Sloan Management Review*, *58*(3), 1-25.

Khanfar, A.A., Kiani Mavi, R., Iranmanesh, M. et al. Determinants of artificial intelligence adoption: research themes and future directions. *Inf Technol Manag* (2024). https://doi.org/10.1007/s10799-024-00435-0

Khrais, L. T., & Shidwan, A. (2020). AI capabilities and organizational performance: A review of the literature. *Journal of Business Research*, *123*, 1-13.

Lee, I., & Shin, Y. J. (2021). AI-driven Big Data Analytics: A Case Study of Its Impact on SMEs' Competitiveness. *Sustainability, 13*(6), 3226.

Patrucco, A. S., Ciccullo, F., & Pero, M. (2020). The impact of digital technologies on procurement and supply chain management: A conceptual framework. *International Journal of Procurement Management*, *13*(1), 1-20.

Perlow, L. A., et al. (2002). The speed trap: Exploring the relationship between decision making and temporal context. *Academy of Management Journal*, *45*(5), 931-955.

Rachinger, M., Rauter, R., Müller, C., Vorraber, W., & Schirgi, E. (2019). Digitalization and its influence on business model innovation. *Journal of Manufacturing Technology Management*, *30*(8), 1143-1160.

Ransbotham, S., Kiron, D., Gerbert, P., & Reeves, M. (2018). Reshaping Business with Artificial Intelligence. *MIT Sloan Management Review*.

Salvi, A., et al. (2021). Digital ecosystems: A systematic literature review. Journal of Business Research, 123, 255-267. Velinov, E., et al. (2020). The role of digital transformation in international business. *Journal of International Business Studies*, *51*(5), 715-734.

Venkatesh, V., Morris, M. G., Davis, G. B., & Davis, F. D. (2003). User Acceptance of Information Technology: Toward a Unified View. MIS Quarterly.

Vial, G. (2019). Understanding digital transformation: A review and a research agenda. *The Journal of Strategic Information Systems*, *28*(2), 118-144.

Wessel, L., et al. (2020). Digital transformation: A multidisciplinary review and research agenda. *Journal of Business Research*, *123*, 1-13.

Zhang, H., et al. (2021). Multi-Agent Reinforcement Learning: A Review. *Journal of Artificial Intelligence Research* (JAIR).

A METHOD TO IDENTIFY MISALIGNMENTS OF BUSINESS MODELS AND BUSINESS PROCESSES

Philipp Url, Wolfgang Vorraber and Siegfried Vössner
Institute of Engineering and Business Informatics, Graz University of Technology
Kopernikusgasse 24/III, 8010 Graz, Austria

ABSTRACT

Business models and business processes represent key concepts when describing the architectural and implementation level of an enterprise supporting the realization of the business strategy. Both levels, that are often seen and treated independently of each other, are changed and adapted in daily business – either due to market needs or by the adoption of various kinds of innovation. This often makes it very difficult to align both levels initially and even more challenging to keep these two levels aligned over time so as to ensure optimal business performance and resource utilization. This paper presents a method to systematically identify misalignments of business models and business processes as a first important step toward aligning them. The method includes a mapping based on the Business Model Canvas (BMC) and practically relevant business process modeling concepts based on the Business Process Model and Notation (BPMN). The alignment analysis of these two concepts is described in a structured procedure. Its application is demonstrated and evaluated by means of a real-world industrial case study and its results are presented and discussed.

KEYWORDS

Business Models, Business Processes, Alignment, Business Model Innovation, Business Process Modeling

1. INTRODUCTION

Business models (BM) as defined by Magretta (2002), Al-Debei & Avison (2010), Chesbrough (2002), Osterwalder et al. (2005), or Zott et al. (2011) and business processes (BP) as defined by Davenport & Short (1990), Hammer & Champy (1993), Scheer (1994), or Weske (2012) are both important concepts to describe the architectural and implementation level of an enterprise (see Figure 1) in order to share the information among relevant stakeholders as a basis for analysis and continuous improvements (Teece, 2018).

Both concepts undergo constant changes in an enterprise in order to achieve targets such as growth or staying competitive. These changes are driven by various types of innovation (Schumpeter, 1939), such as product innovation (Dougherty, 1992; Danneels, 2002), process innovation (Davenport & Short, 1990; Davenport, 1993), socio-technical innovation (Trist, 1981), and technological innovation, such as the steam engine in the late 1700s, electric light in the 1800s, or information technologies in the 1990s.

On the one hand, these types of innovation act as drivers for business model innovation and may result in new or adapted business models (Mitchell & Coles, 2003; Chesbrough, 2010; Teece, 2010; Amit & Zott, 2010). On the other hand, they act as drivers for business process redesign (Davenport & Short, 1990), business reengineering (Hammer & Champy, 1993), business process engineering (Scheer, 1994), all important aspects of business process management (Weske, 2012). Hence, changes on the mentioned levels of an enterprise often occur separately from each other and therefore may lead to misalignments between business models and business processes. These misalignments could lead to issues in an enterprise, such as not achieving its strategic goals (Boubaker et al., 2014; Di Valentin et al., 2015).

Whereas extensive research exists on both, business models and business processes, less attention is paid to the interconnection between these two concepts (Betzwieser et al., 2020; Lara Machado et al., 2023). First approaches to closing this gap exist, but lack details (Solaimani & Bouwman, 2012), lack practical relevance as they do not focus on the most common meta-models (Schief et al., 2012), only focus on one direction, top-down (Suratno et al., 2018, Lara Machado et al., 2024) or bottom-up (Boubaker et al., 2014), focus on lower implementation levels (Zacarias & Martins, 2012), or only focus on specific industries or domains (Kharmoum et al., 2019).

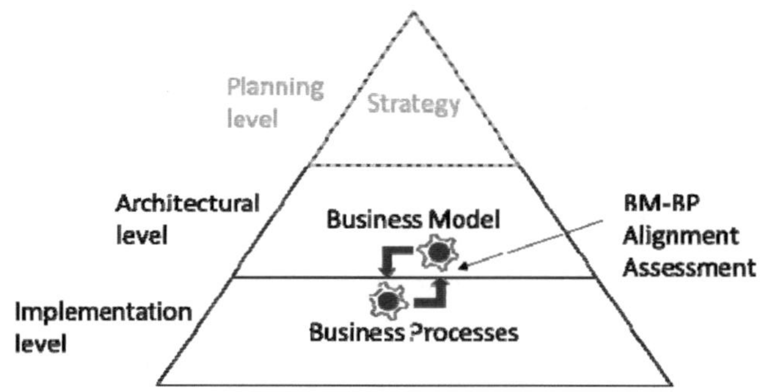

Figure 1. The BM-BP Alignment Assessment Method in the context of the Business Logic Triangle based on Osterwalder & Pigneur (2002)

To address these issues, we propose a new method that is aimed at practitioners in order to identify misalignments of the business model and the business processes in an enterprise as an important first step toward aligning them. For demonstration and evaluation purposes, we applied the method in an industrial case study.

The remainder of this paper is structured as follows: Section 2 explains the concepts of business models and business processes, including the state of the art regarding the alignment of these two concepts. Section 3 describes our research design. The method itself is described in section 4. Its application in a case study follows in section 5. Section 6 concludes the paper, discussing the results, the contributions to research and practice, and limitations.

2. BACKGROUND AND RELATED WORK

In this section the two concepts business models and business processes are briefly discussed and the state of the art concerning the alignment of both concepts is described, focusing on identified issues in existing frameworks and methods in this field of research.

2.1 Business Models and Business Processes

The research on business models gained a great deal of attention from the late 1990s and early 2000s onwards (Osterwalder et al., 2005, Wirtz et al., 2022). Recent theoretical grounding has been established by Magretta (2002), Chesbrough (2002), Osterwalder et al. (2005), Al-Debei & Avison, (2010), and Zott et al. (2011), among others. Al-Debei et al. (2008) summarized the various definitions as follows: "The business model is an abstract representation of an organization … of all core interrelated architectural, co-operational, and financial arrangements … as well as all core products and/or services the organization offers, or will offer … to achieve its strategic goals and objectives." Various approaches exist to describe business models, such as the REA accounting model by McCarthy (1982), e3-value by Gordijn & Akkermans, (2001), STOF by (Bouwman et al., 2008), or the Business Model Canvas (BMC) by Osterwalder & Pigneur (2010). These concepts serve to describe the architectural level of an enterprise (see Figure 1).

The first concepts of business processes appeared in the early 1990s and deal with the redesign of business processes to improve the performance of an enterprise (Davenport & Short, 1990). As defined by Davenport & Short (1990), business processes are "a set of logically-related tasks performed to achieve a defined business outcome." The concept of business processes was further investigated in the context of business reengineering (Hammer & Champy, 1993) and business process engineering (Scheer, 1994). The overarching research field, namely business process management (BPM), as stated by Weske (2012), covers "concepts, methods, and techniques to support the design, administration, configuration, enactment, and analysis of business processes." The explicit representation of business processes, considered as the basis of BPM (Weske, 2012), is addressed by the field of business process modeling and includes many concepts focusing on describing the implementation level of an enterprise (see Figure 1) (Aldin & De Cesare, 2011). Important concepts in this field are process landscapes (PL), representing the top-level part of the process architecture (Dijkman et al., 2016, Dumas et al., 2018), the Business Process Model and Notation (BPMN) (Object Management Group, 2015), and Event Driven Process Chains (EPCs) (Scheer, 2002).

2.2 Alignment of Business Models and Business Processes

The topic of aligning business models and business processes targets the interrelation of these concepts. It first arose in 2000 and reached a peak in terms of the number of publications between 2010 and 2012 (Betzwieser et al., 2020). Since then the topic has been continuously addressed in the context of business model and business process management research (Solaimani & Bouwman, 2012; Heyl, 2014; Betzwieser et al., 2020; Lara Machado et al., 2023). Business models are the link to the strategy, that contains an enterprise's strategic goals and business objectives, and form the basis for designing the business processes (Al-Debei & Avison, 2010; Betzwieser et al., 2020). Existing business model frameworks, as mentioned above, describe how to design or refine business models but pay only little or no attention to their implementation. The challenge of implementing a business model on a process level remains (Solaimani & Bouwman, 2012). Business process management is an ongoing iterative process (Van Der Aalst, 2013) and involves continuously analyzing and reengineering business processes. This alone does not ensure that business processes do not deviate from higher level business objectives (Boubaker et al., 2017). Here, the challenge still exists of keeping the business processes and the business model aligned over time to ensure the execution of strategic decisions and the achievement of strategic goals (Boubaker et al., 2014, Di Valentin et al., 2015).

To address these challenges, systematic transformation and/or alignment approaches between business models and business processes are required. Currently, conceptual proposals to align business models with business processes do exist, but they lack structured and procedural information on how to perform the alignment in detail. This research gap is confirmed by authors such as Heyl (2014), Betzwieser et al. (2020), and Lara Machado et al. (2023). To identify relevant publications and analyze this research gap in detail, a systematic literature review was carried out, as described in section 3. As a result, we identified the following issues in existing frameworks. The first issue is that some of the frameworks are only on a conceptual level and lack details on how to perform the alignment in a structural and procedural manner (e.g. Di Valentin et al., 2012, 2015; Schief et al., 2012; Solaimani & Bouwman, 2012). Second, we identified a lack of practical relevance concerning the selection of meta-models for business model or business processes representation. Most of the identified frameworks do not consider the direct mapping of the BMC and BPMN concepts (e.g. Bonakdar et al., 2013; Boubaker et al., 2014, 2017; Di Valentin et al., 2012, 2015; Hotie & Gordijn, 2019; Iacob et al., 2012; Kharmoum et al., 2019; Meertens et al., 2012; Schief et al., 2012; Skersys et al., 2012; Suratno et al., 2017, 2018). The third issue is the focus on lower implementation levels. These frameworks focus on the alignment of business processes with either work practices (e.g. Zacarias & Martins, 2012) or State Diagram Models and Class Diagrams (e.g. Melouk et al., 2020; Rhazali et al., 2015). The fourth issue is the focus on a specific industry or domain. Identified frameworks either focus specifically on the software industry (e.g. Bonakdar et al., 2013; Di Valentin et al., 2015; Kharmoum et al., 2019; Melouk et al., 2020; Rhazali et al., 2015; Schief et al., 2012) or only pay attention to service-dominant business (e.g. Suratno et al., 2017, 2018). The fifth issue identified is the consideration of only one direction. Except for Di Valentin et al. (2015), all identified frameworks either consider a top-down or a bottom up approach, as opposed to both. The sixth and final issue is that existing frameworks do not consider the status quo of an enterprise's business model and business processes as they do not assess the alignment of the existing business model and existing business processes (e.g. Lara Machado et al., 2024).

Existing frameworks and methods which cover aspects of interrelation and alignment between business models and processes lack both systematic approaches and practically relevant methods to support enterprises with systematic guidance in identifying relevant misalignments of their existing business model and business processes. Our research addresses this gap by developing a method that systematically uncovers relevant problems in the alignment of the business model and business processes of an enterprise by identifying misalignments from both perspectives: from business model to business processes, as well as from business processes to business model.

3. RESEARCH DESIGN

Our research was guided by design science research (DSR) (Hevner et al., 2004) and the related process model by Peffers et al., 2007 with the aim of developing a new method (see section 4) as an addition to the knowledge base and systematically identifying misalignments of a business model and business processes, an as yet unsolved problem. We expect the method to be applicable in situations where enterprises seek to understand whether their existing business model and business processes are aligned. The following specific research activities have been conducted based on the process model by Peffers et al., 2007:

Identify Problem & Motivate: To ensure the rigor of our work and to understand the problem in detail, a systematic literature review was conducted. Its main result, the identification of issues with existing frameworks and methods, is described in section 2.2. Further, its results were used in the design and development of the method. Our literature review is based on Webster & Watson (2002) and vom Brocke et al. (2015). It included a structured material collection, a review of each selected publication, and the compilation of a concept matrix supporting the identification of issues in existing frameworks and methods. The databases used for material collection were Scopus and Web of Science. A search in "Title," "Abstract," and "Keywords" was conducted to identify the most relevant publications. The following search term was applied to cover variations of the terms "Business model," "Business process," and "aligning": (Business Model* OR Value Model*) AND (Business Process* OR Process Management OR Process Model* OR Business Operations) AND (align* OR implement* OR link* OR bridg* OR transf* OR base* OR integrat* OR map*). To narrow down the area of investigation, only the following publications were included: conference papers and journal articles, starting from 2012 (continuing the work by Solaimani & Bouwman (2012), that included a literature review to that date), in English or German language. The abstract screening was conducted with the following screening inclusion criteria: Publications that investigate the alignment or similar concepts (see search term) of business models and business processes and was followed by a full text review.

The search yielded 1613 unique publications for abstract screening (as of Sept. 26, 2024). The abstract screening resulted in 205 selected publications for full text review. The full text read resulted in 54 selected publications. One of the reasons for exclusions in the full text review was that many publications do not distinguish between "business model" and "business process" concepts. Although they use the term "business modeling," they actually perform "business process modeling." A backward and forward search based on Wohlin (2014) was conducted on the selected publications, applying the same screening procedure and selection criteria and revealed an additional 14 publications, resulting in a total of 68 publications. The evaluation of the collected publications and the resulting research gap is summarized in section 2.2.

Defining Objectives of a Solution: The knowledge gained from the literature review was used to define the design objectives for our method. Our method was to provide systematic guidance for identifying relevant misalignments of business model and business processes in enterprises. The identification of misalignments was to support enterprises in tackling the challenge of aligning their business model and business processes to ensure the achievement of their strategic goals and business objectives over time. To ensure the relevance of our method, a further design objective was to use meta-models or concepts for representing business models and business processes of high theoretical and practical relevance to enterprises.

Design & Development: To fulfill the design objectives, we developed a method that addresses the identified issues (see section 2.2) of existing frameworks and methods. We designed the initial version based on the knowledge gained from the literature review. This included a selection and mapping of theoretically and practically relevant concepts for representing business models and business processes (see section 4.1) and the design of a procedure that covers a top-down and bottom-up analysis of the alignment of a business model and business processes to identify relevant misalignments (see section 4.2). To test the initial version of the method, it was first applied in a pre-study with data collected from a research project. Insights from the pre-study were used to further improve the method. The resulting method is described in section 4.

Demonstration & Evaluation: For demonstration and evaluation purposes, the method was applied in a case study based on Yin (2009). The target was to test the method's validity and utility (Gregor & Hevner, 2013) in a relevant environment. Therefore, the case study was conducted with an Austrian SME. SMEs represent a very relevant group of enterprises as in Austria 99.6% (Federal Ministry of Labour and Economy, 2021) and in the European Union 99% (European Commission, 2024) of all enterprises belong to this category. As the method is not tailored to a specific domain, no restrictions on selecting the enterprise were imposed concerning its domain. The results of the method's application were reviewed with the business expert from the enterprise. Each identified misalignment was reviewed concerning its relevance for the enterprise. The application of the method in the case study, its results and evaluation are described in section 5.

4. THE BM-BP ALIGNMENT ASSESSMENT METHOD

To improve the alignment of business models und business processes, we addressed the identified issues in existing frameworks and developed the method described in this section. It is aimed at practitioners to identify misalignments between the business model and the business processes in an enterprise. In general, a misalignment occurs if a business model-level element does not correspond to a business process-level element or vice versa. Based on the ideas of model transformation of existing frameworks (e.g. Boubaker et al., 2017; Kharmoum et al., 2019), a manual qualitative mapping approach was defined as described by Di Valentin et al. (2012), Di Valentin et al. (2015), Skersys et al. (2012), Iacob et al. (2012), and Meertens et al. (2012), supported by an additional alignment analysis procedure, including a top-down and bottom-up analysis, of business model and business process concepts. The additional alignment analysis procedure is required to overcome the semantic gaps between business model and business process concepts. A mapping approach alone would be insufficient, as stated by Hotie & Gordijn (2019).

As a first step, appropriate meta-models were selected according to their theoretical and practical relevance: The selection of the BMC is confirmed by Boubaker et al. (2017), Iacob et al. (2012), Meertens et al. (2012), Solaimani & Bouwman (2012), and Szopinski et al. (2022). The selection of the BPMN, in turn, is confirmed by Glassey (2008), Hotie & Gordijn (2019), Kharmoum et al. (2019), Melouk et al. (2020), Muehlen et al. (2007), Rhazali et al. (2015), Skersys et al. (2012), Solaimani & Bouwman (2012), and Suratno et al. (2017).

Due to the vast number of concepts within BPM and BPMN and as suggested by Di Valentin et al. (2012), a selection of theoretically and practically relevant concepts was made. These concepts are the process landscape (Dijkman et al., 2016; Dumas et al., 2018; Weske, 2012,), also referred to as process map in the literature, and BPMN concepts from the core meta-model of ADONIS (BOC Group, 2024b). The process landscape provides a top-level overview of all processes and represents a starting point for process discovery in an enterprise (Dijkman et al., 2016; Dumas et al., 2018), which makes it very appropriate for our method to align business model concepts with business processes. The ADONIS core meta-model based on BPMN2.0 is very common in the practical field of business process modeling (Glassey, 2008) and also strongly corresponds with the BPR framework by Reijers & Liman Mansar (2005). The mapping pairs of the selected concepts are shown in Table 1 (marked with "x") and are further described in the following section.

4.1 Selection and Mapping of Concepts

The following concepts have been selected for defining the correspondence between them. The selected meta-model for the architectural level is the BMC by Osterwalder & Pigneur (2010), that is based on the business model ontology (BMO) by Osterwalder & Pigneur (2002). Hence, the following nine concepts are included (Osterwalder & Pigneur, 2002):

- Value Proposition: "describes the bundle of products and services that create value for a specific customer segment"
- Customer Segments: "defines the different groups of people or organizations an enterprise aims to reach and serve"
- Key Activities: "describes the most important things a company must do to make its business model work"
- Customer Relationships: "describes the types of relationships a company establishes with specific customer segments"
- Channels: "describes how a company communicates with and reaches its customer segments to deliver a value proposition"
- Key Resources: "describes the most important assets required to make a business model work"
- Key Partnerships: "describes the network of suppliers and partners that make the business model work"
- Cost Structure: "describes all costs incurred to operate a business model"
- Revenue Streams: "represents the cash a company generates from each customer segment (costs must be subtracted from revenues to create earnings)"

The selected concepts on the implementation level are divided into two parts and represent theoretically and practically relevant business process modeling concepts. In the first part, the process landscape concept (Dijkman et al., 2016; Dumas et al., 2018; Weske, 2012), that serves as a business processes overview in an enterprise, is selected. Further, business processes are categorized into (according to Porter, 1985 and Dumas et al., 2018):

- Core Processes (value-adding processes)
- Management Processes (value-defining processes)
- Support Processes (value-preserving processes)

In the second part, the following business process modeling concepts stemming from the ADONIS core meta-model (BOC Group, 2024b) are selected:

- Product: As defined by Kotler & Keller (2015): "a product is anything that can be offered to a market to satisfy a want or need, including physical goods, services, experiences, events, persons, places, properties, organizations, information, and ideas." (p. 367)
- Role: "The approach incorporates process owner identification as well as responsibilities for carrying out the individual steps in a process (according to RACI principle). This significantly improves process transparency and allows for tracing accountability." (BOC Group, 2024a)
- Performance Indicator: "The approach integrates process performance metrics into BPMN models, facilitating process monitoring, analysis, and improvement." (BOC Group, 2024a)
- Document: "Documents associate inputs and outputs to processes as a whole, and to specific activities (tasks) within the process. This enables variety of analyses of organization's documents." (BOC Group, 2024a)
- Application: "Integration of BPMN with IT systems is mapped, ensuring a seamless connection between business processes and technological implementations." (BOC Group, 2024a)
- Resource: Any resources that are required for the value creation of the enterprise (Penrose, 1959)

The above-mentioned concepts are mapped as shown in Table 1. The BMC concepts map to the process landscape and vice versa as follows. All concepts except "Customer Segments" map to certain categories of processes, either due to their semantic similarity, such as "Value Proposition" and "Core Processes," or due to the fact that the BMC concepts require processes to either acquire, maintain, or retire them (Bider et al., 2017). "Customer Segments" alone do not imply any processes as this concept simply defines customer groups that may be considered as participating roles in one of the processes.

Table 1. Mapping pairs of BMC concepts and selected business process modeling concepts

	Business Model Canvas Concepts								
BPM Concepts	Value Proposition	Customer Segments	Key Activities	Customer Relation-ships	Channels	Key Resources	Key Partner -ships	Cost Structure	Revenue Streams
Core Processes	x	-	x	x	-	-	-	-	x
Management Processes	-	-	x	-	x	x	x	x	x
Support Processes	-	-	x	-	x	x	x	x	-
Product	x	-	x	-	-	-	-	-	x
Performance Indicator	x	x	x	x	-	-	-	x	x
Role	x	x	x	x	x	x	x	x	x
Document	x	x	x	x	x	x	x	x	x
Application	x	x	x	x	x	x	x	x	x
Resource	-	-	-	-	-	x	-	-	-

The BMC concepts map to the selected business process modeling concepts and vice versa as follows. Due to the fact that all BMC concepts except "Customer Segments" map to processes, these concepts also map to specific roles, documents, and applications in the context of the described BMC concept. Also, "Customer Segments" map these business process concepts as various customer groups imply specific roles, documents, or applications to represent them on the implementation level. In addition, "Value Proposition," "Customer Segments," "Key Activities," "Customer Relationships," "Cost Structures," and "Revenue Streams" map to "Performance Indicator." Due to their semantic similarity, "Key Resources" maps to "Resource." As "Value Proposition" and "Key Activities" include the value-creating aspects of the business, and as this value is transferred to customers as products through certain "Customer Relationships" and generates a "Revenue Stream," these four concepts map to "Product."

4.2 Alignment Analysis Procedure

The procedure consists of five sequential steps (see Figure 2), including a top-down and bottom-up analysis of a BMC and the corresponding description of an enterprise's business processes. Step 1 and step 2 cover the top-down analysis from the BMC to the PL and the process description. Step 3 and step 4 cover the bottom-up analysis from the PL and the process description to the BMC. Step 5 analyzes the PL and the process description to provide insights on the completeness of the business process documentation. The analysis results in the identification and classification of misalignments between the business model and the business processes. The identified misalignments are qualitatively classified in three categories (minor, medium, and major) indicating the potential business impact of the misalignment, similar to the classification of nonconformities in quality audits (ISO 19011:2018).

As a starting point, the alignment analyst needs to retrieve the completely filled BMC and the business process documentation from the enterprise to be analyzed. Then the analysis is conducted solely by the alignment analyst according to following procedure:

In **Step 1** a top-down analysis of the BMC and the processes on the process landscape is conducted. The content of each BMC concept is compared with the corresponding concept in the process landscape according to the defined mapping (see Table 1). Each misalignment is documented on the process landscape and classified as follows:

- In case the content of a BMC concept does not correspond to any existing process in the process landscape, the misalignment is classified as "Missing in PL [major]."
- In case a corresponding process can be identified in the process landscape, but the correspondence and/or the naming of the corresponding process is ambiguous (e.g. too generic), the misalignment is classified as "Not specific enough in PL [medium]."
- In case a BMC concept corresponds to a process in the process landscape, but the categorization of the process is incorrect, the misalignment is classified as "Wrong categorization in PL (Mgmt., Core, Support) [minor]."

In **Step 2** a top-down analysis of the BMC and the process descriptions is conducted. Again, the content of each BMC concept is compared with the elements of the corresponding concepts of the process description according to the defined mapping (see Table 1). Each misalignment is documented in the process description and classified as follows:

- In case the content of a BMC concept does not correspond to any element of the process description, the misalignment is classified as "Missing in Process Description [major]."
- In case a corresponding element of the process description can be identified, but the correspondence and/or the naming of the potentially corresponding element is ambiguous (e.g. too generic), the misalignment is classified as "Not specific enough in Process Description [medium]."

In **Step 3** a bottom-up analysis of the process landscape and BMC is conducted. Each process of the process landscape is compared with the content of each BMC concept according to the defined mapping (see Table 1). Each misalignment is documented in the BMC and classified as follows:

- In case a process does not correspond to any content of the BMC concepts, the misalignment is classified as "Missing in BM concept [major]."

In **Step 4** a bottom-up analysis of the process description and BMC is conducted. Each element of the process description is compared with the content of each BMC concept according to the defined mapping (see Table 1). Each misalignment is documented in the BMC and classified as follows:

- In case an element of the process description does not correspond to any content of the BMC concepts, the misalignment is classified as "Missing in BM concept [major]."
- In case a corresponding content of the BMC can be identified, but the correspondence and/or the description of the potentially corresponding concept is ambiguous (e.g. too generic), the misalignment is classified as "Not specific enough in BM concept [medium]."

In **Step 5** the process landscape and the process description are analyzed to gain insights on the significance of the analysis results of Step 1 to Step 4.

- In case a process is defined in the process landscape, but there is no corresponding process description, the finding is classified as "Missing Process Description [major]."
- In case a process description exists, but there is no corresponding process on the process landscape, the finding is classified as "Missing in PL [medium]."

- In case a process is doubly defined on the process landscape or in the process description, the finding is classified as "Doubly defined [minor]."

The results of the analysis, the identified misalignments, are then reviewed with the business expert to ensure that only relevant misalignments in accordance with the design objectives (see section 3) are included in the final result.

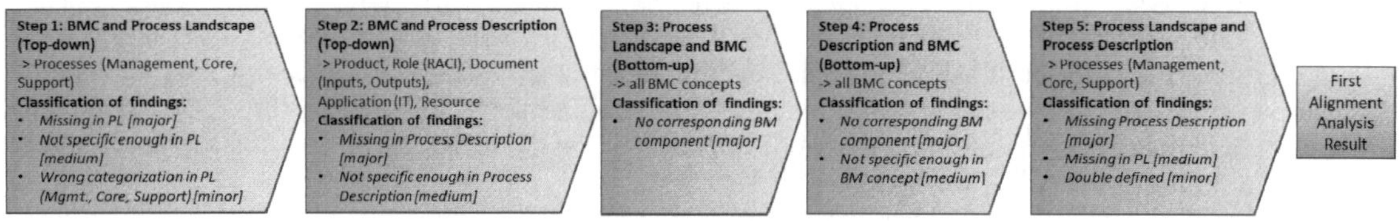

Figure 2. Alignment analysis procedure

5. DEMONSTRATION AND EVALUATION

The method was demonstrated and evaluated with an industrial case study at an Austrian SME with the objective of testing its validity and utility in a relevant environment. Its utility is evaluated by assessing how many of the identified misalignments are relevant from a business expert's perspective. As already stated in section 3, SMEs represent a very relevant group of enterprises in Austria and the European Union. The selected enterprise is a young and growing enterprise which trades Golfcarts for various purposes, including the provision of related services. The CEO wishes to find out if there are any things he has forgotten to formalize, either in the business model or in the business process documentation. Due to the size of the enterprise, the CEO acts as the business model designer and process designer and has profound knowledge on both levels. This makes him an ideal candidate for acting as the business expert in the study. We assumed the role of alignment analyst. In the first meeting we introduced our method to the CEO and collected the existing business model description (in the form of a BMC) and the existing business process documentation (PL and process descriptions) for the analysis. The next step was to conduct the alignment analysis according to our defined procedure. In the final step, we conducted a workshop with the CEO in which all our findings were reviewed and evaluated according to their relevance from the perspective of the CEO. The results are presented in the following section. The data provided for analysis by the enterprise was in German. Therefore, the presented examples in the following section have been translated into English.

Table 2 shows the numbers of identified misalignments in the first analysis and the remaining relevant misalignments after the review for each analysis step and in total. The table entry "-" means that this classification is not applicable in this specific step.

Table 2. Overview of the alignment analysis results

	First analysis result / Final analysis result after review					
Step	1	2	3	4	5	**Total**
# Total findings	**14/12**	**48/46**	**4/4**	**0/0**	**10/9**	**76/71**
Major	7/6	42/40	4/4	0/0	3/3	56/53
Medium	6/5	6/6	-	0/0	2/2	14/13
Minor	1/1	-	-	-	5/4	6/5

71 out of 76 identified misalignments were assessed as relevant by the business expert, which indicates a high utility of the method. The following excerpts from the case study illustrate how misalignments were identified in each step:

Step 1 - BMC and Process Landscape: The analysis of the following content of "Key Activities" led to the identification of two misalignments: *"Make purchases: Purchasing plays an important role in retail, especially in the area of larger order quantities, not only larger discounts, but also cost savings in transportation are possible." "Make purchases"* is clearly stated as a "Key Activity." No corresponding process could be identified in the PL. Therefore, this misalignment was classified as *"Missing in PL [major]."* For the statement *"cost savings in transportation,"* the corresponding process *"Transportation*

& Logistics" was identified. The process was categorized as a supportive process in the PL. As the statement is part of the key activities and as the enterprise is in the trading industry, there are arguments for categorizing this process as a core process. Therefore, this misalignment was classified as *"Wrong categorization in PL (Mgmt., Core, Support) [minor]."*

In the "Value Proposition," the *"Fulfillment of special requests through tailor-made special conversions"* is stated. No corresponding process that covers this value proposition could be identified in the PL. Therefore, this misalignment was also classified as *"Missing in PL [major]."*

Step 2 - BMC and Process Description: The further analysis of the statement *"Fulfillment of special requests through tailor-made special conversions"* in the BMC concept "Value Proposition" reveals the absence of the product *"Special requests"* and a missing performance indicator that indicates the *"Degree of fulfillment of special requests."* Therefore, these misalignments were classified as *"Missing Process Description [major]."*

In "Customer Segments," the terms "Private persons" and "Industry" are mentioned. The corresponding element *"Customer"* was identified in the process description. As *"Customer"* does not distinguish between the two terms mentioned in the BMC, this misalignment was classified as *"Not specific enough in Process Description [medium]."* In addition, no "Application" could be identified in the process description that supports the customer relationship management. Therefore, this misalignment was classified as *"Missing Process Description [major]."*

In "Channels," social media including *"Instagram," "Facebook," "LinkedIn,"* and *"YouTube"* are mentioned. The process description contained the corresponding "Applications" Instagram and Facebook. *LinkedIn* and YouTube were missing. Therefore, this misalignment was classified as *"Missing Process Description [major]."*

Step 3 - Process Landscape and BMC: The four processes *"Renting," "Carry out repair, service and assembly work," "Offer aftersales,"* and *"Repairs under guarantee/warranty"* have no representing elements in the respective concepts of the BMC. Therefore, these misalignments were classified as *"Missing in BM concept [major]."* These processes create value for the customer and should therefore be represented in the "Value Proposition" and/or "Key Activities" of the BMC.

Step 4 - Process Description and BMC: No misalignments were identified in this step. All defined elements correspond to the described BMC concepts.

Step 5 - Process Landscape and Process Description: Three defined processes lacked a process description. Two described processes were missing on the process landscape. And four processes were doubly defined in the provided process documentation. As this indicates that the process documentation was incomplete, the analysis, especially in step 3 and 4, has to be interpreted as incomplete as well.

6. DISCUSSION AND CONCLUSION

Misalignments of business models and business processes may lead to issues in an enterprise, such as not achieving its strategic goals (Boubaker et al., 2014; Di Valentin et al., 2015). Therefore, we developed a method for identifying such misalignments, addressing the identified issues of existing approaches in this field of research (see section 2.2) as a first important step toward the alignment of these two levels. The method was applied in a relevant environment (see section 5) and the evaluation of the analysis result (identification of 71 relevant misalignments) clearly indicates that the method identifies relevant misalignments of a business model and business processes in an enterprise. The identified misalignments in step 1, 2, and 3 indicate that a top-down and bottom-up analysis is relevant in this context, even though step 4 did not encounter any misalignments. This might be explained by the result of step 5, which analyzes the PL and the processes description and indicates that the business process documentation is incomplete.

Our proposed method contributes to the understanding of the relationship of business models and business processes and to further development of methods and tools to assess the alignment of business models and business processes by using DSR. The systematic literature review reveals issues with existing frameworks and methods and elaborates how business models and business processes are linked (see section 2.2). These insights were used to design and develop a method that addresses the identified issues and provides systematic guidance to identify relevant misalignments of an enterprise's business model and business processes. The result of the method can be used as a starting point for aligning the business model and the business processes.

Despite the very promising results and success of the presented case study, more studies are required to further evaluate the method's general applicability and validity. In its current formulation, the method is based on the underlying concept of the BMC and uses BPM concepts. The integration of other BM representations, such as the REA accounting model (McCarthy, 1982), the e3-value (Gordijn & Akkermans, 2001), or the STOF (Bouwman et al., 2008), and additional BPM concepts could increase its general applicability.

Future research may also focus on investigating the applicability of the framework in large enterprises or even on a business ecosystem level with potentially multiple business models and a vast number of business processes. For this purpose, further research is required to investigate to which extent certain aspects of the analysis can be automated to also tackle the challenge of scalability. Additionally, further quantification of the analysis result, for which the basis has been established by identifying and classifying the misalignments, may be of future interest. A further unanswered question to be systematically addressed is how to properly handle misalignments in order to achieve an alignment of the business model and business processes.

REFERENCES

Al-Debei, M. M., and Avison, D., (2010). Developing a unified framework of the business model concept. *European Journal of Information Systems*, Vol. 19, No. (3), pp. 359–376.

Al-Debei, M. M. et al, (2008). Defining the Business Model in the New World of Digital Business. *AMCIS 2008 Proceedings*. Toronto, Canada.

Aldin, L. and De Cesare, S., (2011). A literature review on business process modelling: New frontiers of reusability. *Enterprise Information Systems*, Vol. 5, No. 3, pp. 359–383.

Amit, R. H. and Zott, C., (2010). Business Model Innovation: Creating Value in Times of Change. IESE Business School Working Paper No. 870.

Betzwieser, B. et al, (2020). At the Nexus of Business Models and Business Processes: A Systematic Literature Review. *Proceedings of Pacific Asia Conference on Information Systems (PACIS)*. Dubai, VAE.

Bider, I. et al, (2017). A fractal enterprise model and its application for business development. *Software & Systems Modeling*, Vol. 16, No. 3, pp. 663–689.

BOC Group, (2024a). ADONIS BPMN Guide. BOC Products & Services AG. https://docs.boc-group.com/adonis/en/bpmn_guide/#about-this-guide

BOC Group, (2024b). ADONIS Method and Metamodel. BOC Products & Services AG. https://docs.boc-group.com/adonis/en/docs/15.0/user_manual/amm-000000/

Bonakdar, A. et al, (2013). Transformative Influence of Business Processes on the Business Model: Classifying the State of the Practice in the Software Industry. *Proceedings of 46th Hawaii International Conference on System Sciences*. Hawaii, USA, pp. 3920–3929.

Boubaker, A. et al, (2014). Value-Chain Discovery from Business Process Models. *The Practice of Enterprise Modeling*, Vol. 197, pp. 26–41.

Boubaker, A. et al, (2017). A pattern-based approach to extract REA value models from business process models. *Intelligent Systems in Accounting, Finance and Management*, Vol. 24, No. 1, pp. 29–48.

Bouwman, H. et al, (2008). *Mobile Service Innovation and Business Models*. Springer, Berlin, Heidelberg.

Chesbrough, H., (2002). The role of the business model in capturing value from innovation: Evidence from Xerox Corporation's technology spin-off companies. *Industrial and Corporate Change*, Vol. 11, No. 3, pp. 529–555.

Chesbrough, H., (2010). Business Model Innovation: Opportunities and Barriers. *Long Range Planning*, Vol. 43, No. 2–3, pp. 354–363.

Danneels, E., (2002). The dynamics of product innovation and firm competences. *Strategic Management Journal*, Vol. 23, No. 12, pp. 1095–1121.

Davenport, T. H. and Short, J. E., (1990). The new industrial engineering: Information technology and business process redesign. *Sloan Management Review*, Vol. 31, No. 4.

Davenport, T. H., (1993). *Process innovation: Reengineering work through information technology*. Harvard Business School Press, Boston, Massachusetts.

Di Valentin, C. et al, (2012). Towards a framework for transforming business models into business processes. *Proceedings of Americas Conference on Information Systems (AMCIS)*. Detroit, USA.

Di Valentin, C. et al, (2015). Analysis of IT-Business models towards theory development of business model transformation and monitoring. *Proceedings of the 5th International Symposium on Business Modeling and Software Design (BMSD)*. Milan, Italy, pp. 171–177.

Dijkman, R. et al, (2016). Business process architectures: Overview, comparison and framework. *Enterprise Information Systems*, Vol. 10, No. 2, pp. 129–158.

Dougherty, D., (1992). A practice-centered model of organizational renewal through product innovation. *Strategic Management Journal*, Vol. 13, No. S1, pp. 77–92.

Dumas, M. et al, (2018). *Fundamentals of Business Process Management*. 2nd ed., Springer, Berlin, Heidelberg.

European Commission, (2024). SMEs—European Commission. Entrepreneurship and Small and Medium-Sized Enterprises (SMEs). https://single-market-economy.ec.europa.eu/smes_en

Federal Ministry of Labour and Economy, (2021). Small and medium enterprises in Austria – facts and figures. Bundesministerium Für Arbeit Und Wirtschaft. https://www.bmaw.gv.at/en/Topics/Business-Location/Small-and-medium-sized-Enterprises-SMEs/SME-in-Austria-facts-and-figures.html

Glassey, O., (2008). A case study on process modelling—Three questions and three techniques. *Decision Support Systems*, Vol. 44, No. 4, pp. 842–853.

Gordijn, J. and Akkermans, H., (2001). Designing and evaluating e-business models. IEEE Intelligent Systems,

Gregor, S. and Hevner, A. R., (2013). Positioning and Presenting Design Science Research for Maximum Impact. *MIS Quarterly*, Vol. 37, No. 2, pp. 337-356.

Hammer, M. and Champy, J., (1993). *Business Reengineering: Die Radikalkur für das Unternehmen*. Campus-Verlag, Frankfurt, Germany.

Hevner, A. R., et al, (2004). Design Science in Information Systems Research. *MIS Quarterly*, Vol. 28, No. 1, pp. 75–105.

Heyl, B. H., (2014). Literature Survey on Business Model-Based Integration of Business and Process Architecture. *Proceedings of the 33rd International Conference of the Chilean Computer Science Society (SCCC)*.

Hotie, F. and Gordijn, J., (2019). Value-Based Process Model Design. *Business & Information Systems Engineering*, Vol. 61, No. 2, pp. 163–180.

Iacob, M. E. et al, (2012). From enterprise architecture to business models and back. *Software & Systems Modeling*, Vol. 13, pp. 1059-1083.

Kharmoum, N. et al, (2019). A method of model transformation in MDA approach from E3value model to BPMN2 diagrams in CIM level. *IAENG International Journal of Computer Science*, Vol. 46, No. 4.

Kotler, P. and Keller, K. L., (2015). *Marketing management (15. ed)*. Pearson Education, London, England.

Lara Machado, P. et al, (2023). Methods that bridge business models and business processes: A synthesis of the literature. *Business Process Management Journal*, Vol. 29, No. 8, pp. 48–74.

Lara Machado, P. et al., (2024). Navigating Business Model Redesign: The Compass Method for Identifying Changes to the Operating Model. *Business & Information Systems Engineering*, Vol. 66, pp. 607–638.

Magretta, J., (2002). Why Business Models Matter. *Harvard Business Review,* Vol. 80, pp. 86-92.

McCarthy, W., (1982). The REA Accounting Model: A Generalized Framework for Accounting Systems Shared Data Environment. *The Accounting Review*.

Meertens, L. O., et al, (2012). Mapping the business model canvas to ArchiMate. *Proceedings of the 27th Annual ACM Symposium on Applied Computing*. Trento, Italy, pp. 1694–1701.

Melouk, M. et al, (2020). An Approach for Transforming CIM to PIM up To PSM in MDA. *Procedia Computer Science*, Vol. 170, pp. 869–874.

Mitchell, D., & Coles, C. (2003). The ultimate competitive advantage of continuing business model innovation. Journal of Business Strategy, 24(5), 15–21.

Muehlen, M. et al, (2007). Business Process and Business Rule Modeling Languages for Compliance Management: A Representational Analysis. *Proceedings of the International Conference on Conceptual Modeling*

Object Management Group, (2015). Business Process Model and Notation (BPMN) Version 2.0.2. https://www.omg.org/spec/BPMN/2.0.2

Osterwalder, A. and Pigneur, Y., (2002). An eBusiness Model Ontology for Modeling eBusiness. *BLED 2002 Proceedings*.

Osterwalder, A. and Pigneur, Y., (2010). *Business Model Generation: A Handbook for Visionaries, Game Changers, and Challengers (First Edition)*. John Wiley and Sons, New York, USA.

Osterwalder, A. et al, (2005). Clarifying Business Models: Origins, Present, and Future of the Concept. *Communications of the Association for Information Systems*, Vol. 16.

Peffers, K., et al, (2007). A Design Science Research Methodology for Information Systems Research. *Journal of Management Information Systems*, Vol. 24, No. 3, pp. 45–77.

Penrose, E. T., (1959). *The Theory of the Growth of the Firm*. Wiley, New York, USA.

Porter, M. E. (1985). Competitive Advantage: Creating and Sustaining Superior Performance. FREE PRESS.

Reijers, H. A. and Liman Mansar, S., (2005). Best practices in business process redesign: an overview and qualitative evaluation of successful redesign heuristics. *Omega*, Vol. 33, No. 4, pp. 283-306.

Rhazali, Y. et al, (2015). A methodology for transforming CIM to PIM through UML: From business view to information system view. *Third World Conference on Complex Systems (WCCS)*. Marrakech, Morocco, pp. 1–6.

Scheer, A.-W., (1994). *Business Process Engineering*. Springer, Berlin, Heidelberg.

Scheer, A.-W., (2002). *ARIS — Vom Geschäftsprozess zum Anwendungssystem*. Springer, Berlin, Heidelberg.

Schief, M. et al, (2012). Transforming Software Business Models into Business Processes: *Proceedings of the 14th International Conference on Enterprise Information Systems*. Wroclaw, Poland, pp. 167–172.

Schumpeter, J. A., (1939). *Business Cycles: A Theoretical, Historical, and Statistical Analysis of the Capitalist Process*. McGraw-Hill Book Company, Incorporated, New York, USA.

Skersys, T. et al, (2012). The enrichment of BPMN business process model with SBVR business vocabulary and rules. *Journal of Computing and Information Technology*, Vol. 20, No. 3, pp. 143–150.

Solaimani, S. and Bouwman, H. (2012). A framework for the alignment of business model and business processes: A generic model for trans-sector innovation. *Business Process Management Journal*, Vol. 18, No. 4, pp. 655–679.

Suratno, B. et al, (2017). Towards operationalization of business models: Designing service compositions for service-dominant business models. 29th International Conference on Advanced Information Systems Engineering, CAiSE 2017, pp. 179–187.

Suratno, B. et al, (2018). A Method for Operationalizing Service-Dominant Business Models into Conceptual Process Models. In B. Shishkov (Ed.), *Business Modeling and Software Design*, Vol. 319, pp. 133–148. Springer International Publishing.

Szopinski, D. et al, (2022). Modeling Business Models: A cross-disciplinary Analysis of Business Model Modeling Languages and Directions for Future Research. Communications of the Association for Information Systems, 51, 774–841.

Teece, D. J., (2010). Business Models, Business Strategy and Innovation. *Long Range Planning*, Vol. 43, No. 2–3, pp. 172–194.

Teece, D. J., (2018). Business models and dynamic capabilities. *Long Range Planning*, Vol. 51, No. 1, pp. 40–49.

Trist, E., (1981). The Evolution of Socio-Technical Systems. Toronto, Ontario: Ontario Ministry of Labour, Ontario Quality of Working Life Centre.

Van Der Aalst, W. M. P., (2013). Business Process Management: A Comprehensive Survey. *ISRN Software Engineering*, Vol. 2013, pp. 1–37.

vom Brocke, J. et al, (2015). Standing on the Shoulders of Giants: Challenges and Recommendations of Literature Search in Information Systems Research. *Communications of the Association for Information Systems*, Vol. 37.

Webster, J. and Watson, R. T., (2002), Analyzing the past to prepare for the future: writing a literature review. *MIS Quarterly, JSTOR*, Vol. 26, No. 2, pp. 8-23.

Weske, M. (2012). Business Process Management. Springer Berlin Heidelberg

Wirtz, B. W. et al, (2022). THE CONCEPT OF BUSINESS MODELS–DEVELOPMENT AND RESEARCH PERSPECTIVES. *International Journal of Innovation Management*, Vol. 26, No. 07.

Wohlin, C., (2014), Guidelines for snowballing in systematic literature studies and a replication in software engineering. *Proceedings of the 18th International Conference on Evaluation and Assessment in Software Engineering*.

Yin, R. K., (2009). *Case study research: Design and methods (Vol. 5)*. Sage.

Zacarias, M. and Martins, P. V., (2012). Aligning Business Processes and Work Practices. *Procedia Technology*, Vol. 5, pp. 234–243.

Zott, C. et al, (2011). The Business Model: Recent Developments and Future Research. *Journal of Management*, Vol. 37, No. 4, 1019–1042.

TOWARDS UNDERSTANDING THE IMPACT OF REPORTING REQUIREMENTS ON IS-ENABLED DYNAMIC CAPABILITIES FOR SUSTAINABILITY

Philipp Staudt[1] and Marie-Claude Boudreau[2]
[1]Carl von Ossietzky Universität Oldenburg
Wirtschaftsinformatik für Umwelt und Nachhaltigkeit, Environmental & Sustainable Information Systems, Department of Computer Science, Germany
[2]University of Georgia
Management Information System Department, Athens, GA, USA

ABSTRACT

The European Union's Green Deal introduced significant sustainability reporting regulations, compelling organizations to develop dynamic capabilities for sustainability. However, the role of information systems in building these capabilities, and the development processes of such capabilities more broadly, remain insufficiently understood. To address this gap, we conducted a case study involving an organization subject to these new regulations. Through an inductive approach, we developed a process-model for the development of IT-enabled organizational capabilities for sustainability and found that information systems-enabled dynamic capabilities strengthen other capabilities. These results broaden our understanding of the role of IS in developing organizational sustainability.

KEYWORDS

Green Information Systems, Digital Sustainability, Dynamic Capabilities, Sustainability Reporting, Case Study

1. INTRODUCTION

Sustainability is central to the political arena on both sides of the Atlantic. In the US, the Inflation Reduction Act promotes sustainable technology (Bistline et al., 2023). In the European Union (EU), large companies are now required to report on their ESG performance in standardized ways under the umbrella of Green Deal regulation (Baumüller and Grbenic, 2021). The objective is to make financial markets aware of potential sustainability risks within these companies and to thereby incentivize them to become more sustainable. This regulation significantly expands the number of companies required to provide mandatory, standardized sustainability reports. The main regulatory reporting effort under the Green Deal is the Corporate Sustainability Reporting Directive (CSRD) (Baumüller and Grbenic, 2021). Depending on the activities of an organization, the CSRD requires companies to report up to over 1,000 data points across 12 sustainability standards (European Parliament and Council of the European Union, 2022). It represents an expansion of existing non-financial reporting requirements. The report is now a mandatory component of the yearly financial report, and managers are liable for incorrect information.

In responding to the CSRD, organizations must develop a range of capabilities, many at the interface of accounting and sustainability. Specifically, some organizations may develop what the literature calls dynamic capabilities for sustainability (Wu et al., 2013). Dynamic capabilities enable companies to repurpose resources in response to a changing environment within their industry (Eisenhardt and Martin, 2000). Organizations are known to invest in such capabilities in environments of high market dynamism and uncertainty (Eisenhardt and Martin, 2000; Felin and Powell, 2016). Examples of dynamic capabilities for sustainability include the development of a proactive sustainability strategy or the design of Green IS with decision support capabilities for new sustainability measures (Mousavi et al., 2018; Wu et al., 2013). Although dynamic capabilities related to sustainability have been recognized (Wu et al., 2013), our understanding of how these capabilities are built, how they interact with one another, and the influence of information systems (IS) within this context remains limited. This knowledge gap is central to our research, anchoring the research question:

What is the role of information systems in the process of developing dynamic capabilities for sustainability?

To address this question, we conducted a study aimed at developing a process model that illustrates the role of IS in the development of dynamic capabilities in the context of Green Deal sustainability reporting regulations. Our approach was positivist, as we employed an objective, well-defined, reproducible approach to collect and analyze our data. It was also inductive as our goal was not to test a theory but to uncover a context-specific process. We employed a qualitative case study method, focusing on an organization facing EU Green Deal reporting directives. The implementation of these regulations creates a unique opportunity to understand the processes that lead to IS-enabled dynamic capabilities for sustainability. Our study has theoretical implications for the literature on dynamic capabilities by describing the possibility of reinforcing relationships among dynamic capabilities. It also contributes to the Green IS literature by describing the role of IS in developing dynamic capabilities for sustainability. Practically, our work provides guidance for organizations as they consider investing in building dynamic capabilities for sustainability.

2. THEORETICAL FOUNDATION

Dynamic capabilities refer to specific ensembles of processes and resources in organizations aimed at reconfiguring their resource base (Winter, 2003). For instance, the autonomy of teams and how they choose to support projects have been described as a dynamic capability (Felin and Powell, 2016). As such, dynamic capabilities are concrete organizational routines that can be observed (Eisenhardt and Martin, 2000; Winter, 2003). Dynamic capabilities must be differentiated from ordinary capabilities, which are needed to operate and improve the core business (Winter, 2003). Dynamic capabilities are typically classified into three types: sensing, seizing, and transforming (Teece, 2007). Sensing describes how new information is incorporated into the firm and disseminated. Seizing relates to the organization's ability to respond to environmental cues and exploit new opportunities. Transforming is the organization's ability to keep business strategy and resources aligned during the evolution of new business models (Teece, 2018).

Several authors have argued that the need for dynamic capabilities depends on the volatility, i.e., dynamism, and uncertainty of the business environment (Eisenhardt and Martin, 2000; Felin and Powell, 2016). This is one reason why IS researchers have long been interested in dynamic capabilities. In markets disrupted by digital technology, even well-developed ordinary capabilities that create a unique competitive advantage may suddenly become obsolete. Another reason is that dynamic capabilities are closely related to knowledge management activities within organizations (Paarup Nielsen, 2006; Prieto and Easterby-Smith, 2006). For instance, knowledge development, recombination, and use have been defined as dynamic capabilities (Paarup Nielsen, 2006). A concrete example of such dynamic capabilities is the use of company-wide social media to disseminate and recombine knowledge (Dwivedi et al., 2022), allowing knowledge exchange between employees (Prieto and Easterby-Smith, 2006). Furthermore, dynamic capabilities have been researched in various IS fields, such as the Internet of Things (Sullivan et al., 2023). Parida et al., (2016) showed a link between ICT use and dynamic capabilities, finding that reported ICT use positively correlates with perceived dynamic capabilities in organizations. The concept of dynamic capabilities in IS has been used in various forms, with a need for more conceptual clarity (Steininger et al., 2022). It is important to note that digital technology itself is not a dynamic capability; rather, dynamic capabilities are combinations of resources and processes. While resources can be quickly acquired, dynamic capabilities must be developed.

3. METHODOLOGY

We conducted a positivist, inductive study aimed at developing a process model illustrating the role of IS in the development of dynamic capabilities and their interdependence within the context of ESG regulation. We employed a qualitative single study approach, focusing on an organization facing regulations associated with the European Green Deal. The organization is a medium-sized consumer goods and manufacturing company from the German SDAX index. To maintain its anonymity, we refer to this organization as SDAX. We chose SDAX as it represents a revelatory case, offering a rare opportunity to observe and analyze a phenomenon that had previously been inaccessible.

3.1 Case Description

SDAX is one of the largest companies in Europe within a specific consumer product market, employing over 3,000 people and generating millions in annual revenue. The company had been reporting according to GRI guidelines for over a decade, with sustainability reporting previously handled by its communications department. We began interviewing employees in April 2024. At that time, the company had not yet selected a supplier for a Green Deal reporting software system but had decided to purchase a specialized software package rather than develop one internally. Our interviews took place throughout the process of selecting a system supplier and hiring a sustainability manager to oversee the reporting process. The new sustainability manager was onboarded at the end of our case study and we were able to interview him as well.

3.2 Data Collection

Using a sample covering all relevant sustainability roles in the company, we conducted 14 semi-structured interviews (see Table 1). To ensure consistency across interviews, we developed a standardized set of questions addressing key areas: sustainability reporting processes, organizational structures supporting these efforts, software tools used for reporting, and the collection and application of sustainability data. Ethical considerations were prioritized by obtaining informed consent and respecting participants' autonomy regarding the use, recording, and interpretation of their responses.

Table 1. Overview of conducted interviews ordered by date

No.	Date	Role	Duration
1	05.04.2024	Former Responsible of Sustainability Reporting	82
2	24.04.2024	Environmental Reporting	47
3	25.04.2024	Head of Environmental Protection	56
4	29.04.2024	Environmental Reporting	46
5	29.04.2024	Head of Regional Production Plant	48
6	30.04.2024	Managing Director Switzerland	58
7	30.04.2024	Technical lead, regional plant	54
8	30.04.2024	Controlling & Finance, Responsible for Tool Selection	57
9	02.05.2024	Board Member Marketing & Communication	56
10	06.05.2024	Head of Communications (responsible for sustainability reporting)	48
11	08.05.2024	Technical lead, regional plant	34
12	15.08.2024	Controlling & Finance, Responsible for Tool Selection 2nd	48
13	16.08.2024	Head of Environmental Protection 2nd	28
14	21.08.2024	New Head of Sustainability (since May 2024)	52

3.3 Coding and Analysis

We developed a coding scheme that included key constructs from the dynamic capabilities literature (see Table 2). After coding the interviews, we summarized the results for each code, emphasizing both the nature of the coded segments and the connections interviewees made between different codes.

Table 2. Coding tree

Code	Reference
Investment in dynamic capabilities	Teece (2007)
- Sensing	Teece (2007)
- - Updating sustainability knowledge base	Wu et al. (2013)
- - Maintaining communication channels with stakeholders	Wu et al. (2013)
- Seizing	Teece (2007)
- - Sustainability governance structure	Wu et al. (2013)
- - Sustainability strategy	Wu et al. (2013)
- - Cross-functional knowledge sharing	Wu et al. (2013)
- Transforming	Teece (2007)
-- Standardized environmental management system	Wu et al. (2013)
-- Sustainability performance measurement	Wu et al. (2013)
-- Organizational learning and training	Wu et al. (2013)

4. RESULTS

We identified four temporal phases in which sustainability reporting was implemented within the analyzed case: Understanding, Preparing, Reinforcing, and Exploiting. Understanding begins with the initial sensemaking process, which involves identifying the relevance of the reporting regulation for the organization, and ends with the first actions taken toward technically fulfilling the regulation. Next, the Preparing phase includes all the preparatory steps, such as materiality and gap analyses and the definition of reporting elements. Reinforcing, begins after the preparation phase and ends with the filing of the first completed report. Last, Exploiting begins after the first report is filed. It remains uncertain whether this process is recurring or one-time, but it is likely that organizations will revisit parts of this process when new products are introduced, regulations are amended, or materiality assessments change. These phases help us in characterizing the establishment of dynamic capabilities over time. The resulting process model is depicted in Figure 1 and its connections and phases are described in the following sections. Dashed lines represent initiated processes, whereas solid lines describe processes that were already observed during the interviews. The greyed-out boxes represent strategic planning that were described but not yet implemented at the time of interviewing. The following paragraphs further elaborate on this figure.

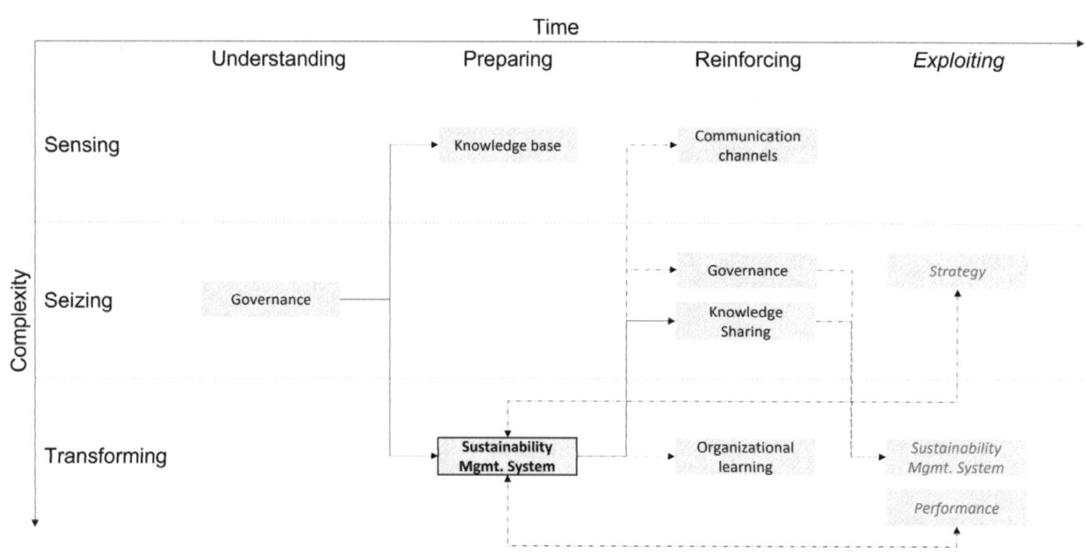

Figure 1. IT-enabled development of dynamic capabilities for sustainability

4.1 Understanding

SDAX began responding to the Green Deal reporting directives by expanding its governance structure to include both the accounting department and the sustainability team ("*So, I'm still relatively new [...]. I started in November in Group Accounting, in the finance department. Our task is to find suitable software for CSRD because we support the sustainability team in this task*", Int.#8). Plans quickly emerged to extend the current sustainability structure with a new head of sustainability ("*We have a sustainability circle in which department heads from various affected departments such as HR, purchasing, environment, IT and logistics come together. It's quarterly, as far as I know [...] The new position for the Head of Sustainability is to be created [...]",* Int.#2). Much of the governance structure depended on the role of the incoming head of sustainability. One interviewee acknowledged that the reporting task "*[...] really is going to be a mammoth task. And we can't do it with our existing resources.*" (Int.#10). While they had been reporting on sustainability activities for over a decade, responsibility for the report still resided in the corporate communications department ("*It used to be in the communications department, but there is to be a new position, a divisional head for sustainability, where this will then be located [...]",* Int.# 2). SDAX expected to dedicate more resources to sustainability reporting ("*And in this respect, yes, more costs for external consultants, more costs for software and more costs for staff development. And perhaps that's not just an increase in staff, it's also an opportunity cost [...]",* Int.# 9). The first step in preparing for the CSRD was conducting the materiality analysis, during which all relevant employees were identified *("[...] when it came to the materiality matrix and the gap analysis, core teams were of course formed.",* Int.# 4). This laid the foundation for the future governance structure for sustainability.

4.2 Preparing

SDAX needed to update its existing knowledge base. One informant remarked, "*We've been doing sustainability reporting for 14 or 15 years. So we're not completely unprepared. But the requirements of the new directive still demand that we do some things differently. For example, we have to show the impact of our activities, the policy behind them, the target definitions and so on*" (Int.#3), highlighting the organization's prior experience while acknowledging the new challenges posed by mandatory standardized reporting.

At the time of the interviews, reporting was still conducted entirely using Excel, but the procurement and implementation of a dedicated sustainability system were planned ("*I'm hoping that the software will eliminate all that a bit, that it will give us a bit more structure and perhaps make it easier for us to calculate the data later on.",* Int.#4). The procurement of the software had been postponed until a head of sustainability was hired, ensuring that their requirements could be included *("[...] someone's coming on June 1st. [...] So I'm going to wait four weeks before we tackle such issues together with the new colleague.",* Int.#10).

The eventual sustainability management system was intended to encompass the entire sustainability organization, including the accounting department ("*It is already planned that the new software should be comprehensive and suitable not only for sustainability, but also for financial reporting such as the EU taxonomy. If possible, everything should be covered by one software*.", Int.#2). The system was necessary to manage the complexity of sustainability reporting ("*At that time, they already knew that the CSRD was coming and that we needed software, as the amount of data we had to record could no longer be displayed and audited in Excel for our auditors.",* Int.#8). This need was reiterated in terms of the audit trails required for reporting and the corresponding governance structure that would need to be represented in the system ("*When the auditor asks for proof, I run off within the company and say: Please give me proof for XY, and I'll put them all together and then have to upload them all*", Int.#1; and "[...] *we're currently looking for software that helps us collect data, but ultimately also maps everything else so that it's audit-proof.",* Int.#3). Auditability was a central aspect of the software procurement specifications for a sustainability management system.

The further integration of the sustainability software within the governance structure was already foreseen ("*Introducing the software wouldn't be a problem at first. Not everyone around me would need to be trained. But of course, if there are data officers who have to provide certain data, I have to show them how important the topic is and that I definitely need the data to write the sustainability report",* Int.#8). An onboarding program was one of the required functionalities in the procurement specifications.

4.3 Reinforcing

The interviewees were already making connections between the eventual system and the governance structure, which had not yet been fully established (*"That's our problem. We're just creating the processes and structures."*, Int.#1; *"Of course, it's not just about a system, but also about a structure behind it, which we don't have yet."*, Int.#3). However, from both a governance and an information systems perspective, the link between sustainability management and financial accounting had already been established (*"So, I definitely know that our finance department isn't quite as aware of this yet. But that's what I'm here for - I have one foot in the finance department and the other in the new sustainability team."*, Int.#8). The employee who made this statement led the software selection committee and coordinated with the head of sustainability (*"We have now, so Group Accounting has now been picked up to the point where they say, okay, we'll take over the controlling of the sustainability indicators, so to speak, and they are now also taking care of the software that we want to introduce."*, Int.#1). This demonstrates how the sustainability management system was already contributing to cross-functional knowledge sharing, even before it was implemented.

There was further evidence that the software would reinforce the governance structure (*"I think that when we move on to the next phase, for example with the software, everyone will be brought together again."*, Int.#2). The sustainability management system was also expected to replace manual data collection processes and connect the relevant employees, requiring the organization to invest in organizational learning (*"So I hope that this will help us in these critical months, because we don't have this additional data collection effort, but our colleagues are forced to enter and maintain the data. Of course, you still have to teach them that."*, Int.#13). Another interview described how the governance structure would be improved (*"And if there's an error or something, you can always ping them again and say: 'Hey, something still needs to be done here. Please upload this for me'."*, Int.#1). Automatic reminder emails from the system and plausibility checks were included in the software specifications. Furthermore, the system was expected to generally help structure the corresponding processes (*"if you don't have a huge department for it, I think it's very helpful to have software that supports you and you can't just memorize everything."*, Int.#1; *"I think the main work that such software has to do is that the process is clearly mapped and the auditor can audit the process."*, Int.#3). The need for organizational learning was also emphasized by the board member, who described the connection between information systems and governance structure (*"That will certainly be a tough learning curve. I think we're going to fall flat on our faces two or three times because we simply won't be able to manage the figures. And then at some point we'll have to think about how we can set things up systemically so that things work differently. And then at some point you'll have pressure to change the structures behind it, which of course have to be right for a system landscape to make any sense at all."*, Int.#10).

Lastly, we found that the investment in the sustainability management system would include efforts to ensure open communication channels with regulatory bodies, ensuring automatic updates of regulatory requirements (*"So if, for example, the limit that something becomes significant or that somehow new data points have to be collected, this is then automatically fed into this CSRD tool* [...]", Int.#14). This was also included in the software specification catalog.

4.4 Exploiting

Respondents offered some insights into how SDAX considered the eventual strategy development and performance measurement. The company expected the eventual sustainability management system to support strategy development (*"I think overall as a company we need to map the entire process, including goal setting, strategy and so on. [...] the software maps this, but we still have to formulate the goals ourselves."*, Int.#3) and wanted to include simulative components (*"So, on the one hand, modeling things and saying where do we actually end up if we update this over a few years or a few months [...]"*, Int.#14). The head of sustainability emphasized that the software is a tool for determining the strategy, but that developing the strategy was a separate microfoundation (*"I believe that, regardless of whether I take the left or the right path, I don't necessarily need the tool itself to develop a strategy. I need to determine where I stand and the tool is a vehicle for that"*, Int.#14). This shows that the sustainability management system not only influences the development of the strategy microfoundation but that the eventual development of this microfoundation already influences the development of the sustainability system microfoundation.

Performance measurement was not a major focus. However, it became clear that, with the arrival of the new head of sustainability, the ability to benchmark and measure performance was added as a requirement in the software search, underscoring a reciprocal relationship ("*He (the incoming head of sustainability) sees the software more as a database that should also cover strategic topics, including benchmarking, visualization options, dashboards, and so on. He wants part of the software to be CSRD compliant so that you can create reports, but he sees the software as a holistic tool that can be used for different purposes",* Int.#12). The need for further system integration was also emphasized in the software specifications provided by the selection committee, which listed necessary interfaces with specific systems. It was also clear that additional steps would be needed to gain a better understanding of how systems could be integrated ("*We can very well imagine that S/4HANA will take on the role of a supplier system in certain areas. [...] But it's a bit of a pipe dream at this point.*", Int.#9). As mentioned earlier, the cross-functional knowledge sharing between sustainability and accounting led to the requirement that the software ensure reliable audit trails.

5. DISCUSSION

A key contribution of this study is identifying the role of IS in the process of developing and implementing dynamic capabilities for sustainability, which we present in Figure 2. This figure shows the emerging dynamic capabilities that are structured by the implementation of the sustainability management system on the left. The right side shows functionality of the system contributing to other dynamic capabilities. This extends our current understanding of the role of IS in dynamic capabilities for sustainability. Steininger et al., (2022) have reviewed the literature on dynamic capabilities in IS research. They describe that in most research, IS are seen as enablers of dynamic capabilities, conceptualized as tools or resources—rather than as microfoundations or dynamic capabilities in themselves. Another set of studies characterizes IS as embedded within dynamic capabilities (Steininger et al., 2022), focusing on the reconfiguration of IT resources within organizations. From these findings, Steininger et al., (2022) propose a nomological network of dynamic capabilities in IS research, connecting resources to dynamic capabilities, which then lead to organizational outcomes.

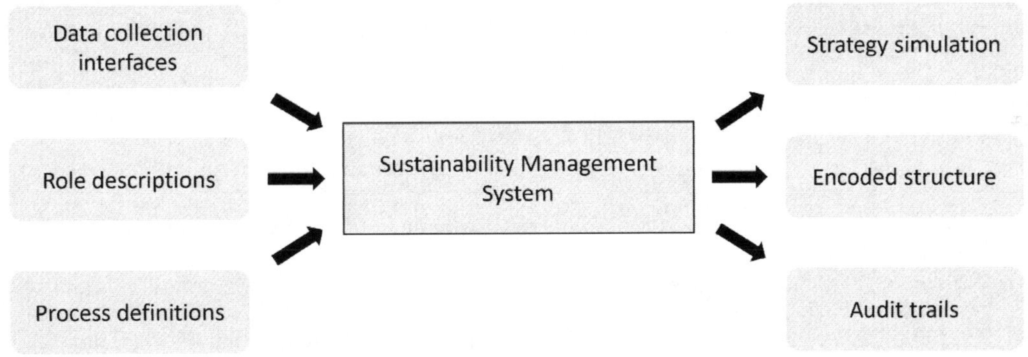

Figure 2. Influence of sustainability management system

Our findings extend this perspective by describing how IS-embedded dynamic capabilities influence other dynamic capabilities through the process of their establishment. Figure 2 is a conceptual view of these processes in the analyzed case. The input required to develop the microfoundation of the sustainability management system leads to the development of other microfoundations, while its output enables or strengthens yet another set of microfoundations. This influence of IS on other dynamic capabilities has not been previously described.

6. CONCLUSION

Sustainability reporting ultimately seeks to describe an organization through its environmental and social metrics, placing it on par with financial reporting. This view of an organization is highlighted as sustainability gains significance across industry, academia, and particularly in the political sphere. In this context, the EU

Green Deal and its related directives offer a unique opportunity to analyze the role of IS in organizational sustainability transformations. These regulations create dynamism and uncertainty in the context of corporate sustainability, as they address a multitude of stakeholders such as regulators, financial institutions, and the broader public. To respond to this uncertainty, many organizations have built dynamic capabilities for sustainability. The SDAX case study allowed us to inductively derive a process model that describes the expansion of dynamic capabilities for sustainability in the organization. We find that the implementation of the sustainability management system, itself a microfoundation for the transforming capability, reinforces a variety of other microfoundations for different dynamic capabilities beyond its main functionality. For instance, the implementation of the system is shown to support the definition of a sustainability governance structure and to further strengthen it throughout its implementation process. Moving forward, our plans include engaging additional organizations to validate the robustness of our preliminary results. Our work adds to the literature on the role of IS for dynamic capabilities by describing its role in supporting other microfoundations particularly in the context of sustainability. Our study has practical implications, as it supports managers in transforming their organizations towards greater sustainability, providing a workable process model and describing the interactions of dynamic capabilities with IS.

REFERENCES

Baumüller, J. and Grbenic, S. O. (2021) 'Moving from non-financial to sustainability reporting: Analyzing the EU Commission's proposal for a Corporate Sustainability Reporting Directive (CSRD)', Facta Universitatis, Series: Economics and Organization, no. 1, pp. 369–381.

Bistline, J., Blanford, G., Brown, M., Burtraw, D., Domeshek, M., Farbes, J., Fawcett, A., Hamilton, A., Jenkins, J., Jones, R. and others (2023) 'Emissions and energy impacts of the Inflation Reduction Act', Science, vol. 380, no. 6652, pp. 1324–1327.

Dwivedi, Y. K., Shareef, M. A., Akram, M. S., Bhatti, Z. A. and Rana, N. P. (2022) 'Examining the effects of enterprise social media on operational and social performance during environmental disruption', Technological Forecasting and Social Change, vol. 175, p. 121364.

Eisenhardt, K. M. and Martin, J. A. (2000) 'Dynamic capabilities: what are they?', Strategic management journal, vol. 21, 10-11, pp. 1105–1121.

European Parliament and Council of the European Union (2022) Directive (EU) 2022/2464 of the European Parliament and of the Council of 14 December 2022 as regards corporate sustainability reporting [Online]. Available at https://eur-lex.europa.eu/legal-content/EN/TXT/?uri=CELEX:32022L2464.

Felin, T. and Powell, T. C. (2016) 'Designing organizations for dynamic capabilities', California management review, vol. 58, no. 4, pp. 78–96.

Mousavi, S., Bossink, B. and van Vliet, M. (2018) 'Dynamic capabilities and organizational routines for managing innovation towards sustainability', Journal of Cleaner Production, vol. 203, pp. 224–239.

Paarup Nielsen, A. (2006) 'Understanding dynamic capabilities through knowledge management', Journal of knowledge management, vol. 10, no. 4, pp. 59–71.

Parida, V., Oghazi, P. and Cedergren, S. (2016) 'A study of how ICT capabilities can influence dynamic capabilities', Journal of Enterprise Information Management, vol. 29, no. 2, pp. 179–201.

Prieto, I. M. and Easterby-Smith, M. (2006) 'Dynamic capabilities and the role of organizational knowledge: an exploration', European Journal of Information Systems, vol. 15, no. 5, pp. 500–510.

Steininger, D. M., Mikalef, P., Pateli, A. and Ortiz-de-Guinea, A. (2022) 'Dynamic Capabilities in Information Systems Research: A Critical Review, Synthesis of Current Knowledge, and Recommendations for Future Research', Journal of the Association for Information Systems, vol. 23, no. 2, pp. 447–490.

Sullivan, Y., Fosso Wamba, S. and Dunaway, M. (2023) 'Internet of things and competitive advantage: a dynamic capabilities perspective', Journal of the Association for Information Systems, vol. 24, no. 3, pp. 745–781.

Teece, D. J. (2007) 'Explicating dynamic capabilities: the nature and microfoundations of (sustainable) enterprise performance', Strategic management journal, vol. 28, no. 13, pp. 1319–1350.

Teece, D. J. (2018) 'Dynamic capabilities as (workable) management systems theory', Journal of Management & Organization, vol. 24, no. 3, pp. 359–368.

Winter, S. G. (2003) 'Understanding dynamic capabilities', Strategic management journal, vol. 24, no. 10, pp. 991–995.

Wu, Q., He, Q. and Duan, Y. (2013) 'Explicating dynamic capabilities for corporate sustainability', EuroMed journal of business, vol. 8, no. 3, pp. 255–272.

ENHANCING SCREEN READER USABILITY: APPLYING USER EXPERIENCE PRINCIPLES FOR IMPROVED ACCESSIBILITY

Solett Smuts and Hanlie Smuts*
University of Pretoria, Pretoria, South Africa

ABSTRACT

Digital technologies are integrated into the ubiquitous computing environment in which users operate. Users engage through digital interactions; however, visually impaired (VI) and visually disabled (VD) users experience digital interactions differently than sighted individuals. In the context of computer-aided drawing systems for the blind (CADB), scholars have expanded our understanding of assistive technologies and how blind and visually impaired (BVI) users, specifically, engage with human–computer interfaces. It is imperative to improve usability and support spatial navigation to apply the potential of human-computer interfaces fully and empower BVI users. This research study was undertaken to investigate and identify user experience (UX) principles for designing screen readers that play a key role in enhancing accessibility for BVI users. Through a systematic literature review of a corpus of 18 papers, thematic analysis yielded 86 sub-themes, categorized into seven primary themes: Navigation, Content Creation Tools, Interactive Technology, UX Design Principles, Evolving Technology, User Needs, and User Skills. The seven primary themes were combined into a conceptual model, providing UX designers and developers with comprehensive guidelines for creating more accessible and user-friendly screen readers. The findings guide the improvement of the digital experience for BVI users, but also contribute to broader inclusivity in digital design, ensuring that assistive technologies meet diverse user needs.

KEYWORDS

User Experience Principles, Screen Readers, Blind Users, Voice Synthesis, Sightless Users, User Theories, Guidelines

1. INTRODUCTION

The internet has emerged as a highly effective medium for educational endeavors, the exchange of information, and communication between individuals (Fernando, 2021). Visually impaired (VI) or visually disabled (VD) users do not have the same digital user experience as sighted users (Kottmeier, 2020). Recent advancements in research and development have accelerated the study of pictorial data representation by blind or visually impaired individuals (BVI) (Fernando, 2021). Such systems must incorporate features that enhance usability, spatial navigation, and shape creation to unlock the complete potential of computer-aided drawing systems for blind people (CADB) (Fernando, 2021).

Studies have investigated how learning can be enhanced for screen readers (Buzzi et al., 2009, Yeh et al., 2008). One study considered three factors for UX principles, including usability, accessibility, and effectiveness (Buzzi et al., 2009). Irrespective of these findings, VI users still experience significant issues when using screen readers; Graham (2015) refers to the emotional experience a blind user faces when using screen readers since most websites are designed for visual interaction. The environment where a screen reader is used can also be considered an issue, i.e., for the user to interact with the screen reader, they must be able to hear, which can prove difficult in a noisy environment (Hlaoui et al., 2019). Using screen readers is also time-consuming due to the inherent nature of how they function (Buzzi et al., 2009).

Therefore, this study aims to investigate the UX principles that can be applied to design a better user experience for blind or VI users using screen readers. User experience (UX) and user interface (UI) design is a broad subject discussed on various platforms and forums (Gonzalez-Holland et al., 2017, Graham, 2015). Notwithstanding previous studies, there is no clear set of guidelines UX designers can follow to ensure their

*0000-0001-7120-7787

product is compatible with screen readers and will provide a good user experience for VI users (Buzzi et al., 2009, Nielsen, 1994, Du Preez et al., 2022). Hence, the question this research investigates is: *What are the user experience principles applied when designing for screen readers?*

The rest of this paper is structured as follows: In Section 2, we provide the background to this research paper, and we describe the research methodology in Section 3. Section 4 contains a discussion of the data analysis and findings, Section 5 describes the study's contribution, and Section 6 concludes the paper.

2. BACKGROUND

When examining UX principles for digital design, it becomes clear that many of these principles are not exclusive to visually impaired (VI) users but can also apply to users without visual impairments. For example, principles such as user control and freedom, as noted by Du Preez et al. (2022), are essential for creating intuitive and effective interfaces for all users, regardless of their visual abilities. Similarly, seminal research by Nielsen (1994) highlights that user control—allowing users to navigate and make corrections easily—benefits VI and non-VI users alike.

However, these principles often lack specificity regarding how they can be tailored to meet the unique needs of VI users or how they should be implemented in the UX design process to enhance accessibility. As a result, existing UX guidelines are insufficient and fail to outline clearly the distinct design considerations necessary for creating inclusive, accessible experiences specifically for VI users. This deficit highlights the need for more targeted UX principles that not only address general usability but also account for the particular challenges and requirements of VI users in digital environments.

2.1 User Experience (UX)

No one definition can be applied to UX as it is influenced by multiple concepts, such as emotions and experimental aesthetic variables (Berni and Borgianni, 2021). In essence, UX comprises experiences in everyday life, how humans interact with products and services, and whether the encounters are meaningful and personal (Law et al., 2009, Hassenzahl, 2013). Furthermore, UX is not just limited to the digital sphere but also applies to all interactions with humans (Law et al., 2009). According to ISO 9241-210, the international standard for the ergonomics of human–system interaction, UX is defined as "a person's perceptions and responses that result from the use or anticipated use of a product, system or service" (ISO, 2024). Hence, UX design broadly encompasses methodologies, tools, and techniques associated with human–computer interaction (HCI) and user-centered design (UCD), representing both distinct and overlapping areas within these fields (Du Preez et al., 2022).

The technical engagement aspects and the emotional, cultural, social, pragmatic, and aesthetic dimensions of the user experience inform the study of HCI (Minichiello et al., 2018). Therefore, HCI recognizes that effective design must consider a holistic view of users' interactions, including their motivations, feelings, and context. Furthermore, UCD emphasizes the user as the central point of the design process, viewing product development as a cyclical, iterative process. The stages of this iterative process, such as analyzing general requirements, conducting contextual task analysis, system prototyping, and user evaluations, are repeated to refine the product continuously (Du Preez et al., 2022). This approach ensures that the final design is not only deeply aligned with the needs, behaviors, and preferences of end-users, but is also technically efficient (Xie et al., 2020, Kuriakose et al., 2022).

2.2 Blind and Visually Impaired Users

Navigation is an important aspect of daily life, whether for work, education, or shopping, and vision plays an important role in enabling movement from one place to another (Kuriakose et al., 2022). Blindness is a medical term used to describe users who cannot observe the visual content of a user interface, whereas visually impaired users cannot view design elements too close in color contrast or when the font size of the interface is too small (Bendaly Hlaoui et al., 2018, Jariwala, 2022). VI and VD users use either or both Braille-based and voice-based (screen reader) computer interfaces (Yeh et al., 2008). Systems that create shapes and drawings are also available for VI and VD users (Fernando, 2021).

Visually impaired users have increasingly adopted assistive technologies for efficient navigation and with the integration of technological advancements in everyday products (Kuriakose et al., 2022, Real and Araujo, 2019). Assistive technologies include devices, equipment, services, systems, and environmental modifications that help individuals overcome physical, social, infrastructural, and accessibility barriers (Xie et al., 2020). By using assistive technologies, visually impaired individuals can participate as equal members of society and lead active, productive, and independent lives (Kuriakose et al., 2022, Xie et al., 2023).

Screen readers refer to assistive technologies designed to help BVI users interact with computers by reading on-screen content aloud, often using a computer-generated voice. In addition, other forms of assistive technologies enhance accessibility through, for example, magnification tools, allowing users to view larger versions of screen elements and, consequentially, enhancing their accessibility (Jariwala, 2022). Screen readers also benefit individuals with learning disabilities, vestibular hypersensitivity, and motion sensitivity, augmenting their effectiveness (Borodin et al., 2010). Screen readers offer users alternative ways to interact with digital platforms, granting access to content and interfaces that would otherwise be inaccessible. In addition to reading the main text, modern screen readers have enhanced features that improve navigation and interaction (Xie et al., 2023). They allow users to engage with different parts of the screen and move efficiently through systems, enabling a more dynamic and seamless experience (Singh, 2012). An example of such a dynamic interaction would be specific hotkeys that can trigger announcements of different types of information, such as alerting users to misspelled words in Microsoft Word (Singh, 2012).

As an assistive technology, screen readers greatly depend on the underlying technologies they interact with, highlighting the importance of designing accessible digital content (Borodin et al., 2010) and optimal browsing strategies for screen reader users (Borodin et al., 2010).

3. MATERIALS AND METHODS

Data were gathered by performing a systematic literature review (SLR), which aims to collect, evaluate, and integrate existing scholarly, practical, and research work toward achieving a specific goal. To achieve optimal outcomes, an SLR follows a meticulous and methodical approach (Biolchini et al., 2005). This study adopted the methodology outlined by Boland et al. (2017), comprising three key phases: planning, execution, and reporting. Planning entails delineating the research question and objectives, formulating a protocol, and establishing criteria for study selection (Boland et al., 2017). Execution encompasses the search for pertinent studies screened based on predetermined criteria, data extraction from included studies, and assessment of study quality (Boland et al., 2017). Reporting involves synthesizing the data from the included studies and presenting findings clearly and concisely (Boland et al., 2017). The search string used was: "User experience principles" AND ("Blind users" OR "Visually Impaired" OR "Sightless users") AND "Screen readers." This search was conducted in academic databases, including *Science Direct, SpringerLink, IEEE Explore, Sage Publications, and Taylor & Francis*. Table 1 summarizes the databases used, and the number of papers found in each database.

Table 1. Various academic databases used during the search phase

Database	*Total papers found*
Science Direct	19
SpringerLink	25
IEEE Explorer	10
Sage Publications	17
Taylor & Francis	24
Other	6
Total	**101**

The inclusion criteria applied in this study were: blind users, visually impaired users, screen readers, and peer-reviewed studies. These included journal papers, conference proceedings, technical reports, and books. Exclusion criteria used in this study were that only papers from after 2010 were included since this study focused on applications of design principles using modern technology such as smartphones. Furthermore, only papers published in English were considered, duplicate papers were removed, and papers behind a paywall were excluded.

Figure 1 visualizes the Preferred Reporting Items for Systematic Reviews and Meta-Analyses (PRISMA) and depicts the outcome of the Conduct Review process step. The search results above produced a corpus of 101 papers for review. Six duplicates were identified, resulting in a corpus of 95 papers. Seventy-two papers were excluded from the initial 101. These were excluded based on language, relevance, paywall-restricted publications, and a paper published in 1968, thereby yielding a corpus of 23 papers for review. One paper, referenced by another reviewed study and considered valuable to the research question, was added to the corpus of full-text papers reviewed. Six of the reviewed full-text articles were excluded based on relevance: One was behind a paywall, and another was a duplicate published under another title. The selected papers resulted in a corpus of 18 papers.

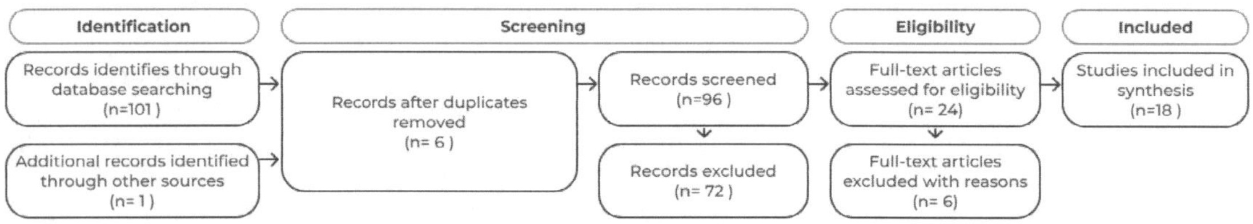

Figure 1. Prisma Flow Chart

Open coding was the first analysis method used to analyze the extracted corpus, as reported in PRISMA, to discover emerging main themes (Leedy et al., 2018), and the second was descriptive codes to classify themes (Welman et al., 2005). Open coding involves categorizing qualitative data into smaller units and assigning a code to each unit (Leedy et al., 2018). This process revealed patterns, themes, and categories, thereby enriching the understanding of the data and how it applies to the research question. Open coding is an iterative process, meaning a researcher revisits data to refine the codes and categories (Leedy et al., 2018). Conversely, descriptive codes condense and classify data within a qualitative research study such as an SLR (Welman et al., 2005). These codes, typically brief phrases or words, encapsulate the essence of the data and are often derived from the data itself (Welman et al., 2005). Descriptive codes aid in organizing the data into meaningful categories and facilitate data analysis (Welman et al., 2005).

4. DATA ANALYSIS AND FINDINGS

The thematic analysis of the identified corpus yielded 86 subthemes, which were grouped into seven main themes, namely *Navigation*, *Content Creation Tool*, *Interactive Technology*, *UX Design Principles*, *Evolving Technology*, *User Needs*, and *User Skills*. Table 2 presents the main themes, subthemes, and references used.

Table 2. Main theme extracted from the literature

Theme Derived	*Subthemes*	*References*
Navigation	Spatial navigation, object detection, Navigation is sequential, Easy navigation / system learning.	(Priscah et al., 2021, Kimogol, 2023, Fernando, 2021)
Content Creation Tool	Shape creation, thermoform plastic, thermal capsule paper, Hands-on exploration of 3D objects.	(Fernando, 2021, Stone and Brown, 2023)
Interactive Technology	User-initiated command-driven interaction, Assistive technologies, Assisting hardware and software, non-visual sensory modalities, Technology, Gesture recognition, Speech processing, Natural language processing techniques, Nontraditional methods of input, Haptic feedback, Voice commands, Vibration feedback, Refreshable braille display, Prerecorded audio, Text-to-Speech convertors, Basic audio feedback, Technology integration, Digital software for learning, Voice assistant feature, Custom voice features, Keyboard shortcut accessibility, Screen readers, Braille embosser, Refreshable braille display, Magnifying devices, User choice of audible features, Audio feedback, Video tutorials,	(Fernando, 2021, Priscah et al., 2021, Muhsin et al., 2024, Kandalan and Namuduri, 2020, Jariwala, 2022, Stone and Brown, 2023, Guerreiro, 2016, Karim et al., 2023, Kimogol, 2023, Zhefan Ye Ye et al., 2021, Nolen, 2015, Lassfolk, 2023, Lahib et al., 2018)

	Multimodal interaction, Voice-overs, Assistive ALT text, Keyboard shortcuts, Voice commands, Using touch and temperature, Voice-over, Tactile feedback, Acoustic feedback, Adapted screen readers, Talking browser, Synchronized audio, and vibration signals	
Evolving Technology	Assisting and adaptive technologies, Smartphone-based assistive applications, Artificial Intelligence, Efficiency of screen readers in scanning, Multivoice assistant feature, Digital Accessibility checkers, Conversational agent, Compatibility of assisting tools, Adaptable screen readers, Refreshable braille display, Sound assigned to objects, Evolving technology, Diverse technology for different groups	(Priscah et al., 2021, Kandalan and Namuduri, 2020, Guerreiro, 2016, Karim et al., 2023, Kimogol, 2023, Nolen, 2015, Lassfolk, 2023, Vollenwyder et al., 2023, Martinez et al., 2022)
UX Design Principles	Ability to learn easily, Support for intended activity, Ability to recover, Ability to manage cognitive load, Ability to personalize, Large UI elements, equitable use, flexibility in use, simple and intuitive use, perceptible information, tolerance for error, low physical effort, and appropriate size and space for use, Consistency in layouts, Font size, Contrast, Discoverability, Repetition, Hierarchy, perceivable, operable, understandable, robust, Sequence and content structure, Accessibility and usage, People first, Clear purpose, Solid structures, Easy interaction, Helpful wayfinding, clean presentations, Plain language, Accessible media, Universal usability, useful, usable, desirable	(Fernando, 2021, Kandalan and Namuduri, 2020, Stone and Brown, 2023, Kimogol, 2023, Lassfolk, 2023, Vollenwyder et al., 2023, Horton and Quesenbery, 2014, Martinez et al., 2022, Bignoli and Stara, 2020)
User Needs	Distinguishing between needs to address challenges, User needs	(Muhsin et al., 2024, Horton and Quesenbery, 2014)
User Skills	Digital skills	(Kimogol, 2023)

The first emerging theme is *Navigation*, which refers to how the software navigates the content on screens, and one of its subthemes is Spatial Navigation. Spatial navigation is the ability to move and determine the environment using cues. Object Detection is another subtheme, referring to how different objects or elements are detected by the technology. Sequential Navigation is another sub-theme derived from the research. The research suggests that most technology used in reading content operates sequentially, which does not allow for quick navigation or scannable content as the technology needs to follow this pattern. The next theme is *Content Creation Tool*, consisting of Shape Creation as one subtheme, which is the recognition and creation of elements using technology for blind and visually impaired users. Other creation tools can also be used to assist blind and VI users in interacting with different elements, utilizing 3D elements created using techniques and objects, such as thermoform plastic and thermal capsule paper.

Interactive Technology is Theme Three, which encompasses multiple subthemes. User-Initiated Command-Driven Interaction is the first subtheme; this allows the user to give commands regarding an expected action to the technology, either orally or in written form. Assistive Technology is a subtheme that includes assistive technology, such as screen readers, magnifiers, text-to-speech, and speech processing. Non-Visual Sensory Modalities form another subtheme and comprise haptic feedback, gesture identification, non-traditional methods of input, vibration feedback, braille embossers, and using touch and temperature. Assistive text alternative (ALT) text adds additional information to describe the object or image and is used by technology to explain context to blind and VI users. Keyboard Shortcuts is a subtheme that allows the user to add shortcuts to their keyboard to perform certain tasks or actions, such as closing a tab or saving an image.

Evolving Technology refers to the continuous development and advancement of technological tools, systems, and processes over time. Technology employed for blind and VI users needs to assist and adapt to new technology and methods; smartphone-based assistive applications utilize the phone's features to assist in identifying text and labels or reading text messages. Artificial Intelligence (AI) is a subtheme of *Evolving Technology*. AI can perform tasks usually requiring human intelligence, which aids blind and VI users in everyday tasks, such as setting the alarm clock or opening the news tab every day at a given time. Screen Readers in scanning and Multivoice Assist features can be viewed as subthemes of evolving technology. Although they emerged from the *Interactive Technology* theme (once these technologies had been developed or were progressing) to perform actions such as scanning content on a page or allowing for multiple voice or audible features, they constitute evolving technology. Digital accessibility checkers are also a form of evolving technology whereby the technology automatically checks if websites conform to digital guidelines. Another subtheme of *Evolving Technology* is refreshable braille displays. This technology uses tiny pins to represent braille dots. Users can run their fingers over these pins to read the content, and these pins are easily lowered or refreshed to display the next set of information.

The next theme is *UX Design Principles*, which encompass vital design considerations when designing digital technologies for blind and VI users, including considerations such as flexible usage, easy interaction, simple and intuitive use, and low physical effort. These guidelines refer to how content is added and the cognitive load on users interacting with such elements. Other guidelines are repetition, consistency in layouts, hierarchy, sequence and content structure, and solid structures, which refer to the structuring of content and the repetition and layout of elements on the screen. The *User Needs* theme pertains to the users' needs and challenges when using technology and the outcomes they expect. The last theme, *User Skills*, focuses on the digital skill level of the technology user. When designing technology for blind and VI users, different skill levels should be included.

5. CONTRIBUTION

A study by Du Preez et al. (2022) produced a model for UX design principles when designing computer interfaces for emotionally vulnerable user groups. The proposed model was enriched with findings from this study (blue text), resulting in the UX principles conceptual model for screen reader design shown in Figure 2. The categorization of the eight themes into the model considered the subthemes of what was identified in Table 2 and used the description of the section indicated in italics and quotation marks to inform their placement.

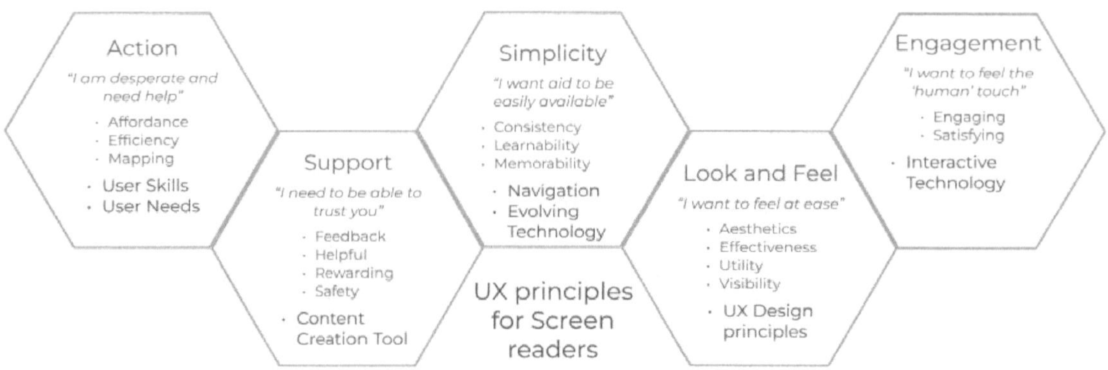

Figure 2. UX Principles Conceptual Model

Figure 2 displays the model used to map the UX principles that can be used in designing for VI users and screen readers. Under the Action section, the researcher added *User Skills* and *User Needs*. *User Skills* refer to the user's digital skills. *User Needs* identifies the challenges from the application. As indicated in Figure 2, Support focuses on trust; the researcher added *Content Creation Tool* to this section. Along with other helpful tools, this should assist the user in their day-to-day lives. We included *Navigation* and *Evolving Technology* under the Simplicity section. *Navigation* informs ease of use and system learning. *Evolving Technology* encompasses several different subthemes, as discussed in Table 2 above. These principles must aid the user in using the system. The researcher added *UX Design Principles* under the Look and Feel section. *Interactive Technology* was categorized under the Engagement section. The designed screen reader would still be used by a human and needs to be engaging to use.

6. CONCLUSION

The internet has transformed education by providing a powerful platform for information exchange and communication. However, visually impaired (VI) and visually disabled (VD) users encounter unique challenges that differ significantly from the digital experiences of sighted users. While discussions about accessibility exist, clear guidelines for UX designers to ensure compatibility with screen readers and enhance the digital experience for VI users remain limited. This study sought to address this gap by investigating the key UX principles necessary for designing better interactions for blind or VI users who rely on screen readers.

Through a systematic analysis of 18 full-text papers, the study identified 86 subthemes, consolidated into seven main themes: *Navigation*, *Content Creation Tool*, *Interactive Technology*, *UX Design Principles*, *Evolving Technology*, *User Needs*, and *User Skills*. These findings provide valuable insights for optimizing UX design to create more inclusive digital environments.

The conceptual model proposed in this study offers a practical framework for guiding UX design, but it requires further testing in real-world settings. In addition, the identified themes should be validated by building prototypes and applying the guidelines across different scenarios. Future research should explore how screen readers are used by VI and BVI users for varying purposes, as well as by non-VI users who rely on assistive technologies for other needs.

REFERENCES

Bendaly Hlaoui, Y., Zouhaier, L. & Ben Ayed, L. (2018). Model driven approach for adapting user interfaces to the context of accessibility: case of visually impaired users. *Journal on Multimodal User Interfaces*, 13, 293-320.

Berni, A. & Borgianni, Y. (2021). From the definition of user experience to a framework to classify its applications in design. *Proceedings of the Design Society*, 1, 1627-1636.

Bignoli, C. & Stara, L. (2020). *Responding to rapid change in libraries: a user experience approach*, Chicago, IL, American Library Association.

Boland, A., Dickson, R. & Cherry, G. (2017). *Doing a systematic review: A student's guide*, Los Angeles, SAGE.

Borodin, Y., Bigham, J. P., Dausch, G. & Ramakrishnan, I. (2010). More than meets the eye: a survey of screen-reader browsing strategies. *Proceedings of the 2010 International Cross Disciplinary Conference on Web Accessibility* (W4A). 1-10.

Buzzi, M. C., Buzzi, M. & Leporini, B. (2009). Accessing e-Learning Systems via Screen Reader: An Example. *International Conference on Human-Computer Interaction*. Springer, Berlin, Heidelberg.

Du Preez, S., Coleman, K. & Smuts, H. (2022). Key user experience principles in designing computer interfaces for emotionally vulnerable user groups. In: Hinkelmann, K. & Gerber, A. (eds.) *Proceedings of the Society 5.0 Conference 2022 - Integrating Digital World and Real World to Resolve Challenges in Business and Society*.

Fernando, S. (2021). *A Formal Approach to Computer Aided 2D Graphical Design for Blind People*. Doctor of Philosophy, Goldsmiths University of London United Kingdom.

Gonzalez-Holland, E., Whitmer, D., Moralez, L. & Mouloua, M. (2017). Examination of the Use of Nielsen's 10 Usability Heuristics & Outlooks for the Future. *Proceedings of the Human Factors and Ergonomics Society Annual Meeting*, 61, 1472-1475.

Graham, G. (2015). A Process and Tool for Evaluation of Accessible User Experience with Websites and Apps for Screen Reader Users who are Blind. Master of Design in Inclusive Design, OCAD University.

Guerreiro, J. P. V. (2016). Enhancing Blind People's Information Scanning with Concurrent Speech. PhD degree in Information Systems and Computer Engineering, Universidade de lisboa instituto superior técnico.

Hassenzahl, M. (2013). User experience and experience design. The encyclopedia of human-computer interaction, 2, 1-14.

Hlaoui, Y. B., Zouhaier, L. & Ayed, L. B. (2019). Model driven approach for adapting user interfaces to the context of accessibility: case of visually impaired users. *Journal on Multimodal User Interfaces*, 13, 293-320.

Horton, S. & Quesenbery, W. (2014). *A web for everyone: Designing accessible user experiences*, Brrokly, New York, Rosenfeld Media.

ISO. (2024). ISO 9241-210:2019 Ergonomics of human-system interaction, Part 210: Human-centred design for interactive systems, Published (Edition 2, 2019), https://www.iso.org/standard/77520.html [Online]. [Accessed].

Jariwala, A. V. (2022). Myaccessible Math: Shining Light on Math Concepts for Visually Impaired Students. Ph.D., Auburn University.

Kandalan, R. N. & Namuduri, K. (2020). Techniques for constructing indoor navigation systems for the visually impaired: A review. *IEEE Transactions on Human-Machine Systems*, 50, 492-506.

Karim, S., Kang, J. & Girouard, A (2023). Exploring Rulebook Accessibility and Companionship in Board Games via Voiced-based Conversational Agent Alexa. In: Byrne, D., Martelaro, N., Boucher, A., Chatting, D., Alaoui, S. F., Fox, S., Nicenboim, I. & Macarthur, C., eds. *Proceedings of the 2023 ACM Designing Interactive Systems Conference*, 10 July 2023 Pittsburgh PA USA. Association for Computing Machinery. New York, NY, United States, 2221-2232.

Kimogol, S. S. (2023). Accessibility of digital teaching materials. Identifying barriers faced by students with visual impairment in digital teaching materials. Master's thesis, Oslo Metropolitan University.

Kottmeier, K. (2020). Who is the average user? How people with visual impairments experience digital services. Master of Arts thesis, Aalto University School of Arts, Designand Architecture.

Kuriakose, B., Shrestha, R. & Sandnes, F. E. (2022). Tools and technologies for blind and visually impaired navigation support: a review. IETE Technical Review, 39, 3-18.

Lahib, M. E., Tekli, J. & Issa, Y. B. (2018). Evaluating Fitts' law on vibrating touch-screen to improve visual data accessibility for blind users. *International Journal of Human-Computer Studies*, 112, 16-27.

Lassfolk, E. (2023). User Experience App Design for Visually Impaired Elderly. Bachelor of Engineering, Metropolia University of Applied Sciences.

Law, E. L.-C., Roto, V., Hassenzahl, M., Vermeeren, A. P. & Kort, J. (2009). Understanding, scoping and defining user experience: a survey approach. *Proceedings of the SIGCHI conference on human factors in computing systems*, 2009. 719-728.

Leedy, P. D., Ormrod, J. E. & Johnson, L. R. (2018). Practical research: Planning and design (11th ed.). *Journal of Applied Learning & Teaching*, 1.

Martinez, R. A., Turró, M. R. & Granollers Saltiveri, T. (2022). Methodology for heuristic evaluation of the accessibility of statistical charts for people with low vision and color vision deficiency. Universal access in the information society, 21, 863-894.

Minichiello, A., Hood, J. R. & Harkness, D. S. (2018). Bringing User Experience Design to Bear on STEM Education: A Narrative Literature Review. *Journal for STEM Education Research*, 1, 7-33.

Muhsin, Z. J., Qahwaji, R., Ghanchi, F. & Al-Taee, M. (2024). Review of substitutive assistive tools and technologies for people with visual impairments: recent advancements and prospects. *Journal on Multimodal User Interfaces*, 18, 135-156.

Nielsen, J. (1994). Enhancing the Explanatory Power of Usability Heuristics. Proceedings of the SIGCHI Conference on Human Factors in Computing Systems. Boston, Massachusetts, USA: Association for Computing Machinery.

Nolen, E. C. (2015). What is architecture without vision? Master of Architecture dissertations-theses, University of Maryland, College Park.

Priscah, C. K., Shem, K. I. & Jane, M. (2021). Establishing Information Seeking Behavior on Access to Digital Resources by Students with Visual Impairment: A Case Study of Nairobi University Library Services, Kenya. *Journal of Education, Society and Behavioural Science*, 34, 95-109.

Real, S. & Araujo, A. (2019). Navigation systems for the blind and visually impaired: Past work, challenges, and open problems. *Sensors*, 19, 3404.

Singh, R. (2012). Blind Handicapped Vs.Technology: How do Blind People use Computers? *International Journal of Scientific & Engineering Research*, 3.

Stone, B. W. & Brown, D. (2023). Anyone Can Learn Universal Design: An Interdisciplinary Course Centered Around Blindness and Visual Impairment. Journal of Postsecondary Education and Disability, 36, 65-74.

Vollenwyder, B., Petralito, S., Iten, G. H., Brühlmann, F., Opwis, K. & Mekler, E. D. (2023). How compliance with web accessibility standards shapes the experiences of users with and without disabilities. International *Journal of Human-Computer Studies*, 170, 102956.

Welman, C., Kruger, F. & Mitchell, B. (2005). Research Methodology, Cape Town, Oxford University Press Southern Africa.

Xie, I., Babu, R., Lee, T. H., Castillo, M. D., You, S. & Hanlon, A. M. (2020). Enhancing usability of digital libraries: Designing help features to support blind and visually impaired users. *Information Processing & Management*, 57, 102110.

Xie, I., Lee, T. H., Lee, H. S., Wang, S. & Babu, R. (2023). Comparison of accessibility and usability of digital libraries in mobile platforms: blind and visually impaired users' assessment. *Information Research an international electronic journal*, 28, 59-82.

Yeh, F.-H., Tsay, H.-S. & Liang, S.-H. (2008). Human computer interface and optimized electro-mechanical design for Chinese Braille display. *Mechanism and Machine Theory*, 43, 1495-1518.

Zhefan Ye Ye, M., Diego López, A. J. D. & Antón García, Á. (2021). Development of a tiflo-application to convert musical notes to Braille. Degree in Video Game Development Degree in Computer Engineering, Universidad Complutemse Madrid.

TOWARDS THE AUTOMATION OF DATA SPACE PRODUCTS THROUGH QUALITY DATA PIPELINES

Asier Garcia-Perez[1], Raúl Miñón[1], Josu Diaz-De-Arcaya[1], Ana I. Torre-Bastida[1], Kosmas Tsiakas[2], Dimitrios Giakoumis[2] and Ekaitz Zulueta-Guerrero[3]
[1]*TECNALIA, Basque Research & Technology Alliance (BRTA), Spain*
[2]*Information Technologies Institute, CERTH, Greece*
[3]*University of the Basque Country (UPV/EHU), Spain*

ABSTRACT

As data becomes a valuable asset for organizations, the challenge is no longer gathering vast amounts of information but refining and managing it to generate value. To this end, there is a growing importance of transforming raw data into high-quality data products within Data Spaces, which are critical components of modern digital ecosystems. The complexity lies not only in the diversity of data sources, formats, and systems but also in the need for data products to remain adaptable and interoperable across various environments. On top of this, Data Spaces often require strict adherence to specific syntaxes and structures. In addition, poor data quality undermines trust and decision-making, and the lack of clear frameworks for processing and consuming data products within these spaces adds technical overhead. The main contribution of this manuscript is a reference architecture designed to facilitate the creation of high-quality, interoperable data products within Data Spaces. Additional contributions include an analysis of the required data types to ensure compatibility with real-world use cases, as well as addressing issues related to data quality, interoperability, and technical integration. The paper concludes with a discussion of future works and potential improvements.

KEYWORDS

Data Spaces, Data Product, Pipelines, DataOps, Architecture, Edge Computing

1. INTRODUCTION

In 2006, Clive Humby, one of the pioneers of data science, famously stated that data is the new oil, underscoring its growing importance in the modern economy (Humby, 2006). However, like crude oil, raw data hold little value until it is processed and refined to extract its true potential. In today's digital landscape, data has become one of the most powerful assets for organizations. However, simply accumulating vast amounts of information is not enough; the real challenge lies in transforming raw data into high-quality products that generate value.

As businesses increasingly rely on data-driven decision-making, the need for efficient ways to manage, process, and deliver data has become more pressing. The complexity arises from the variety of data sources, formats, and systems that organizations must integrate. Furthermore, the rapid evolution of digital ecosystems demands that data products not only maintain high quality, but also remain adaptable and interoperable in diverse environments, ensuring their utility and ability to meet the changing demands of modern enterprises (Raptis, Passarella, & Conti, 2019).

1.1 Problem Statement

Despite the significant potential benefits, developing data products within Data Spaces presents several key challenges. First, raw data must undergo rigorous processing prior to publication, which involves complex transformations and validations to ensure an added-value. Second, maintaining high data quality is crucial to preserve trust and supporting effective data-driven decision making across the ecosystem. Poor-quality data can undermine these processes and diminish the value of shared information. Then, different Data Spaces may enforce a specific syntax and structure, complicating the integration and usability by requiring strict adherence to these conventions, often increasing the technical overhead. Finally, mechanisms for data product consumption are necessary.

1.2 Contribution

This paper presents several key contributions aimed at enhancing the development of data products within Data Spaces:

C1 A reference architecture designed to generate high-quality data products that are fully compatible with Data Space ecosystems, which follows reference architectures such as IDSA (International Data Spaces Association, 2024) or Gaia-X (Noardo et al., 2024).

C2 An analysis of the required data types to support by the reference architecture to be able to fulfill a real use case.

The remainder of this manuscript is organized as follows. Section 2 provides the required background. In Section 3, we analyze similar architectures and tools and evaluate their characteristics. An abstract representation of the required architecture is depicted in Section 4, followed by the concrete implementation of the architecture alongside the datasets considered in Section 5. Finally, conclusions and future work are drawn in Section 6.

2. BACKGROUND

One of the terms that has emerged in the introduction is data products. These data products are essential assets that enable organizations to make informed decisions, streamline operations, and unlock new business opportunities. By transforming raw data into actionable insights, these products facilitate better strategic planning and enhance operational efficiency. The evolution of data management, driven by digital transformation, has shifted organizations from traditional data models to more agile and collaborative approaches, highlighting the importance of continuous improvement and responsiveness to change (Liu & Xu, 2001; Pipino, Lee, & Wang, 2002). In line with this evolution, the Data Mesh approach advocates a decentralized architecture in which each domain manages its data as a product, promoting ownership and accelerating data-driven innovation across the organization (Machado et al., 2022).

However, as companies grow and collaborate within increasingly interconnected ecosystems, data interoperability becomes vital. This interoperability allows different systems and organizations to communicate effectively, fostering collaboration and enabling data-driven decision-making (Kadadi et al., 2014).

In this context, Data Spaces emerge as crucial environments where multiple entities can securely share, integrate, and reuse data while adhering to common standards and regulations. By establishing a secure framework for data exchange, Data Spaces promote trust among participants, ensuring that sensitive information is handled responsibly. This seamless exchange of data not only drives innovation, but also supports growth in a globalized economy, where organizations must adapt quickly to changes and leverage collective intelligence (Curry et al., 2022). The International Data Spaces Association (IDSA) provides a foundational architecture for these ecosystems, ensuring that data sovereignty and security are maintained between participants (Pettenpohl, Spiekermann, & Both, 2022).

A prominent example of this approach is the Gaia-X initiative, which aims to create a European data ecosystem where data sovereignty and interoperability are fundamental (Autolitano & Pawlowska, 2022). This initiative builds on the principles of Data Spaces, fostering cross-border collaboration while ensuring adherence to regulations, such as the General Data Protection Regulation (GDPR) (Scerri et al., 2022). Moreover, standards such as the Data Catalog Vocabulary (DCAT) and the Data Quality Vocabulary (DQV) further support these environments by providing frameworks to describe datasets and evaluate their quality. Utilizing these standards, organizations can ensure that data products shared within Data Spaces meet both interoperability and quality requirements, thus improving their reliability and utility across diverse systems and industries (Albertoni & Isaac, 2021; World Wide Web Consortium, 2014).

To effectively manage and utilize data within these ecosystems, the DataOps methodology has gained prominence as a practice aimed at enhancing agility, data quality, and the continuous delivery of data products. By focusing on collaboration and communication among cross-functional teams, DataOps automates and optimizes data workflows, allowing organizations to efficiently manage the entire data lifecycle, from collection and processing to analysis and decision-making. This approach not only minimizes errors and reduces time to market, but also ensures that data products evolve in response to user needs, thus maximizing their value (Ereth, 2018). Current challenges in implementing DataOps and Data Spaces, such as organizational resistance to change and the integration of legacy systems, continue to influence how organizations adopt these methodologies (Munappy et al., 2020).

The interplay between data products, Data Spaces, and DataOps creates a dynamic environment where organizations can harness the full potential of their data. This ecosystem enables businesses to navigate the complexities of modern data management, enabling them to leverage data as a strategic asset in an increasingly competitive landscape. As organizations continue to innovate, advances in artificial intelligence and machine learning will likely shape the future of data management, further enhancing the capabilities of data products and Data Spaces. In parallel, the integration of edge computing within Data Spaces is gaining traction as the volume of data generated at the edge continues to grow. Edge computing pushes processing and analysis closer to the data sources, reducing latency and enabling real-time decision-making. This shift is particularly relevant in scenarios where rapid responses are critical (Garcia-Perez et al., 2023).

By leveraging edge computing within Data Spaces, organizations can handle sensitive or time-critical data more efficiently and securely. Distributing data processing across edge devices allows computations to occur locally while still complying with the governance frameworks and standards of Data Spaces. This decentralized approach alleviates pressure on central systems and bolsters data sovereignty, ensuring that critical data remains within specific geographic or organizational boundaries. Furthermore, the combination of Data Spaces and edge computing facilitates faster adaptation to dynamic environmental changes, fueling innovation in areas, such as smart cities, autonomous vehicles, and IoT ecosystems. This synergy not only accelerates new business opportunities, but also preserves the trust and interoperability that are the hallmarks of Data Spaces (Kalogeropoulos et al., 2023; Zeiner & Unterberger, 2021).

3. RELATED WORK

Data interoperability and data sovereignty are key requirements that can be met by Data Spaces, but not uniquely, as mentioned in (Otto, 2022). Promoting the value of data products and demanding a quality offer in the form of well-formed data are other key points that these ecosystems must consider. Gaia-X (Noardo et al., 2024) and IDSA (International Data Spaces Association, 2024) specify reference architectures for distributed data infrastructures and Data Spaces, respectively. And it is from its base architectures that innovation must take place, providing new needs, such as monetization, quality assurance, or automation of data product ideation, materialized in the form of derived architectures or components. For example, Datamite architecture (Arjona Aroca et al., 2024) presents a monetization approach. The authors introduce an open-source modular and multi-domain framework that focuses on monetization through interoperability and data exchange. Its modules enable data sharing to a collection of ecosystems like Gaia-X, EOSC or AIoD through a plugin-based approach, proposing a methodology or manner to monetize the data sharing.

In this paper, the focus is set on the combination of two of these necessities: automation and quality, exposing a solution that automates the conceptualization, design and build of data products, while guaranteeing testable quality. To the best of our knowledge, there are no solutions nor frameworks addressing this approach.

In this field, Jeffar et al. (Jeffar & Plebani, 2023) investigate in which extent the principles defined by the Data Mesh paradigm can find valuable support in Gaia-X. From our perspective, the drawback of this approach is that to provide truly valuable data products, they must ensure an acceptable quality degree. This is neither explicitly taken into account nor considered a key challenge in a Data mesh paradigm. However, the authors do expose common ideas regarding the automation of data pipelines.

Finally, we find interesting the work presented by Theissen-Lip et al. (Theissen-Lipp et al., 2023) due to its provision of insights into the definition of the term Data Space and its semantics. In addition, we believe that the extension of this work, including the concept of data product, is necessary since the evolution of Data Spaces requires the ability to define data products and their value. In this article, we have tried to build on Theissen-Lip's conclusions, covering the concept of data products.

4. DATA SPACE PRODUCT GENERATOR

Figure 1 presents the conceptual architecture designed to create data products in the context of Data Space ecosystems. Consequently, this architecture has been conceptualised to enable the creation of data pipelines, through the application of a set of data transformations. Then, a self-description associated with each pipeline is built and published in a Data Space. Finally, this data product can be exposed by a connector to conform a Data Provider in the ecosystem. This chapter expands on the main components showcased in Figure 1, addressing Contribution 1: A reference architecture designed to generate high-quality data products that are fully compatible with Data Space ecosystems, which follows reference architectures such as IDSA (International Data Spaces Association, 2024) or Gaia-X (Noardo et al., 2024).

Data pipelines configurer permits designing data pipelines graphically. For this purpose, a canvas must be supplied where both available data sources and data transformations can be dragged and dropped. There, it must be possible to establish relationships among the entities and configure specific parameters such as the query to perform against a connector or whether transformations are sequentially executed or in parallel. Once the data pipeline is designed, the component generates the definition of the pipeline in a Domain Specific Language (DSL) which, in turn, will be sent to the Pipeline Orchestrator through the Centralised API.

Pipeline Orchestrator is in charge of receiving the definition of the data pipeline and, then, build, deploy, catalog and monitor it. To this end, *Artifact & Code Repository* allocates the software components in charge of performing the defined data transformations. These transformations could be data preparation tasks like anonymization, cleaning, filtering, normalization or data scaling or a process to merge various data sources into one or, indeed, dividing one based on specific characteristics. Furthermore, the Artifact & Code Repository permits the various actors involved in the pipeline definition to include dedicated logic for raising the data quality of the generated data products. This may include specific artifacts aimed at analyzing the quality of incoming data and filtering it if it fails to meet certain quality criteria. Moreover, the repository must establish a set of requirements and guidelines when provisioning data transformations in order to guarantee the whole pipeline compatibility.

Data pipelines can be made up of remote data sources. For this purpose, a specific *connector* must be utilised to properly acquire data. Conversely, *Data Ingestor* component aims to stream data to the platform, which must be registered previously. In this direction, *Data Lake* provides a set of persistence technologies to enable the storage of different types of data like relational, JSON-based or binary files. Meanwhile, *Data Catalog* is responsible for periodically scanning such persistence technologies to offer an updated list of the different data sources available to compose data pipelines. Moreover, a *Schema Registry* is proposed to programatically upload diverse schemas, which, in turn, can be associated with data.

The data arriving at this architecture may originate from edge devices, ensuring that data generated at the edge of the network is seamlessly integrated into the pipeline.

The target of *Data Product Builder* consists in creating self-description documents associated with the built data pipelines. Additionally, this component publishes them in the Data Space ecosystem resource catalog, making the result of data pipelines available in the ecosystem as consumable data products. To this end, the *Data Space Connector* is responsible for serving them to data consumers.

Finally, there is a *Centralised API* to expose the diverse required endpoints to accomplish tasks like data source registration, schema uploading, data pipeline orchestration, etc.

Figure 1. The abstract architecture for the generation of Data Space products

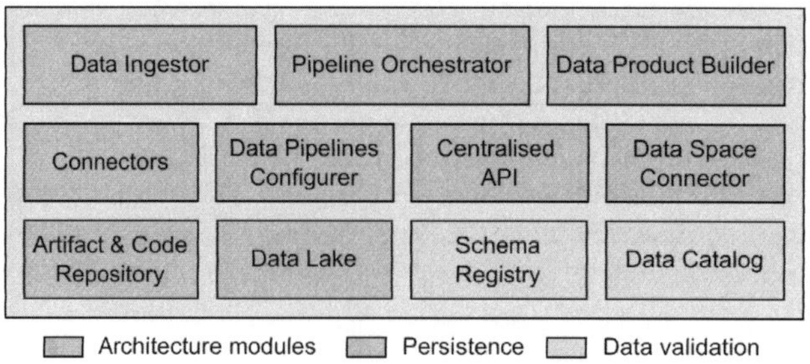

5. IMPLEMENTATION

This section introduces the types of data supported by the proposed architecture and the corresponding datasets, along with the technologies employed for the implementation.

5.1 Considered Datasets

The proposed architecture is designed to serve various types of data, facilitating the multifaceted needs of data products in Data Spaces. In order to define these data types, an analysis of state-of-art datasets for the mobility, healthcare and industrial domains has been performed, leading to the extraction of the essential data formats that are used, as described in Table 1, along with their quality requirements.

The data specifications refer both to online raw data streams and to offline curated datasets of various types. Structured data (e.g., tabular data, sensor readings and analytics) comprise a main source of information for several applications, requiring consistency, completeness and compliance with the specified format. Similarly, semi-structured data, which are commonly represented in a machine-readable format (e.g., JSON files), provide flexibility and promote data interoperability; however, consistency is crucial to allow efficient data exchange. However, unstructured data, including images, audio, video and free text, become increasingly prevalent in diverse domains. This type of data provides insightful and meaningful information; however, they require special quality assessment procedures to ensure their integrity. The reference architecture depicted in Figure 1 facilitates the implementation of data quality and harmonization techniques upon these various data types.

Table 1. The various data types supported by the reference architecture

	Data type	Format	Indicative sources	Indicative applications
DT1	Image	PNG, JPEG	RGB camera Thermal camera Satellite images	Object detection (Deng et al., 2009)
DT2	Video	MP4	Camera stream	Industrial procedure step recognition (Schoonbeek et al., 2024)
DT3	Point cloud	PCD, CSV, JSON, PLY, TXT	LiDAR sensor (x,y,z,intensity) Depth camera	Autonomous driving (Geiger et al., 2012; Yu et al., 2020)
DT4	Time series	CSV, XML, JSON, any machine-readable format	Sensor measurements (e.g., IMU, temperature, etc.) GPS position (lat/lon/alt)	Human activity recognition (Bulbul et al., 2018)
DT5	Audio	MP3, WAV	Text to speech data Human recordings Speech annotation Human-robot interaction	Driver monitoring (Ortega et al., 2020)
DT6	Free text	TXT	Speech to text data Event labels Raw description	Event detection (Singh et al., 2022; Tsiakas et al., 2024)
DT7	Annotations	JSON	2D/3D bounding boxes Classification labels Object/activity tracking Other data-driven task	All the above-mentioned datasets

5.2 Technological Implementation

This subsection details the technologies chosen for implementing the architecture depicted in Figure 1, designed to optimize data product generation within Data Spaces. Airflow was selected as the pipeline orchestrator due to its ability to manage workflows efficiently using scalable and modular Directed Acyclic Graphs (DAGs), making it ideal for automating recurring tasks in DataOps environments. Kafka serves as the data ingestor, enabling real-time, high-volume data ingestion with low latency, which is essential for synchronizing diverse data sources.

For connectors and pipeline configuration, Python-based ad hoc implementations were chosen for their flexibility and use of Domain-Specific Languages (DSLs), allowing intuitive setup and management of complex workflows. GitLab acts as the artifact and code repository, providing robust version control, collaboration tools, and traceability to manage system configurations effectively. The data lake leverages a combination of PostgreSQL for structured data, ElasticSearch for unstructured data with efficient search capabilities, InfluxDB for time-series data, and a filesystem for storing large files, ensuring diverse storage needs are met.

Custom Python solutions facilitate tailored data product creation, while Confluent Schema Registry ensures schema consistency and compatibility throughout the data lifecycle. DataHub enhances governance by offering visibility, traceability, and management of data assets, fostering interoperability. FastAPI provides a centralized API for exposing data products and services through a high-performance interface, and the Eclipse Data Space Connector (EDSC) ensures secure, standards-compliant data exchange across platforms. Together, these technologies enable efficient, interoperable, and high-quality data integration and management within Data Spaces. Table 2 provides a comprehensive overview of the key components and their corresponding technological solutions.

Table 2. Technological implementation of the architecture

Architecture components	Technology	Layer
Pipeline Orchestrator	Airflow (Harenslak & de Ruiter, 2021; Coll Ribas, 2023)	Architecture modules
Data Ingestor	Kafka (Narkhede et al., 2017)	Architecture modules
Connectors	Ad hoc (Fisher & Gruber, 2005; Mernik et al., 2005)	Architecture modules
Data Pipelines Configurer	Ad hoc (Choudhury et al., 2020)	Architecture modules
Artifact & Code Repository	GitLab	Persistence
Data Lake	PostgresSQL; ElasticSearch; Filesystem; InfluxDB (Worsley & Drake, 2002; Andhavarapu, 2017; Naqvi et al., 2017; Fairbanks, 2015)	Persistence
Data Product Builder	Ad hoc	Architecture modules
Schema Registry	Confluent; Schema Registry (Confluent, Inc., 2024; Rooney et al., 2019)	Data validation
Data Catalog	DataHub	Data validation
Centralised API	Ad hoc – FastAPI (Haro Peralta, 2023)	Architecture modules
Data Space Connector	EDSC (Eclipse Foundation, 2022)	Architecture modules

6. CONCLUSIONS AND FUTURE WORK

This manuscript addresses the inherent challenges of Data Spaces and proposes a reference architecture (C1) to streamline data product generation while using the various aspects of data quality in Section 4.1. The supported data types (C2) are described in Table 1. Moreover, a tentative implementation is elaborated in Subsection 5.2.

As per the future work, modules focused on streamlining the seven dimensions of data quality within the pipeline are needed: accuracy, completeness, consistency, timeliness, validity, uniqueness, and relevance. Additionally, mechanisms to detect data quality drift in real-time are to be incorporated, thereby improving the reliability of the generated data products. Future efforts could also better address the challenges of scalability and integration in diverse environments, ensuring that the proposed solutions remain adaptable and effective across varying organizational contexts and technological infrastructures. Furthermore, the validation of the proposed architecture will be addressed as part of the ongoing work within the project, ensuring its feasibility and effectiveness in real-world scenarios.

ACKNOWLEDGEMENT

This work has been supported by the EU Horizon Europe funded project PLIADES under the Grant Agreement No: 101135988.

REFERENCES

Albertoni, R., & Isaac, A. (2021). Introducing the data quality vocabulary (DQV). *Semantic Web, 12*(1), 81–97.

Andhavarapu, A. (2017). *Learning Elasticsearch*. Packt Publishing Ltd.

Arjona Aroca, J., López Osa, M. J., Iturraspe Barturen, U., Siopidis, V., Votis, K., Nikolakopoulos, A., Chondrogiannis, E., Plociennik, M., Himanen, J., Marinakis, A., et al. (2024). Boosting data monetisation with DATAMITE. In *IFIP International Conference on Artificial Intelligence Applications and Innovations* (pp. 33–46). Springer.

Autolitano, S., & Pawlowska, A. (2022). Europe's quest for digital sovereignty: GAIA-X as a case study. *JSTOR*.

Bulbul, E., Cetin, A., & Dogru, I. A. (2018). Human activity recognition using smartphones. In *2018 2nd International Symposium on Multidisciplinary Studies and Innovative Technologies (ISMSIT)* (pp. 1–6). IEEE.

Choudhury, P., Crowston, K., Dahlander, L., Minervini, M. S., & Raghuram, S. (2020). GitLab: Work where you want, when you want. *Journal of Organization Design, 9*, 1–17.

Coll Ribas, X. (2023). *A DataOps reference architecture for Data Science* (B.S. thesis). Universitat Politècnica de Catalunya.

Confluent, Inc. (2024). Schema Registry Overview. Retrieved October 3, 2024, from https://docs.confluent.io/platform/current/schema-registry/index.html.

World Wide Web Consortium. (2014). Data catalog vocabulary (DCAT).

Curry, E., Scerri, S., & Tuikka, T. (2022). *Data Spaces: Design, Deployment and Future Directions*. Springer Nature.

Deng, J., Dong, W., Socher, R., Li, L. J., Li, K., & Fei-Fei, L. (2009). ImageNet: A large-scale hierarchical image database. In *2009 IEEE Conference on Computer Vision and Pattern Recognition* (pp. 248–255). IEEE.

Ereth, J. (2018). DataOps—Towards a definition. *LWDA, 2191*, 104–112.

Fairbanks, K. D. (2015). A technique for measuring data persistence using the ext4 file system journal. In *2015 IEEE 39th Annual Computer Software and Applications Conference, Vol. 3* (pp. 18–23). IEEE.

Fisher, K., & Gruber, R. (2005). PADS: A domain-specific language for processing ad hoc data. *ACM SIGPLAN Notices, 40*(6), 295–304.

Eclipse Foundation. (2022). Eclipse-EDC Connector. Retrieved October 3, 2024, from https://github.com/eclipse-edc/Connector.

Garcia-Perez, A., Miñón, R., Torre-Bastida, A. I., & Zulueta-Guerrero, E. (2023). Analysing edge computing devices for the deployment of embedded AI. *Sensors, 23*(23), 9495.

Geiger, A., Lenz, P., & Urtasun, R. (2012). Are we ready for autonomous driving? The KITTI vision benchmark suite. In *2012 IEEE Conference on Computer Vision and Pattern Recognition* (pp. 3354–3361). IEEE.

Harenslak, B. P., & de Ruiter, J. (2021). *Data pipelines with Apache Airflow*. Simon & Schuster.

Humby, C. (2006). Data is the new oil. *Proc. ANA Sr. Marketer's Summit, Evanston, IL, USA, 1*.

International Data Spaces Association (IDSA). (2024). *International Data Spaces Association*. Retrieved October 2, 2024, from https://internationaldataspaces.org/.

Jeffar, F., & Plebani, P. (2023). Federated data products: A confluence of data mesh and Gaia-X for data sharing. In *International Conference on Service-Oriented Computing* (pp. 107–118). Springer.

Kadadi, A., Agrawal, R., Nyamful, C., & Atiq, R. (2014). Challenges of data integration and interoperability in big data. In *2014 IEEE International Conference on Big Data (Big Data)* (pp. 38–40). IEEE.

Kalogeropoulos, I., Vlontzou, M. E., Psaromanolakis, N., Zarogianni, E., & Theodorou, V. (2023). EdgeDS: Data spaces enabled multi-access edge computing. In *2023 Joint European Conference on Networks and Communications & 6G Summit (EuCNC/6G Summit)* (pp. 424–429). IEEE.

Liu, D. T., & Xu, X. W. (2001). A review of web-based product data management systems. *Computers in Industry, 44*(3), 251–262.

Machado, I. A., Costa, C., & Santos, M. Y. (2022). Data mesh: Concepts and principles of a paradigm shift in data architectures. *Procedia Computer Science, 196*, 263–271.

Mernik, M., Heering, J., & Sloane, A. M. (2005). When and how to develop domain-specific languages. *ACM Computing Surveys (CSUR), 37*(4), 316–344.

Munappy, A. R., Mattos, D. I., Bosch, J., Holmström Olsson, H., & Dakkak, A. (2020). From ad-hoc data analytics to DataOps. In *Proceedings of the International Conference on Software and System Processes* (pp. 165–174).

Naqvi, S. N. Z., Yfantidou, S., & Zimányi, E. (2017). Time series databases and InfluxDB. *Studienarbeit, Université Libre de Bruxelles, 12*, 1–44.

Narkhede, N., Shapira, G., & Palino, T. (2017). *Kafka: The definitive guide: Real-time data and stream processing at scale.* O'Reilly Media.

Noardo, F., Atkinson, R., Bastin, L., Maso, J., Simonis, I., Villar, A., Voidrot, M.-F., & Zaborowski, P. (2024). Standards for Data Spaces Building Blocks.

Ortega, J. D., Kose, N., Cañas, P., Chao, M.-A., Unnervik, A., Nieto, M., Otaegui, O., & Salgado, L. (2020). DMD: A large-scale multi-modal driver monitoring dataset for attention and alertness analysis. In *Computer Vision–ECCV 2020 Workshops* (pp. 387–405). Springer.

Otto, B. (2022). The evolution of data spaces. In *Designing Data Spaces: The Ecosystem Approach to Competitive Advantage* (pp. 3–15). Springer International Publishing.

Haro Peralta, J. (2023). *Microservice APIs: Using Python, Flask, FastAPI, OpenAPI and More*. Simon and Schuster.

Pettenpohl, H., Spiekermann, M., & Both, J. R. (2022). *International Data Spaces in a Nutshell.*

Pipino, L. L., Lee, Y. W., & Wang, R. Y. (2002). Data quality assessment. *Communications of the ACM, 45*(4), 211–218.

Raptis, T. P., Passarella, A., & Conti, M. (2019). Data management in industry 4.0: State of the art and open challenges. *IEEE Access, 7*, 97052–97093.

Rooney, S., Urbanetz, P., Giblin, C., Bauer, D., Froese, F., Garcés-Erice, L., & Tomić, S. (2019). Kafka: The database inverted, but not garbled or compromised. In *2019 IEEE International Conference on Big Data* (pp. 3874–3880). IEEE.

Scerri, S., Tuikka, T., Lopez de Vallejo, I., & Curry, E. (2022). Common European Data Spaces: Challenges and opportunities. In *Data Spaces: Design, Deployment and Future Directions* (pp. 337–357).

Schoonbeek, T. J., Houben, T., Onvlee, H., Van der Sommen, F., et al. (2024). IndustReal: A dataset for procedure step recognition handling execution errors in egocentric videos in an industrial-like setting. In *Proceedings of the IEEE/CVF Winter Conference on Applications of Computer Vision* (pp. 4365–4374).

Singh, G., Akrigg, S., Di Maio, M., Fontana, V., Javanmard Alitappeh, R., Khan, S., Saha, S., Jeddisaravi, K., Yousefi, F., Culley, J., et al. (2022). ROAD: The road event awareness dataset for autonomous driving. *IEEE Transactions on Pattern Analysis and Machine Intelligence, 45*(1), 1036–1054.

Theissen-Lipp, J., Kocher, M., Lange, C., Decker, S., Paulus, A., Pomp, A., & Curry, E. (2023). Semantics in data spaces: Origin and future directions. In *Companion Proceedings of the ACM Web Conference 2023* (pp. 1504–1507).

Worsley, J., & Drake, J. D. (2002). *Practical PostgreSQL*. O'Reilly Media, Inc.

Yu, F., Chen, H., Wang, X., Xian, W., Chen, Y., Liu, F., Madhavan, V., & Darrell, T. (2020). BDD100K: A diverse driving dataset for heterogeneous multitask learning. In *Proceedings of the IEEE/CVF Conference on Computer Vision and Pattern Recognition* (pp. 2636–2645).

Zeiner, H., & Unterberger, R. (2021). Time-aware data spaces: A key computing unit in the edge-to-cloud continuum. In *2021 8th International Conference on Future Internet of Things and Cloud (FiCloud)* (pp. 250–255). IEEE.

Tsiakas, K., Alexiou, D., Giakoumis, D., Gasteratos, A., & Tzovaras, D. (2024). Automated data labelling for pedestrian crossing and not-crossing actions using 3D LiDAR and RGB data. In *2024 IEEE International Conference on Imaging Systems and Techniques (IST)* (pp. 1–6). IEEE.

A SHIP CURVED BLOCK PRODUCTION SCHEDULING METHOD BASED ON ADAPTIVE MESH AND AABB - SAT COLLISION DETECTION

Shaozi Chen[1], Yongjun Ji[2] and Zuhua Jiang[1]
[1]*Shanghai Jiao Tong University, Shanghai, China*
[2]*Shanghai Waigaoqiao Shipbuilding Co., Ltd, Shanghai, China*

ABSTRACT

In block spatial scheduling, the yard resources are relatively scarce and become a bottleneck due to the block's large dimension. Therefore, ship curved block production scheduling (SCBPS) must meet both temporal demands and spatial resource constraints. The coupling of space and time complicates the development of shop-floor plans. A scheduling method for ship curved blocks based on adaptive mesh and Axis-Aligned Bounding Box-Separating Axis Theorem (AABB-SAT) collision detection is proposed. Based on the projection envelope shape of the curved block being a right-angled trapezoid, the algorithm proposes a site resource adaptive mesh method. Considering matching the varying requirements of the block production time intervals, a fast, feasible domain search algorithm is further designed. A precise and efficient AABB-SAT collision detection algorithm is designed with rough and precise collision detection stages. Efficient scheduling of curved blocks can be achieved by employing the scheduling method for ship curved blocks based on adaptive mesh and AABB-SAT collision detection. Finally, the scheduling process of a specific shipyard based on actual data is illustrated.

KEYWORDS

Ship Curved Block, Block Spatial Scheduling, Adaptive Mesh, AABB-SAT Collision Detection

1. INTRODUCTION

As a unique intermediate product in shipbuilding, improving curved block construction capability is vital to the increase in overall shipbuilding capability (Zheng et al, 2012). Currently, shipyards are overwhelmed with orders and need help to keep up with production. However, existing shipyards have long relied on workers' historical experience in scheduling curved blocks (Kwon et al, 2015), leading to long manufacturing cycles, high costs, and uneven utilization of the processing site, which fails to complete the processing tasks. SCBPS under the constraints of limited site space and production time windows has become an urgent problem that needs to be addressed.

In ship curved block scheduling, it is necessary to simplify the shape of the curved blocks. Much work is currently dedicated to studying appropriate curved block modeling methods, such as Lee et al. (1995-1997) assumed that the shape of the blocks is approximately a convex polygon. Wang et al. (2022) further simplified the curved blocks into rectangles (Caprace et al, 2013). However, simplifying into rectangles reduces the difficulty of irregular shape assembly, yet this method does not effectively improve the utilization rate of shipbuilding sites. Therefore, researchers have proposed more precise models. Several paper simplified the curved blocks into right-angled trapezoids but did not design a feasible domain search method based on the characteristics of right-angled trapezoids. Ge et al. (2020) simplified the curved blocks into polygons where all angles are multiples of 15° and proposed a block layout rule based on standard angle filling. Chen et al. (2023) simplified the curved blocks into four shapes, including trapezoids and parallelograms. Further, Du et al. (2019) added pentagons and hexagons. The aforementioned studies can effectively improve the utilization rate of shipbuilding sites. However, complex collision detection issues involving much computation occur due several curved block models.

In collision detection, several scholars have made attempts. Several paper introduced non-occupancy partitioning rectangles to avoid collisions between newly added blocks and existing blocks in the processing site. However, they did not consider right-angled trapezoids' characteristics, treating the curved blocks as rectangles (ZHAO et al, 2010). In comparison, the feasible domain search method for right-angled trapezoids is more complex. Common feasible domain searches are based on a grid of fixed size. To accommodate the diagonal of the right-angled trapezoid, the cell length needs to be very small, resulting in a large number of grid cells and increasing computational costs. Du et al. (2019) determined the positional interference between blocks by judging the positional relationship between the reference points to be divided and the projection polygons of existing divisions. Ge et al. (2020) detected collisions by checking whether the number of intersection points of block positions is greater than 0, whether the number of overlapping edges exceeds 1, and whether the centroid of a block is outside the contour of other blocks. Wang et al. (2022) proposed a collision detection method based on a loop search method. The aforementioned methods are complex and require intricate calculations.

In response to the aforementioned issues and the shortcomings of existing technologies, this paper proposes a scheduling method for ship curved blocks based on adaptive mesh and AABB-SAT collision detection. The paper simplifies the curved blocks into right-angled trapezoids, which not only improves the efficiency of the site utilization but also maintains computational efficiency. Traditional feasible domain search methods must effectively tap into the potential of right-angled trapezoids to enhance site utilization. Therefore, this paper introduces a feasible domain search algorithm based on an adaptive mesh. In traditional fixed-length grid methods, if the unit length is too large, several feasible positions may be overlooked; conversely, if it is too tiny, computational efficiency is compromised. Furthermore, the AABB-SAT collision detection provides efficient and accurate collision detection. Based on the different earliest start times, processing times, projection sizes, and processing sites of the curved blocks, the processing order and location of all curved blocks are determined, achieving a scheduling plan with high computational efficiency.

2. MATHEMATICAL MODELING AND PROCESS OF SCBPS

The problem description is as follows: Arrange N blocks in suitable positions within the site to complete the processing tasks, aiming to maximize the site utilization rate. Given the size information, construction period, earliest start time, and latest completion time of the curved blocks, the issues that need to be determined include the start and completion times of the blocks to be arranged, the construction position of the curved blocks in the processing site, and the construction direction of the curved blocks. The objective is to maximize the site utilization rate.

To establish the mathematical model for the curved block scheduling method, the following parameter definitions are provided: st is the start time of the block scheduling interval; the processing platform $PF = (L, W)$, where L is the length of a certain processing site, and W is the width of a certain processing site; the block $b_i = (u_i, l_i, w_i, a_i), i = 1,2, \cdots N$, represents the upper base length, lower base length, width, and rotation angle of the projected right-angled trapezoid of the curved block respectively. Due to crane constraints, a_i takes the values {0°, 90°, 180°, 270°}, and o_i takes the values {0, 1}, where when a_i is 0° or 180°, o_i is 1, indicating that block b_i is placed horizontally on the processing platform in the length direction; when a_i is 90° or 270°, o_i is 0, indicating that block b_i is placed vertically on the processing platform in the length direction; the block set is $B = \{b_1, b_2, \cdots, b_i, \cdots, b_N\}$, where N is the total number of blocks in the task set; V_{b_i}, V_{b_k} the areas where the projected right-angled trapezoids of blocks b_i and b_k are located, respectively; EST_i, LST_i, LFT_i represent the earliest start time, latest start time, and latest finish time of block b_i, respectively; T_i represents the standard processing cycle of block b_i; PST_i and PFT_i represent the planned start time and planned finish time of block b_i, respectively; the reference point of block b_i, $R_i = (R_{ix}, R_{iy})$, indicates the coordinate point at the bottom left corner of the block, regardless of the angle at which the block is placed on the platform.

The mathematical model is established as follows: Equation (1) represents the objective of the problem, which is to maximize the site utilization rate. The formula represents the site's average utilization rate during the scheduling period, calculated as the sum of the area of each block multiplied by its processing time at the process position divided by the product of the total site area and the scheduling duration.

$$maxF = 1 - \frac{\sum_i (l_i + u_i) \times w_i \times (PFT_i - PST_i)}{\sum_k 2 \times (ET - ST) \times L \times W} \tag{1}$$

Equation (2) indicates that the planned start time for the curved blocks to be arranged should not be earlier than the scheduling start time.

$$PST_i \geq st \quad (2)$$

Equation (3) indicates that the planned start time for the curved blocks to be arranged should not be earlier than the earliest start time of the block, nor later than the latest start time, in order to reduce the inventory accumulation of intermediate pieces from preceding processes and the waiting time for subsequent processes.

$$EST_i \leq PST_i \leq LST_i \quad (3)$$

Equation (4) represents the transformation of the relationship between the placement angle of the curved block and the length direction of the processing site.

$$o_i = 1 - (a_i/(90^{\circ}))\%2 \quad (4)$$

Equation (5) indicates that the curved block does not exceed the processing site boundaries in the x-axis direction.

$$x_i \geq 0 \; and \; x_i + l_i \times o_i + w_i(1 - o_i) \leq L \quad (5)$$

Equation (6) indicates that the curved block does not exceed the processing site boundaries in the y-axis direction.

$$y_i \geq 0 \; and \; y_i + w_i \times o_i + l_i(1 - o_i) \leq W \quad (6)$$

Equation (7) indicates that the curved blocks do not overlap with each other while being in the processing site at the same time.

$$V_{b_i} \cap V_{b_k} = \emptyset \; and \; PST_i < PFT_k \; and \; PFT_i > PST_k \quad (7)$$

Given the NP-hard nature of SCBPS (Zheng et al, 2011), this study adopts a genetic algorithm (GA) to address it. The genetic algorithm is particularly advantageous due to its robust global search capabilities, high tolerance to complex optimization landscapes, and ability to avoid local optima. The GA provides an iterative optimization framework for the surface segment scheduling problem, progressively evolving solutions within the population to approximate the global optimum. The algorithm parameters are set as follows: a population size of 100, a maximum of 50 iterations, a crossover probability of 0.8, and a mutation probability of 0.08. These parameters are designed to balance the algorithm's exploration and exploitation capabilities, enabling it to efficiently identify high-quality approximate solutions within limited computational resources.

Within each generation of the GA, the fitness performance of each individual is assessed based on the average utilization rate of the site, which is evaluated using a one-time scheduling method based on geometry characteristics of curved blocks. The specific steps are as follows: First, collect the processing time of the curved blocks. Determine the geometric shape and size of the processing site boundaries. Sort the curved blocks according to their earliest processing times. Second, based on the current scheduling start time, determine the set of curved blocks that need to be processed currently. Prioritize the curved blocks that have not been successfully processed before. Then, an adaptive mesh will be designed according to the positions of the curved blocks being processed in the processing site, and the feasible domain will be obtained with the feasible domain search algorithm where the current processing site can place the curved block. Next, select a feasible rectangle from the feasible domain according to the maximum area priority rule. Determine the placement position of the curved block using the leftmost bottommost rule, and use the AABB-SAT collision detection algorithm to determine whether the curved block collides with other curved blocks. If a collision occurs, rotate the block until it does not collide; if collisions still occur after all possible rotations, place the block into the set of unsuccessfully arranged blocks for that scheduling start time and proceed to the next block. After all curved blocks for the current scheduling start time have been processed, to eliminate the search for a large number of invalid scheduling start times, update the scheduling start time to the minimum of the two time points, that is, the earliest start time of the remaining curved blocks or the day after the earliest completion time of the curved blocks currently on the site. Continue the above operations until all curved blocks are arranged. Finally, all curved blocks' planned start times and placement positions are outputted.

The fitness values of individuals guide the selection, crossover, and mutation operations. Through iterative optimization, the GA gradually enhances the fitness performance of the population, ultimately identifying the global optimal or near-optimal scheduling plan. This design, which combines the GA with a one-time scheduling method based on the characteristics of the curved block, not only fully considers the geometric features of the curved block but also significantly enhances the scheduling effect through the global search capability of the GA, ensuring efficiency and robustness in complex scenarios.

3. KEY TECHNOLOGIES IN SCBPS

3.1 Feasible Domain Search Algorithm Based on Adaptive Mesh

The Feasible Region Search Algorithm, illustrated in Figure 1, begins by creating an adaptive mesh derived from the processed curved blocks. The algorithm identifies the largest available rectangular space within this mesh. Feasible rectangles are filtered based on the condition that their area must exceed the area of the trapezoid projected by the curved block to be arranged. Rectangles meeting this criterion are added to the feasible region. Finally, the rectangles are sorted in descending order based on their area, resulting in feasible matrices arranged from largest to smallest area.

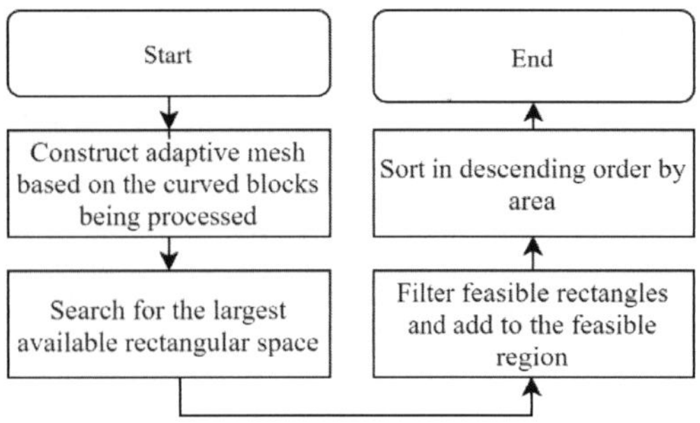

Figure 1. Feasible domain search algorithm

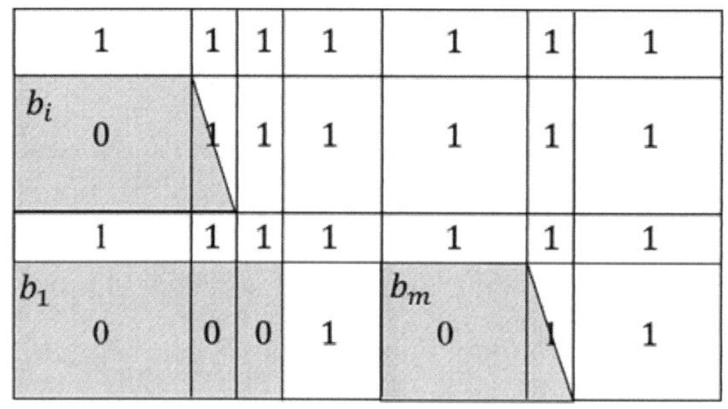

Figure 2. Schematic diagram of adaptive mesh

An adaptive mesh is designed according to the current scheduling start time, the size of the curved block to be processed, and the layout of the curved blocks on the site. Specifically, as shown in Figure 2, the adaptive mesh is determined by drawing horizontal and vertical grid lines parallel to the site boundaries through the vertices of the projected right-angled trapezoids of the curved blocks. Initialize the value of the grid to 1, where 1 indicates that the grid can be used to place curved blocks. Mark the value of the grids that belong to the rectangular part of the right-angled trapezoid as 0, indicating that these grid parts cannot be used to place curved blocks. Among the right-angled trapezoids, the grids marked as 0 represent the areas occupied by the rectangular parts of the trapezoids. The divided triangular sections are marked as 1 to preserve the potential for placing in the other half of the unoccupied triangular area.

The feasible domain search algorithm is used to identify feasible rectangles, reducing a significant amount of invalid search space. Specifically, based on the adaptive mesh marked with 0s and 1s, search for local maximum rectangles within the site containing only grids marked as 1 and determine whether they are feasible. If they are, add them to the feasible domain. The determination method is whether the minimum bounding rectangle of the right-angled trapezoid can fit into the rectangle. Figure 3 illustrates the partial feasible rectangles for the curved block to be arranged.

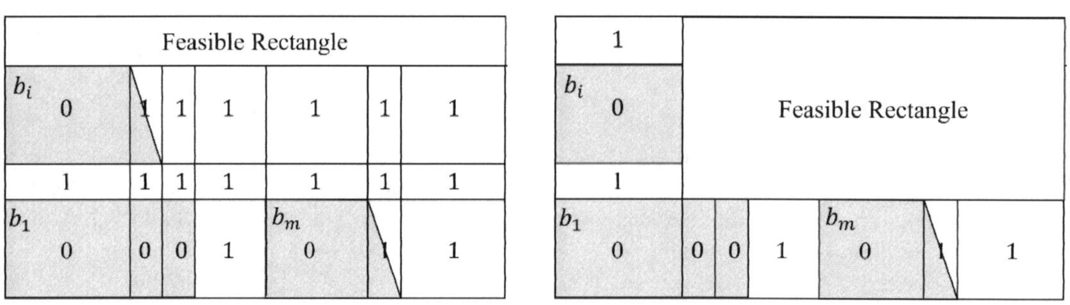

Figure 3. Feasible rectangle schematic diagram

3.2 AABB-SAT Collision Detection Algorithm

The AABB-SAT (Illgen et al., 2022) Collision Detection Algorithm illustrated in Figure 4 is accurate and still efficient. Specifically, collision detection is divided into two stages: rough collision detection and precise collision detection. Rough collision detection quickly excludes two curved blocks that obviously do not collide, while precise collision detection further determines those not excluded. In the first phase, the algorithm computes both curved blocks' Axis-Aligned Bounding Boxes (AABBs). If the AABBs do not overlap, the algorithm concludes that there is no collision, and the process ends. However, if the AABBs overlap, the algorithm moves to the second phase, where it checks for overlaps of the curved blocks' projections on each separating axis. No collision is detected if the projections do not overlap on any axis. Conversely, a collision is confirmed if the projections overlap on all axes. This algorithm effectively detects collisions in right-angled trapezoid by leveraging the efficiency of AABBs alongside the precision of the Separating Axis Theorem (SAT).

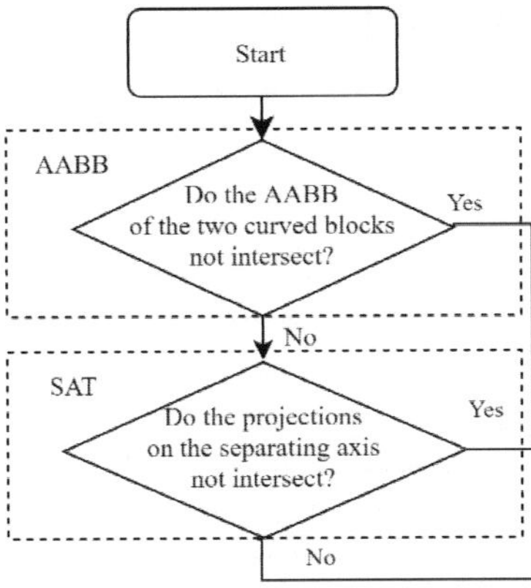

Figure 4. AABB-SAT collision detection algorithm

Rough collision detection is based on the Axis-aligned Bounding Box (AABB) (Bergen, 1997)(Tu, C. and Yu, L, 2009.). Also, the length direction of the processing site is taken as the X-axis, and the direction perpendicular to it is taken as the Y-axis to establish a Cartesian coordinate system. The AABB is a rectangle that wraps the projected right-angled trapezoid of the curved block, with one side parallel to one of the coordinate axes. Only the intersection of the bounding boxes (rectangles) corresponding to the right-angled trapezoids is checked during detection. As shown in Figure 5, if the axis-aligned bounding boxes of two right-angled trapezoids do not intersect, they have not collided.

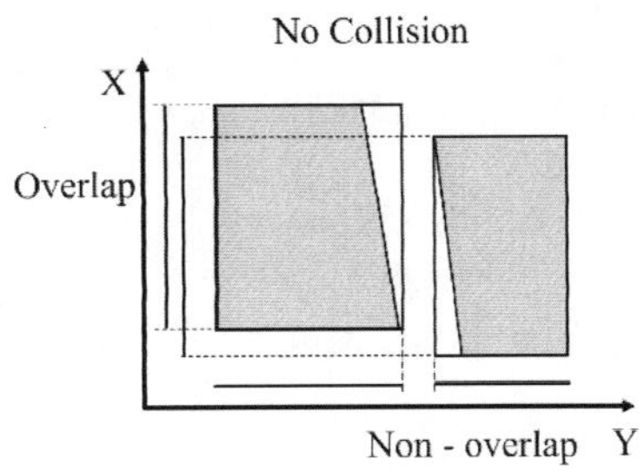

Figure 5. Axis-Aligned bounding box

If the axis-aligned bounding boxes of two right-angled trapezoids intersect, further collision detection is conducted based on the Separating Axis Theorem (SAT)(Liang C, 2015). The SAT states that if the projections of two convex polygons on a particular axis do not overlap, the two convex polygons do not intersect. If projections are made on all axes (the normal vectors of each side), and there is at least one axis on which the projections do not overlap, then the two convex polygons do not intersect. Otherwise, the polygons do intersect, as shown in Figure 6.

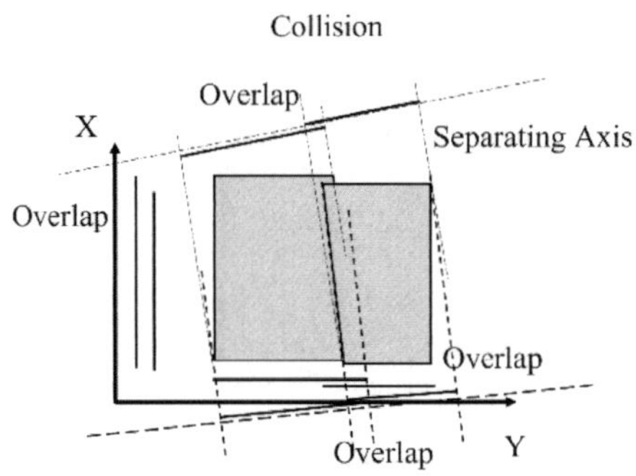

Figure 6. Separating axis theorem

4. CASE STUDY

The site and block information were collected from a large shipyard in Shanghai, with production scheduled between 2022 and 2023. The site's total area is 4500 square meters, for $PF = (L, W)$ and $L = 100m, W = 45m$. There are 200 curved blocks. Parts of the data is shown in Table 1 below.

Table 1. Input information table

Block Number	Processing Time	Upper Base Length	Lower Base Length	Width	Scheduled Start Time	Earliest Start Time	Latest Start Time
H1112-101	30	26	31	10	2022-11-02	2022-10-26	2023-01-11
H1113-101	30	26	31	10	2022-11-02	2022-10-26	2023-01-11
H2420-801	44	15	25	19	2022-11-07	2022-11-06	2023-01-08
H1113-632	14	14	14	18	2022-11-21	2022-11-17	2023-01-20
H1112-101	30	26	31	10	2022-11-02	2022-10-26	2023-01-11

The data is processed through the SCBPS proposed in this paper, based on adaptive meshing and AABB-SAT collision detection. The algorithm is implemented in Python 3.10 using third-party libraries such as NumPy, Matplotlib, Pandas, OpenPyXL, and Timeit. The blocks are sorted in ascending order according to the medium-term schedule start times and arranged sequentially. Based on the changes in the processing site blocks, diagrams of the processing site at different periods are generated. If the site's layout does not change within a certain period, it indicates that no new curved blocks are added and no blocks are completed during that period. Transitioning from one period to the next indicates that either a curved block is completed or a new block is added for processing. The layout results are diagrams of the site layout at different periods, which can be used to query the site's layout on a given day. The average utilization rate of the processing site during the processing time of this batch of tasks is 64.245%, and parts of the layout diagrams for specific periods are shown in Figure 7 below.

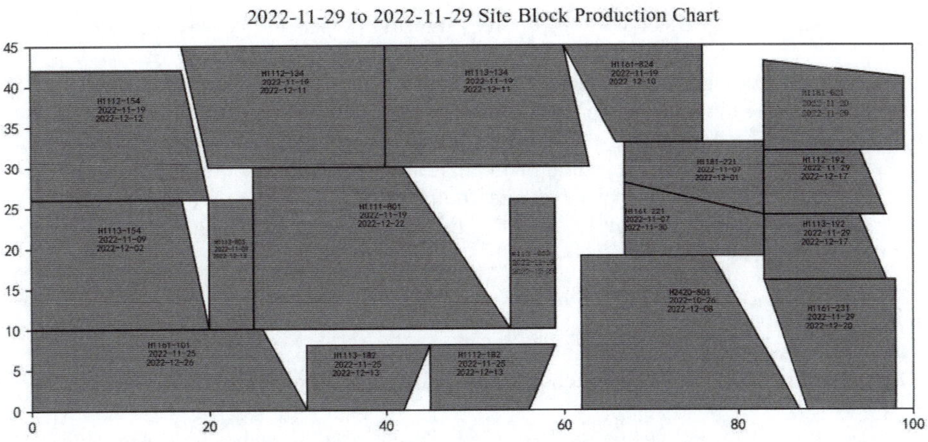

Figure 7. Layout diagram for some time periods

Blocks such as H112-154 are selected from Figure 7, as shown in Figure 8. For block (a), collision detection is conducted after selecting a feasible rectangle, and it is ultimately found that no collision occurs after rotating 270°. Therefore, the space is successfully utilized, but it would have been unusable if the block had been modeled as a rectangle. The unusable space generated by the two blocks is reduced, effectively improving the utilization rate of the processing site.

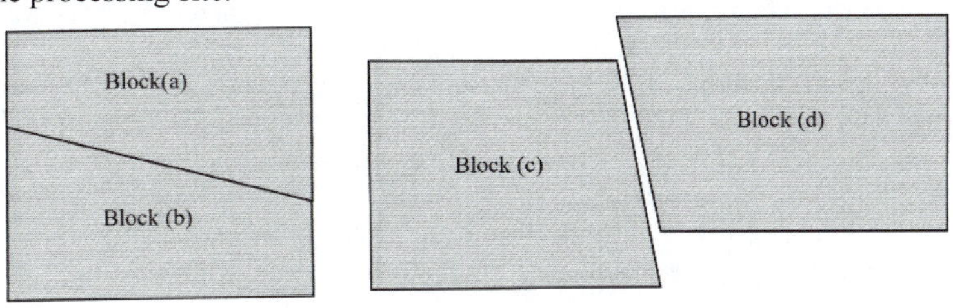

Figure 8. Partial schematic diagram

5. CONCLUSION

This paper proposes a complete, relatively accurate, and efficient surface section scheduling method based on adaptive meshing and AABB-SAT collision detection.

An improved adaptive mesh design method is proposed in response to the issue of traditional grid search having ample search space and low computational efficiency. This method constructs a grid based on the curved blocks processed in the site. Compared to traditional grid methods, it gratifies and updates according to the placement of curved blocks in the site. As the foundation for feasible domain search, the adaptive mesh can reduce invalid grids, thereby reducing several invalid searches and improving computational efficiency.

A feasible domain search algorithm is proposed to address the issue of invalid collision detection in non-feasible spaces affecting computational efficiency. This algorithm obtains all possible maximum non-occupied rectangles by combining grids, effectively finding all unoccupied placement spaces or spaces that may be potentially placed. It filters non-occupied rectangles based on the size of the target-placed curved blocks to determine the feasible domain, reducing blind searches of grids and subsequent heavy collision detection, thus improving computational efficiency.

To address the issue of traditional collision detection needing to be more efficient and accurate, the AABB-SAT collision detection method is proposed. This method offers efficient and high-precision collision detection. This method first uses the AABB collision detection method to quickly exclude curved blocks that do not collide with a minimal amount of calculation. Curved blocks that are not excluded are further detected using the SAT method with high detection precision and low computational complexity.

In future research, a focused analysis on the algorithm's scalability will be conducted to assess its performance with larger sites and complex curved block designs. This includes stress testing and optimization for diverse operational environments. Additionally, the method's general applicability will be verified through testing in various environments, such as different shipyards and construction settings, to evaluate its performance across a broad spectrum of conditions. Furthermore, the development of user-friendly interfaces and tools will be a priority to enhance the practicality and user acceptance of the method. This will involve creating interactive visualization tools and designing interfaces that are intuitive and easy to operate, specifically tailored to simplify the workflow for shipyard operators.

REFERENCES

Bergen, G.V.D. (1997). Efficient collision detection of complex deformable models using AABB trees. *Journal of graphics tools*, 2(4), pp.1-13.

Caprace, J-D. et al, (2013). Optimization of shipyard space allocation and scheduling using a heuristic algorithm. *Journal of Marine Science and Technology*18(3): pp. 404-417.

Chen, Y. et al, (2023). Block workshop spatial scheduling based on cellular automata modelling and optimization. *IET Collab. Intell. Manuf.*, e12075.

Ge, Y., Wang, A. (2020). Spatial scheduling for irregularly shaped blocks in shipbuilding. *Computers & Industrial Engineering*, pp. 106985.

Huynh, J. (2009). Separating axis theorem for oriented bounding boxes. [Online]. Available: www.jkh.me/files/

Illgen, B. et al, (2022). Performant algorithm for spatial scheduling of large structures within computing-intensive simulation projects. *Procedia CIRP*, 107, 167–172.

J. W. Du. et al, (2019). A Simulation-based Dynamic Spatial Scheduling Method of Block Assembly in Shipbuilding. *2019 IEEE International Conference on Industrial Engineering and Engineering Management (IEEM)*, pp. 1491-1495.

Kwon, B. et al, (2015). Spatial scheduling for large assembly blocks in shipbuilding. *Computers & Industrial Engineering* 89(4): pp. 203-212.

Lee, J. et al, (1995). DAS: Intelligent scheduling system for shipbuilding. *AI Magazine*, 16, 78–94.

Lee, J. K. et al, (1997). Developing scheduling systems for Daewoo shipbuilding: DAS project. *European Journal of Operational Research*, 97, 380–395.

Lee, K. J. et al, (1996). A spatial scheduling system and its application to shipbuilding: DAS-CURVE. *Expert Systems with Applications*, 10, 311–324.

Liang, C. et al, (2015). The research of collision detection algorithm based on separating axis theorem[J]. *Int. J. Sci*, 2(10): 110-114.

S. Wang. et al, (2022). A spatial scheduling strategy based on evaluation of the remaining usable area for shipbuilding. *2022 IEEE International Conference on Mechatronics and Automation (ICMA),* pp. 24-29.

Tu, C. and Yu, L., (2009). Research on Collision Detection Algorithm Based on AABB-OBB Bounding Volume. *2009 First International Workshop on Education Technology and Computer Science, 1*, 331-333.

Zhao, M. et al, (2010). Algorithm of Automatic Adjustment in Curved Blocks Building Schedule Subject to Exceptions. J. *Shanghai Jiaotong Univ. (Sci.)*, 44 (03): 428-0432.

Zheng, J. et al, (2011). Spatial scheduling algorithm minimizing makespan at block assembly shop in shipbuilding. *Int.J.Prod.* Res.49(8),2351–2371.

Zheng, J. et al, (2012). Block spatial scheduling modelling and application in shipbuilding. *Int.J.Prod.* Res. 50(10), 2744–2756.

DIGITAL ECOSYSTEMS – NEW OPPORTUNITIES FOR DECISION SUPPORT SYSTEMS

Christer Carlsson and Pirkko Walden
Institute for Advanced Management Systems Research, Turku, Finland

ABSTRACT

Real options valuation is still key to strategic investment decisions but offers challenges for management. Decision-making "on-the go" is losing the insights developed in decision analysis, cleaning out the skills learned through decision support systems and is not mastering the advanced and powerful tools available in decision analytics. Digital ecosystems offer platforms to operate advanced decision analytics models and algorithms to get more insightful and productive decision making.

KEYWORDS

Digital Ecosystems, Decision Analysis, Decision Support Systems, Decision Analytics

1. INTRODUCTION

Some of the more challenging situations for decision makers occur when dealing with options. In the financial world options describe and represent the right to buy or sell a financial value, mostly a stock at an exercise price determined by the market but without any obligation to do so. You exercise the option if the underlying value is higher than the exercise price (call option, the right to buy) or lower than the exercise price (put option, the right to sell). In 1973 Black and Scholes made a major breakthrough by deriving a differential equation that must be satisfied by the price of any derivative security dependent on a non-dividend paying stock. Real options are based on the same principles as financial options, but the options involve "real" assets - to have the possibility for a certain period to either choose for or against making an investment decision, without binding oneself up front (cf. Merton (1973)). The real option rule is that one should invest today only if the net present value is high enough to compensate for giving up the value of the option to wait. Because the option to invest loses its value if the investment is made, the loss is an opportunity cost of investing. The main question for a deferrable investment opportunity is: how long do we postpone the investment, if we can postpone it, up to T time periods? Formulated in this way it is increasingly hard to decide as there is uncertainty about the exact outcome of the investment.

Nevertheless, management must make a decision, and will have to answer for the consequences, either the loss of a major opportunity or the cost of a failed, major investment. Management seeks guidance from classical methods like NPV (net present value) or DCF (discounted cash flow) that are readily available for decision analysis. This does not help much as these methods discount heavily for external uncertainty in the real option and contribute to maybe cancelling interesting and innovative projects because they come with significant uncertainties, often becoming active in some future. Following Leslie and Michaels (1997), real options can be valued using option theories that are the analogue with those developed for financial options and are quite different from the traditional NPV or DCF methods. The real option valuation (ROV) has the following form,

$$ROV = S_0e^{-\delta T} N(d_1) - Xe^{-rT} N(d_2) \qquad (1)$$

$$d1 = (\ln(S_0/X) + (r - \delta + \sigma^2/2)T)/ \sigma\sqrt{T}\ , \ d_2 = d_1 - \sigma\sqrt{T}$$

ROV denotes the current real option value, S_0 is the present value of expected cash flows, X is the (nominal) value of fixed costs, σ quantifies the uncertainty of expected cash flows, and δ denotes the value lost over the duration of the option.

Working out real option valuations (they may want to try several options) management will get guidance for their decisions to exercise options to invest, or to postpone investments, and if so to postpone them T time periods. The problem appears to be that management will have challenges to see the meaning of a "current real option" or to verify that it is correct.

We will use the case of real options to show how information systems support can help management with decision analysis, then how the methods of decision support systems offered more and better support to management and how decision analytics on digital ecosystems platforms now can help modern management to fast and effective decisions despite having to deal with complex and changing uncertainties.

2. DECISION SUPPORT SYSTEMS – FROM DECISION ANALYSIS TO DECISION ANALYTICS

2.1 Decision Analysis

Analytics or Decision Analysis (or Operational Research or Management Science) as it was previously known has not been a major focal point of interest for the Information Systems communities as they are represented at ICIS, ECIS, ACIS and PACIS; at some of these meetings a certain animosity towards the need for mathematics and analytical skills has been visible. This is surprising as analytics is a versatile and effective methodology to handle large and complex industrial and business problems. We also have a tradition in the IS field—since the early days of Decision Support Systems—that we should be able to work with managers to help them work out complex problems and build an understanding with analysed and verified facts. Digitalisation is bringing big data (or "fast data" for streaming big data), which more recently has been claimed to make it impossible to use analytics as huge amounts of data make the algorithms impossible or impractical to use—or it will take too much time as fast decision making in almost real-time is a necessity in the digital economy ("the fast eat the slow" as the slogan goes). In this paper we will argue that if there is time to make bad decisions it should also be time to make good decisions—we only need to know how and what tools to use. Real options are a case in point.

Decision analysis (DA) builds on classical mathematics; linear programming with the simplex algorithm (cf. Dantzig, 1951) offered solutions to real-world problems that can be modelled with a linear objective function and linear constraints. Computer supported algorithms offered possibilities to solve very large problems with hundreds of decision variables and constraints. The field quickly expanded to new forms of programming – goal, integer, multi-objective, stochastic, etc. – with more developed algorithmic support from computers. The programming methods helped formulate operational research as "scientific methods of providing executive departments with a quantitative basis for decisions regarding the operations under their control" (cf. Morse and Kimball, 1951). DA offers a basis in theory and methods to help with the future (1, T) uncertainties in the N(d1) and N(d2) of the ROV equations.

Nevertheless, DA now gets critical evaluations as not being very helpful – a guide to best decisions using decision analysis models handles "uncertainties through subjective probabilities for which the decision maker's attitude to risk is represented by utility functions and the attitude to trade-offs between conflicting aspirations are expressed with multi-attribute value or multi-attribute utility functions" (Wikipedia, non-technical, to avoid lengthy details).

Shortcomings and critical counterexamples have generated reinterpretations of DA and introduced mathematically and computationally more powerful methods and algorithms to meet the challenges from large, complex problems of dynamic, interactive elements (like the case of real options), (cf. Gass and Assad, (2014)). This development offered formal frameworks for important management decisions from 1980'es through the 2020'es. The DA theoreticians were not overwhelmed by the thousands of success stories … "while there may occasionally be justification for such methods in applications (e.g., based on ease of use), decision analysts would argue for multi-attribute utility theory as the gold standard to which other methods should be compared, based on its rigorous axiomatic basis" ((Wikipedia, non-technical). The development of decision support systems (DSS) took issue with the requirements for a rigorous axiomatic basis.

2.2 Decision Support Systems

The origins of the methodology and the information systems platforms for decision support systems (DSS) are often quoted as coming from Keen's and Scott Morton's (1978) linking of management activities with Simon's and Newell's (1958) description of decisions in terms of structured, unstructured, and semi-structured. Decision processes are structured in terms of intelligence ("the search for problems"), design ("development of alternatives") and choice ("analysing alternatives and choosing one for implementation"). In the early days a DSS was described as a computer system developed to deal with a problem in which at least some stage was semi-structured or unstructured and where the judgment of the decision-maker was brought to bear on the unstructured part. A DSS was understood as a human–machine, problem-solving system, where the decision-maker could work with the computer system to work out the problem and find solutions they could understand. This was progress from the DA insistence on anchoring in multi-attribute utility theory (cf. Shim et al (2002)).

One of the key features of DSS was that once the problem is recognized, it is defined in terms that facilitate the creation of models that a decision-maker can understand and use (cf. Bonchek et al (1981). To this was added some supporting features to help decision-makers, (i) sophisticated database management capabilities with access to internal and external data, information, and knowledge, (ii) powerful modelling functions accessed by a model management system, and (iii) powerful, yet simple user interface designs that enable interactive queries, reporting, and graphing functions. Historically, most of the research effort in DA and operational research has been concentrated on development of new algorithms to solve problems faster, which as such do not help decision-makers. However, decision support software developers appear to have incorporated advances in the solution algorithms quite quickly to let users benefit from these enhancements.

Modern forms of DSS include solution software with metaheuristics (which include tabu search, genetic algorithms, simulated annealing, neural networks, and several others) to solve combinatorial problems (cf. Mezei (2017), cf. Carlsson (2018)) and combine techniques from artificial intelligence with analytics to attack large and much larger problems. This offers new challenges, to deliver model solutions in a usable form to describe the problem and the solution. Some help can be found with visualisation tools and with multimedia to highlight solutions or exceptions to norms or to signal infeasibilities.

Modern DSS also benefits from rapid development of human-computer interfacing, research focusing on graphical user interfaces, moving towards mobile phones and wireless devices to dramatically increase the accessibility of the tools to decision-makers wherever they may be (cf. Makkonen (2020)).

Peter Keen (1987) gave DSS research a broad agenda: (i) it should look for areas where the proven skills of DSS builders can be applied in new, emergent or overlooked areas; (ii) it should make an explicit effort to apply analytic models and methods; (iii) it should embody a far more prescriptive view of how decisions can be made more effectively; (iv) it should exploit emerging software tools and AI to build semi-expert systems, and (v) it should re-emphasise the special value of DSS practitioners to understand decision making and information technology. Keen's visions show steps away from the DA insistence on a rigorous axiomatic basis towards active involvement by decision-makers who may not even be trained in more developed forms of analytics. In (Carlsson and Walden (2022)) Keen's visions found a practical implementation. The DW-app 3.0 for smart mobile phones (Android, iOS) registers physical activity exercises carried out, calculates MET-minutes for an activity and registers the results. The DW-app builds on Wellmo, a multi-purpose platform and a 2020'es variation of a DSS, for mobile wellness services developed by a Nokia spin-off. The platform provides the software infrastructure for the DW-app to define user profile and login setup functions including informed consent to allow PA data to be collected. The DW-app was accepted and used by 1000+ young elderly in the *DigitalWells* research program.

In other variations, there has been a steady inflow of methods and algorithms for advanced modelling and the classical AI methods are expanded and enhanced by computational intelligence (cf. Carlsson (2019)), soft computing (cf. Carlsson (2012) and smart systems (cf. Morente-Molinera et al (2016)). Managers, experts, knowledge workers, systems developers, etc. in the 2020s are different from earlier DSS users, with different expectations and requirements on functionality from the support technology and the problem-solving support. Technological proficiency levels of DSS users have improved and appears to continue to increase. Nevertheless, the proficiency may not be enough to fully make use of new advances in technology and information systems support. Actually, the DSS methods could not provide any clear contributions on how to handle the real options case nor offer any insight on "real option valuation" (besides the fact that we deal with differential equations on uncertainty for a flexible time horizon) (cf. Carlsson and Fuller (2003)). DSS builders, who worked closely with the planned users of the systems, found much use for *design science* as a methodology for capturing the needs and problems of actual planning and decision making (cf. Hevner et al (2004)). Actual needs for practical decision support paved the way for design science in systems for which decision analytics contributes the optimization and intelligent systems algorithms (cf. Morente-Molinera et al (2016)).

2.3 Decision Analytics

Analytics represents a shift in focus from both DA and DSS towards developing and delivering critical data, information and knowledge for management and decision-making. Research used for decision analytics (cf. Carlsson (2018)) shows themes like big data, machine learning, business and service analytics, gamification, virtual and augmented reality, visual decision analytics, soft computing, explainable AI, etc. which are described as "hot topics" (cf. *Decision Analytics Track, HICSS,* where these topics are covered in 30+ minitracks).

In decision analytics there are some ways to get new approaches to deal with the dilemma of uncertainties in the case we have for real options valuation. Lotfi Zadeh (*in an HICSS keynote address*) observed that "*you can increase precision if you are willing to give up on relevance or you can increase relevance if you are willing to give up on precision, but you cannot do both at the same time*". It turns out that this can be given forms that managers can work with to tackle uncertainty in real options valuation. The most possible values of the present value of expected cash flows lie in the interval $[s_1, s_2]$, which is the core of the trapezoidal fuzzy number $\hat{S}_0 = (s_1, s_2, \alpha, \beta)$; $(s_2+\beta)$ is the upward potential and $(s_1-\alpha)$ is the downward potential for the present value of expected cash flows. The expected costs are estimated by using a trapezoidal possibility distribution of the form $\hat{H} = (h_1, h_2, \alpha_0, \beta_0)$.

$$\text{FROV} = \hat{S}_0 e^{-\delta T} N(d_1) - \hat{H} e^{-rT} N(d_2) \qquad (2)$$

$$d1 = (\ln (E(\hat{S}_0) / E(\hat{H})) + (r - \delta + \sigma^2/2)T) / \sigma\sqrt{T}, \quad d_2 = d_1 - \sigma\sqrt{T}$$

where, $E(\hat{S}_0)$ denotes the possibilistic mean value of the present value of expected cash flows, $E(\hat{H})$ stands for the the possibilistic mean value of expected costs and $\sigma := \sigma(\hat{S}_0)$ is the possibilistic variance of the present value of expected cash flows.

Now it turns out that if the probabilistic density function in (1) and the possibility distributions of $\hat{S}_0 = (S_0, 1)$ and $\hat{H} = (X, 1)$ are of symmetric triangular form then ROV = E(FROV), that is, the probabilistic real option value coincides with the possibilistic expected value of the fuzzy real option (cf. Carlsson and Fuller (2003)). In the general case, possibility distributions do not satisfy the properties of probabilistic density functions (and vice versa, probability density functions are mostly sub-normal), therefore ROV and E(FROV) can not be compared (since one of them may not be defined). Nevertheless, rigorous probabilistic uncertainty estimates are replaced with upward and downward potentials at selected points of time in [1, T] to give managers tools for their experience and intuitive insights to work out reasonable variations for investment options. There is still the challenge to get managers to adopt and use tools like possibility distributions.

Analytics has gained in importance in business and industry over the last 10-12 years (cf. Sinuany-Stern (2023)), but the introduction of analytic theory and increasingly advanced algorithms also meets with resistance; senior managers and executives are not comfortable with elements of black boxes (such as advanced mathematics) in planning, problem solving and decision making.

Amazon, in a recent article in *IEEE Spectrum*, appears to go against the stream of resistance to push boundaries of what is possible in logistics. Amazon optimises the journey of a package through integration of artificial intelligence (AI) and machine learning (ML) with robotics. The goal is to streamline operations and combine it with minimizing unnecessary packaging. The integration of AI and ML will doubtless have features of the black boxes senior managers resist. Nevertheless, process descriptions make sense and have gained support from Amazon management. Robots work with human operators and are responsible for picking, sorting, and packing millions of products every day. The process generates huge sets of data which is used to train models that enable the robots to pick and package a very diverse and complex range of products. "*At the core of Amazon's robotic systems is machine learning, which allows the machines to "learn" from their environment and improve their performance over time.* (cf. Johnson (2024)).

The use of real-time data is explained as a game-changer in Amazon's packaging operations as it allows Amazon to respond to changes in packaging materials, changes in shipping routes, or feedback from customers. One particularly important application of machine learning is in the handling of unstructured environments " ... *if a robot is tasked with picking a coffee mug from a bin full of diverse items, it needs to use computer vision to identify the mug, understand how to grip it without breaking it, and move it to the correct packaging station*". These tasks may seem simple, but they require advanced ML algorithms and extensive data to perform them reliably at Amazon's scale. The company's AI and ML models are constantly being updated with new data, allowing them to become more accurate and effective over time.

Decision analytics promises to be a game-changer for dealing with the uncertainty that is at the core of real options valuation. The challenge is to get the methods adopted by seasoned managers and experts that can make use of the options markets and find investment opportunities that other potential investors have either missed or been unable to work out. In the next section we will sketch out a digital ecosystem that can take over key DSS functions, offer modern digital support for users and offer an updated platform for decision analytics.

3. DIGITAL ECOSYSTEMS

We understand digital ecosystems as being digital in terms of the infrastructure they are built upon and ecosystems in terms of how they are organized. A digital ecosystem is an open socio-technical system with interoperability of interconnected information technology resources. The digital ecosystem construct we focus on is a platform ecosystem (cf. Koch et al (2022)), *a software system that forms the technical core of a digital ecosystem*. A platform ecosystem enables revenue streams and supports the building and maintenance of databases. Digital platform ecosystems are scalable, interconnect with information technology resources and allow access to a multitude of digital support services (cf. Koch et al (2022)). This also points to development paths to accommodate (e.g.) (i) enhanced modelling with (large) databases for statistics and graphics, (ii) support functions for digital service asset providers and brokers, (iii) applications of analytics tools, and (iv) employment of digital coaching.

In an extensive research project Koch et al (2022) offered a number of criteria for digital ecosystems; among these (DE1), *there is at least one digital ecosystem service; digital ecosystem services mutually exchange data*; (DS1), *the digital platform enables the digital core service activity*; (KP5–openness), *openness is understood as facilitating the system's accessibility in order to enable the "use, development, and commercialization of a technology"*; (KP6–collaboration), *digital ecosystems facilitate collaboration*. We noted that DSS builders, working with the planned systems users, found much use for *design science* as a methodology for systems development. Hevner (cf. (2004)) stated that usable systems solutions can be found through building and implementing designed artifacts. Markus et al (2002) shows that new, innovative, more advanced ICT artifacts extend the boundaries of human problem-solving, which also is one of the aims with digital ecosystems. We will work out the design-science paradigm in some more detail. March and Smith (1995) identified two design processes and four design artifacts for information systems research. The design processes are (i) *build* and (ii) *evaluate*, and the artifacts are *constructs*, *models, methods* and *instantiations*. In design science, artifacts are built for understanding and tackling unsolved problems; artifacts are evaluated to find out how well they contribute to the problem-solving; *constructs* describe problems and solutions and communicate solutions to users; *models* use the constructs to find connections between problems and solution components; *methods* define processes, and *instantiations* show how constructs, models and methods can be implemented into a working system.

In the following, (cf. fig.1), we will work through the TE-DW digital ecosystem design which is worked out for the real options valuation challenge we use as an example and a storyline. The ecosystem is a network of interconnected and collaborating modules D1-D6. Early versions of the TE-DW have been implemented, tested and evaluated in a number of cases (cf. Makkonen et al (2020)).

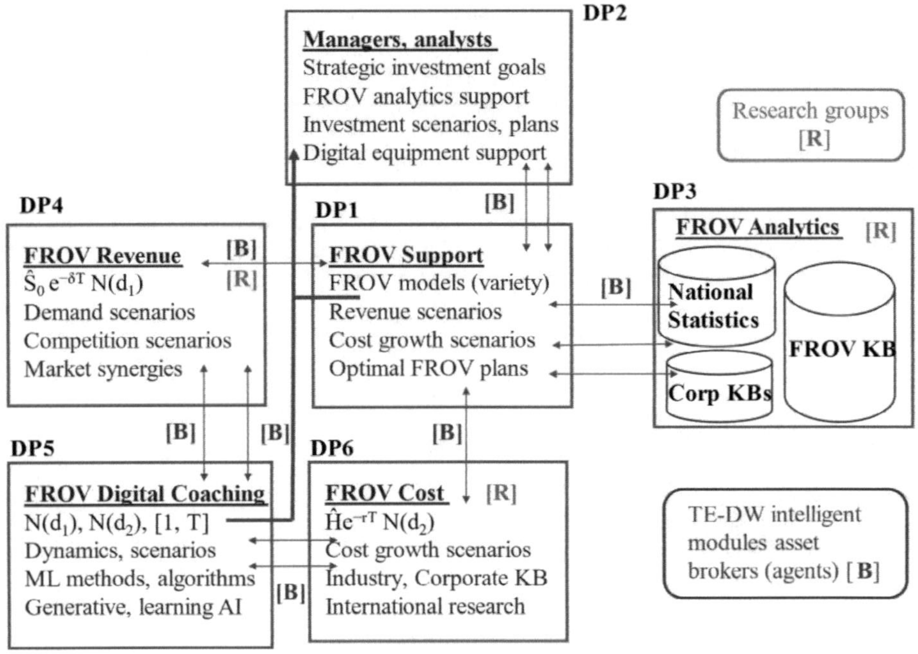

Figure 1. The TE-DW digital ecosystem

The DP1 module supports work with FROV models, allows a user to activate a variety of models for revenue and cost growth scenarios and to select optimal FROV plans. Managers, and analysts (who are not working with DP1), operate the ecosystem through DP2, which supports work on strategic investment goals and sketches on investment scenarios; DP2 describes FROV analytics and supports user operations of the ecosystem with digital pads and smart phones. DP3 collects data and offers data and knowledge bases for FROV analytics. DP4 supports work on revenue streams for selected periods in the interval [1, T] with models for dynamic demand, competition scenarios and macro modelling of market synergies. DP6 supports work on cost growth scenarios for selected periods in the interval [1, T] with access to corporate and industry data, and macro models from international research. DP5 is a digital coaching module to introduce and support the use of dynamic scenario models, machine learning methods and algorithms, and the use of generative and learning AI, which all will be useful for large and complex strategic investment problems.

We will work out some details on the modules DP1-DP6, which in terms of technology are digital platforms (cf. Koch et al (2022)). The TE-DW ecosystem and the modules DP1-DP6 follow the design science principles of *build* and *evaluate*, and use *constructs*, *models*, *methods* and *instantiation elements* to form the digital ecosystem.

- DP1 is the FROV Support platform; methods and models are functionality and support tools; models represent revenue and cost growth scenarios; methods are differential equations or soft computing techniques; models and methods for multiple criteria optimisation help find optimal FROV plans; instantiations – optimal FROV plans.
- DP2 supports managers and analysts with secure communication, team and group support and inter- and intra-group collaboration on digital support tools or smart phones (Android, iOS); DP2 supports models for developing strategic investment goals that fit FROV modelling; DP2 uses (e.g.) simulation tools to describe and explain FROV analytics and to present investment scenarios in usable form for non-professionals; instantiations – strategic investment goals, investment scenarios, investment plans.
- DP3 supports FROV analytics models; DP3 collects data from DP1 and builds a database and a knowledge base for FROV analytics; DP3 collects a corporate database for DP4 and DP6, and collects a national statistics depository for DP4 and DP6; DP3 works with tools for big data and knowledge bases to build a data depository for the TE-DW that adapts to changes in the [1, T] interval; instantiations – depositories.

- DP4 supports FROV revenue modelling; DP4 works with fuzzy modelling for demand and competition scenarios; methods use differential equations, time series with fuzzy parameters or soft computing techniques; market macro models cover market synergies; instantiations – revenue scenarios.
- DP5 formulates and works out digital coaching platforms for the DP1 FROV Support; DP5 offers models for digital coaching on dynamics, scenarios and differential equations; DP5 operates and coaches the use of algorithms, machine learning, generative and learning artificial intelligence; DP5 is activated from/by DP1, DP4 and DP6; instantiations – coaching advice, support.
- DP6 supports FROV cost modelling; DP6 works with fuzzy modelling for cost growth scenarios; methods use differential equations, time series with fuzzy parameters or soft computing techniques; DP6 uses data from DP3 and macro data from international research reports; instantiations – cost growth scenarios.
- The intelligent modules asset brokers [**B**] are intelligent agent-type systems that onboards DP1 FROV Support with managers and analysts on DP2; DP5 on DP4 and DP6; DP3 on DP1, DP4 and DP6.
- Research groups [**R**] can get access to the DP1-DP6 platforms to carry out research programs.
- Corporate user groups collaborate through DP2 to share ideas and comments.

As digital services operate with sensor inputs the TE-DW offers support for decision makers: sophisticated database support, powerful modelling functions and powerful but simple user interface design (digital support tools, smart phones). TE-DW also fits the requirements of Peter Keen's agenda (i) look for areas where the experience and skills of DSS builders and users can get new, emergent forms to be applied in new ways; (ii) apply new forms of analytical models and methods; (iii) exploit emerging software tools and new results on AI methods and instruments; (iv) use the experience of seasoned practitioners for testing the validity and relevance of real options for challenging investment opportunities. The DP2 even supports the modern trends to make decisions – even real options valuations – "on-the-go" as the motto is that "the fast eat the slow". Thus, it appears that we can give the DSS paradigm new forms and opportunities with digital ecosystems platforms.

Several versions of the TE-DW Ecosystem platform have been developed, implemented and used in the (DW) *DigitalWells* research program (cf. Carlsson and Walden (2022, 2023)) that worked to activate young elderly in Finland towards trying out and adopting health-enhancing physical activity (HEPA) programs. As a research tool we developed a digital support platform and application (the most recent version is the DW-app 3.0) that collects PA exercises, shows intensity and duration, logs the results to a cloud-supported database, builds graphical PA reports and shows (weekly, monthly) goal attainment for the user. The DW-program has so far attracted more than 1000 users, who have logged 294 140 PA events from which we have collected PA and HEPA statistics and paired the results with cross-sectional and longitudinal data on experiences with the program. The Metabolic Equivalence (MET) results, which show the effects of individual PA exercises, may not be very precise if compared to lab experiments but will still motivate users, who get a basis to decide that "*the time spent will actually give sufficient health effects*" by comparing the individual efforts with the recommendations we collected in the DW- program.

The development part of the *DigitalWells* followed the design science methodology, (Hevner et al (2004)) with successive iterations of improved constructs based on feedback from users. Gradually, this process firmed up to a process of search for drivers that get potential users to adopt HEPA exercises and turn them into (weekly) routines that extend to monthly or yearly sustained habits (cf. Carlsson and Walden (2022), (2023)). The iterative development of the TE-DW platform and the ecosystem gained support from field studies with the young elderly users. The field studies used several theory frameworks that offered different perspectives on activities, such as Unified Theory of Acceptance and Use of Technology (Venkatesh et al (2012)) and Self-efficacy and Self-Determination Theory (Teixeira et al (2012)), who found that more autonomous forms of motivation support are more effective than traditional group support. The field studies showed (among sets of observations, cf. Carlsson and Walden (2022, 2023)) that performance accomplishment was the main explanation for increased self-efficacy. The increase in self-efficacy for HEPA exercises is important for sustained HEPA when it is reached. The results from field studies suggested – a bit surprising - to widen the search for theory frameworks beyond traditional Information Systems frameworks.

4. CONCLUSIONS

Management makes decisions, and will have to answer for the consequences, either the loss of a major opportunity or the cost of a failed, major investment. Management routinely seeks guidance from classical methods that are readily available for decision analysis, but do not help much. Classical methods guide to discount for external uncertainty and will contribute to maybe cancelling interesting and innovative projects because they come with significant uncertainties that may become active in some future. It was found that real options can be worked out and valued using option theories.

With the use of real option valuations management will get guidance for their decisions to exercise options to invest, or to postpone investments, and if so to postpone them T time periods. Still, there are challenges in real option valuation to see the meaning of a "current real option" or to verify that it is correct.

Shortcomings and critical counterexamples in numerous industrial cases have generated reinterpretations of decision analysis and at the same time introduced more powerful methods and algorithms to meet the challenges from large, complex problems of dynamic, interactive elements (like the case of real options). This development also offered formal frameworks for important management decisions from the 1980'es through the 2020'es.

Decision support systems entered the field in the 1980'es as alternative instruments to the methods and tools of the advanced decision analysis. Managers, experts, knowledge workers, and systems developers in the 2020s are different from earlier DSS users, with different expectations and requirements on functionality from the support technology and the problem-solving support. Technological proficiency levels of DSS users have improved and they appear to continue to increase. Then it has been a bit of surprise that the DSS methods could not provide any clear contributions on how to handle the real options case, nor offer any insight on "real option valuation".

Decision analytics promises to be a game-changer for dealing with the uncertainty that is at the core of real options valuation. The challenge is to get the methods adopted by seasoned managers and experts that can make use of the options markets and find investment opportunities that other potential investors have either missed or been unable to work out. We have proposed that digital ecosystems, that are developed following design science criteria, will offer platforms for operating advanced decision analytics models and algorithms in an understandable form even for "on-the-go" decision support. The TE-DW digital ecosystem has been tested in the *DigitalWells* program.

We showed that the TE-DW digital ecosystem can take over key DSS functions, offer modern digital support for users and offer an updated platform for decision analytics. As digital services, tools and instruments operate with sensor inputs the TE-DW offers support for decision makers: sophisticated database support, powerful modelling functions and powerful but simple user interface design (digital support tools, smart phones).

REFERENCES

Black, F. and Scholes, M. (1973) The pricing of options and corporate liabilities, *Journal of Political Economy, 81, 637-659.*

Bonchek, R.H. et al. (1981*) Foundations of Decision Support Systems*, Academic Press

Carlsson, C. and Fuller, R. (2003). A fuzzy approach to real option valuation, *Fuzzy Sets and Systems*, 139, 297-312.

Carlsson, C. (2012). Soft computing in analytics: handling imprecision and uncertainty in strategic decisions, *Fuzzy Econ. Rev. XVII (2)* (2012) 3–21.

Carlsson, C. (2018). Decision Analytics Mobilised with Digital Coaching, *Intelligent Systems in Accounting, Finance and Management*, ISAF1421, January/March 2018, pp 3-17 DOI: 10.1002/isaf.1421

Carlsson, C. (2019). Combining ANFIS and Digital Coaching for Good Decisions in Industrial Processes, *IFSA/NAFIPS'2019 Proceedings*, Springer Verlag 2019, pp 190-200

Carlsson, C. and Walden, P. (2022) Digital Support Activates Young Elderly to Health-Enhancing Physical Activity, Piet Kommers and Mario Macedo (eds) *Proceedings of the MCCSIS 2022 Conference/E-Health 2022*, July 19-22, 2022, Lisbon, pp 189-196, ISBN 978-989-8704-40-5

Carlsson, C. and Walden, P. (2023) Young Elderly DSS Users – Some Reasons for Sustained and Successful Adoption, in Shafeng Liu, Pascale Zaraté, Daouda Kamissoko, Isabelle Linden, Jason Papathanasiou (eds.) *Decision Support Systems XIII. Decision Support Systems in An Uncertain World: The Contribution of Digital Twins*, ICDSST 2023, LNBIP 474, Springer 2023, pp 252-264

Dantzig, G.B. (1951). Application of the simplex method to a transportation problem. T.C. Koopmans (Ed.), *Activity Analysis of Production and Allocation*, John Wiley and Sons, 359-373

Gass, S.I. and Assad, A.A. (2014). History of Operations Research, *INFORMS Tutorials in Operations Research*, https://doi.org./10.1287/euc.1110.0084

Hevner, A. R. et al. (2004). Design Science in Information Systems Research. *MIS Quarterly*, 28, 75-106.

Johnson, D. Packaging and Robots. How AI and sustainability are transforming the journey from click to delivery at Amazon, *IEEE Spectrum*, November 19, 2024

Keen, P. and Scott Morton, M. (1978). *Decision Support Systems. An Organizational Perspective*, Addison-Wesley Publishing

Keen, P. (1987). Decision Support Systems. The Next Decade, *Decision Support Systems, 3 (3)*

Koch, M., et al (2022). A matter of definition: Criteria for digital ecosystems, *Digital Business*, Vol.2, Issue 2, 1-13

Leslie, K.J. and Michaels, M.P. (1997). The real power of real options, *The McKinsey Quarterly*, 3, 5-22

Makkonen, M., et al (2020). Changes in the Use Intention of Digital Wellness Technologies and Its Antecedents Over Time: The Use of Physical Activity Logger Applications Among Young Elderly in Finland. *Proceedings of the HICSS-54 Conference*, pp 1262-1271

March, S.T. and Smith, G.F. (1995). Design and Natural Science Research on Information Technology, *Decision Support Systems*, 15(4):251-266

Markus, M. L., et al, (2002). A Design Theory for Systems that Support Emergent Knowledge Processes, *MIS Quarterly* (26:3), September, pp. 179-212.

Merton, R. (1973) Theory of rational option pricing, *Bell Journal of Economics and Management Science*, 4, 141-183

Mezei, J., et al (2017). A fuzzy approach to using expert knowledge for tuning paper machines, *JORS 68* (6) (2017) 605–616.

Morente-Molinera, J.A., et al (2016) A linguistic mobile decision support system based on fuzzy ontology to facilitate knowledge mobilization, *Decision Support Systems*, 81 (2016) 66–75

Morse, P.M. and Kimball, G.E. (1951). *Methods of Operations Research,* John Wiley and Sons

Shim, J.P. et al, (2002). Past, present, and future of decision support technology, *Decision support systems* 33 (2), 111-126)

Simon, H.A. and Newell, A. (1958). Heuristic Problem Solving: The Next Advance in Operations Research. *Operations Research*, 6(1), 1-10

Sinuany-Stern, Zilla (2023). Foundations of operations research: From linear programming to data envelopment analysis, *European Journal of Operational Research,* 306, 1069-1080

Teixeira, P.J. et al, 2012. Exercise, Physical Activity and Self-Determination Theory: A Systematic Review, *Int. Journal of Behavioral Nutrition and Physical Activity,* Vol. 9, No.78, pp. 1-30.

Venkatesh, V. et al, 2012. Consumer Acceptance and Use of Information Technology: Extending the Unified Theory of Acceptance and Use of Technology. *MIS Quarterly*, Vol. 36, No. 1, pp.157-178.

X PLATFORM SHARING BEHAVIOR AND MINOR SAFETY INCIDENTS: A DESIGN EFFORT TO LEVERAGE THE POWER OF THE CROWD

Mashael Yousef Almoqbel
Jubail Industrial College
Jubail city, Kingdom of Saudi Arabia

ABSTRACT

This research investigates the effects of several variables on X platform users' likelihood of sharing minor public safety incidents. We conduct a 2 x 2 x 2 repeated measures and between-subjects online experiment. Based on the theory of collective action and prior literature, we examine three manipulations: availability of location information to share the tweet locally, availability of platform authority, and sender (tweeter) authority. We conduct an online experiment with a Qualtrics sample of 246 participants. The study found that location information in public safety tweets did not influence decisions to share incidents. However, when participants decided to share, they were more likely to share incidents locally and increase their exposure. Platform authority did not show a significant effect on decisions to share. Finally, the authority of the tweeter (original poster) significantly affected decisions to share incidents on social media.

KEYWORDS

Social Media, Content Sharing Behavior, Public Safety, Understanding People

1. INTRODUCTION

The number of Americans using social media is growing each year. According to the Pew research center, in 2021, around 81% of the population is using some form of social media (Auxier & Anderson, 2021). An important feature of social media platforms is the ability to easily share content with everyone they choose – people they know vs people they don't know, and in different ways, publicly or privately. In the case of public safety, sharing content on social media increases exposure to it, increases awareness to the raised issue, and may help solve crimes (Heverin & Zach ,2010). Reasons for sharing content in social media have been studied numerously (Dedeoglu, 2018). However, there is a general lack of understanding about reasons to share public safety incidents on social media.

Research in public safety and social media comprises a large part of the literature. Specifically, large scale incidents, due to their high impact, received a lot of attention from researchers in many fields, including computing, CSCW, and HCI (Almoqbel & Xu ,2019; Reuter et al., 2018; Saha & De Choudhury ,2017 ; Zade et al., 2018). Incidents less severe are less studied in the literature (Almoqbel et al., 2020). Minor incidents such as pick pocketing or a closed road are also important to investigate. Therefore, in this research, we focus on incidents of a minor severity and try to understand what affects social media users' decisions to share minor safety incidents on social media, in an attempt to try to influence those decisions to improve public safety.

In this study, we base our investigation on prior literature as well as the theory of collective action. The theory of collective action (Olson ,2009) states that sane and rational individuals will not participate in a public good, unless they are forced to, or there is another incentive on top of the public good that everyone will benefit from. For example, Olson (Olson ,2009) states that people will not pay taxes if there are no rules, regulations, and sanctions from the government to enforce this requirement. Still, everyone will benefit from tax money in terms of public services. In this research, the act of sharing minor public safety incidents on social media to raise awareness and/or to find perpetrators is considered a contribution to public good. Therefore, in an effort to understand users' sharing behavior, with the use of fictitious scenarios, we investigate the effect of three variables on users' decisions to share minor incidents on X, namely: location information, platform authority, and sender (tweeter) authority.

2. BACKGROUND

2.1 Decisions to Share Content on Social Media

Social media users share content on those platforms for many reasons. For example, a study found that retweeting is a prosocial activity that carries underlying motives such as altruism and reciprocity (Lee et al., 2015). The content of the tweets plays a major role in decisions to share those posts. A study found that the number of retweets a post receives does not alter users' intentions to share. Nonetheless, the actual content of the tweet matters (Hung et al., 2015; Park & Kaye ,2019). Research found that the emotional tone of a tweet increases its retweetabbility, or chance to be retweeted (Papachristos et al., 2012). Another similar study conducted on X to understand why users retweet or share content on the platform revealed that users retweet to disseminate and amplify information, inform followers of something, and approve information in those posts, among other reasons (Boyd et al., 2010). In terms of sharing public safety incidents, previous research found that incident severity and location affect people's decisions to report incidents (Huang et al., 2017). Another relevant research that looked at motivations to share disaster- related information on X found that users share those tweets because they wish to provide current and updated information to their community, they desire to share what they believe as relevant information, they want to engage with their community, and they base their sharing decisions on their feelings about the tweet (Nor Athiyah et al., 2017).

2.2 Location Information

Prior research in the field of public safety found that location plays a significant role in terms of information sharing. For example, researchers found that residing in, or living close to a location that was hit by a disaster was highly related to tweeting about the said disaster (Grasso & Crisci ,2016; Smith ,2010). Researchers also found that social media users are more likely to share significant incidents if they are in a close geographic location (Starbird & Palen ,2010). A case in point is when more X users shared information about a disaster when they were closer to the incident than users who lived further away (Kongthon et al., 2014), (Shelton et al., 2014)

Location information was found to be very important in shared tweets about public safety events. Previous research found that authorities and individuals use X hashtags to discuss specified disasters such as the Boston Marathon bombing, the Texas plant explosion, and others (Wukich & Steinberg ,2013). Prior research also found that X users included location information in tweets about specified disasters such as floods and wildfires (Murthy & Gross ,2017; Vieweg et al., 2010). During Hurricane Sandy, a study found that most tweets about the disaster included location related hashtags. The authors found that "five of the top ten hashtag pairs [for Hurricane Sandy] include a storm-related hashtag with a location-related hashtag" (Murthy & Gross, 2017). Moreover, during disasters, X users share location information when tweeting about disasters to allow communicating with other users near the incident and reach out to first responders (Murthy & Gross, 2017; Vieweg et al., 2010).

Prior literature focused on significant incidents and found that location information affects social media users' decisions to share those large-scale incidents (Almoqbel & Xu ,2019). In our inquiry line, we try to understand if location information still affects decisions to share if the severity of the incident is minor. Thus, we hypothesize the following:

- H1. X users who are exposed to location information will be more likely to share incidents on X than users who are not exposed to location information.
- H1.1. When X users decide to share minor incidents on X, they will more likely share using the 'Shield button', which allows for increased local exposure, than the regular X retweet button.

2.3 Coercion

Coercion can be explained as any form of oppression that compels a person to act in a certain way. Coercion can be witnessed as a form of rule, authority, or regulation that includes consequences for violators.

In this research, we introduce two types of coercion in the form of authority: 1. Platform authority in the form of an update to X Terms of Service that requires users to share public safety incidents. 2. A high versus low authority of the tweeter such as an official citizen action group account versus a regular X user.

Tweeter authority: Previous literature found that people perceive law enforcement and other authorities as trustworthy and just entities (Tyler ,2006). Also, prior research found some evidence that when law enforcement accounts on X are transparent with their online community, X aids in increasing perceived legitimacy of those law enforcement accounts (Grimmelikhuijsen & Meijer ,2015). Many research found that legitimacy leads to positive public safety-related behaviors such as compliance with regulations and cooperation with legal entities (Jackson et al., 2012; Murphy et al., 200 ; Papachristos et al., 2012). In the case of public safety, a study used content analysis techniques to understand retweeting behaviors related to the South Korean anti-terrorism regulation (Park & Kaye ,2019). The researchers found that tweets initially created by authorities such as political figures and higher authority individuals were retweeted more than tweets originally posted by regular X users; hence, providing evidence that the tweeter's authority matters in the context of public safety (Park & Kaye ,2019).

Thus, based on previous literature findings, and as a form of cooperation with authorities, we predict that X users will be more likely to share tweets that are tweeted or sent from law enforcement accounts, more than tweets from random people with no legitimate authority. We hypothesize the following:

- H2. X users who are exposed to minor public safety incidents shared by officials on X will be more likely to share those incidents than users who are exposed to minor public safety incidents shared by normal users on X.

Platform authority: Platform authority has the power to instate their own rules in the Terms of Service and have the right to enforce them. Researchers found that people are more likely to obey or adhere to rules and regulations from higher authorities such as law enforcement (Jackson et al., 2012; Tyler 1991 ; Tyler & Fagan 2008). Moreover, previous research found that X users are more likely to share minor public safety incidents if provided with a hypothetical rule from an authority such as the government (Almoqbel et al., 2021).

According to collective action theory, a government rule is considered a form of coercion and is supposed to influence decisions when participating in a public good (Olson ,2009). To test for platform authority, we present participants with consequences that we predict will serve as coercive elements and motivate sharing decisions. We isolate and test the effect of platform authority to understand further if a higher power has more influence on social media in minor public safety incidents. Drawing from collective action theory (Olson ,2009), and previous findings (Almoqbel et al., 2021), we assume X users will be more likely to follow the X platform's rules due to perceived legitimacy in authority and their ability to coerce users to follow appropriate conduct. We hypothesize:

- H3. X users who are exposed to platform authority will be more likely to share incidents on X than users who are not exposed to platform authority.

Due to a lack of studies and literature in this area, we would like to explore any possible interaction between the three manipulations we are studying. We ask the following research question:

- RQ1 Are there any interactions between the main effects?

3. METHODS

3.1 Participants

We needed three different samples to run the study. We recruited two samples for pretesting and later one sample for the online experiment. To indicate the approximate number of participants required for the experiment, we ran a power analysis using G*power software. Since we are using a mixed experimental design, there is no specific formula to calculate the sample for this design to the best of our knowledge. Therefore, we can either use a small effect size (where the formula would suggest a higher number of participants) or assume we will use a between-subjects design. The formula will suggest a large number of participants to be able to see an effect. We first ran the power analysis (power =.80, and p = 0.05) for a complete within-subjects, assuming low effect size. The result suggested a need to have at least 108 participants in total. Then, we re-ran the power analysis assuming a complete between-subjects design. The result suggested recruiting at least 27 participants per group, a total of 217 for the experiment. Thus, in hopes of being able to see better results, and to have a more conservative estimate, we use the latter calculation.

The experiment sample was comprised of adults aged 18 and older residing in the U.S. who are also X users. We used a panel from Qualtrics where a project manager helped with the initial data collection of 256 participants. After the soft launch, we received 10% of the data to check the quality of the data-points and to see if there are variances in the answers and that the treatments are generally causing variance in answers. Then, we continued with the full launch of the experiment. The total number of responses received was 256. After manually checking the results, we identified 29 responses as poor quality. The reasons were answering in a straight-line manner and writing irrelevant text in the open-ended questions. The project manager then ran the experiment and collected 19 more participants. The total responses that were deemed usable are 246. We paid $5 per participant recruited by Qualtrics. The average time spent taking the survey was 7.5 minutes and the data collection was completed in one week.

3.2 Procedure

We choose to conduct a within-subjects and a between-subjects experiment design (mixed design). Since platform authority is difficult to erase after it's introduced to participants, to prevent transferred learning that occurs if the same group is exposed to the no treatment and the treatment, this manipulation will be conducted as a between-subjects experiment, where participants will only either see the treatment or not. Therefore, location information and sender authority will be treated as a within-subjects design, while platform authority will be treated as a between-subjects design, where only half of the participants will be exposed to the treatment.

After testing the posts' content, the proposed design, and the manipulation variables, we conduct the experiment. The experiment is an online experiment with recruits from Qualtrics. We use a 2 (location information vs. no location information) by 2 (authority of tweeter whether official authority or an average person) within-subjects by 2 (coercion from platform authority, no coercion from the platform) between-subjects design experiment. The main dependent variable that we test is likeliness to share minor incidents on X. Our main independent variables are: availability of location information, availability of sender authority, and availability of platform authority.

As part of pretesting, we recruited a total of ten participants and interviewed them about the design of the experiment. Participants were recruited through a snowball method. The interviews were short and took about 15-20 minutes. Participants were asked to give feedback about a fictitious design which is a button that is used to specifically share safety incidents. The material that was tested is in Figure 1. We also showed participants a fictitious message from X that included an update to X Terms of Service that expresses the need to share incidents to raise awareness and find perpetrators (Figure 4), which constitutes coercion and platform authority. The first part of the message includes the fictitious update to X's Terms of Service. The second part contains an original text from the X website that provides information on how the platform enforces its rules (Twitter, 2021). After showing participants the material, we ask them qualitative questions such as how real they think the updates looks and what would they think of the button design. The researchers took notes while participants answered questions about the experiment materials. Most of the comments were related to the language of the X update and some grammatical issues. The author then updated the experiment materials accordingly. Participants were rewarded with $10 for their volunteer participation.

3.2.2 Manipulation 1. For the first manipulation (availability of location information with the incident tweet), we add a fictitious button next to each safety tweet that looks like a shield (Figure 1). We call it the 'Shield' button, which we explain to participants that it utilizes local location-related trending hashtags and automatically attach those hashtags to the tweet's content that the user wants to share. Let's assume that someone is posting about a suspicious van in their street; if another user wants to share this information locally, they can press the Shield button and have the tweet shared in their local location to increase its exposure. When clicking the button, to avoid misuse of the function, the button will quickly run an embedded algorithm to test the topic of the post and ensure that it is safety-related and to circumvent any attempt to advertise one's content, that is not safety related, using the proposed button.

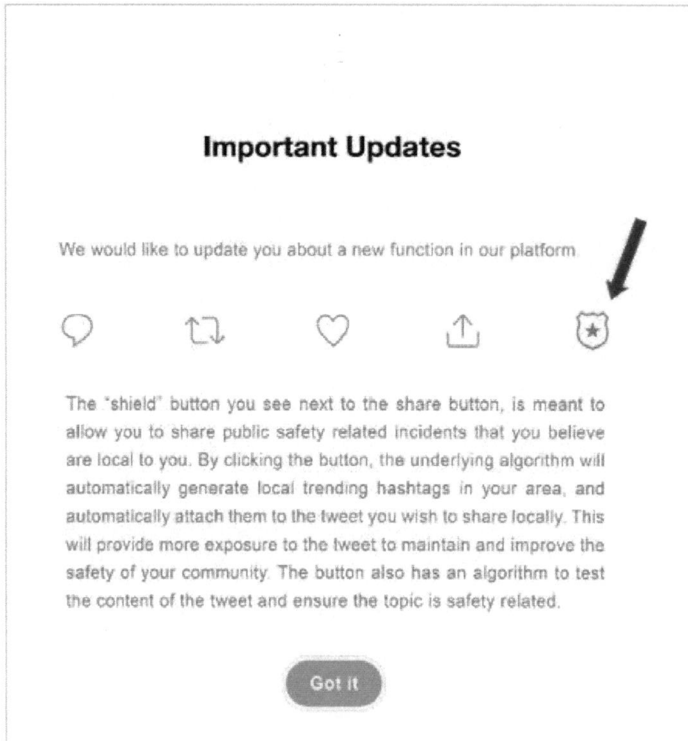

Figure 1. Fictitious update to X that introduces the Shield button

Participants will be asked to read through the instructions (Figure 1). They will see a picture with a red arrow that explains the feature of the Shield button and its function. Participants in the treatment group will be presented with four posts about local public safety incidents that we have used in the pilot study and found suitable and reflect minor safety incidents. The tweets will have more information next to them that reads "happening locally" (Figure 2).

Participants will then be asked to answer a question, as shown below:

- Q1. After viewing the previous tweet, how likely will you share it on X? A Likert-type scale ranging from one (not likely at all) to seven (very likely)
- Q2. How will you share the tweet?
- I will retweet using the X retweet button
- I will retweet using the "Shield" button. (Shield button increases local exposure for public safety tweets).

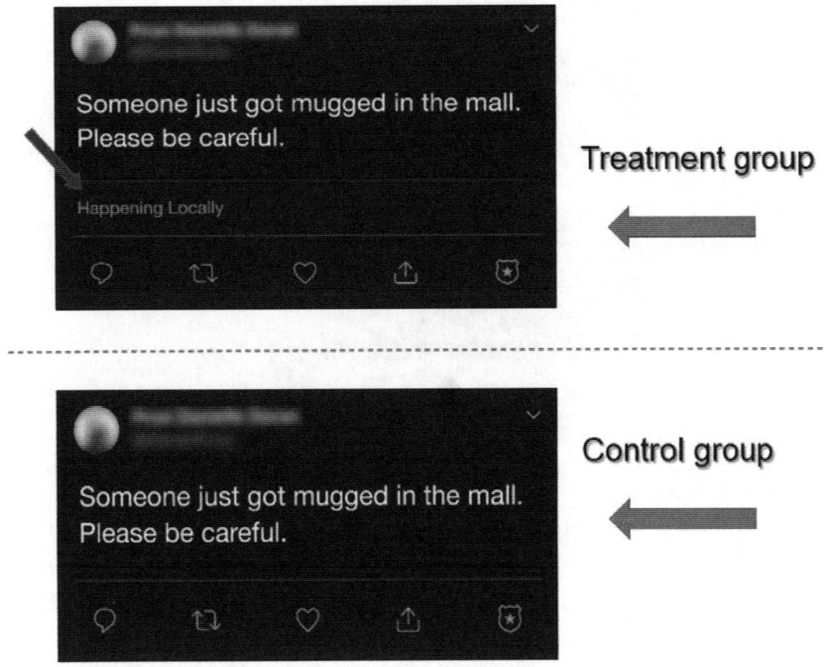

Figure 2. Location Treatment Versus Control Group

The control group will see the same posts but will not have the extra information “happening locally" (Figure 2).

Therefore, not providing them with location information.

Manipulation 2. For the second manipulation (sender authority, whether they are an official authority such as a citizen action group vs. an average person), participants in the treatment group would see four posts from higher authority accounts on X. The sender (tweeter) of this post will be a high authority (Figure 3).

Then, participants will be asked to answer the following question after each tweet: Q1. After viewing the previous tweet, how likely will you share it on X? A Likert-type scale ranging from one (not likely at all) to seven (very likely). The control group will view public safety tweets from regular users who are not officials, which conveys low authority. Participants will see four tweets of minor incidents and will be asked the same question presented for the treatment group. We anticipate that the treatment group will have a higher likelihood to share compared to the control group.

Manipulation 3. The third manipulation (providing a rule that the platform instated, which requires sharing public safety incidents) tests the possible effects of coercion on decisions to share on X through platform authority (Figure 4). According to collective action theory (Olson ,2009), and a previous study conducted in this regard (Almoqbel et al., 2021), coercion affects X users’ tendency to share incidents. We aim to see if the platform can instate something similar to coercion and affects decisions to share. The treatment group will be presented with text that resembles the Terms of Service of X.

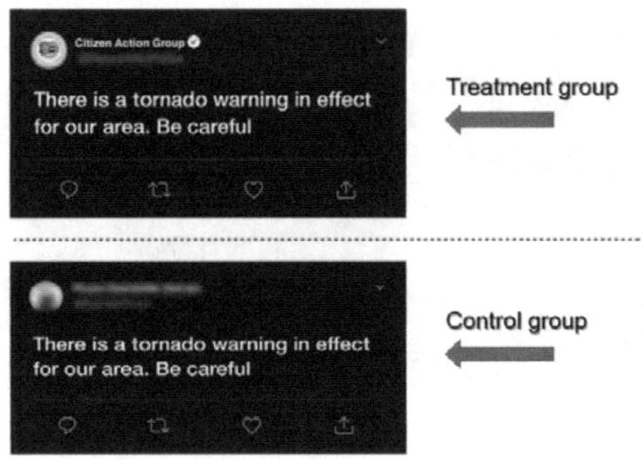

Figure 3. Sender Authority Treatment Versus Control Group

The participants will read that this is an update to X Terms of Service in an attempt to have a more responsible community and a new requirement to abide by law enforcement rules; and that X expects its users to assume a more responsible role to share public safety incidents on X to help maintain and improve public safety for everyone (Figure 4). Then, participants will see four posts about minor public safety, where we expect them to mostly decide to share.

The question they will see after each minor incident tweet will look like this:

- Q1 . After viewing the previous tweet, how likely will you share it on X? A Likert-type scale ranging from one (not likely at all) to seven (very likely)

The control group (Figure 4) will only see the same minor incident tweets (without the Terms of Service update) and will be asked the same question after each tweet, similar to the treatment group.

3.3 Measures

Basic participants demographic data were collected. Our experiment participants' gender demographic was comprised of women (50.4%), men (49.2%), prefer not to say (0.4%). Age was measured using a one to five scale that corresponds to the following values accordingly: 18-27 years old (32.9%), 28-37 years old (7.3%), 38-47 years old (24.8%), 48-57 years old (20.7%), and 58+ (14.2%). Participants reported the following ethnicities: White (80.1%), Black or African American (6.9%), Asian (6.5%), Mixed race (3.7), American Indian or Alaska native (1.6%), Other (1.2%). Basic X usage frequencies were collected.

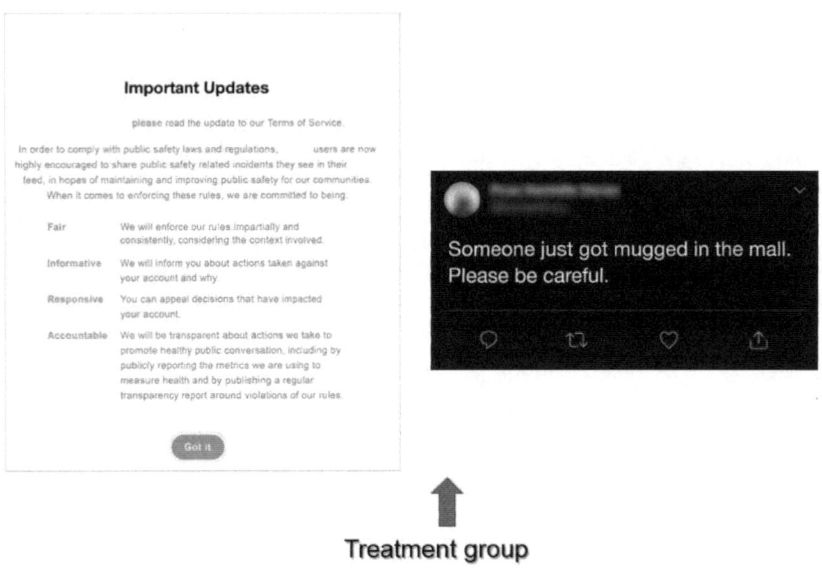

Figure 4. Platform authority treatment group

Participants education (M=18.03, SD=3.9) was reported as a number of years of education they received. We asked how often do you use X? (M=4.15, SD=0.99) and how often do you tweet or retweet? (M=3.18, SD=1.37). The former two questions were measured using a Likert-type scale ranging from one to five, using the following categories: less than once every three months, once or twice every two months, several times a month, several times a week, several times a day. We also asked a number of questions post survey. Participants were asked to answer the following statement: I paid attention throughout the time I was doing the survey, yes (98.4%), No (1.6%). Participants were also asked: Were the instructions and explanations in the survey clear to you? (M=6.49, SD=0.90), and were the questions clear to you? (M=6.49, SD=0.93). The former two questions were measured using a Likert-type scale ranging from one to seven, where 1=Not clear at all, and 7= Very clear.

To check for the attention of participants, we asked them to report the type of content they read. The question included the following options: public safety, nature, education, politics, other. Participants who did not select public safety were removed from the analysis. To test for the sender authority treatment, we asked the question: How much authority did you perceive in the sender of the previous tweet? (M=4.37, SD=1.68), where participants answered using a Likert-type scale ranging from 1=no authority to 7=very high authority. To test for the platform authority treatment, participants were asked: Do you think X as a platform has an authority to influence users about the content they post? Where they answered: Yes (75%), or No (25%).

Figure 5. Platform authority control group

4. RESULTS

To test for the hypotheses, we run full factorial mixed-design ANOVA and paired samples t-tests. One of ANOVA's assumptions is that the dependent variable is continuous. The dependent variables in this study are measured in a scale of 1-7, therefore, considered continuous. Normality of distribution is required by ANOVA and we tested the Kurtosis and Skewness. All values were within -2 and +2 which is considered acceptable and data is not significantly distinguishable from a normal distribution (George & Mallery ,2010). To satisfy ANOVA's assumptions, we run Levene's test which is not significant. We also assume sphericity because we only have two conditions per treatment, therefore, Mauchly's sphericity test is equal to 1.

After running the ANOVA, we found no significant difference between the treatment group viewing location information (M=4.42, SD=1.51) and the control group (M=4.16, SD=1.45). The main effect of location information on sharing was not significant, $F(1, 244) = 0.38$, $p = 0.54$. Therefore, we reject H1. We found a significant difference between the treatment group viewing high sender authority tweets (M=4.36, SD=1.47) and the control group (M=4.14, SD=1.54). The main effect of sender authority of sharing was significant, $F(1, 244) = 13.85$, $p < 0.001$. Therefore, we accept H2. For platform authority, we found no significant difference between the treatment group viewing the X update (M= 4.16, SD= 1.66) and the control group (M= 3.99, SD= 1.75). The main effect of platform authority was not significant ($F(1, 244) = 0.24$, $p = 0.63$). Therefore, we reject H3.

We found no significant interaction between location and platform authority, F (1, 244) = 3.17, p = 0.08. Sender (tweeter) authority and platform authority had no significant interaction, F (1, 244) = 0.02, p = 0.89. Location and sender authority had no significant interaction, F (1, 244) = 0.17, p = 0.68. Location, sender authority, and platform authority had no significant interaction, F (1, 244) = 0.26, p = 0.61.

For H1.1 (When X users decide to share minor incidents on X, they will more likely share using the 'Shield button', which allows for increased local exposure, than the regular X retweet button), we tested using a paired samples t-test. The variables (how likely will you share using the X button, how likely will you share using the Shield button), were measured using a 7-point Likert type scale. The distribution of the variables was not normal, so we computed variables using square root function in SPSS to bring down the Kurtosis to normal levels, between -2 and 2. The resulting four variables adjusted are:

- Likelihood to share tweets that include location information (including the phrase "happening locally") using the Shield button
- Likelihood to share tweets that do not include location information using the Shield button
- Likelihood to share tweets that include location information using the X retweet button
- Likelihood to share tweets that do not include location information using the X retweet button.

The former variables values range from 0.50 to 2.65.

Here, we hypothesized (H1.1) that when X users decide to share an incident, they will share using the Shield button (shares locally by attaching local trending hashtags). There was a significant difference in the scores for sharing tweets with location using the Shield button (M=1.34, SD=0.93) and sharing tweets without location using the Shield button (M=1.24, SD=0.93); t (245) = 2.37, p <0.05. There was also a significant difference between sharing tweets with location using the Shield button (M=1.34, SD=0.93) and sharing tweets with location using the X retweet button (M=0.78, SD=0.88); t (245) = 5.96, p <0.001. For the last pair, there was a significant difference between sharing tweets without location using the Shield button (M=1.24, SD=0.93) and sharing tweets without location using the X retweet button (M=0.82,SD=0.88); t (245) = 4.49, p <0.001. Therefore, we report that H1.1 is supported.

In summary:

- H1 X users who are exposed to location information will be more likely to share incidents on X than users who are not exposed to location information is rejected.
- H1.1 When X users decide to share minor incidents on X, they will more likely share using the 'Shield button', which allows for increased local exposure, than the regular X retweet button is accepted.
- H2 X users who are exposed to minor public safety incidents shared by officials on X will be more likely to share those incidents than users who are exposed to minor public safety incidents shared by normal users on X is accepted.
- H3 X users who are exposed to platform authority will be more likely to share incidents on X than users who are not exposed to platform authority is rejected.
- RQ1 Are there any interactions between the main effects? No found interactions.

5. DISCUSSION

The location of an incident has a major effect on decisions to share that incident on social media (Almoqbel et al., 2020). When we looked at decisions to share using the Shield button (allows for more local exposure to public safety tweets), we saw a significant difference of decisions to share using that button. We were able to see an effect of location on decisions to share perhaps for a number of reasons. The new design addition (Shield button) was explicitly explained to participants in a new update to X. The new button was highlighted to participants before they started the experiment, therefore, participants were very aware of its utility and its presence.

The prior findings suggest that X, and possibly other social media platforms, are able to make design enhancements to improve and maintain overall safety. X already has many safety initiatives. For example, with the COVID pandemic, X updated its Terms of Service and included new policies. Posts such as misleading medical tweets, fake news about cures and vaccines, and others have been blocked (Gadde & Derella, 2020). We saw that X introduced new censorship guidelines to prevent certain content from being viewed by the public, as well as censoring entire users' profiles. X also has a dedicated X handle @XSafety that is dedicated to maintaining safety while using X worldwide. However, there is always opportunities for improvements and we believe that X could utilize the Shield button and pilot test it with a subset of their customer-base and see if the results we found in the self-report experiment are possible in real life situations.

Examining the effect of coercion on decisions to share was interesting. In Olson's collective action theory, it is presumed that rational individuals are inclined to abide by rules and regulations if there is a form of coercion (Olson ,2009). We looked at coercion from the perspective of an authority. For sender (tweeter) authority, we used citizen action group as a source of neutral authority. We presented the source information in a way that may infer authority such as adding a check next to the X handle conveying that the account is authentic. Also, we asked our participants to report how much authority they perceive in the source "citizen action group" ranging from one to seven (highest authority), and they reported a relatively mid to high authority (M=4.37, SD=1.68). When the authority of the original sender of the tweet was high (we used citizen action group), we found that participants were more inclined to share those tweets. This finding is consistent with prior research which found that authority has an impact on compliance (Chiu & Hung ,2020). The finding is also consistent with collective action theory (Olson ,2009), proving that the scope of the theory explains behaviors in social media and in the field of public safety. What is interesting is that the type of authority we had was citizen action group which is a less authority compared with law enforcement. Prior research found that the higher the authority and trustworthiness, the higher the compliance with the said authority (Chiu & Hung, 2020). Thus, when participants decided to share the tweets posted by the citizen action group, they might have done so because of authority or because of perceived trustworthiness of the citizen action group, which might be perceived as a neutral party compared to law enforcement. This is an opportunity for future research to look into different levels of authority and explore whether this difference will have a varying effect on decisions to share incidents.

We speculate a number of reasons of why we did not see a significant difference in some of the tests. The treatment group was exposed to tweets with an extra fictitious information written in blue that says, "happening locally". This addition is not part of the original X design and was not introduced to the participants before the experiment. Perhaps the unfamiliarity of the design change interfered with any possible effects. It is quite possible that participants did not notice this addition and, therefore, inhibited any possible effect on their decisions. Circling back to results in (Almoqbel et al., 2021), we see a clear contradiction. The results of this research found no effect of location on decisions to share based on the ANOVA analysis (although the mean of sharing in closer locations was higher than the mean of sharing with no location information).

Platform authority showed no effect on participants' decisions to share. This finding is possibly due to the kind of treatment we used. We showed participants a page containing text of a fictitious update to X Terms of Service. It is possible that participants did not fully read the text which is the manipulation. A national survey found that 91% of American users skip the Terms of Service and just consent or click 'ok' to proceed and get access to the content (Cakebread ,2017). In fact, an interesting empirical research found that 98% of participants consented on a fake Terms of Service agreement to pay by giving up their first newborn for social media access (Obar & Oeldorf-Hirsch ,2020). Therefore, we speculate that some participants failed to read the presented text, where they will also fail to perceive the authority we predict; therefore, we were not able to see any change in their sharing behavior. It would be interesting for future work to run the study and monitor the time spent on each task, or use eye-tracking tools to ensure that participants were properly exposed to the treatment, to make a better judgement about the effect of platform authority, if any.

We asked a question of whether there are any interactions between the main effects, and we found no interactions. We asked the question to explore possible interactions although there was no research that backs up this assumption. There might not be an interaction, or, due to the design limitations, such interactions were buried and failed to show in the ANOVA. Moreover, the nature of the context we tested was minor incidents. It is possible that participants thought that these tweets are not important enough to warrant a share on social media. Thus, running the study with higher severity incidents might reveal different insights.

6. LIMITATIONS

This study has a number of limitations. The online experiment was based on self-reported data which is not always accurate. Also, running the study in the time of the COVID pandemic could have had an effect on the reported results. Participants' attention and how they view social media and X in particular could have influenced the results. For example, with the rise of the COVID pandemic, the number of fake information and posts on the media skyrocketed and many reports about fake news on social media surfaced. This might have had an effect on decisions to share critical information on social media.

7. CONCLUSION

In this study, we found that location of an incident does not affect decisions to share that incident. Although this finding does not support prior literature, we discuss possible reasons for lack of significant effect. We proposed a design suggestion in the form of a button "we call it the Shield button" that increases exposure to public safety tweets by attaching locally trending hashtags to those tweets. Participants reported using the Shield button significantly more than they used the traditional retweet button. Design implications and possible future research ideas are discussed.

REFERENCES

Almoqbel, M. Y., Alraihan, M. K., & Wohn, D. Y. (2021). Understanding Decisions to Share Minor Public Safety Incidents on Twitter Through a Collective Action Theory Lens. International Journal of Social Media and Online Communities (IJSMOC), 13(1), 76–92.

Almoqbel, M., & Xu, S. (2019). Computational Mining of Social Media To Curb Terrorism. ACM Computing Surveys (CSUR), 52(5), 1–25.

Almoqbel, M., Xun, W., & Hiltz, S. R. (2020). Do I Care Enough? Using A Prosocial Tendencies Measure to Understand Twitter Users' Sharing Behavior for Minor Public Safety Incidents. In 53rd Hawaii International Conference on System Sciences (pp. 1–10). https://hdl.handle.net/10125/64053

Auxier, B., & Anderson, M. (2021). Social Media Use in 2021. https://www.pewresearch.org/internet/2021/04/07/social-media-use-in-2021/

Boyd, D., Golder, S., & Lotan, G. (2010). Tweet, Tweet, Retweet: Conversational Aspects of Retweeting on Twitter. In 43rd Hawaii International Conference on System Sciences (pp. 1–10).

Cakebread, C. (2017). You're Not Alone, No One Reads Terms of Service Agreements. Business Insider. https://www.businessinsider.com/deloitte-study-91-percent-agree-terms-of-service-without-reading-2017-11

Chiu, T., & Hung, Y. (2020). Impacts of Leader Humility Between Authority and Trustworthiness on Compliance: Tests of Three-Way Interaction. Psychological Reports.

Dedeoglu, B. B. (2018). Are Information Quality and Source Credibility Really Important for Shared Content on Social Media? The Moderating Role of Gender. International Journal of Contemporary Hospitality Management.

Gadde, V., & Derella, M. (2020). An Update on Our Continuity Strategy During Covid-19. Twitter Blog.

George, D., & Mallery, P. (2010). SPSS for Windows Step by Step: A Simple Study Guide and Reference (10th Ed.). Pearson Education, Inc.

Grasso, V., & Crisci, A. (2016). Codified Hashtags for Weather Warning on Twitter: An Italian Case Study. PLOS Currents, Disasters, 8. https://doi.org/10.1371/currents.dis.967e71514ecb92402eca3bdc9b789529

Grimmelikhuijsen, S., & Meijer, A. (2015). Does Twitter Increase Perceived Police Legitimacy? Public Administration Review, 75(4), 598–607.

Heverin, T., & Zach, L. (2010). Twitter for City Police Department Information Sharing. Proceedings of the American Society for Information Science and Technology, 47(1), 1–7.

Huang, Y., White, C., Xia, H., & Wang, Y. (2017). A Computational Cognitive Modeling Approach to Understand and Design Mobile Crowdsourcing for Campus Safety Reporting. International Journal of Human Computer Studies, 102, 27–40.

Hung, Y., Hwu, D., Arkenson, C., & Lee, Y. (2015). Designing For Retweets: A Study on Twitter Interface Design Focusing on Retweetability. Procedia Manufacturing, 3, 5496–5503.

Jackson, J., Bradford, B., Hough, M., Myhill, A., Quinton, P., & Tyler, T. (2012). Why Do People Comply with the Law? Legitimacy and the Influence of Legal Institutions. The British Journal of Criminology, 52(6), 1051–1071.

Jackson, J., Bradford, B., Stanko, B., & Hohl, K. (2012). Just Authority?: Trust In the Police in England And Wales. Routledge.

Kongthon, A., Haruechaiyasak, C., Pailai, J., & Kongyoung, S. (2014). The Role of Social Media During A Natural Disaster: A Case Study Of The 2011 Thai Flood. International Journal of Innovation and Technology Management, 11(03), 1440012. https://doi.org/10.1142/s0219877014400124

Lee, M., Kim, H., & Kim, O. (2015). Why Do People Retweet a Tweet? Altruistic, Egoistic, And Reciprocity Motivations for Retweeting. Psychologia, 58, 189–201.

Murphy, K., Tyler, T., & Curtis, A. (2009). Nurturing Regulatory Compliance: Is Procedural Justice Effective When People Question the Legitimacy of the Law? Regulation & Governance, 3(1), 1–26.

Murthy, D., & Gross, A. (2017). Social Media Processes in Disasters: Implications of Emergent Technology Use. Social Science Research, 63, 356–370.

Nor Athiyah, A., Dai, N., Yuko, T., & Yuko, M. (2017). Why I Retweet? Exploring User's Perspective on Decision-Making of Information Spreading During Disasters. In Proceedings of the 50th Hawaii International Conference on System Sciences.

O'connor, C., & Murphy, M. (2020). Going Viral: Doctors Must Tackle Fake News in The Covid-19 Pandemic. BMJ, 369, 10.1136.

Obar, J., & Oeldorf-Hirsch, A. (2020). The Biggest Lie on The Internet: Ignoring the Privacy Policies and Terms Of Service Policies Of Social Networking Services. Information, Communication & Society, 23(1), 128–147.

Olson, M. (2009). The Logic of Collective Action: Public Goods and The Theory of Groups (2nd Ed.). Harvard University Press.

Papachristos, A., Meares, T., & Fagan, J. (2012). Why Do Criminals Obey the Law? The Influence of Legitimacy and Social Networks on Active Gun Offenders. The Journal of Criminal Law and Criminology, 397–440.

Park, C., & Kaye, B. (2019). Expanding Visibility on Twitter: Author and Message Characteristics and Retweeting. Social Media and Society, 5(2).

Reuter, C., Hughes, A. L., & Kaufhold, M.-A. (2018). Social Media in Crisis Management: An Evaluation and Analysis of Crisis Informatics Research. International Journal of Human–Computer Interaction, 34(4), 280–294.

Reuter, C., Kaufhold, M.-A., Spielhofer, T., & Hahne, A. S. (2017). Social Media in Emergencies: A Representative Study on Citizens' Perception in Germany. Proceedings of the ACM On Human-Computer Interaction, 1, CSCW, 1–19.

Saha, K., & De Choudhury, M. (2017). Modeling Stress with Social Media Around Incidents of Gun Violence on College Campuses. Proceedings of the ACM on Human-Computer Interaction, 2, CSCW, 1–27.

Shelton, T., Poorthuis, A., Graham, M., & Zook, M. (2014). Mapping The Data Shadows of Hurricane Sandy: Uncovering The Sociospatial Dimensions of "Big Data." Geoforum, 52, 167–179. https://doi.org/10.1016/j.geoforum.2014.01.006

Smith, B. (2010). Socially Distributing Public Relations: Twitter, Haiti, And Interactivity In Social Media. Public Relations Review, 36(4), 329–335. https://doi.org/10.1016/j.pubrev.2010.08.005

Starbird, K., & Palen, L. (2010). Pass it on?: Retweeting In Mass Emergency. In Proceedings of the 7th International Information Systems for Crisis Response and Management Conference (pp. 1–10). https://doi.org/10.1111/j.1556-4029.2009.01231.x

Twitter. (2021). Twitter's Enforcement Philosophy and Approach to Policy Development. https://help.twitter.com/en/rules-and-policies/enforcement-philosophy

Tyler, T. (1991). Why People Obey the Law. Contemporary Sociology, 20(6), 914. https://doi.org/10.2307/2076190

Tyler, T. (2006). Does The American Public Accept the Rule of Law? The Findings of Psychological Research on Deference to Authority. Depaul Law Review, 56, 661.

Tyler, T., & Fagan, J. (2008). Legitimacy And Cooperation: Why Do People Help the Police Fight Crime in Their Communities? Ohio State Journal of Criminal Law, 6, 231. https://doi.org/10.2139/ssrn.887737

Vieweg, S., Hughes, A., Starbird, K., & Palen, L. (2010). Microblogging During Two Natural Hazards Events. In ACM Conference on Human Factors in Computing Systems (pp. 1–10). https://doi.org/10.1145/1753326.1753486

Wukich, C., & Steinberg, A. (2013). Nonprofit And Public Sector Participation in Self-Organizing Information Networks: Twitter Hashtag and Trending Topic Use During Disasters. Risk, Hazards & Crisis in Public Policy, 4(2), 83–109.

Zade, H., Shah, K., Rangarajan, V., Kshirsagar, P., Imran, M., & Starbird, K. (2018). From Situational Awareness to Actionability: Towards Improving the Utility of Social Media Data for Crisis Response. Proceedings of the ACM On Human-Computer Interaction, 2, CSCW, 1–18.

E-LEARNING FOR MICRO-ENTERPRISES: NEW SWISS FEDERAL ACT ON DATA PROTECTION

Ilya Misyura, Bettina Schneider and Melanie Bühlmann
University of Applied Sciences and Arts Northwestern Switzerland, Switzerland

ABSTRACT

Switzerland, though not being a member of the European Union (EU), implemented a revised data protection law. The new Federal Act on Data Protection (nFADP) has become applicable in September 2023. This regulatory change represents a challenge for micro-enterprises operating in or dealing with personal data, including customer, employee, or supplier data. Small businesses often face hurdles such as limited legal expertise, a lack of dedicated compliance staff, and difficulties adapting complex regulations to their specific needs. To help micro-enterprises navigate the new data protection law, there is a clear need for accessible knowledge and tools to support nFADP compliance. Through qualitative interviews with professional associations and a literature review, existing resources were analyzed, revealing a need for action. Identified research gaps included a lack of condensed, industry-specific guidance, and the absence of practical, step-by-step procedures tailored for small businesses. In response, an interactive online course was developed, offering a targeted, practical approach to nFADP compliance specifically designed for micro-enterprises. This course, which has undergone an initial evaluation, serves as a free resource that not only benefits micro-businesses but also provides a valuable foundation for educators and professionals focused on data protection compliance.

KEYWORDS

E-Learning, Data Protection Compliance, Micro-Enterprises, nFADP

1. INTRODUCTION

Since September 2023, Switzerland has enacted a revised data protection law that imposes strict requirements on how companies must handle personal data (Fedlex, 2023). Businesses have to comply with mandates such as conducting data protection impact assessments and fulfilling data breach reporting obligations. These requirements present a significant compliance challenge for micro-enterprises (MEs), which often operate with limited financial and human resources (Oyetumji, 2024). In the same way that companies outside the European Union (EU) processing personal data of EU residents must comply with the General Data Protection Regulation (GDPR), companies processing personal data of Swiss individuals are also subject to nFADP irrespective of their location (GDPR, Art. 3, 2018; Fedlex, Art. 3c, 2023). To effectively meet the data protection obligations, the first crucial step for MEs is to build a profound understanding of the Swiss law. This requires training that is specifically tailored to their needs, considering factors like duration, language, and instructional style.

Our research shows that MEs in Switzerland are facing considerable challenges in educating and training their employees on the revised data protection law. Interviews with industry representatives (see section 2.2) underscored the difficulties in obtaining industry-specific guidance, coupled with a shortage of available high-quality resources. Furthermore, we analyzed selected existing e-learning resources (see section 2.3) based on their fit for MEs – using the criteria of flexibility and low-cost access to knowledge (Bednarczyk et al., 2012). The analysis revealed a lack of training resources tailored to the specific needs of micro-enterprises operating in Switzerland, as most of the materials either focus on the GDPR or provide inadequate coverage of nFADP (refer to Table 2 in Section 2.3).

Given these inputs, we have decided to create, design, implement, and evaluate an easy-to-access e-learning course for micro-enterprises that would provide clear and targeted materials about nFADP. The approach taken for designing the course can be adapted for creating learning materials regardless of the jurisdiction in which data protection law is applied. The research described in this paper is linked to an

EU/Swiss research project named *Micro-Enterprise Cybersecurity (MECyS).* The international project aims to upskill employees in small businesses confronted with increasing digitalization and bridging the gap in cybersecurity as well as data protection competence (MECyS, 2024a).

The remainder of this paper is structured as follows: Section 2 provides information on European and Swiss data protection laws, characterizes the target group of micro-enterprises, and analyzes the current state of e-learning materials in these topics. Section 3 describes the development process of our e-learning course, including its design principles and implementation, and its evaluation. Section 4 concludes the paper with a summary of key findings and an outlook on future work to refine and enhance the course.

2. BACKGROUND AND RELATED WORK

2.1 Overview of Swiss and European Data Protection Laws

Switzerland has had a Data Protection Act in force since 1993 (Fedlex, 2019). A starting point for discussions on data protection was the desire to guarantee the protection of privacy in the face of technical developments. At this time, computers that allowed to gather, store, and process large amounts of personal data were becoming increasingly important, while simultaneously creating new privacy risks. Much has changed in terms of digitalization since the first data protection law had been introduced. The ubiquity of the internet and smartphones in everyday life has increased and has created the need for regulating privacy in the digital space (Kiss & Szőke, 2015). All this caused a series of refinements of the law and ended in a revised Federal Act on Data Protection in 2020 which came into force on September 1, 2023 (Fedlex, 2023).

Essential changes introduced in nFADP are among other things: the expansion of the definition of sensitive personal data, the incorporation of the concept of profiling, and the introduction of new principles such as "privacy by design" and "privacy by default" (SME Portal, 2024). These expansions mean that companies must be much more vigilant in their data processing and need to take more measures and establish processes to demonstrate compliance. Moreover, even though the Federal Data Protection and Information Commissioner (2024) has published supporting material such as a guide to technical and organizational measures (TOMs), the implementation of new concepts is challenging.

Even though the Swiss nFADP and the EU GDPR are very close to each other and GDPR trainings can serve as a reference, there is a need for nFADP-specific training content. Reasons for that are, for example, that wordings differ on several occasions and might cause confusion (e.g. Verzeichnis der *Be*arbeitungstätigkeiten (Fedlex, Art. 12, 23) vs. Verzeichnis der *Ver*arbeitungstätigkeiten in GDPR (Art. 30). Moreover, certain exemptions for small businesses differ in the two regulations (such as the need to establish a record of processing activities) and the obligation to have Data Protection Officer varies (see Fedlex, Art. 10, 23 and GDPR, Art. 13, 14, 30, 33, 35, 36-39). Also, the handling of fines is different in the two legislations (GDPR, Art. 83, 2018; Fedlex, Art. 59-64, 2023). According to SME Portal (2024), companies that already comply with the GDPR have minimal changes to make. Still, for those businesses, a flexible e-learning course elaborating on nFADP specifics is valuable. Moreover, Swiss MEs that have not yet been affected by GDPR have to build up the knowledge and act upon it from scratch.

2.2 The Profile and Needs of the Micro-Enterprise Target Group

According to the EU legislation (EUR-Lex, 2005), a micro-enterprise is defined as a company that employs fewer than 10 people, while a small enterprise employs less than 50 people. The Swiss Federal Statistical Office (Bundesamt für Statistik, 2017) defines micro-enterprises in the same way, but they mostly talk about Small and Medium-sized Enterprises (SMEs) in general without distinguishing between micro, small, and medium enterprises.

MEs encompass a wide range of small businesses, such as plumbing companies, massage salons, carpentry services, law firms, and many others. According to Benz and Chatterjee (2020), most of them face challenges in adapting to changes in legislation, which stem from various factors, including limited awareness, lack of access to affordable professional legal advice, and the absence of a clear, actionable roadmap to compliance. Many SME managers are confused about basic data security concepts, and despite their willingness to invest in compliance measures, a large number of MEs still struggle to fully comply with legal requirements.

To gain first-hand insight into the challenges MEs face, six organizations were invited for interviews, with three agreeing to participate. One of these organizations not only answered the questions but also expressed interest in the complete training course. Below is a summary of the key feedback received regarding the new data protection legislation.

The first organization, a professional association in Switzerland, highlighted the difficulty in issuing uniform guidelines due to the diverse nature of industries. Some businesses operate online shops, while others do not even have a website. While some core data protection principles have remained unchanged, others have been altered or eliminated, such as the exclusion of company data from protection under the revised law. In response to the new legislation, this association developed a minimal compliance solution, which included a guide and sample documents that businesses could tailor to their own needs. Interestingly, the association reported receiving few inquiries about the new law, offering three possible explanations. First, because they had proactively developed compliance tools ahead of time, members likely did not feel the need for further clarification. Second, the association believes it is unlikely that businesses have ignored the law, given the seriousness with which data protection is treated in Switzerland. Third, it is possible that various industries adapted the association's basic framework to suit their specific needs and shared it with their members. The biggest challenge for MEs, according to the association, is that they must address the new regulations, but in doing so, they often encounter excessive information that is not relevant to their specific context.

The second organization, a healthcare professional association in Switzerland, took a proactive approach by forming a dedicated project team to manage the transition to the new legal framework. Acknowledging the complexity and importance of compliance, they engaged a specialized lawyer to guide the process. Together, they carefully mapped out and agreed on the necessary steps to ensure full alignment with the new data protection regulations. As part of the healthcare sector, they also partnered with a larger, well-resourced organization. This collaboration enabled them to access pre-prepared compliance documents, which they then tailored to fit their specific needs. This strategic partnership not only simplified the transition process but also ensured that they were fully prepared for the regulatory changes in a timely and efficient manner.

The third professional association responded to the interview request but declined to answer the specific questions. Their reasoning was that the organization had already provided its members with a data protection declaration specifically tailored to their industry. This declaration was developed in collaboration with a legal expert and with input from the section presidents of the association. As a result, they felt that there was no further need for additional data protection training, as their members were already equipped with the necessary tools to comply with the new regulations.

In conclusion, the implementation of nFADP has presented various challenges across different industries and SMEs. While some industry associations have been very proactive and provided their members with excellent material—as the healthcare example shows—the interviews reveal a gap in raising awareness and knowledge among micro-enterprises. The experiences of these associations highlight the importance of tailored approaches to data protection education, and this again underscores the need for clear and accessible educational resources to bring understanding and compliance among MEs that are subject to nFADP.

2.3 Analysis of E-Learning Materials on Data Protection in Europe and Switzerland Tailored to Micro-Enterprises

To delve deeper into the needs and gaps in existing data protection e-learning resources for MEs, it is essential to analyze materials available in Europe and Switzerland tailored to this sector. As a starting point, a list of existing tools focusing on data protection selected by the MECyS project team was taken to assess how useful each one can be for MEs (MECyS, 2024a). The list of criteria for the analysis was adapted from one in *MECyS List of Learning Tools* (2024a) and presented in Table 1. In the original document, the criteria were purely descriptive or contained yes/no questions. In our study, the tools were awarded points depending on whether they met the requirements: The more points an instrument receives, the more suitable it is for data protection training, according to the authors' assessment. Depending on the importance of the criterion, between two and a maximum of six points were awarded.

Table 1. Tools assessment criteria

Assessment criterion	Description of the assessment criterion
Type of the tool	The assessment of the format and medium of the tool, without evaluating its content or effectiveness; focus on the structural nature of the tool (game, course, app, LMS, etc.); one point per sub-criterion can be granted (4 maximum): format suitability, user accessibility and compatibility, intuitiveness of interface and usability, technical performance and speed.
Description of the tool	One point per sub-criterion can be granted (4 maximum): clarity of purpose, detailed instruction for use, overview of features and benefits, explicitly mentioned relevance for MEs.
Content type inside the tool	One point can be granted per each type of content included (4 maximum): explanatory content, interactive elements, visual aids, practical exercises.
Learning effect	Assessment of the learning effect on data protection awareness, the relevance and scope of materials (0 points for no effect, 1-4 if only GDPR is covered, 5-6 if both GDPR and nFADP are covered).
Accessibility (open-sourceness)	Assessment of accessibility: Is the tool open-source and can be used in other e-learning products or be adapted (1 point if no, 2 points if yes)?
Transparency of costs	Assessment of costs: 4 points if the tool is free or costs are transparent, 0 points if there are costs but they're not transparently mentioned.
Learning time	Assessment of duration: Is the stated duration of training proportionate to the learning effect and relevant to the tool structure in general (1 point minimum, 2 maximum)?
Available languages	Assessment of language versions: One point for the language available: German, French, Italian (Swiss official languages) and English (for international users), 4 points maximum.
Processing of personal data	Assessment of data protection compliance of the tool: the fact of personal data processing, and if so, the data processing policy is easy to access and written properly (2 points if the tool does not process personal data or, if it does, fulfills the requirements above, 0 if not).

The evaluation showed that most of the tools provide valuable resources in their specific domains and stem from appreciated experts. For example, *Lawpilots* offers e-learning modules on compliance topics, potentially providing significant value to MEs. *DATAK* game engages users by illustrating decisions that might fall under data protection laws, offering an interactive learning experience. *DPIA Tool* is particularly helpful in assessing risks connected with data processing, serving as a good initial step for organizations to identify risks as part of Data Processing Impact Assessment. *GDPR Quiz* is an open-source tool that effectively helps users understand the GDPR providing interactive case-based learning process.

However, having all these advantages, the existing materials do not entirely meet all the requirements defined by assessment criteria, especially concerning having nFADP-related content. For example, *DATAK* game is a great resource for awareness creation, but it is not designed to be a stand-alone knowledge building tool. *GDPR Quiz*, despite its effectiveness and the highest number of assessment points received, does not cover nFADP, making it only partially useful. *DPIA Tool* offers a user-friendly risk assessment process but does not teach the full Swiss or EU data protection law. Other resources, like *Rosenthal's template*, have a dedicated focus on one specific aspect of compliance and do not aim to cover the full law. One comprehensive resource is the offer by *Lawpilots*: it is focused on nFADP; however, it is not available as open-source.

Table 2 shows a summary of each tool assessed, major disadvantages identified and the number of points they received.

Table 2. Assessed tools on data protection in Europe and Switzerland

Name of the tool	Description and main criterion not met	Points
Geiger GDPR Quiz	Interactive quizzes on GDPR-related situations. Focuses only on GDPR, not on Swiss nFADP.	27
Lawpilots	E-learning platform for various compliance topics including data protection. Is not open-source.	25
DATAK	Open-source game with scenarios on data protection. Not designed for knowledge building, but as awareness tool.	22
Geiger DPIA Tool	Data Protection Impact Assessment tool to evaluate risks in data processing. Does not teach specific aspects of Swiss or EU data protection laws.	21
iBarry	Internet security platform by Swiss Internet Security Alliance. No specific resources for employee training on data handling and data protection compliance.	20
GDPR Check by Geiger	Questionnaire-based tool to assess GDPR compliance for SMEs. Focuses only on GDPR, not on Swiss nFADP.	18
Vischer Privacy Score	Questionnaire-based tool to identify data protection compliance gaps. It is focused on assessing and provides recommendations, but not designed for knowledge building.	17
Infoguard	Website with blog articles on security awareness basics. Being a cybersecurity company, it is not designed to focus on nFADP or GDPR.	16
Geiger Virtual Cybersecurity Escape Room	Game-based tool for cybersecurity awareness. Not designed for building knowledge on data protection.	14
Rosenthal Privacy Policy for SMEs	PDF template for creating a privacy statement. Focus is set on one aspect of data protection compliance.	14

In summary, there is a need for easy-to-access open-source, and concise ways for micro-enterprises to educate themselves on the different aspects of nFADP. The evaluated tools offer substantial coverage of data protection and cybersecurity, providing valuable resources in these areas. However, the evaluated tools are in general not specifically designed to build knowledge about nFADP while simplifying the legal aspects and being available as open-source. To address these shortcomings and save resources for micro-enterprises, it is essential to have the necessary information compiled in one place, where it can be easily accessed and organized in a logical, user-friendly manner. This is the gap that our Moodle-based course aims to fill, offering a resource that helps MEs understand and comply with the relevant legal requirements.

3. COURSE DEVELOPMENT

This section aims to elaborate on the development of an e-learning course built upon the insights from the literature reviewed in Section 2. The course structure, design principles, implementation, and evaluation strategies are presented in the following. It is also enriched by integrating insights from the *Swiss National Course Plan* created in scope of the MECyS (2024b) research project.

The course structure is based on one presented in the *Swiss National Course Plan* (MECyS, 2024b). The goal to create a country-specific course plan was to address specific contexts and challenges faced in each project partner's country, including Switzerland. In this document, two distinct learning pathways are presented: one for learners with beginner and intermediate level of knowledge in data protection and cybersecurity, and one for learners with advanced level of knowledge. Since data protection encompasses not just technical measures but also legal, organizational and procedural aspects compared with cybersecurity, the decision was made to follow the advanced pathway which looks like this on a higher level:

1. Risk Assessment and Evaluation
2. Specialized Training
3. Intermediate Assessment
4. Team Communication and Training

5. Final Certification and Improvement

Particularly, our new course adapts steps 1-3 of the MECyS pathway, additionally enriched with a step 0 which covers basics of data protection. Step 4 in our structure is the final certification (in alignment with step 5 from MECyS). Step 4 of the original MECyS pathway, "Team Communication and Training" is referred in the step 2.8 that highlights the moments that can be continuously reviewed both with the ME team and on self-educating level. The learning path steps are structured as follows:

0. Intro/Basics (importance of data protection and its general principles)
1. Data Protection Risk Assessment (using a roadmap to tailor the course to the ME, e.g. if a ME has no web shop, part 2.5 is not mandatory) and Knowledge Evaluation (basic quiz)
2. Training Content
    - 2.1. List
    - 2.2. Risk
    - 2.3. Technical and Organizational Measures (TOMs)
    - 2.4. Data Transfer
    - 2.5. Web Services/Online Shops
    - 2.6. Data Subject Rights
    - 2.7. Data Breaches
    - 2.8. Train and Improve
3. Knowledge Assessment (advanced quiz)
4. Final Certification

3.1 Design of the Course

The core principle during the design phase of our course development was that learners should be able to easily navigate and engage with the content. Each section of the course is accompanied by a set of slides which provide a concise exploration of the specific topic. These slide decks start with the relevant provisions from nFADP and its accompanying ordinance. Alongside these, the corresponding articles or a concise summarization from the GDPR are included. This dual approach not only grounds the learner in the Swiss legal framework but also offers a broader perspective by incorporating the GDPR.

As participants progress through the slides, they encounter highlighted excerpts that underscore the critical aspects of the legislation. These highlights are designed to draw attention to the most significant parts of the laws, ensuring that learners can easily grasp the essential points. Additionally, the slides include overviews that summarize key legal concepts, along with direct links to further legal texts, which allow them to delve deeper into the subject matter if they wish to do so.

Moreover, the course content is enriched with practical applications through the introduction of case studies. For each major topic, two case studies are presented, each accompanied by a series of targeted questions. These questions are crafted to stimulate critical thinking and engage participants. On the subsequent slides, answers to these questions are provided, allowing learners to check their understanding and reflect on the reasoning behind the correct responses. By prompting participants to actively think through the scenarios and formulate answers before revealing the solutions, the course ensures that learners are not merely passive recipients of information but are actively involved in the learning process. This approach enhances comprehension and retention, making learning experience both interactive and effective.

Before participants begin working through the slides, they can take an initial knowledge and data protection risk assessment. The initial knowledge assessment is organized in the form of a quiz. It serves as a valuable step for gauging the current understanding of the data protection topic. Furthermore, the quiz serves as a preview on the style of the second knowledge assessment relevant for certification. The data protection risk assessment is organized in the form of an eight-step-roadmap toward data protection compliance. By self-assessing each of the steps, learners can identify areas that are of higher and lower risk for the ME and following to that tailor the course scope (e.g., if a ME has no web shop, the training content No. 2.5 can be omitted). This initial risk assessment helps learners focus their attention on the sections of the course that might require more in-depth study, making their learning experience more targeted and efficient.

After working through all the relevant training contents, there is one more educational step. It is a test provided at the end of the course. This assessment is designed to measure how much participants have learned and retained throughout the course. By comparing their results from the initial quiz with their performance on the final test, students can see their progress and improvement in understanding the material. This final evaluation not only reinforces the knowledge gained but also provides a sense of accomplishment, confirming that the time and effort invested in the course have resulted in a deeper grasp of the subject. This final assessment is evaluated using a points system, and if the learner reaches a defined points threshold, an online certificate will be issued. For students interested in exploring certain topics further, the course also includes links and references to additional literature, providing opportunities for deeper learning.

3.2 Implementation and Initial Evaluation

Our course is implemented on the Moodle-based platform maintained by MECyS and available via: https://campus.mecys.eu/course/view.php?id=835. It is accessible to all users registered on the platform. The authors have conducted an initial evaluation of the newly developed course, comparing it against the criteria in Table 1. The self-assessment results and qualitative justification are provided in Table 3.

Table 3. Design justification according to assessment criteria

Assessment criterion	Design justification
Type of the tool	The course has the *format* of e-learning easily *accessible* via web, Moodle as LMS platform offers a standardized and *intuitive* interface.
Description of the tool	The *course structure, purpose and user instructions* are introduced to learners at course start supported by a visual roadmap allowing tailoring contents to specific learner needs. The course is visually divided into sections allowing an overview of the *course features* available.
Content type inside the tool	The main part of the course entails *explanatory content* in form of *visually* appealing slides. *Interactive elements* incorporate quizzes allowing learners to check their current level. Throughout the course, two case study examples are providing insights into *practical application* fitting the ME-context.
Learning effect	The course covers nFADP and GDPR. Yet, an evaluation of learning effects on data protection awareness of ME-representatives has to be conducted in near future.
Accessibility (open-sourceness)	The course follows the SCORM standard allowing *integration and adaptation* on other LMS platforms. Ensuring *open-sourceness* is one of the planned future steps.
Transparency of costs	The course is *free to use and adapt.*
Learning time	The course has a planned, *own-paced duration* of 24 hours learning time (3 ECTS). Tailoring the course to the most relevant contents allows learners to decrease the duration *appropriate to their needs.*
Available languages	The course supports the most *common Swiss language*, namely German. Future iteration might lead to French and/or Italian translation.
Processing of personal data	The course is hosted by one of the MECyS project partners *located in the EU.* A *privacy policy* when accessing the course will inform learners about the purposes of data processing.

In addition, the course was tested by one ME-employee located in Germany which is a subject to nFADP since the organization has customers from Switzerland. The feedback was positive in general and confirmed that our suggested format is suitable, and time taken to pass the course is relevant to the learning effect. Still, some downsides of the course were highlighted. Regarding the content, case studies and graphics were found the most beneficial, while theoretical sections, e.g. about "privacy-by-design", were perceived as difficult to comprehend. While the quiz was regarded as useful, the navigation in the multiple-choice questions was not sufficiently clear. Other aspects to improve are the information on the open-sourceness and the target group. Overall, the ME-feedback showed the necessity for balancing engaging and practical content with accessible and easy-to-understand theoretical information, as well as improving the usability of interactive elements.

4. CONCLUSION AND OUTLOOK

Micro-enterprises, being an essential driver of the Swiss economy, face considerable challenges in building knowledge about the revised national data protection law. Achieving nFADP compliance presents a significant burden for small businesses without specialized legal expertise, as the regulations are comprehensive.

Our research examined existing learning materials on data protection, with a particular focus on the Swiss nFADP and the GDPR. Various resources were evaluated based on criteria such as content type, learning effectiveness, language availability, and cost. The aim was to assess how well these materials support MEs in learning about data privacy and to identify gaps.

As the main result, a specialized e-learning course was developed to meet the specific needs of micro-enterprises. The course is designed to simplify the complexities of the nFADP and guide businesses toward compliance, bridging the gap between intricate legal requirements and practical implementation.

Our course provides significant added value as one of the few available that addresses both EU and Swiss data protection laws. This is especially crucial for small businesses operating across borders, as they must comply with both regulatory frameworks. Designed with the limited resources of small enterprises in mind, the course allows for content to be tailored to key topics based on a risk analysis, and it offers the flexibility of self-paced learning.

While the foundational structure of the course has been successfully developed, the next steps are to incorporate the improvements identified in the initial evaluation. An essential task will be an extended evaluation by broader target audience of MEs. Their role will be pivotal in evaluating the course's educational value, accessibility, clarity, and overall user experience. By observing how participants navigate the material and complete the interactive parts, we will gain valuable insights into the course's strengths and areas for improvement. This continuous process of evaluation and refinement will ensure the course not only meets its educational objectives but also provides an engaging, user-friendly learning experience.

REFERENCES

Bednarczyk, H., Koprowska, D. and Bednarczyk, I. (2012) Innovations in educating employees of microenterprises. Polish Journal of Continuing Education 1/2012, pp. 50-63.

Benz, M. and Chatterjee, D. (2020) 'Calculated risk? A cybersecurity evaluation tool for SMEs', *Business Horizons*, 63(4), pp. 531-540. doi:10.1016/j.bushor.2020.03.010.

Bundesamt für Statistik. (2017). *Kleine und mittlere Unternehmen*. [online] Available at: https://www.bfs.admin.ch/bfs/de/home/statistiken/industrie-dienstleistungen/unternehmen-beschaeftigte/wirtschaftsstruktur-unternehmen/kmu.html (Accessed 6 Oct. 2024).

Datak. (2024). *Datak.* [online] Available at: https://www.datak.ch/ (Accessed 6 Oct. 2024).

EUR-Lex. (2005). *Micro-, small- and medium-sized enterprises: Definition and scope*. [online] https://eur-lex.europa.eu/EN/legal-content/summary/micro-small-and-medium-sized-enterprises-definition-and-scope.html (Accessed 6 Oct. 2024).

Fedlex. (2019) *Federal Act on Data Protection (FADP) of 19 June*. SR 235.1. [online] Available at: https://www.fedlex.admin.ch/eli/cc/1993/1945_1945_1945/en (Accessed: 8 October 2024).

Fedlex. (2023). *SR 235.1 — Federal Act on Data Protection.* [online] Available at: https://www.fedlex.admin.ch/eli/cc/2022/491/en (Accessed: 26 September 2024).

GDPR, Legislation Regulation (EU) 2016/679, (EU) 2016/679 (2018). https://eur-lex.europa.eu/legal-content/EN/TXT/PDF/?uri=CELEX:32016R0679 (Accessed: 26 September 2024)

Geiger. *(n.d.). DPIA Tool.* [online] Available at: https://digitaltrust.pages.fhnw.ch/dpia-tool/ (Accessed 6 Oct. 2024).

Geiger. *(n.d.). GDPR-Check.* [online] Available at: https://community.cyber-geiger.eu/games/GDPRcheck-ch/ (Accessed 6 Oct. 2024).

Geiger. *(n.d.). GDPR Quiz.* [online] Available at: https://community.cyber-geiger.eu/games/GDPRQuiz (Accessed 6 Oct. 2024).

Geiger. *(n.d.). Virtual Cybersecurity Escape Room* [online] Available at: https://community.cyber-geiger.eu/games/vcser/ (Accessed: 26 September 2024)

iBarry. (n.d.). *iBarry*. [online] Available at: https://www.ibarry.ch/en/ (Accessed 6 Oct. 2024).

Infoguard. (n.d.). *InfoGuard Know-how Security Awareness*. [online] Available at: https://www.infoguard.ch/en/know-how-security-awareness (Accessed 6 Oct. 2024).

Kiss, A., Szőke, G.L. (2015). *Evolution or Revolution? Steps Forward to a New Generation of Data Protection Regulation.* In: Gutwirth, S., Leenes, R., de Hert, P. (eds) Reforming European Data Protection Law. Law, Governance and Technology Series, vol 20. Springer, Dordrecht. https://doi.org/10.1007/978-94-017-9385-8_13

Lawpilots. (2022). *Effektive Datenschutzschulungen für Unternehmen.* [online] Available at: https://lawpilots.com/de/e-learning/datenschutz/ (Accessed 6 Oct. 2024).

MECyS. (2024a). *Project Results to Improve Small Business Cyber Security: List of Learning Tools* Available at: https://mecys.eu/results/ (Accessed: 23 September 2024)

MECyS. (2024b). *Project Results to Improve Small Business Cyber Security: National Course Plans* Available at: https://mecys.eu/results/ (Accessed: 23 September 2024)

Oyetunji, S.A. (2024). *Investigating Data Protection Compliance Challenges. International Journal of Innovative Science and Research Technology* 9(8), pp.2131-2147. Available at: https://www.ijisrt.com/investigating-data-protection-compliance-challenges (Accessed 6 Oct. 2024).

Rosenthal, D. *(n.d.). Eine einfache, allgemeine Datenschutzerklärung für KMU.* [online] Available at: https://www.rosenthal.ch/downloads/VISCHER-DSE-XS-KMU.pdf (Accessed 6 Oct. 2024).

SME Portal *(n.d.). New Federal Act on Data Protection (nFADP).* www.kmu.admin.ch. Available at: https://www.kmu.admin.ch/kmu/en/home/facts-and-trends/digitization/data-protection/new-federal-act-on-data-protection-nfadp.html (Accessed 6 Oct. 2024).

Vischer *(n.d.). Privacy Score | Fit für das revidierte DSG?* [online] Available at: https://privacyscore.ch/ (Accessed: 26 September 2024)

ANALYSIS OF THE IMPACT OF BLOCKCHAIN TECHNOLOGY ON THE PERFORMANCE OF AN E-VOTING APPLICATION

Sandra Melovic, Darko Stefanovic, Dusanka Dakic and Teodora Vuckovic
University of Novi Sad, Faculty of Technical Sciences,
Trg Dositeja Obradovica 6, Novi Sad, Serbia

ABSTRACT

This paper explores the field of secure digital voting systems, addressing the challenge of balancing data security with performance in mobile e-voting applications. With rising demands for secure, temper-resistant digital voting solutions, blockchain technology offers robust data integrity and security features. However, integrating blockchain can introduce resource demands that impact performance, particulary in mobile contexts. This study presents an in-depth analysis of how blockchain affects memory usage and execution time in an e-voting application developed in Swift. Using Xcode's profiling tools, we conduct a comparative performance assessment before and after blockchain integration. The results indicate a measurable increase in memory consumption and processing time, but these remain within practical limits for real-world application. This work contributes to the development of secure e-voting systems, demonstrating blockchain's visibility in enhancing both data security and system-reliability.

KEYWORDS

Performance Analysis, Blockchain, E-voting, Digital Voting Security, Swift

1. INTRODUCTION

Today, technology is essential across all areas of life, including business, education, healthcare, and politics. Rapid advancements in information technology bring challenges, particularly in optimizing application and programming language performance. As applications grow more complex, users expect high levels of reliability, security, and speed, making optimization a top priority for software engineers. With rising demands for fast, secure applications, especially in fields involving critical data like finance, healthcare, and democratic processes, optimization is increasingly important. Among these applications, e-voting systems have emerged as a transformative solution for modernizing democratic process, offering faster, more efficient, and cost-effective alternatives to traditional voting methods. However, e-voting systems face stringent requirements for security, integrity, and privacy to gain voter trust and ensure electoral credibility (Gibson et al., 2016).

Blockchain technology provides a promising solution to address these challenges. Blockchain, with its decentralized nature, enables the creation of an immutable record of voting data, which prevents manipulation and guarantees that each vote remains credible and secure (Yi, 2019). Blockchain's decentralized ledger ensures that data, once recorded, is immutable, making it suitable for applications requiring high data integrity and security (Taş and Tanrıöver, 2020). As Ivic et al. (2023) point out, in e-government applications, decentralization reduces reliance on centralized authorities and enhances data transparency and security, which are critical for gaining public trust (Ivic et al., 2023). Despite blockchain's potential benefits, its integration with Swift applications faces performance-related challenges. Blockchain transactions can be resource-intensive, impacting application speed and efficiency (Berenjestanaki et al., 2023).

This study addresses the challenge of securing e-voting applications while maintaining optimal performance. By developing a Swift based e-voting application, the research investigates the impact of blockchain on application performance, with a focus on resource consumption and execution time. A comparative performance analysis is conducted using Xcode's profiling tools to evaluate memory usage and processing speed before and after blockchain implementation. Results indicate that, although within practical limits, demonstrating that blockchain can enhance security without significantly compromising performance. This research contributes to the field by providing a detailed assessment of blockchain's impact on Swift applications, thereby supporting the development of secure and efficient e-voting systems. It is intended for developers and engineers seeking to design safe and efficient e-voting systems and researchers exploring blockchain technology in e-governance. Additionally, policymakers and governmental organizations planning to adopt blockchain-based voting platforms can benefit from the findings, which provide insights into the trade-offs between security and performance.

The paper is organized as follows: Section 2 provides the foundational concepts necessary to understand the research. Section 3 describes the methodology used. Section 4 presents the results before and after blockchain implementation. Section 5 discusses the findings, followed by the conclusion in Section 6.

2. FOUNDATIONAL CONCEPTS

E-voting is a modern approach to traditional voting processes, allowing voters to vote electronically. Some report different implementation methods, from e-voting machines to fully online systems accessible from any location (Gawade et al., 2015). The implementation of e-voting systems varies around the world, depending on each country's specific needs, technical capabilities, and legal frameworks. Table 1 shows some examples.

Table 1. E-voting technologies across countries

Country	E-voting technology	Key features	References
Estonia	Online voting system	Digital personal identification cards for authentication; allows citizens to vote online in national elections since 2005.	Johnson (2023)
Belgium	Smart card-based e-voting system	Smart cards for secure voter authentication and vote recording; paper records used for auditing and accuracy verification.	Darmawan (2021)
South Korea	Specialized e-voting machines	Machines enable accurate data entry and quick vote counting.	Lee (2005)
United States	Mixed systems: Direct e-voting (Direct Recording Electronic) and hybrid systems (electronic + paper voting).	Includes blockchain-based platforms like Voatz for remote voting by soldiers and in experimental projects.	Alomari (2016)

E-voting systems aim to increase efficiency, speed, and accessibility, especially for voters in remote or hard-to-reach areas or those with physical limitations. Despite these advantages, e-voting faces several challenges, especially about data protection.

Data protection is a key component in modern information management, especially in critical processes such as elections. It includes all measures to ensure security, integrity, and data privacy (Hossain Faruket al., 2024). Blockchain's core features offer significant opportunities for solving these problems. Though initially associated with cryptocurrency and fintech, blockchain has increasingly been recognized as valuable for applications in other fields. Numerous potential uses have been identified where blockchain's unique features could provide significant benefits (Stefanovic et al., 2023). The resilience and transparency provided by blockchain technology make it a promising solution for secure data management systems outside of cryptocurrency, with applications in areas such as land administration where data integrity is critical (Stefanovic, 2022). For instance, in land administration systems, "data quality in LASs is of utmost importance" due to the legal risks associated with inaccuracies (Stefanovic et al., 2018). The same principles apply to e-voting systems, where blockchain's transparency and immutability are highly beneficial for maintaining data integrity and security. Any attack on the e-voting system, be it hacking, data manipulation, or violation of voter privacy, can have serious consequences for trust in the electoral process (Lauer, 2004). In developing and underdeveloped countries, decentralization is especially critical. In these regions, government corruption can erode public trust. Even in developed nations, where public trust in institutions may not be absolute, blockchain's transparency and security enhance its value as a trustworthy solution (Stefanovic et al., 2022).

The choice of programming language is critical in developing secure, efficient, and user-friendly e-voting systems. Swift, a programming language developed by Apple, was selected for its strong alignment with the project requirements, particularly its integration with Apple's development ecosystem, security-focused design, and performance optimization for iOS devices. While other languages like Java or Kotlin offer specific advantages, Swift's balance of safety, performance, and modern development features made it the ideal choice for implementing an e-voting system targeting Apple platforms. Its memory management and error-handling capabilities contribute to application stability, essential in environments with high user demands. In this context, the key challenge lies in balancing speed and security. E-voting applications must not sacrifice performance for security, nor security for speed, and this is where Swift can prove to be a powerful tool. Swift's security features, including automatic memory management and static typing, help prevent programming errors that could be exploited in attacks (Rahkema and Pfahl, 2023).

Performance analysis is a key component in evaluating the quality of a software system. Performance directly affects user experience, system reliability, and its ability to adequately respond to user expectations, especially in high-load situations. Blockchain technology implementation adds a new layer of complexity to the system and emphasizes the need for thorough performance analysis before and after this integration.

3. METHODOLOGY

This research was conducted between June and September at the Faculty of Technical Sciences, in Novi Sad. The research team consisted of experts in software development, blockchain technology, and mobile application development. Team members included authors of this research. Their combined knowledge with expertise in Swift application development, blockchain integration, and performance optimization enabled the successful implementation and evaluation of the e-voting application.

The research methodology includes three primary aspects: Swift application development, blockchain integration, and performance analysis. Figure 1 illustrates the system architecture of the e-voting application. The approach to developing the e-voting application, the steps and technologies used to integrate blockchain, and the performance analysis techniques are outlined below.

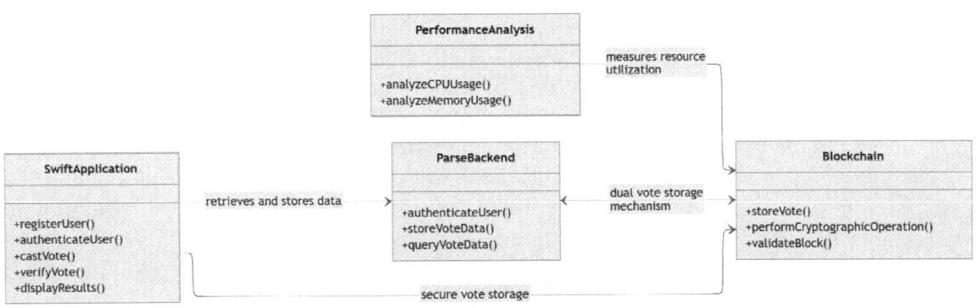

Figure 1. The system architecture of the e-voting application

3.1 Swift Application Development

The development of the e-voting application involved a structured approach to planning, technology selection, and requirements analysis.

The initial step in developing the e-voting system was identifying its key functionalities. These include enabling user registration, authentication, voting, vote verification, and result display, ensuring that voting results are presented accurately and transparently once the voting process is complete.

Several technologies were selected to support the development of the application:

- Xcode: The integrated development environment (IDE) for Apple platforms, used to write, test, debug, and distribute the application. Xcode supports Swift and offers advanced features like performance profiling, version control integration, and simulators for testing.

- SDK (Software Development Kit): Provides tools, libraries, and documentation for developing applications on specific platforms. The SDK aids in integrating functionalities such as camera or GPS access into the application.
- UIKit: The framework used for building the user interface (UI) of the iOS application, providing a wide range of UI components like buttons, tables, and animations, ensuring the application works well across different iPhone and iPad models.
- CocoaPods: A dependency management tool used to simplify the integration of third-party libraries, automating the process of fetching, configuring, and updating dependencies for the application.
- Parse & Back4App: These backend-as-a-service (BaaS) platforms were considered for handling server-side functionalities such as database management, user authentication, and push notifications, reducing the need to manage infrastructure directly.

The Model-View-Controller (MVC) architecture separates the application logic, user interface, and data management. The application's structure is organized into several key components and screens. These include a user-friendly registration and login interface, a main voting screen, a confirmation page to verify vote submission, and an administration view to review results. Each screen is managed by its own view controller, handling interactions and ensuring a responsive experience.

3.2 Blockchain Integration

Given the importance of data integrity and secure access in trustworthy systems, as emphasized by Kijanovic et al. (2024), where the effectiveness of data-driven solutions depends on the underlying data integrity and the robustness of access protocols, blockchain was integrated to enhance the application's transparency and security.

The blockchain's architecture relies on blocks, where each block contains key attributes such as a block index, timestamp, a list of transactions, the previous block's hash, and the current block's cryptographic hash. This structure ensures the unique identification of each vote and maintains the integrity of the entire voting chain. Each new block is validated by verifying that its cryptographic hash matches the previous block's hash, forming a secure chain that prevents unauthorized alterations.

Several technical decisions were implemented to ensure the blockchain's security and functionality. The SHA-256 algorithm from the CryptoKit library was used for hashing, providing a high level of cryptographic security essential for maintaining data integrity. The blockchain begins with a genesis block, which serves as the initial block in the chain. This block is initialized with predefined values and added to the chain only once.

Blockchain's integrity is preserved by validating each added block. Validation involves comparing the current block's calculated hash with the previous block's hash. Any inconsistencies signal potential tampering or corruption, rendering the blockchain invalid. The system also facilitates vote counting in a transparent and immutable manner by tracking how many times a candidate's name appears in transactions across all blocks in the blockchain.

Integration with a Parse backend enables dual storage of votes: one in the blockchain for immutability and transparency, and another in the Parse backend for ease of querying and data access. This dual approach balances the security advantages of blockchain with the efficiency of backend querying. Additionally, the user authentication and vote confirmation processes are tightly integrated with the blockchain and the backend, ensuring that all transactions are valid, transparent, and securely recorded.

3.3 Performance Analysis

Xcode's Instruments tool was selected due to its comprehensive profiling capabilities. Instruments come with several different templates or instruments, each provides specific information about certain aspects of the application. After choosing the technology for analysis, preparation for analysis is carried out, i.e. defining metrics for measuring system performance and creating test scenarios that simulate real conditions of use. The performance of key importance for the e-voting application was CPU usage time and memory usage before and after blockchain integration. Two instruments were used within the Instruments tool, the Time Profiler and Allocations. The Time Profiler instrument identified code segments with high CPU usage, allowing for optimizations in function execution. Metrics such as Total Cycles, Start Function Cycles, and Thread Start Cycles were tracked to detect performance bottlenecks and improve efficiency. The Allocations instruments tracked memory usage, focusing on heap allocations and anonymous virtual memory, to detect issues like memory leaks or inefficient resource management. By observing VM allocations, particularly UILabels managed by CALayer, the analysis helped optimize UI elements and prevent memory-related errors.

Performance testing was conducted in several phases, covering various aspects of the application's operation, to arrive at concrete results including response speed, CPU load, and memory consumption. First, tests were carried out before the implementation of blockchain technology, then, under the same conditions, tests were carried out again, to conclude how blockchain affects the tested performance. The application was tested under normal load and increased load conditions. In the single-user test, only one user performed the operations, whereas in the multiple-user scenario, the same functions were carried out by 10 simultaneous users to simulate concurrent usage.

4. RESULTS

This section aims to present the results obtained during the system performance evaluation.

4.1 Before the Blockchain Implementation

The application is run with a Time Profiler active to collect performance data during critical operations such as registration, voting, and vote processing. The goal was to evaluate how quickly the application responds to user requests under normal load conditions. The profiler provided insight into which functions were consuming the most CPU time, and the results obtained before the blockchain implementation are shown in Table 2.

Table 2. Execution time results obtained by running Time Profiler before blockchain implementation

Metric	Result
Total cycles	4.13 Gc
Start function cycles	4.06 Gc (98.2% of the total)
Cycles of start work queue thread functions	68.10 Mc (1.6% of the total number)
Thread start cycles	2.36 Mc (0.0% of total)

Gc – Giga-cycles; Mc – Mega-cycles

Application resource consumption testing was performed using the Allocations tool. The Allocations instrument was used while performing common user actions, such as registering, logging in, voting, and saving votes. The goal was to monitor how much CPU and memory the application uses during its basic functionalities and evaluate how it reacts under different load levels, such as an increased number of simultaneous users or a larger amount of data in the database. To obtain these data, the application was tested through two cases: when registration, login, and voting are performed by only one user, and by 10 users. The results are shown in Table 3.

Table 3. Memory consumption results obtained by running Allocations before blockchain implementation

Metric	For 1 user	For 10 users
All heap & anonymous VM	o Memory: 24.56 MiB o Allocations: 104,989 o Total size: 507.18 MiB	o Memory: 99.66 MiB o Allocations: 376,525 o Total size: 5.00 GiB
All heap allocations	o Memory: 14.05 MiB o Allocations: 104,783 o Total size: 465.81 MiB	o Memory: 44.35 MiB o Allocations: 375,267 o Total size: 4.69 GiB
All anonymous VM	o Memory: 10.52 MiB o Allocations: 206 o Total size: 41.38 MiB	o Memory: 55.31 MiB o Allocations: 1,258 o Total size: 319.31 MiB
VM: UILabel (CALayer)	o Memory: 3.56 MiB o Allocations: 93 o Total size: 5.44 MiB	o Memory: 21.12 MiB o Allocations: 510 o Total size: 39.91 MiB

VM – Virtual Memory; MiB – Mebibyte; GiB – Gibibyte

4.2 After the Blockchain Implementation

After the successful implementation of blockchain technology, performance testing is performed again to obtain results on the integration impact. The setup for measuring the performance of the e-voting application after the blockchain integration solution was performed in the same way as before the integration. Also, identical metrics were used, and the results are given below. Time Profiler results after the blockchain implementation are shown in Table 4.

Table 4. Execution time results obtained by running Time Profiler after blockchain implementation

Metric	Result
Total cycles	6.35 Gc
Start function cycles	6.24 Gc (98.3% of the total)
Cycles of start work queue thread functions	103.81 Mc (1.6% of the total number)
Thread start cycles	2.17 Mc (0.0% of total)
Additional cycles (Kc), associated with specific blockchain processing (address 0x1fa5e00c3).	57.96 Kc

Kc – Kilo-cycle

Table 5 shows the results of the Allocations tool, for both cases, obtained from the analysis after the blockchain implementation.

Table 5. Memory consumption results obtained by running Allocations after blockchain implementation

Metric	For 1 user	For 10 users
All heap & anonymous VM	o Memory: 24,67 MiB o Allocations: 105,956 o Total size: 798,14 MiB	o Memory: 103,00 MiB o Allocations: 391,215 o Total size: 6,22 GiB
All heap allocations	o Memory: 14,05 MiB o Allocations: 105,760 o Total size: 744,92 MiB	o Memory: 45,67 MiB o Allocations: 389,910 o Total size: 5,79 GiB
All anonymous VM	o Memory: 10,62 MiB o Allocations: 196 o Total size: 53,22 MiB	o Memory: 57,33 MiB o Allocations: 1,305 o Total size: 441,34 MiB
VM: UILabel (CALayer)	o Memory: 4,72 MiB o Allocations: 98 o Total size: 8,33 MiB	o Memory: 21,05 MiB o Allocations: 524 o Total size: 41,19 MiB

5. DISCUSSION

Blockchain integration led to a notable increase in CPU cycles (approximately 53.7%), attributed to the processing needs for cryptographic operations and data validation inherent in blockchain technology. The core execution flow now requires more resources compared to the pre-integration case, and an increase in parallelism management is also observed. However, these increases are only large relative to pre-integration results. Considering these results separately, without any connection with the previous ones, they show that the application remains stable, and the impact on performance is the expected price for the improved security and integrity provided by blockchain technology. This increase suggests that while blockchain adds computational overhead, it is essential for ensuring data integrity and security, especially in e-voting where reliability is critical.

The analysis showed higher memory allocation requirements post-blockchain integration, particularly in managing the application's graphical components and anonymous virtual memory for secure vote storage. Although this increased memory footprint could affect applications with limited resources, the trade-off is justified by enhancing security and data integrity offered by blockchain.

Blockchain implementation in the e-voting application has resulted in significant improvements in security, transparency, and data integrity, but this has come at a cost in terms of performance. Before the introduction of blockchain, the application provided fast response and low resource consumption, which allowed users a smooth and efficient voting experience. After the implementation of the blockchain, a slight increase in transaction processing time and memory consumption was observed, which is a direct consequence of complex cryptographic operations and data distribution through a decentralized network. Performance tests showed that the changed components of the application after the introduction of blockchain maintained stability, while the cost of memory increased within acceptable limits, thus confirming that the system withstanding the additional load that comes with the implementation of blockchain technology.

This finding is highly relevant as it provides empirical evidence on the balance between security and performance in applications where data integrity is paramount, such as e-voting systems. The integration of blockchain, while enhancing security, introduces potential operational costs, including increased computational power and energy consumption. Additionally, scalability challenges, such as handling thousands of simultaneous transactions during national elections, warrant further optimization efforts to ensure broad applicability. However, this research highlights blockchain's practical feasibility for secure, large-scale applications by demonstrating that blockchain integration maintains application stability despite its computational demands. Moreover, this study informs developers and system architects of the potential resource trade-offs in adopting blockchain for security-focused applications. It emphasizes the importance of carefully managing resources, particularly in constrained environments, to support security and usability. Understanding these impacts allows for more informed decisions on blockchain's suitability for various applications, supporting the design of resilient systems and balancing security with efficient performance.

6. CONCLUSION

This research demonstrates that blockchain integration while adding resource demands, allows the e-voting application to maintain stable performance. The finding confirms that blockchain can enhance security and data integrity without severely compromising usability, balancing security needs and acceptable performance levels. The results reveal that the increased CPU cycles and memory usage are manageable within the application's constraints, making blockchain a feasible solution for securing e-voting systems while ensuring a smooth user experience. One of the key contributions of this study is the insight it provides into the practical effects of blockchain on Swift-based applications.

However, there are limitations to consider. The operational costs associated with blockchain integration must be considered, particularly regarding energy consumption and hardware requirements. Cryptographic operations demand significant computational power, which could strain systems operating in resource-constrained environments. These costs may impact the feasibility of deploying blockchain-based e-voting systems in smaller municipalities or developing regions. Exploring lightweight blockchain implementations or energy-efficient consensus protocols could help address these challenges while preserving blockchain's security and transparency benefits.

Additionally, scalability remains a significant concern. Blockchain's decentralized architecture introduces resource demands that may escalate with larger transaction volumes and user bases, posing challenges for large-scale deployments. Also, the study's tests were conducted under controlled conditions with typical load levels, meaning that performance might differ under extreme usage, such as during high-traffic periods with a substantial number of simultaneous transactions. In such cases, latency could become more noticeable, affecting the user experience.

Furthermore, the study focused on a single blockchain configuration; other blockchain implementations or consensus mechanisms might yield different performance outcomes. Future research could evaluate alternative configurations, such as permissioned blockchains or energy-efficient consensus protocols like Proof of Authority or Delegated Proof of Stake. These approaches may optimize performance and reduce operational costs, particularly for mobile and resource-constrained platforms. Expanding performance testing to include stress-testing scenarios that simulate high-concurrency conditions would provide a more comprehensive understanding of scalability and system resilience.

By addressing these challenges, future work can pave the way for the wider adoption of blockchain in security-sensitive applications such as e-voting. This would ensure that systems meet the highest security and transparency standards and remain scalable and cost-efficient for broader use cases.

REFERENCES

Alomari, M.K., (2016). E-voting adoption in a developing country. *Transforming Government: People, Process and Policy*, vol. 10, no. 4, pp. 526–547. doi: https://doi.org/10.1108/TG-11-2015-0046.

Darmawan, I., (2021). E-voting adoption in many countries: A literature review. *Asian Journal of Comparative Politics*, vol. 6, no. 4, pp. 482–504. doi: https://doi.org/10.1177/20578911211040584.

Faruk, M.J.H., Alam, F., Islam, M. and Rahman, A., (2024). Transforming online voting: a novel system utilizing blockchain and biometric verification for enhanced security, privacy, and transparency. *Cluster Computing*, vol. 27, no. 4, pp. 4015–4034. doi: https://doi.org/10.1007/s10586-023-04261-x.

Gibson, J.P., Krimmer, R., Teague, V. and Pomares, J., (2016). A review of E-voting: the past, present and future. *Annals of Telecommunications*, vol. 71, no. 7–8, pp. 279–286. doi: https://doi.org/10.1007/s12243-016-0525-8.

Hajian Berenjestanaki, M., Barzegar, H.R., El Ioini, N. and Pahl, C., (2023). Blockchain-Based E-Voting Systems: A Technology Review. *Electronics*, vol. 13, no. 1, p. 17. doi: https://doi.org/10.3390/electronics13010017.

Ivic, A., Stefanovic, D., Dakic, D., Vuckovic, T., Havzi, S., Sladojevic, S., (2023). Conceptual Framework for the Development of an E-Government Licensing System. *Access Journal - Access to Science, Business, Innovation in the Digital Economy*, vol. 4, no. 2, 27 May 2023, pp. 313–330. doi: https://doi.org/10.46656/access.2023.4.2(11).

Johnson, D. Ed., (2023). *Rethinking Democracy and Governance: Perspectives from the Caribbean*. Taylor & Francis.

Kijanovic, S., Koprivica, S., Taibi, D., Ivic, A., Stefanovic, D., and Komosar, A., (2024). Overview of usage of open government data in building machine learning and AI solutions: a systematic literature review. *Proceedings of the 17th IADIS International Conference Information Systems 2024*, Porto, Portugal, pp. 179-183. doi: https://doi.org/10.33965/IS2024_202401C010.

Lee, H.-W., (2005). Political implications of e-voting in Korea. *Journal of Politics and Policy Studies*, vol. IX, no. 1, pp. 91–107.

Rahkema, K. and Pfahl, D., (2023). Vulnerability Propagation in Package Managers Used in iOS Development. *Proceedings of the 2023 IEEE/ACM 10th International Conference on Mobile Software Engineering and Systems (MOBILESoft)*. IEEE, pp. 60–69. doi: https://doi.org/10.1109/MOBILSoft59058.2023.00015.

Stefanovic, M., Przulj, Dj., and Ristic, S., (2022). Overview of Application of Blockchain Technology in E-Government. *Proceedings on 18th International Conference on Industrial Systems – IS'20*, B. Lalic, D. Gracanin, N. Tasic, and N. Simeunovic (eds). Springer, Cham, pp. 95–102. doi: https://doi.org/10.1007/978-3-030-97947-8_13.

Stefanovic, M., Przulj, Dj., Ristic, S., Stefanovic, D. and Nikolic, D., (2022). Smart Contract Application for Managing Land Administration System Transactions. *IEEE Access*, vol. 10, pp. 39154–39176. doi: https://doi.org/10.1109/ACCESS.2022.3164444.

Stefanovic, M., Przulj, Dj., Stefanovic, D., Ristic, S. and Capko, D., (2023). The proposal of new Ethereum request for comments for supporting fractional ownership of non-fungible tokens. *Computer Science and Information Systems*, vol. 20, no. 3, pp. 1133–1155. doi: https://doi.org/10.2298/CSIS230127038S.

Stefanovic, M., Ristic, S., Stefanovic, D., Bojkic, M., and Przulj, Dj., (2018). Possible Applications of Smart Contracts in Land Administration. *Proceedings of the 26th Telecommunications Forum (TELFOR)*, Belgrade, Serbia, pp. 420–425. doi: https://doi.org/10.1109/TELFOR.2018.8611872.

Taş, R. and Tanrıöver, Ö.Ö., (2020). A Systematic Review of Challenges and Opportunities of Blockchain for E-Voting. *Symmetry*, vol. 12, no. 8, p. 1328. doi: https://doi.org/10.3390/sym12081328.

Yi, H., (2019). Securing e-voting based on blockchain in P2P network. *EURASIP Journal on Wireless Communications and Networking*, vol. 2019, no. 1, p. 137. doi: https://doi.org/10.1186/s13638-019-1473-6.

SYSTEMATIC REVIEW OF IOT TECHNOLOGICAL INTEGRATION APPROACHES INTO PERSONALIZED ONLINE LEARNING

Edlir Spaho and Betim Çiço
Faculty of Architecture and Engineering, Epoka University
Tirana, Vore 1032, Albania

ABSTRACT

The integration of the Internet of Things (IoT) in education has significantly impacted Personalized Online Learning (POL), enabling adaptive, context-aware and learner-centered environments through interconnected devices and real-time data analysis. This systematic review explores various IoT integration technological and pedagogical approaches in POL systems, including context-aware mechanisms, sensors and edge-computing technologies. By examining 61 peer-reviewed studies, the review categorizes IoT technological and pedagogical approaches, evaluates their impact on personalization and identifies challenges such as data privacy and resource constraints. Key findings reveal that IoT-enhanced POL can significantly improve learner engagement, adaptive learning and academic outcomes. However, gaps in interoperability standards and the ethical use of data highlight the need for a unified framework. The paper concludes with recommendations for future research and practical applications, which emphasize IoT's transformative potential in creating intelligent, scalable and inclusive learning environments.

KEYWORDS

Internet of Things, Personalized Online Learning, Technological Approaches, Systematic Review

1. INTRODUCTION

The Internet of Things (IoT) has emerged as a transformative force across various domains, including healthcare, agriculture, manufacturing and education. IoT refers to a network of interconnected devices embedded with sensors and software that facilitate data collection and sharing. In education, IoT enables the creation of smart environments where data from learners and their surroundings can be utilized to enhance teaching and learning processes (Chen and Zhang, 2022).

Personalized Online Learning (POL) represents a paradigm shift from traditional education models by tailoring content, pace and methods to individual learners' needs. POL has gained prominence in addressing the diverse requirements of learners in digital environments. However, its effectiveness heavily depends on the systems' ability to adapt to real-time changes in learner behavior and context. IoT, with its capacity for real-time data collection and contextual awareness, has become a key enabler of advanced POL systems (Tortorella and Graf, 2017; Zhao et al., 2022).

IoT-driven POL systems utilize technologies such as wearable sensors, environmental monitors, and edge devices to gather data on learners' physiological states, engagement levels, and learning preferences. This data feeds adaptive learning algorithms that dynamically adjust instructional content, foster better engagement, improve outcomes for a more inclusive learning experience (Asad et al., 2024).

The objectives of this research are multi-faceted and aim to systematically evaluate the current landscape of IoT integration in POL systems. Specifically, the study seeks to systematically categorize the existing IoT technological approaches, models and methodologies employed in POL, and analyze their impact on learning personalization, engagement and learning outcome, based on the findings to provide actionable recommendations for educators, technologists, and policymakers, to improve the integration of IoT technologies in Personalized Learning (PL) environments.

By achieving these objectives, the research intends to provide a comprehensive overview of the IoT's potential to transform POL, ensuring it is adaptive, inclusive, and effective across diverse educational contexts.

Based on study motivation and objectives, we propose following research question (RQ) to guide the search and selection process:

R.Q.: What are the technological approaches used to integrate IoT in POL systems?

This research question aims to classify and evaluate the range of IoT technologies and approaches used in POL systems, such as Physical Devices and Controllers (Things) used in IoT based POL systems, IoT protocols and communication models, Middleware and IoT Platforms, Data Processing (Cloud, Edge and Fog Computing), IoT Tools and frameworks, Learning Analytics and AI/ML Integration, Security and Privacy (Encryption, Authentication and Authorization, Blockchain).

This review systematically examines peer-reviewed literature on IoT integration in POL, focusing on works published within the last seven years. It incorporates studies that explore the intersection of IoT and POL, excluding those addressing these areas in isolation.

The review methodology follows established protocols to ensure reproducible and credible results, including comprehensive database searches, predefined inclusion criteria and detailed data synthesis.

It contributes by consolidating the theoretical framework of IoT in POL systems, guiding future researches, offering practical insights for educators to enhance learner outcomes and informing policymakers on technological, pedagogical, ethical, and logistical considerations for integration IoT in POL.

Through these contributions, this systematic review seeks to bridge the knowledge gap in IoT-driven personalization of online learning and foster the development of robust, scalable and ethical educational technologies.

2. LITERATURE REVIEW

The increasing adoption of IoT across various domains offers a unique opportunity to transform POL by leveraging real-time data analytics and sensor technology to develop adaptive, context-aware learning environments. Despite promising advancements, the adoption of IoT in educational settings brings different challenges related to technical integration, data privacy, and system interoperability. These challenges prevent the full realization of IoT-enabled POL systems that are capable of truly personalized education delivery.

A study conducted by Betts, et al. (2020) investigated the usage of IoT in creating learner-centered environments, emphasizing data collection, interoperability, and ethical considerations. While not systematic, Betts, et al. (2020) offered a foundation for future reviews by highlighting critical implementation factors. A literature review conducted by Razzaque and Hamdan (2020) focused on aligning IoT technologies with learning outcomes and learning styles in higher education, proposing an interdisciplinary model to improve curriculum design and e-learning experiences, addressing shortcomings in traditional teaching methods. The thematic literature review conducted by Vinayachandra and Prasad (2020) emphasized IoT's transformative impact on POL by enabling customized educational experiences and real-time student monitoring. IoT applications enhance stakeholder interaction, classroom management, and tailored learning paths, allowing educators to adapt content to individual needs and engagement levels.

Despite its potential, IoT integration in POL is still in its early stages. Educational institutions face challenges in implementing IoT due to technical, ethical and financial constraints. Furthermore, existing literature often addresses specific IoT applications without presenting a comprehensive overview of the techniques and their broader implications for POL systems. This creates a need for a systematic review to consolidate knowledge and identify opportunities for further exploration. By conducting a systematic review of existing literature and technological applications, this study identifies and analyzes the effective strategies and significant gaps in the current IoT technological integration approaches. This research is driven by the goal to advance our understanding of IoT's role in education, facilitating the development of more effective, scalable, and learner-centered educational technologies.

3. RESEARCH METHODOLOGY

The objective of this study is to identify the technological approaches used in IoT-based POL systems. Its primary focus is on the intersection of IoT integration approaches and techniques or methods used to implement these techniques. To provide a comprehensive overview of the field, we review IoT in education papers that address POL methods, techniques, and frameworks.

3.1 Systematic Review Protocol

There are different systematic review study guidelines that are available, for example, Kitchenham (2004) and Kitchenham and Charters (2007). However, we selected systematic mapping guidelines identified in Petersen et al. (2015), which consolidated the best practices suggested by other researchers. According to Petersen et al. (2015) a systematic mapping review process begins by formulating research questions (RQs). The next steps involve screening the papers based on their title, abstract, and keyword metadata and then to the full content to answer the RQs. The systematic mapping process we have used in this study is denoted in Figure 1.

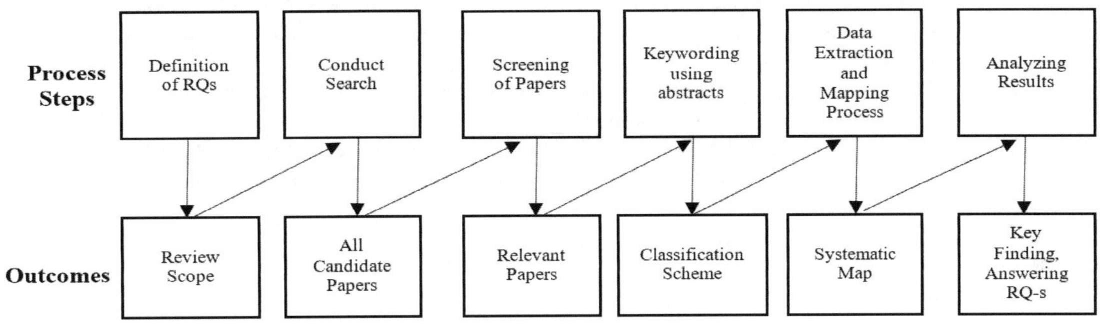

Figure 1. The systematic review process (Petersen et al., 2015)

Identifying the search string of publications was the first step in conducting a systematic review research process. To identify keywords and formulate search string from research questions we followed PICO (Population, Intervention, Comparison and Outcomes) criteria developed by Petersen et al. (2015). These criteria are defined in Table 1.

Table 1. PICO of the study

Dimension	Explanation
Population	Primary studies which integrate IoT in POL systems (both theoretical and empirical studies).
Intervention	Technological approaches utilized within IoT based POL systems.
Comparison	Comparing different technological approaches employed within IoT based POL systems.
Outcome	Evaluation of technological approaches used in IoT based POL systems.

Inclusion criteria focused on peer-reviewed articles published within the last seven years, emphasizing empirical, experimental, or theoretical studies related to IoT integration in POL. Papers that tangentially mention IoT integration in POL are not included in the study. Table 2 provides detailed Inclusion and Exclusion criteria that guided candidate studies selection process.

3.2 Data Collection and Analysis

To explore how IoT is integrated in POL systems in primary studies we formulated a search string that reveals combination of IoT and POL systems. There are three main concepts of the search string “Internet of Things”, “Personalized” and “Online Learning” derived from research question. Our basic string was (Internet of Things AND Personalized AND Online Learning). To extend the scope of research we conducted an investigation of literature for synonyms or interchangeably used terms of identified main concepts. To construct the full string, we used AND Boolean operator to combine main concepts and OR Boolean operator to express synonyms or interchangeably used terms of main concepts.

Table 2. Criteria used for including and excluding research studies

Inclusion Criteria	Exclusion Criteria
Included content of IoT that investigates Educational perspectives to Personalize Online Learning i.e., methods, frameworks and use cases	Duplicate papers from the same study in different databases.
	Mention of IoT is tangential with different scopes not directly related to POL
Published between January 2017 and March 2023.	Publications not written in English
Written in English with full-text available.	Publications not directly related to our topic
Peer-reviewed journal literatures	Full-text is inaccessible
	Books and gray literature

To conduct our research, we implemented the search string in ACM and IEEEXplore digital libraries and on Education Resources Information Center (ERIC) and Springer Link databases. To find latest trends we limited the research from January 2017 to December 2023. Based on the research methodology detailed in this section, the subsequent section presents our findings, highlighting technological approaches employed in IoT based POL systems.

From an initial pool of approximately 6,500 articles retrieved through the search protocol, 61 studies were ultimately selected after applying the inclusion and exclusion criteria.

The following section presents key findings of the systematic mapping study, offering insights that directly reflect the study's objectives. To outline the results, we followed the structure and layout of a systematic mapping study conducted by Cico et al. (2021).

4. RESULTS

4.1 Descriptive Analysis of Results

Table 3 presents the distribution of publications over the years from January 2017 to March 2023 and the distribution of publications across different digital databases and libraries.

Table 3. Distribution of selected studies over years and digital libraries or databases

Publication Year	ACM	ERIC	IEEE	Springerlink
2017	3	5	0	0
2018	0	2	1	4
2019	1	5	4	3
2020	1	6	1	3
2021	2	4	1	2
2022	3	3	1	2
2023	0	1	0	3
Library or Database Total	10	26	8	17

The integration of IoT into POL systems is an interdisciplinary field which includes information technology and education. For this reason, finding nearly 43% of the primary studies in ERIC database makes sense, as this database contains scholarly articles related to education and the integration of different technologies into education to improve the quality of learning. The Springerlink database is the second most utilized source, with 17 publications, representing 28% of the total.

Our research identified that the majority of studies (66%) focused on solution research, emphasizing the development of new frameworks, models, or tools. Evaluation research accounts for 31% of the studies, concentrating on assessing the effectiveness or impact of existing solutions. Validation research, representing only 3%, focuses on rigorously confirming the theoretical underpinnings or assumptions of proposed models or systems. In addition, the results indicate that the majority (64%) of contributions in the study focused on frameworks or methods, emphasizing structured approaches to problem-solving or implementation. Tools accounted for 20%, highlighting practical applications or software developed to support the area of interest.

Meanwhile Models comprised 11%, reflecting theoretical or conceptual structures used to represent processes or systems.

The integration of IoT into POL systems demonstrates a strong interdisciplinary focus on combining education and technology to enhance learning quality. Main trends underscore the field's practical orientation, prioritizing innovative solutions over theoretical validation underscoring the need for more foundational research to establish cohesive theories guiding the integration of IoT into POL systems.

4.2 What are the Technological Approaches and Techniques Used to Integrate Iot?

This systematic review identified a variety of technological approaches and techniques used in IoT-based POL systems. These approaches considered advancements in IoT, machine learning and real-time data analysis to create adaptive and learner-centered educational environments. IoT technological approaches in POL systems are analyzed based on Internet of Things World Forum (IoTWF) reference model architecture to classify implemented approaches. In the context of POL, this model can be applied to create adaptive and responsive educational environments (Hanes, et al., 2017).

4.2.1 Physical Devices and Controllers (Things) used in IoT Based POL Systems

The integration of IoT devices into POL environments involves diverse technologies that enhance educational experiences by implementing real-time data collection and adaptive learning capabilities. Raspberry Pi 3.0 serves as a critical learning edge device due to its compatibility with major broker architectures, offering greater software library support than smaller platforms like Arduino, ESP32 and Photon (Shapsough and Zualkernan, 2020).

Mobile devices play a significant role, particularly in low-income regions, where their widespread possession enables educational access without advanced infrastructure. They are utilized to deliver Augmented Reality (AR) content, facilitating flexible and portable learning experiences, as well as supporting active learning through apps and fieldwork (Whalley et al., 2020). Additionally, smart mobile devices such as iPads and iPhones enhance PL (PL) environments by supporting communication and collaboration between students and tutors, both on and off campus (Mahapatra, Pattanayak, and Pati, 2021).

Wearable devices, including wristbands, smartphones and smartwatches, provide a wealth of data to monitor student physiological and engagement levels during learning activities. Wristbands, for instance, measure heart rate and blood pressure, offering insights into physical and mental states (Zhao et al., 2022). Smartwatches, equipped with biosensors, track metrics like heart rate variability in real-time, ensuring a non-invasive data collection process. Beyond health monitoring, wearable technologies assess engagement levels through methods such as electro-dermal activity and skin temperature analysis, enabling tailored feedback and improving student interaction in digital learning (Ojha, Jebelli and Sharifironizi, 2023).

IoT sensor technologies significantly enhance context awareness in POL. Systems equipped with accelerometers, GPS and ambient light sensors gather data on motion, location and environmental conditions to adapt content formats to suit learner environments (Tortorella and Graf, 2017). Advanced setups include NFC readers and tags, which facilitate interaction between learners and IoT-integrated robots for immersive educational experiences (Cheng et al., 2020). A prototype developed with Arduino Uno R3 and Grove modules measures classroom conditions like temperature, humidity and air quality, transmitting the data online for analysis (Aydin and Göktaş, 2023). Furthermore, multi-touch systems with biometric scanners and interactive whiteboards improve classroom engagement and digital attendance, while RFID technologies streamline campus operations, including attendance and parking management (Shrestha and Furqan, 2020). Sensor networks, including webcams and fitness trackers, collect emotional and behavioral data that inform adaptive learning processes, fostering a holistic educational experience (Kassab and Mazzara, 2020).

The integration of IoT devices into POL environments leverages diverse technologies—ranging from edge devices like Raspberry Pi to mobile, wearable and sensor-based systems—that collectively enhance educational experiences by enabling real-time data collection, adaptive content delivery, physiological monitoring and context-aware learning, ultimately fostering flexibility, engagement and personalized education across varied learning contexts.

4.2.2 Communication Technologies

The use of IoT protocols and communication models are essential to integrate IoT in POL systems. This integration relies on protocols such as MQTT, AMQP, CoAP and XMPP to establish efficient and secure communication frameworks. CoAP is particularly well-known for its resource efficiency in low-power scenarios, while MQTT and AMQP excel in managing large-scale operations and topic hierarchies, making them suitable for expansive educational systems (Shapsough and Zualkernan, 2020), (Bondaryk, Hsi, and Van Doren, 2021), (Adi et al., 2020). Bluetooth Low Energy (BLE) supports seamless, non-intrusive data transmission from wearable devices to connected systems, ensuring that data collection remains distraction-free for learners (Ciolacu, Binder, Svasta, et al., 2019). Furthermore, application-layer protocols like MQTT and AMQP play a crucial role in enabling advanced AI-driven functionalities, such as adaptive and prescriptive learning, by effectively transmitting data to cloud environments for analysis (Adi et al., 2020). Additionally, network infrastructures like 3G mobile networks ensure broad signal coverage for the delivery of educational content, while cloud communication layers enhance overall system responsiveness and scalability in smart learning scenarios (Asad et al., 2024).

The communication models used in IoT-based POL systems use both network-level and device-to-device interaction to ensure dynamic data exchange and system scalability. Publish-subscribe models, supported by protocols like MQTT and AMQP, enable real-time communication between sensors, devices and servers, which is critical for adaptive learning environments (Shapsough and Zualkernan, 2020; Bondaryk et al., 2021).

The integration of IoT into POL systems relies on robust communication models and protocols, such as MQTT, AMQP, CoAP and BLE, which ensure efficient data exchange, scalability and support for adaptive learning functionalities, while network infrastructure enhance responsiveness and system-wide scalability.

4.2.3 Middleware and IoT Platforms

In IoT-based POL, APIs are crucial for integrating advanced functions into learning tools. For emotion recognition, APIs such as Microsoft Cognitive Services-API, Google Cloud Vision-API and CLMtrackr enable the detection of emotions and facial expressions from images and videos, facilitating the personalization of learning content without requiring extensive machine learning expertise (Elkobaisi and Al Machot, 2022). A webcam-based tool leverages these APIs, along with additional features like eye-gaze tracking and heartbeat monitoring, to assess learner emotional states and adapt content to their needs (Kassab and Mazzara, 2020). Additionally, the Dialogflow API is employed to automate data management tasks, such as uploading and updating learning content, streamlining the development process by directly building intents from the database (Reyes et al., 2019).

IoT platforms like MaTHiSiS integrate sensors in devices such as laptops, tablets and smartphones, capturing data on learner affective states to personalize educational content. These systems also leverage mobile and robotic devices, which are equipped with sensors to gather data on student interactions and emotional health (Spyrou and Vretos, 2018). These integrations collectively enhance the ability to provide a responsive and tailored learning experience.

4.2.4 Data Processing (Cloud, Edge and Fog Computing) and Storage

The findings from selected research studies highlight the fundamental role of IoT, edge computing, and cloud-based technologies in enhancing online education systems by providing scalability, flexibility, and cost-effectiveness for PL services.

The Cloud of Things (CoT) framework is utilized to combine IoT with cloud computing, ensuring robust infrastructure for data storage, processing, and service delivery (Mukherjee et al., 2021). Cloud computing enables the deployment of learner models and personalization parameters as web services hosted on various servers, ensuring high availability (Ghallabi et al., 2020). A personal cloud environment bridges the digital divide by enabling learners to access resources without relying on high-end devices. The integration of mobile learning with cloud-based services promotes resource sharing and expands access to educational resources and knowledge exchange while reducing institutional technology burden (Mitra and Gupta, 2020). Real-time synchronization of sensor data and programs through cloud storage allows teachers to monitor student activities, promoting collaboration and cross-user interaction (Bondaryk et al., 2021). The integration of IoT with cloud computing is critical for creating smart educational systems. The cloud layer not only serves as a secure data repository, but also integrates big data analytics to interpret patterns and communicate insights to IoT devices (Asad et al., 2024). Advanced processing services, including affect detection and learning graph adaptation, are hosted in the cloud, enhancing the platform's adaptability, scalability and performance (Spyrou and Vretos, 2018). The use of Content Delivery Network (CDN) ensures efficient distribution of educational materials while maintaining high performance and security through encryption and tokenization processes (Mahapatra et al., 2021).

4.2.5 Tools and Frameworks

The Learning Ecology Framework emphasizes the design of effective Ubiquitous, Mobile and Immersive (UMI) educational scenarios by focusing on space and time considerations. These aspects distinguish UMI scenarios from generic technological tools, ensuring they are integrated into educational contexts with clear differentiation. This framework supports educators in creating environments conducive to adaptive learning (Mavroudi, Fragou, and Goumopoulos, 2019).

A Virtualization Framework is proposed using VMware vSphere Hypervisor-ESXi to establish a technical foundation for mobile cloud learning. It optimizes learning by integrating various educational technologies into a cost-effective, collaborative platform. This framework plays a key role in outcome-based education, enabling efficient knowledge transfer and resource sharing for PL experiences (Mitra and Gupta, 2020).

The Data Analytics Framework addresses the processing and analysis of IoT data from heterogeneous sources. It enables adaptive learning environments by uncovering patterns and supporting knowledge discovery. A notable feature of this framework is its use of an ontology database for knowledge classification and exchange. Smart Objects autonomously exchange knowledge based on inference rules, enhancing adaptability and personalization (Adi et al., 2020). Additionally, Natural Language Processing (NLP) techniques enrich this framework by generating hypothetical rules, such as synonyms and categories, to create dynamic knowledge bases.

A Reinforcement Learning (RL) Framework, named FaiR-IoT, adapts IoT applications to human variability using three levels of RL agents: Multisample RL, Governor RL and Mediator RL. These agents address intra-human, inter-human and multi-human variability, ensuring system fairness and personalization (Elmalaki, 2021).

The Smart Learning Management Frameworks centralize educational components such as lecture materials, assessments, and feedback to streamline education management. This framework provides students with comprehensive access to their learning progress and course content, facilitating a structured and PL experience (Mahapatra et al., 2021). Voas's Primitives Framework outlines IoT scenarios in education through its fundamental components: sensors, communication channels, aggregators, decision triggers and external utilities (Kassab and Mazzara, 2020). This framework facilitates understanding the interactions and dependencies within IoT-enabled learning systems. In addition, a Contextual Bandit Framework is utilized to integrate student and environmental contexts into recommendation systems. By incorporating contextual features, this framework refines decision-making processes, ensuring enhanced personalization in learning recommendations (Prihar et al., 2022).

Adaptive Frameworks in mobile learning tailor content to learner profiles and goals. Context-aware modules are an integral part of these frameworks, considering situational and learner-specific factors to recommend sequences of activities. The Situation, Background, Assessment and Recommendation (SBAR) Framework extends this approach by utilizing machine learning techniques like Adaptive Neuro-Fuzzy Inference Systems (ANFIS) to model context and adaptively organize, present, and facilitate learning interactions in mobile learning. By defining learning paths based on active learner feedback and context, SBAR enhances personalization and active engagement (Muhammad et al., 2018).

The discussed frameworks collectively demonstrate the potential of integrating advanced technologies like IoT, data analytics, RL, and virtualization into educational systems. All of which emphasize personalization, context-awareness and adaptability to enhance learning experiences and foster active engagement in e-learning environments.

4.2.6 Learning Analytics and AI/ML Integration

Machine Learning (ML) plays a crucial role in IoT-based POL, enabling the adaptation of educational content and strategies to meet individual learner needs. Various studies employ ML techniques to classify, predict and analyze student engagement, behavior and knowledge levels using IoT-generated data.

One approach leverages decision trees and rule-based systems, such as OneR, PART and J48 (C4.5), to model and predict student engagement patterns. These methods provide intelligible outputs that aid in understanding and optimizing student interactions within learning environments (Camacho et al., 2020). Similarly, ML algorithms like RNN, RCNN and SOCSW are employed to enhance the Mod-Knowledge agent's ability to classify student responses and questions. The use of supervised and unsupervised methods is determined by the characteristics of the dataset (Trifa, Hedhili, and Chaari, 2019).

Data mining and ML are also used to transform education by tailoring content based on individual preferences and cognitive demands, creating highly PL experiences (Embarak, 2022). Additionally, a ML-based context fusion model processes low-level multi-domain context data to derive high-level contextual information, enabling adaptive intelligence services in IoT environments (Jia et al., 2017). Clustering techniques, such as K-means, are applied to predict clusters of time-based data, providing insights into student behavior and engagement during e-learning sessions (Farhan et al., 2018).

In another study, supervised rule-based learning algorithms are highlighted for their ability to process IoT-generated data, transforming raw input streams into meaningful knowledge. These self-assigned rules play a key role in creating adaptive learning systems (Adi et al., 2020). ML techniques are also integrated with wearable devices to analyze activity data and enhance student health and engagement, promoting healthy behaviors alongside learning (Ciolacu et al., 2019).

Advanced classifiers such as AdaBoost, XGBoost, Gradient Boosting, SVM, KNN and Random Forest are utilized to predict and recommend PL resources based on learner profiles (Soui, Srinivasan, and Albesher, 2022). These algorithms analyze data collected from IoT devices to uncover student learning patterns and behaviors, enabling PL experiences, and provide actionable insights for educators (Shrestha and Furqan, 2020).

Other applications of ML include the development of intelligent guidance and personalized teaching strategies. Adaptive engines, such as the ANFIS, form the foundations for customizing learning content and presentation to the learner needs (Muhammad et al., 2018). AI and ML capabilities embedded in smart mobile devices enable features like voice and face recognition and AR, allowing these devices to act as intelligent tutors that dynamically adjust to individual educational needs and preferences (Whalley et al., 2020).

ML serves as a foundation in IoT-based POL, offering diverse techniques and algorithms—ranging from rule-based systems and clustering methods to advanced classifiers and adaptive engines—that enable the analysis and adaptation of educational content, fostering personalized, context-aware and engaging learning experiences tailored to individual learner needs and preferences.

4.2.7 Security and Privacy

In IoT-based POL systems, various privacy and security techniques are employed to protect user data and ensure system reliability. These techniques focus on securing communication, preserving user privacy and safeguarding sensitive educational information.

The robustness of IoT-based learning platforms is ensured through comprehensive physical and network security measures. Testing procedures include assessing the system's ability to recover from unauthorized shutdowns and implementing encryption techniques to protect user information during data transmission and storage (Wang and Lv, 2022). Firewalls are also utilized to restrict unauthorized access, maintaining the security and integrity of sensitive educational data (Chen and Zhang, 2022).

Advanced privacy-preserving techniques such as Federated Learning (FL) and Differential Privacy (DP) are employed in the development of secure recommender systems. FL allows model training to occur directly on user devices, ensuring that sensitive data remains local and is not transmitted to a central server, thereby enhancing privacy. DP further strengthens the privacy by adding controlled noise to data, making it difficult to identify individual users from aggregated model outputs. Techniques such as gradient clipping and Gaussian noise are employed to safeguard the influence of any single data point on the model's updates, ensuring compliance with privacy standards (Wang et al., 2022).

In addition, encryption methods ensure secure data transmission, while role-based access control restricts unauthorized access, meanwhile blockchain technology offers a decentralized and tamper-resistant approach to safeguarding learner data, enhancing trust in adaptive systems (Kumar, 2021; Elmalaki, 2021; Betts et al., 2020).

In IoT-based POL systems, multi-layered approaches combine encryption, secure communication channels, privacy-preserving methods, differential privacy, and advanced technologies such as blockchain to ensure the protection of sensitive user data, system reliability and compliance with privacy standards, fostering a secure and trustworthy educational environment.

4.2.8 Pedagogical Implications and Impacts of IoT Integration in POL

The integration of IoT in POL has significant pedagogical implications and transformative impacts. By using real-time data from interconnected devices, IoT-based systems create adaptive, learner-centered environments that cater to individual needs. These systems monitor learner physiological and contextual states to tailor content dynamically in order to enhance engagement and academic outcomes (Ciolacu, Binder and Popp, 2019). For instance, IoT-enabled systems can adjust instructional content in real time based on environmental factors, emotional states, or cognitive readiness, fostering a more personalized and inclusive learning experience (Asad et al., 2024).

IoT integration also supports diverse learning styles by enabling personalized content adaptation and dynamic feedback mechanisms. Personalized context-aware recommendation systems analyze behavioral and contextual data to deliver specified learning materials (Yao, 2017). Additionally, adaptive feedback loops ensure that learners receive real-time guidance, enhancing their understanding and motivation (Kumar, 2021).

Active and collaborative learning is another area where IoT makes a substantial impact. By incorporating hands-on and interactive elements such as IoT-enabled sensors and real-time monitoring tools, learners can engage in meaningful activities like project-based and problem-solving tasks (Asad et al., 2024; Shapsough and Zualkernan, 2020). These approaches encourage teamwork, critical thinking, and practical application of knowledge, which foster deeper engagement with the material.

Cognitive load management is an essential pedagogical implication of IoT in POL. IoT systems utilize cognitive load theory to optimize instructional design, balancing cognitive demands to prevent overload and enhance retention. Tailored content delivery ensures that materials are aligned with learner cognitive capacities to better support comprehension and long-term learning outcomes. This alignment is particularly critical in maintaining focus and productivity in digital learning environments (Zhao et al., 2022; Whalley et al. 2020).

Inclusivity and accessibility are enhanced through IoT integration by addressing socio-economic and cultural barriers in education. Mobile IoT devices provide access to tailored educational resources for learners in low-resource settings, promoting equity in learning opportunities (Mohana et al., 2023).

Finally, IoT facilitates scalability and efficiency in POL systems, adapting to diverse educational contexts while optimizing resource utilization (Spyrou and Vretos, 2018; Aydin and Göktaş, 2023).

5. CONCLUSION

The integration of IoT into POL systems demonstrates immense potential to revolutionize education by enabling adaptive, learner-centered experiences. Through real-time data from sensors and smart devices and edge computing, IoT enhances personalization, adaptability, and inclusivity in learning environments by addressing individual preferences, physiological responses, and contextual needs. Despite current challenges such as scalability, data privacy, interoperability issues and the lack of a unified framework for IoT implementation in education, IoT-driven innovations, including context-aware learning systems and wearable biosensors, are transforming traditional education paradigms into dynamic, efficient, and engaging experiences, paving the way for future advancements in Education 4.0.

Our findings emphasize the importance of addressing aforementioned challenges in order to realize the full potential of IoT-enhanced PL systems. Solutions require cross-disciplinary collaboration between technologists, educators, and policymakers to establish robust standards and ethical guidelines. Our review underscores the critical need for scalable IoT systems that are inclusive and adaptable to diverse educational contexts.

Future research in the integration of IoT into POL should prioritize the development of interoperability standards. Establishing universal protocols and frameworks will ensure that IoT devices can seamlessly connect across diverse educational platforms, and enhance system functionality and user experience. Alongside technical standardization, ethical data management practices require significant attention. Advanced encryption methods and anonymization techniques must be explored to address privacy concerns, build trust, and safeguard sensitive learner information in an increasingly interconnected learning ecosystem.

The combination of IoT with artificial intelligence offers a promising avenue for enhancing adaptivity in educational systems. Research should focus on developing real-time adaptive algorithms that respond to learner cognitive and emotional states, providing a truly PL experience. Such systems could dynamically adjust content delivery, pace, and difficulty, thereby fostering more effective and engaging learning outcomes. Furthermore, to make IoT-enhanced systems accessible to a broader audience, scalable implementation strategies must be developed. These strategies should consider various levels of deployment, ranging from individual classrooms to nationwide education systems, ensuring that solutions can be adapted to diverse educational settings.

Another critical area for future exploration is the reasonable adoption of IoT technologies. Cost-effective solutions need to be developed to enable their integration into resource-constrained environments, ensuring that learners in low-income regions can benefit from personalized educational advancements. To validate the effectiveness and practicality of these systems, large-scale, longitudinal studies are essential. These studies should assess the impact of IoT-based learning environments on academic performance, engagement, and overall learner satisfaction, providing empirical evidence to guide further development.

By addressing these research areas, the education sector can move closer to realizing the transformative potential of IoT. Such efforts will enable the creation of intelligent, inclusive, and adaptive learning systems that cater to the unique needs of every learner, fostering equity and innovation in education worldwide.

REFERENCES

Adi, E., Anwar, A., Baig, Z., & Zeadally, S. (2020). Machine learning and data analytics for the IoT. Neural Computing and Applications, 32(20), 16205–16233. https://doi.org/10.1007/s00521-020-04874-y

Asad, M. M., Naz, A., Shaikh, A., Alrizq, M., Akram, M., & Alghamdi, A. (2024). Investigating the impact of IoT-Based smart laboratories on students' academic performance in higher education. Universal Access in the Information Society, 23(3), 1135–1149. https://doi.org/10.1007/s10209-022-00944-1

Aydin, A., & Göktaş, Y. (2023). Examining the Effects of Physical Variables in Classrooms on Students' Attention via the Internet of Things. Participatory Educational Research, 10(1), 160–177. https://doi.org/10.17275/per.23.9.10.1

Betts, A., Thai, K. P., Gunderia, S., Hidalgo, P., Rothschild, M., & Hughes, D. (2020). An ambient and pervasive personalized learning ecosystem: "smart learning" in the age of the internet of things. Lecture Notes in Computer Science (Including Subseries Lecture Notes in Artificial Intelligence and Lecture Notes in Bioinformatics), 12214 LNCS, 15–33. https://doi.org/10.1007/978-3-030-50788-6_2

Bondaryk, L. G., Hsi, S., & Van Doren, S. (2021). Probeware for the Modern Era: IoT Dataflow System Design for Secondary Classrooms. IEEE Transactions on Learning Technologies, 14(2), 226–237. https://doi.org/10.1109/TLT.2021.3061040

Camacho, V. L., Guia, E. D. La, Olivares, T., Julia Flores, M., & Orozco-Barbosa, L. (2020). Data Capture and Multimodal Learning Analytics Focused on Engagement with a New Wearable IoT Approach. IEEE Transactions on Learning Technologies, 13(4), 704–717. https://doi.org/10.1109/TLT.2020.2999787

Chen, L., & Zhang, L. (2022). Computer Teaching System Based on Internet of Things and Machine Learning. Journal of Control Science and Engineering, 2022, 6. https://doi.org/10.1155/2022/3974794

Cheng, Y. W., Wang, Y., Yang, Y. F., Yang, Z. K., & Chen, N. S. (2020). Designing an authoring system of robots and IoT-based toys for EFL teaching and learning. Computer Assisted Language Learning, 34(1–2), 6–34. https://doi.org/10.1080/09588221.2020.1799823

Cico, O., Jaccheri, L., Nguyen-Duc, A., & Zhang, H. (2021). Exploring the intersection between software industry and Software Engineering education - A systematic mapping of Software Engineering Trends. Journal of Systems and Software, 172, 110736. https://doi.org/10.1016/j.jss.2020.110736

Ciolacu, M. I., Binder, L., & Popp, H. (2019). Enabling IoT in Education 4.0 with BioSensors from Wearables and Artificial Intelligence. 2019 IEEE 25th International Symposium for Design and Technology in Electronic Packaging (SIITME), 17–24. https://doi.org/10.1109/SIITME47687.2019.8990763

Ciolacu, M. I., Binder, L., Svasta, P., Tache, I., & Stoichescu, D. (2019). Education 4.0 - Jump to Innovation with IoT in Higher Education. 2019 IEEE 25th International Symposium for Design and Technology in Electronic Packaging (SIITME), 23–26. https://doi.org/10.1109/SIITME47687.2019.8990825

Elkobaisi, M. R., & Al Machot, F. (2022). Human emotion modeling (HEM): an interface for IoT systems. Journal of Ambient Intelligence and Humanized Computing, 13(8), 4009–4017. https://doi.org/10.1007/s12652-021-03437-w

Elmalaki, S. (2021). FaiR-IoT: Fairness-aware Human-in-the-Loop Reinforcement Learning for Harnessing Human Variability in Personalized IoT. IoTDI 2021 - Proceedings of the 2021 International Conference on Internet-of-Things Design and Implementation, 119–132. https://doi.org/10.1145/3450268.3453525

Embarak, O. H. (2022). Internet of Behaviour (IoB)-based AI models for personalized smart education systems. Procedia Computer Science, 203, 103–110. https://doi.org/10.1016/j.procs.2022.07.015

Farhan, M., Jabbar, S., Aslam, M., Ahmad, A., Iqbal, M. M., Khan, M., & Maria, M. E. A. (2018). A Real-Time Data Mining Approach for Interaction Analytics Assessment: IoT Based Student Interaction Framework. International Journal of Parallel Programming, 46(5), 886–903. https://doi.org/10.1007/s10766-017-0553-7

Ghallabi, S., Essalmi, F., Jemni, M., & Kinshuk. (2020). Learner modeling in cloud computing. Education and Information Technologies, 25(6), 5581–5599. https://doi.org/10.1007/s10639-020-10185-5

Hanes, D., Salgueiro, G., Grossetete, P., Barton, R., & Henry, J. (2017). The IoT World Forum (IoTWF) Standardized Architecture. In IoT Fundamentals: Networking Technologies, Protocols, and Use Cases for the Internet of Things (1st ed., pp. 86–91). Cisco Press.

Jia, B., Liu, S., Guan, Y., Li, W., & Ren, W. (2017). The fusion model of multidomain context information for the internet of things. Wireless Communications and Mobile Computing, 2017(1), 8. https://doi.org/10.1155/2017/6274824

Kassab, M., & Mazzara, M. (2020). Towards Designing Smart Learning Environments with IoT. In J.-M. Bruel, M. Mazzara, & B. Meyer (Eds.), Software Engineering Aspects of Continuous Development and New Paradigms of Software Production and Deployment (pp. 152–166). Springer International Publishing. https://doi.org/10.1007/978-3-030-39306-9_11

Kitchenham, B. (2004). Procedures for Performing Systematic Reviews. In Keele University Technical Report. https://www.researchgate.net/publication/228756057

Kitchenham, B., & Charters, S. M. (2007). Guidelines for performing systematic literature reviews in software engineering. In Technical report, EBSE Technical Report EBSE-2007-01 (Issue January 2007). https://www.cs.auckland.ac.nz/~norsaremah/2007 Guidelines for performing SLR in SE v2.3.pdf

Kumar, J. A. (2021). Educational chatbots for project-based learning: investigating learning outcomes for a team-based design course. International Journal of Educational Technology in Higher Education, 18(1), 65. https://doi.org/10.1186/s41239-021-00302-w

Mahapatra, S. K., Pattanayak, B. K., & Pati, B. (2021). Flip learning: A novel iot-based learning initiative. Smart Innovation, Systems and Technologies, 153, 59–67. https://doi.org/10.1007/978-981-15-6202-0_7

Mavroudi, A., Fragou, O., & Goumopoulos, C. (2019). Design Concepts, Principles and Patterns in the Curriculum of the New Computing Education Era. Designs for Learning, 11(1), 141–153. https://doi.org/10.16993/dfl.140

Mitra, S., & Gupta, S. (2020). Mobile learning under personal cloud with a virtualization framework for outcome based education. Education and Information Technologies, 25(3), 2129–2156. https://doi.org/10.1007/s10639-019-10043-z

Mohana, M., Da Silveira, A. C., Subashini, P., Santos, C. A. S., & Ghinea, G. (2023). Technology Enhanced Mulsemedia Learning: Insights of an Evaluation. In H. P. Da Silva & P. Cipresso (Eds.), Computer-Human Interaction Research and Applications. CHIRA 2023 (pp. 24–42). Springer Nature Switzerland. https://doi.org/10.1007/978-3-031-49368-3_3

Muhammad, A., Shen, J., Beydoun, G., & Xu, D. (2018). SBAR: A Framework to Support Learning Path Adaptation in Mobile Learning. In N. Y. Yen & J. C. Hung (Eds.), Frontier Computing (Vol. 422, pp. 655–665). Springer Singapore. https://doi.org/10.1007/978-981-10-3187-8_62

Mukherjee, K., Maurya, S., Mandal, R. K., Thakur, M., & Khatoon, F. (2021). A Novel Methodology for Cloud of Things-Based Secure Higher Education Framework Using Zero Knowledge Proof System. International Journal of Web-Based Learning and Teaching Technologies, 17(4), 1–21. https://doi.org/10.4018/ijwltt.285565

Ojha, A., Jebelli, H., & Sharifironizi, M. (2023). Understanding Students' Engagement in Learning Emerging Technologies of Construction Sector: Feasibility of Wearable Physiological Sensing System-Based Monitoring. In S. Walbridge, M. Nik-Bakht, K. T. W. Ng, M. Shome, M. S. Alam, A. El Damatty, & G. Lovegrove (Eds.), Proceedings of the Canadian Society of Civil Engineering Annual Conference 2021 (Vol. 239, pp. 269–281). Springer Nature Singapore. https://doi.org/10.1007/978-981-19-0503-2_22

Petersen, K., Vakkalanka, S., & Kuzniarz, L. (2015). Guidelines for conducting systematic mapping studies in software engineering: An update. Information and Software Technology, 64, 1–18. https://doi.org/10.1016/j.infsof.2015.03.007

Prihar, E., Haim, A., Sales, A., & Heffernan, N. (2022). Automatic Interpretable Personalized Learning. L@S 2022 - Proceedings of the 9th ACM Conference on Learning @ Scale, 1–11. https://doi.org/10.1145/3491140.3528267

Razzaque, A., & Hamdan, A. (2020). Internet of Things for Learning Styles and Learning Outcomes Improve e-Learning: A Review of Literature. In A.-E. Hassanien, A. T. Azar, T. Gaber, D. Oliva, & F. M. Tolba (Eds.), Proceedings of the International Conference on Artificial Intelligence and Computer Vision (AICV2020) (pp. 783–791). Springer International Publishing.

Reyes, R., Garza, D., Garrido, L., De La Cueva, V., & Ramirez, J. (2019). Methodology for the Implementation of Virtual Assistants for Education Using Google Dialogflow. In L. Martínez-Villaseñor, I. Batyrshin, & A. Marín-Hernández (Eds.), Advances in Soft Computing (pp. 440–451). Springer International Publishing. https://doi.org/10.1007/978-3-030-33749-0_35

Shapsough, S. Y., & Zualkernan, I. A. (2020). A Generic IoT Architecture for Ubiquitous Context-Aware Learning. IEEE Transactions on Learning Technologies, 13(3), 449–464. https://doi.org/10.1109/TLT.2020.3007708

Shrestha, S. K., & Furqan, F. (2020). IoT for Smart Learning / Education. 2020 5th International Conference on Innovative Technologies in Intelligent Systems and Industrial Applications (CITISIA), 1–7. https://doi.org/10.1109/CITISIA50690.2020.9371774

Soui, M., Srinivasan, K., & Albesher, A. (2022). Intelligent Personalized E-Learning Platform using Machine Learning Algorithms. In Machine Learning Methods for Engineering Application Development (pp. 110–126). https://doi.org/10.2174/9879815079180122010011

Spyrou, E., Vretos, N., Pomazanskyi, A., Asteriadis, S., & Leligou, H. C. (2018). Exploiting IoT Technologies for Personalized Learning. 2018 IEEE Conference on Computational Intelligence and Games (CIG), 1–8. https://doi.org/10.1109/CIG.2018.8490454

Tortorella, R. A. W., & Graf, S. (2017). Considering learning styles and context-awareness for mobile adaptive learning. Education and Information Technologies, 22(1), 297–315. https://doi.org/10.1007/s10639-015-9445-x

Trifa, A., Hedhili, A., & Chaari, W. L. (2019). Knowledge Tracing with an Intelligent Agent, in an e-Learning Platform. Education and Information Technologies, 24(1), 711–741. https://doi.org/10.1007/s10639-018-9792-5

Vinayachandra, K., & Prasad K., K. (2020). Application of IoT in the Development of Intelligent Education System – A Thematic Literature Review. International Journal of Management, Technology, and Social Sciences, 5(1), 124–146. https://doi.org/10.47992/ijmts.2581.6012.0086

Wang, M., & Lv, Z. (2022). Construction of personalized learning and knowledge system of chemistry specialty via the internet of things and clustering algorithm. The Journal of Supercomputing, 78(8), 10997–11014. https://doi.org/10.1007/s11227-022-04315-8

Wang, Q., Yin, H., Chen, T., Yu, J., Zhou, A., & Zhang, X. (2022). Fast-adapting and privacy-preserving federated recommender system. VLDB Journal, 31(5), 877–896. https://doi.org/10.1007/s00778-021-00700-6

Whalley, B., France, D., Park, J., Mauchline, A., & Welsh, K. (2020). Developing Active Personal Learning Environments on Smart Mobile Devices. In K. Arai, R. Bhatia, & S. Kapoor (Eds.), Proceedings of the Future Technologies Conference (FTC) 2019 (pp. 871–889). Springer International Publishing. https://doi.org/10.1007/978-3-030-32523-7_64

Yao, C. B. (2017). Constructing a User-Friendly and Smart Ubiquitous Personalized Learning Environment by Using a Context-Aware Mechanism. IEEE Transactions on Learning Technologies, 10(1), 104–114. https://doi.org/10.1109/TLT.2015.2487977

Zhao, Z., Zhao, B., Ji, Z., & Liang, Z. (2022). On the Personalized Learning Space in Educational Metaverse Based on Heart Rate Signal. International Journal of Information and Communication Technology Education, 18(2), 1–12. https://doi.org/10.4018/ijicte.314565

A HYBRID APPROACH INTEGRATING REINFORCEMENT AND SUPERVISED LEARNING FOR INTRUSION DETECTION

Souad Derbali[1], Khaled Jouini[2], Farah Jemili[2] and Ouajdi Korbaa[2]
[1]University of Sousse, ISITCOM, Hammam Sousse
4011, Hammam Sousse, Tunisia
[2]University of Sousse, ISITCOM, MARS Research Laboratory, LR17ES05
4011, Hammam Sousse, Tunisia

ABSTRACT

The rise in sophisticated cyberattacks necessitates advanced and adaptive intrusion detection systems (IDS). Traditional IDS relying on machine learning (ML) often lack flexibility and require significant human intervention. To address this, we propose a real-time IDS that integrates reinforcement learning (RL) and supervised learning (SL) to improve performance and adaptability. This hybrid approach combines RL's ability to make sequential decisions in dynamic environments with SL's precision in intrusion classification. We evaluated several supervised learning methods, such as SVM, LightGBM, and XGBoost, alongside deep reinforcement learning methods, including DQN, DDQN, and PPO, using labeled intrusion datasets. Results show the hybrid SL-RL models outperform traditional ML methods, reducing false positives and negatives while improving generalization to new threats. Key factors include small discount factors and simple reward functions for training RL models. This approach offers a more robust and adaptive defense against evolving cyber threats, promising significant advancements in IDS performance.

KEYWORDS

Hybrid Model (SL-RL), Supervised Learning (SL), Reinforcement Learning (RL), Intrusion Detection System (IDS), Real-time Monitoring

1. INTRODUCTION

Cybersecurity is critical due to increasing sophisticated cyberattacks. Traditional intrusion detection systems (IDS) based on classical machine learning lack flexibility and adaptability, requiring frequent retraining and supervision, and struggle with dynamic threats like DDoS (Academy, 2024a), cloud trust issues, web vulnerabilities, and MitM attacks (Academy, 2024b). To address these limitations, we propose a hybrid approach combining reinforcement learning (RL) for adaptability and supervised learning (SL) for accurate intrusion classification. Using algorithms like DQN, DDQN, D3QN, A2C, SVM, LightGBM, and XGBoost, trained on the CSE-CIC-IDS2018 dataset, our model enhances IDS accuracy, adaptability, and robustness. It incorporates feature extraction, data balancing, hyperparameter tuning, and reward design, achieving high detection accuracy, low false alarms, and better generalization. The study evaluates performance using metrics like accuracy, precision, recall, F1 score, and false positive rate. This hybrid RL-SL method aims to overcome traditional IDS shortcomings, offering improved flexibility and effectiveness. The document is structured as follows: Part 2 reviews previous research, Part 3 covers dataset preparation and model specifics, Part 4 presents numerical results, and Part 5 discusses future prospects.

2. LITERATURE REVIEW

Deep Reinforcement Learning (DRL) and supervised learning adapt to complex environments, optimizing real-time data flows, personalizing medical treatments, and enhancing applications in transportation, logistics, energy, and robotics. Supervised learning predicts market trends and aids early disease detection using annotated data. DRL methods like DQN, DDQN, PG, and PPO optimize decision-making and policies, while supervised algorithms (SVM, LightGBM, XGBoost) excel in classification and prediction. In cybersecurity, combining DRL and supervised learning enhances intrusion detection systems (IDS) using datasets like UNSW-NB15, CTU-13, and CICIDS2018, improving threat detection and defense strategies. The domain of intrusion detection has advanced through machine learning and deep learning. (Mebawondo et al., 2020) developed a lightweight system using information gain and a multilayer perceptron neural network, improving accuracy with UNSW-NB15 but facing dataset dependency. (Abdallah et al., 2022) provided a taxonomy of IDS and supervised learning algorithms, emphasizing feature selection for data imbalance. (Santos et al., 2022) used reinforcement learning, transfer learning, and a sliding window for efficient long-term detection but relied on specific datasets. (Ren et al., 2022) introduced ID RDRL, showing improvements with CSE-CIC IDS2018 but needing validation in diverse environments. (Al-Ibraheemi et al., 2024) used graph convolutional networks and DRL for SDN security, showing improved performance with NSL-KDD but facing implementation challenges. (Vadigi et al., 2023) presented an RL-based model with transfer learning and a sliding window, facing dataset specificity and network traffic evolution challenges. (Badr, 2022) explored dueling double deep Q-learning networks for dynamic environments but was limited by simulated datasets. (Ren et al., 2023) proposed MAFSIDS with DRL and self-feature selection, showing high accuracy but requiring further generalization. (Lopez-Martin et al., 2021) extended RBFNN with offline RL, demonstrating superiority over multiple datasets but facing RL complexity and RBF initialization challenges. Despite progress, gaps remain: supervised learning relies on data quality, limiting unknown attack detection; RL methods face reward complexity and extensive interaction needs; hybrid models struggle with computational complexity and transparency. A new integration technique combining advanced supervised and RL methods with data rebalancing and complexity reduction is proposed, promising more effective, adaptive, and robust IDS for real-time intrusion variability.

2.1 Figures and Tables

Table 1. Comparison of Traditional Methods and Hybrid SL-RL Approach

Methods	Datasets	Advantages	Limitations
Reinforcement Learning (Badr, 2022)	KDD Cup99, ISCX 2012	Adapts to dynamic environments.	Generalization limitations due to simulated datasets.
Deep Reinforcement Learning Auto Feature Selection (Ren et al., 2023)	CSE-CIC-IDS2018 and NSL-KDD	High accuracy via multi-agent framework.	Needs testing for diverse environments and attack scenarios.
RBF Neural Network Reinforcement Learning (Lopez Martin et al., 2021)	Various datasets	Superior performance across datasets.	Complex methods and requires good RBF initialization.
Multilayer Perceptron, Information Gain (Mebawondo et al., 2020)	UNSW-NB15	Improved accuracy.	Dataset-dependent and limited feature set.
Supervised Algorithms, Feature Selection (Abdallah et al., 2022)	KDD '99, NSL KDD, CICIDS2017, UNSW-NB15	Promising performance, emphasizes feature selection.	Lacks implementation details and faces challenges.
Hybrid SL-RL Approach (Our Approach)	CSE-CIC-IDS2018	Combines RL adaptability and SL accuracy.	High computational complexity, needs validation in diverse, real-time environments.

3. METHODOLOGY

The methodology uses the CSE-CIC-IDS2018 dataset as the primary foundation for training and validation due to its comprehensive intrusion scenarios. UNSW-NB15 and NSL-KDD datasets are also included to enhance generalizability and validate robustness across diverse attack scenarios. As illustrated in Figure 1, key steps include data preprocessing, feature normalization (MinMaxScaler, StandardScaler), class imbalance handling (SMOTE), and dimensionality reduction (PCA). Supervised Learning (SL) models (Linear SVM, RBF SVM, LightGBM, XGBoost) and Reinforcement Learning (RL) algorithms (DQN, DDQN, D3QN, A2C, PPO) are evaluated using metrics like accuracy, precision, recall, and false positive rate. While CSE-CIC-IDS2018 is central, integrating additional datasets strengthens cross-validation and result credibility. This combined SL and RL framework ensures optimal intrusion detection performance across diverse and evolving attack patterns.

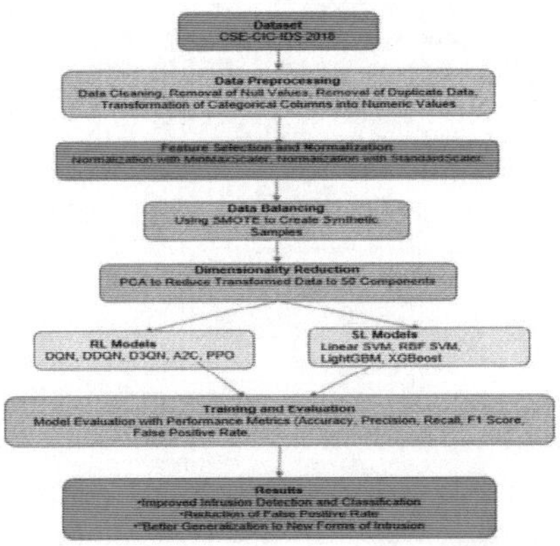

Figure 1. Workflow for an Intrusion Detection System (IDS) based on Supervised Learning and Reinforcement Learning

3.1 Dynamic Hybrid Model (Dynamic Combination of Supervised Learning and Reinforcement Learning)

The combination of supervised learning (SL) and reinforcement learning (RL) for intrusion detection leverages their respective strengths: SL excels with labeled data, while RL adapts to dynamic, uncertain environments. The proposed hybrid model evaluates various SL (SVM, RBF SVM, LightGBM, XGBoost) and RL (DQN, DDQN, D3QN, A2C, PPO) algorithms. SVM and DQN were selected for their effectiveness in classifying static attacks and adapting to evolving threats, crucial in cybersecurity. The implementation demonstrates model initialization, training, and dynamic integration, enabling simultaneous exploitation of both approaches.

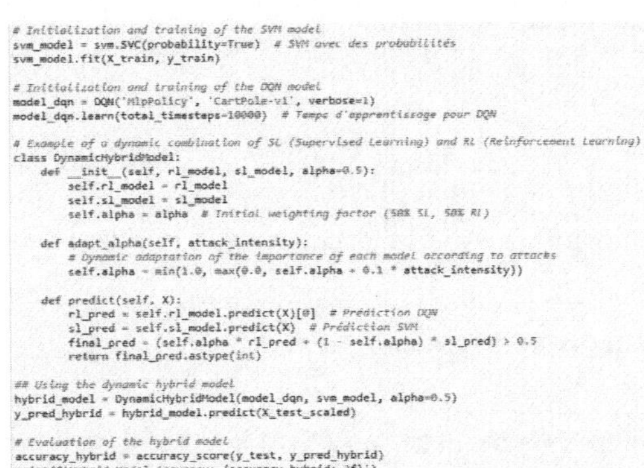

```
# Initialization and training of the SVM model
svm_model = svm.SVC(probability=True)  # SVM avec des probabilités
svm_model.fit(X_train, y_train)

# Initialization and training of the DQN model
model_dqn = DQN('MlpPolicy', 'CartPole-v1', verbose=1)
model_dqn.learn(total_timesteps=10000)  # Temps d'apprentissage pour DQN

# Example of a dynamic combination of SL (Supervised Learning) and RL (Reinforcement Learning)
class DynamicHybridModel:
    def __init__(self, rl_model, sl_model, alpha=0.5):
        self.rl_model = rl_model
        self.sl_model = sl_model
        self.alpha = alpha  # Initial weighting factor (50% SL, 50% RL)

    def adapt_alpha(self, attack_intensity):
        # Dynamic adaptation of the importance of each model according to attacks
        self.alpha = min(1.0, max(0.0, self.alpha + 0.1 * attack_intensity))

    def predict(self, X):
        rl_pred = self.rl_model.predict(X)[0]  # Prédiction DQN
        sl_pred = self.sl_model.predict(X)  # Prédiction SVM
        final_pred = (self.alpha * rl_pred + (1 - self.alpha) * sl_pred) > 0.5
        return final_pred.astype(int)

## Using the dynamic hybrid model
hybrid_model = DynamicHybridModel(model_dqn, svm_model, alpha=0.5)
y_pred_hybrid = hybrid_model.predict(X_test_scaled)

# Evaluation of the hybrid model
accuracy_hybrid = accuracy_score(y_test, y_pred_hybrid)
print(f'Hybrid Model Accuracy: {accuracy_hybrid:.2f}')
```

Figure 2. Dynamic Combination of Supervised and Reinforcement Learning Models for Intrusion Detection

The initialization, training, and dynamic integration of models leverage the strengths of each approach, optimally balancing SVM and DQN weightings to enhance flexibility and threat responsiveness.

3.2 Datasets and Evaluation

The hybrid model's performance is evaluated using prominent cybersecurity datasets, primarily CSE-CIC-IDS2018, for training and validation.

```python
# Load the dataset from CSV file
df = pd.read_csv("C:/Users/mesrs/Downloads/Friday-02-03-2018_TrafficForML_CICFlowMeter.csv")
```

Figure 3. Loading a CSV Dataset Using Pandas in Python

To enhance generalizability, UNSW-NB15 and NSL-KDD datasets are also included. Rigorous cross-validation assesses the SVM model's robustness and classification capabilities, while the DQN model is trained to adapt to diverse simulated attack scenarios in dynamic environments. This approach ensures a comprehensive evaluation, reinforcing the model's credibility and generalizability across various contexts. Integrating additional datasets broadens the tested data spectrum and strengthens cross-validation, highlighting the model's increased robustness and effective generalization to diverse environments and attack types.

```python
# Separation of data into training and test sets
X_train, X_test_scaled, y_train, y_test = train_test_split(X_train_scaled, y, test_size=0.2, random_state=42)

# Initialization and training of the SVM model
svm_model = svm.SVC(probability=True)
svm_model.fit(X_train, y_train)

# Initialization and training of the DQN model
model_dqn = DQN('MlpPolicy', env, verbose=1)
model_dqn.learn(total_timesteps=20000)

# Loading additional datasets from OpenML
unsw_nb15 = fetch_openml(name='UNSW-NB15', version=1)
nsl_kdd = fetch_openml(name='NSL-KDD', version=1)

# Apply cross-validation on each dataset
datasets = {
    "CSE-CIC-IDS2018": (X_train, y_train),
    "UNSW-NB15": (unsw_nb15.data, unsw_nb15.target),
    "NSL-KDD": (nsl_kdd.data, nsl_kdd.target)
}

# Cross-validation and display of results
for name, (X_data, y_data) in datasets.items():
    # Calculating cross-validation scores with SVM
    scores = cross_val_score(svm_model, X_data, y_data.astype(int), cv=5)
    print(f"Cross-validated accuracy for {name}: {scores.mean():.2f}")

# Final display
```

Figure 4. Training and Cross-Validation of SVM and DQN Models on Multiple Intrusion Detection Datasets

3.3 Model Description

This section covers deep reinforcement learning (DRL) and supervised learning. In DRL, an agent learns optimal actions in an unknown environment by maximizing cumulative rewards through states, actions, rewards, and transitions (Figure 5). Key DRL models like PPO, A2C, D3QN, and Double Q-Learning excel in sequential decision-making. In supervised learning, algorithms such as Linear SVM, RBF SVM (effective for non-linear data), LightGBM, and XGBoost (known for speed and efficiency) are widely used for classification and prediction tasks.

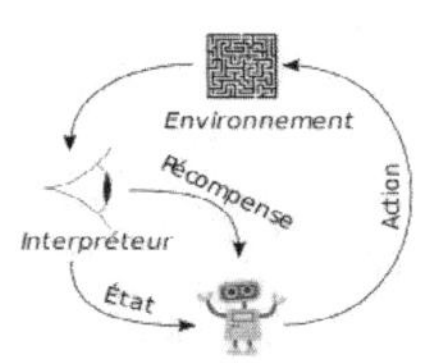

Figure 5. Agent-Environment interaction in the RL model

3.4 Description of Evaluated Models

3.4.1 Q- Learning and Deep Q-Networks (DQN): Overview and Key Mechanisms

Q-Learning aims to find the optimal policy $\pi*$ by maximizing total rewards via the Q function, which estimates rewards for state-action pairs. DQN uses a Deep Neural Network (DNN) with linear activation, mini-batches for training, and an ε-greedy policy to balance exploration and exploitation. Loss is computed using Mean Squared Error (MSE), with a discount factor γ. The ε parameter decreases over time to reduce exploration. The loss function is:

$$MSE = E[(r + \gamma \, max_{a}{}' \, Q(s', a'; \theta^{-}) - Q(s, a; \theta))^2] \quad (1)$$

where θ are the current neural network parameters and $\theta^{-}$are the target network parameters.

3.4.2 Double DQN (DDQN): Enhancing Stability with Dual Networks

DDQN enhances stability over DQN by employing two networks: an online Q network for action prediction and an offline target network for target value calculation, mitigating DQN's "moving target" issue. The loss function is the mean squared error (MSE) between predicted and target values:

$$MSE = E[(r + \gamma \, Q(s', arg \, max_{a}{}' Q(s', a'; \theta); \, \theta^{-}) - Q(s, a; \theta))^2] \quad (2)$$

where θ are the online Q network parameters and $\theta^{-}$are the target network parameters.

3.4.3 Double Dueling Deep Q-Network (D3QN): Enhancing DQN with Advantage Function

D3QN enhances DQN by employing the advantage function A (s, a) to compute Q values, reflecting action quality in a state. The Q values are calculated as:

$$Q(s, a \, ; \, \theta, \alpha, \beta) = V(s \, ; \, \theta, \beta) + A(s, a \, ; \, \theta, \alpha) - \left(\frac{1}{|A|}\right) \textstyle\sum_{a'} A(s, a' \, ; \, \theta, \alpha) \quad (3)$$

Here, V(s;θ,β) is the state value, and A(s,a;θ,α) is the advantage function. The network's final layer computes these separately, combining them to resolve identifiability issues. D3QN training is similar to DDQN, using similar hyperparameters.

3.4.4 Advantage Actor-Critic (A2C): Combining Value and Policy Based Methods

A2C merges value-based and policy-based methods using two networks: an actor network (optimizing policy via policy gradient) and a critic network (evaluating policy via a value function). Both use DNNs with three dense layers. The actor updates parameters through bootstrapping, while the critic uses MSE loss. Training employs mini-batches to form trajectories. The policy update is defined by: $\nabla_{\theta} J(\theta) = \mathrm{E}[\nabla_{\theta} \log \pi_{\theta} (a_t \mid s_t) A(s_t, a_t)]$ (4) where the advantage function $A(s_t, a_t)$ is given by $A(s_t, a_t) = Q(s_t, a_t) - V(s_t)$ (5) The critic's loss function is the mean squared error (MSE), expressed in $MSE = E[(R_t - V(s_t))^2]$ (6) where R_t is the sum of discounted rewards.

3.4.5 Proximal Policy Optimization (PPO): Controlling Policy Updates with Clipping Mechanism

Proximal Policy Optimization (PPO) improves policy updates using a clipping mechanism, employing two networks: a policy network (θ) and a value network (φ). Its objective function combines regular and clipped formulas, leveraging action advantages to reduce variance and enhance accuracy. Predictions occur post-learning. The PPO objective function is: $\min\left(r_{t(\theta)} \cdot A_t, clip\left(r_{t(\theta)}, 1-\varepsilon, 1+\varepsilon\right) \cdot A_t\right)$ (7) where: $r_{t(\theta)} = \frac{\pi\theta(a_t|s_t)}{\pi\theta_{old}(a_t|s_t)}$ is the probability ratio, $A_t$is the estimated advantage, and ε is the clipping hyperparameter. The value function, minimizing variance is : $\mathrm{E}_t = \left[\left(V_t - V_t^{arget}\right)^2\right]$ (8) where V_t^{arget} is the target value.

3.4.6 Linear Support Vector Machines (SVMs): Optimal Hyperplane for Classification

Proximal Linear SVMs are supervised models for classification and regression, finding an optimal hyperplane to separate data by maximizing the margin. The hyperplane is defined by a linear function of input features. Training minimizes a loss function combining classification error and model complexity penalty, expressed as: $\min_{w,b} ||w||^{\,2} + C \sum_i \max\left(0, 1 - y_i(w \cdot x_i + b)\right)$ (9) where w is the weight vector, b is the bias, C is a regularization parameter, x_i are the data points, and $y_i$are the class labels.

3.4.7 Support Vector Machines with Radial Basis Function (RBF) Kernel: Nonlinear Classification

Support Vector Machines (SVMs) with a Radial Basis Function (RBF) kernel improve linear SVMs by mapping data into a higher-dimensional space, enabling effective class separation via a linear hyperplane. The

RBF kernel, defined as : $K(x_i, x_j) = \exp\left(-\gamma \left\|x_i - x_j\right\|^2\right)$ (10) where γ controls data point influence, handles nonlinear classification by identifying optimal hyperplanes in the transformed space. Training minimizes a loss function adapted for the RBF kernel, similar to linear SVMs.

3.4.8 LightGBM: Efficient Gradient Boosting with Leaf- Wise Growth

Light Gradient Boosting Machine (LightGBM) is a highly efficient gradient boosting algorithm that con structs decision trees iteratively. It optimizes logarithmic loss for classification tasks and mean squared error (MSE) for regression tasks, utilizing techniques including leaf-wise growth and feature bundling.

3.4.9 XGBoost: Optimized Gradient Boosting with Regularization

XGBoost is a highly efficient gradient boosting implementation known for its precision and performance. It builds decision trees sequentially, each correcting errors from the previous ones, and uses a regularized objective function to prevent overfitting and enhance generalization. The loss function for XGBoost is defined as: $L = \sum_{\{i=1\}}^{n} l(y_i, \hat{y}_i) + \Omega(f_k)$ (11) where l is loss, y_i is the actual value, Ω is the regularization term, and f_k represents the decision trees. XGBoost effectively manages complex feature interactions through gradient boosting, subsampling, and tree regularization.

4. RESULTS

This study compares the performance of DRL models (DQN, DDQN, D3QN, A2C, PPO) and traditional ML models (linear SVM, RBF SVM, LightGBM, XGBoost) using the CSE-CIC-IDS2018 dataset. Key metrics—accuracy, precision, recall, and F1 score—were evaluated.

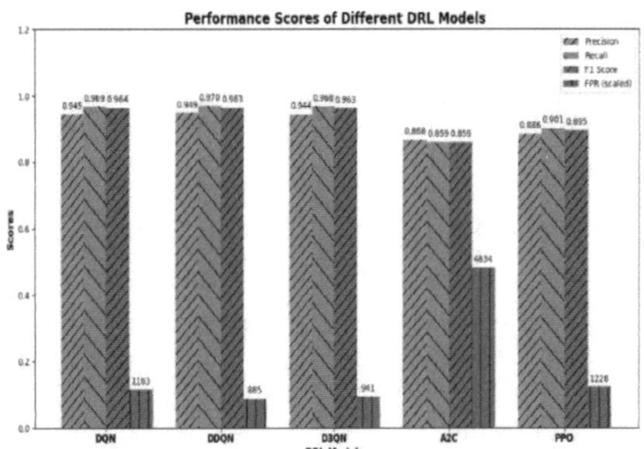

Figure 6. Comparison of DRL Models' Performance Using Precision, Recall, F1 Score, and FPR

To manage computational demands and ensure reliability, stratified sampling maintained attack and benign traffic proportions, with an 80-20 train-test split and fixed random state for reproducibility. Cross-validation validated model reliability and generalizability, demonstrating their robustness and adaptability in diverse intrusion scenarios.

4.1 Simulation 1: Reinforcement Learning

We assess the performance of DQN, DDQN, D3QN, A2C, and PPO under simulated attacks using AUC and confusion matrices. Figure 7 shows ROC curves and confusion matrices for these models. DQN achieves the highest AUC (0.86), followed by D3QN (0.85), DDQN (0.84), A2C (0.83), and PPO (0.80). Confusion matrices reveal true/false positives/negatives, highlighting classification performance. While DQN leads in AUC, all models show misclassifications, indicating vulnerabilities and room for improvement under adversarial conditions.

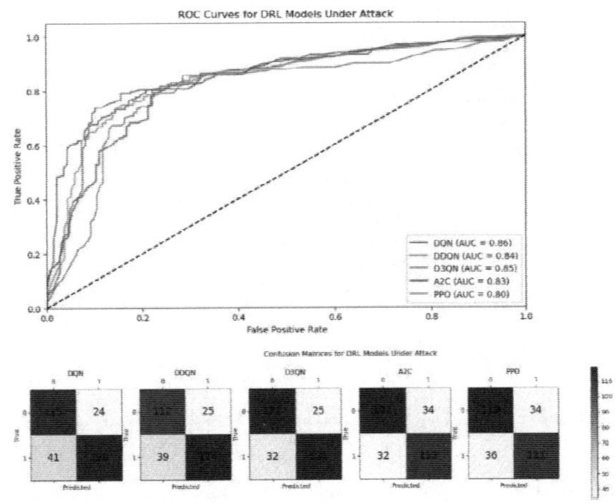

Figure 7. ROC Curves and Confusion Matrices for DRL Models Under Simulated Attacks

4.2 Simulation 2: Supervised Learning

We evaluated Linear SVM, RBF SVM, LightGBM, and XGBoost for intrusion detection, assessing their accuracy and predictive capabilities. Linear SVM performed best with 133 true positives, 135 true negatives, and an AUC of 0.91. RBF SVM followed closely (132 true positives, 131 true negatives, AUC 0.89), as did LightGBM (130 true positives, 127 true negatives, AUC 0.89). XGBoost was slightly weaker (127 true positives, 126 true negatives, AUC 0.86). Linear SVM had the highest AUC, while RBF SVM and LightGBM were competitive, and XGBoost remained effective for intrusion detection.

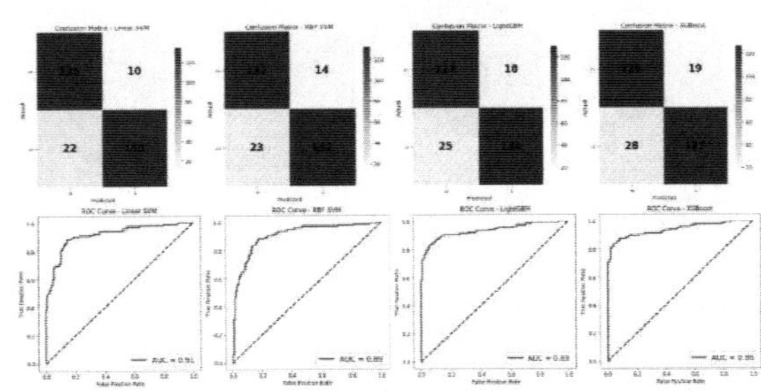

Figure 8. ROC Comparative Performance of Linear SVM, RBF SVM, LightGBM, and XGBoost Models

4.3 Simulation 3: Hybrid Approach: Supervised Learning with Reinforcement Learning

This study proposes a hybrid intrusion detection model combining Deep Q-Network (DQN) and Support Vector Machine (SVM), with a logistic regression meta-model integrating their predictions. Applied to the CSE-CIC-IDS2018 dataset, the approach achieves 0.86 accuracy and 0.92 AUC, with 133 true positives, 124 true negatives, 22 false negatives, and 21 false positives. The model outperforms standalone DQN (AUC 0.84, accuracy 0.87) as reported by Vadigi et al. (2023) and Linear SVM (AUC 0.90, accuracy 0.85) from Abdallah and Otoom (2022), leveraging DQN's adaptability and SVM's classification precision. The results demonstrate the hybrid method's effectiveness in dynamic intrusion detection scenarios.

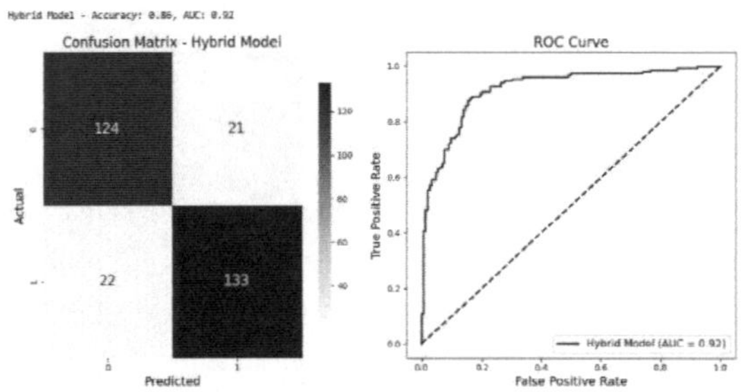

Figure 9. Performance Evaluation of the Hybrid SL-RL Learning Model for IDS

4.4 Simulation 4: Hybrid Approach with Dynamic Combination

A hybrid model combining SVM and DQN was implemented using a dynamic weighting strategy to optimize real-time decision-making under varying threat levels. DQN was prioritized in high-risk scenarios for adaptability, while SVM detected routine patterns in stable environments. The model achieved an accuracy of 0.83 and an AUC of 0.89, with the confusion matrix showing 22 true negatives, 20 true positives, 8 false positives, and 10 false negatives. Despite minor limitations, the model effectively balanced precision and adaptability, leveraging the strengths of both SVM and DQN. Future improvements could enhance its robustness in real-world applications.

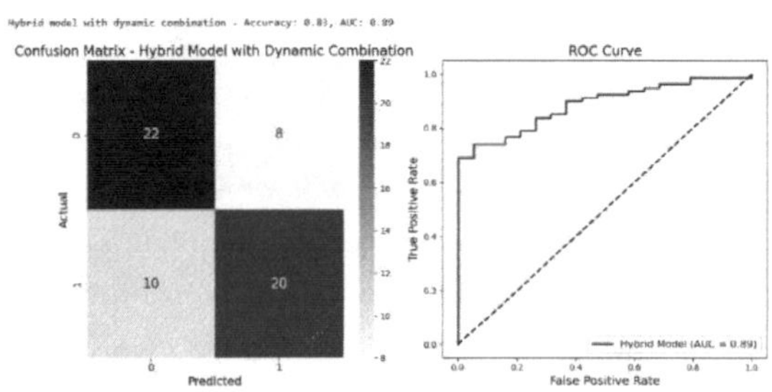

Figure 10. Performance Evaluation of the Hybrid model with dynamic combination

4.5 Analysis and Discussion of Results

DRL and supervised learning models showed performance variations. DQN led DRL methods with an AUC of 0.86, followed by DDQN (0.84) and D3QN (0.85), while A2C (0.83) and PPO (0.80) scored lower. Supervised models outperformed DRL, with Linear SVM (AUC: 0.90) and RBF-SVM (AUC: 0.92) achieving higher accuracy. A hybrid DQN-SVM model with logistic regression achieved an AUC of 0.92 and accuracy of 0.86, surpassing standalone DRL but slightly below supervised models. In Simulation 4, using dynamic weight adjustment, the hybrid model achieved 0.83 accuracy and 0.89 AUC, though confusion matrices revealed detection challenges. The hybrid approach balanced DQN's adaptability and SVM's precision, showing promise for intrusion detection. Future work will refine weighting mechanisms and expand dataset diversity for improved robustness.

5. CONCLUSIONS

This study demonstrated the effectiveness of a hybrid approach combining reinforcement learning (RL) and supervised learning (SL) for intrusion detection, overcoming traditional system limitations by improving flexibility, accuracy, and adaptability. Results showed significant enhancements in detecting intrusions, reducing false positives/negatives, and generalizing across attack types. Algorithms like DQN, DDQN, D3QN, SVM, LightGBM, and XGBoost proved robust in dynamic environments, marking a major advancement in intrusion detection systems.

Table 2

Model	AUC	Accuracy	Notes
DRL (PPO) (Ren et al., 2022)	0.94	0.91	Best AUC in DRL models, high accuracy.
DRL (DDQN) (Lopez Martin et al., 2020)	0.81	0.85	Lowest AUC among DRL models, average accuracy.
DRL (DQN) (Vadigi et al., 2023)	0.84	0.87	Good AUC and accuracy, suitable for discrete scenarios.
Linear SVM (Abdallah et al., 2022)	0.90	0.85	Best AUC and accuracy among super vised models.
RBF-SVM (Lopez Martin et al., 2021)	0.92	0.87	High performance, competitive advanced models.
Hybrid (Supervised + DRL) [Our Study]	0.92	0.86	Combined performance, surpassing standalone DRL models.

6. FUTURE PERSPECTIVES

Future research on hybrid RL-SL intrusion detection could explore diverse datasets for robustness, advanced hyperparameter tuning for accuracy, real-time systems with dynamic updates for emerging threats, optimized detection time and resource use, and multi-agent systems for distributed detection. These steps aim to enhance scalability, efficiency, and resilience in real-world cybersecurity applications.

REFERENCES

Abdallah, E. E., Otoom, A. F., et al., (2022). Intrusion detection systems using supervised machine learning techniques A survey *Procedia Computer Science* Vol 201 pp 205–212

Academy, B., (2024a). What are distributed denial of service (DDoS) attacks? Accessed 2024-06-17

Academy, B., (2024b). What is man-in-the-middle (MITM) attack? Accessed 2024-06-17

Al-Ibraheemi, F. A., Hazzaa, F., Jabbar, M. S., et al., (2024). Intrusion detection in software-defined networks Leveraging deep reinforcement learning with graph convolutional networks for resilient infrastructure *Journal of Information Security and Applications* Vol 15 No 1 pp 78–87

Badr, Y., (2022). Enabling intrusion detection systems with dueling double deep q-learning *Digital Transformation and Society* Vol 1 No 1 pp 115–141

Boullé, M., (2016). Khiops An automatic supervised learning tool for mining large multi-table databases *Proceedings of EGC* pp 505–510

Brim, A., (2020). Deep reinforcement learning pairs trading with a double deep q-network *Proceedings of the 10th Annual Computing and Communication Workshop and Conference (CCWC)* Las Vegas USA pp 222–227 IEEE

Brownlee, J., (2016). *XGBoost with Python Gradient Boosted Trees with XGBoost and Scikit-Learn* Machine Learning Mastery

Coronato, A., Naeem, M., Pietro, G. D., et al., (2020). Reinforcement learning for intelligent healthcare applications A survey *Artificial Intelligence in Medicine* Vol 109 Article 101964

Djeffal, A., (2012). *Using Support Vector Machine (SVM) Methods in Database Analysis* PhD thesis Université Mohamed Khider-Biskra

Fan, J., Wang, Z., Xie, Y., and Yang, Z., (2020). A theoretical analysis of deep q-learning *Proceedings of Learning for Dynamics and Control* pp 486–489 PMLR

Khadka, S. and Tumer, K., (2018). Evolution-guided policy gradient in reinforcement learning *Advances in Neural Information Processing Systems* Vol 31

Kumar, G. V. D., Deepa, V., Vineela, N., et al., (2022). Detection of Parkinson's disease using LightGBM classifier *Proceedings of the 6th International Conference on Computing Methodologies and Communication (ICCMC)* Erode India pp 1292–1297 IEEE

Lopez-Martin, M., Carro, B., and Sanchez-Esguevillas, A., (2020). Application of deep reinforcement learning to intrusion detection for supervised problems *Expert Systems with Applications* Vol 141 p 112963

Lopez-Martin, M., Sanchez-Esguevillas, A., et al., (2021). Network intrusion detection based on extended RBF neural network with offline reinforcement learning *IEEE Access* Vol 9 pp 153153–153170

Mebawondo, J. O., Alowolodu, O. D., et al., (2020). Network intrusion detection system using supervised learning paradigm *Scientific African* Vol 9 p e00497

Merzoug, Z., Laadjal, A., and Houam, L., (2022). *An automatic system for diabetic retinopathy detection based on a supervised learning approach* PhD thesis

Morales, E. F., Murrieta-Cid, R., Becerra, I., et al., (2021). A survey on deep learning and deep reinforcement learning in robotics with a tutorial on deep reinforcement learning *Intelligent Service Robotics* Vol 14 No 5 pp 773–805

Ren, K., Zeng, Y., Cao, Z., et al., (2022). ID-RDRL A deep reinforcement learning-based feature selection intrusion detection model *Scientific Reports* Vol 12 No 1 p 15370

Ren, K., Zeng, Y., Zhong, Y., et al., (2023). MAFSIDS A reinforcement learning-based intrusion detection model for multi-agent feature selection networks *Journal of Big Data* Vol 10 No 1 p 137

Sanchez, J. A. H., Casilimas, K., and Rendon, O. M. C., (2022). Deep reinforcement learning for resource management on network slicing A survey *Sensors* Vol 22 No 8 p 3031

Santos, R. R. D., Viegas, E. K., Santin, A. O., et al., (2022). Reinforcement learning for intrusion detection More model longevity and fewer updates *IEEE Transactions on Network and Service Management*

Shen, R., Zhong, S., Wen, X., et al., (2022). Multi-agent deep reinforcement learning optimization framework for building energy system with renewable energy *Applied Energy* Vol 312 p 118724

Vadigi, S., Sethi, K., Mohanty, D., et al., (2023). Federated reinforcement learning-based intrusion detection system using dynamic attention mechanism *Journal of Information Security and Applications* Vol 78 p 103608

Wang, Y., He, H., and Tan, X., (2020). Truly proximal policy optimization *Proceedings of Uncertainty in Artificial Intelligence* PMLR pp 113–122

THE IMPACT OF USING STATIC CODE ANALYSIS TOOLS ON THE PERFORMANCE OF STUDENT PROJECTS DURING THE EDUCATIONAL CYCLE

Marko Staka, Sara Kijanovic, Danilo Nikolic, Darko Stefanovic and Dusanka Dakic
Faculty of Technical Sciences, University of Novi Sad,
Trg Dositeja Obradovica 6, Novi Sad, Serbia

ABSTRACT

Development in the field of software engineering has led to an expansion of projects, and consequently, projects are becoming increasingly complex, requiring careful attention to code quality. Today, many tools detect various types of issues in code, and their usage is becoming essential. This paper presents the importance of using static code analysis tools, with a focus on their use in education. Student projects at the Faculty of Technical Sciences in Novi Sad were analyzed. The sample included student projects using .NET technology, with one group of projects utilizing the SonarCloud static analysis tool during development, while the other group did not. The research into the quality of these projects showed that the use of static code analysis tools positively influences the development of student projects in the educational process, and such projects, in terms of code quality, are ultimately better than those that do not use tools during development.

KEYWORDS

Education, Student Project Performance, Code Quality, Static Code Analysis

1. INTRODUCTION

The digital era has significantly influenced the implementation of software projects in various areas of social life. The development of new technologies and the digitization of everyday activities have made real-world projects increasingly complex and sophisticated. The expansion of tasks in the field of information technology (IT) has resulted in a significant increase in the number of employees in the IT sector, which has led to a rise in the number of workers with insufficient technical or theoretical education. This issue is explored by Khosrow-Pour (2019), who focus on the challenges in educating future programmers in the context of the expansion of tasks in the IT sector.

Programmers working on software solutions often acquire technical skills through practical projects, while simultaneously lacking adequate theoretical training. In contrast, a study conducted by Ishkov and Krupnov (2024) shows that 91% of surveyed employers highlight the lack of key skills in young professionals, while 55% of graduates report difficulties in finding employment. Therefore, educational institutions play a crucial role in ensuring that future IT engineers not only learn how to write code, but also develop the ability to create high-quality software. Regular revision and reorganization of the educational process at technical universities should aim not only at transferring theoretical knowledge but also at developing practical skills that will facilitate students' transition from academic education to the industrial environment.

The focus of tasks related to information technology in educational institutions is mostly on the functionality of the software being developed. Educational programs are designed to equip future engineers with a range of technologies, ensuring they are well-prepared for the evolving IT market. Code quality is a concept that generally does not receive enough attention (De Araújo et al., 2020), except in courses specifically dedicated to this area. Continuous monitoring of the code quality of each project during the educational cycle represents a significant challenge in terms of time and the availability of technical tools for both students and teaching staff. However, code quality is an important characteristic of software, and for this reason, this topic requires additional attention during the education of IT professionals.

In this paper, an analysis of the code quality of student projects are conducted. The projects were collected from courses in various study programs at the Faculty of Technical Sciences, University of Novi Sad. The analysis covers projects in which static code analysis tools were used, as well as those where such tools were not applied. The research results served as the basis for discussing the importance of using these tools and the consequences of their application in the educational process of future IT professionals. The structure of the paper is as follows: Section 2 provides a review of relevant literature and identifies papers that explore this topic. The research methodology is presented in Section 3, followed by the research results in Section 4. The conclusion and summary of the work are given in Section 5, along with a list of references used in the paper.

2. LITERATURE REVIEW

One of the key approaches for developing practical engineering skills is the project-based learning (PBL) method (Hashiura et al., 2010). However, a common negative consequence of this model is the production of software solutions with insufficient code quality, which can complicate the successful completion of the entire task. Therefore, many researchers, including Hashiura et al. (2010), raise the question of when the optimal time is to introduce learning about code quality. Learning about code quality is crucial from the perspective of functionality and usability, starting with basic exercises before proceeding to the implementation of PBL. Additionally, certain problematic areas that may affect the quality of the implemented solution have been identified. The results of a study conducted by Breuker et al. (2011) show that the code quality of second-year students was not significantly better than that of first-year students. The main reason for this situation is the greater complexity of the projects worked on by second-year students compared to those of first-year students. Software quality characteristics can generally be divided into six categories according to the ISO/IEC 9126-1 standard (Alchimowicz & Nawrocki, 2016).

The most common issues related to code quality that arise in student projects are related to the lack of blank lines between different sections of code (Karnalim et al., 2022). Such deficiencies, as well as unnecessary lines of code, such as import statements, are the most frequent occurrences that affect the readability of student projects. Furthermore, code readability is further compromised by excessively long lines, declaring multiple variables intended for the same operation in a single line, writing multiple programming statements in one line, improperly writing comments, and omitting brackets for conditional statements or loops that contain only one statement, solely because the programming language permits it.

The results of a study investigating the correlation between project code quality and the grades students received in software engineering courses showed that none of the 166 examined characteristics were precise enough to predict the grades (Mierle et al., 2005). Keuning et al. (2017) emphasize that the quality of project code is rarely considered when grading students, which leads to students rarely correcting errors, even when using static code analysis tools during the course.

To address the identified issues, there is a significant number of studies proposing instructional strategies that would help students adhere to coding standards. In these studies, various static code analysis tools, such as SonarCloud (Nikolić et al., 2024), CheckStyle and PMD (Imhmed et al., 2023), were used to propose appropriate strategies for solving these problems. Given the relevance of artificial intelligence, the academic community is particularly investigating the impact, benefits, and challenges of using ChatGPT in the development of student projects (Haindl & Weinberger, 2024).

In order to automatically analyze the source code of exercises, models have been developed (Hashiura et al., 2010). These models enable the provision of feedback to both students and instructors. The implementation of such a tool ensures that students are aware of the quality characteristics of their software. A good practice is for students to have insight into other student projects to check which areas in the code may be problematic from a quality standpoint. These tools also provide benefits to professors, as they help in identifying student projects where errors have been detected, thereby facilitating the monitoring of project codes. Hashiura et al. (2010) emphasize that it is sufficient to point out to students the locations where errors occurred during the process of designing object-oriented systems, without providing specific methods for correction.

It is particularly important to consider the issues related to group work, as projects are typically divided among multiple individuals (Wang & Stalhane, 2005). These challenges often negatively impact code quality, but at the same time, they better prepare students for real work environments in the future industry. Even when attention is paid to code quality during the instructional process of the project, it does not necessarily mean that knowledge and skills will be acquired at the level of individual team members. This situation can lead to knowledge fragmentation, where team members do not fully understand the entire development process. Additionally, there is a risk that responsibility for mistakes is shifted onto other members, rather than collaboratively working on resolving them.

3. METHODOLOGY

The research presented in this paper was conducted in two phases. In the first phase, static code analysis tools were applied to student projects. A total of 506 student projects from seven courses within the domain of information technology at the Faculty of Technical Sciences, University of Novi Sad, were analyzed. Of these seven courses, only one utilized static code analysis tools during the software development process aimed at completing a project task.

For the purposes of further analysis, student projects from two courses where .NET technology was used were considered, as these projects were similar in terms of the number of lines of code. The analysis included 126 projects from final-year students. Of this number, 70 projects were from the course where static code analysis tools were used, while the remaining 56 projects were from the course where such tools were not applied during development. In the continuation of this paper, the projects where static code analysis was applied are referred to as Projects I, while the projects without static code analysis are referred to as Projects II.

For analyzing the code quality of student projects, the SonarCloud tool was used. SonarCloud is a tool for continuous code quality monitoring, enabling automatic analysis and oversight of the code to identify errors, security vulnerabilities, and performance inefficiencies (García-Munoz et al., 2016). This tool was developed by the company SonarSource. According to the authors, SonarCloud has been rated as the most efficient tool for static code analysis (Nikolic et al., 2021). In addition to SonarCloud, the company offers the option to use the SonarQube tool. The difference is that SonarQube is installed on local servers and in private environments, whereas SonarCloud is cloud-based and does not require local installation (*SonarCloud or SonarQube, What's Right for Your Team? | Sonar*, 2024). Both tools provide similar functionalities for code quality analysis, but they differ in terms of implementation and usage.

SonarCloud analyzes the following code quality metrics: bugs, duplicated code, vulnerabilities, code smells, and security hotspots. These metrics will be discussed in detail in the continuation of this study. The results of the analysis indicate the following range of values for the variables examined:

- Bugs (B): from 0 to 201
- Duplication of code (D): from 0 to 18%
- Vulnerabilities (V): from 0 to 24
- Code smells (CS): from 0 to 2000
- Security hotspots (SH): from 0 to 30

Code quality is defined by introducing a new variable, as presented in Hashiura et al. (2010). This variable was created to investigate the impact of the previously mentioned variables on the overall quality of the project. The new variable is called Code Quality (CQ), and its possible outcomes range from 0 to 1. The purpose of this variable is to quantify the quality of the code, with all factors having equal importance. To achieve this, the values of all variables are multiplied by corresponding weight factors (Wb, Wd, Wv, Wcs i Wsh), which are evenly distributed and set at 0,2.

To ensure that the variable's outcome falls within the range of 0 to 1, inverse standardization was applied to each of the mentioned variables. The formula for the inverse standardization of the "bugs" variable is shown below:

$$B_{inverse\ standardized} = 1 - \frac{B - B_{min}}{B_{max} - B_{min}}$$

Where:

- B is the original value of the "bugs" variable,
- Bmin is the minimum value of the "bugs" variable (0),
- Bmax is the maximum value of the "bugs" variable (201).

Where 0 represents the maximum occurrence of the observed variable's value, while 1 represents the variable's minimum value. Inverse standardization was performed for all five variables. Finally, the formula for calculating the Code Quality (CQ) variable is as follows:

$$CQ = B \, x \, Wb + D \, x \, Wd + V \, x \, Wv + CS \, x \, Wcs + SH \, x \, Wsh$$

$$CQ \in [0,1]$$

The CQ variable was calculated for each student project. Following this, the variable was classified using a threshold of 0.5. Values of the CQ variable below this threshold were marked as 0, indicating that the code quality is unsatisfactory. Values equal to or greater than the threshold were marked as 1, implying that the code quality is satisfactory.

4. RESULTS AND DISCUSSION

After classifying the CQ variable, it was determined that all 70 projects in the course where static code analysis tools were used were marked as having satisfactory code quality. In the analysis of projects where static code analysis tools were not used, it was found that 16 out of 56 projects did not meet the criteria for satisfactory code quality. The distribution of projects according to the CQ variable is shown in Figure 1.

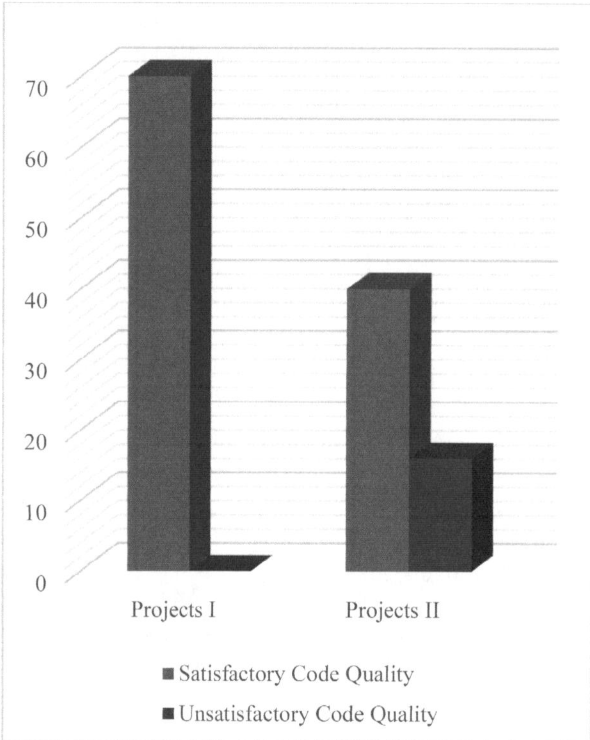

Figure 1. Distribution of satisfactory and unsatisfactory projects

The obtained results are presented in a line diagram in Figure 2. For the purpose of displaying this diagram, the data classification was performed as follows:

$$Q = \begin{cases} 0, & CQ < 0.05 \\ 0.1, & 0.05 \leq CQ < 0.15 \\ 0.2, & 0.15 \leq CQ < 0.25 \\ & \dots \\ 1, & 0.95 \leq CQ \end{cases}$$

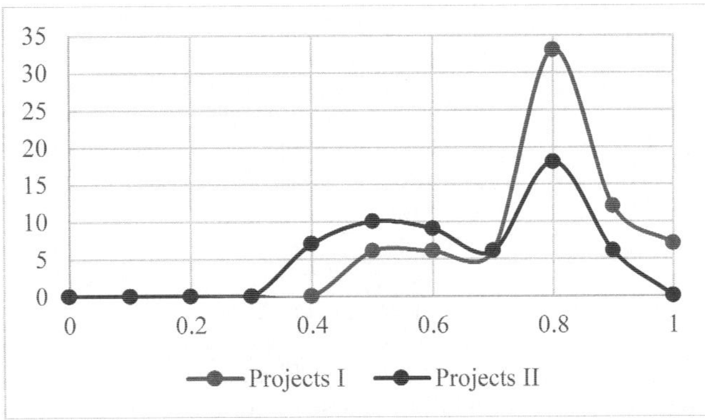

Figure 2. Distribution of projects by Code quality variable value

Based on this diagram, it can be concluded that Projects I have a range closer to a value of 1 compared to Projects II. Projects II exhibit an initial increase, starting from the point of 0.4 (7 projects), and this trend continues up to the point of 0.7. At this point, the results between both projects equalize (value 6). However, after the point of 0.7, Projects I show a significant increase, peaking at 33 at the point of 0.8, while Projects II remains at a lower level, with a value of 18. From the point of 0.8 onward, Projects I maintain its advantage, finishing with a value of 7, while Projects II decline to zero at point 1. These results indicate that Projects I have a higher code quality compared to Projects II.

The minimum, maximum, and average values of the obtained results are presented in Table 1.

Table 1. Minimum, maximum, and average values of the Code quality variable

	Minimum CQ value	Maximum CQ value	Average CQ value
Projects I	0.53	0.98	0.79
Projects II	0.39	0.98	0.72

Based on the data presented in the table, it can be concluded that Projects I demonstrate higher quality compared to Projects II when considering the CQ value. Projects I have a minimum CQ value of 0.53, which is significantly higher than the minimum CQ value for Projects II, which is 0.39. Additionally, the maximum CQ value for Project I is higher, reaching 0.98, while for Projects II it is 0.89.

The average CQ value, which provides an overall insight into project quality, is also higher for Projects I (0.79) than for Projects II (0.72). These data indicate that Projects I maintain a higher level of quality on average, with less variation between the minimum and maximum values, suggesting better standardization of code quality in comparison to Projects II.

5. CONCLUSION

Based on the research results presented in this paper, it can be concluded that the use of static code analysis tools during the development of student projects in the educational process positively impacts code quality. It has been shown that projects in courses utilizing static code analysis tools have higher minimum, maximum, and average values compared to projects where such tools were not used. This indicates a better quality of student projects that implemented these tools. These projects also exhibit less variation in code quality values, suggesting a higher level of standardization in code quality.

Static code analysis tools, such as SonarCloud and SonarQube, have a significant impact on improving the quality of student projects by automatically identifying errors, vulnerabilities, and irregularities in the code at early stages of the development process. These tools provide students with immediate feedback on the quality of their code, allowing them to correct problematic areas before they develop into more serious issues. However, to draw a comprehensive conclusion about the effectiveness of these tools, further research involving the use of other technologies is needed. An analysis of the application of other static code analysis tools in the educational context could be part of future extensions of this research.

By detecting instances of duplicated code, potentially dangerous vulnerabilities, and "code smells," these tools help maintain programming standards and encourage the writing of more readable and maintainable code. This enhances the final project outcome and enables students to develop a deeper understanding of good programming practices that are essential in the software engineering industry. In this way, the importance of code quality is emphasized to students, providing a comprehensive preparation for future engineers to meet the demands of the IT industry. Further research could focus on examining students' experiences with these tools and the knowledge gained, in order to obtain a holistic view of the significance of these tools in the educational process.

This research suggests that integrating static code analysis into educational programs could be crucial for achieving a higher level of quality in student work. Educators and institutions should consider implementing these tools as a standard part of the curriculum, as they aid in identifying code issues and help students better understand the fundamental concepts of good software development practices. A particular challenge is the cost of various static code analysis tools, which may hinder their widespread adoption in educational settings. Such research could influence the availability of higher-quality tools, potentially making them accessible and free for students within the educational process.

A broader application of such tools in education would warrant investigation into whether their use impacts students' ability to identify issues independently, without automated assistance, in a professional environment. Special attention should be given to ensure that the introduction of innovative tools, such as these, does not have adverse effects on the technical skills and education of engineers.

The presented research has certain limitations. It focused solely on one educational context and a relatively limited sample of student projects. Additionally, further investigation into variables such as teamwork, technologies used, and project size opens up opportunities for future research. Analyzing other factors could further explore the potential role of static code analysis tools during the educational process.

ACKNOWLEDGEMENT

This research has been supported by the Ministry of Science, Technological Development and Innovation (Contract No. 451-03-65/2024-03/200156) and the Faculty of Technical Sciences, University of Novi Sad through project “Scientific and Artistic Research Work of Researchers in Teaching and Associate Positions at the Faculty of Technical Sciences, University of Novi Sad” (No. 01-3394/1).

REFERENCES

Alchimowicz, B., & Nawrocki, J. R. (2016). The COCA quality model for user documentation. Software Quality Journal, 24(2), Article 2.

Breuker, D. M., Derriks, J., & Brunekreef, J. (2011). Measuring static quality of student code. Proceedings of the 16th Annual Joint Conference on Innovation and Technology in Computer Science Education, 13–17.

De Araújo, D. M. N., Eler, D. M., & Garcia, R. E. (2020). Teacher Mate: A Support Tool for Teaching Code Quality. In S. Latifi (Ed.), 17th International Conference on Information Technology–New Generations (ITNG 2020) (Vol. 1134, pp. 407–413). Springer International Publishing.

García-Munoz, J., García-Valls, M., & Escribano-Barreno, J. (2016). Improved Metrics Handling in SonarQube for Software Quality Monitoring. In S. Omatu, A. Semalat, G. Bocewicz, P. Sitek, I. E. Nielsen, J. A. García García, & J. Bajo (Eds.), Distributed Computing and Artificial Intelligence, 13th International Conference (Vol. 474, pp. 463–470). Springer International Publishing.

Haindl, P., & Weinberger, G. (2024). Does ChatGPT Help Novice Programmers Write Better Code? Results From Static Code Analysis. IEEE Access, 12.

Hashiura, H., Matsuura, S., & Komiya, S. (2010). A Tool for Diagnosing the Quality of Java Program and a Method for its Effective Utilization in Education. Proceedings of the 9th WSEAS International Conference on APPLICATIONS of COMPUTER ENGINEERING, 277–282.

Imhmed, E., Ceh-Varela, E., & Kilgore, S. (2023). Identifying Code Quality Issues for Undergraduate Students Using Static Analysis and NLP. 2023 International Conference on Computational Science and Computational Intelligence (CSCI), 1527–1533.

Ishkov, A., & Krupnov, Y. (2024). Application of blockchain technologies for creation of innovative ecosystem in higher education. E3S Web of Conferences, 549.

Karnalim, O., Simon, & Chivers, W. (2022). Work-In-Progress: Code Quality Issues of Computing Undergraduates. 2022 IEEE Global Engineering Education Conference (EDUCON), 1734–1736.

Keuning, H., Heeren, B., & Jeuring, J. (2017). Code Quality Issues in Student Programs. Proceedings of the 2017 ACM Conference on Innovation and Technology in Computer Science Education, 110–115.

Khosrow-Pour, D.B.A., M. (Ed.). (2019). Advanced Methodologies and Technologies in Network Architecture, Mobile Computing, and Data Analytics: IGI Global.

Mierle, K., Laven, K., Roweis, S., & Wilson, G. (2005). Mining Student CVS Repositories for Performance Indicators.

Nikolic, D., Stefanovic, D., Dakic, D., Sladojevic, S., & Ristic, S. (2021). Analysis of the Tools for Static Code Analysis. 2021 20th International Symposium INFOTEH-JAHORINA (INFOTEH), 1–6.

Nikolić, D., Stefanović, D., Nikolić, M., Dakić, D., Stefanović, M., & Koprivica, S. (2024). Uncovering Determinants of Code Quality In Education Via Static Code Analysis. IEEE Access

SonarCloud or SonarQube, What's Right for Your Team? | Sonar. (2024, September 24). https://www.sonarsource.com/blog/sq-sc_guidance/

Wang, A. I., & Stalhane, T. (2005). Using Post Mortem Analysis to Evaluate Software Architecture Student Projects. 18th Conference on Software Engineering Education & Training (CSEET'05), 43–50.

VIRTUAL REALITY TO FACILITATE EXPERIENTIAL LEARNING IN COMPUTER SCIENCE

Thomas Schmidt and Thomas Karintholil
Department of Computer Science and Information Systems, Pace University
861 Bedford Rd, Pace University, Pleasantville, NY, 10570
USA

ABSTRACT

This study explores the utility of Virtual Reality (VR) as an experiential learning tool in educational settings. We developed specialized courseware designed to enhance student engagement and learning outcomes through immersive experiences. The effectiveness of the VR courseware was evaluated in a real classroom setting. This study highlights VR's potential to bridge the gap between traditional and experiential learning, engaging more students, particularly neurodivergent students, within the classroom environment.

KEYWORDS

Experiential Learning, Virtual Reality, Data Structures

1. INTRODUCTION

Traditional modes of instruction in education rely on students acquiring information presented narratively (Roberts, 2017) by an instructor and memorizing these concepts before developing a concrete understanding of them (Kolb, 1985). Virtual Reality can open doors to more effective learning by enabling experiential learning. It may be utilized to help students understand the application of concepts before memorizing abstract details.

Data Structures are a concept in Computer Science that could be more effectively understood through experiential learning. The various data structure concepts can be represented visually to enrich students' grasp on their function and efficiency (Duchowski & Davis, 2007). They can also be visualized through the lens of real-world puzzles.

The Towers of Hanoi is one such puzzle that can use the properties of a Data Structure, namely a stack. It is also a very effective problem, when it comes to demonstrating a recursive solution (Benander & Benander, 2008). However, rather than explain the Towers of Hanoi narratively, we built an application that presents the puzzle in 3d with interactive visual objects that may be manipulated by a user. This offers students the chance to learn these concepts by doing rather than through the narration.

2. LITERATURE REVIEW

Experiential learning is a concept that can be traced back to ancient Greek and Chinese philosophy. According to these philosophies, interactive participation supersedes any learning that is predicated on students receiving information rather than gathering it through experience. As Aristotle noted, "These that we have to learn to do, we should learn them by doing them" (Papadakis & Stavrakis, 2017).

However, "Experiential Learning," as a defined educational philosophy came into prominence in the 1960s. According to the lectures of John Dewey, who coined the term, experiential learning fosters "the continuity of experience," which is the quality of wanting to delve further into a subject because of learning experiences that are engaging (Weinstein, 2021). Dewey maintained that a traditional educational setting offers students little in the way of engagement due to passivation in learning. These educational models stifle creativity and student curiosity that would otherwise compel students to pursue a subject further (Dewey, 1938).

Experiential Learning, as described by educational theorist David Kolb, is integral to developing critical thinking skills. Kolb's experiential learning model underscores the active nature of learning, which involves a four-stage cyclical process: Concrete Experience, Reflective Observation, Abstract Conceptualization, and Active Experimentation. This model emphasizes that learning is not a passive absorption of information but an active engagement with experiences that foster critical skills such as analysis, reasoning, and evaluation. Without critical thinking skills to accompany it, the application of knowledge gained from educational instruction would be severely limited (Yefang et al., 2024).

One of the major criticisms of the Experiential learning approach is that it lacks quantitative metrics that can represent its effectiveness. Experiential learning is a cyclical process that takes time and often begins with concrete experience before transitioning to reflection. Additionally, since much of experiential learning happens outside of a test setting or classroom, it is difficult to quickly gauge its effectiveness (Weinstein, 2021). However, VR courseware could bridge the gap between experiential learning and the traditional classroom due to its versatility and realism. VR courseware can allow students to gain concrete experiences prior to, in tandem with, or soon after traditional classroom instruction. It eliminates many of the practical issues with fusing together traditional and experiential learning courseware.

2.1 Stack Data Structure

Stacks are a linear data structure following the Last-In-First-Out principle to store data. Elements are removed from the same end, the top. There are only to possible operations that can be done to modify a stack, pop and push. Elements can be pushed onto a stack or popped (removed) from one. These two operations can only be used to modify the stack's contents. The push operation adds an element on to the top of the stack, whereas the push operation removes the topmost element from the stack. This ensures that the stack maintains its Last in First Out order (Chapter 2 stacks and Queues (no date) Data Structures & Algorithms - Stacks & Queues).

2.2 Recursion

Recursion is a programming technique that relies on a function calling itself multiple times but not returning a value until a base case condition has been met. It is a difficult concept to grasp for students as well as programmers because it can transform code into a less intuitive form, requiring a deeper understanding of execution flow and memory management. This complexity increases when dealing with non-tail recursion, where additional processing occurs after the recursive call, adding layers of abstraction. Conversely, tail recursion, which simplifies memory management and keeps recursive calls as the final operation, is often easier to understand but may require code transformations that obscure the original logic. These challenges make recursion particularly hard to teach and learn, emphasizing the need for systematic teaching methods that gradually introduce its complexities. Starting with simple examples of recursion help build a firmer foundation for learning this concept (Baron, A. & Feitelson, 2024).

2.3 Virtual Reality

Virtual Reality refers to a display capable of projecting 3D information. The popular concept of VR involves immersive Virtual Reality which allows a user to fully experience all of a 3D environment. This may be achieved using a head mounted display that can project a 3D image. In contrast to VR, Mixed reality devices allow users to remain immersed in a 3D world while staying grounded in the real world. It can overlay 3D graphics over a physical environment, thereby straddling the line between the physical and digital worlds (Hamad & Jia, 2022).

HMD VR displays have already become accessible enough to where they are utilized across multiple industries. The technology is also flexible enough to be tailored to specific use cases. For instance, it has already been aimed at improving procedural knowledge of workers in assembly operation. Due to capabilities to recreate situations that are too costly, dangerous or time consuming to simulate in the real world, VR is used in sectors including Industrial, Medical, Healthcare, Training, Manufacturing, and Education. Within education, domains such as engineering and computer science have already begun to use VR to teach skills that require declarative and procedural knowledge (Radianti et al., 2020).

Studies such as the ones by Riviera et al. aimed at simplifying complex material such as Machine Learning demonstrate that it is feasible to create VR courseware that can make such material more approachable, enticing students to engage with the material (Riviera, 2024). Furthermore, VR has been determined to be useful for visualizing challenging concepts in biology, such as point mutations (Vos et al., 2023).

Another study by (Chen et al., 2024) conducted an experiment to investigate the effectiveness of using virtual reality (VR) to provide a more immersive and experiential learning experience for students. The study focused on third-year university students enrolled in a course on gerontology and other aging-related topics. Participants were divided into two groups: one group received traditional instruction through two-dimensional (2D) courseware, while the other group engaged with the material using immersive VR technology. The VR group used head-mounted displays to interact with virtual environments that simulated real-world challenges faced by older adults, including visual impairments and mobility restrictions, as well as barrier-free living environments equipped with assistive technology (AT). In contrast, the 2D group watched pre-recorded videos with the same content but lacked the interactive and immersive elements of the VR experience. The results revealed that the VR group demonstrated significantly greater improvements in knowledge acquisition and practical skills, suggesting that VR can be a powerful tool for teaching complex concepts related to aging and assistive technologies.

Additionally, findings suggest that people respond positively to visualizations that align across multiple dimensions, such as redlining boundaries, racial demographic data, and visual scaling and coloring based on specific data points. This suggests 3D images can translate data into intuitive visualizations that help users gain a deeper understanding of the narrative presented by it (Cogburn & Oyekoa, 2023).

2.4 Neurodivergent

VR is also a promising learning tool for Neurodivergent students. Individuals with neurodiversity include those with ADD/ADHD, ASD, Dyslexia and other learning differences. Although society by and large tends to think of atypical neurological characteristics as a disadvantage, this does not have to be the case. Some researchers contend that having an atypical method of reasoning could turn out to be an advantage rather than a deficit (Dwyer, 2022). For instance, Dyslexic individuals can pull from the strengths of an atypical brain in fields like engineering because they possess global visual-spatial abilities that neurotypical people, people without atypical neurological development lack. Despite this, only 37 percent of students with an atypical neurological condition like ADHD complete their college degrees compared with 51.2 percent of their neurotypical peers. Education and curriculum likely contribute to this underwhelming number (Cogburn & Oyekoya, 2023). There are generally two perceptions held towards neurodiverse people. These attitudes can inform how they are integrated in society. The medical view of Neurodivergent seeks to treat people who are considered to have neurodivergent traits, on the premise that their abnormalities are something to be cured. The Societal paradigm views any "disability" as being caused purely by their environment. In particular, a lack of a neurodivergent friendly environment (Shuck et al., 2024).

VR has experiential learning capabilities that can address the needs of such individuals while drawing out their potential strengths. This may be due to how VR can engage people through multiple sensory channels making them feel more comfortable (Carvalho et al., 2022). This in turn liberates these students to learn the subject matter. As an example, a recent study, by Hite et al., that examined students' attention and learning within a 3D environment, concluded that a VR environment, along with other sensory feedback, such as haptic controls and visual indicators, kept students engaged. Their results revealed that students had a better understanding on how to rotate 3D objects, view them, visualize concepts, and eventually develop a firmer grasp on the subject material (Hite et al., 2024). Another study by Trzinka et al., determined that VR simulations can be used to improve driving skills for drivers with ADHD. A VR simulation enables the researchers to provide students with an immersive environment that can be augmented with specific features such as visual and audible cues to keep their attention focused when necessary or when it lapses (Trzcinka et al., 2023). This study attests to the experiential learning potential of VR and how this in turn could create a learning environment that can support a wide range of learning styles and intelligences.

To further assess VR's utility as an experiential learning tool, we endeavored to create courseware and study its effectiveness in a real classroom setting.

3. METHODOLOGY

With Department approval at Pace University, VR courseware was developed for experimental testing in the CS 241 Data Structures and Algorithms course. This courseware was developed in Unity to simulate the towers of Hanoi. To better understand how VR courseware could affect learning outcomes in Data Structures and Algorithms, two sections of the same course were compared. Students in both sections were asked to take a pre-assessment online, meant to reveal their understanding of the Stack Data Structure & recursion. Two weeks after the pre-assessment, both classrooms were taught about stacks, using the Towers of Hanoi. The students were instructed about the Recursion using the Towers of Hanoi models as well. However, the experimental group section received VR instruction, and all students in the experimental group were given a chance to use the 3D Towers of Hanoi Simulator, running on the metaQuest3, and manipulate the Towers and discs themselves. The amount of moves they made with each disc was recorded and relayed to them. Every student was given the chance to see other students' attempts on a larger screen. The students also had the opportunity to see the complexity increases resulting from adding an additional ring to the simulation. The control group students were provided with traditional courseware. Among the experimental group, only 9 out of a section of 12 students were present for this experiment. This led to an accidental control group with the students who were not present for the experiment becoming another comparison group for the students who 'partook in it. After the experiment each student was given an anonymous questionnaire and asked to fill it. All the students who took the questionnaire indicated that the simulation was helpful for learning a stack data structure. Among the 9, only one student identified as neurodivergent. In the final week of the course, students from both sections completed a post assessment with questions geared at testing their proficiency with concepts surrounding Stack data structures & recursion.

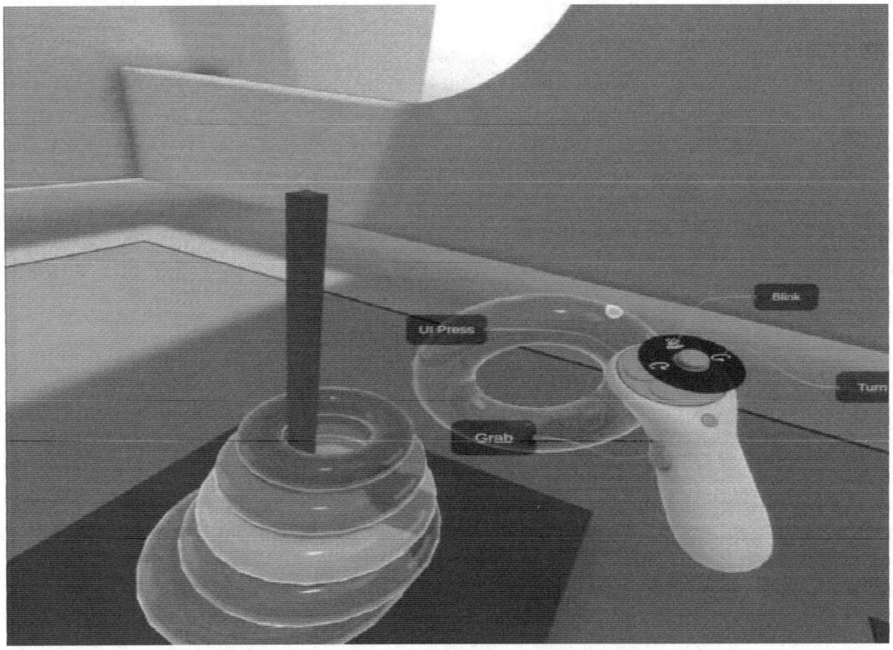

Figure 1. Towers of Hanoi VR Simulation demo

4. RESULTS

Among the students who took the pre-assessment in the control group section, the mean score was 32 percent. Meanwhile, the results from the experimental group revealed a mean score of 32 percent. On the post assessment, the control group achieved a mean score of 98 percent, meanwhile the experimental group yielded a mean score of 100 percent. In the post assessment, questions pertaining to recursion yielded a mean score of 96.85 in the control group as opposed to 100 percent in the experimental. Both the control group and experimental group had mean scores of 100 percent for questions that tested knowledge of stacks. ANOVA T test of means was conducted on both sets, with an alpha $< .05$ indicating significance.

4.1 Anecdotal Experience and Observations

Among the 9 students who took part in the Towers of Hanoi demonstration, only two students reported having prior experience using it. Three of the 9 students expressed that they would like to use the simulation again to learn about stacks or different data structures.

5. DISCUSSION

The results from the CS241 VR courseware experiment underscore the potential benefits of using VR as a supplemental tool in teaching abstract Computer Science concepts and any application that stand to benefit from experiential learning initiatives. However, from anecdotal evidence, we understand that students found the VR simulated courseware to be engaging, many expressing so directly to the experimenters and others detailing this in the post experiment questionnaire. A shortcoming of this semester's experiment was the lack of representation among neurodivergent students as only one of the 9 students was part of the experimental group. Furthermore, the research design was flawed because it did not account for only 9 of the 12 students in the experimental group taking part in the actual experiment. This in turn, left us with a control group within the experimental group. Although this reduces the sample size to a less than adequate size to determine statistical significance, it provides an additional comparison between the control and experimental groups. This could offer future studies a chance to investigate how partial exposure to experiential learning to traditional learning could influence learning outcome. T test of means was used to determine whether there the variance between the two groups' results were statistically significant and not due to random chance. H0 would be there is no difference between the two sections' performance. H1 would be There is a statistically significant difference between section 1 and 2. An ANOVA AB test was considered, however, for ANOVA A B testing, there must be two independent variables being tested for or more than 2 samples. Although the results derived from the sample populations cannot be generalized, the results of this research will offer further insight into how VR may beckon forth experiential learning into the classroom.

6. FURTHER RESEARCH

An area that deserves further inquiry are mixed reality applications (Lee et al., 2023), in experiential learning. Mixed Reality applications offer further opportunity for more intuitive interaction with virtual objects. This cans significantly enhance the learning process. It can promote experiential learning by enabling natural and intuitive interaction with virtual objects, fostering active engagement and improving learning outcomes. Studies show that interactive mixed reality reduces cognitive load and outperforms traditional teaching strategies in areas such as cognitive performance and preparation for high-risk scenarios. For example, mixed reality simulations better equip learners for high-stress situations compared to conventional methods. In cultural heritage education, mixed reality has been used to create engaging museum experiences, increasing interest, enjoyment, and retention compared to standard visits (Almufarreh, 2023). MR may also enhance traditional courseware on offer by making it possible to follow along with an instructor while experiencing 3D visualizations. Very few studies have been conducted and offer experiential learning opportunities for students. Additional research must be conducted to reveal the most effective method to combine experiential learning with traditional instruction to maximize a student's understanding of the subject. Including these methods ensures a robust analysis of the VR intervention's impact on student learning, helping to quantify its benefits over traditional teaching methods and providing evidence for the adoption of such tools in similar educational settings.

REFERENCES

Almufarreh, A. (2023). Exploring the Potential of Mixed Reality in Enhancing Student Learning Experience and Academic Performance: An Empirical Study. *Systems*, [online] 11(6), p.292. doi:https://doi.org/10.3390/systems11060292.

Benander, A.C. and Benander, B.A. (2024). Student Monks – Teaching Recursion in an IS or CS Programming Course Using the Towers of Hanoi. *Journal of Information Systems Education*, [online] 19(4), p.455. Available at: https://jise.org/Volume19/n4/JISEv19n4p455.html [Accessed 9 Dec. 2024].

Baron, A. and Feitelson, D.G. (2024) 'Why is recursion hard to comprehend? an experiment with experienced programmers in python', Proceedings of the 2024 on Innovation and Technology in Computer Science Education V. 1, pp. 115–121. doi:10.1145/3649217.3653636.

Dewey, J. (1938). *Experience and Education*. New York: Macmillan.

Duchowskti, Andrew.T. and Davis, Timothy.A. (2007). Teaching Algorithms and Data Structures through Graphics. In: *Eurographics*. [online] Available at: http://andrewd.ces.clemson.edu/research/vislab/docs/egedu07.pdf [Accessed 6 Oct. 2024].

Chapter 2 stacks and Queues (no date) Data Structures & Algorithms - Stacks & Queues. Available at: https://www.cmpe.boun.edu.tr/~akin/cmpe223/chap2.htm (Accessed: 24 December 2024).

Chen, P.-H., Ho, H.-W., Chen, H.-C., Tam, K.-W., Liu, J.-C. and Lin, L.-F. (2024). Virtual reality experiential learning improved undergraduate students' knowledge and evaluation skills relating to assistive technology for older adults and individuals with disabilities. *BMC Medical Education*, 24(1). doi:https://doi.org/10.1186/s12909-024-05085-y.

Dwyer, P. (2022). The Neurodiversity Approach(es): What Are They and What Do They Mean for Researchers? *Human Development*, [online] 66(2), pp.73–92. doi:https://doi.org/10.1159/000523723.

Filip Trzcinka, Oyewole Oyekoya and Chan, D. (2023). Students with Attention-Deficit/Hyperactivity Disorder and Utilizing Virtual Reality to Improve Driving Skills. ISS Companion '23: Companion Proceedings of the 2023 Conference on Interactive Surfaces and Spaces. ACM, pp.1–4. doi:https://doi.org/10.1145/3626485.3626529.

Hamad, A. and Jia, B. (2022). How Virtual Reality Technology Has Changed Our Lives: An Overview of the Current and Potential Applications and Limitations. *International Journal of Environmental Research and Public Health*, 19(18). doi:https://doi.org/10.3390/ijerph191811278.

Haye, L., Cogburn, C.D. and Oyewole Oyekoya (2023). Exploring Perceptions of Structural Racism in Housing Valuation through 3D Visualizations. ISS Companion '23: Companion Proceedings of the 2023 Conference on Interactive Surfaces and Spaces. ACM, pp.19–23. doi:https://doi.org/10.1145/3626485.3626533.

Hite, R., Childers, G., Jones, G., Corin, E. and Pereyra, M. (2021). Describing the Experiences of Students with ADHD Learning Science Content with Emerging Technologies. *Journal of Science Education for Students with Disabilities*, 24(1), pp.1–34. doi:https://doi.org/10.14448/jsesd.13.0012.

Kolb, D. (1984). *Experiential Learning: Experience as the Source of Learning and Development*. [online] Research Gate. Available at: https://www.researchgate.net/publication/235701029_Experiential_Learning_Experience_As_The_Source_Of_Learning_And_Development.

Lee, H.-D., Huh, Y., Kim, S., Baek, J.-W., Lee, H., Park, S.-M. and Kim, J.-K. (2024). Educational effects of and satisfaction with mixed-reality-based major trauma care simulator: A preliminary evaluation. *Medicine*, [online] 103(1), pp.e36816–e36816. doi:https://doi.org/10.1097/md.0000000000036816.

Papadakis, L. and Stavrakis, M. (2020). Experiential Learning and STEM in Modern Education: Incorporating Educational Escape Rooms in Parallel to Classroom Learning. In: *Learning and Collaboration Technologies. Human and Technology Ecosystems*. Learning and Collaboration Technologies. Human and Technology Ecosystems. Springer, pp.279–295. doi:https://doi.org/10.1007/978-3-030-50506-6_21.

Radianti, J., Majchrzak, T.A., Fromm, J. and Wohlgenannt, I. (2020). A systematic review of immersive virtual reality applications for higher education: Design elements, lessons learned, and research agenda. *Computers & Education*, [online] 147(0360-1315), p.103778. doi:https://doi.org/10.1016/j.compedu.2019.103778.

Rivera, D. (2024). Visualizing Machine Learning in 3D. In: *ACM*. VRST '22: Proceedings of the 28th ACM Symposium on Virtual Reality Software and Technology. pp.1–2. doi:https://doi.org/10.1145/3562939.3565688.

Roberts, P. (2017). Paulo Freire. *Oxford Research Encyclopedia of Education*. [online] doi:https://doi.org/10.1093/acrefore/9780190264093.013.10.

Silva, R., Carvalho, D., Martins, P. and Rocha, T. (2022). Virtual Reality as a solution for Children with Autism Spectrum Disorders: a state of the art systematic review. In: *DSAI '22: Proceedings of the 10th International Conference on Software Development and Technologies for Enhancing Accessibility and Fighting Info-exclusion*. doi:https://doi.org/10.1145/3563137.3563171.

Schuck, Rachel K, et al. "The Neurodiversity Attitudes Questionnaire: Development and Initial Validation." Autism, 28 Apr. 2024, https://doi.org/10.1177/13623613241245756.

Vos, S., Oyekoya, O. and Ogunwobi, O. (2023). Visualization of Point Mutations in Fibronectin Type-III Domain-Containing Protein 3 in Prostate Cancer. In: *ISS Companion '23: Companion Proceedings of the 2023 Conference on Interactive Surfaces and Spaces*. ACM.

Weinstein, N. (2021) 'Experiential Learning', *Salem Press Encyclopedia* [Preprint]. Available at: https://research-ebsco-com.rlib.pace.edu/linkprocessor/plink?id=a2e5703e-d218-3b10-ac22-b46ab3e99c90 (Accessed: 8 December 2024).

Yefang, W., Sereerat, B. - on, Songsiengchai, S. and Thongkumsuk, P. (2024). The Development of an Instructional Model Based on Experiential Learning Theory and Six Thinking Hats to Improve the Critical Thinking Ability of Undergraduate Students. *World Journal of Education*, [online] 14(1), p.66. doi:https://doi.org/10.5430/wje.v14n1p66.

STUDENTS ON LEARNING EMOTIONAL INTELLIGENCE TECHNIQUES VIA ICT AND GAMIFICATION: SOME OF THE FINDINGS OF THE POL-COM PROJECT

Vaiva Zuzeviciute[1], Dileta Jatautaite[2] and Edita Butrime[3]
[1]Mykolas Romeris University, Maironio g. 27, Kaunas, Lithuania
[2]Vilnius University, 3 Universiteto St., LT-01513 Vilnius, Lithuania
[3]Lithuanian University of Health Sciences, A. Mickeviciaus g. 9, LT-44307 Kaunas, Lithuania

ABSTRACT

While the pandemic served as a disrupter for all aspects of life, including educational practices, however, the pandemic also served as an impetus for accelerated learning. Higher education and vocational education teachers have learned to use various information and communications technology (ICT) tools. At least some of the teachers before the pandemic had been reluctant to use due to traditional settings in education or just sincerely had not believed these tools to be useful. This reluctance, maybe sometimes fear, and quite often - a genuine belief in the merit of personal interaction in class - was more prominent for teachers in social sciences or humanities. Nevertheless, due to the pandemic, the practices for teaching and also fostering learning were promptly disrupted and then - changed. On the one hand, the educational landscape in higher education has changed dramatically in recent years. On the other hand, it may be argued that the pendulum has already swung much too far towards ICT domination in the study process for almost all the subjects taught. Even if there is no doubt that these, ICT tools are useful and efficient for acquiring knowledge-orientated and facts-based competencies (which has been evidenced by many studies), it is worthwhile to examine whether the same also applies to the acquisition of other competencies. Namely, for acquiring competencies associated with communication, including emotional intelligence. It is worth noting that law enforcement officers in their professional activities are constantly exposed to stressful, high-pressure situations. However, the field lacks robust attention, and research regarding the place, role, and format of emotional intelligence techniques in their pre-service and in-service training to help them to get equipped to deal with those high-pressure situations. During the implementation of the KA220-VET - Cooperation partnerships in vocational education and training project: A developmental and educational platform and gamified tools for training police officers and similar professionals, with respect to communications, it was identified that the professional field of law enforcement is not yet examined significantly from that perspective (1st phase, 1st quarter of 2024). Then the empirical study (2nd phase, 2nd quarter of 2024; based on experts'/educators' perspectives) showed that there was a great demand for such techniques. The 3rd phase (4th quarter of 2024) is dedicated to examining the perspective of students/future law enforcement officers (the study is outlined in greater detail in the paper further on).

KEYWORDS

Emotional Intelligence, Gamification, E-Learning, Communication Competencies

1. INTRODUCTION

Contemporary education has been dramatically and meaningfully changed by the recent events of the last five years, when during the pandemic teachers have mastered using various information and communications technology, ICT-based tools for teaching and motivating students for learning. While there is no doubt that these tools are useful and quite effective for acquiring knowledge-orientated competencies, it remains to be explored whether the same effectiveness applies to the acquisition of soft competencies (such as skills associated with emotional intelligence and the related aspects). Law enforcement officers constantly deal with extremely stressful, high-pressure situations in their professional lives, because in the majority of cases, law enforcement is called upon when something is wrong, when there is a misfortune in most cases caused by bad actors (though not always, because sometimes the extremely stressful situations are caused by natural causes or are resulted by accidents). Thus emotional intelligence techniques should have a place in pre-service (higher education or vocational education) and also, probably, in in-service training of future law enforcement officers.

However, this field still lacks robust attention and research. While implementing the **KA220-VET - Cooperation partnerships in vocational education and training project: A developmental and educational platform and gamified tools for training police officers and similar professionals, with respect to communications** (The Report on the research of Learning needs of Law-enforcement officers, 2024), it was found that the professional field of law enforcement is not analyzed significantly from this aspect.

This paper **aims** to discuss the concepts of emotional intelligence and to outline the main theoretical considerations on the role and development of emotional intelligence (EI) using gamification, with an emphasis on contextualizing the theoretical concepts within the framework of specific empirical data. The data was collected during the 4th quarter of 2024.

The **RQ**: Can (and how) IT-based gamification be useful for developing educational experiences for learning the aspects related to emotional intelligence from the perspective of students/future law enforcement officers?

Methods of critical analyses of references, theoretical considerations, and empiric study, involving students/future law enforcement officers in Lithuania.

2. LEARNING EMOTIONAL INTELLIGENCE TECHNIQUES VIA ICT AND GAMIFICATION

Gamification via ICT has been the focus of the academic discourse, including the realm of education for almost twenty years now, which was logical considering the ample possibilities that opened up due to developments in the ICT.

Here we would like to note that it is important to remember that while gamification for learning experiences has become accessible and relatively affordable due to the array of offline and online tools in recent decades, this should not overshadow the fact that games have been a part of dedicated educators' toolkits for millennia (here from Teresevicienе, et. al., 2006). During the Modern era especially, the Enlightenment, but also during the Renaissance and even in Ancient Rome and Greece, thinkers, philosophers, and pedagogical theorists called for using activities that were motivating and reflective of a child's needs and maturity. Among those thinkers: Comenius in 17th century, Pestalozzi in 18th century; they emphasized the imperative to develop and offer teaching aids for teaching and especially - learning (textbooks), which are attuned to child' development, which are illustrated and provide children with opportunities for wholesome development (ibid). Due to technological advancements, among which the invention and proliferation of press publishing must not be underestimated, then the developments of digital technologies enhanced the opportunities significantly (ibid). It is just that we, contemporary educators, are privileged. We have at our disposal many more opportunities for gamification in the educational process, that is, using games for various purposes, and of various levels of complexity, duration, and type (single individual or team-focused) in designing and developing educational experiences for learning.

Over the last at least fifteen - seventeen years, more comprehensive research efforts have been designed and implemented to examine the effectiveness of gamification. The theoretical and respective empirical research resulted in the conceptualization of gamification. For example, more than a decade ago Houtari and Hamari (2012) defined gamification as the process when certain processes invoke the same attractiveness as games generally do. These processes may relate to educational, industrial, customer services, or any other realm. Moreover, Hamari et al (2014) noted that gamification is a complex phenomenon, which may be seen as having three main elements: 1) the implemented motivational affordances, 2) the resulting psychological outcomes, and 3) the further behavioral outcomes. That is the motivation is triggered or sustained by immediate positive emotions, which then lead to more sustained outcomes. In more recent years gamification was also implemented in a more structured way for learning skills such as writing (Bharamgoudar, 2018), problem-solving (Cernikovaite, 2023), and even developing creativity (Kalinauskas, 2014).

Numerous recent studies in the field show the general positive effect of using gamification in the educational process, because in many cases it was shown that gamification helps motivation, helps personalization of teaching and especially - learning (see, e.g, Zeybek, Saygı, (2024); may be useful for certain students, especially who maybe a bit shy otherwise, as Smiderle et al (2020) note.

In the context of this paper, where we are interested in how (if?) IT-based gamification can be useful for developing educational experiences for learning the aspects related to emotional intelligence from the perspective of students/future law enforcement officers, the findings of Ares et al (2018), also Jun, Lim (2018) are interesting. While it seems that gamification is quite productive in classes of science, also engineering, however, it remains to be examined whether the same applies in social sciences and humanities, especially, when a specific profession: law enforcement is at focus.

However, researchers noted (at least in the industry) that 'part-time' or rhetoric-only gamification may fail to have any positive effect or may even have the opposite effect (Landers, 2019). Another major concern, which has not been valid previously, when gamification was not ICT-based and became somewhat overemphasized at times probably: is the fact that gamification may be helpful for motivation for students. However, it is not an answer in itself. For example, Hasan et al. (2021) note the need to incorporate wisely the educational tools available for a professional educator; gamification is just one of the tools in the tool kit of a teacher; the variety of teaching methods, attention to learning styles and many other are tools that are as important in the ICT-saturated environment of opportunities today, as they even were.

Regarding emotional intelligence, it must be noted that today emotional intelligence is understood as an ability to perceive, interpret, demonstrate, control, evaluate, and use emotions to communicate with and relate to others effectively and constructively (Goleman, 1998).

It is worth mentioning that, as with almost everything in this world, the ideas regarding the complexity of intelligence, including the role of emotions for reasoning and general guidance for any individual while navigating complex life situations have been discussed for thousands of years (see, e.g., Plato's ideas (here from [3]). However, even in recent the times, there have been attempts to contextualize emotional intelligence, even if the term had not been yet coined back then. The understanding of intelligence has evolved significantly over time, progressing from a simplistic view to a more comprehensive understanding that incorporates emotions as a fundamental aspect. Lewis Terman (here from Nauduziene, 2023) in 1916 argued that intelligence was primarily associated with cognitive skills such as logical reasoning and language proficiency. Not much later - in 1920 - Thorndike offered a broader definition of intelligence; it encompassed not only academic abilities but also emotional and social aptitudes; thus the concept of social intelligence was introduced. Moreover, in 1967 Guilford asserted that intelligence is a complex construct with various facets; yet the acceptance of social intelligence as a crucial component still remained a topic of contention for some time (here from Nauduziene, 2023). Though the concept of emotional intelligence initially emerged in 1964 (here from Davitz, Beldoch (1976)), it gained widespread recognition only following the publication of D. Goleman's bestseller "Emotional Intelligence" in 1995 (here from Goleman, 1998). In his book, Goleman defined emotional intelligence as a set of abilities and traits that are instrumental in enhancing leadership effectiveness, and as encompassing abilities such as self-motivation, perseverance in adversity, impulse control, mood regulation, and empathy. Later, the scholar expanded this definition into twenty-five emotional competencies, including political awareness, service orientation, self-assurance, and achievement drive).

Though the term and its denotations have been in the intellectual-academic market for at least the last thirty years, however, today, there are three primary models of EI. The ability model (Mayer and Salovey, 1997).), mixed models (Bar-On, 1997), and the trait EI model (Petrides et al., 2018). EI as a standard intelligence model denotes a distinct set of mental abilities that (1) are inter-correlated, (2) relate to other extant intelligence, and (3) develop with age and experience (Mayer et al., (2012) also confirmed by Naudužienė (2023) in the Lithuanian context). In contrast, both mixed and trait models define and measure EI as a set of perceived abilities, skills, and personality traits.

Bar-On expanded concept of emotional intelligence (1997, here from 2006) by describing emotional intelligence as a collection of non-cognitive capabilities influencing one's ability to cope with environmental demands, categorizing it into intrapersonal, interpersonal, adaptability, stress management, and general mood competencies. In contrast to the traditional emphasis on academic intelligence, Bar-On's model emphasis was on emotional and social intelligences, as better indicators of life success.

Mayer and Salovey (1997) proposed a hierarchical model of emotional intelligence. Perceiving emotions comprises the first tier; then comes the facilitation of thought; the third tier denotes understanding emotions, and the last one comprises managing emotions. At its core, emotional intelligence involves perceiving and expressing emotions accurately, encompassing the ability to recognize emotions in oneself and others, express emotions effectively, and discern between genuine and misleading emotional expressions. Moving up the hierarchy, emotional intelligence facilitates the integration of emotions into cognitive processes, aiding in intentional focus, judgment formation, and problem-solving approaches. This cognitive-emotional synergy enables individuals to leverage their emotional states to enhance cognitive functioning. Further up, emotional intelligence extends to understanding and analyzing emotions, as well as utilizing emotional knowledge adeptly. This entails the ability to label emotions, interpret the meanings conveyed by emotional expressions, and navigate complex emotional experiences and transitions. At the apex of the emotional intelligence concept authors' visualization placed the reflective regulation of emotions, underscoring self-awareness and self-regulation to promote emotional and intellectual growth. This involves maintaining openness to diverse emotional experiences, skillfully monitoring emotional states, and employing strategies to foster positive emotions while mitigating negative ones. Contemporary researchers, such as Petrides et. al. (2018) state that individuals with strong emotional competencies tend to exhibit positive psychological adjustment, personal well-being, satisfactory interpersonal relationships, and academic achievement, thus making it evident why emotional intelligence is so important in the profession of law enforcement, which adds to our interest in contextualization of the emotional intelligence in police officer's work. Black's assertion that EI is a learned skill reinforces the idea that law enforcement professionals can actively cultivate and enhance their emotional aptitude through deliberate practice and training. By investing in EI development programs, agencies can empower their officers to navigate complex social dynamics, de-escalate volatile situations, and build positive relationships with the communities they serve (Black, 2022).

Therefore, it may be surmised that emotional intelligence serves as a critical tool in law enforcement, especially in managing potentially volatile situations. Without it, negative emotions may take control, leading to unintended escalation. De-escalation begins with regulating one's own emotions, creating some distance in time and perception, which then allows rational thought to prevail over impulses. Recognizing how emotions can quickly cloud judgment and lead to regrettable actions underscores the importance of self-regulation from the outset. Therefore, by improving communication skills, related to emotional intelligence and its aspects, officers can – at least hypothetically - more effectively defuse tense situations and produce rational responses. This ability, we may hypothesize, enhances on-duty interactions, resilience, and interpersonal relationships, contributing to overall effectiveness in law enforcement.

In order to examine whether theoretical considerations are reflected upon and noted by participants of the educational process, a three-phase empiric study was designed and carried out, which is presented further on.

3. FINDINGS FROM AN EMPIRIC STUDY: STUDENTS' PERSPECTIVES

Methodology. A four-phase empirical study was designed, and three phases were already carried out to receive feedback on whether (and how) IT- based gamification may be useful for developing educational experiences related to emotional intelligence. The study was carried out in 2024; it was identified that the professional field of law enforcement had not yet been examined significantly from that perspective (1st phase, 1st quarter of 2024). Then the next phase of the empirical study (2nd phase, 2nd quarter of 2024; based on experts'/educators' perspectives) showed that there was a great demand for such techniques. The findings were shared with the academic community of educators (Zuzeviciute, Jatautaite, Butrime, 2024, Teaching Emotional intelligence techniques via IT and gamification: some of the findings of the POL-COM project; Seville, November. Publication pending). These findings were used to tune the development of curriculum, and teaching aids for educational experiences (on-line Moodle-based course). Then the 3rd phase (4th quarter of 2024) was carried out, with an emphasis on examining the perspective of students/future law enforcement officers; the findings of this (3rd) phase are presented further on.

Participants. In this – 3rd - phase of the study pre-service education students in law enforcement in full-time studies, also some of them acting officers in part-time studies in Lithuania - were invited to review some curriculum materials (examples of gamification; interactive videos; self-assessment quizzes) (approximating 2ECTS). Students were invited to share feedback on whether (and how) the developed elements of the curriculum may be useful for the development of educational experiences for learning the aspects related to emotional intelligence and what suggestions for improvements are necessary.

Students in law enforcement (study programs: law related to criminalistics, to pre-trial investigation; and law and police activities (32), also 4 serving officers in penitentiary law) participated in the study; total No = 36 (of students); total No=8 (of small groups). Full-time students' age varied from 18 to 20 years, part-time – varied from 24 to 29. Thus it is sufficient for the identification of comprehensive and valid insights, though, surely, the limitations of the study stemming from the not numerous number of participants must be taken into account while formulating conclusions with caution.

The process. Students were asked to share their insights, assessment, and critical comments (perspectives) on the curriculum with a general question formulated: What is your perspective on the developed elements of the curriculum for learning the aspects related to emotional intelligence in your future profession (regarding its potential usefulness)? The curriculum was introduced and the reflection sessions were organized in the framework of foreign language teaching and learning (FLTL) for specific purposes (SP). Students had an opportunity to try out the elements of the curriculum (examples of gamification; interactive videos; self-assessment quizzes). Then after the trying-out session, a reflection session was organized. Students were invited to share their perspectives, discuss the advantages and disadvantages of the elements of curriculum, and then provide generalized feedback in the format of written reflection by a group (of 3 to 10 students in each small group). The format of reflection/discussion then followed by written reflection/conclusion was chosen in order to facilitate discussions among students and also to provide some degree of anonymity, because, while the researchers were not directly participating in the discussions, however, they were the teachers of those students thus a certain barrier was a logical precautionary measure to take. The Content analysis of the written reflection/conclusion by each small group was performed; thus the No of specific perspectives is provided in most cases rather than the number of respondents indicating a specific perspective. In some instances, the general perspective/conclusion of a small group is used for discussing specific data, in each case the information regarding the nature of measuring data is provided, for example, it is indicated next to the illustration.

Limitations of the study. On the one hand, the anonymity was secured to some degree, however, the fact that almost all the students were first-year students, thus had been exposed to university experiences just 3 months at the time of the study comprised a major limitation. It was attempted to compensate for the limitation by involving students from three study programmes and from two campuses (in two different cities in Lithuania), thus collecting perspectives from students who had some variety of experiences higher education.

Results. The majority of students indicated that the elements (examples of gamification; interactive videos; self-assessment quizzes) of the curriculum for learning the aspects related to emotional intelligence in their future profession in law enforcement may be useful, Figure 1.

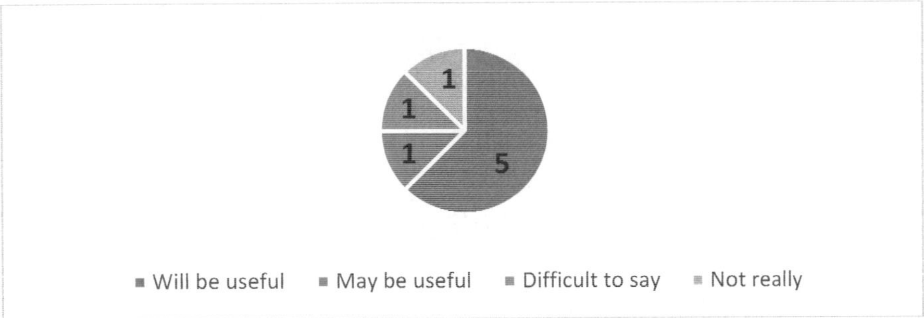

Figure 1. Students on whether the curriculum for learning the aspects related to emotional intelligence in their future profession in law enforcement may be useful (No of small groups)

Out of 8 small groups' the perspective was mainly positive, because students in 5 groups were positive about the usefulness, and in another one were quite positive. However, we also received critical perspectives, because students in 1 small group were hesitant, moreover, there were also students with a negative perspective. The provided explanation regarding negative assessment referred to the perspective that a 'hands-on'/direct practice was more productive for developing such type of competencies.

Students provided examples for usefulness, Figure 2.

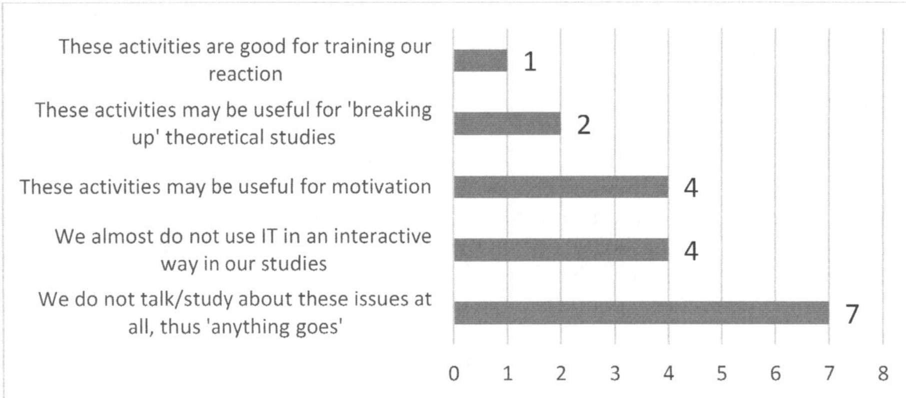

Figure 2. Students on why the elements of the curriculum may be useful (No of categories/ perspectives after Content analysis)

On the one hand, the findings, regarding insufficient attention to emotional intelligence are in line with the findings in other studies in Lithuania (by Zeriukaite, 2024) regarding the specific situation in law enforcement. On the other hand, the findings may to some degree be related to the study limitations, indicated above.

It was found that in general students are quite reflective about their studies, Table 1.

Table 1. Students on why the elements of curriculum may be useful in their studies

Category/perspective (No of contributions, allocated to a specific category)	Examples of contributions within a category/perspective
We do not talk/study about these issues at a thus 'anything goes' (7)	We do not talk/study about these issues at all, thus 'anything goes' (7)
We almost do not use IT in an interactive w in our studies (4)	Teachers give us slides, texts, we use e-tar (*on-line data bases of national legal acts; authors' note*), but legal acts are long texts. Textbooks give tasks we have to answer questions, but not much else
These activities may be useful for motivatio (4)	These quizzes, especially videos with short quizzes are fun; they motivate, but we still learned something
These activities may be useful for 'breaking up' theoretical studies (2)	These activities are good as short breaks in our studies. We study law, we do not expect much fun in studies, but these are very good to have a bit of fun, and also seriously repeat what teachers tell us
These activities are good for training our reaction (1)	Some of the quizzes did not give much time to respond, the Kahoot quiz is colorful, it is fun. But the time for responses is short. That is good, we need quick reaction, so ok. The videos with exercises also are going fast. Good for training the reaction. Also good that there is an option 'repeat'. So we may repeat if really need that.

Students also shared aspects for improving the curriculum for learning the aspects related to emotional intelligence in their future profession in law enforcement. It was noted in one small group reflection that the materials must be aligned with national legal regulations for law enforcement performance. For example: *"<..>in the USA it is allowed to carry a gun, if a person has a permit. But is not allowed, it is against the law here, in Lithuania. The interactive video does not show the situation in Lithuania correctly. It must be clearly indicated that the national law must be followed. The tasks and activities are ok, because they are focused on communication, non-threatening verbal and non-verbal communication. So that is ok; but it is not ok for a citizen to carry a gun in principle. This must be explained, may be in the title?"*

As the curriculum was introduced and the reflection sessions were organized in the framework of foreign language teaching and learning (FLTL) for specific purposes (SP), there were certain findings related to that specific context. For example: *"These activities are good for us because next to learning to communicate in a professional, respectful way, we also learn a foreign language (English - authors' note). But some of the words are new to us, we do not study the informal language...<...> I did not know that 'buddy' means child, this is also good to find out...>".*

The empiric findings showed that the majority of students (N=32) were quite positive about the elements (examples of gamification; interactive videos; self-assessment quizzes) of the curriculum for learning the aspects related to emotional intelligence in their future profession in law enforcement. However, students (N=4) also noted that 'hands-on' practice is best for learning communication. An important comment was made that national legislation regarding the lawful and unlawful behavior of citizens (as noted by students), and by inference (authors' note) – also of law enforcement officers – must be taken into consideration. This important aspect must be surely taken into account while finalizing the curriculum.

4. CONCLUSIONS

Critical analysis of references, led to formulation of conclusion that emotional Intelligence is one of the key components for personal and professional success, as it provides the basis of mental and emotional health, life satisfaction, and general well-being.

While games have been an important part of educators' tools for hundreds if not thousands of years, however, the contemporary focus on gamification is related to advancements in the ICT advancements and thus the ICT-based opportunities. It may be argued that the contemporary focus on gamification is excessive; nevertheless, the role of games in educational settings always remains to foster and motivate learning.

Empiric study (students'/future law enforcement officers' perspectives) revealed that respondents were quite positive about the elements (examples of gamification; interactive videos; self-assessment quizzes) of the curriculum for learning the aspects related to emotional intelligence in their future profession in law enforcement. Respondents noted that ICT- based tools and interactive tasks were not used in their studies too often until the moment of the study (3 months into higher education experiences). Respondents note that interactive activities may foster motivation, and help learn communication competencies, even if a 'hands-on' approach was mentioned as a better alternative for that purpose.

Students also noted the importance of aligning the contents of interactive tasks/activities with the national legal framework. This aspect must certainly be taken into consideration in some format (e.g., in the format of a disclaimer of additional informational packet, while finalizing curriculum).

In conclusion, the study indicates that students' perspective on learning emotional intelligence techniques via ICT and gamification is quite positive, as a means for motivation while studying, however specific issues to be addressed (e.g., attention to the national legal framework) are also indicated. These findings will be incorporated while finalizing the curriculum of the KA220-VET - Cooperation partnerships in vocational education and training project: *A developmental and educational platform and gamified tools for training police officers and similar professionals, with respect to communications*, and then it is planned to carry out the last, fourth phase of this study.

REFERENCES

Ares, A. M., Bernal, J., Nozal, M. J., Sánchez, F. J., & Bernal, J. (2018, July). Results of the use of Kahoot! gamification tool in a course of Chemistry. In *4th international conference on higher education advances (HEAD'18)* (pp. 1215-1222). Editorial Universitat Politècnica de València.

Bar-On, R. (1997). *BarOn emotional quotient inventory (Vol. 40).* Multi-health systems.

Bharamgoudar, R. (2018). Gamification. *Clinical Teacher*, 15(3):268-269. doi:10.1111/tct.12787.

Black, D. (2022). The role of emotional intelligence in public safety. Cordico. Lexipol Team. May 4, 2022. https://www.lexipol.com/resources/blog/role-of-emotional-intelligence-in-public-safety/.

Cernikovaite, M. (2023). Gamification Methods for Adult Learning. In *ICERI2023 16th international conference of education, research and innovation, 13-15 November, 2023, Seville, Spain: conference Proceedings* (pp. 8261-8269). L. Gómez-Chova, G. González-Martínez, J. Lees (Eds.) IATED academy.

Davitz, J.R., Beldoch, M. (1976). The Communication of Emotional Meaning. Greenwood Press.

Goleman, D. (1998). What makes a leader? *Harvard Business Review November-December.*

Hamari, J., Koivisto, J., & Sarsa, H. (2014, January). Does gamification work? -a literature review of empirical studies on gamification. In *2014 47th Hawaii international conference on system sciences* (pp. 3025-3034). Ieee.

Hassan, M. A., Habiba, U., Majeed, F., & Shoaib, M. (2021). Adaptive gamification in e-learning based on students' learning styles. *Interactive Learning Environments*, 29(4), 545-565.

Huotari, K., & Hamari, J. (2012, October). Defining gamification: a service marketing perspective. In *Proceeding of the 16th international academic MindTrek conference* (pp. 17-22).

Jo, J., Jun, H., & Lim, H. (2018). A comparative study on gamification of the flipped classroom in engineering education to enhance the effects of learning. *Computer Applications in Engineering Education*, 26(5), 1626-1640.

Kalinauskas, M. (2014). Gamification in fostering creativity. *Social transformations in contemporary society 2014: international scientific conference for young researchers: June 5-6, 2014: abstract book* / MykolasRomeris University., p. 13-14.

Landers, R. N. (2019). Gamification misunderstood: How badly executed and rhetorical gamification obscures its transformative potential. *Journal of Management inquiry*, 28(2), 137-140.

Mayer, J. D. Salovey, P., (1997) Positive psychology in practice, Emotional Development and Emotional Intelligence: Implications for Educators, In P. Salovey& D. Sluyter (Eds) 3-31. New York: Basic Books.

Mayer, J.D., Caruso, D., Ciarrochi, J., Freedman,J., Gardner,K. J., Hetley, R., Landy,F., Michela, J., Salovey, P. (2012). Emotional Intelligence Information. Site Dedicated to Communicating Scientific Information about Emotional Intelligence, Including Relevant Aspects of Emotions, Cognition, and Personality.

Naudužienė, G. (2023). Emocinio intelekto plėtojimas praktikuojant dėmesingą įsisąmoninimą (Doctoral dissertation).

Petrides, K. V., Sanchez-Ruiz, M. J., Siegling, A. B., Saklofske, D. H., & Mavroveli, S. (2018). Emotional intelligence as personality: Measurement and role of trait emotional intelligence in educational contexts. *Emotional intelligence in education: Integrating research with practice*, 49-81.

Smiderle, R., Rigo, S. J., Marques, L. B., Peçanha de Miranda Coelho, J. A., & Jaques, P. A. (2020). The impact of gamification on students' learning, engagement and behavior based on their personality traits. *Smart Learning Environments*, 7(1), 3.

Tereseviciene, M., Gedviliene, G., Zuzeviciute V., (2006). *Andragogika*, aunas, VMU.

The Report on the research of Learning needs of Law-enforcement officers. (2024). KA220-VET - Cooperation partnerships in vocational education and training project: A developmental and educational platform and gamified tools for training police officers and similar professionals, with respect to communications; https://misehero.cz/pc/ (completed by V. Milasiunaite).

Zeriukaite, G. (2024). *Emocinis intelektas ir policijos pareigūno profesinė veikla*. Mykolo Romerio universitetas.

Zeybek, N., & Saygı, E. (2024). Gamification in education: Why, where, when, and how? —A systematic review. *Games and Culture*, 19(2), 237-264.

PHYGITAL TRANSFORMATION. ENHANCING CUSTOMER EXPERIENCE IN THE DIGITAL SOCIETY

Dalia Gallico
Università San Raffaele Roma, Italy

ABSTRACT

Phygital transformation, the merging of physical and digital dimensions, is revolutionizing customer experience (CX) in e-Business, e-Commerce, and beyond. This paper explores the conceptual framework and practical applications of Phygital strategies, highlighting their role in bridging traditional and digital business models within the e-Society. Drawing on case studies we analyze the advantages of integrating IoT, AR, and AI technologies. The "Discover U" project that I realized exemplifies the transformative potential of Phygital strategies in reshaping the customer experience in fashion. By integrating digital and physical channels, this study explores how neuro-aesthetics, personalized data analytics, and advanced in-store technologies create a seamless, engaging, and customer-centric shopping journey. Leveraging a methodological framework based on customer ontology and real-time data analysis, this research outlines the innovative application of the DY platform in bridging gaps between online and offline channels, enhancing customer satisfaction, and boosting business performance. The findings emphasize the significance of personalized, immersive customer journeys, the challenges of digital transformation, and the implications for future business models.

KEYWORDS

Phygital, Customer Experience, Omnichannel, Neuro-aesthetics, Data Analytics, Retail Innovation

1. INTRODUCTION

The convergence of physical and digital environments, encapsulated in the term "Phygital," is reshaping industries in the era of the e-Society. The rapid evolution of digital transformation necessitates new approaches to engage customers through immersive, seamless experiences. This paper investigates the intersection of technology and customer-centricity, examining how Phygital strategies enhance e-Business, commerce, and societal interactions.

Phygital, derived from "physical" and "digital," encapsulates the integration of real-world and digital interactions. It emphasizes creating seamless customer journeys that transcend traditional boundaries. The key technologies powering the Phygital transition include:

- Internet of Things (IoT): Contributing to smart environments like cities, factories, and retail by enabling connected devices and real-time data sharing.
- Additive Manufacturing: Leveraging 3D printing for personalized and sustainable production processes.
- Augmented Reality (AR): Providing immersive experiences that enhance customer engagement and operational efficiency.
- Simulation: Supporting predictive modeling and scenario analysis for decision-making.
- Horizontal/Vertical Integration: Facilitating seamless information flow across organizational levels and supply chains.
- Machine Learning (ML): Offering predictive analytics to enhance decision-making and operational efficiency.
- Cloud Computing: Enabling scalable, remote access to digital resources, ensuring operational flexibility.
- Cybersecurity: Safeguarding systems and data from digital threats.
- Big Data Analytics: Generating actionable insights to personalize customer experiences and optimize business strategies.

AI plays a crucial role in transforming business operations and customer interactions. Key distinctions include:

- Weak AI: Focused on specific tasks, such as automating processes and enhancing customer interactions through chatbots.
- Strong AI: Aiming to replicate human cognition, offering possibilities for deeper machine learning and decision-making capabilities.

Applications of AI span across domains like supply chain optimization, personalized marketing, and customer service. However, challenges persist, particularly in replicating human empathy and maintaining the human touch in automated processes. Digital transformation integrates emerging technologies into business processes, requiring substantial cultural and strategic shifts. It is characterized by:

- Digitization: Converting physical data into digital formats.
- Digitalization: Optimizing processes using digital technologies.
- Digital Transformation: Overhauling business models and operations to align with the digital era.

To succeed in the digital economy, businesses must innovate their models by incorporating enabling technologies. This involves improving customer experiences, operational efficiency, and overall competitiveness.

2. CUSTOMER EXPERIENCE IN THE PHYGITAL ERA

Customer Experience (CX) has become a critical factor for businesses in the digital society. Evolving consumer behaviors, characterized by heightened expectations and reduced loyalty, emphasize the need for brands to focus on delivering emotionally engaging and personalized experiences. The traditional Funnel Model (Awareness, Consideration, Purchase, and Loyalty) is no longer sufficient to capture the complexities of modern customer journeys. Instead, the Customer Decision Journey proposed by McKinsey presents a circular approach emphasizing continuous engagement through phases like Consideration, Evaluation, Purchase, and Advocacy. The AIDA model (Attention, Interest, Desire, Action), historically a staple of marketing, has given way to frameworks like the Messy Middle. These frameworks better address the dynamic interplay between online and offline touchpoints that influence decision-making. Modern marketing shifts focus from product-centric to experience-centric strategies. Experiential marketing seeks to create sensory, emotional, cognitive, and relational value for consumers, integrating modules like:

- Sense: Engaging sensory perceptions.
- Feel: Establishing emotional connections.
- Think: Stimulating intellectual engagement.
- Act: Encouraging behavioral changes.
- Relate: Fostering social and cultural connections.

The Customer Experience Pyramid, conceptualized by Manning and Bodine, outlines three levels of CX:

1. Functionality: Fulfilling basic needs and ensuring operational efficiency.
2. Ease: Reducing effort for customers through intuitive processes.
3. Emotion: Creating pleasant and memorable interactions.

To measure CX effectiveness, businesses utilize metrics like:

- Customer Satisfaction Score (CSAT): Gauging customer contentment.
- Net Promoter Score (NPS): Assessing loyalty and likelihood of recommendations.
- Customer Effort Score (CES): Evaluating the ease of customer interactions.

Phygital strategies integrate physical and digital dimensions to enhance CX by:

- Offering seamless omnichannel experiences.
- Leveraging data analytics for personalization.
- Strengthening customer relationships through hybrid interactions.

These approaches address the modern consumer's desire for convenience, engagement, and tailored experiences, solidifying the role of CX as a cornerstone of the Phygital era.

3. THE PHYGITAL FRONTIER: A NEW PARADIGM FOR MARKETING

Phygital marketing emerges at the intersection of physical and digital realms, creating unified experiences that engage customers seamlessly across touchpoints. This strategy caters to the growing demand for personalization, immediacy, and immersive interactions. Phygital extends beyond omnichannel integration by emphasizing the fusion of digital efficiency with physical presence. It utilizes tools such as augmented reality (AR), Internet of Things (IoT), and AI to create dynamic, real-time engagements. Several factors contribute to the growing adoption of Phygital strategies:

- Consumer Expectations: The demand for unique, memorable experiences.
- Technological Advancements: The increasing accessibility of IoT, AR, and AI.
- Competitive Advantage: Businesses adopting Phygital models are better positioned to differentiate their brand.

Despite its potential, implementing Phygital strategies presents challenges:

- Infrastructure Investment: Significant costs associated with technology adoption.
- Data Management: Ensuring privacy and security in a hyperconnected ecosystem.
- Employee Training: Equipping staff with the skills to navigate hybrid models.

To implement effective Phygital strategies, businesses must:

- Invest in Technology: Prioritize scalable and interoperable solutions.
- Enhance Customer Engagement: Leverage data insights to personalize experiences.
- Maintain Human Touch: Balance automation with empathy to build trust and loyalty.

Phygital marketing not only transforms customer engagement but also redefines societal interactions by bridging physical and digital divides. It has applications across industries, including education, healthcare, and urban planning, making it a cornerstone of the evolving.

Hybrid business models represent a natural progression in the Phygital landscape. These models:

- Combine e-commerce platforms with physical retail spaces to offer complementary experiences.
- Leverage in-store technologies like smart mirrors and virtual assistants to enhance customer interaction.
- Integrate loyalty programs across channels to unify customer engagement.

Examples of Hybrid Success are Moby Stores (China): Autonomous retail units that bring convenience to remote locations, blending IoT and mobility. Patagonia's Repair Hubs: Physical locations offering product repairs, connected digitally for appointment scheduling and service tracking.

Emerging trends include sustainable Phygital innovations, deeper personalization via AI, and expanding the reach of Phygital strategies to untapped sectors like rural retail and public services.Hybrid business models exemplify the ultimate Phygital convergence, uniting physical and digital strengths to reshape industries. The following elements characterize this revolution:

Core Assets of Hybrid Models

1. In-store Technologies: Smart mirrors, IoT devices, and interactive kiosks enhance physical shopping while seamlessly integrating digital insights.
2. Data Integration: Unified customer profiles across physical and digital platforms ensure tailored experiences and improved service quality.

Building Customer Loyalty through Integration

Hybrid models leverage governance structures to:

- Drive engagement through consistent messaging and integrated rewards systems.
- Enhance loyalty by offering convenience and personalization.

Trends Driving the Hybrid Evolution

- Sustainability: Businesses are integrating environmentally conscious practices into hybrid operations.
- Personalization: AI and big data enable unprecedented levels of customer-specific interaction.
- Scalability: Hybrid solutions extend beyond urban centers, catering to rural and underserved communities.

The hybrid business model underscores a pivotal shift toward a more interconnected, customer-centric economy. Its integration within the Phygital framework offers transformative potential for industries seeking to navigate the complexities of the digital era.

4. PHYGITAL SUCCESS STORIES: INSPIRING APPLICATIONS

The adoption of Phygital strategies has resulted in groundbreaking innovations across industries. These success stories demonstrate the potential of combining physical and digital elements to create impactful customer experiences, setting benchmarks for future applications. Gucci's Virtual 25, a digital-only sneaker line, is a hallmark example of how Phygital strategies redefine luxury. Through augmented reality (AR) and social media platforms, Gucci engaged customers with a product that exists solely in the virtual world. This innovative approach resonates with younger, tech-savvy consumers while aligning with sustainability goals by eliminating physical production. They are not available in physical stores but exclusively online or via the Gucci app, where personalization options are also offered. Launched in collaboration with the app Wanna Kicks, Gucci's first virtual sneakers seamlessly fit into the brand's new strategy of blending fashion with video games to attract and engage new users.

The primary objective is to tap into the gaming phenomenon and engage players by presenting Gucci as their gaming companion. These sneakers, considered beyond reality, evoke an '80s-inspired aesthetic with a contemporary twist. They can only be purchased virtually, allowing users to "try on" their sneakers and interact with their digital avatars within augmented reality and virtual environments.

The Phygital Sustainability Expo exemplifies the integration of digital technologies in the fashion industry to promote sustainable practices. Leveraging IoT, AR, and AI, the event offered interactive experiences that bridged physical exhibits and virtual showcases, enhancing global accessibility and participation. The expo highlighted the power of Phygital strategies in advancing environmental and social goals.

Amazon Go's cashier-less stores showcase the seamless integration of IoT and mobile technologies in retail. Customers enjoy a frictionless shopping experience, bypassing traditional checkouts through IoT-enabled sensors and digital payment systems. This innovation not only enhances convenience but also sets a precedent for future retail models.

DiscoverU integrates in-store technology, web-rooming, and data-driven personalization to transform the customer journey. By combining physical touchpoints with digital insights, the platform creates tailored experiences, fostering deeper customer loyalty and engagement. The success of DiscoverU underscores the potential of Phygital solutions in enhancing business outcomes.

These examples illustrate critical factors that contribute to successful Phygital strategies:

- Customer-Centric Design: Ensuring experiences are intuitive, personalized, and engaging.
- Technological Integration: Employing IoT, AR, and AI to bridge physical and digital interactions.
- Sustainability: Incorporating eco-friendly practices to align with consumer values.
- Scalability: Designing solutions that can be adapted to different industries and market sizes.

The success stories underline the transformative potential of Phygital approaches across sectors. As technology evolves, businesses must continue to innovate by combining the tangible and virtual to create meaningful, scalable, and sustainable experiences.

5. DISCOVER U: A NEW PHYGITAL CUSTOMER EXPERIENCE

The Discover U project realided in Milan originates from the concept of integration in an increasingly Phygital world. The growth of e-commerce has posed significant challenges for physical stores, in some cases leading to closures, prompting strategies for retail channel rationalization. The goal for companies is not to limit sales to a single product but to provide a complete, engaging, and personalized experience tailored to customer needs and desires. The project begins the consumer journey online, utilizing neuro-aesthetics through a gaming test designed to surprise and engage customers. Often, clothing choices are not purely based on personality but are influenced by superficial factors, such as anxiety about appearance. Clothes inevitably characterize us and influence how we present ourselves to others, making selection a challenging process.

The gaming test generates initial sensations, creating an emotional bond that continues through a complex set of brand interactions, culminating in the physical store. Physical shops will not disappear but instead evolve into spaces that offer new, fluid, multimedia-enhanced experiences. The results of the online gaming test generate four suggested outfits aligned with the customer's personality. This platform allows companies to better understand their customers and tailor future purchasing experiences to align with their preferences, bridging the digital and physical shopping worlds to offer a unique and satisfying experience.

Within this framework, the present research provides an innovative contribution to the world of Customer Experience (CX). By creating multiple touchpoints across digital and physical experiences, it aims to optimize conversion rates, seen here as a new lever for sales. As subsequent chapters will show, the project has led to increased sales for the shop by promoting complete outfit purchases, including clothing and accessories. Most importantly, it successfully implemented a new and satisfying CX that generated enthusiasm and contributed to word-of-mouth promotion.

In the store, advanced technologies such as virtual fitting rooms and clienteling tools enhance the shopping experience. Sales associates are equipped with detailed customer profiles, enabling them to provide tailored assistance. The integration of digital and physical tools ensures a seamless transition between online and offline interactions, creating a unified and engaging customer journey.

The implementation of "Discover U" in a pilot store yielded significant results. Conversion rates increased by 75%, with customers more likely to purchase complete outfits rather than individual items. Customer feedback highlighted the convenience and personalization of the shopping experience as key factors driving satisfaction. Additionally, the project enhanced customer retention, with repeat visits increasing by 40% during the pilot phase.

Sales associates reported that the detailed customer profiles provided by the platform allowed them to offer more personalized assistance, strengthening the customer relationship. The integration of virtual fitting rooms reduced decision fatigue and made the shopping process more efficient and enjoyable.

The main objectives of the "Discover U" project are:

To integrate digital tools and physical retail spaces to create a Phygital experience.

To leverage neuro-aesthetic principles to enhance customer engagement and satisfaction.

To boost conversion rates by promoting complete outfit purchases, including clothing and accessories.

To provide businesses with valuable insights into consumer behavior, enabling more effective personalization and inventory management.

To establish physical stores as experiential hubs, complementing the convenience of online shopping.

6. EMERGING BUSINESS TRENDS IN THE PHYGITAL ERA

The rapid integration of physical and digital elements is shaping new business paradigms. Phygital trends are driven by advancements in technology and evolving consumer expectations, pushing industries to innovate continuously.

Hyper-Personalization Businesses are increasingly using AI, big data, and IoT to deliver tailored experiences. This trend focuses on understanding individual customer preferences and offering bespoke products or services.

Sustainable Practices Phygital solutions are incorporating sustainability by reducing waste through digital simulations, virtual products, and streamlined supply chains. This trend aligns with growing consumer demand for eco-conscious choices.

Immersive Technologies Augmented reality (AR), virtual reality (VR), and mixed reality (MR) are reshaping customer interactions. Retailers and service providers use these technologies to create engaging, immersive experiences that blend the physical and digital.

Seamless Integration Phygital models prioritize seamless transitions between online and offline channels. Unified customer profiles and omnichannel strategies ensure consistent branding and experiences.

Phygital trends are influencing various industries, including:

- Retail: Enhanced customer journeys through smart in-store technologies and digital touchpoints.
- Healthcare: Remote monitoring and diagnostics combined with in-person care.
- Education: Hybrid learning environments integrating AR and digital platforms.
- Urban Development: Smart cities leveraging IoT for efficient resource management.

While these trends hold immense potential, challenges include:

- Technological Barriers: High costs and complexity in implementing advanced technologies.
- Data Privacy: Ensuring consumer trust through secure data management.
- Cultural Resistance: Overcoming resistance to change within organizations and among customers.

To capitalize on emerging trends, businesses should:

- Invest in scalable and adaptable technologies.

- Embrace sustainability as a core strategy.
- Focus on customer education to bridge gaps in understanding Phygital solutions.

The future of business in the Phygital era lies in leveraging these trends to create innovative, customer-centric, and sustainable solutions. Businesses that adapt effectively will lead the transformation in the e-Society.

7. EMPIRICAL INSIGHTS INTO PHYGITAL STRATEGIES

The analysis is based on structured interviews with industry leaders, including CEOs, marketing executives, and technology specialists. Participants were selected from diverse sectors such as retail, healthcare, and education to ensure a comprehensive perspective. Key topics included:

- Implementation challenges.
- Benefits observed from Phygital integrations.
- Customer feedback on hybrid experiences.

Phygital strategies significantly improve customer engagement by:

- Personalizing interactions using data analytics.
- Offering seamless transitions between online and offline experiences.

Businesses reported increased efficiency in logistics and supply chain management due to integrated IoT and AI solutions. The introduction of Phygital elements has been linked to higher conversion rates and customer retention, driving revenue growth in competitive markets. PAT Group demonstrated how integrating AI-driven chatbots and in-store kiosks enhanced customer satisfaction and streamlined operations. Banco 31 leveraged Phygital strategies by merging digital campaigns with physical activations, resulting in increased customer acquisition and brand loyalty. Lessons Learned:

- Technology Alignment: Successful implementation requires selecting technologies that align with business objectives.
- Customer-Centric Approach: Understanding customer needs is pivotal to designing effective Phygital experiences.
- Scalable Models: Flexibility in scaling solutions ensures adaptability to diverse markets and industries.

Empirical evidence underscores the need for continuous innovation and strategic planning in the Phygital space. Businesses must focus on integrating emerging technologies, fostering collaboration across departments, and prioritizing customer-centricity to sustain competitive advantages in the evolving e-Society.

8. STRATEGIC IMPLICATIONS AND FUTURE DIRECTIONS FOR PHYGITAL INTEGRATION

Phygital integration is not just a trend but a strategic imperative for businesses aiming to remain competitive in the e-Society. By seamlessly merging physical and digital environments, organizations can meet evolving consumer demands and drive innovation. Phygital strategies foster deeper connections with customers by delivering personalized, engaging experiences that align with their preferences. Organizations leveraging Phygital approaches stand out in saturated markets, creating unique value propositions that attract and retain customers. By integrating IoT, AI, and other digital tools, businesses streamline operations, reduce costs, and improve decision-making processes.

Despite its benefits, Phygital integration poses several challenges:

- Technological Complexity: Implementing advanced technologies requires significant investment and expertise.
- Data Privacy: Managing customer data securely is critical to maintaining trust.
- Cultural Resistance: Organizations must overcome internal resistance to change and adapt to new workflows.

Collaboration between industries can drive innovation, enabling the sharing of best practices and resources to develop scalable Phygital solutions. Incorporating sustainability into Phygital strategies aligns with global priorities and consumer preferences, enhancing brand reputation and long-term viability. Emerging technologies such as 5G, blockchain, and AI will further enhance Phygital experiences, making them more immersive, efficient, and accessible.

To maximize the potential of Phygital strategies, businesses should:

- Invest in continuous learning and development to build technological expertise.
- Foster an innovation-driven culture that embraces change.
- Prioritize customer-centricity by designing solutions that address specific needs and preferences.

Phygital integration represents the future of customer engagement and business operations in the digital age. By adopting strategic, customer-focused approaches, organizations can navigate the complexities of the e-Society and unlock new opportunities for growth and innovation.

The future of the Phygital paradigm lies in its ability to:

- Foster global connectivity and inclusivity.
- Drive cross-industry innovation and collaboration.
- Support sustainable practices aligned with societal and environmental goals.

The Phygital model is more than a business strategy; it is a foundational shift that impacts every aspect of the e-Society. By focusing on customer-centric innovation and leveraging technological advancements, organizations can build a future where physical and digital seamlessly coexist, delivering value and experiences that resonate with the modern consumer.

The integration of Phygital strategies requires a clear roadmap that aligns technological advancements with organizational goals. Key recommendations for businesses include:

Invest in Emerging Technologies Organizations should prioritize the adoption of technologies like IoT, AI, and AR, which are essential for delivering seamless Phygital experiences. These tools enable real-time data collection, personalization, and enhanced customer interaction.

Foster Cross-Departmental Collaboration Successful Phygital integration depends on strong collaboration between marketing, IT, operations, and customer service teams. This ensures cohesive strategies and consistent customer experiences.

Emphasize Customer-Centricity understanding and anticipating customer needs are fundamental. Businesses must leverage data analytics to design personalized and intuitive experiences that resonate with their target audience.

Build Scalable and Flexible Models Phygital solutions should be adaptable to evolving market demands. Scalability allows businesses to expand offerings while maintaining efficiency.

Phygital strategies redefine customer engagement by creating immersive, memorable interactions that bridge physical and digital environments. This transformation enhances brand loyalty and customer satisfaction.

9. CONCLUSION

The "Discover U" project represents a significant step forward in the evolution of retail. By seamlessly integrating digital tools with physical store experiences, the project creates a Phygital Customer Experience that is engaging, personalized, and efficient. The findings from the pilot phase demonstrate the potential for this approach to drive sales, enhance customer satisfaction, and establish physical stores as essential components of the modern retail ecosystem.

Future research and implementation of the "Discover U" platform should explore its scalability across different retail sectors and geographic regions. By continuing to innovate and refine the Phygital experience, businesses can meet the evolving demands of consumers and ensure long-term success in an increasingly competitive market.

This paper has explained the changes brought about by the advent of the Internet and, consequently, the use of devices that have led to new technological and digital applications. This new environment has contributed to the creation of new touchpoints, simplifying the relationships between businesses and customers. The consumer has evolved: they actively interact, are meticulous, and demanding in their choices. It is challenging for companies to predict their moves and anticipate outcomes, especially in the absence of a plan to refine business strategies.

The traditional linear funnel, which for years symbolized the reference model for representing the purchasing process, has now been surpassed by the customer decision journey. This circular model supports businesses in this new context characterized by digital channels and increasingly competitive offerings. The emergence of new consumer-business touchpoints has compelled companies to develop strategies that fully leverage the new relational environment, whether physical or virtual. The integration of different marketing channels facilitates better management of the customer's decision-making experience, making the synergistic management of these channels indispensable.

From a multichannel approach, where each channel independently collects information, employs technologies, and adopts strategies, the shift has been made to an omnichannel approach—seamless and boundaryless. The DY platform, developed demonstrates how the system can be applied to online platforms such as websites, eShops, mobile applications, and integrated into physical stores. This introduces customers to a new, innovative CX (Customer Experience). In addition to increasing sales, it primarily meets consumers' desires and expectations, optimizing not just the sale of a single item but an entire outfit for the company.

From the analysis conducted, omnichannel has emerged as the primary goal most companies strive to achieve. In the context of integrating marketing channels, it is remarkable how the distinction between physical and digital channels is now considered obsolete, even though this is not entirely the case in practice. The DY project aims to break down the barriers that often hinder this integration: first and foremost, the acquisition and collection of consumer data, which is complex and sometimes unattainable—unlike online channels, which rely on effective tools to achieve this goal. On the other hand, the empathetic aspect provided by the physical experience is, of course, preferred by customers.

This process ensures continuity for the customer across interaction channels. For this reason, the two worlds should no longer be considered parallel realities but rather complementary. The study has shown that for the creation of an original customer experience, it is crucial to consider data as the driving force for launching successful projects. Companies must therefore adopt an approach that is not only customer-centric but also data-centric, consistent with the findings of the theoretical analysis.

In conclusion, the integration demonstrated in the project is absolutely essential to achieve genuine digital transformation paths that place the customer and their needs at the center, ensuring full satisfaction and creating a meaningful experience for the customer. The "omnichannel" mindset is, and will continue to be, the primary challenge facing retailers and the entire commercial world in the near future, in response to demands for improved purchasing conditions while always aiming to increase sales profits.

It is essential for companies to continue investing in the development of their "Data Analysis" to collect customer data, analyze their interaction behaviors, and build loyalty by following their preferences.

Omnichannel is an opportunity but also a complex challenge: the change is radical and requires, first and foremost, the adoption of a mindset (or culture) focused on ensuring an experience that meets customer expectations, definitively overcoming the barriers between the physical and digital worlds.

REFERENCES

Alfieri et al., (2018). *Content Strategy.* Egea Milano

Allen K., (2016). *The robots are coming – but we still need human touch in the work-place. T*he Guardian, March 2016

Andreula N, (2020) *Phygital. Il nuovo marketing, tra fisico e digitale.* Hoepli

Angevine et al., (2018). *The secret to making it in the digital sales world: The human touch.* McKinsey&Company. May 2018

Ashton K., (2009). *That "Internet of Things" Thing. In the real world, things matter more than ideas.* RFID Journal, July 2009

Bell, D., Gallino, S., & Moreno, A. (2014), *How to win in an Omnichannel World,* MIT Sloan Management Review

Bentahar A., (2018). *How AI Will Change Marketing asWe Know It.* Forbes, May 2018.

Berger R., (2018). *Artificial Intelligence – A strategy for Europeanstartups.* Ronald Ber-ger GMBH, 2018Bianchi et al., 2016. Omnichannel, no omnishambles. McKinsey Quarterly, December 2016

Berry et al., (2010). *Opportunities for Innovation in the Delivery of Interactive Retail Services.* Journal of Interactive Marketing, May 2010, 24.2, 155-167.

Birke D., (2013). *Social Networks and theirEconomics: Influencing Consumer Choice.* Chinchester, UK: John Wiley &Sons, 2013.

Bloomberg J., (2018). *Digitization, Digitalization, And Digital Transformation: Confuse Them at Your Peril.* Forbes, April 2018.

Bose R, (2002). *Customer relationship management: key components for IT success.* Industrial Management & Data Systems, 2002, 102, 2, 89-97. Boudet

Braga A., (2017). *Digital Transformation.* Milano: Egea

Bryan J., (2018). *What's Your Customer EffortScore? Smarter with Gartner*, July 2018.Chella et al., 2006. A*rtificial Intelligence and Robotics.* Intelligenza Artificiale (3)

Budman M., Khan A., (2017). *Forces of change: Industry 4.0.* A Deloitte series of Indus-try 4.0. Deloitte Insight, 2017

Chen I.J., Popovich K., (2003). *Understanding customer relationship management* (CRM).

ChoudhuryCarboni G., Mangano M., (2018). *Guida alle tecnologie abilitanti. Le guide per l'innovazione digitale* n°2. Camera di Commercio di Ancona, febbraio 2018

De Nobili, F. (2018) *Digital marketing integrato. Strumenti, strategie e tecniche per aumentare le vendite.* Hoepli

Dodson I., (2016). *L'arte del Marketing Digitale.* Milano: Apogeo

Dreyfus H.L., (1992). *What Computers Still Can't Do. A Critique of ArtificialReason.* New York: MIT Press.

Edelman D., Banfi F., (2014). *The funnelis dead. Long live the consumer decisionjour-ney.* McKinsey&Company, February 2014.

Foglio, A. (2001), I*l marketing della moda. Politiche e strategie di fashion marketing,* Franco Angeli,Milano

Fournier et al., (1998). *Preventing the Premature Death Relationship Marketing.* Harvard Business Review, 1998, 76.1, 42-51

Gasparetto W., (2017). *Industria 4.0 per la PMI – Incontro con Fraunhofer. Concetti In-dustria 4.0. Fabbrica intelligente ed industria del futuro.* Confindustria Ud

Gavril M., (2017). *The New Age of Marketing and Digital Transformation.* Forbes, December 2017.

ISA Digital Consulting, febbraio (2018). *Intelligenza Artificiale - Tecnologie e ambiti.*

Kotler P., Keller K.L., (2007). *Il marketing del nuovo millennio.* Milano: Mondadori

Laurita G., Venturini R., (2016). *Strategia Digitale. Comunicare in modo efficace su Internet e sui social media.* Milano: Hoepli

Lemon, K., Verhoef, P. (2016). *Understanding Customer Experience Throughout the Customer Journey.* Journal of Marketing, pp.69-96.

Magone A., Mazali T., (2016). *Industria 4.0. Uomini e Macchine nella Fabbrica Digitale.* Milano: Guerini e Associati.

Mancini P., (2012). *L'evoluzione della comunicazione: vecchi e nuovi media*. Treccani Enciclopedia

Manning H., Bodine K., (2012). *Clienti al centro: Reinventare il business nell'era della Customer Experience.* Milano: Hoepli

Moore S., (2018). *How to Measure Customer Experience. Smarter with Gartner,* June 2018.

Notarnicola G., Carvelli Ma., (2017). *Gestire la transizione nell'era della digital transformation.* Harvard Business Review, settembre 2017.

Pine B.J., Gilmore J.H., (1998). *Welcome to the experience economy.* Harvard Business Review, July-August 1998.

Rezzani A., (2013). *Big Data: Architettura, tecnologie e metodi per l'utilizzo di grandi basi di dati.* Santarcangelo di Romagna (RN): Maggioli Editore

Ricotta F. (2009), *Marketing multicanale,* Pearson Paravia Bruno Mondadori, Padova

Sarzana M. (2016), *App Economy,* Milano: Egea

Schmitt B., (2009). *The concept of brand experience.* Journal of Brand Management, 16.7, 417-419.

Schmitt B., Ferraresi M., (2015). *Marketing esperienziale. Come sviluppare l'esperienza di consumo.* FrancoAngeli

Scholz J., Smith A.N., (2016). *Augmented reality: Designing immersive experiencesthatmaximize consumer engagement.* Business Horizons, 2016, 59, 2, 149-161.

Sniderman et al., (2016). *Industry 4.0 and manufacturing ecosystems. Exploring the world of connectedenterprises.* Deloitte Consulting, 2016.

Stone, M. et al. (2002). *Multichannel customer management: The benefits and challenges.* Journal of Database Marketing, pp. 39-52.

Wigand et al., (2008). *Web 2. 0 and beyond: Implications for electronic commerce.* In-ternational Cost Engineering Council (ICEC), August 2008.

Wilson H.J., Daugherty P.R., (2018). *Collaborative Intelligence: Humans and AI Are JoiningForces.* Harvard Business Review, 2018.

Vietri D., Cappellotto G., aprile (2015). E-*commerce. La guida definitiva. Progettare e realizzare un negozio online di successo*. Milano: Hoepli

Zanotti L., *"Smart retail: il negozio 2.0 diventa sempre più intelligente".*

DIGITAL PLATFORMS AND MENTAL HEALTH: UTILITY AND USABILITY ASSESSMENT OF THE SKYE PLATFORM

Rebeca Mendes[1,2,3], Ana Veloso[1,2], David Sena[2], Diogo Guerra[2], Rodrigo Teixeira[2] and Salvador Luís[2]

[1]*DigiMedia – Digital Media and Interaction Research Centre, University of Aveiro*
[2]*Department of Communication and Art, University of Aveiro*
[3]*Department of Education and Psychology, University of Aveiro*
Campus Universitário de Santiago, 3810-193 Aveiro, Portugal

ABSTRACT

Skye is a digital platform developed to facilitate the professional practice of psychology and support adherence and maintenance of psychotherapeutic intervention in young adults with anxiety problems and disorders. This study aims to evaluate the utility and usability of Skye for psychotherapists, psychologists with training and practice in mental health intervention, and young adults, potential clients of psychotherapeutic interventions in anxiety problems and disorders. It presents exploratory research with mixed methodology, encompassing three phases: (i) preparation, (ii) implementation, and (iii) assessment. Two independent groups of participants were included: (a) therapists who evaluate the professionals' version for desktop, and (b) young adults who evaluate the clients' version for mobile. The study was conducted remotely, using a test version of the Skye platform and an electronic formulary. The analysis retrieved 28 complete responses, six from psychotherapists and 22 from potential clients. The results are predominantly positive regarding the utility and usability of the Skye in both groups. The research supports the adequacy of the work developed and the need for digital resources that aim to support blended psychological intervention for professionals and clients, contributing to the digital transformation in mental health and human-computer interaction.

KEYWORDS

Digital Platforms, Mental Health, Blended Psychological Intervention, Anxiety

1. INTRODUCTION

Skye is a digital platform that seeks to respond to the population's mental health needs by supporting professional blended interventions in anxiety problems and disorders. The platform under development includes features and functionalities that aim to facilitate and personalize the psychotherapeutic intervention process by qualified professionals near their clients.

This paper presents exploratory research with mixed methodology on the utility and usability of the platform Skye in the target populations, and is divided into four parts: (1) Theoretical framework – (1.1) characterizes the mental health context, (1.2) provides information about the psychological intervention supporting the research, and (1.3) presents the Digital Platform concept and functional requirements; (2) Methodology – characterizes the research, population, study design, tools, and participation procedures; (3) Results – introduces the (3.1) Sample characterization, the (3.2) Digital Platform utility results, and the (3.3) Digital Platform usability results; (4) Conclusion – integrates a discussion, the limitations, and suggestions for future studies.

2. THEORETICAL FRAMEWORK

2.1 The Mental Health Context

Mental health consists of physical and psychological well-being and quality of life that allow individuals to feel good about themselves, establish relationships with others, and actively contribute to society (WHO, 2013, 2022a). Mental pathologies – mental disorders, psychosocial deficiencies, mental states associated with significant suffering, functional disability, or risk of self-harm – affect 970 million people worldwide, causing periods of incapacity that can vary between one and six years, and, in severe situations, can reduce average life expectancy by one to two decades (WHO, 2022b). In Portugal, the latest official data on the state of the population's mental health dates to 2019, highlighting the growing trend in the prevalence of mental disorders, warning of the incidence of anxiety, mood, obsession-compulsion, and substance use problems and disorders among younger layers, aged between 10 and 29 (NOFAP, 2021; PNHC, 2019).

Despite the important improvements in access and quality of services observed in the last decade, according to the latest research (Silva *et al.*, 2022) and the Organization for Economic Cooperation and Development (OECD, 2021), around 64% of the Portuguese working-age population has mental health needs that are not currently met, mostly due to financial issues, waiting times for appointments, or travel constraints. Although psychotherapeutic intervention carried out by qualified professionals has proven to help control the impact of mental illness on the Portuguese population and mitigate its negative effects on our society (OPP, 2011), the alarming deficiency in the coverage of specialized mental health intervention professionals continues to contribute to serious insufficiencies in responding to the real needs of the population (NOFAP, 2021; Silva *et al.*, 2022).

Given the situation, it became natural to observe the overload of work on psychotherapists and an inadequate response to the needs of the population, favoring the growing trend of prescribing and using pharmacotherapies for the treatment of mental problems and disorders (NOFAP, 2021; PNHC, 2019).

2.2 The Psychological Intervention Support

Psychological interventions consist of combined strategies and techniques developed by qualified professionals that aim to reduce clinical symptoms of mental problems and disorders and to promote mental health, by transmitting theoretical and practical knowledge and supporting clients in their treatment process (Beck, 2021). In Portugal, the psychological intervention provided demonstrates evidence of reducing healthcare costs both directly, by reducing the demand for services, and indirectly, by increasing productivity, reducing absenteeism, and benefits or social charges associated with the disease, being estimated to allow savings between 20 and 30% of healthcare costs (OPP, 2011). Cognitive-behavioral therapy (CBT) combines cognitive and behavioral strategies and techniques to enhance the effectiveness of the psychotherapeutic intervention (Beck, 2021; Curtiss et al., 2021; Kodal et al., 2018) and has proven to reduce the costs of care and promote a high recovery rate from mental disorders among the Portuguese population (OPP, 2011).

Anxiety is one of the most common disorders among the population (WHO, 2022b, 2022a), and represents a growing incidence among young subjects in Portugal. It is characterized by a persistent and recurrent fear that places the body in a frequent state of alert, causing clinically significant discomfort (APA, 2013). Psychological intervention in anxiety seeks to identify and monitor activating events, negative automatic thoughts, unrealistic beliefs, and maladaptive behaviors, to prevent intrusions, create more coherent cognitive rationales, experience more positive emotions, and facilitate more adaptive behavioral responses (Beck, 2021; Curtiss *et al.*, 2021; Kodal *et al.*, 2018). Among the CBT techniques to intervene in anxiety are the following: psychoeducation – transmission of mental health knowledge that facilitates understanding and overcoming the mental problem or disorder (Baourda *et al.*, 2022); recording and monitoring – recording and monitoring automatic thoughts, emotions, and behaviors resulting from typical clinical patterns of mental disorders; cognitive restructuring – discussion of negative automatic thoughts and unrealistic beliefs that aim to develop critical thinking and generate more positive and adaptive cognitions; relaxation and mindfulness techniques – a set of exercises and techniques that aim to promote relaxation and well-being with a focus on the present; and reinforcement – thoughtful application of incentives that aim to reinforce positive and adaptive thoughts, emotions and behaviors to facilitate the intervention process.

The psychological intervention for anxiety supported by CBT is effective based on empirical evidence but involves adherence and therapeutic maintenance on the part of the client (Beck, 2021). It is the therapist's responsibility to establish a relationship of trust and support that transmits confidence, security, and well-being to the client who suffers from mental problems or disorders (Beck, 2021). However, psychological intervention consists of a process supported mainly by the active participation of the client in their treatment process, with the performance of strategies and techniques defined jointly with the psychotherapist, to achieve the expected results of the therapy (Beck, 2021).

2.3 Digital Platform Concept and Functional Requirements

Considering the national panorama of mental health care, the search for a solution that supported psychological intervention and helped to overcome the problems observed was suggested. Given the growing need for mental health care in the population, the concerns of national health authorities, and the gap in digital resources to assist and support psychotherapeutic interventions, the conception of our digital platform was focused on supporting empirically sustained interventions conveyed through qualified psychotherapists.

Blended care consists of a combination of online and face-to-face psychotherapy, currently being increasingly applied in mental health to achieve optimal benefits retrieved by combining the advantages of these two treatment modalities (Kemmeren *et al.*, 2023; Romijn *et al.*, 2021; Wentzel *et al.*, 2016). To be adequate, blended care should attend to the following (van Gemert-Pijnen *et al.*, 2011; Wentzel *et al.*, 2016): (i) online and presential components should complement each other; (ii) both components contribute to the therapeutic process; (iii) both components can be adjusted and adapted; (iv) both components commit to the treatment protocol established between the therapist and client; and (v) the technological integration should fit the client's needs, capabilities, and agreement.

The idea for Skye focused on the relationship between psychotherapists and their clients, privileging psychotherapeutic intervention carried out by qualified professionals and ensuring the safety and effectiveness of the therapeutic process for the subjects. To achieve this, the digital platform aims to create a single, versatile, simple, and secure resource for professionals to use and personalize for clients, supporting blended interventions. Skye is primarily conceived as a digital platform to assist blended mental health care, with a focus on young adults with anxiety problems and disorders, with a latent potential to cover other psychopathologies, mental disorders, and populations. The digital platform goals are: (1) to facilitate the clinical practice of psychology, (2) to collect data at the moment, (3) to enable the therapist to monitor clients closely, (4) to complement the presential intervention, (5) to promote the clients' engagement with treatment, (6) to increase the clients' responsibility and active participation, (7) to reinforce the relationship between therapist and client, (8) to increase the support given to the client, (9) to mitigate the lack of support between appointments, (10) to increase the clients' knowledge about mental health, and (11) to promote the client's autonomy and self-management.

Skye supports cognitive-behavioral intervention in mental health through the following: (a) the psychotherapist can make new or existing content available for the clients to explore, building a personal database of additional contents supporting psychoeducation; (b) the clients can rate and describe the state of anxiety when they log on or when having an anxious episode, enabling the therapist to monitor and assess the levels of anxiety and potential triggers; (c) the clients can register and share (or not) with the psychotherapist daily episodes and consequent reactions (cognitive, emotional, and behavioral) through the integrated journal; (d) the professional can include existent or create new exercises for relaxation, breathing or other techniques, available for the clients at all the time to help them manage anxiety symptoms; (e) the psychotherapist can add personalized therapeutical goals, established with the client accordance, strengthening the commitment with the therapeutic process; (f) the therapists can also include activities for the clients to perform between appointments, related to the achievement of the therapeutical goals, keeping the clients engaged with the therapeutical process and enabling the psychotherapist monitoring the clients' investment and development; and (g) the professional can reinforce the clients' evolution through the inclusion of a token representing the clients' therapeutic development, working as a positive reinforcement of the clients' efforts during the therapeutic process. Besides the psychotherapeutic features and functionalities, the platform also enables professionals to manage clients and appointments.

The main goal of Skye is to facilitate the intervention of psychotherapists with clients presenting anxiety-related problems and disorders, attending to the principles of blended mental care (van Gemert-Pijnen *et al.*, 2011; Romijn *et al.*, 2021; Wentzel *et al.*, 2016). To ensure the privacy of data and the user's security, the main target of the platform is the psychotherapists, responsible for all the data collection and management, being recommended the previous formal consent of clients to register in the platform. Skye consists of a digital platform supporting two types of versions, one for the psychotherapist in desktop mode, and another for the clients available as an app in mobile mode. The functional requirements are organized through navigation maps for each version of the Skye platform, as presented in Figure 1.

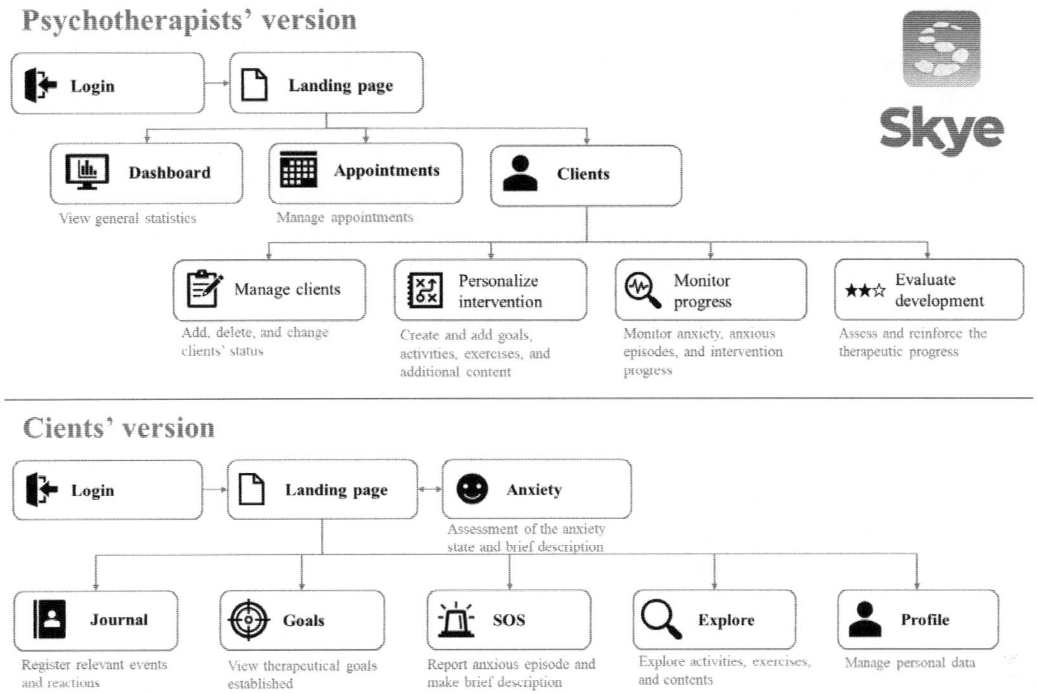

Figure 1. Navigation maps for psychotherapists' (desktop) and clients' (mobile) versions of the Skye platform

3. METHODOLOGY

The present exploratory research is supported by mixed methodology, collecting quantitative and qualitative data to assess the utility and usability of the Skye platform for supporting blended psychological intervention for anxiety within a convenient sample including two groups: (a) psychotherapists, subjects with (at least) a master's degree in psychology and training in mental health intervention, to evaluate the professionals' desktop version, and (b) young adults, from 18 to 29 years old, with (at least) with secondary education, to evaluate the clients' mobile version. Psychotherapists were recruited through an e-mail directed to professionals in Portuguese mental health private clinics, and social media posts on different psychologists' groups. The research encompassed three phases: (i) Preparation – define the research design, create scripts and test versions, and develop the assessment instrument; (ii) Implementation – recruit participants from both groups and implement the research; and (iii) Assessment – process and analyze the data to achieve results.

The study in the implementation phase was conducted at a distance, enabled through a formulary with two different versions, each directed at a group, and both included five parts: (P1) Study presentation and informed consent; (P2) Sociodemographic characterization; (P3) Tasks assignment (psychotherapist/client) – (T1) login/login, (T2) consult patient/report anxiety, (T3) add appointment summary/notice the avatar, (T4) see completed activity/consult ongoing activities, (T5) assign a score to the completed activity/complete one of the ongoing activities, (T6) add a new activity/see the exercises, (T7) add new appointment/open an exercise, and

(T8) see how to add new patient/report anxious episode; (P4) Utility assessment – both groups evaluated the utility of the platform quantitatively through a Likert scale of five points (1 = Very reduced; 2 = Reduced; 3 = Not reduced or elevated; 4 = Elevated; 5 = Very elevated; 6 = Nonapplicable) regarding five different topics based on the platform goals for each version (Psychotherapists – a. clients' management, b. anxiety intervention, c. clients' therapeutic adherence, d. clients' therapy maintenance, and e. overall utility; Clients – a. daily life, b. monitoring mental health, c. therapeutic adherence, d. therapy maintenance, and e. overall utility), and qualitatively through a short open answer retrieving the participants' opinions regarding positive and negative utility aspects; (P5) Usability assessment – psychotherapists and clients evaluated the platform's usability quantitatively through a Likert scale of five points (1 = Strongly agree; 2 = Agree; 3 = Don't agree or disagree; 4 = Disagree; 5 = Strongly disagree) regarding ten different heuristics, established by Nielsen (1994) for the assessment of digital resources (i. visibility of system status, ii. match between the system and the real world, iii. user control and freedom, iv. consistency and standards, v. error prevention, vi. recognition rather than recall, vii. flexibility and efficiency of use, viii. aesthetic and minimalist design, ix. help users recognize, diagnose, and recover from errors, and x. help and documentation), and qualitatively through a short open answer on participants' opinions regarding positive and negative usability aspects.

Participants gave prior informed consent to participate in the study, which included permission to collect, treat, and publish data within the scope of the funded project. Participation took around 30 minutes: 10 minutes to explore the platform, and 20 minutes to respond to the electronic form. Data was collected anonymously and confidentially, respecting the General Data Protection Regulation (GDPR). Participants were warned that participation involved using a digital device for a certain period, not being recommended for subjects with visual problems or limitations, that could cause discomfort to the participant due to exposure to the screen.

4. RESULTS

4.1 Sample Characterization

The research retrieved 29 complete and 70 incomplete responses, from 99 participants with a dropout rate of around 70%. From the sample achieved (N=29), seven (24,14%) participants were psychotherapists and twenty-two (75,86%) were young adults representing potential clients with anxiety problems and disorders. Most participants were from the feminine gender (N=21; 72,41%), with only a few participants from the masculine (N=8; 27,59%). Twenty-two subjects (75,86%) were aged between 18 and 29 years old, two (6,90%) between 30 and 39, three (10,34%) between 40 and 49, and two (6,90%) between 50 and 59 years old. The most prevalent academic level was graduation (N=12; 31,48%), followed by a master's degree (N=10; 34,48%), and secondary level (N=6; 20,69%). Nineteen participants (65,52%) completed all the tasks. Ten participants didn't (34,48%) – eight (27,59%) didn't finish one of the tasks, and two (6,90%) concluded one of the assigned tasks. When attending to the tasks' completion by population type: in the psychotherapists' group (N=7) three participants (42,86%) have completed all the tasks and (42,86%) couldn't perform the last task required, and one (14,29%) couldn't perform any task – subject eliminated from the sample; in the young adults' group (N=22), twelve participants (54,55%) conclude all the tasks, five (22,73%) couldn't perform the fifth task, three (13,64%) couldn't perform the last (eighth) task, one (4,55%) participant completed only three tasks (first, second, and fourth tasks), and another (4,55%) one completed only the fifth task. The final sample comprised 28 participants, 6 psychotherapists, and 22 potential clients.

4.2 Digital Platform Utility Results

Given the different profiles and demo versions each population has tested, the utility assessment of the Skye platform was analyzed by groups – psychotherapists (N=6) and clients (N=22) – each providing quantitative (Figure 2) and qualitative data assessments of Skye's utility, with thirty-eight positive and twenty negative opinions from participants and the respective frequencies presented as following.

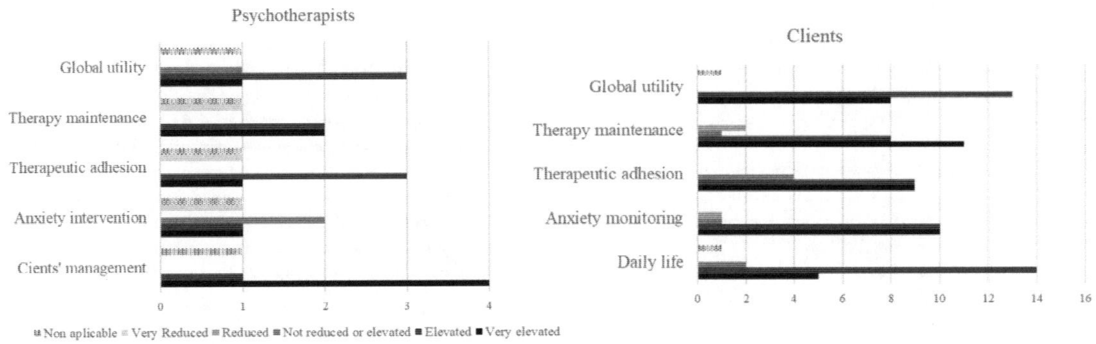

Figure 2. Psychotherapists' (left) and clients' (right) quantitative utility assessment of Skye by topics

Positive utility opinions: mental health support/promotion (7); design/layout (7); monitoring (5); management (4); functioning (3); accessibility (3); communication (2); simplicity (2); practicality (2); therapeutic relationship (1); and personalization (1). **Negative utility opinions**: functioning problems (4); lack of content (3); lack of personalization (2); unclear token (1); potential dependence (1); same as other apps (1); inadequate for seniors (1); demands self-regulation (1); distant intervention (1); lack of motivation (1); confidentiality issues (1); development state of the platform (1); too much information (1); superficial applicability (1). Qualitative assessment of Skye's utility by groups retrieved the following opinions: (a) **psychotherapists** – positive utility aspects (N=6) focus on the potential of the platform and clients' management functions, while negative aspects (N=6) included the state of development of the platform, the reduced content included, confidentiality issues, and applicability concerns; (b) **clients** – positive utility aspects (N=22) focus on design/layout, mental health promotion, and accessibility, while negative utility aspects include mostly the malfunctioning of the version and the lack of different content.

4.3 Digital Platform Usability Results

Usability results are presented through data type – quantitative and qualitative assessment – attending to two analyses – general and by groups. The quantitative assessment provided by the general population (N=28) regarding the platform's usability is presented in Table 1.

Table 1. General usability assessment (frequency and percentage) by heuristics

Heuristics	**General usability Assessment**									
	Strongly agree		Agree		Don't agree or disagree		Disagree		Strongly disagree	
	N	%	N	%	N	%	N	%	N	%
1. Visibility of system status	9	32,1	14	50,0	3	10,7	1	3,6	1	3,6
2. System vs. real world	10	35,7	12	42,9	5	17,9	1	3,6	0	0,0
3. User control and freedom	12	42,9	12	42,9	4	14,3	0	0,0	0	0,0
4. Consistency and standards	15	53,6	9	32,1	4	14,3	0	0,0	0	0,0
5. Error prevention	7	25,0	15	53,6	5	17,9	1	3,6	0	0,0
6. Recognition vs. recall	12	42,9	13	46,4	2	7,1	0	0,0	1	3,6
7. Flexibility and efficiency	13	46,4	12	42,9	2	7,1	0	0,0	1	3,6
8. Aesthetic and design	16	57,1	8	28,5	4	14,3	0	0,0	0	0,0
9. Help users with errors	9	32,1	10	35,7	9	32,1	0	0,0	0	0,0
10. Support and documentation	12	42,9	12	42,9	4	14,3	0	0,0	0	0,0

Skye's quantitative usability assessment by groups is presented in Figure 3.

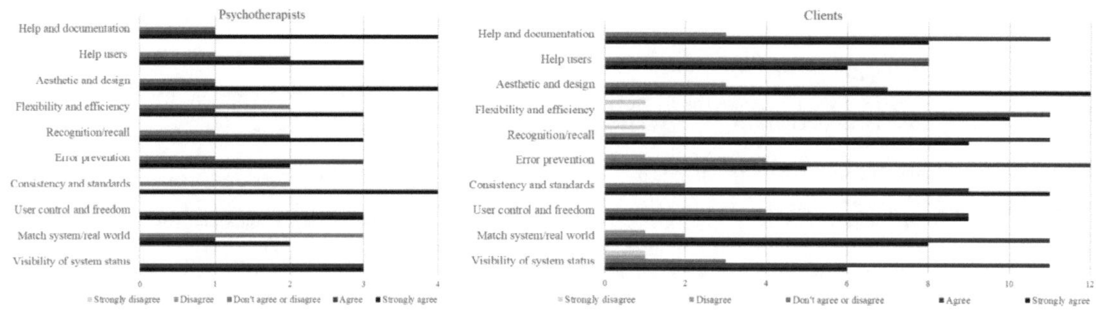

Figure 3. Psychotherapists' (left) and clients' (right) usability quantitative assessment by heuristic

The qualitative usability assessment of Skye retrieved the participants' opinions (N=28) regarding the positive and negative aspects. Fifty-nine positive and twenty-six negative opinions were retrieved. The usability opinions with the respective frequencies are the following: **positive usability opinions** – good design/layout (12), useful (11), easy to use (11), functions (8), good communication (7), good accessibility (3), good performance (3), intuitive (3), and interactive (1); **negative usability opinions** – functioning problems (10), lack of intuition (3), lack of user support (4), lack of content diversity (2), inadequate communication (1), bad accessibility (1), too simple (1), and the adequacy of the token (1). Attending the qualitative assessment of usability between the different populational groups: (a) **psychotherapists** provided positive input (N=6) mostly regarding quick and easy access, the potential of the platform, the facility to keep data together, the good design, and clear communication, and the most negative input (N=6) regarding functional problems, lack of intuitiveness and personalization, and confidentiality issues; and (b) **clients** provided the most positive input (N=22) relating to the utility and practicality, and the simplicity and appeal of the design, and the most negative input (N=20) regarding functioning problems, lack of user support and feedback, and some issues about design.

5. CONCLUSION

This paper presents the assessment of the utility and usability of Skye, a digital platform to support blended mental health interventions for anxiety problems and disorders. Skye's utility and usability were both positively evaluated. Regarding Skye's utility, psychotherapists quantified highly the management functionalities and the support for therapeutic maintenance, probably due to the functionalities included, suggesting the platform can be a utilitarian resource. However, Skye's platform can be improved to promote therapeutic adhesion. Within clients, the most and least appealing utility aspects were the same, including therapeutic maintenance and anxiety intervention. Despite this ambivalence, a strongly positive accordance shows that most clients seem to have benefited from or believed in the potential of the features and functionalities provided. The usability assessment shows that consistency, standards, aesthetics, and minimalist design were the more appealing heuristics of the platform, while recognition rather than recall, flexibility and use efficiency were the lesser. The aesthetics minimalist design, and consistency with treatment were the most appealing usability heuristics of the platform among both groups, but psychotherapists also valued help and documentation. None of the ten usability heuristics presented had a negative quantitative rate, allowing us to conclude that the Skye platform presents good usability for both populations. Conclusions regarding the qualitative assessment of Skye's usability include the correction of functional problems, maintenance of the minimalist design with sharpened details to increase intuitiveness, inclusion of support for users, and addition of more content. The Skye platform seems to have accomplished its goal of supporting blended interventions in mental health based on cognitive-behavior therapy among professionals and potential clients, and the research seems to have contributed to a better understanding of human-computer interaction within blended mental health care. The major research limitation was the dropout rate of around 70%, which might be due to the study being conducted at a distance, or the functional problems reported. Another limitation was the volume and distribution of participants by groups. We recognize the sample is small and has a reduced representation of psychotherapists. The demo version of the Skye platform presented functional problems during the data collection, probably explaining the high dropout rate. Despite these, the results were positive and acted as drivers for improving the platform and developing new technologies and features that might help to support blended or distance interventions in mental health. Future studies with Skye should include the improvement of the platform, the enlargement of the sample, the focus on the psychotherapist population, or different populations, new features, and additional functionalities for other categories of mental problems and disorders.

ACKNOWLEDGEMENT

The present paper was supported by a research grant established between the DigiMedia – Digital Media and Interaction Centre, Department of Communication and Art, University of Aveiro, and the Foundation for Science and Technology, with the reference UI/BD/154591/2022.

REFERENCES

APA. (2013), "Diagnostic and statistical manual of mental disorders: DSM-5™, 5th ed.", *American Psychiatric Association, DSM-5 Task Force*.

Baourda, V.C., Brouzos, A., Mavridis, D., Vassilopoulos, S.P., Vatkali, E. and Boumpouli, C. (2022), "Group Psychoeducation for Anxiety Symptoms in Youth: Systematic Review and Meta-analysis", *The Journal for Specialists in Group Work*, Vol. 47 No. 1, pp. 22–42, doi: 10.1080/01933922.2021.1950881.

Beck, J. (2021), *Cognitive Behavior Theory: Basics and Beyond*.

Curtiss, J.E., Levine, D.S., Ander, I. and Baker, A.W. (2021), "Cognitive-Behavioral Treatments for Anxiety and Stress-Related Disorders", *FOCUS*, Vol. 19 No. 2, pp. 184–189, doi: 10.1176/appi.focus.20200045.

Van Gemert-Pijnen, J.E., Nijland, N., van Limburg, M., Ossebaard, H.C., Kelders, S.M., Eysenbach, G. and Seydel, E.R. (2011), "A Holistic Framework to Improve the Uptake and Impact of eHealth Technologies", *Journal of Medical Internet Research*, Vol. 13 No. 4, p. e111, doi: 10.2196/jmir.1672.

Kemmeren, L.L., van Schaik, A., Draisma, S., Kleiboer, A., Riper, H. and Smit, J.H. (2023), "Effectiveness of Blended Cognitive Behavioral Therapy Versus Treatment as Usual for Depression in Routine Specialized Mental Healthcare: E-COMPARED Trial in the Netherlands", *Cognitive Therapy and Research*, Vol. 47 No. 3, pp. 386–398, doi: 10.1007/s10608-023-10363-y.

Kodal, A., Fjermestad, K., Bjelland, I., Gjestad, R., Öst, L.-G., Bjaastad, J.F., Haugland, B.S.M., *et al.* (2018), "Long-term effectiveness of cognitive behavioral therapy for youth with anxiety disorders", *Journal of Anxiety Disorders*, Vol. 53, pp. 58–67, doi: 10.1016/j.janxdis.2017.11.003.

Nielsen, J. (1994), "10 Usability Heuristics for User Interface Design", available at: https://www.nngroup.com/articles/ten-usability-heuristics/ (accessed 15 July 2024).

NOFAP. (2021), *Mental Health in Portugal: A Brief Epidemiological Portrait.* National Observatory for the Fight Against Poverty.

OECD. (2021), *A New Benchmark for Mental Health Systems*, Organization for Economic Co-operation and Development, doi: 10.1787/4ed890f6-en.

OPP. (2011), *Scientific Evidence on the Cost-Effectiveness of Psychological Interventions in Healthcare*. Order of Portuguese Psychologists.

PNHC. (2019), *No More Time to Waste - Mental Health in Portugal: A Challenge for the Next Decade*. Portuguese National Health Council.

Romijn, G., Batelaan, N., Koning, J., van Balkom, A., de Leeuw, A., Benning, F., Hakkaart van Roijen, L., *et al.* (2021), "Acceptability, effectiveness and cost-effectiveness of blended cognitive-behavioural therapy (bCBT) versus face-to-face CBT (ftfCBT) for anxiety disorders in specialised mental health care: A 15-week randomised controlled trial with 1-year follow-up", *PLOS ONE*, Vol. 16 No. 11, p. e0259493, doi: 10.1371/journal.pone.0259493.

Silva, M., Antunes, A., Azeredo-Lopes, S., Cardoso, G., Xavier, M., Saraceno, B. and Caldas-de-Almeida, J.M. (2022), "Barriers to mental health services utilisation in Portugal – results from the National Mental Health Survey", *Journal of Mental Health*, Vol. 31 No. 4, pp. 453–461, doi: 10.1080/09638237.2020.1739249.

Wentzel, J., van der Vaart, R., Bohlmeijer, E.T. and van Gemert-Pijnen, J.E.W.C. (2016), "Mixing Online and Face-to-Face Therapy: How to Benefit From Blended Care in Mental Health Care", *JMIR Mental Health*, Vol. 3 No. 1, p. e9, doi: 10.2196/mental.4534.

WHO. (2013), "Comprehensive Mental Health Action Plan 2013-2030", *World Health Organization*, p. 40.

WHO. (2022a), *World Mental Health Report: Transforming Mental for All.*

WHO. (2022b), "10 Facts on mental health", *World Health Organization*, July, available at: https://www.who.int/news-room/facts-in-pictures/detail/mental-health (accessed 8 July 2024).

PUBLIC ATTITUDES TOWARD PARTICIPATING IN DISCUSSIONS ON ARTIFICIAL INTELLIGENCE: BEFORE AND AFTER ChatGPT

Yukiko Maruyama
Tokai University
Hiratsuka Kanagawa, Japan

ABSTRACT

Generative artificial intelligence (AI) is rapidly advancing and being adopted by users from many social sectors, engendering diverse social reactions. In this context, public participation is crucial for AI governance. This article focuses on changes in public attitudes toward participation in discussions regarding how to use AI in society before and after ChatGPT was launched. The results suggest that AI has permeated the daily lives of all except those in their 40s and the younger generation has embraced working with the technology. However, little progress has been noted among the 40-somethings. Those who are using AI in their work and daily lives have increased their self-perception of their influence on AI development. On the other hand, it suggested that those who had never used AI as of 2023 indicated that they were not interested in AI and did not understand its value. The results provide considerable insight into promoting collaboration among stakeholders. However, this survey was conducted only in Japan. It is expected that similar surveys will be conducted in other countries in the future.

KEYWORDS

Artificial Intelligence, Public Attitude, Public Involvement, Discussions on Artificial Intelligence

1. INTRODUCTION

Generative AI, represented by ChatGPT launched by OpenAI in November 2022, has rapidly pervaded business activities and daily life. ChatGPT had gained 100 million active users two months after its launch, and the popularity of generative AI foreshadowed its rapid growth and spread to users in most sectors, engendering diverse social responses. As the OECD report (OECD, 2019) mentions, while AI "contributes to better lives and helps people make better predictions and more informed decisions," it "is also fueling anxieties and ethical concerns." Concerns remain about the development and societal implementation of AI, its regulations, and ethical issues with these questions being widely debated. For example, the use of generative AI may conflict with the rights of creators such as painters, illustrators, and actors. Also, the use of ChatGPT in education is controversial. Against this background, public participation in AI governance is essential. In this context, public participation is crucial for AI governance.

Several studies on the public perceptions of AI were conducted before generative AI was developed. Cave et al. (2019) conducted a national survey of the UK population on awareness and perceptions of AI that revealed a negative perception of AI among respondents and feelings that they lacked control over its development. The study authors state that negotiating the deployment of AI requires overcoming these anxieties. Selwyn and Cordoba (2021) surveyed the Australian public regarding their awareness of AI development and how much AI support changed after additional exposure to information. The results revealed that most respondents considered themselves to have limited knowledge of and familiarity with AI and were open to changing their opinions based on additional knowledge. This result suggests that public education on AI is critical. Kelly et al. (2021) surveyed 10,005 respondents from eight countries and six continents regarding their perceptions of AI. They investigated sentiments toward and knowledge of AI, thoughts on its future and impact on society, and opinions on its responsible development and use. Notably, sentiments toward AI differed between countries. Although respondents perceived AI to be transformative, and their expectations of AI-related change were not always positive in all countries, clear differences were observed between countries in terms of future effects. These studies suggest that negative public attitudes and insufficient AI knowledge indirectly affect the development and regulation of AI. This phenomenon suggests that public education on AI is essential. In these studies, the public was not considered an active participant in the discussion, but as externally influencing the debate.

Zhang and Dafoe (2020) investigated American perceptions of 13 types of AI governance and trust in various actors in developing and managing AI development and use. The survey revealed that the respondents considered all AI governance challenges to have high importance and did not unconditionally trust the actors. Zhang and Dafoe mentioned, "As in these other policy domains, we expect the public to become more influential over time in impacting AI policy," and although the public is not a policy maker, they are expected to play a critical role in shaping policies. They considered the public to have a direct influence on the discussions. Ema et al. (2016) stated that AI requires responsible research and innovation (RRI) (Owen et al., 2012) with the collaboration of various stakeholders, including the public, from the early stages. Therefore, they surveyed the attitudes toward AI with various stakeholders, including the public, and aimed to suggest perspectives on future collaboration among stakeholders. Thus, public involvement is critical in discussions on AI development, use, and regulation, particularly as AI becomes increasingly accessible to the public.

However, few studies have focused on public attitudes toward participation in such discussions. Maruyama (2013) investigated the public's support for and intension to participation in the discussions, and factors influence on these their attitude. The results revealed that respondents tended to support public participation but were less willing to participate themselves. This trend was particularly evident among people of 60 and older. Maruyama's research was conducted before ChatGPT was launched and the use of generative AI became widespread in society.

This article focuses on changes in public attitudes toward participation in discussions regarding how to use AI in society before and after the launch of ChatGPT. This study aimed to reveal the differences before and after ChatGPT regarding the following three aspects: The public's involvement with AI, their attitude toward participation in discussions, and factors influencing attitudes. The results provide considerable insight into promoting collaboration among stakeholders.

2. METHOD

Online surveys were conducted in December 2021 and 2023. The respondents were members of an online market research panel with approximately 13 million members. A request to participate in the survey was sent to members of the online market research company until 2000 responses were collected in 2021 and 1000 in 2023. In the end 1976 and 1000 valid responses were collected in each year.

The questionnaire consisted of sets of a series of multiple-choice and open-ended questions. This study addressed multiple-choice questions related to the public awareness of and involvement with AI and attitudes toward public participation in discussions on how to use AI in society. Regarding awareness, the respondents were asked, "Have you ever heard about artificial intelligence (AI)?"

Concerning attitudes toward participation, three items were investigated: support, intention, and self-awareness of influence. Respondents were asked to what extent they agreed with the following statements: "Public should be involved in determining how to use artificial intelligence (AI) in society(support)," "I wish to be involved in determining how artificial intelligence (AI) will be used in society(intention)" and "I think I am able to influence how artificial intelligence (AI) develops in the future (self-awareness influence)."

Six questions (see Table 1) based on Omae et al. (2020) were designed to investigate the factors influencing attitudes toward participation. They evaluated AI educational practices to promote AI-related career development among elementary school students. They defined AI-related career development as "To acquire a desire to contribute toward society through AI." They assumed that educational practices do not promote career development directly but are mediated by improved motivation. Therefore, as stated in Eccles' expectancy-value theory (EVT) (Eccles and Wigfield 2002), they adopted three motivational factors that influence AI-related career development: intrinsic value, attainment/utility value, and the expectation of success. EVT has been extensively used to examine the motivational and achievement-related behaviors of elementary school students, as well as investigate parents' motivation related to involvement in their child's education. Omae et al. mentioned that career development is not equivalent to achievement motivation, but they adopted these three factors because another study (Omae, 2016) revealed the usefulness of EVT in explaining career choices. Their results confirmed that these three factors positively influence AI-related career development.

While the attitudes toward participating in discussions in the study are not the same as achievement motivation, they are akin to contributions to society. This similarity aligns with how Omae et al. define career development. Therefore, these three factors were considered in this study.

Table 1. Questions pertaining to factors associated with attitude toward participation

Intrinsic value
I am interested in artificial intelligence.
I like artificial intelligence.
Attainment/utility value
I think artificial intelligence can be useful to society.
I think artificial intelligence is important to my life.
Expectation of success
I am confident that I can influence the future development of artificial intelligence.
I am confident that I can learn about artificial intelligence.

Furthermore, questions were posed regarding the sources of information on AI and self-assessment of AI-related knowledge; however, this article does not address these responses.

3. RESULTS AND DISCUSSION

3.1 Awareness of and Use of AI

Of the 2021 and 2023 respondents respectively 84.8% and 83.1% indicated that they had heard of AI, with an insignificant difference by year.

Table 2. Responses to questions and statements pertaining to "involvement in AI"

Involvement	Percentage											
Age	All		20-29		30-39		40-49		50-59		60+	
Year	2021	2023	2021	2023	2021	2023	2021	2023	2021	2023	2021	2023
I am/was involved in the development or research of AI technology	2.7	3.7	5.0	8.1	3.8	6.3	2.4	3.0	1.5	2.2	1.1	1.1
I am/was involved in the development and planning of AI-based products and services	3.4	4.6	5.6	6.7	4.1	10.8	4.3	2.4	1.5	1.6	1.9	2.1
I use/have used artificial intelligence in my work or daily activities	4.3	8.1	7.5	14.1	4.4	12.7	4.9	5.5	2.4	7.0	2.5	3.2
I use/have used artificial intelligence in my daily life	9.5	13.7	18.2	18.5	8.2	23.4	10.9	6.7	6.5	14.0	4.4	8.0
I have learned about AI	6.0	7.0	10.7	17.0	7.9	12.7	5.2	3.0	2.6	3.8	4.1	1.6
Other	2.0	1.4	1.6	1.5	1.3	1.3	3.0	2.4	2.6	1.6	1.7	0.5
I have never been involved with AI	80.0	73.6	65.8	57.0	77.3	62.7	80.2	81.7	85.0	75.8	89.8	85.6

Table 2 shows the overall and age-specific percentages of responses to the questions about the respondents' involvement. Responses were multiple-choice questions. Overall, the number of respondents who answered, "I have never been involved with AI" decreased, and those who answered that they were involved in some way increased. The number of respondents in their 20's who answered, "I am/was involved in development or research of AI technology," "I use/have used artificial intelligence in my work or activities" and "I have learned about AI" showed a particular increase. For respondents in their 30's, in all items except "Other" the number of respondents increased but especially for "I use/have used artificial intelligence in my daily life". For respondents in their 50s and the older groups, the number who answered,

"I use/have used artificial intelligence in my daily life" increased. This suggests that AI has permeated daily life for all except the 40's group and the younger generation embraced working with the technology. However, little progress has been made by those in their 40's.

The question regarding involvement was used to narrow the target population in subsequent analyses of public attitudes. In the context of research on AI use, regulation, ethics, etc. the word public is used to address various population groups. In this study, respondents involved in the development or research of AI technology, in the development and planning of AI-based products and services, and who had learned about AI were considered experts. Consequently, respondents, excluding experts and those who answered "Other" were considered "the public" and were subjected to the following analysis. Furthermore, the following analyses were conducted by dividing the target population into two groups: users who responded that they use/have used AI in work and daily life and non-users with no AI contact. Tables 3-6 show the demographic data of the participants used in subsequent analyses. A total of 134 responses in 2021 and 102 in 2023 will be in the user group, and 1334 in 2021 and 612 in 2024 will be in the non-user group.

Table 3. Sex of respondents in the user group

Sex	Frequency	
	2021	2023
Male	73	63
Female	61	39

Table 4. Age of respondents in the user group

Age	Frequency	
	2021	2023
20-29	50	23
30-39	26	21
40-49	23	12
50-59	24	29
60+	11	17

Table 5. Sex of respondents in the non-user group

Sex	Frequency	
	2021	2023
Male	634	286
Female	700	326

Table 6. Age of respondents in the non-user group

Age	Frequency	
	2021	2023
20-29	210	77
30-39	245	99
40-49	264	134
50-59	289	141
60+	326	161

3.2 Attitude Toward Public Participation in Discussion

3.2.1 Support, Intention, And Self-Awareness of Influence

Figures 1 and 2 show the responses to questions about support, intention, and self-awareness of influence on public participation in discussion.

Regarding users group, in each year a very high percentage of respondents answered, "Strongly agree" or "agree" with "Public should participate in determining how to use AI in society". There was almost no change in the responses regarding intention. Concerning self-awareness of influence, the number of respondents who answered "Strongly agree" or "agree" with the question increased in 2023. There was a statistically significant difference in the Mann-Whitney U test between years for self-awareness of influence ($p = 0.047$).

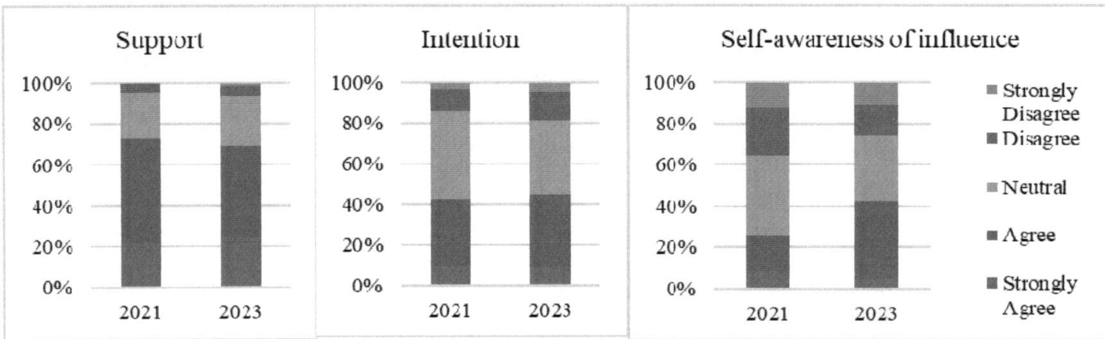

Figure 1. Responses by users group

In the non-users group, there were almost no changes in responses regarding support and self-awareness of influence. Regarding intention, respondents choosing "Strongly agree" and "Agree" decreased in 2023. There was a statistically significant difference in the Mann-Whitney U test between years ($p < 0.010$).

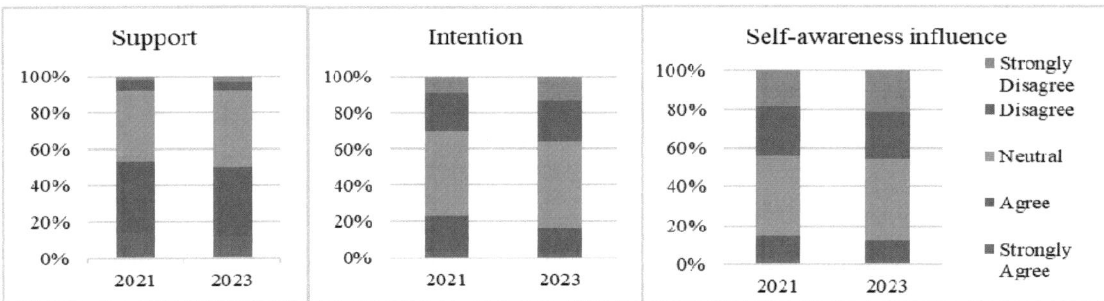

Figure 2. Responses by non-users group

3.2.2 Factors Influencing Support, Intention and Self-Awareness of Influence

Regarding items related to three factors (Table 1), respondents were asked to choose from five options, namely "strongly disagree," "disagree," neutral," "agree," and "strongly agree. "Each response was converted into a score on a Likert-type scale ranging from one to five. The average of the two items categorized for each factor was calculated as the score for each respondent. Tables 7 and 8 present the average scores for each group by year. The Mann–Whitney U test was conducted to investigate the differences in the scores of the three factors by year. The results indicated statistically significant differences in the expectations of success for the users group. Regarding the users group: using AI for work and daily life may have deepened their understanding and given them confidence in their ability to learn about AI, thereby they may have come to believe that they could influence AI's development.

However, there were statistically significant differences in the intrinsic and attainment/utility values for the non-users group. Those who had never used AI as of 2021, but had some understanding of its value, may have started using AI by 2023, owing to the prevalence of generative AI. However, those who have never having used AI as of 2023 may not be interested in it and may not understand its value.

Table 7. Average scores for user group

	Average of scores		
	Intrinsic value	Attainment/utility value	Expectation for success
2021	3.6	3.8	2.9
2023	3.7	3.8	3.2
p-value	0.259	0.95	0.01

Table 8. Average scores of the non-user group

	Average of scores		
	Intrinsic value	Attainment/utility value	Expectation for success
2021	3	3.4	2.6
2023	2.8	3.2	2.6
p-value	<0.001	0.001	0.671

4. CONCLUSIONS

Online surveys were conducted in 2021 and 2023 to reveal changes in public attitudes toward participation in discussions regarding how to use AI in society before and after the launch of ChatGPT. The following three aspects of public engagement were surveyed: their involvement with AI, their attitude toward participation in discussions regarding AI development, and factors influencing attitudes.

AI has permeated daily life in all age-groups except those in their 40s and the younger generation embraced working with the technology after ChatGPT was launched. Those who are using AI in their work and daily lives have increased their self-perception of their influence on AI development. A better understanding of AI through daily use may have led to this change. On the other hand, it suggested that those who had never used AI as of 2023 indicated that they were not interested in AI and did not understand its value.

This survey was conducted only in Japan. It is expected that similar surveys will be conducted in other countries in the future.

REFERENCES

Cave, K. et al., (2019). Scary Robots: Examining Public Responses to AI. *Proceedings of the 2019 AAAI/ACM Conference on AI, Ethics, and Society*. Honolulu, USA, pp 331–337.

Eccles, J. S. and Wigfield, A. (2002). Motivational Beliefs, Values, and Goals. *Annual Review of Psychology*. Vol. 53, No. 1, pp 109–132.

Ema, A. et al., (2016). Future relations between humans and Artificial Intelligence: A stakeholder opinion survey in Japan. *IEEE Technology and Society Magazine*. Vol. 35, No. 4, pp. 68–75.

Kelly, P. G., et al., (2021). Exciting, Useful, Worrying, Futuristic: Public Perception of Artificial Intelligence in eight countries. *Proceedings of the 2021 AAAI/ACM Conference on AI, Ethics, and Society*. Virtual Event, USA, pp. 627–637.

Maruyama, Y., (2023). Public attitude toward Participation in Discussion on Artificial Intelligence in Japan, Proceedings of the International Conferences on ICT, Society, and Human Beings 2023. Porto, Portugal, pp. 116-122.

OECD., (2019). *Artificial Intelligence in Society*. https://doi.org/https://doi.org/10.1787/eedfee77-en

Omae, Y., (2016). Establishment of a Support Environment for Human Resource Development in Science and Technology Based on Machine Learning Analysis (translated by the author). Nagaoka University of Technology, Doctoral Dissertation. (in Japanese)

Omae, Y., et al., (2020). Artificial Intelligence education in elementary school and its evaluation through career development, motivation, and rubrics. *Japan Journal Educational Technology*. Vol. 44, No. 2, pp. 213–223. (in Japanese)

Owen, R. et al., (2012). Responsible Research and Innovation: From Science in Society to Science for Society, With Society. *Science and Public Policy*. Vol. 39, Vo. 6, pp. 751–760.

Selwyn, N., and Gallo Cordoba, B. (2022). Australian Public Understanding of Artificial Intelligence. *AI & Society*. Vol. 37, pp. 1645–1662. https://doi.org/10.1007/s00146-021-01268-z

Zhang, B., & Dafoe, A. (2020). U.S. Public Opinions on the Governance of Artificial Intelligence. *Proceedings of the AAAI/ACM Conference on AI, Ethics, and Society*. New York, USA, pp. 187–193. https://doi.org/10.1145/3375627.3375827

THE IMPACT OF DIGITAL TRANSFORMATION ON ORGANIZATIONAL CULTURE AND BUSINESS: VIEWS OF MANAGERS AND EMPLOYEES

Dijana Vuković[1], Tanja Grmuša[2] and Goran Luburić[2]
[1]*Department for Business Economy, University North, Jurja Križanića 31b, Varaždin, Croatia*
[2]*Marketing and Communication Department, Zagreb School of Business, Ulica grada Vukovara 68, Zagreb, Croatia*

ABSTRACT

Digitalization often requires changes in the organizational structure, including creating new departments, hiring IT and digital technology experts, and creating new roles within the organization. The transformation of business culture also requires additional engagement of leaders who encourage openness to new ideas, experimentation and continuous learning of employees. The second part of the paper presents research conducted on a sample of 150 organizations from various sectors, including retail, manufacturing, healthcare, education and the IT industry. It includes large corporations that have already implemented digital transformation, medium and small companies that are in the transformation phase, and startups that are digitally oriented from the very beginning. To obtain comprehensive and relevant data, surveys were conducted among 500 employees and 50 managers, and additional in-depth interviews with key people responsible for digital strategy and transformation within organizations. Data was collected from various sources within organizations, including internal reports, strategic plans, and public information sources. Thus, the research focused on how digital transformation shapes organizational strategies, structures, and culture, with a particular emphasis on the challenges and opportunities this transformation brings to different types of organizations. These changes require a strategic approach and the integration of digital tools into all aspects of business, to create an organization that is agile, innovative and capable of continuous growth and development in the digital age.

KEYWORDS

Digital Transformation, Organizational Culture, Business, Research, Managers and Employees

1. INTRODUCTION

The pandemic of the COVID-19 virus has resulted in the accelerated digital transformation of numerous organizations to strengthen resilience and competitiveness, as well as visibility on the market. It is no longer just a technical-technological issue, but one that requires a holistic approach and responsible leadership (Pfaff et al., 2023; Jafari-Sadeghi et al., 2023). Digital transformation is often perceived as a threat to established operations and a disruption of business routines. Arguments of opponents of this process are sought in excessive reliance on technologies, slow decision-making, inability to prove business value, lack of operational solutions, fear of losing control, but also fear of the future in general“ (McConnell, 2015).

The results of the research show that,,in 2023, 59 per cent of companies in the EU reached at least a basic level of digital intensity“ (Dokler, 2024), which is far from the European Commission's target for the Digital Decade by 2030, which is 75%. The key obstacles to digitalization are,, limited funding, lack of digital skills, but also resistance to changes within companies“ (Dokler, 2024). However, it is encouraging that Croatia is the leader in the EU in data analytics, but there are also positive developments in the digitalization of small and medium-sized enterprises for which the EU has provided significant funds, and it is worth mentioning the National Recovery and Resilience Plan 2021-2026, which foresees 20% of funds for digitalization. The results for 2023 show two main areas of progress: the increase in experts in the information and communication field, and the digitalization of SMEs and advanced technologies. At the same time, two main shortcomings have been identified - the infrastructure for connectivity and the digitalization of public services. The DESI survey on digital transformation for 2023 showed that Croatia is in 27th place, which indicates a lag in the development of„digital skills and implementation of advanced technologies“ (Croatia Digital Decade Report 2024). This is in line with previous research on workforce readiness for the digital market (Bečić, 2018), as well as comparative reviews of the state of digital transformation in Croatia to developed European countries (Broz et al., 2020; Poljanec-Borić, 2021; Perkov, 2022; Kruljac, 2023). The success of digital transformation depends on readiness for change, perception of costs, awareness of leaders about the digital transformation process, but also education. Namely, „42% of SMEs in the EU have a very low level of digital intensity and only 4% have a very high level“ (Dokler, 2024). Education, as the first step in achieving the organization's digital maturity and realizing its transformational potential (Chanias and Hess, 2016 according to Kruljac and Živković, 2019: 75; Lugavić and Rožajac, 2022: 54), can be implemented based on existing EU funds and digitization vouchers intended for strengthening digital skills. These are forms of informal learning that are often intrinsically motivated, and which can bring multiple benefits to the company, primarily in the context of achieving innovation and productivity.

2. LITERATURE REVIEW

In this chapter, we will present a review of the literature related to the digital transformation process, analyze its impact on organizational culture, and also show how the mentioned process is viewed by key stakeholders – managers and employees.

2.1 Digital Transformation - Definition of the Concept and Characteristics

Perkov (2022) recalls the broad definition of digital transformation depending on the source (EU, OECD), adding that it is a process that conditions the survival of organizations and is no longer a question of choosing a modern business. The digital transformation of an organization includes the following indicators: user experience, business processes and business models (Westerman et al., 2011 according to Turuk et al., 2022: 112). Digitally transformed companies are more competitive, more productive and more open to new business opportunities thanks to digital networking. The concept of digital transformation is associated with the concepts of digitization and digitalization, the confusion of which Lozić (2023) attributes to the linguistic context and similarity of the concepts. While digitization „ converts analog information into digital content without any impact on production processes“ (Lozić, 2023: 112), digitalization refers to the comprehensive use of technology. Furthermore, Lozić uses a third term in explaining digital transformation – digital optimization, which denotes „the process of using digital technology to improve existing operational processes and business models (Patel, 2019)“ (according to Lozić, 2023: 214). This is a short-term activity that seeks to ensure a better market position and progress in the production and sales process. Finally, the author also discusses the concept of digital transformation as a much broader concept that affects the organizational structure. Its goal is to add value to process-oriented management strategies and to ensure support for the organization's core strategies (Lozić 2019 according to Lozić, 2023: 215; Pradana et al., 2022). The end of the digital transformation process is marked by two parallel processes: digital optimization as a continuous process and digital transformation as a prerequisite for further digital optimization (Lozić, 2023: 216), which shows that the digital transformation of an organization is not the end, but the foundation for innovation cycles and the development of new business models.

2.2 The Impact of Digital Transformation on Organizational Culture

Organizational culture refers to a system of values shared by employees that strongly influence the reputation and resilience of an organization (Varlaj et al., 2021; Varlaj et al. 2023). A strong and adaptable organizational culture contributes to easier adoption and implementation of digital technologies (YLan, 2021) and enables organizations to achieve better operational efficiency and greater competitiveness. Pfaff et al. (2023) warn that the relationship between digital transformation and organizational culture has long been viewed only superficially (Feisberger et al. 2022 according to Pfaff et al., 2023) without focusing on its specific values. However, the digital transformation of an organization is not just a technological upgrade, as many superficially understand, but a holistic evolution that requires responsible leadership, understanding of cultural changes and continuous ethical considerations (Omol, 2024) for life in the digital age.

Organizational agility implies the organization's ability to quickly respond to market demands, as well as to effectively implement a digital strategy that represents a bridge between leadership and agility, and must be aligned with the goals for organizational transformation (AlNuaimi et al., 2022). Agile organizations foster environments open to experimentation and continuous learning (from positive and negative outcomes) to thrive in the digital environment (Deep, 2023). It is important to bridge the gap in the adoption of new technologies and the gap in organizational relations to strengthen the organizational culture. A supportive organizational culture contributes to encouraging innovation and adaptability (Omol, 2024). The development of digital culture is one of the prerequisites of digital transformation (Kocak & Pawlowski, 2023; Cardoso et al., 2024), and digital culture rests on the consistent adoption of innovations that can be burdensome and cause resistance for individuals. Some of the challenges in achieving a digital culture are: employee resistance and stepping out of the comfort zone due to facing the new and unknown, highlighting infrastructure costs, inconsistent emphasis on resource allocation, the issue of automation (Forbes, 2022). Accelerating the digital transformation of business is possible through a clear definition digital strategies, clearly defined leadership and division of tasks.

3. RESEARCH METHODOLOGY

The research methodology in this paper is based on a mix of quantitative and qualitative methods to gain comprehensive insight into how digital transformation shapes organizational strategies, structures, and culture. The research was conducted on a sample of 150 organizations from various sectors, including retail, manufacturing, healthcare, education, and the IT industry. The sample includes large corporations that have already implemented digital transformation, medium-sized and small companies that are in the transformation phase, and start-ups that are digitally oriented from the very beginning. The interviews focused on key issues such as leadership in digital transformation, changes in organizational culture, agility and innovation, and strategic orientation. The quantitative approach involved a survey conducted among 500 employees and 50 managers. The study aimed to collect data on the perceptions of employees and managers regarding the implementation of digital tools, changes in the organizational structure, and the impact of these changes on daily business. The survey questions were designed to cover key aspects of digital transformation, including strategy, technology, changes in work processes, and culture.

The research focused on three main aspects of digital transformation:

- *Culture*: How digital transformation affects organizational culture, including changes in the way people work, collaborate, and communicate, and the focus on innovation.
- Structure: How organizational structure changes to support new business models and technologies, and how new roles and departments are created within the organization.
- Strategy: How organizations adapt their strategies in the context of digital transformation, including alignment with market needs and global trends.

The data collected from the survey and in-depth interviews were processed using statistical and qualitative analysis methods. Quantitative data were analyzed using descriptive statistical techniques, while qualitative interview data were interpreted through thematic analysis to identify key patterns and insights.

Their perceptions, experiences, and readiness for change are crucial for the successful implementation of digital transformation. The main objective of this research is to analyze the impact of digital transformation on organizational changes from the perspective of managers and employees. The specific objectives of the research are:

- analyze the obstacles that organizations face during the implementation of digital transformation.
- recognize the possibilities that digital transformation provides for the non-advancement of business and organizational culture processes;
- Determine the key success factors of digital transformation.

The hypotheses of this work are:

Hypothesis H1: An organizational culture that supports innovation and change-oriented leadership significantly contributes to the effective management of business processes.

Hypothesis H2: Optimizing business processes through digital transformation significantly contributes to the development and implementation of strategic orientation.

The research was conducted using a quantitative methodology, where data were collected through a structured survey questionnaire. The questionnaire was designed to assess the perception of employees and managers about the key variables of digital transformation and their impact on strategic orientation.

4. RESEARCH RESULTS

Successfully implementing digital technologies in organizations requires thorough planning, change management, and expertise in applying new tools and solutions. The aim of this research was to gain insight into the real-world challenges, benefits and strategies that experts use when leading digital transformation processes. Our respondents' responses provide a deep understanding of the real-world experiences and strategies that companies use to successfully adapt to the digital era.

What traits and skills do you consider to be key to successfully leading a digital transformation?

Certain traits and skills are essential for successfully leading a digital transformation, enabling leaders to effectively manage change, integrate new technologies, and ensure that the organization remains competitive in the digital environment. Here are a few key traits and skills that I consider to be the most important.

How did you ensure the engagement and support of all levels of the organization during the implementation of digital solutions?

We engaged key stakeholders (managers, executives, and influencers within the organization) from the very beginning, allowing them to actively participate in the selection and implementation of digital solutions. This involvement allowed us to ensure that the solutions being introduced met the real needs of the organization and employees, thereby reducing resistance and uncertainty. Managers were also responsible for communicating the changes within their teams. We paid great attention to training employees in new tools and technologies. We developed a comprehensive training plan that covered different levels of the organization, from basic user training for operational employees to more advanced technical seminars for IT teams.

How did you ensure that the organization's values were aligned with the new ways of working based on digital transformation?

Ensuring that the organization's values were aligned with the new ways of working based on digital transformation required changes in organizational culture, processes, and ways of interacting within the team. To align the organization's core values with new digital tools and technologies, we took several key steps:

- Review and adapt organizational values
- Embed digital principles in the organization's mission and vision
- Promote a culture of openness and innovation
- Work flexibility and support for work-life balance
- Create a shared sense of responsibility and collaboration
- Invest in continuous learning and employee development
- Support leadership in the change process
- Connect new technologies with social responsibilities.

What are the key factors that shaped your digital strategy and how did you align that strategy with the organization's long-term goals?

The key factors that shaped our digital strategy are based on a combination of internal and external factors, as well as on the recognition of changes in market conditions, user needs and technological progress. For the digital strategy to be successful and aligned with the long-term goals of the organization, we have carefully integrated these factors into the development of the strategy and its implementation. One of the key factors was the constant development of new technologies, including artificial intelligence, data analysis, cloud computing, automation and IoT (Internet of Things). We recognized how these technologies can improve our business processes, provide better customer service, optimize operations and enable faster data-driven decision-making.

4.1 Survey Research Results

This chapter discusses the key factors that influence the strategic orientation of organizations in the context of digital transformation. Using a survey that includes variables such as technological development, organizational culture and leadership, business processes and efficiency, and data and analytics, their interrelationships and impact on the ability of organizations to adapt to market changes and achieve competitive advantages were explored. This Research provides a deep understanding of the key variables that shape successful digital transformation and strategic decisions within organizations, with an emphasis on the importance of data and analytics, as well as the need for agile business processes in a dynamic market environment.

Table 1. Descriptive statistics of selected key indicators of digital transformation and reliability of the measuring instrument

Variables	AS	SD	Cronbach Alpha
TECHNOLOGICAL DEVELOPMENT			0.871
It includes the introduction of advanced technologies such as artificial intelligence, blockchain, the Internet of Things (IoT) and 5G, which directly changes the way an organization organizes the business process.	2.67	1.28	
Using advanced analytical tools and big data to make informed decisions and predict trends	2.71	1.26	
ORGANIZATIONAL CULTURE AND LEADERSHIP			0.886
The process involves creating a culture that embraces change, innovation and experimentation. Employees become open to new technologies and ways of working.	3.12	1.26	
Leaders must be prepared to lead change, set a clear vision and strategy, and inspire employees to embrace digital solutions.	3.42	1.21	
ORGANIZATIONAL STRUCTURE			0.916
Organizations must adapt to new market conditions faster than before, which requires reducing bureaucracy and introducing agile methodologies into business processes.	3.14	1.14	
With regard to digital transformation, there is a shift in the functions and responsibilities of employees. New jobs and skills become necessary, and existing positions adapt to new technologies.	3.39	1.10	
BUSINESS PROCESSES AND EFFICIENCY			0.896
Digital transformation enables the optimization of business processes through better resource management, faster decision-making and reduction of disorder.	3.48	0.83	
By introducing digital platforms to monitor and analyze real-time data, organizations can make decisions much faster, with less risk.	3.69	0.91	
DATA AND ANALYTICS			0.914
Digital transformation enables organizations to collect large amounts of data from different channels, which are then analyzed to make better business decisions.	3.69	0.75	
Using advanced analytical tools to predict trends, user behaviour, and future market needs, thereby improving strategic planning.	3.72	0.79	
STRATEGIC ORIENTATION			0.925
Organizations need to develop and implement strategies that integrate digital transformation into every aspect of the business, from marketing to supply chain management.	3.91	0.84	
Organizations that successfully use digital technologies can gain competitive advantages, whether through faster market responses, personalized offerings, or greater efficiency.	3.86	0.87	

Technological development is a key variable in the digital transformation of organizations. According to the data, the introduction of advanced technologies such as artificial intelligence, blockchain, IoT and 5G has a direct impact on the way organizations organize their business processes. The average value for this area is 2.67, with a standard deviation of 1.28, which indicates a diverse perception among employees and managers regarding the implementation of these technologies. These technologies enable organizations to optimize business processes, reduce operating costs and improve efficiency. Furthermore, the use of analytical tools and big data enables better decision-making and forecasting of market trends (average value 2.71, SD 1.26), which makes organizations more agile and able to react quickly to changes in the market. Organizational culture and leadership play a key role in the success of digital transformation. The transformation process requires changes in culture, where employees become open to new technologies and ways of working. The average value for this factor is 3.12, with a standard deviation of 1.26, indicating the relative readiness of organizations to adopt innovations.

Table 2. Multiple regression analysis for the variable predicting strategic orientation

Indicators	
Correlation coefficient R	0.769
Coefficient of determination R^2	0.591
Adjusted R^2	0.588
Standard error	1.948
F ratio	172.971
Sig.	0.000

Independent Variables	b	Beta	t	Sig.
Constanta	2.818		9.250	0.000
Technological development	0.063	0.050	0.986	0.325
Organizational culture and leadership	-0.231	-0.178	-3,499	0.001*
Business processes and efficiency	0.502	0.376	9.640	0.000*
Data and analytics	0.416	0.564	13.880	0.000*

Note: dependent variable – strategic orientation; B – unstandardized coefficient; Beta – standardized coefficient; * - significance at the $p<0.01$ level.

The correlation coefficient (R) is 0.769, which suggests that there is a strong positive relationship between the combination of all independent variables (technological development, organizational culture and leadership, business processes and efficiency, data and analytics) and the dependent variable – strategic orientation. An R-value of 0.769 means that these variables are significantly related to the strategic orientation of the organization. The coefficient of determination (R^2) is 0.591, which means that 59.1% of the variation in strategic orientation can be explained by the variables included in the regression analysis. The adjusted coefficient of determination (adjusted R^2) is 0.588, which is very close to R^2, confirming that all relevant factors are taken into account in the model, without overfitting the model with unnecessary variables. This value indicates that the variables included in the model are justified and contribute to predictive accuracy. The F ratio is 172.971, with a p-value of 0.000. This result confirms that the entire regression model is statistically significant. A high F ratio indicates that the variables included in the model are collectively significant for predicting the strategic orientation of the organization. A p-value of less than 0.01 (0.000) confirms that the model is statistically significant and that we cannot reject the hypothesis that there is a significant relationship between the independent variables and strategic orientation. The coefficient for technological development is positive, meaning that, with increasing technological development, strategic orientation also increases, but it is very weak. However, the p-value of 0.325 indicates that this result is not statistically significant at the 0.01 level.

Table 3. Simple regression analysis for the variable "Successful introduction of digital transformation brings competitive advantage through faster market reactions, personalized offer or greater efficiency

Indicators	
Correlation coefficient R	0.767
Coefficient of determination R^2	0.589
Adjusted R^2	0.588
Standard error	1.922
F ratio	687.909
Sig.	0.000

Independent variables	b	Beta	t	Sig.
Constant	2.382		9.293	0.000
Strategic orientation	0.788	0.767	26.228	0.000*

The aim is to investigate how the strategic orientation of the organization (independent variable) influences the successful implementation of digital transformation as a factor that brings competitive advantages, such as faster market reactions, personalized offers or greater efficiency (dependent variable). The correlation coefficient (R) is 0.767, which shows that there is a very strong positive correlation between strategic orientation and the successful implementation of digital transformation. The coefficient of determination (R^2) is 0.589, which means that 58.9% of the variation in the success of the implementation of digital transformation can be explained by the strategic orientation variable. This result indicates that the model provides a solid explanation of how strategic orientation influences the success of digital transformation, while the rest of the variation may be caused by other factors not included in this model. The adjusted coefficient of determination (adjusted R^2) is 0.588, which is very close to R^2, confirming that the model is good and that the variables in it form a relevant predictor for the dependent variable, without over-adjusting to unnecessary variables. The F ratio is 687.909, and the p-value is 0.000.

5. CONCLUSION

Digital transformation represents a key change that manifests itself through changes in technology, strategy, structure and culture of organizations. The main objective of this research was to analyze the impact of digital transformation on organizational change, focusing on three main aspects: organizational culture, structure and strategy. The results of the research, conducted on a sample of 150 organizations from various sectors, indicate a clear connection between digital innovations and the success of organizational change. The research confirmed that technology and analytics are key factors that enable organizations to optimize business processes and improve efficiency. The use of advanced analytical tools helps organizations make informed decisions and adapt their strategies by market changes, which ensures competitive advantages. Given the high correlation between data use and strategic orientation, it is clear that data plays an increasingly important role in shaping business strategies in the digital age.

However, the results also pointed to the challenges that organizations face. Organizational culture and leadership have proven to be factors that, although crucial for the success of transformation, do not always show a positive impact on the strategic orientation of organizations. Digital transformation is not only a technological change but also a significant impetus for the overall transformation of organizations. In the future, organizations must direct their strategies towards optimizing business processes, encouraging innovation and developing a culture of openness and continuous learning. This research provides the basis for further analysis and development of practices that will enable organizations not only to survive but also to thrive in a fast and complex digital environment.

REFERENCES

AlNuaimi, B. K., Singh Kumar, S., Ren, S., Budhwar, P. and Vorobyev, D. (2022). Mastering digital transformation: The nexus between leadership, agility, and digital strategy, *Journal of Business Research*, Vol. 145, pp. 636-648, https://doi.org/10.1016/j.jbusres.2022.03.038

Asif M, Yang L, Hashim M. The Role of Digital Transformation, Corporate Culture, and Leadership in Enhancing Corporate Sustainable Performance in the Manufacturing Sector of China. *Sustainability.* (2024) Vol. 16. No. 7 2651. https://doi.org/10.3390/su16072651

Bečić, M. (2018). Digitalno gospodarstvo i stanje na tržištu rada Republike Hrvatske. *International journal of multidisciplinarity in business and science*, Vol. 4 No. 6, 2018., pp. 33-40, https://hrcak.srce.hr/clanak/314157 10. 12. 2024.

Bovee, C. L. and Thill J. V. (2012). *Business Communication Today*. Pearson; Eleventh Edition

Broz, T., Butorac, G. and Parežanin, M. (2020). Digital transformation and economic cooperation: The case of Western Balkan countries, *Zb. rad. Ekon. fak. Rij.* Vol. 38., No. 2, pp. 697-722, https://hrcak.srce.hr/file/362817 10. 12. 2024.

Cardoso, A., Sousa Pereira, M., Sá J. C., Powell, D. J., Faria, S. and Magalhães, M. (2024). Digital Culture, Knowledge, and Commitment to Digital Transformation and Its Impact on the Competitiveness of Portuguese Organizations. *Administrative Sciences* 14: 8. https://doi.org/10.3390/admsci14010008

Deep, G. (2023). Digital transformation's impact on organizational culture. *International Journal of Science and Research Archive* Vol. 10, No. 2. pp. 396-401 https://doi:10.30574/ijsra.2023.10.2.0977

Dokler, B. (2024). Možemo dostići ambiciozne EU ciljeve digitalne transformacije do 2030., ali trebamo ubrzati tempo, *Poslovni dnevnik*, Published 17 September 2024, https://www.poslovni.hr/sci-tech/mozemo-dostici-ambiciozne-eu-ciljeve-digitalne-transformacije-do-2030-ali-trebamo-ubrzati-tempo-4455108 10. 12. 2024.

Feliciano-Cestero, M. M., Ameen, N., Kotabe, M., Paul, J. and Signoret, M. (2023). Is digital transformation threatened? A systematic literature review of the factors influencing firms' digital transformation and internationalization, *Journal of Business Research*, Vol. 157, 113546, https://doi.org/10.1016/j.jbusres.2022.113546

Fernandez-Vidal, J., Perotti, A., Gonzalez, R. and Gasco, J. (2022). Managing digital transformation: The view from the top, *Journal of Business Research*, Vol. 152, pp. 29-41, https://doi.org/10.1016/j.jbusres.2022.07.020

Fišter, K. (2024). Vidjeti digitalnu transformaciju – ključne vještine i pristupi, *Bilt. Hrvat. druš. med. inform.* Vol. 30., No. 1, pp. 1 – 4, https://hrcak.srce.hr/file/462080 10. 12. 2024.

Forbes Business Council (2024). 20 Ways To Engage Every Staff Member During A Digital Transformation." https://www.forbes.com/councils/forbesbusinesscouncil/2024/02/16/20-ways-to-engage-every-staff-member-during-a-digital-transformation/ 10. 12. 2024.

Forbes (2022). ‚Digital Transformation And Its Impact on Organizational Culture" https://www.forbes.com/councils/forbeshumanresourcescouncil/2022/07/22/digital-transformation-and-its-impact-on-organizational-culture/ 10. 12. 2024.

Guse, R., Thiebes, S., Hennel, P. and Rosenkranz, C. (2022). How Do Employees Perceive Digital Transformation and its Effects? A Theory of the Smart Machine Perspective. *Conference: Forty-Third International Conference on Information Systems (ICIS),* Copenhagen 2022. https://www.researchgate.net/publication/365293055_How_Do_Employees_Perceive_Digital_Transformation_and_its_Effects_A_Theory_of_the_Smart_Machine_Perspective 10. 12. 2024.

Izvješće za Hrvatsku za digitalno desetljeće (2024). 11. srpnja 2024. https://digital-strategy.ec.europa.eu/hr/factpages/croatia-2024-digital-decade-country-report 10. 12. 2024.

Jafari-Sadeghi, V., Amoozad Mahdiraji, H., Mahabubul Alam, G. and Mazzoleni, A. (2023). Entrepreneurs as strategic transformation managers: Exploring micro-foundations of digital transformation in small and medium internationalises, *Journal of Business Research*, Vol. 154, https://doi.org/10.1016/j.jbusres.2022.08.051

Kocak, S. and Pawlowski, J. (2023). Digital Organizational Culture: A Qualitative Study on the Identification and Impact of the Characteristics of a Digital Culture in the Craft Sector. *SN COMPUT. SCI.* 4, 819. https://doi.org/10.1007/s42979-023-02302-1

Kruljac, Ž. and Knežević, D. (2019). Modeli digitalne zrelosti poduzeća - objašnjenje, pregled literature i analiza, *Obrazovanje za poduzetništvo - E4E: znanstveno stručni časopis o obrazovanju za poduzetništvo,* Vol. 9 No. 2, 2019., pp. 72 – 84, https://hrcak.srce.hr/230577

Lozić, J. (2023). Digitalna transformacija organizacije: putovanje od digitizacije do digitalne transformacije, *Zbornik sveučilišta Libertas*, Vol. 8 No. 9, 2023., pp. 211-223, https://hrcak.srce.hr/312490, 10. 12. 2024., https://doi.org/10.46672/zsl.8.9.14

Lugavić, Z. and Rožajac, A. (2022). Digitalna transformacija: multidisciplinarno upravljanje promjenama, *Tranzicija* 25 (50): Vol. 25. No. 50., 2022., pp. 43-64, https://hrcak.srce.hr/313071 10. 12. 2024.

McConnell, J. (2015). The Company Cultures That Help (or Hinder) Digital Transformation, HBR.org. https://hbr.org/2015/08/the-company-cultures-that-help-or-hinder-digital-transformation 10. 12. 2024.

Omol, E. J. (2024), Organizational digital transformation: from evolution to future trends, *Digital Transformation and Society,* Vol. 3 No. 3, pp. 240-256. https://doi.org/10.1108/DTS-08-2023-0061

Perkov, D. (2022). Izazovi provedbe digitalne transformacije funkcije upravljanja ljudskim potencijalima u mikropoduzećima te malim i srednjim poduzećima Republike Hrvatske, *Zbornik sveučilišta Libertas,* Vol. 7 No. 8, 2022., pp. 85-102, https://hrcak.srce.hr/294118 10. 12. 2024.

Pfaff, M., Wohlleber, A. J., Münch, C., Küffner, C. and Hartmann, E. (2023). How digital transformation impacts organizational culture – A multihierarchical perspective on the manufacturing sector. Computers & Industrial Engineering 183(1):109432. https://doi.org/10.1016/j.cie.2023.109432

Poljanec-Borić, S. (2021). Qualitative Insight into the Characteristics of Digital Enterprise, Content and the State of Digital Transformation in Croatia, *Društvena istraživanja: časopis za opća društvena pitanja,* Vol. 30 No. 1, 2021, pp. 115-134 https://doi.org/10.5559/di.30.1.06, https://hrcak.srce.hr/clanak/369218 10. 12. 2024.

Pradana M, Silvianita A, Syarifuddin S. and Renaldi R (2022) The Implication of Digital Organisational Culture on Firm Performance. *Front. Psychol.* 13:840699. https://doi.org./10.3389/fpsyg.2022.840699

Trenerry B, Chng S, Wang Y, Suhaila ZS, Lim SS, Lu HY and Oh PH. Preparing Workplaces for Digital Transformation: An Integrative Review and Framework of Multi-Level Factors. *Front Psychol.* 2021 Mar 23;12:620766. doi: 10.3389/fpsyg.2021.620766.

Turuk, M., Turčić, I. and Stjepić A. M. (2022). Analiza indikatora digitalnog poduzetništva na primjeru odabranih članica Europske unije, *Zbornik Ekonomskog fakulteta u Zagrebu*, Vol. 20 No. 1, 2022., pp. 111-117, https://hrcak.srce.hr/280445 10. 12. 2024.

Van Der Schaft, A. H. T., Lub, X. D., Van Der Heijden, B. and Solinger, O. N. (2024). How Employees Experience Digital Transformation: A Dynamic And Multi-Layered Sensemaking Perspective. Journal *of Hospitality & Tourism Research*, Vol. 48, No. 5, pp. 803-820. https://doi.org/10.1177/10963480221123098

Varlaj, S., Grmuša, T. and Vuković, D. (2023). The Role of Organizational Values in Creating Reputation and Organizational Resilience // *1th International Communication Digitalization and Society Symposium Proceedings Book* / Akbulut, Deniz (ur.). Istanbul: İstanbul Aydın Üniversitesi İletişim Fakültesi, pp. 189-210.

Varlaj, S., Grmuša, T. and Vuković, D. (2021). The Role of Corporate Values and Corporate Culture in the Untypical Times of the Covid-19 Pandemic // *3rd International conference on decision making for small and medium-sized enterprises: conference proceedings* / Duháček Šebestová, Jarmila; Šperka, Roman; Suchánek, Petr et al. (ed). Opava: Karviná: Silesian University in Opava, School of Business Administration in Karviná, pp. 672-680.

Vuchkovski, D., Zalaznik, M., Mitręga, M. and Pfajfar, G. (2023). A look at the future of work: The digital transformation of teams from conventional to virtual. *Journal of Business Research*, Vol. 163, 113912, https://doi.org/10.1016/j.jbusres.2023.113912

Yildiz, K., Akoğlu, H.E., Emir, E., Angosto, S. and García-Fernández, J. (2024). The perceived effect of digital transformation and resultant empowerment on job performance of employees in the fitness family business", *Journal of Family Business Management*, Vol. ahead-of-print No. ahead-of-print. https://doi.org/10.1108/JFBM-02-2024-0038

Y LAN, P. (2021). Corporate Culture's Role on Digital Transformation, Lesson Learnt for Vietnam Businesses *Proceedings of the International Conference on Emerging Challenges: Business Transformation and Circular Economy (ICECH 2021),* https://www.atlantis-press.com/proceedings/icech-21/125965454, 10. 12. 2024.

Wrede, M., Velamuri V. K. and Dauth, T. (2020). Top managers in the digital age: Exploring the role and practices of top managers in firms' digital transformation. *MDE (Managerial and Decision Economics).* Vol. 41. No. 8, pp 1549-1567, https://doi.org/10.1002/mde.3202

IDRIS – IMPLEMENTATION AND MANAGEMENT OF AN OPEN-SOURCE VIRTUALIZATION PLATFORM FOR DIGITAL TEACHING AT A UNIVERSITY – CASE STUDY

Fulya Ay[1,3], Markus Grüne[1,4] and Pascal Hauch[2]
[1]*Frankfurt University of Applied Sciences, Faculty 3: Business and Law, Nibelungenplatz 1, 60318 Frankfurt am Main, Germany*
[2]*inett GmbH, Altenkesseler Str. 17 / B8, 66115 Saarbrücken, Germany*
[3]*M.Sc.*
[4]*Prof. Dr.*

ABSTRACT

This paper presents IDRIS, an open-source virtualization platform developed at Frankfurt University of Applied Sciences that is used for hosting digital teaching and learning environments. IDRIS is based on Proxmox and is customized with extensions to meet the needs of teachers, learners, and administrators in higher education. This paper describes the high-level architecture of IDRIS, including its user frontends and self-service capabilities, as well as some of the low-level technical architecture and components, although the focus lies on the management perspective. A cost analysis is provided, which shows the initial setup costs and the ongoing operational expenses. Performance metrics are presented to demonstrate the capacity of IDRIS to handle large numbers of concurrent virtual machines. This study also discusses the advantages of IDRIS compared with commercial cloud platforms, including cost efficiency and customizability, while noting some limitations. As an open-source solution tailored for universities, IDRIS offers a blueprint that can be adapted by other institutions to create scalable digital learning environments.

KEYWORDS

Digital Teaching and Learning Environments, Open-Source Virtualization Technology, Higher Education

1. INTRODUCTION

Virtualization platforms, such as Virtual Desktop Infrastructures (VDI) or Cloud Services, play a significant role in e-learning as facilitators of e-learning platforms and digital classrooms, as well as subjects of research and education (Grüne, 2016; Baun et al., 2024). The academic community has extensively examined virtualization in the context of teaching from various perspectives. Certain studies consider virtualization platforms as a means for enhancing data center efficiency and scalability within university settings (Miseviciene et al., 2012; Koratagere, Chandrashekarappa Koppal and Umesh, 2023), while others emphasize the maintenance workload imposed on staff by operating such platforms (Oleksiuk et al., 2021) or the advantages and disadvantages of different open-source virtualization platforms (Oleksiuk and Oleksiuk, 2021). Despite numerous studies on technical aspects, relatively few authors have shared their experiences regarding the cost aspects of establishing or maintaining self-hosted virtualization platforms (Erskine and Füstös, 2013; Wang et al., 2020). Whereas for Cloud Computing users FinOps provides tools for cost management (Storment and Fuller, 2023; Kanumuri and Zeier, 2024). To the best of our knowledge, research presenting a multi-perspective view that integrates managerial, architectural, and functional aspects of the implementation of virtualization platforms for e-learning is lacking. Our paper aims to address this gap by presenting our experience in establishing a virtualization platform customized specifically for teachers and learners in higher education, the Innovative Digital Research and Instruction System (IDRIS) platform. A broader view on our SKILL-ELLE project can be found in our overview paper (Grüne and Ay, 2025).

This study presents the design and implementation of IDRIS, an open-source virtualization platform based on Proxmox (Proxmox Virtual Environment 8.3, 2024), which was developed at Frankfurt University of Applied Sciences in collaboration with inett GmbH, Saarbrücken / Germany within the SKILL-ELLE project. The development of IDRIS prioritized the provision of self-service functionality for teachers, enabling them to manage digital teaching and learning environments (digital classrooms including virtual machines). IDRIS achieved alpha production status by July 2024 and will be utilized in the forthcoming summer semester for numerous courses in Business Information Systems Management at Frankfurt University of Applied Sciences. The source code will be released as open-source software in 2025. This paper will examine the architecture, functionality, and cost structure of IDRIS, offering insights for the academic community and facilitating informed decision-making in the planning and implementation of virtualization platforms for educational purposes.

2. THE IDRIS PLATFORM FOR DIGITAL TEACHING

This section presents the architecture of the IDRIS platform. Requirements for the IDRIS platform were elicited and managed by the SKILL-ELLE team based on prior experience in developing an e-learning platform on Azure (Azure, 2024) while implementation work was planned and executed by the vendor.

IDRIS is based on Proxmox, which has been customized to address the diverse needs of its user groups, for example, through the development of extensions. These extensions include management dashboards for administrators, teachers, and learners. IDRIS will be utilized to provide virtual machines (VMs) to learners and teachers, incorporating preconfigured software packages required for coursework. In this context, learners may utilize, for instance, Windows or Linux desktops with preconfigured software packages. VMs can be granted access to services from other VMs. As an illustration, a learner can employ a client program to access a database on a virtual server to execute SQL queries against the database.

2.1 High-Level Architecture

From a high-level perspective, IDRIS, as a virtualization platform, supports multiple use cases, as shown in Figure 1.

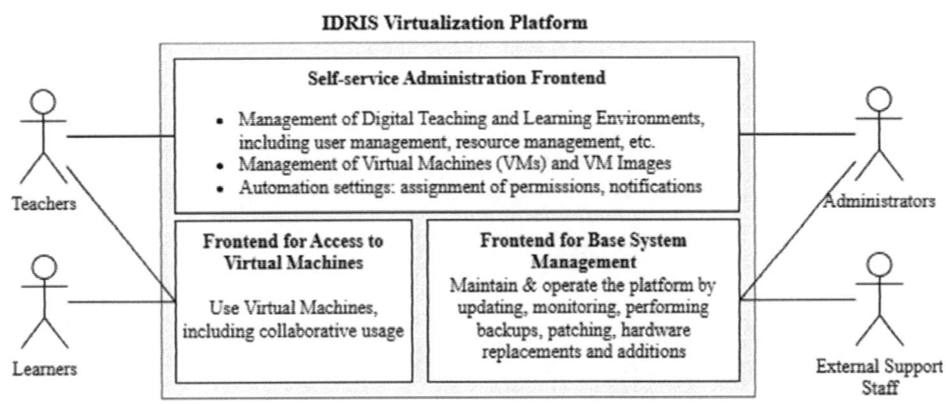

Figure 1. Use Case / Components of the IDRIS Virtualization Platform

The IDRIS platform accommodates multiple user groups: teachers, learners, and administrators, as well as external support staff. Learners access and utilize VMs for their learning activities within a course context. Teachers employ IDRIS as a means for the provision of VMs to their learners and teachers depend on administrators for the installation of VM images that can serve as templates for their courses. Administrators, possessing a fundamental understanding of the platform and its underlying technology, maintain and operate it. External support staff assists administrative team members in maintaining the system and ensuring the platform's continuous functionality through updates and patches.

In IDRIS, the **Self-Service Administration Frontend** contains a series of dashboards that facilitate the management of digital teaching and learning environments (courses) and the underlying infrastructure of IDRIS for teachers and administrators. These dashboards serve as user-friendly interfaces, consolidating technical functionalities into frontends that are easier to understand than the technical frontends provided by the Proxmox base system. The dashboards of the Self-Service Administration Frontend include self-service capabilities for managing the usage times of digital classrooms, user access rights, resource allocation, performance, and VM operations in general and for each course. Specifically, for the creation, modification, and removal of VMs and VM images, including the configuration of computational resources such as CPU, RAM, software, and storage. To support the effective utilization of this functionality, extensive documentation has been developed to guide teachers and administrative staff through various features.

The **Frontend for Access to Virtual Machines** constitutes the user-facing component of the platform, where teachers and learners interact with their virtual machines. It incorporates self-service functionalities that enable users to manage their virtual environments independently. For instance, users can initiate and terminate their own VMs, which are associated with different courses; collaborative use of VMs by multiple users is also possible through the browser-based frontend based on Apache Guacamole (Apache Guacamole, 2024). The Frontend for Access to Virtual Machines also encompasses a landing page that facilitates remote access to virtual machines through a browser-based interface.

The third frontend, the **Frontend for Base System Management**, is utilized to manage the backend operations of the system from a technical perspective. Users comprise technical administrators and external support personnel. The frontend encompasses functions for system maintenance (backup and restore, updating and patching, hardware management, notification, and logging), monitoring the infrastructure in real-time (server performance, virtual machine status, etc.), protecting the system (firewalls to regulate data traffic), and managing resources (e.g., adding or removing hardware components).

2.2 User Frontends in IDRIS

In this section, we will present some of the screen designs for the frontends described in the previous section, as presented in Figure 2.

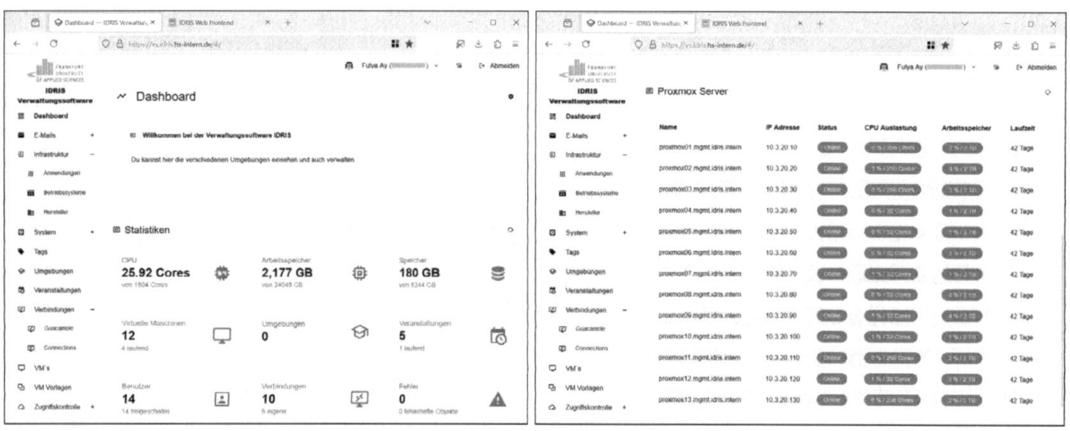

Figure 2. Self-Service Administration Frontends in IDRIS. Browser

After login, users can access the functionality assigned to their roles. At present, frontends are only available in German language. The screens show a menu structure on the left-hand side that allows users to access the functionality in the dashboard. On the first screen, the overall configuration settings, including the number of courses (Veranstaltungen), can be seen. The second screen shows a list of servers running in the Proxmox cluster, including IP addresses, online status, CPU usage, memory utilization, and server uptime.

From an end-user perspective, virtual machines can be accessed through a Web Interface based on Apache Guacamole, as displayed in Figure 3. Apache Guacamole can also be used to display multiple VMs in parallel in one browser window. It is easy to use and ensures that learners and teachers do not need to install additional software for remote access, such as Remote Desktop Protocol (RDP) clients.

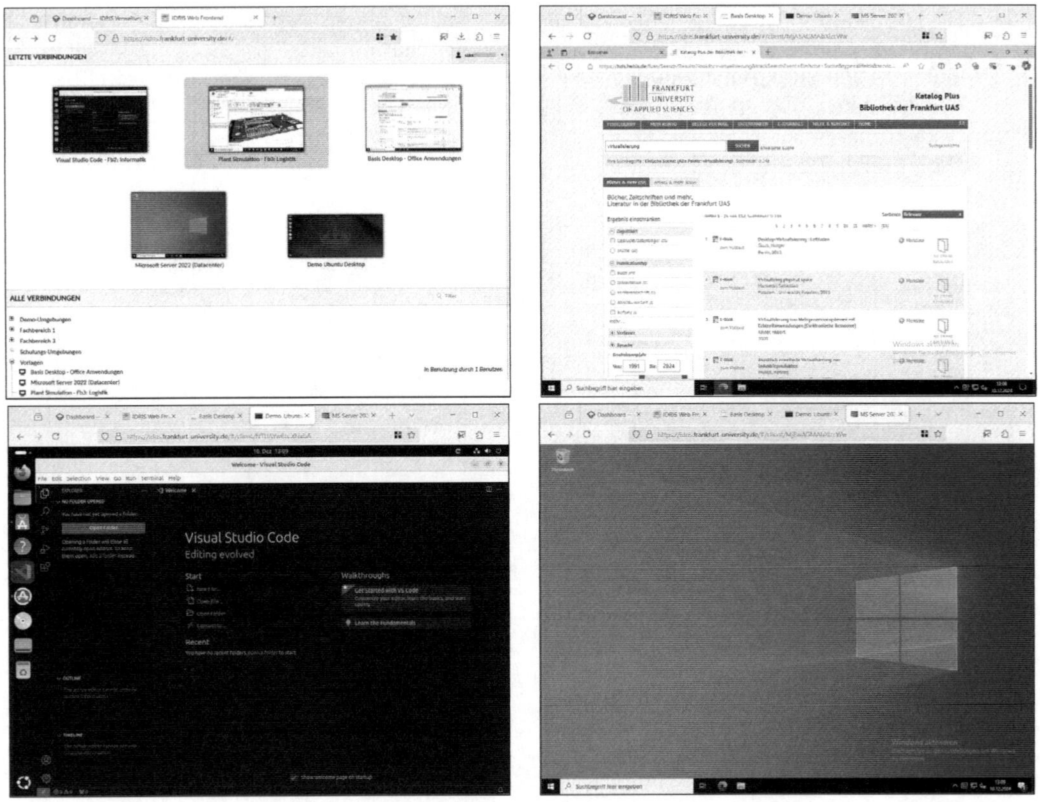

Figure 3. Access to VM through apache guacamole in a browser

In Figure 3 above, the top left screen shows the landing page for teachers and students, the top right and the bottom right screens a Windows desktop running on a VM, and the bottom left represents a Linux desktop. It is possible to host any type of operating system. For Microsoft Windows desktops, additional licenses are needed for the operating system itself and client access licenses for remote access to the desktops.

2.3 Low-Level-Architecture

After discussing the general architecture from a frontend / use case perspective, we will now provide a general review of the technical, low-level architecture of IDRIS depicted in Figure 4 below It comprises several components and software packages, as well as different network segments that together constitute the technical foundation of IDRIS. The IDRIS platform is integrated into the university's IT infrastructure, with its components distributed across distinct networks.

- Virtual machines are hosted in the **Environment Network** and made available to learners, teachers, and personnel directly through the Internet.
- The **Demilitarized Zone Network** is a segregated area in IDRIS used to expose the Self-Administration Frontend. Apache Guacamole is used in this Network to make VMs accessible through a browser. checkmk (checkmk, 2024) was used for network and system monitoring. The network is used by teachers, administrators, and external support staff and can be accessed through the university's intranet or through a Virtual Private Network (VPN) connection.
- The **Management Network** is used for the administration and monitoring of the entire virtualization platform. It hosts Proxmox Virtual Environment (Proxmox VE), Proxmox Backup Server (PBS), and checkmk, a monitoring tool. Access to this network is restricted to administrators and external support personnel. It is accessible only through a separate VPN management network.

- The **Firewall Cluster** – for reasons of simplification depicted within the Management Network – protects the platform against unauthorized access by monitoring and controlling data traffic. OPNsense (OPNsense, 2024) is used as a software product for firewall and routing functionalities. Access is restricted to administrators and external support staff through a separate VPN management network.

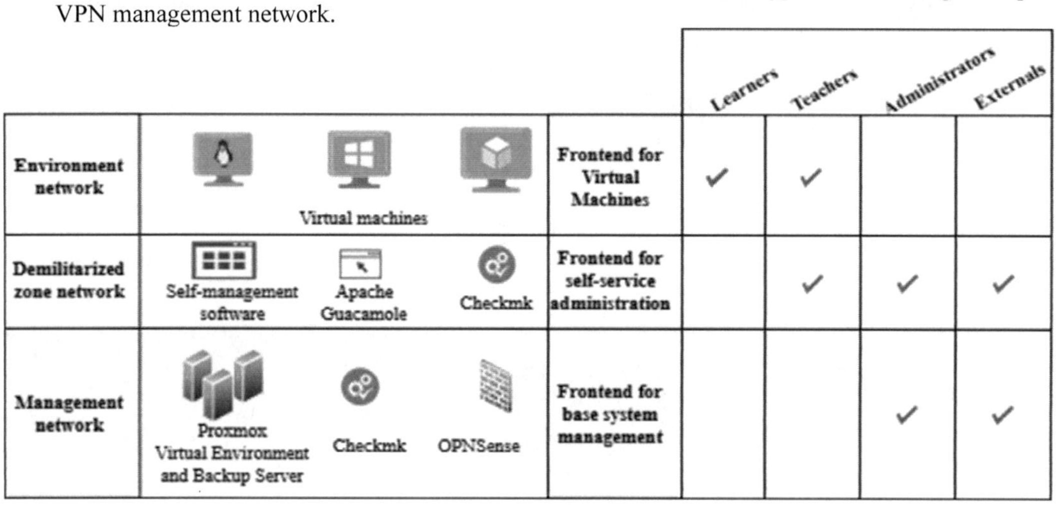

Figure 4. Low-Level-Architecture of IDRIS – Components and Software Products in Use

3. COST AND PERFORMANCE PERSPECTIVE OF IDRIS

Cost is the most important factor for assessing the viability of a platform. The overall costs of a platform can be split into setup costs for development and hardware purchases, as well as ongoing costs for the operation of the platform. In this section, we present the cost profile of the current implementation of IDRIS, not considering overhead costs, such as room rental and electricity. When comparing a self-hosted platform, such as IDRIS, with a cloud platform, these overhead costs must be considered. Fortunately, the implementation of IDRIS was supported by internal and external funds. Table 1 provides an overview of annual operational expenses by cost category.

Table 1. Yearly cost calculation for self-hosted Proxmox platform IDRIS, rounded

Cost block	Annual cost in €, incl. VaT	Comment
Hardware depreciation cost based on total replacement costs of € 315.000 and depreciation 6 years	**€ 52,250**	13 servers with a total of 768 CPU cores, 1.000 TB HDD, 295 TB SSD and 26 TB RAM; no GPUs; 6 switches + 1 backup server
License costs	**€ 16,050**	Proxmox VE + Proxmox Backup Server; OPNsense Business; Checkmk Enterprise
Running costs for teaching and learning environments / VMs	./.	Not figure in. Includes licenses for operation systems for VMs, electricity, etc.
Staff	**€ 78,000**	One staff member with a German salary level of E13. Ideally, 2 per platform.
Support – external consultants / Maintenance and development	**€ 48,000**	Additional expertise sourced from vendor. Maintenance, updates, etc.
Total cost	**€ 194,300**	Monthly: € 16,200

The overall initial setup cost for platform development encompasses expenses for hardware acquisition, vendor contracting, staff involvement in IDRIS development, and additional costs for other teams. Quantifying a fixed cost amount for the initial setup presents significant challenges; however, excluding internal team members, the cost for establishing the environment approximated € 597,000.

As shown in the table, significant costs are incurred through hardware depreciation. It is important to note that the IDRIS setup represents a minimal configuration with all servers located in a single data center. If 24/7 operations are required, the establishment of a failover location is necessary, effectively doubling the depreciation cost block presented in the table. Furthermore, the cost overview assumes the presence of a dedicated staff member for the platform administration. In an optimal scenario, multiple team members should be assigned responsibility for the platform or external staff would need to be recruited to enhance the team's capabilities. The support cost block can be scaled depending on the need for additional support from the vendor.

Table 2 presents a quantitative assessment of the virtualization platform's performance, encompassing parameters such as the number of servers, CPU core count, HDD and SSD storage capacity, and RAM allocation. The table further delineates the resources designated for the operation of the underlying Proxmox base system (system maintenance and redundancy requirements), which must be subtracted from the total capacity available for concurrent user utilization. This comprehensive evaluation facilitates a thorough understanding of the platform's capacity to manage different workloads. The current setup can easily handle 1,000 concurrent VMs with 1.5 CPU cores, 643 GB HDD, 178 GB SSD, and 26 GB of RAM.

Table 2. Performance evaluation of the virtualization platform

Number of servers	CPU cores	Hard disk (GB)	Solid state disk (GB)	RAM (GB)
13	768 (physical)	1,072,000	296,832	26,624
Addition or reduction for base system / Concurrent users	200 % *)	60 %	60 %	100 %
500	3.1	1,286	356	53.25
1,000	1.5	643	178	26.62

**) The system can "produce" more virtual cores from the physical cores. A factor of 200% seems appropriate.*

Table 3 presents the monthly operating costs per user for various numbers of users. The table includes cost projections for 1,000, 1,500, 2,000, 2,500, and 3,000 users. This cost analysis is crucial for understanding the financial implications of scaling the system to accommodate varying user demands. The system possesses the capacity to store approximately 3,000 virtual machines in an activatable state, resulting in a calculated cost per "user" of € 5.40 per month (€ 16,200 / 3,000).

Table 3. Monthly operating costs per user

Number of users / Total cost	1,000	1,500	2,000	2,500	3,000
€ 16,200	€ 16.20	€ 10.80	€ 8.10	€ 6.48	€ 5.40
	Costs per user				

4. CONCLUSION

This study presents our findings from the implementation of the IDRIS platform in the SKILL-ELLE project. The open-source virtualization platform is specifically designed to address the needs of teachers and learners, but it can also be used for the organization of office work environments or research environments. Our aim was to offer a comprehensive overview by detailing the platform's architecture, functionality, and operational expenses.

The platform is currently in use, but further enhancements are required to improve the user interface and ensure system stability. The upcoming summer term at Frankfurt University of Applied Sciences will see an increased adoption of the platform by a larger number of teachers and learners, with plans to host up to 10 separate courses.

At present, the capabilities of IDRIS are limited to providing virtual machines, which is a restriction compared to commercial cloud platforms. However, our solution is cost-effective and can accommodate a high volume of simultaneous users. It may also serve as an alternative to increasingly costly commercial virtualization solutions such as VMWare, which are implementing new licensing models. Nevertheless, commercial systems maintain an edge in GPU computing owing to the limitation of available graphics card drivers for Linux-based virtualization platforms such as Proxmox.

In essence, IDRIS serves as a model system that can be adapted to suit the requirements of other higher education institutions. The system's source code will be made available as Open Source in 2025.

ACKNOWLEDGEMENT

This work was made possible by the Center for Digital Teaching and Learning (SKILL-ELLE), funded by Stiftung Innovation in der Hochschullehre (https://stiftung-hochschullehre.de/projekt/skill/).

REFERENCES

Apache Guacamole (TM) (2024). The Apache Software Foundation. Available at: https://guacamole.apache.org/.

Azure (2024). Microsoft. Available at: https://azure.microsoft.com/en-us/.

Baun, C. et al. (2024) 'Eine Plattform zur Erstellung und Verwendung komplexer virtualisierter IT-Strukturen in Lehre und Forschung mit Open Source Software: Erfahrungen bei der Entwicklung und Nutzung einer neuen Plattform zur Digitalisierung der Hochschullehre', *Informatik Spektrum*, 47(1–2), pp. 38–45. Available at: https://doi.org/10.1007/s00287-024-01559-x.

checkmk (2024). München, Germany: Checkmk GmbH. Available at: https://checkmk.com/.

Erskine, M.A. and Füstös, János T. (2013) 'A Survey of Desktop Virtualization in Higher Education: An Energy- and Cost-Savings Perspective', in. *Proceedings of the Nineteenth Americas Conference on Information Systems*, Chicago, Illinois. Available at: https://core.ac.uk/download/pdf/301360234.pdf.

Grüne, M. (2016) 'Teaching Software Engineering in the Cloud: Applying Cloud Services in E-Business Education', in *BLED 2016 Proceedings*. Bled; Slovenia: AIS, pp. 449–458. Available at: https://aisel.aisnet.org/bled2016/16.

Grüne, M., and Ay, F. (2025). 'Digital Teaching and Learning Environments – Lessons Learned from multiple Projects at a University – Case Study'. *Proceedings E-Society*. 23rd International Conference e-Society 2025, Madeira Island, Portugal.

Kanumuri, S. and Zeier, M. (2024) Scaling cloud FinOps: proven strategies to accelerate financial success. First edition. New York, NY: Apress.

Koratagere, S., Chandrashekarappa Koppal, R.K. and Umesh, I.M. (2023) 'Server virtualization in higher educational institutions: a case study', *International Journal of Electrical and Computer Engineering (IJECE)*, 13(4), pp. 4477–4487. Available at: https://doi.org/10.11591/ijece.v13i4.pp4477-4487.

Miseviciene, R. et al. (2012) 'Educational Infrastructure Using Virtualization Technologies: Experience at Kaunas University of Technology', *Informatics in Education*, 11, pp. 227–240. Available at: https://doi.org/10.15388/infedu.2012.12.

Oleksiuk, V.P. and Oleksiuk, O.R. (2021) 'The practice of developing the academic cloud using the Proxmox VE platform', *Educational Technology Quarterly [Online]*, 2021(4), pp. 605–616. Available at: https://doi.org/10.55056/etq.36.

Oleksiuk, V.P. et al. (2021) 'Some experience in maintenance of an academic cloud', *CTE Workshop Proceedings*, 8, pp. 165–178. Available at: https://doi.org/10.55056/cte.230.

OPNsense(R) (2024). Middelharnis, The Netherlands: OPNsense. Available at: https://opnsense.org/.

Storment, J.R. and Fuller, M. (2023) Cloud FinOps: collaborative, real-time cloud financial management. 2nd edn. Beijing, Boston, Farnham, Sebastopol, Tokyo: O'Reilly.

Wang, B. et al. (2020) 'A survey and taxonomy on workload scheduling and resource provisioning in hybrid clouds', *Cluster Computing*, 23(4), pp. 2809–2834. Available at: https://doi.org/10.1007/s10586-020-03048-8.

POWER WHEELCHAIR VIRTUAL REALITY SIMULATOR

Thomas Keller[1,*], Davide Miceli[1] and Andreas Illenberger[2]
[1]*ZHAW, Winterthur, Switzerland*
[2]*Vivala, Weinfelden, Switzerland*
[*]*[0000-0002-8100-6900]*

ABSTRACT

In recent years, virtual reality (VR) technology has made significant strides, yet its application in special and inclusive education remains limited. This paper explores the critical aspects to consider when integrating VR into special education, specifically focusing on empowering children with disabilities through the simulation of power wheelchair control. The study investigates a user-centered approach, considering both child and caregiver perspectives. The research aims to determine factors influencing the acceptance of VR applications for children with disabilities and the relevant boundary conditions to alleviate caregiver burden.

Employing a design science approach, the study develops a VR application comprising two levels, targeting beginners and advanced users. The wheelchair simulator utilizes a motion platform, a simple joystick, and VR goggles, providing an immersive and interactive learning environment. The research findings highlight positive outcomes, including good usability, observed flow, perceived pleasure, and the acquisition of joystick skills by the children. The study emphasizes the importance of a user-centered approach in VR application development for special education and showcases the potential for improving learning outcomes and motivation in children with disabilities. The implications extend to caregiver relief, indicating the promising role of VR technology in enhancing the effectiveness of therapeutic practices in special education.

KEYWORDS

Virtual Reality, Power Wheelchair Simulator, Special Education

1. INTRODUCTION

In recent years, virtual reality (VR) has established itself as a promising technology and has reached a stable level of development in various areas (Bosse et al., 2022). However, this technology is rarely used in the field of special and inclusive education. For this reason, it is still difficult to assess which characteristics a VR application must have in order to be widely accepted by children with disabilities. This paper examines which aspects and characteristics must be taken into account when using VR in the context of special and inclusive education in order to promote the learning process and create a positive experience for the children. In this study, the learning process is aimed at controlling an electric wheelchair. An application is developed that simulates the use of a power wheelchair. The immersion effect is enhanced with the help of a motion platform. The aim is to facilitate and promote access to the learning process. The power wheelchair is usually of great importance for people with mobility impairments, as it is seen as a way of compensating for the disability.

Physical and cognitive disabilities can have a major impact on the mobility of those affected. Restrictions in mobility have a negative impact on social contact and communication (Sarimski, 2021). As a result, people with physical limitations are often excluded from activities and social interactions. In the context of facilitating the integration of power wheelchair usage among children with mobility impairments, a considerable temporal investment is typically required before these individuals can effectively engage in community activities. The requisite proficiency in operating power wheelchairs necessitates substantial training akin to that undertaken in conventional automotive driving schools. The training regimen is essential for automating and coordinating motor skills. Notably, children with cerebral palsy, confronted by impaired neural networks, undergo a protracted period to establish novel neuronal connections. Unlike their more mobile counterparts, these children undergo distinctive experiential processes that mold their conceptualizations of body image and environmental interactions, necessitating unique skill development approaches (Von Loh, 2017).

Within the framework of developmental psychology, the progression of children through developmental stages is postulated. A theory focused on motor and perceptual skill development delineates a stage wherein the brain formulates the body schema and coordination. Subsequently, children construct a mental representation of visual perception based on these foundations (Ayres, 2013). Consequently, a profound interdependence between motor ability and the interpretation of visual stimuli in the brain is observed.

This interplay manifests in everyday school scenarios wherein children acquiring proficiency in power wheelchair operation require close supervision due to encountering numerous hazardous situations. Despite competence in manipulating the joystick, limitations often arise in their capacity to gauge distances and spatial relationships. Adequate practice spaces are essential for these learners, with conventional classrooms typically proving inadequate. The necessity for close supervision and secure environments imposes temporal constraints on practice sessions. VR technology emerges as a promising avenue for expanding training opportunities for these students.

Observing individuals with mobility impairments who have developed proficiency in assessing distances and spatial relations raises the prospect of alternative pathways for skill acquisition beyond direct motor experiences. While this study does not elucidate the intricacies of neural development, it endeavors to gather observational data. Parameters such as motivation, virtual room mobility, and susceptibility to discomfort are scrutinized to provide initial insights into the potential contributions of VR to the skill development of power wheelchair users.

2. OBJECTIVES

User-centered computing is a paradigm that focuses on considering the needs and requirements of users when developing technologies (Mithun & Yafooz, 2018). In therapeutic pedagogical practice, user-centered computing offers an opportunity to meet the needs of people with disabilities even better (Miesenberger et al., 2008). With the help of VR in particular, user-centered methods can be used to identify and anticipate obstacles and difficulties at an early stage. For example, VR simulations can be used to support people with autism in improving their social skills (Drigas et al., 2022) or to train people with coordination disorders in specific movements (Gonsalves et al., 2015). However, it is important that technologies are developed with the specific needs and abilities of people with disabilities in mind. As mentioned above, this requires a user-centered approach.

The combination of a user-centered approach and VR can also help to increase the interest and motivation of users in therapeutic practice. VR applications can be more exciting and motivating for people with illnesses or disabilities than conventional therapy methods (Winter, 2022). This raises the hope that this can improve the effectiveness of therapy, especially for children. Therefore, the general question can be derived as to whether virtual reality can generate added value compared to conventional therapies.

This study explores two perspectives: On the one hand, the perspective of the child is taken and, on the other, the perspective of the caregiver.

2.1 Child Perspective

The application to be developed is intended for people with disabilities. Therefore, the content of the application is primarily designed with a specific user focus (Nakashima et al., 2010, p. 350). At the same time, the application should support children's lives by trying to promote the learning process (Nakashima et al., 2010, p. 350). It is important that the application motivates the child to train and learn. Based on this aspect, the research question can be formulated as follows:

What factors promote the acceptance of children with disabilities for VR applications that have the purpose of promoting a learning process?

2.2 Caregiver Perspective

Electric Wheelchairs are very expensive. It often takes a long time until a child really has a wheelchair on its own. A VR solution can be made much cheaper and more people can use it. For insurance reasons, it is normally not allowed to “test” an electric wheelchair when the owner doesn’t need it.

Accidents in a virtual environment are less harmful to learners than in real life. A VR setup does not need much room which is considered relevant since space is scarce in schools. It is also possible to let classmates experience an electric wheelchair and get insights how the world looks like from the point of a wheelchair driver.

Based on this aspect, the research question can be formulated as follows:

What boundary conditions are relevant in the context of virtual reality applications in order to give the staff a useful new tool?

3. RESEARCH APPROACH

The research approach is based on the design science approach of Hevner (2010). The "Design and Development Centered Initiation" approach was chosen as the entry point, as it is particularly suitable for the creation of artifacts for specific user fields (Hevner & Chatterjee, 2010). In this study, two iterations were conducted with two children each.

4. RELATED WORK

The literature search revealed that the majority of studies primarily investigated the effectiveness of simulating wheelchair driving in VR in the real world. One example is the studies "Driving performance in a power wheelchair simulator" (Archambault et al., 2012) and "Development and Pilot Test of a Virtual Reality System for Electric Powered Wheelchair Simulation" (Hernandez-Ossa et al., 2017). Various studies show that the simulation of an electric wheelchair in VR has great potential and is therefore effective training for the real world. However, the application's immersion is often only marginally addressed. The development or design of the application itself is not discussed. Most applications are designed to be realistic, while others reproduce real-world environments in the virtual world (Niniss & Inoue, 2006; Vailland et al., 2021). In the studies examined, the applications are often not limited to defined target groups, such as children with disabilities, but are aimed at a broad audience with mobility impairments. Other studies show how the real driving dynamics of an electric wheelchair can be implemented using the Unreal Engine 3 software in order to convey realistic driving dynamics in the application (Herrlich et al., 2010). In some works, large displays are used instead of head-mounted VR glasses, which achieves the immersion effect differently (Niniss & Inoue, 2006). Other studies focus more on barriers and assume that the driver is already partially proficient in wheelchair operation (Pivik et al., 2002).

Arlati (2020) conducted a scoping review on VR-based wheelchair simulators. The study concludes that despite promising results, the high heterogeneity of technological solutions, training programs and their results makes it difficult to draw definitive conclusions on the optimal solution for improving driving skills and thus the effectiveness of power wheelchair simulations. This is precisely where our study comes in, by examining the requirements of an application and attempting to determine which characteristics achieve a high level of acceptance in practice.

Commercial offers for power wheelchair simulators in VR are rare (Koch, 2022). One of the few providers is the non-profit company LIFEtool[1]. LIFEtool offers computer-assisted solutions that support people with disabilities in all areas of life and enable them to communicate independently. One of their projects is the e-wheelchair simulator called WheelSim VR. The application simulates real-life situations, such as fetching parcels, picking up and delivering pizza orders, crossing crosswalks and traffic lights. The terrain reflects real places such as city centers, apartments and stores. From this it can be deduced that the application is primarily aimed at adults who have already been confronted with these activities.

[1] https://www.lifetool.at/en/home/

5. THE WHEELCHAIR SIMULATOR

The hardware consists of a motion platform, a simple joystick and VR goggles. The structure of the seat on the motion platform is based on the restrictions and needs of the user (Figure 1). The joystick is by purpose a very simple version which allows either forward, backward, left and right binary values.

The application consists of two levels whereas each level has several scenes (Keller, 2024). The entire application was programmed with the Unity development environment[2] (version 2021.3.11f1).

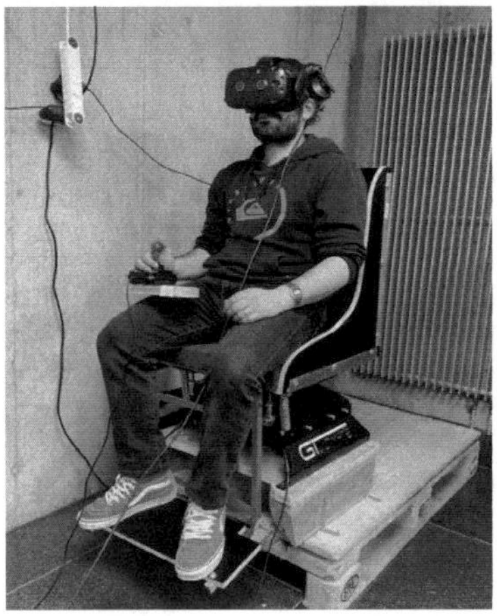

Figure 1. Prototype of the wheelchair simulator consisting of a motion platform, a simple joystick and VR googles

5.1 Level 1: For Beginners

The first level is intended as an introduction to the virtual world and simulates the first attempts at sitting in a power wheelchair. The user shall experience the special immersion effect by the motion platform and be inspired by the fictitious world. At the same time, the first level should be a learning environment that neither overwhelms the user nor distracts them from the subject matter. Above all, the cognitive load must not be too great for the intended user group. An excessive cognitive load could lead to excessive demands and frustration and thus make learning progress much more difficult (Souchet et al., 2022). For this reason, interaction with the virtual world is reduced to a minimum and only permitted if it is relevant to learning so as not to distract the user from the actual learning objective (Orsolits & Lackner, 2020). The focus is on the ability to control a wheelchair. Motor skills, orientation and spatial awareness are crucial for this. This level is primarily aimed at training motor skills whereas the following level aims at more advanced interactions The aim of this level is the ability to maneuver a power wheelchair and what maneuvering options are available. To consolidate motor learning, constant repetition of exercises is essential (Seitz, 2001). In this way, neural connections are formed in the basal ganglia area, which are intuitively accessible after learning (Brandes et al., 2019). In addition, the user should find their personal sitting position in the chair while playing, which is very important for operating a wheelchair (Kopplin, 2008).

The terrain (Figure 2) in the VR application is an island in the open sea. The sea is intended to provide the child with a wide view and thus reinforce the immersion in the virtual world. Mountains are placed on the left and right border of the learning space. Various trees have been placed in two areas to give the landscape more detail and thus maintain the child's curiosity about the surroundings. The learning area is left blank in the first scene so that the focus remains on the action at the beginning of the game. A total of six scenes were created based on this general setting. In the last scene, several additional objects are arbitrarily positioned in the learning area to increase the level of difficulty by requiring the user to avoid colliding with those objects, e.g., trees. All objects have a rigid body to enable collissions and hence, making the game more realistic. If the user drives out into the sea, he or she falls into the depths and the game is restarted.

[2] https://unity.com/

Figure 2. Overview of the learning environment of the beginner's level

The task of the first level is to follow the direction of the arrow (Figure 3). The arrow points in the direction of a sphere. The sphere symbolizes the destination to be reached. If the player consistently follows the arrow, he/she will reach the destination. The arrow then changes direction to the new destination. When the user has reached four destinations in a row, a reward appears. The reward appears in the form of an animated figure (Figure 3). The game flow then switches to the next scene.

Figure 3. Sphere and arrow as a means for orientation within the scene

The scenes differ in the positioning of the intermediate goals. The reason for this is that in this way the user has to go through as many different movement sequences as possible. Thus, it is possible to recognize which movements cause difficulties and which do not. By following the instructions and/or following the arrow, reaction time and sensitivity are increased, similar to an action game (Strahringer & Leyh, 2016, p. 111). In total, the user goes through six different scenes in which they have to achieve twenty-four goals.

5.2 Level 2: For Advanced Users

Level 2 (Figure 4) assumes that the player can maneuver the wheelchair safely. The aim of this level is therefore for the player to be able to decide for themselves in which direction they want to move. The focus is now on training orientation, spatial awareness, decision-making skills and decision-making behaviour. The reward plays a central role in this level, as it is visible in the scene right from the start. This is intended to arouse the user's motivation (Tania Ouariachi et al., 2020). In line with the "freedom to experiment" mediation method (Klopfer et al., 2009), the user should be allowed to take as much time as they want to make a decision on how to act.

Figure 4. The learning environment for level 2

Level 2 is designed as a course consisting of several islands. The islands are connected by bridges or in one case through a tunnel. As the scene progresses, the tasks and the bridges become more and more challenging. As soon as the player successfully passes through the tunnel and makes it to the second island, audio is switched on. On the second island, you the user has to reach a platform. There are two ramps to pass in order to increase the fun as well as to boost the motion platform. Getting onto the second platform is particularly challenging, as you have to drive straight onto the ramp from a right-hand bend so that you have enough momentum to climb the slope. Usually the children had to try several times to find the right approach which fostered their creativity. As soon as you reach the platform, the player is rewarded with a dancing rabbit and music plays at the same time. You then have to descend from the platform in a controlled manner. The player is made aware that the chair accelerates on its own on an incline and that it is important to brake and descend in a controlled manner, just like in the real world. Then the player moves on to the third island. A narrow bridge awaits the player here. After passing the third gate, you have to drive up and down crosswise to reach the playing area of the third island. These passages serve to train manoeuvrability and concentration. On the third island, you have the option of interacting with a ball. Accompanied by music that signals to the driver that they are on the right track, the route continues through the last gate. This is followed by a steep incline, which should ideally be driven on in the middle, as there are dents on the left and right. If the player drives over a dent, the motion platform indicates this by the respective acceleration, i.e., roll, pitch and yaw. When the player reaches the highest platform, a task awaits. The aim is to push five out of 20 balls into the water without falling in. This requires good driving skills. If you succeed, all three familiar characters appear and celebrate with the player to the sound of background music.

6. FINDINGS

The inclusion process comprised two iterations with two children aged 9 and 10 for each level including the responsible remedial teacher. The two children have cerebral palsy with a mobility impairment between level 3 and 4 according to GMFCS[3].

Following criteria have been considered and tried to optimize:

- **Usability/playability**: was perceived as good to very good by children as well as by teacher. Both levels did not need much explanations. The children were able to figure out how to use it themselves.
- **Observed flow**: children were totally immersed both by the stereoscopic view as well as by the motion platform. Both test persons did not show signs of motion sickness.
- **Motivation**: Both test persons showed long lasting concentration on the given tasks. They did not show discouraged when they had an accident. They were eager to practice and soon wanted to play again.
- **Impact**: the use of the joystick was learned by both children. In the beginning, they had problems in level 2: They needed practice to pass obstacles and to stay on the way (otherwise they would fall into the water). Both children soon improved their abilities to move in the virtual environment. The number of accidents decreased quickly. They were able to adapt their visual perception and motor coordination to the virtual environment.

[3] https://cerebralpalsy.org.au/cerebral-palsy/gross-motor-function-classification-system/

When evaluating the hardware factor, it was noticeable that the motion platform was perceived as very positive by both the remedial teacher and the two children. When asked in a subsequent semi-formal interview whether the motion platform had an influence on the effectiveness of the application, the remedial teacher fully agreed. The remedial teacher considered the simple joystick a good choice for the beginning. But depending on the learning progress it should be able to replace it by a more advanced version, ideally with the same model as used for the real power wheelchair. Furthermore, the remedial teacher agreed with the statement that the application in conjunction with the hardware can lead to faster learning success.

Especially in the advanced level, the participants felt joy and positive emotions when they moved along the course and tried the challenges on the islands. The interactions with the ball at the very end in conjunction with the singing and moving toon figures as the reward triggered a big smile and satisfaction. However, they experienced negative emotions when they got stuck along the course, e.g., on a ramp. Nevertheless, they did not ask for help in any situation.

The teacher experienced the children as extremely motivated and with a strong desire to continue the game. When asked about their assessment using the pictograms, both players pointed very close to the green smiley (Keller, 2024).

7. CONCLUSIONS

Current available hardware, e.g., head-mounted display, joystick, motion platform, allows to build a moderately priced wheelchair simulator. Using Unity as a software development environment makes it easy to build virtual worlds that aim at different learning outcomes. This work developed a rather fun oriented course that is designd to be motivating and easy playable. Based on this work various specialized simulators for power wheelchair variants are possible and easily deployed.

REFERENCES

Archambault, P. S., Tremblay, S., Cachecho, S., Routhier, F., & Boissy, P. (2012). Driving performance in a power wheelchair simulator. *Disability and Rehabilitation: Assistive Technology*, *7*(3), 226–233. https://doi.org/10.3109/17483107.2011.625072

Arlati, S., Colombo, V., Ferrigno, G., Sacchetti, R., & Sacco, M. (2020). Virtual reality-based wheelchair simulators: A scoping review. *Assistive Technology*, *32*(6), 294–305. https://doi.org/10.1080/10400435.2018.1553079

Ayres, A. J. (2013). *Bausteine der kindlichen Entwicklung: Die Bedeutung der Integration der Sinne für die Entwicklung des Kindes*. Springer-Verlag. https://books.google.ch/books?hl=de&lr=&id=ryigBgAAQBAJ&oi=fnd&pg=PA1&dq=Ayres,+J.,+Robbins,+J.+(1998):+Bausteine+der+kindlichen+Entwicklung.+Die+Bedeutung+der+Integration+der+Sinne+f%C3%BCr+die+Entwicklung+des+Kindes,+Berlin:+Springer&ots=zQlFSd_20i&sig=xdYUFYW5ko-QjlXjarYkLVzanE8

Bosse, I. K., Haffner, M., & Keller, T. (2022). Virtual Reality for Children with Special Needs. *ICCHP-AAATE 2022 Open Access Compendium "Assistive Technology, Accessibility and (e)Inclusion" Part I.* https://doi.org/10.35011/icchp-aaate22-p1-09

Brandes, R., Lang, F., & Schmidt, R. F. (2019). *Physiologie des Menschen: Mit Pathophysiologie*. Springer-Verlag. https://books.google.ch/books?hl=en&lr=&id=gMCYDwAAQBAJ&oi=fnd&pg=PR5&dq=Physiologie+des+Menschen+lang&ots=rOyzT-8WSF&sig=LEswWTjHaGAFNJ_mGtiy-9IZL2w

Drigas, A., Mitsea, E., & Skianis, C. (2022). Neuro-linguistic programming, positive psychology & VR in special education. *Scientific Electronic Archives*, *15*(1). https://sea.ufr.edu.br/SEA/article/view/1497

Gonsalves, L., Campbell, A., Jensen, L., & Straker, L. (2015). Children with developmental coordination disorder play active virtual reality games differently than children with typical development. *Physical Therapy*, *95*(3), 360–368.

Hernandez-Ossa, K. A., Longo, B., Montenegro-Couto, E., Romero-Laiseca, M. A., Frizera-Neto, A., & Bastos-Filho, T. (2017). Development and pilot test of a virtual reality system for electric powered wheelchair simulation. *2017 IEEE International Conference on Systems, Man, and Cybernetics (SMC)*, 2355–2360. https://ieeexplore.ieee.org/abstract/document/8122974/

Herrlich, M., Meyer, R., Malaka, R., & Heck, H. (2010). Development of a Virtual Electric Wheelchair – Simulation and Assessment of Physical Fidelity Using the Unreal Engine 3. In H. S. Yang, R. Malaka, J. Hoshino, & J. H. Han (Eds.), *Entertainment Computing—ICEC 2010* (Vol. 6243, pp. 286–293). Springer Berlin Heidelberg. https://doi.org/10.1007/978-3-642-15399-0_29

Hevner, A., & Chatterjee, S. (2010). *Design Research in Information Systems*. Springer.

Keller, T. (2024). *E-wheelchair*. https://osf.io/7vnzw/

Klopfer, E., Osterweil, S., & Salen, K. (2009). Moving learning games forward. *Cambridge, MA: The Education Arcade*. https://citeseerx.ist.psu.edu/document?repid=rep1&type=pdf&doi=ee505a90c16adaa764ea15241e4fcca6041b1179

Kopplin, O. (2008). Ein Rollstuhl muss passen wie ein Schuh. *Heilberufe*, *60*(2), 28–30. https://doi.org/10.1007/s00058-008-0028-8

Miesenberger, K., Klaus, J., Zagler, W., & Karshmer, A. (2008). *Computers Helping People with Special Needs: 11th International Conference, ICCHP 2008, Linz, Austria, July 9-11, 2008, Proceedings*. Springer.

Mithun, A. M., & Yafooz, W. M. (2018). Extended user centered design (UCD) process in the aspect of human computer interaction. *2018 International Conference on Smart Computing and Electronic Enterprise (ICSCEE)*, 1–6. https://ieeexplore.ieee.org/abstract/document/8538388/

Niniss, H., & Inoue, T. (2006). Electric wheelchair simulator for rehabilitation of persons with motor disability. *Symposium on Virtual Reality VIII (Proceedings), Belém (PA)*. https://www.researchgate.net/profile/Hafid-Niniss/publication/229040115_Electric_wheelchair_simulator_for_rehabilitation_of_persons_with_motor_disability/links/53f5375a0cf22be01c3f7f36/Electric-wheelchair-simulator-for-rehabilitation-of-persons-with-motor-disability.pdf

Orsolits, H., & Lackner, M. (Eds.). (2020). *Virtual Reality und Augmented Reality in der Digitalen Produktion*. Springer Fachmedien Wiesbaden. https://doi.org/10.1007/978-3-658-29009-2

Pivik, J., McComas, J., MaCfarlane, I., & Laflamme, M. (2002). Using Virtual Reality to Teach Disability Awareness. *Journal of Educational Computing Research*, *26*(2), 203–218. https://doi.org/10.2190/WACX-1VR9-HCMJ-RTKB

Sarimski, K. (2021). *Kinder mit Behinderungen in inklusiven Kindertagesstätten*. Kohlhammer Verlag.

Seitz, R. J. (2001). Motorisches Lernen: Untersuchungen mit der funktionellen Bildgebung. *Deutsche Zeitschrift Für Sportmedizin*, *52*(12), 343–349.

Souchet, A. D., Philippe, S., Lourdeaux, D., & Leroy, L. (2022). Measuring Visual Fatigue and Cognitive Load via Eye Tracking while Learning with Virtual Reality Head-Mounted Displays: A Review. *International Journal of Human–Computer Interaction*, *38*(9), 801–824. https://doi.org/10.1080/10447318.2021.1976509

Tania Ouariachi, Chih-Yen Li, & Wim J.L. Elving. (2020). *Sustainability | Free Full-Text | Gamification Approaches for Education and Engagement on Pro-Environmental Behaviors: Searching for Best Practices*. https://www.mdpi.com/2071-1050/12/11/4565

Vailland, G., Devigne, L., Pasteau, F., Nouviale, F., Fraudet, B., Leblong, E., Babel, M., & Gouranton, V. (2021). VR based power wheelchair simulator: Usability evaluation through a clinically validated task with regular users. *2021 IEEE Virtual Reality and 3d User Interfaces (VR)*, 420–427. https://ieeexplore.ieee.org/abstract/document/9417686/

Von Loh, S. (2017). *Entwicklungsstörungen bei Kindern: Medizinisches Grundwissen für pädagogische und therapeutische Berufe*. Kohlhammer Verlag. https://books.google.ch/books?hl=de&lr=&id=SnYiEAAAQBAJ&oi=fnd&pg=PP1&dq=Von+Loh,+S.+(2017):+Entwicklungsst%C3%B6rungen+bei+Kindern.+Medizinisches+Grundwissen+f%C3%BCr+p%C3%A4dagogische+und+therapeutische+Berufe.+Stuttgart:+Kohlhammer&ots=tN8KIfknJO&sig=YBTO5rfUi3H4bL6hizUhBJSfCoY

Winter, C. (2022). *Evaluation der Verwendung von Virtueller Realität (VR) als Ergänzung zum Laufbandtraining im Rahmen der Behandlung von Gangstörungen bei Patienten mit Multipler Sklerose (MS) und Schlaganfall* [PhD Thesis, Universität Würzburg]. https://opus.bibliothek.uni-wuerzburg.de/frontdoor/index/index/docId/28054

CHALLENGES CONCERNING THE DESIGN OF A NEW BEST PRACTICE USING VIDEO CONFERENCING IN DISCHARGE PLANNING

Malin Hofflander[1] and Lina Nilsson[2]
[1]*Department of Informatics*
[2]*Department of Medicine and Optometry*
Linnaeus University, 39182 Kalmar, Sweden

ABSTRACT

This paper sets out to describe challenges concerning the design of a new best practice using video conferencing in discharge planning sessions. A Participatory Action Research approach was used in the study. Data collection and analysis were carried out through workshop discussions with professionals responsible for discharge planning in hospital and in homecare. The results indicate challenges consisting of two main categories; need of knowledge and competence and need of support, that is of importance in developing new work practices for making the discharge planning session work out using video conferencing in the planning session.

KEYWORDS

Best Practice, Design, Discharge Planning, Participatory Action Research

1. INTRODUCTION

Hospital nurses relate in several earlier studies that discharge planning sessions are complicated and time-consuming, which inhibits the in-depth planning that is needed to render a well-functioning care after discharge (Hayajneh et al., 2020). In an attempt to raise the quality of discharge planning, by enabling the discharge planning sessions to actually take place with less time consumption (Hofflander et al., 2015) and providing the opportunity for both patient and homecare professionals to participate (Krook et al., 2020), the decision was taken, in a region in southeast Sweden, to implement the use of video conferencing in the discharge planning session. This actual implementation process concerning the use of the video conferencing system in discharge planning sessions, has initially been evaluated on the basis of a framework (Hofflander et al., 2015) developed by Nilsen et al. (2010), consisting of various factors that affect the implementation process.

However, when video conferencing is introduced and used in the discharge planning session, the design of a new best practice in everyday work needs to be considered (Hofflander et al., 2013), which is not only about the adoption of a "one-size-fits-all" guideline developed through the lens of evidence-based knowledge (Buikstra et al., 2020). An alternative approach can be that a few individuals at different levels of the organization lead the work of developing context-aware evidence-based practice (Dryden-Palmer et al., 2020). Studies have highlighted that applying standards and clear policies (Mennuni et al., 2017), and evidence-based interventions inspired by best practice guidelines in the discharge planning sessions, can provide better outcome for patients after discharge from hospital (Lobchuk et al., 2021). Enabling interdisciplinary communication between healthcare professionals (Miravitlles et al., 2023) and supporting coordination across various healthcare parties linked to discharge planning sessions, also influences the outcomes for the patient's further care and wellbeing (Flink & Ekstedt, 2017). This need of interdisciplinary, inter professional and inter organizational communication in conjunction with discharge planning sessions is underlined by the fact that social workers and hospital nurses usually focus on the immediate discharge needs rather than on long-term goals and plans for the patient (Gane et al., 2022). Additionally, hospital-based nurses who have not practiced in homecare find it difficult to anticipate patients' needs during the transition from hospital to home and thereafter (Davis et al., 2012). When discharge planning sessions fail, this results in a bad start-up for the patient's further care at home, which in turn often leads to readmission to hospital (King et al., 2023). To improve the discharge planning session using videoconferencing there is need for education in discharge-planning, such as communication and documentation (Roodbeen et al., 2020). The complexity of the discharge planning process, addressing social, cultural, organizational and technological perspectives, highlights the need for more cooperation between the different healthcare professions involved (Krook et al., 2020) as well as the need for enhanced adoption of information and communication technologies as a means of achieving more effective information sharing and communication between different healthcare professionals (Wong et al., 2023). This complexity could increase even more when video conferencing sets out to be a new standard for everyday work practice in discharge planning.

2. AIM

The aim of this study was to investigate involved professionals' perceptions about challenges concerning the design of a new best practice, when video conferencing is implemented in the discharge planning sessions in collaboration between multiple different healthcare professionals in hospital and in homecare.

3. METHODS

This study has a Participatory Action Research (PAR) approach, with in total thirteen professionals working in hospital and in homecare that were involved in discharge planning [Table 1]. All the participants were working either in the hospital or in the homecare sector in the Municipality. Participants were chosen to be part of the research based on having a role in discharge planning as well as being familiar with the use of video conferencing in discharge planning.

Table 1. Compilation of participants in the workshops

Professional	Workplace	Workshop session participation
Nurse A	Hospital	1-5
Nurse B	Hospital	1
Nurse C	Hospital	1
First line manager A	Hospital	1
First line manager B	Hospital	1
First line manager C	Hospital	1
Occupational therapist A	Hospital	2-5
Physiotherapist A	Hospital	2-5
Nurse D	Homecare	1-5
Occupational therapist B	Homecare	1-5
First line manager D	Homecare	1
Physiotherapist B	Homecare	2-5
Social worker A	Homecare	2-5

PAR is a systematic, participatory approach used in this case to enable professionals to extend the understanding of problems or issues regarding discharge planning using video conferencing, as well as to formulate actions that are directed towards the resolution of those problems or issues (Stringer & Genat, 2004). PAR is also an approach to develop research and knowledge - rather than simply a research method - where practitioners and researchers work systematically together, with the aim of exploring issues that directly concern practice. The methodology is based on a conviction of an inherent equality, where the knowledge and experience of the different participants is equally valuable (Stringer, 1999). Traditionally, research is seen as an activity performed by people from different research institutes, with research as part of the profession. However, collaboration between researchers and practitioners in the domain being focused in the research is a way of closing the gap between research and practice (Latour & Woolgar, 1986). All formulations of PAR have in common the idea that research and action should be done 'with' people and not 'on' or 'for' people (Heron & Reason, 2006).

In this study, data was collected through workshop sessions where participants and one of the researchers (MH) got together for in all five sessions. The role of the researcher was to lead the workshop sessions and to facilitate the process by participating in, as well as offering support during, the different phases - look, think and act phases - in PAR (Stringer & Genat, 2004). The looking phase involves gathering of relevant information and defining the research question; the thinking phase involves exploration of the information, together with analyzing and theorization; finally, the acting phase involves planning of the desired change and of how to implement and evaluate it (Stringer & Genat, 2004). By collaborating with the workshop participants in both gathering of the data, and in the analysis phase, the intention was to enable reflection together on the design of a new best practice, using video conferencing, in particular. In PAR, data collection and data analysis go hand in hand during the entire process and is seen as meaningful for the healthcare professionals who were involved in the study as well as for the researchers. Discussions and further analysis of the data were also carried out by the authors between the workshop sessions, to allow deeper issues to surface and be discussed with the workshop participants in the upcoming workshop session.

Ethical considerations

The participants gave written voluntary and informed consent after receiving information about the study. Participants were guaranteed anonymity and the possibility to conclude participation at any time. The authors had a dialogue with the Ethic committee in the Southeast part of Sweden about the study and permission was thereafter given.

4. RESULTS

At the first workshop session, the *looking phase*, first-line managers and discharge planning coordinators working in hospital and in homecare, with an expert role in discharge planning, got together with the purpose of discussing and define a relevant research question to address in the next step of the research.

The participants discussed and agreed that representatives from all the different professionals that participate in discharge planning sessions ought to take part in this kind of work, to collaborate and thus create a more comprehensive and shared view of how the discharge planning sessions ought to be developed. The looking phase resulted in the research question: How can a new work practice be designed, to enable well-functioning discharge planning using video conferencing in discharge planning sessions?

The participants of the first workshop session concluded that the following workshop composition ought to be multi-professional and include participants from every contributing group of professionals, with representatives from both hospital and homecare, with the addition of a social worker from the municipality. This resulted in a reconstruction of the group, where three of the participants from the first workshop continued to be a part of the following workshop group. Those three were one nurse working in hospital, one nurse and one occupational therapist working in homecare. The new participants who joined the group were chosen based on experience and knowledge about discharge planning.

The *looking phase* now shifted over to the next phase, *the thinking phase*, which consisted of three workshops. The new participants in the group were informed by the others and by the group leader about the research question that had been decided on and what it was based on. After the information about the previous workshop had been shared in the new group, the participants started to discuss and reflect on challenges concerning how to design a new best practice, to enable well-functioning discharge planning using video conferencing in discharge planning sessions. This was thus based on the discussions during the looking phase workshop, but also included new contributions from the participants. The group leader took notes during the session and encouraged the participants to share perceptions during the workshop. In the second *thinking phase* workshop, the participants were invited individually, on separate Post-it notes, write down thoughts on how a new work practice ought to be designed, to enable well-functioning discharge planning using video conferencing [Table 2].

Table 2. Examples of Post-it notes during the second thinking phase workshop

Post-it notes
Someone has to lead the session
Well prepared participants are a necessity
Understanding about different roles
Does everybody need to participate every time?
Audio and video = IT needs to work
In what kind of forum can we discuss problems?
Coordinators are needed
Understanding of the whole picture
Understanding of the different roles
What information ought to be written in the system before the session?
Meeting structure
Double time documentation?
What are the expectations concerning the information I share?

The notes were then presented and pasted on the wall by the participants, to allow all workshop members to take part of each other's notes and in the analysis. The participants then discussed and reflected on the content through reflective dialogues, facilitated by the participating researcher and started to cluster the Post-it notes into common themes. The researcher asked naïve questions about issues that the workshop members possibly took for granted, to invite the participants to be questioning the perceptions of the current best practice in discharge planning. After these discussions and critical questions among the workshop members, the Post-it notes were sorted to construct main categories and subcategories.

At the following workshop, the third in the thinking phase, the group leader together with the coauthors, had made a compilation of the discussions and the sorting of the Post-it notes from the previous workshop as a starting point for the continued work. This session was used to review the results from the previous workshop, allowing the participants to reflect and make desired corrections, and discuss the content of the main categories and subcategories where the group leader took notes and put additional questions when necessary to support the analysis process. The workshop participants came to conclusions about what was needed to design a new best practice using video conferencing in the discharge planning sessions. The identified needs could be seen as a cohesive system consisting of two main categories, with underlying subcategories [Table 3].

Table 3. Main categories and subcategories

Need of knowledge and competence	Need of support
Comprehension of the discharge planning process	Support and understanding from managers
Comprehension of the information supplying system	Guidelines elaborated by involved professionals
Comprehension of the wanted information from colleagues	Ability to discuss with colleagues
Comprehension of other professionals' roles in the process	Trust in the video conferencing system

4.1 Need of Knowledge and Competence

The first main category, *need of knowledge and competence*, encompasses the professionals' perceptions of what they need in an interpersonal and inter-professional way, based on different knowledge and competence levels, to design a new best practice using video conferencing in discharge planning. The overall perception was that there was both a lack of knowledge and understanding about the different professionals' roles in discharge planning sessions, and a lack of understanding about what kind of competence the different professionals could contribute with to the process when designing a new best practice. This was stated to be the case not only in discharge planning using video conferencing, but in discharge planning sessions overall.

Comprehension of the discharge planning process

The participants discussed the overall understanding of the discharge planning process and the importance of all involved professionals being aware of the purpose of the comprehensive discharge planning process. The word "comprehensive" seems to disappear when professionals talk about the process in everyday practice. The discharge planning session is rather perceived as something that just has to be done, with short notice and without any possible reflection on when and where the discharge planning session should take place and how the use of video conferencing as a communication tool could enhance the comprehension of the process.

Comprehension of the information supplying system

The workshop participants expressed the importance of the reliability, functionality and usability of the supportive IT systems. This concerns the information supplying system, used to transmit data between hospital, homecare and social welfare, as well as the video conferencing system. The information supplying system is seldom used in its full potential as this information is narrated during the discharge planning session by the professionals from hospital. The design of a new best practice must take into consideration the establishing of a routine for data to be read by involved professionals before the discharge planning session takes place.

Comprehension of the wanted information from colleagues

The participants discussed what kind of information the discharge planning should include between the involved professionals about the patient's further care after discharge. There is no effective agreement or commitment between involved professionals working in hospital and in homecare about what information that would be valuable to transmit. The workshop participants shared the perception that each professional group needs to determine what kind of information that is of importance to be transmitted throughout the whole discharge planning process, to enable the design of a new best practice.

Comprehension of other professionals' roles in the process

The workshop participants expressed that there was a lack of comprehension about the different roles that professions play in the discharge planning process. Professionals working in hospital experience little knowledge about the work environment and work situation in homecare and vice-versa. Despite this, professionals were expected to share information to take well-grounded decisions concerning the continuing care and wellbeing of the patient who was being discharged.

4.2 Need of Support

The other main category, need of support, encompasses the professionals' perceptions of what was needed in the way of support, to design a new best practice using video conferencing in discharge planning. The overall perception of the participants was the need of support and understanding from managers in handling the discharge planning process, as well as the need of reliable support from the IT department concerning the functions of the video conferencing system. This main category was expressed as of central importance not only in discharge planning using video conferencing, but in discharge planning sessions in general.

Support and understanding from managers

The participants discussed the perceived absence of definitions and clarity from managers about what the discharge planning sessions, using video conferencing, should contain. There is a perceived need of understanding from managers about the increased complexity that surrounds the process due to short length of stay in hospital and the fact that patients leaving hospital are in poor condition needing many different arrangements. The calls for participation in discharge planning are sent with short notice, which should be considered when creating a new best practice using video conferencing in discharge planning sessions.

Guidelines elaborated by involved professionals

The workshop participants expressed that the common rules and forms of legislation that regulate the overall discharge planning process mainly regulate the cost allocation between involved stakeholders. The participants expressed the need for involved professionals to collaborate and create a guideline that is correct, based on what is decided upon to be the most important data to transmit before, during and after the discharge planning session takes place. This would mean that only what is deemed as necessary and relevant information for the discharge planning process is transmitted in the information supplying system.

Ability to discuss with colleagues

The participants discussed the need off common arenas, being able to meet and discuss if something after all goes wrong in the discharge planning process. The only time a meeting between involved professionals is held at present, is when there are severe problems. The professionals expressed the need off another, alternative kind of meeting, to enable discussions, negotiations and agreements in a collaborative way. Also, the fact that the discharge planning process is changing over time indicates the need for inter-professional meetings, where representatives participate, with a focus on the overall discharge planning process using video conferencing.

Trust in the video conferencing system

The workshop participants expressed the need of reliability of the video conferencing system to work as intended, to make this a well-functioning way of doing the work. Feelings of uncertainty about the video conferencing system could influence the discharge planning session in a negative way. The participants stated that the video conferencing system creates anxiety among the professionals, as it sometimes is unreliable in its functionality. If a new best practice using video conferencing in the discharge planning session should be designed and successfully implemented, the system itself must be perceived as reliable and well-functioning.

In the final, fifth workshop, which shifted from the *thinking phase* into the *acting phase*, the participants summarized the results from the earlier workshops. The participants had no formal assignment to plan or implement the desired changes at this time, therefor they handed the suggested changes over to the managers in charge for further action.

5. DISCUSSION

This study showed that there is a lack of knowledge and understanding about what specific competence the different professionals could contribute with to the discharge planning process and to designing a new best practice using video conferencing in the discharge planning sessions. Hofflander et al. (2013) and Gane et al. (2022) describe in studies that professionals experienced need for improvement in both communication and understanding between professionals working in hospitals and in homecare in order to develop the discharge planning process. This need for improvement in both communication and understanding between professionals was also described by the participants in this study as lack of comprehension about the different roles that each professional plays in the discharge planning process. The participants expressed that professionals working in hospital had little knowledge about the workplace circumstances in homecare and vice-versa. This unclear understanding of each other's competencies, work practices, work situations and roles is stated by Lokatt et al. (2023) as interprofessional boundaries. Krook et al. (2020) describe similar findings as uncertainty and inequality between different parties' responsibility within the discharge planning process, which creates frustration and troubled feelings among the professionals.

The results of this study also show that involved professionals clearly perceive the need to collaborate and create a standardized guideline to follow, based on what is decided to be the most important information that needs to be transmitted before, during and after the discharge planning session takes place. This would enable only what is perceived as necessary and relevant information is transmitted in the information supplying system, which in turn would enable and encourage involved professionals to read the information beforehand and thus be better prepared. Similarly, Gane et al. (2022) and Mennuni et al. (2017) describe the perceived need to apply standards and clear policies and interventions inspired by best practice guidelines.

The results further indicate a need for support and trust in the video conferencing system. The participants stated that the video conferencing system created anxiety among the participating professionals, as it was unreliable in its functions. If a new best practice using video conferencing in the discharge planning session is to be designed, the video conferencing system itself needs to be reliable. This need of a reliable and well-functioning video conferencing system to be used in discharge planning, has been stated in earlier research by Hedqvist et al. (2023), which is in accordance with the results in this study.

Discussing professionals' perceptions of how to design a new best practice using video conferencing in discharge planning, it is not the new technology *per se* that is in the foreground in the discussions, but rather the work system and the work practices into which the video conferencing is being introduced and implemented. Nor is the existing information system, discussed as a serious problem *per se*; rather it is how it is used or not used, and how it is understood or not understood as a support in and for practice, that surfaces as obstructive to good practice in discharge planning. What needs redesigning from within, it seems, is the socio-technical system (Kuutti & Bannon, 2014) with a focus on the activity of discharge planning sessions and the emergent practices of using video conferencing in this context. And what the participants in this study underlined was the lack of a shared arena for ongoing discussions, negotiations and agreements concerning the cross-organizational activity of discharge planning sessions. The implementation of technology for supporting information and communication processes has increased during recent years, which has created a growing need for understanding how social factors relate to technology (Nilsson, 2014), as well as understanding that using technology cannot compensate for nonfunctioning working routines (Nilsson & Fagerström, 2018). According to Mackenzie & Wajcman (1985) the shaping of these kinds of systems, in what is called the "Social Shaping of Technology" ought to be understood by studying processes and practices of design, development and use of technology, and including political, social and cultural factors in such studies, in contrast to the more traditional approaches and methods of studying technology in society, which focus on the consequences of technological changes.

Methodological considerations

Pragmatic validity is essential in the methodology of PAR. To develop new knowledge which is meaningful and manageable in the work practice and context, professionals need to participate from the very beginning of the process. Ontologically and epistemologically, the assumption of PAR is according to Heron and Reason (2006) that there is a reality, but people interpret this reality differently. By letting the workshop members discuss and reflect on different experiences and knowledge, the discharge planning sessions could be seen and analyzed in a new way. Whether participation in this study will lead to change in everyday work in discharge planning depends on whether the managers in charge are striving towards carrying through the suggested changes. Participatory validity is another aspect which is central in PAR according to Stringer and Genat (2004), who state that a rigorous study requires prolonged engagement and trust. It is difficult to reflect on work practice, since everyday reality often is taken for granted. It requires the researcher to establish relationships and trust to make participants feel secure and have the courage to describe thoughts and perceptions and not what the participants think the researcher wishes to hear. In this research project, the participants created the research question, produced data by telling stories about discharge planning sessions and analyzed the data. This cyclic process provided the participants with an expanded understanding about the discharge panning sessions in general as well as the use of video conferencing in discharge planning in particular. Through continuous dialogues, the participants confirmed the findings by recognizing those in the everyday practice, which is what according to Polkinghorne (2005) is validation of claims.

6. CONCLUSION

Based on the results from this study, it might be useful for the professionals to gain more and deeper understanding of each other's everyday work, and that it would be helpful to develop a corporate and standardized guideline to support the staff in developing new work practices for making the discharge planning session work out well using video conferencing in the planning session. Discharge planning using video conferencing with focus on a short meeting ought to enable fast decisions about appropriate immediate further care, followed by early meet-up by homecare professionals to make assessments and take decisions depending on patients' needs in a more long-term objective.

Further research

In the surges after the Covid-19 pandemic it could be of even greater interest to investigate how video conferencing has affected everyday work practice.

REFERENCES

Buikstra, E., Strivens, E., & Clay-Williams, R. (2020). Understanding variability in discharge planning processes for the older person. *Safety Science*, *121*, 137-146.

Davis, M. M., Devoe, M., Kansagara, D., Nicolaidis, C., & Englander, H. (2012). "Did I do as best as the system would let me?" Healthcare professional views on hospital to home care transitions. *Journal of general internal medicine*, *27*, 1649-1656.

Dryden-Palmer, K. D., Parshuram, C. S., & Berta, W. B. (2020). Context, complexity and process in the implementation of evidence-based innovation: a realist informed review. *Bmc Health Services Research*, *20*(1), 81.

Flink, M., & Ekstedt, M. (2017). Planning for the Discharge, not for Patient Self-Management at Home – An Observational and Interview Study of Hospital Discharge. *International journal of integrated care*.

Gane, E. M., Schoeb, V., Cornwell, P., Cooray, C. R., Cowie, B., & Comans, T. A. (2022). Discharge planning of older persons from hospital: comparison of observed practice to recommended best practice. Healthcare,

Hayajneh, A. A., Hweidi, I. M., & Abu Dieh, M. W. (2020). Nurses' knowledge, perception and practice toward discharge planning in acute care settings: A systematic review. *Nursing Open*, *7*(5), 1313-1320.

Hedqvist, A.-T., Svensson, A., & Larsson, L. G. (2023). Nurses' experiences of person-centred care planning using video-conferencing. *Nursing Open*, *10*(3), 1879-1888.

Heron, J., & Reason, P. (2006). The practice of co-operative inquiry: Research 'with'rather than 'on'people. *Handbook of action research*, 144-154.

Hofflander, M., Nilsson, L., Eriksén, S., & Borg, C. (2013). Discharge planning: Narrated by nursing staff in primary healthcare and their concerns about using video conferencing in the planning session – An interview study. *Journal of Nursing Education and Practice*, *3*(1), 88-98.

Hofflander, M., Nilsson, L., Eriksén, S., & Borg, C. (2015). Framing the implementation process of video conferencing in discharge planning – according to staff experience. *Informatics for Health and Social Care*, *0*(0), 1-18.

King, L., Harrington, A., Nicholls, S., Thornton, K., & Tanner, E. (2023). Towards reduction of preventable hospital readmission: Older people and family members' views on planned self-management of care at home. *Journal of Clinical Nursing*, *32*(15-16), 4599-4613.

Krook, M., Iwarzon, M., & Siouta, E. (2020). The discharge process—from a patient's perspective. *SAGE Open Nursing*, *6*, 2377960819900707.

Kuutti, K., & Bannon, L. J. (2014). *The turn to practice in HCI: towards a research agenda* CHI 2014, Toronto, Canada.

Latour, B., & Woolgar, S. (1986). *Laboratory Life: The Construction of Scientific Facts* (2 nd ed.). University Press.

Lobchuk, M., Bell, A., Hoplock, L., & Lemoine, J. (2021). Interprofessional discharge team communication and empathy in discharge planning activities: A narrative review. *Journal of Interprofessional Education & Practice*, *23*, 100393.

Lokatt, E., Holgersson, C., Lindgren, M., Packendorff, J., & Hagander, L. (2023). An interprofessional perspective on healthcare work: physicians and nurses co-constructing identities and spaces of action. *Journal of Management & Organization*, *29*(6), 1103-1119.

Mackenzie, D., & Wajcman, J. (1985). The Social Shaping of Technology: How the Refrigerator got its hum. *Milton Keynes, Open University Press.*

Mennuni, M., Gulizia, M. M., Alunni, G., Francesco Amico, A., Maria Bovenzi, F., Caporale, R., Colivicchi, F., Di Lenarda, A., Di Tano, G., & Egman, S. (2017). ANMCO position paper: hospital discharge planning: recommendations and standards. *European Heart Journal Supplements*, *19*(suppl_D), D244-D255.

Miravitlles, M., Bhutani, M., Hurst, J. R., Franssen, F. M., van Boven, J. F., Khoo, E. M., Zhang, J., Brunton, S., Stolz, D., & Winders, T. (2023). Implementing an evidence-based COPD hospital discharge protocol: a narrative review and expert recommendations. *Advances in therapy*, *40*(10), 4236-4263.

Nilsen, P., Roback, K., & Krevers, B. (2010). Förklaringsfaktorer för implementeringsutfall - ett ramverk [Implementation, theory and application in health and welfare]. In P. Nilsen (Ed.), *Implementering Teori och tillämpning inom hälso- och sjukvård* (1:st ed., pp. 71-87). Studentlitteratur.

Nilsson, L. (2014). *Social Challenges when Implementing Information Systems in a Swedish Healthcare Organization* (Publication Number 2014:14) Blekinge Institute of Technology]. Karlskrona.

Nilsson, L., & Fagerström, C. (2018). Decision-makers and mediators in a home healthcare digitisation process: nurses' experiences of implementation and use of a decision support system. *Contemporary nurse*, *54*(4-5), 511-521.

Polkinghorne, D. E. (2005). Language and meaning: Data collection in qualitative research. *Journal of Counseling Psychology*, *52*(2), 137-145.

Roodbeen, R., Vreke, A., Boland, G., Rademakers, J., van den Muijsenbergh, M., Noordman, J., & van Dulmen, S. (2020). Communication and shared decision-making with patients with limited health literacy; helpful strategies, barriers and suggestions for improvement reported by hospital-based palliative care providers. *PloS one*, *15*(6), e0234926.

Stringer, E. (1999). *Action Research* (2 ed.). Sage Publications.

Stringer, E., & Genat, W. (2004). *Action Research in Health*. Pearson Education.

Wong, J. H. K., Näswall, K., Pawsey, F., Chase, J. G., & Malinen, S. K. (2023). Adoption of technological innovation in healthcare delivery: a psychological perspective for healthcare decision-makers. *BMJ Innovations*, *9*(4), 240.

SIMULATION OF WI-FI AND TV WHITESPACES TECHNOLOGIES FOR A RURAL CONNECTION TOWARDS COST EVALUATIONS: A NAMIBIAN CASE

Ronald Karon, Nomusa Dlodlo and Alfredo Terzoli
Rhodes University, South Africa

ABSTRACT

Internet connection has the potential to stimulate economic growth in underdeveloped nations; nevertheless, in emerging economies such as Namibia, opportunities for internet access are not evenly distributed. The National Planning Commission of Namibia aimed for 90% broadband access by 2022/2023 as stated in the National broadband Policy. However, over 40% of the country's regions have not yet achieved this goal. The reluctance to establish broadband connections in rural areas is attributable to the high costs faced by telecommunications companies. Moreover, a low Average Revenue per User (ARPU) hampers adequate financing for broadband services in rural areas. Technological alternatives for rural connectivity comprise TV White Space (TVWS) and Wi-Fi. These technologies possess the potential to bridge the digital gap in rural areas by providing affordable broadband connectivity. TVWS is distinguished by its long-range and robust transmission, while Wi-Fi networks are linked to high-speed connections. The problem, however, is that insufficient broadband coverage, including TVWS and Wi-Fi technologies, continues to exist in rural parts of Namibia, attributed to the related telecommunications expenses. This study adopted a positivist research paradigm. For the positivist, the scientific method, in its purest form, is a systematic procedure of experimentation used to examine observations and resolve research questions. The selected paradigm enabled the acquisition of quantitative data through deductive reasoning to address the study's research question. Network simulation experiments were conducted to address the research question of the study. The cost evaluation was based on the network design and coverage predictions for the two simulated networks, TVWS and Wi-Fi. The rural landscape of the Khorixas constituency was identified as the research study area. The TVWS network necessitated three base stations, one situated in each rural community and was hence considered more cost-effective than the Wi-Fi network. Every base station would connect to a fibre optic backhaul network inside the specified research zones. Wi-Fi network simulations indicated the presence of multiple access points, specifically twelve and three, at the healthcare facilities in Fransfontein and Khorixas, respectively, for indoor connectivity.

KEYWORDS

Field Strength, Throughput, Broadband, Telemedicine, Simulation

1. INTRODUCTION

Internet access has the capacity to enhance economic growth in underdeveloped nations, yet, in emerging economies, like Namibia, possibilities for internet access are not equitably dispersed. The National Planning Commission of Namibia has a broadband coverage objective of 90% by 2022/2023 in the National Broadband Policy (MICT, 2022). However, more than 40% of the nation's regions have yet to attain this objective (CRAN, 2022). Consequently, the digital divide persists, especially in rural areas. The sparse population in rural regions significantly complicates and increases the cost of deploying communications infrastructure (Lamola, 2020). The hesitance in the construction of broadband connections in rural regions is related to elevated expenses incurred by telecommunications firms (Lamola, 2020). Furthermore, low Average Revenue per User (ARPU) contributes to the insufficient funding for broadband services in rural regions (Kennedy, et al., 2015). Technology options for rural connectivity include TV White Space (TVWS) and Wi-Fi (Lamola, 2020). These technologies have the capability to bridge the digital divide in rural regions by offering affordable broadband access (Lamola, 2020). TVWS is characterized by long-distance and strong transmission, whereas Wi-Fi networks are associated with fast connections (Lamola, 2020). The problem, however, is that insufficient broadband coverage, including TVWS and Wi-Fi technologies, continues to exist in rural parts of Namibia, attributed to the related telecommunications expenses (Adaptrum, 2018; CRAN, 2022). This study aims to address the research question, “What would TVWS and Wi-Fi networks for cost evaluations look like in a rural Namibian context?”.

2. LITERATURE REVIEW

2.1 Wi-Fi Network

Wi-Fi offers a comparatively economical alternative to the pricey methods of delivering Internet access. The primary drawbacks of Wi-Fi are its limited transmission range and the need for a clear line-of-sight (LOS). Research has been conducted to assess the propagation factors in Wi-Fi to evaluate performance in the presence of obstacles (Lamola, 2020). Propagation studies in both indoor and outdoor scenarios were conducted at a frequency of 2.4 GHz, revealing that Wi-Fi performance diminishes in non-line-of-sight (NLOS) conditions (Lamola, 2020). Further research demonstrated that Wi-Fi exhibits poor performance when obstructed, assessed in the 2.4 GHz and 5 GHz frequencies, which revealed that environmental topography influences radio signal transmission (Lamola, 2020). The overall results indicate that obstacles and environmental features, including vegetation, elevation, and distance, exacerbate route loss and signal attenuation, potentially causing jitter (Lamola, 2020). Other literature experimentally assessed the maximum coverage range of Wi-Fi. This includes studies in Line-of-Sight (LOS) and Non-Line-of-Sight (NLOS) connectivity across various situations. The experimental assessment of Wi-Fi indicated optimal performance, achieving a minimum range of 150 meters under clear line of sight and a maximum range of 225 meters in non-line of sight conditions (Lamola, 2020).

2.2 TVWS Network

Significant interest has emerged about the secondary use of TV bands by using the unoccupied spectrum. Cognitive radio (CR) technology facilitates access to additional licensed television bands, referred to as white spaces (Lamola, 2020). TV Whitespaces (TVWS) are frequencies located between television channels in the Very High Frequency (VHF) and Ultra High Frequency (UHF) ranges (Ifeoluwa, et al., 2015). The Meraka Institute in South Africa provides evidence of ample spectrum in rural regions (Lamola, 2020). Parameters like throughput, latency, and signal-to-noise ratio (SNR) are often examined to assess the suitability of each channel for usage. Research conducted in Malawi indicated that observed throughput and latency are influenced by the distance from the present node to the base station (Lamola, 2020). The measurements obtained across a 7.5 km connection indicate an average SNR of 24.7 dB, a data throughput of 420 kbps, and a latency of 118 ms (Lamola, 2020). The outcomes are followed by an evaluation of the network's performance, whereby the assessments are conducted at a remote secondary school in Malawi, verifying a coverage range of 7.5 km and yielding a maximum throughput of 2 Mbps (Lamola, 2020).

2.3 Network Simulation

Network simulations are widely used for performance assessment in communication systems engineering. It is extensively used for the advancement of novel communication architectures and network protocols. A simulator is software that replicates the behavior of real-world components and serves as a research and development instrument (Silmi, et al., 2020). Various components of the system are represented based on the simulator's intended use. Network simulations save financial resources and time by obviating the need for a test bed, facilitating controlled experimentation with innovative networking protocols, and offering a replicable experimental setting (Silmi, et al., 2020). Research on network simulations raises issues of trustworthiness and scalability (Weingartner, et al., 2009). Moreover, robust network simulations such as NS3 may encounter challenges regarding credibility and scalability (Rampfl, et al., 2013). However, simulation software is progressively enhanced by new developments such as the introduction of Radio Planner 3.0. The software's indented use and the methods for bias mitigation are thus crucial factors. Network simulations enhance study validity by assessing network situations prior to deployment, enabling users to choose permissible experiments, and facilitating comparisons of protocol designs and alterations in network traffic (Heidemann, et al., 2001). Network simulations may accurately forecast real-world outcomes by analyzing dynamic processes on actual networks (Pan, et al., 2012). Simulations delineate the precision trade-offs between bias reduction and accuracy in experimental design and analysis (Eckles, et al., 2014). While real-world experiments are significant, they may be challenging to replicate due to certain networking phenomena, such as wireless radio interference (Silmi, et al., 2020).

2.4 Telemedicine

Telemedicine has become a crucial tool globally for enhancing patient monitoring, mitigating disease transmission, and enabling prompt diagnosis and treatment of the unwell, as seen during the COVID-19 pandemic (Omboni, et al., 2022). Frequent hospital visits may be costly, especially in rural regions, owing to transportation expenses. During the Covid-19 pandemic, while physical contact poses risks, individuals choose telemedicine (Haleem, et al., 2021). Telemedicine services, using video conferencing or other virtual technologies, might effectively diminish the need for medical visits (Haleem, et al., 2021). Telehealth refers to the use of technology to provide healthcare services remotely, including monitoring, triage, diagnosis, treatment, follow-up care, and rehabilitation (Omboni, et al., 2022). Telemedicine may improve patient care, professional practice, and service organization in rural and remote areas (Haleem, et al., 2021; Omboni, et al., 2022). Telemedicine restrictions include unreliable internet connections, difficulties in implementing video translation services, insufficient access to smart devices, and erratic internet availability. The quality of video conferencing using 3G mobile data services was found to be substandard compared to broadband fibre-based solutions. It is crucial to carefully choose and assess telehealth systems before adoption to ensure proper operation (Benjamin, et al., 2021).

3. RELATED WORK

Comparable research was conducted in South Africa in 2020, concentrating on the performance analysis of Wi-Fi and TVWS connections, specifically Wi-Fi in the 5GHz frequency band and TVWS in the UHF, 530-600 MHz frequency bands (Lamola, 2020). This South African investigation used custom-built White Space Mesh Nodes (WSMN) outfitted with Wi-Fi and TV White Space radio interference cards. The research demonstrated that while TVWS had improved propagation characteristics, its performance was inferior to Wi-Fi in scenarios with a clear line of sight and shorter distances. Although the research provided a comprehensive comparison of the performance of the two technologies, the experimental configurations were limited to small lengths of under 300 meters. Furthermore, whereas the studies on Wi-Fi and TVWS connectivity for the South African research included situations like buildings and trees (urban areas), rural settings were excluded. This research paper addressed these exclusions, concentrating on a rural context with a coverage radius of around 20 square kilometers. The performance indications for this research study report were predicated on connections capable of sufficiently supporting video streaming for healthcare services. Finally, cost evaluations based on the network designs were included in this study. Furthermore, other TVWS trial projects were conducted in Africa, namely in Kenya, Nigeria, and Namibia, exhibiting diverse network throughputs (Bakare, et al., 2022). The differing throughputs were based upon various additional factors, including terrain characteristics. The biggest experiment in Africa was done in northern Namibia, covering an area of 9,424 square kilometers, with a channel capacity of up to 10 Mbps (Bakare, et al., 2022). The distinguishing factor for this research paper is the chosen study area. This paper focused on the Khorixas constituency, characterized by its unique terrain elements such as mountainous, in contrast to the mostly flat environment of northern Namibia. The various terrain factors lead to distinct propagation or performance outcomes. In support, Grajek (2024), asserts the need for research specific to regions or countries.

4. RESEARCH METHODOLOGY

4.1 Research Paradigm

The research paradigm selected for this study was a positivist paradigm. A research paradigm signifies the shared perspectives and comprehensions among scientists about their methodology for addressing problems. The positivist paradigm defines a research perspective grounded on the scientific method (Kivunja & Kuyini, 2017). The Positivist paradigm advocates for quantitative research methodologies as essential for researchers to precisely delineate the parameters and coefficients of the gathered, processed, and interpreted data, thereby clarifying the connections embedded within the examined data. For the positivist, the scientific method, in its most unadulterated form, is a systematic procedure of experimentation used to examine observations and resolve research questions (Kivunja & Kuyini, 2017). The chosen paradigm facilitated the collection of quantitative data, using deductive reasoning in addressing the research question of the study. Network simulation experiments were performed to answer the research question of the study. The network simulations facilitated the mapping of necessary infrastructure. The Khorixas constituency's rural environment was designated as the research study area. The data obtained from the simulations facilitated the generation of quantifiable cost efficiency reports.

4.2 Data Analysis

Simulations of TVWS and Wi-Fi broadband networks were performed. The simulations provided the network specifications and required infrastructure. The first phase was the assessment of the research area and network coverage. Secondly, network specifications for the broadband technologies, TVWS and Wi-Fi, were obtained by propagation modelling and coverage simulations using Indoor RadioPlanner 2.0 and RadioPlanner 3.0 software. The third phase included doing a cost assessment based on the network architecture derived from the network designs. Technical network design and subsequent cost evaluations were performed systematically and objectively using quantitative methods.

5. NETWORK DESIGN, SIMULATIONS AND COST EVALUATION

5.1 Network Design

The network design, simulations, and cost assessment pertinent to the study's research question was discussed in this section. This study performed simulations in a remote Khorixas constituency, in the Kunene region. The study used network design and simulations for cost evaluations. Network design and simulations included requirements and configuration parameters. The broadband network design's equipment count and simulation outcomes determined cost evaluations. The Kunene region has the lowest internet penetration in the nation (CRAN, 2022). Network simulations were conducted in Fransfontein, Bampos, and Khorixas rural areas. Broadband consumers included public healthcare institutions. Fransfontein had one public clinic and Khorixas one public hospital. Bampos had no public healthcare. This study focused on rural healthcare as the main client. Other broadband clients not considered for this study were residents, shops and other public institutions like police stations and schools. Wi-Fi network simulations were done using Indoor RadioPlanner 2.0 and TVWS connections with RadioPlanner 3.0. Simulation parameters using Khorixas constituency study area coverage, digital elevation or topography data, and clutter (land use or coverage) data were used. These data allowed exact propagation calculations between base stations and APs, allowing for geographical factors and clutter that affect propagation and cause propagation losses. Custom Digital Terrain Models (DTMs) may be used in RadioPlanner 3.0. This study used a custom DTM since RadioPlanner's default DTM inadequately covered Africa. SRTM from USGS EarthExplorer was used to create the DTM. The research region was plotted using EarthExplorer. Telemedicine, including video connections, was explored since the study's focal customers were healthcare providers. Best-performing network components for telemedicine were studied. For video conference calls, telemedicine needs reliable broadband networks with optimal bandwidth throughput. Internet rates of 5 Mbps or above were classified as optimal speed for High-Definition (HD) video connections

(Coleman, 2020). TVWS used 470-694 MHz spectrum and Wi-Fi 2.4GHz with three non-interference channels of 20MHz. Fibre optic backbone network has POPs in the Khorixas constituency study area. During network node design, many locations were evaluated. These locations underwent propagation and coverage simulations, resulting in many design iterations and access network simulations using RadioPlanner 3.0 and Indoor RadioPlanner,2.0, to optimize network configuration and topology to reduce costs. The next section illustrates TVWS and Wi-Fi design variations.

5.2 Network Simulations

In the TVWS network, over several iterations, the Best Server map shows the transmitter or base station delivering the most robust received signal at each point. The required service threshold for determining the Best Server was a minimum field strength, calculated during the configuration of transmitter settings. The minimum field strength was determined to be 54 dBuV/m. Figure 1 depicts the coverage of the best server downlink for TVWS connections throughout the research locations. Each research area (Fransfontein, Bampos, and Khorixas) had a minimum of one transmitter or base station to provide effective TVWS wireless connectivity. The radio signal strength at reception was 60 dBuV/m and higher. Fibre optic backbone network connection points (POPs) are located in Fransfontein and Khorixas.

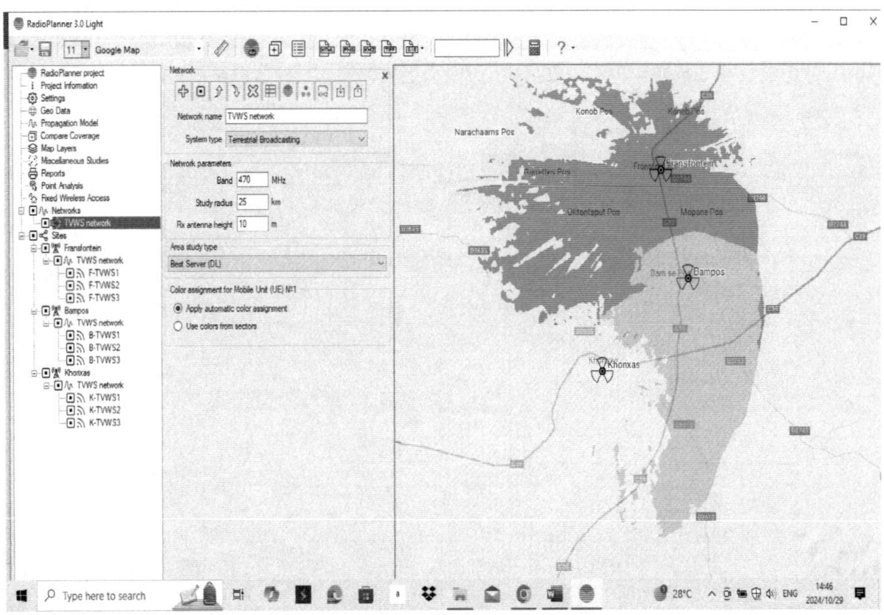

Figure 1. TVWS best server downlink

Following several iterations for the Wi-Fi network at Khorixas, the indoor Wi-Fi network design for a healthcare customer was a hospital, modelled in Figure 2. The floor design is a working prototype and does not precisely represent the real hospital layout in Khorixas. The sample floor layout illustrates the use of twelve access points for coverage. The highest downlink throughput at Khorixas hospital ranged from 98 Mbps to 123 Mbps, with minimum throughputs between 12 Mbps and 24 Mbps. The highest uplink throughput ranged from 60 Mbps to 65 Mbps, with minimum throughputs between 6 Mbps and 19 Mbps.

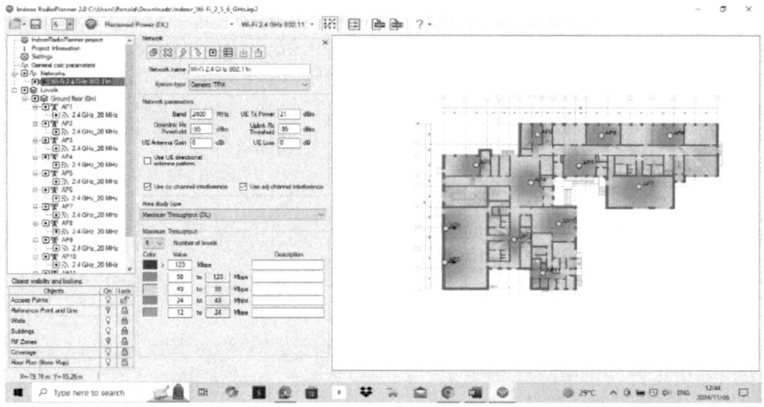

Figure 2. Wi-Fi throughput downlink and uplink for Khorixas hospital

The healthcare client for Fransfontein was a clinic. It is a single structure situated to the west of the rural settlement. Figure 3 illustrates an example floor plan that closely resembles the design and dimensions of the real structure. The maximum downlink throughput is defined as ranging from 98 Mbps to 123 Mbps, with lesser throughputs between 12 Mbps and 24 Mbps. The maximum uplink throughput is indicated as 60 Mbps to 65 Mbps, with lesser throughputs ranging from 6 Mbps to 19 Mbps. Bampos lacked a healthcare facility.

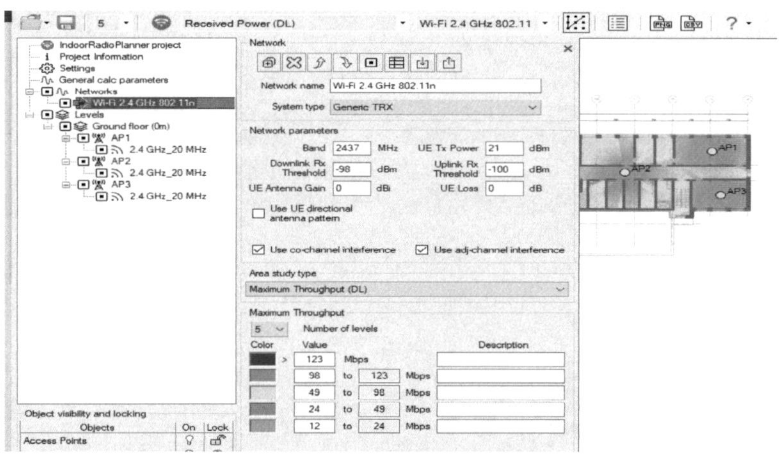

Figure 3. Wi-Fi throughput downlink and uplink for Fransfontein clinic

The coverage predictions for both the hospital and clinic exhibited comparable power downlinks, uplinks, and throughputs. The variation lies in the quantity of access points necessary for adequate coverage, dependent upon the dimensions of the buildings. Predictions for outdoor Wi-Fi coverage in the chosen study area were omitted from this research study. The Indoor RadioPlanner 2.0 user guide states that outside coverage forecast is restricted to a 2 square kilometer range.

5.3 Cost Evaluations

The cost evaluation was predicated on the network design and coverage predictions for the two simulated networks, TVWS and Wi-Fi. The TVWS network required three base stations, one located in each rural community. Each base station would link to a fibre optic backhaul network inside the designated research areas. Wi-Fi network simulations showed several access points at the healthcare institutions in Fransfontein and Khorixas for indoor connectivity. The networks in the study areas are interconnected by the fibre optic network.

6. FINDINGS AND DISCUSSIONS

From the network design and simulations for the TVWS network, a minimum field strength of 54 dBuV/m was calculated from transmission antenna. The simulation calculations of the TVWS network in the research study area revealed that the radio signal strength at reception was 60 dBuV/m or above, exceeding the minimal threshold of 54 dBuV/m. Adequate coverage and performance by the TVWS network was thus attained in the simulations. Long-distance propagation with robust signal penetration, as indicated in the literature, was corroborated by the results of the performed TVWS simulations (Lamola, 2020). The network design shown in Figure 1 was selected as the optimal design from the network iterations. Simulation calculations for the Wi-Fi network showed maximum downlink throughput between 12 Mbps and 123 Mbps, and maximum uplink throughput between 6 Mbps and 65 Mbps. Wi-Fi networks is indicated to provide high-speed throughput, however, possess a limited transmission range and need a clear line-of-sight (LOS), as corroborated in the literature (Lamola, 2020). Nonetheless, sufficient coverage was achieved for the healthcare institutions using the selected designs. Moreover, the chosen TVWS and Wi-Fi network configurations were adequate for the study's sites, since broadband speeds in Namibia were established at 2 Mbps by CRAN (CRAN, 2022). Furthermore, telemedicine services for remote areas would be adequately supported by the networks, as the necessary speeds for high-definition videos were shown to be a minimum of 5 Mbps (Coleman, 2020). Finally, the cost evaluation was based on the required equipment for the two networks as per the network designs. The designs indicated that the TVWS network was more cost-effective than the Wi-Fi network. TVWS required a total of three base stations to provide coverage for the three research areas: Fransfontein, Bampos, and Khorixas. Whereas the Wi-Fi network necessitated 12 access points for Khorixas Hospital and three access points for Fransfontein Clinic to provide optimal indoor coverage. Bampos had no healthcare facility. Moreover, the performance of TVWS demonstrated a greater coverage radius in comparison to Wi-Fi. These results addressed the study's research question: "What would TVWS and Wi-Fi networks for cost evaluations look like in a rural Namibian context?".

7. SIGNIFICANCE OF THE RESEARCH

This research paper aimed to evaluate the cost-effectiveness of TVWS and Wi-Fi technologies. The purpose of the cost evaluations was to provide findings about cost indications based on the necessary equipment derived from the network designs and simulations. The evaluation report may serve as a mechanism to highlight cost efficiency matters associated with the adoption of cost-efficient broadband technologies in rural healthcare connections and perhaps to substantiate the advantages attributed to TVWS in comparison to Wi-Fi technologies. The results from this research could assist multiple stakeholders, including the Ministry of Information and Communication Technology (MICT), public healthcare entities, and telecommunications companies, in making informed decisions about investments and the adoption of TVWS technologies in rural regions of the country. This research contributed to addressing the digital divide about inadequate internet connectivity in rural locations, particularly for healthcare services, by offering cost evaluations using network designs and simulations.

The contributions of this research would yield: 1) a report on network design elements derived from simulations of TVWS and Wi-Fi networks tailored for a rural Namibian context, 2) a resource of essential information to facilitate the planning for the deployment of broadband access networks within national broadband strategies, 3) a means to uncover new insights regarding the cost implications of emerging technologies in rural community environments.

8. CONCLUSION

This study article sought to examine the research question, "What would TVWS and Wi-Fi networks for cost evaluations look like in a rural Namibian context?". The paper presented a technical design overview of network simulations using Indoor RadioPlanner 2.0 and RadioPlanner 3.0 software for a TVWS and Wi-Fi network.

The cost evaluation was predicated on the simulated network design and coverage estimates. The results demonstrated that the TVWS network was economically viable based on the required network equipment for adequate coverage at the selected study locations. The design of the TVWS network indicated that three base stations were necessary for the research location.

The study's limitations were the exclusion of coverage projections for outdoor Wi-Fi in the designated study regions from this research paper. Furthermore, no pricing information for the network equipment was obtained for comprehensive cost estimations. Moreover, no physical network infrastructure was used owing to economic and regulatory (TVWS) constraints. TVWS equipment use is prohibited in Namibia due to regulatory constraints. The research was done in underserved rural parts of the nation, primarily focusing on healthcare services. The justification for the chosen rural location was predicated on low broadband penetration.

Further research is suggested to focus on cost evaluations for the implementation of networks over time, including maintenance and client growth demand considerations. Furthermore, real capital expenditures (CAPEX) and operating expenditures (OPEX) should be included in future research for comprehensive estimates on the cost advantages of broadband networks.

REFERENCES

Adaptrum, (2018). *Case Study: MyDigitalBridge Namibia, Africa Project: Citizen Connect,* s.l.: s.n.

Bakare, B. I., Orike, S. & Ibanibo, T. S., (2022). Design And Simulation of Television White Space Technology for Rural Broadband Connectivity In Nigeria. *Quest Journals Journal of Electronics and Communication Engineering Research,* pp. 15-23.

Benjamin, J. E. et al., (2021). A 15-month experience with a primary care-based telemedicine screening program for diabetic retinopathy. *BMC ophthalmology,* pp. 1-9.

Briglauer, W. & Grajek, M., (2024). Effectiveness and efficiency of state aid for new broadband networks: Evidence from

OECD member states. *Economics of Innovation and New Technology,* pp. 672-700. Coleman, D., (2020). *Designing your wireless network,* s.l.: s.n.

CRAN, (2022). *CRAN market report.* [Online] Available at: https://www.cran.na/yglilidy/2022/03/CRAN-Presentation-Market-Report-Universal-Service-Data-Study-2020-Termination-Rates.pdf

Eckles, D., Karrer, B. & Ugander, J., (2014). Design and analysis of experiments in networks: R. bias from interference.

arXiv:1404.7530, pp. 1-24.

Haleem, A., Javaid, M., Singh, R. P. & Suman, R., (2021). Telemedicine for healthcare: Capabilities, features, barriers, and applications. *Sensors international,* p. 2.

Heidemann, J., Mills, K. & Kumar, S., (2001). *Expanding confidence in network simulations.* s.l., IEEE, p. 15.

Ifeoluwa, O., Nassir, F. & Olayiwola, W. B. A. A., (2015). *Recent trends on TV White Space deployments in Africa.* s.l., Niger J Technol, pp. 556-563.

Kennedy, R., George, K., Vitalice, O. & Okello-Odongo, W., (2015). *TV white spaces in Africa: Trials and role in improving broadband access in Africa.* s.l., IEEE AFRICON.

Kivunja, C. & Kuyini, A. B., (2017). Understanding and applying research paradigms in educational contexts. *International*

Journal of higher education, pp. 26-41.

Lamola, M. M., (2020). *Performance analysis of hybrid WiFi and TV white space links,* s.l.: s.n.

MICT, (2022). *National Broadband Policy for the Republic of Namibia (2018-2022),* Windhoek: MICT.

Omboni, S. et al., (2022). The worldwide impact of telemedicine during COVID-19: current evidence and recommendations for the future. *Connected health,* pp. 1-7.

Pan, B., Demiryurek, U. & Shahabi, C., (2012). *Utilizing Real-World Transportation Data for Accurate Traffic Prediction.*

Brussels, IEEE, pp. 595-604.

Rampfl, S., Wohlfart, F. & Raumer, D., (2013). [Online] Available at: https://citeseerx.ist.psu.edu/document?repid=rep1&type=pdf&doi=d24f94ef148e2bdf269ffa9bde5353a69d08f9f9

Silmi, S., Doukha, Z., Kemcha, R. & Moussaoui, S., (2020). *Wireless sensor networks simulators and testbeds.* s.l., arXiv preprint arXiv:2009.03640, p. 141.

Weingartner, E., Vom Lehn, H. & Wehrle, K., (2009). *A performance comparison of recent network simulators.* s.l., IEEE, pp. 1-5.

TECHNO-ECONOMIC ANALYSIS OF POWER-TO-GAS AND FUEL CELL SYSTEM INTEGRATION IN SOLAR-DIESEL NETWORKS

Eugenia Skepetari, Sotiris Pelekis, Hercules Koutalidis, Christos Ntanos, Alexandros M. Tzortzis, Ariadni Michalitsi-Psarrou and Dimitris Askounis
Decision Support Systems Laboratory, National Technical University of Athens
Iroon Polytechneiou 9, 15772, Zografou, Greece

ABSTRACT

Power-to-Gas (PtG) is an energy storage technology that converts surplus energy from renewable energy sources (RES) into hydrogen via water electrolysis. In this paper, we examine the techno-economic potential of a PtG system investment in a solar-diesel power network in Greece. The suggested methodology utilizes surplus energy during high-RES production periods by converting it into green hydrogen via electrolysis and storing it for later use. This stored hydrogen can be used in fuel cells (FCs) to produce electricity during high electricity demand. A simulation and optimization model has been developed using Python to evaluate the economic and technical viability, minimizing system costs. Three scenarios were simulated: a baseline without PtG, a PtG scenario including current prices, and a PtG scenario reflecting projected cost reductions in 2030. The results demonstrate the techno-economic aspects of integrating PtG into energy systems in areas with significant solar resources in Greece.

KEYWORDS

PtG, Electrolysis, Fuel Cell, Solar, Green Hydrogen, Simulation

1. INTRODUCTION

The increasing electricity demand coupled with the need to address climate change, has led to a rapid development in renewable energy sources (RES) generation. Initiatives to address global warming have been taken through the Paris Agreement (UNFCCC, n.d.) alongside the REPowerEU plan by accelerating the transition to RES, increasing the renewable energy target for 2030 (European Commission, n.d.). In this regard, effective RES integration into the power grid requires robust energy storage systems. These systems can enhance grid stability and reliability by capturing surplus energy from RES when energy demand is low and storing it for later use. Moreover, power grid flexibility (Pelekis et al., 2023a) and accurate load forecasting (Pelekis et al., 2023b) are considered crucial in enabling the grid to adjust to electricity demand fluctuations, thus reducing the risk of imbalances between supply and demand (Pelekis et al., 2023c).

Power-to-Gas (PtG) is a technology that utilizes renewable energy to produce green hydrogen via water electrolysis. Green hydrogen is being promoted as the fuel of the future because of its clean, storable and portable nature (IRENA, 2020). It can be distributed in various forms, such as gas, liquid, or integrated into existing gas networks (Abe et al., 2019; Fambri et al., 2022; Hassan et al., 2021) and stored for long periods with minimal losses (UNIDO et al., 2023). It can also complement renewable electrification using hydrogen fuel cells (Li et al., 2019) and offers solutions for decarbonization in applications such as heavy industry, oil refining, ammonia, methanol, steel, shipping and seasonal energy storage (Ding et al., 2020; IRENA and WTO, 2023).

Several studies have examined the potential of PtG and green hydrogen investments in energy storage systems. Some suggest that PtG and fuel cell systems are more effective than batteries in long-term storage applications (Jacobson, 2024; Pellow et al., 2015), others have analysed the potential of these systems for large-scale and seasonal storage (Mayyas et al., 2020; Petkov and Gabrielli, 2020). Additionally, some studies propose simulation models for wind-turbines/solar panels/fuel cell systems using Matlab/Simulink (Wang and Nehrir, 2008), while others have investigated hybrid systems combining RES with PtG systems, fuel cells and gas turbines (Ding et al., 2020).

This paper contributes to the promotion of green hydrogen and cleaner future energy storage systems. It investigates a PtG system that makes use of green hydrogen produced with a photovoltaic (PV) plant in combination with fuel cells tailored for application in Greece. It extends existing literature by presenting a methodological framework to evaluate the feasibility of PtG and fuel cell investments within a diesel-solar microgrid. Simulation and optimization models have been developed with Python, utilizing real production and consumption data, complementing the tools used in previous research. Unlike prior studies focusing on large-scale and seasonal applications, this study investigates a PtG investment which optimizes green hydrogen storage, minimizing costs, while addressing intra-day energy balancing challenges. Moreover, techno-economic insights about PtG and fuel cell integration are provided, focusing on the potential of green hydrogen to be a viable and affordable storage solution that can improve power system stability and flexibility reducing energy curtailment, and offering an approach to decarbonize important areas of the Greek energy system.

2. METHODOLOGY AND EXPERIMENTAL SETUP

2.1 System Configuration

2.1.1 Materials and Assumptions

The proposed energy system consists of a PV power plant and a diesel generator for backup purposes. This configuration aims to supply electrical power to a community of 5000 inhabitants in Greece. The simulations we conducted entail the following three scenarios: 1) Baseline: no PtG investment; 2) PtG 2023: PtG and fuel cell investment reflecting 2023 costs; 3) PtG 2030: PtG and fuel cell investment with cost projections and emissions pricing adjusted for 2030. The PtG 2023 and PtG 2030 scenarios concern a PtG plant, featuring an electrolysis system, hydrogen storage, and a fuel cell system and they mainly differ in projected reductions in costs, alongside the predicted increase in CO2 emission prices by 2030.

Each scenario simulates a power network that includes a diesel generator, a PV plant, and the electrical demand of the community's population. Regarding model inputs, we used hourly five-year time series of solar energy generation and load consumption data from ENTSO-E covering 2015-10-01 00:00:00 to 2020-09-30 23:00:00 (ENTSO-E, 2024). The file includes the total PV production in the country as well as the total energy demand. For the use cases, the data were modified to reflect our use case. Therefore, the total energy consumption was divided by 2000 to depict said village population, while the solar generation series was normalized to a maximum of 5MW, equal to the installed capacity of the diesel generator. Regarding the diesel generator is set to operate at a technical minimum of 30% to ensure grid stability. This threshold guarantees that the generator can adapt to unexpected changes in demand or generation, while maintaining features like frequency governance and inertia. This is crucial in systems with significant RES integration because of its volatility (Papathanassiou and Boulaxis, 2006). Note here that since such an investment is of 20-30 years duration and the available data is for 5 years, the evaluation of the investment concerns the first 5 years of installation. We consider that the solar power plant and the diesel generator already exist in the grid and have no capital costs, while the whole microgrid is managed by a sole operator.

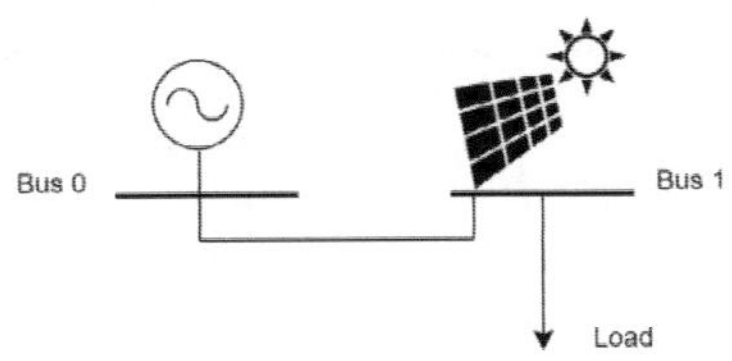

Figure 1a. Baseline Scenario power grid diagram

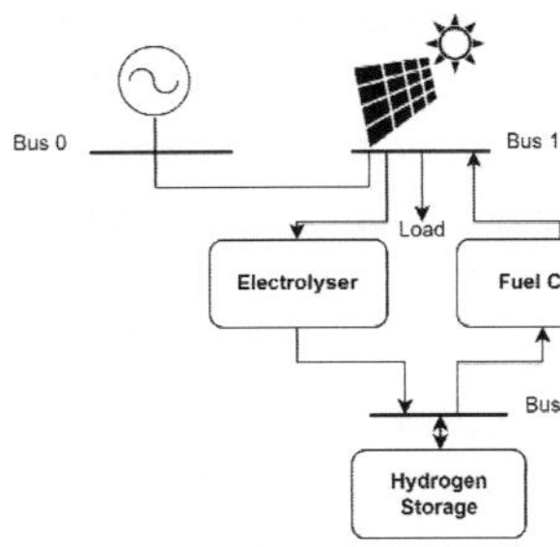

Figure 1b. PtG Scenario power grid diagram

Table 1. Baseline parameters

Parameter	Price 2023	Price 2030	Source
CO2 emissions costs	86€/tCO2	120€/tCO2	(European Commission, 2023)
Diesel generator CO2 emissions factor	0.85tCO2/MWh	0.85tCO2/MWh	(Singh Solanki et al., 2010)
Diesel generator marginal cost	300€/MWh	300€/MWh	(European Commission, n.d.)
Total diesel generator marginal cost	373.1€/MWh	402€/MWh	Equation (1)
Solar Plant marginal cost	10€/MWh	10€/MWh	(IEA, 2023)

2.1.2 Baseline Scenario

The baseline scenario represents an electrical network of a bus (Bus 0), where the diesel generator is attached and a generation bus (Bus 1), where the solar power plant and load are located, as in Figure 1a. Regarding the capital costs, they are zero as we assume that this system already exists, while for the generator's marginal cost, we calculate both the price of the fuel, and the CO2 emissions tax as presented in Table 1 and in the following equation:

$$\begin{aligned} &\textit{Total diesel generator marginal cost} \\ &\quad = (\textit{CO2 emissions costs}) * (\textit{diesel CO2 emissions factor}) + \textit{diesel generator marginal cost} \end{aligned} \quad (1)$$

2.1.3 PtG 2023 Scenario

In PtG 2023, the investment of a hydrogen energy storage system installation in baseline scenario network was studied. In this network excess energy from RES in Bus 1 is converted into hydrogen via electrolysis and this green hydrogen is compressed and stored in a tank in Bus 2. The tank can store it for long periods of time and feed it back to the grid when energy demand is high via a fuel cell (Figure 1b).

The electrolysis system consists of a Proton Exchange Membrane (PEM) electrolyser, water handling units, mass flow controllers, electrolyser handling system, compressor and rectifier. This system is connected to Bus 1 (PV plant), feeds Bus 2 (hydrogen bus), and has the parameters in Table 2. The fixed operating costs (fixed OPEX) include costs such as: maintenance for optimal operation of the electrolyser, staff fees and insurance of the production facilities. Variable operating costs (variable OPEX) include the costs of purchasing energy to balance the plant, i.e. electricity to run the pumps, compressors and temperature control. This amount was set to zero since we assume an operator who manages the whole microgrid and uses the excess electricity generated by the PV plant to power the electrolyser. Note here that, the lifetime of the system is about 20 years, and at 10 years the electrolyser needs to be replaced.

The energy storage system is a hydrogen tank on Bus 2 and its parameters are displayed in Table 2. The fixed operating costs include operation and maintenance costs, while there is no variable operating cost.

The fuel cell system includes fuel cell modules, gas handling units, mass flow controllers, management system and inverter. The system is connected to Bus 2 (hydrogen bus), feeds Bus 1 (PV plant), and has parameters and costs according to Table 2. The capital cost (CAPEX) of the system includes both the fuel cell and inverter costs.

Table 2. PtG nominal power, efficiency and costs parameters for 2023 and 2030

Parameter	PtG 2023	PtG 2030	Source
Electrolysis efficiency	0.64	0.75	(Gorre et al., 2019; IRENA, 2020)
Electrolysis CAPEX	1180€/kWh	665€/kWh	(Gorre et al., 2019; IEA, 2023; IRENA, 2020; Viswanathan et al., 2022)
Electrolysis fixed OPEX	4% CAPEX	3% CAPEX	(Gorre et al., 2019; IRENA, 2020)
Electrolysis variable OPEX	0	0	Own assumption
Hydrogen storage CAPEX	28.25€/MWh	21.19€/MWh	(Gorre et al., 2019; Moran et al., 2024)
Hydrogen storage fixed OPEX	1.5% CAPEX	1.5% CAPEX	(Gorre et al., 2019)
Hydrogen storage variable OPEX	0	0	Own assumption
FC efficiency	0.6	0.65	(Akinyele et al., 2020)
FC CAPEX	1387€/kWh	464€/kWh	(Akinyele et al., 2020; Viswanathan et al., 2022)
FC fixed OPEX	3% CAPEX	3% CAPEX	Own assumption
FC variable OPEX	0	0	Own assumption

2.1.4 PtG 2030 Scenario

The PtG 2030 Scenario replicates the PtG 2023 network; however, we estimate a reduction in capital and operational expenditures for the PtG system, an increase in efficiency as shown in Table 2, and a rise in CO2 emissions costs as shown in Table 1.

2.2 System Simulation and Optimization

The optimization of the network created for each snapshot is performed via Linopy (Hofmann, 2023), using the Simplex algorithm, which is used in the PyPSA library (Brown et al., 2018), and the solver used is GNU Linear Programming Kit (GLPK, 2024), which is designed to solve large-scale linear programming (LP) and mixed integer programming (MILP) problems. The simulations run using TwinP2G (Pelekis et al., 2023d), an optimization tool for power system networks and PtG systems.

Table 3. Simulation and optimization variables

Variable	Unit	Comments	Variable	Unit	Comments
n		Bus	$\lambda_{n,t}$	€/MWh	Marginal cost
r		Generator	$\bar{e}_{n,s}$	MWh	Store nominal energy
s		Energy Storage	$E_{n,s}$	MWh	Energy nominal capacity
κ, l		Branch	$e_{n,s,t}$	MWh	Store dispatch
t		Time	F_l	MW	Branch capacity
w_t	h	Weighting of time t	$f_{l,t}$	MW	Power flow
$g_{n,r,t}$	MW	Generator dispatch	$o_{n,r,t}$	€/MWh	Generator operational cost
$\bar{g}_{n,r}$	MW	Generator nominal power	$o_{n,s,t}$	€/MWh	Store operational cost
$c_{n,r}$	€/MW	Capital cost of extending generator nominal power by one MW	c_l	€/MW	Capital cost of extending branch power by one MW
$h_{n,s,t}$	MW	Storage dispatch	$d_{n,t}$	MW	Electricity demand
$\bar{h}_{n,s}$	MW	Storage nominal power	$\eta_{l,t}$	%	Efficiency
$c_{n,s}$	€/MW	Capital cost of extending storage nominal power by one MW	$\hat{c}_{n,s}$	€/MWh	Capital cost of extending store nominal energy by one MWh

2.2.1 Power Flow Equation

The role of the bus is to enforce the conservation of energy for all components entering and leaving it. The electricity demand $d_{n,t}$ in each bus n must be met at each time t either by the generators and storage or by the flows $f_{l,t}$ from the branches l.

$$\sum_r g_{n,r,t} + \sum_s h_{n,s,t} + \sum_l a_{l,n,t} f_{l,t} = \sum_s d_{n,t} \leftrightarrow w_t \lambda_{n,t} \tag{2}$$

where $a_{l,n,t} = -1$ if branch l starts from the even n, $a_{l,n,t} = 1$ if branch l is a line or transformer and ends at n, and $a_{l,n,t} = \eta_{l,t}$ if l is a link and ends at n. Variable definitions can be found in Table 3.

2.2.2 Objective Function

PyPSA minimizes the total cost of the system, which includes the variable and fixed costs of generation, storage and transmission, given the constraints of each component. The objective function through which the optimization is performed for each snapshot is:

$$\min\left[\sum_{n,r} c_{n,r}\bar{g}_{n,r} + \sum_{n,s} c_{n,s}\bar{h}_{n,s} + \sum_{n,s} \hat{c}_{n,s}\bar{e}_{n,s} + \sum_{l} c_l F_l + \sum_{t} w_t \left[\sum_{n,r} o_{n,r,t}g_{n,r,t} + \sum_{n,s} o_{n,s,t}h_{n,s,t}\right]\right] \quad (3)$$

3. RESULTS

3.1 Baseline Scenario

As illustrated in Figure 2, the PV plant that produces energy during sunlight hours, covers the load during the midday hours, in combination with the generator which operates at its minimum during the midday hours and at its maximum during the evenings when there is no photovoltaic production. It is also observed that there are cuts in RES energy when the generation is larger than the load. These cuts were calculated by the model and are equal to 16,317.11MWh (Table 4).

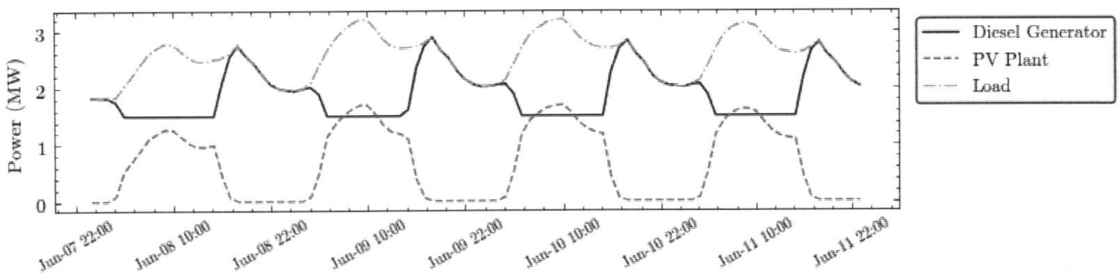

Figure 2. Baseline time series for optimal energy production (diesel and PV plant) and consumption (load)

Table 4. Baseline techno-economic results

Generator	Energy Production (€/MWh)	Energy Cuts (MWh)	Operational Expenditure (€)
Diesel	100446.44	0	37476566.63
PV Plant	26834.55	16317.11	268344.49

3.2 PtG Scenario 2023

Figure 3 illustrates the system's operation over a four-day period in June. The system operates with electrolysis occurring at midday when solar power production is at its peak, resulting in an increase hydrogen tank stored energy in Figure 4. The stored hydrogen is later converted back into electricity by the fuel cell and supplies the grid during insufficient solar production. Thus, energy cuts are reduced and the surplus energy generated is stored for future use.

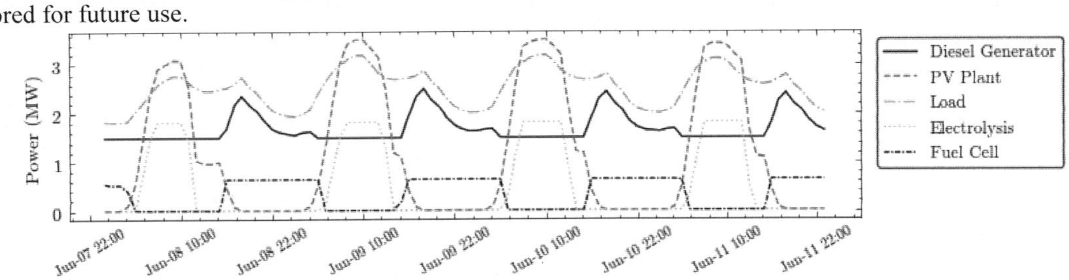

Figure 3. PtG 2023 time series for optimal electric energy production (diesel, PV plant and fuel cell), hydrogen production (electrolysis) and consumption (load) in MW

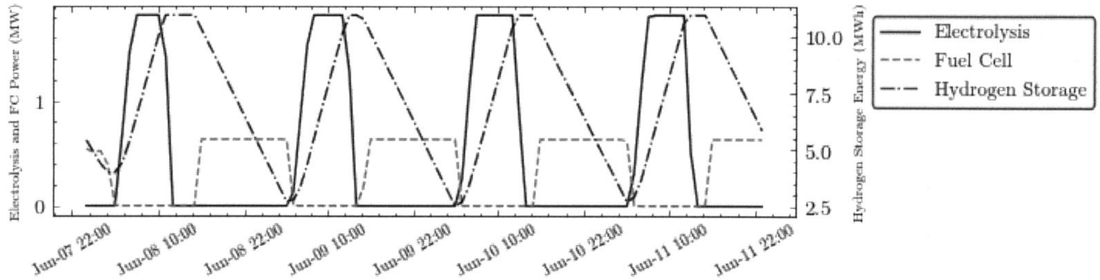

Figure 4. PtG 2023 time series for electrolysis (in MW), fuel cell (in MW) and hydrogen storage (in MWh)

The techno-economic analysis reveals in Table 5 the optimal installed capacities, energy production, CAPEX and OPEX for each component. More specifically, the total cost for the electrolysis system amounts to 557,998.64€ for an electrolyser installation with an optimal nominal power of 1.82MW. Similarly, the total cost for the fuel cell system were calculated 224,413.84€ for the installation of a fuel cell system with a nominal power of 0.63MW. The total cost for the hydrogen storage were calculated 62,671.47€ for the installation of a hydrogen tank with a capacity of 10.93MWh of hydrogen energy.

Table 5. PtG 2023 techno-economic results for network components

Network components	Optimal installed capacity	Energy Production (MWh)	Capital Expenditure (€)	Operational Expenditure (€)
Diesel	5MW	94984.73	0	35438802.45
PV plant	5MW	41624.45	0	410576.59
Electrolysis system	1.82MW	-14223.22	536537.15	21461.49
Fuel cell system	0.63MW	5461.71	217877.51	6536.34
Hydrogen tank	10.93MWh	0	61745.29	926.18

3.3 PtG Scenario 2030

Similar to PtG Scenario 2023, Figure 5 and Figure 6 demonstrate the system's time series for optimal production, transmission and storage. The system operates with electrolysis occurring at midday when solar power production is at its peak, resulting in an increase hydrogen tank stored energy. The stored hydrogen is later converted back into electricity by the fuel cell and supplies the grid during insufficient solar production.

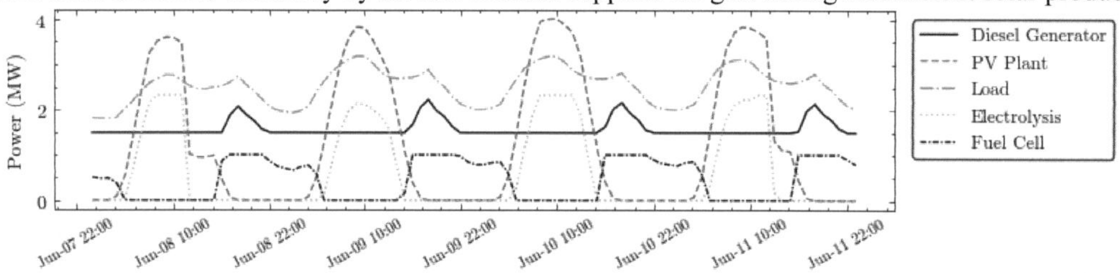

Figure 5. PtG 2030 time series for optimal electric energy production (diesel, PV plant and fuel cell), hydrogen production (electrolysis) and consumption (load) in MW

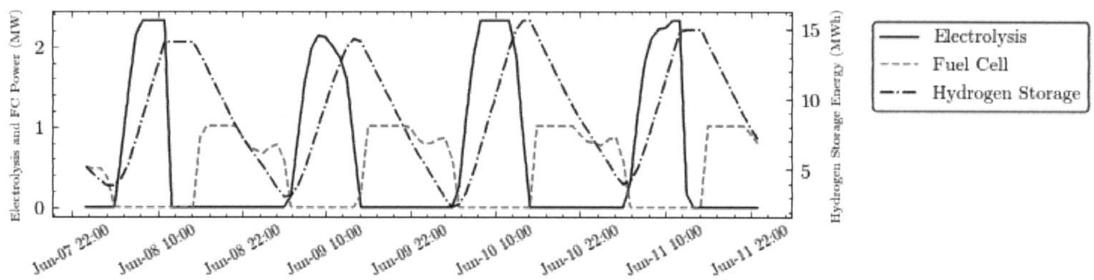

Figure 6. PtG 2030 time series for electrolysis (in MW), fuel cell (in MW) and hydrogen storage (in MWh)

In Table 6 optimal installed capacities, energy production, CAPEX and OPEX for each component are demonstrated. In more detail, the total cost of an electrolysis system of 2.33MW optimal nominal power was calculated 398,293.84€, for a fuel cell system of 1.01MW optimal nominal power was calculated 120,732.15€ and for a hydrogen storage system of 18.67MWh optimal nominal energy capacity was calculated 72,558.3€. Despite the overall reduction in system capital and operating costs in the third scenario, diesel generator costs continue to climb driven by an increase in its marginal cost that leads to a 1.68% increase in overall cost.

Table 6. PtG 2030 results techno-economic results for network components

Network components	Optimal installed capacity	Energy Production (MWh)	Capital Expenditure (€)	Operational Expenditure (€)
Diesel	5MW	92951.09	0	37366339.16
PV plant	5MW	42209.52	0	422095.15
Electrolysis system	2.33MW	-15375.07	386693.05	11600.79
Fuel cell system	1.01MW	7495.36	117215.68	3516.47
Hydrogen tank	16.87MWh	0	71486	1072.3

4. CONCLUSIONS

Investing in PtG and fuel cells systems can be a strategic move towards enhancing energy sustainability. Throughout our analysis, three scenarios were simulated and optimized for a diesel/solar power grid integrating PtG and fuel cell system for a hypothetical community in Greece. In the first scenario, we observed 37.81% energy cuts from the PV plant, alongside the diesel generator's high operating costs and high CO2 emissions. In the second scenario demonstrating the investment and installation of a PtG and fuel cell system, the PV plant production increases by 55.12%, reducing PV energy cuts to 3.54% and using this surplus to produce green hydrogen, while the overall cost -including both CAPEX and OPEX- decreases by 2.78%. In the third scenario where the PtG and fuel cell CAPEX and OPEX have been reduced, the PV plant production increases by 57.3%, reducing PV energy cuts to 2.18%. As a result, the optimal installed capacities of PtG and fuel cell systems increase in comparison to second scenario, highlighting that green hydrogen storage can be a more attractive energy storage solution in the future. We conclude, therefore, that investments in PtG and hydrogen storage technologies are crucial for improving grid efficiency. The main challenge for such investments is the high capital costs of electrolysis and fuel cell systems; these costs are however predicted to decline by 2030, making hydrogen storage an even more attractive solution for stakeholders like investors or transmission system operators (TSOs) who want to invest in energy storage systems in Greece. In summary, investing in PtG and green hydrogen can offer a sustainable, clean, and efficient solution to better utilize renewable energy sources, reduce greenhouse gas emissions, and move closer to achieving energy autonomy.

ACKNOWLEDGEMENT

This work has been funded by the European Union's Horizon Europe research and innovation program under the ENERSHARE project, Grant Agreement No 101069831. The sole responsibility for the content of this paper lies with the authors; the paper does not necessarily reflect the opinion of the European Commission.

REFERENCES

Abe, J. O. et al., (2019). Hydrogen energy, economy and storage: Review and recommendation. Int J Hydrogen Energy 44, 15072–15086. https://doi.org/10.1016/j.ijhydene.2019.04.068

Akinyele, D. et al., (2020). Review of Fuel Cell Technologies and Applications for Sustainable Microgrid Systems. Inventions 2020, Vol. 5, Page 42 5, 42. https://doi.org/10.3390/INVENTIONS5030042

Brown, T. et al., (2018). PyPSA: Python for Power System Analysis. J Open Res Softw 6, 4. https://doi.org/10.5334/jors.188

Ding, X. et al., (2020). Multi-objective optimization for an integrated renewable, power-to-gas and solid oxide fuel cell/gas turbine hybrid system in microgrid. Energy 213, 118804. https://doi.org/10.1016/J.ENERGY.2020.118804

ENTSO-E, (2024). Data Platform – Open Power System Data [WWW Document]. URL https://data.open-power-system-data.org/time_series/latest/ (accessed 3.5.24).

European Commission, (2023). Quarterly report On European electricity markets Market Observatory for Energy DG Energy.

European Commission, (n.d.) REPowerEU [WWW Document]. URL https://ec.europa.eu/commission/presscorner/detail/en/ip_22_3131 (accessed 3.9.24a).

European Commission, (n.d.) HYBRID MODEL-ISLAND OF CRETE [WWW Document]. URL https://energy.ec.europa.eu/system/files/2021-07/2021_derogation_crete_notification_en_0.pdf (accessed 2.27.24b).

Fambri, G. et al., (2022). Techno-economic analysis of Power-to-Gas plants in a gas and electricity distribution network system with high renewable energy penetration. Appl Energy 312, 118743. https://doi.org/10.1016/J.APENERGY.2022.118743

GLPK, (2024). GLPK - GNU Project - Free Software Foundation (FSF) [WWW Document]. URL https://www.gnu.org/software/glpk/ (accessed 2.6.24).

Gorre, J. et al., (2019). Production costs for synthetic methane in 2030 and 2050 of an optimized Power-to-Gas plant with intermediate hydrogen storage. Appl Energy 253, 113594. https://doi.org/10.1016/j.apenergy.2019.113594

Hassan, I. A. et al., (2021). Hydrogen storage technologies for stationary and mobile applications: Review, analysis and perspectives. Renewable and Sustainable Energy Reviews 149, 111311. https://doi.org/10.1016/j.rser.2021.111311

Hofmann, F., (2023). Linopy: Linear optimization with n-dimensional labeled variables. J Open Source Softw 8, 4823. https://doi.org/10.21105/joss.04823

IEA, (2023). World Energy Outlook 2023.

IRENA, (2020). Green Hydrogen Cost Reduction: Scaling up Electrolysers to Meet the 1.5^{0}C Climate Goal, International Renewable Energy Agency. Abu Dhabi.

IRENA, WTO, (2023). International trade and green hydrogen: Supporting the global transition to a low-carbon economy.

Jacobson, M.Z., (2024). Batteries or hydrogen or both for grid electricity storage upon full electrification of 145 countries with wind-water-solar? iScience 27, 108988. https://doi.org/10.1016/j.isci.2024.108988

Li, Z. et al., (2019). A review of the applications of fuel cells in microgrids: opportunities and challenges. BMC Energy 2019 1:1 1, 1–23. https://doi.org/10.1186/S42500-019-0008-3

Mayyas, A. et al., (2020). Hydrogen as a long-term, large-scale energy storage solution when coupled with renewable energy sources or grids with dynamic electricity pricing schemes. Int J Hydrogen Energy 45, 16311–16325. https://doi.org/10.1016/j.ijhydene.2020.04.163

Moran, C. et al., (2024). The hydrogen storage challenge: Does storage method and size affect the cost and operational flexibility of hydrogen supply chains? Int J Hydrogen Energy 52, 1090–1100. https://doi.org/10.1016/J.IJHYDENE.2023.06.269

Papathanassiou, S. A., Boulaxis, N.G., (2006). Power limitations and energy yield evaluation for wind farms operating in island systems. Renew Energy 31, 457–479. https://doi.org/10.1016/J.RENENE.2005.04.002

Pelekis, S. et al., (2023a). Targeted demand response for flexible energy communities using clustering techniques. Sustainable Energy, Grids and Networks 36, 101134. https://doi.org/10.1016/J.SEGAN.2023.101134

Pelekis, S. et al., (2023b). DeepTSF: Codeless machine learning operations for time series forecasting.

Pelekis, S. et al., (2023c). A comparative assessment of deep learning models for day-ahead load forecasting: Investigating key accuracy drivers. Sustainable Energy, Grids and Networks 36, 101171. https://doi.org/10.1016/J.SEGAN.2023.101171

Pelekis, S. et al., (2023d). TWINP2G: A digital twin architecture for optimal power-to-gas planning, in: International Conferences on E-Society and Mobile Learning 2023. pp. 119–126.

Pellow, M.A. et al., (2015). Hydrogen or batteries for grid storage? A net energy analysis. Energy Environ Sci 8, 1938–1952. https://doi.org/10.1039/C4EE04041D

Petkov, I., Gabrielli, P., (2020). Power-to-hydrogen as seasonal energy storage: an uncertainty analysis for optimal design of low-carbon multi-energy systems. Appl Energy 274, 115197. https://doi.org/10.1016/J.APENERGY.2020.115197

Singh Solanki, P. et al., (2010). Distributed Generation to Reduce Carbon Dioxide Emissions: A Case Study for Residential Sector in Oman. The Open Renewable Energy Journal 3, 26–32.

UNFCCC, (n.d.) The Paris Agreement [WWW Document]. URL https://unfccc.int/process-and-meetings/the-paris-agreement (accessed 3.6.24).

UNIDO et al., (2023). Green hydrogen for sustainable industrial development: A policy toolkit for developing countries, IRENA.

Viswanathan, V. et al., (2022). 2022 Grid Energy Storage Technology Cost and Performance Assessment.

Wang, C., Nehrir, M. H., (2008). Power management of a stand-alone wind/photovoltaic/fuel cell energy system. IEEE Transactions on Energy Conversion 23, 957–967. https://doi.org/10.1109/TEC.2007.914200

TECHNICAL GUIDE TO SUPPORT THE DEVELOPMENT OF SECURE RESTFUL APIS

Pedro Pita[1] and Luís Bruno[1,2]
[1]*Polytechnic Institute of Beja, LabSI2, Beja, Portugal*
[2] *INESC-ID, Lisboa, Portugal*

ABSTRACT

This study investigates five critical vulnerabilities from the OWASP Top 10 API Security Risks – 2023 (OWASP, 2023) — API2:2023 (Broken Authentication), API4:2023 (Unrestricted Resource Consumption), API5:2023 (Broken Function Level Authorization), API8:2023 (Security Misconfiguration), and API10:2023 (Unsafe Consumption of APIs). The investigative methodology adopted includes an experimental study, utilizing mixed methods (quantitative and qualitative) for data collection and analysis processes. It presents a practical approach to mitigating these issues through the development of a technical guide and an experimental API. The research emphasizes actionable solutions validated through industry feedback and vulnerability testing, providing a valuable resource for secure RESTful API development.

KEYWORDS

RESTful API, Security, OWASP API Security Top 10, API Development, Vulnerability Mitigation

1. INTRODUCTION

RESTful APIs are central to distributed systems, enabling seamless interaction between services and ensuring interoperability across applications. Designing and implementing APIs has become essential to ensuring system integrity, confidentiality, and availability in the face of potential threats. API security encompasses aspects like authentication, authorization, proper configuration, data validation, and resource abuse prevention. Projects like OWASP (Open Web Application Security Project) (OWASP, 2023) provide guidelines to mitigate common API risks. However, a review of existing literature highlights fragmented solutions, making it difficult for developers to access consolidated knowledge on best security practices.

This article presents a technical guide aimed at mitigating vulnerabilities in RESTful APIs using best practices. It focuses on five high-impact vulnerabilities from the OWASP API Security Top 10 (2023) (OWASP, 2023), including practical examples through a developed API.

This technical guide goes beyond identifying vulnerabilities; it bridges the gap between theoretical knowledge and real-world application. By integrating security into every stage of the API development lifecycle, the guide offers a comprehensive approach to mitigating risks effectively. The five vulnerabilities addressed in detail—API2:2023 (Broken Authentication), API4:2023 (Unrestricted Resource Consumption), API5:2023 (Broken Function Level Authorization), API8:2023 (Security Misconfiguration), and API10:2023 (Unsafe Consumption of APIs)—are accompanied by practical solutions designed to be both accessible and impactful for developers.

The effectiveness and applicability of the guide were validated through structured surveys with industry professionals. The feedback collected emphasized the clarity and practicality of the recommendations, as well as their potential to address common challenges developers face when securing APIs. Suggestions for improvement have been incorporated into the guide, ensuring its usefulness for a broad audience.

By addressing technical, theoretical, and practical aspects, the technical guide seeks to empower developers with the tools and knowledge needed to secure their APIs effectively. The findings underscore the importance of adopting standardized security practices and integrating them into the development process. Moreover, the guide highlights opportunities for future research, including refining existing solutions and exploring new methods to enhance API security further.

This article begins with the related work section, where is compared and analyzed previous studies on API security, as well as the criteria used to select the five vulnerabilities explored in this research. In the methodology section, is outlined the research approach and detail the methodology adopted for the study. The experimental API section describes how the API was developed, with a focus on the techniques implemented to mitigate the identified vulnerabilities. The technical guide section outlines the creation of the technical guide, emphasizing its key characteristics and features. Next, the findings section presents the results of the study and discussing the implications of these vulnerabilities. Finally, the conclusion summarizes the article's key insights, underscoring the importance of secure API development and suggesting directions for future research in this area.

2. RELATED WORK

A comprehensive analysis of the most common API vulnerabilities has identified several sources offering different perspectives on the topic, aligning these analyses with the categories highlighted in the OWASP Top 10 API Security Risks of 2019 (OWASP, 2019) and 2023 (OWASP, 2023). Table 1 provides a consolidated view of these references and the vulnerabilities discussed, highlighting the relationship between the two versions of OWASP. Some vulnerabilities listed in 2019 remain in the 2023 version, underlining the continued relevance of certain risks. For example, Broken Object Level Authorization (API1:2019 and API1:2023) and Security Misconfiguration (API7:2019 and API8:2023) continue to be classified as critical. The persistence of Broken Authentication (API2:2019 and API2:2023) and Broken Function Level Authorization (API5:2019 and API5:2023) further reinforces the importance of rigorous access control and identity protection practices, showing how these concerns have remained unchanged over time.

The study "Development of Vulnerable Web Application Based on OWASP API Security Risks" (M. Idris, et al., 2021) covers all the vulnerabilities described in the 2019 version, including those that remain relevant in 2023. On the other hand, "8 Common API Vulnerabilities" (Mike, 2021) explores most of the 2019 vulnerabilities, except for Security Misconfiguration (API7:2019) and Insufficient Logging & Monitoring (API10:2019). The work titled "Common API Vulnerabilities and How to Secure Them" (P. Team, 2023), while not directly addressing the OWASP lists, discusses issues that clearly correlate with the described categories. For instance, Distributed Denial of Service (DDoS) attacks are related to Lack of Resources Rate Limiting (API4:2019), Unrestricted Resource Consumption (API4:2023), and the absence of protection against brute force attacks, which is associated with Broken Authentication (API2:2019 and API2:2023). It also highlights issues like Insufficient Rate Limiting (API4:2023 and API4:2019) and Man-in-the-Middle attacks, which are linked to Security Misconfiguration (API7:2019 and API8:2023). Additionally, it mentions SQL Injection (API8:2019), emphasizing the importance of mitigation against injection attacks.

The article "Top 5 Most Common API Vulnerabilities You Should Know About" (Reflecdiz, 2022) focuses on issues such as Weak Authentication, directly linked to Broken Authentication (API2:2023). Furthermore, this document also explores flaws like Broken Object Level Authorization (API1:2023 and API1:2019), Excessive Data Exposure (API3:2019), and Security Misconfiguration (API8:2023 and API7:2019), highlighting the challenges in implementing robust security. Similarly, the material "Top API Security Vulnerabilities and How to Fix Them" (Irwin, 2023) analyzes vulnerabilities like Insecure Direct Object References (IDOR), related to Broken Object Level Authorization (API1:2023 and API1:2019), and Broken Authentication issues (API2:2023 and API2:2019). It also addresses flaws like Improper Error Handling and Missing Security Headers, which are linked to Security Misconfiguration (API8:2023 and API7:2019), and Inadequate Rate Limiting, associated with Unrestricted Resource Consumption (API4:2023 and API4:2019). These issues highlight the need for effective measures to mitigate risks like DDoS attacks, ensuring better protection and efficiency in systems.

Moreover, the publication "A Comprehensive Look at API Security and Common API Vulnerabilities" (Williams, 2022) provides a comprehensive analysis covering vulnerabilities such as Broken Object Level Authorization (API1:2023 and API1:2019), Broken Authentication (API2:2023 and API2:2019), Excessive Data Exposure (API3:2019), Mass Assignment (API6:2019), Injection (API8:2019), and various others, demonstrating the broad spectrum of risks faced by APIs. Finally, the contributions "Top API Vulnerabilities and 6 Ways to Mitigate Them" (Maric, 2023) and "6 Serious API Security Vulnerabilities and How to Fix Them" (Malik, 2022) explore vulnerabilities like Broken Object Level Authorization (API1:2023 and

API1:2019), Broken Authentication (API2:2023 and API2:2019), Excessive Data Exposure (API3:2019), Lack of Resources Rate Limiting (API4:2019), and Injection (API8:2019), offering complementary insights into risks and mitigation measures.

Table 1. Mapping of OWASP Vulnerabilities 2019 and 2023 to Articles: An "x" indicates that the vulnerability is addressed in the article, while a "-" signifies its absence

	OWASP 2019/2023	(Idris, et al., 2021	(Mike, 2021)	(Team, 2023)	(Reflecdiz, 2022)	(Irwin, 2023)	(Willias, 2022	(Maric, 2023)	(Malik, 2022)
OWASP 2019/ 2023	API1:2023/API1: 2019 - Broken Object Level Authorization	x	x	-	x	Insecure Direct Object References (IDOR)	x	x	x
	API2:2023/API2: 2019 - Broken Authentication	x	x	CSRF Attack e Credential Stuffing	Weak Authentication	Insufficient Authentication/ Authorization	x	x	x
	API5:2023/API5: 2019 - Broken Function Level Authorization	x	x	CSRF Attack	-	-	-	-	-
	API8:2023/API7: 2019 - Security Misconfiguration	x	-	Man-in-the-middle	x	Improper Error Handling and Missing Security Headers Resources	x	-	-
OWASP 2023	API3:2023 - Broken Object Property Level Authorization	-	-	-	-	-	-	-	-
	API4:2023 - Unrestricted Resource Consumption	-	-	Distributed Denial of Services	-	Inadequate Rate Limiting	-	-	-
	API6:2023 - Unrestricted Access to Sensitive Business Flows	-	-	-	-	-	-	-	-
	API7:2023 - Server Side Request Forgery	-	-	-	-	-	-	-	-
	API9:2023 - Improper Inventory Management	-	-	-	-	-	-	-	-
	API10:2023 - Unsafe Consumption of API	-	-	-	-	-	-	-	-
OWASP 2019	API3:2019 - Excessive Data Exposure	x	x	-	x	x	x	x	x
	API4:2019 - Lack of Resources & Rate Limiting	x	x	Distributed Denial of Services	-	Inadequate Rate Limiting	-	x	x
	API6:2019 - Mass Assignment	x	x	-	-	-	x	-	-

API8:2019 - Injection	x	x	SQL Injection	x	x	x	x	x
API9:2019 - Improper Assets Management	x	x	-	-	-	x	-	-
API10:2019 - Insufficient Logging & Monitoring	x	-	-	-	-	x	-	-

An analysis of these studies shows that most focus on vulnerabilities highlighted by OWASP. Even without explicitly mentioning its categories, they address issues aligned with its principles, reinforcing OWASP's credibility and acceptance in the development community. Therefore, focusing on mitigating vulnerabilities from the latest version of the project is the most effective approach to ensuring API security.

The OWASP Top 10 API Security Risks – 2023 risk assessment model (OWASP, 2023) uses three main factors to evaluate each vulnerability:

- **Threat Agents/Attack Vectors:** Evaluates how easy it is for attackers to exploit a given vulnerability, considering the variety and capabilities of the attackers (threat agents), as well as the methods they use to exploit the vulnerabilities (attack vectors).
- **Security Weakness:** Analyzes the technical causes underlying the vulnerabilities, meaning the security weaknesses in the software that can be exploited by attackers. These include deficiencies in design, configuration, implementation, deployment, or maintenance of applications.
- **Impacts:** Refers to the potential impact of a vulnerability being exploited, evaluating the potential damage it could cause to assets, the organization's reputation, end users, and even legal or regulatory impacts.

It is important to note that these factors are analyzed together to determine the severity and priority of the vulnerabilities listed in the OWASP Top 10 API Security Risks – 2023. In this sense, OWASP documentation provides a detailed analysis of each vulnerability, covering the potential consequences of exploitation and offering practical recommendations for organizations to mitigate them effectively.

In this investigation and analysis of the OWASP Top 10 2023 vulnerabilities (OWASP, 2023), based on OWASP's risk model, was highlighted those whose impacts are classified as "Severe" (critical). This decision was made due to the need to prioritize flaws with the greatest potential to cause significant damage to organizations and end users. Vulnerabilities at this level of impact not only pose a high risk of substantial financial losses but also can compromise an organization's reputation, result in the loss of sensitive data, and expose systems to a higher risk of compromise.

Vulnerabilities with severe impacts require immediate attention and a deep understanding for effective mitigation. Thus, through the technical guide, the aim is to offer concrete and actionable strategies to address them. Specifically, the vulnerabilities with severe impacts include API2:2023 Broken Authentication, API4:2023 Unrestricted Resource Consumption, API5:2023 Broken Function Level Authorization, API8:2023 Security Misconfiguration and API10:2023 Unsafe Consumption of API.

3. METHODOLOGY

To guide and structure the research and investigation process, the principles of the ONDAS Framework (Franco, 2023) methodology were employed. This framework is described as a multidisciplinary theory of "researchology" that provides a comprehensive explanation of the core principles of scientific research. Its primary objective is to explore uncharted areas of knowledge, enabling the discovery of innovative solutions with potential for patentability, ultimately unveiling the secrets of knowledge.

The research methodology adopted includes an experimental study, using mixed methods (quantitative and qualitative) for data collection and analysis processes. The use of tools such as structured surveys and the development of a demonstrative API generates significant results, revealing that the proposed technical guide is useful and practical in the development of RESTful APIs. This study contributes important findings to the existing knowledge, providing a technical guide validated by professionals in the field and filling gaps in security practices for RESTful APIs. These contributions have practical implications for promoting security in the development of distributed systems, web applications, and modern integrations.

4. EXPERIMENTAL API

The API simulates a simplified e-commerce scenario, supporting key operations such as managing users, products, and orders. This business model was chosen for its familiarity, making the concepts discussed in this project more accessible and relevant. Built with Express.js (Express.js, 2010), MongoDB (MongoDB, 2009), and Node.js (NodeJS, 2009), the API ensures scalability and ease of implementation. The source code is available on GitHub (Pita, 2024).

The database structure was designed to be simple, flexible, and to allow readers to practically understand the concepts of security and best practices in API development. Figure 1 illustrates the database schema. MongoDB contains two main collections: Users and Orders. Additionally, it integrates with an external API - DummyJSON API (Muhammad, 2024) - to retrieve product data.

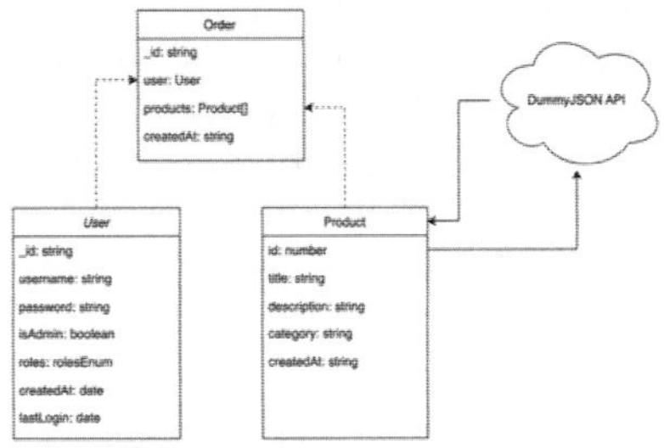

Figure 1. Database structure

The API provides endpoints for managing users, orders, and products, including integration with an external API to retrieve product data. Table 2 summarizes the main endpoints of the RESTful API.

Table 2. All API endpoints and the respective necessary roles to access

Category	Endpoint	Description	Authentication	Admin	Role
Orders	**POST** /orders/add	Create a request with a product list.	X	-	-
Orders	**GET** /orders	List all orders.	X	X	list_all_orders
Orders	**GET** /orders/myorders	List the authenticated user orders.	X	-	-
Orders	**GET** /orders/details/{id}	List the details from an order by ID.	X	X	list_all_orders
Users	**GET** /users	List all users.	X	X	select_user
Users	**POST** /users/register	Register new user.	-	-	-
Users	**POST** /users/login	Authenticate user and return a JWT token.	X	-	-
Users	**GET** /users/{username}	List user details by username.	X	X	select_user
Users	**PUT** /users/promote/{username}	Promote a user by username.	X	X	promote_admin
Users	**POST** /users/roles/{username}	Add or remove roles by username.	X	X	add_roles
Products	**GET** /products	List all available products.	X	-	-
Products	**GET** /products/{id}	List product details by ID.	X	-	-

The API focuses on addressing the five vulnerabilities using the follow techniques:

- **API2:2023 (Broken Authentication):** To mitigate the broken authentication vulnerability, strong password validation rules were implemented to reduce the likelihood of weak credentials. Additionally, token-based authentication was adopted, with token signature validation to ensure proper session management. To protect against brute force and credential stuffing attacks, login attempts were limited, preventing excessive attempts from compromising the system's security.

- **API4:2023 (Unrestricted Resource Consumption):** To address unrestricted resource consumption, rate limiting was introduced to restrict excessive API calls from clients. Furthermore, quotas for resource usage were defined to prevent abuse and denial-of-service (DoS) scenarios, ensuring the system remains available even under high traffic conditions.
- **API5:2023 (Broken Function Level Authorization):** The broken function level authorization vulnerability was addressed by enforcing role-based access control (RBAC), ensuring that API endpoints are only accessible to authorized users with appropriate roles. Endpoint-specific permissions were also configured to minimize the risk of privilege escalation, ensuring that only the appropriate functions could access sensitive resources.
- **API8:2023 (Security Misconfiguration):** To prevent security misconfigurations, secure default configurations were established during the API setup.
- **API10:2023 (Unsafe Consumption of APIs):** To address unsafe consumption of APIs, inputs received from third-party APIs were validated and sanitized to prevent the propagation of malicious data. Additionally, risk assessments for external API integrations were conducted, and fallback mechanisms were implemented to handle failures or vulnerabilities in external APIs, ensuring greater resilience and security.

5. TECHNICAL GUIDE

The development of the technical guide was oriented toward maximizing usability and effectiveness in conveying knowledge about RESTful API security. It targets both professionals who need to understand and mitigate critical vulnerabilities and professionals or students seeking to gain knowledge in the field. Its development considered several aspects to ensure a practical, accessible, and systematic approach to content organization.

Firstly, the segmentation by critical vulnerabilities was based on the five most impactful vulnerabilities from the OWASP API Security Top 10 (2023) (OWASP, 2023). This prioritization allowed for an in-depth focus on key topics, enabling readers to better understand how to minimize the risks associated with these specific threats. Next, the inclusion of a demonstrative API serves to illustrate and support various vulnerabilities and their mitigations, focusing on common operations. This API was specifically developed to demonstrate the mitigation practices for the vulnerabilities under study, effectively bridging the gap between theoretical understanding and practical application.

Thirdly, the organization of the document in a tutorial format facilitates both comprehension and practical application of the concepts. The goal was to achieve a hands-on approach with clear instructions for addressing each vulnerability, illustrated with step-by-step examples that enhance understanding and practical implementation. From this foundation, structured security practices are recommended, presenting specific implementation guidelines for each vulnerability. These include robust authentication, permission- based access control, request rate limiting, and external data validation, ensuring readers grasp best practices. Additionally, specific tools and technologies are recommended, such as JWT for authentication and express- rate-limit for resource consumption management. These tools were carefully selected to simplify the implementation of the security concepts discussed. An interactive index was also designed to provide users with faster and more efficient navigation, allowing them to directly access the specific vulnerability they wish to study. This elevates the reading experience, making it intuitive and seamless. The technical guide can be found in Google Drive (TECHNICAL GUIDE TO SUPPORT THE DEVELOPMENT OF SECURE RESTFUL APIS, 2024).

6. RESULTS

To validate the effectiveness of the technical guide and the implementation of the RESTful API, a survey was developed with the objective of gathering a practical and critical assessment of the guidelines provided in the technical guide, and to ensure, in turn, the clarity, utility, and applicability of the recommended security practices. The analysis follows a mixed methodological approach, integrating both quantitative and qualitative methods within the positivist paradigm with interpretative elements.

A non-probabilistic purposive sample was selected, consisting of five professionals in the API development and security field – three of whom are junior developers with less experience in API development; one is a senior developer, thus having more experience and familiarity with API implementation; and the last is a software architect, offering a broader view of security practices and system architecture – ensuring a diversity of opinions and experiences. The inclusion of each participant followed a deliberate selection logic, including criteria such as technical experience and familiarity with technologies related to RESTful APIs. This strategy aimed to ensure greater relevance of the data to the study's objectives.

To ensure data collection aligned with the study's goals and to maximize the relevance of the responses obtained, the survey was prioritized, then developed using Microsoft Forms (Microsoft, 2024). It is important to note that it was applied in the post-implementation phase of the technical guide, with the aim of evaluating various aspects related to its implementation. These include the ease of implementation, clarity and organization of the guide's instructions, success in identifying issues, and the effectiveness of vulnerability mitigation. Additionally, the utility and usability of the technical guide and the API were also validated, assessing the practical application of the API in real-world contexts.

A total of 16 questions were included, distributed across different response types. Five of these are open- ended, allowing detailed comments from participants; six are dichotomous, with binary options for objective analysis; two are single-choice; one is multiple-choice; and two are ordinal scale questions, evaluating the utility and usability of the technical guide on a scale from 1 (not useful) to 3 (very useful).

Although five participants were selected, only three responded the survey involved three participants – a junior developer, a senior developer, and an architect – representing 60% of the total expected sample, initially composed of five participants with different levels of technical experience. The diversity in responses, represented by different career stages, allowed for a relatively comprehensive and representative analysis of the target audience for the technical guide.

The analysis and comparison of results indicated mostly unanimity – with the exception of the implementation time, which varied significantly depending on the participants' experience. The junior developer took between four to six hours to implement the API, while the senior developer and the architect completed the task within one to three hours. This result highlights the effectiveness of the guide for more experienced professionals. Additionally, the fact that all participants had previous experience with the technologies covered in the guide (Node.js, Express, MongoDB, MongoDB Compass, Visual Studio Code, Postman, and JavaScript) validated the appropriate choice of tools, which proved to be widely used and familiar to the target audience.

Regarding the clarity and organization of the guide, the respondents rated it positively, emphasizing the ease of executing the steps and the absence of technical or compatibility issues during implementation. Furthermore, none of the participants identified vulnerabilities in the API, and all found the explanations about the vulnerabilities and mitigation strategies adequate.

In general, on the scale of utility and usability (1-3), the technical guide received the maximum score of 3 in all responses, standing out as a practical and efficient tool for developing secure RESTful APIs. All suggestions for improvement provided by the participants were carefully analyzed and applied to an improved version of the guide, reinforcing its clarity, accessibility, and alignment with the practical needs of users.

7. CONCLUSION

This research successfully addressed five critical vulnerabilities from the OWASP API Security Top 10 (2023) (OWASP, 2023), combining theoretical insights with practical tools. The dual approach—developing a technical guide and a secure experimental API—bridged the gap between high-level recommendations and actionable solutions. Key contributions include:

- **Practical Solutions:** The experimental API showcased effective implementation of security measures such as robust authentication mechanisms, role-based access control, and rate limiting.
- **Comprehensive Technical Guide:** The guide provided clear instructions for securing RESTful APIs, validated through professional feedback. Its developer-friendly format ensures wide applicability and promotes best practices in API development.
- **Knowledge Contribution:** By addressing gaps in the consolidation of security practices, this work complements OWASP's recommendations with real-world applications.

Despite its successes, the study has limitations, such as the focused scope on five vulnerabilities and the specific use of certain technologies (e.g., Express.js (Express.js, 2010), MongoDB (MongoDB, 2009), NodeJS (NodeJS, 2009)). Future research should explore:

- **Broader Vulnerability Coverage**: Extending the study to include all vulnerabilities from OWASP API Security Top 10.
- **Adaptation to Diverse Architectures:** Testing the guide in microservices, serverless environments, and emerging API standards.
- **Integration with DevSecOps:** Embedding security measures into CI/CD pipelines to ensure continuous protection.

In conclusion, this research provides a robust foundation for enhancing RESTful API security, emphasizing the need for ongoing vigilance and adaptation as API ecosystems evolve.

REFERENCES

OWASP. (2023). OWASP API Security Top 10 2019. Available at: https://owasp.org/API-Security/editions/2023/en/0x11-t10/. [Accessed: 9 January 2025].

OWASP. (2019). OWASP API Security Top 10 2023. Available at: https://owasp.org/API- Security/editions/2019/en/0x11-t10/. [Accessed: 9 January 2025].

Muhammad, O. (2024). DummyJSON API. Available at: https://dummyjson.com/docs. [Accessed: 9 January 2025].

Node.js. (2009). Node.js JavaScript Runtime. Available at: https://nodejs.org/en/docs/ [Accessed: 2025-01-10]. MongoDB. (2009). MongoDB: The Developer DataPlatform. Available at: https://www.mongodb.com/docs/ [Accessed: 2025-01-10].

Sharp, R. (2011). Nodemon: Monitor for Changes in Node.js Applications. Available at: https://nodemon.io/ [Accessed: 2025-01-10].

Express.js. (2010). Express - Fast, Unopinionated, Minimalist Web Framework for Node.js. Available at: https://expressjs.com/ [Accessed: 2025-01-10].

M. Idris, I. Syarif & M. Winarno (2021) Development of Vulnerable Web Application Based on OWASP API Security Risks. In: International Electronics Symposium (IES). [Accessed: 2025-01-10].

Mike (2021). 8 Common API Vulnerabilities. Available at: https://apimike.com/api-vulnerabilities [Accessed: 2025-01- 10].

P. Team (2023). Common API Vulnerabilities and How to Secure Them. Available at: https://www.papertrail.com/blog/common-api-vulnerabilities-and-how-to-secure-them/ [Accessed: 2025-01-10].

Reflecdiz (2022). Top 5 Most Common API Vulnerabilities You Should Know About. Available at: https://www.reflectiz.com/blog/common-api-vulnerabilities/ [Accessed: 2025-01-10].

Irwin, A. (2023). Top API Security Vulnerabilities and How to Fix Them. Available at: https://aptori.dev/blog/top-api-security-vulnerabilities-and-how-to-fix-them [Accessed: 2025-01-10].

Williams, A. (2022). A Comprehensive Look at API Security and Common API Vulnerabilities. Available at: https://www.mimecast.com/blog/a-comprehensive-look-at-api-security-and-common-api-vulnerabilities/ [Accessed: 2025-01-10].

Maric, N. (2023). Top API Vulnerabilities and 6 Ways to Mitigate Them. Available at: https://brightsec.com/blog/top- api-vulnerabilities-and-6-ways-to-mitigate-them [Accessed: 2025-01-10].

Malik, K. (2022). 6 Serious API Security Vulnerabilities and How to Fix Them. Available at: https://www.stackhawk.com/blog/6-serious-api-security-vulnerabilities-and-how-to-fix-them/ [Accessed: 2025 01-10].

Microsoft (2024). Microsoft Forms. Available at: https://forms.office.com/ [Accessed: 2025-01-10].

Daniel José Franco, Apina Lee Omar Khasro Akram (2023). Undergraduate and Graduate Students' Challenges: A Qualitative Study with ONDAS Framework Across Multiple Disciplines and Innovative Research Methodologies Authors. Available at: https://nsuworks.nova.edu/tqr/vol28/iss10/5/ [Accessed: 2025-01-10].

Pita, P. (2024). restapi-example. GitHub. Available at: https://github.com/pedro-pita/restapi-example

TECHNICAL GUIDE TO SUPPORT THE DEVELOPMENT OF SECURE RESTFUL APIS. (2024). Available at: https://drive.google.com/file/d/1ziyciwko5hL0Ky39v3LNEK2jy1RhfrdV/view

OBIA: THE BRAZILIAN AI OBSERVATORY TOWARDS SUSTAINABLE DEVELOPMENT, GOVERNANCE AND POLICY-MAKING

Cristina Godoy Oliveira[1], Tiago Augustini de Lima[1], Alexandre Barbosa[2], Joao Paulo Candia Vieira[1], Luiz Costa[2] and Joao Pita Costa[3]

[1]*CIAAM, C4AI, Univ. of São Paulo, São Paulo, Brazil*

[2]*CETIC, OBIA, São Paulo, Brazil*

[3]*IRCAI, Quintelligence, Ljubljana, Slovenia*

ABSTRACT

Artificial Intelligence (AI) is experiencing rapid expansion, reshaping industries and economies across the globe, with Brazil and the broader South American region playing increasingly influential roles. Recognizing the importance of assessing AI's impact on sustainable development, government involvement, investment, and broader society, the Brazilian Artificial Intelligence Observatory (OBIA) was established. Incorporated into the Brazilian Artificial Intelligence Plan (PBIA) and originally conceived as part of the Brazilian Strategy of AI, OBIA aspires to serve as the premier platform for tracking AI applications within the country. Situated under Axis 5 of the PBIA, OBIA contributes to strengthening AI-related regulations and governance. This paper examines the regional landscape of AI—its current progress, hurdles, and prospects—and evaluates how cutting-edge technologies are shaping economic trajectories, social transformations, and policymaking frameworks across South America, with Brazil at the forefront of innovation. Additionally, it identifies parallels with IRCAI's Sustainable Development Goals (SDG) Observatory, particularly in applying machine learning techniques and harmonizing conventional and crowdsourced data strategies to enhance data collection and analytical methodologies.

KEYWORDS

Artificial Intelligence, Observatory, Survey Data Analysis, Complex Data Visualization, Multidisciplinary Collaboration

1. INTRODUCTION

AI is increasingly influencing the economic and social fabric of Brazil and South America, positioning the region as an emerging center of technological advancement. Despite hurdles such as uneven infrastructure and regulatory complexities, Brazil's progress in AI research and development is helping to clarify and shape how AI affects the broader South American context. Responding to this need, the Brazilian Artificial Intelligence Observatory (OBIA) (MCTI, 2021) provides a platform to guide strategic initiatives and government measures by offering data-driven insights into AI's usage and impact. OBIA's goals involve compiling, recording, and distributing information about AI in Brazil, enabling detailed analyses of its adoption and effects on society. Its mission includes consolidating and disseminating insights on how AI influences various domains, thereby informing policies, strategies, and actions aimed at fostering responsible AI development and deployment, in other words, OBIA serves as a central platform for information, analysis, and guidance an AI adoption, regulation, and social impacts.

In practice, OBIA collects Brazilian data on AI adoption across multiple sectors, including education, industry, government, and healthcare, as depicted in Figure 1. Currently, most indicators rely on conventional data sources, such as surveys and datasets provided to the OBIA team. The initiative's first output, the book "Artificial Intelligence in Healthcare – Potentialities, Risks and Perspectives," was published in July 2024. As a second function, OBIA serves as a repository for key guiding documents in the AI field originating worldwide. Thirdly, OBIA acts as an "information exchange point" among Brazil's AI centers—referred to as the IAX. All gathered indicators are publicly available on the OBIA portal (Costa, *et al*, 2024).

The Center for Artificial Intelligence (C4AI) at the University of São Paulo, funded by FAPESP (São Paulo's state research funding agency) and IBM, contributes to OBIA's work through its humanities division. C4AI provides qualitative analyses in the horizontal focus areas of "Legislation, Regulation, and Ethical Use" and "AI Governance," while also conducting research across the various verticals monitored by OBIA. Its interdisciplinary research team, composed of experts in law, computer science, electrical engineering, sociology, and political science, will thoroughly examine the primary topics monitored by OBIA. This collaborative approach aims to offer a well-rounded understanding of AI's current state in Brazil. Numerous reports, scholarly articles, and datasets will be shared to help OBIA fulfill its mandate. Beyond the involvement of personnel from different NIC.br departments, OBIA maintains a broad network of external partners, including the Center for Management and Strategic Studies (CGEE), the São Paulo State System Data Analysis Foundation (SEADE), C4AI, CIAAM (Center of Artificial Intelligence and Machine Learning), and others. The following sections will highlight C4AI's specific contributions to OBIA through a complementary perspective, focusing on qualitative analyses of decisions by the São Paulo Court of Justice related to AI. In other words, OBIA serves as a central platform for information, analysis, and guidance on AI adoption, regulation, and social impacts.

Thus, the central objective of this paper is to present the progress of two ongoing studies conducted under the scope of OBIA: how the São Paulo State Court of Justice is adjudicating cases involving AI, and how the Brazilian Executive Branch is investing in AI tools, despite the absence of specific legislation on AI systems and tools in Brazil.

2. INVESTIGATING THE REGIONAL LEGAL AND REGULATORY LANDSCAPE OF AI

The research outlined in this paper underpins an initiative aimed at implementing the PBIA strategy (PBIA, 2024), which focuses on monitoring AI regulation and legislation in Brazil. The approach is structured around three key areas—Executive, Judiciary, and Legislative—integrating both traditional and modern data collection methods. In the Executive domain, ongoing monitoring involves regularly scraping data from government transparency websites using a carefully maintained list of AI-related terms. This process helps identify which AI solutions are being procured or utilized by public entities. In the Judiciary sphere, the team examines court rulings from the São Paulo Court of Appeals (TJSP) that touch upon AI-related matters, providing insight into how judges interpret and handle these issues in the absence of dedicated AI legislation (Oliveira, et. al., 2023). As of the most recent data collection in August 2024, over 13,000 relevant court decisions have been found. Regarding the Legislative branch, the group actively follows the debate on Bill 2338/2023, which addresses AI regulation. They participate in public hearings and produce technical notes designed to guide lawmakers. Future plans include expanding this monitoring to state and municipal legislatures, recognizing that many local governments are creating AI-related laws to support the development of "smart cities."

A key component of this research involves compiling a comprehensive list of AI-related terms that informs data scraping and analysis efforts. These terms are drawn from authoritative sources—such as scientific publications, the ISO/IEC 22989:2022 standard (ISO, 2022), and the OECD's report on AI developments (Baruffaldi, 2020) and are updated and refined to ensure relevance and accuracy. By using this carefully curated list, the team conducts monthly web scrapes of TJSP rulings and transparency data from the Brazilian Transparency Portal on the 15th of each month. Scripts developed in Python and R (referencing Jesus Filho's GitHub codebase) facilitate the extraction and processing of these data points. A separate script targets data available in the "Data Download" section of the Brazilian Transparency Portal. To further enhance the analytical process, an automation tool employing natural language processing (NLP) methods is under development. The first stage involves a Named Entity Recognition (NER) model to automatically identify key entities, including involved parties and judicial decisions. Subsequent steps will integrate a classification model to filter out irrelevant data, thereby improving efficiency and accuracy in the analysis.

The selection of AI-related terms follows a rigorous process. Starting with a broad set of 226 AI terms identified by the OECD through its examination of scientific papers, open-source repositories, and patents, the team then incorporates concepts from the ISO/IEC 22989:2022 standard. Experts at the Brazilian Technical Standards Association (ABNT) translate and refine these terms into Portuguese, ensuring only those highly pertinent to AI remain. General terms that might trigger irrelevant results—such as "transparency," which could relate to Brazil's Access to Information Law rather than AI—are excluded. The final roster of 103 bilingual terms (English and Portuguese) guides the data retrieval strategy, ensuring a focused and effective search aligned with the project's research objectives.

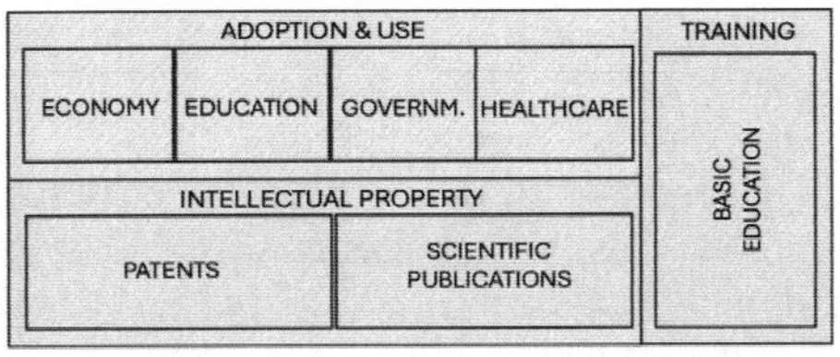

Figure 1. Current Dimensions of OBIA's monitoring topics

As part of the qualitative analysis preparation, we are developing and categorizing repositories that contain reference documents and statistical data. These repositories will be organized around key thematic areas—such as "Legislation, Regulation, and Ethical Use" and "AI Governance"—and will draw on information from sources like the São Paulo Court of Appeals (TJSP), the Transparency Portal, and other pertinent databases. By integrating multiple data-gathering techniques, we enhance both the efficiency and precision of information collection, ensuring that only the most relevant materials are included. In addition, employing web scraping allows us to capture data not available through APIs, resulting in broader and more comprehensive coverage. These repositories are regularly updated and systematically classified based on their relevance to AI terms, creating a dynamic, structured reference resource (see Figure 2), as described in (MCTI, 2023).

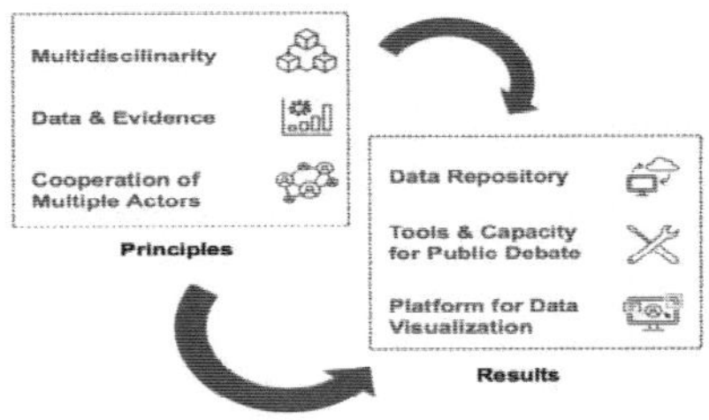

Figure 2. OBIA's guiding principles and expected results (MCTI, 2023)

Building and sustaining cooperation networks calls for active collaboration among interdisciplinary experts from fields such as law, computer science, engineering, sociology, and political science. These networks are crucial for the exchange of insights and methodologies focused on AI monitoring. Employing APIs and web scraping tools ensures access to timely data, enabling ongoing knowledge sharing. Regular activities—such as workshops, webinars, and collaborative research projects—help maintain participant engagement. Disseminating reports, scholarly articles, and datasets further bolsters the network's foundation and supports OBIA's overarching goal of thoroughly monitoring AI advancements.

3. EXECUTIVE BRANCH INVESTMENTS IN AI

The purpose of the research is to analyze how the Three Branches of Government address, evaluate, invest and promote AI systems. For instance, the Judiciary in the State of São Paulo, which is the largest Court system in terms of case volume, has seen a significant influx of cases involving AI systems and similar technology for judicial review. Research in the Legislative Branch has not yet begun. In the Executive Branch, the analysis regarding investment in artificial intelligence systems was carried out through data scraping on the Open Data Portal and Transparency Portal platforms. The Open Data Portal provides a specific Government Procurement API, which facilitates data scraping to analyze categories such as contracts, agreements, purchases made through bidding, exemptions from the bidding process, auctions etc. However, challenges encountered during the scraping process - such as API stability issues - resulted in an unsatisfactory volume of data for the research. As a result, the research team chose to redirect their analysis of the Executive Branch to the Transparency

Portal. On the Transparency Portal, the approach to data scraping followed a similar strategy to that used on the Open Data Portal. The platform offers two primary methods for extracting data: (1) the Data Download Swagger API, which requires the use of a custom script for scraping, and (2) the Dashboard Data Download, which provides comprehensive data for each category in CSV format, necessitating subsequent filtering to extract relevant information. To make this method work, suitable data pre-processing scripts were created to help with the later qualitative analysis of the information. The data collected from the Transparency Portal turned out to be more useful compared to the Open Data Portal, with over 7,000 administrative processes linked to the search terms successfully gathered. This data collection enables the identification of the scale of the Brazilian federal government's investments in AI, highlighting the economic sectors involved and identifying which Executive Branch ministries allocate the most resources to AI technologies for national development.

The qualitative analysis of this data began with the "agreements" category. According to Di Pietro (2020, p. 710), an agreement is defined as a "form of adjustment between the Public Power and public or private entities to achieve objectives of common interest, through mutual collaboration." This instrument of Public Administration is considered a type of promotion when established between public entities or between public and private entities, particularly private initiatives that serve the public interest. When the State does not directly perform a given activity, it can encourage or assist private entities to do so through mechanisms such as financial assistance or subsidies, financing, tax benefits, etc. Agreements are the typical instruments used to implement these incentives (Di Pietro, 2020). A total of 381 agreements were gathered, covering the period from January 1996 to March 2024. The next round of data collection will focus on agreements from April to December 2024. These agreements were signed in nearly all of Brazil's 27 states, except for Alagoas, Piauí, and Roraima. Notably, São Paulo (25.7%), Rio de Janeiro (13.1%), and Rio Grande do Sul (13.1%) accounted for the highest concentration of agreements signed (see Figure 3 on the left).

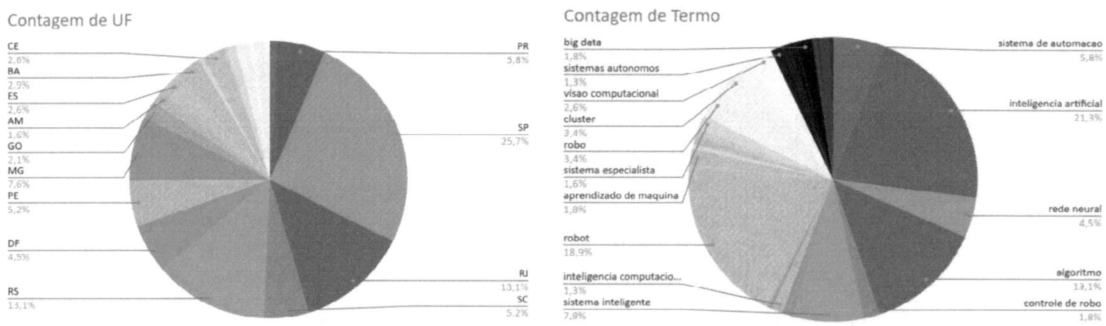

Figure 3. Agreements signed in each State of the Federation (on the left) and data Extraction terms (on the right)

The agreements were identified using 18 specific search terms. Among these, "artificial intelligence" was found in 81 agreements (21.3%), "robot" in 72 (18.9%), and "algorithm" in 50 agreements (13.1%), making them the most frequent terms in this scraping round (see Figure 3 on the right). When it comes to the Executive Branch Ministries involved in agreements related to AI systems, the Ministry of Science, Technology, and Innovation took the lead with 281 agreements (73.8%), mainly through the National Fund for Scientific and Technological Development. The Ministry of Education came next with 37 agreements (9.7%), followed by the Ministry of Integration and Regional Development with 11 agreements (2.9%) - (see Figure 4).

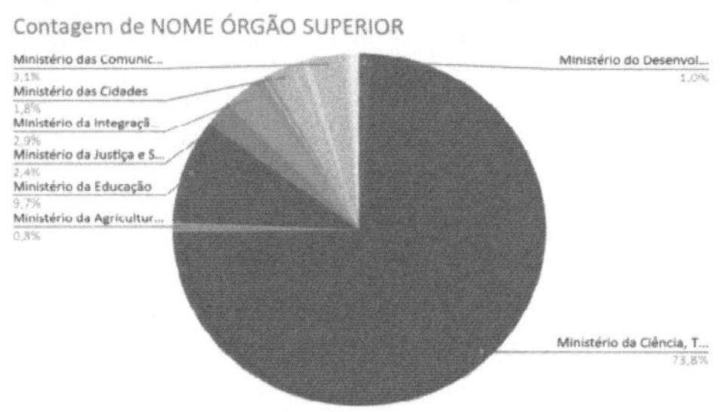

Figure 4. Data Extraction terms

The qualitative analysis of agreements signed with the Federal Executive, as published in the Official Gazette of the Union, began with data from 2024. Between January and March, a total of 13 agreements were identified. The most frequently appearing terms in these agreements were "artificial intelligence," found in 7 instances; "robot/robot," appearing 4 times; and "computer vision" and "neural network," each mentioned once. When it comes to the main bodies behind these agreements, the Ministry of Science, Technology, and Innovation (MCTI) took the lead with 10 initiatives. Next came the Ministry of Human Rights and Citizenship (MDHC) with 2 projects, and the Ministry of Education (ME) with just 1 agreement. In the first three months of 2024, the total funding hit R$ 24,021,405.80. Here's how it was split: the MCTI handled the bulk, with R$ 23,234,371.60 across its 10 projects. The MDHC allocated R$ 539,418.30 for its 2 agreements, while the ME pitched R$ 247,615.93 for its single agreement. Private business entities signed 9 agreements, while non-profit organizations signed 4. The economic areas covered by the 13 agreements, based on their objectives, were: (i) the industrial sector with 4 agreements; (ii) educational robotics with 3 agreements; (iii) AI technology for healthcare with 2 agreements; (iv) AI technology for agribusiness with 2 agreements; (v) the development of AI solutions for education with 1 agreement; and (vi) intelligent monitoring using AI software, possibly linked to the industrial sector, with 1 project. From the analysis of the agreements, it was found that the MCTI enters into agreements in various areas of the economy, even if not related to the technology and innovation sectors. Analysis indicates that the Ministry enters into agreements if the object of the contract is related to science, technology and innovation, regardless of the economic area.

For instance, agreement number 1AAQYB, process number 03.24.0011.00, signed between the MCTI and the private company Safety Diagnostics LTDA, based in Belo Horizonte, Minas Gerais, is focused on using AI to help diagnose neglected diseases and process data to produce real-time epidemiological insights. To do this work, a program or platform for predictive and diagnostic analysis would need to be developed. The agreement is worth R$ 996,360.33, and by May 24, 2024, R$ 372.110.33 — about 37.35% of the total—had already been paid out. However, the appropriate granting body for this initiative should have been the Ministry of Health, not the MCTI. According to Federal Law 14,600/2023, which outlines the basic structure of the Presidency of the Republic and its Ministries, Article 22 specifies the MCTI's responsibilities as follows: national policies for science, technology, and innovation encompass various aspects, including planning, coordinating, supervising, and evaluating activities in these areas. They also include the formulation of policies for digital transformation and automation development, as well as the implementation of the national biosafety policy, space policy, and nuclear policy.

Thus, funding for AI tools and systems would be more effective if each Ministry allocated resources within its area of expertise, while the MCTI (MCTI, 2024) promoted strategic partnerships that integrated sectors and optimized investments in science and technology. Regional development, working in synergy and supported by intersectoral collaborations and technological advancements, is already a reality in countries with significant technological progress, promoting resource efficiency and sustainability in its application (Zhao, 2024). In this way, OBIA could act as a monitor of intersectoral AI initiatives in Brazil, providing data and analyses to assist in the formulation of public policies and strategic alignment between different Ministries, as already occurs in sectors such as health, education, justice, and agriculture.

4. AUTOMATING THE IDENTIFICATION OF AI-RELATED TERMS IN LEGAL DOCUMENTS

As of June 28, 2024, a total of 13,064 decisions from the São Paulo State Court of Justice were retrieved based on selected AI-related terms. Of the 103 terms searched, 45 yielded at least one relevant result. Monthly data distribution is illustrated in Figure 5, while Figure 6 (on a logarithmic scale) presents the frequency of search results by individual AI term. The queries included both Portuguese and English terms. After identifying the top 15 most frequently occurring terms, their use over time was examined, as shown in Figure 7, which depicts their temporal evolution by publication date. A qualitative assessment of 597 decisions from the São Paulo Court of Justice (TJSP) further examined the presence and contextual use of these terms. Specific attention was given to "Facial Recognition" and "Facial Biometrics," which appeared in a variety of legal settings, sometimes straying from their purely technological meaning. Similarly, terms like "Facial Expression Recognition" and "Learning Agent" were often interpreted in psychological or social frameworks rather than in technical contexts.

The methodology combined analytical, comparative, and monographic approaches to discern patterns and contextual factors in these rulings. From the TJSP platform, 597 judgments were reviewed, distributed among the following terms: “Facial Recognition” (1), “Facial Expression Recognition” (1), “Machine Learning” (7), “Artificial Intelligence” in Portuguese (163), “Artificial Intelligence” in English (4), “Machine Learning” in Portuguese (3), “Learning Agent” (1), and “Facial Biometrics” (417). Each ruling followed a standardized structure, and the analysis considered 14 categories, such as the case number, appeal type, presiding judge, judicial district, and the situational context of AI-related terms. Significant findings revealed that “Artificial Intelligence” and “Machine Learning” often appeared in commercial or credit-related disputes, rather than strictly technological scenarios. In these cases, the AI-related terminology did not always reflect technical AI applications but rather served as part of the contract or dispute language.

The analyzed decisions, rendered by collegiate bodies of multiple judges, included a descriptive component outlining the case (appeal type, judicial district, responsible judge, parties), a summary of the decision, a factual report, a majority opinion, and, if present, a dissenting view. For the analysis, each ruling was represented in a single row divided into 14 columns to capture various dimensions—ranging from procedural details to the interpretation and significance of the AI terms used. A recurring theme involved “Facial Biometrics” in loan agreement disputes, where judges often upheld the legality of contracts that employed biometric systems, emphasizing issues around consent and the reliability of these technologies (Baruffaldi, 2020). Nonetheless, inconsistencies emerged, as similar cases sometimes led to different outcomes depending on the presiding judges’ interpretation or comfort with the technology. Overall, the findings highlight several challenges and gaps in the legal framework surrounding AI. Issues related to transparency, fairness, consumer protection, and the need for more consistent legal guidelines were evident, as was the importance of judges having a nuanced understanding of AI’s technical aspects. This research underscores the necessity for clearer standards and improved judicial literacy on AI technologies to ensure equitable and well-informed rulings.

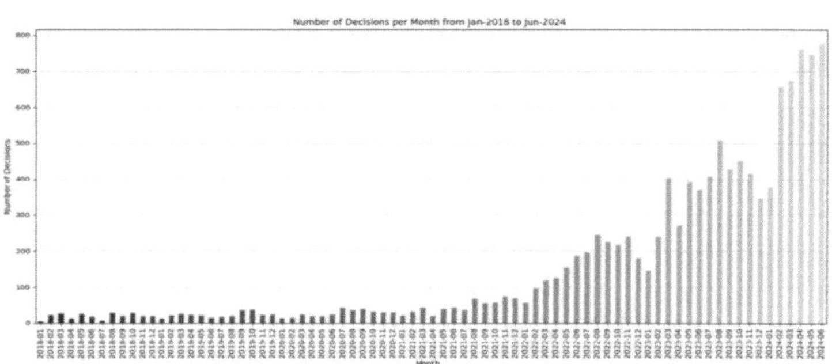

Figure 5. Nr. of Decisions per Month from Jan 2018 to Jun 2024

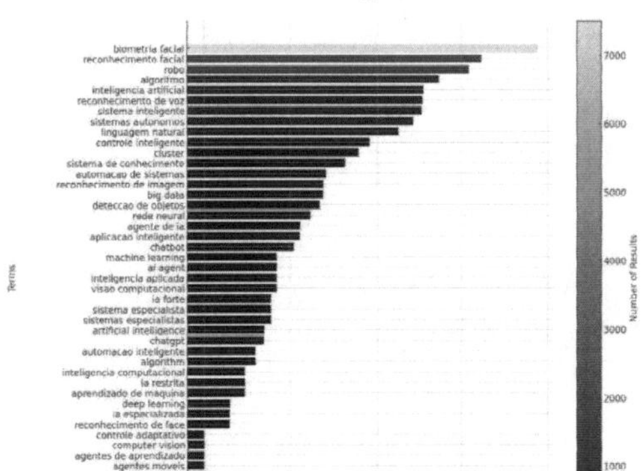

Figure 6. Number of results per AI term

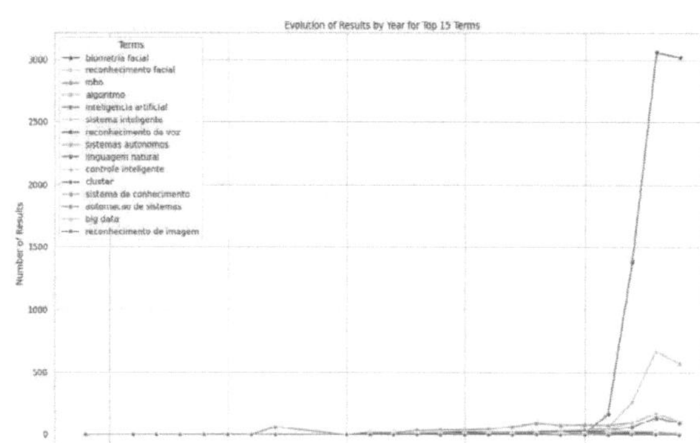

Figure 7. Evolution of results by year for top 15 terms

5. CONCLUSION AND FUTURE WORK

The qualitative research findings from the analysis of court decisions related to AI reveal several key conclusions. AI-related terms such as "Facial Recognition," "Voice Recognition," and "Autonomous Systems" are frequently used in judicial contexts that extend beyond their traditional technological meanings, intersecting with areas like consumer protection, contract law, and fraud. The inconsistency in judicial reasoning and varying outcomes in similar cases highlight the need for clearer legal frameworks and a deeper understanding of AI's technological implications among judges. Furthermore, when analyzing the Brazilian Executive Branch's investments in AI systems, many forms of contracts and agreements are already being implemented across various areas and sectors of the economy, regardless of the absence of specific legislation regulating AI applications in the country. Moving forward, the incorporation of NLP techniques into the analysis will help extract key arguments from judicial decisions, providing deeper insights into the legal discourse on AI. This will enhance the robustness of future research on AI regulation and its implications for public policy, while also enabling us to gather more detailed information from the Executive Branch about AI investments to analyze which areas of the economy receive the most funding for AI systems.

Furthermore, a preliminary analysis of news using the NLP capabilities of the Eventregistry.org system (see Figure 8) show how this source can provide complementary results to the study when, e.g., capturing the attention of media on the terms “criminal law” and “AI” in “Brazil” in the past 12 months, where 1.4% exhibits discussions on Human Rights, and terms like “democracy” and “discrimination” are within the top 30. When performing sentiment analysis over these results we can see large variations after the summer of 2022 with a predominantly negative sentiment regarding this search topic.

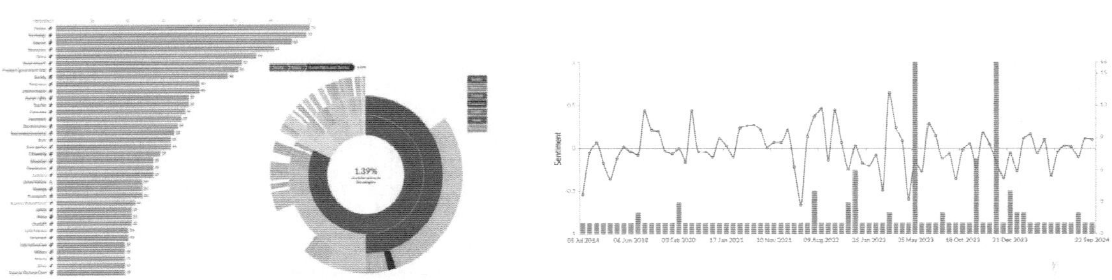

Figure 8. Significance of criminal law and AI in the news

ACKNOWLEDGEMENT

We would like to express our sincere gratitude to the Center for Artificial Intelligence (C4AI) at the University of São Paulo (USP), supported by FAPESP and IBM, for their invaluable support to the AI Observatory team. We thank the CIAAM for their continued collaboration and contributions to this research. We thank the support of the European Commission project ELIAS - Lighthouse of AI for Sustainability (10080425).

REFERENCES

Baruffaldi, S., et al. (2020). *Identifying and measuring developments in artificial intelligence: Making the impossible possible*. OECD.

Costa, L., *et al*. (2024). *The Brazilian Artificial Intelligence Observatory (OBIA)*. Retrieved August 27, 2024, from https://www.obia.nic.br/

Di Pietro, M. S. Z. (2020). *Direito Administrativo* (33ª ed.). Rio de Janeiro: Forense.

ISO. (2022). *Information technology — Artificial intelligence — Artificial intelligence concepts and terminology* (ISO/IEC 22989:2022). Retrieved August 27, 2024, from https://www.iso.org/standard/74296.html/

Ministério da Ciência, Tecnologia, Inovações (MCTI). (2021). *Brazilian Strategy of Artificial Intelligence*. Retrieved September 7, 2024, from https://www.gov.br/ebia-documento_referencia_4-979_2021.pdf

Ministério da Ciência, Tecnologia, Inovações (MCTI). (2023). *OBIA: Observatório Brasileiro de Inteligência Artificial*. Retrieved August 27, 2024, from https://www.gov.br/mcti/pt-br/acompanhe-o-mcti/transformacaodigital/arquivosinteligenciaartificial/1_ebia-reuniao-ro_7_24_05_2023_anexo_2_eixo2-pdf.pdf.

Ministério da Ciência, Tecnologia, Inovações (MCTI). (n.d.). Competências institucionais. Retrieved December 12, 2024, from https://antigo.mctic.gov.br/mctic/opencms/institucional/paginas/Competencias.html

Oliveira, C. G. B., Albuquerque, O. de P., Belotti, E. L., Lopes, I. F., Brandão de A. Silva, R., & Arbix, G. (2023). Intelligent Systems: 12th Brazilian Conference, BRACIS 2023, Belo Horizonte, Brazil, September 25–29, 2023, *Proceedings, Part I*, 18–32.

PBIA. (2024). *Brazilian Artificial Intelligence Plan*. Retrieved September 7, 2024, from https://www.gov.br/mcti/pt-br/acompanhe-o-mcti/noticias/2024/07/plano-brasileiro-de-ia-tera-supercomputador-e-investimento-de-r-23-bilhoes-em-quatro-anos/ia_para_o_bem_de_todos.pdf/view

Zhao, B. (2024). Evaluation of local green supply chain performance using a three-phase data envelopment analysis (DEA) model and Malmquist efficiency framework. *Journal of Digital Information Management, 22*(2), 63-73. https://doi.org/10.6025/jdim/2024/22/2/63-73

READY, SET, KNOW: THE RELATIONSHIP BETWEEN ACTUAL AND PERCEIVED KNOWLEDGE OF CYBERCRIME AND THE INTENTIONS TO ENGAGE IN SELF-PROTECTIVE BEHAVIOUR

Kimberly Bluhm[1], Steven Watson[2], Jurjen Jansen[1,3] and Iris van Sintemaartensdijk[2]
[1]Cybersafety Research Group, NHL Stenden University of Applied Sciences
P.O. Box 1080, 8900 CB Leeuwarden, The Netherlands
[2]Section of Psychology of Conflict, Risk and Safety, University of Twente
P.O. Box 217, 7500 AE Enschede, The Netherlands
[3]Dutch Police Academy
P.O. Box 834, 7301 BB Apeldoorn, The Netherlands

ABSTRACT

This study examined the role of actual and perceived knowledge on individuals' intentions to engage in self-protective behaviour. Participants (N = 222) completed an online questionnaire including an actual knowledge test of cybercrime, protection measures, and items measuring constructs of Protection Motivation Theory. Regression analyses showed that actual knowledge is a predictor for intention to engage in self-protective behaviour and the predictive power was stronger than for perceived knowledge. Overall, we find that both perceived and actual knowledge are crucial constructs for self-protective behaviour, however, they activate different types of efficacy. Perceived knowledge is a stronger predictor for self-efficacy, whereas actual knowledge is a better predictor for response efficacy. Implications for future interventions and research are discussed, in which emphasis should be placed on providing knowledge, increasing user confidence, and the effects of these interventions.

KEYWORDS

Cybercrime, Actual Knowledge, Perceived Knowledge, Protection Motivation Theory, Self-Protective Behaviour

1. INTRODUCTION

Digitalisation has offered society new ways to communicate, and offline activities are transferred into the online domain, including crime. Cybercrime is an umbrella term which includes all forms of crime in which information- and communication technology (ICT) plays a critical role in the execution of the crime (i.e., cyber-dependent and cyber-enabled crimes) (Domenie et al., 2013). In The Netherlands, 16% of the population aged 15 years and older were victim of cybercrime in 2023 (Akkermans et al., 2024). It is imperative that we protect the public against the negative effects of cybercrime. Self-protective measures to achieve online security and to prevent cybercrime victimisation are increasingly available. However, to date, we still observe that even basic measures to increase online security are not taken by individuals (NCTV, 2023). Prior research has indicated that awareness of security threats and coping responses are important predictors of self-protective behaviour and the extent of people's knowledge about relevant security threats and countermeasures is a crucial precursor to adopting self-protective behaviour (Martens et al., 2019). However, studies measuring the effects of awareness on self-protective behaviour, often rely on participants' subjective evaluations of their knowledge. It cannot be assumed that such research accurately estimates participants' actual knowledge of security threats. In this paper, we assess whether objectively rated knowledge has a different effect on security behaviour intentions compared to participants' perceptions of their knowledge.

1.1 Perceived Versus Actual Knowledge

Huang et al. (2011) argue that the lack of knowledge about information security risks can lead to the over- or underestimation of security levels in information systems. Individuals need a certain level of knowledge to engage in appropriate self-protective behaviour. De Kimpe et al. (2022) studied the role of perceived knowledge (i.e., what individuals think they know) in relation to self-protective behaviour and found that as perceived knowledge increased, individuals' intentions to engage in self-protective behaviour against cybercrime victimisation strongly decreased. Therefore, individuals who consider themselves well-informed might believe that they do not (additional) protection measures to protect themselves from cybercrime victimisation, hence creating unsafe situations. Compounding this concern, is the tendency for optimism bias, where people feel they are less likely than others to experience negative events, or have overly positive beliefs in their abilities to avoid negative outcomes (Weinstein, 1980). A recent meta-analysis has shown that such effects do occur with cyber security assessments, and most commonly lead to suboptimal self-protective behaviours (Alnifie & Kim, 2023). Optimism bias implies that perceived knowledge may not accurately capture how well-equipped people are to protect themselves online and the roles of perceived and actual knowledge in self-protective behaviour may even conflict. Therefore, it is necessary to determine whether actual knowledge is a better predictor of self-protective behaviour once these biases are eliminated.

Actual knowledge (i.e., what individuals objectively know about cybercrime) is rarely included in earlier studies, making its effects on intentions unclear (De Kimpe et al., 2022). The role of actual knowledge has been studied in an organisational context, suggesting that as employee's knowledge improved, so did their attitude toward cybersecurity (Roberts, 2021). Therefore, it is likely that actual knowledge plays a crucial role in individuals' engagement in self-protective behaviour, because individuals with high actual knowledge are by definition more aware of threats and countermeasures. Individuals' perceived knowledge might also differ from their actual knowledge, leading them to take different actions to those with greater actual knowledge, because they misunderstand which threats to prioritize and/or suboptimal protection decisions. The limited research examining the role of actual knowledge on self-reported online behaviour suggests it is positively related to safer online behaviour when sharing personal information (Van 't Hoff– de Goede et al., 2019), and there is a positive association between procedural knowledge and self-efficacy (Arachchilage & Love, 2014). Nonetheless, there remains little insight about how actual knowledge affects individuals' willingness to engage in self-protective behaviour to prevent cybercrime victimisation (Haag et al., 2021).

1.2 Protection Motivation Theory

Actual and perceived knowledge likely influence individuals' ability to make more informed decisions about risks. Protection Motivation Theory (PMT) is a dominant model of appraising how individuals make risk decisions related to information security behaviours (De Kimpe et al., 2022; Jansen, 2018). Over the years, PMT has become one of the best explanatory theories for predicting individuals' intention for protective behavior (Floyd et al., 2000). PMT distinguishes two appraisal processes: threat appraisal and coping appraisal. The outcomes of these processes result in protection motivation, i.e., behavioural intentions (Rogers, 1975).

Threat appraisal comprises evaluations of an individuals' perceived vulnerability to negative outcomes, and the perceived severity of those outcomes (De Kimpe et al., 2022). Several studies have suggested that both evaluations are positively associated with individuals' self-protection intentions (Haag et al., 2021; Martens et al., 2019; Rogers, 1975). Coping appraisals capture whether individuals believe they can enact strategies to prevent or reduce threat impacts, and compromises the personal capability to implement security measures (self-efficacy), the extent to which an individual considers these measures as effective (response efficacy), and the relative costs for a given security measure (response costs) (De Kimpe et al., 2022; Haag et al., 2021; Martens et al., 2019; Rogers, 1975). Earlier studies demonstrated that both self-efficacy and response efficacy positively affected individuals' intentions (e.g., De Kimpe et al., 2022; Martens et al., 2019). However, contradictory results were found for the association between response costs and intentions for self-protective behaviour. Gurung et al. (2009) suggested that response costs do not predict self-protective behaviour due to the plethora of free protection measures that is offered. Therefore, we do not include this.

We propose that actual and perceived knowledge serve as distinct antecedents of threat and coping appraisals within an extended PMT framework. Actual knowledge is predicted to be positively related to threat and coping appraisals, because knowledgeable individuals should be aware of both genuine risks and counter measures. Perceived knowledge is expected to be positively associated with coping appraisals, but negatively associated with threat appraisals in line with prior studies. Lastly, we include internet trust as a third antecedent. We define trust as: "The belief that the other party will behave in a socially responsible manner" [p. 106] (Pavlou, 2003). We include internet trust, because too much trust can lead to over-confidence, resulting in careless behaviour (Furnell, 2008). De Kimpe et al. (2022) indicate that internet trust is positively correlated with perceived knowledge and negatively affected perceived severity and perceived vulnerability. A negative relationship between trust and perceived risk, and between trust and protection motivation have also been demonstrated elsewhere (Jansen & van Schaik, 2018). Overall, we expect internet trust to be related to reduced threat appraisal. Thus, the current study focuses on the role of actual knowledge on individuals' intentions to engage in self-protective behaviour. We tested the following sixteen hypotheses:

H1: Perceived severity (1a), perceived vulnerability (1b), self-efficacy (1c), and response efficacy (1d) are positive predictors of intentions toward self-protective behaviour.

H2: Actual knowledge is a positive predictor of perceived severity (2a), perceived vulnerability (2b), self-efficacy (2c), response efficacy (2d), and intentions (2e).

H3: Perceived knowledge is a positive predictor of perceived severity (3a), self-efficacy (3b) and response efficacy (3c), and a negative predictor perceived vulnerability (3d) and intentions (3e)

H4: Internet trust is a negative predictor of perceived severity (4a) and perceived vulnerability (4b).

2. METHODS

2.1 Participants and Measures

In total, 222 participants participated in our study, and the majority were Dutch (56.8%). The age range was between 18 and 67 years (M = 29.9; SD = 12.2). Most participants (145, 65,3%) identified as female, 70 participants (31.5%) identified as male, three participants (1.4%) as non-binary, and one participant (0.5%) did not want to share their gender. Participants were recruited with snowball and convenience sampling procedures. Additionally, the SONA-system of the University of Twente was used, which is a test subject arrangement.

To measure participants' actual knowledge of cybercrime, we used nine questions from the actual knowledge test of Van 't Hoff - de Goede et al. (2019). Participants were asked to select the correct answer, for instance, "*What does it mean if a website is 'infected'?*". Participants received a point for each correct answer (M = 4.74; SD = 1.76), with α = .58. To measure their perceived knowledge, we used two items: (1) "*I feel adequately informed about cybercrime risks*"; and (2) "*I feel adequately informed about how to avoid cybercrime risks.*" (De Kimpe et al., 2022). These items were measured using a five-point Likert Scale (1 = "totally disagree" to 5 = "totally agree"). This construct had a Cronbach's Alpha, α = .86, indicating a good internal reliability (George & Mallery, 2019). This resulted in an average score of M = 3.38 (SD = 0.97).

The items in our questionnaire for internet trust, threat and coping appraisals are derived from previous studies (De Kimpe et al., 2022; Martens et al., 2019) and were adapted to our study (Table 1). Intentions toward self-protective behaviour were measured using items from Anderson and Agarwal (2010). De Kimpe et al. (2022) argue that protections and vulnerabilities against different cybercrimes are often related. Consequently, the measures taken to prevent victimisation typically safeguard individuals against multiple types of cybercrime. Therefore, we studied intentions toward protection measures in general. These items were all measured using a five-point Likert Scale (1 = "totally disagree" to 5 = "totally agree"), except for perceived vulnerability. The items for this construct were reversed, with 1 = "totally agree" to 5 = "totally disagree". We did this to reduce response bias and prevent acquiescence bias (Schriesheim & Hill, 1981). All subscales showed a good internal consistency, except for response efficacy (α = .57)[1] (Tavakol & Dennick, 2011).

[1] We performed additional tests to find an explanation for our low alpha of response efficacy. These tests included a factor analysis, a reliability analysis and correlations between the items. However, the outcomes of these tests do not provide any clarification for this. Additionally, these items are based on items used in earlier studies, in which the alpha for response efficacy was considerably higher.

Table 1. Descriptive Statistics of Items ($N = 222$)

	M	*SD*	*α*
Internet trust	**2.37**	**0.72**	**.78**
I am optimistic about the safety of the internet			
I have every confidence that the internet is safe			
I am satisfied with the safety of the internet			
Perceived severity	**4.33**	**0.59**	**.85**
I believe cybercrime is an important problem/phenomenon			
I believe cybercrime should be taken seriously			
I believe cybercrime is a severe problem			
Perceived vulnerability	**3.33**	**0.89**	**.87**
It is not likely that I become a victim of cybercrime			
It is not probable that I become a victim of cybercrime			
The risk is small that I become a victim of cybercrime			
Self-efficacy	**3.12**	**0.79**	**.76**
Using necessary protection tools against cybercrime is easy			
I feel comfortable using protection tools against cybercrime			
I possess the knowledge and skills to use the necessary protection tools against cybercrime			
Response efficacy	**3.54**	**0.56**	**.57**
Protection tools against cybercrime are effective in preventing cybercrime			
By using protection tools, I can avoid cybercrime			
I am less likely to become a victim of cybercrime if I use protection tools			
Intention toward behaviour	**3.87**	**0.64**	**.74**
I am likely to use protection tools against cybercrime			
I am sure I am going to use protection tools against cybercrime			
I am willing to use protection tools against cybercrime			

2.2 Procedure, and Data Analysis

First, participants read information about the topic and duration of the study. If they consented to participate, they provided their demographics, followed by two items measuring their perceived knowledge. Subsequently, their actual knowledge was tested. Lastly, participants were asked to rate PMT statements and were debriefed about the study. Data collection took place between November and December 2022. Before data collection started, this study was approved by the Ethics Committee of the University of Twente (request number: 221187). We have addressed potential common method bias and the likelihood of participants giving socially desirable answers by guarantying anonymity (Podsakoff et al., 2003).

SPSS (version 28) was used for data analysis. To study the relationships between the constructs, correlations were calculated. The hypotheses were tested using seven regression analyses, which are detailed in the following section.

3. RESULTS

3.1 Correlations

Correlations were calculated to study the relations between the antecedents and the constructs, the antecedents and intentions, and the constructs and intentions (Table 2). A positive correlation was found between actual and perceived knowledge and between perceived knowledge and internet trust, whereas we observed a negative association between actual knowledge and internet trust. Lastly, significant positive associations were found between the original PMT constructs and intentions, except for perceived vulnerability.

Table 2. Pearson Correlations Between Variables

	ACK	PCK	ITR	PSE	PVU	SEE	REE	INT
ACK								
PCK	.21**							
ITR	-.16*	.24***						
PSE	.24***	.09	-.30***					
PVU	.02	-.20***	-.37***	.15*				
SEE	.17*	.45***	.24***	.01	-.30***			
REE	.19**	.12	.07	,01	-.26***	.29***		
INT	.32***	.30***	-.08	.32***	.07	.40***	.20***	

*p <.05, ** p <.01, ***p <.001
ACK = actual knowledge, PCK = perceived knowledge, ITR = internet trust, PSE = perceived severity, PVU = perceived vulnerability, SEE = self-efficacy, REE = response efficacy, and INT = intentions

3.2 Regressions

Seven linear, multiple regression analyses were conducted to study the predictors of threat and coping appraisal, and the intentions toward self-protective behaviour. The standardized regression (β) was reported, as the measurement of the predictor variables differed and we are interested in the relative rather than absolute strength of predictors (Bring, 1994). The first multiple, linear regression included all variables (i.e., the four original PMT constructs, actual knowledge, perceived knowledge and internet trust) to study the predictive power of these variables on intentions (Table 3). This regression shows that self-efficacy was the strongest predictor of intentions.

Table 3. Linear, Multiple Regression

From	To	β	SE	t	ηp2
PSE	INT	.22***	.07	2.69	.17
PVU	INT	.17**	.05	5.17	.05
SEE	INT	.35***	.06	1.68	.20
REE	INT	.10	.07	2.46	.07
ACK	INT	.15*	.02	1.86	.13
PCK	INT	.12	.04	-.70	.13
ITR	INT	-.05	.06	3.59	.07

*p <.05, ** p <.01, *** p <.001
ACK = actual knowledge, PCK = perceived knowledge, ITR = internet trust, PSE = perceived severity, PVU = perceived vulnerability, SEE = self-efficacy, REE = response efficacy, and INT = intentions

The previous regression analysis was followed by six linear, multiple regression analyses that separately assessed the hypotheses (Table 4).

Table 4. Linear, Multiple Regressions with Hypotheses

H	From	To	β	SE	t	ηp2	H confirmed?
1a	PSE	INT	.27***	.07	4.66	.09	+
1b	PVU	INT	.18**	.05	2.92	.04	+
1c	SEE	INT	.42***	.05	6.66	.18	+
1d	REE	INT	.13*	.07	2.02	.02	+
2a	ACK	PSE	.15*	.02	2.23	.02	+
2b	ACK	PVU	-.01	.04	-1.58	.00	ns
2c	ACK	SEE	.12	.03	1.85	.01	ns
2d	ACK	REE	.18**	.02	2.62	.03	+
2e	ACK	INT	.26***	.02	4.05	.07	+
3a	PCK	PSE	.13	.04	1.84	.02	ns
3b	PCK	SEE	.39***	.05	6.02	.19	+
3c	PCK	REE	.06	.04	0.85	.01	ns
3d	PCK	PVU	-.12	.06	-1.76	.01	ns
3e	PCK	INT	.24***	.04	3.74	.06	-
4a	ITR	PSE	-.30***	.06	-4.46	.09	+
4b	ITR	PVU	-.34***	.08	-5.13	.11	+

*p <.05, ** p <.01, *** p <.001
ACK = actual knowledge, PCK = perceived knowledge, ITR = internet trust, PSE = perceived severity, PVU = perceived vulnerability, SEE = self-efficacy, REE = response efficacy, and INT = intentions

Significant, positive relations were found for all original PMT constructs on intentions (i.e. perceived severity (H1a), perceived vulnerability (H1b), self-efficacy (H1c), and response efficacy (H1d)). The relation between actual knowledge and perceived severity (H2a), response efficacy (H2d) and intentions (H2e) were significant, whereas the association between actual knowledge and perceived vulnerability (H2b) and self-efficacy (H2c) was not significant. We found non-significant relations between perceived knowledge and perceived severity (H3a), perceived knowledge and response efficacy (H3c), and perceived knowledge and perceived vulnerability (H3d). The relation between perceived knowledge and self-efficacy (H3b) was significant. Unexpectedly, we found a significant, positive relation between perceived knowledge and intentions (H3e). Lastly, we found significant relations between internet trust and perceived severity (H4a), and internet trust and perceived vulnerability (H4b).

An additional exploratory, multiple regression analysis was performed to determine whether actual and perceived knowledge independently predicted intentions, while also accounting self-efficacy. This variable was included as it was the strongest predictor of intentions, and we hypothesized that there might be conceptual overlap between perceived knowledge and self-efficacy. This analysis showed that actual knowledge ($\beta = .23$, $SE = .02$, $p < .01$, $\eta p^2 = .06$) and self-efficacy ($\beta = .31$, $SE = .06$, $p < .01$, $\eta p^2 = .09$) were significant, positive predictors of intentions, while perceived knowledge was no longer related to intentions after self-efficacy was included ($\beta = .11$, $SE = .06$, $p = .10$, $\eta p^2 = .01$).

4. DISCUSSION

A key finding of this study is that actual knowledge is a crucial indicator for the willingness to engage in self-protective behaviour to prevent cybercrime ealization n. Additionally, actual knowledge was positively related to perceived severity and response efficacy, and negatively correlated with internet trust. On the contrary, perceived knowledge and internet trust were positively correlated. This is in line with the study of De Kimpe et al. (2022). Individuals with high levels of perceived knowledge may overestimate their protection skills, also known as the optimism bias (Slovic, 1987). When they are aware of obvious attempts of cybercrime, they might believe they can identify future other attempts as well, due to their self-perceived knowledge (Martens et al., 2019). Subsequently, they may underestimate the severity of cybercrime risks and mistakenly consider the internet to be safe, which is in line with previous studies (De Kimpe et al., 2022). In contrast, as actual knowledge increases, so does the ealization that susceptibility to risks are high. Actual knowledge was also a stronger indicator for individuals' intentions than perceived knowledge. Furthermore, perceived severity was positively associated with actual knowledge, whereas it was not related to perceived knowledge. Lastly, actual knowledge was negatively associated with internet trust, whereas perceived knowledge was positively associated with this construct. This suggests that being well-informed about cybercrime is more important for protection motivation than the mere perception of being well-informed. Additionally, this indicates that individuals who are well-informed perceived cybercrime as a (more) severe threat, whereas individuals who considered themselves as well-informed lacked this perception. Consequently, individuals may consider themselves as less vulnerable and disregard protection measures, since they believe they are not a target to become a victim, which eventually makes them more vulnerable to become a victim (Drew & Farrell, 2020). Therefore, this study highlights the importance of future cybercrime prevention interventions focusing on increasing individuals' actual knowledge, rather than solely enhancing perceived knowledge.

Both actual and perceived knowledge were positively correlated, indicating that perceived knowledge is likely at least partly derived from actual knowledge. Perceived knowledge has its benefits, as it enhances individuals' capability to engage in self-protective behaviour (De Kimpe et al., 2022). Additionally, it is positively associated with intentions (Huang et al., 2011) and our study shows that as well. However, the association between perceived knowledge and self-protection intentions might be explained by the covariance between perceived knowledge and self-efficacy. Individuals with high levels of perceived knowledge consider themselves well-informed and capable of self-protection, resulting in higher levels of self-efficacy. Our analysis showed that perceived knowledge no longer predicted intentions once self-efficacy was included in the regression model, while actual knowledge continued to independently predict intentions when including self-efficacy. Actual knowledge was not related to self-efficacy, but it was positively associated with response efficacy, suggesting that people who are well-informed view protection measures as effective. Although actual knowledge was a stronger predictor for intentions, it explained only a small part of variance in response efficacy and was not associated with self-efficacy. Simultaneously, perceived knowledge was positively associated with self-efficacy, a critical component of individuals' intentions. This highlights the need for both motivational and factual education, as the two types of efficacy may be based on different types of knowledge.

However, a balance between actual and perceived knowledge should be safeguarded. It is crucial that future interventions (e.g., crime prevention programs or awareness campaigns) focus on increasing individuals' actual knowledge without only awakening perceived knowledge. These two types of knowledge activate different types of efficacy, indicating the need for both factual and motivational elements in education. However, these education programs should be tailored to individuals' level of knowledge (Martens et al., 2019). Indeed, underestimating online threats may encourage individuals to behave unsafely. On the other hand, overestimating the threats can also have negative effects, such as avoiding the usage of internet (Jansen, 2018). It is therefore crucial that this balance between actual knowledge and perceived knowledge will be established.

4.1 Limitations

As we measured intentions toward behaviour in the current study, it is important to note that intentions do not always result in actual behaviour, the well-known behaviour-intention gap (Sheeran, 2002). A longitudinal study, preferably observing or measuring actual behaviour, would allow a direct test of what form of knowledge is most associated with behaviour over time. Moreover, longitudinal or experimental research approaches are necessary to observe cause-and-effect-sequences, as our study is limited to measuring associations at one point in time. Nonetheless, intentions could be a reasonable predictor of behaviour (Scholz et al., 2008).

Another limitation is the validity of the knowledge test used in this study. This test might be one of the scarce measures focusing on actual knowledge. The Cronbach's Alpha for this test was relatively low, but still considered reasonable given the explorative nature of the study. Additionally, it is unclear whether our questions cover the most critical issues for assessing individuals' actual knowledge. Future research could employ a different approach (e.g., a Delphi study) to identify knowledge individuals need to keep themselves safe and use this input for an updated knowledge test. It should also be noted that advice for self-protective behaviour may change over time, potentially limiting the longevity of the construct. Therefore, it is crucial to continually update the measure to validate it or develop a measure that focuses on stable principles rather than details that will likely change over the years.

4.2 Conclusion

Actual knowledge seems to be an important predictor for individuals' willingness to engage in self-protective behaviour to prevent cybercrime victimisation. Additionally, it was positively associated with perceived severity and negatively associated with internet trust. These findings suggest that people who overestimate their knowledge or consider the internet as a safe place are especially vulnerable to become a victim of cybercrime. To motivate users to take concrete protection measures we show that increasing risk perceptions, self-efficacy, and response efficacy are all effective, which aligns with the premise of PMT Additionally, actual knowledge was more effective than perceived knowledge in affecting perceived risks and response efficacy. Perceived knowledge was however most strongly associated with self-efficacy, which plausibly reflects that training requires a motivational and not only a factual element. Studies measuring the success of these interventions should therefore also focus on actual knowledge and not only perceived knowledge to validate whether these interventions are effective. It matters what you know, not only what you think you know.

REFERENCES

Akkermans, M., Derksen, E., Kennis, M., Kloosterman, R., & Moons, E. (2024). Veiligheidsmonitor 2023. https://download.cbs.nl/maatwerk/Veiligheidsmonitor-2023.pdf

Alnifie, K. M., & Kim, C. (2023). Appraising the manifestation of optimism bias and its impact on human perception of cyber security: A meta analysis. Journal of Information Security, 14(02), 93–110. https://doi.org/10.4236/jis.2023.142007

Anderson, & Agarwal. (2010). Practicing safe computing: A multimethod empirical examination of home computer user security behavioral intentions. MIS Quarterly, 34(3), 613. https://doi.org/10.2307/25750694

Arachchilage, N. A. G., & Love, S. (2014). Security awareness of computer users: A phishing threat avoidance perspective. Computers in Human Behavior, 38, 304–312. https://doi.org/10.1016/j.chb.2014.05.046

Bring, J. (1994). How to standardize regression coefficients. The American Statistician, 48(3), 209–213. https://doi.org/10.1080/00031305.1994.10476059

De Kimpe, L., Walrave, M., Verdegem, P., & Ponnet, K. (2022). What we think we know about cybersecurity: an investigation of the relationship between perceived knowledge, internet trust, and protection motivation in a cybercrime context. Behaviour & Information Technology, 41(8), 1796–1808. https://doi.org/10.1080/0144929X.2021.1905066

Domenie, M. M., Leukfeldt, E. R., Van Wilsem, J. A., Jansen, J., & Stol, W. P. (2013). Victimisation in a digitised society: A survey among the members of the public concerning e-fraud, hacking and other high-volume crimes. Eleven International Publishing.

Drew, J. M., & Farrell, L. (2020). A study of cybercrime victimisation and prevention: exploring the use of online crime prevention behaviours and strategies. Journal of Criminological Research, Policy and Practice, 6(1), 17–33. https://doi.org/10.1108/JCRPP-12-2019-0070

Furnell, S. (2008). Securing information and communications systems: Principles, technologies, and applications. Artech House.

George, D., & Mallery, P. (2019). IBM SPSS Statistics 26 Step by Step. https://doi.org/10.4324/9780429056765

Gurung, A., Luo, X., & Liao, Q. (2009). Consumer motivations in taking action against spyware: an empirical investigation. Information Management & Computer Security, 17(3), 276–289. https://doi.org/10.1108/09685220910978112

Haag, S., Siponen, M., & Liu, F. (2021). Protection motivation theory in information systems security research. ACM SIGMIS Database: The DATABASE for Advances in Information Systems, 52(2), 25–67. https://doi.org/10.1145/3462766.3462770

Huang, D.-L., Patrick Rau, P.-L., Salvendy, G., Gao, F., & Zhou, J. (2011). Factors affecting perception of information security and their impacts on IT adoption and security practices. International Journal of Human-Computer Studies, 69(12), 870–883. https://doi.org/10.1016/j.ijhcs.2011.07.007

Jansen, J. (2018). Do you bend or break? Preventing online banking fraud victimization through online resilience. Open Universiteit.

Jansen, J., & van Schaik, P. (2018). Testing a model of precautionary online behaviour: The case of online banking. Computers in Human Behavior, 87, 371–383. https://doi.org/10.1016/j.chb.2018.05.010

Martens, M., De Wolf, R., & De Marez, L. (2019). Investigating and comparing the predictors of the intention towards taking security measures against malware, scams and cybercrime in general. Computers in Human Behavior, 92, 139–150. https://doi.org/10.1016/j.chb.2018.11.002

NCTV. (2023). Cybersecuritybeeld Nederland 2023. https://www.nctv.nl/onderwerpen/cybersecuritybeeld-nederland/documenten/publicaties/2023/07/03/cybersecuritybeeld-nederland-2023

Pavlou, P. A. (2003). Consumer acceptance of electronic commerce: Integrating trust and risk with the technology acceptance model. International Journal of Electronic Commerce, 7(3), 101–134. https://doi.org/10.1080/10864415.2003.11044275

Podsakoff, P. M., MacKenzie, S. B., Lee, J.-Y., & Podsakoff, N. P. (2003). Common method biases in behavioral research: A critical review of the literature and recommended remedies. Journal of Applied Psychology, 88(5), 879–903. https://doi.org/10.1037/0021-9010.88.5.879

Roberts, S. A. (2021). Exploring the Relationships Between User Cybersecurity Knowledge, Cybersecurity and Cybercrime Attitudes, and Online Risky Behaviors. Northcentral University.

Rogers, R. W. (1975). A protection motivation theory of fear appeals and attitude change. The Journal of Psychology, 91(1), 93–114. https://doi.org/10.1080/00223980.1975.9915803

Scholz, U., Schüz, B., Ziegelmann, J. P., Lippke, S., & Schwarzer, R. (2008). Beyond behavioural intentions: Planning mediates between intentions and physical activity. British Journal of Health Psychology, 13(3), 479–494. https://doi.org/10.1348/135910707X216062

Schriesheim, C. A., & Hill, K. D. (1981). Controlling Acquiescence Response Bias by Item Reversals: The Effect on Questionnaire Validity. Educational and Psychological Measurement, 41(4), 1101–1114. https://doi.org/10.1177/001316448104100420

Sheeran, P. (2002). Intention—behavior relations: A conceptual and empirical review. European Review of Social Psychology, 12(1), 1–36. https://doi.org/10.1080/14792772143000003

Slovic, P. (1987). Perception of risk. Science, 236(4799), 280–285. https://doi.org/10.1126/science.3563507

Tavakol, M., & Dennick, R. (2011). Making sense of Cronbach's alpha. International Journal of Medical Education, 2, 53–55. https://doi.org/10.5116/ijme.4dfb.8dfd

Van 't Hoff - de Goede, S., Van der Kleij, R., Van der Weijer, S., & Leukfeldt, R. (2019). Hoe veilig gedragen wij ons online? https://repository.wodc.nl/bitstream/handle/20.500.12832/2433/2975_Volledige_Tekst_tcm28-421151.pdf?sequence=2&isAllowed=y

Weinstein, N. D. (1980). Unrealistic optimism about future life events. Journal of Personality and Social Psychology, 39(5), 806–820. https://doi.org/10.1037/0022-3514.39.5.806

ADVERSARIAL MACHINE LEARNING IN ELECTRICAL POWER AND ENERGY SYSTEMS: A SURVEY

Sotiris Pelekis, Thanos Koutroubas, Afroditi Blika, Evangelos Karakolis, Christos Ntanos and Dimitris Askounis
Decision Support Systems Laboratory, National Technical University of Athens
Iroon Polytechneiou 9, 15772, Zografou, Greece

ABSTRACT

The growing dependence on Artificial Intelligence (AI) within Electrical Power and Energy Systems (EPES) and smart grids introduces vulnerabilities that can be exploited by adversarial attacks threatening their security and reliability. This brief review elaborates on the different aspects of Adversarial Machine Learning (AML) in EPES, namely adversarial attack methodologies, defense mechanisms, and robustness benchmarking procedures. The paper also underlines some of the key practical challenges regarding trade-offs between robustness, computational cost, and accuracy, impacting the feasibility of large-scale deployment of AML methods. In parallel, we attempt to identify current gaps and suggest future research directions to enable robust and secure integration of AI into EPES towards critical infrastructures that are resilient adversarial threats. Focusing on modern power systems and smart grids, our study provides the respective stakeholders (e.g. grid operators, utilities, aggregators) and research community with useful, targeted insights on the specific domain rather than providing generic background that can be disorienting at times.

KEYWORDS

Smart Grid, Power System, Adversarial Machine Learning, Robustness, Cybersecurity

1. INTRODUCTION

In modern Electrical Power and Energy Systems (EPES) and smart grids, Artificial Intelligence (AI) and Machine Learning (ML) are crucial in improving efficiency and energy management (Karakolis et al., 2022, 2023). Processing high volumes of data, such as historical demand patterns, real-time consumption fluctuations, and weather conditions improves load forecasting (Pelekis et al., 2022, 2024; Pelekis, Seisopoulos, et al., 2023), which is a crucial aspect in energy distribution planning which is critical for short, medium, and long-term grid and dispatch planning. Apart from load forecasting, AI also assists the evaluation of grid stability with respect to power, voltage, and frequency (Omitaomu & Niu, 2021), hence enhancing its resilience and reliability guaranteeing, minimizing outages and blackouts (Song et al., 2021). In parallel, it also ensures flexibility and demand response (Michalakopoulos et al., 2024; Pelekis, Pipergias, et al., 2023) alongsied Non-Intrusive Load Monitoring (NILM) (Angelis et al., 2022) and Electricity Theft Detection (ETD). However, this extensive use of AI/ML in power systems, especially within smart grids, introduces potential weaknesses that can be exploited by adversarial attacks. These covert attacks can lead to either random or targeted disruptions (Hao & Tao, 2022) and can impact various areas, resulting in operational disturbances and data security issues (J. Li et al., 2020).

The purpose of this paper is to briefly analyze the current research landscape of AML in EPES including attacks, corresponding countermeasures and targeted evaluation methods for the specific industry sector. Although various surveys have studied the current AML landscape (Finlayson et al., 2019; Hao & Tao, 2022; Machado et al., 2021; Siva Kumar et al., 2020; Vassilev et al., 2024; X. Wang et al., 2019) our study is targeted to power systems providing the respective stakeholders (e.g. Grid operators, utilities, aggregators) and research community with the very specifics of the domain. Contrary to Hao & Tao, which focus on adversarial attacks we contribute by offering the bigger picture of AML in the sector by including defenses and evaluation methods, while also updating the state-of-the-art until mid-2024, when the publications' collection for this paper was terminated.

Section 1 introduced our background and presented the contributions of our paper. Section 2 dives into the literature of adversarial attacks in the EPES domain, while Section 3 presents the corresponding countermeasures accompanied by notes on evaluation. Finally, Section 4, wraps up the document with concluding remarks and future perspectives.

2. ADVERSARIAL LANDSCAPE IN EPES AND SMART GRIDS

Evasion attacks, both white-box and black-box, are the most prevalent forms of attack in the energy sector, largely because the area of poisoning attacks has not been thoroughly researched, resulting in a scarcity of relevant publications in the literature (Hao & Tao, 2022). Furthermore, smart grids are susceptible to privacy attacks since consumer data, such as electricity consumption metrics, are significantly more exposed than in traditional power systems (Omitaomu & Niu, 2021). A summary of the current state-of-the-art in adversarial attacks in EPES and smart grids is given in Table 1.

2.1 Evasion

Evasion attacks can affect various subsystems, including False Data Injection Attacks (FDIA), ETD, demand forecasting, Voltage Stability Assessment (VSA), power quality classification, Event Cause Analysis (ECA), occupancy detection (Yilmaz & Siraj, 2021), and NILM (J. Wang & Srikantha, 2021).

With respect to attacks against FDIA detectors, they primarily use white-box methods against multi-layer perceptrons (MLPs), focusing on undermining the accuracy of ML models employed for FDIA detection. Although ML models have demonstrated effectiveness in recognizing such attacks, they remain susceptible to adversarial attacks. For instance, research indicates that an MLP capable of detecting FDIAs with 99% accuracy can experience a drastic decline in performance, dropping to 20% and 10% after 15 iterations of the Limited-memory Broyden–Fletcher–Goldfarb–Shanno (L-BFGS) attack and the Jacobian-based Saliency Map Attack (JSMA), respectively (Sayghe, Zhao, et al., 2020). Similarly, Sayghe, Anubi, et al. (2020) demonstrate that a 99 % accuracy MLP sees significant performance degradation with the Targeted Fast Gradient Sign Method (TFGSM), dropping to 85% for ϵ=0.1, 40% for ϵ=0.2, and 10% for ϵ=0.3. Additionally, in a study conducted by J. Li et al. (2023), a deep neural network's (DNN) recall drops to as low as 0.9% when subjected to Basic Iterative Method (BIM) attacks with varying perturbations.

Adversaries also focus on ETD usually by altering energy consumption data to evade the respective monitoring system. These attacks typically operate under the assumption that the attacker has access to energy meters, allowing them to manipulate the readings transmitted to the network. Said adversarial attacks can be classified as either white-box or black-box attacks, with black-box methods often being more realistic in real-world use cases. A study (J. Li et al., 2020) evaluated the gradient-based SearchFromFree attack, akin to DeepFool (Moosavi-Dezfooli et al., 2016), on various neural networks (DNN, RNN, and CNN). The findings revealed that adversarial examples could reduce detection accuracy to nearly 0% in white-box and to 20% in black-box settings, highlighting how attackers can successfully bypass detection mechanisms even without comprehensive knowledge of the underlying system.

In addition to ETD, adversaries also focus on load forecasting models, particularly short-term load forecasting (STLF) as manipulating long-term predictions is more challenging due to the greater volume of data and the duration of the attacks. These adversarial actions typically involve introducing adversarial examples to evade ML models, potentially causing significant operational issues. A study (Chen et al., 2019) demonstrated that black-box attack targeting various models including feed-forward NNs, Recurrent Neural Networks (RNNs), and Long Short-Term Memory networks (LSTMs), demonstrated that even slight disturbances in temperature inputs could lead to substantial forecasting errors. Specifically, a mere 4°F increase in temperature readings resulted in a 13% rise in forecasting errors, which could severely impact grid operations by increasing costs or necessitating load shedding.

Adversaries are also focusing on power quality classification models and ECA systems by injecting adversarial examples into voltage signal values to manipulate these evaluation systems. Research (Chen et al., 2018) indicates that adversarial examples can be generated using a technique similar to the Fast Gradient Sign (FGS) attack, in which minor disturbances are added to voltage values to evade detection. Applying this approach to feed-forward NN under black-box setting, it was found that the accuracy of the power quality classifier decreased by 30% when subjected to 40% signal changes with disturbances of ϵ=0.1, showcasing how adversarial attacks can significantly undermine the reliability of power quality assessments.

In the context of VSA, various well-known attacks have been tested by Song et al. (2021) including Fast Gradient Sign Method (FGSM) (Goodfellow et al., 2015), Projected Gradient Descent (PGD) (Madry et al., 2018), DeepFool (Moosavi-Dezfooli et al., 2016), Carlini & Wagner (C&W) (Carlini & Wagner, 2017), and universal perturbations/networks (Moosavi-Dezfooli et al., 2017) on CNN models. These attacks involve adding disturbances to bus voltage values in both white-box and black-box scenarios. The CNN model initially achieved a stability validation accuracy of 99.5%. However, under input-specific white-box attacks, this accuracy significantly dropped to 57.6% when 20 bus voltage measurement points were targeted using the PGD attack and plummeted to 15.5% with 39 points under the C&W attack. In black-box scenarios, the accuracy decline was less severe, with a minimum accuracy of 46.1% observed during the PGD attack. Universal attacks produced comparable results in both settings, resulting in an accuracy decrease to 49.5%.

With respect to ECA attacks, research by Niazazari & Livani (2020) demonstrates that employing FGSM and JSMA attacks on CNN models can achieve a 76% attack success rate (ASR) with a perturbation parameter of ϵ=0.07 in white-box scenarios. Additionally, these attacks demonstrate up to 80% transferability in black-box scenarios when using a substitute model indicating the effectiveness of adversarial examples in deteriorating the performance of ECA systems.

2.2 Poisoning Attacks and Privacy Breaches

The literature on poisoning attacks in EPES, although still limited, reveals significant vulnerabilities within power grid infrastructures, particularly in load forecasting and state estimation (Agah et al., 2024). For example, Qureshi et al. (2022) examined how adversarial disruptions could be implemented on an LSTM load forecasting model. This highlights the security risks associated with federated learning, which, while designed to safeguard user data privacy, creates multiple points of vulnerability if any agents are compromised and send poisoned weights to the central server.

Despite its commonality in other domains, currently the literature on privacy attacks in EPES is also very limited, as no specific studies investigate or report data confidentiality breaches due to models deployed within smart grids. Nonetheless, ML models can be highly vulnerable to model extraction, model inversion, and membership-inference attacks (Kumar et al., 2019) that can allow adversaries to reconstruct sensitive information about the training data or the model itself. This underscores the urgent need for targeted research and practical frameworks that will address these emerging threats.

Table 1. State-of-the-art adversarial attacks in the EPES domain

Ref.	Knowledge	Target Model	Attack Type	Attack Technique	Results
Qureshi et al (2022)	White-Box	MLP	Evasion	L-BFGS, JSMA	L-BFGS: 20% accuracy, JSMA: 10% accuracy
Sayghe, Anubi, et al. (2020)	White-Box	MLP	Evasion	TFGSM	AD: 85% for ϵ=0.1, 40% for ϵ=0.2, 10% for ϵ=0.3
J. Li et al. (2023)	White-Box	DNN	Evasion	BIM	Min. recall 0.9%, Max. recall 18.9%
J. Li et al. (2020)	White-Box, Black-Box	DNN, RNN, CNN	Evasion	SearchFromFree	White-box: 0% accuracy from 86.9% in DNN, Black-box: 20% from 97.5% in RNN
Chen et al. (2019)	Black-Box	FNN, RNN, CNN	Evasion	Adversarial perturbations to temperature values	Max. prediction error: 13% from 1.5% with 4°F deviation in temperature
Chen et al. (2018)	Black-Box	FNN	Evasion	FGS	AD: 67.5% from 97.5% initially with γ=40%, ϵ=0.1
Song et al. (2021)	White-Box, Black-Box	CNN	Evasion	FGSM, PGD, DeepFool, C&W, Universal	White-box: Accuracy 57.6% with l=20 (PGD attack), 15.5% with l=39 (C&W), Black-box: Accuracy 46.1% with l=35 (PGD), 49.5% with l=20 (Universal)
Niazazari & Livani (2020	White-Box, Black-Box	CNN	Evasion	FGSM, JSMA	White-box: 76% ASR with $\ell\infty$, ϵ=0.07 (original accuracy 99.5%), Black-box: 80% transferability with ϵ=0.07 (substitute accuracy 94%)
Qureshi et al (2022)	White-Box	LSTM	Poisoning	Sign flipping attack, additive noise attack	Sign flipping attack significantly reduces the accuracy of load forecasting, resulting in a MAPE of 13.98%

3. DEFENSES AND EVALUATION METHODS

3.1 Countermeasures

To protect EPES and smart grids from adversarial attacks, several defense techniques have been proposed in the literature. Said defenses can be classified into categories such as data pre-processing, model hardening, and runtime detection. The latter is typically executed through auxiliary detection models. Each category addresses specific aspects attack prevention and detection, enhancing the robustness of ML models and maintaining system stability against a variety of adversarial threats. In data pre-processing defenses, techniques such as defensive distillation are employed to manage FDIAs, while Adversarial Perturbation Elimination GAN (APE-GAN) (Jin et al., 2019) is utilized to counter VSA attacks. Model hardening strategies include adversarial training to face FDIAs (J. Li et al., 2023), VSA attacks (Song et al., 2021), and ECA attacks (Niazazari & Livani, 2020). Additionally, gradient masking is implemented to smooth gradients and thwart optimization-based adversarial attacks (Hao & Tao, 2022). Regarding runtime detection, auxiliary detection models enhance defenses through various methods, including adversarial detection for FDIAs, classifier ensembles for identifying adversarial examples in ETD models (Takiddin et al., 2021), and attack detection techniques tailored for smart grid systems (Omitaomu & Niu, 2021).

Beyond the general classification of defense techniques applicable to most NNs, there are specific methods proposed to improve model robustness against particular attacks targeting network malfunctions. For instance, regarding FDIAs, J. Li et al. (2023) examine three traditional adversarial defenses. Techniques such as defensive distillation and adversarial training demonstrate limited effectiveness; the former results in a model that is less sensitive to input perturbations, while the latter struggles to scale effectively with large datasets due to the associated time and cost of training. However, Tian et al. (2019) highlight that adversarial training can significantly improve the robustness of DNNs against FGSM attacks, achieving a test accuracy of 98.4%. Moreover, adversarial detection methods face challenges as they often assume that adversarial examples follow distinct distributions, an assumption that does not hold true for FDIAs. A more effective approach is the implementation of a random input padding framework, which achieves an accuracy of 96% and a recall rate of 95% against ℓ_2-bounded perturbations.

To address Electricity Theft Detection (ETD), Takiddin et al. (2021) introduce an ensemble detector that utilizes auto-encoders with attention mechanisms, Gated Recurrent Units (GRUs), and feed-forward NNs against poisoning attacks. This ensemble detector achieves a high detection rate of 95.2% while maintaining a low false alarm rate of 2.9%, with performance variations of only 1-3% in the presence of poisoning attacks. With respect to VSA, Song et al. (2021) evaluate adversarial training using FGSM and PGD algorithms against various attack methods, including FGSM, PGD, DeepFool, C&W, and Universal Perturbations/Networks in both white-box and black-box scenarios. The results show that PGD adversarial training maintains over 80% accuracy when fewer than 30 bus voltage points are compromised. Additionally, APE-GAN is assessed but proves effective only in white-box settings. In the context of ECA attacks, Niazazari & Livani (2020) investigate adversarial training to develop a robust CNN classifier. Their findings indicate that the adversarially trained model is highly effective, exhibiting only a 5% attack success rate (ASR) even when subjected to perturbations with ϵ=0.3, which is sufficiently large for detection by bad data detectors.

In addition to the previously discussed defenses against evasion attacks, various general data protection methods can contribute in safeguarding ML model data, thereby protecting the privacy of smart grids. These methods not only ensure privacy, which is essential for system security and the robustness of ML models, but they also provide defense against other types of attacks (e.g. FDIA). As noted, energy consumption data in smart grids can be intercepted by attackers, making it crucial to develop techniques for detecting FDIAs without accessing personal consumption data (Cui et al., 2020). One promising solution employs Homomorphic Encryption (HE) to maintain confidentiality and privacy in Convolutional Neural Networks (CNNs) that detect abnormal behavior, achieving an accuracy of 92.67% in ETD (Yao et al., 2019). Furthermore, Federated Learning (FL) enhances data privacy by eliminating the need for data sharing and allowing computations to be performed locally (Cui et al., 2020). In a study by Y. Li et al. (2022), an FL-based FDIA detector integrates FL with a transformer model for attack detection while using HE to protect neural network weights. This approach outperforms traditional DL methods while ensuring user privacy preservation.

A summary of the current state-of-the-art in defenses in EPES and smart grids is given in Table 2.

Table 2. State-of-the-art adversarial defenses in the EPES domain

Ref.	Approach	Defense	Results
Tian et al. (2019)	Model Hardening	Adversarial Training	98.4% test accuracy and average perturbation value 0.14 in FGSM
J. Li et al. (2023)	Model Hardening	Random Input Padding Framework	96% accuracy and 95% recall, in ℓ_2
Takiddin et al. (2021	Runtime Detection	Ensemble Detector	95.2% detection rate and 2.9% false alarm rate, with 1-3% performance variation under poisoning attacks
Song et al. (2021)	Model Hardening	Adversarial Training	Over 80% accuracy for l=20 (with PGD adv training) in all scenarios
Song et al. (2021)	Data Pre-processing	APE-GAN	Over 80% accuracy for l=39 only in the White-box scenario for FGSM, PGD, C&W
Niazazari & Livani (2020)	Model Hardening	Adversarial Training	5% ASR with ϵ=0.3
Yao et al. (2019)	Privacy	HE	92.67% detection rate and data privacy

3.2 Evaluation of Defenses and Model Robustness

3.2.1 Robustness Tradeoffs

In the process of improving a model's robustness, other parameters may be negatively affected, leading to undesirable side effects. Thereafter, specific robustness trade-offs must be considered, as follows:

- **Robustness-Accuracy**: Occasionally, the training and design of a ML system focused on safety can conflict with the objective of achieving high accuracy. Techniques and methods aimed at enhancing the robustness of ML models —and thereby improving safety— may result in reducing the model's accuracy. While theoretical evidence indicates that there is no fundamental trade-off between robustness and accuracy, practical applications often demonstrate that existing methods do not succeed in enhancing both metrics simultaneously (Yang et al., 2020). A closer look on this tradeoff is provided by Yang et al. (2020).
- **Robustness-Computational Cost**: Enhancing robustness typically leads to increased computational costs for both training and testing stages. Adversarial training, for instance, requires more data to improve accuracy and is considerably more resource-intensive compared to standard training methods (Zhao et al., 2022). For example, Raghunathan et al. (2020) demonstrate that achieving a reduction in the standard error of adversarially trained models on CIFAR-10 requires a big amount of data, which is often impractical (Tsipras et al., 2019). Robust training generally focuses on ℓ_p-bounded perturbations, which limits the model's robustness against previously unseen adversarial examples. Additionally, extending robustness to accommodate multiple ℓ_p perturbations remains quite a challenging task at scale (Tramer & Boneh, 2019). As model complexity increases, the computational costs for robustness evaluation also rise, with precise methods struggling to scale effectively for larger models (Katz Guy and Barrett, 2017).
- **Robustness-Training time:** Enhancing model robustness often leads to longer training times, particularly for adversarial training, where new perturbations must be computed at each parameter update (Tsipras et al., 2019). For instance, using the PGD algorithm can require at least 10 additional iterations to generate adversarial examples, leading in a training slowdown of roughly 10x compared to standard training (J. Li, 2019). The RobustBench benchmark (Croce et al., 2021)}underscores that robust models take significantly longer to train. For instance, the most robust model for ℓ_2 on CIFAR-10 achieves 78.80% robust accuracy with a training time exceeding 15 hours. In contrast, the least robust model for ℓ_∞ on ImageNet has a robust accuracy of 25.31% but completes training in just 1.5 hours, again showcasing the trade-off in question.

3.2.2 Robustness Measures

In the EPES domain, the standardized metrics including ASR, Empirical Robustness, Local Loss Sensitivity, and CLEVER score (Weng et al., 2018; Wu et al., 2021) are not commonly used; instead, model performance is evaluated under variable attack sources. Specifically, metrics such as precision, recall, or F1-score are evaluated for various bus systems under attack, where the adversarial measurements should closely match the performance of the original model (Y. Li et al., 2022). In the case of VSA, for instance, any model with detection accuracy below 80\% is considered ineffective (Song et al., 2021). Moreover, for energy forecasting models, the Mean Absolute Percentage Error (MAPE) metric is usually used to evaluate the forecast error and the input feature deviation caused by the simultaneous addition of adversarial perturbations (Chen et al., 2018).

4. CONCLUSIONS

Ensuring the robustness and privacy of AI systems is critical for the reliable operation of EPES and smart grids, which form the backbone of modern energy infrastructure. This review has examined AML within this domain, documenting adversarial attacks alongside the corresponding defenses including evaluation concepts such as robustness measures and tradeoffs. As adversarial threats evolve, stakeholders in the EPES and smart grid ecosystem need to consider proactive, reactive, and adaptive strategies that deal with the resilience of AI systems. In this regard, even though certain progress has been achieved, the ability to attain practical scalable domain-specific solutions for cyber-secure ML in this particular domain still remains an open challenge. It is expected that future research will bridge the gap between theoretical advances and practical deployments, develop frameworks tailored to meet the unique requirements of EPES and smart grids, and ensure secure integrations of AI/ML technologies into these critical infrastructures.

ACKNOWLEDGEMENT

This work is supported by the Smart Networks and Services Joint Undertaking (SNS JU) under the European Union's Horizon Europe research and innovation programme under Grant Agreement No 101139198, iTrust6G project. Views and opinions expressed are those of the author(s) only and do not necessarily reflect those of the European Union or SNS-JU. Neither the European Union nor the granting authority can be held responsible for them.

REFERENCES

Agah, N., Mohammadi, J., Aved, A., Ferris, D., Cruz, E. A., & Morrone, P. (2024). *Data Poisoning: An Overlooked Threat to Power Grid Resilience*. https://arxiv.org/abs/2407.14684

Angelis, G. F., Timplalexis, C., Krinidis, S., Ioannidis, D., & Tzovaras, D. (2022). NILM applications: Literature review of learning approaches, recent developments and challenges. *Energy and Buildings*, *261*, 111951. https://doi.org/10.1016/J.ENBUILD.2022.111951

Carlini, N., & Wagner, D. (2017). Towards Evaluating the Robustness of Neural Networks. *2017 IEEE Symposium on Security and Privacy (SP)*, 39–57. https://doi.org/10.1109/SP.2017.49

Chen, Y., Tan, Y., & Deka, D. (2018). Is Machine Learning in Power Systems Vulnerable? *2018 IEEE International Conference on Communications, Control, and Computing Technologies for Smart Grids (SmartGridComm)*, 1–6. https://doi.org/10.1109/SmartGridComm.2018.8587547

Chen, Y., Tan, Y., & Zhang, B. (2019). Exploiting Vulnerabilities of Load Forecasting Through Adversarial Attacks. *Proceedings of the Tenth ACM International Conference on Future Energy Systems*, 1–11. https://doi.org/10.1145/3307772.3328314

Croce, F., Andriushchenko, M., Sehwag, V., Debenedetti, E., Flammarion, N., Chiang, M., Mittal, P., & Hein, M. (2021). RobustBench: a standardized adversarial robustness benchmark. *Thirty-Fifth Conference on Neural Information Processing Systems Datasets and Benchmarks Track (Round 2)*. https://openreview.net/forum?id=SSKZPJCt7B

Cui, L., Qu, Y., Gao, L., Xie, G., & Yu, S. (2020). Detecting false data attacks using machine learning techniques in smart grid: A survey. *Journal of Network and Computer Applications*, *170*, 102808. https://doi.org/https://doi.org/10.1016/j.jnca.2020.102808

Finlayson, S. G., Bowers, J. D., Ito, J., Zittrain, J. L., Beam, A. L., & Kohane, I. S. (2019). Adversarial attacks on medical machine learning. *Science*, *363*(6433), 1287–1289. https://doi.org/10.1126/science.aaw4399

Goodfellow, I. J., Shlens, J., & Szegedy, C. (2015). *Explaining and Harnessing Adversarial Examples*.

Hao, J., & Tao, Y. (2022). Adversarial attacks on deep learning models in smart grids. *Energy Reports*, *8*. https://doi.org/https://doi.org/10.1016/j.egyr.2021.11.026

Jin, G., Shen, S., Zhang, D., Dai, F., & Zhang, Y. (2019). APE-GAN: Adversarial Perturbation Elimination with GAN. *ICASSP 2019 - 2019 IEEE International Conference on Acoustics, Speech and Signal Processing (ICASSP)*, 3842–3846. https://doi.org/10.1109/ICASSP.2019.8683044

Karakolis, E., Pelekis, S., Mouzakitis, S., Kormpakis, G., Michalakopoulos, V., & Psarras, J. (2023). The I-Nergy Reference Architecture for the Provision of Next Generation Energy Services Through Artificial Intelligence. *International Conferences E-Society 2023 and Mobile Learning 2023*, 95–102.

Karakolis, E., Pelekis, S., Mouzakitis, S., Markaki, O., Papapostolou, K., Korbakis, G., & Psarras, J. (2022). Artificial Intelligence for Next Generation Energy Services Across Europe - The I-Nergy Project. *ES 2021: 19th International Conference e-Society 2021*, 61–68. https://cordis.europa.eu/project/id/101016508

Katz Guy and Barrett, C. and D. D. L. and J. K. and K. M. J. (2017). Reluplex: An Efficient SMT Solver for Verifying Deep Neural Networks. In V. Majumdar Rupak and Kunčak (Ed.), *Computer Aided Verification* (pp. 97–117). Springer International Publishing.

Kumar, R. S. S., Brien, D. O., Albert, K., Viljöen, S., & Snover, J. (2019). *Failure Modes in Machine Learning Systems*.

Li, J. (2019). *Robustness in Machine Learning (CSE 599-M)*.

Li, J., Yang, Y., & Sun, J. S. (2020). SearchFromFree: Adversarial Measurements for Machine Learning-based Energy Theft Detection. *2020 IEEE International Conference on Communications, Control, and Computing Technologies for Smart Grids (SmartGridComm)*, 1–6. https://doi.org/10.1109/SmartGridComm47815.2020.9303013

Li, J., Yang, Y., Sun, J. S., Tomsovic, K., & Qi, H. (2023). Towards Adversarial-Resilient Deep Neural Networks for False Data Injection Attack Detection in Power Grids. *2023 32nd International Conference on Computer Communications and Networks (ICCCN)*, 1–10. https://doi.org/10.1109/ICCCN58024.2023.10230180

Li, Y., Wei, X., Li, Y., Dong, Z., & Shahidehpour, M. (2022). Detection of False Data Injection Attacks in Smart Grid: A Secure Federated Deep Learning Approach. *IEEE Transactions on Smart Grid*, *13*(6), 4862–4872. https://doi.org/10.1109/TSG.2022.3204796

Machado, G. R., Silva, E., & Goldschmidt, R. R. (2021). Adversarial Machine Learning in Image Classification: A Survey Toward the Defender's Perspective. *ACM Comput. Surv.*, *55*(1). https://doi.org/10.1145/3485133

Madry, A., Makelov, A., Schmidt, L., Tsipras, D., & Vladu, A. (2018). Towards Deep Learning Models Resistant to Adversarial Attacks. *International Conference on Learning Representations*. https://openreview.net/forum?id=rJzIBfZAb

Michalakopoulos, V., Sarmas, E., Papias, I., Skaloumpakas, P., Marinakis, V., & Doukas, H. (2024). A machine learning-based framework for clustering residential electricity load profiles to enhance demand response programs. *Applied Energy*, *361*, 122943. https://doi.org/10.1016/J.APENERGY.2024.122943

Moosavi-Dezfooli, S.-M., Fawzi, A., Fawzi, O., & Frossard, P. (2017). Universal Adversarial Perturbations. *2017 IEEE Conference on Computer Vision and Pattern Recognition (CVPR)*, 86–94. https://doi.org/10.1109/CVPR.2017.17

Moosavi-Dezfooli, S.-M., Fawzi, A., & Frossard, P. (2016, June). DeepFool: A Simple and Accurate Method to Fool Deep Neural Networks. *Proceedings of the IEEE Conference on Computer Vision and Pattern Recognition (CVPR)*.

Niazazari, I., & Livani, H. (2020). Attack on Grid Event Cause Analysis: An Adversarial Machine Learning Approach. *2020 IEEE Power & Energy Society Innovative Smart Grid Technologies Conference (ISGT)*, 1–5. https://doi.org/10.1109/ISGT45199.2020.9087649

Omitaomu, O. A., & Niu, H. (2021). Artificial Intelligence Techniques in Smart Grid: A Survey. *Smart Cities*, *4*(2), 548–568. https://doi.org/10.3390/smartcities4020029

Pelekis, S., Karakolis, E., Silva, F., Schoinas, V., Mouzakitis, S., Kormpakis, G., Amaro, N., & Psarras, J. (2022). In Search of Deep Learning Architectures for Load Forecasting: A Comparative Analysis and the Impact of the Covid-19 Pandemic on Model Performance. *2022 13th International Conference on Information, Intelligence, Systems & Applications (IISA)*, 1–8. https://doi.org/10.1109/IISA56318.2022.9904363

Pelekis, S., Pipergias, A., Karakolis, E., Mouzakitis, S., Santori, F., Ghoreishi, M., & Askounis, D. (2023). Targeted demand response for flexible energy communities using clustering techniques. *Sustainable Energy, Grids and Networks*, *36*, 101134. https://doi.org/10.1016/J.SEGAN.2023.101134

Pelekis, S., Pountridis, T., Kormpakis, G., Lampropoulos, G., Karakolis, E., Mouzakitis, S., & Askounis, D. (2024). DeepTSF: Codeless machine learning operations for time series forecasting. *SoftwareX*, *27*, 101758. https://doi.org/10.1016/J.SOFTX.2024.101758

Pelekis, S., Seisopoulos, I.-K., Spiliotis, E., Pountridis, T., Karakolis, E., Mouzakitis, S., & Askounis, D. (2023). A comparative assessment of deep learning models for day-ahead load forecasting: Investigating key accuracy drivers. *Sustainable Energy, Grids and Networks*, *36*, 101171. https://doi.org/10.1016/J.SEGAN.2023.101171

Qureshi, N. B. S., Kim, D.-H., Lee, J., & Lee, E.-K. (2022). Poisoning Attacks against Federated Learning in Load Forecasting of Smart Energy. *NOMS 2022-2022 IEEE/IFIP Network Operations and Management Symposium*, 1–7. https://doi.org/10.1109/NOMS54207.2022.9789884

Raghunathan, A., Xie, S. M., Yang, F., Duchi, J., & Liang, P. (2020). Understanding and Mitigating the Tradeoff between Robustness and Accuracy. In H. D. III & A. Singh (Eds.), *Proceedings of the 37th International Conference on Machine Learning* (Vol. 119, pp. 7909–7919). PMLR. https://proceedings.mlr.press/v119/raghunathan20a.html

Sayghe, A., Anubi, O. M., & Konstantinou, C. (2020). Adversarial Examples on Power Systems State Estimation. *2020 IEEE Power & Energy Society Innovative Smart Grid Technologies Conference (ISGT)*, 1–5. https://doi.org/10.1109/ISGT45199.2020.9087789

Sayghe, A., Zhao, J., & Konstantinou, C. (2020). Evasion Attacks with Adversarial Deep Learning Against Power System State Estimation. *2020 IEEE Power & Energy Society General Meeting (PESGM)*, 1–5. https://doi.org/10.1109/PESGM41954.2020.9281719

Siva Kumar, R. S., Nyström, M., Lambert, J., Marshall, A., Goertzel, M., Comissoneru, A., Swann, M., & Xia, S. (2020). Adversarial Machine Learning-Industry Perspectives. *2020 IEEE Security and Privacy Workshops (SPW)*, 69–75. https://doi.org/10.1109/SPW50608.2020.00028

Song, Q., Tan, R., Ren, C., & Xu, Y. (2021). Understanding Credibility of Adversarial Examples against Smart Grid: A Case Study for Voltage Stability Assessment. *Proceedings of the Twelfth ACM International Conference on Future Energy Systems*, 95–106. https://doi.org/10.1145/3447555.3464859

Takiddin, A., Ismail, M., Zafar, U., & Serpedin, E. (2021). Robust Electricity Theft Detection Against Data Poisoning Attacks in Smart Grids. *IEEE Transactions on Smart Grid*, *12*(3), 2675–2684. https://doi.org/10.1109/TSG.2020.3047864

Tian, J., Li, T., Shang, F., Cao, K., Li, J., & Ozay, M. (2019). Adaptive Normalized Attacks for Learning Adversarial Attacks and Defenses in Power Systems. *2019 IEEE International Conference on Communications, Control, and Computing Technologies for Smart Grids (SmartGridComm)*, 1–6. https://doi.org/10.1109/SmartGridComm.2019.8909713

Tramer, F., & Boneh, D. (2019). Adversarial Training and Robustness for Multiple Perturbations. In H. Wallach, H. Larochelle, A. Beygelzimer, F. d Alché-Buc, E. Fox, & R. Garnett (Eds.), *Advances in Neural Information Processing Systems* (Vol. 32). Curran Associates, Inc. https://proceedings.neurips.cc/paper_files/paper/2019/file/5d4ae76f053f8f2516ad12961ef7fe97-Paper.pdf

Tsipras, D., Santurkar, S., Engstrom, L., Turner, A., & Madry, A. (2019). Robustness May Be at Odds with Accuracy. *International Conference on Learning Representations*. https://openreview.net/forum?id=SyxAb30cY7

Vassilev, A., Oprea, A., Fordyce, A., & Andersen, H. (2024). *Adversarial Machine Learning: A Taxonomy and Terminology of Attacks and Mitigations*. NIST Trustworthy and Responsible AI, National Institute of Standards and Technology, Gaithersburg, MD. https://doi.org/https://doi.org/10.6028/NIST.AI.100-2e2023

Wang, J., & Srikantha, P. (2021). Stealthy Black-Box Attacks on Deep Learning Non-Intrusive Load Monitoring Models. *IEEE Transactions on Smart Grid*, *12*(4), 3479–3492. https://doi.org/10.1109/TSG.2021.3062722

Wang, X., Li, J., Kuang, X., Tan, Y., & Li, J. (2019). The security of machine learning in an adversarial setting: A survey. *Journal of Parallel and Distributed Computing*, *130*, 12–23. https://doi.org/https://doi.org/10.1016/j.jpdc.2019.03.003

Weng, T.-W., Zhang, H., Chen, P.-Y., Yi, J., Su, D., Gao, Y., Hsieh, C.-J., & Daniel, L. (2018). Evaluating the Robustness of Neural Networks: An Extreme Value Theory Approach. *International Conference on Learning Representations*. https://openreview.net/forum?id=BkUHlMZ0b

Wu, J., Zhou, M., Zhu, C., Liu, Y., Harandi, M., & Li, L. (2021). *Performance Evaluation of Adversarial Attacks: Discrepancies and Solutions*.

Yang, Y.-Y., Rashtchian, C., Zhang, H., Salakhutdinov, R. R., & Chaudhuri, K. (2020). A Closer Look at Accuracy vs. Robustness. In H. Larochelle, M. Ranzato, R. Hadsell, M. F. Balcan, & H. Lin (Eds.), *Advances in Neural Information Processing Systems* (Vol. 33, pp. 8588–8601). Curran Associates, Inc. https://proceedings.neurips.cc/paper_files/paper/2020/file/61d77652c97ef636343742fc3dcf3ba9-Paper.pdf

Yao, D., Wen, M., Liang, X., Fu, Z., Zhang, K., & Yang, B. (2019). Energy Theft Detection with Energy Privacy Preservation in the Smart Grid. *IEEE Internet of Things Journal*, *6*(5), 7659–7669. https://doi.org/10.1109/JIOT.2019.2903312

Yilmaz, I., & Siraj, A. (2021). Avoiding Occupancy Detection from Smart Meter Using Adversarial Machine Learning. *IEEE Access*, *9*, 35411–35430. https://doi.org/10.1109/ACCESS.2021.3057525

Zhao, W., Alwidian, S., & Mahmoud, Q. H. (2022). Adversarial Training Methods for Deep Learning: A Systematic Review. *Algorithms*, *15*(8). https://doi.org/10.3390/a15080283

THE FIRST HARDWARE CIRCUIT EMULATING ITALIAN ROAD HOMICIDES LEGAL LOGIC, DAJE!

Grazia Garzo[1] and Alessandro Palumbo[2]
[1]University of Siena, Italy
[2]CentraleSupelec, Inria, Univ Rennes, CNRS, IRISA, France

ABSTRACT

The legal field has increasingly adopted digital technologies in recent years, enhancing efficiency and speed in expert tasks. The integration of these technologies significantly streamlines investigative and decision-making processes, reducing the time and costs traditionally associated with legal procedures. However, this increase in digital system usage necessitates stringent security measures, given that these systems often handle sensitive data requiring strict confidentiality. It is, therefore, crucial to implement safeguards against system tampering and to ensure the privacy of processed information, thereby protecting sensitive data from potential breaches. In this con- text, implementing software functionalities directly on hardware emerges as a promising solution, reducing the exposure to security vulnerabilities typically associated with software. Consequently, we propose the Digital Assurance Judicial Enforcer (DAJE), which, to the best of our knowledge, is the first Boolean-based hardware circuit designed to implement and emulate Italian legal logic for road homicides. DAJE implements 6 LUTs and 24 FFs. Its maximum operating frequency is 642 MHz, with an average power consumption of 89 mW on an FPGA emulation.

KEYWORDS

Boolean Function, Road Homicide, Italian Legal System, Judicial Systems

1. INTRODUCTION

The legal sector has significantly transformed in recent years due to the increasing integration of digital technologies. These cutting-edge tools can potentially revolutionize legal experts' operational methods, enhancing efficiency and expediting decision-making processes (American Bar Association, 2021; Deloitte, 2020). The digitalization of processes leads to substantial savings by reducing the need for physical resources and optimizing the work of judicial personnel, thereby freeing up time for more critical activities. Adopting advanced technologies such as artificial intelligence (AI) and machine learning allows for the automation of numerous repetitive and complex tasks, reducing analysis times and increasing the precision of legal decisions (J. Armour et al, 2022; Legal Futures, 2024). For instance, implementing sophisticated algorithms for legal data analysis can facilitate the search for relevant legal precedents, improve legal risk assessment, and more effectively support investigations (Legal Futures, 2024). Various software solutions employed in the field of justice can be cited. For example, online portals and court management platforms facilitate access to documents and rulings, enhancing the transparency of the judicial system. Using artificial intelligence and advanced algorithms enables the analysis of large volumes of legal data to predict case outcomes and support judges in their decisions. Furthermore, court management software organizes hearings efficiently and monitors the status of cases in real-time, improving the overall management of the court's workload.

Recent technological developments have focused largely on integrating software functionalities into hardware (i.e., ASICs and FPGAs) to boost system performance and reduce power consumption (J. Kim et al, 2023). Generally, a software program executed on a CPU or GPU tends to consume more power than the same function implemented on an FPGA. This is because CPUs and GPUs are designed to be generic and versatile hardware. In contrast, FPGAs can be configured to perform specific operations in a highly parallel manner, with logic optimized for a particular function, thereby reducing the number of unnecessary operations and energy consumption (F. Pacini et al, 2024; M. Qasaimeh et al, 2019). To give some examples, M.S. Brunella et al, 2022 and S. Pontarelli et al, 2019, respectively, networking functions and Linux kernel components have been directly ported to FPGAs. Similarly, K. Arıkan et al, 2022; A. Palumbo et al, 2021; 2023a2023b, microprocessor security functions have been offloaded to dedicated hardware modules. One of the main advantages of hardware-based security is physical isolation, which the software could not provide. Hardware can physically separate sensitive operations from the rest of the system, reducing exposure to common software vulnerabilities such as buffer overflows, malware, or privilege escalation attacks. This isolation reduces the attack surface, making it harder for an adversary to compromise critical security operations. Another key strength of hardware is its tamper resistance: specific hardware designs include mechanisms that can detect and respond to physical tampering, such as erasing sensitive data or shutting down the system if tampering is detected (L. Cassano et al, 2022; P. R, Nikiema et al, 2023. Additionally, secure hardware enclaves (Intel, 2016; ARM 2023) ensure that sensitive operations, such as key generation, occur in a protected environment that software-based attacks can't easily reach (J. Menetrey, 2022).

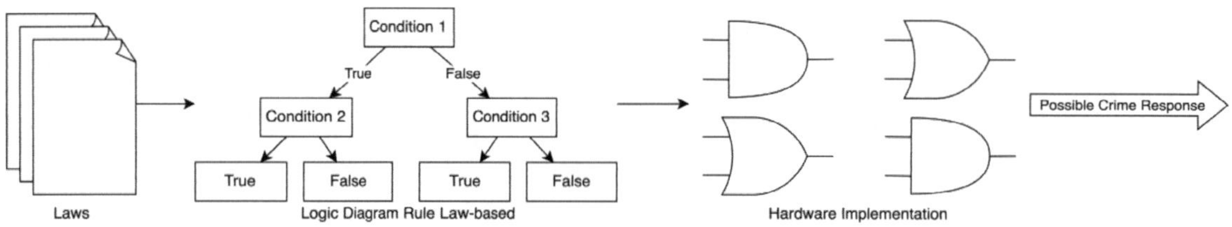

Figure 1. The overview of the proposed approach

Guaranteeing that systems are highly secure with the increasing adoption of digital technologies in the legal domain is critical. Data handled in the legal field is often extremely sensitive, including personal information, judicial evidence, and other confidential data that, if disclosed, could have serious legal and reputational consequences (Deloitte, 2020; GOV.UK, 2022). Consequently, it is essential to implement robust security measures to protect these systems from tampering attempts and ensure the privacy of information as required by privacy regulations such as the General Data Protection Regulation (GDPR) (European Parliament, 2016). Protecting sensitive data requires adopting technologies capable of preventing unauthorized access, protecting against cyber-attacks, and ensuring data integrity throughout its lifecycle (American Bar Association, 2021; GOV.UK, 2022). In this context, functions implemented directly in hardware represent a promising solution to improve the security of software adopted in digital legal systems, offering additional protection due to its physical nature (J. Armour, 2022 GOV.UK, 2022). In addition, if an attacker manages to inject something referred to as malicious software, he/she could potentially compromise and disable the software defenses protecting the system. In contrast, an attacker would likely need physical access to the microprocessor where the hardware circuitry is integrated to sabotage it, making it a more resilient security measure against certain types of attacks. These advantages make hardware solutions particularly suitable for protecting critical information in legal systems while ensuring high performance and reliability (American Bar Association, 2021; Legal Futures, 2024). Given this reality, there is an urgent need to explore preemptively hardware-based methodologies for legal evaluations akin to the approaches already implemented in other domains. Many software functions have been offloaded to dedicated hardware modules to mitigate vulnerabilities. Techniques like DAJE are pioneering examples of how Boolean logic and hardware integration can emulate legal reasoning while offering physical security, tamper resistance, and consistent performance. Judicial systems often experience significant backlogs, resulting in lengthy case resolutions. DAJE-based methodologies can alleviate this burden by automating preliminary analyses and rule-based decision-making, expediting case management while adhering to the transparency and traceability requirements for algorithms mandated by the proposed AI Act (European Commission, 2024).

This manuscript provides a foundation for further exploration of how digital technologies and hardware implementations can be integrated into the legal sector to improve judicial processes' security, efficiency, and reliability, which remain challenging (Legal Futures, 2024; GOV.UK, 2022). To the best of our knowledge, we propose the first hardware-based legal function evaluating crime sciences. The workflow of the presented approach is shown in Figure 1. This paper aims to introduce a novel idea that bridges hardware and legal systems. We are aware that FPGAs are devices well-known for their capability to implement complex functions due to their programmable architecture. The implementation of DAJE on an FPGA is mentioned for demonstrative purposes, serving as a practical example of how these technologies can be utilized to emulate legal logic in judicial applications. Functions implementation on FPGAs lies not only in their superior resilience, reliability, and security compared to software solutions but also in their reprogrammable nature. This adaptability allows the hardware to be updated as new requirements emerge. For instance, the conditions for detecting specific crimes or additional features to monitor can be seamlessly modified or extended through reprogramming. This capability ensures that the system remains future-proof, allowing it to adapt to evolving legal frameworks. In addition, our aim is not to replace human judgment or manage the investigative phase directly. Instead, we seek to lay the foundation for demonstrating to the research community that legal reasoning can be implemented in hardware. This approach offers a resilient methodology to support the legal phase, where the judges evaluate whether the necessary conditions for a crime are met.

The rest of the manuscript is organized as follows: Section 2 examines the works related to our proposal, Section 3 details the proposed methodology, reporting the results and the hardware implementation details. Section 4 concludes the paper.

2. RELATED WORK

Various AI-driven techniques have emerged to facilitate decision-making processes, demonstrating the adaptability of AI. For instance, G. V. Traviani et al, 2022 presents a digital predictive model for assessing the probability of recidivism among convicts, while M. Simmler et al, 2023, an AI-powered tool is used to assist Swiss law enforcement in predicting crime-prone areas.

JudicialTech (J. Barnett et al, 2023) aims to improve access to justice and potentially enhance fairness within the judicial system. Our proposed approach is similar, as we leverage AI for legal decision-making. On the other hand, R. A. Shakh et al, 2020 categorize individuals as acquitted or convicted based on data from criminal cases in the Delhi District Court concerning murder incidents. They use various ML models, achieving accuracies ranging from 85% to 92% and F1 scores between 86% and 92%.

While our study involves a similar number of cases, our methodology differs in terms of feature extraction and decision-making processes. Meanwhile, Chou et al. propose using the Support Vector Machine (SVM) algorithm for document classification, clustering and search to enhance the efficiency of law enforcement departments in managing written criminal judgments. They achieve accuracies ranging from 73.91% to 89.49%, depending on the datasets (S. Chou et al, 2010). Similarly, B. Luo et al, 2017 evaluates different neural networks and SVM implementations to predict criminal charges, achieving high accuracy scores and F1 values, reaching up to 98.97% and 98.51%, respectively, with lower values at 42.9% and 41.16%

B. Strickson et al, 2020 proposes a digital system for predicting legal decisions or judgments. They leverage English documents and supervised learning algorithms, achieving accuracy rates between 49.6% and 69.1%. A similar approach is described in L. Martin et al, 2019, where the authors use a transformer-based judicial algorithm, CamemBERT, to forecast judicial decisions, with an average accuracy of 84.1% and an F1 score of 89.55%.

A detailed empirical study on models designed for legal Natural Language Processing (NLP) tasks to assess the performance of pre-trained language models in the legal context is conducted by D. Song et al, 2022. The reviewed approximately eight distinct legal datasets, whose sizes varied from 900 to 57,000 records. These datasets encompassed five NLP tasks: binary classification, multilabel classification, multiple-choice QA, summarization, and information retrieval. T. Nguyen, 2023 developed a virtual legal assistant based on a modified version of the GPT-3 model, fine-tuned for the legal domain. This assistant was programmed to interactively assist users by answering legal questions, creating legal documents, and providing legal advice.

Q. Huang et al, 2023 present a new method for adapting large language models (LLMs) to specific sectors is proposed, resulting in the development of Lawyer LLaMA, an LLM dedicated to legal applications. During its initial training phase, continuous integration of legal knowledge was prioritized, along with training on legal professional skills through meticulously managed fine-tuning tasks. To reduce errors in content generation, they also added a retrieval module that sources relevant legal articles before the model addresses any queries.

J. Lee, 2023 engineered a legal-specific language model, elaborating on the development of LexGPT models based on the GPT-J architecture and pre-trained using the Pile of Law. This model underwent further enhancement through methods based on human feedback and professional data tuning, ensuring that modifications to the model's code were unnecessary.

S. Icardi, 2020 developed of a Neural Network to predict the risk of life threats in stalking cases is reported, reaching an accuracy of 80%.

The idea for our proposed work was inspired by G. Garzo et al, 2024, where the authors proposed a boolean function to perform legal responses. This manuscript presents the hardware implementation of a similar function. In summary, our research contributes to the expanding body of AI-supported decision-making in the legal realm, offering a unique approach that emphasizes explainability and transparency. This aligns with ongoing advancements in AI and ML (G. Conti, 2020; J. Cui et al, 2023), enriching the landscape of decision-making support in legal contexts. These studies represent an important knowledge base for developing advanced and secure solutions for logical processing. They could have significant applications in the legal field, where a high level of security and privacy in data handling is required, highlighting the potential of advanced digital circuits in enhancing technologically advanced legal infrastructures.

3. METHODOLOGY

Legal, logical reasoning is based on the presence and absence of elements (R. Giovagnoli, 2021). For this reason, we thought a Boolean could be close to emulating it. In the initial phase of our estimation, we identified the most pertinent features describing road homicide scenarios according to the Italian law (G. Musco et al, 2013; R. Giovagnoli, 2023; P. M. Sabella, 2022). Then, we emulated the legal, logical connections using Boolean functions by implementing our Digital Assurance Judicial Enforcer (DAJE) circuit. In the final phase, we tested its accuracy by comparing its responses to judges' verdicts on real road homicide cases that happened in Italy. The test dataset utilized in this research comprises data from 100 incidents of road homicide recorded in Italy. Each incident is represented by a textual description detailing 25 elements characterizing the scene of the crime (such as the type of the victim/defendant violation, if they were driving with a valid driving license, and so on). These elements were delineated in accordance with Italian legislation concerning road homicide incidents (P. M. Sabella, 2022) and are reported in Subsection 3.2. Specifically, we treat these features as binary, indicating their presence or absence at the crime scene.

3.1 Logical Reasoning Fundamentals

When people lose lives on the road following traffic accidents, we can say it is a case of road homicide (detailed definition on the Italian ones by S. Balzani, 2016; G. Musco, 2013; P. M. Sabella, 2022) if a violation of one or more norms of the Italian Road Code law occurs when the obstacle (i.e., the victim) was foreseeable and avoidable (if the defendant had diligent behavior). The logical reasoning for a road homicide crime is according to the occurrence of three conditions (R. Giovagnoli, 2021; 2023):

1. Violation of the Italian Road Code law number 285/1992 norms (e.g., art. 145 penalizing those who fail to comply with a stop signal, art. 146 penalizing those who fail to observe a red light, etc.) or if the act was committed with general recklessness, incompetence, or negligence;
2. The obstacle (i.e., the victim) was foreseeable by the defendant if ordinary diligence had been exercised;
3. The obstacle could have been avoided if the defendant had behaved diligently.

Examining the crime scene and identifying all pertinent factors is crucial for evaluating these conditions. For instance, if the incident occurred during daylight and the victim (i.e., the obstacle to the defendant) was correctly using a crosswalk, the defendant should have been able to foresee and avoid the obstacle. Conversely, if the incident occurred at night and the victim abruptly crossed the road in a non-crosswalk area, the victim would likely not have been easily visible, indicating that the obstacle (i.e., the victim) was neither foreseeable nor avoidable. By applying this logical analysis to the crime scene elements, the investigating judge reconstructs the events and determines whether the three essential conditions were met, thus evaluating the case's circumstances [16].

To test and evaluate our methodology, we selected 100 road homicide cases from open public access Italian portals DeJure Giuffre Francis Lefebvre and Legisway, All-in-One Legal Management Software Wolters Kluwer, both containing texts describing the crime scenes. We referred to road homicide cases that occurred between 2016 and 2024. The data sample was randomly selected. The documents describing the crime scenes were passed to a Large Language Model GPT-based (one by one), asking it to read the text and to build a 25-bit vector for each sample, extracting the 25 predetermined important features. After analyzing all the texts, we built our test dataset containing 100 samples, each with 25 binary values. The last phase of the proposed methodology evaluates the accuracy of the DAJE hardware implementation in predicting the legal response.

3.2 The Digital Assurance Judicial Enforcer Design

The hardware circuit assesses the potential road homicide crimes, evaluating key factors reported in Table 1:

Table 1. Possible Crime True Table

Abrupt defendant driving:	The defendant made a sudden maneuver.
Defendant driving without a valid license	The defendant was driving without a valid license
Defendant fleeing	The defendant fled after the incident.
Defendant invading	The defendant invaded the opposite lane.
Defendant red light violation	The defendant did not stop at the red light
Defendant speeding	The defendant was driving at a speed exceeding legal limits
Defendant stop violation	The defendant did not stop at the stop sign
Defendant vehicles not authorized to operate	The defendant was driving a vehicle that was not insured or not authorized to operate
Defendant with phone	The defendant was using a phone while driving
Drunk or drugged defendant	The defendant was under the influence of alcohol or drugs
Defendant other violation(s)	The defendant violated the road traffic rule (a generic one or considered as another feature
Abrupt victim driving	The victim made a sudden maneuver
Drunk or drugged victim	The victim was under the influence of alcohol or drugs.
No victim reflective jacket	The victim was not wearing reflective clothing to be noticed while he/she was on the road where it was necessary
No victim safety belt	The victim was not wearing a safety belt
Red light victim crossing	The victim crossed during the red light
Victim driving without a valid license	The victim was driving without a valid license.
Victim red light violation	The victim did not stop at the red light
Victim speeding	The victim was driving at a speed exceeding legal limits
Victim stop violation	The victim did not stop at the stop sign.
Victim vehicles not authorized to operate	The victim was driving a vehicle that was not insured or not authorized to operate
Victim other violation(s):	The victim violated the road traffic rule (a generic one or considered as another feature)
Avoidable obstacle by the defendant	The defendant could have avoided the impact on the victim if they had been diligent
Foreseeable obstacle by the defendant	The defendant could have foreseen the victim's approach if they had been diligent

The 25 features could be automatically extracted from crime scene descriptions using advanced NLP techniques in a potential practical application in courts. This extraction process would serve as a preliminary step, feeding the DAJE engine with the necessary data for the subsequent evaluation based on the innovative use of Boolean logic. This approach would integrate artificial intelligence technologies with the efficiency of hardware logic, providing a high-performance system to support judicial decision-making. We treat these features as binary, indicating their presence or absence at the crime scene. The factors in evaluating the possible crime are the Foreseeable Obstacle by the defendant (FO), the Avoidable Obstacle by the defendant (AO), the Defendant's Violation (DV), and the Victim's Violation (VV). For example, in case of safety violations or substance abuse by the defendant (from 1st to 11th features), DV will be set to true; on the other hand, if the victim commits violations (from 12th to 23rd features), VV takes 1. Table 2 reports the boolean function's core decision-making (where 1 means True; 0 corresponds to False). It is worth mentioning that it is impossible to have a scenario where the obstacle is avoidable but not foreseeable (the rows with Crime equal to – in Table 2). DAJE also considered how many violations the defendant and the victim have committed (NDV and NVV, respectively). These cases correspond to the rows with Crime set to $*$ in Table 2: if $NDV \geq NVV$, Crime = 0; otherwise, Crime = 1.

Table 2. Possible Crime Truth Table

FO	AO	DV	VV	Crime
0	0	0	0	0
0	**0**	0	1	0
0	**0**	1	0	0
0	**0**	1	1	0
0	**1**	0	0	–
0	**1**	0	1	–
0	**1**	1	0	–
0	**1**	1	1	–
1	**0**	0	0	0
1	**0**	0	1	0
1	**0**	1	0	1
1	**0**	1	1	*
1	**1**	0	0	0
1	**1**	0	1	0
1	**1**	1	0	1
1	**1**	1	1	1

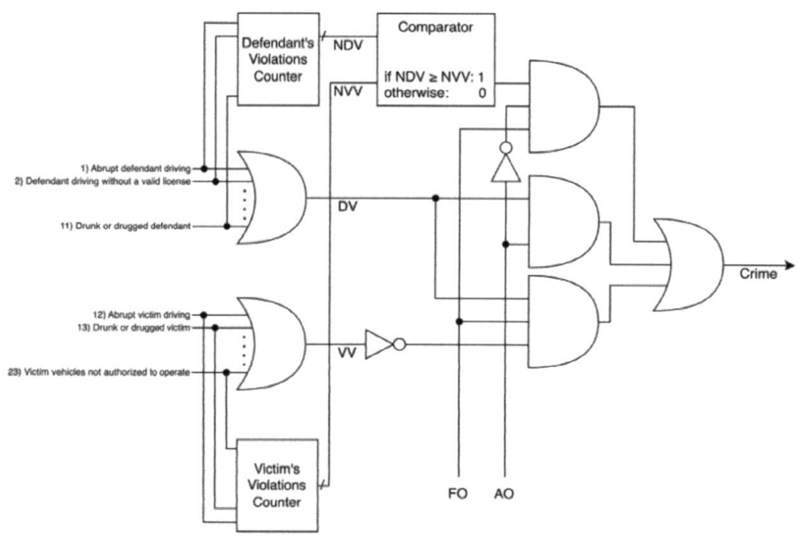

Figure 2. The hardware implementation of DAJE

3.3 The Boolean Rule-Based Hardware Implementation

The whole architecture of DAJE is reported in Figure 2. In particular, DV and VV consist in the output of OR gates, taking in input the respective violations, counted via NDV and NVV counters.

3.4 Evaluation

To test the accuracy of DAJE, we referred to 100 road homicide cases taken randomly from the publicly accessible Italian portals DeJure Giuffrè, Francis Lefebvre and Legisway, All-in-One Legal Management Software Wolters Kluwer. DAJE achieved an accuracy of 86%. In particular, we got True Positive (TP) rate of 73%, corresponding to the cases where DAJE correctly determines that a crime has been committed;

13% ofTrue Negative (TN) corresponding to the cases where DAJE correctly determines that no crime has been committed; 8% of False Positive (FP) rate, when no crime occurred, but DAJE detects one, and 6% of False Negative (FN) rate, indicating cases where a crime occurred, but our DAJE did not detect it.

4. CONCLUSION

We proposed DAJE, the first hardware circuit specifically designed to emulate the legal logic of road homicides according to Italian law. Our proposed hardware solution leverages the inherent advantages of hardware implementations, such as enhanced security and performance, to address these needs. DAJE uses Boolean logic to model the legal reasoning required for road homicide cases in Italy. By encoding the legal conditions and factors involved in such incidents, the DAJE circuit provides a reliable and transparent method for legal decision-making. Our implementation utilizes 6 LUTs and 24 FFs, achieving a maximum operating frequency of 642 MHz and an average power consumption of 89 mW on FPGA emulation. The experimental results demonstrated that DAJE replicates the legal logic applied in real road homicide cases in Italy with an accuracy of 86%. This confirms the viability of hardware-based solutions for legal applications, offering significant potential for improving the security and efficiency of digital legal systems. Applications close to the DAJE paradigm could be useful paradigms that support workers in the justice domain. Indeed, the objective of this paper is not only to introduce a novel concept that bridges hardware and the legal domain but also to inspire future research that explores the intersection between these fields.

In conclusion, DAJE represents a pioneering step towards integrating advanced hardware implementations in the legal sector. We envision this work as the starting point for a new line of research that combines hardware and legal logic, and we hope to serve as pioneers in this emerging field. Furthermore, we encourage the scientific community to delve deeper into this topic, studying and developing other hardware-based solutions that implement legal functions. Future research could expand this approach to other areas of law, refining the hardware design while maintaining the same paradigm on digital systems in legal contexts.

REFERENCES

A. Palumbo and al. (2021). A lightweight security checking module to protect microprocessors against hardware trojan horses. In 2021 IEEE International Symposium on Defect and Fault Tolerance in VLSI and Nanotechnology Systems.

A. Palumbo and al. (2023). Built-in software obfuscation for protecting microprocessors against hardware trojan horses. In 2023 IEEE International Symposium on Defect and Fault Tolerance in VLSI and Nanotechnology Systems (DFT).

A. Palumbo and al. (2023). Improving the detection of hardware trojan horses in microprocessors via hamming codes. In 2023 IEEE International Symposium on Defect and Fault Tolerance in VLSI and Nanotechnology Systems (DFT).

American Bar Association. (2021). Top 5 legal technology trends you need to know. American Bar Association.

Benjamin Strickson and Beatriz De La Iglesia. (2020). Legal judgement prediction for uk courts. In Proceedings of the 3rd International Conference on Information Science and Systems, pages 204–209.

Bingfeng Luo, and al. (2017). Learning to predict charges for criminal cases with legal basis.

Deloitte. (2020). Legal technology transformation: Going beyond risk and compliance. Deloitte United States.

Dezhao Song and al. (2022). On the effectiveness of pre-trained language models for legal natural language processing: An empirical study. IEEE Access, 10:75835–75858.

European Commission. (2024). Proposal for a regulation laying down harmonised rules on artificial intelligence (artificial intelligence act).

European Parliament and Council of the European Union. (2016). Regulation (eu) 2016/679 of the european parliament and of the council of 27 april 2016 on the protection of natural persons with regard to the processing of personal data and on the free movement of such data, and repealing directive 95/46/ec (general data protection regulation).

Federico Pacini and al. (2024). Design and evaluation of cpu-, gpu-, and fpga-based deployment of a cnn for motor imagery classification in brain-computer interfaces. Electronics, 13(9).

Frank McKeen and al. (2016). Intel® software guard extensions (intel® sgx) support for dynamic memory management inside an enclave. In Proceedings of the Hardware and Architectural Support for Security and Privacy.

Giacomo Conti. (2020). Lineamenti di diritto delle piattaforme digitali: volume I: Le tutele del consumatore e dell'utente commerciale nei confronti dei cybermediary. Maggioli.

G-MUSCO E FIANDACA. (2013). Diritto penale parte speciale, vol. ii, tomo i. Zanichelli, Bologna, page 307.

GOV.UK. (2022). Further investment in digital transformation of uk's legal sector.

Grazia Garzo and al. (2024). Opening the black box: How boolean ai can support legal analysis. In 2024 4th International Conference on Computer Communication and Artificial Intelligence (CCAI), pages 269–272.

Guido Vittorio Travaini and al. (2022). Machine learning and criminal justice: A systematic review of advanced methodology for recidivism risk prediction. International journal of environmental research and public health.

J. Lee. (2023). Developing lexgpt models: Enhancing gpt-j with legal data from pile of law. Journal of Legal Technology, 5(3):210–225.

James Menetrey and al. (2022). An exploratory study of attestation mechanisms for trusted execution environments. arXiv preprint arXiv:2204.06790.

Jeremy Barnett, Philip Treleaven, Fredric I. Lederer, Nicolas Vermeys, and John Zeleznikow. (2023). Judicialtech supporting justice.

Jinhyuk Kim and al. (2023). Hardware Accelerators in Embedded Systems, 167–181. Springer International Publishing.

John Armour, Richard Parnham, and Mari Sako. (2022). Augmented lawyering. U. Ill. L. Rev., page 71.

Junyun Cui, Xiaoyu Shen, and Shaochun Wen. (2023). A survey on legal judgment prediction: Datasets, metrics, models and challenges. IEEE Access, 11:102050–102071.

K. C. Wang. ARM TrustZone and Secure Operating Systems, pages 793–845. Springer International Publishing

Kerem Arıkan and al. (2022). Processor security: Detecting microarchitectural attacks via count-min sketches. IEEE Transactions on Very Large-Scale Integration (VLSI) Systems, 30(7):938–951.

Legal Futures. (2024). The game-changer: How legal technology is transforming the legal sector.

Louis Martin and al. (2019). Camembert: a tasty french language model. arXiv preprint arXiv:1911.03894.

Luca Cassano and al. (2022). Is risc-v ready for space? a security perspective. In 2022 IEEE International Symposium on Defect and Fault Tolerance in VLSI and Nanotechnology Systems (DFT), pages 1–6.

M. Ghanem and al. (2021). Crime Scene Processing: Documentation and Evaluation, 15–35. Springer Nature Singapore.

Marco Spaziani Brunella and al. (2022). hxdp: Efficient software packet processing on fpga nics. Commun. ACM, 65(8):92–100.

Monika Simmler and al. (2023). Smart criminal justice: Phenomena and normative requirements. International Review of Administrative Sciences, 89(2):415–432.

Murad Qasaimeh and al. (2019). Comparing energy efficiency of cpu, gpu and fpga implementations for vision kernels. In 2019 IEEE International Conference on Embedded Software and Systems (ICESS), pages 1–8.

Pegdwende Romaric Nikiema and al. Towards dependable risc-v cores for edge computing devices. In 2023 IEEE 29th International Symposium on On-Line Testing and Robust System Design.

Pietro Maria Sabella et al. (2022). Art. 589-ter: Fuga del conducente in caso di omicidio stradale. In Codice Penale: Rassegna di Giurisprudenza e Dottrina, pages 186–187. Giuffre Francis Lefebvre.

Quzhe Huang, Mingxu Tao and al. (2023). Lawyer llama technical report. arXiv preprint arXiv:2305.15062.

Rafe Athar Shaikh and al. (2020). Predicting outcomes of legal cases based on legal factors using classifiers. Procedia Computer Science, 167:2393–2402.

Roberto Giovagnoli. (2021). Manuale di Diritto Penale: Parte Generale. Itaedizioni, Roma, Italia.

Roberto Giovagnoli. (2023). Manuale di Diritto Penale: Parte Speciale. Itaedizioni, Roma, Italia.

Salvatore Pontarelli and al. (2019). Flowblaze: Stateful packet processing in hardware. In Proceedings of the 2019 ACM Symposium on SDN Research (SOSR), pages 1–14.

Shihchieh Chou and Tai-Ping Hsing. (2010). Text mining technique for chinese written judgment of criminal case. In Intelligence and Security Informatics: Pacific Asia Workshop, PAISI 2010, Hyderabad, India, June 21, 2010. Proceedings, pages 113–125. Springer.

Simone Balzani and Alessandro Trinci. (2016). I Reati in Materia di Circolazione Stradale: Con Profili di Diritto Civile e Amministrativo ed Elementi di Tossicologia Forense. Cedam, Padova, Italia.

Simone Icardi. (2020). Predicting the Threat of Death in Stalking Cases Through Artificial Neural Network. University of Ontario Institute of Technology, Oshawa, Ontario, Canada.

T. Nguyen. (2023). A virtual legal assistant based on gpt-3 for interactive legal support. Journal of Artificial Intelligence Research, 70:123–145.

NAVIGATING THE FUTURE OF EDUCATION: EDUCATORS' INSIGHTS ON AI INTEGRATION AND CHALLENGES IN GREECE, HUNGARY, LATVIA, IRELAND AND ARMENIA

Evangelia Daskalaki, Katerina Psaroudaki and Paraskevi Fragopoulou
Foundation for Research and Technology, Institute of Computer Science
N. Plastira 100, Vassilika Vouton, GR-700 13 Heraklion, Crete, Greece

ABSTRACT

Understanding teachers' perspectives on AI in Education (AIEd) is crucial for its effective integration into the educational framework. This paper aims to explore how teachers currently use AI and how it can enhance the educational process. We conducted a cross-national study spanning Greece, Hungary, Latvia, Ireland, and Armenia, surveying 1754 educators through an online questionnaire, addressing three research questions. Our first research question examines educators' understanding of AIEd, their skepticism, and its integration within schools. Most educators report a solid understanding of AI and acknowledge its potential risks. AIEd is primarily used for educator support and engaging students. However, concerns exist about AI's impact on fostering critical thinking and exposing students to biased data. The second research question investigates student engagement with AI tools from educators' perspectives. Teachers indicate that students use AI mainly to manage their academic workload, while outside school, AI tools are primarily used for entertainment. The third research question addresses future implications of AI in education. Educators are optimistic about AI's potential to enhance educational processes, particularly through personalized learning experiences. Nonetheless, they express significant concerns about AI's impact on cultivating critical thinking and ethical issues related to potential misuse. There is a strong emphasis on the need for professional development through training seminars, workshops, and online courses to integrate AI effectively into teaching practices. Overall, the findings highlight a cautious optimism among educators regarding AI in education, alongside a clear demand for targeted professional development to address concerns and enhance skills in using AI tools.

KEYWORDS

AI, K-12 Education, Greece, Hungary, Latvia, Ireland, Armenia

1. INTRODUCTION

Artificial Intelligence (AI) has become prevalent across all levels of education. When we refer to AI in education (AIEd), we include a wide range of systems and tools that mimic human intelligence and serve various educational purposes, like teaching assistants, course creation tools, chatbots, image and video generation, audio, research, animation, text-to-speech, presentations, etc. Understanding teachers' beliefs about AIEd is essential for its effective integration into the educational system. Consequently, numerous studies have emerged in recent years to explore this topic, highlighting both educators' excitement and concerns.

The present survey about AIEd is an overview of teachers' use of AI and examines how AI can effectively support teaching. Conducted from the Greek Safer Internet Center of FORTH (Daskalaki, et al., 2020; Christodoulaki & Fragopoulou, 2010; Kokolaki, et al.,2020; Daskalaki, et al.,2018) in collaboration with the Safer Internet Centers of Hungary[1], Ireland[2], Latvia[3] and Armenia[4], and with the support of the European Network of Safer Internet Centers, Insafe[5], it represents a significant international effort. To our knowledge,

[1] www.gyermekmento.hu
[2] https://webwise.ie/
[3] https://www.drossinternets.lv
[4] https://safe.am/
[5] https://www.betterinternetforkids.eu

this is the first international research supported by Safer Internet Centers from five countries, to investigate the use of AI in education.

This survey aims to guide investigations into various aspects of how AI is integrated into educational settings. While most research on AIEd has focused on technological improvements, according to (Kizilcec, 2024) more research of education technology from a psychological perspective is needed in order to understand what factors shape the way educators perceive, trust, and use education technology in teaching practice, leading to our **first pair of research questions: "***What is the current status of AIEd in the five countries we focus on? How do educators perceive it, and what are their primary areas of skepticism?*" Furthermore, we were also interested in investigating the use of AI by students examining how they interact with AI technologies, their preferences, behaviors, and the impact of these interactions on their learning experiences. This forms our **second research question**: "*What are the patterns, preferences, and impacts of student engagement with artificial intelligence tools in educational settings from the perspective of educators?*". Lastly, the potential for AIEd to revolutionize how we teach, learn, and interact with educational materials is vast. This study aims to uncover potential barriers and opportunities, providing critical insight for the effective implementation of AI education programs. We explore several crucial facets of AI's forthcoming impact in our **third research question:** "*In what ways will AI shape the educational landscape from the perspective of educators?*".

The remainder of the paper is organized as follows: In Section 2. Literature Review, we examine existing research and theories relevant to the study. Section 3. Survey Methods is devoted to the methodology of the survey, including information about the participants involved in the study and the procedures followed during the survey, as well as a description of the questionnaire used, and the measures taken to ensure data reliability and validity. Subsequently, Section 4. Results presents the findings for each main research question of the survey, namely, educators' views on the current state of AI in education, educators' perspectives on the future implications of AI in the educational field, and the future of AI in education. We conclude in Section 6. Discussion and Conclusion, with a summary of key findings, discussing their implications, as well as suggestions for future research.

2. LITERATURE REVIEW

In recent years, numerous researchers have dedicated substantial effort to the study of AIEd. A review of journal articles from 2010 to 2020 (Crompton & Burke, 2022) found four main ways educators used AI to help students learn: monitoring students, managing groups, automated grading, and making data-based decisions. In group management, AI assisted teachers in forming, moderating, and facilitating groups. For students, three major benefits of AI emerged: AI tutors, enhancing student thinking, and personalized learning tailored to each student's strengths, weaknesses, preferences, and interests.

According to Akgun and Greenhow (2022), many teachers believe that introducing AI concepts at an early age can foster critical thinking and problem-solving skills. This early exposure can make children feel more comfortable with technology, becoming at the same time better equipped for their future academic and/or career pursuits.

Roll and Wylie (2016) suggest that AIEd can relieve teachers from the need to acquire all the necessary knowledge and information their students might require. Instead, teachers can focus on providing students with methods to find, discuss, and research information themselves, through team projects or knowledge-building activities. Teachers at present spend a lot of time grading homework and tests, which takes away valuable time from their teaching and quality time with their students (Rasul, et al., 2024).

Indeed, AI tools like intelligent tutor systems, assessment systems, and educational robots can take over these repetitive tasks. This helps reduce the teachers' workload and allows them to focus more on teaching and building relationships with students (Tahiru, 2021). Furthermore, teachers see AI literacy as a way to promote equity in education. As highlighted by (Beverly Park Woolf, et al., 2013) AI can personalize learning experiences, making education more effective by analyzing datasets on teaching behavior, student motivation, and social interactions. This potential for personalization is particularly appealing in elementary education, where students' learning needs can vary widely.

Further research has shown that AI technology can make teaching more efficient. Additionally, AI can provide teachers with more free time and energy for more effective communication with their students, helping them focus on subjects such as morals and skills development. It can also provide teachers with the opportunity to pay more attention to each student's overall physical and mental growth (Tanveer, et al., 2020). It has been noted that teachers have transitioned from a position of providing knowledge to being a medium of facilitating student learning, with a focus on student-centered education, offering at the same time more compassionate care when it is needed.

Teachers who view Generative AI from a positive side are more likely to incorporate it into their daily teaching methods, as indicated by (Kaplan-Rakowski, et al., 2023). The critical factor in this statement seems to be the age of the educators, since the younger ones, particularly those from Generation Z, are more receptive and better adapting to technological advancements (Chan & Lee, 2023).

There are also voices among them who express their concerns regarding AI literacy education. Ally (2019) noted that all the latest technological advances have upgraded the educational system, since they have highlighted new significant alterations in teachers' instructional methods and the way the educators view themselves as a significant part in their role of the learning process. The main concern we should be worried about is the lack of sufficient training and resources. A study surveyed K-12 teachers in Serbia aiming to find out how much they know about AI, how they use it in teaching, and what they think about it (Kuleto, et al., 2022). The results showed that teachers who were more likely to use AI as part of their educational method or expressed their wish to use it in their teaching, were the ones who viewed it more positively. The above finding suggests that had teachers been provided with more training on using AI, they could turn to be more willing to incorporate it into their teaching practices. On the other hand, teachers with less training and exposure to AI technology tend to be more skeptical about using it. The latter often perceive AI literacy as an additional and more complex workload rather than an opportunity to improve their teaching methods and skills. This skepticism is further enhanced by their perception of the complexity of AI tools and the difficulty they will face in making these concepts accessible to young learners.

A scoping review was performed to analyze 16 empirical studies published between 2016 and 2022 (Su, et al., 2023). This review evaluated, examined, and presented research on AI literacy in early childhood education, covering curriculum design, AI tools, teaching methods, research approaches, assessment techniques, and results. The review highlighted several challenges and opportunities related to AI literacy. Key challenges included (1) a lack of AI knowledge, skills, and confidence among teachers, (2) insufficient curriculum design, and (3) a lack of teaching guidelines. Despite these initial hurdles, AI learning has the potential to create educational opportunities and enhance young children's understanding of AI concepts, practices, and perspectives. However, there are still concerns about the fear of overreliance on AI after long-term use, which may undermine traditional teaching methods and pedagogical principles, resulting to uncertain educational outcomes. Moreover, the ethical implications of introducing AI to young children is another concern in the educational community. Teachers are concerned about the existing possibility of AI amplifying issues related to privacy, data security and digital dependency (Institute for Ethical AI in Education, n.d.).

Another report (Schiel, et al., 2024) explored how students in the U.S. use AI tools for school assignments and other activities, their perceptions of the cognitive and academic impacts of these tools, and their views on employing AI to write their college admissions essays. Their findings were that nearly half of the high school students surveyed reported using AI tools, with ChatGPT being the most popular. Among the 54% who hadn't used AI tools, the primary reasons were a lack of interest, distrust of the information provided, and insufficient knowledge about them. Students also used AI tools for entertainment, hobbies, and personalized recommendations. Those with higher academic performance were significantly more likely to use AI tools than those with lower performance. Nearly 74% of students believed that using AI tools would slightly improve their school performance. However, 90% had not considered using AI tools for their college admissions essays, citing concerns about the tools' current limitations in generating high-quality, personalized, original, and authentic content that reflects their skills and unique writing styles. Additionally, students felt that using AI for this purpose would be dishonest and unethical and preferred the sense of accomplishment from writing their own essays.

The integration of AI into education presents a nuanced blend of opportunities and challenges. While several teachers embrace the concept of AI becoming incorporated into teaching and learning experiences, others express concerns regarding further aspects such as its financial implications, specific ethical considerations, and potential impacts on conventional pedagogical methodologies. It is vital to fully understand these divergent perspectives if we want to build new strategies that will empower teachers to harness AI in education effectively and ethically.

3. RESEARCH DESIGN

3.1 Participants and Procedures

The survey was conducted from the members of the Greek Safer Internet Center of FORTH (Daskalaki, et al., 2020; Christodoulaki & Fragopoulou, 2010; Kokolaki, et al., 2020; Daskalaki, et al., 2018) in collaboration with the Safer Internet Centers of Hungary[6], Ireland[7], Latvia[8] and Armenia[9], and with the support of the European Network of Safer Internet Centers Insafe[10].

It took place between October 2023 – March 2024, and the data of the different countries were collected anonymously via online questionnaires. The online questionnaire and its translations were published in the EUSurvey online survey management system. EUSurvey is the official online survey management tool of the European Commission. Its development started under the supervision of DIGIT and is currently available as open-source software under the terms of the EUPL public license. The EUSurvey system adheres to the Web Content Accessibility Guidelines (WCAG) 2.0 Level AA when selected. This setting has been activated in the questionnaires, in order to be inclusive for all.

The survey involved educators from Greece, Hungary, Ireland, Latvia, and Armenia. The online questionnaire was distributed to educators directly from the respective national Safer Internet Centers. Specifically, for Greece, the questionnaire was also communicated to the educators from the Panhellenic School Network, the Greek national network (ISP) of the Ministry of Education which safely interconnects 16K schools of Primary and Secondary education, including educational units abroad, as well as services and entities supervised by the Ministry of Education at central and regional level.

All questions and responses in the questionnaire were provided in the national language of each country to ensure maximal level of clarity and understanding for all participants.

The participants were clearly informed throughout the study that their participation in the research was completely voluntary and anonymous. A total of 1754 educators completed the online survey, of which 1125 were Greek, 298 Hungarian, 130 Irish, 70 Latvian and 131 Armenian educators. The demographic information of the collected sample can be seen in Table 1.

3.2 Questionnaire and Measures

The online questionnaire was released with specific guidelines for educators on how to complete it and included information on the general concepts of AIEd. It was designed to help derive conclusions about AIEd by synthesizing the potential benefits, challenges, and ethical considerations associated with its integration into educational settings. The questionnaire included questions on how AI is used by teachers during the educational process, if and how students use AI tools to support their studies, and the overall attitude of educators towards the use of AI in schools. The goal is to draw recommendations for various stakeholders and target groups such as:

- **Educators:** Teachers and instructors play the most crucial role in implementing AI technologies in the classroom and adapting their teaching methods accordingly.
- **School Administrators:** Administrators at educational institutions are responsible for making decisions regarding the adoption and implementation of AI technologies. They are concerned with improving educational outcomes, increasing efficiency, and managing resources effectively.
- **Policy Makers:** Government agencies and policymakers play a role in regulating the use of AIEd, ensuring ethical and equitable practices, and promoting access to quality education for all students and educators.

---

[6] www.gyermekmento.hu
[7] https://webwise.ie/
[8] https://www.drossinternets.lv
[9] https://safe.am/
[10] https://www.betterinternetforkids.eu

Table 1. Table showing the demographic information of the sample

Measure	Participants		N	%
Country	Greece		1125	64%
	Hungary		298	17%
	Ireland		130	7%
	Latvia		70	4%
	Armenia		131	7%
		Total	1754	100%
Age	Under 25 y.o.		13	0.7%
	26-35 y.o.		156	8.9%
	36-45 y.o.		460	26.2%
	46-55 y.o.		689	39.3%
	Over 55 y.o.		436	24.9%
		Total	1754	100%
Participants' Gender	Female		1220	69.6%
	Male		516	29.4%
	Non-binary		1	0.1%
	I would rather not mention		17	1.0%
		Total	1754	100%
Participants' teaching experience in years	1-4 y.		128	7.3%
	5-10 y.		187	10.7%
	11-20 y.		525	29.9%
	21-30 y.		632	36.0%
	31+ y.		282	16.1%
		Total	1754	100%
Place of Residence	Village		196	11.2%
	Small Town		217	12.4%
	City		684	39.0%
	Large Urban Center		657	37.5%
		Total	1754	100%
Grade(s) educators teach	Preschool age		189	10.7%
	1st-3rd grade		437	24.9%
	4th-6th grade		535	30.5%
	Middle school		651	37.1%
	High School		670	38.1%
	Adults		329	18.7%

- **Parents and Guardians:** Parents and guardians are stakeholders as they are invested in the educational experiences and outcomes of their children. They are interested in how AI technologies are being used to support their children's learning and development.
- **Technology Providers:** Companies and organizations that develop AI technologies for education are stakeholders in the industry. They aim to create innovative solutions that address the needs and challenges of educators and students, while also generating revenue and staying competitive in the market.

The questionnaire comprised both quantitative (close-ended) and qualitative (open- ended) for a total of 33 questions. These included 17 multiple choice questions, two Likert, eight open-ended, and six demographic questions. The qualitative questions were initially concealed and only revealed if the educators had exhausted the provided options but still desired to include their own opinion.

The questionnaire was divided into three thematic parts. The first focused on gathering demographic information about the educators, including their experience, the grades they teach and their place of residence. Table 1 presents the questions, measures, and frequencies for this first part of the questionnaire.

The second part of the questionnaire explored the current landscape of AIEd. Educators were asked about their integration of AI tools into their teaching practices and their individual comfort levels with AI technologies. This part also explored the perceived benefits of AI in enhancing teaching and learning experiences, and the challenges and barriers educators face. Table 2 provides a detailed overview of the questions, responses, and response frequencies from each country for this section.

Finally, the third part focused on the future of AIEd and if it potential to transform teaching and learning. Assumptions of statistical tests were considered prior to analyses. All statistical tests were conducted using the SPSS software, version 29.0.

4. RESULTS

4.1 Results On Current Landscape of AI From Educators' Perspective

Incorporating technology into the educational process can significantly enhance teaching and learning experiences, improving accessibility, and streamlining administrative tasks. Some methods include utilizing e-learning platforms, interactive boards, smart boards, educational apps, and software (Granić, 2022). In one recent survey (Barrett & Pack, 2023) teachers from the USA stated that they like to incorporate innovative technology in the teaching and specifically on the statement "I enjoy using new technologies for teaching" 75% of the teacher either agree or strongly agree. For educators to do so, they need to feel empowered and digital literate.

A very interesting observation arises right from the beginning of the survey, when teachers were asked to do a self-assessment of their digital competences (Clipa, et al., 2023). Responses shown in Table 2, indicate that in Greece 70% consider that their digital skills are adequate, which is also the fact for most Irish teachers (68%) and Latvian teachers (60%). On the other hand, 45% of Armenian teachers believe that their skills need strengthening and 37% of Hungarian teachers believe their digital skills allow them to handle only the basics.

Regarding the frequency of the usage of technology during the educational process most Greek respondents (43%) state that they use technology very often and only 2% state that they do not use it at all. In Ireland, the majority (53%) uses technology very often and 0% not at all. In Latvia 37% use it very often and 39% often, while in Armenia 50% states that they use technology in the educational process very often. Hungarian teachers seem to incorporate technology less. Specifically, 33% percent of teachers, state that they do not use technology at all during the educational process and 22% that they use it rarely. With the exception of Hungary, in all other countries, educators use technology either often or very often in the educational process.

When it comes to AIEd most teachers from Greece, Ireland, and Armenia state that they have used AIEd tools during the educational process (63%, 55% and 50% respectively). 48% of Hungarian teachers and 61% of Latvian teachers state that they have never used tools in the educational process that include AI.

While AIEd tools are increasingly being incorporated into educational settings, the level of understanding among teachers varies widely. Casal-Otero et al. (2023) found that while there is growing interest in teaching AI concepts to students, many teachers themselves lack sufficient understanding of AI. Furthermore, outcomes from research paper (Holmes, et al., 2022) include the recognition that most AIEd researchers are not trained to tackle the emerging ethical questions. This gap in AI literacy among educators is also arising in our survey. In Greece 67% say that they understand how the algorithms of AI methods work, but 22% says that they do not understand. The respective percentages of the other countries are 57% and 27% for Hungary, 76% and 11% for Armenia, and 76% and 5% for Latvia. Interestingly, most Irish educators (53%) claim that they do not understand how AI algorithms work, and that of course is understandable, since AI literacy requires an interdisciplinary and systematic approach, and thus needs a comprehensive educators training (Walter, 2024; Luke Moorhouse, 2024).

Regarding the purpose of the use of AIEd tools (Figure 1), educators from Greece who stated that they use AIEd, report that they use them primarily for their students, namely, to capture the attention of their students (77%), to get them interested in technology (56%), and to help their student become familiar with AI (49%). In Hungary, teachers who use AIEd, do it mostly for their support and training (64%), to capture the attention of their students (60%) and to delve deeper into the lesson (53%).

As far as Ireland is concerned, they also use it mostly for their support and training (72%), but also to make the lesson understandable to all students (individualized education - vulnerable groups) (54%). In Latvia teachers use it for their own support and training (47%) but also in the class to get students interested in technology (40%). Finally, Armenian educators do also use AI tools to delve deeper into the lesson (65%), to entertain their students (60%) and to get them interested into technology (55%).

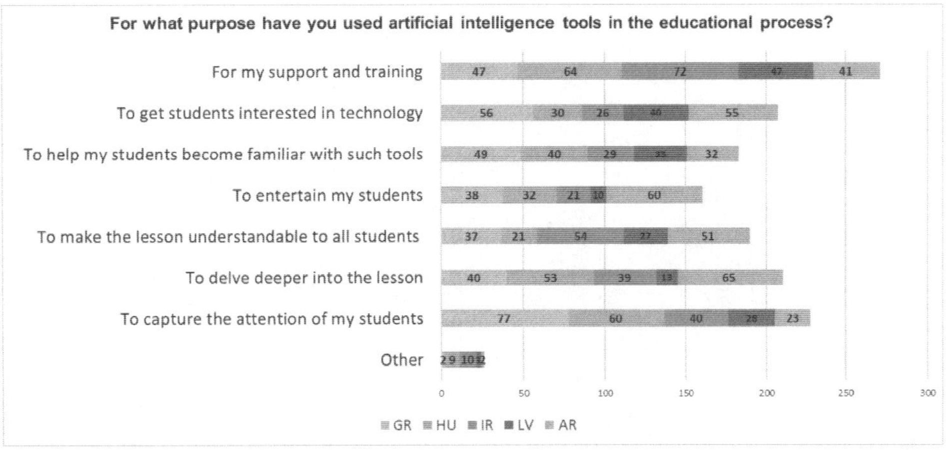

Figure 1. Percentage frequencies of educators' responses from Greece (GR), Hungary (HU), Ireland (IR), Latvia (LV), and Armenia (AR) to the question "For what purpose have you used artificial intelligence tools in the educational process?". The participants could choose multiple options

Although the use of AIEd tools has been reported to be beneficial for students with learning, hearing, visual and mobility impairment (Rakap, 2023), form our survey we can see that only Irish educators rank it as one of their first choices, when stating the purpose of using AI.

Another noteworthy finding is that 10% of the Irish teachers state additional reasons for using AIEd. From their open-ended responses, it is evident that most of them use AI to assist them with writing texts, e.g. “To facilitate my writing as English is not my native language”, “For composing emails and documents”, “Writing story starters, making seating plans, writing lesson plans”.

In the question “Have you noticed whether your students use artificial intelligence tools for their study?” we notice that the majority of Greek teachers (55%) answer “No” and only 15% answers “Yes”. For the other countries, the responses are more balanced. In Hungary, Latvia and Armenia the majority of the educators responded with “Yes” (48%, 41% and 40%), while a significant portion of educators from Ireland responded with “No” (45%). Educators across all countries unanimously agree that students use AI tools for assistance with their academic workload. Specifically, the responses to the statement “To do their homework effortlessly” (shown in Table 2) were as follows: Greece 83%, Hungary 88%, Ireland 83%, Latvia 62%, and Armenia 53%. Another significant reason for students using AI, particularly for Ireland (35%), Latvia (38%) and Armenia (64%) is to acquire additional knowledge. Greek and Latvian teachers also noted the importance of AI “For entertainment and learning at the same time” (41% and 35% respectively).

Beyond school activities, educators also agree that students mostly use AI tools for their entertainment, but also to experiment. These are identified as the top two reasons for students’ engagement with AI tools, as indicated in Table 2.

In our study, teachers highlight the benefits but also the challenges of AIEd (Florence, et al., 2024; Grassini, 2023), emphasizing its potential to enhance teaching efficiency and student engagement, while they also raise concerns about potential risks (Bilstrup, et al., 2020). Specifically, when asked about the potential risks associated with AI tools in education, the majority of educators declared that they are aware of these risks (Greece 53%, Hungary 56%, Ireland 73%, Latvia 49%, and Armenia 52%).

As shown in Figure 2, they agree that the primary risk identified, is students’ tendency to trust the information they find without applying critical thinking (Greece 85%, Hungary 92%, Ireland 90%, Latvia 94% and Armenia 54%). Educators from Hungary, Ireland, Latvia and Armenia also call attention to the fact that students use AI to create and then share material that has been previously tampered with AI tools, which of course encloses the issue of ethical use of AI, a topic extensively discussed in previous surveys (Yusuf, et al., 2024). Educators from Greece (54%) underline that their students expose their own and others' personal data when using these tools, while 71% of Irish teachers state that students are exposed to biased, incorrect or harmful content by using AI tools. Other than that, 49% of Hungarian teachers emphasize that some children might develop emotional bonds with AI robots, perceiving these interactions as real social engagements.

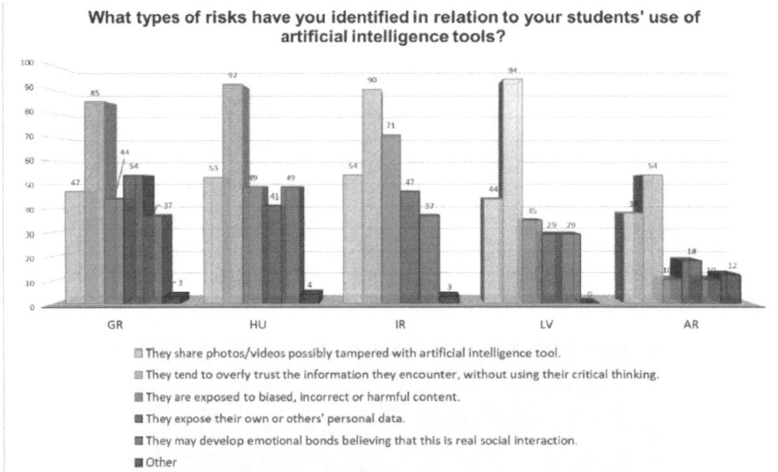

Figure 2. Percentage frequencies of educators' responses from Greece (GR), Hungary (HU), Ireland (IR), Latvia (LV), and Armenia (AR) to the question "What types of risks have you identified in relation to your students' use of artificial intelligence tools?". Participants were allowed to choose more than one option

Furthermore, most educators across all countries state that their schools do not use AI systems for administrative work. Overall, the majority of educators who utilize these systems agree that there are mechanisms in place to ensure that personal and sensitive personal data are adequately protected.

4.2 Results about the Future of AI In Education

Educators assert that AIEd will have a profound impact on the future of education. According to our survey, educators unanimously believe that one of the positive effects AI will have in the future is its potential to support the work of educators. This is a common belief for 75% of Greek educators, 74% of Hungarian, 82% of Irish, 71% of Latvian educators and 64% of Armenian.

Another positive impact is its potential to facilitate personalized learning experiences for students (Chen, et al., 2020). An additional finding derived from our survey, which aligns with other research findings (Ahmad, et al., 2022), indicate that teachers believe AI will reduce their administrative tasks, allowing them to invest more time in teaching and mentoring students (Greece 57%, Hungary 65%, Ireland 72%, Latvia 53%, and Armenia 40%). Other ways AIEd is anticipated to positively affect the educational landscape, is by assisting in the early diagnosis of learning difficulties (Greece 41%, Hungary 35%, Ireland 50%, Latvia 26%, and Armenia 40%) and by offering great potential in educators' trainings (Greece 49%, Hungary 33%, Ireland 61%, Latvia 23%, and Armenia 42%).

It is evident from the results, that educators raise significant concerns about AI in education. Understanding public concerns about AI plays a vital role (Fast & Horvitz, 2017), as public opinion should be incorporated into the process of these regulatory decisions. Having said that, educators most important concern with the raise of AIEd, across all countries, is the failure to cultivate critical thinking (Greece 63%, Hungary 64%, Ireland 70%, Latvia 76%, and Armenia 46%).

For Armenian teachers, the biggest concern is the sharp increase in the incidents of cyberbullying and excessive online use (57%). Greek (51%) and Hungarian educators (49%) are concerned about the absence of social interactions and potential for the children to become emotionally attached to AI systems. In Ireland, 48% of educators worry about the potential exposure of children to misleading or harmful content. Additionally, 27% of Armenian teachers do also consider the risk of insufficient protection of children's personal data. The exploitation of personal content with the use of AI tools, is regarded as a lower risk by the educators (Greece & Hungary 19%, Ireland 9%, Latvia 9%, and Armenia 8%). Finally, teachers from all countries agree on the need for more guidance to enhance their knowledge and skills in using artificial intelligence tools in education (Greece 88%, Hungary 67%, Ireland 99%, Latvia 80%, and Armenia 89%).

Table 2. Questions and responses on artificial intelligence in education

Question	Answers	GR%	HU%	IR%	LV%	ARM%
How familiar are you with technology?	My skills are adequate	70	29	68	60	30
	I can handle the basics	22	37	18	23	25
	My skills need strengthening	8	34	14	17	45
How often do you use technology in the educational process?	0 (Not at all)	2	33	0	0	2
	1	6	22	3	9	4
	2	20	18	12	16	22
	3	29	16	32	39	23
	4 (Very often)	43	11	53	37	50
Have you used tools in the educational process that include artificial intelligence?	Yes	63	41	55	30	50
	No	28	48	41	61	34
	I don't know	8	11	4	9	16
If so, do you understand how the specific algorithms work in order to use the systems efficiently and safely?	Yes	67	57	38	76	76
	No	22	27	53	5	11
	I don't know	11	16	9	19	13
For what purpose have you used artificial intelligence tools in the educational process?	To capture the attention of my students	77	60	40	28	23
	To delve deeper into the lesson	40	53	39	13	65
	To make the lesson understandable	37	21	54	27	51
	To entertain my students	38	32	21	10	60
	To help my students become familiar AI	49	40	29	33	32
	To get students interested in technology	56	30	26	40	55
	For my support and training	47	64	72	47	41
	Other (Please specify)	2	9	10	3	2
Have you noticed whether your students use artificial intelligence tools for their study?	Yes	15	48	35	41	40
	No	55	38	45	33	26
	I don't know	30	14	19	26	34
Why do you think your students use artificial intelligence tools in their preparation and study?	To acquire additional knowledge	21	29	35	38	64
	To address their queries about the course	25	38	20	20	38
	For entertainment and learning	41	25	9	35	28
	To do their homework effortlessly	83	88	83	62	53
	Other (Please specify)	2	6	2	28	2
Have you noticed if your students use artificial intelligence tools outside their school activities?	Yes	20	37	23	26	28
	No	33	28	42	19	8
	I don't know	47	35	35	55	64
What do you believe is the reason your students use artificial intelligence tools beyond their school activities?	To acquire additional knowledge	19	38	41	39	73
	For entertainment	85	80	69	61	54
	For malicious purposes	10	8	14	11	5
	To experiment	67	67	55	61	49
	Other (Please specify)	13	2	0	6	5
Are you aware of any potential risks arising from your students' use of artificial intelligence tools in general?	Yes	53	56	73	49	52
	No	24	23	14	13	31
	I don't know	23	21	13	38	17
What types of risks have you identified in relation to your students' use of artificial intelligence tools?	They share photos possibly tampered.	47	53	54	44	38
	They tend to overly trust the information, without using their critical thinking.	85	92	90	94	54
	They are exposed to biased content.	44	49	71	35	10
	They expose personal data.	54	41	47	29	18
	They may develop emotional bonds..	37	49	37	29	10

5. DISCUSSION AND CONCLUSIONS

AI holds tremendous potential to enhance teaching and learning in education, but its implementation must be guided by principles of equity, transparency, and ethical responsibility. By addressing challenges and ethical considerations while leveraging the benefits of AI technologies, educators and other stakeholders can work towards creating inclusive, empowering, and effective educational experiences for all.

That being said, our survey reveals that while educators from different countries hold varying views about AIEd, they do share common perspectives in certain cases. Regarding our first research question "What is the current status of AIEd in the five countries we focus on? How do educators perceive it, and what are their principal areas of skepticism?" the responses indicate that most educators from Greece, Hungary, Latvia, and Armenia claim to have a good understanding of how AI works and are aware of the potential risks. They are mostly skeptical about cultivating critical thinking in students when using AI tools, and express concerns about students will be exposed to biased data. Another interesting point is that educators mostly use AIEd for their support and training, and in the classroom to capture the attention of their students. Furthermore, educators in all countries state that their schools do not use AI systems for administrative work.

Regarding the second research question "What are the patterns, preferences, and impacts of student engagement with artificial intelligence tools in educational settings from the perspective of the educators?", findings indicate that educators believe students use AI tools in the educational context mostly for their assistance with their academic workload, stating reply "To do their homework effortlessly". Outside of school, educators believe that students predominantly use AI for their entertainment purposes.

Finally, regarding the question "In what ways will AI shape the educational landscape from the perspective of educators?", educators foresee that AI will highly affect the educational process in the future. They express optimism that their work will be supported by AI systems, but also that they will enable personalized learning experiences for their students. However, their primary concern for the future is that the proliferation of AI might hinder the cultivation of critical thinking skills. Last but not least, nearly all educators underline the need for assistance and more guidance to enrich their knowledge and skills in using artificial intelligence tools in education, through training seminars, workshops, but also specialized online courses.

CONFLICT OF INTEREST

No potential competing interest was reported by the authors.

ACKNOWLEDGEMENT

We would like to thank the Safer Internet Centers of Hungary (Király Borbála), Ireland (Jane McGarrigle), Latvia (Maija Katkovska), and Armenia (Narine Khachatryan) for their support in the collection of their national data. We would like to also thank Insafe, the European Network of Safer Internet Centers, especially Karl Hopwood, for its support in disseminating the survey.

FUNDING DECLARATION

This study was supported by Projects DIGITAL EUROPE No. 101081266 (SI4Kids2) 2022-2024, and No. 101146190 (SI4KIDS.GR) 2024-2026.

REFERENCES

Ahmad, S. F. et al., (2022). Academic and Administrative Role of Artificial Intelligence in Education. *Sustainability,* pp. 2071-1050.

Akgun, S. & Greenhow, C., (2022). Artificial intelligence in education: Addressing ethical challenges in K-12 settings. AI Ethics , p. 431–440 .

Ally, M., (2019). Competency Profile of the Digital and Online Teacher in Future Education. *The International Review of Research in Open and Distributed Learning, 20(2).*

Barrett, A. & Pack, A., (2023). Not quite eye to A.I.: student and teacher perspectives on the use of generative artificial intelligence in the writing process. *International Journal of Educational Technology in Higher Education,* pp. 2365-9440.

Beverly Park Woolf, H., Lane, C., Chaudhri, V. K. & Kolodner, J. L., (2013). AI Grand Challenges for Education. *AI Magazine, 34,* pp. 66-84.

Bilstrup, K.-E. K., Kaspersen, M. H. & Petersen, M. G., (2020). *Staging Reflections on Ethical Dilemmas in Machine Learning: A Card-Based Design Workshop for High School Students.* New York, NY, USA, Association for Computing Machinery, p. 1211–1222.

Casal-Otero, L. et al., (2023). AI literacy in K-12: a systematic literature review. *International Journal of STEM Education,* pp. 2196-7822.

Chan, C. & Lee, K., (2023). he AI generation gap: Are Gen Z students more interested in adopting generative AI such as ChatGPT in teaching and learning than their Gen X and millennial generation teachers?. *Smart Learn.*

Chen, X., Xie, H., Zou, D. & Hwang, G.-J., (2020). Application and theory gaps during the rise of Artificial Intelligence in Education. *Computers and Education: Artificial Intelligence,* p. 100002.

Christodoulaki, M. & Fragopoulou, P., (2010). SafeLine: reporting illegal internet content. *Information Management & Computer Security,* pp. 54-65.

Clipa, O., Delibas, C.-S. & Mâță, L., (2023). Teachers' Self-Efficacy and Attitudes towards the Use of Information Technology in Classrooms. *Education Sciences,* pp. 2227-7102.

Crompton, H. & Burke, D., (2022). Artificial intelligence in K-12 education. *SN Soc Sci 2,* p. 113.

Daskalaki, E., Psaroudaki, K. & Fragopoulou, P., (2018). EL-SIC: focus on better and Safer Online Experiences for Kids. *ERCIM NEWS,* pp. 52--53.

Daskalaki, E., Psaroudaki, K., Karkanaki, M. & Fragopoulou, P., (2020). Understanding the online behavior and risks of children: results of a large-scale national survey on 10-18 year olds. *arXiv Preprint.*

Fast, E. & Horvitz, E., (2017). *Long-Term Trends in the Public Perception of Artificial Intelligence.* San Francisco, s.n., pp. 936-969.

Florence, M., Min, Z. & Darlene, S., (2024). Systematic review of research on artificial intelligence in K-12 education (2017–2022). *Computers and Education: Artificial Intelligence,* p. 100195.

Granić, A., (2022). Educational Technology Adoption: A systematic review. *Education and Information Technologies,* pp. 1573-7608.

Grassini, S., (2023). Shaping the Future of Education: Exploring the Potential and Consequences of AI and ChatGPT in Educational Settings. *Education Sciences,* pp. 7-692.

Holmes, W. et al., (2022). Ethics of AI in Education: Towards a Community-Wide Framework.. *International Journal of Artificial Intelligence in Education,* 32(1), p. 504–526.

Institute for Ethical AI in Education, n.d. *Interim report,* s.l.: University of Buckingham.

Kaplan-Rakowski, R., Grotewold, K., Hartwick, P. & Papin, K., (2023). Generative AI and Teachers' Perspectives on Its Implementation in Education. *Journal of Interactive Learning Research, 34(2),* pp. 313-338.

Kizilcec, R. F., (2024). To Advance AI Use in Education, Focus on Understanding Educators.. *International Journal of Artificial Intelligence in Education,* 34(1), p. 12–19.

Kokolaki, E. et al., (2020). Investigating the dynamics of illegal online activity: The power of reporting, dark web, and related legislation. *Computer Law & Security Review,* p. 105440.

Kuleto, V. et al., (2022). The Attitudes of K–12 Schools' Teachers in Serbia towards the Potential of Artificial Intelligence. *Sustainability.*

Luke Moorhouse, B., (2024). Beginning and first-year language teachers' readiness for the generative AI age. *Computers and Education: Artificial Intelligence,* pp. 100-201.

Rakap, S., (2023). Chatting with GPT: Enhancing Individualized Education Program Goal Development for Novice Special Education Teachers. *Journal of Special Education Technology,* pp. 50-62.

Rasul, T. et al., (2024). The role of ChatGPT in higher education: Benefits, challenges, and future research directions. *Ξournal of applied learning and teaching.*

Roll, I. & Wylie, R., (2016). Evolution and Revolution in Artificial Intelligence in Education. *Int J Artif Intell Educ 26,* pp. 582-599.

Schiel, J., Bobek, B. L. & Schnieders, J. Z., (2024). *High School Students' Use and Impressions of AI Tools,* Chicago: ACT Research.

Su, J., Ng, D. T. K. & Chu, S. K. W., (2023). Artificial Intelligence (AI) Literacy in Early Childhood Education: The Challenges and Opportunities. *Computers and Education: Artificial Intelligence.*

Tahiru, F., (2021). AI in Education: A Systematic Literature Review. *Journal of Cases on Information Technology (JCIT),* pp. 1-20.

Tanveer, M., Hassan, S. & Bhaumik, A., (2020). Academic Policy Regarding Sustainability and Artificial Intelligence (AI). *Sustainability.*

Walter, Y., (2024). Embracing the future of Artificial Intelligence in the classroom: the relevance of AI literacy, prompt engineering, and critical thinking in modern education. *International Journal of Educational Technology in Higher Education,* pp. 2365-9440.

Yusuf, A., Pervin, N. & Román-González, M., (2024). Generative AI and the future of higher education: a threat to academic integrity or reformation? Evidence from multicultural perspectives. *International Journal of Educational Technology in Higher Education,* pp. 2365-9440.

DIGIUP: A GAME-BASED APPROACH FOR IMPROVING DIGITAL COMPETENCIES FOR OLDER PEOPLE

Andrej Jerman Blažič and Tanja Pavleska
Laboratory for Open Systems and Networks, Jozef Stefan Institute
Jamova 39, 1000 Ljubljana, Slovenia

ABSTRACT

The advent of digital technologies brought about numerous challenges for diverse groups of citizens, resulting in the so called digital divide. Thus, older adults often struggle with the adaption of digital technologies due to their lack of foundational digital literacy essential for navigating everyday activities. For more than a decade, the EU Digital Skills Strategy and related initiatives have aimed to improve digital skills and competencies of all citizens for a successful digital transformation. Therefore, senior adults are seen as learners who should be treated with patience and care. This study explores the potential of game-based assessment (GBA) and game-based learning (GBL) as innovative approaches for blended learning that aim to bridge the presented gap by fostering digital competencies in a supportive and engaging environment. We developed DiGiUP, a narrative-driven game-based approach for assessing and improving older adults' digital knowledge and skills. To evaluate its performance, we tested and validated DiGiUP within the European Erasmus+ project DIGIBLEND, by involving 45 older adults in structured gameplay sessions, followed by post-game evaluations. Results showed significant improvements in digital skills, particularly in problem-solving and safety, whereas participants reported higher levels of confidence and engagement. Collaborative learning emerged as a key factor in the game's success.

KEYWORDS

Game-Based Assessment, Game-Based Learning, Digital Competences, Blended Learning

1. INTRODUCTION

Digital technology is essential aspect of everyday life, providing opportunities for communication, information access and task management. With the proliferation of digital devices and the internet in most parts of the world, knowledge and skills to use them in everyday life and at work have become crucial for almost everyone. These skills reflect not only the respective knowledge of information and communication technologies (ICT), but also the ability to use the technologies effectively and responsibly. Therefore, the development of digital skills is at the top of the European digital agenda (European Commission, 2024; Sala et al., 2020).

More than a fifth (21.53 %) of the EU population in 2023 was aged 65 and over, with estimation for growth over the next three decades, peaking at 129.8 million in 2050 (Corselli-Nordblad & Strandell, 2020). The lack of digital competence among older adults in the EU is a significant factor for the emergence of the second digital divide. Unlike the first digital divide associated with disparities in economic development, the second is rooted in technological skills and access (Reissmann et al., 2022). On the other hand, only 28% of the European older adults possess basic digital skills, leaving the majority feeling as outsiders in the European digital culture (DESI, 2024). Although this percentage varies across countries, the numbers are important indicator for a significant portion of European citizens not possessing the digital competences needed for regular activities.

The problem of adopting digital skills among older adults is rooted in their prior learning and professional experiences, which lacked exposure to digital technology and internet services (Clark et al., 2016; Schirmer et al., 2023). Thus, they are largely unfamiliar with modern devices despite their usefulness for facilitating social connections and managing daily tasks (Blažič & Blažič, 2020; Oppl & Stary, 2020). Many older adults approach these devices with apprehension, fearing the potential consequences of their lack of digital knowledge (Team, 2020). When faced with the need to use new technologies, they rely on public day centers for assistance with tasks that may seem simple to others but remain challenging for them.

Traditional instructional methods often fall short in addressing the specific challenges faced by older adult learners, as they may not fully accommodate the diverse needs. Research shows that older adults benefit from learning environments that are engaging, non-intimidating, and adaptable to their individual abilities (Casselden, 2023). In this context, game-based assessment (GBA) and game-based learning (GBL) emerge as promising solutions. By blending structured learning objectives with interactive and enjoyable game mechanics, GBA and GBL create a motivating environment that encourages exploration and reduces the fear of failure (Kim & Ifenthaler, 2019). GBA and GBL thus create supportive environments where older adults can build confidence and acquire digital skills at their own pace.

This paper presents an empirically driven GBA approach for development of an educational game for learning digitals skills by older adults, named DiGiUP. The game employs a narrative-driven approach to enhance digital skills among older adults by simulating real-world scenarios where participants apply their digital knowledge to solve challenges. Designed to promote engagement and confidence, DiGiUP combines analog and digital elements to create an interactive learning environment that addresses older adults' unique needs. This study evaluates the game's effectiveness in improving digital competencies, fostering enjoyment, and identifying refinements for future iterations. By leveraging the potential of game-based learning, DiGiUP contributes to bridging the digital divide and promoting lifelong learning and social inclusion among older adults. The study is situated within the framework of the European Commission's DigComp 2.2, which defines digital competence as a multifaceted skill set encompassing information and data literacy, communication, safety, and problem-solving (Vuorikari et al., 2022). These competencies are vital for older adults to navigate today's digital landscape confidently. Yet, existing educational tools often fail to effectively engage this demographic, leaving a gap in practical, scalable solutions.

2. BACKGROUND AND RELATED WORK

The advancement of digital technology has transformed many aspects of modern life, creating a pressing need for digital literacy across all demographics, including older adults. Digital competence is not only a critical skill for accessing information and communication technologies (ICT) but also a key enabler for participation in a rapidly evolving digital society. This section outlines the theoretical foundations that inform the design and evaluation of game-based learning/assessment interventions aimed at evaluating and improving digital skills among older adults.

The advancement of digital technology has transformed many aspects of modern life, creating a pressing need for digital literacy across all demographics, including older adults. Digital competence is not only a critical skill for accessing information and communication technologies (ICT) but also a key enabler for participation in a rapidly evolving digital society. This section outlines the theoretical foundations that inform the design and evaluation of game-based learning/assessment interventions aimed at evaluating and improving digital skills among older adults.

Game based assessment can be defined as the process of evaluating or measuring someone's (digital) knowledge, skills, competencies or progress in a particular area through the use of games (Udeozor et al., 2024). It involves gathering evidence of learning through various methods and making judgments based on that evidence. Games can be an effective tool for several types of assessment: knowledge (A. Pak, 2024; Clark et al., 2016), skills (Behera, 2024; Shute & Ke, 2012), behavior (Landers et al., 2017); and performance assessment (Mislevy et al., 2012).

Digital competence refers to the confident and critical use of ICT for work, leisure, and communication. According to the DigComp Framework (see Figure 1), digital competence encompasses five key areas:

- Information and data literacy: The ability to identify, locate, retrieve, evaluate, and use information effectively.
- Communication and collaboration: Engaging in digital environments for collaboration, interaction, and participation.
- Digital content creation: Creating, editing, and managing digital content.
- Safety: Ensuring online privacy, security, and well-being.
- Problem solving: Innovatively resolving issues using digital tools

For older adults, the focus often centers on *information and data literacy, safety,* and *problem-solving*, as they address critical everyday needs, such as navigating online platforms, protecting personal information, and using digital tools for practical tasks. Furthermore, our work addresses all four assessments types described above: knowledge, skills, behavior, and performance assessment. To do that, the specification of game elements in our approach follows the MDA (Mechanics, Dynamics, and Aesthetics) design framework to define the basic elements of the GBA approach (Hunicke et al., 2004). *Mechanics* represent the main components of the game: rules, actions required by the player in order to play the game, the algorithms and data structures in the game engine, etc. *Dynamics*, on the other hand, are the behaviors manifested during the game-play, as well as the factors affecting players and their "cooperation" during game-play. Finally, *aesthetics* is the emotional responses that the game-play evokes in the player as a result of all other elements.

The last decade brought an increasing number of initiatives and research aimed at enhancing and promoting the social inclusion of older adults in society (Casselden, 2023; Oppl & Stary, 2020; Vuorikari et al., 2022). In their study, Casselden et al. (2023) emphasize the need for a more suitable learning environment for enabling digital literacy training for older adults and reducing their fears in dealing with technology. They highlight the importance and usefulness of simplicity of the learning approach. While an important part in the game's application is the knowledge assessment of players, in order to create positive emotions and better user engagement, emotional signals should be integrated from game design (de Sousa Borges et al., 2014). Researchers have therefore suggested that assessment of emotional reactions should be included in the methodology itself to gauge emotional reaction during game play and provide better motivation and player cooperation (Anolli et al., 2010).

GBL and GBA approaches have significant potential to address the digital divide by offering engaging, low-pressure environments for skill development and retention (Kelli Adam, 2023; Kim & Ifenthaler, 2019; Moeketsi O. Mosia, 2024). GBL integrates instructional content into game mechanics to enhance learning outcomes. It leverages the motivational and interactive game elements, such as feedback and progression, to facilitate active engagement with the learning material. GBA solutions have gained popularity in workplace settings, where the use of serious games (designed for a purpose other than for pure entertainment) are being increasingly applied as important evaluation tools (Dubbels, 2013). In this context, it becomes important for game developers to comprehend how players react when playing games, how GBL scenarios and elements function, and what emotional states are affected during play (al-Qallawi & Raghavan, 2022).

Despite the growing body of work on GBA and GBL, limited studies address the application of these methods to older adults. Much of the current research focuses on youth or general adult learners. Our study contributes to filling this gap by evaluating a game-based approach, DiGiUP, designed explicitly for older adults. By leveraging the DigComp framework and integrating collaborative and adaptive learning elements, this research provides insights into the efficacy of GBA in bridging the digital divide.

3. METHODOLOGY

The combination of the applied GBA approach, followed by the gamified training was based on the selected competence areas from the DigComp 2.2 framework. From the five main areas presented as a digital competence framework for citizens, three were considered as the essential game elements: *Information and data literacy, Safety,* and *Problem solving* (see Figure 1). Each of the three selected competence areas contains several activities, that have been introduced in the game in order to enable GBA and blended learning. As pointed out in Section 2, the specification of the game elements follows the MDA design framework (Hunicke et al., 2004). The game is therefore described through these properties (in Section 3.3) to facilitate the understanding of both the development and the flow of game play. The result is the design and development of an analog game, DiGiUP (Digital Upskill), that allows for assessment and improvement of digital competencies. The game is intended to facilitate the training of older adults' digital skills by making them more confident and successful in acquiring their digital competencies, while allowing for evaluation of players' digital skills and knowledge. The platform that enabled the development, testing and validation of our approach was the Erasmus+ project DIGIBLEND. This led to an evidence-based methodology that is reusable and testable by other researchers and practitioners.

DiGiUP has the shape and properties of a board game that guides the players along a predefined learning path. It was designed as an analog type with the use of playing cards. This type of playing enables the game to run as a step-by-step process, where each step is equipped with a learning material of selected digital knowledge. The use of playing cards bring to players the needed comfort and familiarity, reminding them to the playing of known card games.

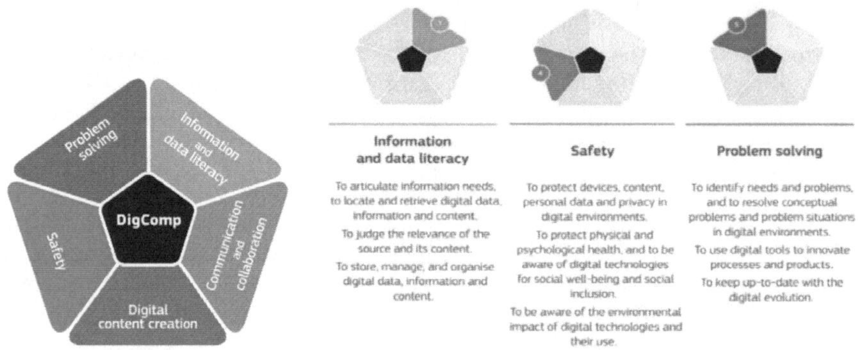

Figure 1. The three DigComp 2.2 competence areas relevant for our work

3.1 Target Group and Research Questions

To ensure successful teaching of the basic digital competencies, it was necessary to assess and acknowledge the needs and abilities of the group of older adults that will play the game. The target group that took part during the game design was clearly defined in terms of the age (65+) and the presence of "common" general educational level. As digital competencies among the members of a group vary, the first challenge in the game development was determining the competence levels of group members. Besides information on age and the existence of some competencies, important issues that were explored were the game mechanics (rules, challenges, competitions, rewards) and dynamics (narratives, storylines). Specification about the real-time actions allowed to the learners' and the behaviors stemming from players' key decisions during the game-specific events were specified and collected. The game aesthetics was also critical and its evolution was also observed during and after the play.

The major research questions we aimed to address during game design and testing are:

- **RQ1**: Is GBA a viable method for digital competence assessment for older adults?
- **RQ2**: Does GBA allow for learning new digital competencies for older adults?
- **RQ3**: Does GBA offer a reusable method for digital competence assessment and learning?

3.2 Data Collection and Analysis

Data collection and analysis were carried out to evaluate the effectiveness of DiGiUP in assessing and improving digital competencies of older adults. The testing involved 45 older adults (34 males and 11 females) between 65-78, recruited from three daycare centers in Slovenia. The game involved 4 sessions, with four players per session, each lasting approximately 65 minutes. Data were collected during game sessions and through post-game evaluations, incorporating both observational and self-reported methods. Participants engaged in structured gameplay sessions moderated by trainers (game masters), who ensured smooth game flow and verified participants' actions and answers. Trainers observed participant behavior, noting levels of engagement, interaction, and progression through game sessions.

3.3 Game Development and Description

DiGiUP delivers an engaging, educational, and collaborative experience through narrative-driven gameplay, providing players with meaningful learning process on topics related to *information and data literacy, safety* and *problem solving*. To provide a systematic outlook of the game elements and the learning process, Table maps DiGiUP's elements onto the MDA framework.

Table 1. The DiGiUP game mapped onto the MDA framework

MDA Framework	DiGiUP Game elements	
Mechanics	*Game-board design*	• A house with 6 rooms (levels): Kitchen, Bathroom, Dining Room, Living Room, Bedroom, and Study Room. • Game-board size is 60 × 90 cm, players progress upward to the top of the house. • Each room contains: 4 question fields and 1 QR field for solving a digital task.
	Player components	• Colored game totems (red, blue, green, yellow) to track individual progress. • Help tiles (12 total), also called trading cards, for assistance during challenges. • Bridging cards (24 total) to "bridge gaps" in knowledge through learning modules.
	Question System	• Questions are categorized by difficulty levels: basic, intermediate, and advanced. • A question book managed by the game master provides quiz content tied to digital competencies in information literacy, safety, and problem-solving.
	Winning conditions	• Players complete all six rooms by answering questions and solving digital tasks. • The first player to reach the top wins, with tiebreakers based on the lowest number of unused bridging cards or a dice roll.
Dynamics	*Progression through levels*	Players answer questions to advance through each room. At the end of a room, they face a mandatory digital task at the elevator to move to the next level.
	Strategic use of help tiles and Bridging cards	• Players use help tiles to 1) request assistance or 2) exchange for bridging cards. • Bridging cards provide access to additional learning modules, enabling players to acquire the knowledge needed to answer difficult questions.
	Collab.problem-solving	Help tiles promote teamwork by encouraging players to assist each other in answering questions or solving digital tasks.
	Player-driven difficulty	Players can choose the level of difficulty for each question, allowing them to tailor challenges to their skill level.
	Competition for progress	Limited help tiles and the scoring system for bridging cards introduce strategic decision-making.
Aesthetics	*Narrative immersion*	• The story revolves around proving digital competency to take care of grandchildren, providing players with a relatable and motivating context. • The narrative creates a sense of purpose as players navigate the rooms and challenges of the house.
	Challenge and mastery	Players face increasing difficulty through the progression of questions and digital tasks, fostering a sense of accomplishment as they overcome each level.
	Collaborative learning	The integration of help tiles and bridging cards encourages teamwork and shared learning, making the experience both interactive and supportive.
	Customizability and inclusivity	The game accommodates varying skill levels through adjustable question difficulties, ensuring accessibility for diverse participants.
	Rewarding learning	Bridging cards transform incorrect answers into opportunities for learning, reinforcing educational goals.
	Competition and strategy	The race to the top of the house creates a sense of excitement and rivalry, while resource management adds a layer of strategic depth.

DiGiUP begins with a relatable scenario: *Players assume the role of grandparents tasked with caring for their grandchildren for a month while their son is away on a business trip. However, the grandchildren, skeptical of their grandparents' digital knowledge, challenge them to prove their competence in digital literacy, safety, and problem-solving by navigating a series of tasks and challenges throughout the family home.* The game unfolds in a house represented on the game board, featuring six distinct rooms, as shown in Figure 2: Kitchen, Bathroom, Dining Room, Living Room, Bedroom, and Study Room. Each room corresponds to a specific set of digital competencies from the DigComp 2.2 framework, with, for instance, the Kitchen and Living Room focusing on information and data literacy, and the Bathroom and Bedroom emphasizing safety skills. The narrative progresses as players move from room to room, starting at the bottom of the house and advancing upwards toward the top floor. To begin, each player selects a totem to represent their progress. Players take turns entering each room and tackling its challenges, which consist of four quiz-style questions (the "traditional steps") and a final digital task (the "digital step"). The questions vary in difficulty from basic, through intermediate, to advanced level. They are presented by the game master, who uses a booklet containing quizzes tailored to each room's topic. Players must choose the difficulty level of each question based on their confidence and strategy.

As players encounter questions, they have the option to answer independently or rely on game resources for assistance:

- If they answer correctly without aid, they progress to the next question and retain any unused help tiles.
- If they struggle, they can use a help tile to request assistance from another player or exchange it for a bridging card.

The bridging cards act as powerful learning tools, offering access to relevant learning modules via QR codes. By scanning the code, players are directed to an online resource that helps them build the knowledge needed to answer the question.

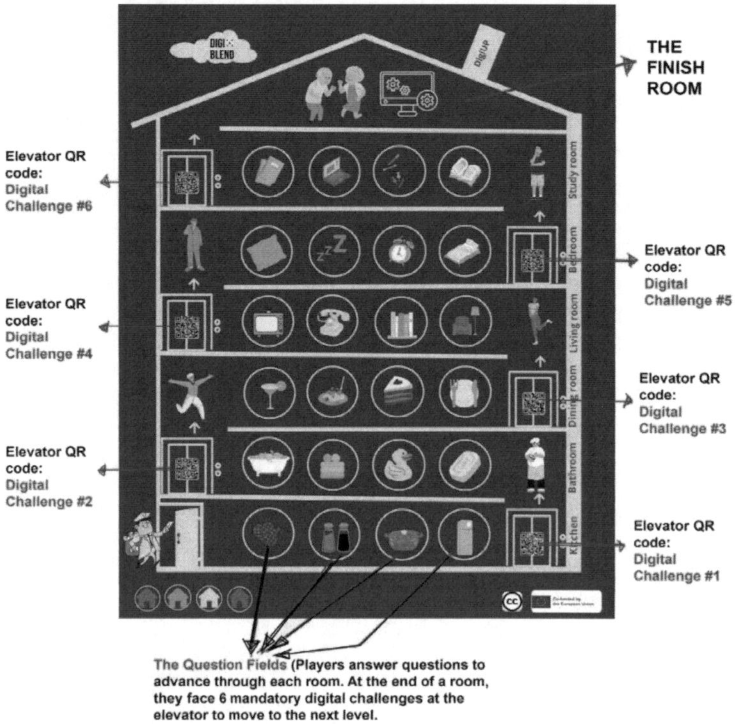

Figure 2. The DiGiUP game board design

Each room culminates in a mandatory digital task at the elevator (represented by a QR field). Only after successfully completing this task can players proceed to the next room. These digital tasks test practical skills aligned with the room's theme, reinforcing learning through application. Players who answer all questions and complete the digital task advance, continuing their journey toward the top of the house. The game's competitive edge comes to life as players strive to reach the final room. The first player to complete all six rooms and solve the last digital task wins. In the case of a tie, the winner is determined by the number of unused bridging cards – rewarding efficient problem-solving and self-reliance. If still tied, a dice roll will ultimate resolve the competition. Such use of bridging cards, customizable question difficulties, and interactive digital tasks, ensures meaningful learning outcomes while fostering a sense of challenge, collaboration, and achievement.

4. RESULTS AND ANALYSIS

DiGiUP provided an engaging and interactive learning experience, yielding valuable insights into its impact on participants. Trainers, who were responsible for facilitating the game's progression, noted that the gameplay effectively stimulated learning and cooperation among players. This was accompanied by an enhanced sense of curiosity, as participants expressed excitement about discovering "what's next" during each stage of the game. Players particularly appreciated the dynamic elements of the game, including the digital challenges and tasks, as well as the incorporation of peer-learning experiences that fostered collaboration.

It is worth noting that participants appeared comfortable during each game session. Moreover, playing encouraged discussions and meaningful interactions among players, making the experience immersive and engaging. Following each session, participants completed a multiple-choice questionnaire to assess their perceptions and learning outcomes. The results, summarized in Figure 3, reveal that majority of players (63%) felt more confident in their knowledge and competencies after playing. This indicates that the game successfully enhanced participants' perception of their digital skills. The most notable improvement was observed in the area of problem-solving, where they demonstrated high gains in competence compared to pre-gaming evaluations. However, improvements in information safety and data literacy were modest. One reason for this is that these areas may require more immersive, real-world simulations, such as identifying phishing emails, cross-checking news sources. Hence, these areas might require additional focus or reinforcement in future iterations of the game. Overall, the fact that 72% of participants reported feeling more confident in their overall digital skills after playing the game testifies of the game's success in achieving its goals.

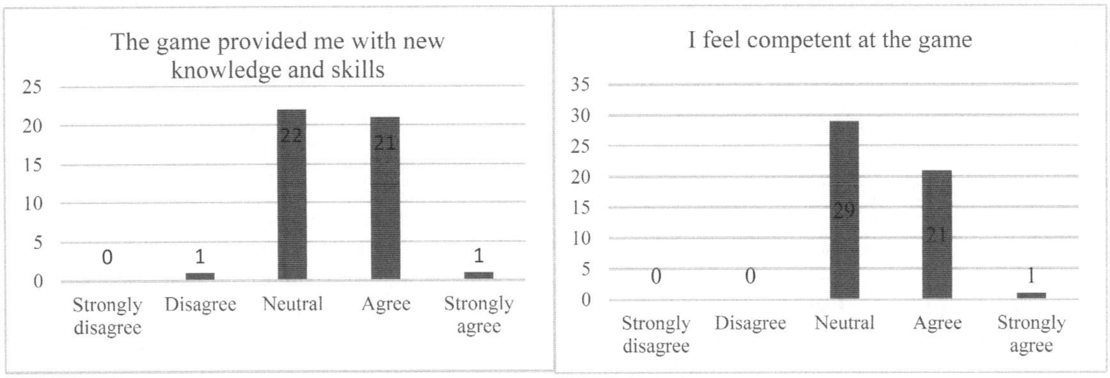

Figure 3. Data from the post-experiment questionnaire of DiGiUP game

Finally, in terms of replayability, the DiGiUP game received strong positive feedback. A total of 67% of players indicated they would choose to play the game again in their free time, highlighting its potential as a sustainable and enjoyable tool.

4.1 Discussion

The testing provided valuable insights into the properties and effectiveness of DiGiUP. The findings reaffirm GBA's potential as a valuable method for assessing and improving digital competencies of older adults. The results showed noticeable improvements in participants' digital skills, particularly in the areas of problem-solving and safety. However, the complexity and longer duration of the game posed challenges. Some participants found it too long and occasionally difficult to follow, suggesting a need for simplified rules and shorter sessions to sustain focus and accessibility.

Another important point is the critical role that trainers played in ensuring the success of the gameplay. They guided participants, tracked their progress, and tailored the experience to individual needs. Over successive sessions, trainers reported needing less intervention, highlighting the games' effectiveness in building participants' confidence and competence. Clearly, the trainer's skill and game understanding can impact the learning effectiveness of DiGiUP. A training program is thus an important part of the pre-learning.

The results and observations allowed us to address the study's primary research questions: **(RQ1)** The results demonstrated that the game effectively assessed digital competencies, offering participants a clear understanding of their skills; **(RQ2)** The game facilitated skill development, particularly in problem-solving and safety competencies, while fostering confidence and curiosity; and **(RQ3)** The game proved to be a reusable tool, adaptable to various learning needs and capable of providing engaging and educational experiences over multiple sessions. The analysis yielded several recommendations to enhance future use:

1. **Simplify mechanics and structure** with rules that are straightforward, ensuring accessibility for participants with varying levels of initial knowledge and skills. Moreover, sessions should be broken into more manageable segments to maintain focus and engagement.

2. **Incorporate interactive and multimedia content** by adding diverse interactive elements to accommodate different learning preferences.
3. **Emphasize collaboration** by keeping peer-to-peer interaction central to the gameplay, leveraging mutual learning as a key benefit for older adults.
4. **Provide trainer support** by continuous guidance to help participants navigate the game and achieve learning outcomes.
5. **Include follow-up activities** through additional resources or sessions to help reinforcement of newly acquired skills.
6. **Train the trainers** to establish a trainer community for best practice exchange. This is especially important considering that personalized training has been proved as one of the most effective methods for learning digital skills for older adults (Pihlainen et al., 2021).
7. **Customize the game for cultural contexts** to suit different cultural and national backgrounds, ensuring relevance and inclusivity for diverse groups.

By addressing these recommendations, future iterations of the game will further improve its accessibility, impact, and adaptability to diverse learning environments.

5. CONCLUSION

As part of the Erasmus+ DIGIBLEND project, we developed an analog card-based game with integrated digital content as a learning tool for older adults of different ages. The testing results have shown that the game offers strong foundational framework for further iterations and improvements. By combining game-based assessment (GBA) with a blended learning approach, the approach offers a sociable, engaging, and low-risk way for older adults to practice digital skills while fostering experimentation and self-guided learning. These factors are particularly significant for older adult learners, as the game provides a safe and enjoyable environment to build confidence and assess their digital competencies without fear of failure.

Our work demonstrated that GBA is a promising approach to bridging the digital divide for older adults, offering an engaging method to integrate them into the digital environment and lifestyle with reduced apprehension or resistance. Through its innovative approach, GBA enables older adults to participate in the rapidly evolving digital world in a friendly, supportive manner. The findings confirm that DiGiUP is an effective and accessible tool for teaching digital competencies to this population, promoting inclusion and fostering lifelong learning.

Future research will focus on validating the study's findings by testing DiGiUP across a broader international context. Planned testing in countries such as Turkey, Italy, Germany, Ireland, Serbia, and Latvia, will provide deeper insights into the game's adaptability and cultural relevance. Moreover, we plan to carry out a longitudinal study in order to investigate the long-term effects of the learning in terms of digital skills retention and maintenance. This enables us to quantify the levels of obtained digital skills and rank them according to the DigComp2.2 proficiency levels. These efforts aim to strengthen the foundation for policy recommendations and create specific guidelines for practitioners involved in game-based and lifelong learning.

REFERENCES

A. Pak, Z. F., I. Sci, Fouzia Sultana, Shabana Ali. (2024). Supplementary Student Support Services for a Blended Learning Environment: A PANT model. *Annals of PIMS-Shaheed Zulfiqar Ali Bhutto Medical University*. https://doi.org/10.48036/apims.v20isuppl-1.775

al-Qallawi, S., & Raghavan, M. (2022). A review of online reactions to game-based assessment mobile applications. *International Journal of Selection and Assessment*, *30*(1), 14–26. https://doi.org/10.1111/ijsa.12346

Anolli, L., Mantovani, F., Confalonieri, L., Ascolese, A., & Peveri, L. (2010). Emotions in Serious Games: From Experience to Assessment. *International Journal of Emerging Technologies in Learning (iJET)*, *5*, 7–16. https://doi.org/10.3991/ijet.v5iSI3.1496

Behera, S. (2024). Innovative Pedagogical Practices In Teacher Education. *International Journal For Multidisciplinary Research*. https://doi.org/10.36948/ijfmr.2024.v06i02.15488

Blažič, B. J., & Blažič, A. J. (2020). Overcoming the digital divide with a modern approach to learning digital skills for the elderly adults. *Education and Information Technologies*, *25*(1), 259–279. https://doi.org/10.1007/s10639-019-09961-9

Casselden, B. (2023). Not like riding a bike: How public libraries facilitate older people's digital inclusion during the Covid-19 pandemic. *Journal of Librarianship and Information Science*, *55*(3), 704–718. https://doi.org/10.1177/09610006221101898

Clark, D. B., Tanner-Smith, E. E., & Killingsworth, S. S. (2016). Digital Games, Design, and Learning: A Systematic Review and Meta-Analysis. *Review of Educational Research*, *86*(1), 79–122. https://doi.org/10.3102/0034654315582065

Corselli-Nordblad, L., & Strandell, H. (2020). *Ageing Europe: Looking at the lives of older people in the EU : 2020 edition*. Publications Office of the European Union. https://data.europa.eu/doi/10.2785/628105

de Sousa Borges, S., Durelli, V. H. S., Reis, H. M., & Isotani, S. (2014). A systematic mapping on gamification applied to education. *Proceedings of the 29th Annual ACM Symposium on Applied Computing*, 216–222. https://doi.org/10.1145/2554850.2554956

DESI. (2024). *Digital Decade DESI visualisation tool*. Shaping Europe's Digital Future. https://digital-decade-desi.digital-strategy.ec.europa.eu/datasets/desi/charts/desi-indicators?period=desi_2024&indicator=desi_dsk_bab&breakdown=y65_74&unit=pc_ind&country=AT,BE,BG,HR,CY,CZ,DK,EE,EU,FI,FR,DE,EL,HU,IE,IT,LV,LT,LU,MT,NL,PL,PT,RO,SK,SI,ES,SE

Dubbels, B. (2013). Gamification, Serious Games, Ludic Simulation, and other Contentious Categories. *Int. J. Gaming Comput. Mediat. Simul.*, *5*(2), 1–19. https://doi.org/10.4018/jgcms.2013040101

European Commission. (2024). *Europe's digital decade: 2030 targets | European Commission*. https://commission.europa.eu/strategy-and-policy/priorities-2019-2024/europe-fit-digital-age/europes-digital-decade-digital-targets-2030_en

Hunicke, R., Leblanc, M., & Zubek, R. (2004). *MDA: A Formal Approach to Game Design and Game Research*. https://www.semanticscholar.org/paper/MDA-%3A-A-Formal-Approach-to-Game-Design-and-Game-Hunicke-Leblanc/2b134e5c46eec50f69c702c0b4aa29687d5d8fba

Kelli Adam, J. D., Robert Lightfoot, Mahjabin Chowdhury. (2023). Cultivating Computational Thinking through Game-Based Learning. *Frontiers in Education Conference*. https://doi.org/10.1109/FIE58773.2023.10342931

Kim, Y. J., & Ifenthaler, D. (2019). Game-Based Assessment: The Past Ten Years and Moving Forward. In D. Ifenthaler & Y. J. Kim (Eds.), *Game-Based Assessment Revisited* (pp. 3–11). Springer International Publishing. https://doi.org/10.1007/978-3-030-15569-8_1

Landers, R. N., Bauer, K. N., & Callan, R. C. (2017). Gamification of task performance with leaderboards: A goal setting experiment. *Computers in Human Behavior*, *71*, 508–515. https://doi.org/10.1016/j.chb.2015.08.008

Mislevy, R. J., Behrens, J. T., Dicerbo, K. E., & Levy, R. (2012). Design and Discovery in Educational Assessment: Evidence-Centered Design, Psychometrics, and Educational Data Mining. *Journal of Educational Data Mining*, *4*(1), 11–48. https://doi.org/10.5281/zenodo.3554642

Moeketsi O. Mosia, F. E. (2024). Sustaining Retentive Memory of Mathematics Concepts in Adolescents Utilising Game-Based Learning: A Case of Repeated Measures. *International Journal of Learning, Teaching and Educational Research*. https://doi.org/10.26803/ijlter.23.7.21

Oppl, S., & Stary, C. (2020). Game-playing as an effective learning resource for elderly people: Encouraging experiential adoption of touchscreen technologies. *Universal Access in the Information Society*, *19*(2), 295–310. https://doi.org/10.1007/s10209-018-0638-0

Pihlainen, K., Korjonen-Kuusipuro, K., & Kärnä, E. (2021). Perceived benefits from non-formal digital training sessions in later life: Views of older adult learners, peer tutors, and teachers. *International Journal of Lifelong Education*, *40*(2), 155–169. https://doi.org/10.1080/02601370.2021.1919768

Reissmann, M., Oswald, V., Zank, S., & Tesch-Römer, C. (2022). *Digitale Teilhabe in der Hochaltrigkeit* (Vol. 6). Bundesministerium für Familie, Senioren, Frauen und Jugend.

Sala, A., Punie, Y., Garkov, V., & Cabrera, M. (2020). *LifeComp: The European Framework for personal, social and learning to learn key competence*. Publications Office of the European Union. https://data.europa.eu/doi/10.2760/302967

Schirmer, M., Dalko, K., Stoevesandt, D., Paulicke, D., & Jahn, P. (2023). Educational Concepts of Digital Competence Development for Older Adults-A Scoping Review. *International Journal of Environmental Research and Public Health*, *20*(13), 6269. https://doi.org/10.3390/ijerph20136269

Shute, V. J., & Ke, F. (2012). Games, Learning, and Assessment. In D. Ifenthaler, D. Eseryel, & X. Ge (Eds.), *Assessment in Game-Based Learning: Foundations, Innovations, and Perspectives* (pp. 43–58). Springer. https://doi.org/10.1007/978-1-4614-3546-4_4

Team, iED. (2020, May 19). *Digital skills for people over the age of 60*. Institute of Entrepreneurship Development. https://ied.eu/project-updates/digital-skills-for-people-over-the-age-of-60/

Udeozor, C., Abegão, F. R., & Glassey, J. (2024). Measuring learning in digital games: Applying a game-based assessment framework. *British Journal of Educational Technology*, *55*(3), 957–991. https://doi.org/10.1111/bjet.13407

Vuorikari, R., Kluzer, S., & Punie, Y. (2022). *DigComp 2.2: The Digital Competence Framework for Citizens - With new examples of knowledge, skills and attitudes*. JRC Publications Repository. https://doi.org/10.2760/115376

DIGITAL TEACHING AND LEARNING ENVIRONMENTS – LESSONS LEARNED FROM MULTIPLE PROJECTS AT A UNIVERSITY – CASE STUDY

Markus Grüne[1] and Fulya Ay[2]
Frankfurt University of Applied Sciences, Faculty 3: Business and Law
Nibelungenplatz 1, 60318 Frankfurt am Main, Germany
[1]Prof. Dr.
[2]M.Sc.

ABSTRACT

This paper explores the use of cloud platforms to modernize IT architectures for digital teaching and learning, drawing from various projects at the Frankfurt University of Applied Sciences (FUAS). Initially, we review the university's status in 2021 and identify the teams involved in creating digital teaching environments. We then provide an overview of several projects, highlighting the establishment of two centralized cloud platforms for digital teaching and the creation of organizational structures to manage these platforms and the demand for digital environments. The second part reviews project outcomes to offer insights for decision-makers, detailing the organization of the central platform management team (SKILL-ELLE) and its connections with other departments. Additionally, we examine the cost structures associated with operating cloud platforms for teaching.

KEYWORDS

Digital Learning Environment, Cloud Migration, Virtualization

1. INTRODUCTION

Since the advent of cloud platforms, the IT landscape has transformed significantly. Companies have integrated cloud platforms into their IT architectures, replacing legacy solutions and custom-built software. Cloud service providers (CSPs) highlight the scalability of cloud services to meet demand. The range of cloud services offered by CSPs has expanded, including virtualized networks (IaaS), platform components (PaaS), software (SaaS), virtual desktop infrastructure (VDI), and serverless functions for building software applications.

Universities have similarly updated their IT infrastructures, though their internal organization differs from companies. German universities, like Frankfurt University of Applied Sciences (FUAS), follow a federal structure, granting faculties autonomy in IT development. Some faculties at FUAS have independently developed their IT solutions, leading to a proliferation of platforms. A 2021 internal survey revealed virtualization platforms such as VMware Horizon, Microsoft Azure, Microsoft Hyper-V, Oracle Cloud Infrastructure, and Proxmox VE. This decentralized development has caused inefficiencies, including limited staff, restricted platform access, lack of central governance, excessive licensing costs, inadequate documentation, and security vulnerabilities.

The Computer Science and Engineering Faculty (FB2) and the Faculty for Business and Law (FB3) at FUAS initiated a project to review and stabilize their IT platforms for digital teaching and learning environments (DTLE). The scope expanded with subsequent projects. The final SKILL project, ending in October 2024 and detailed in Section 2, developed the ELLE center for digital teaching, providing a single contact point for technical and didactical support in DTLE construction. The ELLE team created compliant virtualization platforms with self-service dashboards for managing DTLEs, including student registration and virtual machine (VM) setup processes. SKILL serves as a blueprint for organizational structures in digital learning management and offers insights into university internal structure issues, usage scenarios, and cost perspectives of proprietary and self-built virtualization platforms (SBVP). These insights and advice for decision-makers (central IT, Presidential Board Members, and Deans), are detailed in Section 3, with conclusions presented in Section 4.

Related work – This paper tries to address practical aspects of the implementation of cloud services for teaching purposes. We therefore do not address in this section the general literature available on e-learning or pedagogic aspects of e-learning. Few publications on the implementation of cloud services at universities exist, but studies on their management are scarce. Many articles detail individual cases of courses moved to the cloud and highlight benefits such as cost reduction compared to hardware setups, overcoming time and space constraints, and improvements in security and scalability (Bouyer and Arasteh, 2014; Grüne, 2016; Lin and Chen, 2023). Some works discuss the central role of cloud services in enhancing "Technology Enhanced Learning" (Aggarwal, 2018), their potential to drive the "informatization of education" (Wang and Xing, 2011), and their benefits in developing educational services (Ercan, 2010). However, critical analyses from a management perspective are limited and can be considered as outdated (Abdul Razak, 2009). Technically, there is knowledge on setting up private clouds using virtualization technology (Koratagere et al., 2023). This paper addresses the following gaps: (1) providing a balanced view of cloud services, stating both advantages and risks, (2) identifying useful management structures for constructing and managing cloud services holistically, and (3) offering figures for decision-makers choosing between proprietary cloud services and local virtualization solutions.

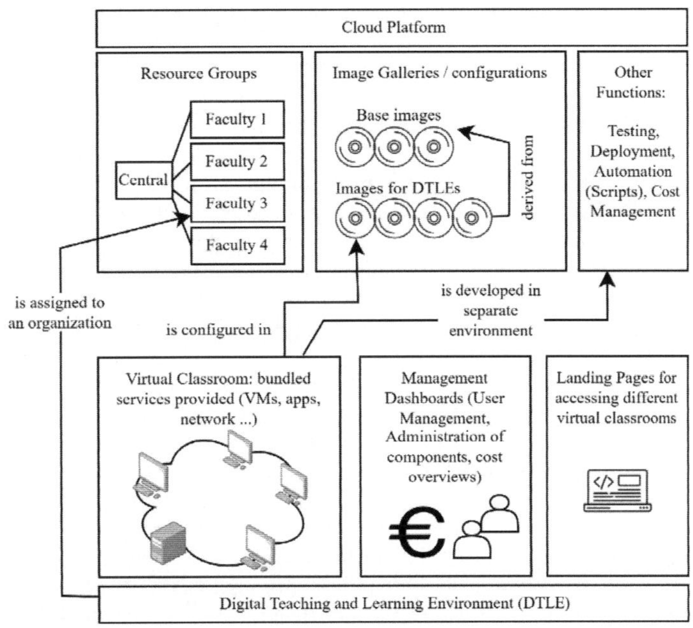

Figure 1. Managing Digital Teaching and Learning Environment (DTLE) on a Cloud Platform

Concepts and definitions – A "digital teaching and learning environment" (DTLE) is defined as a configurable virtual classroom on a cloud platform (CP) or a SBVP, meeting the needs of lecturers and students. Unlike other definitions that include various electronic devices or platforms (Haleem et al., 2022), the DTLE comprises self-service dashboards and landing pages for managing and accessing classroom resources. Each CP-hosted DTLE is managed within a resource group, created for faculties or departments, with a central group for general setup. The digital classroom contains VM instances created from centrally managed images stored in an image gallery, which are reusable and adaptable for future courses. Additional cloud services can be integrated, and for the SBVP/private cloud based on Proxmox VE, services and structures from the cloud platform were reprogrammed, maintaining the overall concept (Figure 1).

2. MANAGEMENT OF DIGITAL TEACHING AND LEARNING ENVI-RONMENTS – A REVIEW OF HISTORICAL PROJECTS AT FUAS

In this section, we will have a short look at some historical projects for the development of strategies for the management of digital teaching and learning environments (DTLE).

2.1 The Need for Consolidation and Early Projects

The VIRTUS Project: In 2019, digital teaching at FUAS was fragmented, with various faculty-level projects delivering software solutions. For instance, the Faculty of Computer Science and Engineering (FB2) provided virtual desktops via VMware Horizon, while the Faculty of Business and Law (FB3) restricted software access to PC pools, and lecturers created their own cloud environments (Grüne, 2016). This fragmentation resulted in multiple issues: solutions were often exclusive to faculty lecturers, lacked documentation and compliance, had insufficient testing, and posed risks for the university. The small application teams were inadequate for comprehensive management, operation, maintenance, and development, sometimes relying on students during staff absences, leading to key person risk. Without architectural guidance and standards, teams developed software independently from the central IT department (CIT), frequently clashing over network security, user authentication, and data center rack space. Consequently, in 2019, the instability led to a search for better organizational methods. FB2 and FB3 collaboratively initiated the VIRTUS project to investigate defects, improve IT platform handling, and explore cloud platforms for virtualization to mitigate technical flaws in the existing VMware Horizon setup.

The project demonstrated, through prototypical implementations on the Azure cloud platform, that managing and hosting DTLEs in the cloud was feasible. For FB3, this allowed software packages for courses, such as SAP clients, to be accessed by students anywhere via cloud-delivered desktops. Besides onboarding Azure, VMware continued to be used for numerous courses, but an internal review revealed several issues (missing support contracts, outdated licensing, lack of documentation, and network vulnerabilities). It became clear that managing the VMware platform required a larger team. One staff member was reassigned, but their lack of experience limited the impact. University-wide questionnaires gathered DTLE requirements from both end users and IT teams. Additional funding was necessary to continue the work.

The DART Project: In 2020, the DART project shifted to implementing cloud solutions for DTLEs, aiming for "full compliance." Strong partnerships were established with CIT, didactical teams, and the legal department. A ticketing system managed DTLE demand. Contracts were secured with the German universities' backbone provider (DFN) for Azure services, and existing solutions were migrated to a new Azure tenant. All software solutions were documented, and integration into internal IT systems, such as user authentication, was completed with the IT department. DART demonstrated that using cloud platforms on a larger scale was feasible but costly and required significant involvement from the DART team. Initially, the team had to enroll users in the DTLEs and acted as the main contact for technical questions, mainly regarding virtual machine restarts, forgotten passwords, and solution limitations. Both VIRTUS and DART revealed, on a small scale, that cloud solutions could streamline the application landscape for courses needing software use in classrooms. During the pandemic, DART played a crucial role in continuing IT-related education requiring classroom software.

2.2 Increasing the Maturity of IT Services for Digital Teaching – the SKILL-ELLE Project

The SKILL-ELLE Project: In late 2020, as the pandemic began in Germany, professors from various faculties combined their digital teaching initiatives into a project proposal for SKILL. After discussions with the Presidential Board, they envisioned the future digital teaching organization and proposed a management structure for it. This vision was to be realized in the SKILL-ELLE subproject at the "ELLE center". The ELLE center aimed to establish the necessary organizational structure for developing digital teaching and learning formats and to foster collaboration among educators in creating innovative technical environments.

Figure 2 illustrates the ELLE center's services (gray boxes) and its connections to secondary services in other departments (white boxes) necessary for delivering DTLEs technically, organizationally, or content-wise. ELLE provided services for (1) onboarding existing DTLEs by migrating them to its cloud platforms, (2) demand management for project prioritization, and (3) Software Delivery Lifecycle (SDLC) management, including design, implementation, testing, and maintenance of solutions. Like the DART team, ELLE was part of the broader university organization and maintained strong ties with other departments and external entities. For example, there was continuous information exchange with CIT, which reviewed architectural blueprints, supported role-based access control/authentication systems, and guided the definition of network architecture and security settings. SKILL-ELLE also continued the customization of cloud platforms for digital teaching.

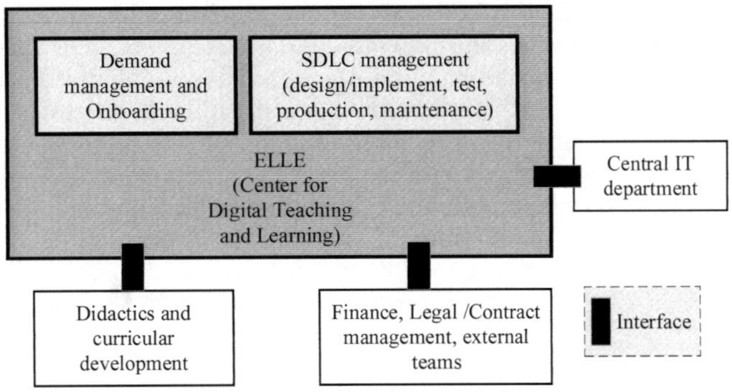

Figure 2. Services of ELLE and interfaces to other departments

Results of SKILL-ELLE: The project team enhanced the cloud platform's architecture by adding a self-service interface for managing DTLEs (see Management dashboards in Figure 1). Students could now access their VMs for various courses through a virtual landing page using their student M365 accounts. Demand management processes were adopted using JIRA and Confluence, replacing costly off-the-shelf services with custom solutions developed by the SKILL-ELLE team. Seeking an alternative to Azure, SKILL-ELLE created a second open-source platform, IDRIS, based on Proxmox VE, aiming to offer low-cost services. This platform is now available for long-running services (servers) and solutions that do not require Microsoft Windows.

The SKILL-ELLE project was confronted with some issues. In the beginning, the acceptance of SKILL-ELLE was low as the departments considered their IT to be unique and did not see a chance in migrating it into a broader framework, such as SKILL-ELLE. In this respect, SKILL-ELLE could demonstrate that especially standard setups of DTLEs could easily be managed centrally. It also became evident that departments faced serious key person risks (unavailability of IT staff) and some operated outdated IT platforms with end-of-life hardware and/or huge financial risks due to foreseeable increases of future licensing costs. Additionally, compliance was a major issue within the departments as most departmental IT solutions were designed at a time when IT documentation and IT compliance requirements were not strictly followed. SKILL-ELLE was able to fill in particular some staffing gaps that persisted in CIT and present the way forward.

At the time of writing, the Presidential Board at FUAS decided to review the university's department and project structures. As a result, existing IT services and digitalization strategies will be bundled in a new department called "Digitalization." The tools, techniques, and services created by SKILL-ELLE were transferred into this department to ensure the continuity of the services. In addition, the number of existing virtualization platforms will be further reduced.

3. LESSONS LEARNED AND RECOMMENDATIONS

In this section, we list our recommendations for future digitalization projects at universities. The information given is based on the learnings during the organizational development of the SKILL-ELLE project and prior projects that were briefly described in Section 2. We split our review into three perspectives, the organizational perspective, the technical perspective, and the financial perspective. In each section, we first review the issues that we saw and provide solution strategies.

3.1 Organizational Perspective

From an organizational and staffing perspective, most issues within FUAS resulted from fragmentation (see Figure 3). Especially, the big number of teams consequently lead to smaller team sizes and less competencies within the teams. Ultimately, ensuring a holistic IT management for the delivery of digital teaching and learning solutions, including compliance with rules and regulations, is almost impossible with small teams. Within the projects we also experienced multiple delays due to the unavailability of secondary services, such as services by HR, Finance, and Legal, which finally led to a long time-to-market.

Recommendations – For the organization of IT services in general and IT services for digital teaching in particular, we recommend a centralization of IT teams. Centralization will lead to the elimination of inefficiencies caused by small team sizes and allow for allocating larger budgets to central solutions. We know that this proposal will find many opponents as this might be seen as "undemocratic" and contradicting the federal organization of German universities. On the other hand, it forces the teams to join forces and can lead to a more efficient handling, e.g., of software licensing, and reduction in workload in the secondary teams. We also recommend integrating non-IT roles within the resulting team and staff who can fill the identified gaps (documentation, testing, and user support) as well as project management roles.

Figure 3. Organizational issues; causes and effects

3.2 Technical Perspective

Overall technical and organizational issues arising from the development of individual, departmental solutions (closed-shop solutions) – The assessment in VIRTUS showed that the services offered by IT teams tried to fulfill the specific requirements of their respective faculty members. For example, software for "Building Information Management" (BIM) which was used in courses for architects, even required GPU processors. However, in most cases the primary use for virtualization platforms lay in the provisioning of virtual Windows desktops with standard software packages. It is evident that there is no one-size-fits-all solution for all potential use cases, but most cases can be accommodated on standard components.

Our recommendation is to conduct an in-depth analysis of individual course requirements for all departments. The analysis should also include the usage patterns for the DTLEs (during the semester or all-year-round, 24x7 versus 8x5) to determine the cost-efficient hosting options. This analysis can also be used to get an overview of the licensing status.

Organizational impact choosing one or more platforms – Relying on a single proprietary cloud platform, can lead to lock-in. Configurations, scripts, and services in these platforms cannot be easily migrated from one platform to another. To mitigate this risk of lock-in, standards such as Docker and Kubernetes can be used to some extent to create virtual computer instances, although this approach is limited to servers. On the other side, as shown in Table 1, the use of proprietary cloud platforms has multiple advantages w.r.t. accessibility, time-to-market, cost clarity, and efficiency. The vast number of services offered can be used to fill gaps instantaneously and to try out recent technologies. For example, media streaming services were employed in one project, which would otherwise have required multiple months to set up an individual media streaming service. It is possible for a university to implement an internal billing process based on consumption and to agree on the distribution of overhead costs (network infrastructure etc.). Cost allocation to originators leads to efficient resource usage. SBVP offer full flexibility and can be adapted to the specific requirements of the university. As costs are distributed across the DTLEs, the individual costs decrease with higher resource usage. If important, the university is in full control of the data kept on the platforms and can thus ensure, e.g., GDPR compliance. From the platform perspective, our general recommendation is to diversify, e.g., by employing a hybrid cloud strategy mixing proprietary cloud solutions with self-hosted virtualization platforms to reap the benefits from both platforms.

Table 1. Technical advantages of proprietary cloud platform and self-built virtualization platforms

	Advantage	Description
Proprietary Cloud Platfom	**Accessibility**	Solutions built on proprietary cloud platforms are accessible from anywhere at any time. They are not "hidden" behind a VPN and can also be opened for external team members and students from other universities.
	Cost Clarity	Cloud platforms provide interfaces for cost analyses, making it easy to identify costs clearly.
	Internal Billing Process	Universities can implement internal billing processes based on consumption.
	Efficient Resource Usage	Cost allocation to the originators of the costs leads to efficient usage of resources.
	Time-to-market / Quick Deployment of New Services	Prefabricated services allow for rapid deployment of new services, such as media streaming. They can also be used for filling gaps and trying out new technologies as the services offered span a wide range.
	Licenses included	License costs are included in the services, if required.
Self-built Virtualization Platform	**Cost efficiency**	Self-built services usually incur lower costs compared to services on proprietary cloud in case of high usage.
	Customization	Allows for tailored solutions specific to the university's needs and requirements.
	Control Over Architecture	Provides the ability to rebuild and re-architect services for optimal performance and cost.
	Open Source	Licensing costs are minimal, and the constructed services can be used by other universities.
	Long-running services	No need for shutting down services. Ideal environment for hosting server-side services.

3.3 Financial Perspective

Overall, the implementation of central platforms for digital learning is costly. Especially, if prior experience is limited. FUAS was able to fund work and initial hardware investments by internal and external projects. As for many projects, the initial investments exceed by far the yearly running costs and should not be underestimated. The overall project budget of ~€2.6 million, from the initial VIRTUS project to the end of SKILL-ELLE, significantly aided in initiating digital learning efforts and covering essential services during the Covid crisis. This section compares the costs between a proprietary cloud platform (Azure) and our self-developed open-source Proxmox platform (IDRIS). This comparison aims to assist decision-makers in their cost calculations and platform selection. To comprehensively assess costs, additional expenses such as overhead for adjacent departments (Legal, Finance, IT), data center costs (electricity, building, cabling), redundancy costs (secondary data center and servers), and extra license costs for virtual desktops and server operating systems must be included. Depending on the university's size, the delivery team structure and ongoing staff costs must be estimated. This analysis focuses on platform costs due to length constraints. Tables 1 and 2 show that staffing consumed most of the budget for all platforms. For Azure, costs stem from service consumption, which can be partially reduced by advance reservations. The self-developed platform incurs significant costs from hardware depreciation and licenses. Some licenses included in Azure services would need to be added if proprietary software is installed. Cost calculations depend on various factors, making it impossible to definitively prefer proprietary cloud platforms over "homegrown" solutions. Both have advantages and disadvantages. For offering virtual desktops to all university students, the open-source solution seems more predictable and affordable, supporting over 1000 students. However, maintaining such a solution requires deep knowledge of its internal architecture, necessitating external expertise.

Table 2. Yearly cost calculation for Microsoft Azure, rounded

Cost block	Annual cost in €, incl. VaT	Comment
Reservation costs for server and services	**€ 10.000**	Reservations help to reduce the overall costs. Cost advantage of up to 60%.
Infrastructure costs	**€ 11.150**	Costs for networks, development environments, log files, public IP addresses, etc.
License costs	./.	Licenses are usually included in the services.
Running costs for teaching and learning environments / VMs	**€ 6.200**	Sample costs for 17 courses with approximately 625 students. The cost depends on the complexity of the environment and the usage patterns of the students.
Running costs for research projects	**€ 2.000**	AI research projects could obtain a separated project space on Azure which they administered on their own.
Staffing	**€ 78.000**	One staff member with a German salary level of E13. Ideally, 2 per platform.
Support – external consultants	**€ 48.000**	Additional expertise sourced from vendor.
Total cost	**€ 155.350**	Monthly: € 12.950

Table 3. Yearly cost calculation for self-hosted Proxmox platform (IDRIS), rounded

Cost block	Ann. cost in €, incl. VaT	Comment
Hardware depreciation cost based on total replacement costs of € 315.000 and depreciation 6 years	**€ 52.250**	13 servers with a total of 768 CPU cores, 1.000 TB HDD, 295 TB SSD and 26 TB RAM; no GPUs; 6 switches + 1 backup server
License costs	**€ 16.050**	Proxmox VE + Proxmox Backup Server; OPNsense Business; Checkmk Enterprise
Running costs for teaching and learning environments / VMs	./.	No. of VMs depending on the config. 1000 VMs: 1.5 CPU, 640 GB HDD, 180 GB SSD, 26 GB RAM / 500 VMs: 3 CPU, 1.3 TB HDD, 350 GB SSD, 53 GB RAM
Running costs for research projects	./.	Not implemented.
Staff	**€ 78.000**	As in Table 1.
Support – external consultants / Maintenance and development	**€ 48.000**	Additional expertise sourced from vendor. Maintenance, updates, etc.
Total cost	**€ 194.300**	Monthly: € 16.200

4. CONCLUSION

In conclusion, this paper provides insights into the challenges and opportunities of implementing digital teaching and learning environments (DTLEs) in higher education institutions. Through a series of projects at Frankfurt University of Applied Sciences, the evolution of our approach to managing DTLEs, from fragmented faculty-level solutions to a centralized, cloud-based platform was demonstrated. The paper highlights the importance of organizational restructuring, technical considerations, and financial planning in successfully implementing and maintaining DTLEs. Key recommendations include centralizing IT teams, adopting a hybrid cloud strategy, and conducting thorough cost-benefit analyses when choosing between proprietary cloud platforms and self-hosted solutions. The experiences and lessons learned presented offer a blueprint for other institutions seeking to enhance their digital teaching capabilities, emphasizing the need for flexibility, collaboration across departments, and ongoing adaptation to technological advancements in the field of education. As more and more organizations follow agile methodologies and the cloud leads to usage-based costing models, universities will have to adapt to a more flexible cost and project handling. A promising way forward could be the adoption of FinOps which "brings financial accountability to the variable spend model of cloud" (Storment and Fuller, 2023).

ACKNOWLEDGEMENT

The Center for Digital Teaching and Learning (SKILL-ELLE) is funded by Stiftung Innovation in der Hochschullehre (https://stiftung-hochschullehre.de/projekt/skill/).

REFERENCES

Abdul Razak, S.F., (2009). Cloud computing in Malaysia Universities. Proc. of the 2009 Innov. Technol. in Intelligent Systems and Industrial Applications, IEEE, Kuala Lumpur, Malaysia, pp. 101–106.

Aggarwal, D., (2018). Leveraging the Power of Cloud Computing for Technology Enhanced Learning (TEL). Proc. 7th Int. Conf. on Reliability, Infocom Techn. and Optimization, IEEE, Noida, India, pp. 391–396.

Beck, K. and Ralph, J., (1994). Patterns Generates Architectures. Proc. of the European Conf. of Object-Oriented Programming. Bologna, Italy, pp. 139-149.

Bodorik P. et al, (1991). Deciding to Correct Distributed Query Processing. *In IEEE Transactions on Data and Knowledge Engineering*, Vol. 4, No. 3, pp. 253-265.

Bouyer, A., Arasteh, B., (2014). The Necessity of Using Cloud Computing in Educational System. *In Procedia - Social and Behavioral Sciences*, Vol. 143, 581–585.

Ercan, T., (2010). Effective use of cloud computing in educational institutions. *In Procedia - Social and Behavioral Sciences*, Vol. 2, 938–942.

Grüne, M., (2016). Teaching Software Engineering in the Cloud: Applying Cloud Services in E-Business Education, in: BLED 2016 Proceedings. AIS, Bled; Slovenia, pp. 449–458.

Haleem, A., Javaid, M., Qadri, M.A., Suman, R., (2022). Understanding the role of digital technologies in education: A review. *In Sustainable Operations and Computers*, Vol. 3, 275–285.

Koratagere, S., Chandrashekarappa Koppal, R.K., Umesh, I.M., (2023). Server virtualization in higher educational institutions: a case study. *In Int. Journal of Electrical and Computer Engineering*, Vol. 13, 4477–4487.

Lin, M., Chen, J., (2023). Practice teaching exploration of Database System based on Huawei Cloud, Proc. 2023 Int. Conf. on Computer Engineering and Distance Learning (CEDL), IEEE, Shanghai, China, pp. 41–45.

Storment, J.R., Fuller, M., (2023). Cloud FinOps – Collaborative, Real-Time Cloud Value Decision Making. 2nd ed., O'Reilly, Sebastopol, USA.

Wang, B., Xing, H., (2011). The application of cloud computing in education informatization. Proc. of the 2011 Int. Conf. on Computer Science and Service System (CSSS), IEEE, Nanjing, China, pp. 2673–2676.

INTERNET SERVICE AVAILABILITY IN HIGH INCIDENCE OF POVERTY: GAPS AND OPPORTUNITIES

Ma. Rowena R. Caguiat and Victorino T. Tolosa II
De La Salle University
2401 Taft Avenue, Manila, Philippines

ABSTRACT

Poverty incidence exists at most 20% of the population of the 48.6% or 783 out of the 1,611 municipalities and cities in the Philippines according to the Philippine Statistics Authority's 2018 Municipal and City Level Poverty Estimate report. This paper aims to gain an understanding on the status, challenges, and potential developments on the state of internet service availability in areas of the Philippines with high levels of poverty incidence from the perspective of stakeholders from individuals in the private sector that have been involved in the delivery of community development services in these communities. The one-on-one interviews from the respondents yielded that there is a perception that the internet service facilities deployment and or lack thereof in the poverty-stricken areas are due to the following reasons: economic motivation, restrictive government policies and security related concerns. Positive impact to educational and knowledge development, economic conditions and health and well-being of the members of the poverty-stricken communities are perceived to be the top results if internet services are made available and affordable. Out of these implications derive the proposition to call on the government to execute stronger measures to fast track the deployment of internet services in the areas with high poverty incidences. The availability of internet services can yield substantial benefits to these marginalized communities, far outweighing any potential drawbacks.

KEYWORDS

Internet Availability, Poverty Incidence, Digital Divide

1. INTRODUCTION

The government organization in this study covers the National Telecommunications Commission (NTC). This office is one of the three attached agencies under the Department of Information and Communications Technology (DICT). The DICT is mandated as the "*primary policy, planning, coordinating, implementing, and administrative entity of the Executive Branch of the [Philippine] government that will plan, develop, and promote the national ICT agenda*"(ntc.gov.ph, n.d.) under the RA 10844 (Republic Act No. 10844, 2015). The NTC has primary responsibility in the regulation and has quasi-judicial functions that relate to the supervision, adjudication, and control of the country's radio communications, telecommunications, and broadcast, including cable television facilities and services (ntc.gov.ph, n.d.). Under the Philippine laws, telecommunications companies require a legislative franchise before it can undertake its full operations in the country. The government entity tasked to regulate the telecommunication industry is the NTC under the mandate of Public Telecommunications Policy Act of the Philippines (Republic Act No. 7925) (Respicio & Co., 2024).

Included in the mandate of the NTC, that is relevant to this research study, is to regulate and supervise the provision of public telecommunication services (Radio Control Law, Act No. 3846, and RA No. 7925). TNTC is collaborating with the Department of Science and Technology (DOST) and DICT to achieve NTC's vision and mission and E-Government Master Plan 2.0 (2016-2022) (EGMP 2.0). The EGMP 2.0 aims to improve government processes, provide better services to citizens and businesses, and promote public participation (dict.gov.ph, n.d.-b).

The Philippines Statistics Authority (PSA) 2020 released the Updated 2015 and 2018 Full Year Official Poverty Statistics that state, "the 2018 poverty incidence among the population, or the proportion of poor Filipinos whose per capita income is insufficient to meet their basic food and non-food needs, is now estimated at 16.7 percent. This translates to about 17.7 million Filipinos living in poverty in 2018" (Mapa, 2020). And in the subsequent year, the PSA released the 2018 Municipal and City Level Poverty Estimate Report. This report produced estimates covering 14 sub-municipalities of the City of Manila, 110 cities and 1,487 municipalities (Mapa, 2021). Another related report included the highlights related to the poverty estimates (Mapa, 2020) that includes the following salient points and figures that are vital in this study; these are shown in the table below:

- Poverty classification refers to the classification level in the report, with level 1 being the highest and level 5 with the lowest percentage of poverty incidence among its population.
- Poverty incidence percentage range per classification refers to the percentage of poverty incidence per classification level in the report.
- Count of municipalities and cities for each classification

The level 5 poverty classification accounts for 48.8% of the total count, which means that 783 out the total 1,611 municipalities and cities with poverty incidences of at most 20%, while 39 % or 629 with poverty incidences of greater than 20% up to 40%, then 6.2% or 100 with poverty incidences of greater than 40% up to 60%, then 5% or 81 with poverty incidences of greater than 60% up to 80%, and 1.1% or 18 with poverty incidences of greater than 80%. These figures and percentages show that poverty exists in every sub-municipality, municipality, and city in the country; 87.6% or 1,412 have poverty incidences up to 40%, while 199 have poverty incidences of greater than 40% of its population as of 2018.

This paper aims to gain an understanding of the status, challenges, and potential developments on the state of internet service availability in areas of the Philippines with elevated levels of poverty incidence from the perspective of stakeholders from individuals in the private sector that have been involved in the delivery of community development and social services in these communities and order established.

This research intends to answer the following research questions:

RQ1: What barriers prevent internet service deployment in poverty-stricken communities?

RQ2: What possible benefits can be achieved if internet services are available and accessible in poverty-stricken communities?

RQ3: What strategies and policies must the state and the private sector co-develop and implement to support the deployment of internet services in poverty-stricken communities?

2. THEORETICAL FRAMEWORK

This paper considers the Digital Divide Theory by analyzing the literature and the qualitative research results. This theory suggests that there is a gap, economically and socially, between the population of a country and their access to technology related to information and communication (communicationtheory.org, n.d.). Also, according to Lythreatis et al. (2022), the digital divide is "*a phenomenon which refers to disparities in Information and Communications Technology access, usage, and outcomes*". Specific to the aim of this study, the technological need by the communities in research is the internet service, which can come in different formats such as wire, which includes copper, coaxial, and fiber optics, and wireless, which may include radio and satellite transmission. In Van Dijk's (2017) article Digital Divide: Impact of Access, he expounded on the relationship between access concerning the concept of the digital divide; he then related that at the initial stages research on the digital divide the term "*access*" meant *"physical access: obtaining the hardware and software of digital media and a connection to the internet*" furthermore he cited that such access was "*correlated with general demographics such as income, level of education, age, gender, and race.* " It worth noting at this point that physical location was not a focal point of the mentioned correlation, however from the perspective of the authors, the distance of the physical location or domicile of users or consumers from town or city centers can be another point of correlation or least can be connected to income level. Van Dijk (2017) further stated that "*obtaining physical access makes no sense when people are not able to use technology*" therefore, "*...skills and competencies are also needed for access."* The authors took note of these points in determining specific communities that is the focus of this research concerning digital divide and likewise in the search for research respondents in this study.

This theory is relevant in this study as it encompasses several factors in determining how the digital divide can be objectively assessed, such as accessibility, utilization, and receptiveness. As stated in Muller and Aguiar's (2022) web article "What is Digital Divide?" indeed, there is no single factor when we talk about the digital divide, while at "*a high level, ...[it] is the gap between those who have internet access and those without it...* [it] *is multifaceted and includes many factors such as access, affordability, quality and relevance*." This theory can help guide developing strategies to address the gaps and take advantage of the opportunities to lessen the digital divide in communities (Colom, 2020), particularly regarding internet service accessibility will be undertaken in this study.

3. RESEARCH METHODOLOGY

The methodology utilized for this paper is qualitative research, focusing on analyzing the themes that emerged from the respondents' answers to the three research questions. The researcher conducted one-on-one interviews with stakeholders who participated in the development of the community (Cabuenas, 2022) and social services in poverty-stricken communities in the country.

The interview respondents comprised community development workers, health workers, social workers, and staff members of organizations providing developmental and social services in poverty-stricken communities. These organizations included formal institutions and volunteer non-profit and non-governmental organizations that have delivered free community development, social work, and health-related services to impoverished communities within the country. To ensure recency and mitigate location or organizational bias, the respondents invited to participate in this study must have served in these communities within the last four years. Additionally, the locations of the communities were not restricted to a single region or province, and the respondents were drawn from a diverse range of organizations and areas of practice.

Since the aim of this study is to look at the perspective of stakeholders from formal and informal non-profit and non-government organizations, this study excluded staff or individuals who are regular employees of telecommunication companies (Telcos), financial services sectors such as banks and financial technology (fintech) organizations, and government entities such as DICT, Department of Social Welfare and Development (DWSD), Department of Interior and Local Government (DILG) and Department of Education (DEPED).

This study employed a qualitative research methodology, utilizing one-on-one interviews for data collection. Depending on the respondents' convenience, interviews were conducted via online video conferencing or face-to-face sessions. Before the commencement of the interviews, respondents were informed that the interview was strictly for this study, and assurances were given that their identities would be anonymized. Their organizations would not be disclosed to ensure data privacy. Respondents were then asked to consent to participate in the study as interviewees responding to the research questions.

4. RESEARCH RESULTS

The one-on-one interviews with qualified respondents were conducted in March, April, and November 2024. There were 11 respondents, and concerning their privacy, their identities were masked with pseudonyms, and their specific organizations were not disclosed.

4.1 Revenue and Profitability

From the respondents' perspective, the primary perceived barriers that impede the deployment of Internet services in poverty-stricken communities are financial considerations by telecommunication companies. These barriers include concerns regarding low revenue generation, a limited subscriber base, and profitability issues. Investing in remote and rural communities necessitates higher expenditures on implementation, logistics, and infrastructure development. Additionally, some respondents indicated that the subscription rates for these services would be low in these areas because community members perceive the costs to be prohibitive. Consequently, they prioritize other basic needs, such as food, over internet subscriptions.:

4.2 Restrictive Processes

Some respondents perceived government processes and procedures to be restrictive, which further complicates the deployment of internet services by telecommunications companies, particularly in remote areas:

4.3 Security Concern

Respondents highlighted that security concerns for telco personnel and facilities present a significant barrier to the deployment of internet services in remote areas of the country. Incidents of facilities being burned by crime groups exacerbate these challenges:

4.4 Educational and Knowledge Development

According to the respondents, internet services can significantly benefit remote and economically challenged communities. These include access to online education and learning resources for students and access to news and essential information, which can facilitate more efficient knowledge development in these areas.

4.5 Economic Opportunities

Respondents emphasized that the availability and accessibility of Internet services in remote or economically disadvantaged communities would primarily facilitate the creation of economic opportunities. This could be achieved through access to online business opportunities, connecting with suppliers and buyers, and improved access to affordable supplies and services.

4.6 Health and Well-Being Improvements

The availability of Internet services is perceived to enable significant benefits related to the health and well-being of community members in remote and poverty-stricken areas. These benefits include faster access to online medical or health interventions and services and more efficient access and delivery of medical supplies. Below are the related responses provided by the respondents:

4.7 Communication with Family and Friends

Some respondents similarly identified the ability to communicate online as a significant benefit for members of communities in economically challenged locations. This capability can help strengthen bonds with kin, family members, and close friends.

4.8 Provision of Internet Services Hubs

The research respondents indicated that collaborative efforts between the government and the private sector are essential for establishing Internet service hubs in impoverished communities. These hubs would facilitate students' access to online classes and educational resources, enable individuals to engage in online business activities, provide access to vital information and health services, and foster communication with family members residing in different locations.

4.9 Policies That Will Help Fast-Track the Deployment and Partnership Between the Government and Private Sector to Lower the Cost of Internet Services

Other respondents emphasized the government's need to provide more efficient processes and enforce policies that expedite the establishment of Internet services and ensure the protection of facilities in remote and impoverished areas.

4.10 Promotion of the Responsible Usage of Internet Services Through Proper Education

Other respondents emphasized that the necessity to provide and enforce policies that promote the proper use of Internet services should be a joint effort by the government and by the private sector.

5. DISCUSSION

As outlined in the research aim and methodology, the research respondents in this study comprise a specific segment of stakeholders engaged with members of marginalized or impoverished communities in our country, either as employees or volunteer staff from NGOs, NPOs, or volunteer organizations.

5.1 Gaps and Challenges

The responses to research question 1 identified several critical factors contributing to the shortage or unavailability of internet service facilities in the country's poor or economically challenged areas. Financial considerations by private companies and telecommunications providers were perceived as primary factors, with revenue generation and profitability being the main drivers for establishing such facilities. Restrictive government policies and processes related to establishing Internet service infrastructure were also seen as significant deterrents. While there are government policies to promote "*sustainable and inclusive development through digital transformation*" under the DICT's digital governance initiatives (NICTDA and DGMP 2023-20288) (dict.gov.ph, n.d.-a) and laws like RA 10844 and RA 10182 to support such mandates and policies (Republic Act No. 10844, 2015) (Republic Act No. 10182, 2011) the respondents in this study has yet to see the benefits of these policies and laws in the communities that they serve. Additionally, some respondents noted unstable or poor internet service or signal even in particular town or city centers; these technical concerns are intended to be addressed under the digital governance initiatives (DGMP 2023-2028) of the government (dict.gov.ph, n.d.-a) at the time of this study such concerns are still present in the communities or areas where our respondents operate and serve. These insights show "*an unequal distribution of resources causes unequal access to digital technologies*"(Van Dijk, 2017).

In remote areas, the physical security of facilities was perceived as another reason for the unavailability of internet services. According to Bauer et al. (2022), barriers to internet infrastructure deployment exist even in an economically advanced country like the United States, including environmental conditions and state or government-related issues. While these barriers are not exactly the same as those in the Philippine context, they indicate that deployment barriers in remote areas for similar facilities or infrastructure are a common challenge.

5.2 Applications

Providing internet hubs to give students easy access to educational materials and enable residents to gain access to online business opportunities is a significant response by the interviewees about research question 3. Government policies that will help fast-track the deployment of internet service facilities alongside stronger government and private sector partnerships that will pave the way to lower the cost of services are also perceived as important recommendations by the research respondents. Another recommendation from the research respondents is to promote the proper use of internet services through appropriate education. These recommendation calls on the government to make more efforts to aid and assist in establishing internet service infrastructure; as discussed by the respondents, it connotes that the private sector will need more government support to deliver internet services in the remote and economically challenged communities faster and more effectively. Proper education on the usage of internet services is also crucial as this will help community members utilize these services and prevent them from being abused by unscrupulous groups or exposed to malicious activities by criminal elements. These calls for government initiatives align with Nandi et al.(2016) article that notes that ICT, in this case, internet services, plays a key role in the "achievement of increased economic and educational exposure, and promotion of global health and wellness through sharing knowledge, technology, and resources" (Nandi et al., 2016).

5.3 Advantages and Opportunities

The positive impact on education and knowledge development is perceived to be the significant benefit of internet service availability in the country's poverty-stricken areas. The positive economic impact on residents in those communities, such as access to online business opportunities and access to goods and raw materials, is also perceived as an essential benefit. The health and well-being of the residents come next as online access to health or medical information is more accessible alongside other information that will improve individual well-being. The research respondents also mentioned that communication with family members and friends, regardless of physical distance, is an essential aspect of the lives of residents and will be hastened by the presence of internet services in these communities.

From consolidated responses by the interviewees related to this study, it is evident that economic factors surrounding the business operations of the telcos coupled with complex and restricted government policies prevent the establishment of internet service facilities in the areas where the economically challenges communities are located. If these factors remain unresolved, they will continuously harm the education and knowledge buildup of the residents in these communities; these may lead to increased vulnerabilities to the individuals in these communities regarding health and physical and financial well-being. Access to essential information on matters of national importance such as health or epidemic, security and safety, and disaster and emergency are delayed or cannot be reached, leading to further marginalization of these communities, thus widening the digital gap even further. On the other hand, if internet services are made available in these areas, it can bring many benefits, such as access to education and correct and reliable information. These will lead to better and less costly access to goods and supplies, better prices for their products, and will help build other business opportunities. This positive condition aligns with the results expected in Colombia, whereby the creation of alternative jobs out of digital ventures or, in our terms, online business opportunities (Arbeláez-Rendón et al., 2023).

6. CONCLUSIONS AND RECOMMENDATIONS

Although this study focused on a specific stakeholder sector servicing economically impoverished communities, and despite the limited number of respondents, the insights gathered are relevant due to their direct and practical engagement with community members. The findings indicate that private companies and telecommunications providers' economic motivation or financial priorities, primarily driven by revenue generation and profitability, pose significant obstacles to providing Internet services in these underserved areas. Regulatory barriers, such as restrictive or bureaucratic government processes, further hinder the establishment of internet service infrastructure, exacerbated by physical security concerns in remote locations. The responses and related literature highlight that the digital divide in economically advanced countries and nations like the Philippines share common challenges, indicating a global issue. To address these challenges, the government and private sector must collaborate to deliver internet services to economically challenged areas. The government should develop policies that incentivize telecommunications companies, enhance public-private ventures, and enforce security measures to protect telecommunication infrastructure in these regions. Additionally, the government should design education and awareness campaigns to ensure the proper use of internet services and create policies to support the establishment of ICT or internet hubs. These initiatives should be integrated into the government's strategic and comprehensive internet service coverage plan.

Given all these insights, the researchers hope that this study encourages all sectors of society, particularly state authorities, to take proactive measures to improve the delivery of internet service facilities in marginalized areas of the country. This can be achieved through various strategies such as government and private sector partnerships, project and operational incentives for private operators, joint physical infrastructure development, and other innovative approaches. The availability of Internet services can yield substantial benefits to these marginalized communities, far outweighing any potential drawbacks. Such collaborative efforts between the government and the private sector will help narrow the digital divide regarding access to internet services in the country. This will improve the country's standing in the World Bank, shifting from a "*worsening digital divide*"(Encarnacion, 2024) to a "narrowed digital divide" shortly. Furthermore, the government must continue to support the telecommunication sector in pursuing telecom infrastructure development initiatives, such as the "*one cell tower serving 4,000 households*"(Galvez, 2020), not only in economic or town centers but also in rural and remote areas.

The response themes indicate that benefits related to educational and knowledge development, economic opportunities, health and well-being improvements, and communication with family and friends positively affect the utilization and receptiveness constructs. In other words, the degree of utilization and receptiveness is likely to improve due to these benefits.

It also suggests that establishing internet service hubs can enhance utilization and receptiveness. Furthermore, policies aimed at expediting deployment to lower service costs can improve utilization while promoting responsible internet usage, enhancing effective utilization and the community members' receptiveness to using internet services appropriately.

ACKNOWLEDGEMENT

The authors of this paper would like to thank the research respondents for sharing their time and insights on this study.

REFERENCES

Arbeláez-Rendón, M., Giraldo, D. P., & Lotero, L. (2023). Influence of digital divide in the entrepreneurial motor of a digital economy: a system dynamics approach. *Journal of Open Innovation: Technology, Market, and Complexity*, *9*(2), 100046. https://doi.org/10.1016/J.JOITMC.2023.100046

Bauer, A., Feir, Donn. L., & Gregg, M. T. (2022). The tribal digital divide: Extent and Explanations. *Telecommunications Policy*, *46*(9), 102401. https://doi.org/10.1016/j.telpol.2022.102401

Cabuenas, J. V. D. (2022, August 15). *Philippine poverty incidence hits 18.1% in 2021, higher than target range*. GMA News. https://www.gmanetwork.com/news/money/economy/841588/philippine-poverty-incidence-hits-18-1-in-2021-higher-than-target-range/story/#:~:text=Preliminary%20data%20released%20by%20the%20PSA%20indicated%20that,Filipinos%2C%20up%20from%2017.67%20million%20recorded%20in%202018.

Colom, A. (2020). The Digital Divide. *Information, Communication & Society*, *23*(11), 1706–1708. https://doi.org/10.1080/1369118X.2020.1781916

Dawadi, B. R., & Shakya, S. (2016). ICT implementation and infrastructure deployment approach for rural Nepal. In *Advances in Intelligent Systems and Computing* (Vol. 463). https://doi.org/10.1007/978-3-319-40415-8_31

dict.gov.ph. (n.d.-a). *DIGITAL GOVERNANCE INITIATIVES*. Https://Pidswebs.Pids.Gov.Ph/CDN/Document/DICT_GreenAndDigital.Pdf.

dict.gov.ph. (n.d.-b). *Mandate, Powers and Functions*. Department of Information and Communications Technology (DICT). Retrieved 13 March 2024, from https://dict.gov.ph/about-us/our-mandate/

Encarnacion, A. (2024, May 2). *Digital divide in PH 'worsening' – World Bank report*. Https://Www.Noypigeeks.Com/Spotlight/Digital-Divide-Philippines-Report-2024/#google_vignette.

Galvez, D. (2020, September 23). One cell tower currently serves 4,000 households — telco official Read more: https://technology.inquirer.net/104264/one-cell-tower-currently-serves-4000-households-telco-official. *Https://Technology.Inquirer.Net/*.

Lee, H. J., Park, N., & Hwang, Y. (2015). A new dimension of the digital divide: Exploring the relationship between broadband connection, smartphone use and communication competence. *Telematics and Informatics*, *32*(1), 45–56. https://doi.org/10.1016/J.TELE.2014.02.001

Lythreatis, S., Singh, S. K., & El-Kassar, A.-N. (2022). The digital divide: A review and future research agenda. *Technological Forecasting and Social Change*, *175*, 121359. https://doi.org/10.1016/j.techfore.2021.121359

Mapa, D. (2020, June 4). *Updated 2015 and 2018 Full Year Official Poverty Statistics*. Https://Psa.Gov.Ph/. https://psa.gov.ph/statistics/poverty/node/162559

Mapa, D. (2021, December 15). *PSA Releases the 2018 Municipal and City Level Poverty Estimates*. Https://Psa.Gov.Ph/. https://psa.gov.ph/content/psa-releases-2018-municipal-and-city-level-poverty-estimates

Muller, C., & Aguiar, J. P. (2022, March 2). *What Is the Digital Divide?* Www.Internetsociety.Org. https://www.internetsociety.org/blog/2022/03/what-is-the-digital-divide/

Nandi, S., Thota, S., Nag, A., Divyasukhananda, S., Goswami, P., Aravindakshan, A., Rodriguez, R., & Mukherjee, B. (2016). Computing for rural empowerment: Enabled by last-mile telecommunications. *IEEE Communications Magazine*, *54*(6), 102–109. https://doi.org/10.1109/MCOM.2016.7498095

Ngwenya, S. O., Heymann, R., Swart, T. G., & Lysko, A. (2023). A COMPARATIVE ANALYSIS OF URBAN AND RURAL BROADBAND PENETRATION AND ACCESS TRENDS IN SOUTH AFRICA. *Proceedings of the International Conferences on ICT, Society, and Human Beings 2023, ICT 2023; and e-Health 2023, EH 2023; Connected Smart Cities 2023, CSC 2023; and Big Data Analytics, Data Mining and Computational Intelligence 2023, BigDaCI 2023*, 64–72.

ntc.gov.ph. (n.d.). *Mandate, Vision & Mission*. National Telecommunications Commission . Retrieved 13 March 2024, from https://ntc.gov.ph/mission-vision/

Panganiban, G. G. F. (2019). E-governance in agriculture: digital tools enabling Filipino farmers. *Journal of Asian Public Policy*, *12*(1), 51–70. https://doi.org/10.1080/17516234.2018.1499479

Republic Act No. 10182, Pub. L. No. REPUBLIC ACT NO. 10182, Congress of the Philippines (2011).

Republic Act No. 10844, Pub. L. No. REPUBLIC ACT NO. 10844, https://www.officialgazette.gov.ph/2016/05/23/republic-act-no-10844/ (2015).

Respicio & Co. (2024, August 28). *Regulatory Requirements of Telecommunications in the Philippines*. Https://Www.Respicio.Ph/Commentaries/Regulatory-Requirements-of-Telecommunications-in-the-Philippines.

Van Dijk, J. A. G. M. (2017). Digital Divide: Impact of Access. In *The International Encyclopedia of Media Effects* (pp. 1–11). Wiley. https://doi.org/10.1002/9781118783764.wbieme0043

Vong, W.-T., Kong, M. L. F., Lai, C. C. E., Then, P. H. H., & Teo, T.-H. (2017). Investigating the Roles of Knowledge Management Practices in Empowering Rural Youth to Bridge the Digital Divide in Rural Sarawak. *Journal of Integrated Design and Process Science*, *21*(1), 61–79. https://doi.org/10.3233/jid-2017-0012

INTERGROUP DYNAMICS IN VIRTUAL REALITY: OBSERVING IN-GROUP PREFERENCES AND INTERGROUP COOPERATION IN A MULTIUSER SOCIAL VR IMMERSIVE ENVIRONMENT

Timor Schwartz Miler and Nili Steinfeld
School of Communication, Ariel University, Israel

ABSTRACT

The study examines intergroup dynamics, biases, cooperation, and competition in social virtual reality (SVR), focusing on the interactions between members of minority and majority groups. A total of 72 Jewish Israeli participants—38 women and 34 men—were recruited from diverse ethnic and religious backgrounds, including Ethiopian and other Jewish ethnicities, as well as ultra-Orthodox and secular communities. These participants were chosen to represent key social dynamics and conflicts within Israeli society. They participated in organized intergroup meetings held in VR. Activities involved team-based cooperation and competition. A qualitative research approach was employed, utilizing open-ended questionnaires and observational methods to examine participant behavior during the session within the framework of participatory action research (PAR). In-group preferences were expressed in participant's choice of partners and spatial proximity to others in some of the groups, whereas in other cases- participants were prone to keep the partners they initially grouped with, regardless of their group identity, throughout the session. We discuss the results and their implications for designing realistic, significant intergroup encounters in SVR.

KEYWORDS

Social Virtual Reality (SVR), Intergroup Contact, Cultural Identity, In-group Bias, Behavioral Observations, Minority-Majority Relations

1. INTRODUCTION

1.1 Intergroup Contact and Prejudice Reduction

Intergroup contact reduces prejudice by fostering understanding and cooperation (Pertiwi et al., 2020). Its effectiveness depends on factors like group status and interaction quality (Bornman, 2016). Allport's (1954) optimal conditions—equal status, cooperation, common goals, and institutional support—are crucial (Di Bernardo et al., 2022). Strong group identifiers may initially show higher prejudice, but meaningful contact reduces bias (Kteily et al., 2019). However, observational studies reveal a preference for in-group interactions, limiting intergroup initiatives (Swyngedouw, 2013).

1.2 A Global Perspective on Intergroup Contact

Intergroup contact is studied worldwide to improve majority-minority relations, addressing tensions over resources, cultural recognition, and political representation. Structured interactions can reduce prejudice and foster understanding through dialogue (Tropp & Pettigrew, 2005; Crisp et al., 2010), but their success depends on design—poorly managed encounters may reinforce stereotypes, while meaningful contact under equality fosters solidarity (Kotzur et al., 2019). Virtual reality (VR) offers a promising tool, enabling controlled interactions across diverse groups.

1.3 Intergroup Contact in Israeli Society: A Case Study

Israel presents a unique case for majority-minority dynamics, involving Arab citizens, Ethiopian-Israelis, the Haredi community, and other minority groups. These groups face systemic inequalities, cultural differences, and historical grievances complicating their inclusion in Jewish society. While structured encounters based on shared goals can reduce prejudice, deeply rooted societal divisions hinder meaningful engagement (Aharon-Gutman, 2010).

Virtual reality simulations provide a controlled, immersive space for engagement across cultural divides. This aligns with Kimmerling's (2001) analysis of Israel's shift to a more diverse society, emphasizing the need for inclusion strategies that balance cultural preservation with integration.

1.4 Contact Between Minority and Majority Groups

Intergroup contact is an effective means of reducing prejudice and fostering positive attitudes toward minorities. Research shows that meaningful interactions yield significant reductions in bias and greater mutual understanding. However, the quality of contact is critical—positive interactions are beneficial, but superficial or poorly managed contact can reinforce negative perceptions (Tropp & Pettigrew, 2005).

Minority group members often experience heightened anxiety during intergroup contact, which can undermine its effectiveness (Crisp et al., 2010). Encounters in majority-dominated spaces may perpetuate exclusion or power imbalances, limiting prejudice reduction (Barlow et al., 2013). To maximize benefits, encounters must foster equality, balanced representation, inclusive environments, and skilled moderation (Kotzur et al., 2019).

Intergroup contact holds promise for solidarity and positive action toward minorities but requires careful facilitation and context sensitivity. Well-structured encounters can challenge societal divides and promote meaningful social change.

1.5 Interpersonal Proximity and Contact Theory

Physical distance between individuals during intergroup interactions shapes outcomes. Seating arrangements and proximity reflect intergroup dynamics and influence success. According to interpersonal proximity theory (Hall, 1963), closer physical proximity enhances positive interactions. This theory defines three personal space zones: intimate (close friends/family), social (acquaintances), and public (impersonal interactions). Four factors contribute to interpersonal closeness: proximity, similarity, exposure, and responsiveness. Increased exposure fosters trust and positive emotions.

In intergroup interactions, individuals tend to seek proximity with their in-group, reflecting interpersonal closeness. However, positive contact can bridge physical gaps across groups (Ryen & Kahn, 1975). This pattern is observable in physical and virtual environments, where minority members often cluster together, indicating insecurity or technological barriers (Tropp & Pettigrew, 2005).

The quality and context of intergroup contact are vital for prejudice reduction and social change. Thoughtfully designed interactions—accounting for social dynamics, group statuses, and facilitation—yield lasting improvements in intergroup relations.

1.6 Social Virtual Reality (SVR)

Social Virtual Reality (SVR) platforms create immersive environments where users interact via avatars, engaging in games and social activities. These platforms simulate realistic behaviors and enable rich social interactions through avatars, virtual spaces, and communication features, including verbal and nonverbal cues (Hasler et al., 2021; Lin & Latoschik, 2022; Torro & Pirkkalainen, 2023; Tassinari et al., 2024). SVR affordances include customizable avatars, object manipulation, spatial sound, and heightened immersion (Slater et al., 2022; Torro & Pirkkalainen, 2023). These features make SVR a promising medium for intergroup contact, particularly for diverse participants unable to meet physically.

VR-based intergroup contact influences empathy, stigmatization, and stereotypes. For example, VR contact with stigmatized groups increases empathy and reduces stigmatization under conditions of strong co-presence (Tassinari et al., 2022b; Stelzmann et al., 2021). Avatar customization and shared identity also affect attitudes and behaviors (Peña et al., 2021). However, most research focuses on one-on-one interactions or non-immersive platforms (Hoter & Shapira, 2022), with few studies examining multiuser dynamics in fully immersive SVR environments.

This study investigates participant behavior in SVR intergroup contact sessions, focusing on how minority group members navigate encounters with the dominant majority in an unfamiliar technological environment. It explores behavioral patterns, including in-group cohesion, hesitation, and leadership tendencies, while examining the impact of technological disparities on interactions and power dynamics.

By analyzing these dynamics, the study underscores SVR's potential as an intergroup contact tool, fostering meaningful exposure to outgroup members and promoting cooperation. The findings contribute to designing inclusive, multicultural SVR environments that address technological barriers, ensure equitable participation, and enhance mutual understanding. Furthermore, this research informs future studies on how environmental and avatar characteristics shape intergroup dynamics, offering guidelines for virtual spaces that bridge social divides and promote social equity.

2. RESEARCH HYPOTHESES

- Participants will perceive intergroup contact in VR as immersive and reflective of realistic conditions.
- Participants in social VR are likely to exhibit in-group biases, as evidenced by preferences for selecting team members from their in-group, maintaining closer proximity to in-group members, and engaging in more frequent or positive communication with in-group members. These in-group preferences will be emphasized for members of minority groups in an interaction featuring majority and minority members.
- Participants engaging in structured intergroup encounters in virtual reality will demonstrate increased positive attitudes toward social diversity and enhanced willingness to collaborate with out-group members in future interactions, as measured through post-session questionnaires and behavioral observations.

3. METHOD

3.1 Participants

The study included 72 Jewish Israeli participants (ages 20–45), with a pilot study (n=8) and a main study (n=64). The pilot assessed feasibility, virtual environments, and intergroup dynamics, involving eight university students (four Ethiopian and four non-Ethiopian Israelis).

In the main study, participants were divided into two demographic groups:

1. Ethiopian origin (n=14; 10 women, 4 men) vs. non-Ethiopian Israelis (n=16; 7 women, 9 men).
2. Ultra-Orthodox (n=16; 8 women, 8 men) vs. non-Haredi Israelis (n=16; 8 women, 8 men).

These groups were chosen to reflect social tensions and minority-majority dynamics in Israeli society. Two participants withdrew due to motion sickness or personal reasons.

Table 1. The number of research participants by group affiliation

	Group affiliation				
	Not Ethiopian	Ethiopian	Secular	Ultra-Orthodox	Total
Male	9	4	8	8	29
Female	7	10	8	8	33
Total	16	14	16	16	62

3.2 Procedure

Participants from the studied groups were recruited for the research: Ethiopian Israelis and non-Ethiopian Israelis, as well as secular and ultra-Orthodox individuals, none of whom were previously acquainted. Approximately two weeks prior to the study, all participants completed a personal details questionnaire and submitted a personal photo. Before the contact activity, each participant was assigned a physical location isolated from others to prevent interaction outside the virtual environment.

During the contact activity, participants used virtual reality headsets and motion controllers to operate within the virtual space. Avatars were designed to reflect participants' gender, ethnic background, and social identity. These visual representations included distinctive cultural and physical markers: dark brown skin tones for Ethiopian-Israeli participants to reflect their ethnic features, traditional religious attire for Haredi participants (including gender-appropriate clothing and head coverings), and contemporary casual dress for secular participants. This design approach ensured culturally sensitive and authentic representation in the virtual environment, acknowledging both visible ethnic characteristics and religious cultural markers.

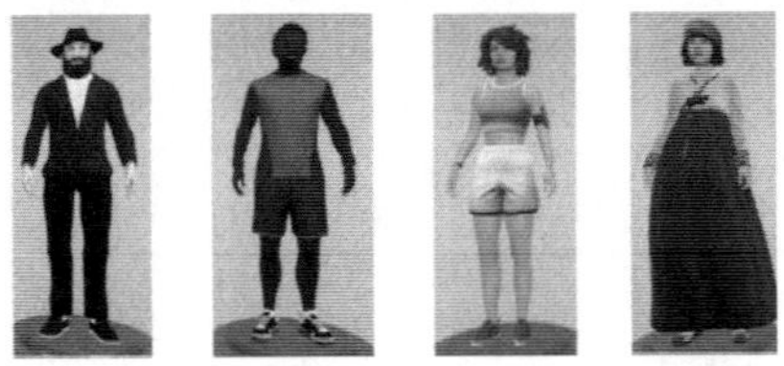

Figure 1. Avatar representations of Israeli ethnic and religious groups

The study was conducted in various locations across Israel. Virtual interactions took place on two different social VR platforms: one for the pilot study and another for the main study. A total of eight research sessions were conducted, each involving eight participants. Four sessions facilitated interactions between ultra-Orthodox and secular participants, while the other four involved participants of Ethiopian origin and non-Ethiopian origin. In each session, participants entered the virtual room simultaneously and interacted with one another. The session began with an introduction to the platform, during which participants practiced navigating their avatars and using virtual tools. The activities included a cooperative task and a competitive game. In the first activity, conducted on both platforms, participants worked in teams in a virtual room equipped with whiteboards and painting tools. They selected a shared value and represented it as a pictorial riddle, fostering collaboration and teamwork. Observations focused on partner selection, dominance, role allocation, listening skills, and technical proficiency.

After the cooperative game, participants were informed that the second part would consist of a competitive game. First, they were asked to select team leaders. Subsequently, they were divided into two groups and instructed to choose with whom they preferred to be on the same team competing against the other group. The competitive game activities varied between the pilot study and the main study.

The pilot study's competitive game *Prison Life,* involved participants as guards or prisoners to observe group competition and cooperation. For the main study, drawing conclusions from the pilot study, we decided to change the environment to a more realistic environment and the competitive game to a more neutral competition game. For the competitive game, participants were divided into teams, chose leaders, and completed a quiz based on memorizing and listing Israeli locations shown in a video. The aim in introducing a competitive activity was to observe how participants choose their partners or team-up with individuals they perceive may assist them in competing with the other group.

Figure 2. Intergroup contact in SVR
Pilot study activity on the first platform

Figure 3. Intergroup contact in SVR
Main study activity on the second platform

3.3 Methodology

The selected methodology was qualitative, integrating observational methods and open-ended feedback. This approach included real-time observations within the framework of participatory action research (PAR) (Savin-Baden et al., 2010) and post-session open-ended questionnaires. To analyze participants' behavior, the sessions were recorded using two VR headset cameras, providing dual perspectives of the virtual space.

A systematic thematic analysis was conducted on the recorded immersive VR sessions, focusing on various thematic elements. These included participants' spatial positioning within the virtual environment, choices regarding proximity to others, task execution requiring technological proficiency with VR controllers, verbal communication styles and content, willingness to lead and actively participate in tasks, and additional behavioral patterns.

Qualitative observations emphasized interactions, team formation preferences, and overall behaviors. Special attention was given to the impact of gender and ethnicity on team selection, with a focus on minority group participants, such as Ethiopian-Israelis and ultra-Orthodox individuals, particularly in their interactions with majority group members. The analysis aimed to uncover patterns of in-group preference and its influence on participants' interactions and behaviors during tasks.

In addition to video analysis, a separate qualitative thematic analysis was performed on participants' written feedback. This analysis examined recurring words and expressions, emotional responses, and references to the physical experience within the virtual environment. Participants' open-ended questionnaire responses explored their subjective feelings, levels of comfort or discomfort, and any observable physical or emotional reactions during interactions in the virtual space.

By combining observational and self-reported data, this methodological approach enabled a comprehensive understanding of both observed behaviors and participants' personal experiences. This provided deeper insights into participants' engagement and social dynamics in the immersive VR setting, as well as their broader attitudes toward social diversity.

4. RESULTS

The findings reveal several key patterns in participant behavior within the Social Virtual Reality (SVR) environment. Participants demonstrated a strong in-group preference, forming and maintaining associations based on familiarity, shared identity, and prior interactions. Rather than actively seeking diverse group engagement, they tended to gravitate toward those with whom they felt most comfortable.

Proximity played a significant role in group selection, often overriding ethnic or social affiliation. Participants primarily chose partners based on their virtual spatial positioning, with new in-group formations emerging as interactions progressed. This indicates that while initial group identities influenced choices, familiarity and prior interaction also shaped partner selection.

Technological adaptation further influenced social dynamics, as participants with greater proficiency in VR tools assumed leadership roles, while those less experienced relied on others for guidance. This created power disparities between technologically adept individuals and those struggling with the medium, particularly among minority participants with limited exposure to VR environments.

In terms of cultural and religious identity, Ultra-Orthodox (Haredi) participants actively used language and symbols to reinforce their identity, integrating religious references into conversations and group decision-making. This behavior suggests that even in virtual spaces, individuals seek ways to preserve their cultural distinctiveness and social cohesion. These behaviors were particularly observed among younger participants. This was especially evident in the group consisting of students aged 20–25, as well as in the group of Ethiopian-origin yeshiva students in the same age range.

Gender roles also influenced participation patterns. Men, particularly from the majority group, were more likely to take on leadership roles, confidently engaging with the virtual environment and directing group activities. In contrast, women often adopted supportive or observational roles, hesitating to assume dominant positions.

Finally, while participants expressed positive attitudes toward intergroup diversity, their behavior indicated hesitation in cross-group collaboration. Despite acknowledging the value of diversity, many defaulted to familiar social circles rather than actively engaging with out-group members.

4.1 Findings in Relation to Research Hypotheses

4.1.1 Hypothesis 1

Participants will perceive intergroup contact in VR as immersive and reflective of realistic conditions.

Findings support this hypothesis, as most participants described the experience as positive, with half reporting that the encounter was engaging and intriguing. Participants experienced a high sense of presence, leading to meaningful social interactions within the virtual environment.

4.1.2 Hypothesis 2

Participants in social VR will exhibit in-group biases, as evidenced by preferences for selecting team members from their in-group, maintaining closer proximity to in-group members, and engaging in more frequent or positive communication with in-group members.

Findings support this hypothesis, as participants demonstrated a clear tendency to prefer partners from their original group, particularly among Ethiopian and Ultra-Orthodox participants, who exhibited a stronger sense of connection to their in-group members. However, it was also found that during the first activity, participants tended to choose partners based on virtual spatial proximity rather than group affiliation. As the activity progressed, new groups formed based on initial collaborations. In the second, competitive activity, participants often chose to continue working with those they had partnered with in the first activity, even if these partners were not part of their original ethnic or religious group. This finding suggests that beyond group identity, prior familiarity and comfort played a significant role in partner selection.

4.1.3 Hypothesis 3

Structured intergroup encounters in VR will increase positive attitudes toward social diversity and intergroup collaboration.

Findings partially support this hypothesis. While participants expressed positive attitudes toward social diversity, their actual behavior reflected a tendency to collaborate within familiar groups rather than seek out intergroup engagement. However, structured activities, such as cooperative tasks, facilitated some intergroup interactions, highlighting the importance of guided facilitation in fostering meaningful collaboration.

5. DISCUSSION

This study investigates the behaviors and interactions of participants in virtual reality (VR) environments, focusing on dynamics within and between majority and minority social groups. The research examines how real-world biases, social hierarchies, and interpersonal behaviors manifest in VR settings. Grounded in contact theory (Allport, 1954), and interpersonal proximity theory (Hall, 1963), the study explores VR's potential to facilitate intergroup understanding while uncovering the challenges inherent in these technologically mediated spaces.

5.1 Study Limitations

Despite its contribution to understanding intergroup dynamics in virtual reality (VR), this study has several limitations. The relatively small sample size and focus on Israeli groups limit the generalizability of the findings to global contexts. Additionally, the variation in technological proficiency among participants often led to unequal power dynamics, emphasizing the need to develop more inclusive VR environments tailored for minority groups.

5.2 Key Findings

The study revealed that real-world biases and group affiliations influence interactions in virtual reality (VR). Participants, particularly Ethiopian-Israelis, displayed in-group favoritism, preferring to engage with members of their own group rather than crossing group boundaries. This bias was particularly pronounced among younger participants aged 18–25, who are in a developmental stage emphasizing group identity and social cohesion (Tajfel & Turner, 1979).

Additionally, some participants preferred newly formed in-groups created during the first activity over their original affiliations, suggesting that VR can facilitate dynamic shifts in social identities (Savin-Baden et al., 2010). During the activities, participants tended to choose partners based on physical proximity within the virtual space. Over time, shared experiences and collaboration contributed to the formation of new in-groups, highlighting the importance of interpersonal comfort over traditional group affiliations.

Gender roles also played a significant role in VR interactions. Men from majority groups assumed dominant roles, leading tasks confidently, while women often adopted supportive or passive roles, reinforcing real-world social stereotypes.

The disparities in technological proficiency observed in this study highlight the importance of providing participants with pre-session training. These disparities often reproduced real-world power dynamics, with technologically skilled participants assuming leadership roles while less proficient participants, particularly from minority groups, relied on others for guidance. Future research should explore how structured technological training can improve intergroup dynamics within VR environments.

Despite challenges, the study highlighted VR's ability to serve as a diverse and inclusive environment, enabling direct intergroup contact and fostering cultural expression. For example, Haredi participants used religious symbols and language in their interactions, showcasing VR as a tool for cultural resilience.

6. SUMMARY AND CONCLUSIONS

This study examines the manifestation of intergroup dynamics within virtual reality (VR) environments, focusing on how real-world social structures and biases translate into virtual spaces. Our findings reveal nuanced patterns of in-group favoritism and gender roles, with technological proficiency emerging as a crucial factor in shaping power dynamics, particularly as minority group participants frequently relied on majority group members for technical assistance.

A particularly notable observation was the development of new "in-group" formations based on prior interactions between participants, rather than pre-existing ethnic or religious affiliations. While spatial proximity influenced these preferences, participants actively sought out previous partners in the virtual space, demonstrating VR's capacity to disrupt traditional group boundaries and facilitate new social connections, especially in deeply segmented societies.

Despite limitations including a relatively small sample size focused on Israeli populations and varying levels of technological expertise among participants, the research underscores VR's potential as a tool for fostering positive intergroup relations and preserving cultural identities. However, the study simultaneously highlights the persistence of real-world biases, power dynamics, and social hierarchies within virtual environments.

The research suggests several important directions for future investigation, including developing concrete strategies for mitigating group-based preferences and technological disparities. These include designing VR environments with built-in mechanisms to encourage intergroup collaboration, targeted technological training programs, and the use of customizable avatars that allow participants to express their cultural identities authentically. Successful implementation of VR-based intergroup interactions requires careful attention to technical support, appropriate training, and the creation of opportunities for meaningful cross-group collaboration.

6.1 Future Research Directions

Future research could focus on developing VR environments that actively promote intergroup equity by incorporating built-in mechanisms to reduce technological barriers and mitigate power imbalances. Additional attention should be given to designing culturally adaptive features, such as customizable avatars, to enhance participants' sense of belonging and identity. Furthermore, exploring the impact of different VR technologies on group dynamics would provide valuable insights for optimizing intergroup interactions.

REFERENCES

Allport, G. W. (1954). *The nature of prejudice*. Addison-Wesley.

Barlow, F. K., Hornsey, M. J., Thai, M., Sengupta, N. K., & Sibley, C. G. (2013). The wallpaper effect: The contact hypothesis fails for minority group members who live in areas with a high proportion of majority group members. *PLoS One*, *8*(12).

Bornman, E. (2016). Intergroup contact experience and frequency as predictors of cross-racial attitudes. *Journal of Psychology in Africa*, *26*(1), 63–69. https://doi.org/10.1080/14330237.2015.1124614

Crisp, R. J., Husnu, S., Meleady, R., Stathi, S., & Turner, R. N. (2010). From imagery to intention: A dual route model of imagined contact effects. *European review of social psychology*, *21*(1), 188-236.

Di Bernardo, G. A., Vezzali, L., Birtel, M. D., Stathi, S., Ferrari, B., Giovannini, D., & Pettigrew, T. F. (2022). The role of optimal conditions and intergroup contact in promoting positive intergroup relations in and out of the workplace: A study with ethnic majority and minority workers. *Group Processes & Intergroup Relations*, *25*(6), 1516–1533. https://doi.org/10.1177/13684302211010929

Hall, E. T. (1963). A System for the Notation of Proxemic Behavior. *American Anthropologist 65*(5): 1003–1026.https://doi.org/10.1080/14330237.2015.1124614

Hasler, B. S., H. Landau, D., Hasson, Y., Schori-Eyal, N., Giron, J., Levy, J., Halperin, E., & Friedman, D. (2021). Virtual reality-based conflict resolution: The impact of immersive 360° video on changing view points and moral judgment in the context of violent intergroup conflict. *New Media & Society*, *23*(8), 2255–2278. https://doi.org/10.1177/1461444821993133

Hoter, E., & Shapira, N. (2022). Simulations in virtual worlds: improving intergroup relations and social proximity. *Intercultural Education*, *33*(4), 435–454. https://doi.org/10.1080/14675986.2022.2080969

Kotzur, P. F., Schäfer, S. J., & Wagner, U. (2019). Meeting a nice asylum seeker: Intergroup contact changes stereotype content perceptions and associated emotional prejudices, and encourages solidarity-based collective action intentions. *British Journal of Social Psychology*, *58*(3), 668-690.

Kteily, N. S., Hodson, G., Dhont, K., & Ho, A. K. (2019). Predisposed to prejudice but responsive to intergroup contact? Testing the unique benefits of intergroup contact across different types of individual differences. *Group Processes & Intergroup Relations*, *22*(1), 3–25. https://doi.org/10.1177/1368430217716750

Pertiwi, Y. G., Geers, A. L., & Lee, Y.-T. (2020). Rethinking intergroup contact across cultures: Predicting outgroup evaluations using different types of contact, group status, and perceived sociopolitical contexts. *Journal of Pacific Rim Psychology*, *14*, e16. https://doi.org/10.1017/prp.2020.9

Pettigrew, T.F., & Tropp, L.R. (2008). How Does Intergroup Contact Reduce Prejudice? Meta-Analytic Tests of Three Mediators. European Journal of Social Psychology. 38. 922 - 934. 10.1002/ejsp.504. Schofield, J. W. (1979). The impact of positively structured contact on intergroup behavior: Does it last under adverse conditions? *Social Psychology Quarterly*, 280-284.

Ryen, A. H., & Kahn, A. (1975). Effects of intergroup orientation on group attitudes and proxemic behavior. *Journal of Personality and Social Psychology*, *31*(2), 302.

Savin-Baden, M., Gourlay, L., & Tombs, C. (2010). Situated learning in virtual worlds and identity reformation. In M. Savin-Baden & R. Wimpenny (Eds.), *Researching learning in virtual worlds* (pp. 179-197). Springer. https://doi.org/10.1007/978-0-85729-361-9_14

Schofield, J. W. (1979). The impact of positively structured contact on intergroup behavior: Does it last under adverse conditions? *Social Psychology Quarterly, 42*(3), 280-284. https://doi.org/10.2307/3033775

Slater, M., Banakou, D., Beacco, A., Gallego, J., Macia-Varela, F., & Oliva, R. (2022). A Separate Reality: An Update on Place Illusion and Plausibility in Virtual Reality. *Frontiers in Virtual Reality*, *3*. https://doi.org/10.3389/frvir.2022.914392

Stelzmann, D., Toth, R., & Schieferdecker, D. (2021). Can Intergroup Contact in Virtual Reality (VR) Reduce Stigmatization Against People with Schizophrenia? *Journal of Clinical Medicine*, *10*(13), 2961. https://doi.org/10.3390/jcm10132961

Tajfel, H., & Turner, J. C. (1979). An integrative theory of intergroup conflict. In W. G. Austin & S. Worchel (Eds.), *The social psychology of intergroup relations* (pp. 33-47). Brooks/Cole.

Tassinari, M., Aulbach, M. B., Harjunen, V. J., Cocco, V. M., Vezzali, L., & Jasinskaja-Lahti, I. (2024). The effects of positive and negative intergroup contact in virtual reality on outgroup attitudes: Testing the contact hypothesis and its mediators. Group Processes & Intergroup Relations, 27(8), 1773-1798. https://doi.org/10.1177/13684302241237747

Tropp, L. R., & Pettigrew, T. F. (2004). Intergroup contact and the central role of affect in intergroup prejudice. In Tiedens & C. W. Leach (eds.), *The social life of emotion: Studies in emotion and social interaction* (pp. 246-269). New York: Cambridge University Press, 2004. (1).

Short Papers

INFORMATION SYSTEM FOR REAL-TIME COLLECTION, SHARING AND UTILIZATION OF DISASTER INFORMATION

Toshihiro Osaragi and Ikki Niwa
Department of Architecture and Building Engineering
School of Environment and Society, Institute of Science Tokyo
2-12-1-M4-1 Ookayama, Meguro, Tokyo 152-8550, Japan

ABSTRACT

In the event of large-scale earthquakes, the rapid collection and utilization of disaster information—such as building collapses, road blockages, and fire outbreaks—are crucial for effective disaster mitigation. In this research, we develop a web application that enables users to gather and share disaster information in real time. The system not only facilitates information sharing among users but also allows for simulations, such as fire spread modeling. A demonstration experiment was conducted with local volunteers to evaluate the system's usefulness and effectiveness in collecting disaster data. Additionally, we analyze delays in information sharing under bandwidth-constrained network conditions and demonstrate the system's overall effectiveness.

KEYWORDS

Disaster Information, Information Collection, Web Application, Real Time, Demonstration Experiment

1. INTRODUCTION

In an era where natural disasters and emergencies are increasingly frequent and severe, the need for robust and efficient information systems to manage disaster response has never been more critical. Effective communication and the timely exchange of information can significantly impact the safety and well-being of communities affected by disasters.

Ngamassi et al. (2017) synthesized existing research on social media visual analytics and visualization toolkits for disaster management, highlighting a substantial increase in the use of social media for disaster response over the past decade (Petersen et al., 2017; Ngamassi et al., 2016; Denis et al., 2014; Hiltz et al., 2014; Hughes, 2014; Yates & Paquette, 2011; Matthew et al., 2010). Other studies have focused on the timely collection of disaster information from large areas by leveraging data submitted to social networking services (SNS). For instance, Stuart et al. (2014) developed a system that extracts disaster-related keywords from Twitter posts in real time and links them to geographical information, enabling the sharing of disaster information through an interactive map.

In this research, we develop a comprehensive cloud-based web application designed specifically for the real-time collection, sharing, and utilization of disaster-related information. This system empowers users, particularly those involved in disaster response and management, to report, share, and analyze critical data in the aftermath of a disaster.

The proposed information system leverages modern technology to facilitate the rapid reporting and dissemination of disaster information. This system is constructed on a foreign-based cloud server (Amazon Web Services EC2, Amazon.com 2017) (Figure 1). It serves as a centralized platform where users can input real-time data concerning various disaster impacts, such as physical damages, road blockages, and fire incidents. The application is designed to be user-friendly, allowing individuals with varying levels of technical expertise to navigate the platform with ease. By harnessing cloud technology, the system ensures that information is readily accessible to all users, enhancing situational awareness and improving response coordination among emergency services and volunteers. One of the system's key advantages is its real-time reporting capability, achieved through the use of Node.js and WebSocket, enabling data synchronization with minimal latency. By designing the system server to be event-driven, the number of simultaneous connections it can handle is significantly increased, allowing for rapid responses to user requests. Furthermore, when the database is updated, the server push-distributes the new information to all active users, ensuring real-time synchronization without requiring users to send data transmission requests. This approach reduces server load and maintains data currency, even in disaster scenarios where transmission networks may be compromised. MongoDB is selected as the database platform due to its ability to process large volumes of data at high speeds, providing enhanced robustness against data currency loss compared to traditional databases.

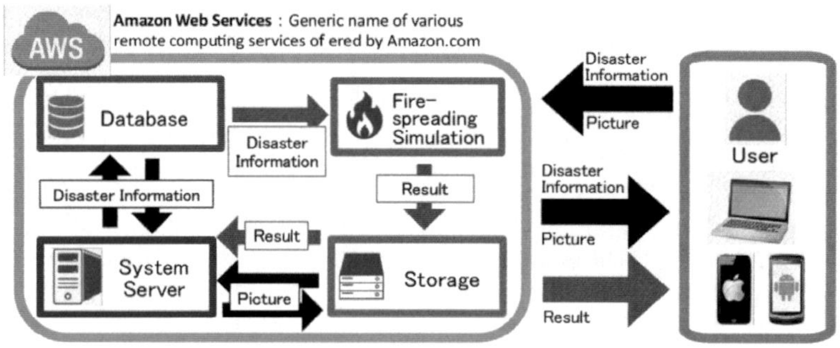

Figure 1. The components of the proposed system

2. KEY FEATURES OF THE SYSTEM

2.1 Real-Time Data Collection, Data Sharing, and Collaboration

The system is equipped with a range of tools that facilitate easy reporting. Users can input details about the nature of the damage, its location, and any additional comments or observations in the form of text or images. This structured approach to data collection ensures that the information submitted is consistent and usable for analysis (Figure 2).

In addition to collecting data, the system promotes the sharing of information among users. Once a report is submitted, it is instantly available to all other users on the platform. This real-time sharing creates a collective knowledge base that enhances situational awareness. For instance, emergency responders can quickly access up-to-date information about hazards, enabling them to plan their operations more effectively. The system also encourages collaboration among users, including volunteers, government agencies, and non-profit organizations involved in disaster response. By fostering a cooperative environment, the system can streamline communication and improve the overall efficiency of disaster management efforts (Figure 3).

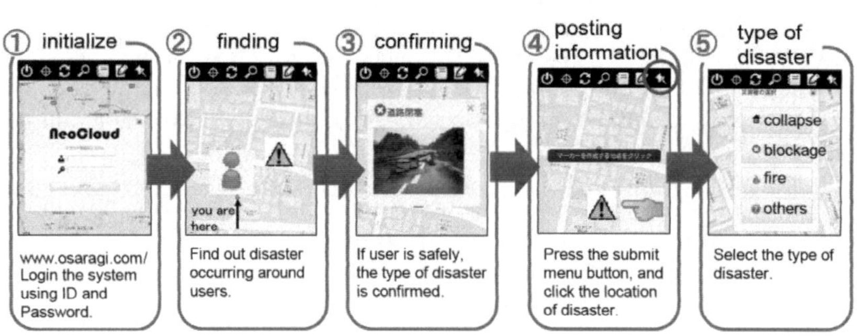

Figure 2. User interface and Web application system

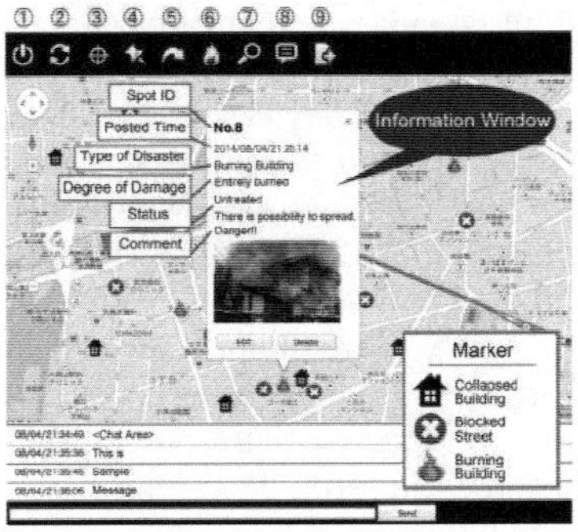

No.	Functions	Details
①	Login	Login using a registered ID and password. Authority to execute functions are set for each account.
②	Reload	Reload the page and initialize the map.
③	Current Location	Show the user's current location based on information by GPS or Wi-Fi network.
④	Post	Select the location of disaster, input some contents, and post the information and picture.
⑤	Correct Position	Correct the location of posted disaster information by dragging the marker on the map.
⑥	Fire-spreading Simulation	Read the result of simulation focused on selected building and show the forecast of fire-spreading.
⑦	Search Name of Places	Search any name input by the user.
⑧	Chat	Chat among online users.
⑨	Output as CSV	Sort information stored in the database in a time-series order and output it as CSV file format.

Figure 3. The components of the proposed system

2.2 Utilization of Collected Data

The information collected through the system is not only valuable for immediate response efforts but also for future planning and preparedness activities. The system includes analytical tools that allow users to process and visualize the data, helping identify patterns, trends, and areas of concern. For example, historical data analysis can inform future disaster preparedness strategies, helping communities better understand their vulnerabilities and develop targeted response plans.

Additionally, the system incorporates secondary applications, such as fire spread simulators, which utilize the collected data to estimate the potential damage from fire incidents. These tools assist emergency responders in making informed decisions about resource allocation and prioritization during disasters.

Figure 4 illustrates the simulated spread of a fire. The spatial distribution of buildings, derived from Tokyo City Planning GIS data (collected from Tokyo's 23 wards), is utilized alongside the fire spread speed equation provided by the Tokyo Fire Department (2001) to model fire propagation between buildings (Hirokawa & Osaragi, 2016a, 2016b). The simulation allows for the adjustment of input conditions, such as season, time, epicenter location, and earthquake intensity, through a straightforward process. Fire spread simulations represent a secondary application of disaster-related information. Our previous studies using multi-agent simulations have shown that providing data on street blockages significantly improves the response time of firefighters to fires (Osaragi et al., 2015; Osaragi & Hirokawa, 2017). Numerous other potential applications for the secondary use of disaster information exist, which will be explored in future reports by the authors.

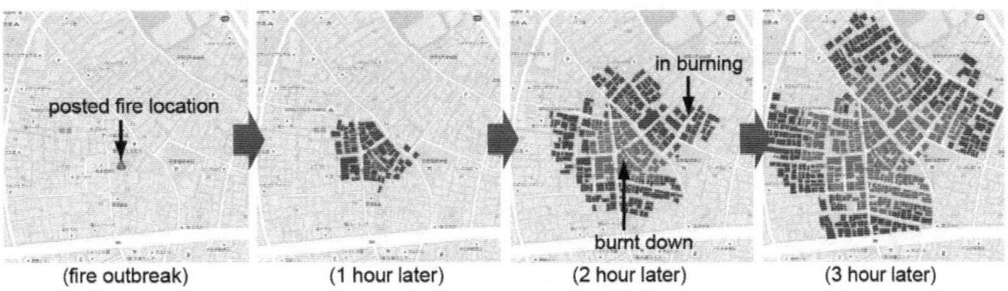

Figure 4. Simulated fire spread images

3. EXPERIMENTAL IMPLEMENTATION

To evaluate the effectiveness of the information system, a series of field experiments were conducted involving disaster prevention volunteers. These volunteers were tasked with using the system to collect disaster information during simulated emergencies. The experiments aimed to assess the accuracy and efficiency of data collection while gauging user experience with the platform.

Locations and types of physical damage (e.g., building collapses, street blockages, building fires) were predefined using simulation results and displayed on participants' smartphone screens as "virtual damage" markers (Figure 5). By displaying virtual damage directly on user devices, the experiment eliminated the need for physical signboards and personnel dispatch, significantly reducing time and labor. This method also enabled the experiment to cover a wider area. Five iterations of the experiment were conducted under varying disaster scenarios to observe participants' learning and adaptation in different and unfamiliar locations.

During the experiments, participants reported approximately 0.7% of the virtual disaster information that was distributed throughout a test region, specifically Setagaya Ward. Figure 6 demonstrates the potential impact of the system on information collection efforts. If a broader user base were to adopt this system—hypothetically, if around 0.2% of the population of Setagaya Ward participated—over 80% of the relevant damage information could be collected. Such comprehensive data collection would significantly enhance the ability of emergency services to respond to and mitigate the effects of disasters.

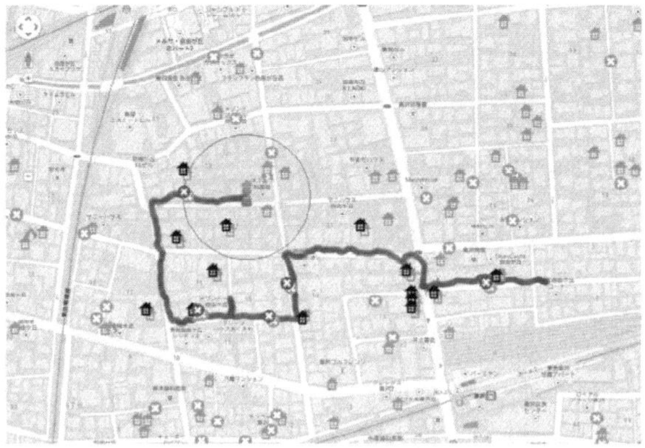

Figure 5. Trajectory of user collecting the virtual damage generated by simulation

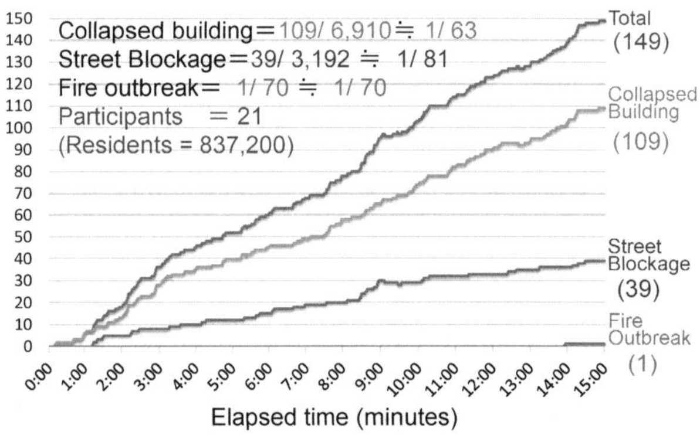

Figure 6. Transition of submission numbers over time

3.1 Impact of the Information Collection Support Function

One notable aspect of the experimental implementation is the use of an information collection support function. This feature prioritizes specific locations for data collection based on simulations of potential damage, thereby improving the efficiency of the data-gathering process.

When participants utilized this support function, they demonstrated an increased ability to gather information about multiple damage events while minimizing the distance they needed to travel (Figure 7). This efficiency is critical during emergencies when time is of the essence and every second counts. By focusing efforts on high-risk areas, the system ensures that crucial information is not overlooked.

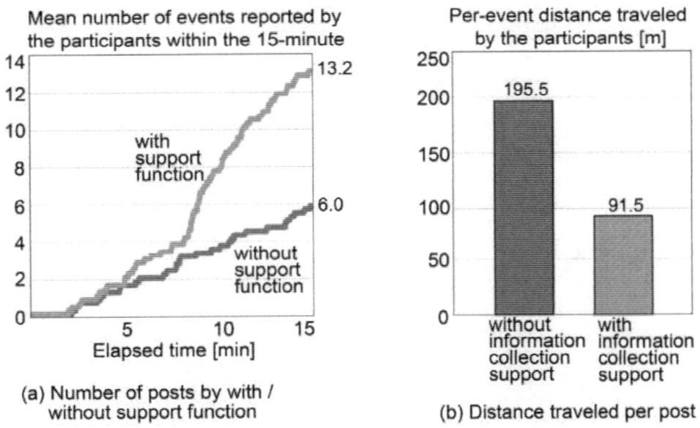

Figure 7. (a) Mean number of events reported within 15 minutes, (b) Per-event distance traveled by participants

3.2 Network Performance and Reliability

In addition to the functionality and usability of the system, its performance in various network conditions is a crucial aspect. To simulate real-world scenarios, additional experiments are conducted to assess the system's ability to synchronize newly submitted disaster information across all users in a network environment compromised by a disaster.

Two transmission speeds are evaluated: 1 Mbps (representative of 3G lines) and 15 Mbps (typical of LTE lines). The simulation included up to 3,000 virtual users, and 100 cycles of the simulation are performed. The results indicate that the mean synchronization times in both networks are less than one second, demonstrating the system's capability to maintain data currency even under challenging conditions (Figure 8).

Further analysis reveals that increasing the number of users has only a minor effect on synchronization delays, with an increase of less than 50 milliseconds. This robustness suggests that the system is well-suited for deployment in real disaster situations where rapid information dissemination is critical. However, the results also highlight the need for additional research and testing to understand the system's performance in actual disaster scenarios. Given the potential for increased user numbers during widespread disasters, strategies to distribute the transmission load and ensure reliable data sharing will need to be explored.

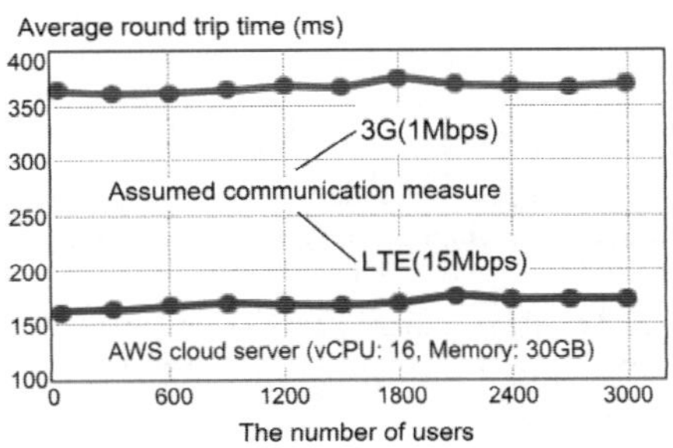

Figure 8. Synchronization time for disaster information submitted by one user to propagate across all other users

4. CONCLUSION AND FUTURE DIRECTIONS

The development of this information system marks a significant step forward in disaster management technology. By facilitating real-time collection, sharing, and utilization of disaster information, the system enhances community resilience and improves response strategies in the face of emergencies.

The experiments conducted thus far have demonstrated the system's effectiveness and potential impact on disaster response efforts. However, continuous improvement is essential. Future directions for this system may include expanding user training to enhance user engagement, developing partnerships with local governments and organizations for broader outreach, and implementing advanced analytics capabilities to further improve data interpretation and visualization.

Ultimately, the goal is to create a more informed and prepared society that can respond swiftly and effectively to disasters, minimizing their impact on communities and saving lives.

ACKNOWLEDGEMENT

This work is part of the research outcomes funded by KAKENHI (Grant Number 23K26347). A portion of this paper was published in Osaragi and Niwa (2018) and presented at IADIS 2024 (Osaragi et al., 2024).

REFERENCES

Amazon.com Inc. (2017). Amazon EC2 Pricing. https://aws.amazon.com/jp/ec2/ [accessed Nov. 9, 2017].

Denis, L., Palen, L., & Anderson, J. (2014). Mastering social media: An analysis of Jefferson County's communications during the 2013 Colorado floods. In *Proceedings of the 11th International Conference on Information Systems for Crisis Response and Management (ISCRAM)*. State College, Pennsylvania.

Hiltz, S., Kushma, J., & Plotnick, L. (2014). Use of social media by U.S. public sector emergency managers: Barriers and wish lists. In *Proceedings of the 11th International Conference on Information Systems for Crisis Response and Management (ISCRAM)*. State College, Pennsylvania.

Hirokawa, H., & Osaragi, T. (2016a). Earthquake disaster simulation system: Integration of models for building collapse, street blockage, and fire spread. *Journal of Disaster Research, Fuji Technology Press Ltd., 11*(2):175-187.

Hirokawa, N., & Osaragi, T. (2016b). Access Time of Emergency Vehicles under the Condition of Street Blockages after a Large Earthquake, *First International Conference on Smart Data and Smart Cities, ISPRS Annals of the Photogrammetry, Remote Sensing and Spatial Information Sciences*, Volume IV-4/W1:37-44.

Hughes, A. (2014). Participatory design for the social media needs of emergency public information officers. In *Proceedings of the 11th International Conference on Information Systems for Crisis Response and Management (ISCRAM)*. State College, Pennsylvania.

Matthew, Z., Mark, G., Taylor, S., & Sean, G. (2010). Volunteered Geographic Information and Crowdsourcing Disaster Relief: A Case Study of the Haitian Earthquake. *World Medical & Health Policy*, *2*(2):7–33.

Ngamassi, L., Malik, A., Zhang, J., & Ebert, D. (2017). Social Media Visual Analytic Toolkits for Disaster Management: A Review of the Literature. In *Proceedings of the 14th International Conference on Information Systems for Crisis Response and Management (ISCRAM)*. Albi, France.

Ngamassi, L., Ramakrishnan, T., & Rahman, S. (2016). Use of Social Media for Disaster Management: A Prescriptive Framework. *Journal of Organizational and End User Computing*, *28*(3).

Osaragi, T., & Hirokawa, N. (2017). A Decision Support System for Fighting Multiple Fires in Urban Areas Caused by Large Earthquakes. *Lecture Notes in Geoinformation and Cartography, Planning Support Science for Smarter Urban Futures*, Springer, Vol. Part I: 77-93

Osaragi, T., Hirokawa, N., & Oki, T. (2015). Information Collection of Street Blockage After a Large Earthquake for Reducing Access Time of Fire Fighters. *Journal of Architecture and Planning (Transactions of AIJ)*, *80*(709): 465-473 (in Japanese).

Osaragi, T. & Niwa, I., (2018). Development of System for Real-Time Collection, Sharing, and Use of Disaster Information, *Lecture Notes in Geoinformation and Cartography*, Springer, pp. 211-229.

Osaragi, T., Hirokawa, N., & Kishimoto, M., (2024). Toward Integrated Disaster Prevention and Mitigation System Linking Disaster Information Collection and Property Damage Simulation, *17th IADIS International Conference Information Systems 2024*, Mar. 2024.

Petersen, L., Fallou, L., Reilly, P. J, & Serafinelli, E. (2017). Public expectations of social media use by critical infrastructure operators in crisis communication, In *Proceedings of the 14th International Conference on Information Systems for Crisis Response and Management (ISCRAM)*. Albi, France.

Stuart, M., Lee, M., & Stefano, M. (2014). Real-Time Crisis Mapping of Natural Disasters Using Social Media, *IEEE Intelligent Systems*, *29*(2):9-17.

Tokyo Fire Department (2001). Development and Application of Evaluation Method for Preventing Ability of Earthquake Fire, The 14th Report of Fire Prevention Council (in Japanese) (in Japanese).

OVERVIEW OF RECOMMENDER SYSTEMS: APPROACHES, APPLICATIONS AND CHALLENGES

Majda El Hassani, Loubna El Faquih and Nadia Machkour
Digital Engineering of Leading Technology and Automation Laboratory (DELTA Lab), ENSAM, Hassan II University of Casablanca, Morocco

ABSTRACT

As the load of information continues to rise to be more overwhelming overtime, recommender systems (RSs) come as efficient tools to alleviate and solve this problem. RSs provide personalized support to users through learning from their previous behaviors and preferences. This paper provides an overview of RSs exploring their basic approaches, including Collaborative Filtering (CF), Content-Based Filtering (CBF), and hybrid systems (HS), alongside AI-driven techniques such as fuzzy logic, natural language processing (NLP), and transfer learning (TL). Additionally, it addresses the various fields of RSs applications with a focus on their significant challenges and limitations besides their potential use in water management.

KEYWORDS

Recommender Systems, Collaborative Filtering, Content-Based Filtering, Hybrid Filtering, Artificial Intelligence, AI-Based Recommender Systems

1. INTRODUCTION

In today's digital age, characterized by an unprecedented flow of information, individuals are continuously confronted with a vast and often overwhelming array of choices (Harper and Konstan, 2016). From browsing millions of products on e-commerce sites to selecting among countless movies, shows, and music on streaming platforms, users are faced with the challenge of shifting through extensive options to find what best suits their needs and preferences. This constant exposure to endless choices can make decision-making difficult, creating a demand for tools that help personalize these experiences. Recommender systems (RSs) have become essential tools for alleviating this cognitive load by assisting users in making more tailored decisions (Geng *et al.*, 2022). These systems use data-driven techniques to filter, prioritize, and tailor information, effectively supporting users in decision-making across various domains such as e-commerce, media streaming, and social networking. This support goes further to serve critical functions through a diverse range of fields beyond traditional applications whether in sectors such as healthcare or water resources management. The two primary techniques of RSs are collaborative filtering and content-based filtering (Barragáns-Martínez *et al.*, 2010). Hybrid systems that combine these techniques aim to improve accuracy by mitigating the limitations inherent in each individual method. However, several challenges still hinder the effectiveness of RSs. Addressing these challenges is crucial for RSs to support decision-making processes across various applications. This paper aims to provide a comprehensive overview of RSs, focusing on their basic methodologies, applications in different fields as well as the role of Artificial Intelligence (AI) in enhancing their decision-support capabilities.

The rest of the paper is organized as follows; Sect. 2 highlights RSs applications across diverse domains, emphasizing the approach employed in each. Following Sect. 3, analyzes the key challenges they encounter. Sect. 4 explores both basic and AI-based RSs approaches. Sect. 5 represents a discussion of findings. Finally, Sect. 6 concludes this paper.

2. APPLICATIONS FIELDS OF RECOMMENDER SYSTEMS

RSs have found applications across various domains. This section focuses on applications in six different fields.

- **E-commerce**: In e-commerce, personalization services analyze user data, product attributes, and external factors to recommend relevant products, enhancing service quality and sales. Collaborative filtering and hybrid recommendations effectively leverage consumer spending patterns to suggest items similar to previous purchases, improving user experience (Hwangbo *et al.*, 2018).
- **Streaming services**: The growth of streaming services like Netflix, YouTube, and Spotify has been driven by RSs that personalize content to simplify user decision-making. For example, Magadum *et al.* (2024) proposed a song recommendation system using dynamic feedback, featuring Backend, Frontend, and Recommender Engine components, built on a dataset of 28,000 Spotify tracks.
- **Education:** Smart education, or e-learning, has gained widespread use in educational settings, particularly following the COVID-19 pandemic. RSs address this by tailoring educational resources to learners goals and interests. Shu *et al.* (2018) proposed a Content-Based Learning Resources Recommendation Algorithm to analyze textual data from materials and predict student-resource rating scores.
- **Tourism:** RSs enhance the travel experience by suggesting destinations, locations, and reviews tailored to user preferences. Kesorn *et al.* (2017) presents a novel technique that uses Facebook check-in data to infer user interests in tourist attractions, offering personalized recommendations based on implicit preferences.
- **Healthcare**: RSs have also evolved to serve critical functions across a diverse range of fields beyond traditional applications such as healthcare. These systems, referred to as health recommender systems (HRS), analyze patient data, medical histories, and treatment outcomes to suggest personalized treatment plans and medications tailored to individual health profiles. In this regard, Valdez *et al.* (2016) identified different usage scenarios for two main user groups: healthcare professionals and end-users and proposed a framework that prioritizes end-user collaboration, privacy, and personalized risk communication
- **Water management and consumption:** Another important field in which RSs play a vital role is water management and consumption. A study by (Dai *et al.* 2016) used a fuzzy logic-based recommendation system (refer to section 4) to personalize daily water intake recommendations using factors like temperature, physical activity, and age. The system adapts to individual needs and aligns with health guidelines. A real-world implementation validated its effectiveness in providing personalized hydration advice.

3. CHALLENGES IN RECOMMENDER SYSTEMS

Despite their widespread adoption, RSs face significant challenges that hinder their performance and user satisfaction. This section provides an overview of the key issues encountered by current RSs.

- Data Sparsity: This relates to the sparsity of user-item interactions, as most users tend to rate only a small fraction of the available items, resulting in a highly sparse ratings matrix. This problem limits the likelihood of finding users with similar rating patterns (Sharma and Suman, 2013). In this context, Ahmadian *et al.* (2022) proposed a four-step recommender system to address data sparsity by assessing and enriching user profiles, refining neighborhoods with temporal confidence measures, and generating recommendations, improving accuracy and reliability.
- Cold Start problem: This refers to the challenge of making accurate recommendations when there is insufficient data available. Typically, the cold start problem includes new community, new item, and new user. The latter aspect is the challenge RSs face when dealing with users who have just started using the system, often called the "new user problem". In this framework, Feng *et al.* (2021) proposed a unified ranking model combining explicit ratings and implicit feedback capturing accurate user and item characteristics to enhance recommendation accuracy.
- Scalability: Growing data volumes causing scalability concerns is a critical issue for RSs. Within this framework, George and Merugu (2005) proposed a scalable co-clustering algorithm that efficiently handles new user and item entries through an incremental and batch hybrid approach, with parallel processing enabling real-time scalability for large datasets.
- Accuracy: RSs face several challenges including handling large volumes of data, which may often include biases or inaccuracies (Chen *et al.*, 2023). Addressing these biases through debiasing strategies is crucial to ensure that recommendations remain fair, precise, and relevant. Effective debiasing techniques help reduce unwanted influences, enhancing the reliability of the system to deliver high-quality recommendations.

- Grey Sheep: This refers to users who have unique preferences that do not fit into the general patterns of other users *(Khusro et al.*, 2016).
- Privacy: Providing personal information to RSs raises concerns about data privacy and security. Users are often hesitant to share their data with systems that lack robust privacy protection (Zhang *et al.*, 2021).

4. RECOMMENDER SYSTEMS APPROACHES

After addressing the main challenges in RSs, this section examines both basic approaches and AI techniques that enhance the effectiveness of these systems.

4.1 Basic Approaches

- Collaborative Filtering (CF) analyzes user behavior to identify similarities and recommend items based on the preferences of similar users (Koren *et al.*, 2022). The CF systems are categorized into two types: memory-based and model-based.
  - Memory-based (or neighborhood-based) systems, divided into user-based and item-based methods, identify patterns among users or similarities between items to estimate item relevance (Ning *et al.*, 2015). Neighborhoods, often formed using K-Nearest Neighbors (K-NN), serve as reference groups for predicting preferences based on shared patterns (Desrosiers and Karypis, 2011).
  - Model-based systems employ machine learning techniques to predict user ratings for unseen items by training models on user-item interaction data (Koren, 2008), aiming to fill gaps in the user-item matrix effectively.

  Though CF remains a popular approach for RSs because it doesn't need domain knowledge, it still encounters several challenges, notably "cold start problem" and grey sheep.
- Content-Based Filtering (CBF) generates recommendations by matching item characteristics to a user's profile based on their preferences. The concept is to profile both the user and the items, creating a "user profile" based on the preferences they have exhibited and an "item profile" that describes the content. While it avoids the user cold-start problem by focusing on individual data, it may limit exposure to new options (Gong and Cheng, 2008).
- Knowledge-Based Systems (KBS) are a type of RSs that relies on available knowledge about the user's requirements or the features of the items. KBS can match specific user preferences or requirements with their knowledge base that incorporates relevant domain knowledge to produce recommendations tailored to the user's stated needs (Aggarwal, 2016).
- Hybrid systems (HS) combine elements of two or more recommendation strategies, leveraging the strengths of each to enhance recommendation accuracy and user satisfaction (Ortega *et al.*, 2013). The most common and popular combination of HS is CF and CBF. Other combinations include other techniques like Knowledge-Based Filtering (KBF), Demographic Filtering (DF) or data mining and machine learning techniques (Son, 2014).

In addition to the previously discussed methods, several other approaches have been highlighted in existing studies such as Demographic-Based, Social Filtering, Context-Aware and Utility-Based RSs (Fayyaz *et al.*, 2020).

4.2 AI-Based Recommender Systems

As AI reshapes industries, its applications transform how people interact with technology, automating tasks and enhancing decision-making. By enabling more personalized recommendations, AI offers significant potential for RSs. This section examines five key AI techniques driving these systems.

- Generative AI: A branch of AI that focuses on developing models that generate synthetic data resembling real-world data. Examples like DALL-E 2, GPT-4, and Copilot are transforming workflows and interactions across industries. Generative AI models, such as Generative Adversarial Networks (GANs) and Variational Autoencoders (VAEs), can generate high-quality and novel content. This capability enhances RSs by improving their ability to make accurate, data-driven recommendations (Feuerriegel *et al.*, 2024).

- Fuzzy Logic (FL): Flexible system that handles uncertainty by allowing values to be partially true and partially false rather than strictly binary, making it useful in in RSs as it can capture the nuances in user preferences, which are often imprecise. Dai *et al.* (2019) proposed a fuzzy logic-based system to recommend daily water intake based on user factors like weight, age, and environmental temperature. Personalized hydration recommendations are displayed on an Android app that syncs with the cup.
- Artificial Neural Networks (ANNs): Enhance RSs by learning complex, non-linear relationships between users and items to predict preferences accurately. ANNs process user and item data through interconnected layers that capture patterns, enabling better generalization of user behaviors. Deep ANNs, specifically, extract high-level abstractions, improving recommendation accuracy. Paradarami *et al.* (2017) developed a hybrid recommender system that combines collaborative and content-based filtering with an ANN, using metadata from review text.
- Transfer Learning (TL): Also known as knowledge transfer, is a machine learning approach that aims to extract knowledge from a source domain to enhance the performance in a target domain. In the context of RSs, TL has shown significant promise by extending recommendations across multiple domains. By leveraging correlations between domains, it enhances user preference mining and mitigates data sparsity or cold start issues (Zhang *et al.* 2021). Following this, Fareed *et al.* (2024) developed a hybrid model, Deep TL and Multimodal Embedding (DTLME), to address cold-start problems. Similarly, Fang (2021) introduced a content-based recommender system using TL and transformer-based deep neural networks.
- Natural Language Processing (NLP): Focuses on enabling computers to understand and generate human language. It plays an important role in RSs by analyzing and identifying keywords, topics, or emotions in a given text in order to capture preferences and sentiment that make more precise recommendations to match the user's specific interests. One of the most significant advancements in NLP is the development of Large Language Models (LLMs) like GPT-4, which have revolutionized text generation, language translation, and sentiment analysis. In the context of RSs, Tarnowska and Ras (2021) proposed an NLP-based recommender system for business decision-makers, using a knowledge-based and text mining approach to analyze business factors such as price competitiveness and staff attitude.

4.2.1 Strengths and Limitations of AI Techniques in Rss

AI techniques have advanced RSs by improving personalization and addressing challenges, but they also introduce new limitations. Both strengths and limitations were found when comparing each method.

Generative AI improves accuracy and diversity but struggles with data realism and high computational costs (Ayemowa *et al.* 2024). FL effectively handles uncertainties but is difficult to scale due to extensive rule-setting (Zhang *et al.* 2021). ANNs excel in complex tasks like cold start problems but lack transparency and face scalability issues (Gabrani *et al.* 2017). TL helps RSs recommend across domains but risks performance drops if domains differ too much (Zhang *et al.* 2021). NLP enhances contextual recommendations but requires significant computing power and struggles with ambiguous language and scalability (Zhang *et al.* 2021).

5. DISCUSSION

In this work, it was observed that while basic approaches in RSs have demonstrated strong performance, they still fall short of addressing key challenges. While effective, CF struggles with sparse user-item interaction data and faces cold start and grey sheep issues. CBF, on the other hand, faces challenges with insufficient item metadata. Both approaches also struggle with scalability as datasets grow. Hybrid methods, which combines multiple techniques, attempt to address these challenges but can increase system complexity and computational demands. KBS are particularly effective in scenarios where interaction data is limited or sparse, such as in niche markets or expert-driven fields. Besides, they are less scalable for dynamic or large datasets and require significant manual input to encode domain expertise. AI-based techniques, particularly Generative AI can enhance the effectiveness of information dissemination in RSs by enabling more personalized content that aligns with the recipient's preferences. Other techniques like TL, ANNs, and NLP offer better solutions by mitigating cold start problems, enhancing prediction accuracy, and processing unstructured data. However,

AI approaches are computationally intensive and raise privacy concerns due to the large amounts of personal data needed for training. RSs are now widely applicable across various domains. However, the adoption of RSs in water field is still in its early stages. Researchers have recognized this potential and have emphasized the importance of raising awareness about water demand through many studies (Rahim *et al.*, 2019). The focus of our future research will be highlighted on designing a machine learning or AI-based recommender system tailored to the field of water resource management, aiming to optimize domestic water usage. The latter will require a large dataset of consumption data to improve the level of accuracy for providing personalized recommendations.

6. CONCLUSION

Over the past few decades, RSs have emerged as one of the key solutions for addressing information and cognitive overload by suggesting relevant and related items to users. Significant advancements have been made in this field to develop high-quality, fine-tuned systems that cater to user needs effectively. This paper offers an overview of RSs applications across various fields and highlights the challenges involved in refining these systems. Moreover, the paper explores basic RSs approaches and showcases how AI has enhanced these techniques enabling systems to better analyze large datasets, predict user behavior with greater accuracy, and provide more personalized recommendations. With the ongoing information explosion, it has become essential to further research and develop new methods capable of delivering recommendations across a wide range of applications while addressing quality and privacy concerns. Consequently, existing RSs require enhancements to meet current demands and future expectations for improved recommendation performance. Further, future work will focus on the application of RSs in water management.

REFERENCES

Aggarwal, C.C. (2016) 'Knowledge-Based Recommender Systems', in Recommender Systems. Cham: Springer International Publishing, pp. 167–197. Available at: https://doi.org/10.1007/978-3-319-29659-3_5.

Ahmadian, S. et al. (2022) 'Alleviating data sparsity problem in time-aware recommender systems using a reliable rating profile enrichment approach', Expert Systems with Applications, 187, p. 115849. Available at: https://doi.org/10.1016/j.eswa.2021.115849.

Ayemowa, M.O., Ibrahim, R. and Khan, M.M. (2024) 'Analysis of Recommender System Using Generative Artificial Intelligence: A Systematic Literature Review', IEEE Access, 12, pp. 87742–87766. Available at: https://doi.org/10.1109/ACCESS.2024.3416962.

Barragáns-Martínez, A.B. et al. (2010) 'A hybrid content-based and item-based collaborative filtering approach to recommend TV programs enhanced with singular value decomposition', Information Sciences, 180(22), pp. 4290–4311. Available at: https://doi.org/10.1016/j.ins.2010.07.024.

Chen, J. et al. (2023) 'Bias and Debias in Recommender System: A Survey and Future Directions', ACM Transactions on Information Systems, 41(3), pp. 1–39. Available at: https://doi.org/10.1145/3564284.

Dai, B. et al. (2016) 'A fuzzy recommendation system for daily water intake', Advances in Mechanical Engineering, 8(5). Available at: https://doi.org/10.1177/1687814016649937.

Dai, B., Chen, R.C. and Ding, Y.Y. (2019) 'A practical approach for estimating human daily water intake', International Journal of Embedded Systems, 11(2), p. 210. Available at: https://doi.org/10.1504/IJES.2019.098297.

Desrosiers, C. and Karypis, G. (2011) 'A Comprehensive Survey of Neighborhood-based Recommendation Methods', in Recommender Systems Handbook. Boston, MA: Springer US, pp. 107–144. Available at: https://doi.org/10.1007/978-0-387-85820-3_4.

Fang, X. (2021) 'Making recommendations using transfer learning', Neural Computing and Applications, 33(15), pp. 9663–9676. Available at: https://doi.org/10.1007/s00521-021-05730-3.

Fareed, A. et al. (2024) 'Elevating recommender systems: Cutting-edge transfer learning and embedding solutions', Applied Soft Computing, 166, p. 112140. Available at: https://doi.org/10.1016/j.asoc.2024.112140.

Fayyaz, Z. et al. (2020) 'Recommendation Systems: Algorithms, Challenges, Metrics, and Business Opportunities', Applied Sciences, 10(21), p. 7748. Available at: https://doi.org/10.3390/app10217748.

Feng, J. et al. (2021) 'RBPR: A hybrid model for the new user cold start problem in recommender systems', Knowledge-Based Systems, 214, p. 106732. Available at: https://doi.org/10.1016/j.knosys.2020.106732.

Feuerriegel, S. et al. (2024) 'Generative AI', Business & Information Systems Engineering, 66(1), pp. 111–126. Available at: https://doi.org/10.1007/s12599-023-00834-7.

Gabrani, G., Sabharwal, S. and Singh, V.K. (2017) 'Artificial Intelligence Based Recommender Systems: A Survey', in, pp. 50–59. Available at: https://doi.org/10.1007/978-981-10-5427-3_6.

Geng, Y. et al. (2022) 'Multi-Feature Extension via Semi-Autoencoder for Personalized Recommendation', Applied Sciences, 12(23), p. 12408. Available at: https://doi.org/10.3390/app122312408.

George, T. and Merugu, S. (2005) 'A scalable collaborative filtering framework based on co-clustering', Proceedings - IEEE International Conference on Data Mining, ICDM, pp. 4–7. Available at: https://doi.org/10.1109/ICDM.2005.14.

Gong, S. and Cheng, G. (2008) 'Mining User Interest Change for Improving Collaborative Filtering', in 2008 Second International Symposium on Intelligent Information Technology Application. IEEE, pp. 24–27. Available at: https://doi.org/10.1109/IITA.2008.385.

Harper, F.M. and Konstan, J.A. (2016) 'The MovieLens Datasets', ACM Transactions on Interactive Intelligent Systems, 5(4), pp. 1–19. Available at: https://doi.org/10.1145/2827872.

Hwangbo, H., Kim, Y.S. and Cha, K.J. (2018) 'Recommendation system development for fashion retail e-commerce', Electronic Commerce Research and Applications, 28, pp. 94–101. Available at: https://doi.org/10.1016/j.elerap.2018.01.012.

Kesorn, K., Juraphanthong, W. and Salaiwarakul, A. (2017) 'Personalized Attraction Recommendation System for Tourists Through Check-In Data', IEEE Access, 5, pp. 26703–26721. Available at: https://doi.org/10.1109/ACCESS.2017.2778293.

Khusro, S., Ali, Z. and Ullah, I. (2016) 'Recommender Systems: Issues, Challenges, and Research Opportunities', in, pp. 1179–1189. Available at: https://doi.org/10.1007/978-981-10-0557-2_112.

Koren, Y. (2008) 'Factorization meets the neighborhood: a multifaceted collaborative filtering model', Knowledge Discovery and Data Mining, pp. 426–434. Available at: https://doi.org/10.1145/1401890.1401944.

Koren, Y., Rendle, S. and Bell, R. (2022) 'Advances in Collaborative Filtering', in Recommender Systems Handbook. New York, NY: Springer US, pp. 91–142. Available at: https://doi.org/10.1007/978-1-0716-2197-4_3.

Magadum, H. et al. (2024) 'Music recommendation using dynamic feedback and content-based filtering', Multimedia Tools and Applications, 83(32), pp. 77469–77488. Available at: https://doi.org/10.1007/s11042-024-18636-8.

Ning, X., Desrosiers, C. and Karypis, G. (2015) 'A Comprehensive Survey of Neighborhood-Based Recommendation Methods', in Recommender Systems Handbook. Boston, MA: Springer US, pp. 37–76. Available at: https://doi.org/10.1007/978-1-4899-7637-6_2.

Ortega, F. et al. (2013) 'Improving collaborative filtering-based recommender systems results using Pareto dominance', Information Sciences, 239, pp. 50–61. Available at: https://doi.org/10.1016/J.INS.2013.03.011.

Paradarami, T.K., Bastian, N.D. and Wightman, J.L. (2017) 'A hybrid recommender system using artificial neural networks', Expert Systems with Applications, 83, pp. 300–313. Available at: https://doi.org/10.1016/j.eswa.2017.04.046.

Rahim, M.S. et al. (2019) 'Predicting Household Water Consumption Events: Towards a Personalised Recommender System to Encourage Water-conscious Behaviour', in 2019 International Joint Conference on Neural Networks (IJCNN). IEEE, pp. 1–8. Available at: https://doi.org/10.1109/IJCNN.2019.8851868.

Sharma, S.K. and Suman, U. (2013) 'An efficient semantic clustering of URLs for web page recommendation', International Journal of Data Analysis Techniques and Strategies, 5(4), p. 339. Available at: https://doi.org/10.1504/IJDATS.2013.058578.

Shu, J. et al. (2018) 'A content-based recommendation algorithm for learning resources', Multimedia Systems, 24(2), pp. 163–173. Available at: https://doi.org/10.1007/s00530-017-0539-8.

Son, L.H. (2014) 'HU-FCF: A hybrid user-based fuzzy collaborative filtering method in Recommender Systems', Expert Systems with Applications, 41(15), pp. 6861–6870. Available at: https://doi.org/10.1016/j.eswa.2014.05.001.

Tarnowska, K.A. and Ras, Z. (2021) 'NLP-Based Customer Loyalty Improvement Recommender System (CLIRS2)', Big Data and Cognitive Computing, 5(1), p. 4. Available at: https://doi.org/10.3390/bdcc5010004.

Valdez, A.C. et al. (2016) 'Recommender Systems for Health Informatics: State-of-the-Art and Future Perspectives', Lecture Notes in Computer Science (including subseries Lecture Notes in Artificial Intelligence and Lecture Notes in Bioinformatics), 9605 LNCS, pp. 391–414. Available at: https://doi.org/10.1007/978-3-319-50478-0_20.

Zhang, Q., Lu, J. and Jin, Y. (2021) 'Artificial intelligence in recommender systems', Complex & Intelligent Systems, 7(1), pp. 439–457. Available at: https://doi.org/10.1007/s40747-020-00212-w

AI IN INFORMATION PROCESSING FOR DECISION MAKING – PERCEPTIONS AND USE INTENTION OF UK MANAGERS

Yanqing Duan[1], Guangming Cao[2], Mark Xu[3], Vincent Ong[4] and Christian Dietzmann[5]
[1]*University of Bedfordshire, Luton LU1 3JU, UK*
[2]*Ajman University, UAE*
[3]*University of Portsmouth, UK*
[4]*Regent's University London, UK*
[5]*University of Leipzig in Germany,and Business Engineering Institute St. Gallen AG, Switzerland*

ABSTRACT

Information processing forms an essential part of any decision making process as it enables decision makers to assess various options, evaluate risks and opportunities to make best choices. In the context of business decision making, information processing also enable managers to make decisions that align with organizational goals and objectives. However, business managers are facing unprecedented challenges in dealing with ever growing abundant data and struggling to make sense of it to make well informed decisions. As Artificial Intelligence (AI) is making profound impact on every aspect of business operations and management, it has the great potential in assisting/replacing business managers' information processing activities Although the use of AI in decision making in general has attracted significant attention from researchers and practitioners, its specific role and impact on business information processing at the individual manager level have not been well explored and examined theoretically and empirically. To address this knowledge gap, the study reported in this short paper aims to empirically investigate the current challenges faced by business managers and their perception and intention in utilising AI for information processing in their decision making process. Three key research questions covering perceived challenges, AI roles and use intention are raised. A questionnaire survey was conducted in the UK to collect data to understand the managers perceptions and use intention. Preliminary data analysis provides very interesting findings and valuable insights. Important implications for theory development and research directions are highlighted.

KEYWORDS

Artificial Intelligence, Information Processing, AI-Human Collaboration, Big Data, Decision Making

1. INTRODUCTION

Data driven decision making is crucial in today's dynamic and competitive business landscape. However, in the era of big data, managers face unprecedented challenges in making sense of overwhelmingly abundant and complex data through information processing. Artificial Intelligence (AI) has the great potential in supporting and/or replacing managers' information processing activities for decision making. Decision making and information processing is inherently individual as personality trait and individual decision making style may significantly affect their decision making behaviour and their intention and action towards seeking support especially from AI systems. Therefore, the benefits of AI can only be realised if the organisational managers are willing to leverage the potential benefit of AI and use AI to assist their decision making in information processing process. Although the use of AI in decision making in general has attracted significant attention from researchers and practitioners, its specific role and impact on business information processing at the individual manager level have not been well explored and examined theoretically and empirically. To address this knowledge gap, the study aims to empirical investigate the current challenges faced by business managers in information processing for decision making and their perception and intention in utilising AI for information processing in their decision making process. This study was an important part a research project on AI and Information Processing. To achieve the research aim, this investigation seeks to address the following questions:

1. *What are the key challenges faced by managers in information processing in the era of Big Data?*
2. *What are the managers' perceived roles of Human-AI collaboration in information processing?*
3. *What are the intentions of managers in using AI for information processing?*

2. LITERATURE REVIEW

The key concept of information processing is considered in this study from a process perspective and defined base on the relevant literature (e.g. Duan, Ong, Xu, & Mathews, 2012; Simon, 1960; Wilson, 1997). It covers three key activities as described below:

- Information acquisition includes information seeking which is solicited searching, or unsolicited receiving from information feeding and automated alerts. It includes receiving information from either pulling information, or being pushed information.
- Information synthesis and analysis includes data integration, data filtering, data manipulation and analysis of data from simple comparison, to statistics and comprehensive analytics.
- Making sense of information includes understanding and interpreting information often leading to action taking e.g. decision making or enhancing individual or collective organization learning.

Using AI for decision making has been one of the most important applications in AI history (Duan, Edwards, & Dwivedi, 2019) because human decision makers face certain constraints on their ability to make optimal choices (Buchanan & O Connell, 2006). Human cognitive capabilities are superior to artificial intelligence, but they also suffer constrains, such as: mental computational power, ability to deal with complex circumstances, limited time, memory capacity, potential bias, which are the strengths of artificial intelligence. Therefore, The key to success with AI is human machine collaboration (Ryder, 2021). However, how can human and AI work together? Researchers and practitioners are continuing debating on how humans and AI can collaborate smartly for the best outcome, e.g. human in charge and AI in the loop or verse visa, AI in charge and human in the loop. According to Ransbotham et al. (2020), there are five modes of Human- AI collaboration ranging from human leads to AI leads:

1. AI generates insights, human uses them in a decision process
2. Human generates, AI evaluates
3. AI recommends, human decides
4. AI decides, human implements
5. Al decides and implements

One of the most notable studies on managers percepion on human-AI collaberation for decison making is by Haesevoets, De Cremer, Dierckx, and Van Hiel (2021). They found that human managers do not want to exclude AI entirely from managerial decisions, but instead prefer a partnership in which humans are in control as they strongly oppose a partnership in which AI provides the most input into the decision-making process.

3. RESEARCH METHOD

A quantitative research method using a survey is employed. A survey questionnaire is developed and used to collect data from a sample of UK companies. The questionnaire survey mainly covers the following areas:

- Respondent's personal and industry profile and decision making level
- Perceived challenges in information processing
- Trust of AI for information processing
- Preferred right combination of human-AI input and Human-AI collaboration mode
- Intention to use AI.

The survey was distributed to managers working in large and medium companies in the selected sectors including Financial Services, Health & Life Insurance, Professional Services, Retail/Wholesale as these four sectors are leading industries in terms of using AI.

4. PRELIMINARY ANALYSIS OF SURVEY RESULTS

A total of 159 valid responses were received. Survey data analysis shows that all respondents are business managers. The decision making levels of their main responsibility cover strategic (4.4%), tactical (42.8%) and operational (52.8%). Figure 1 presents the results regarding the information processing challenges faced by participants. Figure 2 shows the distribution of the preferred Human-AI collaboration modes based on the five mode proposed by Ransbotham et al. (2020). Figure 3 presents the intention to use AI for information processing in decision making among participants.

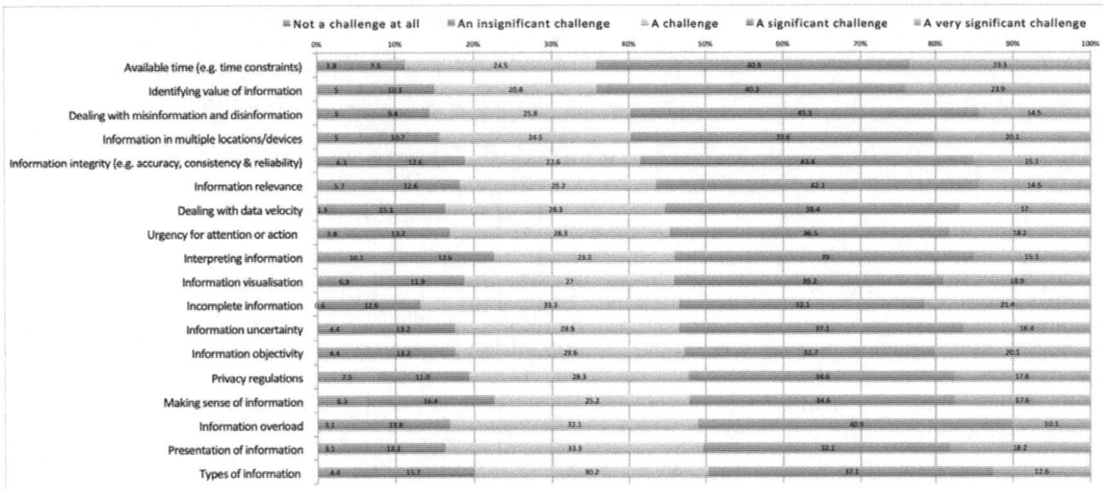

Figure 1. Perceived level of information Processing Challenges (n=159)

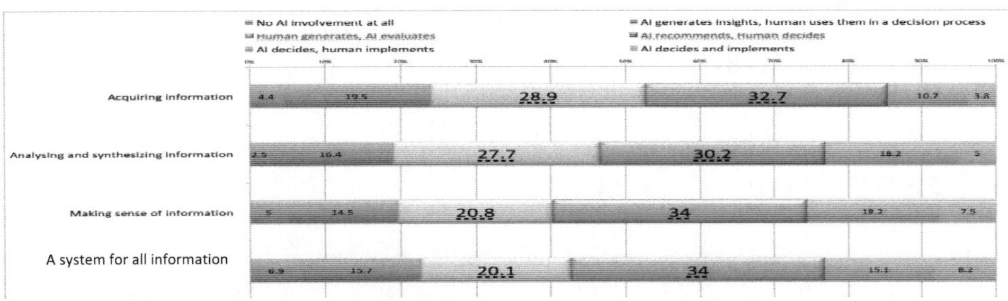

Figure 2. Preferred Human-AI collaboration modes (n=159)

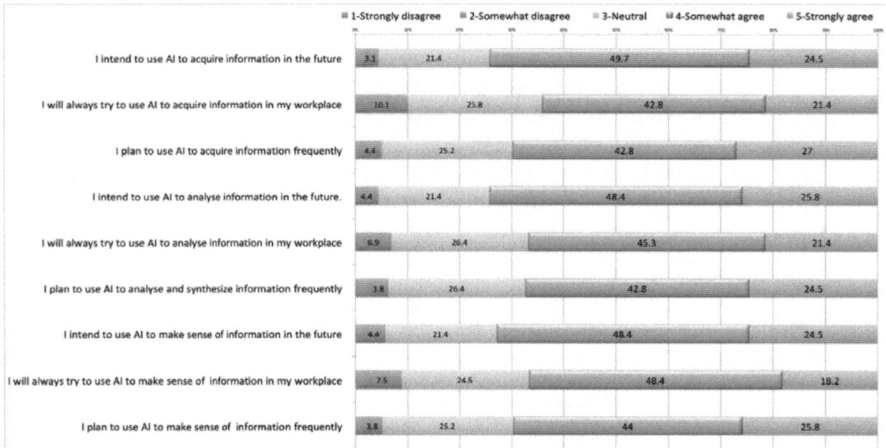

Figure 3. Intention to use AI for information processing in decision making (n=159)

Based on the preliminary data analysis, following important finding are emerged:

- Over 80% managers agree that they face various challenges in information processing. Over 50% managers agree that they face significant or very significant challenges in information processing for decision making. Top challenges include identifying the value of information, time, dealing with misinformation and disinformation, information in multiple locations/devices. However, it is interesting to note that the least challenging areas (23% indicating not a challenge) are interpreting information and making sense of information.
- The preferred right combination of Human –AI collaboration is the equally shared input by both human and AI, i.e. 50% human vs 50% AI. The most preferred Human-AI collaboration modes are AI recommend-human decide and Human generates-AI evaluate.
- Majority of managers (65%-70%) intent to use AI in all stages of information processing.
- Almost all answers are not significantly different among respondents from different sectors and sizes of companies. Almost all answers are not significantly different among managers at different decision making levels except perceived challenge in interpreting information and preferred right combination of human and AI input between strategic and operational level managers.

5. RESEARCH IMPLICATIONS

Insights from our study offer valuable implications for future research. the key implication is that business managers wants human centred AI for information processing. Our findings call for more in-depth investigations to understand the following issues:

- What are the critical factors influencing the acceptance or avoidance of using AI in information processing for decision making
- What are the suitable theoretical models to understand and explain the factors affecting the AI use intention in the context of information process
- How managers are dealing with information processing challenges
- How managers would like to interact with AI and how managers can learn with using AI
- How AI and human can play the strength of each other.

Research should deal with the "dark side" of AI for information processing addressing the following challenges:

- Managers' fears of AI and their personal development concerns
- Consequences and risks of over trusting AI
- Concerns of AI bias and knowing AI limitations
- Ownership and control of AI and AI accessibility and equal opportunity
- Development of AI ethical frameworks and professional bodies to guide and manage

REFERENCES

Buchanan, L., & O Connell, A. (2006). A brief history of decision making. Harvard Business Review, 84(1), 32.

Duan, Y., Edwards, J. S., & Dwivedi, Y. K. (2019). Artificial intelligence for decision making in the era of Big Data – evolution, challenges and research agenda. International Journal of Information Management, 48, 63-71.

Duan, Y., Ong, V. K., Xu, M., & Mathews, B. (2012). Supporting decision making process with "ideal" software agents–What do business executives want? Expert Systems with Applications, 39(5), 5534-5547.

Haesevoets, T., De Cremer, D., Dierckx, K., & Van Hiel, A. (2021). Human-machine collaboration in managerial decision making. Computers in Human Behavior, 119, 106730. doi:https://doi.org/10.1016/j.chb.2021.106730

Ransbotham, S., Khodabandeh, S., Kiron, D., Candelon, F., Chu, M., & LaFountain, B. (2020). Expanding AI's impact with organizational learning. MIT Sloan Management Review and Boston Consulting Group, October 2020.

Ryder, A. (2021). The key to success with AI is human-machine collaboration. MIT Sloan Management Review, 13 January.

Simon, H. A. (1960). The new science of management decision.

Wilson, T. D. (1997). Information behaviour: an interdisciplinary perspective. Information Processing & Management, 33(4), 551-572.

DEVELOPING ORGANISATIONAL SECURITY CULTURE FRAMEWORK FOR NAMIBIAN PUBLIC ENTERPRISES

Hileni Ihambo, Fungai Bhunu Shava and Gabriel Tuhafeni Nhinda
University of Science and Technology
13 Jackson Kaujeua Street, Windhoek, Namibia

ABSTRACT

This study examines cybersecurity practices in Namibian public enterprises, focusing on the challenges of developing a strong security culture. With an increasing reliance on digital infrastructures, public companies face rising security concerns; nonetheless, significant gaps in understanding and leadership participation hinder effective security management. The study employed a mixed-method research design, utilising document analysis, survey and interviews to analyse the security culture within Namibian state companies. The findings show that cybersecurity is impeded by outdated security policies, insufficient employee training, and poor inter-departmental communication. Leadership was highlighted as a critical aspect in driving security culture, but the study discovered inconsistent commitment from senior management, resulting in a reactive rather than proactive security approach. Furthermore, many employees wrongly believe that cybersecurity is entirely the responsibility of the IT department, resulting in low participation and a lack of shared responsibility throughout the firm. Based on the findings, this study created a security culture framework emphasising the importance of updated policies, frequent role-specific training, clear communication channels, and increased leadership engagement. The suggested approach aims to solve these difficulties by combining best practices from the literature with data gathered from document analysis. By integrating cybersecurity with broader organisational goals and promoting active participation from all employees, this framework intends to improve public companies' overall resilience to cyber threats. The study highlights that instilling a security-conscious culture in public companies necessitates a comprehensive, multi-level approach that includes technological solutions, strong leadership, and active employee participation. These findings are helpful for policymakers and organisational leaders aiming to improve cybersecurity policies in the public sector.

KEYWORDS

Organisational Security Culture, Public Enterprises, Namibia, Security Awareness, Training

1. INTRODUCTION

As the digital landscape grows more complex, public enterprises face challenges, including ransomware, data breaches, and espionage, which can potentially disrupt services and compromise national security; as critical drivers of the nation's socio-economic development, Namibian public enterprises are increasingly vulnerable to sophisticated cyberattacks and security threats (Deloitte, 2023). A robust security culture, where security awareness is ingrained in every level of the organisation, is crucial for protecting sensitive data, maintaining operational continuity, and preserving public trust (ISO, 2013). Security culture, a subset of organisational culture, is essential in shaping how an organisation addresses information security challenges. Early research Barney (2002) highlights the importance of shared values and behaviours in creating a competitive advantage. These cultural elements can enhance or undermine an organisation's ability to safeguard assets in security. The theoretical foundation for this research is based on the Theory of Planned Behavior (TPB) and the Protection Motivation Theory (PMT). These theories emphasise the importance of attitudes, subjective norms, and perceived behavioural control in shaping security behaviours. By applying these theories, the study aims to understand how leadership commitment, employee engagement, training, and communication influence the development of a security culture.

Key Elements of a Security Culture

- Leadership Commitment: Effective security culture begins at the top. Leadership must visibly support security initiatives and allocate necessary resources, reinforcing security's importance throughout the organisation (Schein, 2010).
- Employee Engagement: Security is everyone's responsibility. Engaged employees will likely follow security protocols, report incidents, and contribute ideas to improve security measures (International Organization for Standardization, 2013) .
- Training and Awareness: Regular training informs employees about emerging threats and reinforces good security practices .(Barney, 2002).
- Communication: Open channels for discussing security incidents and sharing information about threats help foster trust and proactive engagement across all levels (Willison & Warkentin, 2013).

2. ANALYSIS OF CURRENT PRACTICES

While a positive security culture is critical, many organisations struggle with obstacles such as employee disengagement, inadequate training, and a lack of communication, which can weaken their overall security posture (International Organization for Standardization, 2013).A proactive security culture ensures that employees know security risks and actively engage in preventative measures. It shifts security from being the sole responsibility of IT departments to a shared organisational commitment, which is critical for achieving resilience in the face of evolving threats (Posey, Roberts, & Lowry, 2011).The paper aims to evaluate current security practices within Namibian public enterprises, identify key challenges, and propose a comprehensive framework to foster a proactive security culture. It emphasises the importance of leadership commitment, employee engagement (Dhillon & Backhouse, 2001) , continuous training (European Union Agency for Cybersecurity, 2022). and open communication (Willison & Warkentin, 2013) in building a strong security culture. By addressing these elements, the paper seeks to mitigate security risks, protect critical infrastructure, and promote a shift from viewing security as solely an IT responsibility to a shared organisational commitment, ultimately enhancing the overall security posture of Namibian public enterprises (International Organization for Standardization, 2013)

2.1 Security Practices within Public Enterprises

Public enterprises, especially those in charge of essential infrastructure, play an important role in national security and economic stability. As digital transformation continues, these organisations rely more on technology to provide critical services, making them perfect targets for cyberattacks. Security practices inside public organisations are frequently impacted by legislative requirements and compliance with international standards such as ISO/IEC 27001, which guides information security management systems Dhillon & Backhouse, 2001 . However, (International Organization for Standardization, 2013) have found that security policies in public companies are more reactive than proactive, emphasising responding to problems rather than preventing them. Furthermore, many public organisations struggle to incorporate security into their organisational culture, viewing it as a standalone function of the IT department rather than a shared duty at all levels of the organisation.

3. METHODOLOGY

This study employed a mixed-method approach, utilising qualitative data collection instruments like document analysis, and interviews and the survey quantitative data collection instrument to comprehensively analyse the security culture within Namibian state companies. Document analysis was chosen as the primary method to thoroughly review existing policies, internal reports, guidelines, training manuals, and cybersecurity frameworks used by Namibian state organisations. This approach was appropriate as it allowed for a detailed examination of the existing security practices that reflect the enterprises' security procedures and challenges. The survey was conducted with employees across various departments in the public enterprise The survey aimed to gauge employees' awareness, attitudes, and behaviours regarding cybersecurity as prescribed by the TPB and PMT. It included questions on their understanding of security policies, training effectiveness, and perceived responsibility for cybersecurity. The survey data provided quantitative insights into the security culture within the organisations. Semi-structured interviews were conducted with senior management, IT staff, and non-IT employees to gain deeper insights into the organisation's challenges and perceptions of cybersecurity. The interviews focused on leadership commitment, employee engagement, communication practices, and training programs. Thematic analysis was used for qualitative data and descriptive statistics for quantitative data. This qualitative data complemented the survey findings and provided a comprehensive understanding of the security culture across different levels of the organisation.

4. RESULTS

The document analysis yielded several critical insights into the security culture within Namibian state companies. There were significant disparities in security awareness, with some employees lacking fundamental knowledge of password hygiene and social engineering, highlighting the need for more targeted, role-specific training. Employee participation was found to be poor, as many non-IT employees believed that security was solely the responsibility of the IT department, undermining overall security efforts. Training manuals and internal reports revealed that employee training programs were infrequent and not tailored to specific roles and responsibilities, leaving employees unprepared to handle security incidents effectively. Communication hurdles were also identified, with employees often unwilling to report incidents due to fear of repercussions or confusing protocols. Many of the security policies reviewed were outdated and did not address cybersecurity threats such as social engineering and ransomware. This gap was evident in the National Cybersecurity Policy and internal security protocols, which lacked provisions for emerging threats. Leadership directives and risk management policies showed varying levels of commitment to cybersecurity. Senior management sometimes prioritised compliance over proactive security measures, resulting in insufficient investment in advanced technologies and a lack of accountability. Sections 4.1, 4.2, and 4.3 present the results from the survey and section 4.4 presents the results from the semi-structured interviews.

4.1 Security Awareness Discrepancies

Figure 1 illustrates the percentage of employees who feel confident in identifying specific security risks. It shows that 40% of respondents reported being satisfied with recognising phishing attacks, while 60% felt they understood the malware risks and attacks. A moderate 50% indicate that they practice password hygiene.

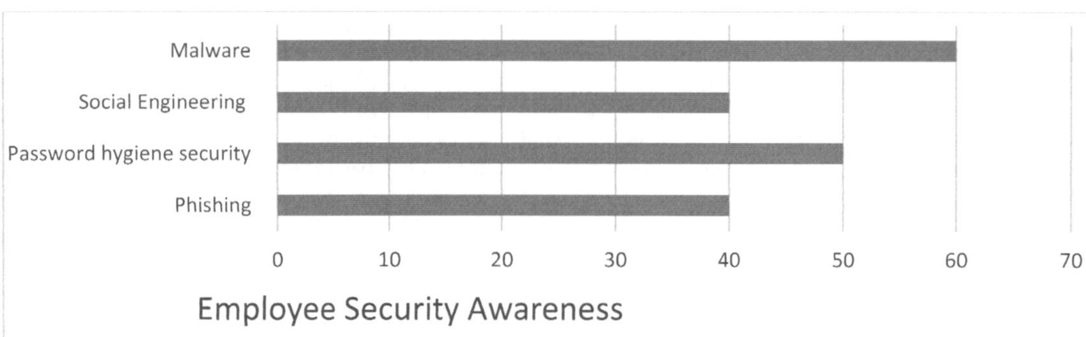

Figure 1. Employee security awareness

4.2 Employee Engagement Challenges

Figure 2 illustrates employees' perception of security responsibility within an organization. It shows that 20% of respondents indicated that security is the responsibility of all employees, 10% felt that it is the responsibility of leadership, while 70% of employees believed that security was solely the responsibility of the IT department, indicating a widespread misperception among the workforces. This view might impede the timely reporting of security issues, weakening the organisation's overall security posture. Encouraging engagement from all employees, not just the IT team, is critical for developing a more resilient and comprehensive security culture. A recurring theme from the survey and interviews was the lack of engagement from non-IT staff. The majority of respondents viewed security as the sole responsibility of the IT department, leading to a lack of ownership across the organisation.

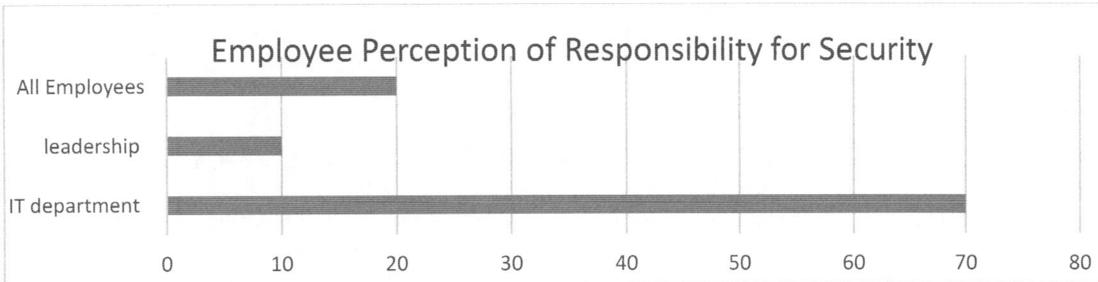

Figure 2. Employee perception of responsibility for security

4.3 Outdated Training Programs

Training programs were found to be infrequent and not tailored to emerging threats. Employees expressed a need for more practical training that addresses real-world risks. The study revealed that existing training programs were outdated and insufficient. Employees desired more frequent, practical training that reflects current threats and security risks.

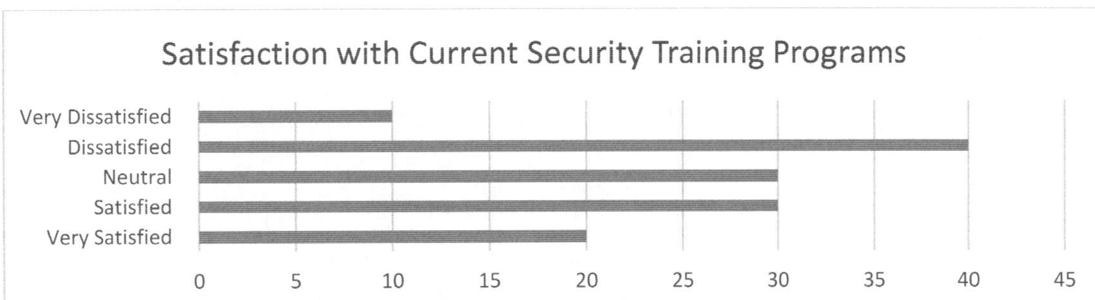

Figure 3. Satisfaction with security training programs

Figure 3 presents employees' satisfaction level with existing security training programs. It indicates that 40% of employees indicated dissatisfaction with the current security training programs, 30% rated it as adequate, and 30% expressed moderate satisfaction but requested more frequent sessions.

4.4 Communication Barriers

Despite having formal reporting channels, employees often hesitate to report incidents due to fear of repercussions or a lack of trust in the process. This underscores the need for transparent and supportive communication systems. Despite having formal channels for reporting security issues, employees were unsure of the reporting process or feared potential repercussions. Interviews confirmed that a clear, open communication channel hindered proactive reporting.

Figure 4. Word Cloud from interview responses on Security Reporting

Figure 4 presents a word cloud that shows frequently mentioned themes from the interviews. Words such as "fear," "uncertainty," and "lack of trust" were common when discussing reporting security incidents. Which from a

5. PROPOSED FRAMEWORK: SECURITY CULTURE FRAMEWORK

This study proposes a comprehensive security culture framework to address identified challenges, consisting of five key components that operate across all organisational levels. It emphasises leadership commitment from the board and management, the IT department's role as the security custodian, effective interaction between IT and staff, integration of security practices across departments, and active staff engagement. The framework aims to foster a cohesive, proactive security culture throughout the organisation.

Policy development and updates include regular review and update of security policies and ensuring that cybersecurity policies are regularly reviewed and updated to address emerging threats and align with best practices. Policy Dissemination: Implement effective methods for communicating updated policies to all employees European Union Agency for Cybersecurity, 2022.

Training and Awareness programs role-specific training: Develop and conduct frequent training sessions tailored to employees' specific roles and responsibilities (Willison & Warkentin, 2013). Continuous Education: Promote ongoing cybersecurity education to inform employees about the latest threats and security practices.

Leadership Engagement Senior Management Commitment: Ensure consistent and proactive involvement of senior management in cybersecurity initiatives. Leadership Training: Train leaders to understand their role in fostering a security-conscious culture (International Organization for Standardization, 2013).

Communication Channels Clear Communication Pathways: Establish and maintain clear channels for communication regarding cybersecurity issues and policies (International Organization for Standardization, 2013) . Feedback Mechanisms: Implement mechanisms for employees to provide feedback and report security concerns.

Shared responsibility Promote a Culture of Shared Responsibility: Encourage all employees to take an active role in cybersecurity (Siponen & Vance, 2010) emphasising that it is not solely the responsibility of the IT department. Recognition and Incentives: Recognise and reward employees who contribute to improving the organisation's cybersecurity posture.

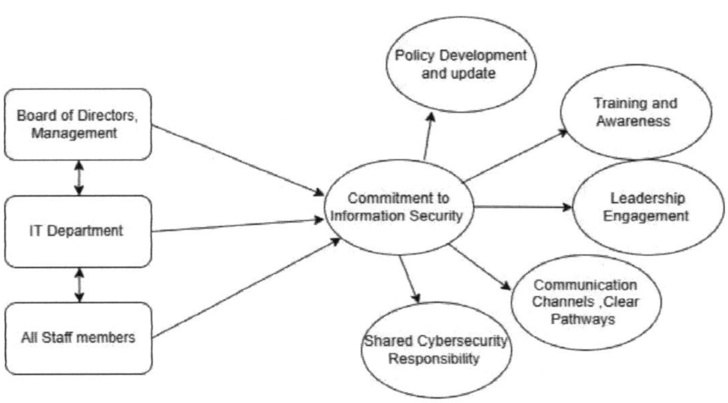

Figure 5. Proposed Organisation Security Culture

By following this framework, Namibian public enterprises can develop a robust cybersecurity culture that addresses current challenges and enhances their resilience to cyber threats. This comprehensive approach involves updated policies, continuous training, strong leadership, clear communication, shared responsibility, alignment with organisational goals, and implementation of advanced technologies.

6. CONCLUSION

This study sought to understand the challenges and existing practices of public enterperises around security then propose a framework to instill a security culture. Establishing a robust security culture within Namibian public enterprises is essential for safeguarding sensitive data, maintaining operational continuity, and preserving public trust. This study identified several critical challenges, including outdated security policies, insufficient employee training, poor inter-departmental communication, and inconsistent leadership commitment. A comprehensive security culture framework was developed by integrating findings from document analysis, a survey, and semi-interviews. This framework emphasises the importance of updated policies, frequent role-specific training, clear communication channels, and increased leadership engagement. Implementing these measures can transform cybersecurity from a reactive to a proactive approach, fostering a security-conscious culture that involves all employees. The insights and recommendations provided by this study are valuable for policymakers and organisational leaders aiming to enhance cybersecurity practices within the public sector, ultimately contributing to the resilience and stability of Namibian public enterprises in the face of evolving cyber threats. Future work could focus on validating and implementing the proposed framework.

REFERENCES

Barney, J. B. (1986). Organisational culture: Can it be a source of sustained competitive advantage? *Academy of Management Review*, *11*(3), 656-665.

Barney, J. B. (2002). Gaining and sustaining competitive advantage. Prentice Hall.

Deloitte. (2023). Cybersecurity predictions. Deloitte Insights.

Dhillon, G., & Backhouse, J. (2001). Information systems security management in the new millennium. *Communications of the ACM*, *44*(7), 80-86.

European Union Agency for Cybersecurity. (2022). Cybersecurity Culture Guidelines.

International Organization for Standardization. (2013). ISO/IEC 27001:2013 Information technology – Security techniques – Information security management systems – Requirements.

Posey, C., Roberts, T., & Lowry, P. (2011). The impact of organisational commitment on insiders' motivation to protect organisational information. *Journal of Management Information Systems*, *27*(1), 193-221.

Schein, E. H. (2010). Organisational culture and leadership.

Siponen, M., & Vance, A. (2010). Neutralisation: New insights into the problem of employee information systems security policy violations. *MIS Quarterly*, *34*(3), 487-502

Willison, R., & Warkentin, M. (2013). Beyond deterrence: An expanded view of employee computer abuse. *MIS Quarterly*, *37*(1), 231-261.

THE DESIGN OF NON-HUMAN PERSONAS

Lene Nielsen[1] and Rike Neuhoff[2]
[1]*IT University Copenhagen, Department of Business IT, Denmark*
[2]*Aalborg University, Department of Architecture, Design and Media Technology, Denmark*

ABSTRACT

This paper examines how descriptions of non-human personas are developed using established templates for human personas as a foundation. The research reveals significant differences in approach: some non-human personas aim to humanize other species, encouraging emotional connections while other descriptions prioritize providing information that is directly relevant to human interests and needs. The study highlights a gap in our understanding of how different elements impact the effectiveness of non-human personas, such as the narrative techniques, the tones of voice, and the levels of anthropomorphism. Additional research in these areas could lead to more engaging and empathy-inducing non-human personas, the development of more effective tools for communication and education, and technological advancements that are more inclusive and ecologically responsible. By exploring these factors, we can potentially create better ways to represent and interact with the non-human world in digital contexts.

KEYWORDS

Personas, Non-Human Personas, Interaction Design, Climate Centered Design

1. INTRODUCTION

It is increasingly clear that technology has a significant impact on both natural ecosystems and the global climate. From large-scale infrastructures, such as data warehouses to single apps – technology increases demands for processing power, drive energy consumption, and carbon emissions. This disturbs and disrupts nature and the climate. These developments highlight the need to rethink systems design practices and processes, ensuring that technological advancement aligns with the needs of our natural ecosystems.

As a consequence, efforts to integrate non-humans in design practices are emerging, but this integration is still in its infancy. One notable field is ICA, animal-computer interaction, which took rise from 2011 (Mancini, 2011), and has since been explored in many projects that design IT systems for animal use and animal monitoring, see e.g. (French et al., 2017) on design for captive elephants. The broader movement to incorporate non-human species into design has led to the development of various conceptual framewords, such as The Participatory Ladder for Non-humans (Hernandez-Santin et al. 2023), The Ecosystema (Tomlinson et al. 2022), and non-human personas (Tomitsch et al., 2021) each addressing different facets of the human-nature-technology relationship. The vocabulary is developing and literature includes concepts such as: *1) More-than-human design* that focuses both on technology and how different technologies communicate, e.g., in internet of things, see e.g. (Giaccardi & Redström, 2020) and on environment (NTNU, Norway & Tarcan, 2022), *2) other-than-human design* that focus on multi-species design (Gatto & McCardle, 2019), *3) life-centred design* that integrates human-centred, environmental, and ethical concerns (Borthwick et al., 2022), *4) planetary-centric design* that takes point of departure in Design Thinking and includes a sustainable approach to product and service design (Poleac, 2023), *5) multi-species design* that is more prominent within urban design (Gatto & McCardle, 2019), and finally 6) *non-human design* that spans the concept of designing conversational agents (Jylkäs et al., 2018) to designing both products and digital concept (Tomitsch et al., 2021). Non-human is often used interchangeably with the term more-than-human (see e.g. (NTNU, Norway & Tarcan, 2022), though for the purpose of this paper, we will employ "non-human" to encompass all entities beyond the human species.

For more than 25 years, personas have been a widely used method for understanding the different human target groups impacted by an IT product or service. Personas have been applied across diverse domains, such as user experience design, healthcare, market research, social media strategy (Guan et al., 2021), and architecture (Nielsen, 2024). Within the field of Information Systems personas have been coupled with use cases (Dittmar & Forbrig, 2019) and used in conjunction with user journeys in agile development processes (Da Silva et al., 2015; Nielsen et al., 2021). The benefits of personas are that they help understand users' needs and contexts; facilitate communication with stakeholders of design projects, guide design decisions, support evaluations, and inform both the design and implementation of solutions (Bashir & Attfield, 2018; Nielsen & Storgaard Hansen, 2014). Furthermore, they align user understanding between stakeholders and design teams (Matthews et al., 2012). One of the key advantages of personas is the ability to foster empathy towards end-users, to help design teams understand users that live different lives and have different needs than those in the design team (Nielsen, 2024).

Over the years, a somewhat standardized style or template has emerged for creating human personas across different domains and products. Most often, personas are displayed on a single page, containing a name, an illustration, either a drawing or a photograph, a catch phrase, and various information about the specific persona (Nielsen et al., 2015; Salminen et al., 2020). This format has become widely accepted for its ability to communicate key user characteristics in a clear and concise manner.

Given the profound impact of technology on non-humans, the concept of personas, a method commonly used in design and IT product development to represent and understand target user groups (Nielsen et al., 2015), has also expanded to include non-human beings allowing designers, innovators, and decision-makers to consider the needs of non-human entities in the design process. In this paper, we examine the nascent attempts to produce non-human personas.

2. METHOD

Methodologically, this paper draws on a literature search and review conducted in the ACM Digital Library and Google Scholar, using the search terms "non-human personas" and "more-than-human personas." The aim of the analysis is to examine how non-human perspectives are represented using personas and to identify opportunities for advancing research in this emerging field. For the analysis, we selected three distinct examples, deliberately chosen to capture variation in content and format, enabling a richer exploration of their approaches to conveying non-human perspectives.

3. THREE EXAMPLES OF NON-HUMAN PERSONAS

The purpose of the first persona description of **"Bees"** (see figure 1) is to support environmental design efforts. The description combines first-person narration with encyclopedic information to inform the reader about specific issues affecting this species. Contrary to human persona descriptions, which often aim at fostering empathy, this description lacks emotional or relatable information. Instead, it prioritizes highlighting the species' ecological significance, as reflected in statements like "humans cannot live without me". The portrayal describes a species rather than a single subject and emphathises the collective behavior of this particular species, which is noted in the shift between the singular "I" and the plural "we". Targeting a human audience, the text offers actionable guidance on supporting the species' needs, as illustrated in recommendations such as "let you garden grow wild".

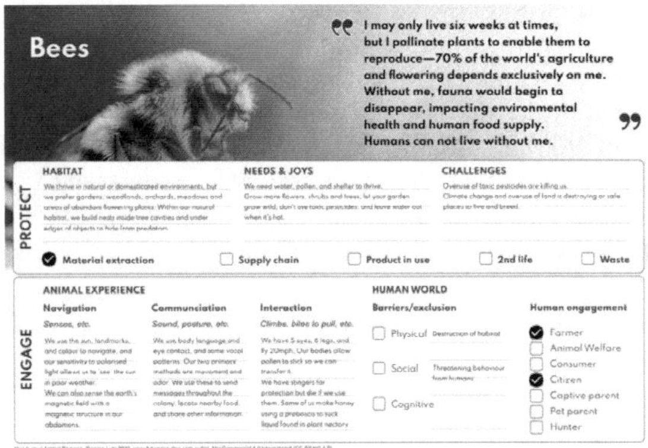

Figure 1. Non-human persona example (Life-Centered Design Lab, n.d.), combining first-person narration and encyclopedic information

Lifestyle / backstory	Beans the possum is usually up during the night while it is quieter and there is less going on around Beans. Compared to during the day when there is plenty of activity from other species, Beans prefers to sleep throughout the day.
Motivations of the persona	Beans usually prefers a place high above the ground away from other species that might harm him. Beans also does his best to stay out the way of others as other possums are very protective of their established territory.
Frustrations the persona experiences	Sometimes Beans is captured by humans and is transported to a location away from where he usually scavenges for food and resides. Being held in an enclosure while Beans is transported and being displaced causes great stress to Beans. These displacements are usually fatal.
Issues faced by persona relating to habitat	It's getting harder for Beans to find a home to rest as trees are being slowly replaced by concrete. The current alternative of a tree to call home is within rooftops of human structures, finding a small opening like a crack to make his way into rooftops. But as Beans is most active at night, he disrupts sleeping humans and this causes humans to attempt to scare Beans out of their house.
Issues faced by persona relating to food	Most of the time Beans can find food he is familiar with, consuming flora and insects around the area located in gardens or in the trees. Occasionally Beans encounters human food and eats it without knowing it may not be healthy for him; sometimes it makes him sick afterwards.

Figure 2. An example of an anthropomorphic non-human persona (Tomitsch et al., 2021)

The second persona description of **"Beans the possum"** (see figure 2) originates from a smart city project and presents the possum using a third-persona narrative. The possum is anthropomorphized through a human-like name "Beans", and expressions that attribute human emotions and experiences, such as references to its "frustrations" and the need for a "tree to call home". These narrative choices are clearly aimed at fostering empathy by encouraging readers to relate to the possum's plight by projecting familiar emotional and experiential qualities onto the non-human subject.

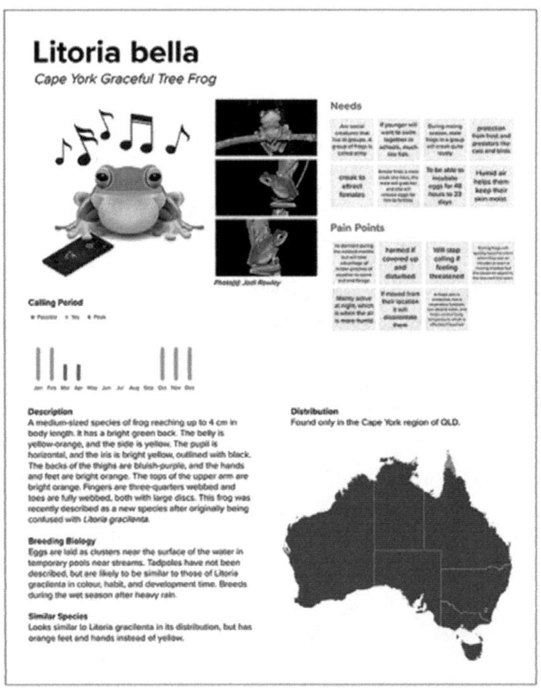

Figure 3. The persona description juxtaposes biological information with a cartoon-like illustration (Tomitsch & Bain, 2023)

The third persona description of **"Litoria bella"** (see figure 3) was developed for use in a citizen science app. The description mainly employs a formal, biological tone, detailing the frog's needs and challenges. However, this narrative choice is juxtaposed with a cartoon-like illustration of a frog using a mobile phone. The contrast between the factual biological information and the playful, anthropomorphic illustration creates a dissonance that blends realism with fantasy.

Collectively, the three examples clearly highlight differences to conveying information, illustrating varying balances between delivering accurate biological details and incorporating more anthropomorphic elements to engage the audience.

4. CONCLUSION

As demonstrated by the three examples, non-human persona descriptions largely build upon established templates used for human persona, incorporating elements like narrative styles and visual illustrations. However, significant variations exist in how non-human personas are constructed. These variations range from factual, encyclopedic representations to anthropomorphic approaches that assign human-like qualities to non-human entities. While some personas aim to foster empathy by humanizing non-human species, others focus more on providing practical information relevant to human interests. Despite these advances, the development and application of non-human personas remain in their early stages. There is a clear need for further research to understand how different narrative techniques, tones of voice, and levels of anthropomorphism impact empathy and engagement. Better understanding and refining these elements, would allow designers to create more effective tools to bridge the gap between human and non-human considerations in design processes, which could eventually contribute to more inclusive and ecologically responsible technological advancements.

REFERENCES

Bashir, E., & Attfield, S. (2018). An International Survey of Practitioners' Views on Personas: Benefits, Resource Demands and Pitfalls. *International Journal on Advances in Software, 11*(3 & 4), 299–310.

Borthwick, M., Tomitsch, M., & Gaughwin, M. (2022). From human-centred to life-centred design: Considering environmental and ethical concerns in the design of interactive products. *Journal of Responsible Technology, 10*(100032), 2666–6596. https://doi.org/10.1016/j.jrt.2022.100032.

Da Silva, T. S., Silveira, F. F., Silveira, M. S., Hellmann, T., & Maurer, F. (2015). A systematic mapping on agile UCD across the major agile and HCI conferences. *Lecture Notes in Computer Science (Including Subseries Lecture Notes in Artificial Intelligence and Lecture Notes in Bioinformatics), 9159*. https://doi.org/10.1007/978-3-319-21413-9_7

Dittmar, A., & Forbrig, P. (2019). Integrating Personas and Use Case Models. In D. Lamas, F. Loizides, L. Nacke, H. Petrie, M. Winckler, & P. Zaphiris (Eds.), *Human-Computer Interaction – INTERACT 2019* (Vol. 11746, pp. 666–686). Springer International Publishing. https://doi.org/10.1007/978-3-030-29381-9_40

French, F., Mancini, C., & Sharp, H. (2017). Exploring Research through Design in Animal Computer Interaction. *Proceedings of the Fourth International Conference on Animal-Computer Interaction*, 1–12. https://doi.org/10.1145/3152130.3152147

Gatto, G., & McCardle, J. R. (2019). Multispecies Design and Ethnographic Practice: Following Other-Than-Humans as a Mode of Exploring Environmental Issues. *Sustainability*, *11*(18), 5032. https://doi.org/10.3390/su11185032

Giaccardi, E., & Redström, J. (2020). Technology and More-Than-Human Design. *Design Issues*, *36*(4), 33–44. https://doi.org/10.1162/desi_a_00612

Guan, K. W., Salminen, J. O., Nielsen, L., Jung, S.-G., & Jansen, B. J. (2021). Information Design for Personas in Four Professional Domains of User Experience Design, Healthcare, Market Research, and Social Media Strategy. *Proceedings of the 54th Hawaii International Conference on System Sciences*, 4446–4455.

Hernandez-Santin, C., Amati, M., Bekessy, S. & Desha, C. (2023). Integrating biodiversity as a non-human stakeholder within urban development. Landscape and Urban Planning, 232, 104678

Jylkäs, T., Aijälä, M., Vuorikari, T., & Rajab, V. (2018). AI assistants as non-human actors in service design. *Proc of DMI Academic Design Management Conference*, 1–2.

Life-centered Design Lab. (n.d.). Non-Human and Non-User Personas. https://lifecentred.design/non-human-personas/non-human-and-non-user-personas

Mancini, C. (2011). Animal-computer interaction: A manifesto. *Interactions*, *18*(4), 69–73. https://doi.org/10.1145/1978822.1978836

Matthews, T., Judge, T., & Whittaker, S. (2012). How do designers and user experience professionals actually perceive and use personas? *Proceedings of the 2012 ACM Annual Conference on Human Factors in Computing Systems - CHI '12*, 1219. https://doi.org/10.1145/2207676.2208573

Nielsen, L. (2024). Personas, Scenarios, Journey Maps, and Storyboards. In C. Stephanidis & G. Salvendy, *User Experience Methods and Tools in Human-Computer Interaction* (1st ed., pp. 71–98). CRC Press. https://doi.org/10.1201/9781003495161-4

Nielsen, L., Hansen, K. S., Stage, J., & Billestrup, J. (2015). A template for design personas: Analysis of 47 persona descriptions from Danish industries and organizations. *International Journal of Sociotechnology and Knowledge Development*, *7*(1), 45–61. https://doi.org/10.4018/ijskd.2015010104

Nielsen, L., Larusdottir, M., & Larsen, L. B. (2021). Understanding Users Through Three Types of Personas. In C. Ardito, R. Lanzilotti, A. Malizia, H. Petrie, A. Piccinno, G. Desolda, & K. Inkpen (Eds.), *Human-Computer Interaction – INTERACT 2021* (pp. 330–348). Springer International Publishing.

Nielsen, L., & Storgaard Hansen, K. (2014). Personas is applicable: A study on the use of personas in Denmark. *Proceedings of the 32nd Annual ACM Conference on Human Factors in Computing Systems*. https://doi.org/10.1145/2556288.2557080

NTNU, Norway, & Tarcan, B. (2022, June 16). *Making-with the environment through more-than-human design*. DRS2022: Bilbao. https://doi.org/10.21606/drs.2022.347

Poleac, D. (2023). Responsive Design Thinking: Transitioning from Human-Centered to a Planetary-Centric Approach to Innovation. Principles and Perspectives. *Springer Proceedings in Business and Economics*, 1–13. https://doi.org/10.1007/978-3-031-19656-0_1

Salminen, J., Guan, K., Nielsen, L., Jung, S., & Jansen, B. J. (2020). A Template for Data-Driven Personas: Analyzing 31 Quantitatively Oriented Persona Profiles. In S. Yamamoto & H. Mori (Eds.), *Human Interface and the Management of Information. Designing Information* (pp. 125–144). Springer International Publishing.

Tomlinson, B., Nardi, B. Stokols, D., Raturi, A. & Torrance A. W. (2022). Returning ecological wealth to nonhuman species through design: the case for ecosystemas. *Ecology and Society* 27, 2:34. https://doi.org/10.5751/ES-13324-270234

Tomitsch, M., & Bain, I. (2023, 12). Non-human personas in practice. *Medium*. https://uxdesign.cc/non-human personas-in-practice-5ad4c7a97799

Tomitsch, M., Fredericks, J., Vo, D., Frawley, J., & Foth, M. (2021). Non-human Personas. Including Nature in the Participatory Design of Smart Cities. *Interaction Design and Architecture(s)*, *50*, 102–130. https://doi.org/10.55612/s-5002-050-007

AFFORDANCES IN ACTION UP TO USER NEEDS: READING DESIGN-ORIENTED SOCIOLOGY IN THE DESIGN OF A RELATIONAL *TRUSTWORTHY GOVERNABLE PLATFORM*

Gianni Jacucci
Department of Information Engineering and Computer Science - DISI - University of Trento. Via Sommarive , 9 I-38123 Povo (TN), Italy

ABSTRACT

This focused and dedicated short research paper examines the architectural design work of a Trustworthy Governable Platform (TGP), that redefines the information paradigm for institutional communication platforms—particularly in relational enterprises—where complex social dynamics are at play. Examples include addressing accountability and ensuring contextual integrity. We adopt a design-oriented sociological perspective to uncover how the platform's creator ensured that its social use and meaning align with the specific situational needs from the outset. The study begins by examining the key features of social interactions that characterise relational enterprises, as identified and articulated by the author of the design process through selected theoretical approaches. Next, we analyse the communicative affordances of technology in action that are necessary to realise these social interaction features. Finally, we explore the design elements of the supporting information and communication infrastructure that the author deemed essential to enable the appropriate options for action. These elements ensure users experience the intended social usage and meaning of the technology in the context of relational enterprises. The purpose of the essay is to stimulate discussion on what we deem a most promising enterprise. TGP has been under active technical development for a number of years and, at the time of writing, is undergoing initial trials for deployment and appropriation.

KEYWORDS

Relational Enterprises, Communications on Information, Entrepreneurial, Management & Organisation Cybernetics, Socio-Cybernetics, Complex Adaptive System and Theory

1. INTRODUCTION

Technologically enhanced forms of social interaction and communication pose a new challenge to social studies: how to apply and integrate sociological insights into the development and design of these technologies. According to [Arminen 2002], design-oriented sociology represents an emerging field within the sociology of technology, addressing the communicative affordances of technologies [Dourish 2001, Hutchby 2001]—that is, the options for action these technologies enable.

The study of affordances focuses on the concrete use of technology, illuminating both its potential and its limitations. This approach enables critical and constructive insights. For example, it identifies limitations when a technology restricts certain actions in specific contexts, such as the computerisation of medical records or the implementation of portable computing devices on construction sites [Heath & Luff 2000] It also highlights shortcomings when technology fails to meet users' needs. Design-oriented sociology contributes to the design process by addressing the relationship between humans and technology, thus serving as a valuable resource. It facilitates the evaluation of design outcomes through what Luff *et al.* [2000] describe as "the reverse engineering of the social usage and meaning of technology in action."

In this paper, we examine the design work of Mike Martin [2024a] on the architecture of a Trustworthy Governable Platform (TGP). This platform revolutionises the information paradigm in institutional communication platforms, particularly in relational enterprises where complex social affordances—such as accountability [Jacucci and Martin 2025] and contextual integrity [Nissenbaum 2010]—are critical. Using a design-oriented sociological lens, we explore how Martin ensured, from the outset, that the social use and meaning of the technology align with situational needs. Of course, any errors or omissions in the design process are subject to evaluation ex post.

The methodology we use in addressing the relationship between human parties and technology is straight forward: we start by considering the key social interaction features characterising relational enterprises, as exposed by the most pregnant theory approaches selected and declared by the author of the design process [Martin 2024a]. We then reason about the communicative affordances of technology in action required to grant the realisation of those key social interaction features. Finally, we consider the aspects of the design of the support information and communication infrastructure the author considered capable of enabling the options for action that deliver to users the correct social usage and meaning of technology in action they need in relational enterprises. Thus, our analytical results are directly compared with those of the author, the prose of which we report in summaries.

Our aim in this review essay is just to frame the recount of the design work, within the design-oriented sociology concept. This will capture in a holistic picture the several intertwined threads of concern that Martin has followed in his original work, striving to serve user's social needs.

We expect in our case that the reverse engineering of the social usage and meaning of technology in action [Arminen 2002] be straight forward, if not null, in terms of limitations or spurious side effects on the social usage and meaning of its technology in action w. r. t. what is needed in the situation, as TGP has been precisely designed for the purpose of respecting them. In particular, as the author's approach has been declaratively design-oriented sociology aware – albeit not in this terminology -, it has been intentionally *exceedingly careful* in selectively designing a socially respectful conversational theory and model.

The final purpose of the essay is to stimulate discussion on what we deem a most promising enterprise. We wish to make clear that the TGP has been under active technical development for a number of years and, at the time of writing, is undergoing initial trials for deployment and appropriation.

2. METHODOLOGY FOR REVIEWING

In Section 3 we describe the key theory elements called upon by the author to play a role in the design of TGP, listed here:

A. He characterises the key social interaction features of relational enterprises [Martin *et al.* 2024].
B. He introduces epistemic registers as a classification into a vertical stack, of the many different related aspects, and level of meaning, in the socio technical arena [Martin & Wilson 2020].
C. He reintroduces the lost paradigm of information to be used in institutional platforms: from Data Processing and Distribution to Information on Communications [Martin & Wilson 2020]
D. He calls upon a cybernetic thinker [Krippendorff 2009] to better define the specific features of the social situation at hand: of outmost cybernetic complexity, in which considering human experience is shown as mandatory.
E. In which authentic communicative action is the norm, as specified by a philosopher [Habermas 1984]. Thus requiring mutual understanding among participants through access to conversations about conversations: a well-known fundamental aspect of human communication and interaction.
F. He examines goal direction in terms of the value of actions [Martin 2024a], and considers its character in relational settings.
G. He examines information privacy and access control, in a systematic approach towards legitimate expectations of reciprocal respect in social interaction, in what is called contextual integrity [Martin 2024].
H. Finally, he recalls key aspects of conversational modelling [Martin 2024a, Martin 2024b], as a quest for order in representing social interaction by language use. Thus opening the way to define a conversation theory and conversation model design aiming at the concrete realisation of the desired affordances of communication technology in action.

From the analysis of these elements, in Section 4 we identify the desired list of theory derived affordances, which satisfy the social usage and meaning of technology in action, designed to supporting users in relational enterprises.

In Section 5 we then check the result against synthesis, by exposing it to a direct, implicit comparison with Martin's complete design work: a work in designing the support infrastructure that in fact localises the application of the entire set of these theory elements together, to the context and structure of relational enterprises, in which human experience is mandatory and authentic communicative action is the norm. For this, we report here, in summary, but in much of his own concepts and approach, the foundational detailed design work of Martin, of which the present paper is a sociological reading. The agnition event of each element, in the overall picture, is a rewarding one, as always.

In Section 6 we let address novelty and significance of Martin's approach to the design of the TGP, introducing a comprehensive view on respecting people's right to participate in deciding policy and goals of purposeful social action [Martin 2025, Martin & Jacucci 2025].

3. MARTIN'S SELECTION OF FLASHES OF THEORY TO BE INVOLVED

A. Relational Enterprises

The key character of relationality is concerned with peoples' experience, not just their interactions. It is direct human experience, requiring both human knowledgeable participation, and evaluation. [Martin *et al.* 2024]. With far reaching consequences. We need explore how relationality could be inscribed in information infrastructures and reflected in the management and governance systems they support. To do this, we must examine how relationality can be appropriately conceptualised and the nature of the information systems in which these conceptualisations could be inscribed and could evolve. Any relationship, whatever its starting point or domains of action, must involve change and learning.

B. Epistemic Registers

The concept of *epistemic registers*, illustrated in a published work on Inter-organisational systems [Martin & Wilson 2020], It serves to examine the stack of epistemic registers of the architectural discourse of socio- technical systems, and operate hermeneutic distinctions in social affairs: a basic factual and constitutive engineering level, an informatics semiotic level above it, an hermeneutic conversational level above it, a fully socio-cultural level above all. A distinction necessary to elaborate and interpret cybernetic meta level concepts, like intention, accountability, and the cultural colouring of social affairs.

C. Sense making of Human Enterprise

The general and exhaustive cybernetic view of sense making in human enterprise requires including, besides actors actions and objectives, also principles, roles, responsibilities: meta issues with respect to functional, first order data, allowing the address of intention and accountability [Martin 2024a, Martin & Wilson 2020, see also Martin *et al.* 2009].

D. Lived experience in relational enterprises: a requirement of determinability of systems

From Krippendorff analysis [Krippendorff 2009] – a cybernetics theorist - of the determinability of generic systems, relationality, as a socio-cultural phenomenon, is characterised as *constitutively determinable;* meaning that:

a. users must take part in its creation and evolution;
b. being experiential – not just observable data -, it must include a second-order cybernetic.

From Krippendorff's distinction comes a disciplinary cross-over: the plan changes from social relationality to informational / behavioural aspects of purposeful, human activity, shifting epistemic register from the conversational to informatics: <u>a second important result</u>, exposing the causality, in why relationality demands a shift in information systems paradigm [Martin 2025].

E. Authentic Communicative Actions

From Habermas definitions [Habermas 1984], authentic, communicative human actions are committed to mutual understanding. Tending to the satisfaction of this commitment requires a most demanding holistic approach to correctly enabling hermeneutic functions.

F. Valuaction

"Valuaction" which Halprin coined [1970], is associated with our concept of relational governance. It recognises that, in creative, relational contexts, adding value, extracting value and evaluation cannot be alienated from each other and associated with different actors: they are all part and parcel of shared conversational work.

G. Contextual Integrity

It is defined by Helen Nissenbaum, while considering privacy, as the right to live in a world where our expectations about the flow of personal information are, for the most part, met; expectations that are shaped not only by force of habit and convention but a general confidence in the mutual support that flows according to key organising principles of social life, including moral and political ones." [Nissenbaum 2010, pp. 231]

H. Conversation modelling

Here, the notion of conversation is analysed, a conversation theory developed and a conversation modelling language and notation presented. The objective is to create an architectural framework for structured communication service definition and to identify the high level requirements on and affordances of any technical service platform which claims to be able to support and sustain relational enterprise and services.

4. DESIRED AFFORDANCES OF TECHNOLOGY IN ACTION

From the corresponding theory elements described in Section 3, we derive the affordances:

A. Relational Enterprises -> The notion that an information system to support relationality must exhibit evolving structures and behaviours, is an important one. Any relational system must be in a constant state of re-determination, capturing and inscribing these developmental changes in its structure and operation, not just in the content that it records and communicates. All this requires that principles of the community and rules of the game be explicitly defined, represented, shared and maintained; actors and actions be also identified and shared, as well as roles and responsibilities in management and in governance; so that intentionality and full accountability be available always.

B. Epistemic Registers -> The introduction of the concept of the vertical stack of epistemic registers is necessary to access and operate hermeneutic distinctions in social affairs. A necessary distinction to elaborate and interpret cybernetic meta level concepts, like intention, accountability, and the cultural colouring of social affairs. In particular, it enables the link of the conversational epistemic register to the underlying informatics one, and it exposes the causality of why relationality demands a shift in information systems paradigm.

C. Sense making of Human Enterprise -> Change paradigm of information on institutional platforms: from Data Processing and Distribution (DPD), to Information on Communications (IC) , for including and tracking besides actors actions and objectives, also principles, roles, responsibilities: meta issues with respect to functional, first order data, allowing the address of intention and accountability. For this we need separating functioning from questioning, executing from learning, acting a simple act from performing a role with responsibility, performance from intention, content from provenance, ability from accountability.

D. Lived Experience -> The social complexity of relational life has unavoidable consequences: here a very generic simple emergent seed (the primordial system) grows and is nurtured as relationality evolves from use, developing TGP a piece at a time (while commercial platforms need be completed to work); the infrastructural architecture here must evolve through experience by user involvement.

E. Authentic Communicative Actions -> An interface set-up expose provenance and content in each turn of conversation, facilitating the performance of conversations on conversations, by allowing direct choice of the object conversation on a basic ground floor, and the deposition of the new conversation act on a dedicated upper floor, thus allowing to keep track in a transparent way – especially in the distribution of roles and responsibilities both for management and governance, what made sense to all, what was agreed, if it still made sense, and how and by whom it was agreed that it be changed

F. Valuaction -> All the conversational activities of, and in, the relational enterprise are valuactions which is equivalent to the normative assertion that all roles should participate, in some way, in governance, and the relational enterprise is necessarily co-creative and co-productive. Realising this assumption involves conversations between sets of participants which produces a two kinds of discourse: Policy and Goals. We refer to the first of these discourses as "Governance" and the second as "Managed Operation".

G. Contextual Integrity -> Access control, and other tactics of relating content to provenance and to intended recipients, helping to reach integral respect of ownership, privacy, and legitimate participation both in management and in governance

H. Conversational Analysis -> Define an appropriate conversation model (publications, sessions, etc.) aiming at the concrete realisation of the desired affordances of communication technology in action of points C, D, E.

5. PUTTING THEORY IN CONTEXT IN MARTIN'S HOLISTIC APPROACH

We take Mike Martin's design work on TGP from three recent publications:

P1: a book chapter entitled: *Moving towards Relational Services – the role of digital service environments and platforms?* [Martin *et al.* 2024]

P2: two related book chapters on: *How and why relationality demands a shift in information systems paradigm.* [Martin 2025, Martin & Jacucci 2025]

P3: an article on: *The Trustworthy, Governable Platform: supporting accountability and governability in complex, multi-party enterprise.* [Martin 2024]

The work described in these publications has two foundational antecedents by the same author:

- in 2009, a paper on the social informatics intervention, theory, method, and practice [Martin *et al.* 2009], in which the cybernetic character of purposeful human action is examined in detail
- in 2020, two papers introducing a new socio-technical approach to information systems [9. 10], in which the development and merging of the communication and computer industry is interpreted along the last forty years or so, explaining a) the surge and establishment, in the present installed base of institutional platforms, of the Data Processing and Distribution (DPD) information paradigm, limited to treating cybernetic first order, functional data; and b) the introduction of the concept of epistemic registers, necessary to access and operate hermeneutic distinctions in social affairs.

We present an overview of the work, taken from P2. In this chapter the purposefulness and goal directed nature of relationality is analysed, from a cybernetic perspective, using Krippendorff's concepts of systems determination [Krippendorff 2009].

The *key arguments* of the Chapter are clear. They are recalled here, with the main results. The key character of relationality and of relational public service is direct human experience, requiring both human knowledgeable participation, and evaluation. Exploring the epistemology of systems as black boxes, systems that are based on human participation are defined *constitutively determinable* by cybernetics scholar Krippendorff [2009], who also indicates that these are by necessity second order cybernetic systems. In fact, authentic, communicative human actions are committed to mutual understanding (Habermas). The conversations taking place in the information infrastructures supporting evolving relationality, involve communicative actions. This implies that a) conversations on conversations will be part of these conversations, and b) they will regard, in addition to other things, second cybernetic order governance of all relational aspects. Krippendorff's argument is here seen to be crucial in linking the socio cultural science of relationality of public service to the logics of informatics and platform engineering of support infrastructures; offering, via the analysis of purposeful human enterprise, the pathway to a theory of relational enterprise, connected to a theory of conversational information communication.

Relevant results:

1. Relational governance and human learning are (re)-institutionalised in public service and infrastructure
2. Causality is exposed of why relationality demands a shift in information systems paradigm
3. Conversations must comprehend conversations on conversations, i. e., second cybernetic order governance
4. Relational socio-technical systems live in co-evolution with their socio-cultural context: they cannot be pre-designed, must emerge and grow from the appropriation of a simple primordial system; emergence with the operation and governance of a community of interest and practice
5. The role of the IT industry changes: from design and development of commercial infrastructure, to supporting user communities in structuring their own infrastructure.

6. CONCLUSION

As indicated at the beginning of the discussion Section 6, because in this paper we have been adopting the design oriented stance, we need underline that in the TGP, the conventional domain of design in the Information System is transferred entirely to the user community and the "technical" design domain is rendered entirely infrastructural, in the form of support services for user defined structured conversations. I.e. the shift from the DPD to the IC systems paradigm. This shows that design-oriented sociology, and its analysis of affordances of technology in action, have two consequences of rank: each TGP community is ultimately responsible of adopting, in social interactions, the degree of emancipation hat it desires, and that it can afford; and, the main known sources for distortion of the will of users, traditional motive for advocating critical system thinking, with TGP have dissolved.

ACKNOWLEDGEMENT

The present author had access to much unpublished as well as published material of, and has enjoyed innumerous discussions with, Professor Mike Martin. For this he wishes to express his deep gratitude.

REFERENCES

Arminen, I. (2002) *Design-oriented Sociology.* Acta Sociologica, 45, 315-321

Dourish, P. (2001) *Where the Action Is: The Foundations of Embodied Interaction.* Cambridge: MIT Press.

Habermas, J. (1984) *Theory of Communicative Action*, trans. Thomas McCarthy, Boston: Beacon Press,

Halprin, Lawrence (1970) *The RSVP cycles; creative processes in the human environment.* George Braziller Inc., New York (1970, c1969) ISBN 0-8076-0557-3

Heath, C. & Luff, P. (2000) *Technology in Action.* Cambridge: Cambridge University Press

Hutchby, I. (2001) *Conversation and Technology from the Telephone to the Internet.* Cambridge: Polity.

Jacucci, G. and Martin, M. (2025) *Advancing Accountability on ICT Platforms to Navigate AI Integration in S-T Systems A New Paradigm for Interplay of Accountability and Interpretation*, UKAIS 2025 Conference, 23-24 April 2025, Newcastle University Business School. Proceedings, to be published.

Krippendorff, K. (2009) *Ross Ashby's information theory: a bit of history, some solutions to problems, and what we face today.* International Journal of General Systems, Vol 47, page 204, Published online: 30 Jan 2009.

Luff, P. Hindmarsh, J. & Heath, C. (eds.) (2000). *Workplace Studies: Recovering Work Practice and Informing System Design.* Cambridge: Cambridge University Press.

Martin M. & Jacucci, G. (2025) *Modelling, reasoning about and providing platforms to enable relational conversations.* Book Chapter to be published in *Futures* .., ibid. see Martin, M. (2025)

Martin, M. & Wilson, R. (2020) *Inter-organisational systems: a neo-socio-technical perspective.* UK Academy for Information Systems Conference Proceedings 2020. 22. https://aisel.aisnet.org/ukais2020/22.

Martin, M. (2024a) *The Trustworthy, Governable Platform: supporting accountability and governability in complex, multiparty enterprise.* Submitted to ITAIS2024 conference, Piacenza, October 11 2024.

Martin, M. (2024b) *A High Level Specification of a Trustworthy Governable Platform.* Submitted to ITAIS2024 conference, Piacenza, October 11 2024.

Martin, M. (2025) *How can relationality and relational enterprise be conceptualised and modelled?* Book Chapter to be published in *Futures in Public Management: The emerging Relational approach to public services.* Volume 8 in the series of *Critical Perspectives on International Public Management.* Rob Wilson, Hannah Hesselgreaves, David Jamieson, Melissa Hawkins, Martin King, Jonathan Kimmitt, eds. Leeds, England: Emeral

Martin, M. Walsh, S. Wilson, R. (2009) *A Social Informatics Intervention: theory, method and practice*" KITE, Newcastle University: http://www.woa.sistemacongressi.com/web/woa2009/papers/Martin_Walsh_Wilson.pdf

Martin, M. Wilson, R. & Jamieson, D. (2024) *Moving towards Relational Services – the role of digital service environments and platforms?* Chapter 11 in S. Baines et al., Co-Creation in Public Services for Innovation and Social Justice. Draft typescript preprint.

Nissenbaum, H. (2010) *Privacy in Context: Technology, Policy, and Integrity of Social Life. Stanford Law Books*

HUMAN-AI INTERACTION IN DECISION-MAKING: A SYSTEMATIC LITERATURE REVIEW AND FUTURE DIRECTIONS

Zhe Zhu and Tero Vartiainen
University of Vaasa
Wolffintie 32, Vaasa, Finland

ABSTRACT

AI helps organizations in decision-making by enhancing data analysis, predictive modelling, and providing insights. However, gaps remain in understanding the phenomenon from a socio-technical aspect. By systematically reviewing 77 articles, the study identifies 21 elements impacting decision-making across six dimensions and suggests future research on task complexity, culture, and ethical frameworks.

KEYWORDS

Artificial Intelligence, Human-AI Interaction, Decision-Making, Socio-Technical Systems, Systematic Literature Review

1. INTRODUCTION

The rapid development of artificial intelligence (AI) has revolutionized decision-making processes, especially within organizational settings (Raji & Buolamwini, 2019). By integrating AI technologies, enterprises are increasingly leveraging its potential to assist in data analysis, predictive modelling, and providing actionable insights to gain a competitive advantage (Steiner et al., 2018). However, despite these notable capabilities, successful and seamless integration of AI into decision-making processes remains challenging for many organizations (Steyvers, 2024). These challenges often result from a lack of understanding of effective human-AI interaction, as well as issues related to trust, transparency, and alignment of AI capabilities with human needs (Mahmud et al., 2022).

Current literature has largely focused on the technical attributes of AI, such as algorithmic improvements and data processing capabilities, while relatively little attention has been given to the broader socio-technical aspects (Steyvers, 2024). While substantial research exists on trust in AI, human-computer interaction, and AI-enabled collaboration, these studies often lack contextualization within organizational decision-making frameworks. This oversight creates a significant research gap in understanding the socio-technical factors that influence the effectiveness of human-AI interaction for decision-making (Puranam, 2021; Shrestha et al., 2019). Key factors include trust, transparency, and user involvement, alongside cultural and infrastructural elements that shape AI's integration into organizational processes (Wu et al., 2022) . Bridging this gap requires a holistic perspective that considers not just the technology but also the social, cultural, and organizational conditions that shape human-AI interaction.

This research aims to fill this gap through a socio-technical perspective by providing a comprehensive understanding of the key elements that influence human-AI decision-making. Specifically, we address the following research questions: (1) What are the key elements that influence the dynamics and effectiveness of human-AI interaction for decision-making? (2) How do technical capabilities and social dimensions interact to shape the outcomes of human-AI decision-making processes across organizational contexts? (3) What are the future directions in this field? To answer these questions, this study identifies and categorizes key elements under a socio-technical framework, exploring their interrelationships and the conditions under which they enhance or hinder decision-making. This framework aims to optimize human-AI interaction by fostering a balance between the technical and social dimensions of decision-making. Ultimately, this research provides actionable insights to guide the integration of AI into decision-making processes, equipping organizations to navigate the complexities of human-AI collaboration effectively and ethically.

2. METHODOLOGY

We conducted a systematic literature review of 77 articles. These articles were identified through a structured process proposed by Madan and Ashok (2013) involving an initial search in major databases (i.e., World of Science, Scopus) with the particular Boolean search string ("machine learning" OR "AI" OR "artificial intelligence") AND ("HAI" OR "human-AI" OR "human-AI interaction") AND ("decision-making" OR "make decision" OR "algorithmic decision-making"), followed by screening for relevance and a detailed full-text review. Inclusion criteria were limited to journal articles or conference papers published in English after 2010 to ensure contemporaneity and rigor. Studies were excluded if they were unrelated to organizational contexts or lacked human involvement. This ensured the review remained relevant to understanding human-AI interaction in decision-making.

A comprehensive search initially identified 154 articles, supplemented by snowball sampling, which added 25 articles through reference examination, resulting in 179 unique studies after duplicate removal. A title and abstract review narrowed the pool to 117 articles. Finally, a thorough full-text review was deployed and 77 were selected for qualitative analysis and synthesis.

We applied the antecedents-phenomenon-consequences logic (Pereira, 2023) to thematically analyze the literature. In this framework, antecedents refer to the problems of AI integration in decision-making, phenomenon refers to the practice of human-AI interaction and its key features, and consequences capture the outcomes of this integration. This process allowed us to distinguish the key elements in decision-making, themes, and relationships under the 'antecedents-phenomenon-consequences' framework while highlighting gaps and opportunities for future research in this field.

3. RESULTS

This systematic literature review identifies twenty-one elements influencing decision-making, categorized into six socio-technical dimensions: people, goals, technology, processes, infrastructure, and culture (see Table 1). These dimensions are grounded in the socio-technical perspective, which emphasizes the interplay between human factors, organizational objectives, technological capabilities, and cultural contexts. The classification based on the socio-technical perspective highlights the interconnected nature of technical and social factors across all dimensions. For instance, the 'people' dimension focuses on trust, cognitive biases, and user involvement. Trust in AI exemplifies a socio-technical issue where transparency and explainability (technical) interact with user training and cultural attitudes (social) to shape its development. Similarly, the 'technology' dimension emphasizes features like explainable AI and adaptive systems, which require alignment with organizational and user needs to ensure effective integration. This classification enables a structured analysis of human-AI decision-making, capturing both technological advancements and the social considerations essential for success.

The *people* dimension is essential for understanding the dynamics of human-AI interaction, focusing on aspects such as trust in AI, cognitive biases, and user involvement. Trust in AI heavily shapes whether users accept or reject AI recommendations, influenced by factors such as system transparency, reliability, and fairness (Gomez et al., 2023). Ensuring users are aware of the AI system's capabilities and limitations is key to maintaining appropriate levels of trust, thereby preventing over-reliance or skepticism, both of which can hinder effective decision-making (Wu et al., 2022). Cognitive biases are another major challenge, with biases such as confirmation bias or overconfidence negatively impacting decision outcomes (Wilson et al., 2019). Addressing these biases through AI designs that prompt users to critically evaluate outputs can mitigate their adverse effects on decision quality. Additionally, direct user participation in AI processes, such as contributing to recommendations and providing feedback, fosters a sense of ownership and satisfaction, which ultimately improves decision outcomes (Gomez et al., 2023). Overall, building trust, minimizing biases, and involving users actively are all essential to creating effective, synergistic human-AI interactions.

Table 1. Key dimensions and elements influencing human-AI decision-making

Dimensions	Key elements	Representative examples
People	Trust in AI	Wu et al., 2022
	Cognitive bias	Wilson et al., 2019
	User involvement	Lin 2024
Goals	Improving decision-making	Steyvers, 2024
	Achieving complementarity	Morrison et al., 2024
	Bias reduction	Schoeffer et al., 2024
	Enhancing transparency and explainability	Shulner-Tal et al., 2024
Technology	AI Models and Tools	Zhou & Khatibi, 2024
	Anthropomorphism	Schelble et al., 2024
	Explainable AI	Shulner-Tal et al., 2024
	Adaptive Systems	Morrison et al., 2024
Processes	Decision Workflow	Lin 2024
	Interaction Pattern	Steyvers, 2024
	Feedback Loop	Shulner-Tal et al., 2024
	Stage of Decision-Making	Felin, 2024
Infrastructure	Data Architecture	Shrestha et al., 2021
	Integration of AI	Felin, 2024
	Scalability and Reliability	Felin, 2024
Culture	Cultural Attitude Towards AI	Shulner-Tal et al., 2024
	Organizational Culture	Wang et al., 2024
	Cross-Cultural Differences	Shulner-Tal et al., 2024

The *goals* dimension describes the broader objectives of human-AI interaction in decision-making, such as improving accuracy, achieving complementarity, reducing biases, and enhancing transparency. Improving decision accuracy is a key motivation for AI integration, as AI excels at processing large volumes of data and identifying patterns that enhance decision quality, particularly in complex situations where human judgment may fall short (Wilson et al., 2019). Achieving complementarity between human intuition and AI capabilities enables the combination of AI's analytical strengths with human contextual insights to optimize decision-making (Felin, 2024). Bias reduction is also an ethical goal for effective human-AI interaction, with AI models designed to recognize and mitigate biases in data or user assumptions, thereby promoting fairness (Schoeffer et al., 2024). Transparency and explainability are equally fundamental to fostering trust and collaboration, as explainable AI (XAI) helps users understand not only the outputs but also the rationale behind AI recommendations, which is vital for confidence in AI-assisted decision-making (Bucinca, 2024). Collectively, these goals support the optimization of human-AI collaboration for improved decision-making in organizational contexts.

The *technology* dimension emphasizes the tools and techniques that enable effective AI-driven decision-making, including AI models and tools, anthropomorphism, explainable AI, and adaptive systems. AI models and tools are vital for enhancing decision-making, providing the computational power and sophisticated algorithms needed to analyze complex datasets (Zhou & Khatibi, 2024). By identifying patterns and generating insights often beyond human capability, AI models significantly improve decision efficiency. Anthropomorphism is another important element, involving the assignment of human-like qualities to AI systems to enhance user engagement (Schelble et al., 2024). However, it must be managed carefully to avoid creating unrealistic expectations. XAI supports transparency by making AI decisions interpretable, which is critical for fostering trust and collaboration (Shulner-Tal et al., 2024). Finally, adaptive systems, as discussed by Morrison et al., (2024), adjust their behaviors to user needs and decision contexts, making them highly effective in dynamic environments by responding to users' actions in real-time.

The key components of the *processes* dimension include decision workflows, interaction patterns, feedback loops, and decision stages. Effective workflows are necessary for smoothly integrating AI into decision processes. Waqar (2024) and Lin (2024) emphasize designing workflows that clearly define when and how AI recommendations should be incorporated, ensuring efficient collaboration between humans and AI. Interaction patterns are also integral to shaping productive human-AI relationships. Structured interaction patterns, as highlighted by Vereschak et al., (2024) and Wang et al., (2024), help foster clear communication and support users in effectively interpreting AI inputs. Feedback loops play an important role in refining AI systems over time. Integrating user feedback allows these systems to continuously adapt and improve, aligning their outputs with human expectations (Waqar, 2024). AI systems should also provide targeted support at different stages of decision-making, from initial data gathering to final recommendations (Felin, 2024).

The *infrastructure* dimension highlights the organizational and technical support needed for effective human-AI integration. Robust data architecture is essential for ensuring AI systems receive reliable and high-quality data (Shrestha et al., 2021). Integrating AI into existing organizational processes requires both technical and cultural readiness (Salimzadeh & Gadiraju, 2024). Organizations must develop the necessary infrastructure to effectively accommodate AI, while ensuring that their workforce is prepared for this transition. Scalability and reliability are also important considerations. AI systems must be designed to scale across diverse contexts while maintaining consistent performance (Zhou & Khatibi, 2024). Scalability enables these systems to handle increasing data loads, whereas reliability ensures effectiveness even under challenging conditions.

The *culture* dimension addresses the social and organizational factors influencing AI adoption. Cultural attitudes towards AI play a significant role in determining user acceptance (Shulner-Tal et al., 2024). Adaptable AI systems that respect local cultural norms are more likely to be trusted and adopted. Similarly, organizational culture has a strong impact on the successful implementation of AI; open, innovation-driven environments are more conducive to effective AI adoption (Wu et al., 2022). Finally, addressing cross-cultural differences is key for AI systems deployed globally—adaptable systems that respect cultural diversity foster greater acceptance and encourage effective human-AI collaboration (Vereschak et al., 2024).

4. FUTURE DIRECTIONS

Several key avenues for future research emerge. First, further exploration is needed to understand how evolving tasks, from routine to complex, affect human-AI collaboration and decision quality. Additionally, more research should focus on how cultural differences, both at the organizational and societal levels, influence trust in AI and the design of culturally sensitive AI systems. New metrics for evaluating AI systems should go beyond accuracy and transparency to include contributions to human creativity and collaborative problem-solving. Furthermore, the role of continuous feedback loops and adaptive learning in AI systems requires deeper examination, as these features can significantly enhance long-term system performance. Finally, research should focus on developing comprehensive ethical governance frameworks to ensure that AI systems operate transparently, accountably, and in alignment with human values, supporting responsible AI integration in decision-making.

5. CONCLUSION

The integration of AI into organizational decision-making offers significant potential but demands careful attention to the factors influencing human-AI collaboration. This study outlines key elements critical to fostering effective collaboration between humans and AI systems. Organizations that consider these elements can maximize the benefits of AI, ensuring that decision-making processes remain aligned with ethical standards and human values, leading to a more effective and supportive decision-making environment.

This study makes a critical theoretical contribution by providing a comprehensive literature review on human-AI decision-making through a socio-technical lens. By synthesizing insights from diverse studies, this review contributes to theoretical development by offering a structured framework that captures the complexity of human-AI collaboration. The findings of this study advance the understanding of human-AI decision-making by shifting the focus from a predominantly technological lens to a holistic socio-technical perspective. By identifying and categorizing key elements across interconnected dimensions, this study provides an organizing framework that captures the interplay between human, organizational, and technological factors. Furthermore, the research highlights how socio-technical factors interact with technological advancements like explainable AI, offering deeper insights into their interdependencies.

Practically, the framework serves as a diagnostic tool for organizations to assess and enhance their human-AI decision-making processes. By identifying potential issues like trust deficits or insufficient user involvement, managers can implement targeted interventions, such as deploying explainable AI or refining feedback systems. This application ensures that decision-making processes remain adaptive and aligned with organizational objectives and ethical standards.

REFERENCES

Buçinca, Z. (2024). *Optimizing Decision-Maker's Intrinsic Motivation for Effective Human-AI Decision-Making*. Paper presented at the Extended Abstracts of the CHI Conference on Human Factors in Computing Systems.

Felin, T., & Holweg, M. . (2024). Theory Is All You Need AI, Human Cognition, and Causal Reasoning. *Strategy Science*.

Gomez, C., Unberath, M., & Huang, C.-M. (2023). Mitigating knowledge imbalance in AI-advised decision-making through collaborative user involvement. *International Journal of Human-Computer Studies*, 172, 102977.

Lin, J., Tomlin, N., Andreas, J., & Eisner, J. . (2024). Decision-Oriented Dialogue for Human-AI Collaboration. *Transactions of the Association for Computational Linguistics*, 12, 892-911.

Madan, R., & Ashok, M. (2023). AI adoption and diffusion in public administration: A systematic literature review and future research agenda. *Government Information Quarterly*, 40(1), 101774.

Mahmud, H., Islam, A. N., Ahmed, S. I., & Smolander, K. (2022). What influences algorithmic decision-making? A systematic literature review on algorithm aversion. *Technological Forecasting and Social Change*, 175, 121390.

Morrison, K., Spitzer, P., Turri, V., Feng, M., Kühl, N., & Perer, A. (2024). The Impact of Imperfect XAI on Human-AI Decision-Making. *Proceedings of the ACM on Human-Computer Interaction*, 8(CSCW1), 1-39.

Pereira, V., Hadjielias, E., Christofi, M., & Vrontis, D. (2023). A systematic literature review on the impact of artificial intelligence on workplace outcomes: A multi-process perspective. *Human Resource Management Review*, 33(1), 100857.

Raji, I. D., & Buolamwini, J. (2019). *Actionable Auditing*. Paper presented at the Proceedings of the 2019 AAAI/ACM Conference on AI, Ethics, and Society.

Salimzadeh, S., & Gadiraju, U. (2024). *"DecisionTime": A Configurable Framework for Reproducible Human-AI Decision-Making Studies*. Paper presented at the Adjunct Proceedings of the 32nd ACM Conference on User Modeling, Adaptation and Personalization.

Schelble, B. G., Lopez, J., Textor, C., Zhang, R., McNeese, N. J., Pak, R., & Freeman, G. (2024). Towards Ethical AI: Empirically Investigating Dimensions of AI Ethics, Trust Repair, and Performance in Human-AI Teaming. *Hum Factors*, 66(4), 1037-1055.

Schoeffer, J., De-Arteaga, M., & Kühl, N. (2024). *Explanations, Fairness, and Appropriate Reliance in Human-AI Decision-Making*. Paper presented at the Proceedings of the CHI Conference on Human Factors in Computing Systems.

Shrestha, Y. R., Krishna, V., & von Krogh, G. (2021). Augmenting organizational decision-making with deep learning algorithms: Principles, promises, and challenges. *Journal of Business Research*, 123, 588-603.

Shulner-Tal, A., Kuflik, T., Kliger, D., & Mancini, A. (2024). Who Made That Decision and Why? Users' Perceptions of Human Versus AI Decision-Making and the Power of Explainable-AI. *International Journal of Human–Computer Interaction*, 1-18.

Steiner, D. F., MacDonald, R., Liu, Y., Truszkowski, P., Hipp, J. D., Gammage, C., . . . Stumpe, M. C. (2018). Impact of deep learning assistance on the histopathologic review of lymph nodes for metastatic breast cancer. *The American journal of surgical pathology*, 42(12), 1636-1646.

Steyvers, M., & Kumar, A. . (2024). Three challenges for AI-assisted decision-making. *Perspectives on Psychological Science*, 19(5), 722-734.

Vereschak, O., Alizadeh, F., Bailly, G., & Caramiaux, B. (2024). *Trust in AI-assisted Decision Making: Perspectives from Those Behind the System and Those for Whom the Decision is Made*. Paper presented at the Proceedings of the CHI Conference on Human Factors in Computing Systems.

Wang, B., Yuan, T., & Rau, P.-L. P. (2024). Effects of Explanation Strategy and Autonomy of Explainable AI on Human–AI Collaborative Decision-making. *International Journal of Social Robotics*, 16(4), 791-810.

Waqar, A. (2024). Intelligent decision support systems in construction engineering: An artificial intelligence and machine learning approaches. *Expert Systems with Applications*, 249, 123503.

Wilson, C. G., Bond, C. E., & Shipley, T. F. (2019). How can geologic decision-making under uncertainty be improved? Solid earth, 10(5), 1469-1488.

Wu, Y., Kim, K. J., & Mou, Y. (2022). Minority social influence and moral decision-making in human–AI interaction: The effects of identity and specialization cues. *New Media & Society*, 26(10), 5619-5637.

Zhou, Y., & Khatibi, S. (2024). A New AI Approach by Acquisition of Characteristics in Human Decision-Making Process. *Applied Sciences*, 14(13), 5469.

PATTERNS OF DEMAND FOR IS TEACHING PROVISION IN TELEMEDICINE: EDUCATIONAL CHALLENGES AND OPPORTUNITIES

Martin Zagar[1], Vladimir Mozetic[2], Marija Banac[2] and Alan Mutka[2]
[1]*RIT Croatia , Don Frana Bulica 6, 20000 Dubrovnik, Croatia*
[2]*Kvarner Health Tourism Cluster, Maršala Tita 188, 51410 Opatija, Croatia*

ABSTRACT

Telemedicine has evolved into a critical element in modern healthcare systems, driven by the integration of Information Systems (IS) and digital technologies. However, the educational infrastructure supporting this evolution has lagged, especially in preparing healthcare professionals to navigate these systems. This paper explores the patterns of demand for IS teaching provision in telemedicine, emphasizing the need for educational reforms to meet this growing demand. By analyzing telemedicine's role in healthcare systems, particularly in countries like Croatia, we discuss the gaps in telemedicine education, the need for micro-credentialing, and the adoption of new teaching models that align with IS advancements.

KEYWORDS

Telemedicine, Information Systems, Education, Digital Health, Micro-credentialing, Healthcare Professionals

1. INTRODUCTION

Telemedicine, defined as the use of Information and Communication Technologies (ICT) to deliver healthcare services remotely, offers numerous advantages, including improved access to care, cost reduction, and increased patient satisfaction, especially in rural and underserved areas (Smith et al., 2020). The expansion of telemedicine has been facilitated by advances in Information Systems (IS), which allow for the secure exchange of patient data, real-time consultations, and the integration of diagnostic and therapeutic tools (Dorsey & Topol, 2020). The growing reliance on telemedicine necessitates the development of digital competencies among healthcare professionals. Studies have shown that effective use of telemedicine depends on healthcare workers' familiarity with digital health technologies, such as electronic health records (EHR), video conferencing tools, and remote monitoring devices (Serper & Volk, 2018). However, many healthcare professionals lack adequate training in these areas, which limits their ability to fully utilize telemedicine systems. For instance, a study by Scott Kruse et al. (2018) highlighted that healthcare providers often struggle with the technical aspects of telemedicine, leading to lower adoption rates and suboptimal use of available technologies.

In countries like Croatia, the integration of telemedicine has been supported by national policies such as the Digital Croatia Strategy, which aims to align healthcare education with the European DigComp framework to improve digital literacy among healthcare professionals (Central State Office for the Development of the Digital Society, 2022). While these policies have provided a foundation for digital health integration, significant gaps remain in the educational infrastructure, particularly in the teaching of IS skills that are crucial for successful telemedicine implementation (Kaufman et al., 2018). Several studies have pointed to the need for a more robust educational framework to support the growing use of telemedicine. For example, a systematic review by Almathami, Win, and Vlahu-Gjorgievska (2020) identified inadequate training as one of the main barriers to telemedicine adoption, particularly in rural settings. The review emphasized the need for healthcare professionals to receive targeted training in telemedicine technologies to ensure effective and sustainable implementation. Additionally, research by George et al. (2019) on the role of micro-credentials in healthcare education suggests that modular, flexible training programs could help healthcare professionals develop the necessary IS skills to navigate telemedicine platforms.

This paper aims to explore the patterns of demand for IS teaching provision in telemedicine, focusing on the Croatian healthcare system. By examining the current state of telemedicine education and identifying gaps in IS training, this study provides insights into how educational reforms can better equip healthcare professionals to meet the challenges of a rapidly evolving healthcare landscape.

2. MATERIALS AND METHODS

This research utilized a mixed-methods approach to explore the patterns of demand for Information Systems (IS) teaching provision in telemedicine education. We conducted study focused on Croatia's healthcare system, particularly the development and implementation of telemedicine education and digital health training. Data collection was based on both quantitative and qualitative methods, capturing information from telemedicine centers, healthcare institutions, and education providers across Croatia.

2.1 Data Sources and Collection

Quantitative and qualitative data were gathered from healthcare institutions and telemedicine centers operating within Croatia's healthcare system. The analysis traced the evolution of telemedicine services in Croatia, with particular attention to the legislative framework supporting these services, the organizational structures involved, and the integration of digital health education into medical training programs.

2.1.1 Quantitative Data

The quantitative data comprised metrics on telemedicine service utilization, the number of telemedicine centers, and the availability of digital health and telemedicine training programs in the healthcare sector. Croatia has established a comprehensive network of telemedicine centers that provide healthcare services across a range of categories, including regular, emergency, and surveillance services. These centers operate with both direct (real-time communication) and indirect (data transfer without direct interaction) service models. Telemedicine services such as remote consultations, diagnostics, and monitoring have been widely implemented, particularly in emergency medical services. Data on telemedicine service utilization indicated that counties such as Primorsko-goranska demonstrated the highest usage rates of telemedicine services, particularly for emergency care. The telemedicine network in these regions is well-developed, with high-speed digital communication infrastructures that enable efficient service delivery. The analysis of these data allowed the study to pinpoint regions with greater telemedicine adoption and identify where the demand for IS training is most pressing.

2.1.2 Qualitative Data

The qualitative component of the study focused on assessing the skills gaps in digital health competencies among healthcare professionals. Information was gathered through surveys and interviews with healthcare workers, administrators, and educators involved in telemedicine operations and education. The analysis identified critical challenges in the implementation of telemedicine education, such as the lack of comprehensive digital health curricula in medical schools and inadequate training on the use of telemedicine technologies. Interviews with telemedicine professionals highlighted the need for more targeted educational interventions to improve digital competencies, particularly in regions where telemedicine adoption is lower due to infrastructure challenges. For example, in some counties, healthcare institutions reported difficulties in accessing technical support for telemedicine platforms, as well as a lack of staff trained to operate these systems efficiently.

2.2 Survey Data

To assess the state of telemedicine education, surveys were distributed to healthcare providers and educators across Croatia. The surveys focused on several key areas:

- Frequency of telemedicine use among healthcare workers.
- Perceived impact of telemedicine on healthcare service delivery.

- Availability of technical support and resources for telemedicine operations.
- Adequacy of training programs in equipping healthcare professionals with digital competencies.
- Perceived need for improvements in telemedicine education within existing medical and nursing curricula.

Survey responses revealed that while telemedicine usage is widespread in counties with well-established telemedicine centers, significant regional disparities remain. In rural and underserved areas, healthcare workers often cited a lack of access to adequate telemedicine training, despite an increasing reliance on remote healthcare delivery. Additionally, educators expressed the need for more structured telemedicine modules within medical school programs and continuing professional development courses to address the growing demand for IS skills.

2.3 Analytical Framework

The analysis was structured around both thematic and statistical approaches. Thematic analysis was used to interpret qualitative data gathered from interviews and surveys, focusing on recurring themes such as the digital literacy gap, challenges in telemedicine implementation, and the role of educational institutions in addressing these gaps. These themes provided insights into the key barriers to effective telemedicine education, such as the absence of mandatory telemedicine courses in medical curricula and the lack of practical, hands-on training for digital tools. For the quantitative analysis, statistical methods were employed to analyze correlations between telemedicine service utilization and the availability of IS training programs. This analysis was critical in identifying regions where there is a high demand for telemedicine services but a lack of corresponding educational infrastructure to support healthcare professionals in utilizing these services. By mapping telemedicine usage data against IS training availability, the study was able to highlight regions and sectors where educational interventions could have the most significant impact.

2.4 Infrastructure and Technical Support

The study also examined the infrastructure supporting telemedicine services in Croatia. Telemedicine centers are part of a national network, with digital communication systems that enable the real-time transfer of medical data and remote consultations. These centers are equipped with high-speed internet connections, which are critical for the effective operation of telemedicine services. However, not all healthcare institutions are connected to this infrastructure, particularly in rural areas where technical support is often lacking. Telemedicine infrastructure in regions with higher adoption rates, such as Primorsko-goranska county, includes advanced telehealth systems capable of handling high volumes of remote consultations and diagnostics. These regions benefit from significant investments in digital infrastructure, including broadband internet and specialized telemedicine equipment. The study explored the correlation between the level of infrastructure development and the availability of IS training, noting that regions with better digital infrastructure were more likely to offer comprehensive telemedicine education programs.

3. RESULTS

The results of the study reveal several key insights into the current state of telemedicine education and the provision of Information Systems (IS) training within Croatia's healthcare system. The analysis covers the utilization of telemedicine services, the digital competency gaps among healthcare professionals, and the availability of telemedicine-specific education programs, highlighting both regional disparities and opportunities for improvement.

3.1 Utilization of Telemedicine Services

The analysis of telemedicine service utilization across Croatia revealed a wide variation between different counties. Regions with more established digital infrastructures, such as Primorsko-goranska county, reported the highest utilization rates of telemedicine services, particularly for emergency healthcare. Data collected from telemedicine centers indicated that the majority of telemedical consultations were related to emergency and diagnostic services, and these centers served as critical hubs for delivering healthcare to remote and underserved populations. For instance, in Primorsko-goranska county, telemedicine services were employed in over 13,000 cases in 2019, demonstrating the significant role these centers play in facilitating remote healthcare delivery. The county has successfully integrated telemedicine into its emergency medical services, with robust digital communication systems in place to support real-time interactions between healthcare providers and patients. Similarly, the Cres, Mali Lošinj, Krk, and Rab islands reported high utilization of telemedicine for emergency care, underscoring the importance of telemedicine in regions with geographic barriers. In contrast, rural areas and counties with underdeveloped digital infrastructures experienced much lower utilization rates. For example, regions in eastern Croatia reported fewer telemedicine interactions, mainly due to inadequate digital infrastructure and limited access to telemedicine training programs for healthcare professionals. This highlights a critical challenge: although telemedicine services are available, their usage is restricted by the lack of infrastructure and skilled personnel to support these services effectively.

3.2 Digital Competency Gaps in Healthcare Professionals

The qualitative analysis revealed significant gaps in the digital competencies of healthcare professionals, which are essential for effective use of telemedicine platforms and IS tools. Surveys conducted among healthcare workers indicated that while many were familiar with the concept of telemedicine, they lacked sufficient training in the use of specific digital health technologies such as Electronic Health Records (EHR), video consultation platforms, and remote diagnostic devices.

The survey results indicated that healthcare professionals in regions with lower telemedicine utilization were less confident in using telemedicine technologies. In rural areas, over 50% of surveyed professionals reported feeling underprepared to handle telemedicine consultations due to limited exposure to IS training. This is particularly problematic in emergency scenarios where real-time digital communication and data sharing are critical. Respondents highlighted the need for more practical training and hands-on experience with telemedicine tools to improve their proficiency.

3.3 Availability of Telemedicine Training Programs

Another key finding from the study was the limited availability of formal telemedicine education and IS training programs within Croatia's medical education system. While telemedicine has been included in the Digital Croatia Strategy (Central State Office for the Development of the Digital Society, 2022) and aligned with the European DigComp framework (European Commission, 2022), the implementation of these programs remains inconsistent across the country. The survey data showed that fewer than 20% of healthcare professionals had access to formal training programs that addressed telemedicine and digital health.

Medical institutions in urban areas, such as Zagreb and Rijeka, have begun integrating digital health modules into their curricula, but these are not yet widespread. For example, several institutions have introduced short-term courses on digital literacy and telemedicine, yet these courses are primarily optional, leaving many healthcare professionals without the necessary skills to operate telemedicine platforms effectively.

In contrast, rural areas reported a near-complete absence of structured telemedicine training. Healthcare providers in these regions stated that any training they received was typically informal, often delivered by peers or self-taught through trial and error. This lack of standardized telemedicine education represents a significant barrier to widespread telemedicine adoption in Croatia, as many healthcare professionals lack both the confidence and the skills required to use telemedicine technologies effectively.

3.4 Regional Disparities in Infrastructure and Access to Training

The study also found that regional disparities in digital infrastructure were closely tied to the availability of telemedicine education and the adoption of telemedicine services. Counties with more advanced digital infrastructures, such as Primorsko-goranska and parts of Istria, had higher levels of telemedicine integration, driven by the availability of high-speed internet, digital medical devices, and trained healthcare professionals.

For example, in Istria, healthcare centers connected to the national telemedicine network reported a high degree of satisfaction with the technical support and training available to them. These centers are equipped with broadband internet connections and advanced telemedicine tools, allowing for seamless data exchange and remote diagnostics. The availability of digital health education in these regions further supports the effective use of telemedicine platforms, with several healthcare institutions offering training programs that align with the European DigComp framework for digital literacy.

However, rural counties, especially in eastern Croatia, lacked both the infrastructure and access to formal telemedicine training programs. Many healthcare providers in these regions expressed frustration with the lack of technical support and cited difficulties in accessing reliable internet connections, which hindered their ability to deliver telemedicine services. The disparity in digital infrastructure between urban and rural areas was a key factor contributing to the uneven adoption of telemedicine across the country.

4. CONCLUSION

The survey highlighted a strong demand for micro-credentialing in IS and telemedicine, particularly among younger healthcare professionals. Many respondents noted that traditional medical education programs are slow to adapt to the rapid pace of technological advancements in telemedicine. They advocated for more flexible, modular training programs that would allow them to gain specialized skills in areas such as digital health, telemedicine platforms, and IS management.

Micro-credentialing, which offers targeted, short-term training programs, was seen as a potential solution to address the gaps in telemedicine education. Healthcare professionals, particularly those in regions with lower telemedicine adoption, expressed interest in pursuing micro-credentials to enhance their digital competencies. These programs would allow them to acquire specific skills relevant to their practice, without the need for extensive retraining or time away from their clinical responsibilities. Finally, the results indicated that several organizational and technical challenges must be addressed to improve the adoption of telemedicine and IS training across Croatia. Many healthcare institutions reported difficulties in integrating telemedicine into their existing workflows, citing a lack of technical support and guidance on how to best utilize telemedicine platforms. Additionally, the absence of clear regulatory guidelines for telemedicine practices further complicated the integration process, particularly in regions where healthcare providers were uncertain about the legal and ethical implications of telemedicine consultations.

REFERENCES

Almathami, H.K.Y., Win, K.T. and Vlahu-Gjorgievska, E., (2020). Barriers and facilitators to the adoption of telemedicine in developing countries: A systematic review. Journal of Medical Internet Research, 22(10), p.e16427.

Central State Office for the Development of the Digital Society, (2022). Digital Croatia Strategy for the period until 2032. Government of Croatia.

Dorsey, E.R. and Topol, E.J., (2020). Telemedicine 2020 and the next decade. The Lancet, 395(10227), pp.859-860.

European Commission, (2022). DigComp 2.2: The Digital Competence Framework for Citizens - With new examples of knowledge, skills and attitudes. Luxembourg: Publications Office of the European Union.

George, P.P., Papachristou, N., Belisario, J.M., Wang, W., Wark, P.A., Cotic, Z. and Car, J., 2019. Online eLearning for undergraduates in health professions: A systematic review of the impact on knowledge, skills, attitudes, and satisfaction. Journal of Global Health, 9(2), p.020426.

Kaufman, N., Kovačić, L., Jelaković, B. and Sarafidis, P., (2018). Telemedicine in the management of patients with chronic kidney disease: An overview of the literature and our experience. Journal of Telemedicine and Telecare, 24(7), pp.507-512.

Kruse, C.S., Krowski, N., Rodriguez, B., Tran, L., Vela, J. and Brooks, M., (2018). Telehealth and patient satisfaction: A systematic review and narrative analysis. BMJ Open, 7(8), p.e016242.

Serper, M. and Volk, M.L., (2018). Current and future applications of telemedicine to optimize the delivery of care in chronic liver disease. Clinical Gastroenterology and Hepatology, 16(2), pp.157-161.

Smith, A.C., Thomas, E., Snoswell, C.L., Haydon, H., Mehrotra, A., Clemensen, J. and Caffery, L.J., (2020). Telehealth for global emergencies: Implications for coronavirus disease 2019 (COVID-19). Journal of Telemedicine and Telecare, 26(5), pp.309-313.

CASE STUDY OF A PORTUGUESE MUNICIPALITY IN A POST-CYBERATTACK CONTEXT

Patrícia Leite[1,2,3], Margarida Antunes[1], Isabel Ferreira[1], Sandro Carvalho[1,2] and Paulo Teixeira[1,2]
[1]*Polythecnic University of Cavado and Ave, Barcelos, Portugal*
[2]*LIACC - Artificial Intelligence and Computer Science Lab. Porto, Portugal*
[3]*2Ai – School of Technology, IPCA, Barcelos, Portugal*

ABSTRACT

Given the importance of the continuous study of cybersecurity methods in the digital context in Portugal, to combat cyber incidents and safeguard fundamental rights, there is an urgent need for the State to develop a document of best practices to guide public services in their protection and recovery processes when targeted by cyber incidents. A technological incident response plan is suggested for the studied Municipal Council, with the objective of facilitating and streamlining the post-cyberattack recovery process, based on the identified need during the analysis conducted after the incident.

KEYWORDS

Fundamental Rights, Digital Universe, Cybersecurity, Incident, Cyberattack, Recovery Process

1. INTRODUCTION

With the rapid advances in technology, it is important to assess whether the fundamental rights of each of us are safeguarded in the digital universe. With this in mind, this paper aims to analyse the following question: How do technological advances compromise fundamental rights?

Technological evolution brings with it the emergence of cyber incidents, namely cyberattacks, which affect both public and private organizations, as well as individuals. To prevent this from becoming increasingly recurrent, it is considered essential to understand cybersecurity.

The focus of this study is on public services, specifically the Local Administration (LA). To this end, a cyberattack that occurred in 2022 in a municipality in the north of Portugal was analyzed, with the aim of exploring the reaction in the process of recovering from the incident and understanding the difficulties it encountered.

In addition to a detailed description of the facts, we identified some questions that we tried to answer. As a contribution to this work, an incident response plan was drawn up so that the Municipality can implement it and make the post-cyberattack process more practical and less time-consuming. Finally, the final considerations of this work are presented.

Ultimately, the basis of this work is essentially the data and studies carried out by the National Cybersecurity Centre (CNCS), legislation on fundamental rights and cybersecurity, as well as documents and information provided by those involved in the Municipality reaction to the cyberattack.

2. RESEARCH STRATEGY

At the beginning of this project, the intention to study fundamental rights and their connection to the advancement of technology was demonstrated. We began by carrying out exploratory research on the subject at the Francisco Manuel dos Santos Foundation (FFMS, 2025) to see if there were any current issues surrounding fundamental rights. After listening to the podcast entitled 'How to guarantee fundamental rights in the Digital Age?', we realised the need to safeguard fundamental rights in the face of technological advances and the importance of cybersecurity in defending them. It was therefore understood that this is one of the problems that most affect us today and it was therefore decided that this topic should also be analyzed and developed in this project. In this sense, this study aims to analyze the following question: How should organizations be prepared to respond to cybersecurity incidents?

During the research, it was emphasized that the Municipality in question had been the target of a major cyberattack that compromised the system for several days. This incident emphasized the need to explore existing vulnerabilities and identify post-attack difficulties. It was therefore decided that the case study for this project would focus on a Municipality in the north of Portugal, with the aim of analyzing in detail the cyberattack that took place, the existing vulnerabilities that led to this incident and the recovery strategy adopted to overcome the damage caused by it. All events relating to the cyber-attack and all the difficulties encountered during the recovery process were analyzed through interviews. Initially, it was suggested to analyze the Municipality's cybersecurity plan before the cyberattack and compare it with the current cybersecurity plan, but this study was not possible due to the confidentiality of the data. Likewise, the main vulnerabilities that led to the computer incident were not mentioned for the same reason. However, during the course of the research there was an interest in seeing some questions answered, such as: 'Shouldn't there be a legally based regulation on the recovery process after a cyberattack?', 'Was the strategy used by the Municipality the right one?' and 'Nowadays, is it necessary to have the orders/opinions of the processes printed out?'. This case study therefore focused on analyzing the data provided in an attempt to answer these questions. The Municipality provided documents to analyze, including statements drawn up to help in the process of recovering from the incident. This allowed for a more detailed analysis of the recovery process and a more consistent answer to the questions initially proposed. As a contribution to this project, a technological incident response plan was drawn up for the Municipality. The project used models of response plans from private cybersecurity companies and chose to collect only the essential information to adapt the plan to this public organization.

Throughout this process, special emphasis was placed on public services, specifically the Local Administration (LA). To this end, a review of the existing literature on fundamental rights and cybersecurity at national level was carried out, based on available reports and analyzing the work carried out by entities dedicated to protecting and securing them.

3. FUNDAMENTAL RIGHTS AND CYBERSECURITY: CONCEPTS, EVOLUTION AND

In the current context, the relationship between cybersecurity and fundamental rights is of great importance, revealing an intrinsic link between these two concepts, since cybersecurity plays a crucial role in protecting and promoting fundamental rights in the digital context. Fundamental rights are defined as the 'basic legal positions recognized by Portuguese, European and international law' that aim to defend the values and interests of natural and legal persons in Portugal and Portuguese citizens living abroad (DR, 2025). The first document to officialize these rights was the Charter of the United Nations in 1945. In the years that followed, documents such as the United Nations Universal Declaration of Human Rights in 1948, the European Convention on Human Rights in 1953, the Constitution of the Portuguese Republic in 1976 and the Charter of Fundamental Rights of the European Union in 2009. Initially, fundamental rights were norms that only analyzed the rights of citizens in relation to each other. However, with technological advances, we have seen not only the creation of new fundamental rights, but also the reformulation and adaptation of existing ones, to guarantee integrity and security in the virtual environment, as evidenced by the Portuguese Charter of Human Rights, which came into force on 17 May 2021, and which approves the Portuguese Charter of Human Rights in the Digital Age, as mentioned in article no. 1 'Object' of the same legal diploma (Lei n.º 27, 2021). All these existing legal regimes provide guidance to citizens on their own rights when interacting with the state, with other people in everyday patterns of behavior or even in the digital environment.

According to Silva (2024), today's fundamental rights have emerged as a response to the needs that have arisen over time, reflecting the need to protect individuals in the face of transformations in the digital universe. As mentioned in Jorge Pereira da Silva's book 'Fundamental Rights for the Digital Universe', 'Fundamental rights are, so to speak, living creatures. They are born, they live, they develop, and in some cases, they wither and die or at least lose much of the importance they had in their heyday'. Regarding the digital world, it is necessary to understand the importance of cybersecurity.

This issue of digital security is presented in Article 15 of the Portuguese Charter on Human Rights in the Digital Age, which states that everyone has the right to security in cyberspace, i.e. to protection throughout virtual space. It also states that the state is primarily responsible for ensuring this security by defining public policies. At the same time, the CNCS co-operates with other entities, helping citizens and companies to prevent threats in cyberspace, offering them training and capacity-building for this purpose. The CNCS therefore has administrative and financial autonomy (Lei n.º 27, 2021).

According to the 'National Cyberspace Security Strategy 2019-2023' document made available by the CNCS, cybersecurity 'consists of the set of measures and actions for prevention, monitoring, detection, reaction, analysis and correction aimed at maintaining the desired security state and ensuring the confidentiality, integrity, and availability of information ...' (CNCS, 2019).

Following a survey carried out by the Directorate-General for Education and Science Statistics (DGEEC) on the use of ICT in municipalities in 2023, various variables were analysed for the 308 Portuguese municipalities (INE, 2024). In analysing this survey, only the most relevant variables for this project were considered, including measures related to the security of the ICT used by these municipalities, who carries out activities related to ICT security, the number of municipalities that have had computer security problems and the consequences of these incidents, and municipalities with insurance against ICT security incidents, the Municipalities that have a defined strategy for guaranteeing information security and what stage of implementation these strategies are at, as well as analysing the stage of implementation of the information security strategy in relation to the General Data Protection Regulation (GDPR) and the stage of implementation of the information security strategy in relation to the Legal Framework for Cyberspace Security (RJSC). In 138 Municipalities (70.1%) the safety plan was drawn up and kept up to date, duly documented and signed by the safety officer, while in 154 Municipalities (78.2%) the annual safety report was drawn up last year and, finally, in a higher number, 183 Municipalities, the communications to the CNCS provided for in Regulation 183/2022 were made, which corresponds to 92.9%.

4. CASE STUDY OF THE MUNICIPALITY

Following the theoretical framework, literature review and analysis of the increase in technological incidents in Portugal over the last few years, this chapter examines the case study of a cyber-attack on the Municipality and analyses its post-cyber-attack reaction and recovery strategy. Next, a technological incident response plan will be presented as a suggestion for the Municipality, with the aim of facilitating and speeding up the recovery process after cyberattacks, given the perception of this need during the analysis of the post-cyberattack process. Subsequently, we will present the questions that arose during this process, which we endeavoured to answer.

In October 2022, the Municipality under study was the target of a cyber-attack that compromised its system for approximately fifteen days, resulting in the closure of its departments and services during this period. This incident led to the partial destruction of crucial information from the various departments, including more than 3 million backup files.

After the incident, the Municipality received a notice demanding a ransom so that all the information could be returned. Regarding the ransom amount, it is not possible to mention exact figures because it is not considered public data. In response to this notification, Municipality understood that it would not pay the ransom, since paying ransoms is not advisable in public services.

In this way, the municipality took the road to recovery. In order to recover from this incident, it was necessary to create an appropriate recovery strategy for each department. At the start of this process, the Municipality identified one of the main difficulties in the post-cyberattack process: the lack of a legal basis for recovering from cyberattacks. Considering this lack of rules, a recovery strategy was drawn up for each of the Municipality's departments, depending on the resources that resisted this cyberattack. In this project, the main focus was on the Urban Planning Department. In this department, a recovery strategy was established and subsequently approved by the Councillor and communicated to the other stakeholders. The established strategy took into account the electronic processing process in place, where all documents and files were received by the department digitally and, after the incident, these files were lost.

Despite the fact that all the Urban Planning Department's files were processed digitally, staff in this sector used to print out an opinion/dispatch for each file. This practice was due to the perception that the services were not sufficiently prepared for this technological evolution.

In addition, the printed document served as a 'guide' for each employee working on the case, because the department operates in a similar way to an industrial production line, where a case passes through several employees and sections.

Therefore, the starting point for recovery in this sector was the dispatches that were printed on the department's premises.

Next, relationships of trust were established where the constituents of each of the files were contacted, asking for more information about their case, since the dispatches only contained a few statements and general information, for example, out of a 200-page document, the dispatch only contained 5.

Next, they needed to contact organizations in the field, such as architectural firms, who were involved in their process to request the required documents. To facilitate the process of retrieving the files, a request was drawn up by the Municipality to submit the lost files. In addition, the Municipality, in collaboration with a certifying body, has drawn up a document with a scheme that simplifies this procedure.

In this document, the first thing to check is whether this is a new procedure or not. If it is new, the documents should be delivered to the One-Stop Shop or to the department's digital platform, e-Urbanismo. On the other hand, if the procedure is old, the recovered documents should be sent to e-Urbanismo or to a read-only digital storage medium.

After this analysis, it was necessary to understand whether or not the project architecture of the process had already been approved and whether there were any specialties in progress. At this stage of the recovery, the following question arose: 'How can we verify the credibility of the information received?'. In other words, with the department in a vulnerable position, clients could send false information for their own gain because some of this information the sector had no way of verifying. In a specific licensing case, the order did not specify the number of floors for the structure in question, so the client, together with their architect, could falsify this information and a license application for a two-story building a year ago could now become a three-story building. To overcome this issue, the first approach was to trust in the good faith of everyone involved and believe that the information received was reliable. In a second step, terms of responsibility were created in which it was stated that the information transmitted was true and all those who sent it had to sign. In addition, the Municipality also developed other declarations such as the project author's declaration of conformity (for re-establishing procedures), the project coordinator's declaration of conformity (for re-establishing procedures without approval), the project coordinator's declaration of conformity (for re-establishing approved procedures) and the project coordinator's declaration of conformity (for re-establishing approved procedures - for the purposes of authorizing use). These declarations were necessary to prove that the legal standards during the recovery process were being complied with and to ensure that all the necessary requirements existed for the process in question to proceed. These declarations are kept to this day so that if there is a problem with these processes, the Municipality will not be held responsible for any false information.

As a contribution to this project, a technology incident response plan was drawn up for the Municipality, with the aim of facilitating and speeding up the recovery process after cyberattacks, given the perception of this need during the analysis carried out.

To draw up this plan, guidance documents on technology incident response plans were consulted. After analyzing these documents, the most appropriate topics were identified for a technology incident response plan for a public entity, specifically a Municipality.

Follow this plan after a cyberattack serves as a 'starting point' for the incident response process. It will also improve the understanding of those involved about the incident and speed up its recovery.

This plan is the basic model for the organization itself, which, based on it and the cyberattack information contained in it, will be able to communicate the occurrence of the incident more clearly and practically to external bodies, particularly the CNCS.

Once the incident has been resolved, this document can also be useful for evaluating what happened and highlighting the points that deserve attention. It also allows comparison with future incidents, helping to identify whether the recent incident was caused by similar reasons to the previous ones.

5. CONCLUSION

At the end of this process, the Municipality's Urban Planning Department raised some questions that they wanted answered.

Based on the information available, we have endeavored to provide an answer to each of these questions in order to draw a better conclusion to this case study. The questions raised were as follows:

- Shouldn't there be a legally based regulation on the recovery process after a cyber-attack?
- Was the strategy used by the Town Planning Department in this municipality the right one?
- In this day and age, is it necessary to have the orders/opinions of the processes printed out?

In the question 'Shouldn't there be a legally based regulation on the recovery process after a cyber-attack?', it was felt that the state should act quickly in this regard.

As analyzed above, the number of cyberattacks has increased dramatically and, despite the help of the CNCS, there is no official document with good practices for the affected entity to follow and make the recovery process quicker and easier, just some reference frameworks (ISO/IEC 27001, 2022; Joel Lanz, 2024).

With regard to the second question raised, 'Was the strategy used by the Town Planning Department in this municipality the right one?', it is worth mentioning that this question can only be answered taking into account the two years that have passed since the incident. What's more, this answer is provisional and temporary, since serious consequences could arise from this strategy at any time.

However, to date, the recovery plan adopted has been very successful and there have been no problems with the information recovered. Furthermore, this strategy is highly praised and has already been used as a reference by departments in other municipalities. With regard to the last question raised, 'Is it necessary to have printed case orders/opinions these days?', it is necessary to evaluate the pros and cons for the department.

With regard to the positive points, it is undeniable that the procedural documents that existed in print were an asset in the post-cyberattack process.

Therefore, one of the advantages of this printing is that the department is always safeguarded in case such incidents happen again. On the other hand, there are some cons, namely the evolution of the system which has shown that these printed dispatches are dispensable in view of technological developments.

Lastly, the cost of printing and the cover can also be a negative point, as it is an expense that is not compulsory. But doesn't the small amount spent on each of these opinions pay off in the event of a cyber-attack? Doesn't the value of these dispatches justify the cost of printing them? It was understood from those who actively participated in the department's recovery process that, from a global perspective, even though the system does not require printed reports, they serve as a guarantee and prevent future problems.

It is agreed that this is an optional practice, but the department continues to adopt it because the difficulties that this cyberattack caused are still very much present and because it recognizes the value of the printed documents that existed at the time of the attack.

Thus, this cyber-attack compromised confidential data of citizens and the municipality itself. This is a real case where fundamental rights, especially the right to privacy, data protection and cybersecurity, mentioned in Law 27/2021, were violated in the digital context.

REFERENCES

CNCS. (2019). Estratégia Nacional de Segurança do Ciberespaço. https://www.cncs.gov.pt/docs/cncs-ensc-2019-2023.pdf

DR. (2025). Direitos fundamentais | DR. https://diariodarepublica.pt/dr/lexionario/termo/direitos-fundamentais

FFMS. (2025). Homepage | Fundação Francisco Manuel dos Santos. https://ffms.pt/pt-pt

INE. (2024). Inquérito à Utilização das Tecnologias da Informação e Comunicação.

ISO/IEC 27001. (2022). Information security, cybersecurity and privacy protection - Information security management systems - Requirements. www.iso.org

Joel Lanz. (2024). The Updated NIST Cybersecurity Framework. The CPA Journal. https://search.proquest.com/openview/cf718e5b24f6e05dea2c90de6fd9448c/1?pq-origsite=gscholar&cbl=41798

Lei n.º 27, Carta Portuguesa de Direitos Humanos Na Era Digital, Diário da República n.o 95/2021, Série I (2021). https://diariodarepublica.pt/dr/legislacao-consolidada/lei/2021-164870244

Silva, J. P. (2024). Direitos Fundamentais da Era Digital. Fundação Francisco Manuel dos Santos.

UNDERSTANDING THE ROADBLOCKS: INVESTIGATING THE BARRIERS TO OPEN BANKING ADOPTION IN THE PHILIPPINES

Jinky T. Dela Torre[1] and Ma. Rowena R. Caguiat[2]
College of Computer Studies, De La Salle University
Manila, Philippines
[1]MBA
[2]Dr., DIT

ABSTRACT

This study examines the slow adoption of Open Banking in the Philippine banking sector despite financial and technological advancements worldwide. Employing the Technology-Organization-Environment (TOE) framework, it identifies key barriers - including limited data sharing between banks and third-party service providers, outdated IT and business models, and consumer trust concerns. The research analyzes the interplay of these factors to uncover conditions that could drive both bank and consumer adoption. A strong emphasis was placed on consumer attitudes, preferences, and behaviors, to highlight how addressing these elements can accelerate Open Banking acceptance. The insights in this working paper are in the process of being developed and will aim to guide policymakers, regulators, and stakeholders in fostering a secure, innovative, and inclusive financial ecosystem, offering a pathway to modernize banking practices and enhance financial accessibility in the Philippines.

KEYWORDS

Open Banking, Adoption, Barriers, Philippines, TOE

1. INTRODUCTION

In modern financial landscapes, the potential for innovation and transformation is vast, yet the Philippine banking sector has shown a notable reluctance to fully embrace the paradigm of Open Banking. To better understand this concept, it's important to define what Open Banking entails. According to Laplante and Kshetri (2021, p.2), Open Banking is a "financial ecosystem that provides third-party financial service providers open access to consumer banking, transaction, and other financial data from banks and nonbank financial institutions through the use of application programming interfaces (APIs)". Building on this foundation, this study delves into the intricate web of factors contributing to the adoption of this phenomenon.

This study embarks on an exploration of the multifaceted interconnections of technological, organizational, and environmental factors, elucidating the complex interplay between technological, institutional, and socio-economic actors. As the landscape of financial services evolves with rapid technological advancements, this paper endeavors to unravel the intricacies of the non-adoption of Open Banking within Philippine banks, shedding light on the dynamics at play and their implications for the financial ecosystem.

The emergence of Application Programming Interfaces (APIs) is a causal factor and technological enabler for Open Banking. As a result, the landscape of modern finance is undergoing a dynamic shift, ushering in fintech entities as potential solutions to address existing consumer challenges. These challenges are intricately intertwined with the notion of data accessibility and data sharing within the financial ecosystem. Data sharing between banks is crucial for efficient financial operations, risk management, and fostering innovation.

This study aims to analyze the barriers that hinder the banks from adopting open banking and from there create the conditions that will influence bank and consumer adoption of open banking in the Philippines through the Technology-Organization-Environment (TOE) framework. Given this research objective, the following research questions were formulated to aid in the research planning, design, and execution:

1.) How do technological, organizational, and environmental factors, along with consumer attitudes and behaviors, influence the non-adoption of open banking by banks in the Philippines?

2.) How do technological, organizational, and environmental factors, including consumer perceptions, influence the non-adoption of open banking by consumers in the Philippines?

The significance of this research lies in its potential to provide a comprehensive and nuanced understanding of the factors that could influence the adoption of open banking by Philippine banks. Central to this investigation is the cyclical nature of consumer and bank adoption, emphasizing that consumer adoption is a factor of equal significance driving banks to adopt open banking. Consumers are more likely to embrace open banking if banks create the necessary conditions, which, in turn, motivates banks to invest further in open banking solutions (Chan et al., 2022). This cyclical and cohesive relationship highlights the interdependence between consumer and bank adoption, offering insights into how banks can strategically foster an environment conducive to widespread open banking acceptance.

2. LITERATURE REVIEW

Socio-economic inequality in any country could be ameliorated by adopting the Open Banking (OB) mechanism. OB is seen to facilitate and improve the lives of customers by providing personalized and convenient experiences (Gonçalves and Araujo 2022; Grassi et al., 2022; Laplante and Kshetri 2021; Premchand and Choudhry 2018). By accessing consumer banking data through OB, banks can quickly assess a customer's borrowing capacity and offer them the best rates and tailored financial products. Also, consumers could also plan and manage their finances effectively since everything is aggregated in one dashboard. This streamlined process eliminates the need for extensive paperwork, as consumers can upload the necessary documents with a single click, making the overall experience faster and more convenient (Assala et al., 2022).

Given these significant advantages, it is crucial to understand the factors influencing the adoption of OB, especially in regions like the Philippines where its implementation has been uneven. This study will utilize the Technology-Organization-Environment (TOE) framework to establish how these three major components are influencing the non-adoption or partial adoption of open banking by banks in the Philippines. According to Tornatzky, Fleischer, and Chakrabarti, who introduced the TOE framework in 1990, the technological context refers to the characteristics and attributes of the technology itself, including its complexity, compatibility, and relative advantage (Tornatzky et al., 1990). The organizational context encompasses the internal factors within an organization, such as its structure, culture, resources, and capabilities, that influence the adoption and implementation of technology. Lastly, central to this environmental dimension are the consumers, influenced by how the organizations are implementing the technological offerings to the public. Furthermore, the environmental context includes external factors such as industry norms, competition, government regulations, and market demands that shape technology adoption decisions (Tornatzky et al., 1990). The TOE framework provides a holistic approach to technology adoption by considering the interplay between these dimensions. In line with this assessment, the literature review highlights the following barriers to open banking adoption from the perspective of banks:

Lack of Consumer Awareness

The environment is the most critical issue in implementing open banking, and one of the possible reasons is the lack of understanding from the public (Daiy et al. 2021). This lack of awareness is a challenge for both the banks and the consumers (Briones de Araluze and Cassinello Plaza 2022; Kassab and Laplante 2022; Nanaeva et al., 2021). Suppose that the public is unfamiliar with the concept and potential benefits of OB. In that case, it may create a barrier to adoption, as banks may perceive limited customer demand or acceptance (Daiy et al., 2021).

Reluctance in Sharing Data

Banks have the most data to share, so they might not have the motivation to do so (He et al., 2023). Specifically, customers' account data is a valuable and essential asset that can serve as a barrier to entry for newcomers in the financial industry when incumbents become unwilling to share them (Borgogno and

Colangelo 2020). Further, data sharing could have a possible effect on an incumbent bank's brand or image (Nanaeva et al., 2021). However, Ciocănel et al. (Ciocănel et al., 2024) demonstrated how trust building through technology and the establishment of power relationships can significantly impact the adoption rates of open banking services, particularly in the context of tenant referencing in the United Kingdom. This indicates that addressing trust issues and fostering strong relationships between stakeholders can mitigate the reluctance of banks to share data, thereby enhancing the adoption of open banking.

Lack of Regulatory Support

Another vital aspect that could be the most influential barrier is governance and regulation. The absence of appropriate rules can create obstacles to establishing and operating open banking systems, hindering their adoption and development (Lynn et al., 2020). One of the areas that need policy regulation is API standardization (Abubakar and Handayani 2022; Aytaş et al., 2021; Premchand and Choudhry 2018).

3. RESEARCH DESIGN AND METHODOLOGY

This study uses a qualitative exploratory design to investigate barriers to Open Banking adoption in the Philippines, offering an in-depth examination of stakeholder perspectives and contextual factors. Interviews will be transcribed for accuracy, with data analyzed using Descriptive Coding to categorize topics and Pattern Coding to identify themes. Applied Thematic Analysis (ATA) and narrative analysis will uncover key patterns and contextual insights. NVivo software will support efficient coding and data management. Structured interview guides designed for banking consumers and executives will gather comprehensive data on challenges, motivations, and conditions for adoption, ensuring a systematic approach to understanding and addressing the barriers to Open Banking.

Interview Guides for Banking Consumers

To establish a foundational understanding, the interview guides will begin with an introduction and background section to gather information on the interviewee's banking habits, familiarity with Open Banking, and demographic details.

Building on this foundation, the guides are designed to gather qualitative data from banking consumers with a focus on uncovering pain points and unaddressed needs, as well as addressing the challenges faced by non-advanced users. For segments that prefer face-to-face interaction, the questions will explore how banks can integrate personal touchpoints into Open Banking offerings. Furthermore, the guides will include questions that gauge consumer interest by illustrating potential benefits, such as expense trackers and tailored financial advice, to better understand their appeal and relevance.

Interview Guides for Bank Executives

The interview guides are designed to gather qualitative data from bank executives, managers, and key stakeholders on their experiences and strategies related to Open Banking. While insights from bank executives have been explored, this study places greater emphasis on understanding consumer perspectives, as their needs and expectations are pivotal in driving Open Banking adoption. Nonetheless, the inclusion of executive insights remains essential to comprehensively address the dimension of organizational factors, such as strategic alignment, technological readiness, and operational adaptability, which are critical for successful Open Banking implementation.

Reliability and Validity

Ensuring reliability and validity is of paramount importance to uphold the quality and credibility of the study's findings. The criteria that will be used to test and validate the findings are construct validity, internal validity, external validity, and reliability. Construct validity is ensuring that operational measures pertaining to the concepts are specifically identified. Internal validity on the other hand, deals with ascertaining that correct causal relationships are established, leading to accurate inferences. As for external validity, this test covers the study's generalizability. Lastly, reliability means the study could be replicated if another researcher would follow the same process (Dul & Hak, 2007; Yin, 2018). A process tracing approach will also be used for this study (Gerring, 2006).

4. PRELIMINARY DATA

Below is the summary of the interviews conducted as of date, with Senior Executives of three (3) banks, 1 traditional and 2 digital banks.

Table 1. Interview Results with CXOs

Banks' reasons in hesitating to adopt open banking	CXO1	CXO2	CXO3	CXO4	CXO5	CXO6
Losing its competitive edge					✓	✓
Still profitable even w/o open banking				✓		✓
Might lose branding						✓
Need to modernize IT architecture	✓	✓	✓		✓	✓
Not yet regulatory mandated						✓

5. CONCLUSION

This Short Paper emphasizes the key technological, organizational, and environmental challenges hindering Open Banking adoption in the Philippines, emphasizing consumer trust and engagement. It highlights the potential of Open Banking to enhance financial service accessibility, improve consumer financial management, and foster innovation. However, these benefits depend on addressing significant barriers, including outdated IT infrastructures, weak regulatory frameworks, and consumer trust issues.

This short paper is currently limited by its concise scope and qualitative approach, but it already provides valuable insights into the adoption barriers specific to the Philippine banking sector. These findings have practical applications, such as guiding policymakers in creating supportive regulations, aiding banks in trust-building strategies, and helping technology providers align innovations with consumer needs. Data collection and analysis is still ongoing but it already establishes a foundation in establishing a secure, inclusive financial ecosystem, contributing to the broader understanding of Open Banking adoption dynamics.

REFERENCES

Abubakar, L., and T. Handayani. (2022). "The Urgency of Open Application Programming Interface Standardization in the Implementation of Open Banking to Customer Data Protection for the Advancement of Indonesian Banking." *Padjadjaran Jurnal Ilmu Hukum* 9 (1): 67–88. https://doi.org/10.22304/pjih.v9n1.a4.

Assala, K., S. et al, (2022). "Assessing Perceptions of Open Banking: The Case of Digital Natives in France." *Gestion 2000* 39 (4): 45–65. https://doi.org/10.3917/g2000.394.0045.

Aytaş, B. et al, (2021). "Open Banking: Opening up the 'Walled Gardens.'" *Journal of Payments Strategy and Systems* 15 (4): 419–31.

Borgogno, Oscar, and Giuseppe Colangelo. (2020). "Consumer Inertia and Competition-Sensitive Data Governance: The Case of Open Banking." SSRN Scholarly Paper 3513514. Rochester, NY: Social Science Research Network. https://doi.org/10.2139/ssrn.3513514.

Briones de Araluze, G.K., and N. Cassinello Plaza. (2022). "Open Banking: A Bibliometric Analysis-Driven Definition." *PloS One* 17 (10): e0275496. https://doi.org/10.1371/journal.pone.0275496.

Chan, Rebecca, et al, (2022). "Towards an Understanding of Consumers' FinTech Adoption: The Case of Open Banking." *International Journal of Bank Marketing*, April. https://doi.org/10.1108/IJBM-08-2021-0397.

Ciocănel, A. et al, (2024). "Open Banking and Data Reassurance: The Case of Tenant Referencing in the UK." *Information Communication and Society*. https://doi.org/10.1080/1369118X.2024.2310481.

Daiy, Alexander Kuan, et al, (2021). "A Hybrid MCDM Model for Evaluating Open Banking Business Partners." *Mathematics* 9 (6): 587. https://doi.org/10.3390/math9060587.

Dul, J., & Hak, T. (2007). *Case Study Methodology in Business Research*. Routledge.

Gerring, J. (2006). *Case Study Research: Principles and Practices*. Cambridge University Press. https://doi.org/10.1017/CBO9780511803123

Gonçalves, Arthur Vilela, and Fernando Oliveira de Araujo. (2022). "The Implementation of Open Banking in Brazil: An Overview from the Perspectives of Professionals from Large Retail Banks." *Brazilian Journal of Operations & Production Management* 19 (4): 1661–1661. https://doi.org/10.14488/BJOPM.1661.2022.

Grassi, Laura, et al, (2022). "How Does a Data Strategy Enable Customer Value? The Case of FinTechs and Traditional Banks under the Open Finance Framework." *Financial Innovation* 8 (1): 75. https://doi.org/10.1186/s40854-022-00378-x.

He, Zhiguo, et al, (2023). "Open Banking: Credit Market Competition When Borrowers Own the Data." *Journal of Financial Economics* 147 (2): 449–74. https://doi.org/10.1016/j.jfineco.2022.12.003.

Kassab, Mohamad, and Phil Laplante. (2022). "Trust Considerations in Open Banking." *IT Professional* 24 (1): 70–73. https://doi.org/10.1109/MITP.2021.3136015.

Laplante, Phil, and Nir Kshetri. (2021). "Open Banking: Definition and Description." *Computer* 54 (10): 122–28. https://doi.org/10.1109/MC.2021.3055909.

Lynn, Theo, et al, (2020). "Exploring Open Banking and Banking-as-a-Platform: Opportunities and Risks for Emerging Markets." In *Entrepreneurial Finance in Emerging Markets: Exploring Tools, Techniques, and Innovative Technologies*, edited by Darek Klonowski, 319–34. Cham: Springer International Publishing. https://doi.org/10.1007/978-3-030-46220-8_20.

Nanaeva, Z. et al, (2021). "Open Banking in Europe: The Effect of the Revised Payment Services Directive on Solarisbank and Insha." *Journal of Payments Strategy and Systems* 15 (4): 432–44.

Premchand, Anshu, and Anurag Choudhry. (2018^). "Open Banking & APIs for Transformation in Banking." In *2018 International Conference on Communication, Computing and Internet of Things (IC3IoT)*, 25–29. https://doi.org/10.1109/IC3IoT.2018.8668107.

Tornatzky, Louis G. et al, (1990). "Processes of Technological Innovation." Lexington Books. https://scholar.google.com/scholar_lookup?title=processes+of+technological+innovation&author=Tornatzky%2C+Louis+G.&publication_year=1990.

Yin, R. K. (2018). *Case Study Research and Applications*. SAGE Publications Inc. https://us.sagepub.com/en-us/nam/case-study-research-and-applications/book250150

DEVELOPMENT OF TRANSITIONAL BUSINESS MODEL FOR SMALL BUSINESSES: A RESPONSE TO ERA OF CONVERGENCE OR COVID-19?

Marko Budler[1] and Katerina Božič[2]
[1]SEB LU, Kardeljeva ploscad 17, Ljubljana, Slovenia
[2]JB Energija, Novo mesto, Slovenia

ABSTRACT

The COVID-19 pandemic has significantly impacted global economies, prompting industries to adapt their operations. Small health-and-sports businesses have been particularly affected by economic uncertainty and operational changes, but little is known about how they managed the uncertainties and changes in their modes of operation. This study uses a qualitative approach to investigate the strategies these businesses adopted through developing transitional business models during the pandemic and era of convergence. Semi-structured interviews were conducted with representatives from small health-and-sports (also: fitness) businesses that faced pandemic-related restrictions. Results show that these businesses used a trial-and-error method (i.e., the development of a transitional business model) to adjust their value offerings and build resilience amid the converging offerings' repertoires in health-and-sports industry. Additionally, maintaining customer perceptions of service quality, and customer loyalty was crucial for retaining clients.

KEYWORDS

Digital, Transitional, Business Model, COVID-19, Convergence, Health Industry

1. INTRODUCTION

The COVID-19 pandemic has forced small fitness businesses to adapt rapidly, addressing unprecedented disruptions within the industry. Limited resources and lack of preparedness have posed significant challenges for these businesses, making necessary adjustments difficult (Akpan, Soopramanien, and Kwak, 2021). Small businesses often rely on specific business models, which can restrict their ability to make adjustments during crises (Clauss et al., 2022). However, the small businesses tend to have the advantage of flexibility, allowing for continuous operations and enhanced customer service (Sullivan-Taylor and Branicki, 2011).

The rapid and unpredictable nature of the pandemic has often prevented businesses from undertaking comprehensive business mode (BM) redesigns. Some researchers suggest "temporary adaptations" as a more practical approach during such disruptions (Witschel et al., 2019). Thus, this study explores the strategies and adjustments adopted by small fitness businesses during the pandemic to refine their value propositions and build resilience.

Understanding these adjustments provides valuable insights for small businesses seeking to enhance their BM resilience and adapt effectively to changing conditions. The current study also adds a response to recent calls for industry-specific research on BM redesigns amid the pandemic (see e.g., Escamilla-Fajardo et al., 2020) by further examining the specific of fitness (health-and-sports) businesses.

2. BUSINESS MODEL APPROACH TO SMALL FITNESS BUSINESSES

Chesbrough and Rosenbloom (2002) describe a business model as a framework that outlines a company's value proposition, target market, revenue structure, value chain configuration, resource assessment, cost structure, profit potential, network position, and competitive strategy. In the fitness industry—encompassing gyms and health services—business models focus on delivering health and wellness products and services to customers (also: clients).

The COVID-19 pandemic forced businesses in health-and-sports industry to rethink and redesign their BMs due to the scale and intensity of disruptions. Adjustments were necessary to implement safety measures like social distancing and strict hygiene protocols aimed at minimizing infection risk for the customers. According to McAlister (2020), nearly two-thirds of small fitness business customers preferred to shift to online or on-demand training options, even though the majority still valued in-person interactions.

To adapt, businesses rapidly transitioned to digital platforms by offering streaming services and online workout programs. This shift also prompted a reevaluation of the business model elements, emphasizing the need for business model resilience, and customer loyalty. To build loyalty, fitness businesses had to accommodate changing customer preferences by incorporating diverse distribution channels and digital solutions. Embracing such change is believe to also allow these businesses to either revert to their traditional models post-pandemic or continue evolving their offerings to meet ongoing customer demands.

2.1 Research Design and Findings: Towards a Transitional Business Model

We employed a qualitative research design to study small fitness businesses during the COVID-19 pandemic. An exploratory approach is particularly effective for investigating complex phenomena and understanding intricate relationships (Corbin and Strauss, 1990; Eisenhardt and Graebner, 2007). Our method relied on abductive reasoning (Creswell, 2013; Mantere and Ketokivi, 2013), where we iteratively engaged initial insights from the data with existing theories to develop explanations for our findings.

To implement this design, we conducted semi-structured interviews, a flexible and effective method of gathering data (Holstein and Gubrium, 1995; Alvesson, 2003). The interview guide included open-ended questions covering: (i) their current business model and experiences with BM re-design; (ii) modifications made in response to COVID-19; (iii) their commitment to customers; and (iv) if relevant, proactive strategies used for BM adjustments (The interview guide can be accessed in the supplementary data).

The study aims to explore specific business model adjustments made during disruptions, using purposeful and theoretical sampling to obtain the most relevant insights (Coyne, 1997; Suri, 2011). In line with this approach (Denzin and Lincoln, 2005), we conducted 12 semi-structured interviews with small fitness businesses identified as successful, well-known, and financially stable before the COVID-19 pandemic but significantly impacted by it. The interviews were carried out over two months, from September 2021 to November 2022. We utilized QDA Miner Lite software for transcription analysis and coding. Following the principles of grounded theory, data collection and analysis were conducted simultaneously, allowing us to identify and discuss emerging patterns and similarities as they arose. Figure 1 shows the data structure that emerged from our analysis.

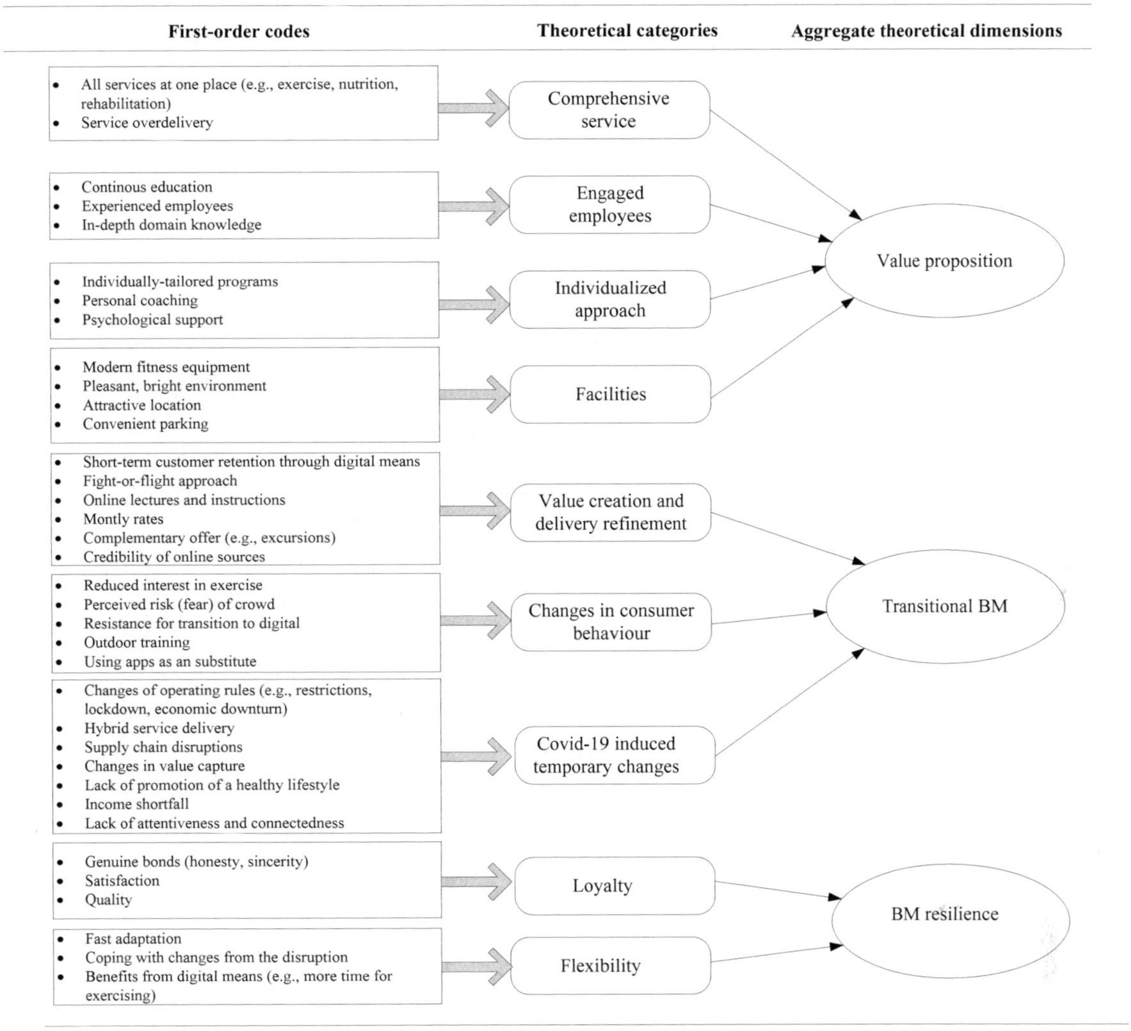

Figure 1. A summary of findings from the semi-structured interviews and focus group

Small fitness businesses have faced increasing pressure to broaden their range of services in response to evolving customer needs, especially amid disruptions like the COVID-19 pandemic. In a competitive market, these businesses must clearly communicate their value propositions to remain relevant. Employees play a critical role in ensuring high-quality customer service, which is essential for retaining clients. Our research supports that engaged and knowledgeable staff significantly impact the overall customer experience, highlighting the importance of ongoing training and professional development.

As customers increasingly seek a sense of community and belonging, small fitness businesses have adapted by offering personalized and engaging approaches to build strong customer relationships. This focus on community not only enhances loyalty but also sets them apart as preferred service providers. The pandemic required a shift in business model elements, prompting small fitness businesses to refine how they create and deliver value. Facilities adjusted their operations to comply with safety regulations, such as limiting in-person activities and allowing only vaccinated clients upon reopening. This shift was necessary to maintain customer trust and adapt to competitors' evolving service offerings. However, these changes also revealed shifts in consumer behavior, as many clients temporarily left the fitness space due to facility closures, disrupting their routines and physical activity levels.

The industry faced substantial income losses, with estimates suggesting a 75% decline in revenue. To counter this, businesses quickly developed or expanded digital options for remote workouts, demonstrating the importance of business model resilience, and adjustments with transitional business model (trial-and-error structure) during crises.

Customer satisfaction remained crucial throughout this period, as the quality of services directly influenced loyalty. When customers perceive that they receive more value than expected, their satisfaction and commitment to the business increase. By maintaining a high level of service and adjusting offerings to meet customer expectations, small fitness businesses could build resilience and sustain customer loyalty during challenging times.

3. CONCLUSION

Several small fitness businesses in our study utilized their existing resources and capabilities to navigate the evolving challenges of the COVID-19 pandemic. Their immediate response involved shifting operations online, but this required modifications to their business models to ensure resilience. The businesses adopted a two-pronged strategy: first, they implemented a trial-and-error approach to sustain operations despite the ambiguity of the pandemic impact and the uncertainty surrounding future business operations. Second, they adjusted their value propositions and built customer loyalty to enhance business model resilience.

Our findings reveal that the need for the adjustments led to the creation of a transitional business model that allowed for experimentation and flexibility. In an environment of limited resources, these businesses had to innovate under pressure, aligning their business models closely with the existing industry structure while modifying value-related dimensions such as distribution channels and customer engagement to increase loyalty. The study also highlights the advantages of small fitness businesses, particularly their flexibility and responsiveness. Unlike larger firms with more complex operations, small businesses can adapt swiftly to external challenges, demonstrating a capacity for rapid learning and adjustment. However, as they expand their service offerings to meet customer demands, the health-and-sports industry is seeing an increasingly blurred line between different types of fitness businesses (i.e., business model convergence).

To enhance business model resilience, small fitness businesses should leverage their strengths by engaging in joint value-creation activities that align their internal capabilities with external market demands. The study suggests that expertise and experience, which emerged as critical internal advantages, can be used to foster value co-creation with other similar businesses.

The findings have several practical applications. First, developing comprehensive services tailored to customer needs can position small fitness businesses as preferred providers in the market. Second, our focus on these businesses reveals their inherent strengths, such as flexibility, and limitations, like resource constraints, illustrating the "duality" of challenges they face. However, the study's scope is limited by its focus on Slovenian small fitness businesses, which may affect the generalizability of findings to other markets and cultural contexts. Additionally, the study did not explore more proactive strategies, such as risk management and agility, which could further influence the effectiveness of BM adjustments in similar scenarios.

ACKNOWLEDGEMENT

The authors would like to acknowledge the financial support of the Slovenian Research Agency (core research project J7-50185).

REFERENCES

Akpan, I.J., Soopramanien, D. and Kwak, D.-H., (2021). Cutting-edge technologies for small business and innovation in the era of COVID-19 global health pandemic. *Journal of Small Business & Entrepreneurship*, *33*(6), pp. 607-617.

Alvesson, M., (2003). Beyond neopositivists, romantics, and localists: A reflexive approach to interviews in organizational research. *Academy of Management Review*, *28*(1), pp. 13-33.

Chesbrough, H. and Rosenbloom, R.S., (2002). The role of the business model in capturing value from innovation: evidence from Xerox Corporation's technology spin-off companies. *Industrial and Corporate Change*, *11*(3), pp. 529-555.

Clauss, T., Breier, M., Kraus, S., Durst, S. and Mahto, R.V., (2022). Temporary business model innovation–SMEs' innovation response to the Covid-19 crisis. *R&D Management*, *52*(2), pp. 294-312.

Corbin, J.M. and Strauss, A., (1990). Grounded theory research: Procedures, canons, and evaluative criteria. *Qualitative Sociology*, *13*(1), pp. 3-21.

Coyne, I.T., (1997). Sampling in qualitative research. Purposeful and theoretical sampling; merging or clear boundaries? *Journal of Advanced Nursing*, *26*(3), pp. 623-630.

Creswell, J.W., (2013). *Research Design: Qualitative, Quantitative, and Mixed Methods Approaches*. Sage Publications.

Denzin, N.K. and Lincoln, Y.S., (2005). Introduction: The Discipline and Practice of Qualitative Research. In *The Sage Handbook of Qualitative Research*, 3rd ed., pp. 1-32. Thousand Oaks, CA: Sage Publications Ltd.

Eisenhardt, K.M. and Graebner, M.E., (2007). Theory building from cases: Opportunities and challenges. *Academy of Management Journal*, *50*(1), pp. 25-32.

Escamilla-Fajardo, P., Núñez-Pomar, J.M., Calabuig-Moreno, F. and Gómez-Tafalla, A.M., (2020). Effects of the COVID-19 Pandemic on Sports Entrepreneurship. *Sustainability*, *12*(20), 8493.

Holstein, J.A. and Gubrium, J.F., (1995). *The Active Interview*. Sage Publications.

Mantere, S. and Ketokivi, M., (2013). Reasoning in organization science. *Academy of Management Review*, *38*(1), pp. 70-89.

McAlister, L., (2020). Here's How COVID-19 Has Changed Fitness. @askmindbody. Last modified May 29, 2020. Available at: https://www.mindbodyonline.com/business/education/blog/heres-how-covid-19-has-changed-fitness.

Sullivan-Taylor, B. and Branicki, L., (2011). Creating resilient SMEs: why one size might not fit all. *International Journal of Production Research*, *49*(18), pp. 5565-5579.

Suri, H., (2011). Purposeful sampling in qualitative research synthesis. *Qualitative Research Journal*, *11*(2), pp. 63-75.

Witschel, D., Döhla, A., Kaiser, M., Voigt, K.-I. and Pfletschinger, T., (2019). Riding on the wave of digitization: insights how and under what settings dynamic capabilities facilitate digital-driven business model change. *Journal of Business Economics*, *89*, pp. 1023-1095.

CHESS AND MUSIC: QUANTITATIVE AND ARTISTIC INTERPRETATION OF INFORMATION

Victor Zheng
North Central College, United States

ABSTRACT

Fork is a framework written in the SuperCollider programming language for algorithmically composing music to chess games in real time in a way that meaningfully conveys the progress of the game in a musically coherent manner. Fork is intended to serve as a dynamic, immersive soundtrack to app-based chess where the players have direct control over the resulting generation, thus turning chess itself into a musical endeavor alongside its normal gameplay. The principles behind Fork straddle the boundary between more traditional note structures and compositional use of uniquely electronic parameters such as timbre and spatialization in musically effective sonification of data.

KEYWORDS

Music, Music Informatics, Algorithmic Music, Supercollider, Chess, Chess Sonification, Interactive Music, Data Sonification, Data in Music

1. INTRODUCTION

Fork seeks to provide a simple yet immersive interaction with chess where each change in the sound is immediately tangible and musically coherent while being intuitively relatable with the impact of the move. It also seeks to be unpredictable, where identical sequences of moves will not inherently produce the same musical result.

2. RELATED PROJECTS

Many projects have been done with the aim of sonifying data taken from chess games. "Chess sonification" yields many results on Google and YouTube. They generally involve a system of converting each individual move into sound, accounting for factors such as piece being moved and/or captured, position on board, and progression of the game. For a more immersive musical result, sonification must also incorporate some level of autonomy, wherein some sound is constantly present, not only dependent on each move. Such autonomy can be controlled via algorithms that interpret the game and affect ongoing sound in response. Several prominent, well documented projects are below.

Stefan Höller's approach as described in *Data-Driven Soundtracks for Chess* (2019) uses the Stockfish engine to identify key moments including decisive moves and mistakes as well as the momentum of a game, all of which determine the progression of the soundtrack. Two soundtrack models are described. The first is a precomposed rock inspired soundtrack divided into several stages, through which the music progresses based on the Stockfish evaluation of the game's progress. The second involves a more subtle harmonic background track without melody or rhythm which can be looped indefinitely, while key moments are marked with short sound cues.

Musical Chess, developed by Ian Clester, John Casun, Qianyi Sun, Jiarui Xu, and Nikhil Ravi Krishnan (2022) similarly uses Stockfish to evaluate the position of the game. Through using synthesizers and controllable sonic parameters, Musical Chess is able to use timbre as well as pitch in its sonifications. The eight squares of each rank and column are mapped to a diatonic scale, with timbre evolving as it evaluates the progression of the game.

Zugzwang (2021), developed by Francesco Ardan Del Rì and Raul Masu, integrates instrumental performance and improvisation with gestural interpretation of chess data. The sonification process of Zugzwang maps spaces on the board to individual pitches under a central mode, using different timbres to identify the pieces being moved. Separately, each move will choose one of four different abstract graphics to be displayed on screen. The choice depends on the time taken to make each move; these graphics are to be interpreted freely by improvising human performers independently of the sonified chess moves.

3. DATA INTERPRETATION

Fork draws its data from the interactions between opposing pieces. At each move of the game, Fork tracks the number of attacks, capture value, and presence of checks resulting from the move. The number of attacks represents the number of pieces on either side initiating an attack at any point. They are represented by the variables `wAtk` (attacks initiated by White) and `bAtk` (attacks initiated by Black). The difference between the combined `wAtk` and `bAtk` values caused by each move is represented by the variable `atkDel`.

Also present are the *stability* and *emphasis* parameters. The stability (`stab`) parameter begins at 3 and is incremented by 1 whenever a move does not result in a capture or check. When `stab` is 3 or greater, then the game is interpreted to be in a stable state. `stab` is reset to 0 whenever a capture or check takes place.

A move is marked with the emphasis (`emph`) Boolean being set to true whenever a high value capture (a rook or a queen) takes place. In such cases, `stab` is also reset to 0.

Below is the opening of a game illustrating the behavior of the various parameters at each move.

Figure 1. Starting position

```
wAtk = 0;
bAtk = 0;
atkDel = 0;
stab = 3;
```

Figure 2. 1. e4

```
wAtk = 0;
bAtk = 0;
atkDel = 0;
stab = 4;
```

Figure 3. 1...d5

```
wAtk = 1; //d5
bAtk = 1; //e4
atkDel = 2;
stab = 5;
```

Figure 4. 2. exd5

```
wAtk = 0;
bAtk = 1; //d5
atkDel = 1;
stab = 0;
```

4. DIRECT CONTROL

The *direct* component of the soundtrack comprises the immediate sonic response to each move.

A *direct tone* plays at every move. The frequency is determined by the move's `atkDel` parameter, corresponding to an overall C Dorian mode. When `atkDel` is equal to 0, this indicates a stable game state, and the resulting tone will be derived from the i triad, translating to C, E♭, and G in C Dorian. At higher levels of `atkDel`, the resulting tones shift in probability towards the VII triad, comprising the notes B♭, D, and F in C Dorian.

The reason for using atkDel to control the pitch is to deliberately choose a parameter that is straightforward as well as central to the game's state, but not so obvious as to be overly predictable. The concept of an attack is simple enough for any novice to understand, and indeed protecting one's pieces is essential to effective chess playing. However, a piece such as the queen is able to initiate many attacks all at once if surrounded by pieces, and counting the actual number of attacks is not a priority for most chess players.

To a similar end, easily decodable elements of each move such as the identity or value of the piece being moved and its starting point and destination have no effect on the sound. By separating the most obvious parameters factoring into a chess player's moves and tactical decisions from the resulting sound, a player will not very easily be able to predict each following note, nor will it get repetitive through normal gameplay. The exceptions are a delay effect and extra notes added to the direct tone for rook captures, queen captures, and checks – such events are both sparing and pivotal enough to warrant musical emphasis.

5. AUTONOMY

Separate from the direct tone are the autonomous components that run continuously, its parameters reacting to each move.

All direct tones are fed into a list and replayed in random order at a rapid tempo in the middle register. This forms the *background melody* component. Simultaneously, they are also played in the order in which they came, in a slower tempo and higher register, the *high melody*. These two components form the main melodic element of the soundtrack; the subtle shifting of its notes between the i and VII triads depending on the behavior of the direct tone influences the stability and character of the melody in reflection of the game state.

In harmonic support is a system of possibilities for the root of the underlying harmony. The root of the chord begins on scale degree 1 (C) and progresses in response to the `stab` parameter.

When a capture or check takes place, `stab` resets to 0, resulting in a *progression* of the chord root and step towards instability. Any move that does not capture or check increases `stab` by 1, and when `stab` reaches 3, a *resolution* of the chord results, restoring stability. A progression or resolution is determined by two maps of possible paths a chord root can take. For example, as represented by the arrows in Fig. 5 below, C can progress towards D, E♭, F, G, and B♭. All possibilities are equally likely, minimizing the chance of predictability even in the exact same sequence of captures and checks.

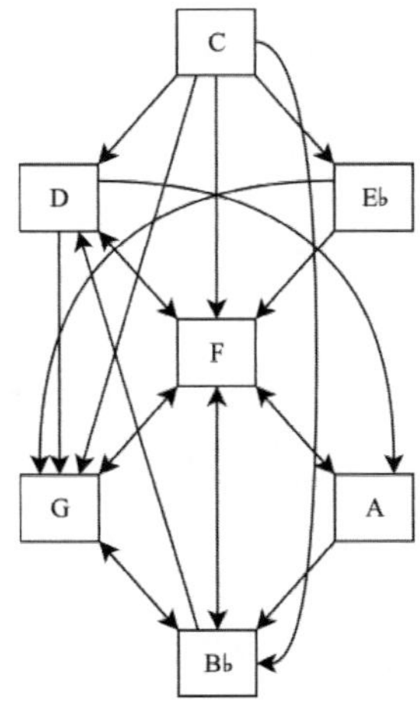

Figure 5. Progression map. All chords have one or more choices in progressing. Progression paths are reminiscent of tonic to predominant motion in common practice harmony, primarily avoiding leading tone dominant-tonic motion except when reaching B♭, which are treated by the direct tone and melody as inherently unstable

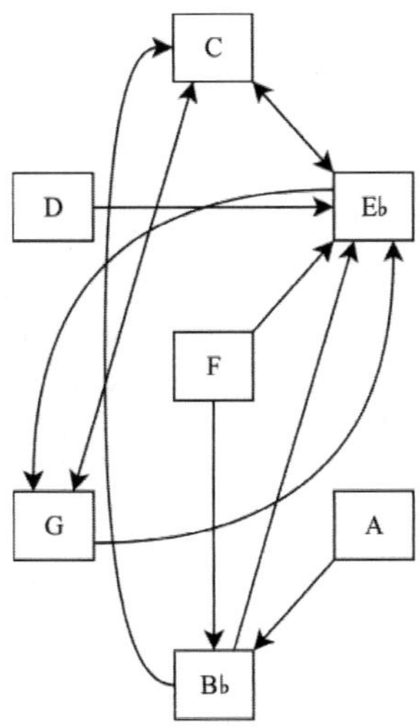

Figure 6. Resolution map. Far fewer choices are available with resolution than with progression, using the C, E♭, G, and B♭ chords as possible destinations. Leading tone dominant-tonic motion is more emphasized in cases of B♭ and E♭, but the inclusion of more indirect resolution paths such as C to E♭ and back maintains a balance between the four possible resolution endpoints

What determines a chord's function with regards to progression and resolution is the nature of the motion (see detailed descriptions under Fig. 5 and Fig. 6), not the identity of the chord itself. This allows for the music to resolve effectively on to any one of the four possible resolution endpoints, and in doing so using the other possible endpoints as in a progressive function.

The harmony, deriving from the root, is executed by several autonomous elements. At all times, the root and the notes that form a third and fifth from it play as long, continuous tones, ensuring that a complete *chord* is always in place. Separately, the notes that comprise the chord are also played separately in random order at a fast tempo, forming the *bass rhythm*. Intermittently, notes from the chord also play a fast, percussive pattern in a high register as the *high percussion* component.

All autonomous components operate continuously without need for player input, thereby avoiding the possibility of interruption of the soundtrack.

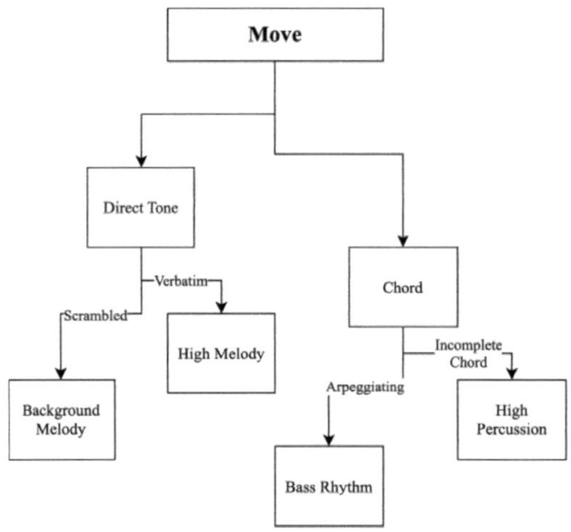

Figure 7. Hierarchy of control. A player does not need to alter any aspect of their chess-playing technique to control the soundtrack compellingly. Their move is their only control vector on the soundtrack, but its effect on the music is propagated through a hierarchy to control an ultimately deep, diverse range of musical parameters.

6. EVALUATION AND IMPACT

Fork taps into the strengths of both the worlds of chess and of music, ensuring that both are operating in their element without compromise.

Existing chess sonification models that emphasize direct control of each move on the sound are vulnerable to overreliance on direct mapping of obvious parameters such as piece identity and board location, resulting in predictable and simple musical output. This predictability is exacerbated by the nature of chess, a game that features no shortage of standardized openings, midgame, and endgame scenarios.

Those sonification models that feature more elaborate musical composition in their structure also suffer from predictability, as traditionally composing the soundtrack results in inflexibility and limited control by the player over the music. Each rendition will only feature small variations and overall follow the same structure.

Fork and the hierarchy of control it affords a player allows each move to control the music both directly and indirectly, bringing flexibility and variability to the music and its realization. Such flexibility is critical to ensuring that the music can be trusted to behave compellingly regardless of the skill of a player.

The musical structures of Fork rely primarily on a variation of classical functional harmony, where chords and notes move between zones of stability and instability. This has ramifications for both melody and harmony and serve as an effective determiner for the notes generated. The harmony, being the slower moving of the two entities, serve to determine the larger-scale structure of the music. Thus, effective variance is ensured on both the micro and macro levels of the music through the maintenance of a coherent musical grammar.

Fork presents a viable framework for the sonification of chess in a musically effective way that reacts dynamically to the myriad possibilities of a game. It will provide an immersive, new musical experience for any chess application that transcends the current compositional practices of game music.

REFERENCES

Clester, I., Kasun, J., Sun, Q., Xu, J., Krishnan, N. R. (2022). *MusicalChess*. GitHub. https://github.com/RoseQSun/MusicalChess

Dal Rì, F., & Masu, R. (2021). Zugzwang: Chess Representation Combining Sonification and Interactive Performance. *Proceedings of the 16th International Audio Mostly Conference*. 89–92. https://doi.org/10.1145/3478384.3478394

Höller, S. (2019). *Data-Driven Soundtracks for Chess* [Master's thesis]. University of Applied Sciences Upper Austria

CONTINUOUS LEARNING OF BIG DATA ANALYTICS OF EMPLOYEES: INTEGRATING UTAUT AND SITUATED EXPECTANCY–VALUE BELIEFS

Seula Lee[1], Hyewon Lee[2] and Youngsang Cho[3]
[1]*Management of Technology, Yonsei University, Seoul, 03722, South Korea*
[2]*Be My Career. Co, Gyeonggi Startup Lab (AI), Gyeongi-do, 16824, South Korea*
[3]*Department of Industrial Engineering, College of Engineering, Yonsei University, Seoul, 03722, South Korea*

ABSTRACT

Despite recognizing the importance of big data analytics capabilities for competitive advantage, the understanding of employees' skill development remains limited. While situated expectancy-value theory (SEVT) is useful for identifying factors influencing learning intention, it lacks actionable strategies for organizations to foster learning environments. Integrating the unified theory of acceptance and use of technology (UTAUT) with SEVT, this ongoing study addresses the gap in understanding how employees enhance their skills to use big data analytics effectively among semiconductor manufacturing engineers. Data were collected from 144 engineers at a semiconductor manufacturing company in South Korea. Partial least squares structural equation modeling was used to analyze the relationships between the constructs. The results show that performance expectancy, effort expectancy, and social influence positively affect continued intention to use big data analytics applications, except facilitating conditions. Secondly, continued intention to use and social norms as supportive environments of learning positively influence intrinsic motivation, mediated by factors such as self-efficacy and perceived usefulness. Understanding these factors provides actionable insights into how technological investment creates learning environments that facilitate the continuous development of big data analytics capabilities. By focusing on mechanisms that foster continuous learning, this study offers strategic guidance for organizations that aim to drive data-driven innovation and maintain a competitive advantage in high-tech industries.

KEYWORDS

Big Data Analytics Capability, Capability Development, Continued Intention, Situated Expectancy-Value Theory, UTAUT

1. INTRODUCTION

Big data analytics (BDA) applications refer to the tools and technologies used to collect, store, process, and analyze large volumes of data from diverse sources. These applications enable the transformation of big data into valuable strategic assets for future innovation (Sabharwal and Miah, 2021). In the semiconductor manufacturing industry, BDA is crucial for optimizing production efficiency through techniques such as equipment failure prediction, automated process control, and yield optimization (David et al., 2024). To fully realize the benefits of BDA, it is essential to develop internal BDA capabilities that enhance operational performance and maintain competitive advantage (Kim and Cho, 2022; Shabbir and Gardezi, 2020). However, previous studies have focused on BDA adoption and implementation (Wang et al., 2022), so there is limited understanding of how employees continuously develop these capabilities, which is critical for sustaining data-driven innovation in such high-tech industry.

Research in information system focuses on the acceptance and usage of BDA applications, with less emphasis on the continuous development of skills. On the other hand, in the field of education, Chai et al. (2020) and Seufert et al. (2019) addressed the impact of technology environments on individual learning motivation and behavioral intentions, but they have not been sufficiently validated in the workplace context and do not provide specific requirements for technology environments, limiting their strategic use in organizations.

To address this gap, we integrate the integrated unified theory of acceptance and use of technology (UTAUT) and the situated expectancy-value theory (SEVT), providing a comprehensive framework to explain both the behavioral and motivational mechanisms that support the continuous development of BDA capabilities. We investigate the factors that influence employees' continued intention to use BDA applications, as sustained usage is not only a measure of technology adoption but also a critical factor for the development of BDA skills. Additionally, this study explores how the use of BDA applications influences employees' learning through the mediation of expectancy-value beliefs, emphasizing the role of motivational factors in shaping continuous learning behaviors. We aim to explain mechanisms that support the development of BDA skills and provide actionable insights for driving data-driven innovation and maintaining a competitive advantage.

2. PREVIOUS LITERATURE

2.1 Unified Theory of Acceptance and Use of Technology

UTAUT is a comprehensive model explaining the acceptance and use of technology. UTAUT identifies four core factors that influence acceptance and usage behaviours: performance expectancy, effort expectancy, social influence, and facilitating conditions (Venkatesh et al., 2016). BDA applications have fundamentally different characteristics from incumbent systems, so Venkatesh (2022) suggests that it is necessary to modify the existing factors of UTAUT or add new factors to understand the adoption of BDA applications. Recent studies have highlighted user resistance as a key factor that negatively affects the acceptance of BDA applications because these systems demand a completely new way of working (Cabrera-Sánchez and Villarejo-Ramos, 2020; Soon et al., 2016). In this study, we used a unified model that considers UTAUT and user resistance to examine the determinants affecting the adoption of BDA within a semiconductor manufacturing company.

2.2 Situated Expectancy-Value Theory

Situated Expectancy-Value Theory (SEVT) offers a valuable framework for understanding how environmental and contextual factors impact learning motivation (Eccles and Wigfield, 2024). Wang et al. (2023) found that infrastructural technology such as big data analytics applications serve as a supportive environmental factor in the learning intention of big data analytics. Insights from research on learning in education could be applied to the business context, where continuous learning of big data analytics knowledge and skills is important for maintaining and improving competitiveness (Pancić et al., 2023), so that the environmental factors of SEVT can help companies design more effective strategies for fostering a culture of continuous learning.

3. RESEARCH MODEL AND HYPOTHESES

This study aims to understand the intention of employees to voluntarily acquire knowledge and skills to utilize big data analytics resources in the workplace, thereby strengthening the organization's big data capabilities.

In the technology acceptance theory, continued intention (CI) is used for reflecting both an individual's initial behavior and their future participation (Ahmad et al., 2022). Performance expectancy (PE), effort expectancy (EE), and social influence (SI) represent psychological factors shaped by cultural and environmental contexts, while facilitating conditions (FC) reflect technological factors (Venkatesh et al., 2016). Understanding these factors provides strategic insights into fostering continued using intention (CI), as each factor has been shown to have a positive. Based on the above studies, the following hypotheses are proposed in this study:

- H1. PE is positively related to CI.
- H2. EE is positively related to CI.
- H3. SI is positively related to CI.
- H4. FC is positively related to CI.

In the SEVT framework, while previous studies have used learning intention as the dependent variable, our research extends this perspective by incorporating future participation, reflecting the necessity for companies to continuously develop big data analytics capabilities. Accordingly, we define continued learning intention (LI) as employees' voluntary engagement in developing their competencies to utilize newly introduced technologies, and used it as the final dependent variable.

Wang et al. (2023) conceptualized supportive environments through technological and social factors, measuring technological factors using facilitating conditions (FC) and social factors using social norms (SN), both of which were used as independent variables. However, in this study, we adopt CI as a more comprehensive measure of the supportive technological environment, reflecting the interactive effect of multiple factors rather than just resource availability. In the UTAUT, FC does not act in isolation but interacts with other psychological factors to influence continued using intention (CI) (Venkatesh et al., 2016). Based on this perspective, CI may be conceptualized as the collective outcome of technological environmental factors and serves as a comprehensive indicator for measuring supportive technological environments. In contrast, social environments are measured using social norms (SN), following prior research without modification.

Expectancies and subjective task values act as mediators that positively influence the relationship between supportive environments and learning outcomes. Expectancies, measured as self-efficacy (SE), reflect how confident individuals feel about completing a task, while subjective task values, measured as perceived usefulness (PU), represent how useful or important they perceive the task to be (Eccles and Wigfield, 2020). When employees utilize big data in a supportive environment with sufficient technological and social resources, they are more likely to develop strong beliefs in their ability to use BDA applications (SE) and recognize their value for achieving professional goals (PU), which, in turn, enhances their continued learning intention (LI). Based on these theoretical foundations, the following hypotheses are proposed.

- H5-1. SE mediates the relationships between CI and LI.
- H5-2. SE mediates the relationships between SN and LI.
- H6-1. PU mediates the relationships between CI and LI.
- H6-2. PU mediates the relationships between SN and LI.

Figure 1 presents our research model, which integrates UTAUT and SEVT to explore external factors that influence the CI of BDA applications. We can also examine how internal motivation affects the continuous learning of big data analytics by analyzing the effects of CI and social norms as supportive environments.

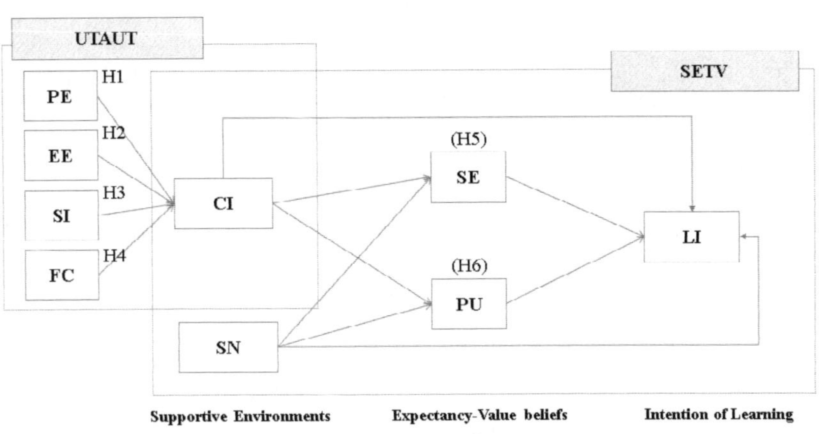

Figure 1. The research model framework

4. RESEARCH METHODOLOGY

4.1 Data Collection

The survey questionnaires have 30 indicators. For making survey questionnaires easily understood, firstly we got response from 10 employees who frequently use big data analytics application and have big data analytics capability, then got feedback from each participant and reviewed the survey questionnaires. Then, for the actual survey and analysis, we chose a semiconductor manufacturing company in South Korea that has implemented big data analytics platforms and developed its employees' big data analytics capability. Most employees of this company use big data and related analytics tools to perform their work at least once a month, on average. At this early phase of the ongoing research, data has been obtained from only manufacturing engineers, and the objective is to develop a base model that can later be extended with additional variables. With the help of each division's big data competency development teams, we randomly selected 990 employees from different team units and organizational positions and distributed the survey questionnaires. A total of 144 usable responses were obtained. The male-to-female ratio was 76:24, and 57% of respondents were between the ages of 30 and 40. 19% of respondents were junior with up to 5 years of experience, 49 % had work experience of 5-10 years, and 32% had work experience over 10 years. 4.2 Partial Least Squares Structural Equation Modeling.

Our research model has a complex structure and includes many constructs, so we chose partial least squares structural equation modeling (PLS-SEM), which is known as an alternative to covariance-based structural equation modeling (CB-SEM) (Hair et al., 2019). PLS-SEM accounts for the total variance and uses it to estimate parameters. It can perform robustness checks for internal consistency reliability, as well as convergent and discriminant validity (Hair et al., 2019).

5. RESULT

5.1 Scale Validation

Cronbach's alpha of all variables is reliable at 0.7 or higher and composite reliability's rule has same result. Each latent variables' average variance extracted (AVE) are higher than 0.5. The square root of the AVE of each latent variable is greater than the highest value of the correlation between other, which satisfies the Fornell-Larcker criterion for discriminant validity. These results indicate that the constructs are distinct from one another, demonstrating that each construct is measuring a unique aspect within the model. Thus, we can confirm that the internal consistency reliability and convergent validity are suitable for analysis.

5.2 Result of Hypotheses Testing

The estimation results are summarized in Table 1. Estimated coefficients for PE→CI (β=0.179), EE→CI (β=0.212) and SI→CI (β=0.217) are statistically significant and they are all positive except UR→CI. As a result, H1, H2 ansH3 are all accepted as like Sekaran and Bougie (2016). However, FC does not significantly affect CI, so H4 is rejected. The estimated coefficients of CI→PU (β=0.598), CI→SE (β=0.569), CI→LI (β=0.485), SN→PU (β=0.277), SN→SE (β=0.348), PU→LI (β=0.211), and SE→LI (β=0.166) are all positive and statistically significant ($p < 0.05$). Therefore, H5-1, H5-2, H6-1 and H6-2 are accepted. Given that estimated coefficient for SN→LI is not statistically significant, we can say that PU and SE are likely to fully mediate rather than partially mediate the relationship between SN and LI.

Table 2. The estimation results

Latent Variables	CI	PU	SE	LI
PE	0.179(2.426)**			
EE	0.212(3.236)***			
SI	0.217(2.585)**			
FC	0.079(1.129)			
CI		0.598(8.082)***	0.569(9.001)***	0.485(6.92)***
SN		0.277(2.726)***	0.348(5.350)***	0.094(1.199)
PU				0.211(2.147)**
SE				0.166(1.937)*

Note 1: The figures in parentheses represent the t-value.
Note 2: *, **, and *** indicate significance levels of 10%, 5%, and 0.1%, respectively.

5.3 Discussion

The results show that the continued intention to use BDA application in the high-tech company is influenced by four factors. First, PE, EE and SI have a positive affect the continued intention to use BDA applications, as demonstrated in previous studies (Cabrera-Sánchez and Villarejo-Ramos, 2020; Wan et al., 2020). Second, FC is not statistically significant, as it is more strongly associated with actual usage behavior rather than with continued intention to use BDA application (Khan and Qudrat-Ullah, 2021).

In this study, we also found that continued intention to use BDA applications and supportive social norms positively impact the motivational factor for learning BDA, using SEVT. Especially, the positive effect of PU on LI is relatively greater than that of SE on LI, and this result is consistent with previous findings (Eccles and Wigfield, 2020; Wang et al., 2023). In this study, PU and SE were observed to play a full mediating role in the relationship between SN and CI. This suggests that it is important to emphasize the usefulness of a BDA tool and ensure that its benefits are fully recognized when a company utilizes it.

6. CONCLUSION

This study provides several strategic implications for high-technology industries where BDA is an important asset, such as semiconductor manufacturing. Firstly, understanding the influence on the CI of using BDA application makes companies' recognition of BDA infrastructure and organizational strategies important. In particular, this means the necessity for strategies that make the interface of BDA more convenient, improve perceived usefulness, and provide necessary resources such as training and a supportive environment to support continuous use of BDA application by employees. Additionally, by improving big data quality and data-driven culture, addressing user resistance can prevent potential risks in technology adoption. Second, we found the positive role of SN and strategies for CI of BDA in promoting learning intentions. Creating a culture that values continuous learning and using can enhance employees' internal motivation to develop competencies. Organizations might consider fostering an environment that supports knowledge sharing and the development of big data competencies.

The integration of UTAUT and SEVT contributes to a deeper understanding of the relationship between the intended continuous use of BDA and the development of BDA skill. Furthermore, this study challenges and extends existing theory by suggesting that continued intention to use BDA applications is a critical variable for studying not only technology adoption but also its educational impact. Our findings enrich the theoretical landscape by highlighting the importance of motivational factors such as self-efficacy, which have been often overlooked in traditional UTAUT literature. This suggests that future developments in technology acceptance study might better consider psychological factors to more effectively explain their significant influence on learning outcomes. These theoretical insights pave the way for future research to explore the interdependencies between technology acceptance and the development of human resources.

While this study provides valuable insights, it does not fully address the cultural dimensions that shape BDA adoption and learning outcomes. In particular, organizational characteristics, such as differences in work structures and leadership styles, may impact the effectiveness of BDA strategies. Future research should explore how these cultural and organizational dynamics interact with the technological and motivational factors examined in this study. Understanding these interdependencies will be crucial for designing more effective strategies for BDA adoption and competency development in diverse workplace settings.

REFERENCES

Ahmad, M. O. et al, (2023). An empirical investigation on business analytics in software and systems development projects. *Information Systems Frontiers*, Vol. 25, No. 2, pp 917-927.

Cabrera-Sánchez, J. P. And Villarejo-Ramos, A. F., (2020). Factors affecting the adoption of big data analytics in companies. *Revista de Administração de Empresas,* Vol. 59, pp 415-429.

Chai, C. S. et al, (2020). An extended theory of planned behavior for the modelling of Chinese secondary school students' intention to learn artificial intelligence. *Mathematics,* Vo.8, No. 11, 2089.

David, J. et al, (2024). New paradigm of Yield analysis in Big Data and AI Era in Semiconductor Manufacturing. *IEEE Electron Devices Technology & Manufacturing Conference*, Bangalore, India, pp. 1-3.

Eccles, J. S. And Wigfield, A., (2020). From expectancy-value theory to situated expectancy-value theory: A developmental, social cognitive, and sociocultural perspective on motivation. *Contemporary educational psychology,* Vol. 61, 101859.

Eccles, J. S. and Wigfield, A., (2024). The Development, Testing, and Refinement of Eccles, Wigfield, and Colleagues' Situated Expectancy-Value Model of Achievement Performance and Choice. *Educational Psychology Review*, Vol. 36, No. 2, pp 1-29.

Hair, J. F. et al, (2019). When to use and how to report the results of PLS-SEM. *European business review*, Vol. 31, No. 1, pp 2-24.

Khan, R. A. et al, (2021). Technology adoption theories and models. *Adoption of LMS in Higher Educational Institutions of the Middle East*, Dubai, UAE, pp 27-48.

Kim, D. and Cho, K., (2022). Digital transformation characteristics of the semiconductor industry ecosystem. *Sustainability*, Vol. 15, No. 1, 483.

Pancić, M. et al, (2023). Business intelligence (BI) in firm performance: role of big data analytics and blockchain technology. *Economies*, Vol. 11, No. 3, 99.

Sabharwal, R. and Miah, S. J., (2021). A new theoretical understanding of big data analytics capabilities in organizations: a thematic analysis. *Journal of Big Data*, Vol. 8, No. 1, 159.

Sekaran, U. and Bougie, R., (2016). *Research Methods For Business: A Skill Building Approach*, John Wiley & Sons, Hoboken, NJ, USA

Seufert, S. et al, (2019). A pedagogical perspective on big data and learning analytics: A conceptual model for digital learning support. Technology, *Knowledge and Learning*, Vol. 24, pp 599-619.

Shabbir, M. Q. and Gardezi, S. B. W., (2020). Application of big data analytics and organizational performance: the mediating role of knowledge management practices. *Journal of Big Data*, Vol. 7, No. 1, 47.

Soon, K. W. K. et al, (2016). A study of the determinants affecting adoption of big data using integrated Technology Acceptance Model (TAM) and diffusion of innovation (DOI) in Malaysia. *International journal of applied business and economic research*, Vol. 14, No. 1, pp 17-47.

Venkatesh, V., (2022). Adoption and use of AI tools: a research agenda grounded in UTAUT. *Annals of Operations Research*, Vol. 308, No. 1, pp 641-652.

Venkatesh, V. et al, (2016). Unified theory of acceptance and use of technology: A synthesis and the road ahead. *Journal of the association for Information Systems*, Vol. 17, No. 5, pp 328-376.

Wan, L. et al, (2020). Toward an understanding of university students' continued intention to use MOOCs: When UTAUT model meets TTF model. *Sage Open*, Vol. 10, No. 3, 2158244020941858.

Wang, F. et al, (2023). University students' intentions to learn artificial intelligence: the roles of supportive environments and expectancy–value beliefs. *International Journal of Educational Technology in Higher Education*, Vol. 20, No. 1, 51.

IMPLICATIONS OF CYBER-STALKING LAW ON MALE VICTIMS: EVALUATING THE SOCIOLOGICAL PERSPECTIVE

Ameema Miftha, Marc Conrad and Marcia Gibson
Institute For Research in Applicable Computing
The University of Bedfordshire, University Square, Luton, Bedfordshire, UK

ABSTRACT

Cyberstalking is an increasingly prevalent form of harassment in the digital age. On the outside, it has laws and regulations that are designed to protect victims. However, the sociological implications of these laws, particularly as they pertain to male victims, have received limited attention. This conference paper aims to shed light on the challenges faced by male victims of cyberstalking and to evaluate the sociological impact of existing laws and regulations. Based on an in-depth analysis of the experiences of male victims, this paper would explore the ways in which gender norms, stereotypes, and societal perceptions intersect with cyberstalking laws and their enforcement.

KEYWORDS

Cyberstalking, Male Victim, Sociological, Cyberstalking Law, Woman Cyberstalker, Woman Accused

1. INTRODUCTION

Cyberstalking can be seen as persistent harassment and intimidation of individuals through electronic communication channels (Vasiu, 2013). This has emerged as a significant societal issue in the digital age. While legal frameworks have been established to address cyberstalking, there is a noticeable gap in understanding its sociological implications (Mathur, 2017). This is especially more visible with the male victims (Masoodi, 2016). This paper seeks to explore the sociological consequences of cyberstalking laws for male victims and how societal norms and stereotypes intersect with these legal measures.

The research conducts a 'desk research' by examining secondary data which already makes relevant observations in the area of research (Martins, da Cunha, & Serra, 2018). Theoretically, this gives a head-start to the research by presenting important insights available with government offices, public libraries and market reports. This however needs considerable effort in terms of fine-tuning and rationalizing the existing findings for the given context (Martins, da Cunha, & Serra, 2018). The research outcome showed that being a male victim to cyberstalking is just as problematical as being a female victim. The landscape on cyberstalking for male victims speaks of a dubious and challenging socio-legal perspective. There are evidence of gender-based discrimination, sexist mentality, lack of sensitization, ambiguity with the law and the society's absolute disregard to female culpability in cyberstalking.

2. DRAWING THE SOCIO-LOGICAL LEGAL PERSPECTIVE

An overview is being done of the existing cyberstalking laws and regulations, and how they work in society. This section emphasizes the need for a gender-neutral approach to ensure equal protection for all victims. The paper also analyzes the enforcement and effectiveness of these laws in cases involving male victims. The sociological impact of cyberstalking laws on male victims are being explored for factors which are critical, yet less talked about:

2.1 Sexist Mentality and Discrimination

'*It is not possible, you must have done something to provoke her*', this is what the male cyber-stalking victims get to hear when they file an First Information Report (FIR) in the police station (Malik, 2022). India is full of prejudices when it comes to cyberstalking landscape. Just as the female victims face unexpected scenarios if they take the legal course, the male victims are equally besieged. The prejudices within the society are such that they wouldn't believe that even a man can be a victim to cyberstalking (penacclaims, 2019). This is reflective of the 'sexist mentality' in the country's social fabric where a lot of discrimination is done on the basis of gender. Just as homophobic and racist, the laws in India can also be seen as sexist (Arora, 2020). According to the police, they cannot be very tough on a girl (penacclaims, 2019). Even the family-members of the girl, the perpetrator, would claim that the girl is being falsely implicated, or the man is taking revenge as she refused his proposal. There are an 'n' number of ways where a male victim is denied justice just because the cyberstalker is a girl. This was evident with the case of Aakash, a South-Delhi Resident, when the police denied his FIR report just because they believed that a girl could never do this and in fact, the victim, Aakash, would have done something to provoke her (Mathur, 2017). Same is the case with another cyber-stalking victim, Vijay Nair, who was being flooded with 'suggestive' social media messages by a woman. Despite having substantial evidence about him being cyberstalked, the legal recourses available to him were negligible (Mathur, 2017).

2.2 Lack of 'Sensitization'

It has been argued that the law on cyberstalking in India, and particularly for man, is completely non-existent (Malik, 2022). There is an evident need to sensitize the people, community and the law enforcement people about how cyberstalking is actually a crime. The legal recourses are either sexist or numb about victim's grief (Arora, 2020). Men, as victims, have no other option but to make an amicable settlement with the woman stalker, as happened with Vijay Nair (Mathur, 2017). One can also argue about the lack of resources in cyber-stalking laws which make it very difficult for male victims to fight it out legally. One of the experts has argued that the IT Act needs to be amended so as to include cyberstalking in it (Neha, Bhatt, & Pareshkumar, 2021). In an infamous case of cyberstalking a husband, the male victim, was spied by his wife for over three months. In the course, his emails and phone numbers were unethically hacked by his son so as to reveal his location as he moved. The husband could not prove anything in the court as, given the Evidence Act, he could not prove the hacking or the use of electronic devices. The complexities here make cyberstalking a very loosely governed crime where the perpetrators have multiple options to get away. And even if the male victims have enough evidences to prove cyberstalking, the police would let go the woman Cyberstalker smilingly with a soft rebuke, 'बेटा अब आगे से परेशान मत करना' (kiddo, do not play any such mischief with the boy from now onwards) (Mathur, 2017). One can sense the seriousness around cyber-stalking when a police-officer says so to a woman Cyberstalker where even the evidence is present to prove her crime.

2.3 No Textual References for 'Male Victim' in the Law

One can further sense the gravity of the problem when it is reported that fifty percent of the cyberstalking cases now have male victims. The statistics do also prove the fact that just a few years back a majority of the cyber-stalking cases had female victims, but the scenario has changed fast. Today, fifty percent of the cyberstalking cases have male victims. Despite it being a 50:50 ratio, the laws around cyberstalking still keep it inclined to woman as 'victim' (Khare, 2018). The law absolutely denies approving the fact that even women cyberstalkers do also exist (Arya, 2019). Apparently, for the law, this is a territory which only men trespass. Section 67 of the IT Act and Section 354D of the IPC have wordings that see woman as 'victim' and man as 'accused' (Sethi, 2022). Ironically, in one such case, the police asked the male victim to tell the section under which to book the female Cyberstalker. Apparently, they went through Section 354D of the IPC and Section 67 of the IT Act and could not understand what sections would apply in this case. The reason is clear with the wordings of the criminal law (Amendment Act, 2013), '*stalking is an offence under Section 354D of the IPC (Indian Penal Code). When a man is trying to communicate with a woman without her interest over the internet via email, instant messages or any other electronic communication is the offence of stalking*'. One can see that the policy wordings state it clearly, *when a man is trying...*

Meanwhile the male victim was sitting on the bench searching on Google about what case should apply for his case so that a FIR can be actually lodged against the woman Cyberstalker.

Significant other references do also talk about the fact that voyeurism has been outlawed under Section 354C of the IPC, however its provisions only apply if the victims is a 'woman' (Masoodi, 2016). A common resentment is that the scope of Section 354C is restricted and its reach is far narrower. However, the male victims can still see some respite with Section 66E which states that 'the victim might be anybody'. The role of gender under Section 66E does not apply in determining culpability (Masoodi, 2016). However, the section is less talked about and the even the police doesn't consider it so often when dealing with male cyberstalking victims (Sethi, 2022).

2.4 Deficiencies with the Existing Law on Cyberstalking

Further research into the area shows that woman, as 'accused', would only come to scene when there are cases of extortion and criminal intimidation. If the experts are to be believed then the male victims need to wait for criminal intimidation or extortion so that the legal course can start to take its course (Masoodi, 2016). The existing Indian laws on cyberstalking do not have any 'clearly written provisions' on cyberstalking by women (Dhaka, 2014). In case, the woman Cyberstalker goes on to commit fake impersonation, identity theft or cheating, only then it amounts to be a crime by a woman. Here, Section 506 mentions that, only if there is cyberstalking coupled with extortion, threatening message, obscenity or intimidation, the law can invoke relevant section' (Arora, 2020). One can argue the fact that cyberstalking is actually not considered a crime until and unless it comes with other 'criminal' adjunctions (Keswani, 2017). One can actually see this with the case of Delhi where a 27-year-old marketing professional was constantly harassed by repeated calls and messages on all of his social media accounts by a girl. When he approached the local police station, the authorities told him to go as there was no crime done (penacclaims, 2019). Apparently in India, a male victim has to wait for something more unlawful before the police would take charge (Halder & Jaishankar K., 2017).

Also, the infrastructure on cyberstalking complaint is comparatively better laid out for a woman as compared to a man (Sethi, 2022). In case a woman wants to file a complaint on cyberstalking, a dedicated cybercrime unit is therefore in every city. Also, the government has formed Cyber Cells to immediately take note of woman grievances on cyberstalking. The complaints are lodged on digital registers and the Criminal Investigation Department (CID) is sensitized on every such matter. In case there is no Cyber Cell or Cybercrime Unit nearby, the woman victim can instantly lodge an FIR with the local police station. However, the problem is that no such facilities are available for the male victims (Bhasin & Mehta A., 2019). There have been instances where the Cyber Cells struggled to formally register a complaint as they didn't know under which section they would write the male victim's grievance of cyberstalking (Sethi, 2022).

2.5 Gendered Nature of Cyberstalking and Underreporting

Cyberstalking is often perceived as a gendered issue where women are typically considered the primary victims (Malik, 2022). This perception can lead to under-reporting of cyberstalking cases involving male victims. Also, this underreporting can be linked to societal expectations of male strength and emotional resilience (Keswani H. , 2017). Examining the gendered nature of cyberstalking is therefore crucial for understanding the unique experiences and challenges faced by male victims. Also, there is a certain socio-logical perspective that speaks about the stereotypes and male victims. The evidence tell that societal stereotypes about masculinity and strength can affect male victims' willingness to report cyberstalking incidents (Mathur, 2017). Clearly, there is a role of stigma and emasculation in male victims' experiences. It therefore becomes important to study the perceptions of vulnerability. This requires analysis of societal perceptions of vulnerability in the context of male victims of cyberstalking. Also, there is need to study how the societal norms around gender roles and expectations intersect with cyberstalking experiences for men (Myneni, 2021). This should reveal more about the impact of these norms on male victims' coping mechanisms and support networks.

3. CONCLUSIONS AND FUTURE WORK

One can therefore conclude that there are no clear provisions to deal with the accused women cyber-stalkers. In India, there is an absolute lack of clearly stated laws on cyberstalking for male victims. What makes it further complicated is the sociological perspective where even the lawmakers or the law enforcement bodies would not see this as a serious crime. It is either taken very lightly or they would find it difficult to see the criminal side of it. Section 67 of the IT Act does make a mention of cyberstalking, but it is based entirely on transmission or publication of obscene material. Similarly, Section 354D is there for the cyberstalking victims, but the police finds no mention of female accused or male victim in its language. The scenario on cyberstalking is therefore very challenging for the male victims. The legal and social complexities leave them open to this kind of abuse, completely unguarded and defenseless.

Extensive studies need to be done in the future that highlight the vulnerability of male cyberstalking victims. This requires analysis of societal perceptions of vulnerability in the social and legal context of male victims of cyberstalking. Also, there is need to study how the societal norms around gender roles and expectations intersect with cyberstalking experiences for men. This should reveal more about the impact of these norms on male victims' coping mechanisms and support networks.

REFERENCES

Arora, N. (2020). Cyberstalking and its Legal Aspects. New Law College, Bharati Vidyapeeth University, Pune.

Arya, N. (2019). "Cyber Crime Scenario in India and Judicial Response". Pub. By (ijtsrd), ISSN: 2456-6470, Volume-3 Issue-4, June 2019.

Bhasin, D., & Mehta A. (2019). Cyber Stalking: New Age Terror, IJLMH Volume 2, Issue 1 2019 ISSN: 2581- 5369

Dhaka, A. (2014). Cyberstalking: Issues and Regulations. Retrieved from 2021 JETIR October 2021, Volume 8, Issue 10.

Halder, D., & Jaishankar K. (2017). Cyber Crimes against Women in India. Sage Pub. India Pvt Ltd ISBN: 978-93-859-8577-5.

Keswani, H. (2017). Cyber Stalking: A Critical Study. Bharti Law Review April-June.

Khare, C. (2018). Laws Punishing Cyber Stalking and Online Harassment. Retrieved from https://blog.ipleaders.in/cyber-stalking/

Malik, M. (2022). Both men and women vulnerable to online harassment in India: Amidst rising online harassment victims seek strict action. Retrieved from https://mediaindia.eu: https://mediaindia.eu/society/both-men-and-women-vulnerable-to-online-harassment-in-india/

Martins, F., da Cunha, J., & Serra, F. (2018). Secondary Data in Research – Uses and Opportunities. Ibero American Journal of Strategic Management (IJSM), 17(4), 01-04. doi:10.5585/ijsm. v17i4.2723.

Masoodi, A. (2016). For victims of cyberstalking, justice is elusive. Retrieved from https://www.livemint.com: https://www.livemint.com/Politics/St93190XdGvpiclGWwnX0I/For-victims-of-cyber-stalking-justice-is-elusive.html

Mathur, A. (2017). Cyberstalking Law: Ill-equipped to protect women, non-existent for men. Retrieved from https://timesofindia.indiatimes.com:https://timesofindia.indiatimes.com/city/delhi/cyberstalking-law-ill-equipped-to-protect-women-non-existent-for-men/articleshow/59179132.cms

Myneni, S. (2021). Information Technology Law (Cyber Laws). 2nd Edition Asian Law House Page No. 545.

Neha, K., Bhatt, D., & Paresh Kumar, D. D. (2021). Legislative and Judicial Responses to Cyberstalking Against Women: An India Perspective. GAP Indian Journal, ISSN – 2582-8177.

penacclaims.com. (2019). Cyberstalking and its Legal Aspects. Navya Arora New Law College, Bharati Vidyapeeth University, Pune, Volume 11, July 2020 ISSN 2581-5504 www.penacclaims.com.

Sethi, P. (2022). Cyber-stalking in India. Retrieved from https://lawbhoomi.com: https://lawbhoomi.com/cyber-stalking-in-india/#:~:text=Section%2066E%20of%20the%20Information%20Technology%20Act%20of%202000%20might,of%20this%20provision%20as%20well.

Vasiu, L. (2013). Cyberstalking Nature & Response Recommendations, AJOIS Vol.2, No.9 Oct.2013 EISSN 2281-4612, Mcser Pub. Rome Italy.

E-SUPPLY CHAIN MAPPING: ILLUMINATING THE NETWORK'S CYBER PHYSICAL RISKS

Sandor Boyson
R. H. Smith School of Business, University of Maryland, USA

ABSTRACT

Through a multi-year series of sponsored research activities, our research team has aimed to develop and refine an integrated IT supply chain mapping methodology to help enable risk analysts, financial executives, information officers and operations managers to visualize, analyze and prioritize the risks in their organization's cyber physical supply chains. The highly granular information generated by integrated supply chain mapping can enable sophisticated risk scoring of production and service locations; and criticality analyses not only at the site level but also across both the supply chain network and industry levels. Single sources of failure for critical parts and services can become more transparent; and mitigation activities can increasingly aim at enhancing the resilience of those assets/sites with the highest corporate revenue at risk or highest mission-criticality. This research was supported by both public and private sector sponsors, including the U.S. National Institute of Standards & Technology (NIST); the General Services Administration (GSA); and Microsoft and Resilinc Corporations.

KEYWORDS

Cybersecurity, Cyber Supply Chain Risk Management, Supply Chain Mapping

1. URGENT NEED FOR VISIBILITY INTO CYBER PHYSICAL SUPPLY CHAIN RISKS

The cyber supply chain is an end to end process that includes software and hardware production, IT network deployment and systems integration services. Boyson, Corsi and Rossman (2009) pointed out that "the cyber supply chain includes the entire set of key actors and their organizational and process-level interactions that plan, build, manage, maintain, and defend an information system." Similarly, Simpson (2010) defined the IT system supply chain as an internationally distributed and dynamic collection of people, process and technology.

Whether its sourcing code from India or electronic components from China, It's obvious that rapid globalization has changed the operating dynamic of the cyber supply chain. For IT managers and system integrators of all kinds, there have been new efficiency gains and operational flexibilities to be realized from these global arrangements. But there has been a serious downside as well: the lack of visibility and loss of control caused by rapid globalization has become a major business liability. Goertzel (2010) pointed out that "today, most software is acquired from a complex supply chain of OTS vendors, open source repositories, and contractors whose identities, locations, and trustworthiness are often unclear or unknown (and possibly unknowable)". Highly publicized examples of such software supply chain attacks have included Dell Power Servers shipped with malicious malware; and routers shipped to the Pentagon infected with report-back mechanisms to a foreign intelligence agency. In addition to cyber threats, global IT supply chains also face a spectrum of business & operating risks such as weather disruption: The 2011 flooding in Thailand, the world's second largest hard disk drive (HDD) producer after China, led to large-scale destruction of production capacity, pushed up prices 20-40 percent and hobbled PC sales worldwide. A flood event of similar proportion in Shenzhen China would impact 90% of world consumer electronics production. Researchers have long noted that such location-specific events have impacts that cascade globally because most supply chains were not designed with overall redundancy and resilience as key criteria (Haraguchi and Lall, 2015).

For governments, this heightened exposure to the uncertainties and threats of the global supply chain has created a crisis of confidence in the integrity of the very systems that government relies upon to conduct its operations. This research paper builds on the strategies, methodologies and controls defined in NIST's "Cyber Supply Chain Risk Management Practices For Systems & Organizations" (May, 2022) and the NISTIR 8179, "Criticality Analysis Process: Helping Organizations Decide Which Assets Need To Be Secured First (April 11, 2018). A key finding of these documents is that "risks are associated with an enterprise's decreased visibility into and understanding of how the technology they acquire is developed, integrated and deployed"; and "there are no known models or algorithms which adequately fulfil the needs of federal departments and agencies in measuring cyber-security risk related to supply chain interdependencies." A basic motivation of our research has been to help federal managers gain visibility into their cyber supply chain network structures: map the hubs and nodes of their networks; identify their critical suppliers in Tiers 1, 2, 3 and beyond; graph the extent of interdependencies between the tiers; and analyze the risk-scores of suppliers. As part of of our research effort with NIST, we surveyed 200 key IT vendors of the federal government; mapped over 60 public and private standards & practice initiatives; and created a set of portal-based enterprise assessment tools that were field tested by over 200 companies. We also collaborated with Resilinc Corporation to learn to apply machine learning techniques to very large datasets from its enterprise supply chain customers (as demonstrated in section III). Our objective was to help generate better mapping/ filtering technology to help managers more quickly hone in on supply chain locations with highest/lowest value at risk and highest/lowest risk response capabilities.

2. METHODOLOGY FOR INTEGRATED E-SUPPLY CHAIN MAPPING

2.1 Building the Representations Layer

Step 1 of this methodology is building a Supply Chain Representations Layer. Supply chain visibility begins with the creation of a Base Map. This involves the construction of a map that geo-codes (by latitude/longitude) the locations of significant hardware production assets, product warehousing/distribution sites, software development/testing centers and network/data operations sites. Map creation can be outsourced to commercial application providers (such as Resilinc, Interos or Everstream,etc); or developed by industry users themselves who collect and display their own cyber supply chain network data in open source Google or Drupal Base Layer GIS Maps. Overlayed on to this base map are site location data on business processes, geo-political, climate, cyber risks etc.

In addition, real time threat data generated by IT network traffic analysis can be integrated into a command center view that can visualize & richly display these flows. Network mapping tools, such as those from KMD and Splunk/ Intermapper, enable the user to auto-generate network maps in real time for traffic analysis & threat monitoring purposes. Other tools from sources such as www.shadowserver.org enable the tracking of the number of malicious network connections an enterprise is experiencing by mapping network traffic and tracking cyber-attacks across supply chain networks in real time; by storing historic malicious connections; and by having extensive data sharing partnerships with industry, government and law enforcement. Other sources enable the identification of persistent threats hidden and resident in corporate systems. For example, Team Cymru at hhttp://www.team-cymru.org/ tracks advanced persistent threats not readily sensed or discovered within the enterprise. As part of our research, our team built such a console for NIST- a cyber supply chain dashboard. A portal front-end, a user-interface that aggregated and filtered risk data from business sources such as Bloomberg, SEC/Edgar and cyber threat data. The dashboard enabled the user to create and navigate risk performance profiles of their own and peer organizations; its Information Architecture is shown below:

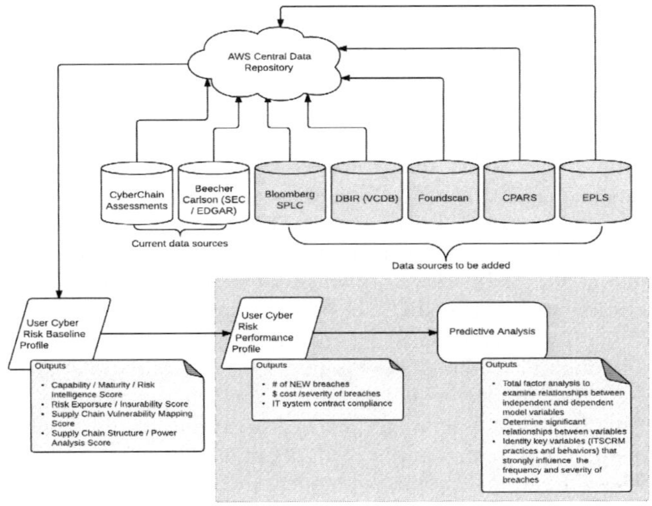

Figure 1. Information architecture for the cyber-risk portal

These assessment tools enabled risk diagnosis of current and prospective vendors, their IT supply chain "trouble spots" and areas for improvement based on NIST guidelines. `Organizations that completed our portal's enterprise assessment received an Aggregate Risk Score that analyzed the organization's alignment with NIST Cyber Security Framework; its IT Supply Chain's riskiness : its exposures and susceptibility to attacks along the chain; and it's operating distance from current best practice.

2.2 Conducting Supply Chain Dependency Analysis

Step 2 of this methodology is conducting an Supply Chain Dependency Analysis : users will examine the extent of inter-dependencies among hubs and nodes represented in **Step 1**. This means analyzing the number and size of relationship dependencies between cyber physical supply chain hubs and nodes; and visually graphing the extent of inter-dependencies. Supply chains are ultimately about relationships: the complexity of supply chains are linked to the total number of suppliers from which the Acquirer or OEM sources; and the financial and operational relationships between them. Boyson and Paraskevas developed and scaled algorithms to measure an Original Equipment Manufacturer's percentage of total cost of goods spent with each supplier and the percent of each supplier's revenue attributable to those OEM purchases. This Supply Chain Power dependency metric is a particularly helpful financial and operations risk indicator as it directly assesses leverage/power between supply chain actors. Dependency analyses increasingly needs to look beyond an individual organization/company supply chain and go deeper into datasets that provide insights into **an industry's shared but hidden supply chain vulnerabilities.** Mckinsey Global Institute pointed out that IT leaders Dell and Lenovo shared suppliers in many cases and were unaware of their common risks: "Network analysis can reveal some of the hidden dependencies lurking within supplychains;75 percent of Dell's 20 most connected suppliers are shared with Lenovo, and 70 percent of Lenovo's 20 most connected suppliers are shared with Dell. Foxconn, IBM, and Microsoft are hardware and software suppliers to both companies—and are highly connected in both networks. Should one become disrupted, it would not only affect Dell and Lenovo's existing operations but also limit their ability to secure alternative sourcing." (Source: Mckinsey Global Institute, "Risk, Resilience and Rebalancing in Global Value Chains", January, 2020). SEMI, the industry association serving the global electronics manufacturing and design supply chain is seeking to help its members avoid these hidden dependencies by leveraging industry supply chain mapping efforts to provide visibility over 95% of the supply chain mapped down to the supplier, sub-tier, part-site, and commodity levels (Source: Globe Newswire, Milpitas, CA, May 02, 2023).

2.3 Performing Criticality Analyses on Large Scale Supply Chain Risk Data

Step 3 of this methodology is performing Supply Chain Criticality Analyses: users will filter network locations and supply chain relationships to target specific sites & suppliers for special risk management attention and investment. Boyson, Guntuka & Gerst engaged in research with Resilinc Corporation, harnessing machine learning to map and analyze a supply chain network spanning 10,000 supplier locations in the U.S. and Asia with a predominance of high tech and electronics industry sites. For each geo-coded supply chain location in our test sample, critical risk management overlays/ filters were applied. Each of the sites were screened and benchmarked against other sites for indices such as number/severity of risk events, availability of alternate suppliers, revenue at risk, time to recover (TTR) from events and business continuity planning levels (BCP). Using machine learning, we processed the sites' associated data points not only to gain deeper supply chain risk insights about individual sites, but network vulnerability or resilience as a whole. Our findings included some of the following comparative performance indicators for our test sample of 10,000 sites: **Revenue at Risk:** 35% of the total production sites under study had high levels of revenue at risk and represented critical financial risks for the corporate customer sourcing from these locations. **Business Continuity Risks:** High business continuity risks due to the absence of actual response plans and training exercises affected the majority of sites in the sample: 74% of all sites and 72% of highest-revenue sites did not have a Business Continuity Plan (BCP). They were unprepared for disruptions to their operations**. Alternative Suppliers:** Almost 90% of the sites did not have not identified arrangements in place with alternate suppliers in event of a disaster .Conversely, we used machine learning to pinpoint the most advanced network sites that demonstrated the highest degree of preparedness: sites that combined mature, active Business Continuity Programs and aggressive alternate site identification (Source: https://hbr.org/2022/05/how-exposed-is-your-supply-chain-to-climate- risks).

3. CONCLUSIONS

Our proposed three step methodology encourages users to create a base map of the cyber physical supply chain; then overlay business, climate and cyber risk data upon the geo-coded supply chain locations. Each hub or node location might have a record with the following associated information:

-Latitude/longitude coordinates
-Six digit ICT NAICS codes (311111-339999); and other industry descriptors
-Financial performance/contribution to corporate revenue
-Business/operations risks
-# and severity of risk events
-Cyber risk data
-Process complexity (# of manufacturing/software development/ data center processes)
-Supply chain relationships (# of external sourcing or distribution relationships)
-Unknown or grey market sources of supply
-Ownership/foreign threat level
-Dependency on energy utility grid
-Telecom network reliability

We have demonstrated that the information generated by this methodology can enable sophisticated risk scoring of supply chain locations and also deeper machine learning/insight generation across both the extended enterprise and industry supply chains. Single sources of failure for critical parts and services can become more transparent; and mitigation activities might then increasingly aim at enhancing the resilience of assets/sites with the highest revenue at risk or highest mission-criticality. As Linnenlueke, Ambulkar and Angkiriwang have noted, accelerated decision making is a fundamental characteristic of flexible and adaptive supply chains. The integration of data collected from multiple sources representing both supply chain and IT risks in a centralized repository can bring heightened executive-level risk awareness; better insights into systemic risk; and shorter decision-paths to prioritizing and implementing risk mitigation actions.

REFERENCES

Ambulkar, S., Blackhurst, J. and Grawe, S., (2015). Firm's resilience to supply chain disruptions: Scale development and empirical examination. Journal of operations management, 33, pp.111-122.

Angkiriwang, R., Pujawan, I.N. and Santosa, B., (2014). Managing uncertainty through supply chain flexibility: reactive vs. proactive approaches. Production & Manufacturing Research, 2(1), pp.50-70.

Boyson, Sandor, (2014). Cyber Supply Chain Risk Management: Revolutionizing the strategic control of critical IT systems", Technovation, Vol.34 Issue 7, July, 2014.

Boyson, Sandor, Corsi, Thomas and Patrick Paraskevas John, (2022). Defending Digital Supply Chains: evidence from a decade long research program Technovation, Volume 118, December 2022,102380.

Boyson, Sandor, Corsi Thomas and Paraskevas John, (2008). Critical Metrics for Evaluating Supplier Performance: A Statistical Analysis for The Manufacturing and Industrial Base Office of The U.S. Secretary of Defense, 2008.

Goertzel, Karen, (2010). Supply Chain Risk Management and the Software Supply Chain, Conference Presentation at OWASP AppSec DC, November 2010. https://www.owasp.org/images/7/77/BoozAllen-AppSecDC2010-sw_scrm.pdf

Linnenluecke, M. K., Griffiths, A. and Winn, M., (2011). Extreme Weather Events and the Critical Importance of Anticipatory Adaptation and Organizational Resilience in Responding to Impacts. Business Strategy and the Environment, 21(1), 17–32. doi: 10.1002/bse.708

Masahiko Haraguchi and Upmanu Lall, (2015).Flood Risks and impacts: ACase Study Of Thailand's Floods in 2011 and research questions for supply chain decision making International Journal of Disaster Risk Reduction, Volume 14, Part 3, December 2015, Pages 256-272

Simpson, Stacy, (2010). Software Integrity Controls: An Assurance-Based approach to Minimizing Risks in the Software Supply Chain. Arlington, VA: SAFECode, June 14, 2010. http://www.safecode.org/publications/SAFECode_Software_Integrity_Controls0610.pdf.

U.S. Department of Commerce, (2022). Assessment Of the Critical Supply Chains Supporting the U.S. Information and Communications Technology Industry, U.S. DOC/U.S.DHS, February 23, 2022.

PERCEIVED EMPLOYABILITY IN AN AI-DRIVEN WORLD: LIFELONG LEARNING FOR GENERATIONS X, Y AND Z

Sabina Lissitsa and Chen Sabag-Ben Porat
Ariel University, Kiryat Hamada, Ariel, 40700, Israel

ABSTRACT

The rise of AI is reshaping labor markets and employability across generations. This study examines how AI competence, human capital, and social capital impact career resilience among Generations X, Y, and Z. Using a large-scale online survey (N=723) and hierarchical regression analysis, findings reveal that Generation X relies on professional networks, Generation Y balances AI skills and networking, while Generation Z struggles to translate AI proficiency into career benefits. These digital labor ruptures underscore the importance of both technological adaptation and social capital in employment outcomes. Policy recommendations highlight the need for AI upskilling programs, intergenerational learning, and structured career support to foster workforce resilience. By addressing generational differences and promoting adaptable career strategies, this research enhances understanding of employability in the AI-driven era.

KEYWORDS

Perceived Employability, Human Capital, Social Capital, Generational Cohorts, Lifelong Learning

1. INTRODUCTION

The rapid pace of globalization and technological innovation, coupled with shifts in organizational structures, has profoundly redefined career trajectories in contemporary society (Forrier and Sels, 2003). Employability, framed as an individual's ability to secure positions in both internal and external labor markets, is not merely a static quality but a dynamic interplay of human and social capital (Sullivan and Baruch, 2009, Lissitsa and Chachashvili-Bolotin, 2019). Theories of human capital stress the accumulation of skills, competencies, and knowledge (Becker, 2009), while social capital emphasizes the role of networks and connections (Adler and Kwon, 2002). Together, they highlight how individuals must leverage both to thrive in an environment where careers are increasingly non-linear and subject to constant flux.

In this context, the imperative for lifelong learning becomes more pronounced (Lissitsa and Chachashvili-Bolotin, 2020). Lifelong learning, therefore, is not merely an option but a strategic necessity. It equips individuals to respond proactively to the evolving demands of the AI-driven market, ensuring that they remain relevant amidst technological disruption (Poquet and De Laat, 2021). Lifelong learning and adaptability to technology are profoundly shaped by career stages (Lissitsa et al., 2017) and the differing values associated with each generational cohort (Lissitsa, 2024). For instance, Generation X, often characterized by their focus on stability and long-term career progression (Erickson, 2010), may approach the necessity of AI competence with a desire to augment their existing skills to maintain relevance. In contrast, Generation Y (Millennials) and especially Generation Z, who entered the workforce during periods of intense technological transformation, may exhibit greater flexibility in adopting AI-related skills, perceiving them as integral to their professional identities (Chan and Lee, 2023). These variations highlight the importance of understanding how different generations prioritize and integrate technological competencies into their employability strategies.

The current study, therefore, explores the patterns in which human and social capital variables, particularly AI competence, impact perceived employability among different generations.

2. BODY OF PAPER

2.1 Methodology

The study was conducted through an online survey of 723 respondents aged 18-58. The sample included 168 respondents from Gen X, aged 45-58, 222 respondents from Gen Y, aged 29-44 and 333 respondents from Gen Z, aged 18-28. Based on national statistical data, quotas were imposed for age, sex, and residential area. The response rate was about 70%.

Variables

Dependent variable

Perceived employability was measured using a self-reported index based on responses to five statements such as: "The skills you have acquired in your current job will be attractive to potential future employers,"rated on a 5-point Likert scale (see Rothwell and Arnold, 2007).

Independent variables

Human capital variables were measured by *formal education and perceived AI competence*. The last was measured using a 10-item self-reported index, based on responses to statements such as: "You are able to create AI-based solutions to solve problems," rated on a 5-point Likert scale (see Carolus et al., 2023).

Perceived social capital in career self-management was measured using a 2-item self-reported index, based on responses to statements such as: "You established or maintained connections with people who can assist you professionally," rated on a 5-point Likert scale.

Findings

Descriptive findings

Our descriptive findings show that AI competence among "digital immigrants"- Gen X, (Mean = 3.06, SD = 0.97) was significantly lower compared to "digital natives" Gen Y (Mean = 3.31, SD = 0.84), and Gen Z (Mean = 3.41, SD=0.87). The employability of young career employees - Gen Z (Mean = 3.67, SD = 0.78) was significantly lower compared to mid-career Gen Y (Mean = 3.81, SD = 0.77) and Gen X (Mean = 3.81, AD = 0.82).

Multivariate analysis

To address the study's aim, we ran three models of hierarchical regression separately for each generation (see Table 1).

Table 1. Predicting perceived employability – hierarchical regression findings

	Generation Z		Generation Y		Generation X	
	B	Beta	B	Beta	B	Beta
(Constant)	3.13**		1.89**		2.73**	
Genger (male)	0.01	0.01	-0.14	-0.09	-0.07	-0.05
Locality (center)	0.06	0.04	0.00	0.00	-0.05	-0.03
Age	-0.01	-0.02	0.01	0.04	0.00	0.01
Religiosity	-0.06	-0.07	0.04	0.05	0.00	0.00
Social capital	**0.15****	0.23	0.10	0.13	**0.21****	0.27
AI competence	0.10	0.12	**0.16****	0.18	0.13	0.16
Education	-0.04	-0.05	**0.20****	0.26	-0.01	-0.01
R^2	0.086		0.13		0.132	

3. CONCLUSION

The findings from this study offer crucial insights into the differential impacts of AI competence and social capital on perceived employability across generations. These results illuminate not only generational disparities in the integration of AI into career trajectories but also the varying mechanisms through which human and social capital influence employability.

Firstly, the pronounced role of social capital in enhancing employability among Generation X and Generation Z highlights the continued importance of networking and relational resources, even in a technology-driven labor market. For Generation X, who are often digital immigrants, social capital may act as a compensatory mechanism for their lower levels of AI competence. This suggests that while technological skills are critical, the value of human connections, mentorship, and professional networks cannot be overstated. Generation X workers may rely on established professional relationships to maintain their employability in industries increasingly dominated by younger, more tech-savvy professionals. This finding resonates with the social capital theory, which posits that the strength of one's professional networks can provide access to job opportunities and resources, thus bolstering employability (Adler & Kwon, 2002).

For Gen Z, their reliance on social capital might be attributed to their relative lack of professional experience. Although they are considered digital natives, their early career stages make professional connections particularly valuable as they navigate the initial stages of their careers.

In contrast, the findings for Generation Y demonstrate that human capital variables, formal education, and AI competence play a more significant role in shaping their perceived employability. This generation is often seen as being in the midst of their careers, where the accumulation of skills and qualifications—especially those related to technological proficiency—becomes essential for maintaining competitiveness in the labor market. The positive effect of AI competence on employability for Generation Y aligns with human capital theory, which emphasizes the role of education and skills in enhancing labor market value (Becker, 2009). Generation Y workers, many of whom entered the workforce during a period of rapid technological advancement, may have internalized the necessity of continuous upskilling, particularly in areas such as AI, as part of their professional identity. The ability to leverage these advanced competencies, therefore, positions them as attractive candidates in a competitive, rapidly evolving job market.

The generational differences observed in the relative importance of AI competence and social capital underscore the need to view employability through a multifaceted lens. Employability is not only a reflection of individual skill sets but is also shaped by broader social and relational dynamics. This interplay between human and social capital highlights the complex ways in which individuals across different career stages navigate the labor market. For older generations, leveraging social capital may serve as a buffer against technological gaps, whereas for younger, more tech-savvy cohorts, social capital complements human capital in facilitating career advancement.

Furthermore, the growing impact of AI on employability highlights the broader societal and organizational shifts that are reshaping career development. As AI continues to permeate industries, the ability to adapt to and work alongside intelligent systems will become increasingly integral to career success. Lifelong learning, therefore, emerges not merely as an individual responsibility but as an organizational imperative. Employers should consider embedding AI-related skills development into their learning and development strategies, ensuring that employees across all generations are equipped to navigate the AI-driven future of work. The findings also reinforce the importance of fostering a culture of continuous learning, where employees are encouraged to view skill acquisition as an ongoing process rather than a one-time investment.

In conclusion, this study contributes to a deeper understanding of how generational differences shape the relationship between AI competence, social capital, and perceived employability. It underscores the need for tailored career development strategies that recognize the unique challenges and strengths of each generation. By integrating insights from human and social capital theories, this research offers a more nuanced perspective on employability in the context of rapid technological change, and it provides actionable recommendations for both individuals and organizations striving to remain competitive in an AI-driven labor market.

REFERENCES

Adler, P. S. & Kwon, S.-W. (2002). Social capital: Prospects for a new concept. *Academy of management review,* 27, 17-40.

Becker, G. S. (2009). *Human capital: A theoretical and empirical analysis, with special reference to education*, University of Chicago press.

Carolus, A., Koch, M. J., Straka, S., Latoschik, M. E. & Wienrich, C. (2023). MAILS-Meta AI literacy scale: Development and testing of an AI literacy questionnaire based on well-founded competency models and psychological change-and meta-competencies. *Computers in Human Behavior: Artificial Humans,* 1, 100014.

Chan, C. K. Y. & Lee, K. K. W. (2023). The AI generation gap: Are Gen Z students more interested in adopting generative AI such as ChatGPT in teaching and learning than their Gen X and millennial generation teachers? *Smart learning environments,* 10, 60.

Erickson, T. J. (2010). *What's next, Gen X?: Keeping up, moving ahead, and getting the career you want*, Harvard Business Press.

Forrier, A. & Sels, L. (2003). The concept employability: A complex mosaic. *International journal of human resources development and management,* 3, 102-124.

Lissitsa, S. (2024). Generations X, Y, Z: the effects of personal and positional inequalities on critical thinking digital skills. *Online Information Review.*

Lissitsa, S. & Chachashvili-Bolotin, S. (2019). The effect of digital variables on perceived employability in an ethnic minority and the hegemonic group. *Israel Affairs,* 25, 1082-1104.

Lissitsa, S. & Chachashvili-Bolotin, S. (2020). It's not what you know but where you come from: Cognitive skills, job autonomy and latent discrimination of ethnic minorities in Israel. *International Review of Education,* 66, 341-362.

Lissitsa, S., Chachashvili-Bolotin, S. & Bokek-Cohen, Y. A. (2017). Digital skills and extrinsic rewards in late career. *Technology in Society,* 51, 46-55.

Poquet, O. & De Laat, M. (2021). Developing capabilities: Lifelong learning in the age of AI. *British Journal of Educational Technology,* 52, 1695-1708.

Rothwell, A. & Arnold, J. (2007). Self-perceived employability: Development and validation of a scale. *Personnel review,* 36, 23-41.

Sullivan, S. E. & Baruch, Y. (2009). Advances in career theory and research: A critical review and agenda for future exploration. *Journal of management,* 35, 1542-1571.

OPPORTUNITIES AND CHALLENGES IN USING LARGE LANGUAGE MODELS AND GENERATIVE AI FOR ICD CLINICAL CODING

Alberto Freitas, Fernando Lopes and João Vasco Santos
RISE-Health, MEDCIDS, Faculty of Medicine, University of Porto
Alameda Prof.
Hernâni Monteiro, 4200-319, Porto, Portugal

ABSTRACT

The adoption of Large Language Models (LLMs) and Generative AI in healthcare is increasing due to their potential to improve clinical coding processes. This paper reviews existing literature on applying LLMs and Generative AI to support International Classification of Diseases (ICD) clinical coding. Key benefits include improving coding accuracy, reducing administrative workload, and enhancing decision-making support. However, data privacy, interpretability, and the need for domain-specific adaptation persist. This review highlights the potential of these technologies and emphasises key aspects of their effective integration into clinical workflows.

KEYWORDS

Large Language Models, Clinical Coding, ICD-10, Data Quality

1. INTRODUCTION

Clinical coding plays a critical role in healthcare systems, translating medical diagnoses and procedures into standardised formats such as the International Classification of Diseases (ICD) 10th version (ICD-10). These data are essential for several purposes, including billing, quality management, epidemiological surveillance and research. Accurate coding ensures proper hospital reimbursement and supports practical data analysis. However, clinical coding processes face ongoing challenges, including the increasing complexity of medical records, high workloads on clinicians and coders, the shortage of health professionals, and frequent updates to coding standards.

Additional challenges arise from variability in documentation practices, inconsistent coding guidelines across institutions, and reliance on outdated tools. For example, discrepancies in information across different parts of a medical record or the need for clearer, concise summaries can hinder the coding process. Coders often need more time to address incomplete or ambiguous documentation (Alonso, 2020).

Recent advancements in artificial intelligence (AI), particularly in Large Language Models (LLMs) like GPT-4 and Generative AI systems, offer promising solutions to these challenges (Klang, 2024). These technologies can process unstructured clinical narratives, extract relevant diagnostic and procedural information, and map them to ICD-10 codes with improved accuracy and efficiency (Falis, 2024). AI-driven tools can revolutionise the clinical coding process, reducing the workload for coders, potentially enhancing consistency, and minimising errors associated with manual coding practices.

This paper explores the applications, benefits, challenges, and future opportunities of integrating LLMs and Generative AI into ICD-10 clinical coding. It highlights how these tools can address existing barriers, improve accuracy, and enhance workflows to create a more efficient and reliable coding system.

2. METHODS

This paper synthesises findings from the scientific literature on using LLMs and Generative AI for clinical coding. Searches were conducted using terms related to LLMs (e.g., "Large Language Models," "generative AI") and clinical coding (e.g., "ICD-10," "medical coding"). Articles were identified through academic databases, focusing on studies that reported empirical findings or discussed applications of LLMs in healthcare. This narrative review concisely summarises key insights without following systematic review protocols.

3. BACKGROUND AND APPLICATIONS OF LLMS IN CLINICAL CODING

Natural Language Processing (NLP) techniques have evolved significantly, from rule-based methods to advanced deep learning models like LLMs (e.g., GPT and BERT). While generic NLP performs well in general language tasks, fine-tuning with domain-specific datasets is essential to address the complexity and terminology of clinical coding tasks (Dai, 2024). Large Language Models (LLMs), such as GPT and BERT, are advanced AI models designed to process and understand human language, trained on extensive datasets containing diverse text inputs. These models excel at tasks like generating coherent text, summarising lengthy documents, and classifying language into meaningful categories. Their ability to recognise patterns, context, and relationships within the data enables highly accurate and efficient performance across a range of applications. Generative AI builds upon the foundation of LLMs, interpreting and analysing text while creating new, contextually relevant content learned during training. This expanded capability allows for a broad spectrum of innovative uses, including content generation, conversational agents, and specialised applications in healthcare and clinical coding (Chen, 2022).

LLMs have been adapted in healthcare to analyse clinical narratives, identify diagnostic and procedure terms, and map them to ICD-10 codes. A recent evaluation of GPT-based systems in emergency departments demonstrated superior specificity and precision compared to human coders within a subset of 200 cases with coding discrepancies. Human reviewers preferred GPT-4-generated codes over human-coded ones by a significant margin ($p<0.001$), highlighting the potential of AI to improve coding quality in clinical contexts (Klang, 2024). Techniques such as fine-tuning with domain-specific datasets have further improved the accuracy of these models in medical applications (Liu, 2022).

Examples of Applications of LLMs in Clinical Coding

Automated coding: LLMs can map clinical notes directly to ICD-10 codes. Fine-tuned models can achieve high accuracy in predicting codes from electronic health records (EHRs), significantly improving the efficiency and reliability of the coding process (Liu, 2023). These models reduce the need for manual intervention, enhancing efficiency and minimising errors in repetitive coding tasks.

Assisted decision-making: rather than replacing human coders, AI systems using LLMs provide intelligent coding suggestions to assist decision-making. These tools reduce the cognitive load on coders by highlighting potential matches or resolving ambiguities in clinical documentation, allowing coders to focus on more complex cases. This assistance improves workflow efficiency, enhances accuracy, and minimises errors, particularly for less experienced coders (Soroush, 2024).

Integration with EHRs: AI-driven tools integrated into EHR systems enable real-time coding suggestions during documentation. This integration enhances operational efficiency, reduces administrative burdens on clinicians and coding staff, and ensures accuracy and consistency in real-time coding tasks (Falis, 2024). These systems also support compliance with evolving coding standards, helping healthcare organisations maintain up-to-date practices.

4. ADVANTAGES OF USING LLMS FOR ICD-10 CODING

Automation and efficiency: the adoption of LLMs and Generative AI represents significant progress in automating clinical coding tasks, transforming a traditionally labour-intensive and error-prone process. AI-driven systems process large volumes of clinical narratives with minimal human intervention, efficiently extracting diagnostic and procedural terms. These tools accelerate the coding process, reduce administrative burdens, and allow healthcare professionals, particularly coders and administrative staff, to focus on more complex and specialised tasks. Empirical evidence supports these benefits; for instance, GPT-4 demonstrated superior precision and specificity compared to human coders in emergency department records (Klang, 2024). These advances enhance productivity and improve the quality of healthcare services, but further research is needed to assess their impact on metrics such as time efficiency and cost reduction.

Accuracy: LLMs are effective in identifying patterns and understanding the context of data, allowing them to make accurate coding suggestions even with incomplete or unclear clinical documentation (Zhang, 2020). They can help reduce the risk of manual errors caused by misinterpretation, fatigue, or lack of training, leading to consistent coding. Improved accuracy in coding benefits processes such as billing, epidemiological surveillance, and monitoring or evaluation of healthcare quality.

Scalability: LLMs are inherently capable of managing large volumes of data, making them particularly suitable for healthcare environments with extensive clinical documentation needs (Liu, 2023). Their scalability ensures consistent performance across several departments/specialities, enabling hospitals and large healthcare systems to optimise operations effectively.

These advantages – the combination of automation, enhanced accuracy, and scalability offered by LLMs and Generative AI – provide substantial benefits for clinical coding, addressing some of the common challenges.

5. CHALLENGES AND LIMITATIONS

5.1 Challenges

Ambiguous cases and rare conditions: one of the primary challenges for LLMs in clinical coding is managing ambiguous or rare cases. Medical documentation often lacks specificity, uses abbreviations, or contains incomplete information, complicating the assignment of precise ICD-10 codes. Furthermore, rare conditions or less commonly encountered scenarios may not be adequately represented in training datasets, leading to gaps or inaccuracies in coding (Dai, 2024).

Semantic and contextual understanding: clinical coding requires a detailed understanding of medical semantics, context and reasoning. Despite their advanced capabilities, LLMs need help interpreting the complexities of medical terminology, the broader context of clinical documentation and relationships/associations between conditions or health service context. For instance, differentiating between primary and secondary diagnoses or recognising a disease's progression may require domain-specific fine-tuning, which is often insufficient in general-purpose models.

Interpretability: LLMs frequently operate as black-box systems, which makes it challenging to understand the rationale behind their coding recommendations. This lack of transparency can hinder trust and adoption in clinical workflows. Explainable AI techniques are, therefore, critical to enhancing the interpretability and reliability of AI-driven coding systems (Liu, 2022).

Domain-specific adaptation: general-purpose LLMs are not inherently optimised for medical applications. Fine-tuning these models with medical datasets is essential for achieving accurate and reliable performance in clinical coding. However, limited access to annotated and domain-specific data poses a significant obstacle to developing high-performing models. Although promising results have been reported, such as improved specificity and accuracy in certain coding scenarios, the generalizability of these findings across different medical domains and workflows remains unclear.

Privacy and ethics: ensuring data privacy and security is paramount in the use of sensitive clinical data, requiring strict adherence to regulations such as the Health Insurance Portability and Accountability Act (HIPAA) and the General Data Protection Regulation (GDPR). Robust mechanisms, including federated learning, are essential to protect patient information while supporting model training and deployment. Additionally, AI-driven systems must address ethical and legal concerns, such as potential biases in coding recommendations and accountability for errors. Establishing clear ethical guidelines and frameworks is critical to ensuring these technologies' fair and responsible deployment, mitigating risks associated with incorrect or biased coding.

5.2 Limitations

Generalizability: the performance of LLMs often depends on the quality and diversity of their training datasets. It remains a significant challenge to generalise their application across different medical specialities, healthcare settings, and versions of ICD coding systems (e.g., the transition between ICD versions). Models trained on one dataset may underperform when applied to different domains, departments, or specialities with unique coding practices.

Data quality: LLMs effectiveness relies on access to comprehensive, accurate, and up-to-date medical datasets for training. However, such datasets are often challenging to obtain due to privacy concerns, data-sharing restrictions, and variability in clinical documentation practices (Souza, 2022). Limited data availability can restrict LLMs ability to deliver reliable and consistent results.

6. FUTURE DIRECTIONS

Assisted decision-making is a key application of LLMs in clinical coding. These systems offer suggestions and help resolve unclear or complex parts of medical records, reducing the workload and increasing accuracy for human coders. The combination of AI and human expertise enhances efficiency and consistency. This section examines how LLMs contribute to this process and their effects on clinical coding practice.

Improve domain-specific performance: future efforts should focus on fine-tuning LLMs using domain-specific datasets such as medical literature, clinical notes, and annotated coding records. This specialised training would enhance their understanding of medical terminology and the complexities of clinical coding systems, ensuring greater accuracy and contextual relevance.

*Expand coverage to rare and complex c*ases: to increase the utility of LLMs in diverse healthcare settings, their capabilities should be enhanced to cover a broader range of diseases, including rare and complex conditions. Future research should explore advanced methodologies such as no-shot and few-shot learning, which can be particularly effective in this context. No-shot learning enables models to infer appropriate ICD codes for conditions without specific training data, relying on their understanding of medical terminology and context. Few-shot learning allows models to generalise from small, specialised datasets, improving their ability to handle uncommon coding challenges. Combined with continuous validation in real-world environments, these techniques could significantly enhance the generalizability of LLMs to less frequent clinical scenarios and rare diseases (Sen, 2021).

Integration with other coding frameworks: combining LLMs with other coding systems like SNOMED-CT could create a more comprehensive and detailed approach to clinical documentation and coding. This integration would improve precision and support interoperability across various healthcare platforms and systems.

Multimodal AI solutions: research should investigate multimodal AI systems that combine text-based analysis with additional data sources such as imaging and lab results. Such systems can provide a deeper understanding of patient information, leading to more accurate and reliable coding recommendations.

Continuous improvement: real-world validation is critical to ensure that LLMs meet practical healthcare needs. Pilot programs in clinical environments can help identify barriers and refine performance (Klang, 2024). Continuous learning mechanisms should also be incorporated, allowing models to adapt to updates in medical knowledge, evolving coding standards, and user feedback.

Ethical and transparent deployment: guidelines and regulatory frameworks must be developed to ensure responsible use of AI in clinical coding. These should address potential biases, maintain transparency in model recommendations, and establish accountability for errors. Such measures are essential to build trust and ensure the safe adoption of AI in healthcare.

7. CONCLUSION

LLMs and Generative AI hold significant promise for transforming ICD-10 clinical coding, improving accuracy, efficiency, and scalability. These technologies offer substantial benefits, including automation and enhanced consistency, reducing healthcare professionals' administrative burden. Their integration into healthcare systems has the potential to enhance workflows and improve coding practices (Liu, 2023).

However, several challenges remain. Data privacy, interpretability, and ethical concerns require careful attention. Additionally, models must address the complexities of ambiguous cases, ensure robust contextual understanding, and overcome limitations in generalizability across different specialities and settings.

Future efforts should focus on refining models through domain-specific fine-tuning, validating their effectiveness in real-world clinical environments, and expanding their applications to cover rare and complex cases (Liu, 2022). Collaborative efforts involving clinicians, researchers, developers, managers, and policymakers are essential to align AI tools with healthcare needs and address ethical and regulatory considerations.

The future of clinical coding relies on the responsible and innovative use of AI, leading to more efficient, accurate, and reliable healthcare delivery. Ongoing development and interdisciplinary collaboration can help these technologies overcome existing challenges and realise their full potential to transform healthcare workflows (Soroush, 2024).

REFERENCES

Alonso, V. et al, (2020). Problems and barriers during the process of clinical coding: A focus group study of coders' perceptions. *Journal of Medical Systems*, Vol. 44, 62. https://doi.org/10.1007/s10916-020-1532-x

Chen, P.F. et al, (2022). Training a Deep Contextualized Language Model for International Classification of Diseases, 10th Revision Classification via Federated Learning: Model Development and Validation Study. *JMIR Medical Informatics*, Vol. 10, No. 11, e41342. https://doi.org/10.2196/41342

Dai, H.J. et al, (2024). Evaluating a Natural Language Processing-Driven, AI-Assisted International Classification of Diseases, 10th Revision, Clinical Modification, Coding System for Diagnosis-Related Groups in a Real Hospital Environment. *Journal of Medical Internet Research*, Vol. 26, e58278. https://doi.org/10.2196/58278

Falis, M et al, (2024). Can GPT-3.5 generate and code discharge summaries? *Journal of the American Medical Informatics Association*, Vol. 31, No. 10, pp. 2284–2293. https://doi.org/10.1093/jamia/ocae132

Klang, E. et al, (2024). Assessing Retrieval-Augmented Large Language Model Performance in Emergency Department ICD-10-CM Coding Compared to Human Coders. medRxiv. https://doi.org/10.1101/2024.10.15.24315526

Liu, L. et al, (2022). Hierarchical Label-Wise Attention Transformer Model for Explainable ICD Coding. *Journal of Biomedical Informatics*, Vol. 133, 104161. https://doi.org/10.1016/j.jbi.2022.104161

Liu, L. et al, (2023). Automated ICD Coding Using Extreme Multi-Label Long Text Transformer-Based Models. *Artificial Intelligence in Medicine*, Vol. 144, 102662. https://doi.org/10.1016/j.artmed.2023.102662

Sen, C. et al, (2021). From Extreme Multi-Label to Multi-Class: A Hierarchical Approach for Automated ICD-10 Coding Using Phrase-Level Attention. CoRR. https://arxiv.org/abs/2102.09136

Soroush, A. et al, (2024). Large Language Models are Poor Medical Coders – Benchmarking of Medical Code Querying. *NEJM AI*, Vol. 1, No. 5. https://doi.org/10.1056/AIdbp2300040

Souza, J. et al, (2022). Multisource and temporal variability in Portuguese hospital administrative datasets: Data quality implications. *Journal of Biomedical Informatics*, Vol. 136, 104242. https://doi.org/10.1016/j.jbi.2022.104242

Zhang, Z., Liu, J., Razavian, N., (2020). BERT-XML: Large Scale Automated ICD Coding Using BERT Pretraining. In *Proceedings of the 3rd Clinical Natural Language Processing Workshop*. Association for Computational Linguistics, pp. 24–34. https://aclanthology.org/2020.clinicalnlp-1.3

GAVIN: TOWARDS GDPR-COMPLIANT BLOCKCHAIN-BASED ACADEMIC CERTIFICATION

Luis Anido-Rifón, Christian Delgado-von-Eitzen, Manuel J. Fernández-Iglesias,
María Ruiz-Molina, Pablo Molina-Martínez, Martín Llamas-Nistal and Fernando A. Mikic-Fonte
atlanTTic Research Center – University of Vigo
EE Telecomunicacion, Campus Universitario s/n, Vigo (Pontevedra), Spain

ABSTRACT

The fragmentation of academic credentialing systems poses significant challenges for verifying educational qualifications. This paper identifies the main challenges that need to be addressed to create a blockchain-based system to support academic certification management fully compliant with the European General Data Protection Regulation (GDPR). This work is based on a previous conceptual model proposed by the authors that relies on keeping personal data off the blockchain while allowing for effective verification through an encrypted salted hash mechanism with additional access control measures. The main contribution of this paper is the identification of the three key technical challenges found that are common to any blockchain-based solution that intend to be fully GDPR-compliant: (1) access control mechanisms to limit access to data stored on blockchain platforms; (2) scalability and inter-blockchain communication, which require the integration of multiple private blockchains managed by different organizations, as well as connection to a consortium blockchain; and (3) the need for a private reliable backup system in case an institution ceases operations.

KEYWORDS

Blockchain, GDPR, Data Protection, Academic Certificates

1. INTRODUCTION AND MOTIVATION

As the demand for proof of skills and qualifications grows, so does the prevalence of fraudulent academic certificates, which can originate from various sources: (i) Degree mills selling fake qualifications; (ii) Fabricated documents from non-existent institutions (Muzammil, 2010). ; (iii) Altered authentic documents with false information; (iv) Counterfeit records produced by dishonest employees at legitimate institutions; (v) Incorrect translations of genuine documents for use in different countries.

The rise of fake credentials poses a significant threat in our interconnected society. Compounding the issue, there are no universal standards for academic information or centralized record-keeping systems. Additionally, if an educational institution ceases operations, its records may disappear, making it impossible to verify the credentials of its alumni. This lack of traceability further exacerbates the challenges of authenticating academic achievements.

A possible approach to overcome these problems is the use of Blockchain technology. Blockchain is the underlying technology of Bitcoin (Nakamoto, 2008). It consists of a time-sequenced series of blocks, each cryptographically linked to the previous one, creating a secure chain. This decentralized and distributed ledger stores blocks as reliable digital records that are practically unchangeable yet easily verifiable. In a blockchain network, there is no central authority; instead, information is shared among a network of peers.

Since 2013, the educational sector has been exploring blockchain technology to protect academic information through various initiatives and projects (Delgado-von-Eitzen et al, 2021a). While the number of blockchain-based applications in education is increasing, most remain in the early stages of development, with only a few being actively used by academic institutions and their stakeholders. Many initiatives have already explored the use of Blockchain storing a hash digest of the actual data, using a combination of off-chain and blockchain systems.

Of paramount relevant in the case of Europe is the compliance with the General Data Protection Regulation (GDPR) (GDPR, 2016) (e.g., data portability, accountability of accesses and operations, data modification support, right to be forgotten, etc.) is not fully addressed by any of the initiatives investigated (Delgado-von-Eitzen et al, 2021a). In this paper we outline a proposal for a GDPR-fully compliant blockchain-based academic certification system and identify the main challenges that need to be addressed with the current technologies available. The main contribution is the identification of the practical difficulties to go from a conceptual model to a real implementation using the state-of-the-art blockchain technology. The next section outlines the proposal, section 3 identifies the challenges of this ongoing work. Finally, some conclusions and hints to solve these challenges are presented in section 4.

2. THE PROPOSAL: GAVIN

This section presents the conceptual model for the GAVIN (GDPR-compliant blockchain-based architecture for universal learning, education and training information management) proposal [Delgado-von-Eitzen et al, 2021b]. The proposed conceptual model (c.f. Figure 1) outlines a system for validating documents or data records issued by service providers (e.g., financial institutions, educational organizations) using blockchain technology. In this model, an institution issues a document containing academic information to a data subject, who can then share it with a third party for verification through blockchain infrastructure.

The most relevant features of the above model include:

- Secure Off-Chain Storage: Private information is stored securely off-chain, under the control of data subjects and service providers (E), while proof of authenticity ("Verification data") is permanently recorded on one of the private blockchains and then transferred to consortium blockchain.
- Verification Process: The issuer structures the academic information from the original document as a Merkle Tree (Liu, X. et al., 2021) and stores the root as an encrypted salted hash on one of the private blockchains. The data subject is provided with all the information including the salts and decryption key for verification purposes. A third party can verify the document by decrypting the root, computing a hash with the provided salts, and comparing it to the retrieved hash.

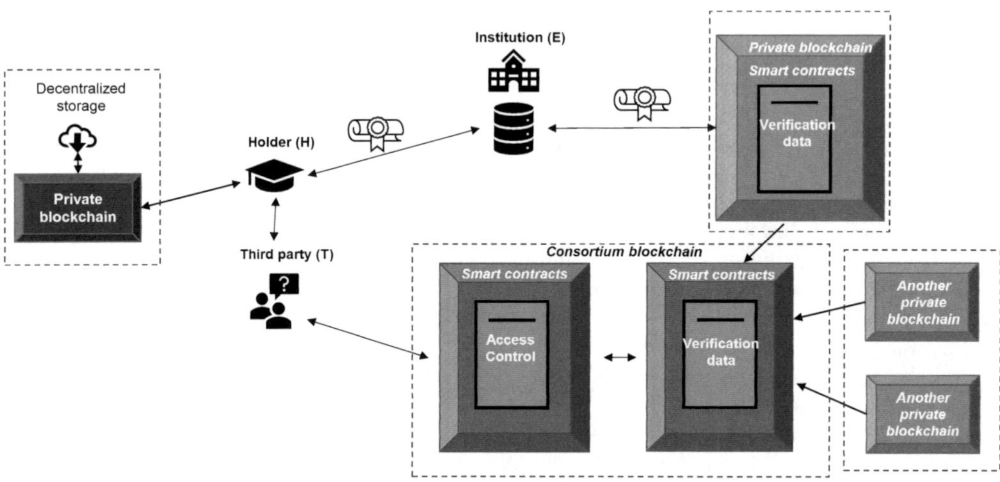

Figure 1. Proposed conceptual model

- GDPR Compliance: The model adheres to GDPR regulations by ensuring no personal data is stored on the blockchains, maintaining anonymity, and allowing for data subjects' rights, including the right to be forgotten.
- Consortium Blockchain: The system suggests using a consortium blockchain to control access, as it will be later explained, where only trusted and permissioned nodes can participate. This ensures that only the issuer and the data subject have full access to the verification data.

- Scalability: The model can be implemented on a consortium blockchain with the potential for branch blockchains to enhance scalability and accommodate various organizational needs.

The model accommodates three use cases: one where the data subject securely shares the complete academic certificate for verification, a second one where the holder shares only parts of the academic information for verification and a third one where a third party is granted access to retrieve the complete academic information directly from the issuing institution, and then permission to verify it. This system offers a reliable way to verify data authenticity while ensuring data protection and compliance with existing regulations. In all the use cases, the third party cannot access the information to verify the academic data without explicit consent from the holder, which will be recorded on the consortium blockchain. The holder will also be able to revoke access to the verification data at any time.

3. CHALLENGES

This section identifies the three main technical challenges that need to be address in order to implement the conceptual model presented in the previous section:

3.1 Challenge 1: Access Control

The first challenge lies in the consortium blockchain (cf. Figure 1). We need to address the difficulty of creating a blockchain-based system that allows holders of academic information to grant or revoke access permissions to third parties for verification purposes. If a third party does not have permission, they should not be able to access the information under any circumstances, nor should they be able to do so if the holder explicitly withdraws permission. As shown in Fig. 1, the consortium blockchain consists of two blockchains: one contains a smart contract responsible for access control, allowing or denying third parties the ability to consult the verification data, which is securely stored in the second consortium blockchain. When a third party (T) wants to consult the verification information of a certain holder (H), the system first checks that (H) has granted (T) permission to access it. If so, the smart contract on the first consortium blockchain queries the second blockchain, returning the required information. If at any point (H) withdraws permission from (T), the access control smart contract will deny access to the information. The model includes provisions, as required by the GDPR, to ensure that all access and permission changes are properly recorded. The reason for separating the consortium blockchain into two is that currently, no existing blockchain technologies allow for the dynamic and flexible permission configuration required by this model at account level, as each holder (H) may change permissions at any time. Frameworks such as Hyperledger Fabric and GoQuorum offer access control mechanisms, but they do not provide the necessary granularity for this model at the level of individual accounts. While they enable private transactions, these are limited to interactions among nodes. In this case, we require access control at the account level. Thus, the division into two interconnected chains presents a new approach that poses a technical challenge but resolves the requirement for flexibility.

3.2 Challenge 2: Scalability and Inter-Blockchain Communication

The process of issuing academic degrees is not constant throughout the academic year, so there are certain moments when peaks are reached. If we take into account these requirements and that the capacity of a blockchain platform to process information is limited, this technology can be an impediment. To solve it, one approach is the one proposed in challenge 2, given that the project requires sufficient scalability to register a large number of academic records. To achieve this, it proposes multiple private blockchains maintained by different organizations, which will register verification data for the academic information before sending it to the consortium blockchain. While blockchain interconnection is still developing, the project will leverage Ethereum technology and a Firewall for secure connections (Steichen, M., Hommes, S., & State, R, 2017).

Challenge 2 focuses on unidirectional data flow from private blockchains (the green ones included in Figure 1) to the consortium blockchain, making it simpler than Challenge 1, which involved also executable transactions, that are not necessary in this case. The solution involves using Inter-Blockchain Communication (IBC) (Qasse, I. A. et al., 2019) to connect the consortium blockchain with the private ones (Kan, L. et al., 2018), enabling the easy transfer of data. IBC technology is still in the development and improvement phase.

3.3 Challenge 3: An Institution Disappears

In the event that an institution disappears, and a user loses their certificate, there must be a reliable backup system to preserve this information (see Fig. 1). The issuing entity should upload the details of all its issued certificates to this backup before ceasing operations, allowing users to retrieve their information if it is lost.

The technology used for this backup must be sufficiently decentralized to ensure that users retain ownership of their stored data (Khalid et al, 2023). In this model, academic information is stored in a decentralized storage controlled by a private blockchain as a control access secure mechanism, although it could be done with a decentralized storage system only if it allows the confidentiality of the information entered to be protected. The academic information, stored in this decentralized storage will be only accessible to the data holder through an authorized account. This ensures that users can retrieve their information while preventing unauthorized access to all records on the decentralized storage. Additionally, the data of the Academic Information will be encrypted with a key known to the owner thereof, so if it is destroyed, from the point of view of the RGPD it is considered that the data has been deleted since it cannot be access or decrypt. Thanks to the implementation of this challenge 3, once the owner of the information manages to recover it, he can continue sharing it in whole or in part thanks to the proposed model as already described. It is important to note that challenge 3 is only necessary in those cases in which the owner of the data loses the academic information, since if this is not the case and even if the educational institution has disappeared, the designed model allows the academic degree to continue to be verified without incident.

4. CONCLUSION AND FUTURE WORK

The GAVIN model presents a promising solution to address obstacles of academic credential verification using blockchain while keeping fully GDPR compliance. By leveraging blockchain technology, the proposed system addresses the vulnerabilities associated with traditional academic data management. GAVIN offers secure off-chain storage mechanism while keeping fully compliance with GDPR regulations. Although no personal data is stored in the blockchain, an access control mechanism is added to prevent massive queries from being made and, although it is not personal data, conclusions can be drawn or information inferred through advanced analysis.

The identification of key challenges—access control, inter-blockchain communication, scalability, and the need for a robust backup system—highlights the complexities involved in transitioning from a conceptual model to a practical implementation. Addressing these issues through innovative technological solutions, such as Inter-Blockchain Communication (IBC) and decentralized storage, will be critical for realizing the full potential of the GAVIN architecture.

Future work includes the implementation of these challenges and its validation in a heterogeneous academic environment including formal, informal and non-formal education.

ACKNOWLEDGEMENT

This study was funded by the European Union (Next Generation Funds) and the Spanish Ministry of Science and Innovation (Agencia Estatal de Investigación) under 'Plan de Recuperación, Transformación y Resiliencia' in the call 'Proyectos de Transición Ecológica y Transición Digital'. Grant number TED2021- 130828B-I00 (GDPR-compliant blockchain-based architecture for universal learning, education and training information management).

REFERENCES

Delgado-von-Eitzen, C., Anido-Rifón, L., & Fernández-Iglesias, M. J. (2021). Blockchain applications in education: A systematic literature review. *Applied Sciences*, *11*(24), 11811. DOI: 10.3390/app112411811

Delgado-von-Eitzen, C., Anido-Rifón, L., & Fernández-Iglesias, M. J. (2021). Application of blockchain in education: GDPR-compliant and scalable certification and verification of academic information. *Applied sciences*, *11*(10), 4537. DOI: 10.3390/app11104537

GDPR, G. D. P. R. (2016). General data protection regulation. Regulation (EU) 2016/679 of the European Parliament and of the Council of 27 April 2016 on the protection of natural persons with regard to the processing of personal data and on the free movement of such data, and repealing Directive 95/46/EC.

Kan, L., Wei, Y., Hafiz Muhammad, A., Siyuan, W., Gao, L.C., & Kai, H. (2018) A Multiple Blockchains Architecture on Inter-Blockchain Communication, IN *Proceedings. of the 2018 IEEE International Conference on Software Quality, Reliability and Security Companion (QRS-C)*, Lisbon, Portugal, 2018, pp. 139-145, DOI: 10.1109/QRS-C.2018.00037.

Khalid, M. I., Ehsan, I., Al-Ani, A. K., Iqbal, J., Hussain, S., & Ullah, S. S. (2023). A comprehensive survey on blockchain-based decentralized storage networks. *IEEE Access*, *11*, 10995-11015.

Liu, H., Luo, X., Liu, H., & Xia, X. (2021) Merkle Tree: A Fundamental Component of Blockchains, In *Proceedings of the 2021 International Conference on Electronic Information Engineering and Computer Science (EIECS)*, Changchun, China, 2021, pp. 556-561. DOI: 10.1109/EIECS53707.2021.9588047.

Muzammil, M. (2010). Corrupt schools, corrupt universities: What can be done? Compare: A Journal of Comparative and International Education, 40(3), 385–387. DOI: 10.1080/03057921003703934

Nakamoto, S. Bitcoin: A Peer-to-Peer Electronic Cash System. 2008. Available online: https://www.bitcoin.org/bitcoin.pdf.

Qasse, I. A., Abu Talib, M., & Nasir, Q. (2019, March). Inter blockchain communication: A survey. In *Proceedings of the ArabWIC 6th Annual International Conference Research Track* (pp. 1-6). DOI: 10.1145/3333165.3333167

Steichen, M., Hommes, S., & State, R. (2017, September). ChainGuard—A firewall for blockchain applications using SDN with OpenFlow. In 2017 Principles, Systems and Applications of IP Telecommunications (IPTComm) (pp. 1-8). IEEE. DOI: 10.1109/IPTCOMM.2017.8169748.

WEB3-BASED E-HEALTH: SECURITY AND PRIVACY CHALLENGES AND SOLUTIONS

Vladimir Oleshchuk
University of Agder, Kristiansand, Norway

ABSTRACT

While Web3 technologies promise to revolutionize e-health systems, significant security and privacy e-health critical issues remain unaddressed. This paper explores key gaps, including privacy-preserving technologies, key management, consent revocation, off-chain data handling, and the scalability of security protocols, benefits of large language models. Addressing these issues is critical to unlocking the full potential of Web3 in healthcare.

KEYWORDS

Web3, E-Health, Security, Privacy, Blockchain

1. INTRODUCTION

The advent of Web3 technologies introduces a paradigm shift in internet architecture, emphasizing decentralization, transparency, and user control. Web3 technologies, leveraging decentralization and blockchain, aim to enhance e-health security and privacy. While these features promise enhanced autonomy and trust, they also expose critical vulnerabilities in the security of information systems and various unresolved challenges that could hinder adoption. This paper discusses key cybersecurity challenges and mitigation strategies in Web3, with a focus on threats to blockchain protocols, smart contracts, and decentralized storage systems, and outlines these challenges and possible solutions, emphasizing areas requiring further research and innovation.

2. WHY PRIVACY-ENHANCING TECHNOLOGIES ARE ESSENTIAL FOR E-HEALTH IN WEB3?

E-health systems manage sensitive patient data, making them attractive targets for cyberattacks. Traditional centralized systems are vulnerable to data breaches and unauthorized access. Web3, with its decentralized architecture, promises improved security. However, blockchain's transparency (by design) conflicts with the privacy needs of sensitive health data. Achieving privacy in transparent blockchain systems remains challenging (Zyskind, Nathan and Pentland, 2015). Privacy-Enhancing Technologies (PETs) address these challenges by ensuring secure data sharing, processing, and storage while maintaining privacy.

E-health systems require robust privacy mechanisms to protect sensitive health data and ensure regulatory compliance. Web3 technologies, through decentralized architectures, offer enhanced security but still face challenges in privacy. Privacy-Enhancing Technologies (PETs), such as Zero-Knowledge Proofs (ZKPs), homomorphic encryption, and secure multi-party computation (SMPC), provide the tools to meet stringent privacy and security requirements in e-health. This paper explores how PETs are used, why they are essential, and what specific PETs are applied in Web3-based e-health systems.

Since blockchain's transparency can inadvertently expose sensitive health data, PETs can allow secure interactions without revealing private information (Gupta et al., 2021).

E-health often involves sharing and analyzing patient data for research. PETs could ensure this can be done without compromising privacy (Zhang, R., et al., 2022).

In the following sections we briefly describe above mentioned essential elements of PETs.

3. WHAT PETS ARE USED IN WEB3 FOR E-HEALTH?

ZKPs enable verification of a statement without revealing underlying data. Examples of applications in e-health include verifying patient eligibility for clinical trials without exposing medical history (Bünz et al., 2020) and securely proving compliance with health protocols.

Homomorphic encryption allows computations on encrypted data without decrypting it. Examples of applications include secure medical data analysis by researchers without accessing raw data (Aono et al., 2017) and processing encrypted patient records for personalized treatment recommendations.

SMPC allows multiple parties to compute a function over their inputs while keeping them private. Examples of applications include enabling collaborative medical research without exposing patient data and secure voting mechanisms for decentralized healthcare governance (Yao, 1986).

Differential privacy ensures aggregate data analysis does not reveal individual records. Examples of applications include publishing anonymized health statistics from patient data and preserving privacy in machine learning models for predictive healthcare (Dwork, 2006).

More specific blockchain introduces unique PETs for privacy are mixing protocols that hiding transaction metadata, useful for anonymizing health payments and access to health records and Off-Chain storage with On-Chain proofs can be used to store sensitive health data off-chain while maintaining verifiable integrity on-chain.

4. HOW PETS ENFORCE REQUIREMENTS IN E-HEALTH

Data Confidentiality, Data Integrity and Patient Control and Interoperability are security critical requirements in e-health applications. PETs enforce data confidentiality by encrypting and anonymizing health data, ensuring only authorized entities can access it. Blockchain immutability ensures data integrity, while PETs add cryptographic assurance of data correctness. PETs like ZKPs and SMPC enable dynamic consent mechanisms, allowing patients to manage data sharing securely. To ensure interoperability, standards such as Decentralized Identifiers (DIDs) and Verifiable Credentials (VCs) have been proposed to integrate PETs into interoperable systems for e-health (World Wide Web Consortium (W3C), 2019).

5. PRIVACY-PRESERVING IDENTITY MANAGEMENT

Pseudonymous blockchain identities risk revealing user activity patterns. Web3 technologies introduce decentralized identity management, shifting control from centralized authorities to users. While this provides greater security and control, ensuring privacy remains challenging. Advanced zero-knowledge identity solutions can be a solution (Jain et al., 2021).

Privacy-preserving identity management (PPIM) in Web3 aims to secure user identity while maintaining anonymity and enabling verifiability. This paper explores methodologies including zero-knowledge proofs, self-sovereign identities, and attribute-based encryption, highlighting their roles in enhancing privacy in decentralized ecosystems.

Let us consider key approaches that can be useful to implement privacy-preserving identity management (PPIM) in Web3 environments. Zero-knowledge proofs ((ZKPs)) allow one party to prove knowledge of information without revealing the information itself. This can validate user attributes or credentials in identity verification. Examples of applications in Web3 include validating age, citizenship, or health status without revealing additional data (Bünz et al., 2020). Protocols such as zk-SNARKs and zk-STARKs are being used for blockchain-based authentication systems.

6. SELF-SOVEREIGN IDENTITY

Self-Sovereign Identity (SSI) represents a paradigm shift in digital identity management, aligning with Web3's principles of decentralization, user control, and privacy. By leveraging DIDs, VCs, and blockchain,

SSI offers a robust framework for secure and interoperable identity systems. Self-Sovereign Identity (SSI) enables individuals to own and control their digital identities without relying on centralized authorities. Frameworks such as DID (De- centralized Identifiers) and Verifiable Credentials (VCs) provide standards for Web3 identity systems (Lundkvist et al., 2017). Blockchain ensures tamper-proof storage, while off-chain verifiable data registries enhance privacy.

Digital identity management has traditionally been dominated by centralized systems, leading to issues such as data breaches, identity theft, and lack of user control. Self-Sovereign Identity (SSI) emerges as a solution by decentralizing identity management and giving individuals full ownership of their digital identities (Lundkvist et al., 2017). This aligns seamlessly with Web3's nature of decentralization, privacy, and user empowerment.

Self-Sovereign Identity (SSI) empowers users to control and manage their digital identities without reliance on centralized entities. In Web3, SSI leverages decentralized technologies such as blockchain and cryptographic protocols to provide privacy, security, and interoperability. The idea of SSI is aimed to deal with some challenges in traditional identity systems such as centralization risks where centralized identity systems are prone to single points of failure, making them vulnerable to data breaches; lack of user control when users have limited control over how their personal data is stored and shared; and fragmentation that requires users to maintain multiple identities across platforms, leading to inefficiency and security risks (Allen, 2016).

Adopting SSI in Web will provide the following benefits:

- User Control and Privacy: Users own and control their identity, deciding when, how, and with whom to share their information.
- Decentralization: Blockchain ensures a tamper-proof, decentralized registry of identifiers, reducing reliance on central authorities.
- Interoperability: Standards such as Decentralized Identifiers (DIDs) and Verifiable Credentials (VCs) facilitate cross-platform identity verification (World Wide Web Consortium (W3C), 2019).
- Security: Cryptographic techniques protect against identity theft and unauthorized access (Stocker, 2019).

7. HOW SSI IS IMPLEMENTED IN WEB3?

Decentralized Identifiers (DIDs) are unique identifiers stored on a blockchain that users control without dependence on centralized authorities. DIDs enable verifiable and secure identity interactions across platforms (Lundkvist et al., 2017).

Verifiable Credentials (VCs) are cryptographically signed documents that verify claims about an individual's identity or attributes without revealing sensitive information. For example, a VC can confirm that a person is over 18 without exposing their date of birth (World Wide Web Consortium (W3C), 2019).

Blockchain serves as the backbone provides an immutable, decentralized ledger for storing identity-related metadata and enabling trustless verification. SSI systems leverage blockchain for store cryptographic proofs or public keys securely (as Anchor Points) and for registering and resolving DIDs globally (as Decentralized Registries) (Stocker, 2019).

SSI employs advanced cryptographic techniques, such as Zero-Knowledge Proofs (ZKPs), to enable selective disclosure of information. This ensures users can verify their identity or credentials without exposing unnecessary details (Bünz et al., 2020).

Access control is an crucial part of any e-health system, Attribute-Based Encryption (ABE) allows access control based on attributes rather than user identity. In Web3 setting it means that ABE can restrict access to specific services based on user attributes while preserving anonymity (Goyal et al., 2006). By combining ABE with blockchain ensures secure access control without exposing sensitive user data.

Examples of already existing implementations are platforms such as uPort and Sovrin that use a combination of blockchain and cryptographic techniques to enable privacy-preserving identity management. uPort offers decentralized identity and user authentication using Ethereum smart contracts (uPort Foundation, 2017), while Sovrin implements SSI with verifiable credential issuance and storage in a privacy-respecting manner (Stocker, 2019).

Future research should focus on integrating advanced cryptographic tech- niques and creating user-friendly interfaces to facilitate adoption. Privacy-preserving identity management is critical for Web3's success. By leveraging technologies like ZKPs, SSI, and ABE, Web3 ecosystems can provide secure, private, and user-centric identity solutions.

8. LLMS IN WEB3 E-HEALTH

Web3 e-health systems aim to decentralize healthcare services and improve privacy by leveraging blockchain and cryptographic technologies. However, the complexity of managing and securing sensitive health data requires advanced AI capabilities. Large Language Models (LLMs) can assist in tasks such as privacy-preserving data handling, automated consent management, and threat detection (Brown et al., 2020; Liu et al., 2023). In this section we outline how LLMs can complement Web3 frameworks to ensure robust security and privacy in e-health and explore what LLMs can do and how they can be applied to enforce robust security and privacy measures in decentralized e-health ecosystems.

LLMs such as GPT have emerged as powerful tools for natural language processing, providing capabilities like contextual understanding, data synthesis, and intelligent automation. In Web3 e-health systems, LLMs can play a pivotal role in enhancing security and privacy.

8.1 What Can LLMs Do in Web3 E-Health?

LLMs can used to parse and interpret healthcare policies, regulatory frameworks, and smart contract terms, automating compliance verification (Liu, X., et al., 2023). For example, they can automate GDPR or HIPAA compliance checks for smart contracts or simplify user interactions with decentralized applications (dApps) through natural language interfaces.

By leveraging synthetic data generation and differential privacy techniques, LLMs can anonymize patient data for research while preserving utility or generate synthetic datasets to train healthcare models without exposing sensitive information (Abadi et al., 2016).

Integrating LLMs with blockchain-based monitoring systems can help to identify suspicious patterns in transactions and access logs and predict and mitigate potential data breaches or insider threats (Calder et al., 2021).

LLMs can help to interpret user input and automate the creation and enforcement of dynamic consent mechanisms in e-health systems. For instance, by translating user preferences into enforceable blockchain-based smart contracts and providing contextual explanations of consent terms to patients (Jain et al., 2021).

8.2 LLMs for Security and Privacy in Web3 E-Health

LLMs can analyze and verify user credentials, integrating with Decentralized Identifiers (DIDs) to enhance authentication systems. This includes both verifying the authenticity of Verifiable Credentials (VCs) issued in healthcare (World Wide Web Consortium (W3C), 2019) and detecting inconsistencies or fraudulent activities in identity claims.

They can be utilized to analyze data from decentralized networks and external sources to generate threat intelligence reports in real-time and suggest mitigation strategies for emerging threats to e-health systems. Thay can also assist in drafting and verifying privacy-preserving data sharing protocols using natural language specifications for smart contract creation and AI-driven verification to ensure compliance with privacy stan- dards like GDPR. Through conversational AI interfaces, LLMs can enable secure communication between patients and healthcare providers in Web3 applications and help to clarify terms and conditions of data sharing agreements in a privacy-aware manner.

Large Language Models (LLMs) provide versatile tools to enhance security and privacy in Web3 e-health systems. By automating tasks such as consent management, threat detection, and policy compliance, LLMs can address critical gaps in current decentralized healthcare ecosystems. Their integration into Web3 frameworks promises a more secure and user-friendly e-health environment.

9. CONCLUSION

Securing Web3 systems requires a multifaceted approach, combining robust technical solutions with rigorous regulatory frameworks. By addressing vulnerabilities in protocols, smart contracts, and storage systems, Web3 can achieve its vision of a decentralized yet secure digital ecosystem to ensure secure and privacy-preserving systems for the future of e-health.

REFERENCES

Abadi, M., et al., (2016). Deep learning with differential privacy. *Proceedings of the 2016 ACM SIGSAC Conference on Computer and Communications Security*, pp. 308–318.

Allen, C., (2016). The path to self-sovereign identity. *Coindesk*.

Aono, Y., et al., (2017). Homomorphic encryption for privacy-preserving medical analysis. *Journal of Biomedical Informatics*, 80, pp. 107–120.

Brown, T., et al., (2020). Language models are few-shot learners. *Advances in Neural Information Processing Systems*, 33, pp. 1877–1901.

Bünz, B., et al., (2020). Zether: Towards privacy in a smart contract world. *Proceedings of the 2020 IEEE Symposium on Security and Privacy*, pp. 393–408.

Calder, C., et al., (2021). AI for cybersecurity: State of the art and research challenges. *ACM Computing Surveys*, 53, pp. 1–38.

Dwork, C., (2006). Calibrating noise to sensitivity in differential privacy. *Proceedings*, pp. 265–284.

Goyal, V., et al., (2006). Attribute-based encryption for fine-grained access control of encrypted data. *Proceedings of the 13th ACM Conference on Computer and Communications Security*, pp. 89–98.

Gupta, D., et al., (2021). A decentralized framework for medical data privacy and access control. *Journal of Biomedical Informatics*, 120, p. 103857.

Jain, A., et al., (2021). Blockchain for privacy-preserving identity management in healthcare. *IEEE Transactions on Network and Service Management*, 18, pp. 1012–1024.

Liu, X., et al., (2023). Trustworthy AI in healthcare: Challenges and opportunities. *Nature Biomedical Engineering*, 7, pp. 114–126.

Lundkvist, C., et al., (2017). Decentralized identifiers and verifiable credentials. *W3C Credentials Community Group*.

Stocker, A., (2019). Sovrin: Digital identities in the blockchain era. *Ledger*, 4, pp. 1–12.

uPort Foundation, (2017). uPort: A platform for self-sovereign identity.

World Wide Web Consortium (W3C), (2019). Decentralized identifiers (DIDs) v1.0.

Yao, A.C.-C., (1986). Protocols for secure computations. *Foundations of Computer Science*, pp. 160–164.

Zhang, R., et al., (2022). Security and Privacy for Healthcare Blockchains. *IEEE Transactions on Services Computing*, vol. 15, no. 6, pp. 3668-3686,

Zyskind, G., Nathan, O. and Pentland, A.S., (2015). Decentralizing privacy: Using blockchain to protect personal data. *Proceedings*, pp. 180–184.

OBSERVING THE IMPACT OF AI IN THE PROGRESS OF THE SUSTAINABLE DEVELOPMENT GOAL 11

Joao Pita Costa[1], Leonardo Barrionuevo[2] and Maša Kovič Dine[3]
[1]*International Research Centre for Artificial Intelligence under the auspices of UNESCO, Institute Jozef Stefan, Jamova cesta 39, 1000 Ljubljana, Slovenia*
[2]*MetAmazonia Academy, AMAGroup, Avenida Anita Garibaldi 850, 80540-400 Curitiba, Brazil*
[3]*Faculty of Law, University of Ljubljana, Poljanski nasip 2, 1000 Ljubljana, Slovenia*

ABSTRACT

With Artificial Intelligence (AI) playing an increasingly pivotal role in shaping global development, it becomes imperative to thoroughly monitor and enhance its influence on the progress of the United Nations' Sustainable Development Goals (SDGs). This study undertakes a comprehensive analysis by implementing a SDG 11-focused AI-based Observatory offering a comprehensive framework for monitoring and evaluating the contributions of AI to sustainable development targeting topics that can enhance sustainable cities and communities worldwide. Drawing from four primary data sources—worldwide news, scientific publications, policy documents, and educational resources—the Observatory provides a multifaceted perspective on key issues such as urban planning, public transportation, circular economy, and civic engagement. Through the use of AI tools, the Observatory analyzes these data streams to support capacity building, policy development, and equitable access to AI, while identifying emerging trends and biases. The study highlights the growing significance of AI in shaping sustainable communities, with particular emphasis on the increased discussions for Community resillience. Global trends reveal a focus on ecosystem management, machine learning, and digital data, while regional case studies, such as the selected use case of the Brazilian Amazon, demonstrate a shift toward environmental preservation and leadership in climate-related initiatives supported by technological transformation. The findings underscore the need for region-specific approaches to sustainable development, ensuring that AI technologies themselves are aligned with Human Rights and equity considerations, as well as them being used in a way to contribute to respect them by urban stakeholders. The proposed framework goes beyond mere analysis by delivering actionable insights, equipping policymakers and innovators with the tools they need to drive future advancements. Ultimately, this work contributes to a more informed understanding of how AI can be strategically leveraged to accelerate progress toward achieving the SDG 11 goals, ensuring that technological innovation aligns with the global sustainability of cities and communities.

KEYWORDS

Sustainable Cities & Communities, SDG 11, Artificial Intelligence, Smart Cities, Published Science Data-Driven Policy

1. INTRODUCTION

The pursuit of sustainable communities has become a central objective in global development strategies, as underscored by the 11th United Nations' SDG 11, emphasizing the enhancement of inclusive, safe, resilient, and sustainable communities worldwide. As cities continue to grow and face increasing pressures from climate change, resource constraints, and social inequality, innovative data-driven decision-making solutions are needed to ensure that urban development is sustainable and equitable. AI is emerging as a powerful advantage for addressing these challenges, offering new ways to optimize resource use, improve public services, and enhance community resilience (Leal Filho, 2024). The newly launched SDG 11 Observatory, developed by the International Research Center for Artificial Intelligence under the auspices of UNESCO (IRCAI), offers a platform designed to monitor and evaluate AI's impact on sustainable urban communities, providing real-time insights that can guide data-driven, inclusive and equitable decision-making. It serves also as a data-driven collaboration platform engaging its stakeholders. In the current landscape, AI has been applied to urban sustainability through various smart community initiatives. These include AI-driven systems for optimizing energy use, reducing pollution, improving public transportation, and enhancing civic engagement. The unequal distribution of AI technologies across regions and populations raises concerns about inclusivity, especially in underserved communities. However, AI-driven systems may, if designed correctly, ensure a more targeted outreach, by identifying underrepresented groups and proactively invite them to engage with the system.

Numerous SDG observatories have been established globally to monitor progress toward the SDGs, collecting, visualizing, and disseminating data on key SDG indicators. Notable examples include: (i) worldwide initiatives such as the UN's SDG Global Observatory (UNDP, 2024); (ii) as well as continent-wide such as the EU SDG Observatory by Eurostat (Eurostat, 2024) tracking SDG progress within European nations, and the Africa SDG Observatory (UNECA, 2024) providing insights into sustainability trends across the continent; and (iii) additionally, national observatories, such as in Brazil (IBGE,2024). Together, these observatories enhance transparency and accountability, equipping policymakers with data for evidence-based interventions aimed at achieving the goals of SDG 11. IRCAI's SDG 11 Observatory goes beyond existing tools by focusing on SDG 11 and providing a dynamic classification system that identifies emerging trends, challenges, and opportunities in the pursuit of sustainable communities. This AI-based system processes vast amounts of data, offering detailed insights into community-specific issues such as resource efficiency, climate resilience, and social inclusion. Moreover, the *Bias Board* view provides an overall understanding of the potential biases in the data, ensuring that AI applications do not perpetuate or exacerbate social inequalities, following (Gupta and Degbelo, 2023). This focus on transparency and equity makes the SDG 11 Observatory a crucial tool for cities aiming to foster truly sustainable and inclusive communities, aligning technological innovation with the principles of fairness and social justice.

2. DATA AND METODOLOGY

The key research question this paper seeks to address is: How much can be captured by the SDG 11 Observatory's enhancing our understanding of AI's role in promoting sustainable, inclusive communities, and what are the implications for policymakers? By exploring the SDG 11 Observatory's potential to provide actionable insights, this paper will contribute to the growing discourse on how AI can be used to create more sustainable and equitable urban and community environments. The SDG 11 Observatory's findings offer practical recommendations for policymakers and urban planners, ensuring that AI technologies are not only effective but also aligned with the broader goal of fostering resilient and inclusive communities in line with the SDG 11 scope, based on good practices for creating sustainable cities and to nurture international cooperation. This shows to be particularly relevant in the context of the use case of the Brazilian Amazon, brought into this study by the digital transformative effort led by AMAGroup, named *MetAmazonia* (AMAGroup, 2024), that leverages international research collaboration on AI and ESG over data sourced on the biggest private natural reserve, hosting urban spaces and multiple ethnicities, including indigenous groups, aiming to boost climatetech through crowdsourcing at a global level (Köhl et al, 2023).

Table 1. Data ingested into the SDG11 Observatory from worldwide news (indicating the language coverage), published scientific articles, and related legal and regulatory landscape

Concepts	2024 News	Lang. Coverage	Science	Policies
Air quality index	447	(28)	18,184	98
Circular Economy	6097	(48)	9,366	62
Urban Planning	44306	(76)	198,672	1,249
Civic engagement	2759	(11)	25,900	215
Public Space	8434	(39)	47,725	452
Municipal Wastewater	9775	(64)	57,604	35
Smart City	7433	(41)	9,527	167
Public Transport	29120	(69)	28,766	401
Gentrification	1959	(51)	3,124	56
Suburban	2848	(78)	17,725	12

The SDG 11 AI-based Observatory integrates multiple data sources to provide comprehensive insights into sustainable cities and communities. It draws from four primary sources: (1) real-time worldwide news, with data coming from a vast multilingual pool of one million news articles ingested daily, offering timely updates on global events and trends; (2) published scientific articles, tapping into over 126 million research papers to capture academic knowledge on SDG 11-related topics; (3) AI-related policies, providing a legal and regulatory perspective on the application of AI in sustainable urban development; and (4) educational resources, specifically curated from VideoLectures.net. These diverse data streams are analyzed using Natural Language Processing (NLP) such as wikifier.ijs.si that can identify *Wikidata* concepts present in the ingested documents through text similarity and use the multilingual coverage in Wikipedia to perform the analysis across languages (Leban et al, 2014). Table 1 presents the data ingested into the SDG 11 Observatory, covering various key concepts related to sustainable urban development. It aggregates information from worldwide news sources (in collaboration with the AI-based multilingual news engine *Event Registry*), scientific publications, and policy documents, while also indicating the language coverage for each concept. In this study we consider topics such as "Urban Planning", widely discussed across all data sources, with significant representation in news (44,306 articles), scientific literature (198,672 publications), and policies (1,249 documents). Other critical concepts, such as "Public Transport" and "Municipal Wastewater," also show substantial presence, particularly in scientific discourse. The table highlights the comprehensive nature of the data sources, with some topics like "Circular Economy" and "Smart City" being covered across a wide range of languages and scientific discussions. Interestingly, topics like "Civic Engagement" and "Gentrification," while crucial for sustainable community development, have comparatively lower visibility in policy documents, indicating potential areas where greater policy focus may be needed. Overall, the table underscores the Observatory's ability to track a broad spectrum of urban sustainability issues, drawing from diverse global sources.

3. DISCUSSION OF RESULTS

This study underscores the growing significance of AI in shaping sustainable communities, empowering their crowdsourced intelligence from open data and open science, as evidenced by the trends and good practices captured in the SDG 11 Observatory. The analysis of the ingested data highlights a marked increase in discussions related to AI and sustainable urban development, particularly after 2020, which likely corresponds to the increased adoption of AI technologies during the COVID-19 pandemic. The prominence of topics such as digital data and machine learning reflects AI's multifaceted role in addressing key urban challenges, including resource management, public health, and environmental sustainability. Notably, the comparison between global discussions and those focused on the particular case of the Brazilian Amazon guided by the efforts and expertise of the global *MetAmazonia* initiative, reveals a distinct focus on environmental preservation, biodiversity, and climate-related concerns in the latter, suggesting that AI's application in sustainable development varies significantly depending on regional priorities and challenges. These results provide valuable insight into how AI could be tailored to meet the specific needs of diverse urban as well as rural environments, reinforcing the importance of contextualized approaches in sustainable development.

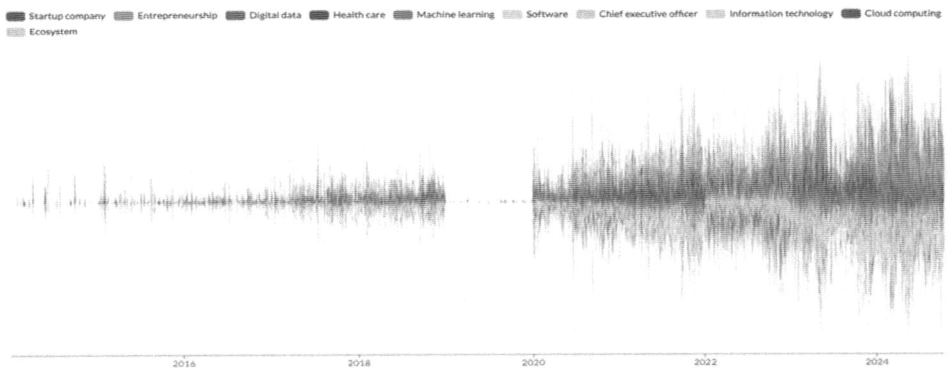

Figure 1. Graph of trends captured in the news on sustainable communities and AI worldwide

The graph in Figure 1 illustrates trends in news coverage related to sustainable communities and AI over the past decade, showing a marked increase in the frequency of discussions across various topics, particularly from 2020 onwards. The growing intensity and frequency of these topics after 2020 likely reflect the accelerating integration of AI technologies into sustainable development initiatives, particularly as cities and communities began leveraging AI to tackle complex challenges like urban planning, resource management, and public health during the COVID-19 pandemic. The visible spikes suggest periods of heightened attention, possibly corresponding to major advancements, innovations, or global events highlighting the role of AI in sustainable communities. Overall, the graph highlights the increasing relevance of AI in shaping sustainable community development and urban ecosystems over time. When comparing the most common concepts discussed in news related to sustainable communities and AI globally with those specific to the Brazilian Amazon region we see that the most prominent topics include "Ecosystem" (57.5%), "Digital Data" (46.2%), and "Startup Company" (41.1%), reflecting a broader focus on technological innovation and infrastructure development for sustainable urban environments. In contrast, discussions surrounding the Amazon focus heavily on "Ecosystem" (56.8%), "Chief Executive Officer" (55.9%), and "Agriculture" (51.6%), highlighting regional concerns related to environmental sustainability, biodiversity, and leadership in sustainability initiatives. The Amazon-related news places greater emphasis on climate-related concepts such as "Deforestation" (46.2%) and "Renewable Energy" (47.1%), reflecting the unique ecological and social challenges faced in this region. This contrast demonstrates how global narratives around AI and sustainability are more technology-focused, while local discussions in the Amazon center around environmental preservation and leadership in mitigating climate change. However, both indicate that an area where more attention is needed is the intersection of human rights and AI. AI technologies have the potential to enhance urban environments by improving infrastructure, public services, and community resilience. However, these advancements must be implemented in ways that respect and promote human rights, particularly the right to privacy, freedom from discrimination, right to a clean, healthy and sustainable development (UNGA, 2022), access to adequate standard of living, as well as plethora of other economic, social and cultural rights (UN General, 1976). A two-prong approach should be taken in this regard. Firstly, AI systems used in urban planning and governance must be designed to be transparent, inclusive, and equitable to ensure that human rights violations do not occur with their use, such as sharing of private information or providing racially biased outcomes (Cugurullo, 2024). Secondly, AI systems can be an extremely helpful tool in ensuring public participation and civic engagement in urban decision-making, contributing to an increasing respect of human rights by the urban authorities. As several smart city models of public participation around the world have shown, AI systems enable a scalable, inclusive and targeted engagement of local residents and communities, thus ensuring that their needs and desires related to the urban living are being heard (Kovič Dine, 2024). These almost always relate to the respect of economic, social and cultural rights, like the right to housing, access to drinking water, access to education, right to play or to a healthy urban environment, and hence facilitate the prevention of the marginalization of vulnerable populations. By aligning AI-driven urban solutions with human rights, we can create cities that not only thrive technologically, but also uphold the dignity, equality, and well-being of all citizens in a sustainable and resilient manner, as in (Sirmaçek et al, 2023).

4. CONCLUSION AND FUTURE WORK

This study has provided an in-depth discussion of the SDG 11 Observatory design and its role in leveraging AI to promote sustainable and inclusive communities through the adaptive AI-based domain-specific classification and real-time data analysis, particularly in Community-related contexts. The findings reveal that AI has become a key enabler of Smart Community initiatives, from optimizing energy consumption and public services to enhancing civic engagement and addressing social inequalities. The growing global focus on ecosystem management, digital data, and startup-driven innovations highlights the potential of AI to address complex urban challenges. Moreover, regional case studies, such as the Brazilian Amazon, demonstrate that local narratives focus on environmental preservation and leadership in sustainability efforts, underscoring the need for region-specific approaches to sustainable development. IRCAI's unique approach is aligning with the *MetAmazonia Academy* priorities to equip policymakers and innovators with the AI-related expertise and tools to make informed decisions that align technological innovation with global sustainability objectives. Looking forward, future work will further explore the knowledge extraction and natural language interaction potential of large language models, informed by the ingested data in a Retrieval-Augmented Generation (RAG) approach, expanding the SDG 11 Observatory's capabilities by incorporating more localized data to better capture domain and region-specific challenges and solutions. Additionally, we will continue refining the bias-detection capabilities to ensure greater accuracy and fairness in AI-driven decision-making. Moreover, the SDG 11 Observatory could be improved with a Human Right component to map out an AI-related human rights index, that could provide information whether solutions are in line with Human Rights obligations. Collaborations between stakeholders in different global and regional SDG initiatives will be strengthened to share best practices and harmonize data collection and analysis efforts. Ultimately, ongoing research and development in AI and its applications in urban sustainability will be crucial in accelerating progress toward achieving the SDGs, ensuring that cities and communities worldwide can thrive in an inclusive and sustainable manner. Based on the findings of this initial study, we are launching a worldwide Youth Challenge on AI and SDG 11 with UNESCO, aimed at engaging young innovators in developing AI-driven solutions for the sustainable cities and communities they know well and are part of, following (Zaouini, 2024).

ACKNOWLEDGEMENT

This research was partially funded by the European Commission's Horizon research and innovation program under grant agreement 101135800 (RAIDO - Reliable AI and Data Optimisation) and 10080425 (ELIAS - Lighthouse of AI for Sustainability) and by the Public Agency for Scientific Research and Innovation of the Republic of Slovenia within the framework of the research project J5-3107 (Development and use of artificial intelligence in the light of negative and positive obligations of the state to guarantee the right to life).

REFERENCES

AMAGroup (2024). MetAmazonia. [online]: https://www.metamazonia.io/ (accessed in 4.10.2024).

Cugurullo F. (2024) 'Urban Artificial Intelligence: From Automation to Autonomy in the Smart City'. 2 Frontiers in Sustainable Cities 1-14.

Eurostat (2024) EU SDG Observatory [online]: https://www.eesc.europa.eu/en/sections-other-bodies/observatories/sustainable-development-observatory (accessed in 4.10.2024)

Gupta S. and Degbelo, A., 2023. An empirical analysis of AI contributions to sustainable cities (SDG 11). *In The Ethics of Artificial Intelligence for the Sustainable Development Goals* (pp. 461-484). Cham: Springer.

Instituto Brasileiro de Geografia e Estatística - IBGE (2024) Indicadores Brasileiros para os Objetivos de Desenvolvimento Sustentável [online]: https://odsbrasil.gov.br/ (accessed in 4.10.2024)

Köhl M. et al. "Physical process assessments-Amazon Forest dieback." *Hamburg Climate Futures Outlook 2023: The plausibility of a 1.5° C limit to global warming-social drivers and physical processes*. Cluster of Excellence Climate, Climatic Change, and Society (CLICCS), 2023. 152-157.

Kovič Dine M. (2024). AI and Public Participation: Can the Smart Cities' models be Applied to the Right to Participate in Environmental Decision-Making with implications for the Right to Life?, In *V. Sancin (ed.), Artificial Intelligence and Human Rights: From the Right to Life to A Myriad of Diverse Human Rights Implications*, Litteralis.

Leal Filho W. et al (2024). The role of artificial intelligence in the implementation of the UN Sustainable Development Goal 11: Fostering sustainable cities and communities. *Cities*, *150*, pp.105021.

Leban G., Fortuna B., Brank J. and Grobelnik M. (2014) *Event registry: learning about world events from news*. In: *Proceedings of the 23rd International Conference on World Wide Web*, 107-110.

Sirmaçek B. et al (2023). The potential of artificial intelligence for achieving healthy and sustainable societies. In *The ethics of artificial intelligence for the sustainable development goals* (pp. 65-96). Cham: Springer.

UN Development Programme UNDP (2024) SDG Global Observatory [online]: sdgs.un.org (accessed in 4.10.2024)

UN Economic Commission for Africa – UNECA (2024) Africa UN Data for Development Portal [online]: https://ecastats.uneca.org/africaundata/ (accessed in 4.10.2024)

UNGA, The human right to a clean, healthy and sustainable environment, A/RES/76/300 (28 July 2022).

UN General (1976) Int. covenant on economic, social and cultural rights. United Nations, Treaty Series, 993(3).

Zaouini M., Pita Costa J. et al (2024) Addressing Water Sustainability Challenges in North Africa with Artificial Intelligence. *In the Proceedings of the Slovenian Conference on Data Mining and Data Warehouses.*

Reflection Papers

LEVERAGING BEHAVIOUR SEQUENCE ANALYSIS (BSA) IN INFORMATION SYSTEMS: EXAMINING MALICIOUS INSIDER THREAT AS AN EXAMPLE

Monica T. Whitty
Monash University
Department of Software Systems and Cybersecurity, Clayton Campus, Wellington Road, Melbourne, Australia

ABSTRACT

This paper explores the application of Behaviour Sequence Analysis (BSA) in Information Systems (IS) research. BSA is a methodological approach originating from criminology that examines the temporal order and structure of behaviours to uncover patterns. This paper argues for its utility in IS research, particularly in examining socio-technical challenges that involve temporal dynamics. Drawing from a previous application to an IS problem on insider threat, the paper illustrates how BSA can uncover complex behavioural pathways, combining technical and human factors. Beyond insider threats, this paper highlights the potential of BSA to optimise workflows in enterprise systems, enhance ransomware detection, and analyse user interactions with IS platforms. By bridging IS's technical and social dimensions, BSA offers researchers a dynamic and innovative tool to tackle some of the field's most pressing challenges.

KEYWORDS

Behaviour Sequence Analysis, Information Systems, Insider Threat, Cybersecurity, Work Efficiency, Healthcare

1. INTRODUCTION

Information Systems (IS) is a multifaceted field that examines the interaction between technology, individuals, and organisations. Researchers in this field examine challenges such as information systems design, implementation, and management. Notably, IS has been formally defined as research "primarily concerned with socio-technical systems that comprise individuals and collectives that deploy digital information and communication technology for tasks in business, private, or social settings" (Recker, 2021; p.3). Given this focus, this paper makes the case for employing Behaviour Sequence Analysis (BSA) as a methodology in IS Research. Notably, BSA is a method developed by criminologists and has mainly examined pathways that lead to identifying perpetrators (e.g., stalkers and murderers) (see Keatley et al., 2019). However, this paper proposes that it is also a valuable method for IS researchers. The paper makes the case by demonstrating the application of the technique to examine malicious insider threats. It then suggests how this methodology might be applied to other problems typically examined by IS researchers.

2. BEHAVIOUR SEQUENCE ANALYSIS (BSA)

Behaviour Sequence Analysis is a methodological approach that examines the temporal order and structure of behaviours to uncover patterns and relationships with sequences of actions. By focusing on the progression of behaviours over time, BSA provides insights into the processes underlying various phenomena (Keatley, 2018).

At its core, BSA involves coding individual actions and analysing their sequential relationships. The method allows researchers to identify recurring patterns, transitions, and structures within behavioural data and provides opportunities to add psychological aspects to the analysis. For instance, in a cold case, this method has opened new lines of inquiry for police by examining behaviours and evidence (e.g., fingerprinting) (Keatley and Clarke, 2020).

By examining the order in which behaviours occur, BSA offers a dynamic perspective that statistical analyses may overlook. Traditional approaches, for example, focus on individual risk factors that are tested in statistical approaches such as hierarchical regression models or multilevel modelling. Whilst these statistical methods are essential and often critical, they have limited value when examining temporal problems. For example, BSA has been employed to investigate the lives of serial killers, tracing pathways from childhood abuse to methods of murder. This work revealed significant links between early abuse and later criminal behaviours, highlighting the sequential nature of criminal development (Marono et al., 2020).

2.1 Employing BSA to Examine IS Problems

In researching for this paper, it became apparent that IS researchers do not typically employ BSA. The only instance appears to be examining malicious insider threats (Whitty et al., 2023; 2024). However, IS researchers consider temporal problems that consider social and technical events. For example, Robey and Newman (1996) researched the process of developing and implementing a materials management system in one company over 15 years. They identified 44 events and patterns of repeated failures. More recently, De Smedt et al. (2019) examined critical behavioural patterns that can predict outcomes for improving decision-making in organisational workflows. This paper now considers, by way of an example, how BSA might be applied to examine malicious insider threats.

Malicious insider threats pose significant challenges to the security and integrity of information systems. These threats originate from individuals within an organisation who misuse their authorised access to harm system functionalities, steal sensitive data or disrupt operations. These threats can be at least as harmful as external threats (Whitty, 2021). Research has focused on the use of AI and ML to detect insider threats and tools, such as Darktrace, Sureview, and Spector 360, that create records of employees' digital behaviours and employ AI to learn what are normal online activities and deviations from the norm (Gheyas and Abdallah, 2016; Whitty et al., 2024). These methods can have a high false-positive rate (Al-Mhiqani et al., 2022). Researchers in Information Systems argue that pathway models are needed to improve detection (Shaw and Sellers, 2015; Shaw and Stock, 2011) and that these models also need to consider human behaviours (Cappelli et al., 2012). BSA results could be combined with AI and ML tools to improve detection.

2.2 Methodology

This example of BSA, drawn from my previous work (see Whitty et al., 2023, 2024), will explain its utility as a method and the steps involved so that IS researchers might consider employing BSA to examine this and other research problems. In the study, we examined 86 IF theft cases from court documents. The details in each case include the insider's role, the type of organisation targeted, and a description of the offending with each step involved over time.

2.2.1 Grounded Theory

Prior to the BSA, we conducted a grounded theory analysis (Strauss and Corbin, 1988), which aligns with previous applications of this methodology (Keatley, 2018). The grounded theory analysis allowed us to uncover socio-technical variables. We drew from previous work (MITRE, 2023; Whitty, 2021) and identified new variables.

2.2.2 Behaviour Sequence Analysis

Next, a Behaviour Sequence Analysis (BSA) was conducted to investigate pathways to insider IP theft. The steps are described below.

The first step in the BSA was *parsing.* Parsing involves segmenting behavioural episodes into discrete actions or events. This process requires meticulous examination to identify clear boundaries where one behaviour concludes and another commences (Keatley, 2018). This example might include beginning work at an organisation, taking on new roles, or granting security access.

The second step involved *categorising*, where similar behaviours are grouped into overarching categories or codes. This process involved developing a coding scheme that reflected the theoretical framework or research objectives guiding the analysis. In this case, examples of categories included misuse of access privileges, conducting presentations, and taking photographs. Establishing reliable categories facilitates the identification of patterns and ensures consistency in the analysis.

The final stage is *analysing*, which entails statistically examining the sequences to uncover patterns, transitions, and relationships between categorised behaviours. Coded sequences involve strings of events. Techniques such as transition frequency matrices and state diagrams (see Figure 1, taken from the Whitty et al., 2023 paper) are employed to visualise and interpret the flow of events over time. The BSA provides findings in state transition diagrams, which typically highlight stronger (i.e., those with higher frequency and Standardized Residual) pairings in the data. End-users and novice readers can easily interpret these flow-type diagrams.

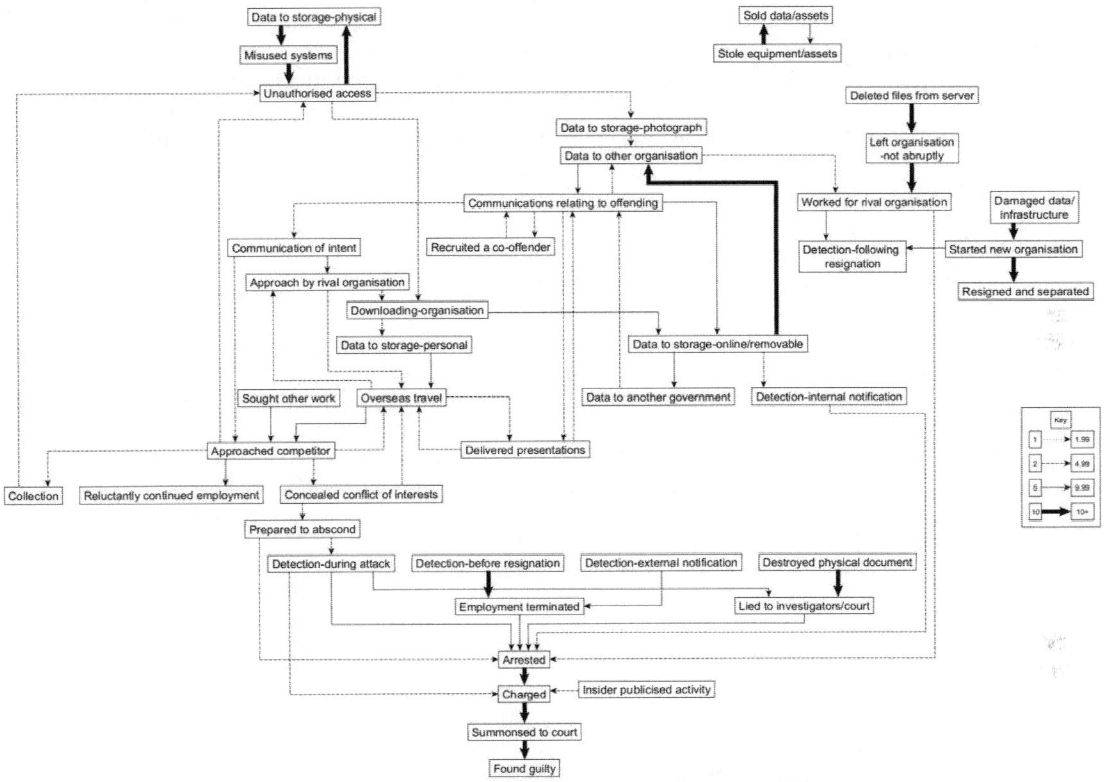

Figure 1. State transition diagram of behaviours and events leading to IP theft (Whitty et al., 2023; p. 385)

From this example, the state transition diagram (Figure 1) shows the complexity of IP theft. It also highlights socio-technical events. This work demonstrates the importance of considering the combination of technical and behavioural systems, which is the objective of IS researchers. Contrary to previous understandings of IP theft, multiple pathways were found, which were not all linear. For example, approaches to a competitor were an antecedent to overseas travel (n = 4, SR = 3.57), concealment of a conflict of interest (n = 3, SR = 4.78), and unauthorised access (n = 6, SR = 3.30). Approaches by a rival organisation were also both antecedents - to overseas travel (n = 3, SR = 4.64) and communications relating to offending (n = 4, SR = 1.92) and a sequitur to behaviours. These findings could be combined with technical tools to improve the detection of insider threats.

3. BSA – A NOVEL METHOD FOR IS RESEARCHERS TO CONSIDER

This paper recommends that BSA is applicable well beyond criminal concerns. Although it has only been applied in IS research to examine insider threats, it may have great potential for examining other IS problems. This section provides *hypothetical examples* of how BSA might be employed to study other IS problems.

Recker (2021) highlights numerous research questions that she claims scholars in information systems are investigating. Some of these include: "How can societal issues be resolved through information technology? How can healthcare be assisted through information technology?... What role does information technology play in global markets and local governments?... How can information technology contribute to the greening of the planet?" (p3-4). These questions arguably have a technical and social component and could be considered temporally. Below are some hypothetical IS problems that could be researched using BSA.

Problem 1. Organisations rely on information systems to streamline workflows and improve efficiency. BSA allows researchers to consider human and temporal aspects that AI overlooks or struggles to interpret. BSA could be used to analyse employee interactions with enterprise software, such as Customer Relationship Management (CRM). In a CRM system, sales representatives might interact with the system by:

1. Searching for a client (A)
2. Logging interaction notes (B)
3. Scheduling follow-ups (C)
4. The client does not respond (D)
5. Becoming stressed when clients do not respond (E)
6. Employing new methods to engage clients (F)

Using BSA, patterns of inefficient workflows could be identified, such as repeated back-and-forth between logging notes and scheduling follow-ups or the client not responding and the employee becoming stressed. This could lead to system redesigns to simplify processes, reduce redundant steps, or suggest automated solutions.

Problem 2. Businesses of all sizes increasingly experience ransomware attacks. They follow a sequence of behaviours by attackers and responses by the organisation, such as network reconnaissance, file encryption, and ransom demands. BSA might analyse logs and observations of human behaviour to identify these sequences in the attack lifecycle. For example:

1. Gain initial access through phishing or vulnerability exploitation (A)
2. Deploy ransomware payload (B)
3. Encrypt critical files (C)
4. Send ransom demand (D)
5. Organisation opts not to pay the demand (E)

Analysing server or endpoint logs might reveal early ransomware indicators, such as repeated privilege escalation attempts or abnormal file encryption patterns. Understanding the outcome may also help inform organisations how to approach a ransomware attack.

Problem 3. Information technology can potentially improve lifelong health illnesses, such as diabetes. BSA might analyse the following events to identify ways to improve their healthcare:

1. Patient recognises symptoms (e.g., fatigue, excessive thirst) (A)
2. Patient searches online to understand the causes (B)
3. Patient uploads symptoms and glucose level data for an appointment (C)
4. Patient stressed by needing to wait a week for an available time slot (D)

Analysing patients' concerns and patterns of seeking help may reveal a more effective pathway for patients to seek appropriate support and information about their illness.

4. CONCLUSIONS

This paper has highlighted BSA's potential as a novel and powerful methodological approach for Information Systems (IS) research. While BSA originates from criminology, its application to IS problems offers a new dimension of analytical depth and relevance.

This paper has demonstrated the steps and value of BSA by using the example of malicious insider threats. In brief, the method first employs a grounded theory approach to identify socio-technical variables, followed by parsing, categorising, and analysing. The method also encourages visualisations so lay audiences can understand and interpret the findings. Such insights provide actionable intelligence for organisations, allowing them to develop targeted interventions and improved security protocols.

BSA's potential applications extend far beyond insider threats. BSA's ability to reveal dynamic behavioural patterns and transitions over time makes it particularly suitable for addressing temporal and complex IS challenges, such as understanding the impact of IT systems on healthcare, environmental sustainability, and global markets. In this paper, I considered hypothetical examples, such as healthcare, workplace and efficiency, and ransomware attacks, to highlight the potential uses of BSA for IS researchers. By leveraging this methodology, IS researchers can tackle some of the most pressing challenges in the digital age, developing innovative solutions that consider both the social and technical dimensions of technology use. The insights gained from employing BSA could lead to more effective system designs, better security practices, and improved decision-making frameworks, ultimately advancing the IS research field.

REFERENCES

Al-Mhiqani, M.N., Ahmad, R., Abidin, Z.Z., Abdulkareem, K.H., Mohammed, M.A., Gupta, D., & Shankar, K, (2022), "A new intelligent multilayer framework for insider threat detection", *Computers & Electrical Engineering,* 97, pp. 1-23, doi: 10.1016/j.compeleceng.2021.107597.

Cappelli, D. M., Moore, A. P., and Trzeciak, R. F. (2012), *The CERT guide to insider threats: how to prevent, detect, and respond to information technology crimes (Theft, Sabotage, Fraud)*, Addison-Wesley, Upper Saddle River, NJ.

Gheyas, I. A., & Abdallah, A. E., (2016). Detection and prediction of insider threats to cyber security: A systematic literature review and meta-analysis. *Big Data Analytics, 1,* article 6. doi.org/10.1186/s41044-016-0006-0

Keatley, D. A. (2018). *Pathways in crime: An introduction to behaviour sequence analysis.* Palgrave Macmillian.

Keatley, D., & Clarke, D. D. (2020). A timeline toolkit for cold case investigations. *Journal of Criminal Psychology, 10(*2), 47-63. https://doi.org/10.1108/JCP-09-2019-0039

Keatley, D. A., Sheridan, L., & Whitty, M. T. (2019). "The road not taken": Understanding and mapping complexity in threat assessment. *Journal of Threat Assessment and Management, 6*(3-4), 198-201. https://psycnet.apa.org/doi/10.1037/tam0000132

Marono, A., Reid, S., Yaksic, E., & Keatley, D. (2020). A behaviour sequence analysis of serial killers' lives: From childhood abuse to methods of murder. *Psychiatry, Psychology and Law, 27*(2), 1-12. http://dx.doi.org/10.1080/13218719.2019.1695517

MITRE: ATT&CK Matrix for Enterprise (2023). Available at: https://attack.mitre.org/matrices/enterprise (accessed 2 April 2023).

Recker, J. (2021). *Scientific research in information systems: A beginner's guide*. Springer.

De Smedt, J., Deeva, G., & De Weerdt, J. (2019). Mining behavioral sequence constraints for classification. *IEEE Transactions on Knowledge and Data Engineering, 32*(6), 1130-1142. https://doi.org/10.1109/TKDE.2019.2897311

Robey, D., & Newman, M. (1996). Sequential patterns in information systems development: An application of a social process model. *ACM Transactions on Information Systems (TOIS), 14*(1), 30-63. https://doi.org/10.1145/214174.214178

Shaw, E. D., and Sellers, L. (2015), "Application of the critical-path method to evaluate insider risk", *Studies in Intelligence*, *59,* pp.1–8.

Shaw, E. D., and Stock, H. V. (2011), *Behavioral risk indicators of malicious insider theft of intellectual property: Misreading the writing on the wall. White Paper*, Symantec, Mountain View, CA. (2011).

Strauss, A., and Corbin, J. (1988), *Basics of qualitative research: Grounded theory procedures and technique*. Sage, London.

Whitty, M. T. (2021). Developing a conceptual model for insider threat. *Journal of Management & Organization, 27*(5), 911-929. doi:10.1017/jmo.2018.57

Whitty, M. T., Ruddy, C., Keatley, D., Butavicius, M. & Grobler, M. (2024). The prince of insiders: A multiple pathway approach to understanding IP theft insider attacks. *Information & Computer Security, 32*(4), 509-522. https://doi.org/10.1108/ICS-11-2023-0210

Whitty, M. T., Ruddy, C., & Keatley, D. A. (2023). To catch a thief: Examining socio-technical variables and developing a pathway framework for IP theft insider attacks, Human Aspects of Information Security and Assurance. HAISA 2023. *IFIP Advances in Information and Communication Technology, 674.* Springer, Cham. https://doi.org/10.1007/978-3-031-38530-8_30.

INCREASING THERAPY ADHERENCE THROUGH EMOTIONALIZATION

Mirella Moser and Thomas Keller
ZHAW School of Management and Law, Winterthur, Switzerland

ABSTRACT

Chronic pain is a widespread global health issue, affecting approximately 20% of the population. Effective management of chronic pain relies heavily on patients' adherence to treatment plans, but maintaining long-term engagement remains a challenge. While digital interventions have been developed to support therapy adherence, they often fall short in sustaining user commitment due to limited emotional connection and motivation. This paper proposes an emerging approach that utilizes emotionalization through personalized metaphorical representations, enhanced by generative AI and extended reality (XR) technologies. By integrating these personalized digital models into the treatment process and involving trusted individuals, the proposed solution aims to foster a deeper emotional bond between patients and their health, thereby improving long-term adherence. This strategy, though initially tested with orofacial pain, has the potential to be applied to a wide range of chronic conditions, offering a novel, emotionally engaging method to enhance therapy adherence.

KEYWORDS

Therapy Adherence, Emotionalization, Generative AI, Extended Reality, Chronic Disease

1. INTRODUCTION

Chronic pain disorders represent a global health issue characterized by prolonged and often difficult-to-treat pain conditions. According to the International Association for the Study of Pain (IASP), 20% of the global population suffer from chronic pain, accounting for nearly one in five physician visits (International Association for the Study of Pain, n.d.). The World Health Organization (WHO) defines chronic pain as pain that persists or recurs for more than three months, continuing beyond the normal healing process and involving both biological and psychosocial components. Chronic headaches and chronic orofacial pain occur on at least 50% of days over a minimum of three months (WHO, n.d.).

Therapy adherence, defined as the degree to which patients follow prescribed medical advice, is a key factor for successful pain management. A high level of adherence is often associated with improved health outcomes (DiMatteo, 2004). In the context of chronic pain, maintaining adherence is especially important. Managing chronic pain typically involves long-term use of medication and/or therapeutic interventions, making consistent adherence to the treatment plan essential for achieving positive therapeutic results (Turk & Okifuji, 2002). However, in practice, many patients struggle to consistently follow their treatment regimens.

Digital interventions play an essential role in the treatment of chronic diseases and in supporting therapy adherence. However, the long-term use of mobile applications in particular often falls short of expectations, possibly due to a lack of user-friendliness or feedback (Portelli & Eldred, 2016). Future research should prioritize the development and evaluation of digital tools specifically designed to enhance therapy adherence. These tools should incorporate innovative approaches that provide long-term support while engaging and motivating users over time.

2. RELATED WORK

As pointed out, digital interventions play an essential role in the treatment of chronic diseases and in supporting therapy adherence. One example is the "Digital Companion" project, which has investigated an integrated system designed to enhance therapy adherence for chronic conditions (Yoker, 2023). This system combines practice management software with a patient-facing app, enabling data collected between consultations to be seamlessly integrated into physicians' systems, making it available during subsequent consultations. Other examples of digital support for chronic illnesses include monitoring systems for conditions like diabetes and chronic obstructive pulmonary disease (COPD), where health metrics are continuously tracked, displayed, and trigger alerts as needed (Vitodata, n.d.). Chronic inflammatory bowel disease is also monitored through specialized software that facilitates documentation and disease management (ibid.). Additionally, cancer patients can benefit from apps that function as interactive therapy assistants or diaries, providing vital support throughout their treatment journey (Scholz & Teetz, 2021).

Various initiatives and providers focus on managing chronic pain using diverse digital tools with different emphases and combinations. Immersive technologies, e.g., XR, have shown positive results by providing pain patients with distraction and coping strategies (Lavine, 2020). Additionally, artificial intelligence is utilized, particularly in diagnosis and therapy management (Rejula et al., 2021). Digital tools and devices are also employed for remote patient monitoring (RPM) and digital therapy (ibid.). Digital therapy involves software, mobile applications, sensors, and other digital approaches as therapeutic interventions for various medical issues. RPM focuses on patient monitoring between consultations. Mobile applications like 'Branch,' 'Curable,' and 'Pathways Pain Relief' use these approaches, offering features ranging from pain tracking and connecting with medical teams to mindfulness exercises and personalized therapy plans. Advanced apps like 'KaiaHealth', 'Wave,' and 'What's Up' utilize interactive biofeedback training and AI-based analyses to identify behavioral correlations and integrate therapies like Cognitive Behavioral Therapy (CBT) and Acceptance and Commitment Therapy (ACT) (US Pain Foundation, 2021). In the realm of orofacial pain, digital solutions primarily enhance doctor-patient communication (Digital Society Initiative, 2022), utilize imaging techniques for precise diagnoses (University of Zurich, n.d.-c), employ CAD/CAM technologies in dentistry (University of Zurich, n.d.-a), and support computer-assisted surgery (University of Zurich, n.d.-b).

A recent master thesis explored a principle not yet addressed by existing digital tools: enhancing therapy adherence through emotionalization (Moser, 2024). Emotionalization was achieved using metaphorical images representing patients' personal health situations, derived from self-assessments. The study focused on patients with chronic orofacial pain, allowing them to alter and beautify their metaphorical representations by engaging in beneficial therapy measures and adhering to the treatment. A metaphorical image of a life tree has been chosen, which changed in form and color based on stress and pain levels. Like a Tamagotchi, patients were encouraged to care for the life tree and, indirectly, for themselves. Qualitative results indicated the effectiveness of the principle of self-assessment, and patients found the metaphorical representation generally intriguing. The web application aided patients in developing better self-awareness. However, significant improvement in therapy adherence was not achieved. Patients felt insufficiently motivated by the possibility of beautifying their "tree of life". Additionally, not all patients emotionally connected with this metaphorical representation of their situation. Some preferred alternative forms, such as a small human figure, or desired the tree to encompass more aspects of their health.

3. EMOTIONAL CONNECTIONS – AN EMERGENT APPROACH

Building on the findings of related work and existing digital solutions, it is evident that successful tools must be both engaging and motivating to foster sustained therapy adherence. A promising approach to achieving this involves enhancing emotionalization aspects. To strengthen these aspects, several future development directions were identified. First, the metaphorical representation of the health situation should be individualized to achieve stronger emotional connection. Additionally, the sense of responsibility for this figurative representation should be reinforced. These goals can be achieved by using generative AI to create personalized metaphorical images and scenes tailored to each patient, and by involving close and convincing third persons who provide the patients with these personalized metaphorical images as a gift. Next, the human-computer interaction must be further enhanced to accommodate various devices. While smartphones should remain as everyday tools, expanding to XR applications can enhance presence, emotionalization, and therapy adherence through immersion. Finally, involving healthcare professionals in the process is crucial. Therefore, the system has to be integrated with regular consultations with pain specialists, enabling healthcare professionals to analyze the collected data and provide valuable insights.

4. PROPOSED SOLUTION

The proposed solution introduces a novel intervention mechanism: a personalized, emotionally engaging 'gift' presented to the patient by a trusted individual, such as a responsible healthcare professional. This virtual gift can take various forms, such as a pet, a plant, or a digital artwork as 3D model. It will be created through generative AI and is displayed using XR technology. The patient will be responsible for taking care of this personalized virtual gift, which also represents his or her specific health situation.

The goal of this intervention is to foster a sense of responsibility and emotional connection in the patient, thereby enhancing therapy adherence. Through positive behavior and adherence to prescribed therapeutic measures, the patient can take care of and improve the condition of the 3D model. For instance, a pet might grow healthier and more vibrant as the patient engages in beneficial activities, or a plant might flourish (see Figure 1).

Figure 1. Possible states of a virtual plant and a cat generated by ChatGPT 4o

This approach aims to create a tangible and emotionally resonant incentive for the patient to follow their treatment plan. The integration of generative AI allows for the creation of highly individualized models that can adapt and respond to the patient's actions and progress. XR technologies will further enhance the immersive experience, making the interaction with the model more engaging and impactful. By involving a trusted individual in presenting the gift, the intervention also leverages social support, which is known to play a significant role in managing chronic pain (Gong et al., 2024).

The USP of this solution lies in its ability to potentially achieve stronger therapy adherence through emotional engagement. By caring for their Tamagotchi-like health representation, patients indirectly care for themselves, breaking the common cycle of short-term app use and ensuring long-term engagement. However, potential risks, such as increased distress or gamification addiction (Yang & Li, 2021) are acknowledged. Integrating with healthcare systems ensures patients maintain regular contact with professionals, which is vital for managing chronic conditions and addressing these risks. Unlike current patient tools that often operate as closed systems independent of healthcare provider systems, this solution fosters continuous professional supervision and support. Since the approach of emotionalization is not restricted to the chosen use case of orofacial pain it is applicable to all chronic diseases, emphasizing consistent and long-term adherence to treatment plans.

The system targets four main use cases as depicted in Figure 2. First, the healthcare professional together with the patient elaborates a virtual 3D model (as illustrated in Figure 1) with a strong meaning to the patient. The model is then handed over to the patient as a 'gift' or 'challenge' (UC1). Second, this gift evolves based on the patient's self-assessment (UC2). Third, patients are additionally encouraged to maintain the well-being of this 3D model by engaging in beneficial activities such as breathing exercises (UC3.1) and physical practices (UC3.2), which positively affect the state of their gift. Fourth, before a consultation and/or in the time between consultations, the healthcare professional can review, analyze and monitor the patient's self-assessment data and the activities performed (UC4), enabling more personalized and informed care. It is also conceivable that a person close to the patient, rather than the healthcare professional, could be responsible for the virtual gift.

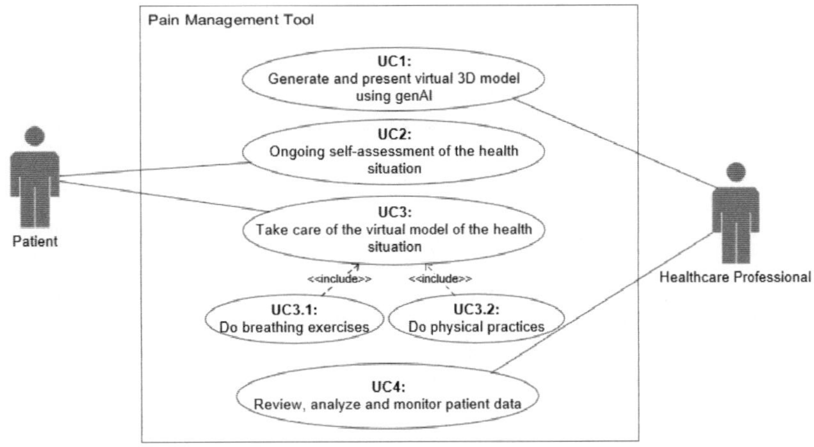

Figure 2. Use Case Diagram

5. CONCLUSIONS

Traditional digital tools often fail to sustain long-term engagement, highlighting the need for solutions that foster a deeper emotional connection between patients and their treatment. The proposed approach of personalized, metaphorical health representations, supported by generative AI and XR technologies, may offer a promising avenue. While the emotionalization strategy was initially tested with orofacial pain, its potential applicability across various chronic conditions emphasizes its broader relevance and impact.

The following key components of the proposed approach should be highlighted:

Emotional Engagement: The use of personalized metaphorical images and XR technologies may significantly enhance patients' emotional engagement with their treatment plans. This emotional connection may be crucial for maintaining long-term adherence.

Personalization and Social Support: Tailoring digital interventions to individual patients' needs and involving trusted individuals in the process may create a more supportive and motivating environment. This approach leverages social support, which is a key factor in managing chronic pain and chronic conditions in general.

Technological Integration: The integration of generative AI and XR technologies offers additional ways to create dynamic and interactive health representations. These technologies can adapt to patients' progress and provide real-time feedback, making the treatment process more engaging.

Healthcare Professional Involvement: Continuous involvement of healthcare professionals is essential for the success of these digital interventions. Regular consultations and professional supervision ensure that patients receive personalized and informed care.

While the proposed approach is promising, its implementation raises several questions that need to be addressed for successful integration. The specific role of healthcare professionals remains to be defined, including when and how often they should engage in the process to provide meaningful support without overburdening their schedule. The nature of patient interaction with the virtual models also requires clarification to ensure that these models remain engaging and meaningful over time. The adaptability of the virtual models is another critical factor. They need to be dynamic enough to maintain motivation over time while avoiding the risk of encouraging unrealistic expectations or addictive behavior. A balance must be found that maintains patient interest and motivation without creating dependency. These issues highlight the need for further investigation and refinement to ensure that the proposed solution can be effectively implemented and scaled in practice.

REFERENCES

Digital Society Initiative. (2022, April 4). Interdisziplinäres Projekt: Digitale visuelle Informationstherapie (DigiVisIn) bei orofazialen Schmerzen. http://www.dsi.uzh.ch/de/current/news/archive/2020/DigiVisin.html

DiMatteo, M. R. (2004). Variations in patients' adherence to medical recommendations: A quantitative review of 50 years of research. *Medical Care*, *42*(3), 200–209. https://doi.org/10.1097/01.mlr.0000114908.90348.f9

Gong, C., Shan, H., Sun, Y., Zheng, J., Zhu, C., Zhong, W., Guo, J., & Chen, B. (2024). Social support as a key factor in chronic pain management programs: A scoping review. *Current Psychology*. https://doi.org/10.1007/s12144-024-06233-9

International Association for the Study of Pain. (n.d.). Revision of the International Classification of Diseases (ICD-11). International Association for the Study of Pain (IASP). Retrieved June 27, 2024, from https://www.iasp-pain.org/advocacy/icd-11-pain-classification/

Lavine, G. (2020, December 22). Using Virtual Reality to Treat Real Pain. https://heal.nih.gov/news/stories/virtual-reality

Moser, M. (2024). No Pain is Gain—Digital support of pain therapy for chronic orofacial pain. https://doi.org/10.17605/OSF.IO/NYSTV

Portelli, P., & Eldred, C. (2016). A quality review of smartphone applications for the management of pain. *British Journal of Pain*, *10*(3), 135–140. https://doi.org/10.1177/2049463716638700

Rejula, V., Anitha, J., Belfin, R. V., & Peter, J. D. (2021). Chronic Pain Treatment and Digital Health Era-An Opinion. *Frontiers in Public Health*, 9. https://doi.org/10.3389/fpubh.2021.779328

Scholz, P. D. S. S., Laura, & Teetz, L. (2021, July 21). So finden chronisch Kranke gute Medizin-Apps. Apotheken Umschau. https://www.apotheken-umschau.de/e-health/gesundheitsapps/so-finden-chronisch-kranke-gute-medizin-apps-840195.html

Turk, D. C., & Okifuji, A. (2002). Psychological factors in chronic pain: Evolution and revolution. *Journal of Consulting and Clinical Psychology*, *70*(3), 678–690. https://doi.org/10.1037/0022-006X.70.3.678

University of Zurich. (n.d.-a). Center of Dental Medicine—CAD/CAM. Retrieved November 17, 2023, from http://www.zzm.uzh.ch/en/research/topics/04/02.html

University of Zurich. (n.d.-b). Center of Dental Medicine—Computer-assisted surgery. Retrieved November 17, 2023, from http://www.zzm.uzh.ch/en/research/topics/04/03.html

University of Zurich. (n.d.-c). Center of Dental Medicine—Imaging. Retrieved November 16, 2023, from https://www.zzm.uzh.ch/en/research/topics/04/01.html

US Pain Foundation. (2021, January 6). 10 best apps for people with chronic pain. https://uspainfoundation.org/blog/10-best-apps-for-people-with-chronic-pain/

Vitodata. (n.d.). Chronische Krankheiten Monitoring mit Software vitomed. Retrieved April 16, 2024, from https://www.vitodata.ch/de/digitale-arztpraxis/disease-management-medizinisches-monitoring

WHO. (n.d.). ICD-11 for Mortality and Morbidity Statistics. Retrieved November 10, 2023, from https://icd.who.int/browse11/l-m/en#/http://id.who.int/icd/entity/1581976053

Yang, H., & Li, D. (2021). Understanding the dark side of gamification health management: A stress perspective. Inf. Process. Manage., 58(5). https://doi.org/10.1016/j.ipm.2021.102649

Yoker, Ü. (2023). Der digitale medizinische Begleiter erinnert an Diät und Training. Impact ZHAW. https://impact.zhaw.ch/de/artikel/der-digitale-medizinische-begleiter-erinnert-an-diaet-und-training

A BRIEF REFLECTION ON THE CONVERGENCE BETWEEN GAMING AND GAMBLING[1]

Joan Arnedo-Moreno[1], Joan Josep Pons[2], Daniel Aranda[1] and Alexandra Samper-Martínez[3]
[1]*Universitat Oberta de Catalunya, Spain*
[2]*Tecnocampus Universitat Pompeu Fabra, Spain*
[3]*Euneiz Universidad Vitoria-Gasteiz, Spain*

ABSTRACT

This paper explores the convergence between gaming and gambling, focusing on how gambling practices in video games or eSports may serve as potential gateways for young people to develop gambling behaviors. Through a comprehensive review of scientific literature, the study examines the incorporation of gambling-like activities (GLA) into video games—such as loot boxes, roulette simulations, and casino-style features—and the growing normalization of gambling within the eSports ecosystem. Central to this analysis is the concept of "*gamblification*," which underscores the reciprocal influence between gaming and gambling: gambling products increasingly mimic game-like aesthetics, while video games integrate gambling-themed elements. Although correlations between problematic video game use and gambling behaviors are observed, definitive causality remains unproven. The paper concludes by emphasizing the importance of media literacy initiatives tailored to young people, equipping them with critical tools to navigate and mitigate the risks associated with these intertwined activities.

KEYWORDS

Gaming, Gambling, E-Sports, Convergence, Gamblification

1. INTRODUCTION

According to Newzoo's Global Games Market Report (2024), the video game sector will reach 3,42 billion players (an increase of 4,5% in comparison with the previous year) and the industry will generate $187,7 billion (2,1% more than in 2023). While these data are often mentioned with a certain degree of triumphalism within the sector, especially emphasizing that they exceed the figures of industries as powerful and recognized as film or music, it is very important to contextualize them. Actually, nowadays, the video game industry receives more income from microtransactions (or MT, a business model where users can purchase in-game virtual goods with micropayments) than from the purchase of games properly. Only from 2023 to 2024 the revenues from MTs have grown from $73,27 billion to $80,88 billion, and is expected to keep a steady growth in the upcoming years, according to some reports[2]. In most cases, even though downloading the game is free, users require some virtual internal currency, bought with real money, to acquire in-game items or advantages (Schwiddessen & Karius, 2018). The introduction of this monetization strategy has led the industry to develop some mechanics where virtual currency is spent in what could be considered gambling-like activities (GLA). A clear example are loot boxes (or loot crates, or gacha), where the acquired article is not known a priori, but chosen at random by the video game once it has been paid. The key aspect is that, in most cases, the odds are different for each possible virtual good - the better the item, the lower the odds of obtaining it. At the present time, there is intense debate about this type of game dynamics, especially within consumer groups, educators and researchers in video game studies, who are concerned about their possible effects on the population. Even so, the surrounding legislation is less than that regarding gambling in general. The main reason argued by lawyers and legislators for considering these practices not gambling and, therefore, being unnecessary to act, is that there is no direct

[1]Paper developed in the framework of the project *"Gamblification, youth and video games: research to promote responsible gaming practices"*, funded by the Ministry of Social Rights, Consumption and Agenda 2030 of the Government of Spain
[2]https://www.thebusinessresearchcompany.com/report/online-microtransaction-global-market-report

monetary benefit, unlike in other traditional gambling practices (e.g. lotteries, casinos, slots). There are only a few examples of countries that have chosen to legislate to limit their use, especially among minors. From making the sample of the probabilities of obtaining each prize mandatory, in China (and now around the world), to the total prohibition of loot boxes, in the emblematic case of the Netherlands.

Another element that is considered relevant in the normalization of gambling as part of having fun within the context of video games, would be eSports (always understood as regulated competitions by professional players teams) betting, similarly to other professional sports of popular consumption. It should be borne in mind that eSports consumption has ceased to be niche and is a booming sector, especially among the youngest and thanks to continuous streaming platforms. To get an idea of its current relevance and the clear generational relay that they represent, it is enough to contrast the total of prizes offered within the most popular eSports tournament, The International from DOTA TV, with other mainstream sports. In 2021 the prize was 40 million dollars, whereas those of the recognized tennis tournaments of Roland Garros and Wimbledon, the same year, were 46 and 48 million respectively. In this case, the simile is much more direct, since bets on eSports often follow the same model as other types of sports bets, and used as a tool by betting houses that want to attract a young audience. The only differences from traditional sports betting are the type of competition, and what is being betted, such as the use of virtual goods instead of money ("skin gambling"), that can be later turned into money or online store credits through gray markets. The aim of this paper is to carry out a critical reflection based on the current scientific literature on the topic, in order to try to evidence the practices linked between video game consumption and traditional gambling. The final goal is, based on the analysis of the scientific evidence accumulated over the last few years, to be able to answer the research question (RQ): *"Is the problematic use of GLA in video games, and bets on eSports, an initiation process among young people towards other types of gambling?"* From the answer to this RQ, it is possible to propose recommendations focused on giving young people critical tools in order to understand the risks associated with these possible links between video games or eSports, and traditional gambling, so they can act more freely in this environment and, therefore, benefit from them.

2. DISCUSSION

The study of factors linked to problems in the use of video games and participation in gambling usually correspond to the identification of two officially recognized types of behaviour disorder within the "Diagnostic and Statistical Manual of Mental Disorders" (DSM) of the American Association of Psychology (APA, 2013). On the one hand, the disorder in the use of Internet games (Internet Gaming Disorder, or IGD) and, on the other hand, gambling disorder (Gambling Disorder, or GD), respectively. The most important aspect to consider in this regard is the "gamblification", understood as the effects of the current convergence between certain monetization models and gambling mechanisms within the video games themselves (Macey & Hamari, 2024). This creates the possibility that a player can experience a problem with gambling ("problem gambling") within a video game, without this implying any effect of gateway towards other "traditional" gambling systems (e.g. slots, lottery) or digital gambling (e.g. casinos or online poker), which incorporate typical elements of video games to their interface to capture players. Therefore, it is not always clear where one issue ends and the other begins. Normally, to try to trace a border, it is considered that in the case of "problem gaming" the simplest metric to consider is the time spent on the activity, although not all authors agree (Vadlin et al., 2018), while in "problem gambling", it is the total expenditure on money.

According to the current literature, although many lawmakers do not consider GLA in video games gambling per se, in their legal definition, they do consider them to have obvious similarity patterns, from a psychological perspective (Drummond, 2018; Fauth-Bühler, 2017). This fact is aggravated by what is known as the "gamblification" of society, with the media convergence between gambling activities, more based on chance, and game-like activities (such as video games), more skills-based (Macey & Hamari 2020). Furthermore, its continuous and unsupervised availability towards adolescents in their digital format, the suspicion that this type of dynamics normalizes gambling with money expenditure as part of the fun grows. And as a result, it ends up generating gateway processes between the world of video games and traditional gambling houses. Since age restrictions are more strictly and broadly enforced for gambling activities than for video games, and legal frameworks only classify gambling as such when there is explicit monetary involvement, many individuals who eventually engage in gambling start playing video games at a younger age.

As a result, it is plausible that those who transition from problematic video game use to gambling habits—whether or not classified as problematic according to established assessment instruments—are predisposed to addictive behaviors. The manifestation of such behaviors may be moderated by age. The convergence trend is also evident in two key ways: an increasing number of gambling products adopting video game-like interfaces, and the integration of gambling-themed mechanics based on chance within video games themselves, with loot boxes serving as the most emblematic example. Additionally, the extensive use of related advertisements and incentives designed to attract players to games involving gambling systems with monetary outcomes further blurs the boundaries between gaming and gambling. This evolving ecosystem, in effect, "normalizes" gambling as a standard component of entertainment within the broader gaming experience.

Starting from this point, and to provide a brief summary of what the scientific literature reveals about this topic in response to the research question raised in the introduction, it can be indicated that suspicions of a correlation between problematic video game use or eSports betting and gambling-related behaviors in other contexts are confirmed. However, studies consistently emphasize—and this is crucial—that it is not possible to establish causality. Importantly, neither the simple habit of playing video games nor being an eSports spectator is inherently problematic. The risks appear only when specific behaviors, such as excessive engagement or interactions involving gambling-like mechanics, come into play (Spicer, 2022; Gibson, 2022; McCaffrey, 2023; Richard, 2023). A key factor in understanding what we talk about when referring to "problems or habits with gambling" is the impact that certain dynamics driven by video game developers, mainly loot boxes, have. In this sense, the problem is often not in a gateway effect towards other gambling (especially in online format, but also in "traditional") format, but in new mechanics based on microtransactions incorporated into video games. Additionally, there are other aspects to consider, such as the type of advertising associated with ads integrated into games, or eSports competitions (gambling houses, online casinos). In this context, Delfabbro (2020) provides a comprehensive summary of the current landscape concerning the convergence between video games and gambling. He underscores the absence of a clear causal link between video game use and gambling behavior, highlighting that some issues traditionally associated with gambling problems may, in fact, be better understood as video game dependency issues. This dependency is not driven by the pursuit of pleasure or escapism, but rather by an overwhelming need to acquire virtual items essential for progressing or outperforming other players in the game. This distinction further complicates the understanding of gambling-related risks in the context of modern video games.

3. CONCLUSION

The most relevant conclusion inferred from this reflection is that, given the unlikely intervention of regulators (with occasional exceptions in certain countries), it becomes essential to raise awareness among adolescents about "*gamblification*" practices already embedded in many modern video games. Fostering a critical mindset is crucial to help them recognize that these mechanisms are not merely gameplay features designed for entertainment, but rather manipulative strategies driven by economic interests, which may evolve into risky behaviors. Promoting media literacy and consumer awareness can serve as a preventive approach to mitigate potential harm. Among other the recommendations that can be proposed as a result of this study, in order to carry out actions with young people, we list:

- Communicate clearly the nature of current monetization models and their underlying economic motivations to stimulate critical thinking. Emphasize that modern video games already incorporate manipulative mechanisms commonly associated with gambling.
- Utilize evaluation tools identified in the literature to assess risk situations, either through educators or self-assessment by adolescents, regarding video game use and gambling behaviors.
- Consider gender differences in intervention strategies. For boys, focus on channeling competitive impulses and risk-taking tendencies into healthier, active pursuits. For girls, where the behavior is often linked to emotional escape, adopt a support-focused approach centered on emotional coping strategies.

Recalling Johan Huizinga's seminal work Homo Ludens (1938), in which he offered one of the earliest definitions of play, including a particularly significant phrase:

"Play is a free activity, standing quite consciously outside 'ordinary' life as being 'not serious', but at the same time absorbing the player intensely and utterly. It is an activity connected with no material interest, and no profit can be gained by it. It proceeds within its own close boundaries of time and space, according to fixed rules and in an orderly manner" (p.28)

REFERENCES

American Psychiatric Association (APA) (2013). Diagnostic and statistical manual of mental disorders (5th Ed.). Am Psychiatric Assoc Pub.

Delfabbro, P. & King, D. L. (2020). Gaming-gambling convergence: evaluating evidence for thegateway hypothesis. *International gambling studies. 20*(3), 380–392. https://doi.org/10.1080/14459795.2020.1768430

Drummond, A., & Sauer, J. D. (2018). Video game loot boxes are psychologically akin to gambling. *Nature human behaviour, 2*, 530–532. https://doi.org/10.1038/s41562-018-0360-1

Fauth-Bühler, M., & Mann, K. (2017). Neurobiological correlates of internet gaming disorder: Similarities to pathological gambling. Addictive Behaviors. https://doi.org/10.1016/j.addbeh.2015.11.004

Gibson, E., Griffiths, M. D., Calado, F., & Harris, A. (2022). The relationship between videogame micro-transactions and problem gaming and gambling: A systematic review. Computers in Human Behavior, 131, 107219.

Huizinga, J. (1938 originally, 1955 edition). *Homo Ludens: A Study of the Play Element in Culture*. Beacon Press.

Macey, J., & Hamari, J. (2020). GamCog: A measurement instrument for miscognitions related to gamblification, gambling, and video gaming. *Psychology of Addictive Behaviors, 34*(1), 242–256. https://doi.org/10.1037/adb0000526

Macey, J., & Hamari, J. (2024). Gamblification: A definition. New Media & Society, 26(4), 2046-2065. https://doi.org/10.1177/14614448221083903

McCaffrey, M. (2023). Loot boxes, problem gambling, and problem gaming: a critical review of the emerging literature. Communications of the Association for Information Systems, 52(1), 132-163.

Newzoo (2024). Global Games Market Report. https://newzoo.com/resources/trend-reports/newzoos-global-games-market-report-2024-free-version (accessed in Dec 2024)

Richard, J., & King, S. M. (2023). Annual Research Review: Emergence of problem gambling from childhood to emerging adulthood: a systematic review. Journal of Child Psychology and Psychiatry, 64(4), 645-688.

Schwiddessen, S., & Karius, P. (2018). Watch your loot boxes!–recent developments and legal assessment in selected key jurisdictions from a gambling law perspective. *Interactive Entertainment Law Review 1*(1), 17-43. https://doi.org/10.4337/ielr.2018.01.02

Spicer, S. G., Nicklin, L. L., Uther, M., Lloyd, J., Lloyd, H., & Close, J. (2022). Loot boxes, problem gambling and problem video gaming: A systematic review and meta-synthesis. New Media & Society, 24(4), 1001-1022.

Vadlin, S., Åslund, C., & Nilsson, K. W. (2018). A longitudinal study of the individual-and group-level problematic gaming and associations with problem gambling among Swedish adolescents. Brain and Behavior. https://doi.org/10.1002/brb3.949

Posters

CYBER PHYSICAL SYSTEM SECURITY ROADMAP FOR CRITICAL INFRASTRUCTURES

Mike Mekkanen[1], Tero Vartiainen[1], Chen-Wei Yang[2] and Valeriy Vyatkin[2]
[1]University of Vaasa, Wolffintie 32, FI-65200 Vaasa, Finland
[2]Laboratorievägen 14, SE-97187 Luleå, Sweden

ABSTRACT

Critical infrastructures (CIs) such as energy, transportation, and healthcare are being digitalized constantly. CI systems are cyber-physical systems consisting of software that steers physical parts (cf. dams). The digitalization process exposes CIs to cyber-attacks and there is need to develop cybersecurity of CIs. For this purpose, we develop a roadmap for development and research of cybersecurity of CIs.

KEYWORDS

Critical Infrastructures, Cybersecurity, IT-OT Convergence

1. INTRODUCTION

Critical infrastructures (CIs) are undergoing a major digital transformation through combining the digital and physical worlds. This transformation brings cybersecurity vulnerabilities that need proactive and protective protection to mitigate the impact of different incidents such as failures or cyber-attacks (Simos et al 2023). Were the obscurity of the transformed CIs, in turn, affects daily life activities, society and economy by providing critical services such as healthcare and energy. The challenges can be tackled with the help of the options that the security and risk management decision-makers must update upgrade existing security management's initiatives to include cyber-physical security (CPS) and using new technological methods and tools (Fischer-Preßler et al. 2024; Masi et al. 2023). A reliable resilient and sustainable CI is achieved through a comprehensive security management initiative that includes CPS (Yosef et al. 2017). Achieving the goal requires supporting both the technological development of the CI operational technology (OT) network and the securing of the application of information technology (IT) network through different parties' cooperation, investments programs for both networks and regulations. We argue that development of cybersecurity of CI need a practical roadmap. For this development work, we adopted an interpretative approach as our methodology. This approach involves classifying people's perceptions and synthesizing insights. In our case, we gathered perceptions from professionals and conducted a literature review. We organized a small workshop in March 2024 and conducted interviews with professionals (n=5). Additionally, we examined literature on cybersecurity and critical infrastructure. We then categorized the collected perceptions into meta-level factors influencing the cybersecurity of critical infrastructure. The next section presents the resulting roadmap.

2. ROADMAP

Our roadmap consists of the following factors (Figure 1): 1) Understanding and built-in knowledge of the CI assets and their security posture in which that allows to effectively evaluate, identify and prioritize the required optimization steps. 2) Understanding of CI operation and define their risk vectors, security counter-measures metrics. 3) Methods and tools for evaluating conditions of security in real time as well as analytically to assist in risk management decision-making. 4) CI operators must establish self-assessment and autonomous correction operations applying assigned tools and procedures. 5) Real-time security state monitoring tools that link to the self-assessment and autonomous operation activates for self-healing actions, while allowing the operators to override them, if necessary. 6) Cyber environments would benefit from additional knowledge gained from threats that have been identified and resolved to prevent recurrences in future. 7) Modelling and simulation tools for system and threat modeling in real-time to test and assess the holistic CI monitoring, detecting and protection systems. 8) Critical infrastructure subsectors could likewise profit from real-time monitoring and protection due their coherent interdependences, 9) Promoting awareness, fostering a security culture, and providing ongoing professional training should receive special focus.

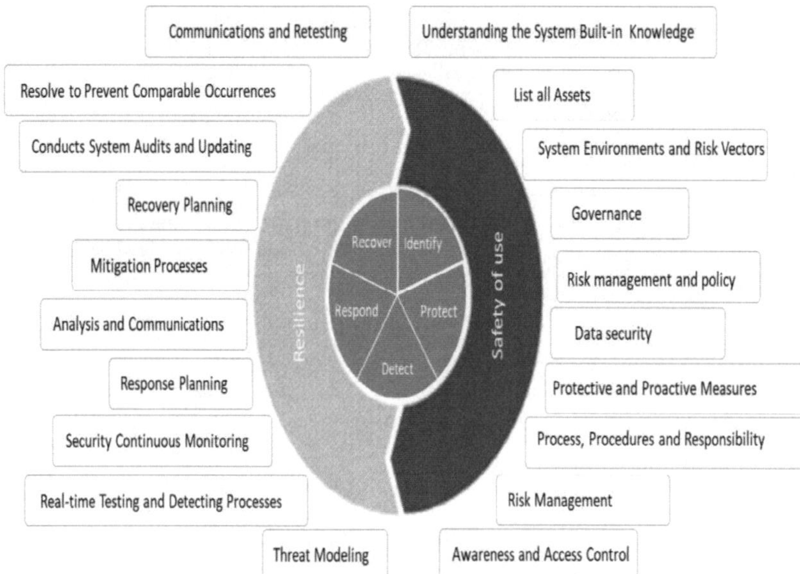

Figure 1. The topics of CI development

ACKNOWLEDGEMENT

This study was funded by Interreg Aurora, European Union.

REFERENCES

Fischer-Preßler, D., Bonaretti, D., & Bunker, D. (2024). Digital transformation in disaster management: A literature review. *The Journal of Strategic Information Systems*, 33(4), 101865. https://doi.org/10.1016/j.jsis.2024.101865

Marcelo Simoes, Mohammed Elmusrati, Tero Vartiainen, Mike Mekkanen, Mazaher Karimi, Sayawu Diaba, Emmanuel Anti, Wilson Lopes, (2023). *Enhancing data security against cyberattacks in artificial intelligence based smart grid systems with crypto agility*. [online] https://arxiv.org/abs/2305.11652

Masi, Massimiliano, Giovanni Paolo Sellitto, Helder Aranha, and Tanja Pavleska. "Securing Critical Infrastructures with a Cybersecurity Digital Twin." *Software and Systems Modeling* 22, no. 2 (April 1, 2023): 689–707.

Yosef Ashibani, Qusay H. Mahmoud. (2017). Cyber physical systems security: Analysis challenges and solutions. The *Journal of computer and security*, Vol 68, pp81-97.

MODELLING RESPIRATORY INFECTIONS IN KHARKIV REGION (UKRAINE) UNDER THE CONFLICT

Dmytro Chumachenko[1,2], Sergiy Yakovlev[3,4], Alexander Kirpich[5], Lyudmila Kirichenko[3], Pavel Skums[6], Gerardo Chowell[5] and Tetyana Chumachenko[7]

[1]*National Aerospace University "Kharkiv Aviation Institute", Vadym Manko str., 17, 61070 Kharkiv, Ukraine*

[2]*Balsillie School of International Affairs, 67 Erb St. W, N2L 6C2, Waterloo, ON, Canada*

[3]*Lodz University of Technology, ul. Żeromskiego 116, 90-924 Lodz, Poland*

[4]*V.N. Karazin Kharkiv National University, Svobody sq 4, 61022 Kharkiv, Ukraine*

[5]*Georgia State University, 33 Glimer St., SE Atlanta, GA 30303, USA*

[6]*University of Connecticut, 371 Fairfield Way, Storrs, CT 06269-4155, USA*

[7]*Kharkiv National Medical University, Nauky ave, 4, 61001 Kharkiv, Ukraine*

ABSTRACT

The full-scale Russian invasion of Ukraine has significantly disrupted public health systems, impacting the dynamics of influenza and acute respiratory tract infections (ARTIs) in Kharkiv Oblast. This study employed a long short-term memory (LSTM) model to analyze monthly disease incidence data from 2013 to 2023. Pre-invasion data revealed distinct seasonal trends, with peaks during winter months and declines during summer. However, the post-invasion period witnessed a dramatic drop in reported cases, likely due to population displacement, healthcare breakdowns, and reporting disruptions rather than actual infection declines. The LSTM model demonstrated high accuracy in pre-invasion, achieving mean absolute percentage errors (MAPE) of 1.83% for ARTIs and 6.39% for influenza. However, post-invasion predictions deviated sharply, with MAPE exceeding 800%, underscoring the limitations of traditional models in conflict settings. These findings highlight the need for adaptive modelling and robust public health systems to mitigate the effects of crises on disease dynamics.

KEYWORDS

Epidemic Model, Infectious Disease, Influenza, Acute Respiratory Tract Infection, War, Deep Learning

1. INTRODUCTION

The full-scale invasion of Ukraine by Russia has precipitated a humanitarian and health crisis with significant implications for public health. Armed conflicts are well-documented disruptors of healthcare systems, exacerbating the spread of infectious diseases such as influenza and acute respiratory tract infections (ARTIs) (Chumachenko et al., 2024). The ongoing war in Ukraine has created an environment where respiratory infections and other communicable diseases pose a substantial public health challenge.

The dynamics of infectious disease outbreaks in emergencies often deviate significantly from those observed under normal conditions (Marou et al., 2024). While effective in stable environments, traditional epidemiological models may lack the adaptability required to capture the complex interplay of factors in conflict zones (Goniewicz et al., 2021). Data analytics and machine learning advances, including long short-term memory (LSTM) networks, provide an alternative by modelling temporal dependencies in epidemiological data. These approaches enable more accurate forecasting and dynamic decision-making during crises, addressing the limitations of traditional models.

This study focuses on Kharkiv Oblast, a region severely affected by the conflict, to estimate the impact of the invasion on the dynamics of influenza and ARTIs. Using an LSTM-based methodology, the research aims to analyze how war-induced disruptions influence disease dynamics and contribute to public health management strategies during emergencies. By examining these patterns, the study contributes to understanding the broader implications of war on epidemiological processes and health outcomes.

2. MATERIALS AND METHODS

This study utilized monthly data on influenza and ARTIs in Kharkiv Oblast from January 2013 to December 2023, provided by the Kharkiv Oblast Center for Disease Control and Prevention. Preprocessing steps involved normalizing the data to ensure comparability across different scales and splitting it into training (2013–2020), validation (2021), and testing (2022–2023) subsets.

LSTM networks were employed to model disease dynamics. The model used the preceding 12 months of data as input to predict case counts for the following month. This design allowed the network to identify trends and seasonal patterns while accounting for disruptions caused by the war. The LSTM architecture consisted of a single-layer network with 64 hidden units, followed by a dense output layer. The model was trained using the Adam optimization algorithm with a learning rate of 0.001, and the mean squared error (MSE) was employed as the loss function to minimize prediction errors.

The training process involved iterative learning with early stopping applied to prevent overfitting. Cross-validation was performed to validate the model's performance and ensure robustness. The final model was tested on the 2022–2023 data, representing the period of active conflict, to assess its predictive accuracy. Mean absolute percentage error (MAPE) was used to evaluate forecast quality.

Forecasted values were compared against recorded data for the conflict period to identify deviations attributable to war-induced disruptions, such as population displacement, healthcare system breakdowns, and reduced disease reporting.

3. RESULTS

The incidence of ARTIs in Kharkiv Oblast displayed distinct seasonal trends from January 2013 to February 2022. Monthly case counts varied significantly, with peaks occurring during colder months, such as January and February, and lower values during summer. For instance, the winter months of January and February 2022 recorded 45,659 and 53,374 cases, respectively. Historically, the highest peaks were observed during the 2015–2016 season, with 28,720 cases in January 2016 and 31,636 cases in December 2016. These fluctuations generally reflect the expected seasonal variation in ARTIs, with high transmission rates in cold weather due to increased indoor crowding and favourable conditions for viral spread.

However, the full-scale Russian invasion of Ukraine, starting on February 24, 2022, marked a significant turning point in the ARTIs dynamics. Following the invasion reported cases plummeted drastically, with only 3,426 cases in March 2022, and further declined to as low as 1,631 cases in July 2022. These values are among the lowest recorded for the entire study period. This sharp decline likely reflects disruptions in healthcare infrastructure, population displacement, and a breakdown in reporting mechanisms rather than an actual reduction in infections. A partial recovery in reported cases was observed later in 2022, with 9,482 cases in September and 12,440 cases in February 2023. However, the patterns have not returned to their pre-war consistency, highlighting the ongoing impact of the conflict.

Influenza incidence in Kharkiv Oblast followed similar seasonal trends to ARTIs but occurred on a much smaller scale. Between 2013 and early 2022, influenza cases showed clear peaks during winter months, with the highest incidences recorded in February 2016 (244 cases) and January 2016 (201 cases). Notably, influenza activity significantly decreased during 2020 and 2021, coinciding with the COVID-19 pandemic, likely due to the widespread use of face masks, social distancing, and other public health measures that suppressed influenza transmission.

The post-invasion period saw a sharp decline in reported influenza cases, with zero cases recorded from March to September 2022. A modest resurgence was observed in late 2022 and early 2023, including 135 cases in January 2023 and 131 in February 2023. While higher than other post-invasion months, these figures remain far below the pre-war peaks. As with ARTIs, the decline in influenza incidence after the invasion likely reflects disruptions in disease surveillance and healthcare access rather than a genuine reduction in cases.

The LSTM model was employed to forecast ARTIs and influenza cases, leveraging pre-invasion data. The model demonstrated strong performance in the validation phase, achieving a MAPE of 1.83% for ARTIs and 6.39% for influenza. These results highlight the model's ability to capture seasonal and long-term trends under stable conditions.

However, when applied to the post-invasion period, the LSTM model's predictions deviated dramatically from observed data, with MAPE exceeding 800% for both diseases. This stark difference reflects the war's profound impact on disease dynamics and reporting systems. Factors such as damaged healthcare infrastructure, mass displacement, and a breakdown in disease surveillance contributed to the model's failure to predict case counts in this unprecedented context accurately.

These results underscore the limitations of using pre-war data to model disease dynamics in conflict zones. While the LSTM model effectively predicted ARTIs and influenza trends under normal circumstances, it could not account for the external disruptions introduced by the war. This highlights the need for real-time data integration and adaptive modelling approaches to address the unique challenges posed by conflict settings.

4. CONCLUSION

This study demonstrates the significant impact of the Russian invasion of Ukraine on the dynamics of ARTIs and influenza in Kharkiv Oblast. Both diseases showed a dramatic reduction in reported cases after February 2022, reflecting disruptions in healthcare access, population displacement, and data reporting rather than actual infection declines. The pre-invasion LSTM model effectively predicted disease dynamics with high accuracy; however, post-invasion deviations exceeding 800% highlight the profound influence of conflict on epidemiological trends. These findings underscore the importance of context-specific modelling and robust healthcare systems to manage public health during crises.

ACKNOWLEDGEMENT

The study was partially supported by the IMPRESS-U program, an international collaboration between the United States, Poland, and Ukraine (NSF grant OISE-2412914; NCN grant 2023/05/Y/ST6/00263).

REFERENCES

Chumachenko, D., et al. (2024). Methodology for assessing the impact of emergencies on the spread of infectious diseases. *Radioelectronic and Computer Systems*, 2024(3), pp.6–26. doi: 10.32620/reks.2024.3.01.

Goniewicz, K., et al. (2021). The Influence of War and Conflict on Infectious Disease: A Rapid Review of Historical Lessons We Have Yet to Learn. *Sustainability*, 13(19), p.10783. doi: 10.3390/su131910783.

Marou, V., et al. (2024). The impact of conflict on infectious disease: a systematic literature review. *Conflict and health*, 18(1). doi: 10.1186/s13031-023-00568-z.

OPTIMIZATION OF MOBILE MEDICAL SERVICE LOCATIONS BASED ON PREDICTIVE ANALYTICS IN CRISIS SCENARIOS

Sergiy Yakovlev[1,2], Lyudmyla Kirichenko[1], Olha Matsyi[1], Alexander Kirpich[3] and Dmytro Chumachenko[4,5]

[1]*Lodz University of Technology, ul. Żeromskiego 116, 90-924 Lodz, Poland*

[2]*V.N. Karazin Kharkiv National University, 4 Svobody sq., 61022 Kharkiv, Ukraine*

[3]*Georgia State University, 33 Gilmer St, SE Atlanta, GA 30303*

[4]*Balsillie School of International Affairs, 67Erb St, W, N2L 6C2, Waterloo, ON, Canada*

[5]*National Aerospace University "Kharkiv Aviation Institute", 17 Vadyma Manka St, 61070 Kharkiv, Ukraine*

ABSTRACT

The optimization of mobile medical service locations is essential for enhancing emergency response efficiency during crises such as pandemics, natural disasters, and armed conflicts. This study develops a maximum coverage model that integrates predictive analytics using geospatial data to define demand regions and exclude areas unsuitable for deployment, such as natural obstacles or active conflict zones. Medical data on infection dynamics are incorporated to forecast disease spread and guide the allocation and configuration of service areas. The model dynamically adapts to changes in service territories, ensuring effective resource utilization and maximizing coverage. A test scenario demonstrates the practical application of this methodology, highlighting its relevance for crisis management and public health optimization in complex and rapidly evolving environments.

KEYWORDS

Mobile Medical Service Location, Infection Spread Prediction, Military Conflict, Optimization Model, Maximum Coverage Location Problem

1. INTRODUCTION

The optimization of mobile medical service locations is a critical component in enhancing healthcare delivery, particularly in crisis scenarios. Whether responding to the spread of infectious diseases like COVID-19 or addressing the needs of populations in conflict zones, effective location planning ensures equitable access to care while maximizing resource efficiency. This study emphasizes the role of predictive analytics in the optimization process, allowing decision-makers to anticipate and respond to dynamic conditions in crisis scenarios. For instance, during a pandemic, predictive models can forecast infection hotspots, guiding the strategic placement of mobile medical facilities to maximize coverage and reduce transmission rates. Similarly, in armed conflict situations, location optimization must account for safety constraints, accessibility challenges, and population displacement patterns, all of which can be informed by data-driven predictions.

The integration of optimization techniques and predictive analytics within the framework of E-Society creates new opportunities for improving healthcare infrastructure:

- *Data-Driven Decision-Making:* Leveraging geospatial analytics, epidemiological forecasts, and real-time data enables the precise identification of optimal locations.
- *Inclusivity and Accessibility*: Models can prioritize underserved populations, ensuring medical services reach the most vulnerable.
- *Adaptability in Crisis:* Dynamic and flexible planning allows for rapid reconfiguration of healthcare services in response to evolving crises.

The paper of Hezam, I. M. et al. (2021) presents a systematic literature review on mathematical models of humanitarian logistics. Optimization models are classified into three main domains: facility location, aid distribution, and mass evacuation, where each problem includes both deterministic and non-deterministic models. Current research demonstrates the value of combining mathematical modeling with GIS for solving complex location problems. Among the many modern publications close to the subject of our research, we note the articles by Alisan O. et al. (2023) and Hashemi S.E. et al. (2022).

2. MATERIALS AND METHODS

2.1 Problem Description

In crisis scenarios, such as the spread of infectious diseases or armed conflicts, optimizing the locations of mobile medical services becomes a critical challenge. This task involves several interconnected components:

- *Crisis Scenario Predictions:* Predictive models are utilized to forecast infection spread, identify high-risk zones for disease transmission, and analyze areas affected by occupation, active combat, or other factors limiting accessibility.
- *Restricted Zones:* Prohibited areas are defined by natural, logistical and security constraints.
- *Resource Constraints:* Mobile units are constrained by the availability of personnel, equipment, and medical supplies, which collectively determine the service radius of each unit. Resources can be predefined or treated as variables depending on the scenario.
- *Optimization Objectives:* The goal is to develop an optimal placement strategy for mobile units that maximizes population coverage, minimizes location-associated risks, and efficiently allocating limited resources.
- *Dynamic Problem Characteristics:* The optimization models must account for evolving crisis scenarios, enabling adaptive reconfiguration of mobile facility locations, such as those associated with combat zones, mining and demining of areas, etc. Service areas should dynamically reflect resource availability, and geospatial analytics and predictive modeling must be integrated to manage the complexity of location constraints.

This problem is structured as a constrained optimization task with the following objectives:

- *Maximizing Coverage:* Ensuring the largest possible population within the effective service areas of facilities is served.
- *Ensuring Safety and Accessibility:* Avoiding restricted zones defined by safety, and logistical factors.
- *Resource Efficiency:* Allocating limited resources to achieve maximum impact.

The complexity of the task underscores the importance of developing advanced optimization approaches that integrate local and global methods, predictive analytics, and geospatial data.

2.2 Modeling and Optimization

We formulate the problem as follows. There is a demand zone (region) S_0 and a family of service areas $S_1, ..., S_n$. Each service area S_i is associated with a point c_i, which called a centroid and relative to which such area will be defined. The problem is to find such a position of service area centroids c_i in order to provide the optimal service of the demand zone S_0 according to a given criteria. It is assumed that the shape and sizes of the demand zone and service areas are specified. Restrictions can be imposed on the position of centroids, which determine their allowable location. As optimality criteria, we will consider the maximum coverage area of the demand zone.

Yakovlev S. et al. (2023) proposed a generalized formulation of such a problem taking into account the arbitrary shape of both the demand zone and the family of service areas. In general, the problem is formulated as a unconstrained nonlinear optimization problem:

$$\varphi(\mathbf{p}, \mathbf{m}) \to max$$

subject to $\mathbf{p} \in D$, where $\mathbf{p} = (p_1, ..., p_n)$ is the vector of parameters determining the location of service areas $S_1, ..., S_n$; $\mathbf{m}$ is the vector of metric parameters determining their sizes; D denotes the feasible set of admissible parameters $(\mathbf{p}, \mathbf{m})$.

As a rule, when considering such a class of problems, it is assumed that the service areas have a circular shape, and the centroids coincide with their centers with coordinates $p_i = (x_i, y_i)$. In this case, $\mathbf{m} = (r_1, ..., r_n)$. To calculate the radii r_i of circles $S_i(p_i)$, methods are known that take into account the volume of resources, population density of the region, disease statistics, etc. There may be options when the radii are fixed $r_i = \hat{r}_i$ or are variables $r_i = r_i(x_i, y_i)$ depending on the location of the service areas $S_i(p_i)$. The radii can be stationary or dynamically changing taking into account forecasts of the spread of infectious diseases, population displacement in the event of military operations, etc.

For circular service areas, we propose a so-called extended elastic model that allows us to present optimality criteria in the form

$$\varphi(\mathbf{p}, \mathbf{m}) = \sum_{i=1}^{n} \mu_{i0}(p_i, r_i) - \sum_{i=1}^{n-1} \sum_{j=i+1}^{n} \mu_{ij}(p_i, r_i, p_j, r_j) \,,$$

where $\mu_{i0}(p_i, r_i)$ is the area of intersection of S_0 and S_i; $\mu_{ij}(p_i, r_i, p_j, r_j)$ is the area of intersection of S_i and S_j, which are calculated according to known formulas.

The feasible set D is defined based on constraints governing the location of service areas. Geospatial data are utilized to identify prohibited zones, which are transformed into an analytical form using a system of inequalities. These zones include both natural barriers (e.g., rivers, lakes, or buildings) and dynamic restrictions influenced by military operations. Additional constraints, such as transportation logistics and resource limitations, are incorporated. The formalization of such constraints is well-documented in the literature. Constraints on the centroids' locations can be either stationary (e.g., natural barriers) or dynamic (e.g., military strategies). For dynamic models, predictive analytics provide data for fixed time points, defining both the parameters of service areas and the formation of prohibited zones.

The complexity of the problem arises from its high dimensionality and the multi-extremal nature of the objective function. Our methodology combines local and global optimization techniques. Gradient-based methods are employed for local optimization, while metaheuristic algorithms are utilized during the global optimization stage to explore and rank local extrema effectively.

2.3 Case Study

We applied the proposed approach to optimize the placement of mobile vaccination centers in the Kharkiv region (Ukraine) during military operations. A distinctive feature of this region is that it comprises both occupied and recently deoccupied territories. To address the challenges, we utilized infection spread models (e.g., for COVID-19) to forecast demand levels and define the service areas of mobile centers. Additionally, geospatial data were employed to identify prohibited zones, including natural obstacles and dynamically changing conflict zones (combat action, minefields, etc.). Due to restrictions on access to the relevant datasets, we cannot disclose the specific initial data or the detailed solutions obtained. Therefore, the presented example is illustrative (Figure 1). In this example, prohibited zones are represented as ellipses, while service areas are depicted as circles. The radii of the service areas were calculated based on population density, disease incidence rates, and the availability of medical personnel.

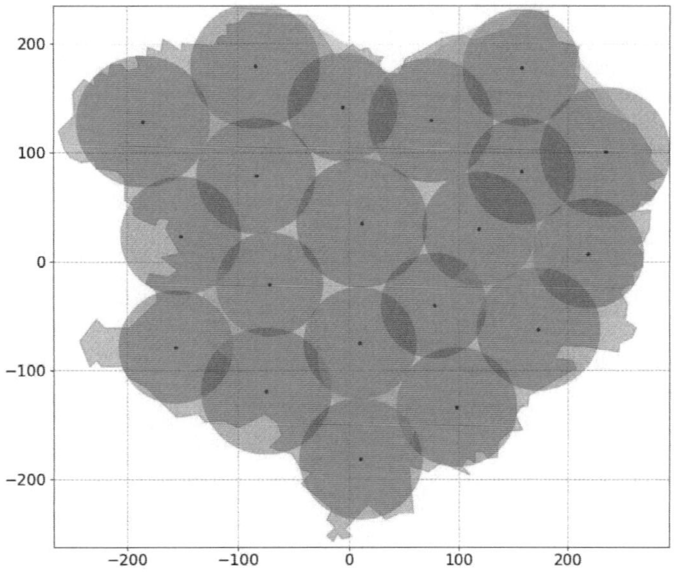

Figure 1. An illustrative example of the optimal location of service areas

3. CONCLUSION

This study proposes a coverage-based optimization model adapted for crisis scenarios. The model uses predictive analytics to define the service radius of mobile health units based on the volume of services required, while restricting potential locations to areas that meet safety and accessibility criteria. Practical applications include: optimizing the location of vaccination sites or testing centers based on infection spread forecasts; ensuring safe access to health services in conflict zones for displaced populations while reducing risks to health care providers. By integrating digital technologies and optimization models, this approach strengthens the resilience of healthcare systems within E-Society. It highlights how predictive analytics can transform crisis management, ensuring efficient resource allocation and equitable access to care, even in the most challenging conditions.

ACKNOWLEDGEMENT

The study was partially supported by the IMPRESS-U program, an international collaboration between the United States, Poland, and Ukraine (NSF grant OISE-2412914; NCN grant 2023/05/Y/ST6/00263).

REFERENCES

Alisan, O., et al. (2023). Location selection of field hospitals amid COVID-19 considering effectiveness and fairness: A case study of Florida. *International Journal of Disaster Risk Reduction*, 93:103794. doi:10.1016/j.ijdrr.2023.103794

Hashemi, S.E., et al. (2022). An Efficient Greedy Randomized Heuristic for the Maximum Coverage Facility Location Problem with Drones in Healthcare. *Applied Sciences*, 12(3):1403 doi: 10.3390/app12031403

Hezam, I. M., et al. (2021). A Systematic Literature Review on Mathematical Models of Humanitarian Logistics. *Symmetry*, 13(1): 11. doi:10.3390/sym13010011

Oksuz, M.K., and Satoglu, S.I. (2020). A Two-Stage Stochastic Model for Location Planning of Temporary Medical Centers for Disaster Response. *Int. Journal of Disaster Risk Reduction*, 44: 101426. doi: 10.1016/j.ijdrr.2019.101426

Yakovlev, S., et al. (2023). Maximum Service Coverage in Business Site Selection Using Computer Geometry Software. *Electronics*, 12(10): 2329. doi:10.3390/electronics12102329

Doctoral Consortium

THE ROLE OF INTELLECTUAL PROPERTY IN DRIVING BUSINESS SUCCESS FOR PROPTECH COMPANIES IN THE 4TH AND 5TH INDUSTRIAL REVOLUTIONS

Marijana Ribičić
DOBA Business School
Prešernova 1, 2000 Maribor, Slovenia

ABSTRACT

This paper, part of a doctoral dissertation, explores the role of intellectual property (IP) in the Property Technology (PropTech) sector. It examines the business success of companies applying technological innovations in an increasingly digital society. PropTech companies are key innovators, creating smart solutions and advancing technologies. The aim of this research is to encourage PropTech companies to achieve greater business success and drive the development of new technological solutions, aligning with the focus of conferences such as business management and e-Society. Through the analysis of 5,535 PropTech companies to investigate the link between IP and business success, a categorization of over 250 companies, and 10 case study interviews, this research assesses the economic and strategic implications of IP in enhancing competitiveness and fostering technological development. The paper offers insights into the impact of IP on sector-specific innovations, highlighting potential pathways for industry growth and sustainability.

KEYWORDS

Property Technology, Intellectual Property, Smart Cities, Digital Transformation, Internet of Things, Augmented Reality

1. INTRODUCTION

A PropTech is characterized by the massive implementation of new technologies such as home matching tools, drones, virtual reality, building information modeling (BIM), data analytics tools, artificial intelligence (AI), the Internet of Things (IoT), and blockchain, smart contracts, crowdfunding in the real estate sector, real estate-related fintech, smart cities, regions, smart homes, and the sharing economy. The rapid digital transformation within the real estate industry has led to the emergence of Property Technology (PropTech), where innovative digital solutions redefine traditional real estate operations (Siniak et al., 2020).

According to Merkel (2019), the first generation of PropTech emerged in the UK and the USA due to increasing data processing capabilities in the early 1980s and the introduction of personal computers in the late 1970s and early 1980s. The second generation of PropTech created a new wave of innovations within the commercial real estate market, starting in the mid-1990s, focusing on development in investments and entrepreneurship, primarily through the enhancement of existing technologies. This technology becomes increasingly important for the real estate market as it is applicable in every household with a data connection, especially in the areas of smart measurement and building automation. The third and current generation of PropTech is tackling the challenges of AI. After connecting properties, buildings, and equipment, artificial intelligence (AI) technologies can independently analyze and manage data.

Can we say that the development of the third generation of PropTech aligns with the Fourth Industrial Revolution (4IR), and can we anticipate that the future fourth generation of PropTech will correlate with the Fifth Industrial Revolution (5IR)? On November 1, 2024, we searched for articles on the development of the fourth generation of PropTech using Google Scholar, but we did not find many scientific articles on the topic. However, what does the development of 4IR and 5IR tell us?

The Fifth Industrial Revolution (5IR), according to George & George (2020), will bring transformation to the manufacturing sector that could spur a new industrial revolution. 5IR is expected to represent an evolution of modern manufacturing processes that enable people and machines to work together, combining the unique cognitive abilities of workers and the precise technical knowledge of robots to foster an innovative culture in the workforce. 5IR aims to create customer satisfaction and open new markets. It will be characterized by collaboration between machines and humans, with the goal of enhancing production further by creating customized products that meet consumer demands. In the scientific work of Pizon et al. (2022), the possibilities of implementing collaborative robots (cobots) for performing manual tasks in human-cobot collaboration teams are described, with the aim of reducing waste within manufacturing systems from the perspective of 5IR.

As we can see, the development of 5IR emphasizes the collaboration between humans and robots/cobots, which could also be applicable in PropTech companies—particularly architectural companies (ConTech). Such an example is mentioned in the scientific work of Pizon et al. (2022). To illustrate the proposed implementation model, a conceptual case study was developed that corresponds to the actual furniture production process. The identification of space for the use of cobots was verified using value stream mapping, and the possibilities of implementation were analyzed using simulation software. The production process was mapped in a value stream map and simulation software, demonstrating potential time savings in executing the production process and possible increases in average production volume. Therefore, the possibilities for implementing the presented concept were positively verified. This approach lays the foundation for innovative solutions based on an interdisciplinary combination of organizational, managerial, and technical aspects from the perspective of cobot usage. This provides an opportunity to develop a cost-effective solution for implementing modern cobot technology to reduce waste in accordance with lean management principles. The concept opens perspectives for many questions regarding how and when to implement cobot solutions within an organization, which is particularly relevant from the perspective of companies operating in specific industries that utilize selected technologies and methods of work organization. This example is ideal for developing fourth-generation PropTech, especially when compared to the development of 5IR. This is particularly relevant from the perspective of specific PropTech companies utilizing selected technologies and methods of work organization. The implementation of cobot solutions should be tailored to the organization's ecosystem. A change in the organization's business strategy that includes the implementation of 5IR solutions or, ultimately, the application of lean management techniques should be aligned with its sustainable development, corporate social responsibility (CSR), and even ESG (environmental, social, and governance factors) while being economically justified.

The rapid digital transformation within the real estate industry has led to the emergence of Property Technology (PropTech), where innovative digital solutions redefine traditional real estate operations. As PropTech companies integrate technologies such as IoT, AI, and 3D modeling, the management and protection of intellectual property (IP) becomes critical for maintaining competitive advantage and fostering innovation.

Those novel digital solutions are reshaping the real estate industry through advancements in smart buildings, architectural design, and real estate management platforms. In such a rapidly evolving field, does intellectual property (IP) play a pivotal role in protecting innovation and fostering competitive advantage? There is limited research examining the specific types of IP leveraged by PropTech companies and the impact of these assets on business success, especially for emerging startups within this sector.

This study seeks to address this gap by exploring the types of IP used by PropTech companies and analyzing how IP influences their business success. Our research is guided by several core questions:

IP1: What types of intellectual property are utilized by PropTech companies?

IP2: Does IP affect the business success of PropTech companies, particularly innovative startups? If so, how?

IP3: What is the resource-based differences (RBV) among PropTech companies in their use of industrial property and unregistered IP, such as copyrights and trade secrets? Why do companies choose one form over another, or opt for no IP at all?

Our hypotheses were structured to test the relative importance of various IP types across different PropTech segments. For companies specializing in smart buildings, patents were anticipated to be crucial (H1a), while industrial design was expected to be most relevant for architectural companies (H1b). Trademarks were likely to dominate IP usage among real estate platforms (H1c). For innovative PropTech startups, trademarks were projected to be more significant than patents (H1d). Additionally, we hypothesized that patents (H2a) and registered industrial property (H2b) would positively correlate with business success among more established PropTech companies, whereas trademarks would have a greater impact on the success of startups, with patents playing a less influential role (H2c).

Lastly, the third research question (IP3) was explored through a qualitative approach, allowing for in-depth analysis of the resource-based choices in IP utilization across PropTech companies. This study thus aimed to provide a comprehensive understanding of IP's role within the PropTech sector, offering insights that could guide companies in strategically managing intellectual property for enhanced innovation and market success. Through both statistical and qualitative analyses, the paper sought to provide a comprehensive understanding of IP's impact on PropTech's growth and long-term sustainability.

2. METHODOLOGY

We used a combined quantitative and qualitative approach to enable systematic data analysis and quantify the relationships among variables. Analyses were conducted using the Jamovi software (2024, version 2.5) and QDA Miner.

a) From the OrbisIP program, we exported samples of **5.535 PropTech companies** to analyze the patented solutions entered the IPC_code "Building" along with keywords related to the PropTech industry, identified through QDA Miner, to systematically analyze data using to answer on H2 hypotesis.

b) From the website Unissu, we sampled **200 European PropTech companies** and conducted qualitative and quantitative analyses to answer H1 hypotesis.

c) From Y Combinator (with some data also taken from Unissu), we selected **50 startup companies** for quantitative and qualitative analysis to answer H1d and H2c hypotesis.

d) We interviewed 10 successful **PropTech companies**, including 5 that use industrial property and 5 that do not. These companies were exhibitors at the MBF conference in Rovinj.

The study categorizes PropTech companies into three main areas:

1. **Smart PropTech Companies** - developing automation systems (e.g., IoT, AI, Smart Homes).
2. **ConTech Companies** - utilizing digital solutions like BIM and 3D modeling.
3. **Property Management Companies** – software for property, asset, and investment management.

2.1 Results and Analysis

This research utilizes Jamovi, QDA Miner to analyze data of 5.535 PropTech companies. Methods include descriptive statistics, correlation, and ANOVA for statistical analysis, and word-phrase analysis for qualitative insights.

Most patents were registered by companies **H1a**, which is why we confirm the above hypothesis. Architectural companies mostly registered a trademark, not an industrial design, so we reject hypothesis **H1b**. Real estate platforms also registered the most trademarks, thereby confirming the **H1c** hypothesis.

Business success is measured by total revenue, net profit, and the number of employees, based on our work framework. Based on the analysis conducted, we can confirm hypothesis **H2a**: Patents positively correlate with the business success of PropTech companies. The Pearson's r is consistently above 0.5, indicating strong correlation effects, with $p < .001$. Although we could have included other variables representing business performance, we also displayed two variables where Pearson's $r < .1$, showing trivial values, specifically for ROCE and ROE.

Hypothesis **H2b** is confirmed, as registered industrial property positively correlates with the business success of PropTech companies. Specifically, in the previous example, we saw that patents were included, while the second table are trademarks and registered designs (see doctoral dissertation).

Based on these results, hypothesis **H2c** cannot be confirmed, as there are not enough companies in the sample using trademarks or patents to establish a clear correlation with business success. Given that patents are not present in the companies within this sample, we can suggest that patents do not play a role in the business success of these companies, at least at this stage.

Interviews have been conducted with ten PropTech companies. Four companies are in the Smart category, four are in ConTech, and two are in property management. The findings are as follows:

Table 1. Coding frequency

	Count	% Codes	Cases	% Cases
PropTech category				
MICRO COMPANY	4	6,2%	4	40,0%
SMALL COMPANY	1	1,5%	1	10,0%
MIDDLE COMPANY	1	1,5%	1	10,0%
BIG COMPANY	4	6,2%	4	40,0%
H1a	4	6,2%	4	40,0%
H1b	4	6,2%	4	40,0%
H1c	2	3,1%	2	20,0%
PATENT	1	1,5%	1	10,0%
TRADE MARK	6	9,2%	6	60,0%
IND. DESIGN	2	3,1%	2	20,0%
COPYRIGHT I TRADE SECRET	10	15,4%	9	90,0%

The interview participants were founders, directors, and representatives of PropTech companies. The categorization of companies was based on criteria from the European Union and the United States, with 40% of participants belonging to micro-enterprises, 10% to small enterprises, 10% to medium-sized enterprises, and 40% to large companies. It is important to note that one company is a franchisee, and two companies are representatives of large PropTech companies registered in the United States. Additionally, only one small Croatian PropTech company holds two registered forms of intellectual property, an industrial design and a trademark, while its affiliated company holds a registered patent, which was required for an EU grant application.

All companies possess unregistered IP (copyright and/or trade secrets). The research question on the differences based on RBV resources in the use of industrial property and unregistered IP yielded the following answer: All large companies, with revenues ranging from 50 million to 7.5 billion euros, have registered trademarks, while none of the micro companies have registered any form of IP or industrial property.

3. CONCLUSION AND DISCUSSION

The findings confirmed several hypotheses regarding IP registration and its correlation with business performance. Most notably, hypothesis H1a was validated, demonstrating that patents were predominantly registered by PropTech companies of the first category, indicating their significance in the industry. However, hypothesis H1b was rejected, as architectural companies (second category) favored trademarks over industrial designs. Additionally, hypothesis H1c was confirmed, as real estate platforms primarily registered trademarks, reflecting their strategic emphasis on brand protection.

Further analysis focused on business success metrics—total revenue, net profit, and number of employees. Hypothesis H2a was substantiated, showing a strong positive correlation between patents and business success, with a Pearson's r consistently above 0.5 and $p < .001$, indicating significant statistical relevance. Similarly, hypothesis H2b was confirmed, as registered industrial property also positively correlated with business success among PropTech companies. In this context, the analysis revealed the notable presence of patents and trademarks, emphasizing their roles in driving business outcomes.

To confirm the hypothesis H2c, further research would be needed, perhaps with a larger sample of companies that use trademarks and patents and examining their connection to business success. However, it can also be assumed in the future that, in any representative sample, there will always be a small number of start-ups using industrial property, as the patent registration process takes 18 months, and start-ups require more time to develop new ideas, innovations, and file patent applications.

Regarding our research question of how patents are related to business outcomes, our analysis shows that, although there is a significant relationship between company size (measured by the number of employees, revenue, and net profit) and its patent activity, this does not directly correlate with immediate financial benefits for ROE and ROCE. This indicates that simply having a larger number of patents does not necessarily lead to better financial returns or efficiency in the use of equity. While patents may reflect innovation capacity, they do not directly influence measures of financial performance, or it may take more time for such effects to manifest. Some factors could include the time lag between patent grants and commercial success, varying quality and market potential of different patents, or other strategic factors affecting financial performance. This underscores the complexity of the innovation economy, where the quantity of patents is not a direct indicator of financial success, return of investments.

Finally, research question Q3 remains ongoing, suggesting that further exploration is needed to fully understand the complexities of IP utilization within the PropTech sector. The reason why other large PropTech companies have registered trademarks is unclear, but we can conclude that there is a revenue difference between PropTech companies with trademarks and those without.

Although the research included a statistically significant number of companies the results are based on data collected over a specific period. Longitudinal studies are needed to assess how the relationship between IP and business success evolves over time. The qualitative part of the research is based on interviews with a limited number of PropTech companies, which may lead to bias. A larger number of interviews or additional methods, such as focus groups, could enhance the understanding of IP strategies in the sector.

Future research could focus on incorporating temporal variables to ascertain causality, specifically to determine whether financial growth is driven by the registration of industrial property or if other factors contribute to this success. Overall, this study contributes valuable insights into the relationship between IP and business performance, guiding PropTech companies in strategically managing their IP portfolios to enhance innovation and achieve market success.

ACKNOWLEDGEMENT

I would like to express my gratitude to my supervisor, Dr. Ana Hafner, for her invaluable guidance and support throughout this research.

REFERENCES

George, A. S., & George, A. S. H. (2020). Industrial Revolution 5.0: The Transformation of the Modern Manufacturing Process to Enable Man and Machine to Work Hand In Hand. *Journal of Seybold Report.*

Merkel, M. J. (2019). Key technologies and evolution of PropTech companies. *Zarządzanie. Teoria i Praktyka*, *1*, 37–41. https://www.ceeol.com/search/article-detail?id=892855

Pizoń, J., Cioch, M., Kanski, L., & García, E. S. (2022). Cobots Implementation in the Era of Industry 5.0 Using Modern Business and Management Solutions. *Advances in Science and Technology Research Journal*, *16*(6), 166–178. https://doi.org/10.12913/22998624/156222

Siniak, N., Kauko, T., Shavrov, S., & Marina, N. (2020). The impact of proptech on real estate industry growth. *IOP Conference Series: Materials Science and Engineering*, *869*(6). https://doi.org/10.1088/1757-899X/869/6/062041

AUTHOR INDEX

International Association for Development of the Information Society (IADIS)
Rua Sao Sebastiao Da Pedreira
No. 100, 30, 1050-209
Lisbon, Portugal

ISBN 979-8-3313-1620-4

9 798331 316204

CURRAN ASSOCIATES INC.
proceedings.com